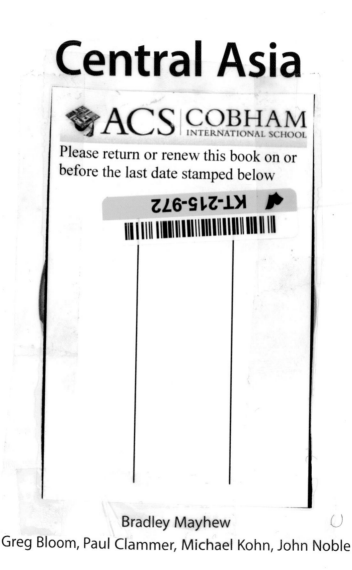

lonely planet

Central Asia

ACS | COBHAM
INTERNATIONAL SCHOOL

Please return or renew this book on or
before the last date stamped below

KT-215-972

Bradley Mayhew

Greg Bloom, Paul Clammer, Michael Kohn, John Noble

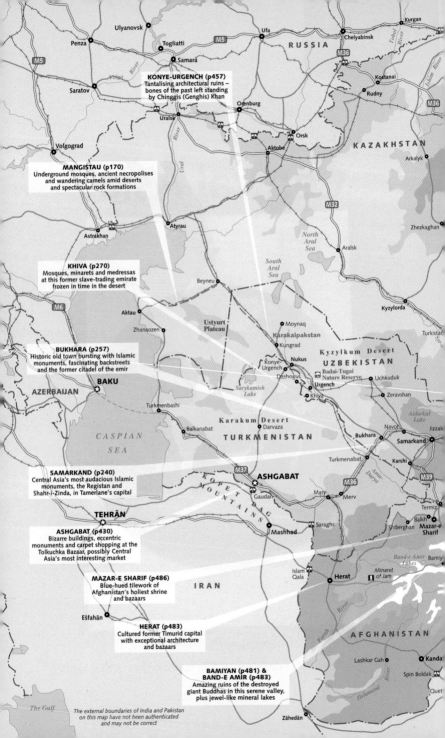

KONYE-URGENCH (p457)
Tantalising architectural ruins –
bones of the past left standing
by Chinggis (Genghis) Khan

MANGISTAU (p170)
Underground mosques, ancient necropolises
and wandering camels amid deserts
and spectacular rock formations

KHIVA (p270)
Mosques, minarets and medressas
at this former slave-trading emirate
frozen in time in the desert

BUKHARA (p257)
Historic old town bursting with Islamic
monuments, fascinating backstreets
and the former citadel of the emir

SAMARKAND (p240)
Central Asia's most audacious Islamic
monuments, the Registan and
Shahr-i-Zinda, in Tamerlane's capital

ASHGABAT (p430)
Bizarre buildings, eccentric
monuments and carpet shopping at the
Tolkuchka Bazaar, possibly Central
Asia's most interesting market

MAZAR-E SHARIF (p486)
Blue-hued tilework of
Afghanistan's holiest shrine
and bazaars

HERAT (p483)
Cultured former Timurid capital
with exceptional architecture
and bazaars

**BAMIYAN (p481) &
BAND-E AMIR (p483)**
Amazing ruins of the destroyed
giant Buddhas in this serene valley,
plus jewel-like mineral lakes

The external boundaries of India and Pakistan
on this map have not been authenticated
and may not be correct

ASTANA (p172)
Spectacular 21st-century architecture in Kazakhstan's booming new capital

**KOCHKOR (p335) &
SONG-KÖL (p339)**
Hire horses, stay in yurts and live the nomad life on the high pastures

ALMATY (p126)
Booming, cosmopolitan city, with fine mountain scenery just an hour outside the city

INYLCHEK GLACIER (p334)
A long trek or short helicopter flight to outrageous views of Khan Tengri, one of the world's most beautiful peaks

AROUND KARAKOL (p325)
Lovely alpine scenery, mountain pastures and fine trekkinhg a stone's throw from Lake Issyk-Köl

**TORUGART PASS (p346) &
IRKESHTAM PASS (p362)**
The most exciting mountain routes into Central Asia

FAN MOUNTAINS (p396)
Great trekking past a string of turquoise mountain lakes

PAMIR HIGHWAY (p411)
One of the world's classic road trips, past sublime high-altitude scenery

WAKHAN VALLEY (p488)
Silk Road forts, high altitude treks and views of the Hindu Kush in this spectacular valley shared by Afghanistan and Tajikistan

ELEVATION

7000m
5000m
3000m
1000m
500m
200m
0m

LEGEND

Freeway
Primary Road
Secondary Road
Tertiary Road
Unsealed Road

0   300 km
0   180 miles

On the Road

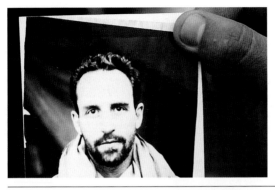

BRADLEY MAYHEW
Coordinating Author
After reading about Afghanistan for close to 20 years, the biggest thrill of this trip was finally making it there. Watching traditional glass-makers in Herat (p483), following my armed guard along the city walls of Balkh (p487) and making the beautiful overland trip through Afghan Badakhshan (p494) were moments to treasure. This photo was taken in Faizabad by an old-school portrait photographer.

MICHAEL KOHN The month of August is bloody hot in Kyrgyzstan and I was relieved to finally reach the cool mountain retreat of Arslanbob (p352). I am sitting at a chaikhana perched over the white-water stream that rushes through town. My travel mate and I had just ordered up some *plov* (pilaf) and chai; one of the best meals I had in Kyrgyzstan.

GREG BLOOM At the door of Bukhara's 'second' synagogue, I was greeted by the rabbi's adorable granddaughters, quite possibly the last of Bukhara's Bukhara Jews (p262). With their frocks, cardigans and leggings, they appeared to have stepped right out of a 19th-century photograph. The elder took this with my 21st-century camera.

JOHN NOBLE Kazakhstan has just one work of classic old Central Asian architecture, the Yasaui Mausoleum (p158) at Turkistan. The beauty of its Timurid tilework is a real lift.

PAUL CLAMMER The first sight of the Band-e Amir lakes (p483) robs your breath. In a land the colour of dust, it beggars belief that anything could be deeply blue. But it's a truly Afghan blue too, confirming what the ancients always knew: this country should be the source of the world's lapis lazuli. *(Reflections from an earlier trip.)*

For full author biographies see p548

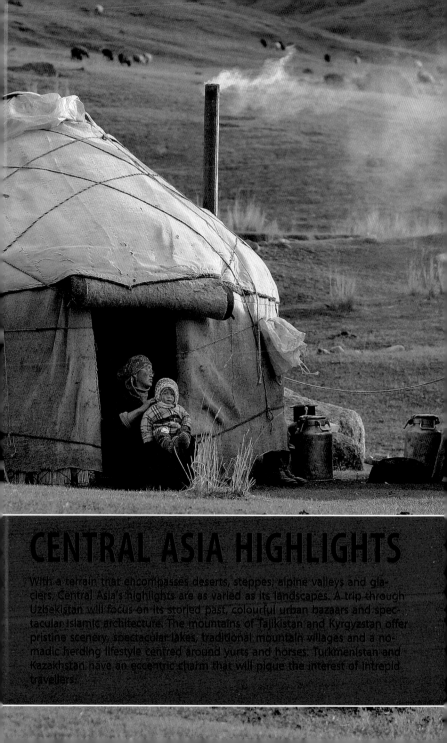

CENTRAL ASIA HIGHLIGHTS

With a terrain that encompasses deserts, steppes, alpine valleys and glaciers, Central Asia's highlights are as varied as its landscapes. A trip through Uzbekistan will focus on its storied past, colourful urban bazaars and spectacular Islamic architecture. The mountains of Tajikistan and Kyrgyzstan offer pristine scenery, spectacular lakes, traditional mountain villages and a nomadic herding lifestyle centred around yurts and horses. Turkmenistan and Kazakhstan have an eccentric charm that will pique the interest of intrepid travellers.

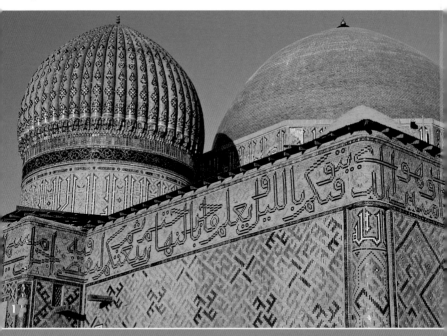

ARCHITECTURE

Central Asia's architectural gems owe everything to its shared Persian heritage. From the Timurid blue domes and tilework of Samarkand and Herat to the urban ensembles of Bukhara and Khiva, nothing connects Central Asia to its past like its magnificent buildings.

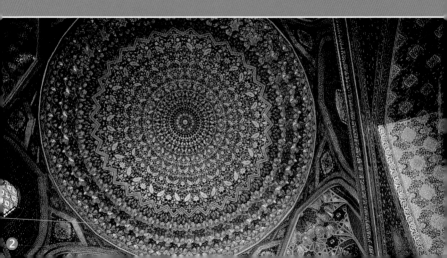

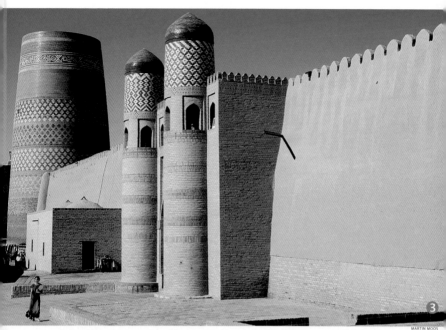

MARTIN MOOS

❶ Yasaui Mausoleum, Turkistan, Kazakhstan

Easily Kazakhstan's most beautiful building (p158), this Timurid-era Sufi shrine is a rare architectural gem in a land ruled by restless nomads.

❷ Registan, Samarkand, Uzbekistan

Not one but three massive medressas (p243) make this the most spectacular ensemble in Central Asia. Climb the corkscrew minarets for awesome views over Timur's showcase city.

❸ Khiva's Ichon-Qala, Uzbekistan

The former khanate of Khiva (p272) is an entire walled city of traditional architecture, frozen in time in the desert wastes of the Karakum. Royal palaces, blue-tiled tombs and mud-baked city walls recall a slave-trading past.

❹ Kalon Minaret, Bukhara, Uzbekistan

This towering minaret (p261) stopped Chinggis (Genghis) Khan in his tracks 800 years ago; chances are the beautiful brickwork, impressive mosque and neighbouring blue-domed medressa will do the same to you.

❺ Shah-i-Zinda, Samarkand, Uzbekistan

Central Asia's head-spinning turquoise-blue Timurid tilework doesn't get any better than this spectacular street of royal tombs (p244).

❻ Lyabi-Hauz, Bukhara, Uzbekistan

Gentrification has cleaned up this gorgeous plaza around a pool (p259) but the teahouse is still one of the nicest places in Central Asia to adapt to the chaikhana pace of life.

❼ Gur-e-Amir Mausoleum, Samarkand, Uzbekistan

Timur's resting place (p244) is a suitably beautiful construction, from the floating ribbed dome to Timur's jade tombstone.

❽ Shrine of Hazrat Ali, Mazar-e Sharif, Afghanistan

Dazzling chocolate-box tilework, holy white doves and open-air evening prayers make Mazar's holiest shrine (p486) a pilgrimage site of peace and power.

❾ Herat, Afghanistan

Herat (p483) is arguably Afghanistan's most beautiful city, packing an architectural double shot with the stunning Friday Mosque and the massive and magnificently restored citadel.

CULTURE & TRADITION ON THE SILK ROAD

From the sublime to the ridiculous, it's the daily details of travel in Central Asia that quickly get under the skin. From chaikhanas and carpet shops to the ubiquitous taste of mutton kebabs, these are the ingredients from which Silk Road dreams are made.

CHRISTOPHER HERWIG

❶ Shashlyk

The ever-present roadside grills define travel across Central Asia. A round of kebabs served up with hot nan bread and a generous portion of fat and grease is the classic culinary experience.

❷ Bazaars

Haggling for carpets, camels or car parts is perhaps the quintessential Central Asian activity. Ashgabat (p435), Samarkand (p249), Khojand (p390), Andijon (p240) and Urgut (pictured; p250) all have epic markets.

❸ Fragrant melons and golden peaches

Central Asian bazaars groan with ripe fruit in July and August. From the world's best melons and peaches to *kishmish* grapes and fresh mulberries, it's a summertime delight.

❹ Chaikhana culture

Central Asia without teahouses (p89) is like Britain without pubs. Recline on a shady tea bed and join the white-bearded locals in conversation over a reviving pot of green tea.

❺ Tash Rabat, Kyrgyzstan

Kyrgyzstan's superbly remote Tash Rabat (Stone Caravanserai; p346) epitomises the romance of the Silk Road. Set high in the Tian Shan, it offered shelter to traders and caravans for centuries.

MARTIN MOOS

❻ Carpets

Souvenirs don't get classier than a Bukhara-style Central Asia carpet. Turkmenistan (p435) and Afghanistan (p492) are the best places for serious carpet shoppers.

❼ Blue burqas

The light-blue shuttlecock shape of a woman's burqa has come to define Afghanistan, the only place in Central Asia where you'll see sizeable numbers of women veiled.

ACTIVITIES

Central Asia offers adventurers some of the world's great trekking, biking and mountaineering. This isn't Nepal – expect to work for your adventure or employ a local company for logistical support – but once here there's an excellent chance you'll have the spectacular mountain valleys, yurt camps and snowy peaks to yourself.

ANDREW PEACOCK

❶ Horse Trekking
Kyrgyzstan is the prime place to saddle up and trek out to summer pastures, mountain lakes and remote yurt camps, such as Sarala-Saz (pictured; p339), but Tajikistan and Turkmenistan also offer equestrian adventures (p108).

❷ Hiking
The mountains of Kyrgyzstan (such as the Ak-Say Canyon, pictured; p313), southern Kazakhstan and Tajikistan offer fantastic hiking (p108), from lake-studded valleys to rich walnut forests, sometimes just a few miles from the capital city.

❸ Cycling the Silk Road
Whether you decide to pedal the desert road to Samarkand or the tough (but paved) Pamir Hwy (pictured), be prepared for the two-wheeled adventure of a lifetime (p110).

❹ Fan Mountains
Tajikistan's prime trekking destination (p397) is a stone's throw from Samarkand and offers spectacular turquoise lakes, homestays and mountain meadows.

❺ Climbing
Central Asia offers the highest peaks outside the Himalayas. Experts will aim for stunning Khan Tengri (7010m) or Pik Lenin (7134m), but easier options abound in the valleys south of Bishkek and Almaty. See p110.

❻ Heli-skiing
Soviet choppers can drop you atop mountains (p112) of pristine dry powder for dream downhills far away from a lift queue or even a marked run. Tashkent (p230) and Bishkek (p314) are the main centres.

❼ Trekking the Tian Shan
The town of Karakol in Kyrgyzstan is the gateway to lush forested valleys, rushing streams and snowcapped Alpine peaks (p323), with classic treks lasting from two days to a week.

❽ Jeeping the Pamir Hwy
One of the world's great road trips, Tajikistan's Pamir Hwy (p411) takes you across the roof of the world, past epic views, sky-blue lakes and remote Kyrgyz yurt camps.

TOP: MOSAFER/ALAMY / BOTTOM: BRADLEY MAYHEW

NOMADIC TRADITIONS

Mosques and minarets are only half the story in Central Asia. Horses have dominated the region for millennia and to really get to grips with the nomadic past you have to saddle up, and ride out to a yurt for a taste of the freshest yoghurt you've ever had.

CHRISTOPHER HERWIG

❶ Eagle Hunting
It's hunting *with* eagles, not *of* eagles, that truly recalls Central Asia's nomadic past. Several places in Kyrgyzstan offer a close-up look or come in winter for an authentic hunt (p332).

❷ Buzkashi
Imagine a game of rugby, on horseback, with a decapitated goat's corpse instead of a ball (p64). From Kyrgyz pastures to the Afghan steppe, you'll need spare camera batteries.

❸ Overnight in a yurt
Big on midnight stars and low on indoor plumbing, a yurtstay (p498) is a quintessential inner Asian experience, whether a remote Pamiri herder's camp or a Kazakh-style yurt in the Karakum desert.

❹ Afghan Wakhan Valley
The Afghan side of the Wakhan Corridor (p488) ranks as one of the most remote and beautiful spots on earth, where Central Asia's most traditional lifestyles remain largely untouched

7/3/11

*915
.8
MAY*

Contents

Regional Map Contents

Destination

For decades – centuries even – much of the world has regarded Central Asia as little more than a blank on the map, synonymous not with the centre of Asia but with the middle of nowhere. Yet for two millennia, the deserts, grasslands, oases and mountain ranges between the Caspian Sea and China were a thoroughfare for Silk Road traders, nomadic empires and migrating invaders, tying together Europe and Asia on the Eurasian steppes.

Central Asia's storybook history, from Alexander the Great to the khans of Khiva, litters the land at every turn. At times the storied caravan stops of Samarkand and Bukhara, with their exotic skyline of minarets and medressas, seem lifted directly from the days of Marco Polo and Chinggis (Genghis) Khan. Even today you'll get powerful whiff of the Silk Road downwind of an Uzbek kebab seller and glimpse a hint of a nomadic past in the eyes of a Kazakh businessman.

East of the desert and steppe rise the snowcapped Pamirs and Tian Shan mountains of Kyrgyzstan and Tajikistan, hosting fantastic trekking and mountain adventures. Community-based tourism projects bring you face to face with nomadic Kyrgyz herders, meeting them in their yurts and on their terms. The region's little-visited oddities, namely Turkmenistan and parts of Kazakhstan, offer an offbeat interest all of their own.

For the people of ex-Soviet Central Asia it's been a turbulent 20 years since independence. Since then the Central Asian republics have forged differing paths, but have shared many challenges. All have grappled with economic collapse, population shifts and resurgent Islam and have re-invented their past, rehabilitated historical heroes and reinforced their national languages in an attempt to redefine and shore up what it means to be Central Asian.

But there are major differences. Turkmenistan and Kazakhstan are the only republics which seem to have bright economic possibilities – sitting pretty on enormous reserves of oil and gas. Tajikistan is the only one which has experienced the horror of civil war, whereas the others are all in dread that they will be next to succumb to Islamic fundamentalism and political meltdown. Uzbekistan and Turkmenistan have faced this challenge by sliding into pariah states, where political abductions, torture and trumped-up charges are commonplace.

Tensions persist among the claims of Central Asian fraternity. Disputes over water, electricity and gas supplies bubble under the surface and the lack of regional trust means that big issues such as the Aral Sea, the drug trade and economic cooperation don't even make it on to the table. All are destabilised to some extent by Afghanistan's political instability to the south. With Afghan poppy lords churning out 90% of the world's heroin, it's no surprise that drug smuggling and soaring rates of domestic drug use are a particular regional problem.

But it's not all political dictatorships and economic hardship. After the confusion and social turmoil of the 1990s life has settled for many Central Asians. Economies are finally growing and standards of living are gradually rising. Grassroots community tourism projects are flourishing in much of the region. International crossings have been retied with China, Afghanistan and Iran, opening up new opportunities for both trade and tourism and retying the region to the rest of the world.

Investment and nationalism are reshaping the very face of Central Asia. Cities across the region have been brought up to date by the arrival of

'Central Asia's storybook history, from Alexander the Great to the khans of Khiva, litters the land at every turn'

Turkish supermarkets, new restaurants and international standard hotels and Kazakhstan has built an entire new capital, Astana, from scratch.

All this reflects the redrawing of Central Asia. Where once Tashkent and Ashgabat looked north to distant Moscow for economic and political direction, modern Central Asians now turn also to China, Turkey, Iran, Europe and the US, all of whom are equally intent on redefining spheres of influence long blocked by the Iron Curtain. The US-led War on Terror has only raised the stakes in a geopolitical game that stretches from transcontinental gas pipelines to Islamic extremism.

In many ways Afghanistan remains the odd man out in this book's coverage of Central Asia. Never a part of the Soviet Union, its recent history has been tied to 30 years of relentless conflict, from the Soviet invasion and ensuing civil war to Taliban rule, political turmoil puts the country out of reach to most visitors. When travellers are able to return, they will find Timurid architecture to rival Samarkand, mountain beauty to match the Pamirs and a rich culture that has much in common with ethnic kin to the north.

As Central Asia's new economic and cultural ties strengthen, oil routes open and Silk Roads are redrawn, this little-understood region will undoubtedly become increasingly important to the security, economy and politics of Russia, Asia and the world beyond. The challenge for the governments of Central Asia is to meet the religious, secular and economic desires of its people, while treading the tightrope between authoritarianism and Islamisation.

Whether you want to explore the architectural gems of Bukhara or horse trek across the high Pamirs, the region once known as Transoxiana, Turkestan or Tartary offers something for everyone. And everywhere you'll be greeted with instinctive local hospitality, offering a shared meal, a helping hand or a place to stay. Add to this the intrinsic fascination of a forgotten region fast emerging as a geopolitical pivot point and you have one of Asia's most absorbing and hidden corners.

'Everywhere you'll be greeted with instinctive local hospitality, offering a shared meal, a helping hand or a place to stay'

Getting Started

Central Asia isn't the easiest place to travel through. You'll need to invest some serious time tracking down visas, permits and the latest travel information, preferably months before you depart. You won't meet crowds of travellers on the road and there are certainly no video cafes serving banana muesli. But for a certain type of traveller this is all part of the attraction of a land that has been largely off-limits to travellers for the last 2000 years.

Yet, two decades after independence, travel is generally getting easier every year, with ever-improving accommodation options from boutique B&Bs to rural homestays, vastly improved food and a network of shared taxis that will shuttle you around cheaply and in relative comfort. Do your research on Central Asia's epic history in particular and you'll find the region quickly addictive. The more you put in, the more you'll get out of this Asian heartland.

WHEN TO GO

Central Asia has an extreme continental climate, resulting in burning hot summers and freezing cold winters. At lower elevations spring and autumn are the overall best seasons, in particular April to early June and September through October. In March/April the desert blooms briefly and the monotonous ochre landscapes of Turkmenistan, Uzbekistan and Kazakhstan become a Jackson Pollock canvas of reds, oranges and yellows. Late summer is maximum harvest time, when market tables heave with freshly picked fruit.

Summer (mid-June to early September) is ferociously hot in the lowlands of Tajikistan, Uzbekistan, Turkmenistan and Afghanistan, with sizzling cities and desert temperatures as high as 40°C or more. July through August is the best time to visit the mountains of Kyrgyzstan, Tajikistan and southeast Kazakhstan, and to trek (earlier and later than that, herders and other summer residents will have returned to the lowlands).

Winters (November to March) are bitterly cold everywhere, especially in the mountains but also in the desert. Snow starts to fall in November and mountain passes fill with snow until April or even May. Even Bishkek and Almaty might have snow in April. Northern Kazakhstan is comfortable right through the summer but freezes in the sub-Siberian winter.

See Climate Charts (p499) for more information.

For more details see the Climate and When to Go sections of the individual country chapters.

You might want to time your visit with the region's two major celebrations – Navrus (around 21 March) and the various independence days (around September/October). See the Holiday sections in each country's Directory for specific dates.

COSTS & MONEY

By travelling with a friend, staying in homestays, eating in chaikhana (teahouses) and hiring the odd taxi when there is no public transport, you can

---

ALL CHANGE

Please note that travel details in Central Asia change frequently and without warning. Central Asian embassies shift location like restless nomads, visa regulations change with the wind and transport rates oscillate wildly with the price of petrol and supply of vehicles. Expect prices for all things in this guide to jump (or even fall) each year; rates in this book, especially for transport, are therefore an indication rather than absolute values.

get around Central Asia for around US$15 to US$20 per person per day (more like US$25 to US$45 in Kazakhstan). For a minimum of comfort you'll probably have to part with US$20 for a hotel in bigger towns. In order of expense, the cheapest countries are Kyrgyzstan, Uzbekistan, Tajikistan, Kazakhstan and (most expensive) Turkmenistan. Budget accommodation costs are highest in Kazakhstan, transport costs are highest in the Pamirs of Tajikistan.

You can shave down costs by eating in bazaars, staying in private homes and the occasional bottom-end place, sharing hotel rooms with other travellers, getting around town by local bus instead of taxi and spending less time in (expensive) cities.

Trekking trips start at around US$100 per person per day with professional trekking agencies but you can arrange a trip for a fraction of this through community tourism organisations such as Community Based Tourism (CBT) in Kyrgyzstan (p302) and Murgab Ecotourism Association (META) in the Pamir region of Tajikistan (p414).

For midrange travel in Uzbekistan, you'll be looking at spending US$15 to US$30 per person for a stylish B&B; throw in US$10 per day for taxi hire between towns. Where there are any, four-star hotels in Central Asia are fairly poor value at around US$100 per double.

Don't forget to factor in visa and permit costs, which can mount up, and of course long-haul transport to get you to and from Central Asia.

Money is best brought in a combination of cash in US dollars (perhaps around two-thirds of your funds), a credit card (and PIN) and a few emergency travellers cheques (which are the least useful form of currency in this destination).

TRAVEL LITERATURE

See the boxed texts at the start of the individual country chapters for recommended books on specific republics.

Lonely Planet's coverage of neighbouring countries includes *China; Pakistan & the Karakoram Highway; Iran; Georgia, Armenia & Azerbaijan; Trans-Siberian Railway;* and *Russia*. Lonely Planet also produces a dedicated *Central Asia* phrasebook.

Beyond the Oxus; Archaeology, Art & Architecture of Central Asia by Edgar Knobloch is an oddly appealing book for a specialist cultural and architectural history of Central Asia (including Afghanistan), perhaps because it's so rich in all the background information, reconstructions, floor-plans and close-ups that nobody in Central Asia seems to know about any more.

The Great Game by Peter Hopkirk is a fast-paced, very readable history of the Great Game – the 19th-century cold war between Britain and Russia – as it unfolded across Europe and Asia. It's carried along in Hopkirk's trademark style, in a series of personal stories – all men, all Westerners, all resolute and

---

TRAVELLING SAFELY IN CENTRAL ASIA

In general Central Asia is a pretty safe place to travel despite the media's presentation of the region as a hot spot of environmental disaster, human rights violations and Islamic insurgency. The main exception to this is Afghanistan, where travel is currently not advised (see the boxed text on p469). And in 2010 the political situation in Kyrgyzstan was particularly volatile – see p295.

Most travellers eventually come face to face with crooked officials, particularly policemen, as checks are endemic throughout the region. You shouldn't have any problems as long as your documents are in tip-top shape. You will find general advice on travelling safely on p500, with specific country information in the Directory section of each individual country chapter.

DON'T LEAVE HOME WITHOUT...

- A fistful of visas (see p510 and the Visas sections of the individual country chapters) and plans set in motion for any travel permits (p510) you might need

- The latest government travel warnings (p501), plus a small pinch of salt

- A sun hat, sunglasses and sunscreen for the strong desert and mountain sun, plus a torch (flashlight) for overcoming iffy electricity supplies and toilet trips in the countryside

- Water purification – if you plan to trek or get off the beaten track

- Floss – to get the mutton out from between your teeth

- A sleeping bag – very useful in winter or for rural Kyrgyzstan and Tajikistan in summer

- Mementos from home (eg postcards and photos) and gifts to help break the ice at homestays and yurtstays

- Long, baggy, nonrevealing clothes. These will win you friends in Islamic Central Asia, particularly in rural areas. Central Asia is not the place to get a suntan. See p70.

- A Russian phrasebook and a paperback novel – there are very few English-language bookshops in Central Asia

- A good insurance policy, especially if headed to Afghanistan (p492)

square-jawed, with Victoria Crosses for everybody – real *Boys' Own* stuff; melodramatic, but essentially true.

Setting the East Ablaze, also by Peter Hopkirk, takes up where *The Great Game* stops – a gripping cloak-and-dagger history of the murderous early years of Soviet power in Central Asia, and communist efforts to spread revolution to British India and China.

The Lost Heart of Asia by our favourite travel writer Colin Thubron is a worthwhile read – the author is deservedly praised for his careful research, first-hand explorations, delicate observations and baroque prose. *Shadow of the Silk Road* is Thubron's follow-up a decade later, covering a transcontinental trip from Xi'an to Antioch, via Kyrgyzstan, Uzbekistan and Afghanistan.

From the Peter Hopkirk school of history, *Tournament of Shadows* by Karl Meyer looks at some lesser-known Great Game characters and brings the game up to date with the present scramble for oil in the Caspian Sea. A modern regional follow-up by the same author is *Dust of Empire.*

Inside Central Asia, by Dilip Hiro, is the most up-to-date and accessible political portrait of modern Central Asia, starting from the arrival of the Russians and then proceeding separately with each of the independent ex-Soviet republics. A fine introduction to the region.

Of the dozens of wonderful antique travelogues dealing with Central Asia, one of the most accessible is *Turkestan Solo: A Journey Through Central Asia* by Ella Maillart, an account of the indomitable Swiss traveller's forays around Kyrgyzstan and Uzbekistan in the 1930s, which has been reprinted in paperback.

By contrast, *Silk Road to Ruin* by Ted Rall is a rollicking, subversive and satirical portrait of the region that is part travelogue, part graphic novel. It's fresh and edgy and neatly captures the realities of travel in the region.

If you fancy some fiction, try Tom Bissell's *God Lives in St Petersburg,* a collection of six well-crafted short stories set in Samarkand, Tashkent, Kazakhstan and Kyrgyzstan. Also check out Uzbekistani author Hamid Ismailov's novel *The Railway* (see p81) or something by the Kyrgyz writer Chinghiz Aitmatov (p296). Pack Dostoyevsky's hefty *The Brothers*

'STANS AT A GLANCE

Afghanistan The 'Crossroads of Asia', fractured by 30 years of almost continual war. Central Asian–style cities like Herat and Mazar-e Sharif in the north, spectacular mountain scenery in northeastern Badakhshan and turbulent Pashtun areas in the south and east. Check the security situation.

Kazakhstan One of the last great blanks on the map, with interesting and quirky sites separated by vast amounts of nothing. Good hiking in the southeast and increasingly popular ecotourism options. Sub-Siberian Russian cities and steppe in the north.

Kyrgyzstan Vowel-challenged republic of Alpine mountains, yurts and high pastures. The best place in Central Asia for hiking and horse riding. Community tourism programs and a wide network of homestays give you a grass-roots adventure on the cheap. Plus it'll give you a gazillion points at Scrabble.

Tajikistan The region's most outlandish high-altitude scenery, home to Central Asia's best road trip, the stunning Pamir Hwy. Fabulous trekking, the region's most humbling hospitality and the gateway to the Afghan Wakhan Corridor. This is the cutting edge of adventure travel.

Turkmenistan The 'North Korea of Central Asia'. Hard to get into (tourist visas require you to hire a guide) but a real curiosity once you are there, not least for the bizarre personality cult of former president Turkmenbashi. Reforms following the death of President Niyazov in December 2006 have been glacially slow.

Uzbekistan Home to historic Silk Road cities, epic Islamic architecture and the region's most stylish private guest houses. The shashlyk-scented heart of Central Asia. Don't miss it.

Karamazov for the long train trip up to Semey in northeastern Kazakhstan, where the author served in the army for five years and began his famous novel.

There are dozens of suburb travelogues on Afghanistan (see p474). If we were limited to just one it would be Jason Elliot's beautiful and moving modern classic *An Unexpected Light: Travels in Afghanistan.*

INTERNET RESOURCES

Some of the best Central Asian websites are those of the major local travel agencies (see p511), Central Asian embassies abroad (also on p511) and US embassies in Central Asia.

For country-specific sites see the Internet Resources headings in the relevant country Directories.

Abandon the Cube (www.abandonthecube.com) Good travel blog covering Uzbekistan, Turkmenistan and southern Kazakhstan, amongst others.

Asie-centrale (www.asie-centrale.com, in French) News, cultural articles and general tourist information.

Central Asia News (www.centralasianews.net) Regional news service.

Discovery Central Asia (www.centralasia.travel) Engaging website of regional publishers, full of interesting articles and cultural details from across Central Asia.

EurasiaNet (www.eurasianet.org) News and cultural articles, with resource pages for each country.

Ferghana.ru (www.ferghana.ru) Regional news service.

Jamestown Foundation (www.jamestown.org) Another good site for Central Asian political analysis and news; click on the 'Eurasia Daily Monitor'.

Lonely Planet (www.lonelyplanet.com/thorntree) The dedicated Central Asia branch of the Thorn Tree forum is one of the best places anywhere to get up-to-date info on visas, border crossings and more.

Oriental Express Central Asia (www.orexca.com) Lots to explore in this virtual travel guide focusing on Uzbekistan, Kyrgyzstan and Kazakhstan.

Pamirs (www.pamirs.org) Superb travel site with up-to-date travel information on the Pamir mountain range of Tajikistan.

Radio Free Europe/Radio Liberty (www.rferl.org) Click on 'News by Country' for a range of interesting reports. There's also a weekly news report on Central Asia at http://rfe.rferl.org/reports/centralasia/, which you can get by email.

Silk Road Seattle (http://depts.washington.edu/uwch/silkroad) Online maps, virtual art collections, historical texts and articles on traditional culture, architecture and anything else Silk Road–related.

Silk Road Society (www.travelthesilkroad.org) Book reviews, travel information and links to the online *Open Central Asia* magazine (www.ocamagazine.com). You need to be a member, which is free.

Turkic Republics & Communities (www.khazaria.com/turkic/index.html) Music, books and excellent links for the entire Turkic world.

There are many good political blogs on Central Asia. Our favourites include:

New Eurasia (www.neweurasia.net) Great collection of Central Asia bloggers.

Registan.net (www.registan.net) News and views on Central Asia, including Afghanistan.

Roberts Report (www.roberts-report.com) Biting political blog from US Central Asia expert Sean Roberts, with an emphasis on Kazakhstan.

World Affairs Blog Network (http://centralasia.foreignpolicyblogs.com) Current affairs.

TRAVELLING RESPONSIBLY

Tourism is still relatively new to Central Asia, so please try to keep your impact as low as possible and create a good precedent for those who follow you.

One of the best ways to ensure your tourist dollars make it into the right hands is to support community tourism projects, such as CBT (p302) in Kyrgyzstan, META (p414) in Tajikistan and several programs in Kazakhstan

---

PERSONAL HIGHS & LOWS OF CENTRAL ASIA *Bradley Mayhew*

Favourites

- Sitting in a teahouse with a cold Tian-Shansky beer, kebabs and hot nan bread – magic!
- Shared taxis, when you score the front seat.
- Finally crossing the Torugart Pass. Yes!
- A crowd of white-bearded *aksakals* (literally 'white beard', revered elders) resplendent in stripy cloaks and turbans.
- Turquoise-blue domes and mesmerising Timurid tilework.
- Trekking, almost anywhere.
- Central Asian handshakes, with a slight bow and a hand on the heart.
- Overnighting in a yurt in Kyrgyzstan or Tajikistan or a traditional courtyard house in Uzbekistan.
- Central Asian melons and grapes, and Kyrgyz *kaimak* (sweet cream) and honey (for breakfast).

Pet Peeves

- The taste of congealed mutton fat on the roof of your mouth.
- Local bus trips that take seven hours to go 100km, or Soviet-era taxis that require stream water every 200m to cool the engine.
- Getting turned back at the Torugart or Qolma Passes.
- Aggressive drunks who think you are Russian.
- Soviet hotel architecture.
- Pugnacious 'Bride of Frankenstein' receptionists with dyed cherry-red hair, all mysteriously called Svetlana.
- The fifth vodka toast to 'international friendship', with the sixth lined up behind it…
- Visa hassles and *militsia* (police) checks.
- The smell of Soviet-era canteens and finding there's nothing on the menu. Except goulash. Again.

(see p125). Elsewhere try to engage local services and guides whenever possible and choose companies that follow ecofriendly practice (eg Ecotour in Bishkek, see p304).

The following are a few tips for responsible travel:

- Be respectful of Islamic traditions and don't wear singlets, shorts or short skirts in rural areas or the Fergana Valley.
- Don't hand out sweets or pens to children on the streets, since it encourages begging. Similarly, doling out medicines can encourage people not to seek proper medical advice. A donation to a project, health centre or school is a far more constructive way to help.
- You can do more good by buying your snacks, cigarettes, bubble gum etc from the enterprising grannies trying to make ends meet rather than from state-run stores.
- Don't buy items made from endangered species, such as Marco Polo sheep and snow leopards. Don't accept Marco Polo sheep meat in the Pamirs.
- Don't pay to take a photo of someone and don't photograph someone if they don't want you to. If you agree to send someone a photo, make sure you follow through with it.
- Discourage the use of scarce fuels such as firewood and *tersken* (high-altitude bush) in the eastern Pamirs (see p380).
- If someone offers to put you up for the night make sure you don't put your host under financial burdens. Don't let them sacrifice an animal in your honour (common in the Pamirs) and try to offer money or a gift in return for your host's hospitality. See also p70 for more hints on responsible travel and p90 for cultural tips on visiting someone's house or sharing a meal.
- Don't let your driver drive too close to archaeological sites and try to stick to existing tracks when driving off road.
- Try to give people a balanced perspective of life in the West. Point out that you are only temporarily rich in Central Asia and that income and costs balance out in Amsterdam just as they do in Almaty. Try also to highlight the strong points of the local culture – strong family ties, comparatively low crime etc.
- Make yourself aware of the human rights situation in the countries you travel through; don't travel blindly.

Itineraries
CLASSIC ROUTES

SILK ROAD CITIES OF UZBEKISTAN   10 to 14 Days

Fly into **Tashkent** (p212) and get a feel for the big city before taking a domestic flight to Urgench and then a short bus or taxi ride to **Khiva** (p270), comfortably seen in a day. Then take a taxi for an overnight trip to one or two of the desert cities of **ancient Khorezm** (p270), around Urgench.

From Urgench take the long bus or taxi ride down to **Bukhara** (p257), which deserves the most time of all the Silk Road cities. Try to budget a minimum of three days to take in the sights and explore the backstreets.

From here take the golden (actually tarmac) road to **Samarkand** (p240) for a day or two. Soak in the glories of the Registan and Shah-i-Zinda and, if you have time, add on a day trip to **Shakhrisabz** (p251), the birthplace of Timur (Tamerlane).

An alternative to this route is to tack on Turkmenistan, visiting **Konye-Urgench** (p457) from Khiva before crossing the desert to **Ashgabat** (p430) and then travelling to Bukhara via the Mausoleum of Sultan Sanjar at **Merv** (p451).

This loop route through Uzbekistan and Turkmenistan, starting and finishing in Tashkent, is a historical and architectural tour that links Central Asia's most popular tourist sites. You'll need at least 14 days if you tack on Turkmenistan.

OVER THE TORUGART – LAKES, HERDERS & CARAVANSERAIS   Two Weeks

This trip takes in fabulous mountain scenery, a taste of life in the pastures and the roller-coaster ride over the Torugart Pass to Kashgar. There are lots of opportunities for trekking or horse riding on this route.

From easy-going **Bishkek** (p298) head east to the blue waters and sandy beaches of **Issyk-Köl** (p315), the world's second-largest alpine lake. Take in a couple of days' trekking or visiting the alpine valleys around **Karakol** (p320). The idyllic valley of **Altyn Arashan** (p326) offers great scope for horse riding or a short trek to alpine Ala-Köl and the glorious Karakol Valley. If you have time you can explore the little-visited southern shore en route to Kochkor. If you are low on time head straight to Kochkor from Bishkek.

In small and sleepy **Kochkor** (p335) take advantage of the Community Based Tourism (CBT) program and spend some time in a yurt or homestay on the surrounding *jailoos* (summer pastures). This is one of the best ways to glimpse traditional life in Kyrgyzstan. Try to allow three days to link a couple of yurtstays by horse, although most can be visited in an overnight trip. The most popular trip is to the herders' camps around the peaceful lake **Song-Köl** (p339), either by car or on a two-day horseback trip. The pastures are popular with herders and their animals between June and August.

From here head to **Naryn** (p340) and then the Silk Road caravanserai of **Tash Rabat** (p346), where you can stay overnight in yurts and even take a difficult horse trip to a pass overlooking Chatyr-Köl. From Tash Rabat it's up over the Torugart Pass *(insha'Allah)* to wonderful Kashgar.

If you want to experience traditional life in the high pastures while enjoying stunning scenery, take this trip through Kyrgyzstan from Bishkek to Kashgar, over the Torugart Pass.

CENTRAL ASIA OVERLAND – THE SILK ROAD   Three Weeks

There are dozens of different route options for traversing Central Asia. Much of this itinerary follows ancient Silk Road paths.

Western roads into Central Asia lead from Mashhad in Iran to Ashgabat in Turkmenistan, or from Baku in Azerbaijan (by boat) to Turkmenbashi, also in Turkmenistan. If you only have a three-day transit visa for Turkmenistan you can travel from Mashhad to Mary (to visit the World Heritage-listed ruins of Merv) in one long day via the crossing at Saraghs, giving you more time at Merv and bypassing Ashgabat.

From **Ashgabat** (p430) the overland route leads to **Merv** (p451) and the Silk Road cities of **Bukhara** (p257), **Samarkand** (p240) and **Tashkent** (p212). From here head into the Fergana Valley and swing north along the main road to relaxed **Bishkek** (p298). From Bishkek cross the border into Kazakhstan to cosmopolitan **Almaty** (p126) and make some excursions from the city before taking the train (or bus) to Ürümqi in China.

An alternative from Bishkek is to arrange transport to take you over the **Torugart Pass** (p346) visiting the *jailoos* around **Kochkor** (p335) and Song-Köl and the caravanserai at **Tash Rabat** (p346), before crossing the pass to Kashgar. You can then continue down into Pakistan to join the main overland trail into India and Nepal.

A third alternative if you are in a hurry is to travel from Tashkent to Andijon, cross the border to **Osh** (p356) and then take a bus or a combination of bus and taxi over the **Irkeshtam Pass** (p361) to Kashgar.

The trip from Mashhad/Baku to Ürümqi/Kashgar fits nicely into an overland route from the Middle East to Asia. Much of this trip follows ancient Silk Road paths and can be completed in three weeks.

SAMARKAND TO OSH VIA THE PAMIR HWY   Three Weeks

Take in the architectural glories of **Samarkand** (p240) before taking a shared taxi across the border into Tajikistan. Check out the Sogdian archaeological site of **Penjikent** (p393) and then either hire a car for a day trip up to the Marguzor Lakes or arrange a taxi through the mountains to scenic lake **Iskander-Kul** (p396).

Continue the taxi ride through stunning vertical scenery to Tajikistan's mellow capital **Dushanbe** (p381), where you should budget a day or two to arrange the flight, shared jeep, or hired car for the long but impressive trip along the Afghan border to **Khorog** (p404) in Gorno-Badakhshan.

You can drive from Khorog to Murgab in a day, but there are lots of interesting detours here, especially the beautiful **Wakhan Valley** (p409) and its storybook 12th-century Yamchun Fort (and the nearby Bibi Fatima Springs). Nearby Abrashim Qala, another fort, offers amazing views across to Afghanistan's Wakhan Corridor. With your own transport, you can connect from **Langar** (p410) to the Pamir Hwy and continue to Murgab.

There are loads of side trips to be made from **Murgab** (p412), so try to budget a few days here to visit a local yurt camp in the surrounding high pastures. Headed north, **Kara-Kul** (p416) is a scenic highlight and worth a least a lunch stop or picnic. Once over the border in Kyrgyzstan, at Sary Tash, it's worth detouring 40km to **Sary Moghul** (p361) for its fine views of towering Pik Lenin (Koh-i-Istiqlal).

From here you can continue over the mountains to the Silk Road bazaar town of **Osh** (p356) or better still exit Central Asia via the **Irkeshtam Pass** (p361) to Kashgar.

This wild three-week jaunt ranks as one of the world's most beautiful and remote mountain road trips and is not one to rush. Hire a vehicle for at least part of the way and do the drives in daylight.

ROADS LESS TRAVELLED

AFGHANISTAN: FOR BETTER DAYS   Four Weeks

For this itinerary we'll put on our rose-coloured spectacles in anticipation of an outbreak of peace in Afghanistan. Here's to better days.

After flying in to the booming capital of **Kabul** (p476), visit Babur's Gardens, what's left of the Kabul Museum, and the city's bird market, Ka Faroshi.

Drive northwest to **Bamiyan** (p481), where the destroyed Buddhas still command a power in their absence and the valley is one of the most beautiful in the country. It's just a few hours to the surreal blue lakes of **Band-e Amir** (p483) and the site of Afghanistan's first national park.

Drive back to Kabul and fly to Herat or invest an extra week and continue on the hardcore overland route via the fabled, remote **Minaret of Jam** (p483).

Herat (p483) is perhaps the most interesting city in Afghanistan, if not the region, so budget several days to see the restored fort, the stunning Friday Mosque, bazaars and the remnants of the Timurid-era Musalla Complex.

Fly from Herat to **Mazar-e Sharif** (p486), avoiding the unadvised overland trip via Maimana. The day trip to the city's namesake Shrine of Hazrat Ali is a must, as is a day trip to historic **Balkh** (p487).

Overland eastwards via Taloqan and Kunduz to **Faizabad** (p487), and continue through stunning mountain scenery to the remote Afghan **Wakhan Corridor** (p488). Continue to **Sarhad-e Broghil** (p489) and experience Central Asia's wildest trekking, or cross into Tajikistan at Ishkashim to link up with the Samarkand to Osh via the Pamir Hwy itinerary (p28).

At the time of press it was not safe to travel in Afghanistan so consider this an armchair itinerary to dream about, for the time being at least.

SOUTHERN KAZAKHSTAN   Two weeks

You can start this trip anywhere in northwestern Kazakhstan. If you're headed from Russia, then start in Aktobe; if coming by boat from the Caucasus, start in Aktau. Either way, start with a long train ride to Aralsk, or fly there from Almaty.

The fishing port of **Aralsk** (p161) is a long way from any fish but it's a fine springboard for a visit to the Aral Sea, and the town's beached fishing boats are a powerful icon of environmental disaster.

From Aralsk take the train along the Syr-Darya river, keeping your eyes peeled for a rocket launch as you pass near Baykonur Cosmodrome. Stop off at **Turkistan** (p157) to soak up Kazakhstan's only architectural masterpiece, the 14th-century Timurid tomb of Kozha Akhmed Yasaui. Keep the historical vibe going with a detour to the nearby ruined Silk Road city of **Sauran** (p159) and a visit south to **Otrar** (p156), the spot where Chinggis (Genghis) Khan's troops first attacked Central Asia and where Timur (Tamerlane) breathed his last.

Vibrant **Shymkent** (p151) is the place to stock up on supplies before heading out for some rural hiking, horse riding and tulip-spotting at **Aksu-Zhabagyly Nature Reserve** (p155) or **Sayram-Ugam National Park** (p156), both of which have enough homestays and ecotourism programs to keep you busy for days.

Back at Shymkent, continue the 'Silk Road by rail' theme by running the rails to **Almaty** (p126), Kazakhstan's largest city. There is plenty to do here, including visiting the iconic Scythian-era Golden Man and soaking in the wonderful Arasan Baths, before hitting the Kazakh club scene. Walk off the next day's hangover on a hike to **Bolshoe Almatinskoe Lake** (p144), set in the lovely spurs of the Tian Shan.

This Kazakh taster takes you by train along the southern belly of Kazakhstan, through the country's most historic and Central Asian–scented cities.

TRANSCASPIA   Two Weeks

There are three major excursions inside Turkmenistan; to the north, to the west and to the east. For a shorter trip, pick just one of the following three spokes.

Headed from **Bukhara** (p257), make for Mary and base yourself there for day trips to **Merv** (p451) and Gonur (p453). Budget a couple of days in **Ashgabat** (p430), visiting the city's monuments, remaining statues of former president Turkmenbashi and the National Museum. Don't miss **Tolkuchka Bazaar** (p435) and the cable car into the **Kopet Dag Mountains** (p435). Then visit an Akhal-Teke farm for a half-day of horse riding.

From Ashgabat, visit **Nissa** (p441), **Gypjak** (p441) and the **Köw Ata Underground Lake** (p443) before visiting **Nokhur** (p443), a friendly and photogenic village that offers good hiking in the mountains. Most visitors spend two nights here, sleeping in a guesthouse. From Nokhur, continue west to the pilgrimage site of **Parau Bibi** (p443), and then remote **Dekhistan** (p445), one of many cities decimated by the Mongols. From the city of Balkanabat, head north to scenic **Yangykala Canyon** (p445), before driving back to the capital. Alternatively continue to the sleepy port town of **Turkmenbashi** (p446) and fly or train back from there.

The third leg leads into northern Turkmenistan. From Ashgabat travel to the spectacular **Darvaza Gas Crater** (p442). If you are well equipped it's possible make a desert excursion to a remote Turkmen settlement, overnighting in a yurt. From Darvaza, continue north to see the ruins of **Konye-Urgench** (p457), once capital of Khorezm, before heading into **Khiva** (p270), Uzbekistan (or flying back to Ashgabat).

This route through Turkmenistan begins and ends in Uzbekistan. You can easily do it in reverse or even exit at Turkmenbashi on the ferry to Azerbaijan. If you fly in and out of Ashgabat you'll have to do some backtracking but domestic flights are cheap.

TAILORED TRIPS

COMMUNITY TOURISM

Kyrgyzstan leads the world in small-scale ecotourism projects that connect travellers with local families, guides and shepherds.

Kochkor (p335) is a fine place to find a homestay, watch your host make *shyrdaks* (felt carpets) and arrange a horse and guide for the two-day trek to

Song-Köl (p339), where real shepherds will put you up in a real yurt.

In the little-visited pastures of the **Talas Valley** (p349) and **Suusamyr Valley** (p348) are two other ecotourism projects; hardy travellers are guaranteed to have these to themselves.

Two great places to combine hiking and mountain hospitality are the **Marguzor Lakes** (p396 and the boxed text on p395) and **Geisev** (see the boxed text, p407) regions in Tajikistan. Hike between turquoise lakes in mountain scenery, overnighting in traditional village homestays.

In spectacular high-altitude Tajikistan, **Murgab** (p412) has a good tourism program that can arrange homestays and jeep hire for trips to local archaeological sites, high-altitude lakes and remote yurt camps.

Kazakhstan's best ecotourism option is probably **Aksu-Zhabagyly Nature Reserve** (p155). Overnight horse trips into the mountains are very pleasant. Another homestay and hiking option is at **Korgalzhyn Nature Reserve** (p179), where you can spot the world's northernmost community of pink flamingos.

OFFBEAT CENTRAL ASIA

First stop is wacky Turkmenistan, 'the North Korea of Central Asia'. In **Ashgabat** (p430), stroll past the 'Ministry of Fairness' and visit the Turkmenbashi World of Fairytales amusement park – imagine Disneyland but without any of the fun.

The dinosaur footprints at **Kugitang Nature Reserve** (p456) are off the wall, but nothing compares to the burning desert around the **Darvaza Gas Craters** (p442), especially at night. Check with travel agents to see whether the craters' fires have been extinguished, as decreed by the president.

Bizarre future Turkmen attractions include a huge US$9 billion artificial lake in the middle of the desert. Until then, you'll have to settle for a surreal swim in the underground lake of **Köw Ata** (p442).

In **Moynaq** (p280) or, better, outside **Aralsk** (p161), see beached fishing boats 150km from what's left of the Aral Sea. If the steppes of Kazakhstan appeal, go to **Aktau** (p167), 300km from…anywhere. From here track down the underground mosques of **Mangistau** (p170) and then bump across the steppe to reach the appropriately titled Valley of Balls.

Alternatively, visit the new Kazakh capital, **Astana** (p172), to stare open-mouthed at the world's largest tent (150m tall) and the excellent collection of 4th-century-BC pickled horse intestines at the Presidential Culture Centre.

WORLD HERITAGE SITES

The following sites have all made it onto Unesco's list. Kazakhstan's honours include its most spectacular building, the **Mausoleum of Kozha Akhmed Yasaui** (2003; p158) at Turkistan, as well as the **Petroglyphs at Tamgaly** (2004; p148). A recent addition is the **Steppe and Lakes of Saryarka** (2008; p179), focusing on the Naurzum and Korgalzhyn nature reserves and their migratory waterbirds.

Turkmenistan offers the five historic cities of **Ancient Merv** (1999; p451), and one of the medieval world's great cities. From here it would be a shame not to visit the former Parthian capital of **Nissa** (2007; p441) or the architectural remains of **Konye-Urgench** (2005; p457), ancient Gurganj, near the Uzbekistan border.

Uzbekistan has arguably the most spectacular World Heritage sites, including **Khiva's old city** (1990; p270) and the historic cities of **Bukhara** (1993; p257), **Shakhrisabz** (2000; p251) and **Samarkand** (2001; p240).

The most recent addition to the Unesco list is Kyrgyzstan's **Solomon's Throne** (2009; p358) in Osh, a somewhat underwhelming choice despite its status as a regional pilgrimage spot.

Afghanistan boasts the **Minaret of Jam** (2002; p483) and the **Archaeological Remains of the Bamiyan Valley** (2003; p481), both of which have been included on the list of World Monuments in Danger.

ACTIVITIES

The austere **Fan Mountains** (p396) have long been one of Central Asia's premier trekking destinations. Easily visited from Samarkand, they offer a wide range of route options.

The alpine valleys of the Tian Shan around **Karakol** (p320) offer great versatility for trekking and horse trips and are probably the most popular trekking destination in the region. The **Zailiysky Alatau range** (p145), an hour south of Almaty, also has great trekking.

For true adventurers, the Afghanistan side of the **Wakhan Corridor** (p488) now offers homestays, guides, porters and donkeys for a once-in-a-lifetime trek to the Roof of the World.

Horse riding is the natural way to traverse the pastures around **Kochkor** (p335), where community-based tourism groups can arrange horse treks to places such as Song-Köl.

Nothing conjures up the spirit of the Silk Road like travelling by camel. For the desert experience try **Lake Aidarkul** (p256) or **Ayaz-Qala** (p270) in Uzbekistan; for Bactrian camel trekking try **Rang-Kul** (p414) in the Pamirs.

Mountaineers who know what they are doing can tackle **Pik Lenin** (p362), one of the world's easier 7000m peaks. Few mountain amphitheatres can compare to basecamp on the **Inylchek Glacier** (p334), where ascents can be made to peaks around Khan Tengri.

History

Central Asia is perhaps the best place on earth to explore the reality of the phrase 'the sweep of history'. Populations, conquerors, cultures and ideas have traversed the region's steppes, deserts and mountain passes for millennia. Nothing symbolises Central Asia's role as a conduit between cultures better than the Silk Road, through which the great civilisations of the East and the West first made contact. But Central Asia was, and is, more than just a middle ground, and its cultural history is far more than the sum of the influences brought from the East and the West.

See www.orientarch.
uni-halle.de/ca/bud/
bud.htm for more on the
archaeology of southeast-
ern Central Asia.

Here in the heart of the largest landmass on earth, vast steppes provided the one natural resource – grass – required to build one of this planet's most formidable and successful forms of statehood, the nomadic empire. The grass-fed horses by the millions and mounted archers remained the unstoppable acme of open-ground warfare for more than 2500 years. How the settled civilisations on the periphery of Eurasia interacted with successive waves of mounted nomadic hordes is the main theme of the story of Central Asia.

EARLY HISTORY

Cultural continuity in Central Asia begins in the late 3rd millennium BC with the Indo-Iranians, speakers of an unrecorded Indo-European dialect related distantly to English. The Indo-Iranians are believed to have passed through Central Asia and Afghanistan on their way from the Indo-European homeland in southern Russia. From Central Asia, groups headed southeast for India and southwest for Iran. These peoples herded cattle, forged iron, invented the wheeled chariot, and buried their dead nobles in burial mounds (kurgans). The Tajik people are linguistic descendants of these ancient migrants. One of these subsequent Indo-European groups was the Sakas (part of a people known as Scythians), who have left kurgans, rock carvings and other remains across Central Asia. The most spectacular Saka-era remnant is Kazakhstan's famous 'Golden Man' find, dating from a 5th-century kurgan outside Almaty (see p132).

Central Asia is strewn
with ancient petroglyphs,
some of the best of which
can be visited at Saim-
aluu Tash in Kyrgyzstan
(p344) and Tamgaly in
southeastern Kazakhstan
(p148).

Central Asia's recorded history begins in the 6th century BC, when the large Achaemenid empire of Persia (modern Iran) created client kingdoms or satrapies (provinces) in Central Asia: Sogdiana (Sogdia), Khorezm (later Khiva), Bactria (Afghan Turkestan), Margiana (Merv), Aria (Herat), Saka (Scythia), Arachosia (Ghazni and Kandahar) and Gandhara (Kabul Valley). Sogdiana was the land between the Amu-Darya and Syr-Darya, called Transoxiana (Beyond the Oxus) by the Romans, where Bukhara and Samarkand would later flourish. Khorezm lay on the lower reaches of the Amu-Darya, south of the Aral Sea, where one day the 19th-century khans

TIMELINE

100,000–40,000 BC	2nd millennium BC	6th century BC
Remains of Neanderthal man found at Aman-Kutan cave near Samarkand.	Saka/Scythian tombs in the Pamirs and the tomb of Sarazm (western Tajikistan) date from this period.	The Central Asian prophet Zoroaster (also known as Zartosht or Zarathustra) is murdered in Balkh, after founding one of the great monotheistic religions, Zoroastrianism.

ALEXANDER THE GREAT

In 330 BC this former pupil of Aristotle, from Macedonia, led his army to a key victory over the last Achaemenid emperor, Darius III, in Mesopotamia. With the defeat of his Persian nemesis, Alexander (356–323 BC) developed a taste for conquest. By 329 BC, aged 28, he had reached modern-day Herat, Kandahar and Kabul. Ascending the Panjshir Valley and crossing the Hindu Kush in winter he pressed northward to Bactria, crossed the Oxus (Amu-Darya) on inflated hides and proceeded via Cyropol/Cyropolis (Istaravshan) and Marakanda (Samarkand) towards the Jaxartes (Syr-Darya), which he crossed in order to crush Saka defenders. Perhaps in celebration he founded his ninth city, Alexandria Eskhate (Farthest Alexandria), on the banks of the Jaxartes, where today's Khojand stands.

Alexander met the most stubborn resistance of his career in the Sogdians, who in concert with the Massagetes, a Scythian clan, revolted and under the leadership of Spitamenes held the mountains of Zerafshan (Zeravshan) until 328 BC. After an 18-month guerrilla war, the rebels' fall was a poignant one: attacked and defeated after Greek troops scaled the cliffs of their last redoubt, the 'Rock of Sogdiana' (its location today in the Hissar Mountains remains a mystery). Their leader eventually yielded both the fortress and the beautiful Bactrian princess Roxana (Roshanak), whom Alexander married in Balkh in 327 BC.

The brilliant Macedonian generalissimo's three-year sojourn in Central Asia was marked by a growing megalomania. It was at Marakanda (modern Samarkand) that Alexander murdered his right-hand general, Cleitus. He tried to adopt the dress and autocratic court ritual of an Oriental despot, until his Greek and Macedonian followers finally refused to prostrate themselves before him.

When he died in Babylon in 323 BC, Alexander had no named heir (despite siring a son with Roxana). But his legacy included nothing less than the West's perennial romance with exploration and expansion.

EAST MEETS WEST

The aftermath of Alexander's short-lived Macedonian empire in Central Asia saw an explosion of East–West cultural exchange and a chain reaction of nomadic migrations. The Hellenistic successor states of the Seleucid empire in Bactria disseminated the aesthetic values of the classical world deep into Asia. Hellenistic cities and Buddhist monasteries of the 2nd century BC, such as Ai-Khanoum, Takht-i-Sangin and Kobadiyan on the borders of Tajikistan, Uzbekistan and Afghanistan (former Bactria), reveal a fascinating fusion of Greek, Persian and local art forms. Ai-Khanoum, known to Alexander as

Alexander the Great (Iskander or Sikander) is a popular figure, after whom several lakes and mountains are named. His troops are blamed for the occasional blond-haired blue-eyed Tajik or Nuristani, although this is more the result of Aryan influence.

Balkh, the 'Mother of All Cities', is the oldest recorded city in Afghanistan. It's served as the birthplace of Zoroaster, campaign headquarters of Alexander the Great, a rest stop for Marco Polo and Timur's coronation site.

The Sogdians (from modern Tajikistan and Uzbekistan) were the consummate Silk Road traders, so much so that their language became the lingua franca of the Silk Road.

THE SILK ROAD

For centuries, the great civilisations of East and West were connected by the Silk Road, a fragile network of shifting intercontinental trade routes that threaded across Asia's highest mountains and bleakest deserts. Geographically there's no such thing as a single 'Silk Road', nor was there much traffic from one end to the other; most caravanners were short haul.

Silk Routes

Routes changed over the years according to local conditions. At any given time any portion of the network might be beset by war, robbers or natural disaster: the northern routes were plagued by nomadic horsemen and a lack of settlements to provide fresh supplies and mounts; the south by fearsome deserts and frozen mountain passes.

Though the road map expanded over the centuries, the network had its main eastern terminus at the Chinese capital Ch'ang-an (modern Xi'an) and divided at the Jade Gate, skirting north and south of the dreaded Taklamakan Desert before meeting again in Kashgar, from where the trail headed up a series of passes into and over the Pamirs and Tian Shan (two such passes in use today are the Torugart and Irkeshtam, on the Chinese border with Kyrgyzstan).

Beyond the mountains, the Fergana Valley, long famed for its horses, fed westward through Kokand, Samarkand and Bukhara, past Merv and on to Iran, the Levant and Constantinople. Another route wound from Tashkurgan, through the Pamirs, Bactria (Balkh) and Aria (Herat) to Iran. In the middle of the network, major branches headed south over the Karakoram range to India and north via the Zhungarian Gap and across the steppes to Khorezm and the Russian Volga.

Caravans & Trade

Silk was certainly not the only trade on the Silk Road but it epitomised the qualities required for such a long-distance trade; light, valuable, exotic and greatly desired. China's early need for horses to battle nomads on its northern border was actually a more significant reason for the early growth of the Silk Road.

Though the balance of trade was heavily stacked in favour of China (as it is today!), traffic ran both ways. China received gold, silver, ivory, lapis, jade, coral, wool, rhino horn, tortoise shell, horses, Mediterranean coloured glass (an industrial mystery originally as inscrutable to the Chinese as silk was in the West), cucumbers, walnuts, pomegranates, golden peaches from Samarkand,

Alexandria-Oxiana, boasted not only Greek-style baths, but also a theatre and gymnasium, right on the banks of the Amu-Darya.

Several thousand kilometres east, along the border of Mongolia and China, the expansion of the warlike Xiongnu (Hsiung-nu) confederacy (probably the forebears of the Ephalites, or Huns) uprooted the Yuezhi of western China. The Yuezhi ('Yüeh-chih') were sent packing westward along the Ili River into Saka, whose displaced inhabitants in turn bore down upon the Sogdians to the south.

The Xiongnu were also irritating more important powers than the Yuezhi. Although protected behind its expanding Great Wall since about 250 BC,

107 BC	105 BC	AD 78–144
Chinese armies arrive in the Fergana Valley.	Parthia and China exchange embassies and inaugurate official bilateral trade along the caravan route that lay between them. With this the Silk Road is born.	King Kanishka rules the Kushan empire from capitals at Kapisa (Bagram) and Peshawar. Buddhist monasteries bloom in Afghanistan, southern Uzbekistan and Tajikistan as the first human images of Buddha are created.

sesame, garlic, grapes and wine, plus – an early Parthian craze – acrobats and ostriches. Goods arriving at the western end included silk, porcelain, paper, tea, ginger, rhubarb, lacquerware, bamboo, Arabian spices and incense, medicinal herbs, gems and perfumes.

And in the middle lay Central Asia, a great clearing house that provided its native beasts – horses and two-humped Bactrian camels – to keep the goods flowing in both directions. The cities of Bukhara and Samarkand marked the halfway break, where caravans from Aleppo and Baghdad met traders from Kashgar and Yarkand. *Rabat* (caravanserais) grew up along the route, offering lodgings, stables and stores. Middlemen such as the Sogdians amassed great fortunes, much of which went into beautifying cosmopolitan and luxuriant caravan towns such as Gurganj, Merv and Bukhara. The cities offered equally vital services, such as brokers to set up contracts, banking houses to set up lines of credit, and markets to sell the goods.

The Cultural Legacy

The Silk Road gave rise to unprecedented trade, but its true legacy was the intellectual interchange of ideas, technologies and faiths that formed the world's first 'information superhighway'. It's curious to note that while the bulk of trade headed west, religious ideas primarily travelled east.

Buddhism spread along the trade routes to wend its way from India to China and back again. It's hard to imagine a Central Asia dotted with Buddhist monasteries. Today only the faintest archaeological evidence remains; at Adjina-Tepe in Tajikistan, Kuva in the Fergana Valley, Fayoz-Tepe and the Zurmala Stupa around Termiz in Uzbekistan and the rock-carved stupa of Takht-e Rostam in northern Afghanistan.

Musical styles and instruments (such as the lute) crossed borders as artists followed in the wake of traders, pilgrims and missionaries. The spread of Buddhism caused Indian, Chinese, Greek and Tibetan artistic styles to merge and fuse, forming the exquisite Serindian art of Chinese Turkestan and the Gandharan art of Pakistan and Afghanistan.

To religion and art, add technology. The Chinese not only taught Central Asia how to cast iron but also how to make paper. Prisoners from the Battle of Talas (see p41) established paper production in Samarkand and then Baghdad, from where it gradually spread into Europe, making it culturally the most important secret passed along the Silk Road.

China eagerly sought tranquillity on its barbarian frontier. In 138 BC, the Chinese emperor sent a brave volunteer emissary, Zhang Qian, on a secret mission to persuade the Yuezhi king to form an alliance against the Xiongnu.

When he finally got there, 13 years later, Zhang found that the Yuezhi had settled down in Bactria/Tokharistan (southern Tajikistan and northern Afghanistan) to a peaceable life of trade and agriculture, and no longer had an axe to grind with the Xiongnu. But Zhang Qian's mission was still a great success of Chinese diplomacy and exploration and the stage had been set for the greatest of all East–West contacts; the birth of the Silk Road (see p36).

226–651	440–568	630
Sassanid empire.	The Hephthalites (White Huns) migrate from the Altai region to occupy Transoxiana, Bactria, Khorasan, and eastern Persia, conquering the Kushans and eventually carving the Buddhas at Bamiyan.	Chinese Buddhist pilgrim Xuan Zang travels to India via Issyk-Köl, Tashkent, Samarkand, Balkh and Bamiyan in search of Buddhist texts. En route he visits the summer capital of the Blue Turks at Tokmok (Tokmak), Kyrgyzstan.

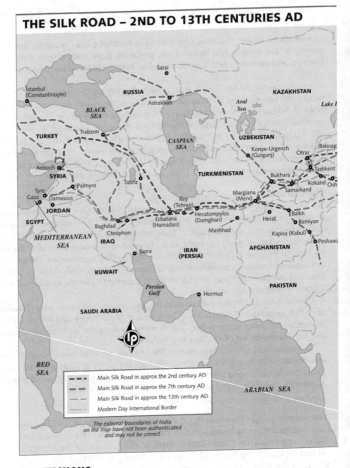

THE SILK ROAD – 2ND TO 13TH CENTURIES AD

Main Silk Road in approx the 2nd century AD
Main Silk Road in approx the 7th century AD
Main Silk Road in approx the 13th century AD
Modern Day International Border

The external boundaries of India on the map have not been authenticated and may not be correct

THE KUSHANS

The peaceable, put-upon Yuezhi finally came into their own in the 1st century BC when their descendants, the Kushan dynasty, converted to Buddhism. The Kushan empire (250 BC–AD 226) grew to control northern India, Afghanistan and Sogdiana from its base at Kapisa, near modern-day Bagram

642–712	747	751
Arab conquest of Central Asia by the general Qutaybah ibn Muslim brings Islam to the region. Central Asia is called Mawarannahr in Arabic – the 'Land Beyond the River'.	Chinese army battles Tibetans in the Wakhan Valley of the high Pamirs.	Tang dynasty Chinese forces are routed by Arab, Turkic and Tibetan forces at the Battle of Talas, limiting Chinese expansion in Central Asia.

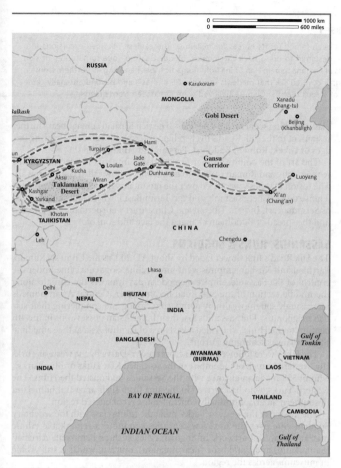

in Afghanistan. At its height in the first three centuries after Christ, it was one of the world's four superpowers, alongside Rome, China and Parthia.

Vigorous trade on the Silk Road helped fuel and spread Kushan and Buddhist culture. Excavations at Kapisa (Bagram) have revealed Chinese lacquerware, Greek bronzes, Indian-style carved ivory panels and Egyptian

787–850	9th–10th centuries	858–941
Life of Central Asian mathematician Al-Khorezmi (Latinised as Algorismi), who gave his name to algorithm, the mathematical process behind addition and multiplication. The title of his mathematical work, *Al-Jebr*, reaches Europe as algebra.	The heyday of the Samanid dynasty in Bukhara. Its greatest ruler, Ismail Samani, is buried in a beautiful tomb in Bukhara and is celebrated as Tajikistan's founding father.	Life of Rudaki, court poet of the Samanids, born near modern Penjikent in Tajikistan, considered the founder of Tajik/Persian literature.

DRAGON HORSES

Central Asia has been famed for its horses for millennia. The earliest Silk Road excursions into the region were designed to bring back the famous 'blood-sweating' (due to parasites or skin infection) horses of Fergana to help Han China fight nomadic tribes harassing its northern frontier. Much of the highly coveted silk that made its way into Central Asia and beyond originally came from the trade of steeds that the Chinese believed were descended from dragons.

---

glass depicting scenes from *The Illiad*. The rich Kushan coinage bears further testament to the Silk Road's lively religious ferment, with coins bearing images of Greek, Roman, Buddhist, Persian and Hindu deities.

The art of the empire further fused Persian imperial imagery, Buddhist iconography and Roman realism to create what is now called Gandharan art. The fusion of styles was carried over the mountains to the furthest corners of Transoxiana, Tibet, Kashmir and the Tarim Basin, where it became termed as Serindian art. Indian, Tibetan and Chinese art were permanently affected and the spread of Buddhism changed the face and soul of Asia.

The Silk Road Foundation (www.silkroadfoundation.org) has articles on Silk Road cities and travel, as well as information on workshops, lectures and music, plus a fine online journal.

SASSANIDS, HUNS & SOGDIANS

The Silk Road's first flower faded by about AD 200, as the Chinese, Roman, Parthian and Kushan empires went into decline. Sogdiana came under the control of the Sassanid empire of modern-day Iran. As the climate along the middle section of the Silk Road became drier, Central Asian nomads increasingly sought wealth by plundering, taxing and conquering their settled neighbours. The Sassanids lost their Inner Asian possessions in the 4th century to the Huns, who ruled a vast area of Central Asia at the same time that Attila was scourging Europe.

The Huns were followed south across the Syr-Darya by the western Turks (the western branch of the empire of the so-called Kök Turks or Blue Turks), who in 559 made an alliance with the Sassanids and ousted the Huns. The western Turks, who had arrived in the area from their ancestral homeland in southern Siberia, nominally controlled the reconquered region.

The history of the Silk Road is neither a poetic nor a picturesque tale; it is nothing more than scattered islands of peace in an ocean of wars.

LUCE BOULNOIS, SILK ROAD: MONKS, WARRIORS & MERCHANTS ON THE SILK ROAD

The mixing of the western Turks' nomadic ruling class with the sedentary Sogdian elite over the next few centuries produced a remarkable ethnic mix and beautiful artwork in Sogdian cities such as Penjikent, Afrosiab (Samarkand) and Varakhsha (near Bukhara), much of which is still visible in museums across the region.

THE ARRIVAL OF ISLAM

When the western Turks faded in the late 7th century, an altogether new and formidable kind of power was waiting to fill the void – the army of Islam. Exploding out of Arabia just a few years after the Prophet Mohammed's

973–1046	980–1037	986
Life of scientist Al-Biruni, from Khorezm, the world's foremost astronomer of his age, who knew 500 years before Copernicus that the earth circled the sun and estimated the distance to the moon to within 20km.	Life of Abu Ali ibn-Sina (Latinised as Avicenna), from Bukhara, the greatest medic in the medieval world, whose Canon of Medicine was the standard textbook for Western doctors until the 17th century.	The Russians, in search of a religion, contact Muslim missionaries from Khorezm, but decide not to adopt Islam, opting instead for Orthodox Christianity.

death, the Muslim armies rolled through Persia in 642 to set up a military base at Merv (modern Turkmenistan) but met stiff resistance from the Turks of Transoxiana. The power struggle to control the lands between the Amu-Darya and Syr-Darya ebbed and flowed but Arab armies under the brilliant General Qutaybah ibn Muslim gradually gained ground, taking Bukhara in 709 and Samarkand in 712.

China, meanwhile, had revived under the Tang dynasty and expanded into Central Asia, murdering the khan of the Tashkent Turks as it flexed its imperial muscles. It was perhaps the most costly incident of skulduggery in Chinese history. The enraged Turks were joined by the opportunistic Arabs and Tibetans; in 751 they squeezed the Chinese forces into the Talas Valley (in present-day Kazakhstan and Kyrgyzstan) and sent them flying back across the Tian Shan, marking the limits of the Chinese empire for good (see the boxed text, p41).

After the Battle of Talas, the Arab's Central Asian territories receded in the wake of local rebellions. By the 9th century, Transoxiana (now known by the Arabic name Mawarannahr, or the 'Land Beyond the River') had given rise to the peaceful and affluent Samanid dynasty. It generously encouraged development of Persian culture while remaining strictly allied with the Sunni caliph of Baghdad. It was under the Samanids that Bukhara grew into a vanguard of Muslim culture to rival Baghdad, Cairo and Cordoba, garnering it the epithet 'The Pillar of Islam'. Some of the Islamic world's best scholars were nurtured in the city's 113 medressas and the famous library of Bukhara shone as one of the world's great centres of intellectual development.

Samanid Central Asia produced some of history's most important scientists, as well as great writers like court poet Rudaki. Bukharan native and court physician Abu Ali ibn-Sina (Latinised as Avicenna; 980–1037) was the greatest medic in the medieval world and laid the foundations of modern medicine, while Al-Biruni (973–1046), from Khorezm, was the world's foremost astronomer of his age, estimating the distance to the moon to within

Do a search for 'Central Asia' at www.loc.gov/exhibits/empire for wonderful old photos of Central Asia from the Prokudin-Gorskii collection.

LOST BATTLE, LOST SECRETS

The Chinese lost more than just a fight at the Battle of Talas in 751. The defeat marked the end of Chinese expansion west and secured the future of Islam as the region's foremost religion. But to add insult to injury, some of the Chinese rounded up after the battle were no ordinary prisoners: they were experts at the crafts of papermaking and silkmaking. Soon China's best-kept secrets were giving Arab silkmakers in Persia a commercial advantage all over Europe. It was the first mortal blow to the Silk Road. The spread of papermaking to Baghdad and then Europe sparked a technological revolution; the impact of this on the development of civilisation cannot be underestimated.

998–1030	1009	mid-11th century
Mahmoud (the Great) rules Central Asia from Ghazni (southern Afghanistan), which becomes one of the greatest cities in the Islamic world. The Ghaznid empire rules from Calcutta to the Caspian.	Persian poet Firdausi finishes his great epic poem, the Shah Name (Book of Kings), presenting it to Mahmoud of Ghazni.	The Karakhanid (Qarakhanid) empire splits in two: one rules over Western Turkestan (Transoxiana), the other over Eastern Turkestan (the Tarim Basin).

20km. Confused schoolchildren around the world can thank mathematician Al-Khorezmi (Latinised as Algorismi; 787–850) for the introduction of algebra (*Al-Jebr* was the title of one of his mathematical works), as well as the algorithm, the mathematical process behind addition and multiplication.

KARAKHANIDS TO KARAKITAY

By the early 10th century, internal strife at court had weakened the Samanid dynasty and opened the door for two Turkic usurpers to divide up the empire: the Ghaznavids in Khorasan and modern-day Afghanistan, south of the Amu-Darya; and the Karakhanids in Transoxiana and the steppe region beyond the Syr-Darya. The Karakhanids are credited with finally converting the populace of Central Asia to Islam. They held sway from three mighty capitals: Balasagun (now Burana in Kyrgyzstan) in the centre of their domain, Talas (now Taraz in Kazakhstan) in the west, and Kashgar in the east. The Ghaznavids under Mahmoud the Great ruled Afghanistan, Samarkand and Bukhara from Ghazni in southern Afghanistan and are credited with snuffing out Buddhism in the region and introducing Islam to India.

The Karakhanids and Ghaznavids coveted each other's lands. In the mid-11th century, while they were busy invading each other, they were caught off guard by a third Turkic horde, the Seljuqs, who annihilated both after pledging false allegiance to the Ghaznavids. In the Seljuqs' heyday their sultan had himself invested as emperor by the caliph of Baghdad. The empire was vast: on the east it bordered the lands of the Buddhist Karakitay, who had swept into Balasagun and Kashgar from China; to the west it extended all the way to the Mediterranean and Red Seas.

An incurable symptom of Inner Asian dynasties through the ages was their near inability to survive the inevitable disputes of succession. The Seljuqs lasted a century before their weakened line succumbed to the Karakitay and to the Seljuqs' own rearguard vassals, the Khorezmshahs. From their capital at Gurganj (present-day Konye-Urgench), the Khorezmshahs burst full-force into the tottering Karakitay. At the end of the 12th century the Khorezmshahs emerged as rulers of all Transoxiana and much of the Muslim world as well.

And so Central Asia might have continued in a perennial state of forgettable wars. As it is, the Khorezmshahs are still remembered primarily as the unlucky stooge left holding the red cape when the angry bull was released.

MONGOL TERROR, MONGOL PEACE

Chinggis (Genghis) Khan felt he had all the justification in the world to destroy Central Asia. In 1218 a Khorezmian governor in Otrar (modern-day Kazakhstan) received a Mongol delegation to inaugurate trade relations. Scared by distant reports of the new Mongol menace, the governor assassinated them in cold blood. Up until that moment Chinggis, the intelligent khan of the Mongols who had been lately victorious over Zhongdu (Beijing), had been

One major Silk Road industry rarely mentioned is the trade in slaves. Slaves dominated the global workforce between the 8th and 11th centuries and nomadic Turkmen slave raiders kept the slave markets of Khiva and Bukhara stocked well into the 18th and 19th centuries.

The Karakitay lent their name to both Cathay (an archaic name for China) and Kitai (the Russian word for China).

For more on the Mongols see the excellent book *Storm from the East*, by Robert Marshall.

1136	1148–1215	1218
Shrine of Hazrat Ali constructed in Mazar-e Sharif, allegedly to entomb the body of Ali.	The Ghorid empire pillages India and Iran, enriches its capitals at Firuzkoh and Herat and creates Herat's Friday Mosque (1201) and the enigmatic Minaret of Jam (1194).	The foolhardy execution of Mongol envoys by the Khwarezmian Shah Muhammad deflects the Mongol armies westwards into Central Asia.

carefully weighing the alternative strategies for expanding his power: commerce versus conquest. Then came the crude Otrar blunder, and the rest is history.

In early 1219 Chinggis placed himself at the head of an estimated 200,000 men and began to ride west from his stronghold in the Altay. By the next year his armies had sacked Khojand and Otrar (the murderous governor had molten silver poured into his eyes in Chinggis' presence), and Bukhara soon followed.

It was in that brilliant city, as soldiers raped and looted and horses trampled Islamic holy books in the streets, that the unschooled Chinggis ascended to the pulpit in the chief mosque and preached to the terrified congregation. His message: 'I am God's punishment for your sins'. Such shocking psychological warfare is perhaps unrivalled in history. It worked and news eventually filtered back to Europe of the Tartars, an army of 'Devil's Horsemen', sent from the Gates of Hell (Tartarus) to destroy Christendom.

Bukhara was burned to the ground, and the Mongol hordes swept on to conquer and plunder the great cities of Central Asia – Samarkand, Merv, Termiz, Urgench, Herat, Kabul, Balkh, Bamiyan, Ghazni – and, eventually under Chinggis' generals and heirs, most of Eurasia. No opposing army could match their speed, agility and accuracy with a bow.

Settled civilisation in Central Asia took a serious blow, from which it only began to recover 600 years later under Russian colonisation. Chinggis' descendants controlling Persia favoured Shiite Islam over Sunni Islam, a development which over the centuries isolated Central Asia even more from the currents of the rest of the Sunni Muslim world.

But there was stability, law and order under the Pax Mongolica. In 20th-century terms, the streets were safe and the trains ran on time. The resulting modest flurry of trade on the Silk Road was the background to several famous medieval travellers' journeys, including the most famous of them all, Marco Polo (see the boxed text, p44).

On Chinggis Khan's death in 1227, his empire was divided among his sons. By tradition the most distant lands, stretching as far as the Ukraine and Moscow and including western and most of northern Kazakhstan, would have gone to the eldest son, Jochi, had Jochi not died before his father. They went instead to Jochi's sons, Batu and Orda, and came to be known collectively as the Golden Horde. The second son, Chaghatai, got the next most distant portion, including southern Kazakhstan, Uzbekistan, Afghanistan and western Xinjiang; this came to be known as the Chaghatai khanate. The share of the third son, Ogedei, seems to have eventually been divided between the Chaghatai khanate and the Mongol heartland inherited by the youngest son, Tolui. Tolui's portion formed the basis for his son Kublai Khan's Yuan dynasty in China.

Unlike the Golden Horde in Europe and the Yuan court in Beijing, the Chaghatai khans tried to preserve their nomadic lifestyle, complete with the khan's roving tent encampment as 'capital city'. But as the rulers spent more

Genetic testing has revealed that over 16 million men in Central Asia have the same Y-chromosome as Chinggis (Genghis) Khan, who can therefore somewhat perversely be considered among history's most prolific lovers.

The Persian historian Juvaini summed up the Mongol invasions succinctly: 'They came, they sapped, they fired, they slew, they looted and they left'.

The Great Horde roamed the steppes of the Zhetisu region (Russian: Semireche), north of the Tian Shan; the Middle Horde occupied the grasslands extending east from the Aral Sea; and the Little Horde took the lands west of there, as far as the Ural River.

1220–21	1275–6?	1336–1405
Chinggis Khan's army destroys Bukhara, killing 30,000, before taking Herat. That city rebels and 160,000 of its inhabitants (contemporary records say 1.5 million) are killed in a week. Another 200,000 are massacred in Balkh.	Marco Polo travels through Herat, Balkh and the Wakhan en route to China, writing of Badakhshani rubies, sheep and the high Pamir plateau.	Life of Timur (Tamerlane), whose campaigns resulted in the deaths of more than one million people. He became infamous for building towers or walls made from the cemented heads of a defeated army.

THE TRAVELLING POLOS (1271–98) *Bradley Mayhew*

In the 1250s, Venice was predominant in the Mediterranean and looking for new commercial routes. In this context the Venetian brothers Nicolo and Mafeo Polo set out to do some itinerant trading; sailing from Constantinople with a cargo of precious stones, they made their way to the Crimea. Choice business deals followed and took them gradually up the Volga (they stayed a year at the Mongol encampment at Sarai), eastward across the steppes, south to Bukhara (for an enforced three-year stay), then across Central Asia in the company of a Mongol envoy to Karakoram (now in Mongolia), the seat of Kublai Khan, grandson of Chinggis.

Kublai welcomed the Europeans warmly and questioned them at length about life and statecraft in Europe, finally making them ambassadors to the pope in Rome with the request that the pope send him 100 of his most learned priests to argue the merits of their faith over others. If they succeeded, Kublai said, his whole empire would convert to Christianity. It took the Polos three difficult years to get home; when they arrived, no one believed where they had been.

Marco Polo, teller of the world's most famous travel tale, was not yet born when his father Nicolo and uncle Mafeo set out on their journey. When they returned he was a motherless teenager. A couple of years later the elder Polos set off once more for Kublai's court, this time taking 20-year-old Marco.

The pope had supplied only two monks, and they stayed behind in Armenia, perhaps after their first taste of shashlyk. (It is tempting to conjecture how the fate of Eurasia might have been different if the requested 100 doctors of religion had shown up at Karakoram and converted the entire Mongol empire.)

The Polos made their way to Balkh, and on through the Hindu Kush, Badakhshan and the Pamirs, then on past Kashgar, Yarkand and the southern route around the Taklamakan Desert, reaching China via Dunhuang and the Gansu Corridor. They found the khan dividing his time between Khanbaligh (now Beijing) and his nearby summer capital of Shangdu (the Xanadu of Samuel Taylor Coleridge's poem).

Marco was exceptionally intelligent and observant, and Kublai took a great liking to him. He was soon made a trusted adviser and travelling representative of the ageing khan, bringing the khan news of his far-flung and exotic empire, little of which Kublai had actually seen.

The three Polos spent about 16 years in China. They were only allowed to go home when they agreed to escort a Mongol princess on her way to be married in Persia. To avoid long hardship, the party took the sea route from the east coast of China around India and up the Gulf. Back in Venice, in 1295, no one recognised the Polos and still no one believed their tales.

Many years later, during a war with Genoa, Marco Polo was captured in a naval battle. While in prison he dictated the story of his travels. The resulting book has become the world's most widely read travel account, though some question its authenticity. If Marco really did travel to China, why did he omit any mention of the Great Wall and the customs of drinking tea and binding feet? And why do Chinese imperial records fail to make any mention of Polo?

Hounded all his life by accusations that the exotic world he described was fictitious, Marco Polo was asked to recant on his deathbed. His answer: 'I have not told the half of what I saw'.

In 2009-10 Bradley retraced the footsteps of Marco Polo, travelling overland from Venice to Xanadu via Iran and Afghanistan as part of a five-hour TV documentary for Arte and SWR.

1407–47	**1424–29**	**late 15th century**
Timur's son Shah Rukh rules the Timurid empire from Herat during a golden age of poetry, painting and architecture. His wife Ghowar Shad is one of most remarkable women in the history of Islam.	Shah Rukh's son Ulugbek builds an observatory in Samarkand, before he is beheaded in 1449 as part of a religious backlash.	The decline of the overland trade routes, including the Silk Road, due to a new emphasis on trade by sea.

and more time in contact with Muslim collaborators who administered their realm, the Chaghatai line inevitably began to settle down. They even made motions towards conversion to Islam. It was a fight over this issue, in the mid-14th century, that split the khanate in two, with the Muslim Chaghatais holding Transoxiana and the conservative branch retaining the Tian Shan, Kashgar and the vast steppes north and east of the Syr-Darya, an area collectively known as Moghulistan.

TIMUR & THE TIMURIDS

The fracturing of the Mongol empire immediately led to resurgence of the Turkic peoples. From one minor clan near Samarkand arose a tyrant's tyrant, Timur ('the Lame', or Tamerlane). After assembling an army and wresting Transoxiana from Chaghatai rule, Timur went on a spectacular nine-year rampage which ended in 1395 with modern-day Iran, Iraq, Syria, eastern Turkey, the Caucasus and northern India smouldering at his feet.

All over his realm, Timur plundered riches and captured artisans and poured them into his capital at Samarkand. The city grew, in stark contrast to his conquered lands, into a lavish showcase of treasure and spectacle. Much of the postcard skyline of today's Samarkand dates to Timur's reign, as do many fine works of painting and literature. Foreign guests of Timur's, including the Spanish envoy Ruy Gonzales de Clavijo, took home stories of Oriental enchantment and barbarity which fed the West's dreams of a remote and romantic Samarkand.

Timur claimed indirect kinship with Chinggis Khan, but he had little of his forerunner's gift for statecraft. History can be strange: both conquerors savagely slaughtered hundreds of thousands of innocent people, yet one is remembered as a great ruler and the other not. The argument goes that Timur's bloodbaths were insufficiently linked to specific political or military aims. On the other hand, Timur is considered the more cultured and religious of the two men. At any rate, Timur died an old man at Otrar in 1405, having just set out in full force to conquer China.

For more on the extraordinary life of Timur see *Tamerlane: Sword of Islam, Conqueror of the World* by Justin Marozzi.

Important effects of Timur's reign can still be traced. For instance, when he pounded the army of the Golden Horde in southern Russia, Timur created a disequilibrium in the bloated Mongol empire which led to the seizure of power by its vassals, the petty and fragmented Russian princes. This was the predawn of the Russian state. Like the mammals after the dinosaurs, Russia arose from small beginnings.

For a scant century after Timur's death his descendants ruled on separately in small kingdoms and duchies. A Timurid renaissance was led by Timur's son Shah Rukh (1377–1447) and his remarkable wife Gowhar Shad, who moved the capital from Samarkand to the cultured city of Herat, populated by fine architects, musicians, miniature painters and poets. The Sufi poetry of Jami and Alisher Navoi (see p81), the miniature paintings of Bihzad (which

1501–07	1526	1592
The Sheybanid Uzbeks capture Samarkand, Bukhara and Herat, bringing to an end the Timurid dynasty and forcing Babur to flee south to Kabul.	Babur captures Delhi and founds the Mughal empire in India. His famous gardens and tomb still exist in Kabul.	Khiva made capital of Khorezm.

THE MONGOL KISS OF DEATH

Alongside the exchange of silk, jade, paper and Buddhism, historians rank disease as one of the Silk Road's less salubrious gifts to the world. One school of thought has it that the Black Death plague spread in 1338 from a diseased community of Nestorian Christians at Issyk-Köl in current Kyrgyzstan. Disease-ridden rat fleas then followed merchant caravans along Silk Road trade routes to the Mongol capital of Sarai in the Russian Volga.

By 1343 Mongol Khan Jani Beg of the Golden Horde was famously catapulting the plague-riddled corpses of his dead soldiers over the city walls of Kaffa, in the Crimea peninsula, in one of the world's first examples of biological warfare. The outbreak caused the Genoese population to flee by boat to the Mediterranean coast, spreading the disease deeper into Europe.

In the ensuing six years the Black Death pandemic went on to kill between 30% and 60% of Europe's population – around 100 million people. It was the Mongols' farewell kiss of death to the world.

had a huge influence on subsequent Persian and Mughal miniatures) and the grand architecture commissioned by Gowhar Shad still rank among Central Asia's greatest cultural legacies.

From 1409 until 1449, Samarkand was governed by the conqueror's mild, scholarly grandson, Ulugbek (Ulugh Bek). Gifted in mathematics and astronomy, he built a large celestial observatory and attracted scientists who gave the city a lustre as a centre of learning for years to come.

In addition to Persian, a Turkic court language came into use, called Chaghatai, which survived for centuries as a Central Asian lingua franca.

UZBEKS & KAZAKHS

Modern Uzbekistan and Kazakhstan, the two principal powers of post-Soviet Central Asia, eye each other warily across the rift dividing their two traditional lifestyles: sedentary agriculture (Uzbeks) and nomadic pastoralism (Kazakhs). Yet these two nations are closely akin and parted ways with a family killing.

The family in question was the dynasty of the Uzbek khans. These rulers, one strand of the modern Uzbek people, had a pedigree reaching back to Chinggis Khan and a homeland in southern Siberia. In the 14th century they converted to Islam, gathered strength, and started moving south. Under Abylkayr (Abu al-Khayr) Khan they reached the north bank of the Syr-Darya, across which lay the declining Timurid rulers in Transoxiana. But Abylkayyr had enemies within his own family. The two factions met in battle in 1468, and Abylkayyr was killed and his army defeated.

After this setback, Abylkayyr's grandson Mohammed Shaybani brought the Uzbek khans to power once more and established Uzbek control in Transoxiana; modern-day Uzbekistan. Abylkayyr's rebellious kinsmen became the forefathers of the Kazakh khans.

When Chinggis Khan's grandson Mutugen was murdered at the citadel of Shahr-e Zohak in the Bamiyan Valley in 1222, the Mongol retribution was so bloody that the nearby fort was christened Shahr-e Gholghola, the City of Screams.

1635–1758	1717	1731
Zhungarian (Oyrat) empire terrorises Kazakhstan, Kyrgyzstan and China.	First Russian expedition to Khiva ends in a massacre of 4000 Tsarist troops and the decapitated Russian leader's head is sent to the Emir of Bukhara as a gift.	Lesser Kazakh Horde places itself under Russian protection, opening up the ensuing annexation of Kazakhstan by Tsarist forces and settlers.

The Uzbeks gradually adopted the sedentary agricultural life best suited to the fertile river valleys they occupied. Settled life involved cities, which entailed administration, literacy, learning and, wrapped up with all of these, Islam. The Shaybanid dynasty, which ruled until the end of the 16th century, attempted to outdo the Timurids in religious devotion and to carry on their commitment to artistic patronage. But the Silk Road had withered away, usurped by spice ships, and Central Asia's economy had entered full decline. As prosperity fell, so did the region's importance as a centre of the Islamic world.

The Kazakhs, meanwhile, stayed home on the range, north of the Syr-Darya, and flourished as nomadic herders. Their experience of urban civilisation and organised Islam remained slight compared with their Uzbek cousins. By the 16th century the Kazakhs had solidly filled a power vacuum on the old Scythian steppes between the Ural and Irtysh Rivers and established what was to be the world's last nomadic empire, divided into three hordes: the Great Horde, the Middle Horde and the Little Horde.

One effect of the Shaybanid expansion was to force Andijon-born ruler Zahiruddin Babur (1483–1530) out of Fergana and Samarkand and into exile in Kabul. In 1526 Babur continued into India, adding his name to the long list of empire builders who have driven armies over the Khyber Pass, where he ultimately founded the magnificent Mughal empire. The word Mughal (a corruption of 'Mongol') is not the only legacy of Babur's rule in India; you don't have to look too hard to see the shape of a Central Asian medressa in the lines of the Taj Mahal.

Babur never returned to his beloved Fergana Valley and his memoirs, the *Baburnameh*, are full of nostalgic laments to the joys of his lost homeland (mostly melons and women, in that order). After his death in 1530, Babur's body was returned to Kabul and was buried in his famous gardens. You can still visit Babur's Gardens today (p479), recently restored after decades of neglect.

THE ZHUNGARIAN EMPIRE

The Oyrats were a western Mongol clan who had been converted to Tibetan Buddhism. Their day in the sun came when they subjugated eastern Kazakhstan, the Tian Shan, Kashgaria and western Mongolia to form the Zhungarian (Dzungarian or Jungarian) empire (1635–1758). Russia's frontier settlers were forced to pay heavy tribute and the Kazakh hordes, with their pasturage filling the mountain gap known as the Zhungarian Gate, were cruelly and repeatedly pummelled until the Oyrats were liquidated by Manchu China.

Reeling from the Zhungarian attacks, the Kazakhs (first the Little Horde, then the Middle Horde, then part of the Great Horde) gradually accepted Russian protection over the mid-18th century.

The Russians had by this time established a line of fortified outposts on the northern fringe of the Kazakh Steppe. However, it appears that there was

The Caspian region of Central Asia is sitting atop an estimated 200 billion barrels of crude oil. Kazakhstan's Kashagan oil field alone holds probably the world's second-largest concentration of oil.

When Buddhist pilgrim Xuan Zang visited the Bamiyan Valley in the 7th century he wrote of 10 monasteries, 1000 monks and a third sleeping Buddha over 1000ft long. Archaeologists are currently still searching for Bamiyan's last remaining Buddha.

1747	1758	1776
Ahmad Shah Durrani crowned, beginning the creation of modern Afghanistan.	Oyrats defeated by Manchu China and Kyrgyzstan nominally under Chinese rule.	Kabul becomes capital of Afghanistan.

no clear conception in St Petersburg of exactly where the Russian Empire's frontier lay. Slow on the uptake, Russia at this stage had little interest in the immense territory it now abutted.

THE KHANATES OF KOKAND, KHIVA & BUKHARA

In the fertile oases now called Uzbekistan, the military regime of a Persian interloper named Nadir Shah collapsed in 1747, leaving a political void which was rapidly occupied by a trio of Uzbek khanates.

The three dynasties were the Kungrats, enthroned at Khiva (in the territory of old Khorezm), the Mangits at Bukhara and the Mins at Kokand; all rivals. The khans of Khiva and Kokand and the emirs of Bukhara seemed able to will the outside world out of existence as they stroked and clawed each other like a box of kittens. Boundaries were impossible to fix as the rivals shuffled their provinces in endless wars.

Memory of the Oyrat legacy has been preserved in epic poetry by the Kazakhs and Kyrgyz, who both suffered under the Oyrats' ruthless predations.

Unruly nomadic clans produced constant pressure on their periphery. Bukhara and Khiva vainly claimed nominal control over the nomadic Turkmen, who prowled the Karakum desert and provided the khanates with slaves from Persia and the Russian borderlands. Kokand spread into the Tian Shan mountains and the Syr-Darya basin in the early 19th century, while Bukhara further exercised nominal control over northern Afghanistan and much of modern-day Tajikistan.

The khans ruled absolutely as feudal despots. Some of them were capable rulers; some, such as the last emir of Bukhara, were depraved and despised tyrants. In the centuries since Transoxiana had waned as the centre of Islam, the mullahs had slipped into hypocrisy and greed. The level of education and literacy was low, and the *ulama* (intellectual class) seems to have encouraged superstition and ignorance in the people.

It was no dark age, however – trade was vigorous. This was especially true in Bukhara, where exports of cotton, cloth, silk, karakul fleece and other goods gave it a whopping trade surplus with Russia. Commerce brought in new ideas, with resulting attempts to develop irrigation and even to reform civil administrations. European travellers in the 19th century mentioned the exotic architectural splendour of these distant glimmering capitals.

In none of the three khanates was there any sense among the local people that they belonged to a distinct nation – whether of Bukhara, Khiva or Kokand. In all three, *sarts* (town dwellers) occupied the towns and farms, while clans who practised nomadism and seminomadism roamed the uncultivated countryside. *Sarts* included both Turkic-speaking Uzbeks and Persian-speaking Tajiks. These two groups had almost identical lifestyles and customs, apart from language.

In many respects, the three khanates closely resembled the feudal city-states of late-medieval Europe. But it is anybody's guess how they and the Kazakh and Kyrgyz nomads might have developed had they been left alone.

1837	1839–42	1842
Herat is the scene of battle between Russian-assisted Persians and British-backed Afghans. It is an initial skirmish in the Great Game, as Herat becomes known as 'the Gateway to India'.	British occupation of Afghanistan ends in disastrous retreat from Kabul.	British officers Conolly and Stoddart beheaded in front of the Ark by the Emir of Bukhara.

THE RUSSIANS ARE COMING!

By the turn of the 19th century Russia's vista to the south was of anachronistic, unstable neighbours, who had a nasty habit of raiding southern settlements, even taking Christian Russians as slaves. Flush with the new currents of imperialism sweeping Europe, the empire found itself embarking willy-nilly upon a century of rapid expansion across the steppe.

The reasons were complex. The main ingredients were the search for a secure, and preferably natural, southern border, nagging fears of British expansion from India, and the boldness of individual tsarist officers. And probably, glimmering in the back of every patriotic Russian's mind, there was a vague notion of the 'manifest destiny' of the frontier.

The first people to feel the impact were the Kazakhs. Their agreements in the mid-18th century to accept Russian 'protection' had apparently been understood by St Petersburg as agreements to annexation and a few decades later Tatars and Cossacks were sent to settle and farm the land. Angered, the Kazakhs revolted. As a consequence, the khans of the three hordes were, one by one, stripped of their autonomy, and their lands were made into bona fide Russian colonies, sweet psychological revenge, no doubt, for centuries of invasion by nomadic armies from the east. In 1848, as the USA was gaining land stretching from Texas to California, Russia abolished the Great Horde, ending the last line of rulers directly descended, by both blood and throne, from Chinggis Khan. Kokand was the first of the three Uzbek khanates to be absorbed, followed by Bukhara (1868) and then Khiva (1873).

The last and fiercest people to hold out against the tsarist juggernaut were the Tekke, the largest of the Turkmen clans. Of all nomad groups, the Tekke had managed to remain the most independent of the khanates. Some Turkmen clans had asked to be made subjects of Russia as early as 1865, for convenient help in their struggle against the Khivan yoke. But none were in a mood to have their tethers permanently shortened as Russia expanded into their territory.

Much blood was spilled in the subjugation of the Tekke. The Russians were trounced in 1879 at Teke-Turkmen, but returned with a vengeance in 1881 with a huge force under General Mikhail Dmitrievich Skobelev (who famously rode a white horse and dressed only in white). The siege and capture of Geok-Tepe, the Tekkes' last stronghold, resulted in the death of around 15,000 Tekke and only 268 Russians.

With resistance crushed, the Russians proceeded along the hazily defined Persian frontier area, occupying Merv in 1884 and the Pandjeh Oasis on the Afghan border in 1885. It was the southernmost point they reached. Throughout the conquest, the government in St Petersburg agonised over every advance. On the ground their hawkish generals took key cities first and asked for permission later.

> 'Russia has two faces, an Asiatic face which looks always towards Europe, and a European face which looks always towards Asia.'
> BENJAMIN DISRAELI

1862–84	1877	1890
Tsarist Russia takes Bishkek (1862), Aulie-Ata (1864), Tashkent (1865), Samarkand (1868), Khiva (1873), Kokand (1877) and Merv (1884).	German geographer Ferdinand von Richthofen coins the term 'Silk Road' to describe the transcontinental network of trade routes between Europe and China.	Captain Francis Younghusband thrown out of the Pamirs by his Russian counterpart, much to the outrage of British hawks.

When it was over, Russia found it had bought a huge new territory – half the size of the USA, geographically and ethnically diverse, and economically rich – fairly cheaply in terms of money and lives, and in just 20 years. It had not gone unnoticed by the world's other great empire further south in British India.

THE GREAT GAME

What do two expanding empires do when their ill-defined frontiers draw near each other? They scramble for control of what's between them, using a mix of secrecy and stealth.

The British called the ensuing struggle for imperial power the 'Great Game'; in Russia it was the 'Tournament of Shadows'. In essence it was the first cold war between East and West. All the ingredients were there: spies and counterspies, demilitarised zones, puppet states and doom-saying governments whipping up smokescreens for their own shady business. All that was lacking was the atom bomb and a Russian leader banging his shoe on the table. Diplomatic jargon acquired the phrase 'sphere of influence' during this era.

The phrase 'Great Game' was first coined by British officer Arthur Conolly (later executed in Bukhara) and immortalised by Kipling in his novel *Kim*.

The story of the Great Game would be dull as dishwater except that its centre arena was some of the world's most exotic and remote terrain. The history of Central Asia's international relations from the beginning of the 19th century to the present day can be seen in the context of the Great Game, for this was the main reason for Russian interest in the region.

As the Russians spread into Central Asia, the British turned towards Afghanistan. In 1836 British officer Alexander 'Bukhara' Burnes visited Kabul to woo the Emir Dost Mohammed but when the emir also entertained a Russian envoy from Moscow, the British decided the emir must go and a friendlier ruler installed in his place. The British invaded from the south via Kandahar and Ghazni and took Kabul, settling into imperial garrison life, as a tribal revolt formed in the mountains. The spark of violence was the murder of Burnes, when a mob burst into his house in Kabul and hacked him to death. As events spun out of control, the British retreated. On 5 January 1842, 4500 British soldiers and their families and 12,000 camp followers headed towards Peshawar in the dead of winter. Within five days 12,000 were dead, lost to the winter cold and the *jezails* (muskets) of the local Ghilzai tribes. Three days later a sole survivor, one Dr William Brydon, limped into the garrison at Jalalabad on a half-dead pony to bring back news of the disaster. It was an ignominious end to the first Anglo-Afghan War. Rudyard Kipling's famous poem 'The Young British Soldier' captured the horror in words that still resonate strongly today:

> When you're wounded and left on Afghanistan's plains,
> And the women come out to cut up what remains,
> Jest roll to your rifle and blow out your brains,
> An' go to your Gawd like a soldier.

1893	1916	1917
The 1640-mile Durand Line is drawn between Afghanistan and British India. The line still marks the current border but is still crossed at will by everyone from Pashtun smugglers to Taliban militants.	An uprising over forced labour conscription during WWI leads to over 200,000 Kazakhs fleeing to China.	The Bolshevik October Revolution in Russia leads to the creation of the Tashkent Soviet.

By 1848 the British had defeated the Sikhs and taken control of the Punjab and the Peshawar valley. With a grip now on the 'Northern Areas' Britain began a kind of cat-and-mouse game with Russia across the vaguely mapped Pamir and Hindu Kush ranges. Agents posing as scholars, explorers, hunters, merchants – and even Muslim preachers and Buddhist pilgrims – criss-crossed the mountains, mapping the passes, spying on each other, courting local rulers, staking claims like dogs in a vacant lot. In 1882 Russia established a consulate in Kashgar. A British agency at Gilgit (present day Pakistan), which had opened briefly in 1877, was urgently reopened when the *mir* (hereditary ruler) of Hunza entertained a party of Russians in 1888.

Imperial tensions continued with the Russian annexation of Bukhara and Samarkand but it was the Russian occupation of Merv in 1884 that really sent blood pressures through the roof in Britain and India. Merv was a crossroads leading to Herat, an easy gateway to Afghanistan, which in turn offered entry into British India. The British government finally lost its cool the following year when the Russians went south to control Pandjeh.

Then in 1890, Francis Younghusband (later to head a British incursion into Tibet) was sent to do some politicking with Chinese officials in Kashgar. On his way back through the Pamirs he found the range full of Russian troops, and was told to get out or face arrest.

This electrified the British. They raised hell with the Russian government and invaded Hunza the following year; at the same time Russian troops skirmished in northeast Afghanistan. After a burst of diplomatic manoeuvring, Anglo-Russian boundary agreements in 1895 and 1907 gave Russia most of the Pamirs and established the Wakhan Corridor, the awkward finger of Afghan territory that divides the two former empires.

The Great Game was over. The Great Lesson for the people of the region was: 'No great power has our interests at heart'. The lesson has powerful implications today.

For more on that quintessential Great Gamester, Francis Younghusband, read Patrick French's excellent biography *Younghusband*.

COLONISATION OF TURKESTAN

In 1861, the outbreak of the US Civil War ended Russia's imports of American cotton. To keep the growing textile industry in high gear, the natural place to turn to for cotton was Central Asia. Other sectors of Russian industry were equally interested in the new colonies as sources of cheap raw materials and labour, and as huge markets. Russia's government and captains of industry wisely saw that their own goods could not compete in Europe but in Central Asia they had a captive, virgin market.

In the late 19th century, European immigrants began to flood the tsar's new lands, a million in Kazakhstan alone. The new arrivals were mostly freed Russian and Ukrainian serfs hungry for land of their own. Central Asia also offered a chance for enterprising Russians to climb socially. The first

1919	1919–29	1920
Third Anglo-Afghan War results in Afghan independence from Britain.	King Amanullah attempts modernist reform program in Afghanistan, resulting in tribal rebellion.	Soviet troops seize Khiva and Bukhara, replacing the respective khanate and emirate with People's Soviet Republics.

mayor of Pishpek (Bishkek) left Russia as a gunsmith, married well in the provinces, received civil appointments, and ended his life owning a mansion and a sprawling garden estate.

Work began on the Trans–Caspian railway at Krasnovodsk in 1880 and reached Samarkand in 1888. The Orenburg–Tashkent line was completed in 1905. This was also the golden age of Russian exploration in Central Asia, whose famous figures – Semenov, Przewalski and Merzbacher – are only today starting to get credit abroad.

'The out-
break of
WWI in 1914
had disas-
trous conse-
quences in
Central Asia.'

The Russian middle class brought with them straight streets, gas lights, telephones, cinemas, amateur theatre, charity drives, parks and hotels. All these were contained in enclaves set apart from the original towns. Through their lace curtains the Russians looked out on the Central Asian masses with a fairly indulgent attitude. The Muslim fabric of life was left alone, as were the mullahs, as long as they were submissive. Development, both social and economic, was initially a low priority. When it came, it took the form of small industrial enterprises, irrigation systems and a modest program of primary education.

In culture it was the Kazakhs, as usual, who were the first to be influenced by Russia. A small, Europeanised, educated class began for the first time to think of the Kazakh people as a nation. In part, their ideas came from a new sense of their own illustrious past, which they read about in the works of Russian ethnographers and historians. Their own brilliant but short-lived scholar, Shokan Ualikhanov (Chokan Valikhanov), was a key figure in Kazakh consciousness-raising.

THE 1916 UPRISING

Resentment against the infidel Russians ran deep and occasionally boiled over. Andijon in Uzbekistan was the scene of a rebellion, or holy war, from 1897 to 1898, which rocked the Russians out of complacency. After the insurrection was put down, steps were taken to Russify urban Muslims, the ones most under the influence of the mullahs and most likely to organise against the regime.

The outbreak of WWI in 1914 had disastrous consequences in Central Asia. In Zhetisu/Semireche (southeastern Kazakhstan), massive herds of Kazakh and Kyrgyz cattle were requisitioned for the war effort, whereas Syr-Darya, Fergana and Samarkand provinces had to provide cotton and food. Then, in 1916, as Russia's hopes in the war plummeted, the tsar demanded men. Local people in the colonies were to be conscripted as noncombatants in labour battalions. To add insult to injury, the action was not called 'mobilisation' but 'requisition', a term usually used for cattle and materiel.

Exasperated Central Asians just said no. Starting in Tashkent, an uprising swept eastwards over the summer of 1916. It gained in violence, and attracted harsher reprisal, the further east it went. Purposeful attacks on Russian militias and official facilities gave way to massive rioting, raiding and looting. Colonists were massacred, their villages burned, and women and children carried off.

1920–26	1921	1928–30
Basmachi rebel movement in Central Asia reaches a peak, with as many as 16,000 armed men fighting the Soviet army.	Creation of Turkestan Soviet Socialist Republic (SSR).	Latin script replaces Arabic script in Central Asia, rendering millions illiterate overnight, to be replaced again by Cyrillic script in 1939–40.

The resulting bloody crackdown is a milestone tragedy in Kyrgyz and Kazakh history. Russian troops and vigilantes gave up all pretence of a 'civilising influence' as whole Kyrgyz and Kazakh villages were brutally slaughtered or set to flight. Manhunts for suspected perpetrators continued all winter, long after an estimated 200,000 Kyrgyz and Kazakh families had fled towards China. The refugees who didn't starve or freeze on the way were shown little mercy in China.

REVOLUTION & CIVIL WAR

For a short time after the Russian Revolution of 1917, which toppled the tsar, there was a real feeling of hope in some Central Asian minds. The Central Asian society which the West, out of ignorance and mystification, had labelled backward and inflexible had actually been making preparations for impressive progress. The Young Bukharans and Young Khivans movements agitated for social self-reform, modelling themselves on the Young Turks movement which had begun transforming Turkey in 1908. The Jadidists, adherents of educational reform, had made small gains in modernising Uzbek schools. The Bolsheviks made sure, however, that we will never know how Central Asia might have remade itself.

In 1917 an independent state was launched in Kokand by young nationalists under the watchful eye of a cabal of Russian cotton barons. This new government intended to put into practice the philosophy of the Jadid movement: to build a strong, autonomous Pan-Turkic polity in Central Asia by modernising the religious establishment and Westernising and educating the people. Within a year the Kokand government was smashed by the Red Army's newly formed Trans-Caspian front. More than 5000 Kokandis were massacred after the city was captured. Central Asians' illusions about peacefully coexisting with Bolshevik Russia were shattered as well.

Bolshevik Conquest

Like most Central Asians, Emir Alim Khan of Bukhara hated the godless Bolsheviks. In response to their first ultimatum to submit, he slaughtered the Red emissaries who brought it and declared a holy war. The emir conspired with White (anti-Bolshevik) Russians and even British political agents, while the Reds concentrated on strengthening party cells within the city.

For more on Nazaroff's cat-and-mouse exploits on the run in Central Asia from the Bolsheviks, read his *Hunted Through Central Asia*.

In December 1918 a counter revolution broke out, apparently organised from within Tashkent jail by a shadowy White Russian agent named Paul Nazaroff. Several districts and cities fell back into the hands of the Whites. The bells of the cathedral church in Tashkent were rung in joy, but for the last time. The Bolsheviks defeated the insurrection, snatched back power, and kept it. Nazaroff, freed from jail, was forced to hide and flee across the Tian Shan to Xinjiang, always one step ahead of the dreaded secret police.

1930s	1936	1941–45
Stalin's genocidal collectivisation programs strike the final blow to nomadic life. Around 20% of the Kazakh population leave the country, with a similar number dying in the ensuing famine.	Stalin's 'Great Purge' results in the arrest and execution of political leaders across the Soviet Union, including Central Asia.	Over 22 million Soviet citizens die in WWII, known locally as the Great Patriotic War. Kazakhstan and Uzbekistan each receive over one million refugees.

The end came swiftly after the arrival in Tashkent of the Red Army commander Mikhail Frunze. Khiva went out with barely a whimper, quietly transforming into the Khorezm People's Republic in February 1920. In September, Mikhail Frunze's fresh, disciplined army captured Bukhara after a four-day fight. The emir fled to Afghanistan, taking with him his company of dancing boys but abandoning his harem to the Bolshevik soldiers.

'Undeveloped Central Asia had no shortage of bright, sincere people willing to work for national liberation and democracy'

THE SOVIET ERA

From the start the Bolsheviks ensured themselves the enmity of the people. Worse even than the tsar's bleed-the-colonies-for-the-war policies, the revolutionaries levied grievous requisitions of food, livestock, cotton, land and forced farm labour. Trade and agricultural output in the once-thriving colonies plummeted. The ensuing famines claimed nearly a million lives; some say many more.

Forced Collectivisation

Forced collectivisation was the 'definite stage of development' implicit in time-warping the entire population of Central Asia from feudalism to communism. This occurred during the USSR's grand First Five Year Plan (1928–32). The intent of collectivisation was first to eliminate private property and second, in the case of the nomadic Kazakhs and Kyrgyz, to put an end to their wandering lifestyle.

The effect was disastrous. When the orders arrived, most people simply slaughtered their herds and ate what they could rather than give them up. This led to famine in subsequent years, and widespread disease. Resisters were executed and imprisoned. Millions of people died. Evidence exists that during this period Stalin had a personal hand in tinkering with meagre food supplies in order to induce famines. His aims seem to have been to subjugate the people's will and to depopulate Kazakhstan, which was good real estate for Russian expansion.

The *basmachi* (Muslim guerrilla fighters, literally 'bandits'), in twilight for some time, renewed their guerrilla activities briefly as collectivisation took its toll. It was their final struggle.

Political Repression

Undeveloped Central Asia had no shortage of bright, sincere people willing to work for national liberation and democracy. After the tsar fell they jostled for power in their various parties, movements and factions. Even after they were swallowed into the Soviet state, some members of these groups had high profiles in regional affairs. Such a group was Alash Orda, formed by Kazakhs and Kyrgyz in 1917, which even held the reins of a short-lived autonomous government.

1948	1954	1957
Ashgabat destroyed in an earthquake; 110,000 perish.	Virgin Lands campaign in Kazakhstan leads to Slav immigration and, eventually, massive environmental degradation.	Minaret of Jam 'rediscovered' by French-Afghan expedition. At the time it is the world's second-tallest minaret.

By the late 1920s, the former nationalists and democrats, indeed the entire intelligentsia, were causing Stalin serious problems. From their posts in the communist administration they had front-row seats at the Great Leader's horror show, including collectivisation. Many of them began to reason, and to doubt. Stalin, reading these signs all over the USSR, foresaw that brains could be just as dangerous as guns. Throughout the 1930s he proceeded to have all possible dissenters eliminated. Alash Orda members were among the first to die, in 1927 and 1928.

Thus began the systematic murder, called the Purges, of untold tens of thousands of Central Asians. Arrests were usually made late at night. Confined prisoners were rarely tried; if any charges at all were brought, they ran along the lines of 'having bourgeoisie-nationalist or Pan-Turkic attitudes'. Mass executions and burials were common. Sometimes entire sitting governments were disposed of in this way, as happened in Kyrgyzstan (see p294).

Construction of Nationalities

The solution to the 'nationality question' in Central Asia remains the most graphically visible effect of Soviet rule: it drew the lines on the map. Before the Russian Revolution the peoples of Central Asia had no concept of a firm national border. They had plotted their identities by a tangle of criteria: religion, clan, valley or oasis, way of life, even social status. The Soviets, however, believed that such a populace was fertile soil for dangerous Pan-Islamism and Pan-Turkism. These philosophies were threats to the regime.

Ultimately, each nation became the namesake for a Soviet Socialist Republic (SSR). Uzbek and Turkmen SSRs were proclaimed in 1924, the Tajik SSR in 1929, and the Kazakh and Kyrgyz SSRs in 1936.

So, starting in about 1924, nations were invented: Kazakh, Kyrgyz, Tajik, Turkmen, Uzbek. Each was given its own distinct ethnic profile, language, history and territory. Where an existing language or history was not apparent or was not suitably distinct from others, these were supplied and disseminated. Islam was cut away from each national heritage, essentially relegated to the status of an outmoded and oppressive cult, and severely suppressed throughout the Soviet period.

Some say that Stalin personally directed the drawing of the boundary lines (see p392). Each of the republics was shaped to contain numerous pockets of the different nationalities, and each with long-standing claims to the land. Everyone had to admit that only a strong central government could keep order on such a map. The present face of Central Asia is a product of this 'divide and rule' technique.

World War II

'The Great Patriotic War Against Fascist Germany' galvanised the whole USSR and in the course of the war Central Asia was drawn further into the Soviet fold. Economically the region lost ground from 1941 to 1945 but a

1966	1973	December 1978
Tashkent levelled in earthquake, leaving 300,000 homeless.	Daoud overthrows King Zahir Shah, declares Afghanistan a republic.	Soviet army invades Afghanistan and installs new regime.

THE REBIRTH OF THE SILK ROAD

The two decades since the fall of the USSR has seen a mini-revival in all things Silk Road in Central Asia. The re-establishment of rail links to China and Iran (and plans for links to Afghanistan), the growth of border trade over the Torugart, Irkeshtam, Qolma and Khunjerab passes, the rebuilding of bridges to Afghanistan and the increase in oil piped along former silk routes have all reconnected the 'stans with their ethnic and linguistic relatives to the south and east, while offering a means to shake off ties with Moscow. Goods from Turkey, Iran and, especially, China now dominate local bazaars as they did centuries ago. Camel trains may have been replaced by Kamaz trucks and silk replaced by scrap metal, but the Silk Road remains as relevant as it ever was.

---

sizable boost came in the form of industrial enterprises arriving ready-to-assemble in train cars: evacuated from the war-threatened parts of the USSR, they were relocated to the remote safety of Central Asia. They remained there after the war and kept on producing.

Other wartime evacuees – people – have made a lasting imprint on the face of Central Asia. Koreans, Volga Germans, Chechens and others whom Stalin suspected might aid the enemy were deported from the borderlands and forcibly relocated en masse. They now form sizable minority communities in all the former Soviet Central Asian republics.

For many wartime draftees, WWII presented an opportunity to escape the oppressive Stalinist state. One Central Asian scholar claims that more than half of the 1.5 million Central Asians mobilised in the war deserted. Large numbers of them, as well as prisoners of war, actually turned their coats and fought for the Germans against the Soviets.

Agriculture

The tsarist pattern for the Central Asian economy had been overwhelmingly agricultural; so it was with the Soviets. Each republic was 'encouraged' to specialise in a limited range of products, which made their individual economies dependent on the Soviet whole. Tajik SSR built the world's fourth-largest aluminium plant but all the aluminium had to brought in from outside the region.

The Uzbek SSR alone soon supplied no less than 64% of Soviet cotton, making the USSR the world's second-largest cotton producer after the USA. Into the cotton bowl poured the diverted waters of the Syr-Darya and Amu-Darya, while downstream the Aral Sea was left to dry up. Over the cotton-scape was spread a whole list of noxious agricultural chemicals, which have wound up polluting waters, blowing around in dust storms, and causing serious health problems for residents of the area. For further details, see p100.

March 1979	1979–89	8 December 1991
Ismail Khan leads a rebellion in Herat, killing dozens of Russian advisors and their families. The Russians carpet bomb the city in response, leading to the death of 24,000 civilians.	Mujaheddin fight holy war against Soviet army resulting in the death of 15,000 Soviets, 1.5 million Afghans, and the exodus of six million refugees, over half the country's population.	Collapse of the Soviet Union, as Russia, Ukraine and Belarus found the Commonwealth of Independent States (CIS). Two weeks later the Central Asian ex-Soviet republics join and Gorbachev resigns three days later.

Another noxious effect of cotton monoculture was what's known as the 'cotton affair' of the Brezhnev years. A huge ring of corrupt officials habitually over-reported cotton production, swindling Moscow out of billions of roubles. When the lid finally blew off, 2600 participants were arrested and more than 50,000 were kicked out of office, including Brezhnev's own son-in-law.

In 1954 the Soviet leader Nikita Khrushchev launched the Virgin Lands campaign. The purpose was to jolt agricultural production, especially of wheat, to new levels. The method was to put Kazakh SSR's enormous steppes under the plough and resettle huge numbers of Russians to work the farms. Massive, futuristic irrigation schemes were drawn up to water the formerly arid grassland, with water taken from as far away as the Ob River in Siberia. The initial gains in productivity soon dwindled as the fragile exposed soil of the steppes literally blew away in the wind. The Russians, however, remained.

Benefits of the Soviet Era

In spite of their heavy-handedness, the Soviets made profound improvements in Central Asia. Overall standards of living were raised considerably with the help of health care and a vast new infrastructure. Central Asia was provided with industrial plants, mines, farms, ranches and services employing millions of people (never mind that no single republic was given the means for a free-standing economy, and that most operations were coordinated through Moscow). Outside the capitals, the face of the region today is still largely a Soviet one.

Education reached all social levels (previously education was through the limited, men-only network of Islamic schools and medressas), and pure and applied sciences were nurtured. Literacy rates hit 97% and the languages of all nationalities were given standard literary forms. The Kyrgyz language was given an alphabet for the first time.

Soviet women had 'economic equality' and although this meant that they had the chance to study and work alongside men *while* retaining all the responsibilities of homemakers, female literacy approached male levels, maternity leave was introduced and women assumed positions of responsibility in middle-level administration as well as academia.

Artistic expression was encouraged within the confines of communist ideology and cinemas and theatres were built. The Central Asian republics now boast active communities of professional artists who were trained, sometimes lavishly, by the Soviet state. And through the arts, the republics were allowed to develop their distinctive national traditions and identities (again, within bounds).

If the Central Asian republics were at all prepared when independence came, they were prepared by the Soviet era.

From the Mongol destruction of irrigation canals to the Russian harnessing of water for cotton production and the death of the Aral Sea, the control of water in the deserts of Central Asia has been central to the region for centuries and will continue to be a source of future contention.

Central Asia's old Arabic alphabet was replaced by the Soviets with a Latin one, and later with a Cyrillic script. Several republics (Turkmenistan and Uzbekistan) have shifted back to a Latin script, meaning older people are using alphabets incomprehensible to the youth.

April 1992	1992–97	1994–6
Mujaheddin factions capture Kabul, triggering a civil war. Over the next four years the city is bombed, shelled and all but destroyed by the shifting mujaheddin alliances, as 50,000 Kabulis lose their lives.	Civil war in Tajikistan claims 60,000 lives and displaces 500,000.	Tailban capture Kandahar, Herat and finally Kabul, ruling Afghanistan until 2001. Their first act in the capital is to lynch former President Najibullah.

The Soviet-Afghan War

In 1979 the Soviet army invaded Afghanistan, determined to prop up a crumbling communist regime on their doorstep. In retrospect, someone should have consulted the history books beforehand, for the lessons of history are clear; no one wins a war in Afghanistan. Of the 50,000 Soviet troops engaged in Afghanistan, up to 20,000 were Central Asians, mainly Tajiks and Uzbeks, drafted into the war to liberate their backward relatives. They faced a poorly equipped but highly motivated guerrilla force, the mujaheddin, united for once in their jihad against the godless invaders.

Funding soon poured in from the USA, determined to bleed the USSR and create a 'Soviet Vietnam'. The biggest covert CIA operation of all time funnelled funds through the Pakistan secret service, the Inter Service Agency (ISA) and the Afghans quickly found themselves in the middle of a proxy Cold War.

Peshawar became home to mujaheddin, arms dealers, journalists, spies, CIA agents and gem dealers, who brought donkeyloads of Badakhshani lapis and rubies over the high mountain passes in exchange for weapons. Resistance by guerrilla commanders like Ahmad Shah Massoud (see p472) was boosted by the arrival of helicopter-crunching Stinger missiles. Gradually the tide turned.

In the end, after 10 years of brutal guerrilla war that claimed the lives of 15,000 Soviets and 1.5 million Afghans, the Soviets finally pulled out, limping back over the Amu-Darya to Termiz. They weren't quite massacred to a man as the British before them but the strains of war indelibly contributed to the cracking of the Soviet empire. Over six million Afghans had fled the country for refugee camps in neighbouring Iran and Pakistan. Afghanistan was shattered and the USSR would never recover.

POST-SOVIET CENTRAL ASIA

One Russian humorist has summed up his country's century in two sentences: 'After titanic effort, blood, sweat and tears, the Soviet people brought forth a new system. Unfortunately, it was the wrong one'.

By the spring of 1991 the parliaments of all five Central Asian republics had declared their sovereignty. However, when the failure of the August coup against Gorbachev heralded the final end of the USSR, none of the republics was prepared for the reality of independence.

With independence suddenly thrust upon them, the old Soviet guard was essentially the only group with the experience and the means to rule. Most of these men are still in power today. All the Central Asian governments are still authoritarian to some degree, running the gamut from pure *ancien regime*-style autocracy (Turkmenistan), to a tightly controlled mixture of neocommunism and spurious nationalism (Uzbekistan), to a marginally more enlightened 'channelled transition' to democracy and a market economy (Kazakhstan and Kyrgyzstan).

Ghost Wars by Steve Coll is a gripping and intricately researched history of the CIA's covert funding of the Afghan mujaheddin and the spawning of Al-Qaeda in Afghanistan.

When the Soviets invaded Afghanistan in December 1979 there were already 8000 Soviet troops and 4000 Soviet advisers in the country.

For a look at the Afghanistan war from the Soviet perspective try *The Hidden War: A Russian Journalist's Account of the Soviet War in Afghanistan* by Artyom Borovik or *Afghanistan: A Russian Soldier's Story* by Vladislav Tamarov.

1998	2001	2003
USA sends cruise missiles to destroy Osama bin Laden's Al-Qaeda bases in Afghanistan, in retaliation to the bombings of US embassies in Kenya and Tanzania.	The Taliban destroy the Bamiyan Buddhas and loot Kabul Museum. On 9 September Ahmad Shah Masoud is assassinated by Al-Qaeda. Operation Enduring Freedom defeats the Taliban and the Northern Alliance regains power.	US defence secretary Rumsfeld declares an 'end to major combat' in Afghanistan...

In some ways, not much changed. In most of the republics the old Communist Party apparatus simply renamed itself using various (unintentionally ironic) combinations of the words 'People', 'Party' and 'Democratic'. Political opposition was completely marginalised (Turkmenistan), banned (Uzbekistan), or tolerated but closely watched (Kazakhstan, Kyrgyzstan and Tajikistan). Kazakhstan suddenly found itself with a space program and nuclear weapons (which it promptly handed back to Russia, making it the only country ever to voluntarily return to nuclear-free status). All the republics swiftly formed national airlines from whatever Aeroflot planes happened to be parked on their runways on the day after independence.

Yet in most ways, everything changed. The end of the old Soviet subsidies meant a decline in everything from economic subsidies to education levels. The deepest economic trauma was/is in the countryside, but even today in the cities wages for many professionals remain low as US$35 a month. Most heart-rending were the pensioners, especially the Slavs whose pensions were made worthless overnight with the devaluation of the rouble. Throughout the 1990s, one of the most common sights across Central Asia was watery-eyed *babushkas* (old women) sitting quietly on many street corners, surrounded by a few worthless possessions for sale, trying not to look like beggars. Suddenly the Soviet era began to look like a golden age.

> The collapse of the Soviet Union sent the Central Asian republics into an economic collapse estimated at three times greater than the Great Depression of 1930s America.

QURANS & KALISHNIKOVS: THE TALIBAN IN AFGHANISTAN

With Soviet troops out of Afghanistan, the Great Powers packed up their bags, washed their hands and walked away from the country. In the gun-soaked and mine-strewn vacuum the mujaheddin commanders turned on each other, carving out private fiefdoms based on ethnic lines and fighting over the country like frenzied players in a *buzkashi* match. Kabul was shelled and pulverised in the struggle.

With the US and Russia temporarily off stage, the creation of the newly independent ex-Soviet Central Asian states added new players to the Afghan game. Uzbekistan supported the ethnic Uzbek warlord Dostum, while Tajikistan offered Massoud a home base and Iran offered support to its Shiite co-religionists the Hazaras. Even neutral Turkmenistan eyed the country as a conduit for its gas pipelines.

By 1994 a new force, the Taliban, spread through the country. Fired with religious zeal from the Deobandi medressas of Pakistan and flush with Pakistani funds and support, the black-turbaned Taliban took Kandahar, Herat and finally Kabul, pushing the mujaheddin commanders to the edges of the country.

The Taliban were initially received as heroes for bringing security and peace to a war-weary people, but their one-eyed leader Mullah Omar's real agenda was the creation of the world's purest Islamic state. Women were swiftly banned from work and public education, the burqa became

> *Taliban* by Ahmed Rashid is the definitive bestselling history of that movement. Rashid's most recent title, *Descent Into Chaos*, links Afghan opium, Taliban insurgency, Uzbek torture, US rendition and Pakistan's tribal areas, in a searing depiction of the West's failures in the region.

2004	13 May 2005	2005
New Afghan constitution created by *loya jirga*, a tribal grand council. After three years as interim leader, Hamid Karzai is elected president in the country's first elections.	Massacre of between 200 and 1000 unarmed protestors by government troops in Andijon, Uzbekistan. The incident sours relationships between Uzbekistan and the USA and Europe, and Uzbekistan swings back politically towards Russia.	Kyrgyzstan's Tulip Revolution sweeps President Akaev from power, forcing curbs on the new president's power.

PIPE DREAMS – THE NEW GREAT GAME

Central Asia and the Caspian region is a mother lode of energy and raw materials, representing perhaps the most concentrated mass of untapped wealth in the world, a wealth measured in trillions of dollars. It is this fact that quietly drives many countries' Central Asian and Afghanistan policies.

All eyes are on Kazakhstan, Central Asia's brightest economy, sitting pretty on what is estimated to be the word's third largest oil reserves, but don't forget Turkmenistan, which boasts the world's fourth largest reserves of natural gas. Kazakhstan and Uzbekistan also have major natural gas reserves.

As Western energy firms jockey to strike high-stake deals in a region of interlocking interests, this scramble is taking on a geopolitical significance. Russia, the US, China, the UK, Europe, Iran, Turkey, India and Pakistan all have vital strategic interests in securing both energy resources and control over their supply.

Russia's traditional stranglehold on supply routes has been challenged recently. Turkey has built a pipeline across the Caspian to Ceyhan, while Europe is proposing a second link, the Nabucco pipeline, through the Caucasus and Turkey, once again to bypass Russia. Other pipe dreams include the TAPI line from Turkmenistan to Afghanistan, Pakistan and India, originally conceived by the US company Unocal. In 1997 the Americans even invited Taliban leaders to Texas, where they met with Unocal's Afghan representative, one Hamid Karzai. Security in Afghanistan has long been a prerequisite for American pipe dreams.

China has also become a major player in the scramble for influence. It recently spent billions of dollars to become the main shareholder of PetroKazakhstan and is currently building a 3000km-long pipeline to Ürümqi. There are epic plans to continue this along the former Silk Road to Japan, making China the energy corridor of the east.

Governments are well aware of the dangers of laying major oil pipelines through volatile Central Asia but the strategic need to ensure fuel supplies and the financial rewards are simply too fantastic to walk away from. This superpower competition for oil and gas in the region – dubbed 'round two of the Great Game' – can only intensify and it is a rivalry which will have increasing resonance over the ensuing decades.

Items 'Tali-banned' (banned by the Taliban) included music, movies, nail polish, lipstick, playing cards, neckties, photography, long hair, shaving, kites and paper bags (lest they accidentally carry verses from the Quran).

compulsory, men were forced to grow beards and the Taliban 'Department to Propagate Virtue and Eliminate Vice' banned everything from music to kite-flying as un-Islamic. As they dragged Afghanistan back to the 8th century, the Taliban wiped away traces of the country's rich pre-Islamic past, including the remarkable 1500-year-old Buddhas of Bamiyan.

During the 1980s over 30,000 foreign fighters from Pakistan and the Middle East had joined the Afghan jihad against the Soviets. Some of these now turned on their former arms suppliers, the US, in a classic case of what the CIA terms 'blowback'. Afghanistan became a base not only for Osama bin Laden and Al-Qaeda but also a training centre for regional Islamist groups like the Islamic Movement of Uzbekistan (IMU) and Islamist guerrillas engaged in a brutal civil war in neighbouring Tajikistan. Afghanistan had become a ticking bomb.

2005	2006	2006
Parliamentary elections held in Afghanistan.	Turkmenistan's 'President for life' Niyazov (Turkmenbashi) dies, ending one of the modern era's great personality cults.	NATO takes responsibility for Afghan security; widespread violence across the south.

CENTRAL ASIA & THE WAR ON TERROR

The September 11 2001 attacks on New York changed everything in Central Asia. Citing Afghan rules of hospitality, the Taliban refused to handover Osama bin Laden. As war was waged from 30,000ft the Taliban simply took off their turbans and melted away, as did Bin Laden, lost somewhere in the caves of Tora Bora. When the dust settled Hamid Karzai was elected as Afghanistan's interim head and an International Assistance Force (ISAF) rushed to provide security, first in Kabul and then across the country.

The early years after 2001 saw 4.5 million Afghan children return to school (including girls), five million refugees return home, a reduction in the numbers of arms and an economic rebirth in Kabul, alongside a war-weary and traumatised population and a shattered infrastructure. As the Iraq war gradually diverted American effort and attention away from Afghanistan, the warlords, drug mafia and then the Taliban quietly crept back. Suicide bombings, previously unseen in Afghanistan, began to rock Afghan cities. The security situation worsened in the south, reconstruction programs ground to a halt, and public support started to crumble amidst talk of massive corruption, collateral damage and 'foreign invaders'.

Financed by a multibillion dollar opium trade, the Taliban can afford to play a waiting game, hoping the foreign invaders will lose heart, as foreign invaders always have in Afghanistan. Afghanistan's nickname, 'the graveyard of Empires', has proved prophetic throughout history. US and NATO troops are currently hoping to beat the odds, but they are stuck in a nasty conundrum: there can be no reconstruction and development without peace and there can be no long-term peace without development.

The Central Asian republics (particularly Uzbekistan) look south to Afghanistan's chaos in horror, using the perceived threat of Islamic insurgency to justify their increasing repressive policies. Separate bombings in Uzbekistan, Kyrgyzstan and Tajikistan in 2009 underscored the threat but it's hard to say whether armed attacks are the cause for repression, or rather a result of it. The region's political tensions also remain deep, as evidenced by the street demonstrations and violence that unseated Kyrgyz president Bakiev and pushed Kyrgyzstan to the brink of civil war in 2010.

In the words of journalist Ahmed Rashid, the West is 'losing' Afghanistan and Central Asia. As long as the issues of reform, reconstruction, poverty, development and corruption remain unaddressed across the entire region, Central Asia will likely be a fertile breeding ground for dissent of all kinds for years to come.

Presidents Nazarbaev (in power since 1989), Karimov (1990) and Rakhmon (1994) continue to rule without active opposition. President Niyazov of Turkmenistan upped the ante further, proclaiming himself 'president for life' in 1999. Only his death in December 2006 forced him out of office.

All the Central Asian countries ranked in the bottom 20% of Transparency International's 2008 Corruption Perceptions Index, with Uzbekistan and Afghanistan reckoned the most corrupt.

2009	2010	June 2010
Disputed Afghan elections between Pashtun incumbent Hamid Karzai and Tajik foreign minister Abdullah Abdullah; Karzai eventually wins, amid allegations of fraud.	Violent street demonstrations force Kyrgyz president Bakiev from office, leaving over 70 dead.	At least 200 killed and 400,000 displaced in ethnic clashes between Kyrgyz and Uzbeks in Osh in the Kyrgyz Fergana Valley. Tens of thousands of Uzbek refugees flee to the Uzbekistan–Kyrgyzstan border.

People

From gold-toothed Turkmen in shaggy, dreadlocked hats to high-cheekboned Kyrgyz herders whose eyes still carry the glint of a nomadic past, Central Asia presents a fascinating collection of faces and peoples. The total population of the former Soviet Central Asia is about 57 million, with another 28 million in Afghanistan. Few areas of its size are home to such tangled demographics and daunting transitions.

Each republic inherited an ethnic grab bag from the Soviet system. Thus you'll find Uzbek towns in Kyrgyzstan, legions of Tajiks in the cities of Uzbekistan, Kazakhs grazing their cattle in Kyrgyzstan, Turkmen in Uzbekistan – and Russians and Ukrainians everywhere. Given the complicated mix of nationalities across national boundaries, Central Asia's ethnic situation is surprisingly tranquil. The most noticeable divide (and a largely amicable one) is between the traditionally sedentary peoples, the Uzbeks and Tajiks, and their formerly nomadic neighbours, the Kazakhs, Kyrgyz and Turkmen.

PEOPLES OF THE SILK ROAD

Centuries of migrations and invasions, and a location at the crossroads of Asia have added to Central Asia's ethnic diversity. A trip from Ashgabat to Almaty reveals an absorbing array of faces from Turkish, Slavic, Chinese and Middle Eastern to downright Mediterranean – surmounted, incidentally, by an equally vast array of hats.

Before the Russian Revolution of 1917, Central Asians usually identified themselves 'ethnically' as either nomad or *sarts* (settled), as Turk or Persian, as simply Muslim, or by their clan. Later, separate nationalities were 'identified' by Soviet scholars as ordered by Stalin. Although it is easy to see the problems this has created, some Kazakhs and Kyrgyz say that they owe their survival as a nation to the Soviet process of nation building.

In many ways Afghanistan is less a country than a patchwork of ethnic groups that spill over regional borders, a fact that is key to an understanding of recent conflict. Afghan society splintered violently along ethnic fault lines during the civil war of the 1990s, with Uzbek, Tajik and Hazara warlords battling each other and the Pashtun Taliban for control.

The following sections are a summary of the peoples of Central Asia.

Central Asian identity has always centred as much around oases (such as Bukhara, Merv, Herat, Tejend and Khorezm) as it does around the concept of a modern nation state.

KAZAKHS

KAZAKHS
Kazakhstan: 10 million
China: 1.4 million
Russia: 600,000
Uzbekistan: 500,000
Mongolia: 140,000
Turkmenistan: 80,000
Kyrgyzstan: 40,000

The Kazakhs were nomadic horseback pastoralists until the 1920s; indeed the name Kazakh is said to mean 'free warrior' or 'steppe roamer'. Kazakhs trace their roots to the 15th century, when rebellious kinsmen of an Uzbek khan broke away and settled in present-day Kazakhstan. They divide themselves into three main divisions, or *zhuz*, corresponding to the historical Great (southern Kazakhstan), Middle (north and east Kazakhstan) and Little (west Kazakhstan) Hordes (see p119). To this day family and ancestry remain crucial to Kazakhs. 'What *zhuz* do you belong to?' is a common opening question.

Most Kazakhs have Mongolian facial features, similar to the Kyrgyz. Most wear Western or Russian clothes, but you may see women – particularly on special occasions – in long dresses with stand-up collars or brightly decorated velvet waistcoats and heavy jewellery. On similar occasions men may sport baggy shirts and trousers, sleeveless jackets and wool or cotton robes. This outfit may be topped with either a skullcap or a high, tasselled felt hat resembling nothing so much as an elf's hat.

Kazakh literature is based around heroic epics, many of which concern themselves with the 16th-century clashes between the Kazakhs and Kalmucks, and the heroic *batyr* (warriors) of that age. Apart from various equestrian sports (see the boxed text, p64, and p367), a favourite Kazakh pastime is *aitys*, which involves two people boasting about their own town, region or clan while running down the other's, in verses full of puns and allusions to Kazakh culture. The person who fails to find a witty comeback loses.

Kazakhs adhere rather loosely to Islam. Reasons for this include the Kazakhs' location on the fringe of the Muslim world and their traditionally nomadic lifestyle, which never sat well with central religious authority. Their earliest contacts with the religion, from the 16th century, came courtesy of wandering Sufi dervishes or ascetics. Many were not converted until the 19th century, and shamanism apparently coexisted with Islam even after conversion.

Having a longer history of Russian influence than other Central Asian peoples, and with international influences now flooding in thanks to Kazakhstan's free-market economy and oil wealth, Kazakhs – in the cities at least – are probably Central Asia's most cosmopolitan people. The women appear the most confident and least restricted by tradition in Central Asia – though the custom of bride-stealing (with or without her collusion) has not altogether disappeared in rural areas and the more Kazakh-dominated towns in Kazakhstan's south.

> Kazakhs and Kyrgyz share many customs and have similar languages, and in a sense they are simply the steppe (Kazakh) and mountain (Kyrgyz) variants of the same people.

The 10 or so million Kazakhs have only recently become a majority in 'their' country, Kazakhstan.

KYRGYZ

The name Kyrgyz is one of the oldest recorded ethnic names in Asia, going back to the 2nd century BC in Chinese sources. At that time the ancestors of the modern Kyrgyz are said to have lived in the upper Yenisey Basin (Ene-Sai, or Yenisey, means 'Mother River' in Kyrgyz) in Siberia. They migrated to the mountains of what is now Kyrgyzstan from the 10th to 15th centuries, some fleeing wars and some arriving in the ranks of Mongol armies.

Many Kyrgyz derive their name from *kyrk kyz*, which means '40 girls', which fits with oral legends of 40 original clan mothers. Today, ties to such clans as the Bugu (the largest clan), Salto (around Bishkek), Adigine (around Osh) and Sary-Bagysh remain relevant and politicised. Clans are divided into two federations, the Otuz Uul (30 Sons) of the north and the Ich Kilik of southern Kyrgyzstan. The southern and northern halves of the country remain culturally, ethnically and politically divided, as demonstrated in the violent political upheaval of 2010 (see p294).

> **KYRGYZ**
>
> Kyrgyzstan: three million
> Tajikistan: 300,000
> Uzbekistan: 180,000
> China: 143,000
> Afghanistan: 3000

During special events older Kyrgyz women may wear a large white wimple-like turban (known as an *elechek*) with the number of windings indicating her status. Kyrgyz men wear a white, embroidered, tasselled felt cap called

---

HOLY SMOKE

In markets, stations and parks all over Central Asia you'll see gypsy women and children asking for a few coins to wave their pans of burning herbs around you or the premises. The herb is called *isriq* in Uzbek, and the smoke is said to be good medicine against colds and flu (and the evil eye), and a cheap alternative to scarce medicines. Some people also burn it when they move into a new home.

an *ak kalpak*. In winter, older men wear a long sheepskin coat and a round fur-trimmed hat called a *tebbetey*.

Most Kyrgyz now live in towns and villages but herders still do make the annual trek with their yurts up to *jailoos* (summer pastures). Traditions such as the Manas epic (see p296), horseback sports and eagle hunting (p331) remain important cultural denominators. One lingering nomadic custom is that of wife stealing (p293), whereby a man may simply kidnap a woman he wants to marry (often with some collusion, it must be said), leaving the parents with no option but to negotiate a *kalym* (bride price).

In 1979 there were around 30,000 Kyrgyz nomads in the Little Pamirs of the Afghan Wakhan. With the arrival of war in 1980 the community packed up its yurts and fled to Gilgit, finally relocating to eastern Turkey three years later after a failed attempt to emigrate to Alaska. Around 1500 Kyrgyz are left, maintaining a semi-nomadic lifestyle herding yaks, sheep and Bactrian camels.

The Kirghiz and Wakhi of Afghanistan: Adaptation to Closed Frontiers and War by Afghan anthropologist Nazif Shahran describes the traditional life and challenges faced by the inhabitants of the remote Wakhan.

TAJIKS

With their Mediterranean features and the occasional green-eyed redhead, Tajiks like to tell visitors that their land was once visited by Alexander the Great and his troops, who are known to have taken local brides. Whether that blood is still visible or not, the Tajiks are in fact descended from an ancient Indo-European people, the Aryans, making them relatives of present-day Iranians. The term 'Tajik' is a modern invention. Before the 20th century, *taj* was merely a term denoting a Persian speaker (all other Central Asian peoples speak Turkic languages).

BUZKASHI

In a region where many people are descended from hot-blooded nomads, no one would expect badminton to be the national sport. Even so, *buzkashi* (literally 'grabbing the dead goat') is wild beyond belief. As close to warfare as a sport can get, *buzkashi* is a bit like rugby on horseback in which the 'ball' is the headless carcass of a calf, goat or sheep (whatever is handy).

The day before the kickoff the *boz* (carcass) has its head, lower legs and entrails removed and is soaked in cold water for 24 hours to toughen it up. The game begins with the carcass in the centre of a circle at one end of a field; at the other end is a any number of wild, adrenaline-crazed horsemen, known as *chapandazan*. At a signal it's every man for himself as they charge for the carcass. The aim is to gain possession of the *boz* and carry it up the field and around a post, with the winning rider being the one who finally drops the *boz* back in the circle. All the while there's a frenzied horsebacked tug-of-war going on as each competitor tries to gain possession; smashed noses and wrenched shoulders are all part of the fun.

Not surprisingly, the game is said to date from the days of Chinggis (Genghis) Khan, a time when it enforced the nomadic values necessary for collective survival – courage, adroitness, wit and strength, while propagating a remarkable skill on horseback. The point of the game used to be the honour, and perhaps notoriety, of the victor, but gifts such as silk *chapan* (cloaks), cash or even cars are common these days.

Buzkashi takes place mainly between autumn ploughing and spring planting seasons, in the cooler months of spring and autumn, at weekends, particularly during Navrus or to mark special occasions such as weddings or national days. Mazar-e Sharif in Afghanistan is the number-one place to find authentic *buzkashi* but if you are lucky you might catch local versions in the Wakhan Valley, Faizabad or Lake Shewa in Afghanistan, in Kyrgyzstan (where it's known as *ulak-tartysh*), Uzbekistan *(kupkari)* and Kazakhstan *(kokpar)*. Navrus is the best time to find a game on, especially in Mazar-e Sharif, Hissar (outside Dushanbe) or the hippodrome at Shymkent in Kazakhstan.

Tracing their history back to the Samanids, Bactrians and Sogdians, Tajiks consider themselves to be the oldest ethnic group in Central Asia and one that predates the arrival of the Turkic peoples. Some Tajik nationalists have even demanded that Uzbekistan 'give back' Samarkand and Bukhara, as these cities were long-time centres of Persian culture.

There are in fact many Tajik subdivisions and clans (such as the Kulyabis and Khojandis), which is one reason why the country descended into civil war after the fall of the USSR.

Badakhshani or Pamir Tajik (sometimes called mountain Tajiks) are a distinct group, speaking a mix of languages quite distinct from Tajik and following a different branch of Islam. Most Tajiks are Sunni Muslims, but Pamiri Tajiks of the Gorno-Badakhshan region belong to the Ismaili sect of Shiite Islam, and therefore have no formal mosques. Most Badakhshani define themselves primarily according to their valley (Shugni, Rushani, Yazgulami, Wakhi and Ishkashimi), then as Pamiris, and finally as Tajiks.

Traditional Tajik dress for men includes a heavy, quilted coat *(chapan)*, tied with a sash that also secures a sheathed dagger, and a black embroidered cap *(tupi)*, which is similar to the Uzbek *dopy*. Tajik women could almost be identified in the dark, with their long, psychedelically coloured dresses *(kurta)*, matching headscarves *(rumol)*, striped trousers worn under the dress *(izor)* and bright slippers.

There are almost eight million Tajiks in northern, western and northeastern Afghanistan (about one quarter of the population). Afghani Tajiks follow a code of conduct called Abdurzadagai, similar to the Pashtun Pashtunwali but share closer ties to their valley than their ethnic group. Their language Dari (very similar to Tajik) served as the language of government for centuries, even while the reigns of government were dominated by Pashtuns. Tajiks, led by the war hero Ahmad Shah Massoud, dominated the mujaheddin and Northern Alliance governments in the 1990s.

There are also around 33,000 Sarikol and Wakhi Tajiks in China's Tashkurgan Tajik Autonomous County. Wakhi Tajiks also live in northern Pakistan.

TURKMEN

Legend has it that all Turkmen are descended from the fabled Oghuz Khan or from the warriors who rallied into clans around his 24 grandsons. Most historians believe that they were displaced nomadic horse-breeding clans who, in the 10th century, drifted into the oases around the Karakum desert (and into Persia, Syria and Anatolia) from the foothills of the Altay Mountains in the wake of the Seljuq Turks.

Turkmen men are easily recognisable in their huge, shaggy sheepskin hats *(telpek)*, either white (for special occasions) or black with thick ringlets resembling dreadlocks, worn year-round on top of a skullcap, even on the hottest days. As one Turkmen explained it, they'd rather suffer the heat of their own heads than that of the sun. Traditional dress consists of baggy trousers tucked into knee-length boots, and white shirts under the knee-length *khalat*, a cherry-red cotton jacket. Older men wear a long, belted coat.

Turkmen women wear heavy, ankle-length velvet or silk dresses, the favourite colours being wine reds and maroons, with colourful trousers underneath. A woman's hair is always tied back and concealed under a colourful scarf. Older women often wear a *khalat* thrown over their heads as protection from the sun's rays.

The Turkmen shared the nomad's affinity for Sufism, which is strongly represented in Turkmenistan alongside the cult of sheikhs (holy men), amulets, shrines and pilgrimage. The Turkmen language (also called Turkmen)

TAJIKS

Tajikistan: 4.4 million

Afghanistan: 7.7 million

Uzbekistan: 630,000

Kazakhstan: 100,000

China: 33,000

Kazakhs make up 56% of Kazakhstan, Tajiks 65% of Tajikistan, Kyrgyz 66% of Kyrgyzstan, Uzbeks 80% of Uzbekistan and Turkmen 85% of Turkmenistan.

TURKMEN

Turkmenistan: 3.6 million

Iran: one million

Afghanistan: 650,000

is closest to Azeri. Interestingly, there was a Turkmen literary language as early as the mid-18th century.

UZBEKS

UZBEKS

Uzbekistan: 18 million

Tajikistan: 1.6 million

Afghanistan: 2.6 million

Kyrgyzstan: 690,000

Kazakhstan: 457,000

Turkmenistan: 396,000

China: 14,700

The Uzbek khans, Islamised descendants of Chinggis Khan, left their home in southern Siberia in search of conquest, establishing themselves in what is now Uzbekistan by the 15th century, clashing and then mixing with the Timurids. The Uzbek Shaybanid dynasty oversaw the transition from nomad to settler, although the original Mongol clan identities (such as the Kipchak, Mangits and Karluks) remain.

The focal point of Uzbek society is still the network of tight-knit urban *mahalla* (districts) and *kishlak* (rural villages), where neighbours attend one another's weddings, celebrations and funerals. Advice on all matters is sought from an *aksakal* (revered elder, literally 'white beard'), whose authority is conferred by the community. In general Uzbeks resisted Russification and emerged from Soviet rule with a strong sense of identification and their rich heritage.

Uzbek men traditionally wear long quilted coats tied by a brightly coloured sash. Nearly all wear the *dopy* or *doppilar,* a black, four-sided skullcap embroidered in white. In winter, older men wear a furry *telpek*. Uzbek women are fond of dresses in sparkly, brightly coloured cloth *(ikat)*, often as a knee-length gown with trousers of the same material underneath. One or two braids worn in the hair indicate that a woman is married; more mean that she is single. Eyebrows that grow together over the bridge of the nose are considered attractive and are often supplemented with pencil for the right effect. Both sexes flash lots of gold teeth.

There are around 1.3 million Uzbeks in northern Afghanistan, north of the Hindu Kush, who have historically grown cotton or traded in karakul fleeces. Ties to the local *arbab* (landlord) are still strong in this region. Afghanistan's most famous Uzbek is strongman, militia leader and warlord General Abdul Rashid Dostum, who fought both for and against the Soviets in the 1980s and currently holds a post in the Afghan government.

Check out www.oxuscom.com/uzbeks.pdf for more information on the Uzbek people.

SLAVS

Russians and Ukrainians have settled in Central Asia in several waves, the first in the 19th century with colonisation, and the latest in the 1950s during the Virgin Lands campaign (see p57). Numerous villages in remoter parts of Central Asia were founded by the early settlers and are still inhabited by their descendants.

Many Slavs, feeling deeply aggrieved as political and administrative power devolves to 'local' people, have emigrated to Russia and Ukraine. At the height of the migration more than 280,000 Russians left Kazakhstan and 200,000 left Tajikistan in a single year, most of them well-educated professionals. Some have returned, either disillusioned with life in the motherland or reaffirmed in the knowledge that Central Asia is their home, like it or not. Some 3.8 million Russians and 333,000 Ukrainians live in Kazakhstan alone.

PASHTUNS

PASHTUNS

Pakistan: 26 million

Afghanistan: 12 million

Pashtuns are the largest ethnic group in Afghanistan, making up around 42% of the population. The most ancient Aryan texts refer to them as the Paktua, while Herodotus talks of the Paktues; the British preferred the name Pathans. Many Pashtuns (also known as Pashtos or Pakhtuns, depending on the regional pronunciation) live over the border in Pakistan's lawless Tribal Areas.

Pashtuns are divided starkly along clan lines, the largest of which are the southern Durranis and southeastern Ghilzai, though there are dozens of others subclans (known as *khel*) such as the Wazir, Afridi, Khattak and Shinwari. President Hamid Karzai is a Pashtun of the Popolzai clan. Kandahar is considered the centre of Pashtun culture and it was from here that Mullah Omar ruled Afghanistan during the Taliban years.

Traditional Pashtuns live by a moral code called Pashtunwali that stresses deep-rooted notions of *siali* (equality), *badal* (revenge), *melmastia* (hospitality), *nang* (honour) and *nanawatai* (sanctuary). Blood vendettas are common. Over the centuries they have been stereotyped as loyal, honest, brave, independent and wily, with a love of freedom and guns, perpetually waiting in ambush on some craggy bluff.

> For two decades Afghans made up the world's largest single group of refugees, primarily in Iran (about 2.5 million) and Pakistan (5 million). Five million have returned home since the fall of the Taliban.

OTHER PEOPLES

Dungans are Muslim Chinese who first moved across the border in 1882, mainly to Kazakhstan and Kyrgyzstan, to escape persecution after failed Muslim rebellions. Few still speak Chinese, though their cuisine remains distinctive.

Over half-a-million Koreans arrived in Central Asia as deportees in WWII. They have preserved little of their traditional culture. They typically farm vegetables and sell their pickled salads in many bazaars.

A further half-a-million Germans were deported in WWII from their age-old home in the Volga region, or came as settlers (some of them Mennonites) in the late 19th century. Most have since departed to Germany but pockets remain, and you'll come across the occasional village in Central Asia with a German name, such as Rotfront in Kyrgyzstan. Likewise, most Jews, an important part of Bukharan commerce since the 9th century, have moved to Israel (and Queens, New York). The chief rabbi of Central Asia remains in Bukhara, though – see p262.

> The first census in Afghanistan for 30 years is planned for 2010, if the security situation permits.

Karakalpaks occupy their own republic in northwest Uzbekistan (see p276) and have cultural and linguistic ties with Kazakhs, Uzbeks and Kyrgyz.

Kurds are another WWII-era addition to the melting pot, with many living in Kazakhstan. Estimates of their numbers in Central Asia range from 150,000 to over a million. Meskhetian Turks have groups in the Fergana (the largest concentration), Chuy and Ili Valleys. It is estimated that there are half a million Uyghurs in the former Soviet Central Asian republics (having moved there from Xinjiang after heavy Chinese persecution in the late 19th century), with about half of these in Kazakhstan.

BODY LANGUAGE

A heartfelt handshake between Central Asian men is a gesture of great warmth, elegance and beauty. Many Central Asian men also place their right hand on the heart and bow or incline the head slightly, a highly addictive gesture that you may find yourself echoing quite naturally. Afghan men in particular are great huggers.

Good friends throughout the region shake hands by gently placing their hands, thumbs up, in between another's. There's no grabbing or Western-style firmness, just a light touch. Sometimes a good friend will use his right hand to pat the other's. If you are in a room full of strangers it's polite to go around the room shaking hands with everyone. Don't be offended if someone offers you his wrist if his hands are dirty. Some say the custom originates from the need to prove that you come unarmed as a friend.

Women don't usually shake hands but touch each others' shoulders with right hands and slightly stroke them. Younger women in particular will often kiss an elder woman on the cheek as a sign of respect.

THE UNSEEN FACES OF AFGHANISTAN

Attitudes to women in Afghanistan are radically different from ex-Soviet Central Asia, so much so that crossing the border from Tajikistan into Afghanistan feels like stepping back through the centuries. It's quite easy for male travellers to travel for weeks in conservative Afghanistan without ever seeing a woman's face.

To most Afghan men women are a powerful symbol of family honour, and society seeks to minimise contact between unrelated men and women. The hijab (veil) covers the hair of all Afghan women and unlike in the ex-Soviet republics, the blue shuttlecock-shaped burqa (or *chaderi*) is a frequent sight. The much-maligned burqa has become a particularly powerful symbol of women's status in Afghanistan, though its role is also much misunderstood in the West.

In the early 1970s women strolled the streets of Afghanistan wearing skirts, a sight inconceivable just a decade later. The darkest days came during the Taliban era, when women were forbidden from working, attending school after the age of eight, appearing in public without a male companion (a particularly cruel prohibition considering Afghanistan's tens of thousands of war widows), or receiving medical help from a male doctor. Resistance took place in the form of home tuition and even home beauty parlours.

Today the statistics for female health and education make for grim reading. Around 87% of Afghan women are illiterate, while the average life expectancy for a woman in Afghanistan is just 44 and infant mortality ranks amongst the highest in the world. Forced marriage and domestic abuse are common.

There has been progress in recent years. Thousands of girls schools reopened after the fall of the Taliban (though many schools have been threatened and attacked in the wake of the Taliban resurgence) and in 2005 for the first time a woman became governor of an Afghan province (Bamiyan). Still it's hard to say whether women are really that much better off compared to a decade ago.

Bushy beards and Kalashnikovs are only half the story in Afghanistan. To dig a little deeper the following books offer powerful insights into the unseen faces of Afghan women:

Three Women of Herat: A Memoir of Life, Love and Friendship in Afghanistan (Veronica Doubleday) An intimate portrait of women in the 1970s, a world now largely lost.

Afghanistan, Where God Only Comes to Weep (Siba Shakib) Powerful novel depicting the struggles of a defiant Afghan woman, by the Iranian-German author.

Kabul in Winter: Life Without Peace in Afghanistan (Ann Jones) A well-written look at the lives of Afghan women, with a journalist's eye.

Veiled Threat: The Hidden Power of the Women of Afghanistan (Sally Armstrong) Journalistic look at a cross-section of Afghan women's lives during Taliban rule.

You may see colourfully dressed South Asian–looking women and children begging or working as fortune-tellers. These are Central Asian gypsies, called *luli (chuki)*, who number around 30,000, speak Tajik and originate from areas around Samarkand, southern Tajikistan and Turkmenistan.

Hazaras are the third-largest ethnic group in Afghanistan, totalling about 2.5 million in the mountainous centre of the country. Descendants of Mongol troops, they have high-cheekboned Mongolian faces. As Dari-speakers and followers of Shia Islam, they have long been supported by co-religionists Iran but discriminated against inside Afghanistan, especially under the Taliban who tried to bomb and starve the Hazaras into submission.

Out of Steppe: The Lost Peoples of Central Asia follows author Daniel Metcalfe through five of the 'stans searching for lost communities of Karakalpaks, Bukharan Jews, Germans, Afghan Hazaras and Sogdians.

The fair-skinned and blue-eyed Nuristanis of northeast Afghanistan were once known as the *kafir* (infidels) because of their polytheistic belief system. Most were converted to Islam in the late 19th century. They have close connections to the Kafir Kailash of Pakistan.

Afghanistan has around three million pastoral nomads known as Kuchi, generally considered a Pashtun tribe. You might see Kuchi caravans on their annual migration to pastures around remote Lake Shewa in Badakhshan.

Many Kuchis have lost much of their livestock in recent years to droughts and land mines. Other nomads include the Dari-speaking Aimaq in central and western Afghanistan.

Other ethnic groups in Afghanistan include Baluchis, who span the southern border with Pakistan and Iran.

DAILY LIFE

It's been a social rollercoaster in Central Asia since independence: the overall birth rate is down, deaths from all causes are up, economies have plummeted, crime has skyrocketed, life expectancies have dropped and migration (most especially emigration) is on the rise. Many older Central Asians lost their social and cultural bearings with the fall of the Soviet Union. Health levels are plummeting, drug addiction is up and alcoholism has acquired the proportions of a national tragedy.

But it's not all bad news. Traditional life is reasserting itself in today's economic vacuum and tourism projects are encouraging traditional crafts, sports and music. Communities remain strong and notions of hospitality remain instinctual despite the economic hardships. After 20 years of uncertainty, most people have started to find their way in the new order.

> Afghans share a particular love of competitive games, from fighting partridges to duelling kites and even egg fighting. One curious BBC headline from 1999 read 'Six Killed in Afghan Egg Fight', after the Taliban tried to break up an un-Islamic egg fight by using rocket launchers.

TRADITIONAL CULTURE

In Islam, a guest – Muslim or not – has a position of honour not very well understood in the West. If someone visits you and you don't have much to offer, as a Christian you'd be urged to share what you have; as a Muslim you're urged to give it all away. Guests are to be treated with absolute selflessness.

For a visitor to a Muslim country, even one as casual about Islam as Kazakhstan or Kyrgyzstan, this is a constant source of pleasure, temptation and sometimes embarrassment. The majority of Central Asians, especially rural ones, have little to offer but their hospitality, and a casual guest could drain a host's resources and never know it. And yet to refuse such an invitation (or to offer to bring food or to help with the cost) would almost certainly be a grave insult.

All you can do is enjoy it, honour their customs as best you can, and take yourself courteously out of the picture before you become a burden. If for some reason you do want to decline, couch your refusal in gracious and diplomatic terms, allowing the would-be host to save face. As an example, if you are offered bread, you should at least taste a little piece before taking your leave.

If you are really lucky you might be invited to a *toi* (celebration) such as a *kelin toi* (wedding celebration), a *beshik toi* (nine days after the birth of a child), or a *sunnat toi* (circumcision party). Other celebrations are held to mark the birth, name giving and first haircut of a child.

Afghans are the region's most deeply conservative and religious people, mixing great grace, hospitality and pride. (On arriving in Afghanistan in 1933, Robert Byron famously quipped 'Here at last is Asia without an inferiority complex'.) Thirty years of war, combined with the exodus and return of millions of refugees, has fractured natural ties and traditional lifestyles throughout the country, yet most Afghans maintain traditional lifestyles and deeply conservative attitudes to family, religion and the role of women. Foreign women are often treated as an 'honorary male' by local Afghan men.

While most Central Asians have adopted Western dress (especially tracksuits) with enthusiasm, almost all Afghan men regardless of ethnicity wear

DOS & DON'TS

- Dress codes vary throughout Central Asia. Outside of Afghanistan, the main place where you should dress conservatively is Uzbekistan's Fergana Valley (see p282). Western-style clothes are acceptable in the capital cities and in large towns such as Samarkand, which see a lot of tourist traffic.

- Working mosques are generally closed to women and often to non-Muslim men, though men will likely be invited in outside of prayer times. In Kazakhstan women can visit many working mosques but may be restricted to a special women's gallery. When visiting a mosque, always take your shoes off at the door, and make sure your feet or socks are clean. It is polite to refer to the Prophet Mohammed as such, rather than by his name alone. Never walk in front of someone praying to Mecca.

- When you visit someone's home, take your shoes off at the door unless you are told not to. You will often find a pair of undersized flip-flops waiting for you at the door. (Traditional Central Asian footwear consists of overshoes, which can be taken off without removing the *massi*, soft leather under boots.) Avoid stepping on any carpet if you have your shoes on. See p90 for tips on food etiquette.

- Try not to blow your nose in public; it's considered rude.

- Central Asian society devotes much respect to its elderly, known as *aksakal* (white beards). Always make an effort to shake hands with an elder. Younger men give up their seats to *aksakal*, and foreigners should certainly offer their place in a crowded chaikhana (teahouse). Some Central Asians address elders with a shortened form of the elder's name, adding the suffix 'ke'. Thus Abkhan becomes Abeke, Nursultan becomes Nureke, and so on.

the traditional *pirhan tonban* – a knee-length shirt over super-baggy trousers, better known in neighbouring Pakistan as a *shalwar kameez*. Pashtuns wear a pancake-shaped beret known as a *pakul*, and carry a *pattu* (multipurpose shawl/scarf/blanket/hat), while traditional Afghans of all ethnic groups wear a turban, or *lungi*.

Religion

With the exception of rapidly shrinking communities of Jews and Russian Orthodox Christians, small minorities of Roman Catholics, Baptists and evangelical Lutherans, and a few Buddhists among the Koreans of the Fergana Valley and Kyrgyzstan, nearly everyone from the Caspian Sea to Kabul is Muslim, at least in principle. The years since independence have seen a resurgence of a faith that is only beginning to recover from 70 years of Soviet-era 'militant atheism'.

ISLAM
History & Schisms

In AD 612, the Prophet Mohammed, then a wealthy Arab of Mecca in present-day Saudi Arabia, began preaching a new religious philosophy, Islam, based on revelations from Allah (Islam's name for God). These revelations were eventually compiled into Islam's holiest book, the Quran.

Islam incorporates elements of Judaism and Christianity (eg heaven and hell, a creation story much like the Garden of Eden, stories similar to Noah's Ark) and shares a reverence for many of the same prophets (Abraham/Ibrahim, Moses/Musa, Jesus/Isa), but treats these prophets simply as forerunners of the Prophet Mohammed. While Jews and Christians are respected as People of the Book (ahl al-Kitab), Islam regards itself as the summation of and last word on these faiths.

In 622 the Prophet Mohammed and his followers were forced to flee to Medina due to religious persecution (the Islamic calendar counts its years from this flight, known as Hejira). There he built a political base and an army, taking Mecca in 630 and eventually overrunning Arabia. The militancy of the faith meshed nicely with a latent Arab nationalism and within a century Islam reached from Spain to Central Asia.

Succession disputes after the Prophet's death (632 AD) soon split the community. When the fourth caliph, the Prophet's son-in-law Ali, was assassinated in 661, his followers and descendants became the founders of the Shiite sect. Others accepted as caliph the governor of Syria, a brother-in-law of the Prophet, and this line has become the modern-day orthodox Sunni sect. In 680 a chance for reconciliation was lost when Ali's surviving son Hussain (Hussein) and most of his male relatives were killed at Kerbala in Iraq by Sunni partisans.

About 80% of all Central Asians are Muslim, nearly all of them Sunni (and indeed nearly all of the Hanafi school, one of Sunnism's four main schools of religious law). The main exception is a tightly knit community of Ismailis in the remote western Pamirs of Gorno-Badakhshan in eastern Tajikistan (see p401).

A small but increasingly influential community of another Sunni school, the ascetic, fundamentalist Wahhabi, are found mainly in Uzbekistan's Fergana Valley.

About 80% of Afghans are followers of Sunni Islam, with the Hazara making up most of the 19% Shiite minority.

Practice

Devout Muslims express their faith through the five pillars of Islam (see the boxed text, p72).

Devout Sunnis pray at prescribed times: before sunrise, just after high noon, in the late afternoon, just after sunset and before retiring. Prayers

The oldest Quran, the Osman Quran, is kept in Tashkent (p218). It was written just 19 years after the death of the Prophet Mohammed and was later brought to Central Asia by Timur.

The word Islam translates loosely from Arabic as 'the peace that comes from total surrender to God'.

To learn more about Ismailism, try the scholarly Short History of the Ismailis: Traditions of a Muslim Community, or The Isma'ilis: Their History and Doctrines, both by Farhad Daftary.

are preceded if possible by washing, at least of the hands, face and feet. For Ismailis the style of prayer is a personal matter (eg there is no prostration), the mosque is replaced by a community shrine or meditation room and women are less excluded.

The melancholy sounding Arabic azan (call to prayer) translates roughly as 'God is most great. There is no god but Allah. Mohammed is God's messenger. Come to prayer, come to security. God is most great'.

Just before fixed prayers a muezzin calls the Sunni and Shiite faithful, traditionally from a minaret, nowadays often through a loudspeaker. Islam has no ordained priesthood, but mullahs (scholars, teachers or religious leaders) are trained in theology, respected as interpreters of scripture, and are sometimes quite influential in conservative rural areas, especially in Afghanistan.

The Quran is considered above criticism: it is the direct word of God as spoken to his Prophet Mohammed. It is supplemented by various traditions such as the Hadith, the collected acts and sayings of the Prophet Mohammed. In its fullest sense Islam is an entire way of life, with guidelines for nearly everything, from preparing and eating food to banking and dress.

Sufism

The original Sufis were simply purists, unhappy with the worldliness of the early caliphates and seeking knowledge of God through direct personal experience, under the guidance of a teacher or master, variously called a sheikh, Pir, *ishan, murshid* or *ustad*. There never was a single Sufi movement; there are manifestations within all branches of Islam. For many adherents music, dance or poetry were routes to trance, revelation and direct union with God. Secret recitations, known as *zikr*, and an annual 40-day retreat, known as the *chilla*, remain cornerstones of Sufic practice. This mystical side of Islam parallels similar traditions in other faiths.

The Bakhautdin Naqshband Mausoleum (p268) in Bukhara is Central Asia's most important Sufi shrine. Afghanistan's holiest Sufi shrine is probably the tomb of poet and mystic Khoja Abdullah Ansari, at the Gazar Gah complex outside Herat.

Sufis were singularly successful as missionaries, perhaps because of their tolerance of other creeds. It was largely Sufis, not Arab armies, who planted Islam firmly in Central Asia and the subcontinent. The personal focus of Sufism was most compatible with the nomadic lifestyle of the Kazakh and Kyrgyz in particular. Although abhorred nowadays in the orthodox Islamic states of Iran and Saudi Arabia, Sufism is in a quiet way dominant in Central Asia. Most shrines you'll see are devoted to one Sufi teacher or another.

When Islam was itself threatened by invaders (eg the Crusaders), Sufis assumed the role of defenders of the faith, and Sufism became a mass movement of regimented tariqas (brotherhoods), based around certain holy places, often the tombs of the tariqas' founders. Clandestine, anticommunist tariqas helped Islam weather the Soviet period, and the KGB and its predecessors never seemed able to infiltrate.

The moderate, non-elitist Naqshbandiya tariqa was the most important in Soviet times, and probably still is. Founded in Bukhara in the 14th century, much of its influence in Central Asia perhaps comes from the high profile of Naqshbandi fighters in two centuries of revolts against the Russians in the Caucasus. In 1944 large Chechen and Ingush communities were deported

FIVE PILLARS OF ISLAM

- The creed that 'There is only one god, Allah, and Mohammed is his prophet'.
- Prayer, five times a day, prostrating towards the holy city of Mecca, in a mosque (for men only) when possible, but at least on Friday, the Muslim holy day.
- Dawn-to-dusk fasting during Ramadan.
- Making the haj (pilgrimage to Mecca) at least once in one's life (many of those who have done so can be identified by their white skullcaps).
- Alms giving, in the form of the zakat, an obligatory 2.5% tax.

to Siberia and Kazakhstan. When, after Stalin's death, the survivors were permitted to return to their homeland, they left behind several well-organised Sufi groups in Central Asia. A number of well-known 1930s *basmachi* (Muslim guerrilla fighters) leaders were Naqshbandis, as were several of Afghan's mujaheddin.

Another important Sufi sect in Central Asia is the Qadiriya, founded by a teacher from the Caspian region. Others are the Kubra (founded in Khorezm, p457) and Yasauia (founded in the town of Turkistan in Kazakhstan). All these were founded in the 12th century.

Jihad: The Rise of Militant Islam in Central Asia, by Ahmed Rashid (2002), is a review of how and why Islamic militant groups rose in the Fergana Valley from the ashes of the Soviet Union.

Islam in Central Asia

Islam first appeared in Central Asia with Arab invaders in the 7th and 8th centuries, though it was mostly itinerant Sufi missionaries who converted the region over the subsequent centuries.

Islam never was a potent force in the former nomadic societies of the Turkmen, Kazakhs and Kyrgyz, and still isn't. Islam's appeal for nomadic rulers was as much an organisational and political tool as a collection of moral precepts. The nomad's customary law, known as *adat*, was always more important than Islamic sharia.

The Central Asian brand of Islam is also riddled with pre-Islamic influences – just go to any important holy site and notice the kissing, rubbing and circumambulation of venerated objects, women crawling under holy stones to boost their fertility, the shamanic 'wishing trees' tied with bits of coloured rag, the cult of Pirs (saints) and the Mongol-style poles with horse-hair tassels set over the graves of revered figures. Candles and flames are often burned at shrines and graves, and both the Tajiks and Turkmen jump over a fire during wedding celebrations or the Qurban (Eid al-Azha) festival, traditions that hark back to fire-worshipping Zoroastrian times. The Turkmen place particular stock in amulets and charms. At Konye-Urgench Turkmen women even roll en masse down a hillside in an age-old fertility rite (p459).

There is also a significant blurring between religious and national characteristics. The majority of Central Asians, although interested in Islam as a common denominator, seem quite happy to toast the Prophet's health with a shot of vodka.

Some archaeologists believe that the Bronze Age site of Gonur Depe (see p453) was the birthplace of the world's first monotheist faith, Zoroastrianism, while others believe it to be Balkh in northern Afghanistan.

The Soviet Era

The Soviet regime long distrusted Islam because of its potential for coherent resistance, both domestically and internationally. Three of the five pillars of Islam (the fast of Ramadan, the haj and the zakat tax) were outlawed in the 1920s. The banning of polygamy, child marriage, the paying of bride price and the wearing of the paranja (veil) possibly pleased many women but the banning of Arabic script, the holy script of the Quran, was much less popular. Clerical (Christian, Jewish and Buddhist as well as Muslim) land and property were seized. Medressas and other religious schools were closed down. Islam's judicial power was curbed with the dismantling of traditional sharia courts (which were based on Quranic law).

From 1932 to 1936 Stalin mounted a concerted antireligious campaign in Central Asia, a 'Movement of the Godless', in which mosques were closed and destroyed, and mullahs arrested and executed as saboteurs or spies. By the early 1940s only 2000 of its 47,000 mullahs remained alive. Control of the surviving places of worship and teaching was given to the Union of Atheists, which transformed most of them into museums, dance halls, warehouses or factories.

During WWII things improved marginally as Moscow sought domestic and international Muslim support for the war effort. In 1943 four Muslim

The percentage of practising Muslims in the ex-Soviet republics ranges from 47% in Kazakhstan to 75% in Kyrgyzstan, 85% in Tajikistan, 88% in Uzbekistan and 89% in Turkmenistan.

Religious Boards or 'spiritual directorates', each with a mufti (spiritual leader), were founded as administration units for Soviet Muslims, including one in Tashkent for all of Central Asia (in 1990 one was established for Kazakhstan). Some mosques were reopened and a handful of carefully screened religious leaders were allowed to make the haj in 1947.

But beneath the surface little changed. Any religious activity outside the official mosques was strictly forbidden. By the early 1960s, under Khrushchev's 'back to Lenin' policies, another 1000 mosques were shut. By the beginning of the Gorbachev era, the number of mosques in Central Asia was down to between 150 and 250, and only two medressas were open – Mir-i-Arab in Bukhara (p261) and the Imam Ismail al-Bukhari Islamic Institute in Tashkent.

Perhaps the most amazing thing though, after 70 years of concerted Soviet repression, is that so much faith remains intact. Credit for any continuity from pre-Soviet times goes largely to 'underground Islam', in the form of the clandestine Sufi brotherhoods (and brotherhoods they were, being essentially men-only), which preserved some practices and education – and grew in power and influence in Central Asia as a result.

Islam Today in the Ex-Soviet Republics

Since independence, Central Asia has seen a resurgence of Islam, and mosques and medressas have sprouted like mushrooms across the region, often financed with Saudi or Iranian money. Even in more conservative Uzbekistan and Tajikistan, those new mosques are as much political as religious statements, and the rise of Islam has as much to do with the search for a Central Asian identity as it does with a rise in religious fervour.

Most Central Asians are torn between the Soviet secularism of the recent past and the region's deeper historical ties to the Muslim world, but few have a very deep knowledge of Islam. Only the Fergana Valley regions of Uzbekistan and southern Kyrgyzstan can be considered strongly Muslim, and only here do women commonly wear the hijab (headscarf).

All the Central Asian governments have taken great care to keep strict tabs on Islam. Only state-approved imams (preacher or religious leader) and state-registered mosques are allowed to operate in most republics. Tajikistan's Islamic Revival Party is the only Islamist party in the region not to be outlawed.

Central Asia has experienced a taste of Islamic extremism, in the form of the Islamic Movement of Uzbekistan (IMU), which launched a series of armed raids and kidnappings in 1999 to 2001 in an attempt to establish an Islamic state in Uzbekistan. The movement largely disappeared when its Al-Qaeda-supplied bases in Afghanistan were destroyed and its enigmatic leader Juma Namangani killed, but there are fears that extremists may return to Tajikistan and Uzbekistan if squeezed out of Afghanistan.

Under the cloak of the War on Terror, the Uzbek government has arrested thousands of Muslims as 'extremists', most of them from the Fergana Valley. Some, but not all, are members of the peaceful but radical organisation Hizb-ut-Tahrir (Movement of Liberation), which hopes to establish a global Islamic caliphate and has support across the region.

Turkmenistan also keeps tight controls on Islam. Turkmen mosques have quotations from former President Niyazov's book the *Ruhnama* engraved next to quotations from the Quran. The former chief cleric of Turkmenistan was charged with treason and sentenced to 22 years in prison after refusing to accept the Turkmen president as a messenger of God.

With the old communist ideals discredited, democracy suppressed and economic options stagnating, the fear is that radical Islam will provide

By 1940, after Stalin's attacks on religion, only 1000 of Central Asia's 30,000 mosques remained standing and all 14,500 Islamic schools were shut.

Before the arrival of Islam, Central Asia sheltered pockets of Zoroastrianism, Manichaeism, Judaism, Nestorian Christianity and an ancient tradition of Buddhism. In the 8th century there were even Nestorian bishoprics in Herat, Samarkand and Merv.

an alluring alternative for a Central Asian youth left with few remaining options.

Islam in Afghanistan

Afghanistan is a far more fervently devout country than any of the ex-Soviet republics and Islam is in fact one of the few things (aside from an invading army) able to unite the Afghan peoples. The village mosque plays a central role in the lives of Afghans and mullahs, *sayyid* (descendents of the Prophet Mohamed) and wandering holy men *(malang)* wield considerable influence. The Naqshbandi and Qaddirriyah Sufi orders in particular have deep roots in the country. Afghanistan has hundreds of shrines *(ziarat)* of local holy men and Sufi saints, including the famous shrine of Hazrat Ali at Mazar-e Sharif. Afghans also pray at the graves of war martyrs *(shahid)*, the most famous of whom is the iconic Ahmad Shah Massoud.

Radical Islam has traditionally played little part in Afghan culture and only appeared when society started to fracture during a quarter-century of war. It was largely Arab jihadists and Afghan refugees schooled in medressas in Pakistan who introduced the ultra-orthodox Wahhabi and Deobandi schools of Islam favoured by Osama bin Laden and the Taliban. The Taliban brand of radical and austere Islam in fact runs counter to much of traditional Afghan belief.

The Taliban did their utmost to create what they considered a 'pure' Islamic emirate, enforcing sharia Islamic law, while persecuting Shiite Hazaras, suppressing Sufi Islam and banning pre-Islamic festivals such as Navrus (Nauroz). Afghanistan has been an Islamic republic since 1992.

Most Muslims believe Ali was buried in Najaf (Iraq) but Afghan tradition says his body was brought to Balkh on a white camel and later entombed in Mazar-e Sharif's Shrine of Hazrat Ali.

Afghanistan's most sacred relic is the cloak and beard hair of the Prophet Mohammed (housed in Kandahar). Taliban leader Mullah Omar famously wrapped himself in the holy cloak, declaring himself 'Commander of the Faithful'.

Arts

Uzbekistan: Heirs to the Silk Road, by Johannes Kalter and Margareta Pavaloi, is a beautiful hardback look at the art of the region.

Set astride millennia-old trade and migration routes, Central Asia has long blended and fused artistic traditions from Turkic and Persian, Islamic and secular, settled and nomadic worlds, creating in the process an indigenous Central Asian aesthetic.

Whether it be the architectural glories of Samarkand, the other-worldly performance of a Kyrgyz bard, the visual splendour of an Afghan carpet or the exotic musical sounds blasting from your taxi driver's stereo, artistic expression lies at the heart of the Central Asian identity and will follow you on your travels through the region.

ARCHITECTURE

Central Asia's most impressive surviving artistic heritage is its architecture. Some of the world's most audacious and beautiful Islamic buildings grace the cities of Bukhara, Khiva and especially Samarkand (all in Uzbekistan). Few sights evoke the region better than the swell of a turquoise dome, a ruined desert citadel or a minaret framed black against a blazing sunset.

Due largely to the destructive urges of Chinggis (Genghis) Khan, virtually nothing has survived from the pre-Islamic era or the first centuries of Arab rule. The Bolsheviks further destroyed many of Central Asia's religious buildings, except those of architectural or historical value.

Early Influences

Monuments of Central Asia: A Guide to the Archaeology, Art and Architecture of Turkestan, by Edgar Knobloch, is an excellent overview of the region's architectural heritage, including Afghanistan.

Central Asian architecture has its roots in Parthian, Kushan and Graeco-Bactrian desert citadels, whose structure was defined by the demands of trade, security and water. Iranian, Greek and Indian art blended in the 2000-year-old desert cities of Toprak Qala, Nissa and Termiz, among others.

Environmental constraints naturally defined building construction. The lack of wood and stone forced Central Asian architects to turn to brickwork as the cornerstone of their designs. Tall portals, built to face and catch the prevailing winds, looked fabulous but also had a cooling effect in the heat of summer. The influence of a nomadic lifestyle is particularly relevant in Khiva, where you can still see the brick bases built to house the wintertime yurts of the khans.

Several important technological advances spurred the development of architectural arts, principally that of fired brick in the 10th century, coloured tilework in the 12th century and polychrome tilework in the 14th century.

Without the seemingly insignificant squinch (the corner bracketing that enables the transition from a square to an eight-, then 16-sided platform), the development of the monumental dome would have stalled. It was this tiny technology that underpinned the breathtaking domes of the Timurid era.

Timurid Architecture

For an in-depth look at the Timurid architecture of Samarkand try www.oxuscom.com/timursam.htm.

Most of the monumental architecture still standing in Central Asia dates from the time of the Timurids (14th to 15th centuries); rulers who combined barbaric savagery with exquisite artistic sophistication. During his campaigns of terror Timur (Tamerlane) forcibly relocated artisans, from Beijing to Baghdad, to Central Asia, resulting in a splendid fusion of styles in textiles, painting, architecture and metal arts.

ARCHITECTURAL HIGHLIGHTS

The following are our picks of the architectural highlights of Central Asia:

Ismail Samani Mausoleum (p262; 900–1000) In Bukhara: mesmerising brickwork.

Kalon Minaret (p261; 1127) In Bukhara: Central Asia's most impressive minaret, 48m high.

Mausoleum of Sultan Sanjar (p452; 1157) In Merv: huge double-domed Seljuq monument.

Minaret of Jam (p483; 1194) Part of ancient Ghor in central Afghanistan: this enigmatic and perplexingly remote 65m Ghorid spire was the world's tallest for over seven centuries.

Friday Mosque (p485; 1200) In Herat: astounding Ghorid monument, with four portals ablaze in mosaic colour.

Shah-i-Zinda (p244; 1300–1400) In Samarkand: features Central Asia's most stunning and varied tilework.

Bibi-Khanym Mosque (p244; 1399–1404) In Samarkand: Timur's intended masterpiece, so colossal that it collapsed as soon as it was finished.

Gur-e-Amir Mausoleum (p244; 1404) In Samarkand: exquisite ribbed dome, sheltering the tomb of Timur.

Musalla Complex (p485; 1417) In Herat: neglected remains of a once-great religious complex includes four remaining minarets and a tomb that looks lifted from Samarkand.

Ak-Saray Palace (p251; 1400–50) In Shakhrisabz: tantalising remains of Timur's once-opulent palace.

Shrine of Khoja Abu Nasr Parsa (p487; 1460s) In Balkh: famous for its elegant Timurid ribbed dome and twin corkscrew pillars, currently under renovation.

Shrine of Hazrat Ali (p486; 1480) In Mazar-e Sharif: chocolate box with every square inch covered in dizzying blue tiles.

Registan (p243; 1400–1600) In Samarkand: epic ensemble of medressas; the Sher Dor (1636) flaunts Islamic tradition by depicting two lions chasing deer, looked down upon by a Mongol-faced sun.

Lyabi-Hauz (p259; 1600) In Bukhara: delightful complex featuring a pool, *khanaka* (pilgrim resthouse) and medressa.

Char Minar (p263; 1807) In Bukhara: quirky ex-gateway, resembling a chair thrust upside down in the ground.

The Timurids' architectural trademark is the beautiful, often ribbed and elongated, azure-blue dome. Other signature Timurid traits include the tendency towards ensemble design, the monumental *pishtak* (arched entrance portal) flanked by tapering minarets, and exuberant, multicoloured tilework, all evident in the showiest of showpieces, the Registan (p243) in Samarkand.

Architectural Design

The traditional cities of Bukhara and especially Khiva reveal the most about traditional urban structure. The distinction between *ark* (fortified citadel), *shahristan* (inner city with wealthy residential neighbourhoods, bazaars and city wall) and outlying *rabad* (suburbs) has formed the structure of settlements since the first Central Asian towns appeared 4000 years ago. A second outer city wall surrounded most cities, protecting against desert storms and brigands.

Apart from the Islamic monuments mentioned below, secular architecture includes palaces (such as the Tosh-Hovli, p274, in Khiva), *ark* or *bala hissar* (forts), *hammam* (multidomed bathhouses), *rabat* (caravanserais), *tim* (shopping arcades), *tok* (or *tak;* covered crossroad bazaars) and the local *hauz* (reservoirs) that supplied the city with its drinking water.

Check out the wonderful 360-degree photos of Central Asian architectural and archaeological sights at www.world-heritage-tour.org. Click on 'Central Asia' on the world map.

MOSQUES

Islam dominates Central Asian architecture. *Masjid* (mosques) trace their design back to the house of the Prophet Mohammed, though later designs vary considerably. Common to most is the use of the portal, which leads into a colonnaded space and a covered area for prayer. Other Central Asian mosques, such as the Bolo-Hauz Mosque (p262) in Bukhara, have, instead, a flat, brightly painted roof, supported by carved wooden columns, while

CENTRAL ASIAN MONUMENTS IN DANGER

The **World Monuments Fund** (www.wmf.org) 2010 list of 'world monuments in danger' includes the old city of Herat, the desert castles of Khorezm (p268) in Uzbekistan and the architecture of Saryarka in Kazakhstan. Previous lists have warned about the fragility of the twin minarets of Ghazni (p490), the No Gombad Mosque (p487) outside Balkh and the Minaret of Jam (p483; all in Afghanistan); the ancient ruins of Merv (p452) and Nisa in Turkmenistan; and Bukhara's Abdul Aziz Khan Medressa (p259) in Uzbekistan.

still others, such as the Juma Mosque (p273) in Khiva, are hypostyle, that is with a roofed space, divided by many pillars.

Whether the place of worship is a *guzar* (local mosque), serving the local community, a *jami masjid* (Friday mosque), built to hold the entire city congregation once a week, or a *namazgokh* (festival mosque), the focal point is always the mihrab, a niche that indicates the direction of Mecca. Central Asia's largest modern mosque is at Gypjak in Turkmenistan (see p441).

MEDRESSAS

These Islamic colleges, normally two-storeys high, are set around a cloistered central courtyard, punctuated with *aivan* (or *aiwan*; arched portals) on four sides. Rows of little doors in the interior facades lead into *hujra* (cell-like living quarters for students and teachers) or *khanaka* (prayer cells or entire buildings) for the ascetic wandering dervishes who stayed there. Most medressas are fronted by monumental portals. On either side of the entrance you will normally find a *darskhana* (lecture room) to the left, and mosque to the right.

The niches in the medressas' front walls were once used as shopkeepers' stalls.

MAUSOLEUMS

The *mazar* (mausoleum) has been popular for millennia, either built by rulers to ensure their own immortality or to commemorate holy men. Most *mazars* consist of a *ziaratkhana* (prayer room), set under a domed cupola. The actual tomb may be housed in a central hall, or underground in a side *gurkhana* (tomb). Popular sites offer lodging, washrooms and even kitchens for visiting pilgrims. Tombs vary in design from the classic domed cupola style or the pyramid-shaped, tentlike designs of Konye-Urgench (p457) to whole streets of tombs as found at the glorious Shah-i-Zinda (p244) in Samarkand.

Afghanistan's No Gombad (Nine Domes) Mosque (p487), outside Balkh, is the oldest surviving mosque in Central Asia and thought to be one of world's oldest, dating from the 9th century.

MINARETS

These tall, tapering towers were designed to summon the faithful during prayer time, so most have internal stairs for the muezzin to climb. They were also used as lookouts to spot invaders, and even, in the case of the Kalon Minaret (p261) in Bukhara, as a means of execution. Some minarets (eg at Samarkand's Registan, p243) exist purely for decoration.

The best surviving caravanserai in Central Asia is the Tash Rabat (Stone Caravanserai; p346), high in the pastures of central Kyrgyzstan, near the border with China.

Decoration

Tilework is the most dramatic form of decoration in Central Asia, instilling a light, graceful air into even the most hulking of Timurid buildings. The deep cobalts and turquoise ('colour of the Turks') of Samarkand's domes have inspired travellers for centuries.

Decoration almost always takes the shape of abstract geometric, floral or calligraphic designs, in keeping with the Islamic prohibition on the representation of living creatures. Geometric and knot (*girikh*) designs were closely linked to the development of Central Asian science – star designs were a favourite with the astronomer king Ulugbek. Calligraphy is common, either in the square, stylised Kufi script favoured by the Timurids or the more scrolling, often foliated thulth script.

Tiles come in a variety of styles, either stamped, faience (carved onto wet clay and then fired), polychromatic (painted on and then fired) or jigsaw-style mosaic. Tiles are still manufactured by hand at a traditional workshop inside Herat's Friday mosque.

Take time also to savour the exquisite details of Central Asia's carved *ghanch* (alabaster), patterned brickwork, and intricately carved and painted wood.

Each of Uzbekistan's historic cities has its own colour; greens are most common in Khorezm, khakis in Bukhara and blues in Samarkand.

FILM

Central Asian cinema isn't exactly high profile, but two films well worth checking out are *Luna Papa*, by Tajikistan's Bakhtyar Khudojnazarov, and *Beshkempir*, by Kyrgyz director Aktan Abdykalykov.

AFGHANISTAN'S LOST TREASURES

As caretakers pried open the sealed vaults of the Afghan National Bank in March 2004, no one was optimistic enough to hope for much, let alone for hidden treasure. What they eventually found deep in the vault, individually wrapped in tissue paper, were 20,000 pieces of gold, including one crown alone made of 2000 gold pieces. One golden brooch depicted Aphrodite sporting Bactrian-style wings and Indian features, while Greek-style laurel leaf designs complemented Scythian bear and deer motifs from Siberia – all potent symbols of Central Asia's position astride the Silk Road.

What the staff had rediscovered was the fabled Bactrian Gold, originally unearthed in 1978 at Tillya Teppe (near Balkh) in Afghan Turkestan but lost in the confusion of the Soviet invasion before it could be catalogued. The magnificent discovery was compounded five months later by the unveiling of the Bagram ivories, a spectacular series of 1800-year-old Kushan panels originally unearthed from what was essentially an old Silk Road warehouse.

The rediscoveries were a rare piece of good news for Afghanistan's battered and bruised cultural heritage. Since the 1980s archaeological sites across the country have been looted, treasures have been stolen and ancient sites have been bombed. Thousands of priceless Graeco-Bactrian coins disappeared during the long civil war, only to eventually turn up for sale on the underground art market.

Even the contents of Kabul Museum were not safe. In 1993 a mujaheddin shell crashed through the roof of the museum and before long mujaheddin fighters had looted the building. The priceless Gandharan statues that survived were later smashed to pieces by the iconoclastic Taliban in 2001, just days after they dynamited the fabled Buddhas of Bamiyan. Ingenious staff at Kabul's National Gallery managed to save the gallery's portraits from destruction by hastily painting over them with a layer of water colours, turning portraits into temporary landscapes. The Taliban also turned their rockets on the Minar-e Chakri Buddhist pillar, as part of their attempts to wipe away all traces of pre-Islamic 'idolatry'.

Herat's famous Musalla Complex, the brainchild of Timurid Queen Gowhar Shad, is in a similarly sorry state. After surviving earthquakes, deliberate destruction by British canons in 1885 and a direct hit from a Soviet artillery shell in the 1980s, the remaining five of the original 15 minarets totter in critical danger, held up by cables that will eventually slice them in half, like wire cutting through cheese.

These days saving cultural treasures has taken a back seat to establishing security, but work is underway. The **Aga Khan Trust for Culture** (www.akdn.org/agency/aktc.html) is doing great work restoring Herat's fort and Kabul's Babur's Gardens, as well as supporting music schools and retraining mosaic tilemakers, while the **Turquoise Mountain Foundation** (www.turquoisemountain. org) works to conserve traditional architecture in Kabul.

After years of neglect and destruction, it's all part of an effort to recast and represent Afghanistan's breathtaking cultural heritage, not only to the world but, critically, to the Afghans themselves.

CELLULOID AFGHANISTAN

Bollywood 'masala' movies dominate the cinemas of Afghanistan but DVD audiences abroad have the choice of several great art-house films and documentaries on the country:

- *Afghan Star* (2008) Documentary about the Afghan version of Pop Idol and the polarised local response to it, ranging from adoration to threats of assassination. See www.afghanstardocu mentary.com.
- *The Kite Runner* (2007) Hollywood version of the popular novel by Khalid Hosseini.
- *Osama* (2003) Afghanistan's first post-Taliban film was a heartbreaking story of a young girl who has to disguise herself as a boy to work in Taliban-era Kabul. Golden Globe-winning director Siddiq Barmak discovered his star begging outside a cinema in Kabul.
- *Kandahar* (2002) Iranian director Mohsen Makhmalbaf's tale of an Afghan exile returning home to save her friend from suicide. The film met such international acclaim that even George W Bush apparently requested a special screening.
- *The Boy who Plays on the Buddhas of Bamiyan* (2001) Phil Grabsky's award-winning documentary is a touching account of a Hazara family living in the shadow of the destroyed monuments.
- *Rambo III* (1988) Afghanistan's unlikeliest cinematic outing. Sylvester Stallone goes jihad, joining the mujaheddin to kick the butts of bad Russians (with even worse accents), destroying Soviet helicopters with his bow and arrow, and taking in a game of *buzkashi* (polo-like game) in breaks between epic bouts of destruction. It's not half as much fun as it sounds.

Kazakhstan has emerged as the powerhouse filmmaker in the region, offering such recent coproduction spectaculars as *Mongol* and *Nomad,* as well as the Oscar-shortlisted silent movie *Kelin* (2009) and the documentary-style art-house hit *Tulpan,* the latter a fitting elegy to life on the Kazakh steppe. Kazakhstan-born filmmaker Timur Bekmambetov (director of *Night Watch* and *Wanted*) is perhaps the most famous Kazakhstani after Borat. Kazakhstan's annual Eurasia Film Festival exists to promote Central Asian film.

FOLK ART

Central Asian folk art developed in tune with a nomadic or seminomadic way of life, focusing on transport (horses) and home (yurts). Designs followed the natural beauty of the environment: snow resting on a leaf, the elegance of an ibex horn, the flowers of the steppe. Status and wealth were apparent by the intricacy of a carved door or a richly adorned horse. Yet art was not merely created for pleasure; each item also had a practical function in everyday life. From brightly coloured carpets used for sleeping and woven reed mats designed to block the wind, to leather bottles used for carrying *kumys* (or *qymyz;* fermented mare's milk); many of today's souvenirs in Kyrgyzstan and Kazakhstan are remnants of a recent nomadic past.

With such emphasis on equestrian culture it is not surprising that horses donned decorative blankets, inlaid wooden saddles, and head and neck adornments. Men hung their wealth on their belts with daggers and sabres in silver sheaths, and embossed leather purses and vessels for drink. Even today the bazaars in Tajikistan and the Fergana Valley are heavy with carved daggers and *pichok* (knives).

Nomads required their wealth to be portable and rich nomadic women wore stupendous jewellery, mostly of silver incorporating semiprecious stones, such as lapis lazuli and cornelian (believed to have magical properties).

Some of the best examples of Central Asian folk art can be seen at Tashkent's Museum of Applied Arts (p219).

The Arts and Crafts of Turkestan, by Johannes Kalter, is a detailed, beautifully illustrated historical guide to the nomadic dwellings, clothing, jewellery and other 'applied art' of Central Asia.

To remain portable, furnishings consisted of bright quilts, carpets and *aiyk kap* (woven bags), which were hung on yurt walls for storing plates and clothing. *Kökör* (embossed leather bottles) were used for preparing, transporting and serving *kumys;* these days empty cola bottles suffice.

Most Central Asian peoples have their own traditional rug or carpet styles. The famous 'Bukhara' rugs – so called because they were mostly sold, not made, in Bukhara – are made largely by Turkmen craftsmen in Turkmenistan and northwestern Afghanistan. Deep reds and ochres are the primary palate, with the stylised *gul* (flower) a common motif. The Kyrgyz specialise in *shyrdaks* (felt rugs with appliquéd coloured panels or pressed wool designs called *ala-kiyiz*); see p339. Kazakhs specialise in *koshma* (multicoloured felt mats).

Afghan carpets have long been in a league of their own but during the war the Afghan carpet industry moved wholesale to Pakistan and has since struggled to recapture its past glories. Andkhoi in northern Afghanistan, near the Turkmen border, is the country's traditional centre of carpet production. One quintessentially Afghan innovation is the 'war rug', popular in the 1980s for its woven folk images of tanks, Kalashnikovs and helicopter gunships. Other notable Afghan crafts include Herat's famous hand-blown blue glass and Mazar-e Sharif's *karakul* (fleece) hats, famously modelled by President Hamid Karzai.

Further north, Uzbeks make silk and cotton wall hangings and coverlets such as the beautiful *suzani* (embroidery; *suzan* is Persian for needle). *Suzani* are made in a variety of sizes and used as table covers, cushions and *ruijo* (a bridal bedspread), and thus were important for the bride's dowry. Generally using floral or celestial motifs (depictions of people and animals are against Muslim beliefs) an average *suzani* requires about two years to complete. Possibly the most accessible Kazakh textile souvenir is a *tus-kiiz* (*tush-kiyiz* in Kyrgyzstan), a colourful wall hanging made of cotton and silk.

The colourful psychedelic tie-dyed silks known as *ikat* or *khanatlas* are popular throughout the region. Take a close-up tour of how the cloth is made at the Yodgorlik Silk Factory (p238) in Margilon.

If you are into carpets, don't miss a visit to Ashgabat's Carpet Museum (p434), which showcases the world's largest hand-tied carpet.

To view some fine examples of Afghan 'war rugs' see www.warrug.com and http://rugsofwar.wordpress.com.

LITERATURE

The division into Kazakh literature, Tajik literature, Uzbek literature and so on, is a modern one; formerly there was simply literature in Chaghatai Turkic and literature in Persian. With most pre-20th-century poets, scholars and writers bilingual in Uzbek and Tajik, literature in Central Asia belonged to a shared universality of culture.

Take for example Abu Abdullah Rudaki, a 10th-century Samanid court poet considered the father of Persian literature, who also stars in the national pantheons of Afghanistan, Iran and Tajikistan (he is buried in Penjikent) and is also revered by Uzbeks by dint of being born in the Bukhara emirate. Omar Khayam (1048–1131), famed composer of *rubiayyat* poetry, although a native of what is now northeast Iran, also has strong ties to Balkh and Samarkand, where he spent part of his early life at the court of the Seljuq emir.

Uzbekistan's national poet is Alisher Navoi (1441–1501), who pioneered the use of Turkic in literature. Born in Herat in modern-day Afghanistan, Navoi served the Timurid court of Hussain Baiqara, commissioning public buildings, advising on policy and writing *divan* (collections) of epic poetry.

Afghanistan, it has been said, is a nation of poets. It is particularly rich in Sufi poetry, much of it in the form of *ghazal* (rhyming couplet) and mystical in nature, dealing with the themes of spiritual love. Best known to Western audiences is Mawlana Rumi (1207–73), born in Balkh (or Vakhsh in Tajikistan – both places claim his birth site) and still today said to be the

Uzbekistan is the world's third-largest producer of silk. For the opportunity to see traditional silk production in Uzbekistan, see p238.

For a fictionalised account of the life of Persian poet Omar Khayam, check out Amin Maalouf's imaginative novel *Samarkand,* partially set in Central Asia.

most widely read poet in the United States. Most Afghans can quote you lines from Rumi, Ansari (1006–88) or the Timurid poet Jami (1414–92), who wrote alongside Alisher Navoi during Herat's cultural heyday. Afghans also lay claim to Iran's national poet Firdausi, who composed his epic *Shah Nama* (Shahnameh; Book of Kings) while court poet for the 11th-century Ghaznavid dynasty. Uzbeks, Tajiks and Afghans from across the region all know the *Shah Nama*'s telling of Rostam and Sohrab, in which the tragic hero Rostam kills his son in a case of mistaken identity.

A strong factor in the universal nature of Central Asian literature was that it was popularised not in written form, but orally by itinerant minstrels in the form of songs, poems and stories. Known as *bakshi* or *dastanchi* in Turkmen and Uzbek, *akyn* in Kazakh and Kyrgyz, these storytelling bards earned their living travelling from town to town giving skilled and dramatic recitations of crowd-pleasing verse, tales and epics to audiences gathered in bazaars and chaikhanas. With their rhythms, rhymes and improvisation, these performers share much in common with rap artists in the West (but with fewer women in g-strings and considerably less bling).

The most famous epic is Kyrgyzstan's *Manas* (p296), said to be the world's longest, and recited by a special category of *akyn* known as *manaschi*, though other epics include the Uzbek *Alpamish* and Turkmen *Gorkut*. Certain bards are folk heroes, regarded as founders of their national literatures, and memorialised in Soviet-era street names (eg Toktogul, Zhambyl and Abay, see p191). Soviet propagandists even used *akyns* to praise Lenin or popularise the latest directive from party central. Bardic competitions are still held in some rural areas, these days with cash prizes.

State opera houses in Tashkent (p225), Almaty (p138) and Dushanbe (p387) stage classics like Aida for just a dollar or two in classy surroundings. Most productions break over summer.

It was only with the advent of Bolshevik rule that literacy became widespread. Unfortunately, at the same time, much of the region's classical heritage never made it to print because Moscow feared that it might set a flame to latent nationalist sentiments. Instead writers were encouraged to produce novels and plays in line with official Communist Party themes. While a number of Central Asian poets and novelists found acclaim within the Soviet sphere, such as Tajik Sadruddin Ayni (1878–1954), and Uzbeks Asqad Mukhtar and Abdullah Kodiri, the only native Central Asian author to garner international recognition was Kyrgyz Chinghiz Aitmatov (1928–2008), who had novels translated into English and other European languages. His works have also been adapted for the stage and screen, both in the former USSR and abroad.

One interesting modern work is the exiled Uzbek writer Hamid Ismailov's *The Railway* (2006), a satirical novel that mixes anecdote and fantasy to depict life in the fictional end-of-the-line town of Gilas in Soviet Uzbekistan. The novel was swiftly banned in Uzbekistan.

MUSIC

Anyone interested in the music of the region should pick up *The Hundred Thousand Fools of Gold: Musical Travels in Central Asia,* by Theodore (Ted) Levin. The book is part travel, part ethnomusicology and comes with a CD of on-site recordings.

Although visual arts and literature succumbed to a stifling Soviet-European influence (which they're presently struggling to shrug off), the music of Central Asia remains closely related to the swirling melodies of Anatolia and Persia. The instruments used are similar to those found in this region; the *rabab* (*rubab;* six-stringed mandolin), *dutar* (two-stringed guitar), *tambur* (long-necked lute), *dombra/komuz* (two-stringed Kazakh/Kyrgyz guitar), *kamanche* (Persian violin, played like a cello) and *gijak* (upright spiked fiddle), *ney* (flute), *doira* (tambourine/drum) and *chang* (zither). Most groups add the ubiquitous Russian accordion, while Afghan music reflects Indian influence through the use of the *sarinda* (upright fiddle), harmonium and tabla drum.

In the past the development of music was closely connected with the art of the bards, but these days the traditions are continued by small ensembles of musicians and singers, heavily in demand at weddings and other *toi* (celebrations). In Uzbek and Tajik societies there's a particularly popular form of folk music known as *sozanda*, sung primarily by women accompanied only by percussion instruments such as tablas, bells and castanets. There are also several forms of Central Asian classical music, such as the courtly *shash maqam* (six modes) tradition of Uzbekistan, most of which are taught through the traditional system of *ustad* (master) and *shakirt* (apprentice). Central Asia has a strong tradition of the performer-composer, or *bestekar*, the equivalent of the singer-songwriter, who mixed poetry, humour, current affairs and history into music.

Musical traditions in remote regions like the Pamirs are sometimes preserved in just a few individuals, a situation the Aga Khan Trust for Culture is trying to redress through its dozen or so music schools scattered throughout Central Asia and Afghanistan.

> The art of the Kyrgyz bards and the classical Tajik-Uzbek music known as *shash maqam* are both included on Unesco's list of 'Masterpieces of the Oral and Intangible Heritage of Humanity'.

PAINTING

Rendered in a style that foreshadows that of Persian miniature painting, some splendid friezes were unearthed in the excavations of the Afrosiab palace (6th to 7th centuries), on the outskirts of Samarkand, depicting a colourful caravan led by elephants. You can view copies at Samarkand's Afrosiab Museum (p245). Similar Silk Road–era wall frescoes were discovered at Penjikent and Varakhsha, depicting everything from panthers and griffins to royal banqueting scenes.

The Arab invasion of the 8th century put representational art in Central Asia on hold for the better part of 1300 years. Islam prohibits the depiction

> To listen to British DJ Andy Kershaw's musical travels through Turkmenistan, visit www.bbc.co.uk/radio3/ worldmusic/onlocation/ turkmen.shtml.

CENTRAL ASIAN DISCOGRAPHY

The following recordings offer a great introduction to Central Asian music and are our personal favourites.

City of Love (Real World; www.realworld.co.uk) By Ashkabad, a five-piece Turkmen ensemble. Superb and lilting, with a Mediterranean feel. Recommended.

Music of Central Asia Vol. 1: Mountain Music of Kyrgyzstan (Smithsonian Folkways; www.folkways. si.edu) Collection of evocative Kyrgyz sounds by Tengir-Too, featuring the *komuz* and Jew's harp, with a section from the *Manas*.

Music of Central Asia Vol. 3: Art of the Afghan Rubab (Smithsonian Folkways; www.folkways.si.edu) By Afghan émigré Homayun Sakhi, featuring three ragas that demonstrate Afghanistan's strong musical links to India. Other volumes in the Smithsonian series cover bardic divas and music from Badakhshan.

Rough Guide to the Music of Central Asia (World Music Network; www.worldmusic.net) Excellent introduction to the sounds of the Silk Road, from Tajik rap to Kyrgyz folk melodies. Artists include classical singer Munadjat Yulchieva, the Kambarkan Folk Ensemble, Sevara Nazarkhan, Ashkabad, Yulduz Usmanova and Uzbek *tambur* player Turgun Alimatov.

Secret Museum of Mankind, the Central Asia Ethnic Music Classics: 1925-48 (Yazoo; www. shanachie.com) Twenty-six scratchy but wonderfully fresh field recordings of otherwise lost music.

The Selection Album (Blue Flame; www.blueflame.com) Career retrospective from Uzbek pop superstar Yulduz Usmanova.

The Silk Road – A Musical Caravan (Smithsonian Folkways; www.folkways.si.edu) 'Imagine if Marco Polo had a tape recorder' runs the cover note for this academic two-CD collection of traditional recordings by both masters and amateurs, from China to Azerbaijan.

Yol Boisin (Real World; www.realworld.co.uk) By Sevara Nazarkhan, a very accessible Uzbek songstress given a modern production by Hector Zazou. Sevara supported Peter Gabriel on tour in 2007. Her most recent recording is *Sen*.

of the living, so traditional arts have developed in the form of calligraphy, combining Islamic script with arabesques, and the carving of doors and screens. Textiles and metalwork took on floral or repetitive, geometric motifs.

Archaeology magazine offers several articles on Kabul Museum and the attempts to save Afghanistan's remaining cultural heritage. See www.archaeology.org/ afghanistan.

Painting and two-dimensional art were only revived under the Soviets who introduced European ideas and set up schools to train local artists in the new fashion. Under Soviet tutelage the pictorial art of Central Asia became a curious hybrid of socialist realism and mock traditionalism – Kyrgyz horsemen riding proudly beside a shiny red tractor, smiling Uzbeks at a chaikhana surrounded by record-breaking cotton harvests. You'll see a good selection of these at most regional museums.

Almaty has Central Asia's most vibrant contemporary arts scene: Tengri Umai (p139) is a good gallery to start your visual explorations.

Food & Drink

Food should not be the main reason you come to Central Asia. Most restaurants and cafes serve only standard slop, which somehow seems to taste (and smell) indelibly of the old USSR. The situation has improved in recent years, particularly in the cities, with a rush of pleasant open-air cafes, fast-food joints and particularly Turkish restaurants. The best way to appreciate regional cuisines, and the region's extraordinary hospitality, is still at a meal in a private home.

For country-specific specialities, see the Food & Drink entries in the individual country chapters.

In the heavily Russian-populated cities of northern Kazakhstan and in all the Central Asian capitals, the dominant cuisine is Russian.

STAPLES & SPECIALITIES

Central Asian food resembles that of the Middle East or the Mediterranean in its use of rice, savoury seasonings, vegetables and legumes, yoghurt and grilled meats. Many dishes may seem familiar from elsewhere – *laghman* (similar to Chinese noodles), *plov* (similar to Persian rice pilafs), nan (flat breads found all over Asia), and *samsa* (the samosa of India). Others are more unusual, such as Kazakh horsemeat sausage.

The cuisine falls into three overlapping groups. First, there's the once-nomadic subsistence diet found in large areas of Kazakhstan, Kyrgyzstan and Turkmenistan – mainly meat (including entrails), milk products and bread. Second, there's the diet of the Uzbeks and other settled Turks, which includes pilafs, kebabs, noodles and pasta, stews, elaborate breads and pastries. The third group is Persian, ranging from southern Uzbekistan and Tajikistan into Afghanistan, which is distinguished by subtle seasoning, extensive use of vegetables, and fancy sweets.

Seasoning is usually mild, although sauces and chillies are offered to turn up the heat. Principal spices are black cumin, red and black peppers, barberries, coriander and sesame seeds. Common herbs are fresh coriander, dill, parsley, celeriac and basil. Other seasonings include wine vinegar and fermented milk products.

Food Culture in Russia & Central Asia, by Glenn Mack & Asele Surina, is a detailed look at everything from *plov* (pilaf) to *piroshki* (fried potato or meat pies).

Ingredients

Mutton is the preferred meat. Big-bottomed sheep are prized for their fat, meat and wool, and fat from the sheep's tail actually costs more than the meat. The meat-to-fat ratio is generally stacked heavily in favour (and flavour) of the fat and you will soon find that everything smells of it. Sheep's head is a great delicacy, which may be served to honoured guests in some homes.

Produce is at its most bountiful around September. In general, May is the best time for apricots, strawberries and cherries, June for peaches and July for grapes and figs. Melons ripen in late summer, but are available in the markets as late as January.

You can find caviar and seafood dishes in western Kazakhstan, near the Caspian Sea. Dried and smoked fish are sold near Issyk-Köl.

Even Marco Polo raved about Afghan melons, stating that Sapurgan (Shebergan) had 'the very best melons in the world... When dry they are sweeter than honey, and are carried off for sale all over the country'.

Standards

The ubiquitous shashlyk – kebabs of fresh or marinated mutton, beef, minced meat (*farsh* or *lyulya kebab*) or, in restaurants, chicken – is usually served with nan and vinegary onions. The quality varies from inedible to addictively delicious. Liver kebabs are known in Turkic as *jiger*. Afghan kebabs come in the slightly different form of *sikh kebabs* (like shashlyk), *kofteh* (minced meat) or *chapli kebab*, a type of Pashtun hamburger.

Plov (*pilau* in Tajikistan, *pilao* in Afghanistan) consists mainly of rice with fried and boiled mutton, onions and carrots, and sometimes raisins, quince, chickpeas or fruit slices, all cooked up in a hemispherical cauldron called a *kazan*. *Plov* is always the *pièce de résistance* when entertaining guests and Uzbekistan is the artery-clogged heart of Central Asian *plov*. Afghanistan's national dish is Qabli *pilao*, a variant with grated carrot, raisins and almonds.

Stout noodles *(laghman)* distinguish Central Asian cuisine from any other. *Laghman* is served everywhere, especially as the base for a spicy soup (usually called *laghman* too), which includes fried mutton, peppers, tomatoes and onions. Korean, Uyghur and Dungan noodles are generally the best.

Other soups include *shorpo* (*shurpa* or *sorpo*; *shorwa* in Afghanistan), boiled mutton on the bone with potatoes, carrots and turnips; *manpar* (noodle bits, meat, vegetables and mild seasoning in broth); and Russian borsht (beetroot soup).

Nan (*non* to Uzbeks and Tajiks; *lepyoshka* in Russian), usually baked in a *tandyr* (tandoori) oven, is served at every meal. Some varieties are prepared with onions, meat or sheep's-tail fat in the dough; others have anise, poppy or sesame seeds placed on top. Afghan versions are thinner and larger but equally delicious. Nan also serves as an impromptu plate for shashlyk. Homemade breads are often thicker and darker than normal nan. Boring, square, white-flour Russian loaves are known simply as *khleb*.

Salads are a refreshing break from heavy main courses, although you'll soon tire of the dreaded *salat tourist* (sliced tomatoes and cucumbers). Parsley, fresh coriander, green onions and dill are served and eaten whole.

Breakfast (*zaftrak* in Russian) generally consists of tea or instant coffee, bread, jam, some kind of eggs, and maybe yoghurt, cream or semolina.

> The safest way to get a taste of Afghanistan is to try a recipe from the comprehensive book *Noshe Djan: Afghan Food and Cookery* by Helen Saberi.

Snacks

There are four other variations on the meat-and-dough theme – steamed, boiled, baked and fried. *Manty* or *mantu* (steamed dumplings) are a favourite from Mongolia to Turkey. *Chuchvara* (*tushbera* in Tajik, *pelmeny* in Russian) are a smaller boiled cousin of *manty*, served plain or with vinegar, sour cream or butter, or in soups. Both are sometimes fried.

One of the most common and disappointing street foods are *piroshki*, greasy Russian fried pies filled with potatoes or meat.

Fruits are eaten fresh, cooked, dried or made into preserves, jams and drinks known as *kompot* or *sok*. Central Asians are fond of dried fruits and nuts, particularly apricots and apricot stones, which when cracked open have a pith that tastes like pistachios. At any time of year you'll find delicious walnuts, peanuts, raisins and almonds, plus great jams (sea-buckthorn jam is a real treat) and wonderful mountain honey. Afghanistan has particularly good pomegranates, melons and fresh mulberries *(tut)*.

> A favourite snack is the *samsa* (*sambusa* in Tajik), a meat pie made with flaky puff pastry, and baked in a tandoori oven – at their best in Kyrgyzstan.

NASVAI

Throughout Central Asian and Afghanistan you might notice some men chewing and copiously spitting, or talking as if their mouth is full of saliva. *Nasvai* (also known as *nasvar, naswar* or *noz)* is basically finely crushed tobacco, sometimes cut with spices, juniper or lime. As a greenish sludge or as little pellets, it's stuffed under the tongue or inside the cheek, from where the active ingredients leach into the bloodstream, revving up the user's heart rate. Amateurs who fail to clamp it tightly in place, thus allowing the effluent to leak into the throat, might be consumed with nausea.

Milk Products

Central Asia is known for the richness and delicacy of its fermented dairy products, which use cow, sheep, goat, camel or horse milk. The milk itself is probably unpasteurised, but its cultured derivatives are safe if kept in hygienic conditions.

The fresh yoghurt served up to guests in the mountain pastures of Kyrgyzstan and Tajikistan will be the best you've ever tasted. Yoghurt can be strained to make *suzma*, which is like tart cottage or cream cheese, and used as a garnish or added to soups. *Ayran* is a salty yoghurt/water mix, the Russian equivalent is called *kefir*; don't confuse this with the Russians' beloved *smetana* (sour cream). *Katyk* is a thinner, drinkable yoghurt. Many doughs and batters incorporate sour milk products, giving them a tangy flavour.

The final stage in the milk cycle is *kurut*, which is dried *suzma* (often rolled into marble-size balls), a rock hard travel snack with the half-life of uranium. Scrape away the outer layer if you're uneasy about cleanliness.

Tvorog is a Russian speciality, made from soured milk, which is heated to curdle. This is hung in cheesecloth overnight to strain off the whey. The closest Central Asian equivalent is *suzma*. *Kaimak* is pure sweet cream, skimmed from fresh milk that has sat overnight. This wickedly tasty breakfast item, wonderful with honey, is available in many markets in the early morning, but sells out fast, usually by sunrise.

Central Asians of every ethnic group love ice cream (*morozhenoe* in Russian). You'll find a freezer of the stuff almost anywhere.

Turkish Food

Turkish restaurants are popping up everywhere in Central Asia and most are excellent value. *Pides* are similar to thin-crust pizzas; *lahmacun* is a cheaper, less substantial version. Kebabs are popular, especially Adana kebabs (minced-meat patties) and delicious Iskander kebabs (thinly sliced mutton over bread, with yoghurt and a rich tomato sauce). Meanwhile *patlıcan* (aubergine) and *dolma* (stuffed peppers) are the most common vegetable dishes. *Çaçık* is a delicious yoghurt, cucumber and mint dip and makes a great snack with *lavash*, a huge bread similar to nan but lighter. Turkish desserts include baklava (light pastry covered in syrup) and *sütlaç* (rice pudding).

The culinary techniques of samosas and tandoori cooking (baking in a *tandyr* or clay oven) followed the Emperor Babur from Central Asia to the Indian subcontinent in the 15th century.

Holiday Food

A big occasion for eating is Navrus (see p503), a celebration of the spring equinox. Along with *plov* and other traditional fare, several dishes are served at this time in particular. The traditional Navrus dish, prepared only by women, is *sumalak* – wheat soaked in water for three days until it sprouts, then ground, mixed with oil, flour and sugar, and cooked on a low heat for 24 hours. *Halim* is a porridge of boiled meat and wheat grains, seasoned with black pepper and cinnamon, prepared just for men. *Nishalda* (*nishollo* in Tajik) – whipped egg whites, sugar and liquorice flavouring – is also popular during Ramadan. To add to this, seven items, all beginning with the Arabic sound 'sh', are laid on the dinner table during Navrus – *sharob* (wine), *shir* (milk), *shirinliklar* (sweets), *shakar* (sugar), *sharbat* (sherbet), *sham* (a candle) and *shona* (a new bud). The candles are a throwback to pre-Islamic traditions and the new bud symbolises the renewal of life.

A special holiday dish in Kazakhstan and Kyrgyzstan is *beshbarmak* (*shilpildok* in Uzbek, *myasa po-kazakhsky* in Russian), large flat noodles with lamb and/or horsemeat and cooked in vegetable broth (the Kazakh version serves the broth separately). It means 'five fingers' since it was traditionally eaten by hand.

Uzbek men usually stay out of the kitchen but are almost always in charge of preparing *plov*; an *oshpaz*, or master chef, can cook up a special *plov* for thousands on special occasions.

DRINKS
Tea

Chay (чай; *choy* to Uzbeks and Tajiks, *shay* to Kazakhs) is drunk with reverence. Straight green tea (*kok* in Turkic languages; *zelyony* in Russian; *chai sabz* in Afghan Dari) is the favourite; locals claim it beats the heat and unblocks you after too much greasy *plov*. Black tea (*kara* in Turkic languages; *chyorny chay* in Russian; *chai siaa* in Dari) is preferred in Samarkand and Urgench, and by most Russians. Turkmen call green tea *gek* and black tea *gara*.

Western Turkmen brew tea with camel's milk and Pamiris use goat's milk. Kazakh tea is taken with milk, salt and butter – the nomadic equivalent of fast food – hot, tasty and high in calories.

Other Nonalcoholic Drinks

Don't drink the tap water. Cheap bottled mineral water is easy to find, but it's normally gassy and very mineral tasting. Modern joint-venture brands are more expensive but taste a lot better, though most are carbonated. Companies such as Coca-Cola have bottling plants in all the Central Asian countries (including Afghanistan) and their products are everywhere.

Tins of cheap imported instant coffee can be found everywhere; hot water (*kipitok*) is easy to drum up from a hotel floor-lady or homestay.

Alcoholic Drinks
VODKA & BEER

Despite their Muslim heritage, most Central Asians drink. If you don't enjoy hard booze and heavy drinking, make your excuses early. Like the Russians who introduced them to vodka, Central Asians take their toasts seriously and a foreign male guest may be expected to offer the first toast.

Given the depth of Central Asian hospitality it's impolite to refuse the initial 'bottoms up' (Russian – *vashe zdarovye!*), and/or abstain from at least a symbolic sip at each toast. But there's usually heavy pressure to drain your glass every time – so as not to give offence, it is implied – and the pressure only increases as everybody gets loaded. It's worth knowing that while Russian dictionaries define *chut chut* as 'a little bit', when applied to a shot of vodka it would appear to mean 'up to the rim'.

Apart from the endless array of industrial-strength vodkas, you'll find a wide range of Russian and European beers (*pivo*) for around US$1 to US$2 a bottle or can. St Petersburg's Baltika is the brew of choice and comes in a wide range of numbers from 0 (nonalcoholic) to 9 (very strong). Baltikas 3 and 6 are the most popular. Popular beers on tap include Tian-Shansky, Shimkent (both Kazakh), Sim Sim (Dushanbe) and Siberian Crown (Russian). The first time you order a local Berk Beer in Turkmenistan always seems to raise a smile. 'Draft' beer is advertised in Russian as *na razliy, razlivnoe* or *svezhey pivo* (fresh beer).

The Taliban famously crushed the contents of the Kabul Intercontinental Hotel's wine cellar under their tank tracks and it remains illegal for Afghans to drink. Alcohol is sporadically available in Kabul for the international community, much of it smuggled from the northern border with Uzbekistan.

KUMYS & OTHER ATTRACTIONS

Kumys (properly *kymys* in Kyrgyz; *qymyz* in Kazakh) is fermented mare's milk, a mildly (2% to 3%) alcoholic drink appreciated by Kazakhs and Kyrgyz, even those who no longer spend much time in the saddle (nonalcoholic varieties are also made). It's available only in spring and summer, when mares are foaling, and takes around three days to ferment. The milk is put into a *chelek* (wooden bucket or barrel) and churned with a wooden plunger called a *bishkek* (from where that city derives its name).

Locals will tell you that *kumys* cures anything from a cold to TB but drinking too much of it may give you diarrhoea. The best *kumys* comes from the herders themselves; the stuff available in the cities is sometimes diluted with cow's milk or water.

Kazakhs and Kyrgyz also like a thick, yeasty, slightly fizzy concoction called *bozo,* made from boiled fermented millet or other grains. Turkmen, Kazakh and Karakalpak nomads like *shubat* (fermented camel's milk). An early morning glass of breakfast *chal* (camel's milk) in Turkmenistan will wake you up faster than a double espresso.

WHERE TO EAT & DRINK

You can eat in streetside stalls and cafes, private and state-run restaurants and chaikhanas and, best of all, in private homes. There has recently been an explosion of private restaurants in larger towns and you can now eat well and cheaply, a great improvement on a few years ago. In smaller towns, restaurants can be pretty dire, if they exist at all, and hotels may have the only edible food outside private homes.

A few restaurants (*meyramkhana* in Kazakh and Kyrgyz, *oshhona* in Uzbek) in bigger cities offer interesting Central Asian, Turkish, Chinese, Georgian, Korean or European dishes and earnest service.

Outside the cities, Russians and Russified locals don't expect good food from restaurants. What they want at midday is a break. What they want in the evening is a night out – lots of booze and gale-force techno music or a variety show. Even if there's no music blasting when you come in, the kind staff will most likely turn on (or turn up) the beat especially for the foreigners.

The canteen (столовая; *stolovaya*) is the ordinary citizen's eatery – dreary but cheap, with a limited choice of cutlets or lukewarm *laghman.*

Certain old-town neighbourhoods of Tashkent and Samarkand have home restaurants offering genuine home-style cuisine. There is rarely a sign; family members simply solicit customers on the street; the competition can be intense.

Midrange and top-end restaurants are limited to Tashkent, Bishkek, Dushanbe and Almaty. The food is generally well-prepared European cuisine, with the occasional Siberian salmon or black caviar to liven things up.

The most common eatery in Afghanistan is the chaikhana, which often also doubles as a cheap hostel for travellers. Larger towns like Herat and Mazar-e Sharif have more formal restaurants and local fast-food joints, while Kabul has many restaurants catering to the expat community.

Self-Catering

Every sizable town has a colourful bazaar (*rynok* in Russian) or farmers market with hectares of fresh and dried fruit, vegetables, walnuts, peanuts, honey, cheese, bread, meat and eggs. Private supermarkets across the region now sell a decent range of European and Russian goods, with a better selection though slightly higher prices than the bazaars.

> Don't misread meat prices on menus in fancier restaurants – they are often given as per 100g, not per serving (which is often more like 250g to 400g).

> Bear in mind that many Russian main dishes are just that and you'll have to order garnishes (rice, potatoes or vegetables) separately.

TEAHOUSES

The chaikhana (teahouse; transliterated as *chaykhana* in Turkmen, *chaykana* in Kyrgyz, *choyhona* in Uzbek and Tajik, *shaykhana* in Kazakh) is male Central Asia's essential sociogastronomic institution, especially in Uzbekistan and Afghanistan. Usually shaded, often near a pool or stream, it's as much a men's club as an eatery – although women, including foreigners, are tolerated. Old and young congregate to eat or to drink pot after pot of green tea and talk the day away.

Traditional seating is on a bedlike platform called a *tapchan,* covered with a carpet and topped with a low table. Take your shoes off to sit on the platform, or leave them on and hang your feet over.

Perhaps the best opportunity to sample authentic Kyrgyz, Dungan and Tartar specialities is Kyrgyzstan's Festival of National Cuisine and Folklore (p329), held near Issyk-Köl on the last Sunday in July.

Korean and Dungan vendors sell spicy *kimchi* (vegetable salads), a great antidote for mutton overdose. Russians flog *pelmeny, piroshki* (deep-fried meat or potato pies) and yoghurt. Fresh honey on hot-from-the-oven nan makes a splendid breakfast.

Don't be afraid to haggle (with a smile) – everybody else does. As a foreigner you may be quoted twice the normal price or, on the other hand, given a bit extra. Insist on making your own choices or you may end up with second-rate produce. Most produce is sold by the kilo.

The odd state food store *(gastronom)* exists here and there, stocked with a few bits of cheese and dozens of cans of Soviet-made 'Beef in its own Juice' stacked up along the windowsill.

VEGETARIANS & VEGANS

Central Asia can be difficult for vegetarians; indeed the whole concept of vegetarianism is unfathomable to most locals. Those determined to avoid meat will need to visit plenty of farmers markets.

'Without meat' is *etsiz* in Turkmen, *atsiz* in Kazakh and Kyrgyz, *goshsiz* in Uyghur, *gushtsiz* in Uzbek, and *bez myasa* in Russian.

In restaurants, you'll see lots of tomato and cucumber salads. *Laghman* or soup may be ordered without meat, but the broth is usually meat-based. In private homes there is always bread, jams, salads, whole greens and herbs on the table, and you should be able to put in a word to your host in advance. Even if you specifically ask for vegetarian dishes you'll often discover the odd piece of meat snuck in somewhere – after a while it all seems a bit of a conspiracy.

HABITS & CUSTOMS

There are a few social conventions that you should try to follow.

Devout Muslims consider the left hand unclean, and handling food with it at the table, especially in a private home and with communal dishes, can be off-putting. At a minimum, no one raises food to the lips with the left hand. Try to accept cups and plates of food only with the right hand.

Bread is considered sacred in Central Asia. Don't put it on the ground, turn it upside down or throw it away (leave it on the table or floor cloth). If someone offers you tea in passing and you don't have time for it, they may offer you bread instead. It is polite to break off a piece and eat it, followed by the *amin* (see the boxed text, below). If you arrive with nan at a table, break it up into several pieces for everyone to share.

The *dastarkhan* is the central cloth laid on the floor, which acts as the dining table. Never put your foot on or step on this. Try to walk behind, not in front of people when leaving your place at the *dastarkhan* and don't step over any part of someone's body. Try not to point the sole of your shoe or foot at anyone as you sit on the floor. Don't eat after the *amin*. This signals thanks for and an end to the meal.

Hospitality

If you're invited home for a meal this can be your best introduction to local customs and traditions as well as to local cuisine. Don't go expecting a quick bite. Your host is likely to take the occasion very seriously. Uzbeks, for example, say *mehmon otanda ulugh,* 'the guest is greater than the father'.

AMIN

After a meal or prayers, or sometimes when passing a grave site, you might well see both men and women bring their cupped hands together and pass them down their face as if washing. This is the *amin,* a Muslim gesture of thanks, common throughout the region.

TEA ETIQUETTE

Tea is the drink of hospitality, offered first to every guest, and almost always drunk from a *piala* (small bowl). From a fresh pot, the first cup of tea is often poured away (to clean the *piala*) and then a *piala* of tea is poured out and returned twice into the pot to brew the tea. A cup filled only a little way up is a compliment, allowing your host to refill it often and keep its contents warm (the offer of a full *piala* of tea is a subtle invitation that it's time to leave).

Pass and accept tea with the right hand; it's extra polite to put the left hand over the heart as you do this. If your tea is too hot, don't blow on it, but swirl it gently in the cup without spilling any. If it has grown cold, your host will throw it away before refilling the cup.

It's important to arrive with a gift. Something for the table (eg some fruit from the market) will do. Better yet would be something for your hosts' children or their parents, preferably brought from your home country (eg sweets, postcards, badges, a picture book). Pulling out your own food or offering to pay someone for their kindness is likely to humiliate them (although some travellers hosted by very poor people have given a small cash gift to the eldest child, saying that it's 'for sweets'). Don't be surprised if you aren't thanked: gifts are taken more as evidence of God's grace than of your generosity.

You should be offered water for washing, as you may be eating with your hands at some point. Dry your hands with the cloth provided; shaking the water off your hands is said to be impolite.

Wait until you are told where to sit; honoured guests are often seated by Kyrgyz or Kazakh hosts opposite the door (so as not to be disturbed by traffic through it, and because that is the warmest seat in a yurt). Men (and foreign women guests) might eat separately from women and children of the family.

The meal might begin with a mumbled prayer, followed by tea. The host breaks and distributes bread. After bread, nuts or sweets to 'open the appetite', business or entertainment may begin.

The meal itself is something of a free-for-all. Food is served, and often eaten, from common plates, with hands or big spoons. Always eat, offer and accept food with your right hand, never your left. Pace yourself – eat too slowly and someone may ask if you're ill or unhappy; too eagerly and your plate will be immediately refilled. Praise the cook early and often; your host will worry if you're too quiet.

Traditionally, a host will honour an important guest by sacrificing a sheep for them. During these occasions the guest is given the choicest cuts, such as the eyeball, brain or meat from the right cheek of the animal. Try to ensure that your presence doesn't put your host under financial hardship. At least try to leave the choicest morsels for others.

If alcohol consumption is modest, the meal will end as it began, with tea and a prayer.

> The cuts of meat served are often symbolic; the tongue is served to someone who should be more eloquent and children get the ears, to help them be better listeners.

EAT YOUR WORDS

We have used mostly Russian words and phrases in this section.

Useful Phrases in Russian

I can't eat meat.	*ya ni em maysnovo*	Я не ем мясного.
I'm a vegetarian.	*ya vegetarianka* (female)/	Я вегетарианка./
	ya vegetarianets (male)	Я вегетарианец.
Can I have the menu please?	*daytye, pazhalsta, myenyu*	Дайте, пожалуйста, меню?
How much is it/this?	*skol'ka eta stoit*	Сколько это стоит?
May I have the bill?	*schyot, pazhalsta*	Счёт, пожалуйста?

Menu Decoder

A typical menu is divided into *zakuski* (cold appetisers), *pervye* (first courses, ie soups and hot appetisers), *vtorye* (second or main courses) and *sladkye* (desserts). Main dishes may be further divided into *firmennye* (house specials), *natsionalnye* (national, ie local, dishes), *myasnye* (meat), *rybnye* (fish), *iz ptitsy* (poultry) and *ovoshchnye* (vegetable) dishes. The classiest places always dedicate a page for cigarettes and vodka.

Don't be awed by the menu; they won't have most of it, just possibly the items with prices written in.

GARNISHES

grechka	гречка	boiled buckwheat
kartofel fri	картофель фри	French fries, chips
kartofel pure	картофельное пюре	mashed potato
makarony	макароны	macaroni, pasta
ris	рис	rice

MEAT, POULTRY & FISH

antrecot	антрекот	steak
befstroganov	бефстроганов	beef stroganoff
bifshteks	бифштекс	'beefsteak', glorified hamburger
bitochki	биточки	cutlet
farel	форель	trout
frikadela	фрикаделька	fried meatballs
galuptsi	голубцы	cabbage rolls stuffed with rice and meat
gavyadina	говядина	beef
gulyash	гуляш	a dismal miscellany of meat, vegetables and potatoes
kotleta po-Kievski	котлета по-киевски	chicken Kiev
kuritsa	курица	chicken
lyulya kebab	люля кебаб	beef or mutton meatballs
ragu	рагу	beef stew
shashlyk farshurabanniya	шашлык фаршурабанния	minced-meat (Adana) kebab
shashlyk iz baraniny	шашлык из баранины	mutton kebab
shashlyk iz okorochkov	шашлык из окорочков	chicken kebab
shashlyk iz pecheni	шашлык из печени	liver kebab
sosiski	сосиски	frankfurter sausage
sudak zhareny	судак жареный	fried pike or perch

SALADS

agurets	огурец	cucumber
chuisky salat	чуйский салат	spicy carrot salad in vinaigrette
Frantsuzky salat	Французский салат	beetroot, carrots and French fries
gribi	грибы	mushrooms
kapusty salat	капустный салат	cabbage salad
kartoshka	картошка	potato
mimosa salat	салат мимоза	fish and shredded-potato salad
morkovi salat	морковный салат	carrot salad
olivye salat	салат оливье	potato, ham, peas and mayonnaise

pomidor	помидор	tomato
salat iz svezhei kapusty	салат из свежей капусты	raw cabbage salad
salat tourist	салат турист	sliced tomatoes and cucumbers
stolichny	столичный	beef, potatoes, eggs, carrots, mayonnaise and apples

SNACKS

chuchvara	чучвара	dumplings
kolbasa	колбаса	sausage
laghman	лагман	noodles, mutton and vegetables
manty	манту	large meat ravioli, often served with sour cream
non	нон	bread
pelmeni	пельмени	small dumplings in soup
plov	плов	pilaf rice
samsa	самса	samosa (meat pie)

SOUPS

borshch	борщ	beetroot and potato soup, often with sour cream
manpar	манрар	noodle bits, meat, vegetables and mild seasoning in broth
mastoba	мастоба	rice soup
okroshka	окрошка	cold or hot soup made from sour cream, potatoes, eggs and meat
rassolnik s myasam	рассольник с мясом	soup of marinated cucumber and kidney
shorpo	шорпо	soup of boiled mutton on the bone with potatoes, carrots and turnips

Food Glossary
DAIRY & BREAKFAST

amlet	omelette
ayran	salty yoghurt/water mix
barene	jam
blini/bliny	pancakes
kaimak	sweet cream
kasha	porridge
khleb	bread
kurut	dried suzma (see below)
masla	butter
myod/assal	honey
non	bread
sakhar	sugar
sir	cheese
smetana	sour cream
sosiki	hot dog sausage
suzma	strained yoghurt, like tart cottage or cream cheese
tvorog	curd with cream and sugar
yaichnitsa	fried egg
yitso	egg
yitso barennye	boiled egg
yitso zharennye	fried egg

DRINKS

bozo	beverage made from fermented millet
chay	tea
kafe	coffee
kafe s slivkami	coffee with milk
katyk	thin, drinkable yoghurt
kompot	juice
kumys	fermented mare's milk
mineralnaya vada	mineral water
piva	beer
shubat	fermented camel's milk
sok	juice/fruit squash
stolovaya vada (biz gaz)	still water (no gas)

FRUIT

abrikos	apricot
arbuz	watermelon
persik	peach
vinagrad	grapes
vishnya	cherry
yablaka	apple

MEAT, POULTRY & FISH

beshbarmak	chunks of meat served atop flat squares of pasta
farel	trout
gavyadina	beef
jiger	liver
karta	horsemeat sausage
kazy	smoked horsemeat sausage
kolbasa	sausage
kury gril	roast chicken
kuurdak	fatty stew of meat, offal and potato
shashlyk	kebab

Environment

THE LAND

The Central Asia of this book includes Afghanistan and also Kazakhstan, which in Soviet parlance was considered a thing apart. It is true that Kazakhstan's enormous territory actually extends westward across the Ural River, the traditional boundary between Europe and Asia, but Kazakhstan still shares many geographic, cultural, ethnic and economic similarities and ties with Central Asia 'proper'.

A quick spin around the territory covered in this book would start on the eastern shores of the oil-rich Caspian Sea (actually a salt-water lake). Then dip southeast along the low crest of the Kopet Dag Mountains between Turkmenistan and Iran before heading south to the mighty Hindu Kush of Afghanistan and the southern Dasht-e Margo (Desert of Death) bordering Iran and Pakistan. Head north along the rugged maze-like mountains bordering Afghanistan and Pakistan (keeping an eye out for Osama Bin Laden) and follow the Panjshir Valley until you recross the snowcapped Hindu Kush.

Back on the Turkestan plains, follow the Amu-Darya river along the desert border with Uzbekistan and Tajikistan along its headstream, the Pyanj River, into the high Pamir plateau. Round the eastern nose of the 700m snow peaks of the Tian Shan range; skip northwestward over the Altay Mountains to float down the Irtysh River and then turn west to plod along Kazakhstan's flat, farmed, wooded border with Russia, ending in the basin of the Ural River and the Caspian Sea.

Central Asia, as defined by this book, occupies 4.65 million sq km, of which almost 60% belongs to Kazakhstan.

The sort of blank which is drawn in the minds of many people by the words 'Central Asia' is not entirely unfounded. The overwhelming majority of the territory is flat steppe (arid grassland) and desert. These areas include the Kazakh Steppe, the Betpak Dala (Misfortune) Steppe, the Kyzylkum (Red Sands) desert and the Karakum (Black Sands) desert. The Kyzylkum and Karakum combined make the fourth-largest desert in the world.

Central Asia's mountains are part of the huge chain which swings in a great arc from the Mongolian Altay to the Tibetan Himalaya. Central Asia's high ground is dominated by the Pamirs, a range of rounded, 5000m to 7000m mountains known as the 'Roof of the World', which stretch 500km across Tajikistan. With very broad, flat valleys, which are nearly as high as the lower peaks, the Pamirs might be better described as a plateau (*pamir* roughly means 'pasture' in local dialects). The roof of the Pamir, Tajikistan's 7495m Koh-i-Samani, is the highest point in Central Asia and was the highest in the USSR (when it was known as Kommunizma). The Pamirs is probably the least explored mountain range on earth.

Uzbekistan is one of only two countries in the world defined as double landlocked, ie surrounded by countries which are themselves landlocked.

Varying from 4000m to more than 7400m, the crests of the Tian Shan form the backbone of eastern Central Asia. Known as the Celestial Mountains, the Chinese-named Tian Shan (the local translation is Tengri Tau) extend over 1500km from southwest Kyrgyzstan into China. The summit of the range is Pobedy (7439m) on the Kyrgyzstan–China border. The forested alpine valleys and stunning glacial peaks of the range were favourites among such Russian explorers as Fedchenko, Kostenko, Semenov and Przewalski.

These two mountain ranges hold some of the largest glaciers and freshwater supplies on earth (around 17,000 sq km) and are one of the region's most significant natural resources. The 77km-long Fedchenko Glacier (the longest in the former USSR) allegedly contains more water than the Aral Sea.

The Caspian Sea is called either the world's biggest lake or the world's biggest inland sea. The Caspian Depression, in which it lies, dips to 132m below sea level. Lake Balkhash, a vast, marsh-bordered arc of half-saline water on the Kazakh Steppe, is hardly deeper than a puddle, while mountain-ringed Lake Issyk-Köl in Kyrgyzstan is the fourth-deepest lake in the world. Other glacially fed lakes dot the mountains, including Song-Köl in Kyrgyzstan and stunning Kara-Kul, first described by Marco Polo, in Tajikistan.

Some residents of massive Kazakhstan live about as far away from Vienna as they do from Almaty. Tashkent is closer to Kashgar and Tehran than to Moscow or Kiev.

Most of Central Asia's rainfall drains internally. What little water flows out of Central Asia goes all the way to the Arctic Ocean, via the Irtysh River. The Ili River waters Lake Balkhash; the Ural makes a short dash across part of Kazakhstan to the Caspian Sea. The region's two mightiest rivers, the Syr-Darya (Jaxartes River) and Amu-Darya (Oxus River), used to replenish the Aral Sea until they were bled dry for cotton (p100). There is evidence that the Amu-Darya once flowed into the Caspian Sea, along the now-dry Uzboy Channel.

Afghanistan is dominated by the mighty Hindu Kush (Killer of Hindus) mountains, which rise in a great knot south of the Pamirs as the westernmost outpost of the Great Himalayan Range. The range marks the watershed between the Oxus (Amu-Darya) and the Indus Rivers, which in cultural terms translates as the divide between the Central Asian and Indian-influenced worlds. The range's Salang Pass north of Kabul links northern and southern Afghanistan, while the Khyber Pass to the east has long enticed invading troops as the gateway to the Indian subcontinent. North of the Hindu Kush is the flat Turkestan plain, a major thoroughfare for Silk Road traders and ethnically, culturally and geographically tied to Central Asia.

Southern Afghanistan is dominated by arid hills and harsh *dasht* (deserts), where a network of man-made underground irrigation channels allows the existence of agriculture. Southern rivers like the Helmand drain into a series of lakes on the Iranian border or simply disappear into the thirsty desert sands.

Beautifully illustrated *Realms of the Russian Bear* (John Sparks) focuses on the flora and fauna of the old URRS, including that of the Tian Shan and Central Asia's steppes, deserts and seas.

GEOLOGY

The compact, balled-up mass of mountains bordering Tajikistan, Kyrgyzstan, China and Afghanistan is often called the Pamir Knot. It's the hub from which other major ranges extend like radiating ropes: the Himalaya and Karakoram to the southeast, the Hindu Kush to the southwest, the Kunlun to the east and the Tian Shan to the northeast. These young mountains all arose (or more correctly, are arising still) from the shock waves created by the Indian subcontinent smashing into the Asian crustal plate more than a hundred million years ago. Amazing as it seems, marine fossils from the original Tethys Sea have been found in the deserts of Central Asia as a testament to the continental collision. The Tian Shan are currently rising at the rate of around 1cm per year.

Botanists say that the modern apple has its genetic origins in Kazakhstan; revealingly the largest city Almaty translates as 'Father of Apples'.

Central Asia and Afghanistan is therefore unsurprisingly a major earthquake zone. Ashgabat was 80% destroyed by a massive earthquake in 1948 that killed 110,000 and Tashkent was levelled in 1966. More recently, devastating earthquakes hit the Tajikistan–Afghanistan border in 1997 and 1998, while central and eastern Afghanistan were hit by powerful quakes in 2002, 2008 and 2009.

WILDLIFE

Central Asia is home to a unique range of ecosystems and an extraordinary variety of flora and fauna. The ex-Soviet Central Asian republics comprised only 17% of the former USSR's territory, but contained over 50% of its variety in flora and fauna.

The mountains of Kyrgyzstan, Kazakhstan, Tajikistan and Afghan Badakhshan are the setting for high summer pastures known as *jailoo*s. In summertime the wild flowers (including wild irises and edelweiss) are a riot of colour. Marmots and pikas provide food for eagles and lammergeiers, while the elusive snow leopard preys on the ibex, with which it shares a preference for crags and rocky slopes, alongside the Svertsov ram and argali or Marco Polo sheep. Forests of Tian Shan spruce, ash, larch and juniper provide cover for lynxes, wolves, wild boars and brown bears. Lower down in the mountains of southern Kyrgyzstan, Uzbekistan, Tajikistan, Turkmenistan and northern Afghanistan are ancient forests of wild walnut, pistachio, juniper, apricot, cherry and apple. Arslanbob in Kyrgyzstan is home to the world's largest walnut grove.

The steppes (what's left of them after massive Soviet cultivation projects) are covered with grasses and low shrubs such as saxaul. Where they rise to meet foothills, the steppes bear vast fields of wild poppies (including some opium poppies) and several hundred types of tulip, which burst into beautiful bloom in May and June.

Roe deer and saiga, a species of antelope, have their homes on the steppe. The saiga (see Poaching, p102) is a slightly ridiculous-looking animal with a huge bulbous nose that once roamed in herds 100,000 strong. The ring-necked pheasant, widely introduced to North America and elsewhere, is native to the Central Asian steppe, as are partridges, black grouse, bustards, and the falcons and hawks that prey on them. Korgalzhyn Nature Reserve in Kazakhstan is home to the world's most northerly colony of pink flamingos.

Rivers and lake shores in the flatlands create a different world, with dense thickets of elm, poplar, reeds and shrubs known as *tugai*, where wild boar, jackal and deer make their homes. Over 90% of *tugai* environment along the Amu-Darya has been lost over the years.

In the barren stony wastes of the Karakum and Kyzylkum you'll need a sharp eye to catch a glimpse of the goitred gazelle (zheyran). Gophers, sand rats and jerboas feed various reptiles, including (in Turkmenistan) vipers and cobras.

Turkmenistan's wildlife has a Middle Eastern streak, understandable when you consider that parts of the country are as close to Baghdad as they are to Tashkent. Leopards and porcupines inhabit the parched hills. The *zemzen* or *varan* (desert crocodile) is actually a type of large lizard that can grow up to 1.8m long (see p429).

Central Asia has been famed for its horses since Chinese reports of the 'blood-sweating' horses of Fergana, that Han China needed to fight the nomadic tribes harassing its northern frontier. Today's most famous horses are the Akhal-Teke of Turkmenistan, the forefather of the modern Arab thoroughbred. There are only around 2000 thoroughbred Akhal-Teke in the world, of which 1200 are in Turkmenistan.

Thirty years of war have affected Afghanistan's wildlife as much as its people. The remote mountainous Badakhshan and Nuristan regions of Afghanistan still boasts brown bears, snow leopards, markhors (easily identified by their corkscrew twisted horns) and even a few rhesus macaques, the only (non-human) primates in Central Asia. Afghanistan also forms an important corridor for migrating waterbirds, with species flying over the Salang Pass in spring and winter en route to or from their winter habitat in the southern deserts.

Chiy, a common bulrush-like grass with whitish, canelike reeds, is used by Kyrgyz and Kazakh nomads to make decorative screens for their yurts.

The New York–based Wildlife Conservation Society (www.wcs.org) leads the way in the Afghan Pamirs, surveying wildlife, working with local communities and lobbying for protected status for the region.

Endangered Species

The mountain goose, among other rare species, nests on the shores of Kyrgyzstan's mountain lakes, but the population has shrunk over the years to fewer than 15 pairs worldwide.

RETAIL THERAPY FOR SNOW LEOPARDS

At Ak Shyrak and Inylchek (Engilchek), two villages in Kyrgyzstan's remote Central Tian Shan, the US-based Snow Leopard Trust is trying to help people increase their household income in a way that also helps protect snow leopards and their habitat.

Together with local partners, the Snow Leopard Trust provides herders with training and equipment to produce handicrafts like felt rugs, handbags and slippers, using wool from their livestock. These products are then marketed through the Snow Leopard Trust's website (www.snowleopard.org). Members pledge not to kill snow leopards or wild sheep and goats (the snow leopard's most important large prey) and to follow sustainable herding practices. About half of households in Ak-Shyrak, bordering the Sarychat-Ertash Reserve, currently participate in the program, which has been expanded to Eki Naryn and Tash Bashat in the Naryn area.

Since the 1930s Caspian seal numbers have dropped from over a million to 100,000.

The population of snow leopards in Central Asia and the Russian Altay is estimated at about 1000, out of a global population of around 7000. These secretive and solitary animals are a keystone species, keeping others in balance and check. There are thought to be between 150 and 500 leopards in Kyrgyzstan, with more in the Pamirs of Tajikistan and a similar number in the Wakhan region of Badakhshan (and possibly in the Nuristan region) in Afghanistan. Only 5% of these magnificent creatures' habitat is currently protected.

The marshlands of the Amu-Darya region of Uzbekistan and Afghanistan was once home to the Turan (Caspian) tiger but these became extinct when the last known survivor was shot in 1972. Wild Bactrian camels, once the quintessential Silk Road sight, are now only found in remote areas of Afghanistan (though they're sometimes seen from the Tajikistan side of the Wakhan Valley). Perhaps 1000 remain. Domestic camels are common in Kazakhstan.

Locals have blamed Vozrozhdenie (p101) for the terrifying sudden deaths of half a million saiga antelope (one-third of the global population) on the Turgay Steppe, northeast of the Aral, in 1988.

There has been some good news, though: eight Przewalski's horses were recently reintroduced into Kazakhstan's Altyn-Emel National Park after being extinct in the region for 60 years.

Over the last decade Bukhara (Bactrian) deer have also been relocated to reserves in Uzbekistan and Kazakhstan, including Altyn-Emel National Park, raising regional numbers from just 350 to over 1000. You can pat yourself on the back for this; the Altyn-Emel project was partly funded with money generated by ecotourism.

NATIONAL PARKS

Many of the region's approximately three-dozen nature reserves (zapovednik) and protected areas (zakazniki) and dozen or so national parks (gosudarstvenny natsionalny prirodny park) are accessible for tourists.

The existing system of national parks and protected areas, one of the positive legacies of the USSR, is nevertheless antiquated and inadequate. All suffer from a chronic lack of government funding and are under increasing pressure from grazing, poaching, firewood gathering and even opium-poppy plantations.

In Kyrgyzstan just 2.5% of the country's area is dedicated to land conservation, of which most is only semiprotected and commercially managed, often as hunting reserves. This is well below the minimum 10% recommended by the World Conservation Union but things are improving. Kazakhstan's new Irgiz-Turgay nature reserve in the northwestern steppes is part of a planned 60,000-sq-km system of protected areas known as the Altyn Dala (Golden Steppe) Conservation Initiative.

The protected areas that are easiest to visit include the following:

Aksu-Zhabagyly Nature Reserve (p155) High biodiversity in southern Kazakhstan, famed for its beautiful tulips, it also has an established ecotourism program and offers excellent mountain hiking and birdwatching.

Ala-Archa National Park (p311) Offers fine hiking and climbing just outside Bishkek.

Badai-Tugai Nature Reserve (p270) In Karakalpakstan, it protects a strip of *tugai* riverine forest on the eastern bank of the Amu-Darya. Once off limits, today it welcomes foreign tourists, as the entry fee pays for food for a Bukhara deer–breeding centre.

Ile-Alatau National Park (p144) Good mountain hiking on Almaty's doorstep.

Karakol Valley (p327) Alpine ecosystem in the Tian Shan, southeast Issyk-Köl, with superb scenery and fine trekking routes.

Kugitang Nature Reserve (p456) The most impressive of Turkmenistan's nature reserves, focused around the country's highest peak, is home to the rare markhor mountain goat and several hundred dinosaur footprints.

Sary-Chelek Biosphere Reserve (p351) Remote trekking routes cross this Unesco-sponsored reserve, centred on a large mountain lake.

Sayram-Ugam National Park (p156) Ecotourism programs include hikes and horse treks.

Ugam-Chatkal National Park (p230) Unesco-sponsored biosphere reserve, with juniper forests, wild boars, bears and snow leopards, plus some fine hiking and rafting.

Afghanistan's only national park protects the azure-blue mineral lakes and travertine cliffs of Band-e Amir, popular amongst local visitors. The 570-sq-km park was established on paper as early as 1973 but only became a reality in 2009. Uncontrolled fishing has been halted (the mujaheddin liked to fish with hand grenades) and a New Zealand–funded ecotourism program has been established to help manage a potential future growth in tourism. The region is home to wolves, ibex, urial (a type of wild sheep) and the Afghan snow finch, thought to be the only bird found exclusively in Afghanistan. The last snow leopard disappeared from the region in the early 1980s.

Plans also exist to formalise the nearby Ajar Valley Wildlife Reserve, a former royal hunting park, and the Big Pamir Reserve in the Wakhan region of Afghanistan. Both currently exist on paper only.

ENVIRONMENTAL ISSUES

Central Asia's 'empty' landscapes served as testing grounds for some of the worst cases of Soviet megalomania. Land and water mismanagement and the destruction of natural habitat were part of a conscious effort to tame nature ('harness it like a white mare', as the propaganda of the day had it). The results are almost beyond belief and on a staggering scale.

Even casual students of the region are familiar with some of the most infamous catastrophes of Soviet environmental meddling: the gradual disappearance of the Aral Sea and the excessive levels of radiation around the Semey (Semipalatinsk) nuclear testing site (see p124). Add to this the consequences of Khrushchev's Virgin Lands scheme (p57), which was planned to boost grain production but which ended up degrading hundreds of thousands of square kilometres of Kazakh steppe.

In the economic malaise of the post-Soviet years, the environment has taken a back seat. Whether it is poaching, hunting tours or pollution from gold-mining operations, the promise of hard-currency in an otherwise bleak economic landscape means that nature is often the victim.

The extreme continental climate of Central Asia is particularly susceptible to global climate change, and glaciers in the Pamirs and Tian Shan are already shrinking by around 15m a year.

Water is in fact the only major resource in Tajikistan and Kyrgyzstan and both countries plan a series of giant hydroelectric dams, much to the concern of downstream Uzbekistan and Turkmenistan who consider water supplies vital to their cotton-based economies. You can expect water issues to become increasingly pressing over the next few decades, as Central Asia's future becomes increasingly defined by two of nature's greatest gifts: oil and water.

For news articles on environmental issues, go to the Environment Department website (www.eurasianet.org).

Extremes along the Silk Road, by Nick Middleton, devotes one-third of the book to Kazakhstan, with a trip out to the former biological weapons site at Vozrozhdenie Island in the Aral Sea.

The Aral Sea

The Aral Sea straddles the border between western Uzbekistan and southern Kazakhstan. It's fed by the Syr-Darya and Amu-Darya Rivers, flowing down from the Tian Shan and Pamir mountain ranges. Back in the 1950s these rivers brought an average 55 cubic km of water a year to the Aral Sea, which stretched 400km from end to end and 280km from side to side, and covered 66,900 sq km. The sea had, by all accounts, lovely clear water, pristine beaches, plenty of fish to support a big fishing industry in the ports of Moynaq and Aralsk, and even passenger ferries crossing it from north to south.

The best places to view the Aral disaster are Moynaq (p280) in Uzbekistan and Aralsk (p161) in Kazakhstan, both of which display fishing trawlers rusting in the salty desert.

Then the USSR's central planners decided to boost cotton production in Uzbekistan, Turkmenistan and Kazakhstan, to feed a leap forward in the Soviet textile industry. But the thirsty new cotton fields, many of them on poorer desert soils and fed by long, unlined canals open to the sun, required much more water per hectare than the old ones. The irrigated area grew by only about 20% between 1960 and 1980, but the annual water take from the rivers doubled from 45 to 90 cubic km. By the 1980s the annual flow into the Aral Sea was less than a tenth of the 1950s supply.

Production of cotton rose, but the Aral Sea sank. Between 1966 and 1993 its level fell by more than 16m and its eastern and southern shores receded by up to 80km. In 1987 the Aral divided into a smaller northern sea and a larger southern one, each fed, sometimes, by one of the rivers.

The two main fishing ports, Aralsk (Kazakhstan) in the north and Moynaq (Uzbekistan) in the south, were left high and dry when efforts to keep their navigation channels open were abandoned in the early 1980s. Of the 60,000 people who used to live off the Aral fishing industry (harvesting 20,000 tons of fish a year), almost all are gone. These days the rusting hulks of beached fishing boats lie scattered dozens of kilometres from the nearest water.

In parts of Karakalpakstan more than one in 10 babies die (compared to one in 100 or more in Britain), a rate largely attributable to health problems caused by the Aral Sea disaster.

There are hardly any fish left in the Aral Sea: the last of its 20-odd indigenous species disappeared in about 1985, wiped out by the loss of spawning and feeding grounds, rising salt levels and, very likely, residues of pesticides, fertilisers and defoliants used on the cotton fields, which found their way into the sea. For years only introduced species such as the Black Sea flounder remained in the briny water, though recently a dozen freshwater species have begun to return to the northern sea via the Syr-Darya.

The Aral Sea's shrinkage has devastated the land around it. The climate around the lake has changed: the air is drier, winters are colder and longer, and summers are hotter. The average number of rainless days has risen from 30 to 35 in the 1950s to between 120 and 150 today. Salt, sand and dust from the exposed bed is blown hundreds of kilometres in big salt-dust sandstorms, which also pick up residues of the chemicals from cultivated land. Locals talk of a new Akkum (White Sands) desert forming an unholy trinity with the Kyzylkum (Red Sands) and Karakum (Black Sands) deserts. A visit to anywhere near the sea is a ride into a nightmare of blighted towns, blighted land and blighted people.

The website www.cawater-info.net has info on the Aral Sea and other water-related issues in Central Asia.

In human terms, the worst-affected areas are those to the Aral Sea's south – as far as northern Turkmenistan – and east. (The areas north and west of the Aral Sea are very sparsely populated.) The catalogue of health problems is awful: salt and dust are blamed for respiratory illnesses and cancers of the throat and oesophagus; poor drinking water has been implicated in high rates of typhoid, paratyphoid, hepatitis and dysentery; and the area has the highest mortality and infant mortality rates in the former USSR, as well as high rates of birth deformities. In Aralsk, tuberculosis is common.

Humans are not the only ones affected by the disaster. Of the 173 animal species that used to live around the Aral Sea, only 38 survive.

Especially devastating has been the degradation of the big Amu-Darya and Syr-Darya deltas, with their diverse flora and fauna. The deltas have supported irrigated agriculture for many centuries, along with hunting, fishing, and harvesting of reeds for building and papermaking. The dense *tugai* forests, unique to the valleys of these desert rivers, have shrunk to a fifth of their old size, causing a catastrophic drop in the once-abundant water bird population.

The local name for the Aral is the Aral Tenghiz, or Sea of Islands. Barsakelmes (Place of No Return) Island, a nature reserve protecting the saiga antelope, goitred gazelle and the rare kulan or Asiatic wild ass, is no longer an island and has reportedly become an unviable habitat because it is now so arid.

Nor can matters have been helped by the use of Vozrozhdenie Ostrov (ironically translating as Rebirth Island) as a Soviet biological warfare testing site (anthrax and plague were both released at the Aralsk-7 site) until it was abandoned in 1992. In 2002 the 'island's' secrets were joined to the mainland by the exposed seabed.

The Aral isn't the only body of water drying up. Lake Balkhash in Kazakhstan, which gets its water from the Ili River, has shrunk by 1000 sq km since the 1970s.

LONG-TERM SOLUTIONS

Dozens of inquiries, projects and research teams have poked and prodded the Aral problem; locals joke that if every scientist who visited the Aral region had brought a bucket of water the problem would be over by now. The initial outcry over the disaster seems to have largely evaporated, along with the sea, and the focus has shifted from rehabilitating the sea, to stabilising part of the sea and now stabilising the environment around the sea.

To restore the Aral would require irrigation from the Amu-Darya and Syr-Darya to cease for three years, or at least a slashing of the irrigated area from over 70,000 to 40,000 sq km; in other words, a complete restructuring of the economies of Uzbekistan and Turkmenistan. No one is seriously considering this.

A 600-year-old mausoleum recently discovered on the dried-out bed of the Aral Sea has indicated that Aral levels might be cyclical to some degree.

Finally in 1988 a gradual increase in water flow to the sea was ordered, to be achieved by more efficient irrigation and an end to the expansion of irrigation. However, early promises of cooperation and money from the Central Asian leaders bore little fruit. The now annual Aral Sea convention of Central Asian leaders has achieved little, except to highlight conflicting claims to sections of the Amu-Darya. A US$250-million World Bank scheme aims to clean up water supplies, improve sanitation and public health, restore some economic viability and biodiversity to the Amu-Darya delta, and stabilise the Aral's northern sea.

In 2003 the little channel still connecting the northern and southern seas was blocked by a 12.8km-long dike, preventing further water loss from the northern sea (see the boxed text, p163), but condemning the southern sea to oblivion. The northern sea is now expected to rise almost 3.5m and should reach a state of equilibrium by about 2025, sooner if a second dam is constructed by 2014 as planned. But if recent rates of depletion continue, the southern sea is expected to split again into western and eastern parts. The eastern part will receive the Amu-Darya and is expected eventually to stabilise into three lakes with the construction of small dikes, but the western part will go on shrinking.

The Aral Sea was once the world's fourth-largest lake. It is now recognised as the world's worst manmade ecological disaster.

Longer-term efforts may focus on building more dikes around parts of the sea, rehabilitating the blighted region around the sea and stabilising its fragile environment, improving water management and building up local institutions to manage these projects. Whether the will exists among Central Asia's politicians to introduce less water-intensive irrigation methods, or even less thirsty crops than cotton, remains to be seen.

Overgrazing & Deforestation

Overgrazing and soil degradation are major problems affecting all the Central Asian republics. The steady rise in livestock grazing has unhinged delicate ecosystems and accelerated desertification and soil erosion. From 1941 to 1991 the population of sheep and goats more than doubled to 5.5 million in Turkmenistan and quadrupled to 10 million in Kyrgyzstan, while a third of Kyrgyzstan's available grasslands have disappeared.

In Kazakhstan much of the semi-arid steppe, traditionally used as pasture over the centuries, was put to the plough under the Virgin Lands campaign (see p57). Wind erosion in the steppes of north Kazakhstan has accelerated soil depletion.

Soil degradation is also activated by failure to rotate crops and excessive use of chemicals, and aggravated by irrigation-water mismanagement. In Kazakhstan, 40% of rangeland is considered to be overused, and will need 10 to 50 years to be restored to its original fertility. In Kyrgyzstan an estimated 70% of pastureland suffers erosion above acceptable levels. In Tajikistan the productivity of summer pastures in the mountains has dropped by 50% over the last 25 years and large areas of the Pamirs are threatened by desertification.

All of Afghanistan's forests are threatened; it's thought that in the last 30 years the amount of forest has dropped sixfold to a critical 0.5% of the country's landmass. Afghanistan's heavily wooded eastern provinces of Nuristan, Konar and Paktika, bordering Pakistan, unfortunately made easy targets for clear-cutting and timber smuggling into Pakistan by mujaheddin groups. To compound the problem, government control in these regions remains patchy at best.

Pollution

Cotton is to blame for many of Central Asia's ills. Its present cultivation demands high levels of pesticides and fertilisers, which are now found throughout the food chain – in the water, in human and animal milk, in vegetables and fruit, and in the soil itself. In the Osh region of Kyrgyzstan 94% of soils contain DDT.

Search the website of the UN Environment Programme (www.grida.no) for reports on the state of Central Asia's environment.

Kazakhstan, the third-largest industrial power in the Commonwealth of Independent States (CIS), suffers particularly from industrial pollution, the worst culprits being power stations running on low-grade coal, and metallurgical factories. Lake Balkhash has been polluted by copper smelters established on its shores in the 1930s; bird and other lake life here is now practically extinct. An added threat comes from a planned nuclear power station on the shores of the lake. There are also concerns about oil and other pollution draining into the Caspian Sea (see p125) and radioactive seepage from Soviet-era uranium mines in Kyrgyzstan.

Mining techniques are inefficient, outdated and environmentally hazardous. In 1998 almost two tonnes of sodium cyanide destined for the Kumtor gold mine in Kyrgyzstan was spilled into the Barskoön River, which made its way into Issyk-Köl.

Poaching

The unfortunate combination of economic hardship, a crisis in funding for wildlife protection and the opening of borders with China (the region's main market for illegal trafficking in animal parts) saw a huge rise in poaching after the fall of the Soviet Union, both as a food source and for trophies to sell for hard currency. Afghan's lawlessness has also contributed to poaching in that country.

For more on the plight of the saiga antelope, visit www.saiga-conservation.com.

Tens of thousands of critically endangered saiga antelope are killed every year by poachers, who sell their horns to Chinese medicine makers. Over the last decade, saiga numbers have declined from more than 1 million to a shocking 40,000. Musk deer, currently found in Kyrgyzstan, Kazakhstan and Russia, are killed for their musk glands. Around 160 deer are killed for every 1kg of musk, making the musk worth three to four times its weight in gold. Tens of thousands of the deer have been killed in the last 20 years and numbers in Russia have fallen by 50%.

Poaching birds of prey to be sold in the Gulf is a particular problem in Afghanistan. The Taliban went as far as to build an airstrip in the Registan Desert Reserve to attract rich Gulf Arabs who came to hunt houbara bustards – a favourite pursuit of Osama Bin Laden, amongst others. Saker falcons face a similar problem in Kazakhstan, where over 1000 birds are poached a year.

Several private and government travel agencies run hard-currency hunting expeditions. The high prices charged for trophies (US$7500 for a Marco Polo sheep) could, in theory, fund wildlife protection and discourage local poaching by adding broader value to local endangered species. Ironically, one of the few places in Tajikistan not to have seen a dramatic drop in the number of ibex and Marco Polo sheep in recent years is the Jarty-Gumbaz hunting camp, where local poaching has almost completely ceased under the increased protection of the hunting camp.

Marco Polo sheep are named after the Italian traveller who wrote of them after visiting the Pamirs: 'There are… wild sheep of great size, whose horns are a good six palms in length.'

Activities

The soaring peaks, rolling pasturelands and desert tracts of Central Asia offer some of Asia's finest active adventures. Make like the Kazakh hordes on a horse trek across the Tian Shan, explore the Pamirs on foot like the first Russian imperial explorers, or live the Silk Road dream on a camel trek across the Kyzylkum desert – these are just some of the ways to get under the skin and into the landscapes of Central Asia.

With few facilities, tricky paperwork and modest traveller infrastructure, the 'stans aren't the easiest place for do-it-yourself adventurers. The good news is that the ever-increasing network of community-based tourism projects offers thrilling new opportunities to get off the map and meet locals on their own terms. Once the exclusive playing fields of Soviet scientists and Eastern European alpinists, these days you are almost guaranteed to have the magical alpine valleys and remote corners of Central Asia to yourself. See the Itineraries chapter (p32) for a variety of trips available throughout the region.

For an overview of trekking options in Tajikistan, check out the excellent trekking section of www.pamirs.org.

TREKKING

Central Asia is not only one of the world's great trekking destinations but also one of its best-kept secrets. Kyrgyzstan, Tajikistan and southeastern Kazakhstan hold the cream of the mountain scenery, thanks to the mighty spurs of the Tian Shan and Pamir ranges. See below for a list of the most popular trekking destinations and cross-references to coverage in this book.

With many established routes and excellent trekking companies to offer support, Kyrgyzstan is probably the best republic for budget trekking. Treks here have the added bonus of adding on a visit to an eagle hunter or a night or two in a yurt en route.

Tajikistan packs a double whammy, with the Fan Mountains in the west and high Pamirs in the east. The former offers a wide range of route options and difficulties, passing dozens of turquoise lakes. Treks in the Pamirs are more hardcore and anyone but the most experienced trekkers will really need some kind of professional support for these remote, demanding routes. See p417 for a rundown of the easier Pamir trek options.

In Kazakhstan, the mountains south of Almaty conceal some great mountain scenery just an hour's drive from the city, though sadly the transborder treks to Issyk-Köl in Kyrgyzstan are now off limits due to border restrictions.

TOP TREKKING AREAS

- **Fan Mountains** (p397), Tajikistan – routes from three days to two weeks.
- Alpine-like valleys of the **Tian Shan** (p328), around Karakol, Kyrgyzstan.
- Walnut forests and waterfalls around **Arslanbob** (p353), Kyrgyzstan.
- High-altitude lakes of the **Zarosh-Kul** loop (p412), Pamirs, Tajikistan.
- **Khan Tengri** and **Inylchek Glacier** – from Kyrgyzstan (p334) or Kazakhstan (p148).
- Around **Almaty**, Kazakhstan – either from Ozero Bolshoe Almatinskoe or Chimbulak (see p145) or further away in the Kolsay Lakes region (p146).
- **Ala-Archa National Park** (p313), Kyrgyzstan – just two hours from the capital.
- **Wakhan Corridor** and **Little Pamir**, Afghan Badakhshan (p488), Afghanistan.

Other less-visited regions in Kazakhstan include the Altay Mountains in the far northeast.

For some off-the-beaten-treks in Kyrgyzstan, not covered in this guide, try the three-day trek from Sokuluk Canyon to Suusamyr Valley (p348); from the Shamsy Valley south of Tokmok to yurtstays at Sarala-Saz (p339); or from Kyzyl-Oi to Köl Tör lake (p339). Another option is the trek from Chong-Kemin Valley to Grigorievka or to Jasy-Köl and back; arrange horses in Kaindy (p314).

In Tajikistan there are several interesting short trekking routes in the western Pamirs that combine trekking with rural homestays (see p407), including at Bodomdara and Rivak.

Adventurers can also consider Afghanistan's Wakhan Corridor, in the remotest high northeastern corner of the country. Only a handful of trekkers have explored the area since Marco Polo passed through in the 13th century. Treks into the Little and Big Pamir ranges run from a few days to a couple of weeks, visiting Chaqmaqtin Lake and the famous Broghil Pass on the border with Pakistan. Security is good as long as you visit as a side trip from Tajikistan, rather than from Kabul. For information on routes see the excellent websites www.mockandoneil.com/wakhan.htm, www.juldu.com and www.mountainunity.org/trekking.html.

What Kind of Trek?

Self-supported trekking is possible but not always easy in Central Asia. There are no trekking lodges like the ones you would find in Nepal and few porters, so you will have to carry all your own food for the trek. Public transport to the trailheads can be patchy, slow and uncomfortable so it's generally worth shelling out the extra money for a taxi. Some trekking areas are at the junction of several republics, requiring you to carry multiple simultaneous visas and a fistful of different currencies. It is possible to hire donkeys at many trailheads (eg in the Fan Mountains) and hire horses in Kyrgyzstan (for around US$10 per day) and the Tajikistan Pamirs (US$20 per day). Organisations like CBT in Kyrgyzstan (see the boxed text, p106), and META and PECTA (p404) in Tajikistan can often offer logistical support.

You can hire simple tents, sleeping bags and stoves from Bishkek and Karakol (p323) in Kyrgyzstan and in Penjikent and Khorog in Tajikistan, but in general, good gear, particularly sleeping bags, is hard to find in the region. A multifuel (petrol) stove is most useful, though you will need to clean the burners regularly as local fuel is of extremely poor quality. Camping gas canisters are generally available in Karakol.

Karakol is the main centre of trekking. The tourist information centre here sells 1:100,000 topo maps and has a folder detailing trekking routes. Several companies here offer a range of logistical support.

Trustworthy local knowledge, and preferably a local guide, are essential for trekking in Central Asia. The various branches of CBT (p302) in Kyrgyzstan can put you in touch with a general guide for US$10, though for someone with a guaranteed knowledge of mountain routes you are better off arranging this with a trekking agency for around US$20 per person per day. Trekking and horse guides are available for around US$20 to US$35 through community tourism programs in the Fan Mountains and in Afghanistan's Wakhan Corridor.

There are lots of competent trekking agencies in Central Asia that can arrange a full service trek. See the list on p113, for the most reliable. Treks organised through local trekking agencies cost from US$50 per person per day, far cheaper than international companies.

For more on the issues behind community-based tourism, see www.unesco.org/culture/ecotourism.

Trekking in Russia & Central Asia by Frith Maier has 77 pages of Central Asia route descriptions, plus chapters of useful background and planning info. Unfortunately it's seriously dated, as it was written in 1994.

Foreign trekking companies such as **Himalayan Kingdoms** (www.himalayanking doms.com), **Explore Worldwide** (www.explore.co.uk), **Exodus** (www.exodus.co.uk), **KE Adventure** (www.keadventure.com) and **World Expeditions** (www.worldexpeditions.com) run treks in the Inylchek/Khan Tengri region and the Fan Mountains. **Wild Frontiers** (www. wildfrontiers.co.uk) operates treks in the Afghan Wakhan.

COMMUNITY-BASED TOURISM IN CENTRAL ASIA

At the end of the 1990s, with few economic options left to Kyrgyzstan, development organisations started to look to new sources of income to support remote communities, starting with tourism. The idea was to help connect intrepid tourists to a series of local service providers, from drivers to herders, in a fair and mutually beneficial way, while supporting local craft production and sustainable tourism practices.

The phenomenon started in Kochkor in central Kyrgyzstan with Swiss help (Helvetas) and has since rapidly spread throughout the region. Today these community-based tourism organisations offer some of Central Asia's best and most exciting experiences, at fantastic value. Plus you can sleep better in your yurtstay at night knowing that your money is going directly to the family you are staying with, rather than a middleman in Bishkek or abroad. See the boxed text on p107 for our pick of the best community tourism adventures in Central Asia.

Community Based Tourism (CBT; p302; www.cbtkyrgyzstan.kg) in Kyrgyzstan is the region's leader, with a network of a dozen locations across the country, sometimes overlapping with original organisation Shepherd's Life. Most towns in Kyrgyzstan have CBT-inspired homestays and the organisation now offers everything from homestays and horse treks (see p108) to folk music concerts and horse-racing festivals.

In Tajikistan, **Murgab Ecotourism Association** (META; p414; http://phiproject.free.fr) offers fantastic adventure in the Pamirs and can put you in touch with remote yurtstays, fixed-price 4WD hire and English-speaking guides in a region devoid of any formal tourist infrastructure. **Mountain Societies Development & Support Project (MSDSP)** in Khorog has helped establish homestays in the eastern Pamir, including the popular homestay and hiking program in the Geisev Valley (see p407).

The hub for ecotourism in Kazakhstan is the **Ecotourism Information Resource Centre** (EIRC; p130; www.eco-tourism.kz), which offers similar grassroots adventures and homestays, from flamingo-watching at Korgalzhyn Nature Reserve to horse riding in Sayram-Ugam National Park, though at higher prices than elsewhere in the region. See the boxed text, p125 for the main ecotourism locations in Kazakhstan, including horse treks and nature trips at Aksu-Zhabagyly Nature Reserve (www.wildnature-kz.narod.ru).

Community-based tourism is starting to make its way into Uzbekistan through a Unesco-supported program in the **Nuratau-Kyzylkum Biosphere Reserve** (p257; www.nuratau.com).

Even Afghanistan offers a network of homestays, trekking guides and pack animals for visits to the remote (and safe) Wakhan Corridor (p488). The program is organised by the Aga Khan Foundation and offers some of the world's remotest treks. See www.wakhan.org and www.mountainunity.org for more details.

In addition to gung-ho adventures, most community-tourism organisations offer a range of cultural activities. CBT can organise displays of felt-making or eagle-hunting. EIRC arranges fun workshops making *kumys* (fermented mare's milk) and concerts of traditional Kazakh music.

Program coordinators at CBT or META sustain themselves through a 15% commission or, in the case of Shepherd's Life, a small coordinator's fee. A few teething problems remain to be addressed, including issues with nepotism, reliability and the tendency for service providers to break away and found their own rival businesses, and most of the organisations are not yet financially self-supporting. Remember also that these are not professional tourism companies, so be sure to pack a sense of humour and expect some delays and schedule changes during your trip.

Community-based tourism projects are a fantastic resource for independent travellers and deserve your support. Expect the experience to rank amongst the highlights of your travels.

TOP 10 COMMUNITY TOURISM ADVENTURES IN CENTRAL ASIA

The following adventurous trips can be arranged by community-tourism programs (p106) in Kyrgyzstan, Tajikistan and the Afghan Wakhan and offer exciting ways to get off the beaten track without blowing your budget.

- Two- or three-day horse trip across the *jailoo* (summer pasture) from Kyzart or Jumgal to Song-Köl, Kyrgyzstan (p340).
- Four-day trek from Arslanbob to the holy lakes of the Köl-Mazar, Kyrgyzstan (p353).
- Trek through a Unesco Biosphere from Kara-Suu to Lake Sary-Chelek, Kyrgyzstan (two to three days; p351) or go wild on the five-day Talas/Leninopol to Lake Sary-Chelek trek.
- Horse trek from Kazarman to the petroglyphs at Sailmaluu Tash, Kyrgyzstan (p344).
- Three-day trip from Kochkor to Köl Ükök lake, Kyrgyzstan (p339).
- Hunting with eagles in Bokonbayevo, Kyrgyzstan (p332).
- Camel trekking for three days on the Roof of the World (p414).
- Horse trek for a week past a chain of high-altitude Pamiri lakes, on the Zarosh-Kul loop (p412).
- Trek from homestay to homestay up the outrageously remote Afghan Wakhan and hike up to the historic Broghil Pass, Afghanistan (p488).
- Excursion to Chatyr-Köl from Tash Rabat – day hike/horse trip or overnight at the lake, Kyrgyzstan (p346).

When to Go

The best walking season is June to September, but be ready for bad weather at any time. Most high-altitude treks or climbs take place in July or August; lower areas can be scorching hot during these months.

Trekking Permits & Problems

Permits are needed for some border areas of Kazakhstan, including the Central Tian Shan and the Altay region. These take up to 45 days to procure (see p198) so apply ahead of time if you plan to trek in these regions.

In Kyrgyzstan any place within 50km of the Chinese border (such as the Inylchek Glacier, the Alay Valley, the Turkestan range or Pik Lenin) requires a military border permit which is fairly easy to obtain through a trekking agency.

While most commonly used trekking routes are quite safe, mountain routes on the borders of southeastern Kyrgyzstan and Tajikistan have been off-limits for much of the last decade since American climbers were kidnapped in this region in 2000. Some border areas around here are mined. Discuss your route with a trekking agency before you wander off into these hills, and take a local guide.

Maps

The following trekking/climbing maps for Central Asia are published and available abroad:

Central Tian Shan (EWP; www.ewpnet.com) 1:150,000; Inylchek Glacier and surroundings.
Fan Mountains (EWP; www.ewpnet.com) 1:100,000; Fan Mountains in Tajikistan.
Pamir Trans Alai Mountains (EWP; www.ewpnet.com) 1:200,000; Pik Lenin and the Fedchenko Glacier.
Pik Lenin (Gecko Maps; www.geckomaps.com) 1:100,000; topographical map of the mountain.
Geoid (see p299 and p368) in Bishkek sells useful maps of major central Tian Shan trekking regions for the equivalent of about US$3 each. You can buy 1:100,000 topo maps of the trek routes around southeast Issyk-Köl at the Tourist Information Centre (p320) at Karakol.

The website http://mountains.tos.ru/kopylov/pamir.htm is an excellent climbing resource, with route descriptions, plans and schematic maps. This link is for the Pamir mountain range, follow the index links for other Central Asian regions.

Geo (p127) in Almaty sells a wide variety of topographic and trekking maps from 1:25,000 to 1:100,000, as well as more general maps.

The following 1:100,000 Uzbek topographical maps, printed in 1992, are essential for trekking, if you can track them down.

Bisokiy Alay Treks from Shakhimardan, Khaidakan and the Sokh Valley in southern Kyrgyzstan.

Fannsky Gory Tajikistan's Fan Mountains.

Matcha Palmiro-Alay Tsentralnaya Chast Treks from Vorukh and Karavshin Valley, southern Kyrgyzstan.

Note that on Russian maps, passes marked Unclassified (N/K) or 1A are simple, with slopes no steeper than 30°; glaciers, where they exist, are flat and without open crevasses. Grade 1B passes may have ice patches or glaciers with hidden crevasses and may require ropes. Passes of grade 2A and above may require special equipment and technical climbing skills.

Hiking

Hiking (as opposed to trekking, which is multiday) is a major outdoor pursuit for Almaty residents and there are fine hikes from Chimbulak (p145), among others. The Sayram-Ugam National Park (p156) and Aksu-Zhabagyly Nature Reserve (p155) are two beautiful areas of hiking country on the fringes of the Tian Shan between the southern Kazakhstan cities of Shymkent and Taraz. Rakhmanovskie Klyuchi in far east Kazakhstan (p189) is the starting point for hikes up the sublimely beautiful Altay valleys that fall off the slopes of Mt Belukha. Zapadno-Altaysky (Western Altay) Nature Reserve near Ust-Kamenogorsk is also good for hiking – see p188 for more information.

> The websites www.mountain.ru/eng and www.adventuretravel.ru/eng have some articles on trekking and climbing in Central Asia. The Kyrgyz Alpine Club (www.kac.centralasia.kg) is another good resource.

You can make nice day hikes from bases in Ala-Archa National Park, near Bishkek, and Altyn Arashan, near Karakol, both in Kyrgyzstan. The Wakhan and Pshart valleys in the Pamirs of Tajikistan offer superb valley walks, as does the Geisev Valley (p407), where you can leave the tent behind and overnight in village homestays. If you're in Dushanbe for the weekend in summer tag along with the weekly day hikes led by Goulya's Outdoor Adventures (p385).

Uzbekistan has less potential, though Chimgan has some nice hikes. Walks in the mountains around Nokhur are possible in Turkmenistan. Most of the trekking regions mentioned earlier offer fine day-hikes.

Local hiking clubs are an excellent way to get out of the cities for the weekend, get some mountain air and meet up with local expats. One good bet is the twice-monthly excursions of the Tashkent Hiking Club (p221).

HORSE TRIPS

Kyrgyzstan is the perfect place to saddle up and explore the high pastures. CBT and Shepherd's Life coordinators (p106) throughout the country arrange overnight horse treks to *jailoo* (summer pastures) around central Kyrgyzstan, or longer expeditions on horseback lasting up to two weeks. Horse hire costs the equivalent of around US$13 per day, or around US$50 per person per day with a guide, yurtstay and food.

Horseback is the perfect way to arrive at Song-Köl. Trips can depart from either Jangy Talap, Chayek, Jumgal or Chekildek and take around three days, staying in yurts en route. The six-day horse trek from Song-Köl to Tash Rabat via the Mazar Valley is an adventurous choice.

There are also good horse treks from Karakol (Altyn Arashan offers some lovely day trips) and Tamga (on the southern shores of Issyk-Köl), as well as Naryn, Arslanbob, Kazarman and Ak-Terek north of Özgön. Kegeti canyon, east of Bishkek, is another popular place for horse riding. See p107 and p364 for other horse-trek ideas.

The Pamirs of Tajikistan and Kyrgyzstan are also sublime places for a horse trek; see p412 for details of horse treks from Bachor. The **Pamir Trek Association** (www.pamirtrek.com) is an association of horse guides from the Tajikistan Pamirs and Kyrgyzstan Pamir Alai valley that offers horse treks in these regions.

For organised trips in Kyrgyzstan, the following private local companies are also recommended:

AsiaRando (☎ 3132-47710/1, 517-73 97 78; www.asiarando.com; Padgornaya 67, Rot Front, Chuy Oblast) Horse-riding trips to Song-Köl from its base in Rotfront village. Contact Gérard and Dominique Guillerm.

Pegasus Horse Trekking (p318) Trip from Cholpan-Ata into the mountains on the north side of Issyk-Köl, including the Ornok Valley and Grigorievka.

Shepherds Way (p330; www.kyrgyztrek.com) Excellent treks into the Terskey Alatau south of Barskoön, ranging from three to 30 days.

Foreign companies that offer horse-riding trips in Kyrgyzstan include **Wild Frontiers** (www.wildfrontiers.co.uk), the **Adventure Company** (www.adventurecompany.co.uk) and **High and Wild** (www.highandwild.co.uk).

If you know what you're doing, there's nothing at all to stop you buying your own horse, though you'll be haggling with some wily horse traders. You can buy a horse in Karakol's animal bazaar for around US$400 to US$500.

For a classy ride, you can't do better than astride a thoroughbred Akhal-Teke in Turkmenistan. A couple of stables in the Geok-Dere region outside Ashgabat (see p436) offer short rides and some travel agencies can arrange multiday horse treks. **DN Tours** (www.dntours.com) offers an 11-day desert ride on Akhal-Tekes, with camping and the opportunity to stay in local villages. **Stantours** (www.stantours.com) offers a week-long horse-riding trip through the Kopet Dag Mountains.

Kan Tengri (see p113) offers horse treks through the desert landscapes of Altyn-Emel National Park and also in the central Tian Shan. There are further horseback options in the ecotourism centres of Aksu-Zhabagyly Nature Reserve and Sayram-Ugam National Park (ride between them in three days), at the Kolsay Lakes in southeast Kazakhstan and at Zapadno-Altaysky (Western Altay) Nature Reserve near Ust-Kamenogorsk (see p188). These are generally more expensive than in neighbouring Kyrgyzstan.

The German company **Kasachstan Reisen** (☎ in Kazakhstan 701-407 9611, in Germany 030-4285 2005; http://kasachstanreisen.de) offers interesting horse-riding, 4WD and trekking trips in Kazakhstan in partnership with local Kazakh agencies.

If you're content to watch rather than ride, the colourful weekly horse races at Ashgabat Hippodrome (spring and autumn) and the annual At-Chabysh and Murgab horse festivals will be a highlight. Summer equestrian fun and games take place in select high pastures across Kyrgyzstan; CBT (p302) in Kyrgyzstan has the details.

For an inspirational look at adventure treks and travels in the Pamirs of Tajikistan and the Afghan Wakhan, check out photographer Matthieu Paley's site at www.pamirknot.com.

CAMEL TREKKING

If you've got Silk Road fever and imagine a multiday caravan across the wastes of Central Asia, you could be in for a disappointment. Bukhara travel agencies arrange camel treks north of Nurata around Lake Aidarkul (p256) and there are also possibilities at Ayaz-Qala in northwest Uzbekistan (p281) but these are mostly short jaunts from comfortable tourist yurts (with electricity, plumbing and three-course meals). The best time for low-altitude desert camel trekking is from March to May, when the spring rains turn the floor of the Kyzylkum into a Jackson Pollock canvas.

For the full-on 'Marco Polo' experience, META in Tajikistan offers one- to three-day treks on Bactrian camels in the high-altitude Rang-Kul region of the eastern Pamirs (see p414).

MOUNTAIN BIKING & CYCLING

Several tour companies offer supported biking trips over the Torugart Pass, although die-hard do-it-yourselfers will find the Irkeshtam crossing logistically easier. The Kegeti canyon and pass in northern Kyrgyzstan is another biking location favoured by adventure-travel companies. In the past Dostuck Trekking (p114) has offered an amazing mountain-biking itinerary to Merzbacher Lake in the central Tian Shan.

In Kyrgyzstan the Karkara Valley offers quiet country back roads. From here you can cycle around the southern shore of Issyk-Köl and then up into central Kyrgyzstan. Karakol's Kyrgyz Tours (p321) is a cooperative of guides that can take you on five-day mountain bike trips from Karakol if you bring your own bike.

Bike tours on offer in Kazakhstan include two-week MTB trips from Almaty to Lake Issyk-Köl via the Karkara Valley, with Arnai Tours or Kan Tengri (p130), and steppe tours with Karaganda-based Nomadic Travel Kazakhstan (p184). Most travellers on multiday trips bring their own bikes.

A growing number of die-hards organise their own long-distance mountain-bike trips across Central Asia. The most popular route is probably the Pamir Hwy in Tajikistan, which is a spectacular but hard trip. Cyclists who have done the route recommend transporting your bike to Khorog and starting from there. The highway is paved but winds can make pedalling hard work. Several cyclists have been harassed and extorted in border areas, including by border guards. Still it's one of the world's great bike trips. For tips and bike travelogues around Central Asia see the following websites:

- www.tandemtoturkestan.com
- www.trans-tadji.info
- www.silkroadbybike.com
- www.timbarnes.ndo.co.uk
- www.crazyguyonabike.com/doc/standiet

You can rent mountain bikes for local trips in Bishkek, Naryn and Murgab. You can get some bike parts in Bishkek (see p309).

KE Adventure Travel (www.keadventure.com) operates mountain bike itineraries in Kyrgyzstan and Kazakhstan that even include some heli-biking.

RAFTING

Intrepid rafters and kayakers have stared to explore Central Asia's remote white water but commercial operations are still limited.

For rafting in Kyrgyzstan, see p365. For Kazakhstan, see p130.

Hamsafar Travel in Tajikistan (p382) can help with information on kayaking and rafting in Tajikistan.

Tashkent operators run fairly tame rafting trips in September and October on the Syr-Darya river. There's plenty of exciting whitewater nearby on the Ugam, Chatkal and Pskem Rivers: talk to Asia Raft (p231) in Tashkent.

MOUNTAINEERING & ROCK CLIMBING

Central Asian 'alpinism' was very popular during the Soviet era, when climbers dragged their crampons from all over the communist bloc to tackle the region's five impressive 'Snow Leopards' (peaks over 7000m).

Top of the line for altitude junkies are Khan Tengri, Pik Pobedy and other peaks of the central Tian Shan in eastern Kyrgyzstan (p333) and southeast Kazakhstan (p148). Khan Tengri is a stunningly beautiful peak. Massive Pobedy is the world's most northern 7000m-plus peak and the hardest of Central Asia's 7000m-plus summits.

Several Almaty and Bishkek tour agents can arrange trips to this region, including helicopter flights to the base camps during the climbing season

The blog 'Paddling in the Pamirs' (http://pamirs.wordpress.com) has useful information on kayaking Tajikistan's rivers.

The website www.kayakussr.com offers a wealth of information on paddling rivers in the Pamirs, Tian Shan and Altay ranges.

For details of the first Afghan ascent of Noshaq in 2009, see www.noshaq.com.

from the end of July to early September. There are two approaches, via the
northern Inylchek Glacier from Kazakhstan and along the southern Inylchek
Glacier from Kyrgyzstan. Even if you aren't a climber, these are fine treks
that lead into a breathtaking mountain amphitheatre. You will need a border
zone permit (p365) for either side and a mountaineering permit (US$105)
on the Kyrgyz side to climb here.

The other prime high-altitude playground is the Pamir in southern
Kyrgyzstan and eastern Tajikistan, especially Pik Lenin (Koh-i-Istiqlal in
Tajik), accessed from the north side at Achik Tash base camp (p362). Lenin
is a non-technical climb and is considered one of the easiest 7000m summits,
yet it has claimed the most lives. The season is July and August. Companies
like Tian Shan Travel and Asia Travel operate commercial expeditions from
base camps at Achik Tash.

Peaks Koh-i-Samani (Kommunizma; 7495m) and Korzhenevskaya
(7105m) are much less known and both accessed from Moskvin Glade base
camp to the west.

The most accessible climbing is in Ala-Archa National Park, just outside
Bishkek, where popular routes from the Ak-Say glacier require just a couple
of days. Mt Korona, Mt Uchityel and Mt Free Korea are the most popular
peaks here. The **Alpine Fund** (p304; www.alpinefund.org) in Bishkek is a good resource
for this region.

Other 4000m-plus peaks include Pik Sayram in the Aksu-Zhabagyly
Nature Reserve and Mt Belukha in east Kazakhstan's northern Altay
Mountains. Experienced climbers will find that plenty of unclimbed sum-
mits await, especially in the Kokshal-Tau range near the border with China.

Some of the best rock climbing is in the Turkestan range in Kyrgyzstan's
southern arm, in particular the Karavshin and Liailiak regions, often called
'the Patagonia of Central Asia' due to its towering rock spires. The action
focuses on Mt Pyramid (5509m) and the 2km vertical wall of Mt Ak-Suu
(5335m). Trips to this once volatile region are best organised by a travel
company.

Kyrgyzstan: A Climber's Map & Guide, by Garth Willis and Martin
Gamache, and published by the American Alpine Club, is a map and mini-
guide that covers Ala-Archa, the western Kokshal-Tau and Karavshin regions.
See p107 in this chapter for more climbing maps.

Jagged Globe (www.jagged-globe.co.uk) is one foreign company that has in the
past offered supported climbs on Khan Tengri. Most of Almaty and Bishkek's
trekking agencies arrange mountaineering expeditions, as does Moscow-
based **RusAdventure** (www.rusadventure.com).

Mountaineering equipment is hard to find in the region so you should
bring your own gear, though you might find basic equipment at the Leader
office in Karakol (no rope).

Afghanistan's Wakhan Corridor is a potential playground for mountaineers set on exploring the 7000m peaks of the Hindu Kush bordering Pakistan.
Peak Noshaq (7492m) is probably the real prize for hard-core mountaineers,
though there are dozens of unnamed and unclimbed summits here. *Peaks
of Silver and Jade,* by Carlo Alberto Pinelli, is a comprehensive climbing
guide to the range, available in Faizabad through the Aga Khan Foundation.

WINTER SPORTS

Central Asia's ski season is approximately November to April, with local
variations. The region's best-known and best-equipped downhill area is
Chimbulak (Shymbulak; p143; www.shimbulak.kz), a day-trip from Almaty. February
is the best time to be there. A day lift pass costs around US$34. The new Ak
Bulak and Tabagan (www.tabagan.kz) resorts near Talgar, 90 minutes from

Robert Craig's *Storm and
Sorrow in the High Pamirs*
chronicles the tragic
1974 climbing season on
Pik Lenin, during which
all eight members of a
Soviet women's climbing
team perished on the
mountain.

For more on summits in
Central Asia, visit www.
summitpost.com and
start with a search for
'Snow Leopards'.

In 1990 an earthquake-
induced avalanche killed
43 people on Pik Lenin in
mountaineering's worst
single accident.

Almaty, both have good facilities. Almaty and Astana will host the 2011 Asian Winter Games (upgrading facilities in the run-up) and Almaty made an unsuccessful bid to host the 2014 Winter Olympics.

Skiing is still in its infancy in Kyrgyzstan, but there are several options in the Kyrgyz Alatau valleys (especially Ala-Archa), south of Bishkek (p313) and at Karakol (p329). It's possible to rent skis and boards in Bishkek through ITMC Tien Shan (p305), as well as in Karakol. The relatively modern Karakol Ski Base (www.karakol-ski.kg) in Karakol has chair lifts, accommodation and rental equipment between November and March.

Nearly every sports-related agency in Central Asia offers heli-skiing, in which old Aeroflot MI-8 helicopters drop you off on remote high peaks and you ski down. Most guarantee from 3000 to 4000 vertical metres per day for descents of up to 5km but require a group of 12 to 15 people. The Kyrgyz Alatau range behind Bishkek is one of the cheapest places to try out heli-skiing (p314).

Heli-skiing is also awesome in Uzbekistan's Chimgan and Chatkal ranges behind Tashkent from January to May. While the Chatkals aren't huge, they are blanketed in some of the driest, fluffiest powder you'll find anywhere and the winter weather is relatively stable, lessening the chances of getting grounded for days on end. But the best part is the price – US$500 per day for about 6000 vertical metres, much less than what you'll pay in North America. Book heli-skiing through Asia Adventures (p217), as most other agencies go through them.

Kazakhstan's pristine Altay Mountains are renowned for cross-country skiing; the best place to do this is Rakhmanovskie Klyuchi (p189). Cross-country skis are also available for hire at Arslanbob in southern Kyrgyzstan.

A few travel firms in Kazakhstan and Kyrgyzstan offer ski-mountaineering trips in central Tian Shan in July and August, and in the Zailiysky Alatau and Küngey Alatau ranges from February to April.

The Medeu ice rink (p143) just outside Almaty is one of the largest speed-skating rinks in the world; larger than a football pitch. It's open to the public daily from November to April.

Sports fans might want to watch Uzbekistan's best football team FC Pakhtakor Tashkent at their home stadium in Tashkent. In winter catch Kazzinc Torpedo, Central Asia's best ice-hockey team, in Ust-Kamenogorsk's Dvorets Sporta stadium.

FOUR-WHEEL DRIVE TRIPS

The back roads of Kyrgyzstan, and particularly Tajikistan's Badakhshan region, offer great scope for adventure travel in an indestructible Russian UAZ jeep. Four-wheel drives can be hired from around US$0.45 per kilometre in both countries.

In Kyrgyzstan one possible 4WD itinerary leads from Talas over the Kara Bura Pass into the Chatkal river valley and then around to Lake Sary-Chelek. Other tracks lead from Naryn to Barskoön, and Barskoön to Inylchek, through the high Tian Shan.

It's well worth hiring a 4WD from Murgab in the eastern Pamirs for trips out to such gorgeously remote places as Shaimak, Jalang and Zor-Kul (see p414).

More 4WD fun, of a slightly sandier nature, is possible in Turkmenistan. One exciting itinerary is the trip from Yangykala Canyon across the Karakum desert to the Darvaza Gas Craters. Expect plenty of dune bashing, sleeping under starry skies and stops for tea in remote Turkmen villages.

OTHER ACTIVITIES

Several companies organise caving trips, especially around Osh, in Kyrgyzstan, and Chimgan, north of Tashkent in Uzbekistan. It's possible to scuba dive in Lake Issyk-Köl, but some of the equipment used looks like props from a 1960s Jacques Cousteau documentary.

There are some fine opportunities for nature spotting. The wetlands of Kazakhstan's Korgalzhyn Nature Reserve lie at the crossroads of two major bird migration routes, attracting 300 species including the world's most northerly flamingo habitat (between April and September). The tulips of Aksu-Zhabagyly Nature Reserve are world famous and several local and foreign companies run tours to this area in spring. **Kan Tengri** (see p113) offers birdwatching and botanical tours in Kazakhstan and **East Line Tours** (www.birdwatching-uzbekistan.com, www.eastlinetour.com) runs bird-watching trips in Uzbekistan. The website www.kazakhstanbirdtours.com is a great resource for bird-watching in Kazakhstan and also runs birding tours. Foreign companies include **Naturetrek** (www.naturetrek.co.uk), which runs botanical and bird-watching tours of Kazakhstan, and US-based **Wings** (www.wingsbirds.com), which offers a 'Birding the Silk Road' tour of Uzbekistan and Kazakhstan in May. All these websites have good background info on the type of birds you might spot.

A day spent with a Kyrgyz *berkutchi*, or eagle hunter (a man who hunts with eagles, not a man who hunts eagles), is an unforgettable experience. Authentic hunts take place in winter but it's possible to watch and even take part in a demonstration hunt during the summer months at Kadji-Sai (p332) and Bokonbayevo (p332) in Kyrgyzstan.

> You can hunt with eagles or just watch a hunting display at several places in Kyrgyzstan, including at Kadji Sai and nearby Bokonbayevo on the southern shore of Issyk-Köl.

Odyssey Travel (www.odysseytravel.com.au), in Australia, operates archaeological tours to the Khorezm region of Uzbekistan, during which you'll spend two weeks on an archaeological dig, followed by a short general tour of the country.

Sport fishing is an option in the Ili delta in Kazakhstan. Spelunkers will get a kick from exploring the miles of twisting tunnels that make up the Karlyuk Caves, Central Asia's largest, deep underneath Turkmenistan's Kugitang Nature Reserve (p456).

Extreme golfers with balls of steel can play a round at **Kabul Golf Club** (www.kabulgolfclub.com). Be prepared for 'greens' that are actually browns, made of sand and engine oil, and roughs that are *very* rough. On the plus side, all nine holes are now mine-free…

ADVENTURE TRAVEL OPERATORS IN CENTRAL ASIA

The following travel companies all offer adventure trips in the region, whether it be a full tour or partial logistical support for your own trip.

Afghanistan

Afghan Logistics & Tours (p495; www.afghanlogisticstours.com) Badakhshan trekking and kayaking.
Great Game Travel (p; www.greatgametravel.com) Wakhan trekking.

> See p490 for more information on Afghanistan activities.

Kazakhstan

A13 (p130) Various southeast Kazakhstan activities.
Altai Expeditions (p188;altai_expeditions@dvn.kz) Wide range of active trips and nature tours in the Altay. Email for the current trip list.
Asia Discovery (☎ 250 81 08;www.asia-discovery.nursat.kz; office 19, Abai 61, Almaty) Experienced group-orientated adventure agency offering treks, horse riding, rafting and bird-watching tours lasting one to two weeks.
Kan Tengri (p130; www.kantengri.kz) Kazakhstan's top adventure-travel company.
Karlygash (Karla) Makatova (p130; www.asia-adventuretours.com) Independent one-woman operator who offers day hikes, treks and climbs, plus kayaking.
Nomadic Travel Kazakhstan (p184; www.ecotourism.kz) Dynamic outfit offers trips by bicycle, foot, horse or minibus to some really offbeat destinations in central Kazakhstan.
Tour Asia (p131;www.tourasia.kz) Specialises in expeditions in the central Tian Shan and the Pamirs.

> See p193 for more information on Kazakhstan activities.

Kyrgyzstan

See p364 for more information on Kyrgyzstan activities.

Ak Sai (p304;www.ak-sai.com) Trekking, mountaineering, biking and heli-skiing. Operates base camps at Inylchek, Achik Tosh/Pik Lenin and Karavshin, and owns the Red Fox camping store (p309).

Alp Tour Issyk Köl (p323) This professional company offers a range of treks around the Tian Shan, including Khan Tengri base camp, and can supply border permits, guide/cooks, porters and climbing guides. The staff will also support your own long-distance treks.

Alptreksport (p358) Contact Yury Lavrushin. Two brothers, veterans of the International Mountaineering Camp Pamir (IMC Pamir), organise mountaineering, trekking and caving trips, including some around Sary-Chelek, Achik, Jiptik Pass (4185m) and Sary Moghul in the Alay Valley.

Asia Mountains (p304; www.asiamountains.net) Runs a base camp at Achik Tash and a guesthouse in Bishkek (p306).

Dostuck Trekking (p304; www.dostuck.com.kg) Offers ascents to peaks, treks, helicopter transport and border permits.

Edelweiss (p305; www.edelweiss.elcat.kg) All kinds of adventures.

International Mountaineering Camp Pamir (IMC Pamir; p305; www.imcpamir.netfirms. com) Trekking and mountaineering programs and operates the Achik Tash base camp at the foot of Pik Lenin.

Issyk-Kul Travel (p322; www.issykkultravel.com) Specialises in cultural, trekking and horse trips around Issyk-Köl, especially the Karkara Valley.

ITMC Tien-Shan (p305; www.itmc.centralasia.kg) Competent adventure-travel operator offering package and piecemeal help, including mountaineering (with base camps at Khan Tengri, Achik Tash – for Pik Lenin – and Koh-i-Samani), trekking, heli-skiing and mountain biking.

NoviNomad (p304; www.novinomad.com) Horse treks, mountain bikes and trekking with an environmentally responsible company. Can book CBT trips.

Tien-Shan Travel (p305; www.tien-shan.com) Ex-cartographers with expedition gear and a menu of set group tours into the mountains.

Top Asia (p305; www.topasia.kg) Trekking, mountaineering and horse riding, especially around Tash Rabat.

Tour Khan Tengri (p323; www.tour-khantengri.com) Experienced outfitter with a camp in the Inylchek Valley.

Turkestan (p321; www.turkestan.biz) Professionally-run treks and mountaineering trips to Khan Tengri, horse treks into the Küngey Alatau mountains north of Issyk-Köl and great helicopter trips to Inylchek Glacier. In winter they operate heli-skiing trips. Contact Sergey Pyshnenko.

Tajikistan

See p416 for more information on Tajikistan activities.

Asia Discovery (☎ 237 91 76; www.asiadiscovery.tj; Apt 33, 126 Somoni, Dushanbe) English-speaking trekking, paragliding, mountaineering and rock climbing.

Hamsafar Travel (p382; www.hamsafar-travel.com) Treks to the interesting Yagnob region and the Fan Mountains and support for most other adventures you can dream up.

Mountain Adventure Travel (☎ 221 18 12; www.matt.tj; Dushanbe) Trekking specialists Surat Toimastov and Dilshod Karimov operate top-notch trekking, jeep and skiing trips, strong in the Pamirs but also with trips to the little-visited south. Treks cost around US$100 to US$120 per day for small groups. Formerly Pamir Adventure and Azimuth Travel.

Pamir Silk Tour (p404; pst_pamirs@yahoo.com) Horse treks in the Pamirs and Wakhan trekking.

Pamir Travel (p394; www.travel-pamir.com) Good for Fan Mountain and Zerafshan Valley treks, with an office and guest house in Penjikent and branch in Dushanbe.

Turkmenistan

See p461 for more information on Turkmenistan activities.

Ayan Travel (p433; www.ayan-travel.com) Wildlife watching, horse treks, hikes, camel treks, 4WD desert tours.

DN Tours (p433; www.dntours.com) Horse riding.

Stantours (p433; www.stantours.com) Based in Kazakhstan but offering such adventures as camel treks across the Karakum desert, markhor-watching and climbing in Kugitang and a week-long expedition on Akhal-Teke horses in the Kopet Dag mountains.

Uzbekistan

Asia Adventures (p217; www.asad.uz) Adventure travel specialist offers mountaineering and other trips across Central Asia. It's the exclusive operator of heli-skiing tours in Chimgan.

Asia Travel (www.asia-travel.uz) Trekking and climbing specialists, with mountain biking and camel trekking in central Uzbekistan, horse riding from Arkit, heli-skiing.

Asian Specialized Tours (p217; www.ast.uz) Guide Boris Karpov knows the local mountains like the back of his hands.

Sogda Tour (p243; www.sogda-tour.com) Trips include to the caves and mountains around Darbent/Boysun.

See p281 for more information on Uzbekistan activities.

Kazakhstan
Казахстан

The world's ninth-biggest country has finally edged into global consciousness. Long regarded as little more than a big blank space in the middle of Asia, Kazakhstan has made it onto the map thanks to the judicious use of its vast mineral resources in its two decades as a nation, with a little helping hand – since all publicity is good publicity – from that pseudo-Kazakh Borat Sagdiyev and his 2006 calumnies upon its people.

The most economically advanced of the 'stans', Kazakhstan has reinvented itself since the Soviet collapse as a uniquely prosperous and modern Eurasian nation. The commercial and social hub, Almaty, has an almost European feel with its boutiques, chic cafes and avant-garde arts and club scene. Astana, in the north, has been transformed into a 21st-century capital with a profusion of stunning futuristic architecture. President Nazarbaev, who has ruled Kazakhstan since Soviet times, certainly doesn't encourage political opposition but has managed to forge a peaceful, confident, multiethnic nation – which makes him by and large pretty popular.

The country's southern fringe, on old silk routes and the edge of the Tian Shan, has always attracted a flow of Central Asia travellers. Today, with better transport and better facilities of every kind, it's easier than ever before to soak up the soulful rhythms of the boundless steppe, to watch flamingos on salty inland lakes, or to discover mysterious underground mosques near the Caspian Sea. Homestay programs in some of the most beautiful areas help to offset the fact that Kazakhstan is overall the most expensive country in Central Asia.

Travellers are still rare enough here for a foreign guest to be treated not as just another tourist but with real warmth and hospitality. Enjoy it while it lasts!

FAST FACTS

- **Area** 2.7 million sq km
- **Capital** Astana
- **Country code** ☎ 7 (the same as Russia)
- **Famous for** oil, steppe, Borat
- **Languages** Kazakh, Russian
- **Money** tenge (T); US$1 = 145T; €1 = 200T
- **Off the map** Beket-Ata, Sauran
- **Phrases** *salemetsiz be* (hello); *rakhmet* (thanks)
- **Population** 16 million

HOW MUCH?

- **Snickers bar** US$0.60
- **100km bus ride** US$2
- **One-minute phone call to the USA/ UK** US$0.70
- **Internet per hour** US$1.70
- **Traditional hat** US$10
- **1L petrol** US$0.65
- **1L bottled water** US$0.55
- **Bottle of local beer** US$0.70
- **Shashlyk** from US$2

HIGHLIGHTS

- **Almaty** (p126) Leafy, sophisticated metropolis with spectacular mountains on its doorstep.
- **Aksu-Zhabagyly Nature Reserve** (p155) Hikes, homestays and horse rides amid gorgeous mountain scenery.
- **Astana** (p172) Twenty-first-century fantasy architecture in a brand-new capital.
- **Turkistan** (p157) Beautiful Timurid architecture at the country's holiest site.
- **Mangistau** (p170) Remote desert country honeycombed with canyons, weird rock outcrops, underground mosques, ancient necropolises and wandering camels.

ITINERARIES

- **Three days** Explore Almaty by foot, taking in Panfilov Park (p131), the Central State Museum (p131) and the Kok-Tobe cable car (p132), and make a trip into the mountains south of the city (p144). If you're travelling on to Kyrgyzstan in summer, use the Karkara Valley crossing (p147).
- **One week** Extend the three-day itinerary with time in southern Kazakhstan – Shymkent (p151), lovely Aksu-Zhabagyly Nature Reserve (p155) and the splendour of Turkistan (p157) – or head for Astana (p172), Kazakhstan's spectacular capital-under-construction.
- **Two weeks** The extra week allows for a more leisurely exploration of the one-week options, adding in the magnificent central Tian Shan (p148) in Kazakhstan's southeastern corner or explorations of the central steppe (p184) or the mountain country out of Ust-Kamenogorsk (p188).

- **One month** You can get around the whole country, taking in more adventurous destinations such as the Aral Sea (p162), the strange underground mosques and dramatic rock formations of the deserts outside Aktau (p170), or the pristine, gorgeously beautiful Altay Mountains (p188) in the northeast.

CLIMATE & WHEN TO GO

Like the rest of Central Asia, Kazakhstan has hot summers and very cold winters. During the hottest months, July and August, average daily maximums reach the high 20°Cs in Almaty and Astana.

In Almaty, temperatures typically remain below freezing for much of December, January and February. The ground is snow-covered for an average 111 days a year. In sub-Siberian Astana there's frost from October to April, with temperatures lurking between -10°C and -20°C from December to February.

Annual precipitation ranges from less than 100mm a year in the deserts to 1500mm in the Altay Mountains.

You can travel at any time of year with the right preparation and logistics, but the most comfortable months are May to September. July to September is best for trekking in the southeastern and eastern mountains. See p499 for an Almaty climate chart.

HISTORY

Kazakhstan as a single entity with defined boundaries was an invention of the Soviet regime in the 1920s. Before that, this territory – apart from the far south, which was within the ambit of the settled Silk Road civilisations of Transoxiana – was part of the domain of nomadic horseback animal herders that stretched right across the Asian steppe and into eastern Europe. Some of the various peoples here at times fell under the sway of regional or continental potentates; at other times they were left to sort themselves out. A people who can be identified as Kazakhs emerged in southeastern Kazakhstan in the 15th century. Over time they came to cover a territory roughly approximating modern Kazakhstan, though some of this territory continued to be governed periodically from elsewhere and/or occupied by other peoples. The borders of Kazakhstan established by its Soviet rulers excluded some Kazakh-populated areas and included some areas with non-Kazakh populations.

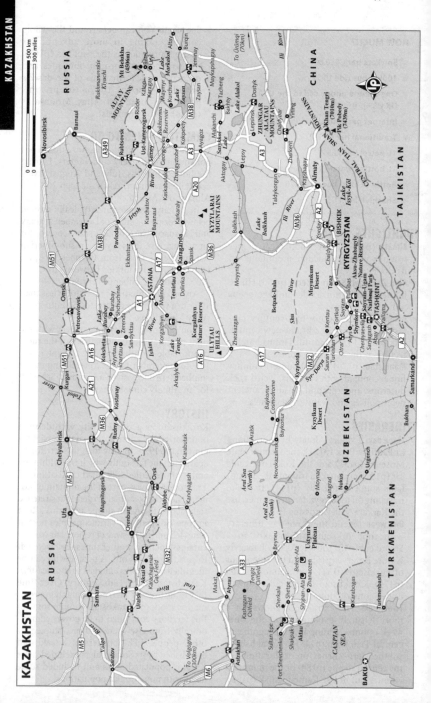

RECOMMENDED READING

▪ *In Search of Kazakhstan* (also published as *Apples Are From Kazakhstan*) by Christopher Robbins (2007). Highly readable portrait of the country, built around extensive travels and meetings with many remarkable Kazakhstanis, not least President Nazarbaev.

▪ *The Kazakhs* by Martha Brill Olcott (1995). Authoritative tome of nearly 400 detailed pages that will sort your Abylays from your Abylqayyrs.

▪ *The Silent Steppe* by Mukhamet Shayakhmetov (published in English 2006). First-hand account of the horrors of collectivisation and WWII.

▪ *The Oil and the Glory* by Steve Levine (2007). The scramble for Caspian oil.

▪ *Modern Clan Politics and Beyond: The Power of 'Blood' in Kazakhstan* by Edward Schatz (2005). Investigates the ongoing influence of the traditional Kazakh *zhuz* (hordes).

Early Peoples

The early history of Kazakhstan is a shadowy procession of nomadic peoples, most of whom swept into the region from the east and left few records. By around 500 BC southern Kazakhstan was inhabited by the Saka, part of the vast network of Scythian cultures that stretched across the steppes from the Altay to Ukraine. The Saka left many burial mounds, in some of which fabulous relics have been found – above all, the Golden Man (see p132), a superb warrior's costume discovered near Almaty that has become a Kazakhstan national symbol.

From 200 BC the Huns, followed by various Turkic peoples, migrated here from what are now Mongolia and northern China. The early Turks left totemlike carved stones known as *balbals,* bearing the images of honoured chiefs, at sites used for burials, worship and sacrifices. These can be seen in many museums in Kazakhstan today. From about AD 550 to 750 the southern half of Kazakhstan was the western extremity of the Manchuria-based Kök (Blue) Turk empire.

The far south of Kazakhstan was within the sphere of the Bukhara-based Samanid dynasty from the mid-9th century, and here cities such as Otrar and Yasy (Turkistan) developed on the back of agriculture and Silk Road trade. The Karakhanid Turks from the southern Kazakh steppe ousted the Samanids in the late 10th century, taking up the Samanids' settled ways (as well as Islam) and constructing some of Kazakhstan's earliest surviving buildings (in and around Taraz).

Chinggis (Genghis) Khan

Around AD 1130 the Karakhanids were displaced by the Khitans, a Buddhist people driven out of Mongolia and northern China. The Central Asian state set up by the Khitans, known as the Karakitay empire, stretched from Xinjiang to Transoxiana, but in the early 13th century it became prey to rising powers at both extremities. To the west, based in Khorezm, south of the Aral Sea, was the Khorezmshah empire, which took Transoxiana in 1210. To the east was Chinggis Khan, who sent an army to crush the Karakitay in 1218, then turned to the Khorezmshah empire, which had misguidedly murdered 450 of his merchants at Otrar. The biggest-ever Mongol army (200,000 or so) sacked the Khorezmian cities of Otrar, Bukhara and Samarkand, then swept on towards Europe and the Middle East. All of Kazakhstan, like the rest of Central Asia, became part of the Mongol empire.

On Chinggis Khan's death in 1227, his enormous empire was divided between his sons. The lands most distant from the Mongol heartland – north and west from the Aral Sea – went to the descendants of his eldest son Jochi and came to be known as the Golden Horde. Southeastern Kazakhstan was part of the Chaghatai khanate, the lands that went to Chinggis' second son Chaghatai. In the late 14th century far southern Kazakhstan was conquered by Timur from Samarkand.

The Kazakhs

The Kazakh story starts with the Uzbeks, a group of Islamised Mongols named after leader Özbeg (Uzbek), who were left in control of most of the Kazakh steppe as the Golden Horde disintegrated in the 15th century.

In 1468 an internal feud split the Uzbeks into two groups (see p46). Those who ended up south of the Syr-Darya ruled from Bukhara as the Shaybanid dynasty and ultimately gave their name to modern Uzbekistan. Those who stayed north remained nomadic and became the Kazakhs, taking their name from a Turkic word meaning free rider, adventurer or outlaw. The Kazakh khanate that resulted was a confederation of nomadic peoples that by the 18th century stretched over most of southern, western and central Kazakhstan, descendants of the Mongols and earlier Turkic inhabitants.

The Kazakhs grouped into three 'hordes' *(zhuz)*, with which Kazakhs today still identify: the Great Horde in the south, the Middle Horde in the centre, and the Little Horde in the west. Each was ruled by a khan and comprised a number of clans whose leaders held the title *axial*, *bi* or *batyr*.

The Zhungars (Oyrats), a warlike Mongol clan, subjugated eastern Kazakhstan between 1690 and 1720 in what Kazakhs call the Great Disaster. Abylay Khan, a leader of the Middle Horde who tried to unify Kazakh resistance to the Zhungars after 1720, was eventually elected khan of all three hordes in 1771, but by that time they were well on the way to being Russian vassals.

The Russians Arrive

Russia's expansion across Siberia ran up against the Zhungars, against whom they built a line of forts along the Kazakhs' northern border. The Kazakhs sought tsarist protection from the Zhungars, and the khans of all three hordes swore loyalty to the Russian crown between 1731 and 1742. Russia later chose to interpret these oaths as agreements to annexation, and gradually extended its 'protection' of the khanates to their ultimate abolition, despite repeated Kazakh uprisings. By some estimates one million of the four million Kazakhs died in revolts and famines before 1870. Meanwhile, the abolition of serfdom in Russia and Ukraine in 1861 stimulated peasant settlers to move into Kazakhstan.

In 1916 Russian mobilisation of Kazakhs as support labour behind the WWI front caused a widespread uprising. It was brutally quashed, with an estimated 150,000 Kazakhs killed and perhaps 200,000 fleeing to China.

The Communist Takeover

In the chaos following the Russian Revolution of 1917, a Kazakh nationalist party, Alash Orda, tried to establish an independent government,

based in Semey. As the Russian Civil War raged across Kazakhstan, Alash Orda eventually sided with the Bolsheviks, who emerged victorious in 1920 – only for Alash members soon to be purged from the Communist Party of Kazakhstan (CPK). Meanwhile many thousands more Kazakhs and Russian peasants had died in the civil war, and several hundred thousand fled to China and elsewhere.

The next disaster to befall the Kazakhs was denomadisation, which happened between 1929 and 1933. The world's biggest group of seminomadic people was pushed one step up the Marxist evolutionary ladder to become settled farmers in new collectives. They slaughtered their herds rather than hand them over to state control and, unused to agriculture, died in their hundreds of thousands from famine and disease. Those who opposed collectivisation were sent to labour camps or killed. Kazakhstan's population fell by more than two million.

'Development' & Unrest

In the 1930s and '40s more and more people from other parts of the USSR – prisoners and others – were sent to work in labour camps and new industrial towns in Kazakhstan. Camp inmates included entire peoples deported en masse from western areas of the USSR around the time of WWII. A further wave of 800,000 migrants arrived in the 1950s when Nikita Khrushchev decided to plough up 250,000 sq km of north Kazakhstan steppe to grow wheat in the Virgin Lands scheme (see p172).

Although the labour camps were wound down in the mid-1950s, many survivors stayed on. Yet more Russians, Ukrainians and other Soviet nationalities arrived to mine and process Kazakhstan's coal, iron and oil. The population of Kazakhs in Kazakhstan dwindled to less than 30%.

During the Cold War the USSR decided Kazakhstan was 'empty' and 'remote' enough to use for its chief nuclear bomb testing ground (the Semipalatinsk Polygon; see p124). In 1989 Kazakhstan produced the first great popular protest movement the USSR had seen: the Nevada-Semey (Semipalatinsk) Movement, which forced an end to nuclear tests in Kazakhstan.

Independent Kazakhstan

Nursultan Nazarbaev, born into a rural Kazakh peasant family in 1940, began to rise up the CPK ranks in the 1970s. He became first secretary (party leader) in 1989 and has ruled Kazakhstan ever since. In 1991 Nazarbaev did not welcome the breakup of the USSR, and Kazakhstan was the last Soviet republic to declare independence. He soon renounced the opportunity for Kazakhstan to become a nuclear power by transferring all 1410 Soviet nuclear warheads on Kazakh soil to Russia. Kazakhstan's first multiparty elections, in 1994, returned a parliament favourable to Nazarbaev, but there were complaints of ballot rigging and the arbitrary barring of candidates.

The parliament, however, turned out to be a thorn in Nazarbaev's side, obstructing his free-market economic reforms, which one deputy called 'shock surgery without anaesthetics'. Nazarbaev dissolved parliament in 1995 and soon afterwards won an overwhelming referendum majority to extend his presidential term until 2000. New parliamentary elections returned an assembly favourable to Nazarbaev.

In 1997 Nazarbaev moved Kazakhstan's capital from Almaty to Astana, then a medium-sized provincial city in the central north, citing Astana's more central and less earthquake-prone location, and greater proximity to Russia. Despite incredulity at first, Astana has been transformed at great cost into a capital for the 21st century with some spectacular new buildings. The new capital is just part of Nazarbaev's vision of Kazakhstan as 'a Central Asian snow leopard', which will use its huge natural-resource wealth to build a diversified, hi-tech economy, with a trilingual (Kazakh, Russian and English) populace, by the year 2030. He has forged friendly relationships with the main Western powers and Russia, and developed a working relationship with China (one of the major investors in Kazakhstan), while also rubbing along OK with Kazakhstan's Central Asian neighbours.

Western companies paid vast amounts to get a slice of Kazakhstan's large oil and gas reserves, mainly near and beneath the Caspian Sea, where the Tengiz field, already operative, and the Kashagan field, expected to start flowing in 2012, have reserves almost as big all the USA's oilfields combined. Kazakh oil production in 2009 was 1.5 million barrels a day, making it the world's 21st biggest producer. Kashagan alone is expected to be producing that much before 2020, and Kazakhstan hopes to be in the world's top 10 producers as early as 2015.

In 1999 Nazarbaev was assured of victory in new presidential elections after the main opposition leader, Akezhan Kazhegeldin, was barred from standing. Nazarbaev argued openly that democratic reform could only succeed on the back of economic progress – something that was certainly happening as the country posted 9% to 10% growth year after year, which helped to maintain ethnic harmony, too. Nazarbaev won a further seven-year presidential term with over 90% of the vote in the 2005 elections. His political rivals and critics were frequently sacked, jailed or even, in two cases in 2005 and 2006, found shot dead. The government denied any involvement in the deaths.

Nazarbaev's eldest daughter, Dariga Nazarbaeva, a powerful media owner and previously a mild critic of her father, merged her own political party, Asar, with his, Otan, in 2006. The combined political giant, Nur-Otan, then won every seat in the lower house of parliament in 2007. International observers described the elections as flawed, as they had done every election held in post-Soviet Kazakhstan.

CURRENT EVENTS

Nazarbaev's presidential term ends in 2012. Assuming that he remains healthy, there is nothing to stop him standing again. In 2007 parliament removed any limits on the number of terms he could serve. There is no apparent strategy in place for a transition to multiparty democracy, nor any obvious heir apparent. One would-be candidate was removed from the scene in 2007–08 when Rakhat Aliev, a multimillionaire businessman and politician, and husband (since divorced) of Dariga Nazarbaeva, was sacked as ambassador to Austria and then sentenced *in absentia* to two 20-year sentences for plotting a coup, and kidnapping and running a criminal gang. He denied the charges.

Nazarbaev remains very popular among the population at large. Criticism of the country's lack of genuine democracy comes chiefly from the middle class and abroad. The issue came into particular focus in 2010, when Kazakhstan held the one-year presidency of the Organization for Security & Co-operation in Europe (OSCE), a multicountry body designed to promote security, democracy and human rights.

Critics of Nazarbaev continue to be put out of action. In 2009, prominent human-rights activist Yevgeny Zhovtis received a four-year manslaughter sentence in a trial condemned as unfair by rights groups. The media rights body Reporters Without Borders ranked Kazakhstan 142nd out of 175 countries in its 2009 Press Freedom Index, characterising Nazarbaev as a predator of press freedom. Insulting the president or government officials is a criminal offence in Kazakhstan.

Most of this won't matter too much to the bulk of Kazakhstanis as long as the economy stays on track. In 2009 Kazakhstan devalued the tenge and bailed out two of its biggest banks as falling commodity prices and the world banking crisis struck. Fortunately it was able to use US$10 billion from its sovereign wealth fund – oil revenues stashed away for just such an emergency – to fund the bail-out and launch a recovery program. With the giant Kashagan oilfield expected to start flowing in 2012, and commercial deposits of almost every known valuable mineral scattered around the country, the economic future remains bright.

The new wealth, however, tends to be concentrated in the major cities and areas where the resources are located. Rural areas and cities in resource-poor areas are falling behind. Even by official figures 12% of the population is living below the poverty line. Nazarbaev himself is reckoned one of the world's richest men.

Corruption remains a barrier to a true free-market economy: Kazakhstan ranked 120th out of 180 countries on the 2009 Corruption Perceptions Index of Transparency International (TI), despite a high-profile government anticorruption drive.

PEOPLE

Although Kazakhs now form the majority of Kazakhstan's population, it is a multiethnic country where economic progress is encouraging other groups to think of themselves as Kazakhstanis as well as ethnic Russians, Ukrainians, Koreans, Uzbeks, etc.

Kazakh culture, rooted in oral tradition, survives at its strongest in the countryside, although urban Kazakhs are showing a growing interest in their roots too, now that there is no Soviet regime to tell them that nomadic culture and the Kazakh language are symbols of a backward past. City-dwellers enjoy hanging out in the yurts and *kymyzkhanas* (*kymyz* stalls) that spring up all round the country in summer, and they often still decorate their homes with colourful, yurt-style carpets and tapestries.

Family, respect for elders and traditions of hospitality remain very important to Kazakhs. Ancestry determines both a person's *zhuz* (horde) and clan. The best ancestor of all is Chinggis Khan, and right up to the 20th century the Kazakh nobility consisted of those who could trace their lineage back to him. Traditionally, Kazakhs may not marry anyone descended from males going back seven generations on the father's side of their family. Kazakhs often don colourful traditional garb for weddings, and the practice of bride stealing (with or without the bride's consent) has not altogether disappeared in rural areas and the more Kazakh-dominated towns in the south.

Kazakh tradition is most on display during the spring festival Nauryz (Navrus; the spring festival on 22 March; see p195), when families gather, don traditional dress, eat special food, and enjoy traditional music and games rooted in their equestrian traditions such as *kokpar* (see the *buzkashi* boxed text, p64), *audaryspak* (horseback wrestling) and *kyz kuu* (a boy–girl horse chase – if he wins he gets to kiss her; if she wins she gets to beat him with her riding whip). Falconry (hunting with birds of prey) is another still-beloved Kazakh tradition.

Population

Southern areas are about 90% Kazakh, while in some northern towns the majority population is Russian. Over half the people now live in urban areas.

Of the 16 million population, 63% are Kazakhs – a big upward swing from Soviet times, aided by emigration of two million Russians, Germans and Ukrainians after independence and the arrival of hundreds of thousands of *oralman* (ethnic Kazakhs repatriating from other countries). The total population is still down by over a million since the early 1990s.

Other main ethnic groups are Russians (24%), Uzbeks (3%), Ukrainians (2%), and Germans, Tatars and Uyghurs (1% to 1.5% each). There are more than 100 other nationalities.

RELIGION

Kazakhs have never been deeply religious and extremism is notable by its absence. Islam, their predominant faith, is at its strongest in the south, especially around Taraz, Shymkent and Turkistan. Pilgrimages to the mausoleum of Kozha Akhmed Yasaui at Turkistan and the desert shrine of Beket-Ata, east of Aktau, are important ways for Kazakh Muslims to affirm their faith. Most Muslims are of the Sunni denomination. The Russian Orthodox Church claims more than 40% of the population. The government stresses Kazakhstan's tradition of religious tolerance.

ARTS
Film

The seeds of Kazakhstan's feisty film industry were sown when Stalin relocated the main Soviet film studios to Almaty during WWII. The biggest recent productions have been two lavish historical epics aimed at fostering national pride – *Nomad* (2005) and Oscar-nominated *Mongol* (2007). Young Kazakhstani directors are also making thought-provoking movies tackling more sensitive realities. The best include Sergey Dvortsevoy's *Tulpan* (2008), about a young man returning from the Russian navy to a shepherd's life in the Betpak-Dala; *Song from the Southern Seas* (2008), directed by Marat Sarulu, focused on contemporary Kazakh–Russian interethnic relations; and the Oscar-shortlisted *Kelin* (2009) by Ermek Tursunov, a silent movie whose erotic scenes upset some in Kazakhstan.

The highest-grossing Kazakh film ever (US$1 million) was Akhan Sataev's *The Racketeer* (2007), about a young man drawn into the post-Soviet gangster world in Almaty. Sadly, many other Kazakh-made films, despite garnering awards at international festivals, are largely ignored by their home audiences, who much prefer Hollywood productions. Globally better known than anyone working in Kazakhstan is Timur Bekmambetov, who was born in Atyrau in 1961 but has made his film career in Moscow and Hollywood, directing international successes *Night Watch*, *Wanted* and *9*. Bekmambetov is however scheduled to return to Kazakhstan to make a new national blockbuster, *The Golden Warrior*.

The annual Eurasia Film Festival, held in Astana, showcases recent films from throughout Central Asia.

Music & Literature

Foreign tastes prevail in popular music too, with Western-style or Russian pop, electronica and rock being many people's preferred listening. However, Kazakh traditional music is equally popular as Kazakhs reconnect with their roots. The national instrument is the *dombra*, a small two-stringed lute with an oval box shape. Other instruments include the *kobyz* (a two-stringed primitive fiddle), whose sound is said to have brought Chinggis Khan to tears, and the *sybyzgy* (two reed or wood flutes strapped together like abbreviated pan pipes). The music is largely folk tunes, handed down like the area's oral literature through the generations; short on pounding excitement, it captures the rhythms of nomadic life on the steppe. A good place to catch traditional Kazakh concerts is Almaty's State Philharmonia (see p138). Keep an eye open for the Sazgen Sazy and Otrar Sazy folk orchestras, whose members wear colourful traditional garb to go with their music. Urker, Roksonaki and Ulytau are groups that provide an interesting crossover between indigenous sounds and imported rhythms like rock, pop and jazz.

The most skilled singers or bards are called *akyns*. Undoubtedly the most famous and important form of Kazakh traditional art is the *aitys*, a duel between two *dombra* players who challenge each other in poetic lyrics. You might catch one of these during Nauryz (p195) or other holidays such as 9 May (Victory Day) or 16 December (Independence Day), as well as on TV. The national bard Abay Kunanbaev (1845–1904; see p191) invented Kazakh written literature and still stands head and shoulders above all others in the literary pantheon.

Art & Crafts

Kazakhs are also rediscovering their identity through contemporary art, which has gone through a rapid process of catching up with international trends such as performance and video art and installations. Wacky Rustam Khalfin is probably the leading avant-garde creator. The film *Kazakhstan Swings* (www.zc-zfilms.com) documents some of the wilder excesses of this movement. Meanwhile painters and graphic artists are producing lot of bright and very attractive work – check Almaty's Tengri Umai gallery (p139).

In pre-Soviet times the Kazakhs developed high skills in the crafts associated with nomadic life – brightly woven carpets and wall hangings for yurts, jewellery, ornate horse tackle and weaponry, and splendid costumes for special occasions. You can admire these in almost any museum in the country.

ENVIRONMENT
The Land
Except for the strings of mountains along its southern and eastern borders, Kazakhstan is pretty flat. At 2.7 million sq km, it's about the size of Western Europe. It borders Russia to the north, Turkmenistan, Uzbekistan and Kyrgyzstan in the south, and China in the east. It has a lengthy shoreline of about 1900km on the Caspian Sea.

Southeast Kazakhstan lies along the northern edge of the Tian Shan, where Mt Khan Tengri (7010m) pegs the China–Kazakhstan–Kyrgyzstan border. Kazakhstan's eastern border, shared with China, is a series of mountain ranges culminating in the Altay, where some peaks top 4000m.

The north of the country is flat, mostly treeless steppe, with much of its original grassland now turned over to wheat or other agriculture. Further south and west the steppe is increasingly arid, becoming desert or semidesert. A surprising number of lakes, especially in the north, and scattered ranges of hills, break up the steppe.

The most important rivers are the Syr-Darya, flowing across the south of Kazakhstan to the Little Aral Sea; the Ural, flowing from Russia into the Caspian Sea; the Ili, flowing out of China into Lake Balkhash; and the Irtysh, which flows across northeast Kazakhstan into Siberia. Lake Balkhash in the central east is now (following the demise of the Aral Sea) the largest lake in Central Asia (17,000 sq km).

Wildlife
Kazakhstan's mountains are rich in wildlife, including bear, lynx, argali sheep, ibex, wolves, wild boar, deer, and the elusive snow leopard, of which perhaps only 30 remain in the Altay, the mountains south of Almaty and the Aksu-Zhabagyly Nature Reserve. Two types of antelope, the saiga and the goitred gazelle (zheyran), roam the steppe in much smaller numbers than they used to. At least the saiga, whose numbers fell from over a million in the 1970s to about 40,000 by 2002, is staging a comeback, thanks largely

to a combined government–NGO program to conserve steppe habitats in the centre of the country – check out www.saiga-conservation.com and http://acbk.kz for more. In Altyn-Emel National Park, Przewalski's horses, extinct in Kazakhstan since 1940, have been reintroduced from zoos in Europe.

The golden eagle on Kazakhstan's flag is a good omen for ornithologists. Hundreds of bird species are to be seen, from the paradise flycatcher of Aksu-Zhabagyly to the Himalayan snowcock and the relict gulls of Lake Alakol. Thousands of flamingos spend summer at Korgalzhyn Nature Reserve, 150km southwest of Astana. See www.kazakhstanbirdtours.com for good bird background.

Environmental Issues
Because of its vast size and relative emptiness, Kazakhstan was forced to endure the worst excesses of the Soviet system – a fearful legacy it is still grappling with. The Aral Sea catastrophe is well known (see p100 and p163), but the country also continues to suffer from the fallout, literal and metaphorical, of Soviet nuclear tests, conducted mainly near Semey. Industrial air pollution, especially from metallurgical plants, is still bad in cities such as Karaganda, Ust-Kamenogorsk (Oskemen), Ekibastuz and Kostanay. Growth in car ownership has brought increasing traffic pollution to Almaty.

NUCLEAR TESTS
During the Cold War, far from both Moscow and the eyes of the West, some 460 nuclear tests were carried out at the Polygon, as the testing ground near Semey was known. Although looking empty on the map, the region around the Polygon certainly wasn't uninhabited: villagers living close by were given virtually no protection or warning of the dangers.

The end for the Polygon came about as a result of the Nevada-Semey Movement, a popular protest launched in the wake of two particular tests in 1989. Within a few days more than a million signatures were collected on Kazakhstan's streets calling for an end to the tests. President Nazarbaev finally closed the site in 1991, announcing compensation for the victims. The tragic effects linger, however: genetic mutations, cancers, weakened immune systems and mental illness continue to destroy lives and occupy hospitals and clinics in and around Semey, and may do so for years to come. The UN Development Programme says that over 1.3 million people have been adversely affected by the tests.

THE CASPIAN SEA

As the Kashagan underwater oilfield approaches lift-off, and other fields around the Caspian are already being pumped, the environmental future of the world's largest lake sits in the balance.

Oil operations have already brought environmental problems around the Kazakh section of the Caspian shore, including leaks from wells that have been submerged by rises in the level of the sea. Oil in the Tengiz field has a very high sulphur content, which has been blamed by some locals for human illnesses in the area. The region around Aktau, also an oil producer and the scene of uranium mining and a large chemical-metallurgical complex in Soviet times, suffers high levels of respiratory disease.

Signs of trouble are visible among the Caspian's more than 400 fish species, including the famous beluga (white) sturgeon, source of the world's best caviar. The giant beluga's last natural breeding ground is around the Ural delta, and there are fears that exploitation of the Kashagan oilfield nearby could put paid to the fish. The same area is also a breeding ground for the poor Caspian seal, whose numbers have dwindled from over a million to under 100,000 since the 1930s, from water pollution, disease, hunting, and a recent jellyfish plague that killed off much of the seal's staple fish diet. Rising temperatures have already reduced the thickness of winter ice where the seals gather to mate, so the prospects for one of the world's smallest seals look pretty bleak.

FOOD & DRINK

The food culture of Kazakhstan is one of the strongest indications of Kazakhs' nomadic roots. Nomads eat the food most readily available, and in most cases this meant horses and sheep. The Kazakh national dish is *beshbarmak,* chunks of long-boiled mutton, beef, or perhaps horse meat and onions, served in a huge bowl atop flat squares of pasta. The broth from the meat is drunk separately.

In bazaars and a growing number of restaurants you'll come across horse meat in various forms. Menus may offer a plate of cold horse meats as a starter, and 'horse steak' as a main dish. *Kazy, shuzhuk/shuzhak* and *karta* are all types of horse-meat sausage, with horse intestine used as the casing. *Kuurdak* (also *kurydak*) is a fatty stew of potatoes and meat and offal from a horse, sheep or cow (including lungs and heart), boiled in a pot for two to three hours.

Across the country you'll also find ubiquitous Central Asian dishes such as shashlyk, *laghman* (long, stout noodles), *manty* (steamed dumplings), *plov* (pilaf) and *samsa*

ECOTOURISM & CBT IN KAZAKHSTAN

Ecotourism and community-based tourism (CBT) have taken root in Kazakhstan and provide economical ways to enjoy several of the country's most attractive areas. The Ecotourism Information Resource Centre (EIRC) in Almaty (see p130) can provide information, bookings and practical help for visiting a dozen ecotourism and CBT programs around the country.

These programs offer homestays, guided hikes, treks and horse rides, and a variety of other activities from wildlife-spotting to concerts of traditional Kazakh music. Average homestay prices are 3000T to 5000T per person per night including three meals – good value for Kazakhstan. You'll typically spend about the same again on guides, park fees, horses, vehicle transfers and other expenses.

Top sites include the following:

Aksu-Zhabagyly Nature Reserve (p155) Beautiful mountain country at the northwest extremity of the Tian Shan, with high biodiversity.

Sayram-Ugam National Park (p156) Near Aksu-Zhabagyly, with similar attractions.

Korgalzhyn Nature Reserve (p179) Steppe lakes and exciting birdwatching; the world's most northerly flamingo habitat.

Kokshetau (p181) Village life, walks and rides amid unspoiled northern countryside with lakes, woodlands and rocky hills.

(pastry pies with various fillings). Kazakhs make a sweet *plov* with dried apricots, raisins and prunes, while *plov askabak* is made with pumpkin. In summer open-air beer and shashlyk bars spring up in every town. Anywhere with a glowing (or flaming) grill out front will be serving shashlyk.

A local snack is *baursaki*, fried dough balls or triangles, not unlike heavy doughnuts. Kazakh apples are also famous in Central Asia (Almaty and its old name, Alma-Ata, literally mean 'Father of Apples').

The cuisines of some non-Kazakh ethnic groups – Russian, Korean, Uyghur, Dungan – are also prominent. A sign with Arabic script is usually a mark of a Uyghur restaurant and of good *laghman* to be had inside. The major cities have their share of international restaurants too.

Kymyz (fermented mare's milk) is popular. You can buy it, as well as *shubat* (fermented camel's milk, with a less salty taste), in some city supermarkets as well as in markets and out in the countryside.

Most midrange and top-end restaurants add a 10% service charge to the bill, which doesn't go to those who provide the service, so you should provide a tip as well. The 'business lunch' *(biznes lanch, kompleksny obed)* offered by many city restaurants is usually a good-value set meal, typically comprising soup or salad, a main course, a dessert and a drink.

ALMATY АЛМАТЫ

☎ 727 / pop 1.4 million / elev 850m

Kazakhstan's economic success is most palpable here in its biggest city, where at times you could almost believe you are in Europe, such are the numbers of expensive international shops lining the streets and of Mercedes, Audis and BMWs negotiating the peak-hour jams. This leafy city with a backdrop of the snowcapped Zailiysky Alatau has always been one of the most charming Russian creations in Central Asia. Today Almaty's large middle class have expensive suburban apartments, 21st-century shopping malls, Western-style coffee lounges, fine restaurants, chic bars, dance-till-dawn nightclubs and new ski resorts to help them enjoy life to the full. No one even seems too bothered that Almaty has been replaced by Astana as Kazakhstan's capital.

This is Kazakhstan's main transport hub and a place many travellers pass through rather than linger, but stay a few days and you'll find that Almaty is a surprisingly sophisticated and hedonistic place – one for enjoying green parks and colourfully illuminated fountains, for visiting excellent museums, theatres, shops and markets, and for eating, drinking and partying in Central Asia's best selection of restaurants, bars and clubs. And great mountain hiking and skiing are right on the doorstep.

The perfect times to visit are mid-April to late May, and mid-August to mid-October, when it's neither too cold nor too hot.

HISTORY

Almaty was founded in 1854, when the Kazakhs were still nomads, as a Russian frontier fort named Verny, on the site of the Silk Road oasis Almatu, which had been laid waste by the Mongols. Cossacks and Siberian peasants settled around it, but the town was almost flattened by earthquakes in 1887 and 1911. In the late 19th and early 20th centuries it was a place of exile, its best-known outcast being Leon Trotsky.

Renamed Alma-Ata (Father of Apples), it became the capital of Soviet Kazakhstan in 1927. The Turksib (Turkestan–Siberia) railway arrived in 1930 and brought big growth – as did WWII, when factories were relocated here from Nazi-threatened western USSR and many Slavs came to work in them. Large numbers of ethnic Koreans, forcibly resettled from the Russian Far East, arrived at the same time.

In the 1970s and '80s Kazakhstan's leader Dinmukhamed Kunaev, the only Central Asian member of the Soviet Politburo, managed to steer lots of money southeast from Moscow to transform Alma-Ata into a worthy Soviet republican capital. Hence the number of buildings in relatively adventurous late-Soviet styles such as the Arasan Baths and Hotel Kazakhstan, and stately piles such as the Academy of Sciences and the old parliament, now the Kazakh-British Technical University.

In 1991 Almaty was the venue for the meeting where the USSR was finally pronounced dead, when all five Central Asian republics, plus Azerbaijan, Armenia and Moldova, joined the Commonwealth of Independent States founded by Russia, Ukraine and Belarus. The name Almaty, close to that of

---

ALMATY MUST-SEES

Kok-Tobe Smooth cable-car ride to the best views in town (p132).

Central State Museum All Kazakhstan's history under one roof (p131).

Ozero Bolshoe Almatinskoe Turquoise lake in a high-elevation mountain bowl (p144).

Abay State Opera & Ballet Theatre Quality theatre at a bucket-shop price (p138).

Barakholka This market is a vast melange of junk and gems (p139).

---

the original Silk Road settlement, replaced Alma-Ata soon after.

Almaty lost its status as Kazakhstan's capital in 1998 but remains the country's economic, social and cultural hub. Despite a blip in the building boom during the 2008–10 *krizis*, office towers, apartment blocks and shopping centres continue to push skyward, especially in the south of the city.

ORIENTATION

Some find a lack of distinctive landmarks on Almaty's long, straight streets confusing. Keep in mind that the mountains are to the south, and that the city slopes upward from north (650m) to south (950m). The walking tour on p133 will help you to identify key reference points for navigating the city.

The downtown area stretches roughly from the Green Market (Zelyony Bazar) in the north to Respublika alangy in the south. South of here the new business district is developing along streets like Al-Farabi.

Many street names were changed after independence, but two decades later many local people are still more familiar with the Soviet names, so you'll find the most important of these given in brackets on the Almaty map. In the centre, the main north–south streets are Dostyk (Lenina), Konaev (Karl Marx), Furmanov, Abylay Khan (Kommunistichesky), Zheltoksan (Mira) and Seyfullin. The key east–west streets are Zhibek Zholy (Gorkogo), Gogol, Tole Bi (Komsomolskaya), Abay and Satpaev.

The airport is 13km north of the centre, and the Sayran long-distance bus station is 5km west. The main train station, Almaty-II, and the Sayakhat regional bus station are on the northern edge of the central area.

INFORMATION
Bookshops & Maps

The Hyatt, InterContinental and Dostyk hotels have bookshops with titles in English and German, including books on Kazakhstan.

Akademkitap No 1 (☎ 273 78 18; Furmanov 91; 10am-8pm Mon-Fri, to 7pm Sat & Sun); No 2 (☎ 272 79 81; Furmanov 139; 10am-7pm) Has a range of dictionaries, phrasebooks and books; No 1 is good for city and hiking maps.

GEO (☎ 243 34 35; Satpaev 30B; 9.30am-6pm Mon-Fri) Sells topographic maps of regions of Kazakhstan published at various times from the 1970s onwards; 1:200,000 maps are 700T, 1:500,000 are 800T. Also has a range of city, country and hiking maps.

Hotel Otrar (☎ 250 68 08; Gogol 73; 9am-noon) The newsstand here has a good map selection.

Emergency
Ambulance (☎ 03)
Fire service (☎ 01)
Police (☎ 02)

Internet Access

Many hotels and some cafes and restaurants offer wi-fi access (often free).

Cafemax (☎ 260 99 99; Timiryazev 1A; per hr 300T; 8am-2am Sun-Thu, 24hr Fri & Sat) Fast connections on lots of computers, and a cafe on the spot. You can also send faxes and make photocopies.

Kazaktelekom (☎ 233 11 50; Zhibek Zholy 100; per hr 220T; 8am-midnight) An inexpensive, recently renovated facility with plenty of computers.

Online Club (Silk Way City, Tole Bi 71; per hr 250-350T; 24hr) Good facility upstairs in this shopping mall.

Webclub Net (Ramstor; Furmanov 226; per hr 350T; 9am-midnight) Another shopping-mall facility.

Medical Services

Pharmacies (Kazakh: *darikhana*; Russian: *apteka*) all over Almaty sell many Western medicines.

International SOS (☎ 258 19 11; www.international sos.com; Lugansky 11; 9am-7pm Mon-Fri, to 1pm Sat) International-standard clinic with 24-hour emergency service; very expensive for nonmembers with a 62,716T administrative fee (valid for a week), plus costs of consultations (17,940T for a standard consultation) and medicines. Take your credit cards.

Interteach (☎ 320 02 00; www.interteach.kz; Furmanov 275D) International clinic with some English-speaking GPs, dentists and specialists available noon to 5pm Monday to Friday; 1st/2nd consultation 2800/1700T; one-week membership including ambulance service and in-patient treatment available.

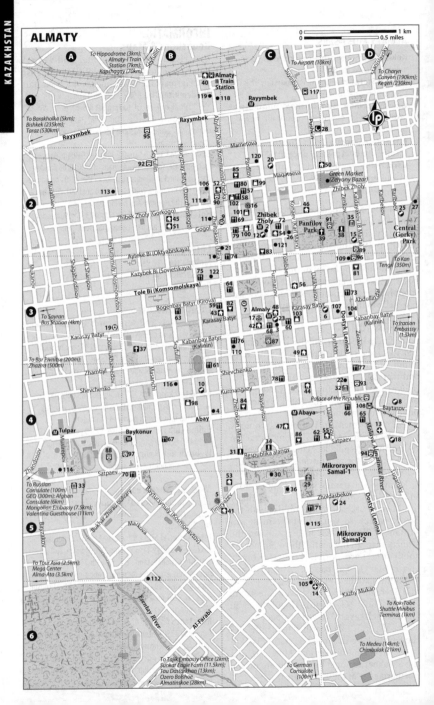

ALMATY

0 — 1 km
0 — 0.5 miles

To Hippodrome (3km);
Almaty-I Train
Station (7km);
Kapshagay (70km)

To Airport (10km)

To Charyn
Canyon (190km);
Kegen (230km)

Almaty-
II Train
Station

Rayymbek

To Barakholka (5km);
Bishkek (235km);
Taraz (530km)

Rayymbek

Rayymbek

Mametova

Green Market
(Zelyony Bazar)
Zhibek Zholy

Panfilov
Park

Central
(Gorky)
Park

Zhibek Zholy (Gorkogo)

Gogol

Zhibek
Zholy

To Kan
Tengri (350m)

Ayteke Bi (Oktyabrskaya)

Kazybek Bi (Sovietskaya)

Tole Bi (Komsomolskaya)

To Sayran
Bus Station (4km)

Bogenbay Batyr (Kirova)

Karasay Batyr

Karasay Batyr

Almaty

Karasay Batyr

Abdullin

To Iranian
Embassy
(1.5km)

To Bar Pivnitsa (200m);
Zhazira (500m)

Kabanbay Batyr
(Kalinin)

Kabanbay Batyr
(Kalinin)

Zhambyl

Shevchenko

Shevchenko

Palace of the Republic

Abay

Kurmangazy

Abaya

Baykonur

Tulpar

Respublika alangy

Satpaev

Mikrorayon
Samal-1

To Russian
Consulate (100m);
GEO (300m); Afghan
Consulate (6km)
Mongolian Embassy (7.5km);
Valentina Guesthouse (11km)

Satpaev

Zholdasbekov

Mikrorayon
Samal-2

To Tour Asia (2.5km);
Mega Center
Alma-Ata (3.5km)

To Kok-Tobe
Shuttle Minibus
Terminus (1km)

Al-Farabi

To Medeu (14km);
Chimbulak (21km)

To Tajik Embassy Office (2km);
Sunkar Eagle Farm (11.5km);
Tau Dastarkhan (13km);
Ozero Bolshoe
Almatinskoe (28km)

To German
Consulate
(100m)

Money

There are exchange kiosks at the transport terminals and on most main streets. Avoid kiosks in other very public places, such as the Green Market, to minimise the risk of theft.

An ATM is never too far away: look for 'Bankomat' signs. The airport, all shopping malls, the TsUM department store, most banks and some supermarkets and smaller shops have them.

Post

Central post office (Bogenbay Batyr 134; 8am-7pm Mon-Fri, 9am-5pm Sat & Sun)

DHL (298 02 76, 258 85 88; www.dhl.kz; Gogol 99; 9am-7pm Mon-Sat)

Registration

Migration Police (254 46 84; Karasay Batyr 109A; 10am-noon & 5-6.30pm Mon-Wed & Fri) If you need to register with the migration police and you choose to do it in person, this is where you must come. The entrance is actually from Baytursynuly: the building is a blue one set back off the street between Baytursynuly 61 and Baytursynuly 63. Be there before 10am because queues/scrums often form. You will have to fill in a form in Russian or Kazakh and hand over your passport, migration card, the address of your hotel (don't give a private address) and 1000T. You will normally be able to pick up your passport and migration card the same afternoon – again it's advisable to be there before opening time. See p196 for more on the important subject of registration.

Telephone & Fax

Kazaktelekom Panfilov (☎ 297 56 03; Panfilov 129; 🕑 8am-7pm Mon-Fri, 9am-3pm Sat); Zhibek Zholy (☎ 233 11 50; Zhibek Zholy 100; 🕑 8am-midnight) You can phone from these offices. The Panfilov branch has fax and photocopying too.

Tourist Information

Almaty Info Centre (☎ 278 05 26, 279 81 46; www. almaty-info.net; Zheltoksan 71; 🕑 9am-1pm & 2-6pm) Run by the Kazakhstan Tourist Association, this centre is combined with the Ecotourism Information Resource Centre and offers maps, leaflets and tourist information. You can request information by email too.

Ecotourism Information Resource Centre (EIRC; ☎ 278 05 26; www.eco-tourism.kz; ecocentre.kz@gmail. com; Zheltoksan 71; 🕑 9am-1pm & 2-6pm) Helpful, English- and German-speaking information and booking centre for community ecotourism programs in Kazakhstan (see the boxed text, p125); can help with travel arrangements to ecotourism villages. Also offers car excursions with English-speaking guides, and places on weekend bus trips with Russian-speaking guides, to numerous places of interest around southeast Kazakhstan. One-day weekend bus trips cost 1400T to 3500T.

Travel Agencies

There are a number of general travel agencies useful for travel tickets, hotel bookings, visa support, outings from the city and longer tours. The following are particularly well geared up for independent travellers:

Stantours (☎ 705-118 4619; www.stantours.com) Expert operation with excellent personal service, and is a specialist in visas for the whole region. Also provides air and train tickets, and can book accommodation and tours throughout Central Asia, including Turkmenistan tours and active tours to offbeat locations. Prices are reasonable. Contact Stantours by email or phone.

Valentina Guesthouse (☎ 295 86 20, 777-668 6399; http://valentina-gh.narod.ru; Zhabaev 62A, Akzhar) This guesthouse (see p135) also functions as a travel agency, providing ticketing, accommodation bookings, inexpensive tours and visa support for guests and nonguests alike.

Arrangements can be made by email. Day trips from Almaty are typically around US$140 plus US$10 per person; overnight trips are US$150 to US$200 per day plus US$50 per person for accommodation and meals.

Other useful travel and tour agencies include the following:

Arnai Tours (☎ /fax 267 40 77; www.arnaitours.kz; Abay 59) This experienced, English- and German-speaking agency offers group, individual, short, long, conventional and active trips, including Baykonur Cosmodrome launch trips (see p159). A two-week Kazakhstan and Kyrgyzstan mountain bike trip is €990/1454/1807 per person for six/four/two people (bring your own bikes).

Jibek Joly (☎ 250 04 45; www.jibekjoly.kz; Hotel Zhetisu, Abylay Khan 55) Runs rural cottage accommodation in several places in southeast Kazakhstan, offers tours to Altyn-Emel National Park and other southeastern destinations, provides visa support and sells ISIC cards.

Otrar Travel (☎ 250 68 36, 24hr reservations centre 250 68 50; www.otrar.kz; Hotel Otrar, Gogol 73) Established agency for air and train tickets, hotel bookings, visa support and tours; also has branches in 16 other Kazakhstan cities.

Transavia (www.transavia-travel.kz) Airport (☎ 270 33 01; 🕑 24hr); Dostyk (☎ 261 04 14; Dostyk 85; 🕑 9am-8pm); Zheltoksan (☎ 258 33 06; Zheltoksan 104, entrance on Ayteke Bi; 🕑 9am-8pm) Useful for tickets on less prominent airlines such as SCAT, S7 and Kam Air.

The following specialise in active trips, and can usually also organise visa support and accommodation:

A13 (☎ 333 52 13; www.a13.travel, www.expats.kz; Zheltoksan 87) This bright agency run by young travel and adventure enthusiasts is geared towards independent travellers and can set up most trips and activities you might fancy in southeast Kazakhstan, including rafting on the Chilik River, biking, birdwatching and paragliding, at good prices.

Kan Tengri (☎ 291 02 00, 291 08 80; www.kantengri .kz; Kasteev 10) Kazakhstan's top adventure-travel company, highly experienced and respected in mountain tourism. Kan Tengri focuses on climbs, trekking and heli-skiing in the central Tian Shan (including Mt Khan Tengri) and Zailiysky Alatau. Also offers horse treks, mountain biking, birdwatching and botanical tours. Most trips last between one and three weeks. A two-week trek typically costs around €1000 per person. Minimum group size is six. The company's director is Kazbek Valiev, the first Kazakh to scale Mt Everest.

Karlygash (Karla) Makatova (☎ 701-755 2086; www.asia-adventuretours.com; kmakatova@yahoo.com) Independent one-woman operator who has long organised trips for the expat community and travellers – day hikes, treks, climbs, drives, kayaking, helicopter flights and more. Her trips are spirited, not too expensive, and a good way to meet locals and expats. Contact Karla by email or phone.

Tour Asia (☎ 376 57 13; www.tourasia.kz; Baikadamov 30-1) Long-established company offers trekking and mountaineering in the central Tian Shan, the mountains south of Almaty and the Pamirs, plus horse riding, mountain-bike trips and horse treks in Aksu-Zhabagyly. Located 5km southwest from the centre.

DANGERS & ANNOYANCES

Almaty is a pretty safe town, but you should still exercise normal precautions (see p193 and p500). The most common emergencies for Westerners here concern late-night activities – people robbed in taxis after emerging inebriated from bars and nightclubs, and the like.

Scams

Watch out for the 'Wallet Full of Dollars'. Someone finds a wallet on the ground as you pass, opens it and finds a lot of money inside. They offer to share the loot with you and if you start to get involved, another person appears, claiming the wallet is theirs and that it originally contained much more money. They then demand compensation or threaten to take you to the police. To avoid trouble, ignore anyone who 'finds' or 'loses' a wallet, and keep walking without hesitation.

SIGHTS
Panfilov Park

This large and popular rectangle of greenery, in the lower (northern) part of the centre, was first laid out in the 1870s and focuses on the candy-coloured **Zenkov Cathedral**, Almaty's nearest (albeit distant) rival to St Basil's Cathedral. Designed by AP Zenkov in 1904, the cathedral is one of Almaty's few surviving tsarist-era buildings (most others were destroyed in the 1911 earthquake). Although at first glance it doesn't look like it, the cathedral is built entirely of wood (including the nails). Used as a museum and concert hall in the Soviet era, then boarded up, it was returned to the Russian Orthodox Church in 1995 and has been restored as a functioning place of worship, with colourful icons and murals. Services are held at 8am and 5pm Monday to Saturday, and 7am, 9am and 4 or 5pm Sunday.

The park is named for the Panfilov Heroes, commemorated at the fearsome **war memorial** east of the cathedral. This represents the 28 soldiers of an Almaty infantry unit who died fighting off Nazi tanks in a village outside Moscow in 1941. An eternal flame commemorating the fallen of 1917–20 (the Civil War) and 1941–45 (WWII) flickers in front of the giant black monument of soldiers from all 15 Soviet republics bursting out of a map of the USSR.

Museums

Almaty's best museum stands 300m up Furmanov from Respublika alangy. The **Central State Museum** (☎ 264 46 50; Mikrorayon Samal-1, No 44; admission 100T; ☽ 9.30am-6pm Wed-Mon, last entry 5pm) takes you through Kazakhstan's history from Bronze Age burials to telecommunications and the transfer of the capital to Astana, with many beautiful artefacts. It's just a pity that signage in nonlocal languages is limited to 'Don't touch, please!'. A large replica of the Golden Man (see p132) stands in the entrance hall. Downstairs, hall 1 deals with archaeological finds and early history up to Chinggis Khan (with *balbals* and models of some of Kazakhstan's major monuments). Next to it is the 'Open Collection', an exhibit of outstanding ancient gold adornments found in Kazakhstan, mainly from Scythian burials between the 6th and 3rd centuries BC, which requires a special 1300T ticket (you do get a tour in English, Russian or Kazakh for your money). The ethnographic display in hall 2, upstairs, features a finely kitted-out yurt and some beautifully worked weaponry and horse and camel gear, plus musical instruments and exotic costumes going back to the 18th century. Halls 3 and 4 on the upper floors deal with the 20th and 21st centuries, with exhibits on some of Kazakhstan's many ethnic groups, heroes of WWII and independent Kazakhstan. Get there by bus 2, 63 or 86 up Furmanov.

In a striking 1908 wooden building (another work of cathedral architect Zenkov) at the east end of Panfilov Park is the **Museum of Kazakh Musical Instruments** (☎ 291 69 17; Zenkov 24; admission 200T; ☽ 9am-1pm & 2-6pm Tue-Sun), the city's most original museum. It has a fine collection of traditional Kazakh instruments – wooden harps and horns, bagpipes, the lutelike two-stringed *dombra* and the violalike *kobyz*. Tours in English are available for 200T (except Saturday): you'll hear tapes of the instruments and, if lucky, see someone strum the *dombra*.

The **Kazakhstan Museum of Arts** (☎ 247 83 56; Musirepov 22; admission 200T; ☽ 10am-6pm Tue-Sun, closed last day of month) has the best art collection in the country, with Kazakh, Russian and Western European art. It includes some Soviet-era works that were banned at the time. Particularly interesting are the room of modern Kazakh handicrafts and the large collection of paintings by Abylkhan Kasteev (1904–73). Kasteev's clear portraits, landscapes and scenes of Soviet progress (railways, hydroelectricity, collective farming) obviously toed the party line but his technique is fabulous.

The intriguing **Geology Museum** (☎ 261 52 83; Dostyk 85; admission 100T; ☉ 10am-5pm Mon-Fri) is in the bowels of a building opposite the Hotel Kazakhstan. The country's mineral wealth is on display, with relief maps and touch-screen computers to provide quick geology lessons in English.

Kok-Tobe

This 1100m hill (Green Hill) on the city's southeast edge is crowned by a 372m-high TV tower visible from far and wide, and affords great views over the city and the mountains, plus an assortment of attractions at the top. The easy way up is by the smooth **cable car** (one-way/return 800/1500T; ☉ every 15min 11am-10pm Mon-Thu, to 11pm Fri-Sun), which glides up in six minutes from beside the Palace of the Republic on Dostyk. Like the cable car, the facilities at the top were recently modernised, and now include assorted cafes and restaurants, Kazakh craft shops, a climbing wall, a roller coaster, a minizoo, a children's playground – and life-

sized bronze statues of the four Beatles, placed here on the initiative of local fans in 2007. The work of Almaty sculptor Eduard Kazaryan, this is claimed to be the world's only monument showing all the Fab Four together. You can sit beside a guitar-strumming John on the bench.

The cable car and other facilities may close early, or not open at all, in poor weather. The cheaper way to get there is by bus 95 (from Ramstor on Furmanov) or 99 (south up Abylay Khan then east on Abay and south on Dostyk) to the terminus on Omarova, from which a shuttle minibus (one-way/return 300/500T, every few minutes from 10am to 10pm) runs up to the top of Kok-Tobe.

Respublika Alangy

The focal point of this broad, Soviet-created ceremonial square at the high southern end of central Almaty is the tall **Monument to Independence**. The stone column is surmounted with a replica Golden Man standing on a winged snow leopard. Around its base are statues of a Kazakh family (a man, a woman and two colt-mounted children); behind is a semicircular wall of low-relief bronze sculptures depicting 10 scenes from Kazakhstan's history, from Golden Man times at the left end to Nazarbaev at the right. Overlooking the square from the south is the neoclassical-style **city government building**. Southeast of here, opposite the Central State Museum, is a large official **Presidential Residence** (Furmanov 205). At the top of Zheltoksan, the striking **Dawn of**

THE GOLDEN MAN

The Golden Man (Zolotoy Chelovek in Russian, Altyn Adam in Kazakh) is a warrior's costume from about the 5th century BC that was found in 1969 in a Scythian tomb about 60km east of Almaty, near Yesik (Issik). It is made of more than 4000 separate gold pieces, many of them finely worked with animal motifs, and has a 70cm-high headdress bearing skyward-pointing arrows, a pair of snarling snow leopards and a two-headed winged mythical beast. Though the person who wore this costume may have no genetic connection with modern Kazakhs, the Golden Man has become modern Kazakhstan's favourite national symbol.

The conventional wisdom is that the skeleton found inside the costume was that of a young Scythian prince killed in battle. Archaeologist Jeannine Davis-Kimball, however, argues in *Warrior Women* (2002) that it was too badly damaged for its gender to be determined, and that other goods found there suggest the Golden Man was in fact a Golden Woman. Apparently 20% of graves with armaments from the Scythian cultures were of women.

The original Golden Man is apparently kept safe in the National Bank building in Almaty, but replicas adorn museums all over the country and a stone version stands atop the Independence Monument on Almaty's Respublika alangy (square). A copy was even unveiled by President Nazarbaev in front of the Kazakhstan embassy in Washington, DC, in 2006.

Freedom monument honours those killed and injured on Respublika alangy on 17 December 1986 during the first unrest unleashed in Central Asia by the Gorbachev era of *glasnost*. Thousands had gathered to protest against Dinmukhamed Kunaev's replacement as head of the Kazakhstan Communist Party by the Russian Gennady Kolbin. A counterdemo of workers armed with metal bars turned the protest into riots, police opened fire and possibly as many as 250 people were killed. Zheltoksan (meaning December) is the post-Soviet name for a street that was previously called Mira (Peace).

You can reach Respublika alangy on bus 41 up Seyfullin, or bus 2, 63 or 86 up Furmanov.

Central (Gorky) Park

Central Almaty's biggest **recreational area** (admission 35T; [clock] 24hr), at the eastern end of Gogol, is still known as Gorky Park. It has boating lakes, funfair rides, an **Aquapark** (adult/child 3500/2800T; [clock] 11am-10pm Jun-Sep), a rather sad zoo, a cinema and several cafes and shashlyk and beer stands. It's busiest on Sunday and holidays. Trolleybuses 1 and 12 run along Gogol to the entrance.

St Nicholas' Cathedral

The pale turquoise **Nikolsky Sobor** (Baytursynuly 51), with its gold onion domes, stands out west of the centre. The cathedral was built in 1909 and was later used as a stable for Bolshevik cavalry, before reopening in about 1980. It's a terrifically atmospheric place, like a corner of old Russia, with icons, candles and restored frescoes inside and black-clad old supplicants outside. For the best impression, visit at festival times such as Orthodox Christmas Day (7 January) or Easter for the midnight services.

ACTIVITIES

At the **Arasan Baths** ([phone] 272 46 71; Tolebaev 78; admission Mon-Fri 1500T, Sat & Sun 2000T; [clock] sessions every 2hr, 8am-8pm) you can choose from Russian or Finnish baths, each with men's and women's sections. Go with a friend or two and you'll find it's an enjoyable and truly relaxing experience. A shop in the lobby sells soap, towels, and flip-flops for walking around in, or you can bring your own. Also available are *veniki* (bunches of oak and birch leaves) so that you can stimulate your circulation with a good thrashing. Massage is available too. Built in

the early 1980s in a modernistic Soviet style, this is the finest bathhouse in Central Asia.

ALMATY WALKING TOUR

Respublika alangy (**1**; p132) is the best place to start an Almaty walk: it's all downhill from here, and on a clear morning the square provides a panoramic view of the snowcapped mountains. Head east along Satpaev and turn

---

WALK FACTS

Start Respublika alangy
Finish Central mosque
Distance 8km
Duration Four hours

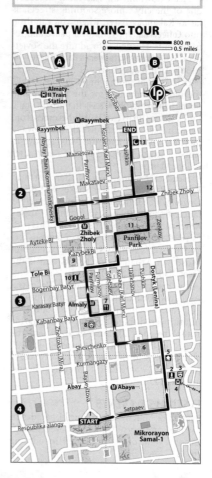

ALMATY WALKING TOUR

down Dostyk. Behind the large **statue (2)** of the iconic writer Abay Kunanbaev is the **Palace of the Republic (3)**, a concert hall. From here you could detour for a ride on the **Kok-Tobe cable car** (**4**; p132) for great views across the city.

A block north of the 26-floor **Hotel Kazakhstan** (**5**; Dostyk 52), a Soviet-era landmark built in 1977, turn west along Shevchenko to the magnificent **Academy of Sciences** (**6**; cnr Shevchenko & Konaev), one of the true gems of Soviet monumental architecture. Fountains and parks around the building make this a cool spot to linger in summer. Check out the 'Eastern Calendar' fountain with Chinese zodiac creatures on the east side of the academy.

Head downhill on tree-lined Tolebaev, one of the city's more soothing streets, as far as Kabanbay Batyr, where you can drop into **Coffeedelia** (**7**; p136) for a pause and refreshments. Head west to admire the Soviet-neoclassical **Abay State Opera & Ballet Theatre** (**8**; p138). Two blocks north of here is a small park in front of another imposing Soviet pile, the old parliament, now the **Kazakh-British Technical University** (**9**; Tole Bi 59). In the park you'll find a **statue (10)** to two WWII heroines from western Kazakhstan, Manshuk Mametova (a machine gunner) and Alia Moldagulova (a sniper), which replaced one of Lenin after independence.

Head east along Tole Bi then north to **Panfilov Park** (**11**; p131). Strike west along Gogol, which is lined with some of the city's fanciest shops, then head north on Abylay Khan and east along Zhibek Zholy. This pedestrianised street, with cafes, a few buskers and artists, is Almaty's (sort of) version of Moscow's Arbat. A few blocks east is the **Green Market** (**12**; p139), the city's most colourful market, with a true flavour of Central Asia. Just north of the market along Pushkin you can (except on Friday) visit Almaty's multitowered, blue-domed, white-marble **central mosque (13)**, built in 1999 and the largest in the country, with space for 3000 worshippers in the finely decorated main prayer hall (women must cover their heads, arms and legs here).

FESTIVALS & EVENTS

Nauryz (22 March) sees colourful parades in the city, and horse racing and even the occasional game of *kokpar* at the Hippodrome (p139).

There's an international **jazz festival** (www.jazz. kz) in April, with the concerts in recent years at the **Palace of Schoolchildren** (☎ 264 14 49; Dostyk 114; tickets 1000-2000T), followed by jams at the Cinema Bar (p139).

SLEEPING

Room prices continue to escalate in Almaty and some midrange establishments here charge 25,000T for two people. For those who are probably not paying their own bills there's no shortage of excellent top-end hotels. Agencies can be useful for making reservations when calling a hotel yourself is getting you nowhere.

Budget

Third Dormitory (Obshchezhitie No 3; ☎ 262 01 61; Satpaev 5; dm 1000T) The 4th floor of an accommodation block of the national agricultural university functions as a cheap hotel. Rooms have two or four beds and are basic but clean enough, as are the shared bathrooms. Enter beneath a 'Kazkholodmash Almaty' sign, go up one flight of one stairs, and 'reception' is the first room on the left.

Gostinitsa/Konak Uy (☎ 296 11 15; Almaty-II Station; dm 2000T) This is upstairs from the international hall of Almaty-II train station, to the left as you enter the building. Dorms have hard beds and shared bathrooms, but are acceptable if you arrive late. You can have a bed for one hour for 500T, or from morning to evening for 1500T.

Hotel Saulet (☎ 267 11 75; Furmanov 187; dm 2600T, tr with private bathroom 10,000T) The Saulet has bare, clean dorms with four single beds, a toilet and basin, and shared showers. It's handy for billiard players as there are several tables downstairs. The sign above the door just says 'Konak Uy Gostinitsa' ('hotel' in Kazakh and Russian).

Hotel Turkistan (☎ 266 41 36; www.turkistan-hotel. kz; Makataev 49; s with shared shower 3000T, s/d with private bathroom 5000/6500T, lux tr 8000T; 🖳 🛜) This hotel opposite the Green Market, used by many regional traders, is reasonable value but security is not the tightest. Standard rooms are well used and have TV, phone and small bathtub.

Midrange

Hotel Zhetisu (☎ 250 04 07; www.zhetysuhotel.kz; Abylay Khan 55; s with shared bathroom 3000T, s/d with private bathroom from 5500/8200T) This is a dowdy Soviet-era survivor that doesn't lift the spirits, but at least the staff have lightened up a bit. The location is pretty central and the rooms are clean, reasonably big and equipped with satellite TV. Rates include breakfast. Trolleybuses 5 and 6 from Almaty-II station go past the door.

So Young's Guesthouse (☎ 701-731 6096; sisyoungs@ hotmail.com; Dom 5, Ayteke Bi 153; per person US$30; 🖳 🛜) Friendly, English-speaking, piano-playing South Korean expat So Young Lee can accommodate up to five in her bright, clean, modern downtown apartment. Hot showers, washing machine, internet and kitchen use are all included in the price. Call or email first. The street entrance is shared with Assalom Aleykum Shaykhana.

Valentina Guesthouse (☎ 295 86 20, 777-668 6399; http://valentina-gh.narod.ru; Zhabaev 62A, Akzhar; per person US$35; 🖳) About 14km southwest of the centre, friendly Valentina's has a green garden and four clean, sizeable guest rooms sharing two bathrooms. It's not exactly convenient for the city centre but it offers transfers to/from transport terminals, helpful ticket-booking services, and all sorts of trips out of the city, at good prices. English-speaking manager-guide Marat is a former mountain rescuer and knows the region like the back of his hand. Buses 11 and 44 go close to the guesthouse: check the website for exact directions. A taxi from the centre (around 1000T) can take anywhere from 20 minutes to an hour or longer depending on traffic. Breakfast is included.

Top End

Hotel Uyut (☎ 279 55 11; http://hotel-uyut.kz; Gogol 127/1; s 10,900-21,000T; d 17,000-24,000T; 🅿 🛏 🖳) Right next door to the Kazzhol and with an almost identical layout, this hotel comes off second best in almost every department but is still welcoming and fine. Breakfast is included.

ⓞⓤⓡⓟⓘⓒⓚ Hotel Kazzhol (☎ 250 89 41; www. kazju.kz; Gogol 127/1; s 11,900-28,000T; d 19,500-31,000T; 🛏 🖳 🛜 🌊) This friendly, efficient, sparkling-clean hotel on a quiet lane between Gogol and Zhibek Zholy is the best value at this sort of price. Desk staff speak English, and the smart rooms all have writing desks and international satellite TV. Rates include a good buffet breakfast, and the fitness centre has a 20m pool. Airport and station transfers available at reasonable prices.

Hotel Alma-Ata (☎ 272 00 70/47; www.hotel-alma-ata.com; Kabanbay Batyr 85; s 15,000-20,000T; d 20,000-32,000T; 🅿 🛏 🖳 🛜) This large pile opposite

APARTMENTS

Valentina Guesthouse (p135) offers one-/two-bedroom central apartments for US$60/90 per night – book ahead. Stantours (p130) can provide central apartments for up to three people for US$110 to US$120 per night, with a two-night minimum and an obligatory airport or station transfer (US$30). Karlygash Makatova (p130) has apartments from US$60 per person and, subject to availability, accommodation with families for US$25 per person.

the opera theatre must have seemed futuristic when built in 1967. It provides plain but pleasing pine-furnished, renovated rooms with gleaming bathrooms and satellite TV, plus restaurant, wine bar, hairdresser and ATMs. The amiable reception staff speak some English. Breakfast is included.

Hotel Saya (☎ 272 32 65; www.saya-hotel.kz; Furmanov 135; r/half lux 15,600/19,600T; 🅿 🛏 🛜) Helpful, Russian-speaking staff and just 12 unexciting if well-equipped rooms. A spartan breakfast is included. It's half-price for 12 hours, and they have been known to slash rates by 30% when business is slow.

Hotel Tien Shan (☎ 393 05 99; Konaev 151; s/d 21,250/25,000T; 🅿 🛏 🖳 🛜) Three-star branch of the Tien Shan Grand Hotel (p136), with very big, bright, comfortable, well-equipped rooms, and breakfast and fitness room access included in the price.

Hotel Otrar (☎ 250 68 06; www.group.kz; Gogol 73; s/d from 28,600/30,800T; 🅿 🍴 🛏 🖳 🛜) Facing Panfilov Park, the well-situated Otrar has spick-and-span rooms with satellite TV, a fitness room and a good help-yourself breakfast (included in rates) in a fancy dining room.

Holiday Inn (☎ 244 02 55; www.ichotelsgroup.com; Timiryazev 20; s/d from 30,000/36,000T; 🅿 🍴 🛏 🖳 🛜) If you're after international-chain ease and familiarity, this recently opened hotel is bright and comfy, and its rates are about half those of nearby five-star options.

Hotel Ambassador (☎ 250 89 89; www.ambassadorhotel.kz; Zheltoksan 121; s/d 30,000/40,000T; 🛏 🖳 🛜) Very good medium-sized hotel in the heart of the city, in a modernised 1930s building with classical decor. Free airport pickups are offered, and there are often massive discounts on Saturday and Sunday. Breakfast is included.

Tien Shan Grand Hotel (☎ 244 96 99; www.ts -hotels.kz; Bogenbay Batyr 115; s/d from 33,000/37,000T; P ⊠ ⊠ ⬛ ⬛ ⬛) An elegant hotel in the handsome former Geology Ministry building, with attractive, good-sized rooms. It has an excellent spa with saunas and a good pool – included in rates, as is breakfast.

Hotel Dostyk (☎ 258 22 70; www.dostyk.kz; Kurmangazy 36; r from 44,800T; P ⊠ ⬛ ⬛ ⬛) A multiyear upgrade has given this 1980s Communist Party hotel an elegant, contemporary style and a full range of in-house services, including spa and gym. The Italian-designed rooms are stylish though not large. Buffet breakfast is included.

InterContinental Almaty (☎ 250 50 00; www. intercontinental.com; Zheltoksan 181; r from 69,440T; P ⊠ ⊠ ⬛ ⬛ ⬛) Just southwest of Respublika alangy, this glitzy high-rise hotel is widely known by a former name, the Ankara. It has plenty of five-star amenities, including seven restaurants, cafes and bars, and a costly business centre. Glass lifts glide up and down the 12-storey atrium. Rooms are very comfy. Breakfast is not included.

EATING

You won't find a better range of good restaurants anywhere else in Central Asia. A large range of international cuisines is represented and some places have great design and ambience too.

Cafes

ourpick 4A Coffee (☎ 271 82 37; coffees, cakes & pastries 200-600T; Zhibek Zholy 81; ❤ 8am-9pm; ⊠) This attractive, American-run coffee house in a leafy side street just off pedestrianised Zhibek Zholy is a great place to drop in or hang out. It has a fine selection of real coffees and irresistible lemon meringue pie, carrot cake and raspberry tarts.

Coffeedelia (coffees, juices, cakes & pastries 200-900T; ⊠ ⬛); Kabanbay Batyr (☎ 272 64 09; Kabanbay Batyr 79; ❤ 8am-midnight Mon-Thu, 8am-1am Fri, 9am-1am Sat, 9am-midnight Sun); Zheltoksan (☎ 261 26 80; Zheltoksan 117; ❤ 8am-midnight) Fashionable coffee house with a relaxed atmosphere, fabulous cakes and pastries, good coffees, teas, juices and breakfasts, and free wi-fi. The Kabanbay Batyr branch, the original, is trendier (but not overwhelmingly so) and busier; the Zheltoksan site hosts live jazz, rock, world music or film presentations at 9pm most Tuesday, Thursday and Saturday evenings.

Restaurants

Dastarkhan Food Self-Service (☎ 267 37 37; Nauryzbay Batyr 122/124; mains 200-600T; ❤ 24hr; ⊠ ⬛) A slightly upmarket cafeteria with a big choice including salads, *laghman*, *plov*, Uzbek *shorpa* (mutton and vegetable soup) and *bifstroganof*. You'll get a good feed for 600T to 800T. Huge queues at lunchtimes Monday to Friday.

Kimep Grill (☎ 237 47 57; Abay 4; mains 300T; ❤ 8am-8pm Mon-Fri, to 2pm Sat; ⊠) The bright, clean cafeteria of the Kazakhstan Institute of Management, Economics & Strategic Research is open to all and serves out good-value soups, salads, *laghman*, *manty*, *plov* and meat dishes.

Kaganat (mains 300-500T; ❤ 24hr; ⊠); Abylay Khan (☎ 261 75 22; Abylay Khan 105); Bogenbay Batyr (☎ 267 60 96; Bogenbay Batyr 148); Dostyk (☎ 264 02 46; Dostyk 108); Satpaev (☎ 255 86 82; Satpaev 7A) This very popular cafeteria chain will feed you satisfactorily and cheaply any time of day or night. Soups, salads, breads, assorted hot mains and desserts are on offer.

Zhazira (☎ 375 40 46; Zhambyl 175; mains 400-550T; ❤ 10am-10pm; ⊠) There's very good Dungan (Chinese Muslim) food at this clean and efficient spot, at good prices. You can't go wrong with the *guyru* or *suyru laghman* (the *suyru* has larger strips of meat) or the *guyru-to-myan* (fried *laghman*). Four people could share the spicy chicken-and-potato dish *dapan-dzhi*.

Traktir Zhili-Byli (☎ 250 75 13; Kurmangazy 43; mains 650-1800T; ❤ noon-midnight; ⊠ ⬛ ⬛) Good-value Russian food from pancakes to 'pork in a fur', in a rustic, log-walled setting.

Bombolo (☎ 273 44 99; Zhibek Zholy btwn Abylay Khan & Panfilov; mains 700-1300T; ❤ 11am-2am Mon-Wed, 11am-4am Thu-Sat, 2pm-2am Sun; ⊠ ⬛) A nice place to eat outdoors in the summer, with shashlyk, pancakes and an international selection of meat dishes and salads.

Restoran Printsessa (Princess; ☎ 261 06 27; Tolebaev 53; dishes 800-2500T; ❤ noon-midnight; ⊠) Come to this large, bustling restaurant just off Gogol for a filling Chinese meal. The menu offers a big choice including a good chicken, chilli and peanuts dish.

Namaste (☎ 292 24 84; cnr Satpaev & Baytursynuly; mains 900-3000T; ❤ 11am-midnight; ⊠ Ⓥ) A small, tranquil restaurant that does excellent Indian, Thai and Chinese food – great for vegetarians.

Zheti Kazyna (☎ 273 25 87; Abylay Khan 58A; mains 900-4000T; ❤ noon-midnight; ⊠ ⬛) This exotically decorated, Central Asian–themed restaurant is a place to come for quality regional cooking. Old favourites such as *manty, laghman,* shashlyk, *samsa* and spicy Dungan noodles are styled for the Western palate, and there are Kazakh specialities including *beshbarmak* (flat noodles with meat or vegetable broth) and horse steaks. On the same premises are equally popular European and Japanese-Chinese eateries, and you can order from any of the three menus in any part. Two courses will cost a minimum of 1400T, and you can easily spend a whole lot more. The entrance is actually on Makataev.

Koreana (☎ 260 65 04; Masanchi 98; mains 1000-1600T; ☯ noon-midnight; ✖ Ⓔ) Neat, unpretentious and entered through a food shop, Koreana is one of the best of Almaty's several Korean restaurants, and definitely not the most expensive. Try the *bulfogi* (marinated beef), *bibimpab* (a rice, egg, meat and vegetable dish) or *kimchi* (marinated cabbage) and try to leave room for the *tedjantige*, a meat, vegetable, tofu and bean paste soup, eaten at the end of the meal. Bowls of Korean salads come free with most main dishes.

Mama Mia (☎ 273 38 73; Gogol 87; dishes 1000-2100T; ☯ 11am-midnight; ✖) A bright, relaxed, little pizza/pasta/salad house, with efficient service and a good choice of tasty food.

Samba Grill (☎ 279 94 15; Abylay Khan 83; rodizio 1500T; ☯ 24hr; ✖) The thing to order at this popular place is the Brazilian-style *rodizio*, which comprises soup, salads and grilled meats that keep coming to your table till you can manage no more. A band plays rock and samba in the evenings, and the outdoor terrace is nice on a summer night.

Safran (☎ 293 83 83; Dostyk 36; mains 1500-3700T, set lunch Mon-Fri 1500-1800T; ☯ noon-midnight; ✖ Ⓔ) Flavoursome Middle Eastern food in a beautiful Middle Eastern setting makes Safran a great place to head when you have 6000T to 8000T to spend on dinner. Tasty dishes range from hummus and falafel to Moroccan chicken with pumpkin-and-ginger sauce.

L'Affiche (☎ 272 10 92; Kabanbay Batyr 83; mains 2000-5000T; ☯ 9am-1am Mon-Thu, 9am-4am Fri, 11am-4am Sat, 2pm-1am Sun; Ⓔ ✖) This elegant Euro-style cafe-restaurant has large-scale Gauguin reproductions covering its ceiling. It's good for anything from a coffee-and-dessert stop to a salad or an *haute-cuisine* dinner of pumpkin cream soup and baked lamb shank.

Thai (☎ 291 01 90; Dostyk 50; mains 4000-10,000T; ☯ 11am-11pm; ✖ Ⓔ) A very swish restaurant with a pleasant outdoor summer terrace, spe-cialising in high-quality Thai and Japanese dishes. The emphasis is on fish and seafood.

Self-Catering

There are plenty of large, well-stocked supermarkets with many Western imports on their shelves.

Yubileyny (☎ 250 75 50; cnr Gogol & Abylay Khan; ☯ 24hr) One of the biggest central supermarkets, with a deli. There are several quick-eat and take-away food options out the front, too, with inexpensive doughnuts, *bliny* (pancakes), *plov, baursaki* and more.

Stolichny (☎ 266 55 75; cnr Abylay Khan & Kabanbay Batyr; ☯ 24hr) Best-quality goods of any downtown supermarket, a huge wine section and a good deli counter.

Green Market (Zelyony Bazar, Kok Bazar; ☎ 273 89 61; Zhibek Zholy 53; ☯ 8am-6pm Tue-Sun) Stalls at this large, two-level central market are piled with nuts, fresh and dried fruit, smoked fish, spices, fruit jams and preserves, ready-made Korean salads, vegetables, medicinal herbs, cheeses, sausages and enormous hunks of fresh meat. You can get *kymyz, shubat* and freshly squeezed pomegranate juice here too. Cafes dotted around the place will serve you a bowl of *laghman* or *plov* with tea and bread for less than 400T.

Two good supermarkets are in the **Silk Way City** (☎ 267 74 74; Tole Bi 71; ☯ 24hr) and **Ramstor** (☎ 258 75 75; Furmanov 226; ☯ 9am-11pm) shopping centres.

DRINKING

Finding a drink for any budget isn't difficult in Almaty, as the distinction between cafes, restaurants and bars is blurred to say the least. Beer gardens under sunshades sprout around the city in summer.

Staut (www.staut.kz; beer 0.4L/1L 334/774T, business lunch Mon-Fri 660T, mains 600-1500T; ☯ 24hr; ✖); Makataev (☎ 273 51 66; Makataev 81); Abylay Khan (☎ 272 68 80; Abylay Khan 147) Brewing its own German-style beers, Staut has several bars around town, and they get packed in the evenings mainly with locals aged in and around their 20s. Live-band nights from 9pm Friday and Saturday at the ample Makataev establishment are hugely popular. Plenty of reasonably priced food too.

ᴼᵁᴿᴾᴵᶜᴷ Shtab (☎ 272 24 40; Zheltoksan 132; beer 1L 280-1400T; ☯ 10am-midnight; ✖) A quaint little beer bar opposite Hotel Ambassador, with a dozen tables and a big choice of local and foreign draft beers including arguably Kazakhstan's best, Shymkentskoe.

Bar Pivnitsa (Zhambyl 174; beer 0.5L 220-300T; ☻noon-midnight; ✗) No 'Irish' decor, no expat prices, no loud music – this local beer bar is pretty close to an actual pub. You can sit and chat over any of dozens of sensibly priced local and foreign brews, and that's just what the predominantly local clientele enjoy doing.

Soho (☎ 267 03 67; Kazybek Bi 65; admission free Sun-Thu, 1000T Fri & Sat; ☻noon-1am Sun-Thu, to 3am Fri & Sat; ✗) Expats and locals pack Soho every night for tankards of beer, international food and crowded dancing to the good resident rock-blues band. It's got a sort of urban-global theme, with pictures of New York mixed in with flags for every nationality. Some of the local girls are sex workers, some aren't.

Mad Murphy's (☎ 291 28 56; Tole Bi 12; ☻ 10.30am-1am) This Irish pub is the most consistently popular expat haunt for stout, pub grub (dishes 1600T to 3000T), darts, football on the screens and the Friday-night rock band.

Vogue (☎ 264 16 99; Satpaev 11; cocktails 1000-4000T; ☻noon-5am; ✗ 🛜) Fashionable preclub lounge bar with lipstick-red decor and face control, celebrated for fatal cocktails like the 'Anglichanin' (Englishman) – beer, Red Bull, lemon and cherry juice and brandy.

ENTERTAINMENT

If you can make some sense of Russian (or have an online translation tool), *Time Out Almaty* (www.timeout.kz) is a great source of listings, reviews and contact details.

Concerts, Ballet & Opera

Almaty has a good theatre and musical scene, and it's well worth catching at least one performance while you're here. Keep an eye open for concerts by the **Sazgen Sazy** (www.sazgen-sazy.kz) or Otrar Sazy folk orchestras.

Abay State Opera & Ballet Theatre (☎ 272 79 34; www.gatob.kz; Kabanbay Batyr 110; admission 400-1700T; ☻ ticket office 10am-1pm & 2-6pm) Almaty's top cultural venue, with three or four performances a week at 5pm or 6.30pm. Some get sold out a week or more ahead. Classics such as *Swan Lake*, *La Bohème*, *Aida* and *Carmen* are a few of the regular shows. Also look out for Kazakh operas such as *Abay* and *Abylay Khan*.

State Philharmonia (☎ 291 80 48; www.philharmonic.kz; Kaldayakov 35) Offers a range of performances including symphony, chamber, jazz, organ and traditional music.

Gay & Lesbian Venues

There is a gay scene in Almaty but bars often open and close quickly. The gay community tries to get together at parties at varied venues – they're publicised on www.gay.kz (in Russian), which also has info on gay support organisations, culture and meeting places, and blogs, chat and small ads.

Real Club (☎ 233 57 26; Rayymbek 152; men Sun-Thu free, Fri & Sat 600T, women Sun-Thu 500T, Fri & Sat 1000T; ☻ 11pm-6am) Though closed for renovations at research time, this is the only long-running gay club. It has shows on Friday and Saturday nights. You need to go with someone who is known there, and should travel by taxi – attacks have happened on nearby streets.

Da Freak (p138) is gay-friendly.

Live Music

Zhest (☎ 292 70 17; www.zhest.kz; Abay 44B; admission 500-2000T; ☻ 10pm-8am Thu-Sat) This Nissen-hut-like building (the name means Tin) on the east side of the Central Stadium is a legendary live-rock venue. Top Kazakh, Russian and occasional international bands (eg Nazareth) rock the joint every weekend. Be sure to stay on the bouncers' good side.

Guns & Roses (☎ 291 91 77; Dostyk 52/2; admission free; ☻ 2pm-3am) Assorted combos of rock, blues, and jazz musicians, most featuring the talented Indian Mark, play good music nightly except Monday from 9pm in this large expat pub in the Hotel Kazakhstan. There's expat pub food (dishes 1000T to 3000T), space to dance and usually a good crowd in. Happy hour is 5pm to 8pm Monday to Thursday.

Soho (left) has a polished rock and blues band nightly from 10pm.

Nightclubs

Almaty's educated and aware students and 20-somethings have spawned a hedonistic nocturnal scene. Flyers will get you in cheap to some clubs and there are lots of special events and parties (check http://partyzan.kz). *Time Out Almaty* has fairly comprehensive but bizarrely organised listings in Russian. Three-day raves happen during summer full moons out at Lake Kapshagay, with DJs flown in from Europe, and tickets and bus transport sold in the city at places like Meloman (p139).

our pick Da Freak (☎ 273 13 37; Gogol 40; admission Fri 1500T, Sat 2000T; ☻ 11pm-6am Fri & Sat) The best electronic club in town, Freak has two dance floors, the country's top DJs and sometimes guests from Moscow or Western Europe. The clientele is a cool, 20ish, local crowd with a smattering of international 20s-to-35s in there too. The entrance is round the back of Zhuldyz restaurant in Panfilov Park.

Cinema Bar (☎ 291 87 44; Kazybek Bi 20; admission 1500T; ☼ 6pm-2am Tue-Sun) This lounge-style boutique cinema – with soft seating, sofas and cushions – turns into a packed party club from around 10pm Friday and Saturday when DJs and live bands play dance, rock and jazz. The crowd is mostly local and a bit arty. Well worth checking out.

Copacabana (☎ 279 78 53; www.copacabana.kz; Zheltoksan 66; admission 2000T; ☼ 5pm-1am Tue, to 2am Wed, to 3am Thu, to 5am Fri, to 6am Sat, to midnight Sun) Head to hot Copacabana for wild nights of dancing to live Latin bands, Cuban dancers and DJs spinning Latino and Latino house. Be ready to fork out 20,000T to 40,000T if you want a table on Thursday, Friday or Saturday (all food and drinks included in the fee). There are dance classes most nights at 7pm.

Esperanza (☎ 299 66 99; www.esperanza.kz; Seyfullin 481; admission per club men 0-2000T, women 0-500T; ☼ 10pm-6am) With two nightclubs, a restaurant, two cafes and even a hotel all in one building (oh yes and a strip club, not an uncommon feature of Almaty nightlife), some people joke that you could live your whole life in Turkish-owned 'Esperanza City'. One club plays R&B and house; the other, '80s pop. The venues attract a mixed crowd and are among the few places still alive after 2am early in the week. On Friday and Saturday they get jam-packed and can be fun. Tables, with dinner included, start at 8000T.

Sport

Hippodrome (☎ 294 86 00; Zhansugirov) Horse races and occasionally *kokpar* (see Buzkashi, p64), take place several kilometres north of the centre. Get someone to call ahead and see what's on.

Central Stadium (☎ 292 47 10; Abay 48) Club and international soccer matches are played here, though the internationals will be less frequent now that Astana has a new national stadium.

SHOPPING

Stalls inside the Central State Museum (p131) and the Kazakhstan Museum of Arts (p131) are good places to look for Central Asian crafts and carpets. A 2m-by-3m Kazakh carpet typically costs around 60,000T to 75,000T.

TsUM (☎ 273 29 51; Zhibek Zholy 85; ☼ 10am-9pm Mon-Sat, to 8pm Sun) Visit this large, crowded, central department store for the experience as well as to buy. It deals in electronic goods, clothes, cosmetics, glass, china and gifts, and prices are reasonable. On the ground floor you'll find a bigger variety of mobile phones than you've ever seen in one place, and the top floor has probably the best range of kitsch souvenirs and gifts in the country – ornamental swords and horse whips, fur and felt hats, traditional jewellery and miniature yurts, camels and Golden Men.

Tengri Umai (☎ 273 57 66; www.tu.kz; Panfilov 103; 10am-6pm Mon-Sat) This gallery has probably the country's best selection of contemporary art, by artists from Kazakhstan and other former Soviet republics. There's some innovative and appealing work here, and exhibits include video, photography and installations. To find it, go through an arch from Panfilov, pass building 101 on your right, and it's at the far corner of the next building, 103.

Meloman (☎ 273 10 24; Gogol 58; ☼ 24hr) A good place for CDs of all kinds of music and DVDs in Russian and Kazakh (some with English subtitles). It's a national chain, with several other branches in Almaty.

For sports gear, including mountain bikes and winter sports equipment, head to **Yeti** (☎ 272 68 59; Kabanbay Batyr 73/3; ☼ 10am-7pm) or **Limpopo** (☎ 261 70 61; Seyfullin 534; ☼ 10am-7pm Mon-Sat, to 6pm Sun).

Almaty's middle class shops at modern supermarkets and malls stocked with expensive, often imported, goods, and at international stores such as Zara, Yves Rocher and Benetton, which are dotted all around the city centre. The main malls include **Silk Way City** (☎ 267 74 70; Tole Bi 71; ☼ 24hr), **Ramstor** (☎ 258 75 75; Furmanov 226; ☼ 9am-11pm) and the biggest, **Mega Center Alma-Ata** (☎ 249 65 63; Rozybakiev 247A).

Markets

Watch out for pickpockets in these places.

Green Market (Zelyony Bazar, Kok Bazar; Zhibek Zholy 53; ☼ 8am-6pm Tue-Sun) A sprawling place with two levels indoors and vendors spread outside, too. Much of it is devoted to food (see p137), but there are stalls with clothing and other goods.

Barakholka (☼ 8am-5pm Tue-Sun) This huge, crowded flea market is on the ring road in the northwestern outskirts. Uzbeks, Chinese,

KAZAKHSTAN

Uyghurs and others converge here to sell everything from animals, fridges and cars to fur hats, jeans and felt slippers, at very good prices. Chinese goods predominate. Weekends, especially early Sunday morning, are the busiest times. Take any 'Barakholka' bus westbound on Rayymbek.

GETTING THERE & AWAY

Almaty is Kazakhstan's main air hub and is linked to most major Kazakhstan cities by daily trains. Minibuses and shared taxis run to many places in the southeast of the country. Buses reach cities in southern, northern and eastern Kazakhstan, but a long haul is usually more comfortable by train.

For information on international connections, see Transport in Kazakhstan (p199) and Transport in Central Asia (p515).

Air

The **airport** (☎ 270 33 33; www.almatyairport.com; Maylin 2) is 13km north of the centre; schedules and daily flight information are given on its website.

Air Astana flies at least once daily to the cities of Aktau (23,250T), Aktobe (15,000T), Astana (10,500T), Atyrau (33,000T), Karaganda (16,500T), Kyzylorda (13,500T), Pavlodar (17,750T), Shymkent (14,250T), Uralsk (32,500T) and Ust-Kamenogorsk (15,750T). Note: these fares are the cheapest generally available; close to departure, you may have to pay more. SCAT flies two or three times a week to Aktau (27,000T), Astana (15,500T), Kokshetau (17,000T), Semey (20,500T), Shymkent (15,000T), Taraz (7000T) and Ust-Kamenogorsk (17,400T). A further five weekly flights to Semey go via Semeyavia. See p199 for a listing of international connections.

AIRLINE OFFICES

You can buy air tickets at many travel agencies and *aviakassy* (air-ticket offices) around town including several in the **Gorodskoy Aerovokzal** (City Air Terminal; Zhibek Zholy 111; ☯ 9am-8pm Mon-Sat, to 7pm Sun).

The following airlines were flying from Almaty at the time of writing:

Air Arabia (☎ 272 66 81; www.airarabia.com; Kermet Travel, Kabanbay Batyr 49/76) Flies to/from Sharjah.

Air Astana (☎ 244 44 77; www.airastana.com; Furmanov 273; ☯ 24hr) Many domestic and international destinations.

Air Baltic (☎ 273 13 13; www.airbaltic.com; Cross Way, Zheltoksan 59) Flies to/from Riga, June to October.

Asiana Airlines (☎ 270 32 34; www.flyasiana.com; Aksunkar Hotel, Airport) Flies to/from Seoul.

BMI (☎ 272 40 40; www.flybmi.com; Dostyk 43) Flies to/from London.

China Southern Airlines (☎ 230 04 86; www.cs-air.com; Tole Bi 23A) Flies to/from Ürümqi.

Czech Airlines (☎ 299 92 22; www.csa.cz; Zheltoksan 144) Flies to/from Prague.

EgyptAir (☎ 239 70 36; www.egyptair.com; Satpaev 7A) Flies to/from Cairo.

Etihad Airways (☎ 334 12 10; www.etihad.com; Makataev 127/9) Flies to/from Abu Dhabi.

Kam Air (www.flykamair.com; tickets sold by Transavia, p130) Flies to/from Kabul.

KLM (☎ 250 77 47; www.klm.com; Makataev 127/9) Flies to/from Amsterdam.

Lufthansa (☎ 333 50 25, 250 50 52; www.lufthansa.com; Hyatt Regency Almaty, Satpaev 29/6) Flies to/from Frankfurt.

Rossiya (☎ 292 44 25; www.rossiya-airlines.com; Ros Uni Sky, Seyfullin 577) Flies to/from St Petersburg.

S7 (www.s7.ru; tickets sold by Transavia, p130) Flies to/from Novosibirsk.

SCAT (www.scat.kz; tickets sold by Transavia, p130) Flies to/from several domestic and regional destinations.

Semeyavia (Tickets sold at Gorodskoy Aerovokzal, p140) Flies to/from Semey.

Tajik Air (☎ 257 11 55; www.tajikair.tj; Office 235, Hotel Aksunkar, Airport) Flies to/from Dushanbe.

Transaero (☎ 273 23 76; www.transaero.ru; Furmanov 53) Flies to/from Moscow.

Turkish Airlines (☎ 333 38 49; www.turkishairlines.com; Furmanov 100) Flies to/from İstanbul.

Turkmenistan Airlines (Tickets sold at Gorodskoy Aerovokzal, p140) Flies to/from Ashgabat.

Uzbekistan Airways (☎ 272 33 10; www.uzairways.com; Office 40, Tole Bi 69) Flies to/from Tashkent.

Ukraine International Airlines (www.flyuia.com; tickets sold by agencies) Flies to/from Kiev.

Bus, Minibus & Taxi

Long-distance buses use **Sayran bus station** (☎ 276 26 44; cnr Tole Bi & Utegen Batyr), 5km west of the centre. Destinations (schedules subject to change) include Astana (4680T, 16 hours, 2pm and 10.30pm), Karaganda (4285T, 20 hours, 2pm, 10pm and 10.30pm), Shymkent (1800T, 12 hours, three buses between 8pm and 11pm), Taraz (1440T, 10 hours, eight daily, mostly departing 8pm to 11pm), Turkistan (2200T, 15 hours, 5pm), Ust-Kamenogorsk (4000T, 22 hours, two daily) and also Zharkent (1000T, six hours, five daily). For buses to Bishkek

(Kyrgyzstan) and Ürümqi (China), see p200 and p200, respectively.

Quicker minibuses to some not-so-distant destinations wait at the front of the Sayran bus station building, and even quicker shared taxis wait at the front or on Utegen Batyr at the side of the bus station. To Taraz it's 2000T (eight hours) by minibus and 4000T (seven hours) by taxi.

Most nearby destinations are served by the ramshackle **Sayakhat bus station** (☎ 230 25 29; Rayymbek). Minibuses to Bayankol (1500T, eight hours), Kegen (1000T, five to six hours), Narynkol (1500T, eight hours), Saty (2000T, eight hours) and Zhalanash (1500T, six hours) leave between 7am and 9am, when they get enough passengers.

Car

Self-drive rates for one or two days start around 7500T per day. See p202 for a few tips on driving and renting in Kazakhstan. Companies offering self-drive rentals include the following:

Dixie Travel (☎ 279 28 08; www.dixie.kz; Zheltoksan 59) This firm allows cars to be driven anywhere in Kazakhstan.

Hertz (☎ 245 88 51; www.hertz.kz; Office 15/3B, Timiryazev 42)

Rent A Car Ivan (☎ 317 2850, 327 29 69; www. rentacar.ar.kz; Furmanov 230-86)

Train

Nearly all main long-distance trains stop at **Almaty-I station** (☎ 296 33 92), 8km north of the centre at the end of Seyfullin, but fortunately most continue to the more convenient **Almaty-II station** (☎ 296 15 44), at the end of Abylay Khan on the northern edge of the central area. There are several train ticket offices in the centre, including in the **Gorodskoy Aerovokzal** (City Air Terminal; ☎ 279 01 65; Zhibek Zholy 111; ☾ 9am-7pm). Ticket offices in the stations, and on Abylay Khan just south of Almaty-II, are open 24 hours. You need to show your passport when buying tickets.

Destinations served at least daily (in some cases several times daily), with typical *kupeyny* (2nd-class) fares, include Aktobe (6800T, 40 to 46 hours), Aralskoe More (Aralsk; 5300T, 32 to 37 hours), Astana (4500T, 20 to 22 hours), Atyrau (7900T, 50 to 51 hours), Karaganda (3950T, 16 hours), Kokshetau (5300T, 27 to 34 hours), Kyzylorda (4225T, 24 to 28 hours), Petropavlovsk (5700T, 31 hours), Semey

(3400T to 3700T, 20 to 22 hours, daily from Almaty-I, every two days from Almaty-II), Shymkent (2660T to 2870T, 13 to 16 hours), Taraz (2400T, 9½ hours), Turkistan (3400T, 16 to 17 hours), Uralsk (8440T, 52 hours) and Ust-Kamenogorsk (3400T, 24 hours). Trains for Mangyshlak (Aktau; 8730T, 67 hours) depart every second day.

For Karaganda and Astana you can take the Talgo, a sleek, Spanish-built, fast overnight train with lovely clean bathrooms. Unfortunately it can't travel at full speed because the Kazakh track isn't up to that. Train 1 departs Almaty-II just after 7pm (it doesn't stop at Almaty-I), reaching Astana at 8am. The one-way fare in 3rd/2nd/1st class to Astana is 10,300/15,100/18,700T (2nd class is a two-person compartment).

The only direct train to Moscow (35,800T) is train 7, leaving at 6am on even dates and taking 80 hours via Shymkent, Aktobe, Uralsk and Saratov. You can get there half a day quicker by changing trains two or three times en route. There are also daily trains to Novosibirsk.

GETTING AROUND
To/From the Airport

The airport bus stop is 400m along the street, outside the parking area. Several city buses (50T) run from here through the city centre (a 30- to 40-minute ride). They operate from about 6.30am to 11pm. All of these pass Sayakhat bus station; routes from there are as follows:

Bus 32 Green Market, west on Makataev, south on Nauryzbay Batyr to Abay.

Bus 79 Green Market, west on Gogol, south on Furmanov, west on Abay.

Bus 86 Green Market, west on Makataev, south on Furmanov, west on Al-Farabi.

Bus 92 West on Rayymbek, south on Nauryzbay Batyr, west on Abay.

Returning to the airport, buses 32 and 92 head north on Zheltoksan instead of Nauryzbay Batyr.

A taxi from the airport to the centre should cost 1500T, although drivers may try for much more. You can get a cab for 1000T or so by walking about 100m along the street outside the airport – you'll find drivers waiting just past the first corner. You can call a taxi from reliable **Almaty Taxi** (☎ 255 53 33; ☾ 24hr; no English spoken) for 1500T going to or from the airport.

Bus, Tram & Trolleybus

Almaty has a vast network of bus, trolleybus and tram routes (all 50T), running from about 6.30am to 11pm. They can get very crowded, so if you have much baggage or are short of time, it's simpler to take a taxi. All services mentioned here follow the same routes in both directions unless stated. Charts of the bus routes are available on the Russian-language section of the city government website, www.almaty.kz, under 'Transport'. Tram and trolleybus routes are often shown in telephone directories.

BUS STATIONS

From Sayran bus station, buses 37 and 94 run east along Tole Bi to the centre. The 94 turns north on Konaev, then east on Gogol to Gorky Park. The 37 turns north on Zheltoksan then east on Rayymbek to Sayakhat bus station; going out to Sayran it heads south on Nauryzbay Batyr instead of Zheltoksan. Tram 4 heads east from Sayran along Tole Bi, then south on Baytursynuly, east on Shevchenko, north on Konaev and east on Makataev.

Many routes including buses 29, 32, 37 and 79 pass Sayakhat bus station: just look for one saying 'Sayakhat' and heading in the right direction.

TRAIN STATIONS

From Almaty-II, trolleybuses 5 and 6 head south on Abylay Khan, then west on Abay to the Central Stadium and beyond.

From Almaty-I, buses 2 and 73 run to Sayakhat, the Green Market and Gogol, then south on Furmanov as far as Ramstor.

OTHER USEFUL ROUTES

In the central area, Furmanov is the main artery for north–south routes, along with Naurybay Batyr (southbound) and Zheltoksan (northbound). Gogol and Abay are the principal east–west arteries. In addition to the routes from the airport and bus and train stations already mentioned, useful routes are those listed below:

Bus 29 Sayakhat bus station, Pushkin, Makataev, Kaldayakov, Bogenbay Batyr (Kabanbay Batyr northbound), Dostyk, Butakovka.

Bus 48 Tole Bi eastbound, Dostyk, Zholdasbekov, Furmanov, Kazhy Mukan

Bus 63 Rayymbek, Nauryzbay Batyr (Seyfullin northbound), Makataev, Pushkin, Gogol, Furmanov, west on Al-Farabi to Navoi.

Bus 65 Kaldayakov, Tole Bi, Dostyk, Abay to Central Stadium

Bus 66 Gogol (north side of Panfilov Park), Kaldayakov, Kazybek Bi, Dostyk, Abay, Zhandosov.

Bus 105 Sayakhat bus station, Pushkin, Gogol (Makataev eastbound), Furmanov, Abay, Baytursynuly, Timiryazev

Trolleybus 1 Gorky Park, Gogol, south on Auezov to Timiryazev.

Trolleybus 2 Green Market, Pushkin, Gogol, Auezov, west on Abay.

Metro

Almaty's new metro was due to open at the end of 2010. The first stretch of line runs from Rayymbek station, near Almaty-II train station, about 3km south beneath Furmanov as far as Abay, then 4km west beneath Abay to Alatau station. There are five intermediate stations on this line (see the Almaty map for locations). Metro construction originally started in 1988 but work proceeded in fits and starts until major funds were allocated in 2005.

Taxi

There are some official taxis – marked with chequerboard logos or other obvious signs – but many private cars also act as taxis. Just stand at the roadside with your arm out and you'll rarely have to wait more than six or eight cars before one stops. Say where you're going and how much you're offering. If you can't agree on a price, let the car go and wait for another. A ride in the centre of Almaty should cost 200T to 400T, depending on distance (sometimes a bit more at night). You can call a cab from **Almaty Taxi** (☎ 255 53 33; ⊗ 24hr; no English spoken): minimum fare is 500T.

AROUND ALMATY

There are some great outings to be made right on Almaty's doorstep, notably into the Zailiysky Alatau range, a beautiful spur of the Tian Shan to the south of the city. The main access routes into the Zailiysky Alatau foothills are the Malaya (Little) Almatinka valley, where the winter sports centres Medeu and Chimbulak are found, and the Bolshaya (Big) Almatinka valley, leading up to Ozero Bolshoe Almatinskoe (Big Almaty Lake).

If you're heading high into the mountains, make sure you have a good map and/or a guide. There is year-round avalanche danger wherever you see snow. See the Trekking Warning boxed text, p145.

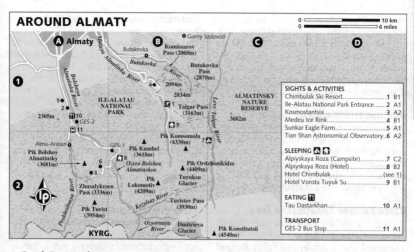

AROUND ALMATY

0 — 10 km
0 — 6 miles

SIGHTS & ACTIVITIES	
Chimbulak Ski Resort..................1 B1
Ile-Alatau National Park Entrance......2 A1
Kosmostantsia..............................3 A2
Medeu Ice Rink...........................4 B1
Sunkar Eagle Farm.......................5 A1
Tian Shan Astronomical Observatory..6 A2
SLEEPING
Alpiyskaya Roza (Campsite)...........7 C2
Alpiyskaya Roza (Hotel)................8 B2
Hotel Chimbulak........................(see 1)
Hotel Vorota Tuyuk Su..................9 B1
EATING
Tau Dastarkhan...........................10 A1
TRANSPORT
GES-2 Bus Stop..........................11 A1

Good Russian-language maps covering the area are sold at Akademkitap and GEO (p127). *Turistskie Marshruty g. Almaty-oz. Issyk-Kul* (Astana, 2000) covers the whole area between Almaty and Lake Issyk-Köl and grades all the passes in the region. (For more on mountain grades see p107).

Medeu & Chimbulak

These are Almaty's playgrounds in the Malaya Almatinka valley, both easily visited on a day trip from the city. The winter sports facilities here were upgraded for Almaty's co-hosting (with Astana) of the 2011 Asian Winter Games. Medeu, at 1700m, is a scattering of buildings around the huge Medeu ice rink, about 15km southeast of central Almaty. Chimbulak, at 2200m, is Central Asia's top skiing centre. Medeu is always several degrees cooler than Almaty, and Chimbulak is cooler still. Except in summer, rain in Almaty means snow and zero visibility at the higher elevations.

The 10,500-sq-metre **Medeu ice rink** (☎ 727-386 95 36; www.medey.kz; admission adult/under 13yr 800/400T; ♾ noon-4pm & 6-11pm Mon-Fri, 11am-4pm & 5-11pm Sat, 10am-4pm & 5-11pm Sun approx Nov-Apr), built in 1972, is made for speed skating and many champion skaters have trained here. Even when the rink is closed people come to relax at the shashlyk and drink stands, and to take a walk in the surrounding valleys and hills. You can rent skates for 800T per two hours, though you need to leave your passport or 10,000T as deposit.

What looks like a dam in the main valley above the ice rink (about 3km by road or 800-odd steps on foot) is actually there to stop avalanches and mudslides. The road climbs a further 4.5km from this barrier to the **Chimbulak ski resort** (☎ 727-258 19 99; www. shimbulak.kz), which has ski runs for all levels and a total drop of 900m (and a bowling alley for evening diversion). The ski season runs from about November to April. Skis and snowboards rent for 3500T to 15,000T per day depending on condition: it's much cheaper to rent in Almaty at shops such as Yeti (p139) if you can manage to lug the gear up to Chimbulak.

Day lift passes are 5000T, with individual lift tickets at 600T. It takes three lifts to reach the top of the runs at the Talgar Pass.

SLEEPING & EATING

Hotel Vorota Tuyuk Su (☎ 727-264 03 25; www.alpina. kz; r with shared bathroom 9000-12,000T, with private bathroom 11,000-35,000T; ℗) Two kilometres up the road past Chimbulak, this handsome stone lodge has 22 comfortable rooms in attractive wooden cottages, plus a restaurant with mainly Russian food, a bathhouse and a billiards room. Rates include breakfast. They'll provide transfers from Almaty for 11,000T round trip.

Hotel Chimbulak (☎ 727-258 19 99; http://shimbulak .kz; r/half lux/lux 10,000/15,000/30,000T) The large lodge at the Chimbulak resort has a great location at the foot of the ski lift, but most of the rooms are unrenovated and not very exciting. Discounts of about 40% are given on the cheaper rooms outside the skiing season.

Food options at Medeu and Chimbulak are mainly limited to cafes doling out shashlyk, *manty*, soups, salads and maybe *plov*, though the Samal opposite the skating rink at Medeu does some Turkish and Asian fare too.

GETTING THERE & AWAY

From Almaty, buses 6 and 6A go to Medeu (30 minutes) every few minutes from Dostyk, opposite the Hotel Kazakhstan. The last buses back leave Medeu about 10pm. Taxis from Medeu to Chimbulak cost around 1500T, or 500T per person on a shared basis.

Ozero Bolshoe Almatinskoe Area

West of the Malaya Almatinka valley lies its 'big sister', the Bolshaya Almatinka valley. The paved road south up this valley starts at a large roundabout on the southern edge of Almaty where Al-Farabi meets Navoi. You pass many roadside cafes and restaurants before reaching, after 7.5km, the entrance to the **Ile-Alatau National Park** (admission per person 330T). Immediately before the park gate is the **Sunkar eagle farm** (☎ 727-255 30 76; admission 200T; ⊙ daylight). It also keeps hunting dogs and is worth a look any time, but the real attraction is the entertaining display of trained raptors in flight (1000T), at 4pm or 5pm daily except Monday. It has a restaurant and shashlyk stands too.

About 1.5km past the park gate is the restaurant complex **Tau Dastarkhan**. The road forks 250m past here, at a spot known as GES-2 after a small hydroelectric station nearby. The paved right branch heads to the settlement of Alma-Arasan (4km). The unpaved left branch follows the Bolshaya Almatinka River upstream, passing another small hydroelectric station, GES-1, after 8km, and reaching 2500m-high **Ozero Bolshoe Almatinskoe** (Big Almaty Lake) after a further 7km. (From GES-1 hikers normally shortcut the road by following the water pipe straight uphill to the lake.) The picturesque, 1.6km-long lake, resting in a rocky bowl, is frozen from November to June and only takes on its famous turquoise tinge once the summer meltwater has drained away. It's a good birdwatching spot, especially during the May migration.

Two kilometres up the track to the west from the lake (about a 40-minute walk), at 2750m, is the outlandish **Tian Shan Astronomical Observatory**, sometimes still referred to by its Soviet-era acronym, GAISh. The observatory has the second-biggest telescope in the former USSR, with magnification of around 600 times, installed in 1991. It only operates at part-capacity now due to lack of funding, and a former radar dish is used as a TV receiver. It's possible to stay here (see below), and to take tours (in Russian) of the working sections for 500T.

At the head of the Zhusalykezen Pass (3336m), 6km southwest from the observatory, is the **Kosmostantsia**, a group of mostly wrecked buildings belonging to scientific research institutes.

SLEEPING & EATING

Tian Shan Astronomical Observatory (☎ 727-276 21 67; per person incl meals €40) This unique lodging has prime lake and mountain views, and the rooms have electric heaters for warmth. You need to reserve for weekends and any time between May and September.

Alpiyskaya Roza (☎ 727-264 03 25; www.alpina.kz; r with shared bathroom 7000-9500T, with private bathroom 9000-35,000T; ℗) This mock Swiss chalet–style hotel is halfway between GES-1 and the lake. Rooms are clean and comfortable, breakfast is included, and the atmospheric bar has house-brewed beer. It offers all sorts of guided mountain trips. Transfers from Almaty are 11,000T, round trip.

The **Tau Dastarkhan** (☎ 727-270 57 29; www.tau-dastarkhan.kz) complex offers half a dozen midrange and top-end restaurants in a pretty water-garden setting; it's a good spot for a meal in the Bolshaya Almatinka valley. One of the best options is **Avlabar** (☎ 727-270 56 46; mains 1000-2300T; ⊙ 10.30am-2am, to midnight in winter), serving savoury Georgian specialties from *khachapuri* (big, warm cheese pies) to *chanakhi* (a lamb, potato, eggplant and tomato dish), plus good Georgian wine, of course. If it's chilly staff come round with tiger-stripe rugs to wrap yourself in.

GETTING THERE & AWAY

From central Almaty, bus 63 runs south on Furmanov and along Al-Farabi to the roundabout where it meets Navoi. Here you can switch to bus 28, heading up the valley about every 15 minutes from 7am to 7.30pm, as far as the GES-2 fork. To walk from GES-2 to the lake takes four or five hours, with a rise of nearly 1100m. But there are easier ways of getting there: you can get an Almaty city taxi for 3000T to 4000T to GES-1 (after which the road deteriorates), and almost any Almaty travel agency can organise a day trip to the lake and probably the observatory for 25,000T to 35,000T.

Even better news: the road to the lake has been undergoing a major upgrade, which should make it passable for all vehicles right up to Kosmostantsia, possibly as soon as 2011.

Hikes & Treks

The higher reaches of the Zailiysky Alatau have many peaks over 4000m, lots of glaciers, and Tian Shan firs on the steep valley sides. In summer the valleys are used as summer pasture. Sadly the Kazakhstan–Kyrgyzstan 'green border' – foot trails through the mountains, without border posts – is now closed, with border guards patrolling the access routes, so it's no longer possible to trek all the way across the mountains to Lake Issyk-Köl. But it is still possible to take a hike of one or several days in the Zailiysky Alatau. Officially a permit is needed to enter the border zone, which starts at the north end of Ozero Bolshoe Almatinskoe (camping is not allowed beside the lake), but there are good routes that avoid the border zone, and a good guide can smooth the way if you do pass through it.

Agents such as Valentina Guesthouse, A13, Karlygash Makatova, Arnai Tours and Khan Tengri (see p130) can provide guides and organisational support for mountain treks. A13 charges around €30 per person per day, including car transfers and camping gear, for three- or four-day mountain treks with English-speaking guides.

DAY WALKS FROM CHIMBULAK

In summer, it's a 3km hike (or ride on the ski lift!) up to the Talgar Pass at 3163m, where you can see glacier-flanked Pik Komsomola (4330m) rising 3km to the south. Or you can head on up the valley road from Chimbulak. It continues upward for 8km, paved most of the way, to end at about 3500m beneath the glaciers ringing the top of the valley. If you are going up to these high elevations it's advisable to spend a night acclimatising at Chimbulak (it's possible to camp here).

GES-2–OZERO BOLSHOE ALMATINSKOE–KOSMOSTANTSIA–GES-2 LOOP

This is a fine trek of about 35km. For acclimatisation reasons it's best done in two days,

TREKKING WARNING

On any mountain hike or trek, you *must* be equipped for bad conditions. The trekking season lasts from about mid-May to mid-September; July and August have the most reliable weather, but at any time it can rain or snow in the mountains, even when it's warm in Almaty. If you're caught unprepared by a sudden storm, it could be fatal. There is also year-round avalanche danger wherever you see snow. And acclimatisation is essential: altitude sickness can affect anyone who ascends rapidly above 2500m, so spending a night on the way up is highly advisable.

with a night at the Tian Shan Observatory or Alpiyskaya Roza, even if you take a vehicle part of the way.

You can start where bus 28 terminates at GES-2, or save 8km by taking a taxi to GES-1. Here climb the metal steps beside the broad water pipe rising sharply up the gorge, then walk up the pipe for the most direct route to Ozero Bolshoe Almatinskoe (two to three hours). From the lake, follow the road uphill to the right to the observatory (40 minutes). From the observatory it's about 2½ hours up the road to Kosmostantsia at the Zhusalykezen Pass (3336m), from which you can descend west to the Prokhodnaya valley (three to four hours) and walk 8km down the valley past Alma-Arasan back to GES-2. If you have enough energy and time to play with, from the Zhusalykezen Pass you can detour 2km north to Pik Bolshoe Almatinsky (3681m), which affords great views back down to Almaty (smog permitting); or 2km south to Pik Turist (3954m), which is easier walking though higher. Alternatively, get a vehicle all the way to the Zhusalykezen Pass and summit either peak in more leisurely fashion!

CHIMBULAK TO OZERO BOLSHOE ALMATINSKOE

This longer, more demanding, three-day route crosses high-level passes and runs through the border zone, so you should definitely take a guide. Start with a night at Chimbulak, then hike (or ride the ski lift) up to the Talgar Pass (3163m) and descend to the Levy (Left) Talgar River, where you can camp overnight at the Alpiyskaya Roza campsite. Next day hike up the Levy Talgar and camp on the grass beneath the Dmitrieva or Turist glaciers at about 3500m. On the third day cross the Turistov Pass (3930m) and descend to Ozero Bolshoe Almatinskoe, where guides should have a vehicle waiting for you.

SOUTHEAST KAZAKHSTAN

The region from Almaty to Lake Balkhash is known as Zhetisu (Russian: Semirechie), meaning Land of Seven Rivers. There are actually more than 800 rivers, many fed by glaciers in the mountains along the Kyrgyz and Chinese borders. This is one of Kazakhstan's most varied regions, with plenty to see and do using Almaty as a base.

KOLSAY LAKES ОЗЁРА КОЛЬСАЙ

These three pretty lakes lie amid the steep, forested foothills of the Küngey Alatau, 110km southeast of Almaty as the crow flies, but almost 300km by road via Chilik (Shelek) and Zhalanash.

The lakes are strung along the Kolsay River, about 1800m to 2800m high, southwest of the village of Saty. From Saty it's about 12km by road to the 1km-long Nizhny (Lower) Kolsay lake at 1800m. On the way you pay a national park entrance fee of 240T per person. The Sredny (Middle) Kolsay lake at 2250m is the

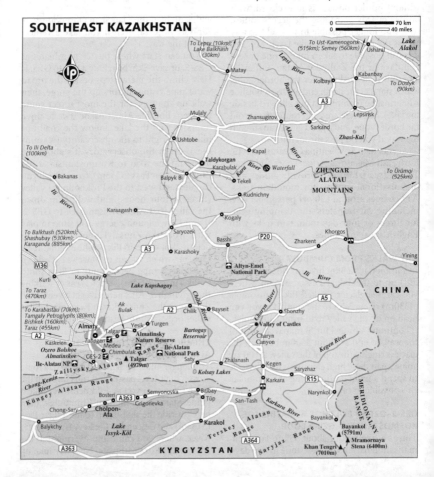

biggest and most beautiful, 5km from the lower lake via a hike of about three hours. From the middle lake to the smaller Verkhny (Upper) Kolsay lake at 2800m, where the forests give way to alpine grasslands, is about 4km and three hours' walking. It's no longer permitted to hike south from the upper lake over the Sarybulak Pass to Kyrgyzstan, thanks to the closure of the 'green border' between the two countries.

Sleeping & Eating

The EIRC (p130) can book you into one of seven **homestays** (per person incl 3 meals 3500T) in Saty. The families can provide cars or horses to the lower lake, and horses from there to the middle lake, at around 1000T for a car and 3000T to 5000T per day for a horse. It's possible to ride from Saty to the middle lake and back in one day.

Jibek Joly (p130) has three six-room wooden **cottages** (per person 4400-8850T, equipped kitchen per day 4850T), with two- and four-bedrooms, on a hillside above Nizhny Kolsay lake.

There's also a **yurt camp** (yurts Mon-Fri 5000T, Sat & Sun 10,000T) 1km below the lower lake. These yurts have four comfortable beds, kettle and electric heater!

Camping is not allowed in the lakes area.

Getting There & Away

A minibus to Saty (2000T, eight hours) normally leaves Almaty's Sayakhat bus station at or soon after 7am. Alternatively, take one to Zhalanash and find a ride for the 25km to Saty. Jibek Joly charges about 3000T to carry a carload of clients from Zhalanash to Saty, or around 25,000T for a transfer from Almaty (one-way).

Many people visit the lakes on two-night tours: an economical option is weekend bus trips, which you can book through the EIRC. These cost around 9000T including accommodation, food and excursions. The first night is in the bus, travelling from Almaty.

Another interesting and much more demanding option, offered by A13 (p130) among others, is to trek five days to the lakes across the mountain passes from Almaty.

CHARYN CANYON
ЧАРЫНСКИЙ КАНЬОН

The swift Charyn (Sharyn) River has carved a 150m- to 300m-deep canyon into the otherwise flat and barren steppe some 200km east of Almaty, and time has weathered this into all sorts of weird and colourful rock formations, especially in the branch canyon known as the Valley of Castles (Dolina Zamkov). This is no Grand Canyon, but it's worth a trip. You can take a long day trip from Almaty for around 25,000/35,000T per car/vanload through agencies, or 2200T per person on weekend bus trips through the EIRC (p130). Overnight camping (free) offers a more relaxed pace. April, May, June, September and October are the best months to come: it's too hot in summer. There's a 300T-per-person national park fee to enter the canyon area, which is not always enforced.

Getting here by public transport is possible, but you may not be able to get back the same day. Take a 7am bus or minibus from Almaty's Sayakhat bus station heading to Kegen or Narynkol, and get out at the signposted turn off to the canyon about 190km from Almaty, just before the road starts descending into the Charyn valley. From here it's 10km east along a fairly flat dirt road to a parking area and then 3km (about one hour) down through the Valley of Castles to the river. If you're lucky you might get a taxi or a lift to the parking area; if not, it's a walk!

Don't try to swim in the river, which is deceptively fast.

KARKARA VALLEY
КАРКАРАНСКАЯ ДОЛИНА

The beautiful, broad valley of the Karkara River is an age-old summer pasture for herds from both sides of what's now the Kazakhstan–Kyrgyzstan border.

From Kegen, 250km by road east of Almaty, a scenic road heads south up the valley to Karkara village, and then on to the border post about 28km from Kegen. The road, which is normally open from about April to October, then veers west towards Tüp and Lake Issyk-Köl in Kyrgyzstan. No public transport reaches the border, but minibuses leave Almaty's Sayakhat bus station at about 7am daily for Kegen (1000T, five to six hours), and from Kegen you can get up the valley and into Kyrgyzstan either by hitching or by taxi. At San-Tash, 19km into Kyrgyzstan, you can find a bus or a shared jeep to Tüp or Karakol. Be sure to get your Kyrgyz entry stamp at the border. Almaty travel agencies such as Stantours and Valentina Guesthouse (p130) offer Almaty–

Karakol transfers by this route for US$350 to US$450 per vehicle.

From late June to late August, mountain-tourism company Kan Tengri (p130) maintains a summer **base camp** (full board €50) at about 2200m on the Kazakh side of the international border. Primarily a staging post for treks and climbing expeditions to the central Tian Shan, the camp offers tent accommodation to all comers, with hot showers, a cafe and a bar. A three-day trip from Almaty, including a helicopter flight to Khan Tengri, costs €300 per person: contact the company at least one week in advance and ask about the paperwork needed, as the track to the camp passes through some Kyrgyz territory, and a border-zone permit may be needed for the helicopter trip.

For information on the Kyrgyz side of the Karkara Valley, see p319.

CENTRAL TIAN SHAN
ЦЕНТРАЛЬНЫЙ ТЯНЬ ШАНЬ

Kazakhstan's highest and most magnificent mountains rise in the country's far southeastern corner where it meets Kyrgyzstan and China. Khan Tengri (7010m) on the Kyrgyz border is widely considered the most beautiful and demanding peak in the Tian Shan, and there are many more 5000m-plus peaks around it, including Mramornaya Stena (Marble Wall, 6400m) on the Kazakh–Chinese border, and Pik Pobedy (7439m) south of Khan Tengri on the Kyrgyz–Chinese border.

Khan Tengri is flanked by two long, west-running glaciers, the North Inylchek Glacier on its Kazakh side and the South Inylchek glacier on its Kyrgyzstan side.

The Almaty-based mountain-tourism firm Kan Tengri (p130) offers a variety of exciting one- to three-week treks and full-scale mountaineering expeditions in and around this area in July and August, using base camps on the Inylchek glaciers and at Bayankol (Ak-Kol) to the north, all at altitudes of around 4000m. Access is often by helicopter, using the Karkara Valley base camp as a staging and acclimatisation post. A typical two-week trek costs around €1000; a three-week trek with a bit of 'easy' climbing should be around €1400. Check the company's website for current offerings. Many treks include helicopter flights around the main peaks and glacier hikes to

the foot of Khan Tengri and/or Pik Pobedy. Also possible are heli-skiing trips with descents from peaks as high as 5800m. Karlygash Makatova (p130) can arrange two-day flying visits with a night at one of the Inylchek camps and a Khan Tengri fly-past.

See p333 for information on the Kyrgyz part of the Central Tian Shan.

TAMGALY PETROGLYPHS
ПЕТРОГЛИФЫ ТАМГАЛЫ

The World Heritage–listed Tamgaly petroglyphs are the most impressive of many petroglyph groups in southeastern Kazakhstan. Situated in a lushly vegetated canyon in an otherwise arid region near Karabastau village, 170km northwest of Almaty, they number more than 4000 separate carvings from the Bronze Age and later, in several groups. The varied images include sun-headed idols, women in childbirth, bull sacrifice, hunting scenes and a big variety of animals, and are best seen in the afternoon when most sunlight reaches them. The canyon was a ritual site for nomadic peoples from at least 3000 years ago, and there are also ancient burial mounds here. Many Almaty agencies can organise day trips: 25,000T per carload is a fair price with an English-speaking guide.

ALTYN-EMEL NATIONAL PARK
НАЦИОНАЛЬНЫЙ ПАРК АЛТЫНЕМЕЛЬ

Though quite time-consuming and potentially expensive to visit, this large, 4600-sq-km national park stretching northeast from Lake Kapshagay is worth considering if you appreciate beautiful desolation and some unusual natural and archaeological attractions. It's famous for the **Singing Dune**, which hums like an aircraft engine when the weather is suitably windy and dry, but archaeology fans will be absorbed by the **Terekty petroglyphs** and the 31 **Besshatyr burial mounds**, which are one of the biggest groups of Scythian tombs known anywhere. Wildlife enthusiasts can hope to see rare goitred gazelles (zheyran), argali sheep, wild ass *(kulan)* and possibly Przewalski's horses.

Several simple visitor **cottages** (per person 2500-5000T, meals extra) and **camping areas** (per person 1500-2300T) are scattered around the park. Organising an independent visit can be complicated and expensive: overall the best bet is to arrange a tour with an Almaty agency (see p130). A typical price for a three-day jaunt is about 75,000T for a vehicle and a driver, plus about 35,000T per person, slightly less if you camp.

Information on the park is available at its **Almaty office** (☎ 727-250 04 51; Hotel Zhetisu, Abylay Khan 55; ⏱ 9am-6pm Mon-Fri).

LAKE BALKHASH
ОЗЕРО БАЛХАШ

Now Central Asia's biggest lake, following the demise of the Aral Sea, Lake Balkhash covers 17,000 sq km, but is only 26m at its deepest point. The western end, fed by the Ili River, is fresh water; the eastern end is salty. A good way to explore the lake area is with Karaganda-based Nomadic Travel Kazakhstan (p184), which can take you boating on the lake as well as to the Shunak meteorite crater (over 3km in diameter) and the Bektau-Ata pluton (an unerupted volcano). The EIRC (p130) can arrange homestays in Shashubay village, just east of Balkhash city.

There are fears that Lake Balkhash may be shrinking because of interference with the flow of the Ili River. Critics blame the Kapshagay hydroelectric dam, built on the river in the 1960s, and increasing diversion of the Ili's waters in China.

SOUTHERN KAZAKHSTAN

Today this is the most Kazakh part of Kazakhstan: Kazakhs are generally the great majority in the population, having been settled here in large numbers during Soviet collectivisation. It is also the only region of Kazakhstan that was within the sphere of the Silk Road and the settled civilisations of Transoxiana in medieval times. It's a fascinatingly varied region, whose chief attractions begin in the Aksu-Zhabagyly Nature Reserve with its pristine mountain country, great hiking and homestays. Shymkent is the atmospheric main city. At Turkistan, the Mausoleum of Kozha Akhmed Yasaui is Kazakhstan's most sacred Muslim shrine and a fine piece of Timurid architecture.

TARAZ ТАРАЗ
☎ 7262 / pop 406,000

Taraz is one of Kazakhstan's oldest cities, although only limited evidence of this is visible thanks to its near-total destruction by Chinggis Khan. Today it's a mostly Soviet-built place with leafy boulevards, one of Kazakhstan's biggest, most bustling markets and an excellent museum.

Medieval Taraz reached its peak in the 11th and 12th centuries as a wealthy Silk Road stop and capital of the Turkic Karakhanid state which ruled Bukhara for a while. It was comprehensively levelled by the Mongols and effectively disappeared until the existing town was founded in the 19th century, as a northern frontier town of the Kokand khanate, with the name Aulie-Ata.

The Soviet regime settled many internal exiles here, renamed the town Dzhambul after the locally born Kazakh bard Zhambyl Zhabaev. Following independence, the name changed back to Taraz. After bleak years in the 1990s Taraz has staged a comeback based to a large extent on trade and commerce, situated as it is on the most direct route from Tashkent to Bishkek and Almaty.

Orientation & Information

The meeting of east–west Tole Bi with north–south Abay is the centre of town. West from here a government square, Dostyk alangy, stretches along Tole Bi.

ATF Bank ATM (Suleymenov 9) For Visa, Visa Electron, MasterCard, Maestro and Cirrus cards.

Kazaktelekom (☎ 45 38 54; Abay 124; internet per hr 280T; ⏱ 8am-10pm) You can also phone from here.

Sights

Taraz' **Regional Museum** (☎ 43 25 85; Tole Bi 55; admission 150T; ⏱ 9am-1pm & 2-6pm Tue-Sun) – painted pink like most buildings on Dostyk alangy – was completely renovated for the city's official 2000th anniversary celebrations in 2002 and is one of the best local museums in the country. Its pride and joy is the domed rear building housing an impressive collection of *balbals*, totemlike stones bearing the carved faces of honoured warriors or chieftains, dating from the 6th to 9th centuries AD. Nomadic early Turks left these monuments at many sacred sites in southern Kazakhstan.

A wooded **park** (⏱ 9am-6pm) off eastern Tole Bi contains reconstructions of two small medieval mausoleums and a medieval mosque, and is well worth a look. Both mausoleums contain cloth-covered sarcophagi and all three buildings are Islamic holy sites; leave shoes outside. The **Karakhan Mausoleum**, originally built in the 12th century, marks the grave of a revered Karakhanid potentate known as Karakhan or Aulie-Ata (Holy Father). The **Dauitbek Mausoleum**, for a 13th-century Mongol viceroy, is said to have been built lopsided in revenge for the man's infamous cruelty. Behind Dauitbek is a new reconstruction of the 9th- to-12th-century **mosque** in which Aulie-Ata is believed to have prayed. The dim-lit prayer hall with wooden pillars and a low wooden roof has a beautifully medieval and peaceful atmosphere.

Just east of here begins Taraz' **Green Market** (Zelyony Bazar, Kok Bazary; 9am-6pm Tue-Sun), which stretches for 500m and is a fascinating wander, with as much of a Silk Road bazaar feel as at any market in the country. You can buy anything from a *dombra* or Chinese silk to a phone or a decorative loaf of nan bread. The heart of medieval Taraz lies beneath this market.

Sleeping & Eating

Hotel Taraz (☎ 43 34 91; Zhambyl 75A; s 4500-6000T, d 5000-10,000T) The cheap option, though inconveniently placed 1.5km north of the centre,

Hotel Taraz has simple but adequate rooms, friendly staff and a restaurant. From the bus station, buses 10 and 26 pass by; from the train station, take marshrutka 077. To the centre, take marshrutka 038.

Hotel Zhambyl (☎ 45 25 52; hotel-zhambyl@nursat. kz; Tole Bi 42; s 6660-10,000T, d 12,100-14,400T;) With helpful staff and an in-house tour office, this upgraded Soviet-era survivor provides comfortable rooms with a rather drab buffet breakfast included. You get the room for 24 hours whatever time you check in.

Hotel Gazovik (☎ 43 32 33; hotel_gazovik@mail.ru; Suleymenov 7A; s 9500-14,000T, d 17,000-22,000T;) The best hotel is a modern, 21-room affair just off the central square. The good, carpeted rooms boast paintings, international satellite TV and bathtub. Reception staff speak some English and there's a good Russian/European restaurant (dishes 750T to 1400T) downstairs. Breakfast is included.

Madlen (☎ 45 57 77; Kazybek Bi 144A; cakes & snacks 100-500T; 10am-11pm) Stop into this spotless cafe, with waitresses in long German-style skirts, for great cakes, coffee, quiche, croissants and salads.

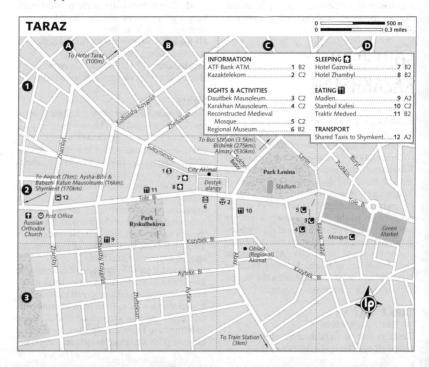

TARAZ

INFORMATION	**SLEEPING**
ATF Bank ATM....................1 B2	Hotel Gazovik......................7 B2
Kazaktelekom....................2 C2	Hotel Zhambyl.....................8 B2
SIGHTS & ACTIVITIES	**EATING**
Dauitbek Mausoleum...........3 C2	Madlen...............................9 A2
Karakhan Mausoleum..........4 C2	Stambul Kafesi...................10 C2
Reconstructed Medieval	Traktir Medved..................11 B2
Mosque.........................5 C2	
Regional Museum................6 B2	**TRANSPORT**
	Shared Taxis to Shymkent......12 A2

0   500 m
0   0.3 miles

To Hotel Taraz (100m)

To Airport (7km); Aysha-Bibi & Babazhi Katun Mausoleums (16km); Shymkent (170km)

To Bus Station (3.5km); Bishkek (275km); Almaty (530km)

City Akimat
Dostyk alangy
Park Lenina
Stadium
Park Ryskulbekova
Post Office
Russian Orthodox Church
Oblast (Regional) Akimat
Mosque
Green Market

Kolbasshy Koygeldi
Zheltoksan
Suleymenov
Zhaparov
Tole Bi
Kazybek Bi
Ayteke Bi
Aytiev
Zhambyl
Zheltoksan
Abay
Sukhe Bator
Lenin
Pushkin
Buryl
Tole Bi
Bayzak Batyr

To Train Station (3km)

Stambul Kafesi (☎ 45 25 29; Abay 117; dishes 300-700T; ⏰ 11am-10pm) A small Turkish cafe serving excellent doners and kebabs.

Traktir Medved (Tole Bi 56; mains 400-1000T; ⏰ 11am-2am) This Russian-tavern-style restaurant, with a warm atmosphere and efficient service, prepares pretty good meat dishes, vegetarian shashlyk, soups and salads.

Getting There & Away

Taraz' **Aulie-Ata airport** (☎ 31 61 26), 8km from the centre off the Shymkent road (800T by taxi), has three SCAT flights a week to Almaty (7000T) and four to Astana (22,000T).

The **train station** (☎ 96 01 15; Baluan Sholak) is 4km south of the centre. At least five daily trains run to Almaty (2400T, 9½ hours) and six or more to Shymkent (1440T, four hours). There's at least one a day to Astana, Turkistan and Aralsk.

From the **bus station** (☎ 92 26 70; Zhambyl), 4km northeast of the centre, minibuses leave when full for Almaty (2000T, eight hours, until 6pm) and Shymkent (700T, three hours, until about 6pm). Shared taxis to Almaty (4000T, seven hours) leave from outside the bus station during daytime. Shared taxis to Shymkent (1500T, 2½ hours) wait on Zhambyl just north of Tole Bi. See p200 for transport to Bishkek.

The road to Almaty is mostly in decent condition except for the badly potholed 160km stretch skirting the Kyrgyz border between Merki and Korday.

Getting Around

Marshrutkas 01 and 47 (40T) from the train station, and 46 from the bus station, run to the intersection of Abay and Tole Bi; marshrutka 077 from the train station heads up Abay then goes west on Kaybek Bi.

AROUND TARAZ
Aysha-Bibi & Babazhi Katun Mausoleums

Near Aysha-Bibi village, 16km west of Taraz on the Shymkent road, are the tombs of two 11th- or 12th-century women, legendary protagonists of a Kazakh *Romeo and Juliet* tale. The main facade of the Mausoleum of Aysha-Bibi is probably the only authentically old building around Taraz. Made of delicate terracotta bricks in more than 50 different motifs forming lovely patterns, the building looks almost weightless. The

story goes that Aysha, daughter of a famed scholar named Khakim-Ata, fell in love with Karakhan, the lord of Taraz, but Aysha's father forbade them to marry. The lovers swore a secret pact and Aysha eventually set off for Taraz with her companion Babazhi Katun. Aysha collapsed from exhaustion, sickness or snake bite (versions differ); Babazhi Katun rushed to Karakhan, who raced to his beloved just in time to hear her before she expired. Karakhan had her tomb built on the spot, adding later the Mausoleum of Babazhi Katun, with its unusual pointed, fluted roof. Today the site is an obligatory stop for local wedding groups to pray and take photos.

The mausoleums are about 300m (signposted) south off the main road in the village. Shymkent-bound minibuses from Taraz will take you to Aysha-Bibi or you can hire a taxi in Taraz.

SHYMKENT ШЫМКЕНТ
☎ 7252 / pop 462,000 / elev 510m

Southern Kazakhstan's most vibrant city, with bustling bazaars and a lively downtown, Shymkent (Russian: Chimkent) has more of a Central Asian buzz on its leafy streets than anywhere else in the country. Stop here to soak up the atmosphere, eat well and head out to nearby places of interest, including Turkistan and the Aksu-Zhabagyly Nature Reserve.

The Mongols razed a minor Silk Road stop here; the Kokand khanate built a frontier fort in the 19th century; Russia took it in 1864; and the whole place was rebuilt in Soviet times. Shymkent smelts lead, makes cigarettes and refines oil, but it's perhaps best known for Kazakhstan's best local beer, Shymkentskoe Pivo. The population today is just over half Kazakh and about 15% Russian and 15% Uzbek.

Mosquitoes can be an irritant from June to August.

Orientation

Two shopping centres, the modern Mega Shymkent and the older TsUM, are located opposite one another on the main downtown street, Tauke-Khan. These are prime landmarks and meeting places. The several bus stations are scattered around the city fringes, the most important being Samal, 4km north of the centre, and Ayna, 3km northeast. The train station is at the end of Kabanbay Batyr,

1.5km southeast of Ordabasy ploshchad, a busy intersection.

Information

You'll find ATMs in **Mega Shymkent** (🕙 10am-10pm) and **TsUM** (🕙 10am-8pm), among other places. Exchange offices at the train station and on Tauke-Khan between Kazybek Bi and Dulati trade Uzbek, Kyrgyz and Russian cash at widely varying rates.

Kazaktelekom (Turkistan; 🕙 24hr) You can phone from here.

Mega Net Club (cnr Tauke-Khan & Konaev; internet per hr 150T, with Skype & webcam 200T; 🕙 10am-11pm) Good, modern internet facility in the Meloman store inside Mega Shymkent.

Sights

MUSEUMS

The **Regional Museum** (☎ 53 02 22; Kazybek Bi 13; admission 100T; 🕙 9am-6pm Tue-Sun) has excellent exhibits on Shymkent's history as a caravan town, plus material on old Otrar and Aksu-Zhabagyly Nature Reserve, as well as displays upstairs on the Russian, Soviet and post-independence eras. Spot the photos of Shymkent's best-known daughter – the 1970s gymnast Nellie Kim, who grew up and trained here.

The small **Museum of Victims of Political Repression** (Sayasi kugyn-surgin kurbandarynyn muzeyi; ☎ 21 00 25; Ryskulbekov; admission 100T; 🕙 9am-6pm Mon-Sat) was Kazakhstan's first museum of its kind when it opened in 2001. Photos and documents on Soviet oppression in Kazakhstan and its most celebrated victims surround a central sculpture showing freedom-striving figures restrained by a Soviet banner. Explanatory material is in Kazakh but a 200T booklet with some English text gives a little help in understanding what's here.

MARKETS

The **Central** or **Upper Bazaar** (Ortalyk bazar, Verkhny bazar; Tashenov; 🕙 8am-8pm Tue-Sun) is now rather diminished after the conversion of its outlying sprawl into parks. But it still makes for an interesting wander and is a reminder of Shymkent's long trading history. Of several new markets around the city fringes, the biggest and most interesting is **Bazar Samal** (Ryskulov), next to Samal bus station, which

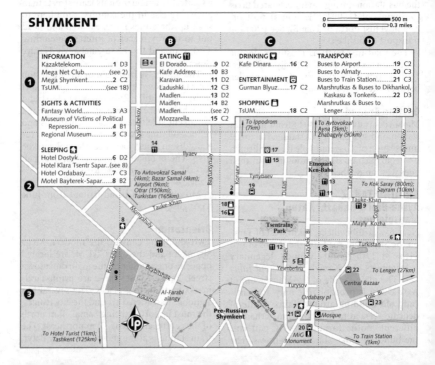

SHYMKENT

0 — 500 m
0 — 0.3 miles

INFORMATION	
Kazaktelekom	1 D3
Mega Net Club	(see 2)
Mega Shymkent	2 C2
TsUM	(see 18)

SIGHTS & ACTIVITIES	
Fantasy World	3 A3
Museum of Political Repression	4 B1
Regional Museum	5 C3

SLEEPING	
Hotel Dostyk	6 D2
Hotel Klara Tsentr Sapar	(see 8)
Hotel Ordabasy	7 C3
Motel Bayterek-Sapar	8 B2

EATING	
El Dorado	9 D2
Kafe Address	10 B3
Karavan	11 D2
Ladushki	12 C3
Madlen	13 D2
Madlen	14 B2
Madlen	(see 2)
Mozzarella	15 C2

DRINKING	
Kafe Dinara	16 C2

ENTERTAINMENT	
Gurman Blyuz	17 C2

SHOPPING	
TsUM	18 C2

TRANSPORT	
Buses to Airport	19 C2
Buses to Almaty	20 C3
Buses to Train Station	21 C3
Marshrutkas & Buses to Dikhankol, Kaskasu & Tonkeris	22 D3
Marshrutkas & Buses to Lenger	23 D3

To Ippodrom (7km)

To Avtovokzal Ayna (3km); Zhabagyly (90km)

To Avtovokzal Samal (4km); Bazar Samal (4km); Airport (9km); Otrar (150km); Turkistan (165km)

Etnopark Ken-Baba

To Kok Saray (800m); Sayram (10km)

Tsentralny Park

To Lenger (27km)

Central Bazaar

To Hotel Turist (1km); Tashkent (125km)

Al-Farabi alangy

Pre-Russian Shymkent

Ordabasy pl

Mosque

MiG Monument

To Train Station (1km)

has a particularly colourful array of rugs and textiles.

OTHER SIGHTS

Central Shymkent's several parks, including the amusement park **Fantasy World** (pr Respubliki; rides 70-400T; ☉ 10am-midnight Thu-Tue, noon-midnight Wed, shorter hr in winter), are popular hangouts, especially on summer evenings. Southeast of Fantasy World is the ceremonial square **Al-Farabi alangy**, and southeast of here, across the small Koshkar-Ata canal, you'll find the few remaining streets of **pre-Russian Shymkent** – a quiet, villagelike area of one- and two-storey wooden houses.

Festivals & Events

Shymkent's **Nauryz** celebrations, on 22 March, are among the biggest in the country. *Kokpar*, horse races, *audaryspak* (horseback wrestling) and *kyz kuu* all happen at the Ippodrom (Hippodrome) on the northern edge of the city.

Sleeping

Hotel Turist (☎ 56 02 31; pr Respubliki 43; s 1500-5000T, d 2000-7000T; ✖) The cheapest rooms in this partly renovated old Soviet hotel provide a reasonable budget option. They're bare and dilapidated but have private bathrooms and hot showers. The Turist is set back from Pr Respubliki opposite the corner of Gagarina; bus 5 comes here from the train station via Tauke-Khan.

Hotel Ordabasy (☎ 53 64 21; fax 53 56 82; Kazybek Bi 1; s 3000-7000T, d 5000-8400T; ✖) A good semibudget option with amiable staff, although the street-side rooms get traffic noise. All rooms are a good size, with bathroom and multichannel satellite TV. Breakfast is included.

Motel Bayterek-Sapar (☎ 33 75 55; kcs2005@mail.ru; pr Respubliki 4; s 3900-4900T, d 4900-5900T; ✖ ✖) Good-value, clean, air-conditioned rooms of varied sizes, inside the Klara-Tsentr-Sapar shopping mall. Bathrooms are shared (with squat toilets and hot showers) but are spotless. Breakfast and an hour in the sauna are included in the rates.

Hotel Dostyk (☎ 53 99 73; www.hoteldostyk.kz; Adyrbekov; s/d from 6600/10,500T; P ✖ ▢) The rooms aren't as spiffy as the lobby but they're modern and quite OK, with satellite TV, apricot paint, air-conditioning, and have touches like tea, coffee, kettle and dressing gowns. Rates include breakfast.

Hotel Klara Tsentr Sapar (☎ 23 23 33; kcs2005@mail.ru; pr Respubliki 4; s 7900-14,900T, d 9900-16,900T; ✖ ▢ ☎) A bright hotel with good, English-speaking service. The comfortably furnished rooms boast cable TV and original paintings. Rates include breakfast and an hour in the sauna.

Eating

Ladushki (Turkistan 12; items 30-125T; ☉ 8am-9pm) With decor like a kids' restaurant, Ladushki is actually a very popular cafeteria where you can get a serve of *manty* or *bliny*, or two pastries and a coffee, for under 200T.

Madlen (☎ 21 06 91; Ilyaev 17; coffees & desserts 200-500T; ☉ 10am-midnight Thu-Tue, 11am-midnight Wed) Great coffee house with delicious cakes and desserts, and pavement tables too. Has other branches in Ethnopark Ken-Baba and Mega Shymkent mall.

Kafe Address (☎ 53 43 00; Momyshuly 3; dishes 250-650T; ☉ 10am-midnight; ☎ E) Bright Turkish cafe rapidly serving *pide* (similar to pizza), shashlyk, doner, kofta and more, including some vegetarian options.

Karavan (☎ 54 52 83; Etnopark Ken-Baba; mains 250-700T) Karavan specialises in Uyghur food and there's plenty of choice, but those in the know come for the very tasty *burro-laghman* (fried *laghman*).

our pick **Kok Saray** (☎ 43 22 30; Zholdasbekov 22; mains 400-800T) This atmospheric restaurant serves the best Uzbek food in town (and in Kazakhstan, claim aficionados). Don't miss the perfect *plov* (*tashkentsky* with white rice, *andizhansky* with black) or the superb *samsas*, which include a delicious pumpkin *(s tykvoe)* variety. Located just off the north side of Tauke-Khan: you can't miss its bright lights after dark.

Also recommended:

El Dorado (Tauke-Khan 82; dishes 400-1000T; ☉ 24hr) Pizza and mayonnaise-free salads. There's no sign: it's next to BTA bank.

Mozzarella (☎ 30 05 57; cnr Ilyaev & Shaymerdenov; mains 800-1500T; E) A slick Italian job.

Drinking & Entertainment

Look for '*Razlivnoe pivo*' signs to track down draft Shymkentskoe Pivo. Shymkent also has a microbrewery producing the good, unfiltered, Bavarian-style Sigma beer, available in several places around town.

Gurman Blyuz (Ilyaev 47; mains 400-500T; admission for music 500T; ☉ 10am-midnight) The Wednesday jazz

KAZAKHSTAN

sessions, starting at 8pm, at this small restaurant are a Shymkent highlight, with excellent live music and an offbeat crowd. There's also often live rock here at 8pm Saturday.

Kafe Dinara (Konaev; ☻ noon-midnight) The most popular central place among all ages to grab an inexpensive beer, and shashlyk if you like (both cost 120T to 150T).

Getting There & Away

AIR
From the **airport** (☎ 53 52 95), 10km northwest of the centre, there are flights to Almaty (14,000T to 20,000T) and Astana (23,500T to 26,500T) daily, and to Kyzylorda, Atyrau, Aktau and Moscow a few days a week.

BUS, VAN & TAXI
For Almaty, comfortable air-conditioned buses (1000T to 2000T depending on the bus and where you sit, 12 hours) depart from **Avtovokzal Samal** (☎ 45 12 41; Ryskulov), 4km north of the centre, every half-hour from 6pm to 8pm; from **Avtovokzal Ayna** (cnr Zhibek Zholy & Aymautov), 3km northeast of the centre, at 6.30pm, 7pm and 7.30pm; from the train station at 6.30pm; and from beneath the MiG plane monument opposite Ordabasy ploshchad at 7pm. You can go and book seats for all of these earlier in the day.

For Taraz, marshrutkas (700T to 1000T, three hours) depart Samal from 7am to 7pm. Shared taxis (1500T) go from just outside Samal's entrance.

For Turkistan there are marshrutkas (500T, two hours) and eight daily buses (350T, three hours, 9am to 6.20pm) from Samal.

Buses to Kyzylorda (1000T, eight hours, four daily) go from Samal.

For road transport to Tashkent see p201; for a bus to Bishkek see p200.

TRAIN
From the **train station** (☎ 95 21 20) at least five trains a day go to Almaty (2660T to 2870T, 13 to 16 hours), Kyzylorda (2120T, nine to 10 hours), Taraz (1440T, four hours) and Turkistan (1335T, four hours) and three or more to Aralsk (3400T, 16 to 18 hours), and at least two to Aktobe (5040T, 28 to 31 hours). The best service to Almaty is train 12 at 6pm. There are also trains to Astana and Aktobe at least daily, to Moscow most days and to Mangyshlak (Aktau) every two days. Trains to Tashkent (8½ hours) go in the

early hours of Monday (3130T) and Thursday (5780T).

Getting Around
Fleets of buses (35T) and marshrutkas (40T) trace over 100 routes around Shymkent's streets. A taxi from the airport to the centre costs around 1000T. In the city, almost any car will stop if you hold your hand out, and take you anywhere for 300T to 400T.

Some useful buses and marshrutkas (all running both directions along their routes):

Bus 5 Train station, Ordabasy ploshchad, Tashenov, Tauke-Khan, Pr Respubliki

Bus 12 Airport, Tauke-Khan, Kazybek Bi, Ordabasy ploshchad, train station

Bus 69 Ordabasy ploshchad, Kazybek Bi, Tauke-Khan, Baytursynuly, Ryskulov, Samal bus station

Bus 111 Ordabasy ploshchad, Turkistan, Momyshuly, Tauke-Khan, Pr Respubliki

Marshrutka 101 Train station, Ordabasy ploshchad, Kazybek Bi, Ayna bus station

AROUND SHYMKENT

Sayram
pop 40,000

About 10km east of Shymkent, the busy little town of Sayram was a Silk Road stop long before Shymkent existed: in fact it's one of the oldest settlements in Kazakhstan, dating back possibly 3000 years. Kozha Akhmed Yasaui (see p157) was born here, and Sayram is a stop for many pilgrims en route to his mausoleum at Turkistan. Sayram's population today is almost entirely Uzbek.

Most of the main monuments can be seen in a walk of about 1½ hours starting from Sayram's central traffic lights (ask marshrutka conductors for the Tsentr stop). Walk up Amir Temur, away from two mosque domes, and take the first street on the right. About 100m along, in a small fenced field on your right, is the circular, brick-built **Kydyra Minaret**, about 15m high and probably dating from the 10th century. You can climb up inside to view the Aksu-Zhabagyly Mountains away to the east. Return to the central crossroads and continue straight ahead, passing the bazaar on your left. Just after the bazaar, on the right, is the 13th-century **Karashash-Ana Mausoleum**, where Akhmed Yasaui's mother lies buried beneath the central tombstone. Continue 200m, passing the modern **Friday Mosque** on your right, to the large **Mirali Bobo Mausoleum**, where a leading 10th-century Islamic scholar lies buried.

Now turn back and take the street to the left, Botbay Ata, before the Friday Mosque. Fork right after 150m, and the street ends at a larger street, Yusuf Sayrami. Head left here and you'll reach a green and yellow sign marking the spot where, according to legend, Kozha Akhmed Yasaui's mentor Aristan Bab handed him a sacred persimmon stone, given to Aristan Bab by the Prophet Mohammed (the gap of five centuries between the lives of the Prophet Mohammed and Akhmed Yasaui is spanned by the belief that Aristan Bab had an extremely long life). About 200m past this spot, turn left into a cemetery to the three-domed **Abd al Aziz-Baba Mausoleum**. Its occupant is believed to have been a leader of the Arabic forces that brought Islam to the Sayram area way back in AD 766. Pilgrims come here for help in averting misfortune and the 'evil eye'. From here head back to the central crossroads, where you can take a taxi to the small 14th-century **Ibragim Ata Mausoleum** on the northern edge of town, where Akhmed Yasaui's father lies. A modern mosque and medressa are attached.

Several chaikhanas around the central crossroads serve inexpensive shashlyk, tea, soups and *plov*. Marshrutkas to Sayram (50T, 30 minutes) leave from Shymkent's Ayna bus station about every 15 minutes or so until around 7pm.

Aksu-Zhabagyly Nature Reserve

This beautiful 1319-sq-km patch of valleys and mountains climbing to the Kyrgyz and Uzbek borders east of Shymkent is the longest established (1926) and one of the easiest visited of Kazakhstan's nature reserves. The reserve, at the west end of the Talassky Alatau range (the most northwesterly spur of the Tian Shan), stretches from the edge of the steppe at about 1200m up to 4239m at Pik Sayram. The main access point is the village of Zhabagyly, 70km east of Shymkent as the crow flies.

In this area where mountains meet steppe there's a great diversity of life. The bright-red Greig's tulip, which dots its alpine meadows in April and May, is one of 1312 flowering plants known here. Wildlife you stand a chance of spotting includes ibex, argali sheep, red marmots, paradise flycatchers, golden eagles, various vultures – and bears (most likely in

spring). The scenery, a mix of green valleys with rushing rivers, snowcapped peaks and high-level glaciers, is gorgeous. You can visit at any time of year, but the best months to come are April to September.

From Zhabagyly village it's 6km southeast to the nearest reserve entrance, then 6km (about 1½ hours' walk) to Kshi-Kaindy, a mountain refuge near a waterfall at 1700m, then a further 6km to Ulken-Kaindy, a second refuge. From Ulken-Kaindy it's 10km to a group of some 2000 stones with petroglyphs of up to 900 years old, below a glacier descending from the 3800m peak Kaskabulak. A good way to visit these sites is by horse, spending two nights at Ulken-Kaindy. More demanding treks will take you over 3500m passes with nights spent in caves. Another great spot is the 300m-deep Aksu Canyon at the reserve's western extremity, a 25km drive from Zhabagyly village. In September and early October the canyon is a busy raptor migration route.

Obligatory fees for entering the reserve are 1860T per person per day, plus 1700T per group per day for an accompanying ranger. Local accommodation options will deal with these for you and all offer a range of well-run trips in the reserve and further afield, for specialists and nonspecialists alike (their websites are great information sources for the area). Typical trip prices include: English-speaking guide 6000T a day; horse 500T to 600T per hour or 4000T to 5000T per day; 4WD vehicle to Aksu Canyon and back 12,000T; camping in the reserve including meals 6500T per person. Wild Nature's director Svetlana Baskakova is a highly knowledgeable biologist and great guide who speaks excellent English. Yevgeny Belousov of Zhenja & Lyuda's is another highly experienced biologist and English-speaker. If you want to head for the real high country including Pik Sayram (no technical climbing but you need to be in good condition), Misha Norets is your man.

SLEEPING

It's best to contact these places in advance to give them time to make plans for your visit. The EIRC (p130) can also make reservations for you.

   Homestay Ruslan (☎ 72538-5 55 85, 701-431 6327; www.zhabagly.com; Abay 24, Zhabagyly; tent 1200T, per person with 0/3 meals 2500/5000T, yurts per person with 3 meals 7000-15,000T) Run by a Kazakh-Dutch family,

Ruslan has beds for 11 in six good rooms in two buildings, with clean shared bathrooms.

Wild Nature (Dikaya Priroda; ☎ /fax 72538-5 56 86, ☎ 701-279 9155; www.wildnature-kz.narod.ru; Taldybulak 14, Zhabagyly per person with 3 meals 5000T) This NGO runs one of Kazakhstan's longest-running and best-organised community tourism programs, offering comfortable homestays with hot showers and local meals.

Misha Norets (☎ 701-693 15 47; Tulkibas; per person with 3 meals 5000T) In Tulkibas, 18km west of Zhabagyly, English-speaking Misha and his friendly family offer homestay accommodation with good meals. Misha is a good guide for the high country.

Zhenja & Lyuda's Boarding House (☎ 72538-5 55 84, 701-717 5851; www.aksuinn.com; Abay 36, Zhabagyly; per person with 3 meals US$35-40) Biologist Yevgeny Belousov has transformed his home on Zhabagyly's main street into a cosy small hotel. Rooms have two single beds and private bathroom. Yevgeny has been in the business since 1990 and knows his job well.

GETTING THERE & AWAY

Marshrutkas to Zhabagyly village (300T, two hours) leave Shymkent's Ayna bus station around 11am and 2pm. Alternatively, there are marshrutkas about every half-hour, 7.30am to 3pm, from Ayna to Turar-Ryskulov (also called Turarkent or Vanovka; 250T, 1½ hours) on the Taraz highway, where you can get a taxi from the market for the 20km trip to Zhabagyly (200/800T per seat/vehicle). Transport to Tulkibas is also available at Turar-Ryskulov.

You can also take a train from Almaty, Taraz or Shymkent to Tulkibas and arrange with your accommodation to be picked up from there (usual cost to Zhabagyly: 1600T). Train 11, departing Almaty-II station at about 5pm daily, reaches Tulkibas (2660T) at about 5am. Or come by bus or taxi from Taraz or Almaty and get out at Akbiik, 7km east of Turar-Ryskulov, then take a taxi (around 500T) for the 12km trip to Zhabagyly.

Accommodation options also offer car transfers to/from Turar-Ryskulov or Akbiik, and even Shymkent or Taraz (6000T to 7000T).

Sayram-Ugam National Park

This park abutting the Uzbek border immediately southwest of the Aksu-Zhabagyly reserve is less well known and cheaper to visit, but offers similar attractions and biodiversity. A community-tourism program provides homestays in the villages of Kaskasu, Dikhankol and Tonkeris and the town of Lenger, all near the park's northern boundary. You can even combine Aksu-Zhabagyly with Sayram-Ugam via a 60km, two- or three-day foot or horse trek between Zhabagyly and Tonkeris or Kaskasu.

Good outings into the hills by foot or horse are to Kaskasu Canyon and Ak-Mechet Gorge (day trips), and Susingen Lake (two or three days, camping). Community-tourism prices are 2000T per day for a guide, 600T per hour for an English translator, 2000T per day per horse, 3500T per person for homestays including meals, and 4000T per person for overnight camping in the park, including meals. There's a park entrance fee of 450T per person.

Homestays are slightly more basic than at Zhabagyly, with outside toilets (except at Lenger). At Kaskasu and Lenger you can stay in yurts (per person with meals 3800T).

Make arrangements through the **Regional Ecotourism Centre** (☎ 72547-6 13 48, 701-111 8192, 701-222 0328; a3ugam@mail.ru; www.ugam.kz), in Kafe Kara-Kia, an internet cafe in the centre of Lenger.

Lenger is 27km southeast of Shymkent; Dikhankol is 47km, Kaskasu is 57km and Tonkeris (close to the western boundary of the Aksu-Zhabagyly reserve) is 70km. The community-tourism people offer car transfers for 40T per kilometre. Marshrutkas (150T, 30 minutes) and buses (100T) to Lenger both leave about every half-hour from Tole-Bi near Shymkent's Central Bazaar. For Dikhankol, Kaskasu and Tonkeris there are marshrutkas (400T to 500T, one to 1½ hours, every two to three hours) and buses (around 300T, 1½ to two hours, three or four times daily) from Tashenov near the Central Bazaar. Shared taxis leave from the same stops.

Otrar

About 150km northwest of Shymkent lie the ruins of Otrar, the town that brought Chinggis Khan to Central Asia. Much of the rest of Asia and Europe might have been spared the Mongols if Otrar's Khorezmshah governor had not murdered the great khan's merchant-envoys here in 1218. A thriving Silk Road town at the hub of a fertile agricultural area, it was mercilessly trashed by Chinggis' forces in 1219 in reprisal for the envoy outrage. It was rebuilt afterwards but eventually abandoned around 1700 after being trashed again by the Zhungars (Oyrats). Today it's just a large dusty mound, known locally as Otyrar-Tobe, 11km north of the small town of Shauildir, but recent excavation and conservation work have revealed some interesting bits of what lies below the surface.

En route from Shymkent, stop at the good little **Otrar Museum** (☎ 72544-2 17 22; Zhibek Zholy 1; admission 100T; ☉ 9am-6pm) in Shauildir. Worthwhile tours in English cost only 100T. At **Otyrar-Tobe** (admission 100T; ☉ 8am-dusk) you can inspect low walls and pillar stumps of the 14th-century Palace of Berdibek (where that other great pillager Timur died, en route to conquer China, in 1405), along with the palace mosque and a bathhouse, and a small residential area and a section of city wall from the 10th to 12th centuries. In its heyday Otrar spread over nearly 10 times the area of the mound where these remains have been uncovered.

Two kilometres from the ruins is the **Aristan-Bab Mausoleum**, the tomb of an early mentor of Kozha Akhmed Yasaui. The existing handsome, domed, brick building here dates from 1907 and is a stop for pilgrims heading to Turkistan.

Buses (350T, 2½ hours) and marshrutkas (600T, two hours) to Shauildir leave about hourly, 8am to 6pm, from Shymkent's Samal bus station. From Turkistan, Shymkent-bound marshrutkas can drop you at Tortkol, where you can pick up a Shauildir-bound marshrutka (250T, 45 minutes) or taxi. A taxi from Shauildir to Otyrar-Tobe, Aristan-Bab and back shouldn't cost more than 1500T round trip. You can also take trains from Shymkent or Turkistan to Timur, 7km east of Shauildir, and a taxi from there.

TURKISTAN ТУРКИСТАН
☎ 72533 / pop 112,000

At Turkistan, 165km northwest of Shymkent in the Syr-Darya valley, stands Kazakhstan's greatest architectural monument and its most important site of pilgrimage. The mausoleum of the first great Turkic Muslim holy man, Kozha Akhmed Yasaui, was built by Timur in the late 14th century on a grand scale comparable with his magnificent creations in Samarkand. Turkistan has no rivals in Kazakhstan for man-made beauty. It's an easy day trip from Shymkent.

Turkistan was already an important trade and religious centre (under the name Yasy) by the time the revered Sufi teacher and mystical poet Kozha Akhmed Yasaui was born at Sayram, probably in 1103. Yasaui underwent ascetic Sufi training in Bukhara, but lived much of the rest of his life in Turkistan, dying here about 1166. He founded the Yasauia Sufi order and had the gift of communicating his understanding to ordinary people through poems and sermons in a Turkic vernacular, a major reason for his enduring popularity.

Yasaui's original small tomb was already a place of pilgrimage before Timur ordered a far grander mausoleum built here in the 1390s. Timur died before it was completed and the main façade was left unfinished – it remains today bare of the beautiful tilework that adorns the rest of the building, with scaffolding poles still protruding from the brickwork. From the 16th to 18th centuries Turkistan was the capital of the Kazakh khans.

Orientation & Information

Coming by road from Shymkent, you'll enter Turkistan from the southeast and the mausoleum will loom into view on your left. The town's main street is Sultanbek Kozhanov. The bus station is about 2km west of the centre, just before the large, busy market in the bustling, down-at-heel, nonmonumental part of town where most people live, and the train station is 3km southwest of there.

There are Visa, MasterCard and Maestro ATMs in the gable-roofed building opposite Hotel Yassy on Tauke Khan. **Internet Klub** (Amir Temir; internet per hr 150T; ☉ 24hr) is upstairs in a building just behind a bus stop about 500m from the mausoleum.

Sights

Before visiting the Yasaui Mausoleum itself, it's worth seeing the recently renovated **museum** (admission 200T; ☉ 9am-7pm), 250m to its northeast. This has some English-language labelling and helpful English-speaking staff. It contains some archaeological displays but most of the material focuses on Kozha Akhmed Yasaui, Sufism and Islamic learning. There are models of the Yasaui Mausoleum, the Aristan Bab Mausoleum (p157) and the Hilvet semi-underground mosque to which Yasaui retired late in life, plus books of his poetry.

lonelyplanet.com

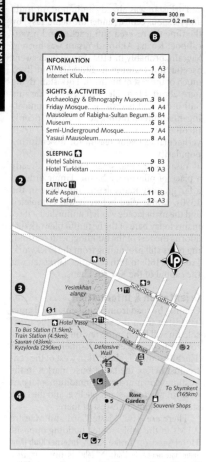

TURKISTAN

The main approach to the Yasaui Mausoleum is through a lovely **rose garden**, past which is a replica of the small 15th-century **Mausoleum of Rabiga-Sultan Begum** (the original was torn down for tsarist building material in 1898). Rabiga-Sultan Begum was Timur's great-granddaughter and wife of Abylkayyr Khan, a 15th-century leader of the then-nomadic Uzbeks. It was Abylkayyr who put the finishing touches to the structure (but not decoration) of the Yasaui mausoleum's facade – note the distinct brickwork at the top of the arch. He was killed in the 1468 feud that split the Uzbeks and effectively gave birth to the Kazakh people (see p46).

The **Yasaui Mausoleum** (admission free; daylight) itself has a slightly museumlike feel despite

being a place of pilgrimage. Visitors don't usually remove shoes though women normally wear headscarves (available at the entrance). The main chamber is cupped with an 18m-wide dome, above a vast, 2000kg, metal *kazan* (cauldron) for holy water, given by Timur. Around this central hall are 34 smaller rooms on two floors. Yasaui's tomb lies beyond an ornate wooden door at the end of the chamber: you can view it through grilles from corridors on either side. The right-hand corridor contains the tomb of Abylay Khan, leader of Kazakh resistance to the invading Zhungars in the 18th century. Don't miss the mausoleum's carpeted mosque, with its beautifully tiled mihrab.

The glorious blue, turquoise and white tiling on the outside of the building merits close inspection. Note the particularly lovely fluted rear dome, above Akhmed Yasaui's tomb chamber.

A number of other monuments, all with free admission, stand nearby. To the south, on a small hill, are the wood-pillared, 19th-century **Friday Mosque** and, next door, the 12th- to 15th-century **Hilvet semi-underground mosque**, with the cell to which Yasaui is said to have withdrawn towards the end of his life. Just east of the mausoleum, built into its defensive wall, the **Archaeology & Ethnography Museum** (admission free; 9am-7pm) has material on old Turkistan and some of the many other ancient and medieval settlements in this fertile part of the Syr-Darya valley.

Sleeping & Eating

Hotel Sabina (3 14 05; Sultanbek Kozhanov 16; s/d downstairs 1500/2000T, upstairs 2500/3000T;) Turkistan's budget option has eight smallish but clean and decent rooms, sharing bathrooms. Those upstairs are bigger and brighter, with TVs and a better bathroom.

Hotel Turkistan (4 21 97; fax 4 14 26; Sultanbek Kozhanov; r 4500) The nicest choice, with a rather grand domed lobby, original oil paintings, thick red carpets, well-looked-after rooms and helpful staff. The restaurant (dishes 300T to 400T) is fine too.

Kafe Safari (Bayburt 21A; dishes 120-300T; 9am-11pm) This little family-run establishment serves up good shashlyk and other staples (*manty, laghman, plov*) in a nice little summer courtyard or an interior dining room.

Kafe Aspan (Sultanbek Kozhanov; dishes 150-400T; 10am-1pm Jun-Aug, noon-midnight Sep-May) A neat and tranquil spot on the main street, with good salads, soups and meat dishes.

Getting There & Around

From the bus station, buses run to Shymkent (350T, three hours) about hourly from 9am to 6pm, while marshrutkas (800T, four hours) and shared taxis (2000T) head to Kyzylorda up to midafternoon. Marshrutkas for Shymkent (500T, two hours) go from a yard 200m east of the bus station until late afternoon.

The train station has at least six daily trains northwest to Kyzylorda (1580T, six hours), three to Aralsk (2870T, 14 hours) and two to Aktobe (4500T, 25 hours), four or more daily southeast to Almaty (3400T, 17 hours) and Shymkent (1335T, four hours), and trains five days a week to Tashkent (5600T, 8½ hours).

Marshrutka 2 (30T) runs between Sultanbek Kozhanov and the bus and train stations.

SAURAN САУРАН

Northwest of Turkistan stands the best preserved and most atmospheric of all the many ruined Silk Road cities in the Syr-Darya valley. Sauran was capital of the Mongol White Horde in the 14th century and remained inhabited until the 18th century. Sixteenth-century writers described it as a 'pleasant' and 'cheerful' city with two high minarets and a sophisticated water-supply system. Its circuit

of limestone walls, plus remains of some bastions and gates, still stand despite conquerors and the elements. Excavations inside have revealed brick walls and areas of patterned stone paving. Sauran is visible as a long, low mound about 2.5km southwest from the Turkistan–Kyzylorda highway, a little over 40km out of Turkistan and about 13km past the village of Sauran. The access track goes under the railway that parallels the road here. Closer up, the ruins loom like something out of *The Lord of the Rings* (but remember: this is Sauran, not Sauron). They are normally unsupervised. A taxi from Turkistan should cost around 3000T round trip: ask for Krepost (Fortress) Sauran to distinguish it from Sauran village.

KYZYLORDA КЫЗЫЛОРДА

☎ 7242 / pop 186,000

On the Syr-Darya 290km northwest of Turkistan, Kyzylorda (Red Capital) became capital of Soviet Kazakhstan in 1925 but was replaced by cooler Almaty when the Turksib railway reached there in 1929. Rice is grown on irrigated steppe around Kyzylorda (so mosquitoes are a pest here), but oil and gas operations in the South Turgay Basin, mainly Chinese-owned, are what underpin the city's growing prosperity today. Kyzylorda's chief role for most travellers is as a staging post for Aralsk or Baykonur.

BAYKONUR COSMODROME

The Baykonur Cosmodrome, a 6717-sq-km area of semidesert about 250km northwest of Kyzylorda, has been the launch site for all Soviet and Russian manned space flights since Yury Gagarin, the first human in space, was lobbed up here in 1961. In fact the cosmodrome is 300km southwest of the original town of Baykonur, but the USSR told the International Aeronautical Federation that Gagarin's launch point was Baykonur, and that name also stuck to the real site. The Russian military town built to guard and service the cosmodrome, formerly called Leninsk, has now acquired the name Baykonur too. The Kyzylorda–Aralsk road and railway pass between the town and the cosmodrome, some of whose installations are visible (the whole site stretches about 75km north). The town's train station is called Toretam.

Since the collapse of the USSR, Kazakhstan has leased the cosmodrome and the town to Russia, and the current lease runs to 2050. Baykonur today has nine launch complexes and sends up astronauts from many countries, including space tourists, as well as unmanned spacecraft. Following the end of the USA's space shuttle program in 2010, Baykonur is the world's only launch centre for human space flight apart from China's Jiuquan.

Visitors to the cosmodrome and Baykonur town require advance permission from the Russian space agency, **Roscosmos** (www.federalspace.ru), and the only practicable way in is to organise a visit well in advance through a well-connected travel agency. One of the few agencies offering visits on a regular basis is Arnai Tours in Almaty (p130). Three-day trips (per person for 5/10 people €1129/891) are planned to coincide with launches: dates are known three to six months ahead and you need to start the paperwork at least two months in advance.

KAZAKHSTAN

KAZAKHSTAN BY HORSE

Australian adventurer Tim Cope spent three years (2004 to 2007) riding horses across the steppes from Mongolia to Hungary, following in the hoofmarks of Chinggis (Genghis) Khan and his hordes. Fifteen months of his trip were spent crossing Kazakhstan from the Altay Mountains to the western Russian border, via Lake Balkhash, the Betpak-Dala desert, Aralsk and Atyrau – a unique experience of the country's steppe heartland.

How has Kazakh culture survived Sovietisation and the international influences of the last two decades? As an indicator of how much has changed in the last century, in 1897 nomads comprised 93% of the population. Nowadays about 9.6% of Kazakhs work on the land, and probably less than half of 1% carry on a nomadic or seminomadic way of life.

The destruction of the nomad way of life between 1928 and 1931, then the collapse of the Soviet system, left rural Kazakhs in a particularly hard situation: they no longer had the knowledge or skills to return to a traditional lifestyle and were equally unable to adapt to private farming. Up to 80% of livestock disappeared in the 1990s in many areas – largely through mismanagement, economic collapse and massive mafia-linked meat export. Many people who had moved nomadically even under Soviet rule were forced to live sedentary lives, turning to subsistence farming, grazing small herds of sheep, cattle, horses and camels.

But even though most Kazakhs are not nomadic, there is a revival of nomadic traditions. The oral traditions in remote villages were something that I savoured, and I came to view many of the Kazakh men singing melancholy songs to their *dombras* as dormant nomads. If they had enough animals they would be back out there on the steppe at the first opportunity.

The most striking survivor of nomadic culture is hospitality. In old times it was bad luck for any Kazakh to allow a traveller to pass without inviting them in for at least a cup of tea. They say that guests bring good luck into the home. All the 70-odd families that helped me in my journey understood that first and foremost my horses needed to be looked after. Even when grain, fodder and pasture were very scarce, they always gave all they had.

How do genuine nomads live? Some families still migrate with the seasons to the same pasturelands as their ancestors did. They live in a traditional *kstau* (mudbrick hut) in winter, and yurts for the rest of the year, reaching the *jailoos* (summer pastures) at the height of summer. I met one family of nomads who migrate along a 600km round route each year from the Muyunkum Desert in the south across the Betpak-Dala almost as far as Zhezkazgan. They were the envy of many village Kazakhs because they had enough livestock to be able to move.

Mangistau is renowned as the area where the Kazakh nomad way of life has been preserved more than anywhere else.

Is the steppe really empty? It is perhaps more empty now than it has been for centuries. Marginal pastures have been abandoned and often tombs are the only reminder that nomads were once

In the city centre the worthwhile **Regional Museum** (☎ 27 62 74; Auezov 20; admission 160T; ☻ 9am-1pm & 3-7pm Tue-Sun) spreads over 14 rooms, ranging from abandoned Silk Road cities and the Aral Sea to renowned local musicians and sporting champions.

About 175km out of Kyzylorda, beside the road to Aralsk, rises the atmospheric **Korkyt Ata Monument** (☻ 9am-7pm), dedicated to a legendary medieval *kobyz* player who supposedly died from snakebite beside the nearby Syr-Darya. The ground plan of the whole thing represents a *kobyz*, and the wind blowing through metal pipes inside one *kobyz*-like structure makes a sound like *kobyz* music.

Sleeping & Eating

Hotel Samruk (☎ 26 24 40; Auelbekov 24; r from 6000T; ☒) This small hotel is towards the cheap end of the scale here but has good, modern rooms with air-con and satellite TV. It faces the WWII monument, 700m straight ahead from the train station.

Hotel Asetan (☎ 27 79 59; asetan@mail.ru; Ayteke Bi 28; s/d 12,000/13,000T; ☒ ☐) Centrally located Asetan, remodelled a few years ago, provides big rooms with stately wallpaper, comfortable furnishings and Jacuzzi-style showers. Breakfast is included.

Remet (☎ 26 21 41; cnr Ayteke Bi & Auezov; pizzas 550-1250T; ☻ 10am-2am) A cool little hangout with there. The massive herds of saiga that roamed the steppe have also largely disappeared, because of the trade in male saiga horns in China, where they are used as a flu remedy.

But the steppe is not an empty wasteland. By horse especially, one comes to appreciate the constantly changing moods of the land, from vast plains of wormwood and *ak shi* (tall, tussocky 'white grass') to haunting saksaul forests, and the magic of vast salt lakes contrasting with hidden pockets of soft grassland and dunes. The steppe is not a destination, but a mood, a feeling, an entity that must be allowed to seep into your veins unrushed.

What temperature extremes did you encounter in your travels and how did you deal with them? The coldest I experienced while riding and camping was probably -40°C. Summer temperatures reached over 50°C. In the summer in central Kazakhstan the only way to survive the heat was to travel exclusively at night and hope to find shelter by morning. In the far southwest approaching the Caspian Sea Kazakhs live in half-underground huts to survive the conditions, and without their help it would have been impossible to travel in summer.

Despite the cold, winter was the preferable season to travel. I knew that my horses could eat the snow, and they didn't sweat much, reducing the risk of saddle sores. Camping out was a bit chilly, but with the right sleeping bag, petrol stove, tent, and cold-weather clothing and boots, it was possible to survive.

Do you like kymyz, shubat and horse meat? I developed a love for *shubat* that helped cool me down in the hot summer, and horse meat that filled me and kept me warm in the winter months. At first it was difficult to watch horses being slaughtered in the winter *sogim* (meat harvest) rituals, but I came to appreciate that without horses, life just wouldn't be possible on the steppe. By partaking in the flesh of the horse, Kazakhs believe they are respecting that animal.

How did this trip change you? I was able to live by the rhythms of the land, measuring time by seasons, the rise and fall of the sun, and the availability of grass and water. The journey made me more patient, more tolerant, and more appreciative of the fine balance between humans and nature. I also learnt to appreciate the value of family and friends as never before, and the Kazakh saying 'Mountains never meet, but people do'.

You can read Tim's diary of his trip at www.timcopejourneys.com. Tim, who speaks Russian, has also completed a TV documentary series about his journey for ARTE and ZDF in Europe and ABC Australia. DVDs are available through his website. A book about his journey will be released by Bloomsbury (Allen & Unwin in Australia) in 2011. An award-winning adventurer, Tim is also coauthor of *Off the Rails: Moscow to Beijing By Bicycle*, and often writes for magazines and newspapers about his travels.

decent pizza, inexpensive draft beer and tables in the front yard in summer.

Getting There & Away
Air Astana flies daily to Almaty (13,500T) and Astana (24,000T); SCAT heads once or twice weekly to Aktau, Atyrau and Shymkent. The **train station** (Auelbekov), with the same services as Turkistan (see p159), is on the northern edge of the centre. Buses to Aralsk (1200T, seven hours) go at 11am, 3.30pm and 9pm from the south side of the square in front of the station, where you may also find shared taxis. Five daily buses to Turkistan (700T, five hours) and Shymkent (1000T, eight hours), and marshrutkas to Turkistan

(800T, four hours), go from the shabby **bus station** (Bokeykhan), 3.5km south of the centre.

ARALSK (ARAL)
АРАЛЬСК (АРАЛ)
☎ 72433 / pop 37,000

Four decades ago Aralsk, 450km northwest of Kyzylorda, was an important fishing port on the shores of the Aral Sea, with a population twice its current size. A large mosaic in its train station depicts how in 1921 Aralsk's comrades provided fish for people starving in Russia. Today a large part of the Aral Sea is gone, victim of Soviet irrigation schemes that took water from its lifelines, the Syr-Darya and the Amu-Darya, and pushed the shoreline

60km out from Aralsk (see p100). If you want to witness the Aral Sea environmental disaster firsthand, Aralsk is easier to visit, and more interesting, than similarly defunct ports in Uzbekistan. Nor is everything quite so gloomy here: efforts to save part of the sea are succeeding (see boxed text, p163) and a small-scale fishing industry has started up again.

BTA Bank (main square) has an **ATM** (9am-12am) for Visa, Visa Electron and MasterCard. You can get online at **Internet** (Abilkayyr Khan; internet per hr 200T; 24hr), on the main street.

Sights & Activities

Four **fishing boats** stand on pedestals beside the former harbour, just along the street from the hotel. They were brought here and painted in 2005, as a tribute to fallen heroes. Also close to the harbour is the old fish-processing plant, **Aralrybprom**, which stayed alive 20 years after the Aral Sea departed by canning fish from the Baltic and Vladivostok, but eventually went bankrupt in the late 1990s.

The small **history museum** (Yesetov; admission 150T; 9am-1pm & 3-7pm Mon-Sat) has a few desiccation photos and some imaginative oil paintings on the Aral Sea theme – including *Zhalanash Port,* showing a woman in bathing costume striding towards what looks like a desert. There's also a large diorama of a battle between Bolshevik and White forces near Aralsk in 1919.

Near **Zhalanash** (Zhambyl), a former fishing village 45km west of Aralsk, you can still see a **ship cemetery**, where four abandoned hulks rust in the sand, often providing shelter for those other ships of the desert, the area's ubiquitous wandering camels. A few years ago there were more ships, but several have been reduced to nothing by scrap-metal scavengers.

The NGO **Aral Tenizi** (2 22 56, 2 36 91, 701-662 7163; www.aralsea.net; zmakh@mail.ru; Makataev 10; office 9am-noon & 2-6pm Mon-Fri), which works to revive the Aral fishing industry, can arrange jeeps and drivers to visit the sites. Ask for English-speaking Serik Duisenbaev. A half-day trip to the Zhalanash ship cemetery and the sea costs 10,000T for one or two people, 15,000T for three or four. A day trip to Tastubek, 25km west of Zhalanash, the nearest village to the seashore, is 15,000T for up to four people (you can swim here and camp overnight if you wish). A day trip to the Kok-Aral Dam, 220km from Aralsk (about 3½ hours each way), is 20,000T for up to four. Aral Tenizi charges all

clients a US$20 membership fee per group. Try to contact them ahead, to allow time to make your arrangements.

Sleeping & Eating

Aral Tenizi (2 22 56, 2 36 91, 701-662 7163; www.aralsea.net; zmakh@mail.ru; Makataev 10; per person with breakfast/meals 2000/3000T; office 9am-noon & 2-6pm Mon-Fri) The NGO Aral Tenizi offers clean and comfortable host-family accommodation, with running water and usually squat toilets.

Aral Hotel (2 14 79; Makataev 14; r 4000-7000T;) Aralsk's hotel is a couple of doors from the Aral Tenizi office. It's basic and a bit dilapidated, but the more expensive rooms do have hot showers; the cheaper ones have cold or no showers.

For meals, the best bets are **Chin-Son** (Makataev; mains 300-650T; 11am-3am), opposite the Aral Tenizi office, with Kazakh, Russian and spicy Korean dishes; and **Infiniti** (Abilkayyr Khan; mains 150-300T; 11am-1.30am), on the main street, with an evening admission fee of 200T and good *plov, manty* and meat dishes.

Getting There & Around

Aralsk's **train station** (9 50 72), called Aralskoe More, is 1km northeast of the central square. There are at least three daily departures northwest to Aktobe (2100T, 10½ hours), six or more southeast to Kyzylorda (1900T, seven to nine hours) and Turkistan (2870T, 14 hours), and four or more to Shymkent (4000T, 17 hours) and Almaty (5300T, 32 hours), plus trains to Tashkent (10,750T, 23 hours) five days a week. In July and August tickets can be brutally hard to come by here, often selling out a week in advance, so try to buy onward or return tickets before arriving.

Buses to Kyzylorda (1200T, seven hours) go at 11am, 3.30pm and 9.30pm from the train station. They're occasionally cancelled in winter. No public transport runs along the very poor 600km road to Aktobe. Aral Tenizi (p162) can provide taxis to or from Kyzylorda (30,000T, six hours).

WESTERN KAZAKHSTAN

Kazakhstan's biggest oil and gas fields – Tengiz (oil), Karachaganak (gas) and the offshore oil of Kashagan beneath the Caspian Sea – have brought boom times to the west's four main cities, but elsewhere the human population is sparse and the landscape is chiefly desert and steppe. For those with a taste for adventurous exploring, the deserts east of Aktau, dotted with underground mosques, ancient necropolises, wandering camels and spectacular rock formations, are just the ticket.

Western Kazakhstan – so far west that the part beyond the Ural River is in Europe – is a gateway to Central Asia from Azerbaijan and the Volga and Ural regions of Russia, and there are even flights from Western Europe to Atyrau and Uralsk. Overland drivers and riders should take careful soundings about the current state of highways in this region. The roads from Atyrau to Aktobe and from Karabutak (220km east of Aktobe) to Aralsk still had long stretches in appalling condition at time of writing. Improvement works are underway, but until they are completed, drivers between Atyrau and Aktobe go via

Uralsk, and if Almaty is your goal, the route via Kostanay and Astana is in much better condition than the one via Aralsk. The region is one hour behind Astana, Almaty and the rest of the country.

AKTOBE АКТӨБЕ

☎ 7132 / pop 290,000 / elev 220m

Aktobe (formerly Aktyubinsk), on the main railway to Moscow about 100km from the Russian border, is a growing commercial hub that has experienced an influx of oil and gas companies operating in the region's fields, and an accompanying facelift. As a gateway to Kazakhstan from Russia, it makes a favourable impression. The centre focuses on north–south-running Abilkayyr Khana. The older part of the city, with the train station, is about 3km east. You can get online and use Skype at @i.net (Abilkayyr Khana 43; internet per hr 250T; ⏱ 9am-2am), opposite Hotel Aktobe.

THE ARAL SEA: ON ITS WAY BACK TO ARALSK

Nearly four decades after they last saw the Aral Sea in their harbour, the people of Aralsk have real hope that it will be back soon.

Helped by international aid agencies and lenders such as the World Bank, Kazakhstan has revived the northern part of the Aral, now severed from the remnants of its southern body.

A mud dyke was built across the last channel connecting the northern and southern parts of the sea in the 1990s. With no outlet to the south, the North Aral started to fill again with water from the Syr-Darya. The dyke collapsed in 2002 but a sturdier, 10m-high concrete replacement, the Kok-Aral Dam, was completed by 2005. With rehabilitated waterworks along the Syr-Darya also helping by increasing the flow of water into the sea, by 2010 the North Aral had crept back to within 23km of Aralsk and attained a depth of 20m.

Now, a new dyke, 4m higher than the Kok-Aral Dam, is to be built across the mouth of Saryshyganak Bay, the northeastern arm of the sea that used to reach Aralsk. At the same time a new channel from the Syr-Darya will be cut to feed water into Saryshyganak Bay. The new dyke is scheduled to be ready by 2014, and it is hoped that the waters will reach Aralsk in 2015. Zhalanash, site of the 'ship cemetery' and currently about 10km from the water, may again become a real fishing village.

In the 1990s the fishing catch in the North Aral was limited to flounder, a flatfish that proved to be the only species able to survive the Aral's extreme salinity then. Since 2005, 15 types of freshwater fish have returned to the North Aral. Fishers travel from their villages, often now 25km or 30km from the shore, to take out small boats from which they catch carp, catfish, pike and the valuable pike-perch, which is exported to Russia. The remaining flounder are now so small, because of the freshness of the water, that they are usually thrown back. The total annual catch is around 2000 tonnes, about one-tenth of what the Aral used to provide.

Locals also hope that revival of the North Aral and Saryshyganak Bay will reduce the noxious sandy, salty windstorms that plague communities such as Aralsk.

The Kok-Aral Dam has condemned the South Aral to accelerated evaporation, but most experts consider the supersaline, fishless South Aral already a lost cause, with no hope of an increase in water from its main source, the Amu-Darya, which flows through Turkmenistan and Uzbekistan. Indeed satellite photos show that the once-far-bigger South Aral may already be smaller than the North Aral.

Sights

The beautiful new **Nur Gasyr Mosque** and the Russian Orthodox **Khram Svyato-Nikolsky** (St Nicholas' Church), both topped with masses of gold, straddle Abilkayyr Khana between the new and old towns. Both were opened jointly by Kazakhstan's President Nazarbaev and Russia's President Medvedev in a symbolic act of solidarity in 2008. They are normally open to visitors when their doors are open. A new park is being built between them. Also worth a look is the unique **Nurdaulet complex** (Abilkayyr Khana 46), which is a shopping centre, amusement park, zoo and mosque all rolled into one.

The **Regional Museum** (☎ 21 13 67; Altynsarin 14; admission 100T; 9am-1pm & 2-6pm Wed-Mon), in the old town, has fairly typical displays of stuffed wildlife and history, which become more interesting if English-speaking curator Rosa is there to give you a tour.

The **Alia Moldagulova Museum** (☎ 52 15 98; Moldagulova 47; admission 50T; 10am-1pm & 2-6pm Tue-Sun) honours a locally born WWII sniper who notched 91 Nazi scalps before being killed in action herself. A block west of the museum, a statue of Alia provides a contemporary interpretation of her significance.

Sleeping & Eating

Hotel Ilek (☎ 96 01 01; www.ilek.kz; Ayteke-bi 44; s/d with shared bathroom 2500/4200T, r with private bathroom 6000-18,000T;) Just two blocks from the train station, the Ilek is a large-ish, mostly renovated hotel offering a budget option of small, unrenovated rooms with shared bathrooms. The other rooms are decent but unexceptional. Breakfast and air-con are included with the more expensive rooms.

Hotel Aktobe (☎ 56 28 29; hotel@aktobe.kz; Abilkayyr Khana 44; s/d from 4500/5600T;) A central Soviet-style hotel with a large range of clean rooms equipped with CNN, bathroom, fridge and, in the more expensive ones, air-con. The lobby has a bar, an ATM, a hairdresser and air- and train-ticket kiosks.

Hotel Amsterdam (☎ 52 01 06; http://amsterdamhotel.kz; Zhubanova 50A; r 13,000-25,000T;) An attractive building with a host of facilities and good service, the Amsterdam is well located just off Abilkayyr Khana. Rooms are discreetly comfy, with large beds.

our pick **Taksim** (☎ 57 30 20; Abilkayyr Khana 64; mains 700-1600T; 10am-3am;) Bright, contemporary Taksim, on the main downtown intersection,

serves up a range of great breakfasts, burgers, salads, *zakuski* (Russian appetisers), steaks, kebabs, pastas, pizzas and desserts. Free wi-fi too, and outdoor beanbag seating in summer!

Chindalle (☎ 54 91 50; Abilkayyr Khana 55B; mains 1200-3000T; sushi 800-1200T;) This polished Japanese-Korean restaurant, almost opposite Hotel Aktobe, does fine sushi. The waitresses' outfits are charming.

Entertainment

FK Aktobe (Ortalyk Stadion, cnr Abilkayyr Khana & Moldagulova; www.fcaktobe.kz; admission 600-1200T) Kazakhstan's passionately supported, most successful soccer club, which regularly makes it into the early rounds of the UEFA Champions League. The domestic season runs from March to October.

Getting There & Around

Flights go to Almaty (15,000T) and Astana (28,700T) daily, Aktau (23,000T) and Atyrau (23,000T) daily except Monday, and Moscow three times weekly.

Trains from the **station** (Ualikhanov; ☎ 21 17 77) run at least once daily to Almaty (6800T, 40 to 46 hours), Aralsk (2100T, 11 hours), Moscow (19,000T, 37 hours), Orenburg (Russia, seven hours), Shymkent (5000T, 31 hours) and Uralsk (1920T, 12 hours). Trains to Uralsk, including the Moscow-bound 7 and 387, duck into Russia en route and require a Russian visa and possibly a double-entry Kazakhstan visa. Bus 15 (25T) from the station runs the full length of Abilkayyr Khana and back.

Intercity buses leave from **Avtostantsia Ekspress** (☎ 55 02 26; 312 Atkyshtar Diviziyasy No 9Zh). Daily destinations include Astana (6000T, 26 hours), Uralsk (2250T, eight hours) and Russian cities including Orenburg (1700T, six hours), Orsk (1500T, 3½ hours) and Samara (4500T, 14 hours). The best places to find taxis to Orenburg (per person/vehicle 5000/20,000T), Orsk (per vehicle 12,000T), Samara (50,000T) or Uralsk (6000/25,000T) are outside the train station or at **Avtovokzal Sapar** (312 Atkyshtar Diviziyasy No 4).

The local motorbike club, **Asar Motor Aktobe** (☎ 22 83 53, 701-339 7714; zobenko1969@mail.ru; Aviagorodok 124), near the airport, offers a very helpful free check over of travellers' motorbikes, cars or jeeps, space to work on vehicles, and information on routes and road conditions. Ask for Gennady Zobenko.

Taxis in town cost 300T to 500T.

URALSK (ORAL) УРАЛЬСК (ОРАЛ)

☎ 7112 / pop 260,000 / elev 35m

Closer to Vienna than Almaty and sitting on the European bank of the Ural River, Uralsk is the first or last city for some Central Asia overlanders. It's also a base for expat oilmen hauling themselves out to the pumping stations at Karachaganak, 150km east. Founded by Cossacks in the 17th century, Uralsk has its roots in Russia, as is clear from the beautiful, traditional Russian architecture throughout the leafy centre.

The main boulevard, Dostyk, running 6km north–south, has two Russian Orthodox cathedrals and is very prettily lit at night. Pedestrianised Dina Nurpeyisova (formerly Teatralnaya), crossing Dostyk, is Uralsk's mini version of Moscow's Arbat. Nightclubs such as **Aysberg** (cnr Dostyk & Temir Masin) and **Maximum** (Dina Nurpeyisova) compete for the custom of Uralsk's glamorous under-25s.

A famous Russian serf rebellion was launched in 1773 from a log house that is now the **Pugachyov Museum** (☎ 26 49 86; Dostyk 35; admission 100T; ⏰ 10am-6pm Tue-Sun). Yemelyan Pugachyov led a group of Cossacks and hundreds of thousands of serfs in a revolt against the autocratic Catherine the Great that spread to the Ural Mountains and along the Volga. The museum is in Uralsk's oldest district, Kureni, at the south end of town, easily reached by bus 35 (35T) along Dostyk. Features include a replica of the cage in which Pugachyov was held after capture, and a spooky portrait with Catherine's eyes and hair seemingly growing out of Pugachyov's head.

Sleeping & Eating

Hotel Oral (☎ 51 30 20; Kurmangazy 80; s/d with shared bathroom 2700/3000T, with private bathroom 5000/7000T; ⏰) The cheaper rooms in the large, green Oral are an acceptable, basic, budget option. Staff are quite friendly and there's also a 24-hour cafe.

Hotel Sayakhat (☎ 51 30 03; sayahat38@mail.ru; Temir Masin 38; s/d from 7000/8000T; P ⏰) Rooms in this remodelled Soviet hotel, on the corner of Dostyk, are smallish but cosy. A reasonable breakfast is included. Some staff speak English.

Plenty of restaurants are dotted along Dostyk. **Camelot** (☎ 50 39 01; Dostyk 185; mains 1100-2400T; ⏰ noon-midnight; E), right in the centre, is the classiest, great for varieties of the local

sturgeon and the highly imaginative names of its dishes. **Dixie Pub** (Atrium Mall, Dina Nurpeyisova 17; mains 1500-2800T; ⏰ noon-2am; E) serves everything from fried calamari to a good burrito, in absolutely American-sized portions.

Getting There & Around

Uralsk has flights to Aktau (29,000T to 32,000T), Astana (22,000T to 26,000T) and Atyrau (17,000T to 22,000T); to Almaty (32,000T to 46,000T) five times weekly and to Moscow (43,000T) twice a week. There's a weekly Air Astana flight to/from Amsterdam.

From the **train station** (☎ 51 86 47), at the north end Kurmangazy, there are daily trains to Aktobe (1920T, 12 hours), Almaty (8440T, 52 hours) and Moscow (12,935T, 26 hours, via Saratov). Trains to Aktobe and Almaty pass through Russia en route, meaning you need a Russian visa. You may also need a double-entry Kazakhstan visa: check at the station or with a travel agent.

From the **bus station** (☎ 28 31 09; Syrym Datuly), 6km east of the centre (500T by taxi), there are buses to Aktobe (2250T, eight hours, 9am), Atyrau (2500T, nine hours, four daily) and, in Russia, Samara (1750T, six hours, five daily) and Saratov (2850T, nine hours, 8am). Minibuses to Atyrau (3500T, five hours) leave the train station when they fill up with passengers – make a morning start. Shared taxis to Aktobe (6000T, five hours), Atyrau (5000T, five hours), Samara (5000T, five hours) and Saratov (7000T, seven hours) go from the train and bus stations.

Bus 12 (35T) runs between the airport and city centre via the bus and train stations.

ATYRAU АТЫРАУ

☎ 3122 / pop 160,000 / elev -25m

Atyrau, 30km up the Ural River from its mouth on the Caspian Sea, began as a Russian fort in the 16th century and today acts as command station for the Tengiz oilfield 200km south. Tengizchevroil, the multibillion-dollar joint venture exploiting the field, has its headquarters in this predominantly Kazakh town.

Atyrau is a possible entry point into Kazakhstan, but unless you are here to work there's not very much reason to linger. However, the expat scene does make for a good selection of places to eat, drink and dance.

Orientation & Information

The Ural River meanders through the town, marking the border between Asia and Europe. The train station is 4km northeast of the centre; the airport is 6km west. You'll find **Atyrau shopping mall** (Satpaev; ☺ 10am-11pm) convenient for many needs, including ATMs, public internet (per hour 150T), train and

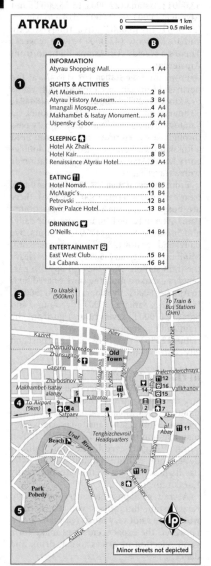

air ticket offices and the well stocked Ideal supermarket.

Sights

The modernised **Atyrau History Museum** (☎ 22 29 12; Azattyk 9B; admission 400T; ☺ 10am-1pm & 2-7pm Tue-Sun) has some interesting displays including a replica of the local 'Golden Man' – a 2nd-century-BC Sarmatian chief with a gold-plated tunic, found in 1999 at Araltobe, 200km east of Atyrau – and a room on Sarayshyk, an old trading centre and capital of the Nogai Horde (one of the successors to the Golden Horde), 50km north of Atyrau. English-language museum tours are available for 1000T.

Opposite the History Museum is the **Art Museum** (☎ 25 48 03; Azattyk 11; admission 200T; ☺ 10am-1pm & 2-7pm Tue-Sun), worth a look for its collection of paintings on Atyrau life.

On Satpaev 900m west of the bridge, beside the large square Makhambet-Isatay alangy, is the handsome, blue-and-white **Imangali Mosque**, opened in 2000. The 19th-century Russian Orthodox **Uspensky Sobor** (Dormition Cathedral; Isatay 16), restored in 2000, emerges like a jewelled finger from the shabby 'old town' north of here.

Sleeping

There's no shortage of good hotels – at a price.

Komnaty Otdykha (☎ 95 56 05; Train Station; dm 2000T, s/d 3400/6000T) The cheapest sleep is the railway retiring rooms, entered from the station platform. They're basic, with shared bathrooms, and short on security, but clean – and half-price for less than 12 hours.

Hotel Kair (☎ 25 43 86; Atambaev 19A; s/d from 4200/6000T; ✸) A relatively inexpensive, well-kept place south of the river; no food or bar, though.

Hotel Ak Zhaik (☎ 32 78 81/2; www.akzhaikhotel. com; cnr ploshchad Abay & Azattyk; s/d 10,000/18,000T; Ⓟ ✸ ▢ ⧢) This very central hotel has comfy rooms and a slew of useful facilities including an ATM, a train ticket office, a pub with wi-fi internet and a good lobby cafe. Breakfast is included.

Renaissance Atyrau Hotel (☎ 90 96 00; www.renaissancehotels.com/guwbr; Satpaev 15B; r from 24,640T Fri-Sun, from 44,690T Mon-Thu; Ⓟ ✕ ✸ ▢ ⧢ ⧉) Elegant international-class luxury Marriott hotel with all the facilities you could hope for.

Eating

McMagic's (☎ 25 54 45; Makhambet 116A; dishes 300-750T; ☺ 10am-midnight; ⧢) In the big Daria store building, this is a reasonable Western-style burger and pizza bar.

River Palace Hotel (☎ 35 52 39; Ayteke Bi 55; pizzas 1000-1800T) The pizzeria in this Italian-run top-end hotel is as good as you'd hope, and in the evening from about May to September they have tables on the roof terrace, with expansive river views.

Hotel Nomad (☎ 25 29 02; Azzatyk 75B; mains 1000-2500T; ☻ 7-10am, noon-2pm, 6-10pm; **V**) With an Indian manager and an Indian chef, the little restaurant at this hotel serves a big choice of great Indian food, and not bad Tex-Mex either.

ourpick Petrovski (☎ 32 10 92; Azattyk 2; dishes 1300-2200T; ☻ 8am-1am) Very tasty European and Thai dishes are served at this stylish but informal, pop-art-decked little place. Top breakfasts, too.

Drinking & Entertainment

The pick of several expat-style pubs is wood-panelled, stained-glassed **O'Neills** (☎ 99 60 96; Zheleznodorozhnaya; ☻ 9am-2am), which serves good pub food and heaves at happy hour (6pm to 8pm Friday and Saturday). You can dance to a funky Latin band at the Mexican-themed restaurant **La Cabana** (☎ 99 60 96; Azattyk) from 7pm Wednesday and 9pm Friday and Saturday. Or dance to electronic rhythms at **East West Club** (☎ 32 85 40; Azattyk 6; admission 1000-2000T, women free Wed; ☻ from 10pm Wed, Sat & Sun), all metal piping, mirror globes and scantily clad dancing girls.

Getting There & Away

From the **airport** (☎ 20 92 92) there are direct flights to Aktau (17,000T), Astana (from 24,500T) and Uralsk (17,000T to 22,000T) daily; to Aktobe (23,000T), Almaty (38,000T) and Amsterdam (from 117,000T) most days; and to Baku (29,000T), Moscow (from 47,000T) and İstanbul (68,000T) two or three days a week.

Atyrau lies on a main railway from Russia through western Kazakhstan to Uzbekistan. From the **station** (☎ 95 55 49; Vokzalnaya 1) trains go daily to Aktau (Mangyshlak; 2900T, 20 hours), Aktobe (2300T, 16 hours), Almaty (7900T, 50 hours), Astrakhan (Russia; 4300T, 16 hours) and Kungrad (Uzbekistan; 3300T, 19 hours); to Moscow and Volgograd five days a week; to Nukus (Uzbekistan) and Saratov (Russia) four days a week; to Samarkand three days a week; and to Tashkent twice a week.

From the bus station, next door to the train station, there are four daily buses to Uralsk (2500T, nine hours) and two to Astrakhan (2500T, eight hours), plus minibuses (3500T) and shared taxis (5000T) to Uralsk from early morning to early evening, both taking five hours.

Getting Around

Taxis to or from the airport should cost 600T but you may have to pay more coming into town. City buses cost 45T. Bus 21 runs between the airport and the train station via Satpaev, Abay and Makhambet. Buses 14 and 15 also travel between Satpaev, Abay and the station. Bus 2 from the station runs down Azattyk south of Abay.

AKTAU АКТАУ
☎ 7292 / pop 183,000

Perched between the desert and the Caspian, hundreds of kilometres from anywhere else of any size, with all its water derived from desalination, Aktau is perhaps the most oddly situated of all the weirdly located places scattered across the former USSR.

Local uranium and oil finds were the reason Soviet architects began to lay out a model town of wide, straight streets here in 1958. The uranium, from an open-cast mine 30km to the northeast, fed the Aktau's nuclear fast breeder reactor, which generated Soviet Aktau's electricity, powered its desalination plant and produced uranium concentrate for military purposes. Thanks to the sandy beaches on the blue Caspian and temperate climate (several degrees above zero in January), the place was also developed as an elite Soviet holiday resort.

Uranium mining, nuclear power and associated chemical and metallurgical operations were wound down in the 1990s, leaving an apocalyptic industrial wasteland around Aktau's fringes. But oil and gas have given Aktau a new lease of life as a centre for both onshore and offshore operations, and with its seaside location, low-key summer tourism and reasonable standard of living, it's a pleasant town in which to spend a day or two. More of a reason to come here, though, are the natural and man-made wonders of the surrounding region, Mangistau (p170).

Orientation

The only significant street with a name is Kazakhstan Respublikasy Prezidentininy

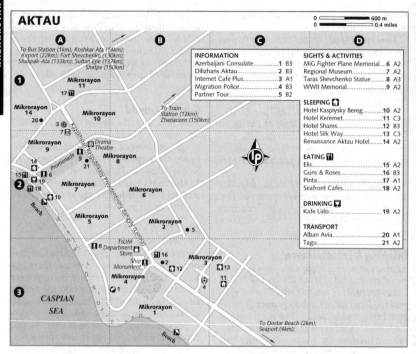

AKTAU

INFORMATION
Azerbaijani Consulate..............1 B3
Dilizhans Aktau...................2 B3
Internet Cafe Plus................3 A1
Migration Police..................4 B3
Partner Tour......................5 B2

SIGHTS & ACTIVITIES
MiG Fighter Plane Memorial....6 A2
Regional Museum..................7 A2
Taras Shevchenko Statue.......8 A3
WWII Memorial....................9 A2

SLEEPING
Hotel Kaspiysky Bereg..........10 A2
Hotel Keremet....................11 C3
Hotel Shams......................12 B3
Hotel Silk Way...................13 C3
Renaissance Aktau Hotel......14 A2

EATING
Elis.............................15 A2
Guns & Roses.....................16 B3
Pinta............................17 A1
Seafront Cafes...................18 A2

DRINKING
Kafe Lido........................19 A2

TRANSPORT
Alban Avia.......................20 A1
Tagu.............................21 A2

dangyly. Not surprisingly, many people still call it Lenina. Aktau addresses are based on *mikrorayon* (microdistrict) and *dom* (building) numbers: 4-17-29 means Microdistrict 4, Building 17, Apartment 29.

Information

Internet Cafe Plus (Dom 22, Mikrorayon 9; internet per hr 290T; 24hr) In the building with a huge painting of Abylay Khan on its street end.

Migration Police (Dom 123, Mikrorayon 3; 9am-noon Tue, Wed, Fri & Sat) Deals with registration matters.

Partner Tour (52 60 88; partnertour@nursat.kz; Office 5, Dom 12, Mikrorayon 2; 10am-1pm & 2-7pm Mon-Fri, to 5pm Sat) This well-organised agency can set up guided trips from one to seven days around the sights of Mangistau. English- and German-speaking guides are available.

Sights

To best savour Aktau's atmosphere, stroll along the pedestrian walk from the large **WWII Memorial** beside Kazakhstan Respublikasy Prezidentininy dangyly to the **MiG fighter plane memorial** at the seaward end of the street. From the MiG you can descend steps to the

breezy **seafront**, a mixture of low cliffs, rocks and thin sandy strips, with assorted cafes and bars that are lively in summer (when some of them double as open-air discos), but fairly desolate during the rest of the year. A narrow street followed by a pedestrian promenade parallel the coast for 1km south from here, at the end of which you can climb steps to a landmark **statue of Taras Shevchenko** (for details on Shevchenko see p171). The wider, more popular **Dostar Beach** (admission 100T) is about 4km southeast of here.

The **Regional Museum** (Dom 23A, Mikrorayon 9) was closed for rebuilding at research time.

Sleeping

Hotel Keremet (50 15 69; Dom 20, Mikrorayon 3; s/d 2000/3500T, r half lux/lux 4000/5000T;) Rooms at this budget option are bare and worn, and the cheapest have share bathrooms, but all have air-con. Staff are amiable and there's also a cafe.

Hotel Kaspiysky Bereg (Caspian Shore Hotel; 52 26 28; Mikrorayon 7; s 6000-10,000T, d 10,000-15,000T) This homey small hotel near the seashore has good-sized rooms sporting glassed-in showers and attractive Chinese silk 'paintings'. Breakfast is included.

Hotel Shams (☎ 50 07 36; Dom 70, Mikrorayon 2; r 7000T; ✷) The small, recently renovated Shams offers attractive rooms with carpets, pine furnishings and international TV channels, despite an unpromising entrance up the steps at the back of the building next to Shams Kafe.

Hotel Silk Way (☎ 50 59 09; Dom 25A, Mikrorayon 3; www.silkwayaktau.com; r 14,000-20,000T; ❂ ✷ ☎) A new hotel providing spacious, impeccable and well-equipped, if bland, rooms. It also has an international restaurant, and breakfast is included in rates.

Renaissance Aktau Hotel (☎ 30 06 00; www.renaissancehotels.com/scobr; Mikrorayon 9; r from 49,200T; ❂ ✗ ✷ ⌨ ☎ ✋) Aktau's Marriott hotel provides superstylish modern rooms and suites, most with sea views, plus a heated pool, two elegant eateries and a host of other facilities.

Eating, Drinking & Entertainment

Several seafront cafes below the MiG monument serve up fried chicken, *manty* and meat, fish or vegetable shashlyk (400T to 1400T), and have outdoor tables in summer. The rooftop of **Kafe Lido** (✹ 4pm-3am) is packed for summer night drinks.

Guns & Roses (☎ 52 49 41; Kazakhstan Respublikasy Prezidentininy dangyly, Dom 66, Mikrorayon 2; dishes 950-3000T; ✹ 10am-2am Sun-Thu, to 4am Fri & Sat) A large and festive 'English' pub, Guns & Roses serves generous burgers, curry, steaks and the like. There's sport on TV and a tight rock band plays Wednesday, Friday and Saturday nights.

Elis (☎ 43 85 02; Mikrorayon 7; dishes 1000-2500T; ✹ noon-2am) The two bars at this multitasking venue on the coastal embankment serve a range of good international food. There's live rock and pop in the upstairs bar (past the Beatles and Elvis photos) from 10pm nightly, while the lower bar has a nice outdoor terrace. You can bowl and play billiards here, too.

Pinta (☎ 31 17 40; Dom 8, Mikrorayon 11; mains 1100-2200T; ✹ noon-3pm & 6pm-1am; E) A cosy, small restaurant with a Russian-international menu specialising in pork, chicken and fish.

Kofeynya Tetti (✹ 9am to 11pm; dishes from 250T; ☎), adjoining Pinta, is a great cafe for coffee, cakes and breakfast,.

Getting There & Away

A useful air and train ticket agency is **Dilizhans Aktau** (☎ 50 83 38; West Wing, Hotel Aktau, Mikrorayon 2; ✹ 9am-8pm). The **airport** (☎ 46 80 96), 23km north of the centre, has an always-open **air-ticket office** (☎ 46 80 52; ✹ 24hr).

Air Astana (☎ 60 97 57; Airport) flies daily to Almaty (23,250T) and Atyrau (17,000T), with connections for Astana (37,000T) at Atyrau. SCAT goes to Atyrau (12,000T to 14,000T) and Uralsk (29,000T to 32,000T) daily, to Aktobe (23,000T) five times weekly, to Astana (30,000T) four times weekly, and to Almaty (27,000T), Kyzylorda and Shymkent twice a week. SCAT also operates trans-Caspian flights to Baku (23,500T) four times weekly, to Astrakhan (22,500T) and Tbilisi (24,500T) three times a week, and to Yerevan (30,500T) once a week, as well as flying to İstanbul and southern Russian cities a few times weekly. Azerbaijan Airlines, represented by **Alban Avia** (☎ 42 74 00; Dom 59, Mikrorayon 14), flies to Baku six days a week. There are three weekly flights to Moscow by Transaero.

Aktau's **train station** (☎ 46 52 50), called Mangyshlak, is 12km east of the centre. It lies near the end of a branch line off the Atyrau–Uzbekistan line, so journeys to anywhere are l-o-n-g. Trains leave daily for Aktobe (2400T, 26 hours) and Atyrau (2900T, 20 hours); every two days for Almaty (8730T, 68 hours, via Aralsk and Shymkent) and Astana (4500T, 47 hours); and on Sunday and Thursday for Kungrad (Uzbekistan; 22 hours). Change trains at Beyneu for connections to Uzbek destinations on other days.

From the **bus station** (Mikrorayon 28), in the north of town, minibuses leave when full, until about 7pm, to Shetpe (400T, two hours) and Zhanaozen (420T, two hours), and several times daily to Fort Shevchenko. Shared taxis to these destinations, charging around 800T per person, go from the street just south of here. See p201 for information on transport from Zhanaozen to Turkmenbashi in Turkmenistan.

A ferry to Baku (Azerbaijan) leaves irregularly from the **seaport** (☎ 44 51 25) in the southeast of town. It's a cargo ship that carries some passengers and a small number of vehicles, and there can be anything from two days to two weeks between sailings. Cabin fares for the scheduled 18-hour crossing run from 8100T to 10,500T. **Tagu** (☎ 51 39 89; www.tagu.ucoz.ru; tagu@mail.kz; Dom 12, Mikrorayon 7; ✹ 9am-1pm & 2-6pm Mon-Sat, 10am-3pm Sun) provides information and tickets, and you can put your name on the passenger list there. Take food for the voyage.

Getting Around

City buses cost 25T. Bus 3 runs north up Kazakhstan Respublikasy Prezidentininy dangyly then east to the bus station, and vice versa. From the train station, bus 101 runs to the centre; from the port, bus 4.

Taxis within town should cost 200T. For the train station expect to pay 400T or 500T, and for the airport 1500T.

AROUND AKTAU

The stony deserts of **Mangistau**, the region of which Aktau is capital, stretch 400km east to the border with Uzbekistan. This labyrinth of dramatic canyons, weirdly eroded, multicoloured rock outcrops, surprising lakes, mysterious underground mosques and ancient necropolises is only beginning to be explored, even by archaeologists. A minor branch of the Silk Road once ran across these wastes, and sacred sites, some with strong Sufic associations, are located where people buried their dead or where holy men dwelt. The underground mosques may have originated as cave hermitages for ascetics who retreated to the deserts.

A few sites, including Beket-Ata and Fort Shevchenko, can be reached by public transport of various sorts, but for most places you need a knowledgeable driver with a 4WD vehicle (non-4WDs won't make it along some of the rough tracks). Getting to these places across the surreal desert, with only the occasional herd of camels or sheep for company, is part of the fun. Partner Tour (p168), in Aktau, and Stantours (p130) are experienced operators offering trips. Day trips from Aktau in a 4WD for up to four passengers generally cost 40,000T to 60,000T; itineraries of several days, camping most nights, are also available.

Koshkar Ata

All of Kazakhstan is dotted with picturesque cemeteries or necropolises set outside villages and towns, and Mangistau has a notable concentration of them: locals boast the figure 362. Many of them date back to nomadic times, when tribes would bury their dead at special sites. Fascinating carvings adorn many of the older stone monuments in the necropolises – the commonest forms are the *kulpytas*, a

---

THE PILGRIMAGE TO BEKET-ATA

Beket-Ata, 285km east of Aktau, is an underground mosque to which the clairvoyant, healer and teacher Beket-Ata (1750–1813) retreated in the later part of his life, ultimately dying and being buried here. A Mangistau native, Beket-Ata studied in Khiva and on his return he is believed to have set up four mosques, including this one where he founded a Sufi school. Every day dozens of pilgrims – and on holidays, hundreds – make the bumpy journey across the deserts to pray and receive Beket-Ata's inspiration. The underground mosque (three caves) is set in a rocky outcrop, overlooking a desert canyon. You won't quickly forget the journey here across otherworldly desertscapes or the pilgrimage atmosphere that touches all visitors.

Aktau tour companies run two-day trips to Beket-Ata costing around 80,000T to 100,000T for up to four people. To do it independently, start by taking a minibus from Aktau bus station to the oil town of Zhanaozen (420T, two hours), 150km by paved road. From Zhanaozen bus station get a taxi to the bazaar (100T), where jeeps leave in the morning for Beket-Ata, charging 3500T per person or 14,000T for the vehicle, round trip. You'll spend most of the five- or six-hour trip to Beket-Ata (135km) lurching and bumping along steppe and desert tracks. En route, vehicles stop at Shopan-Ata, an underground mosque and large necropolis dating back to at least the 10th century, where Shopan-Ata, a disciple of Kozha Akhmed Yasaui (see p157) and inspiration to Beket-Ata, dwelt. Most groups sleep (free) in the pilgrim hostel–cum–mosque–cum–dining hall at Beket-Ata, before leaving early the next morning. Zhanaozen has hotels in the street along the east end of the bazaar, including **Hotel Lyuks** (☎ 72934-3 25 57; Mikrorayon Shanirak; r 4000-10,000T; ⊠) and the more dilapidated **Hotel Zhansa** (☎ 72934-3 49 29; Mikrorayon Shanirak; r 1500-2300T; ⊠). Best in town is **Hotel Aruana** (☎ 72934-6 33 88; Satpaev 2; s/d 12,135/13,635T; ℗ ⊠).

On arrival at Shopan-Ata and Beket-Ata all visitors are expected to purify themselves by using the squat toilets. If you're travelling with pilgrims, be ready to join in prayers and ritual walks around sacred trees. You may be invited to join meals of the Kazakh national dish *beshbarmak* (flat noodles with meat or vegetable broth), sitting round big bowls of food, eating with the right hand only.

carved stone column; the *koitas*, a stylised ram; the *koshkar-ta*s, a more realistic ram; and the sarcophaguslike *sandyk-tas*. One of the most interesting necropolises is **Koshkar Ata**, at Akshukur, 15km north of Aktau on the Fort Shevchenko road. Its skyline of miniature domes and towers resembles some fairytale fantasy city, and just inside the entrance is a fine example of an old *koshkar-tas*.

Fort Shevchenko

The dusty little town of Fort Shevchenko stands 130km north of Aktau near the tip of the Mangyshlak Peninsula. The **Local Museum** (admission 100T; ☺ 9am-noon & 2-6pm), in a yurt-shaped building near the minibus and taxi stand, includes material on the region's necropolises and underground mosques, but the best reason to come here is the **Shevchenko Museum** (admission 100T; ☺ 9am-noon & 2-6pm), behind the Local Museum. The great Ukrainian poet and artist Taras Shevchenko (1814–61) spent seven years in exile here in the 1850s, and the museum, housed in the old Russian military commandant's house, exhibits many of Shevchenko's penetrating landscapes, local scenes, portraits and self-portraits. Beside the house is the cellarlike **zemlyanka** (admission 100T; ☺ 9am-noon & 2-6pm), a half-underground room where the sympathetic commandant permitted Shevchenko to live and work.

Kafe Aybi (Abdikhalykov; dishes around 250T; ☺ 10am-midnight), by Fort Shevchenko's minibus stand, serves salads, *manty* and other local standards.

About 5km beyond Fort Shevchenko, the coastal village of **Bautino** is a service base for offshore oil and gas operations.

Minibuses to Fort Shevchenko (400T, two hours) leave from Aktau's bus station at 9am, 11am, 2pm, 5pm and 7pm (more frequently on Saturday and Sunday). The last one back to Aktau leaves Fort Shevchenko at 7pm.

Shakpak-Ata & Sultan Epe

Shakpak-Ata is perhaps the most intriguing of all Mangistau's underground mosques – a cross-shaped affair with three entrances and four chambers, cut into a cliff close to the Caspian coast. It's 133km north of Aktau and 37km northwest of the village of Taushik – the final 11km, north from the Taushik–Fort Shevchenko road, is down a stony, bumpy track. Shakpak-Ata probably dates back to the 10th century, and its walls are adorned with deeply incised Arabic inscriptions, sculpted

columns, weirdly weathered niches and drawings of horses and hands. The cliff is peppered with burial niches, and there's a necropolis of similar age below it, with more than 2000 tombs.

The signposted turning to Sultan Epe, another underground mosque and necropolis pairing, is 7km past the Shakpak-Ata turning on the Taushik–Fort Shevchenko road. You first reach the Kenty-Baba Necropolis, 7km from the road, with two towerlike mausoleums and other carved monuments. Sultan Epe is about 1km beyond, on the edge of a deep canyon. The necropolis – tomb of holy man Sultan Epe, considered the protector of sailors – is rich in carvings, while the underground mosque, of similar age to Shakpak-Ata, comprises several small rooms and low passages.

You can also reach these two sites by travelling east from Fort Shevchenko along the Taushik road, which is being improved.

Around Shetpe

The small town of Shetpe is 150km northeast of Aktau by paved road, and 70km east of Taushik. Seven kilometres towards Shetpe from the crossroads where the Shetpe and Taushik roads divide, you pass Torysh or the **Valley of Balls**, which is scattered with hundreds of giant stone balls, some over 2m wide. The awesome 332m chalk outcrop **Sherkala** (Lion Rock) rises mysteriously from the desert about 22km northwest of Shetpe, looking from some angles like a giant yurt. The paved road there from Shetpe passes between impressive uplands. A short detour en route leads to the remains of the medieval Silk Road town of **Kyzylkala**. At the foot of Sherkala's north side are the faint remains of a medieval caravanserai fort. You could reach Sherkala independently by taking a minibus from Aktau to Shetpe and then finding a taxi in Shetpe. In a 4WD it's possible to combine this area with Shakpak-Ata and Sultan Epe in one longish day trip.

NORTHERN KAZAKHSTAN

This is the most Russified part of Kazakhstan but it's also the location of the new capital, Astana, chief crucible of the prosperous, multiethnic Kazakhstan of the future and a spectacular exercise in capital-city creation that has to be seen to be believed.

The northern steppes also harbour surprising areas of natural beauty: the flamingo-filled lakes of Korgalzhyn; the hills, forests and lakes around Burabay; and the verdant countryside and tranquil villages southwest of Kokshetau.

Until the 19th century, this region was largely untouched except by Kazakh nomads and their herds. As Russia's hand stretched southwards, Russian and Ukrainian settlers came to farm the steppe – a million or more by 1900. In Soviet times, the Kazakhs were forced into collective farms and industrial cities such as Karaganda and Kostanay, which sprouted to exploit coal, iron ore and other minerals, and in the 1950s huge areas of steppe were turned over to wheat in Khrushchev's Virgin Lands scheme. More settlers, deportees and prisoners arrived from other parts of the USSR to work all the new projects. Ironically half the new wheatlands were abandoned by the 1980s because of wind erosion.

In the 1950s most of the labour camps were closed, but a lot of the survivors stayed. After the Soviet collapse many ethnic Germans, Russian and Ukrainians left, but Kazakhs still number less than one-third in several areas.

The climate is sharply continental and the most pleasant months to travel are May to September. In January and February *average* temperatures in Astana range between -11°C and -22°C, and bitter steppe winds can make it feel much colder still.

ASTANA АСТАНА

☎ 7172 / pop 620,000 / elev 350m

The country's spectacular new capital has risen fast from the northern steppe and is already a showpiece for 21st-century Kazakhstan. It is scheduled to go on rising and spreading into a city of over 1 million people by 2030. Its skyline grows more fantastical by the year as landmark buildings in a variety of Asian, Western, Soviet and wacky futuristic styles, many of them by leading international architects, sprout on vast acreage south of the Ishim River. Several spectacular structures are open to visitors and no one fails to be amazed by both the buildings themselves and the very concept of the place.

Just a medium-sized provincial city known for its bitter winters when President Nazarbaev named it out of the blue in 1994 as Kazakhstan's future capital, Astana replaced Almaty in 1997. The old centre lives on as a commercial and services centre. To the south, governmental and business buildings are going up, and also cultural, sports and leisure centres, hotels, a university and eye-catching residential developments. Around US$12 billion (some 30% of it from the government) had already been spent on building the new Astana by 2010. Some have dubbed it the 'Dubai of the steppe'.

Astana was founded in 1830 as a Russian fortress called Akmola (Kazakh for 'white tomb'). In the 1950s Akmola became the headquarters of the Virgin Lands scheme and was renamed Tselinograd (Virgin Lands City) in 1961. After the USSR collapsed, Akmola got back its old name. But Nazarbaev's plan to shift the capital attracted cynical comments that Akmola would be the president's own political 'white tomb'. Thus the place became simply Astana – Kazakh for 'capital'. Reasons cited by Nazarbaev for the change were Astana's location, more central and less earthquake-prone than Almaty's, and better transport links with Russia. Others have speculated that he may also have wanted to head off secessionist sentiments among the north's ethnic Russian population.

Astana is now a nexus of people from all over Kazakhstan. Some find it an impersonal place, but the country's ambitious and talented are increasingly drawn here. It's easy to question the spending of billions on prestige architecture, but many citizens are clearly proud of their new capital. As an exercise in nation building its merits are obvious.

Orientation

The Ishim River (Yesil in Kazakh) flows roughly southeast–northwest across the city. The old city is north of the river, known as the right bank (*pravy bereg* in Russian). The city centre, and most hotels, restaurants and other services, are still here. The showpiece governmental hub of Kazakhstan is growing up fast to the south (mostly on the left bank, *levy bereg*), on land that was once just a scattering of *dachas* (holiday bungalows) for the folk of Tselinograd.

The train and bus stations are side by side, 3km north of centre. The airport is 14km south.

Information

Internet Kafe Best (☎ 21 11 67; pr Respubliki 8; internet per hr 200T, Skype per hr with/without camera 500/300T; ⊙ 9am-midnight)

Main post office (Auezov 71; 🕐 8am-7pm Mon-Fri, 9am-4pm Sat, 10am-3pm Sun)
Online Club (☎ 79 09 51; Mega Astana, Korgalzhinskoe shosse 1; internet per hr 350T; 🕐 10am-midnight)
Otrar Travel (☎ 21 32 21; www.otrar.kz; pr Respubliki 9; 🕐 9am-10pm) Leading airline-booking and travel agent.

Sights & Activities

OLD CITY

The right bank is a mix of Soviet and post-independence architecture, plus a few now historic-looking tsarist-era houses. The yurt-shaped, blue-domed **Presidential Culture Centre** (☎ 22 33 08; pr Respubliki 2; admission free; 🕐 10am-5pm Tue-Sun) houses the high-quality main museum. Tours in English are available for 50T. The ground floor holds traditional Kazakh items: a brightly decked yurt, colourful carpets and costumes, elaborate horse tackle. The 2nd floor is devoted to archaeology, including *balbals* and models of some of the country's most important medieval buildings. Side rooms on this level hold outstanding collections of Kazakh jewellery and of 'gold and gold-makings', the latter including replicas of the Golden Man and the 'second Golden Man' from western Kazakhstan (see p166), gold jewellery from the Scythian burial mounds at Berel (p189), a bejewelled replica of a horse from the Berel tomb, and real 4th-century-BC horse innards pickled in formaldehyde! The 3rd floor covers Kazakhstan from the 15th to 20th centuries, and the 4th floor is mainly devoted to the history of Astana.

The **Contemporary Art Museum** (☎ 21 54 33; pr Respubliki 3; admission 200T; 🕐 10am-6pm Tue-Sat, to 5pm Sun) has a permanent collection with some striking works, and stages regular temporary exhibitions.

The **President's Museum** (☎ 75 12 14; Beibitshilik 11; admission free; 🕐 tours 10.30am, noon, 2.30pm & 4pm Tue-Sun) is a fascinating peep into the pomp and circumstance surrounding the country's leader. Housed in the former presidential palace, it's a succession of supremely lavish galleries and halls decked with beautiful gifts to President Nazarbaev from foreign governments and grateful citizens. Check out the bank of Cold War–style direct-line phones in the antechamber to the presidential office itself. Obligatory tours are in Russian but it's normally OK to stray from the group. The entrance is on Abay.

NEW CITY

City Park & Around

The large **city park** on the south side of the river is reached by a footbridge from the south end of Zheltoksan. At its south end you'll find the **Monument to the Dead of the Totalitarian Regime** (a mound topped with a giant Kazakhstan flag) and the **Atameken** (☎ 22 16 36; admission 200T; English-language tours 500T; 🕐 9am-10pm), a 200m-long, walk-around country map with models of major buildings – quite fun. Adjacent is **Duman** (☎ 24 22 22; www.duman.kz; adult/child 100/50T, oceanarium 1000/500T; 🕐 10am-8pm Tue-Sun), a modern leisure centre most worth visiting for its oceanarium, which has over 2000 creatures from the world's oceans and a 70m shark tunnel. Opposite Duman are the UFO-shaped **Circus** and the shiny new Mega Astana shopping centre.

Khan Shatyr

The extraordinary **Khan Shatyr** (www.khanshatyr.com; Turan) rises 1.5km south of Mega Astana. This 150m-high, transparent, leaning, tentlike structure is made of a special heat-absorbing material that produces summer temperatures inside even when it's -30°C outside. Expected to open by late 2010, its multilevel interior includes botanical gardens, minigolf, shops, cafes, a concert and events area and, near the top, an aquapark with a large pool, slides and great views. It was designed by celebrated British architect Norman Foster.

The Khan Shatyr marks, for the moment, the western end of the main axis of new Astana. To its east, across a park, stands the grand headquarters of the state energy company, **KazMunayGaz**.

Nurzhol bulvar

East of KazMunayGaz begins **Nurzhol bulvar**, the central showpiece boulevard of Kazakhstan's new governmental and administrative zone, a 2km line of gardens and plazas that leads east to the presidential palace and is flanked by large and imaginative buildings in various stages of construction. First up on the north side is the tall, copper-and-glass **Transport & Communications Ministry** – dubbed the 'Lighter' for its form by irreverent locals. Detour a block south here to the **Islamic Centre** (🕐 9am-8pm), which has a beautiful four-minaret mosque opened in 2005. The mosque's interior is an exquisite multidomed space with inscriptions and

KAZAKHSTAN

ASTANA

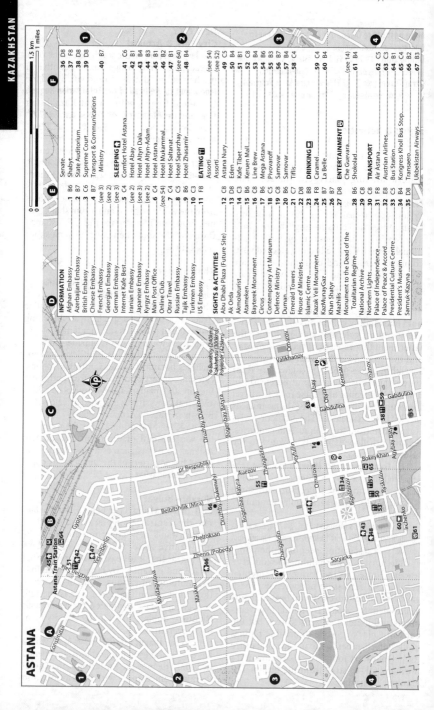

INFORMATION		
Afghan Embassy	1	B6
Azerbaijani Embassy	2	B7
British Embassy	3	C6
Chinese Embassy	4	B7
French Embassy	(see 3)	
Georgian Embassy	(see 2)	
German Embassy	(see 3)	
Internet Kafe Best	5	C4
Iranian Embassy	(see 2)	
Japanese Embassy	(see 3)	
Kyrgyz Embassy	(see 2)	
Main Post Office	6	C4
Online Club	(see 54)	
Otrar Travel	7	C4
Russian Embassy	8	B6
Tajik Embassy	9	B6
Turkmen Embassy	10	C3
US Embassy	11	F8
SIGHTS & ACTIVITIES		
Abu Dhabi Plaza (Future Site)	12	C8
Ak Orda	13	D8
Akmolaturist	14	C3
Atameken	15	B6
Bayterek Monument	16	C8
Circus	17	B6
Contemporary Art Museum	18	C5
Defence Ministry	19	C8
Duman	20	B6
Emerald Towers	21	C7
House of Ministries	22	D8
Islamic Centre	23	B8
Kazak Yeli Monument	24	F8
KazMunayGaz	25	B7
Khan Shatyr	26	B7
Mazhilis	27	D8
Monument to the Dead of the		
Totalitarian Regime	28	B6
National Archive	29	C8
Northern Lights	30	C8
Palace of Independence	31	F8
Palace of Peace & Accord	32	E8
Presidential Culture Centre	33	C5
President's Museum	34	B4
Samruk-Kazyna	35	D8

Senate	36	D8
Shabyt	37	F8
State Auditorium	38	D8
Supreme Court	39	D8
Transport & Communications		
Ministry	40	B7
SLEEPING 🛏		
Comfort Hotel Astana	41	C6
Hotel Abay	42	B1
Hotel Altyn Dala	43	B4
Hotel Altyn-Adam	44	B3
Hotel Astana	45	B1
Hotel Mukammal	46	B2
Hotel Saltanat	47	B1
Hotel Saparzhay	(see 64)	
Hotel Zhasamir	48	B4
EATING 🍴		
Assorti	(see 54)	
Assorti	(see 52)	
Astana Nury	49	C5
Eden	50	B4
Kafe Tibet	51	B1
Keruen Mall	52	C8
Line Brew	53	B4
Mega Astana	54	B6
Pivovaroff	55	B3
Samovar	56	B7
Samovar	57	B4
Tifis	58	C4
DRINKING 🍷		
Caramel	59	C4
La Belle	60	B4
ENTERTAINMENT 🎭		
Che Guevara	(see 14)	
Shokolad	61	B4
TRANSPORT		
Air Astana	62	C5
Austrian Airlines	63	C3
Bus Station	64	B1
Kongress Kholl Bus Stop	65	C4
Transaero	66	B2
Ukbekistan Airways	67	B3

0   **1.5 km**
0   **1 miles**

To Burabay (240km);
Kokshetau (300km);
Pavlodar (425km)

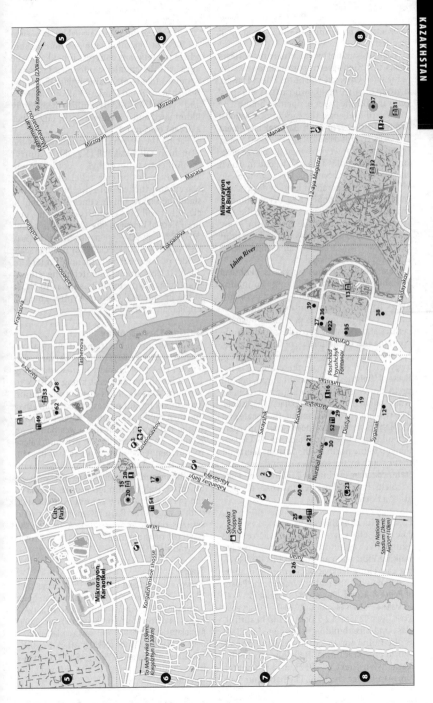

geometrical patterning in blue, green, gold and red.

Back on Nurzhol bulvar admire the **Northern Lights**, three light-green apartment towers with wavy sides. Opposite will be the **Emerald Towers**, a group of office blocks whose tops will splay outward like the pages of opening books. The boulevard leads past the egg-domed **National Archive** to the 97m-high **Bayterek monument** (☎ 24 08 35; adult/child 500/150T; ♥ 10am-11pm), a white latticed tower crowned by a large glass orb. This embodies a Kazakh legend in which the mythical bird Samruk lays a golden egg containing the secrets of human desires and happiness in a tall poplar tree, beyond human reach. A lift glides visitors up inside the egg, where you can ponder the symbolism, enjoy expansive views and place your hand in a print of President Nazarbaev's palm while gazing eastward towards his palace.

East along Nurzhol bulvar is **ploshchad Poyushchykh Fontanov** (Singing Fountains Square), where music-and-water performances happen about 9pm on summer evenings. Twin golden-green, conical business centres stand east of here: the southern one contains the headquarters of **Samruk-Kazyna**, Kazakhstan's sovereign wealth fund. Curving away left and right from these towers is the **House of Ministries**, and straight ahead, behind pretty flower gardens, stands the blue-domed, white-pillared presidential palace, the **Ak Orda**. The two houses of parliament, the **Senate** and the **Mazhilis**, rise behind the left-hand ministerial building. The space before the Ak Orda is flanked to the north by the **Supreme Court** and to the south by the spectacular and large new **State Auditorium** (architects: Manfredi and Luca Nicoletti, Italy), whose design evokes the petals of a flower.

East of Nurzhol Bulvar

The new city's axis continues across the Ishim River behind the Ak Orda. To save walking 2km you can hop on bus 40, heading east along Dostyk or north or Orynbor, to Astana's unmistakable pyramid, the **Palace of Peace & Accord** (Dvorets Mira i Soglasya; ☎ 74 47 44; Manasa 57; tours adult/child 500/300T; ♥ tours every 45min, 10am-12.15pm & 2-5.45pm). This beautiful, glass-and-steel building was opened in 2006 as the home for the triennial Congress of World and Traditional Religions, hosted by Kazakhstan (next in 2012), and is another Norman Foster creation. The half-hour tour

(English-speaking guides available) shows you a 1300-seat opera hall, the 3rd-floor atrium where the religions congress is held, and the apex with its circular conference table and windows filled with stained-glass doves (by British artist Brian Clarke). Full of symmetry and symbolism, the pyramid is beautifully illuminated and a highlight of the city. It has a decent cafe, too.

Facing the pyramid across Manasa is the 91m-high tall **Kazak Yeli** (Kazakh Country) monument, topped by a golden eagle and with a 5m bronze relief of President Nazarbaev tucked into its base. Behind stand the **Shabyt**, a high, concave ring of blue glass that will house an arts university, and the **Palace of Independence** (Dvorets Nezavisimosti; ☎ 70 03 89; tours 400T; ♥ 10am-1pm & 2-6pm Tue-Sun), well worth a visit especially for its huge scale model of how Astana is planned to look in 2030. It also holds an interesting ethnographic hall with exhibits similar to those at the Presidential Culture Centre. Tours in English are available.

Getting There & Away

Bus 21 runs from the train station south on Zhenis, west on Abay, south on Saryarka and Turan, east past Duman then south along Kabanbay Batyr and east along Dostyk to Bayterek. Bus 42 starts at the train station and runs south on pr Respubliki from Abay and then south on Kabanbay Batyr. Returning to the old town, catch these westbound on Konaev. To go direct to the pyramid/Palace of Independence area you can use bus 40, which starts at the train station, heads south on Zhenis and east across the old town on Seyfullin, wiggles through eastern Astana to the pyramid and then continues to Dostyk, with a stop at the Bayterek monument (and returns on the same route). A taxi to the Bayterek or the pyramid from the old town is around 700T.

Tours

Travel agency **Sayat** (☎ 36 52 52; http://sayattravel. kz) has a kiosk outside the train station, open summer only, where you can join a two-hour city bus tour (in Russian) for 800T. **Akmolaturist** (☎ 33 02 07/04; www.akmolatourist.com; Office 22, Hotel Abay, pr Respubliki 33) offers English-speaking guides at 13,700/15,800T for two-/three-hour city tours if you provide the transport.

Sleeping

Hotel prices in Astana are high. The more economical lodgings cluster near the train and bus stations and are not great value.

Hotel Astana (☎ 93 28 97; Gyote 1; dm 2000-2500T; r 8000T) Upstairs in the west end of the train station, the Astana is bare bones but clean and has friendly staff. Dorms have up to six beds and shared bathrooms.

Hotel Saparzhay (☎ 38 11 36; Gyote 9; r 2400-5000T) Dreary digs in the bus station, though the receptionists are friendly enough. The cheapest rooms share bathrooms.

Hotel Abay (☎ 93 32 96; Birzhan-Sala 3A; s 3000-7000T, d 5000-10,000T; 🞩) Well-used lodgings in a short sidestreet 1½ blocks out the front of the train station. The rooms are mostly good sized, with phone, bathroom and TV. Half-price for under 12 hours.

Hotel Saltanat (☎ 38 31 21; Yesenberlin 13; r 5000-9000T) The Saltanat, 500m from the train station (turn left at the intersection with the large Opera & Ballet Theatre), has neat, decent-sized rooms in pastel shades. Discounts for under 12 hours.

Hotel Altyn-Adam (☎ 32 77 24; altyn.adam@mail.ru; Seyfullin 26; s 7000-11,000T; d 12,000-13,000T; lux 15,000-18,000T; 🅿 🞩 🛜) The 'Golden Man' is a modern, central hotel with rooms that are nothing fancy but well sized and perfectly comfortable. It has a good little cafe/restaurant, where you'll eat your included breakfast before the snarling stares of a stuffed wolf and lynx. It offers around one-third off the price for stays under 12 hours. Staff speak no English.

Hotel Zhasamir (☎ 32 33 97; www.jasamir.kz; Kenesary 17; s/d 10,000/17,000T; 🅿 🞩 🖥 🛜) The Zhasamir has good-sized rooms low on clutter but curiously big on sparkle and frills. But it's not a 'love hotel', and the prices are good for Astana. Breakfast is included.

Hotel Mukammal (☎ 30 29 06; www.mukammal.kz; Zhenis 53/1; s 12,000-17,500T, d 24,000T; 🅿 🞩 🖥 🛜) This well-run, 40-room hotel halfway to the train station provides friendly attention, cosy, carpeted rooms in golden tones, sparkling bathrooms, and a good little Kazakh and European restaurant. Breakfast is included and there are good discounts on Friday to Sunday nights.

Hotel Altyn Dala (☎ 32 33 11; www.altyndala.kz; Bigeldinov 8/1; s 13,000-20,000T, d 18,000-26,000T; 🅿 🞩 🛜) The Altyn Dala has a newer, more expensive building at the front and the original, cheaper one behind; both have cosy rooms. Rates include both breakfast and lunch, although the meals are nothing to get too excited about. Reception staff are always courteous.

Comfort Hotel Astana (☎ 22 10 21; www.comfortho tel.kz; Kosmonavtov 60; s/d 26,600/40,000T; 🅿 🞩 🞩 🛜) South of the river, the two-storey Comfort lives right up to its name. With a quiet lobby lounge, an international restaurant and attentive, professional service it's a tasteful retreat from the city hustle. Rates include breakfast; half-price deals are often available at weekends.

Eating

Kafe Tibet (Birzhan-Sala; mains 300-450T; 🕙 8am-10pm; 🇪) This neat and bright little restaurant near the train station does good *laghman, manty, plov* and chicken and beef dishes at very good prices. Try the slightly spicy *guyru laghman*, with meat and veggies. Some staff even speak English.

Samovar (mains 400-1000T; 🇪); Old Town (☎ 32 43 16; Kenesary 24; 🕙 24hr); Left Bank (☎ 97 41 71; Kabanbay

---

ASTANA: MUCH MORE TO COME

The Palace of Peace & Accord, currently near the southeast edge of the city, is conceived as Astana's symbolic centre, and by 2030 it will be near the geographical centre too. The southern part of the city is planned to spread far beyond its current extents.

Landmark projects in the pipeline include Batygai, a self-contained 'indoor town' for 10,000 people west of the Khan Shatyr; 'Mini-Venice', a residential complex with canals, west of Batygai; and Abu Dhabi Plaza, a cluster of towers south of the Bayterek Monument, which will be Astana's tallest building (372m) and is yet another Norman Foster project.

The design of the new National Library (architects: Bjarke Ingels Group, Denmark), south of the State Auditorium, is based on a Möbius strip. It may look like a giant metallic doughnut.

On the airport road 3km south of Nurzhol bulvar, the 30,000-seat National Stadium, with a retractable roof, opened in 2009.

Batyr 25; ☾ noon-2am) A cheerful Russian restaurant-cafe where helpful, red-silk-shirted waiters serve a good range of fare from breakfasts, *bliny* and soups to lunch and dinner mains.

Eden (☎ 32 43 16; Kenesary 24; mains 800-2300T; ☾ noon-midnight) Tasteful and slightly formal, the Eden restaurant is a good choice if you want to converse over a good dinner. It's strong on Russian and European meat and fish dishes.

Astana Nury (☎ 22 39 22; pr Respubliki 3/2; mains 1000-4000T; ☾ noon-1am; ☎ **E**) This top-class Azerbaijani restaurant has two lovely summer decks overlooking the river and an inside dining room with beautiful Azeri decor. The many varieties of shashlyk and Azeri *pilaw* (rice) dishes are among the best on the menu and at its cheaper end.

Pivovaroff (☎ 32 88 66; Beibitshilik 24; lunch buffet 1280T, mains 1100-3500T; ☾ noon-2am; **E**) Office workers pile into this beer cellar for the buffet of good fresh salads, soups and hot main dishes, available noon to 4pm Monday to Friday. Á la carte, there are good sausages, steaks and shashlyk – as well as house-brewed, unfiltered Staronemetskoe (Old German) beer.

Tiflis (☎ 22 12 26; Imanov 14; mains 1500-4000T; ☾ 11am-2am; ✕ **E**) This upscale Georgian restaurant has gone all out with its decor, right down to the hay carts and staff decked out in traditional garb. The Georgian food is pretty good too, and the roaring log fire is wonderful in winter.

Line Brew (☎ 23 63 73; Kenesary 20; mains 1700-4000T, 0.5L beer 460T; ☾ noon-2am; **E**) You can't miss Line Brew's large, red-brick castle building, and the interior is, well, like the inside of a castle, with a tavern atmosphere. The food runs a gamut from Greek salad to Angus or horse steaks, grilled pike-perch or homemade pasta. A shashlyk grill flames in the middle of the room, and a nice pop/rock/jazz band plays nightly except Monday. There are plenty of Belgian and other beers too.

SHOPPING CENTRES

Mega Astana (Korgalzhinskoe shosse 1) and **Keruen Mall** (Nurzhol bulvar) both have convenient **food courts** (dishes 400-800T; ☾ 10am-midnight) and branches of **Assorti** (☾ noon-midnight; mains 1100-3000T); Mega Astana (☎ 79 14 71); Keruen Mall (☎ 79 53 97), which does fine pizzas and grills in a relaxed ambience.

Drinking & Entertainment
COFFEE LOUNGES
Caramel (☎ 22 25 41; Imanov 10A; cake & coffee around 1000T; ☾ 9am-11pm Mon-Thu, 10am-1am Fri-Sun; ✕ ☎) A tasteful, spacious and relaxed coffee house that's great to drop in to for a caffeine-and-sugar pick-me-up.

La Belle (☎ 23 06 00; Irchenko 12; coffees, cakes & desserts 400-800T; ☾ noon-2am; ☎) This dim-lit, well-heeled lounge is a place to sink into sofas or big leather chairs and while away at least one hour. You can order almost any coffee concoction, with or without ice cream or liquor. Alcoholic beverages are the go in the evening.

BARS & NIGHTCLUBS
our pick Che Guevara (☎ 701-257 0909; admission usually free; pr Respubliki 33A; ☾ 8pm-4am) This cool bar/club attracts an artsy-professional 20s and 30s crowd, with DJs spinning assorted sounds from deep house to funk or soul. You can just go for a drink or food, or stay around after it livens up around midnight.

Shokolad (Chocolate; ☎ 99 00 33; Saryarka 2; ☾ noon-3am Mon-Thu, 10pm-6am Fri & Sat, 6pm-6am Sun) In the bowels of the Radisson Hotel, on Friday and Saturday nights Chocolate is the hottest club in town. If you get past the face control (look your best) you'll have a wild time dancing to electro, house and R&B DJs. Admission varies from free upwards but for a table (with food) you're looking at a minimum of 50,000T.

Getting There & Away
Astana has increasingly good connections with the rest of the country and the rest of the world. The official city website (www.astana.kz) helpfully gives train and air schedules in English.

AIR
At the **airport** (☎ 70 29 99; www.astanaairport.kz), Air Astana flies at least four times daily to Almaty (18,000T to 20,000T), once daily to Aktobe (20,000T to 24,000T), Atyrau (29,000T; with connections for Aktau, 37,000T), Kyzylorda (20,000T), Uralsk (22,000T to 26,000T) and Ust-Kamenogorsk (17,000T to 20,000T), and four times a week to Pavlodar (8500T), Petropavlovsk (8500T) and also Semey (16,000T). SCAT goes to Shymkent (23,500T to 26,500T) daily, and Aktau (30,000T) and Taraz (22,000T) twice or more weekly.

See p199 for international flights.

Airline Offices

Air Astana City (☎ 59 14 04; Office 9, 2nd fl, Ramstor, Dom 11, Mikrorayon Samal; 🕙 9am-9pm); Airport (☎ 28 64 65; 🕙 24hr)

Austrian Airlines City (☎ 39 00 00; Hotel Ramada Plaza, Abay 47); Airport (☎ 77 73 04)

Lufthansa (lufthansaastana@dlh.de; Airport; 🕙 8-10pm Mon, Wed & Sat, 11pm-2am Tue, Thu & Sun)

Transaero City (☎ 91 14 00; Druzhby 7); Airport (☎ 77 72 66)

Turkish Airlines (☎ 77 70 20/21; Airport)

Uzbekistan Airways (☎ 23 60 43; Room 17, Saryarka 31)

TRAIN

From the **train station** (☎ 38 07 07; Gyote 7), trains go to Karaganda (1440T, four hours) at least 12 times daily, to Almaty (4500T, 13 to 22 hours) at least six times daily, to Kokshetau (600T to 1600T, five hours) at least five times daily and to Petropavlovsk at least three times daily (2100T, eight to 11 hours). The speedy, comfortable Talgo (train 2) to Almaty (13 hours) leaves at 7.15pm, costing 10,300/15,100T in 3rd/2nd class, but can get booked up days in advance. There are also daily trains to Moscow, Pavlodar and Shymkent, and trains to Aktobe, Atyrau, Omsk, Semey and Yekaterinburg at least every two days. Train 54 to Ürümqi, China (17,300T, 33 hours) leaves on Tuesday; train 53 to Astana departs Ürümqi on Friday.

BUS, MINIBUS & TAXI

From the **bus station** (☎ 38 11 35; Gyote 9) buses and minibuses run to many destinations including Almaty (4300T, 17 hours, three daily), Karaganda (800T, 4½ hours, 30 or more daily), Kokshetau (1200T, five hours, nine daily), Pavlodar (1600T, seven to eight hours, seven daily), Petropavlovsk (2200T, 10 hours, five daily), Semey (3400T, 15 hours, five daily) and Ust-Kamenogorsk (4000T, 17 hours, two daily). There's a daily service to Omsk and Novosibirsk in Russia.

Private minibuses and taxis to Burabay (see p181), Karaganda (minibus/shared taxi 1200/1500T, 2½ hours) and Kokshetau (1500/2000T, 3½ hours) wait outside the bus station.

Getting Around

Astana has an excellent city bus (60T) and marshrutka (65T) network; check www.astana .kz for route maps in English.

Bus 10 runs about every 15 minutes, from around 6am to midnight, between the bus station and the airport (a one-hour trip), via Yesenberlin, Beibitshilik, Seyfullin, Respubliki and Konaev (and vice versa). A taxi between the airport and centre is usually 2000T. Buses 25 and 31 run from the train station to the Kongress Kholl (Congress Hall) stop in the city centre, then south on pr Respubliki at least as far as Ramstor.

Taxi drivers ask 500T for rides in the central area. You can often flag down a passing car for less.

AROUND ASTANA

During the Stalin years **Malinovka** (also called Akmol), 35km west of Astana, housed ALZhIR, a notorious camp for wives and children of men who were interned elsewhere as 'betrayers of the motherland'. The **Museum of Victims of Repression** (admission 120T; 🕙 10am-5pm Tue-Sun) conveys something of life in the camp and documents Soviet repression in Kazakhstan. A memorial alley behind the museum is lined by plaques with the prisoners' names. Akmolaturist (p176) will take a minibus-load with an English-speaking guide for 13,000T.

Further west past Malinovka, **Korgalzhyn Nature Reserve** is a Unesco World Heritage Site (part of the Steppe and Lakes of Saryarka), with numerous steppe lakes at the crossroads of two major bird migration routes. The more than 300 bird species recorded here include pelicans and cranes, and from April to September salty Lake Tengiz supports the world's most northerly flamingo colony (several thousand of these birds migrate to the Caspian Sea during winter). A good new **visitors centre** (Madina 20; admission 300T; 🕙 9am-6pm Wed-Sun) in the small town of Korgalzhyn, 130km from Astana, has a cafe, a library and exhibits on birds, migration and the local area. The town also has a community ecotourism program offering simple but clean **homestays** (per person incl 3 meals 5000T) and guided birdwatching trips outside the reserve itself but still with plenty of lakes and interesting birdlife (guides cost around 400T per hour). To make arrangements contact the EIRC in Almaty (p130), the local NGO **Rodnik** (☎ 71637-2 10 43, 701-602 8751; oorodnik@mail.ru; Madina 20; 🕙 9am-6pm Mon-Fri), or homestay owners **Timur and Kenzhe Iskakov** (timur_iskak@mail.ru) or **Bibinur and Marat Alimzhanov** (nursultan32@mail.ru).

For permits and guides in the reserve itself, contact the **reserve office** (☎ 71637-2 16 50), also in the visitors centre building. Alternatively, Akmolaturist (p176) has **cabins** (per person 3500T; May-Sep) beside Sultankeldy Lake in the reserve, and will be able to sort out permits and guides (2250T per hour).

Buses to Malinovka (255T, one hour) and Korgalzhyn (1000T, 2½ hours) leave Astana bus station eight times daily between 10am and 7.40pm. A taxi to Korgalzhyn is around 5000T. The Korgalzhyn ecotourism people can arrange car transfers for 10,000T each way. Akmolaturist offers a minibus for 30,000T return.

LAKE BURABAY ОЗЕРО БУРАБАЙ
☎ 71630

Lake Burabay, some 240km north of Astana, is the focus of **Burabay National Nature Park** (www.gnpp.kz, in Russian), a picturesque 835-sq-km area of lakes, hills, pine forests and strange rock formations. The repository of several Kazakh legends and with recently much-improved facilities, the park is well worth a visit for anyone who's in the north. President Nazarbaev has a summer holiday home beside little Lake Karasie.

The roughly circular Lake Burabay is 15km north of Shchuchinsk, which lies on the Astana–Kokshetau road and railway. The small town of Burabay (formerly Borovoe) stretches about 2.5km along the lake's northeast shore. The brightly revamped **Visitor Centre & Nature Museum** (Vizit-Tsentr & Tabigat Murazhayy; Kenesary; admission 370T; 10am-8pm Tue-Sun Jun-Aug, 9am-6pm Tue-Sun Sep-May), on the main road in the town, contains a diverse display of stuffed wildlife from Kazakhstan's national parks, a 3-D model of the park and two ATMs. The *otdel turizma* (tourism department) here can give you a park map and may be able to answer questions in English. Next door and included in the admission price is an outdoor zoo with two Przewalski's horses, several deer (including a pair of maral) and various raptors, bears, wolves and raccoons in small enclosures.

A well-made **walking path** parallels the road for 9km from the lake's southeast corner to the northwest corner via Burabay town. Heading west from the town it's a 4km walk (or 500T taxi) to the picturesque **Goluboy Zaliv** (Blue Bay), a place with a specially mystical aura for Kazakhs. The most celebrated

Burabay legend links **Zhumbaktas**, the Sphinx-like rock sticking out of the lake here, with **Okzhetpes**, the striking 380m-tall rock pile rising behind it. While Abylay Khan's army was fighting the Zhungars back in the 18th century, a beautiful princess was captured and brought to Burabay, where many Kazakh warriors fancied her as a wife. The princess agreed to give her hand to the first warrior who could shoot an arrow to the top of Okzhetpes. All failed, hence the name Okzhetpes, which means 'Unreachable by Arrows'. The distraught princess then drowned herself in the lake, thus creating Zhumbaktas (Mysterious Stone).

You can rent a **rowing boat** (per 30/60 min 1000/2000T) in front of the large Hotel Abilay Khan at Goluboy Zaliv to paddle out to Zhumbaktas. Continue 1.75km further round the lake and you reach **Polyana Abylay Khana** (Abylay Khan's Clearing), where the warrior hero reputedly once assembled his forces during his Zhungar campaigns. A tall, eagle-topped monument, with good old Ab astride a snow leopard, stands in the clearing; a large, flat-topped rock known as Abylay Khan's Throne hides in the trees behind. A path from the back of the clearing leads up 947m **Mt Kokshetau**, the highest peak in the park (about 1½ hours to the top).

A shorter and gentler climb, with good views of both Lake Burabay and the larger Lake Bolshoe Chebachie to its north, is **Mt Bolektau**. This takes about half an hour by the track heading up to the right just before the Km 4 post heading west from Burabay town.

Local agencies offer a variety of group trips in the park, usually with Russian-speaking guides. Possibilities include horse riding to Kenesary's Cave (Peshchera Kenesary) on the south side of Lake Burabay (1700T, three hours), hiking Mt Kokshetau (1500T, three hours) and climbing Okzhetpes (1700T). Gentle gradients make the area good for **cycling**: to rent a bike look for '*Prokat Velosipedov*' signs along the main road in Burabay.

Sleeping

The choice of hotels in and near Burabay town is wide and good. It's also fairly easy to rent rooms, cabins, apartments or even yurts for 1000T to 2000T per person: look for signs saying '*sdam komnati/domiki/kvartiry/yurty*' along the main street, Kenesary.

Baza Otdykha Akmolaturist No 1 (☎7 15 11; Kenesary 55; per person 1500T) By the roundabout at the entrance to Burabay from Shchuchinsk, this friendly little place provides cosy rooms for up to six people, with a shared kitchen and clean shared bathrooms. Meals are available for 2500T per person. You can book through Akmolaturist (p176) in Astana.

Hotel Nursat (☎7 13 01; www.bereke-burabai. com; Kenesary 26; r 6000-9000T; P) This red-brick hotel, almost opposite the Nature Museum, has large, bright and comfy if plain rooms. Breakfast is included.

Hotel Kokshebel (☎7 11 97; www.kokshebel. com; Kenesary 2A; cabins 8000-12,000T; r 22,000-32,000T; P 🖿 🕿) This is a well-built, well-run, new hotel with attractive pine-wooded grounds stretching down to the lakeshore (with private beach) at the west end of town. The rooms are comfortable and well equipped, with breakfast included. The cosy wooden cabins, holding up to five people, are under the pines close to the lake.

Eating

Burabay's main smattering of nonhotel eateries is along Kenesary near the central bus and taxi stop.

Kafe Dostar (Kenesary 10A; mains 500-800T; 🕙9am-2am) This pleasant, semiopen-air restaurant a short walk west of the bus stop serves up steaks and carp as well as the more usual shashlyk, *plov, manty* and *laghman*.

Kafe Alina (☎7 20 20; Kenesary 23; mains 500-900T; 🕙9am-1am; 🗶) Done out in pinks and purples, Alina is just east of the bus stop and turns out respectable salads and meat dishes. It has a nice summer terrace.

ourpick Kafe Taranchi (Kenesary; mains 600-800T; 🕙10am-2am) The Taranchi has an unmissable castlelike exterior, almost opposite Kafe Dostar. Good Uyghur *laghman, plov* and *toshkan* (a spicy meat, onion and noodles dish), and some Russian dishes, are served in an interior that conjures up an old caravanserai: gourds dangle from a wood-and-matting ceiling, and pseudocrumbling white brick walls are hung with interesting art and ikat.

Getting There & Around

Minibuses (1300T to 1500T, three hours) and shared taxis (2000T, 2½ hours) to Burabay leave from outside Astana's bus station when full. Daytime departures are plentiful in summer and at weekends. In Burabay the bus and taxi stop is just off the main street, Kenesary, towards the west end of town. To and from Kokshetau there are three buses or minibuses (450T, two hours) per day; shared taxis are 500T. More plentiful transport (at least 22 buses) runs from both Astana and Kokshetau to Shchuchinsk, from where buses or minibuses (150T, 30 minutes) run every 40 minutes (7am to 7pm) to Burabay. Shared/charter taxis between Shchuchinsk and Burabay are 200/800T.

KOKSHETAU КОКШЕТАУ
☎7162 / pop 134,000

Though one of Kazakhstan's less affluent cities, Kokshetau, 290km north of Astana, is a friendly and pleasant enough jumping-off point for community-tourism homestays in the pretty rural area to its southwest. The town has half a dozen universities and teaching colleges, and makes a lot of bread. Have a stroll around the central area between Abay and Auezov, where you'll find several green park areas.

Contact the community-tourism organisation **Ekos** (☎/fax 26 64 60; http://ecos.koks.kz; Chapaeva 37), at the west end of town, to set up a trip to the villages of Zerenda (40km southwest of Kokshetau), Sandyktau, Ayyrtau and Imantau (all 80km to 90km southwest). The main attraction here is the experience of village life amid unspoiled countryside with lakes, woodlands, rocky hills and walking and riding routes. Kazakh music and dance performances and outings to local historic sites are also on offer. The **homestays** (per person incl 3 meals 3000-5000T) are mostly in modernised village family homes. Only a few have indoor toilets but most have Russian bathhouses and all can provide hot water. Trail guides cost 4400T per day (English- and German-speaking guides are available in Ayyrtau and Zerenda), horse rides cost 1500T per day, and local taxis cost 70T per kilometre. A 48-hour visit normally adds up to between 12,000T and 25,000T per person in total. Buses or marshrutkas run several times daily from Kokshetau bus station to Imantau (420T, two hours), Sandyktau (390T to 460T, two hours), Zerenda (220T to 250T, one hour) and to Lobanovo (360T), from which it's a 500T taxi ride to Ayyrtau (total two hours). Ekos can organise a taxi for you for around 3000T to or from Zerenda or 6000T for the other villages.

Sleeping & Eating

Hotel Kokshetau (☎ 25 64 27; Abay 106; r 3600-11,000T; **P**) This Soviet-era hotel has dowdy rooms and a smoky smell throughout, but helpful and friendly staff and a very central location.

Hotel Zhekebatur (☎ 26 96 34; qulshat_z@mail.ru; Auezov 184; s/d from 6500/9000T; **⬛**) The best hotel, with comfy rooms sporting satellite TV, plus a restaurant, and a sauna with a spring-fed pool. Breakfast is included.

Novinka Fast Food (Kuybysheva 31; dishes 300-750T; ◷ 10am-11pm) Bright Turkish cafe with the best pizzas in town, good doners and burgers. No alcohol.

Kafe Piramida (☎ 25 56 88; Kuybysheva 93; mains 500-1000T; ◷ noon-1am; ✗) With a small pyramid on its roof, this central spot has a cool little cafe downstairs and a restaurant with big windows upstairs. You can get salads, meat and fish dishes, *bliny* and real coffee in both parts.

Getting There & Around

The train and bus stations are at the end of Abay, 2km east of the centre. Shared taxis to Petropavlovsk (2000T, two hours), and mini-buses/shared taxis to Astana (1500/2000T, 3½ hours) wait in front of the train station. At least three daily trains go to Astana (600T to 1600T, five to six hours) and Petropavlovsk (1500T, four hours). Buses dawdle at least 12 times daily to both places. Bus 1 (35T) runs between the stations and the town centre. Taxis in town are 400T.

PETROPAVLOVSK (PETROPAVL)
ПЕТРОПАВЛОВСК
(ПЕТРОПАВЛ)
☎ 7152 / pop 207,000 / elev 140m

Just 60km from the Russian border, Petropavlovsk is as much a part of Siberia as of Kazakhstan, and has a high Russian population. It's a reasonably prosperous and attractive place, older and architecturally more diverse than many cities in Kazakhstan. It was founded as a Russian fort in the 1750s and later developed as a trade, railway and industrial centre.

Orientation

The main downtown axis, Konstitutsii Kazakhstana, runs northwest–southeast and is attractively tree lined and pedestrianised – a popular hangout. The train and bus stations are about 2.5km southeast of the heart of town, off Satpaeva.

Sights

The new **Abylay Khan Residence Museum** (☎ 49 21 32; Sutyusheva 1B; admission 180T; ◷ 10am-6pm Tue-Sun) is devoted to the 18th-century Kazakh leader who spearheaded resistance to the invading Zhungars. This 19th-century building (restored at a cost of 606T million) stands on the site of an earlier wooden residence built for Abylay by the Russians. Two richly decorated rooms are set up as Abylay's private chamber and throne room. Other features include a model of the Yasaui mausoleum at Turkistan (Abylay's burial place), Abylay's family tree tracing his lineage back to Zhanibek (the founder of the Kazakh khanate in the 15th century) and a grand diorama of Kazakh and Zhungar cavalry armies charging into each other. No English-language explanatory material or tours, unfortunately. To reach the museum walk to the northwest end of Konstitutsii Kazakhstana (1.5km from Hotel Kyzyl Zhar), go one block to the left, and then 500m to the right along Sutyusheva.

The modernised **Regional Museum** (☎ 46 84 78; Konstitutsii Kazakhstana 48; admission 180T; ◷ 10am-6pm Tue-Sun) occupies two of several attractive 19th-century red-brick buildings along Konstitutsii Kazakhstana. Downstairs are natural history, archaeology and Kazakh culture; upstairs it's the region's story from Petropavlovsk's origins as a Cossack fort.

The large **market** (cnr Buketova & Astana; ◷ 8am-6pm), between the centre and the stations, makes for an interesting wander.

Sleeping

Hotel Kyzyl Zhar (☎ 46 11 84; Konstitutsii Kazakhstana 54; s 2600-8000T, d 4000-15,000T; **P**) Clean rooms and friendly staff make this large Soviet-era block, smack-bang in the centre, a sound option for a range of budgets.

Hotel Skif (☎ 46 88 07; hotel_skif@mail.ru; Parkovaya 118; s 5000-20,000T, d 7000-22,000T; **P** 🛜 **⬛**) Large, comfy rooms with contemporary fittings and good bathrooms, and an excellent restaurant serving large breakfasts (included in rates), make this well-run hotel a fine midrange choice. It's downtown, 500m southwest of Konstitutsii Kazakhstana.

Eating & Drinking

Arabika (☎ 46 57 32; Konstitutsii Kazakhstana 18A; hot drinks 250-500T; ◷ 10am-1am) A real coffee lounge, with real coffee, soft jazz, comfy chairs at low tables, and photos of Einstein and Russian bard Vladimir Vysotsky. There's a full range of alcoholic beverages too.

Slavyansky Dvor (Konstitutsii Kazakhstana 52; mains 1000-1400T; noon-midnight; E) In a period brick building in front of Hotel Kyzyl Zhar, this atmospheric bistro serves excellent fish, pork, lamb and salads amid heavy wood tables and iron fixtures. To get into the Kazakh mood, you could start with the *shuzhak* (sliced horsemeat sausage with mustard). In summer you can eat outside in courtyard booths.

Getting There & Around

Air Astana flies to Astana (7500T) four times weekly. SCAT flies to Almaty (20,000T) five times a week.

From the **train station** (38 34 34) trains leave at least three times daily to Astana (3000T, nine to 10 hours) and Kokshetau (1500T, four hours) and once or more to Almaty (5700T, 31 hours). They also head to many Russian cities including daily services to Moscow (31,000T to 35,000T, 41 to 46 hours), Omsk (4800T, 4½ hours), Yekaterinburg (Sverdlovsk; 8850T, 15 hours) and even Vladivostok (five days). Rail timetables here use Moscow time (two hours behind local time in summer, three hours in winter).

There are 10 daily buses to Kokshetau (800T, 3½ hours), seven to Astana (2200T, 10 hours) and two each to Omsk (1430T, six hours) and Tyumen (2000T, 8½ hours) from the **bus station** (33 03 69). Taxis here charge about 20,000T to Astana, 2000T (shared) to Kokshetau and 25,000T to Omsk.

It's a 300T taxi ride from the stations to the centre, or take trolleybus 2 or 4 (30T).

KARAGANDA (KARAGANDY)
КАРАГАНДА (КАРАГАНДЫ)
7212 / pop 450,000 / elev 550m

Smack in the steppe heartland, 220km southeast of Astana and 1000km northwest of Almaty, Karaganda is most famous for two things: coal and labour camps. The two are intimately connected, as the vast 'KarLag' network of Stalin-era camps around Karaganda was set up to provide slave labour for the mines. Prison labour also built much of Karaganda itself. Oddly enough given this history, the city centre is still endowed with two large Lenin statues.

During the depressed 1990s many of Karaganda's ethnic-German residents (descendants of Stalin-era deportees) departed for Germany. But Karaganda has bounced back and today it has a lively buzz, with tree-lined avenues and a downtown full of shopping malls, cafes, restaurants and theatres.

Coal mining is still key to the area's economy. The world's biggest steel company, ArcelorMittal (controlled by British-Indian billionaire Lakshmi Mittal), owns eight mines, with 24,000 employees, to fire its steelworks at Temirtau.

Orientation

The train and bus stations are beside each other at the south end of the city centre. Bukhar Zhyrau, the main street, heads north through the centre from here. Parallel to Bukhar Zhyrau are Yerubaev and Gogol, one and two blocks east, respectively. Main streets off Bukhar Zhyrau include Abdirov, heading east 1km north of the stations, and Beibitshilik (Mira), heading east after 2.25km.

Information

Internet Kafe Traffik (Bukhar Zhyrau 46; internet per hr 240T; 9am-9pm) Efficient, comfortable place along a lane beside the Benetton shop.

Tourist Information Centre (41 33 44; Bukhar Zhyrau 47; 9am-7pm Mon-Fri) Inside the Ecological Museum.

Sights & Activities

The **Karaganda Ecological Museum** (41 33 44; http://ecomuseum.kz; Bukhar Zhyrau 47; admission 100T, tour for 1 person 400T, for 2 or more 300T; 9am-7pm Mon-Fri, by arrangement Sat), run by a dedicated, campaigning environmental NGO, has to be the most imaginative museum in the country. Everything can be touched, and this includes large rocket parts that have fallen on the Kazakh steppe after Baykonur space launches, and debris collected from the Semipalatinsk Polygon (p192). The guided tours, available in English, are well worth it. The entrance is beneath an 'Ortalykkazzherkoynany' sign at the side of the building.

The recently modernised **Karaganda Oblast Museum** (56 31 21; Yerubaev 38; admission 200T; 9am-6pm) has ample and interesting displays on local and regional history, including a section on KarLag. Guided tours (300T), available in English, add significantly to the interest.

The main entrance to the leafy **Central Park** is off the west side of mid–Bukhar Zhyrau. The park stretches over 2km from north to south, with a large lake at its heart.

Tours

Nomadic Travel Kazakhstan (☎ 43 38 83, 705-250 4256; www.ecotourism.kz; Karaganda Ecological Museum, Bukhar Zhyrau 47; ☻ 9am-7pm Mon-Fri) This dynamic outfit run by a small group of young Kazakhstani travel enthusiasts offers trips by bicycle or minibus to some really offbeat destinations in central Kazakhstan, lasting from one to 10 days. If you want to explore the steppe heartland, climb its hills, visit remote archaeological and historic sites and experience vast panoramas, with English-speaking guides, these are your people. Accommodation is in village homestays, tents or herders' huts. Typical prices for the longer trips are around €120 per person per day for groups of two and €60 to €100 for groups of four. One- or two-day trips are around €70/40 per person per day for groups of two/four. Destinations include:

Kyzylarai mountains Around 300km southeast of Karaganda, with walks, horse rides, 3000-year-old stone necropolises, the steppe's highest mountain (1565m Aksoran) and homestays in the felt-making village of Shabanbay Bi.

Lake Balkhash area (see p149)

Semipalatinsk Polygon (see p192)

Ulytau hills North of Zhezkazgan, with Bronze Age petroglyphs and the mausoleums of Chinggis Khan's eldest son, Jochi, and Alasha-Khan, considered the founding father of the Kazakh people.

Sleeping

Bakhytty Hostel (☎ 51 99 24, 705-113 6554; http://bakhyttyhostel.narod.ru; bakhyttyhostel@yahoo.com; Garibaldi 52; per person 1100T; 🖥 ☎) Kazakhstan's only travellers' hostel occupies an old-fashioned one-storey house in the Zhana-Meshet district, about 2km east of the train and bus stations. Accommodation is in single and double rooms. There's a communal kitchen and shared showers. Bakhytty is run by the Kazakhstan representative of WWOOF (p199) and the hospitality network Servas. Contact them in advance: they'll pick you up on arrival.

ourpick Hotel Ar-Nuvo (☎ 42 02 84; www.arnuvo.kz; Beibitshilik 4A; s/d 15,000/17,000T; 🅿 🗙 ☎) An attractive new hotel with solidly comfy rooms, welcoming desk staff, a good restaurant and 40% discount on Saturday and Sunday nights. Breakfast is included. The entrance is on a lane heading east off Bukhar Zhyrau between Nos 20 and 22.

Also recommended:

Hotel Gratsia (☎ 41 24 59; fax 41 24 43; Voynov-Internatsionalistov; s/d with shared shower 2500/5000T, r with bathroom 6000-8000T) A decent-value budget place, the Gratsia is located behind the City Mall on Bukhar Zhyrau.

Hotel Karaganda (☎ 42 52 05; Bukhar Zhyrau 66; r with shared bathroom 4000T, with private bathroom 7000-11,500T; ☎) With a range of rooms at different prices, this central Soviet survivor suits many people.

Eating

Askhana (Alikhanov 14A; lunch 300-400T; ☻ 11am-3pm Mon-Fri) You can get a reasonable soup, salad, hot main dish and tea at a very good price at this clean, cafeteria-style place, across from the ArcelorMittalbuilding up the street, opposite the Ecological Mmuseum.

Uyghurskaya Kukhnya (Balkhashskaya 75; mains 700-800T; ☻ 10am-midnight Mon-Sat) Probably the best place in town for Central Asian staples like *laghman*, *manty* and *plov*; salads and meat dishes are served too. It's on the corner of Balkhashskaya and Bukhar Zhyrau, three bus stops south from the train station along Bukhar Zhyrau.

Assorti (☎ 91 17 07; City Mall, Bukhar Zhyrau 59/2; mains 1100-3000T; ☻ noon-2am; 🗙 🇪) This bright restaurant on the top floor of City Mall (opposite Hotel Karaganda), with good views over Bukhar Zhyrau, is part of a quality national chain. It's a fine place for pizzas, soups, salads and grills.

In summer, open-air **shashlyk-and-beer cafes** are strung all along Abdirov.

Entertainment

Vision (☎ 31 97 40; www.music-club.kz; Yerubaev 50A; ☻ 8pm-2am) Also known by its former name Elvis, this is a fun place to listen to live rock and roll, jazz or blues (nightly from 10pm), drink some beer and eat good food – especially in the open air in summer.

Getting There & Around

Karaganda's **airport** (☎ 42 85 42; www.karaganda-airport.com), 24km southeast of the centre (2000T by taxi), has daily Air Astana flights to Almaty, twice weekly flights to Ust-Kamenogorsk with SCAT, and three Transaero flights a week to Moscow.

The **train station** (☎ 43 36 36; cnr Bukhar Zhyrau & Yermekova) has at least 11 daily trains to Astana (1440T, four hours) and six to Almaty (3950T, 16 hours). There are also daily trains to Petropavlovsk and Shymkent, and less frequent departures as far as Semey, Novosibirsk and Moscow. It's best to try to book ahead as Karaganda is a midroute station.

Destinations from the **bus station** (☎ 43 18 18; www.avokzal.kz; Yermekova 58/6) include Almaty (4280T, 20 hours, three daily), Astana (800T, 4½ hours, every half-hour or hour, 6.30am to 8.30pm), Pavlodar (2300T, 10 hours, eight daily), Semey (2800T, 15 hours, one daily) and Shymkent (3890T, 20 to 27 hours, two daily). Minivans (1200T) and shared taxis (1500T) outside the bus station will whisk you to Astana in 2½ hours. Daily buses head as far as Petropavlovsk, Bishkek and Novosibirsk.

For bus 1 travelling north from the stations, walk under the flyover and wait at the stop to the left. The bus runs along Bukhar Zhyrau then east along Beibitshilik.

AROUND KARAGANDA

Spassk, 35km south of Karaganda on the Almaty highway, was the site of a KarLag camp where foreign prisoners of war were kept after WWII. Beside the highway is the mass grave of some 5000 prisoners, with eerie groups of three crosses scattered around the site, and monuments installed in the 1990s by several countries whose nationals died here. A taxi to Spassk and back should cost around 1500T from Karaganda.

Dolinka village, 50km southwest of Karaganda, was the administrative headquarters for the whole KarLag system. A modest **KarLag Museum** (☎ 72156-5 82 22; admission 100T; ☼ 9am-6pm Mon-Fri) is housed in the old KarLag hospital. Guides (200T) can give you a village tour including the grandiose KarLag headquarters building (into which the museum plans to move), the old officers' club (now the village's main shop), the soldiers' barracks and the children's cemetery. Get to Dolinka by Shakhtinsk-bound bus 121, leaving Karaganda bus station about every 15 minutes. Get off at the Vtoroy Shakht stop after about one hour (120T), take a taxi into Dolinka (200T, 1.5km) and ask for the *muzey* (museum).

Nomadic Travel Kazakhstan (p184) takes trips to both of these sites for €63 to €70 per group of up to five.

EASTERN KAZAKHSTAN

Ust-Kamenogorsk, a relatively prosperous regional capital, is the gateway to a large and mostly unspoiled region of mountains, lakes and villages with good hiking, horse riding, biking, rafting and other activities. The Altay Mountains, at its eastern extremity, are one of the most beautiful corners of Kazakhstan but you must plan well ahead to get the necessary border-zone permit if you want to visit them (see p188).

The region's other main city, Semey, still suffers from the effects of Soviet nuclear testing nearby but is one of Kazakhstan's most historically interesting places.

UST-KAMENOGORSK (OSKEMEN)
УСТЬ-КАМЕНОГОРСК (ӨСКЕМЕН)
☎ 7232 / pop 348,000 / elev 280m

Ust-Kamenogorsk (Kazakh: Oskemen), 800km north of Almaty, is a lively and progressive city with generally low-key Soviet architecture, at the confluence of the Irtysh and Ulba Rivers. It is gaining a name as something of an 'ecotourism' centre. Founded as a Russian fort in 1720, it has grown from a small town since the 1940s, when Russians and Ukrainians began arriving to mine and process the area's copper, lead, silver and zinc. These industries still keep Ust out of the economic doldrums, but are bad news for air quality.

Orientation & Information

Central Ust-Kamenogorsk is focused on pretty Park Zhastar. The main streets are Kazakhstan, running north from the Irtysh bridge to the bustling bazaar; Kirova, two blocks west; and Ordzhonikidze, which crosses them both leading to the main bridge over the Ulba. The bus station is a short distance west of the Ulba along Abaya, while the main train station, Zashchita, is 6km northwest along Nezavisimosti, and the airport is 3km further in the same direction.

Triada (Ordzhonikidze 52; internet per hr 120T; ☼ 10am-8pm) provides reasonably central internet access with lots of computers.

Sights

Clustered around **Park Zhastar** (☼ daylight) are some of Ust-Kamenogorsk's oldest buildings and several worthwhile museums, though a modernisation program means that some may still be temporarily closed. The **Ethnography Museum** (admission per branch 100T; ☺ 9am-6pm); Korpus No 1 (☎ 26 31 59; Gorkogo 59); Korpus No 2 (☎ 26 82 97; Kaysenova 67) is in two buildings facing opposite corners of the park. Korpus 1 exhibits the traditional culture of the Kazakhs of the East Kazakhstan region; Korpus 2 is devoted to the many other ethnic groups in the region, from Chechens to Koreans. The good **History Museum** (☎ 25 54 60; admission 150T; Kaysenova 40; ☺ 9am-5pm Wed-Mon) has a natural-history section with stuffed regional wildlife, including a snow leopard and a giant maral deer, and human history exhibits that reveal a huge number of ancient burial mounds in the region. In the park itself is a replica **Russian pioneer village**

(admission 250T; ☺ variable) of log cabins, furnished and decorated in period style.

It's nice to take a walk to the **Strelka**, where the Irtysh and Ulba meet, marked by a large Heroes of the Soviet Union memorial.

Sleeping

Hotel Alyans (☎ 22 29 45; Abaya 20; dm 1500T, d 3000T) This fairly friendly budget option, 1km north of the bus station, sits on the 7th floor of a seven-storey green building bearing the word 'Nursat'. Rooms are clean and hold either two or four; all have a shower, some have private toilets.

Hotel Ust-Kamenogorsk (☎ 26 18 90; www.hotel -oskemen.kz; Kabanbay Batyra 158; r 3500-11,500T; 🐾) A large Soviet-era hotel whose rooms, even the

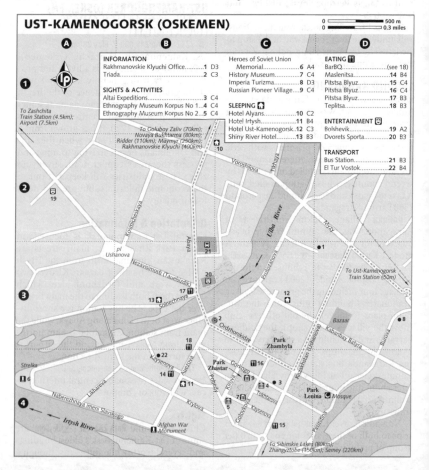

UST-KAMENOGORSK (OSKEMEN)

0 ———— 500 m
0 ———— 0.3 miles

INFORMATION	
Rakhmanovskie Klyuchi Office	1 D3
Triada	2 C3

SIGHTS & ACTIVITIES	
Altai Expeditions	3 C4
Ethnography Museum Korpus No 1	4 C4
Ethnography Museum Korpus No 2	5 C4
Heroes of Soviet Union Memorial	6 A4
History Museum	7 C4
Imperia Turizma	8 D3
Russian Pioneer Village	9 C4

SLEEPING	
Hotel Alyans	10 C2
Hotel Irtysh	11 B4
Hotel Ust-Kamenogorsk	12 C3
Shiny River Hotel	13 B3

EATING	
BarBQ	(see 18)
Maslenitsa	14 B4
Pitstsa Blyuz	15 C4
Pitstsa Blyuz	16 C4
Pitstsa Blyuz	17 B3
Teplitsa	18 B3

ENTERTAINMENT	
Bolshevik	19 A2
Dvorets Sporta	20 B3

TRANSPORT	
Bus Station	21 B3
El Tur Vostok	22 B4

To Zashchita Train Station (4.5km); Airport (7.5km)

To Goluboy Zaliv (70km); Novaya Bukhtarma (80km); Ridder (110km); Maymyr (250km); Rakhmanovskie Klyuchi (400km)

To Ust-Kamenogorsk Train Station (50km)

Voroshilova

Ulba River

Myri

pl Ushanova

Nezavisimosti (Täuelsizdik)

Proletarskaya

Kosmicheskaya

Abaya

Bazaar

Solnechnaya

Ordzhonikidze

Park Zhambyla

Park Zhastar

Kaysenova

Auezova

Pobedy

Kirova

Gorkogo

Park Lenina   Mosque

Tokhtarova

Kazakhstan (Ulanova)

Kabanbay Batyra

Burova

Feruniny

Kaysenova

Golovnoy

Strelka

Likhareva

Naberezhnaya imeni Slavskogo

Krylova

Irtysh River

Afghan War Monument

To Sibinskie Lakes (80km); Zhangyztobe (150km); Semey (220km) cheapest, unrenovated ones, are in decent condition. All have bathrooms.

Hotel Irtysh (☎ 25 29 12; travel@ukg.kz; Auezova 22; s/d from 6000/8000T; **P** **⚅**) Another Soviet-era establishment – a bit cosier and more accustomed to foreigners than the Ust-Kamenogorsk, and with breakfast included. Rooms are all renovated, and fitted out in shades of brown.

Shiny River Hotel (☎ 76 65 25; www.shinyriverhotel.kz; Solnechnaya 8/1; s 11,000–25,000T, d 14,000–29,000T; **P** **⚅** **🖥** **📶**) This excellent modern hotel overlooking the Ulba has tasteful, very comfy rooms, two bars and a classy restaurant (main dishes 1100T to 2700T, English-language menu available) with multinational fare. Breakfast is included.

Eating

Maslenitsa (☎ 25 09 00; Kaysenova 117A; mains 230-530T; ⌚ 9am-11pm; **V**) The house speciality, ham-and-cheese-stuffed *bliny*, are unique in this neck of the woods. It's an informal two-level place, decorated in pine from the counter to the rafters, and does a big choice of good *bliny*, soups, salads, cakes and main dishes. Order at the counter and your choice arrives at your table in no time.

Pitstsa Blyuz (Pizza Blues; pizzas 300-800T; ⌚ 9am-11pm; Gorkogo (☎ 24 81 67; Gorkogo 56); Nezavisimosti (☎ 76 51 01; Nezavisimosti 1); Kazakhstan (☎ 25 23 66; Kazakhstan 64) Highly popular local chain serving pretty good pizzas and salads, and great cakes, in clean, bright surroundings. Also at the Gorkogo and Kazakhstan locations are Kofe Blyuz, a slightly more expensive cafe-restaurant with real coffee and wi-fi.

ourpick **Teplitsa** (☎ 20 89 59; Auezova 43; meals 500-1200T; ⌚ 9am-11pm) Yet another arm of the Pizza Blues empire, Teplitsa (Greenhouse) is a stylish update on the old *stolovaya* (canteen) concept. There's plenty of freshly prepared food to choose from, and it's hard to beat the tasty sausages grilled to order in front of you.

In the same building as Teplitsa is the slickly contemporary **BarBQ** (☎ 20 89 60; mains 800-1000T; ⌚ 9am-11pm), doing grills and sushi.

Entertainment

Bolshevik (☎ 47 54 37; Nezavisimosti 37; admission up to 800T; ⌚ from 11pm) This giant dance club in an old cinema is the nocturnal venue of the moment. The motif is retro Soviet, with red flags and Lenin busts; the music is pop and dance, with regular theme parties. Generally free entry for women before about 1am. Take a taxi.

From September to April, don't miss **Kazzinc Torpedo** (www.kazzinc-torpedo.kz) at the **Dvorets Sporta** (☎ 76 62 50; Abaya 2; admission 250-400T). Frequent Kazakhstan ice hockey champions, Torpedo is also the only Kazakhstan team playing in the Russian Major League (Russia's second-best league). It has produced a number of NHL players. Look for posters outside the stadium: face-off is usually at 6.30pm.

Getting There & Away

From the **airport** (☎ 54 34 84) Air Astana flies daily to Almaty (26,000T) and Astana (20,000T); SCAT flies to Semey (2000T) three times weekly, to Karaganda (10,000T), Katon-Karagay (2000T) and Kyzylorda (22,000T) twice a week, and to Bayan-Olgii (Mongolia; 25,500T) and Novosibirsk (Russia; 19,000T to 27,500T) on Wednesday. S7 Airlines flies twice weekly to Moscow. Buses 2 and 39 (40T) run to the airport from Auezova in the centre. A taxi to the airport costs around 1500T. A good ticket agency is **El Tur Vostok** (☎ 25 76 22; Kaysenova 80; ⌚ 8.45am-7pm Mon-Sat, 9am-5pm Sun).

From the **bus station** (☎ 76 66 26; Abaya) buses run five times daily to Semey (950T to 1100T, four hours), and two or three times to Almaty (4000T, 22 hours), Astana (4000T, 17 hours), Barnaul (3000T to 3500T, 12 hours), Katon-Karagay (1500T, nine hours), Pavlodar (2500T, 11 hours) and Novosibirsk (6300T, 17 hours). Shared taxis to Semey from the bus station cost 2000T – most leave in the morning.

Buses to China also go from the bus station. Departures are on Wednesday and Sunday, at 6pm to Altay (5250T, 20 hours) via the border at Maykapshagay, and at 6.15pm to Ürümqi (9000T, 30 hours) via Bakhty.

Ust-Kamenogorsk's main train station is **Zashchita** (☎ 50 27 37), off Nezavisimosti 7km northwest of the centre. One daily train heads south to Almaty (3400T, 24 hours). Other trains from Zashchita, including one every two days to Semey, head north into Russia to meet the Semey–Novosibirsk line: at the time of writing foreigners are not allowed to take these trains (although they can cross the same border, north of Shemonaykha, by bus!). For other trains heading south, get a bus (700T, three hours) or a taxi (shared/charter 2000/8000T, 2½ hours) from Ust-Kamenogorsk bus station to Zhangyztobe, 150km southwest. From here there are three or four trains a day to Almaty (17 to 19 hours). You can buy train tickets at **El Tur Vostok** (☎ 25

OUT AND ABOUT FROM UST-KAMENOGORSK

Even if you have left it too late to get the border permit needed to visit the Altay Mountains proper, there's still plenty of beautiful country within reach of Ust-Kamenogorsk that's good for hiking, horse or bike riding, rafting or just exploring. Public transport around the region is limited; it's easier if you organise trips through a good Ust-Kamenogorsk agency such as the following:

- **Altai Expeditions** (☎ /fax 7232-24 57 09; www.altaiexpeditions.kz, nomad@altaiexpeditions.kz; Office 115, Gorkogo 46; ☽ 10am-7pm Mon-Fri) Run by enthusiastic, English-speaking Andrey Yurchenkov, Altai Expeditions offers a big range of active trips and nature tours in the Kazakh, Russian and Mongolian Altay and areas nearer to Ust-Kamenogorsk, including day trips. A wide-ranging two-week Altay tour starts at around US$700/1300 per person for six/two people. Custom itineraries are available.

- **Imperia Turizma** (☎ 7232-26 11 08; www.imper-tour.kz; Burova 20) Offers foot or horse trekking in the Ridder and Belukha areas, rafting on various rivers near Ust-Kamenogorsk, and more. Limited English spoken, however.

The mining town of **Ridder** (formerly Leninogorsk), 110km northeast of Ust-Kamenogorsk, is the gateway to beautiful mountain country abutting the Russian border, including the **Zapadno-Altaysky (Western Altay) Nature Reserve**. This area is good for camping, hiking, horse riding, mountain biking, rafting and skiing. Imperia Turizma offers three days' trekking in the Ridder area from 7000T per person including meals. The EIRC (p130) can fix you up with a homestay in Ridder or a wooden guesthouse in the forests. **Klimovka Recreation Centre** (☎ office 72336-2 22 75; tklimova@mail.ru; Lenin 16-72, Ridder; cabins 12,000-20,000T), 32km beyond Ridder, provides attractive and comfortable cabins with excellent meals included, and can organise all activities. Eleven buses a day run to Ridder (700T, three hours) from Ust-Kamenogorsk bus station. Note: foreigners are not allowed to cross into Russia by the road heading east from Ridder.

Within easy day-trip distance south of Ust-Kamenogorsk are the five beautiful **Sibinskie Lakes**, between stark, rocky mountains; the **Akbaur** Bronze Age astronomical complex; and the ruins of the **Ablainskit** Buddhist monastery. Altai Expeditions knows these remote destinations well.

About 200km east of Ust-Kamenogorsk, **Maymyr** village is a good base for hikes and rides around the broad Naryn valley and the high mountains to the south. Ask Altai Expeditions about Aleksey Mekhnin's comfy cottages and yurts, and good horses. A further 60km east, the EIRC (p130) can put you in homestays in villages around the quaint little town of **Katon-Karagay**, some of them within **Katon-Karagay National Park**. Two daily buses head from Ust-Kamenogorsk to Maymyr and Katon-Karagay. There are also two weekly SCAT flights from Ust-Kamenogorsk to Katon-Karagay for just 3000T.

92 72; Kaysenova 80; ☽ 8am-7pm Mon-Sat, to 5pm Sun); tickets from Zhangyztobe are only available on the day of departure.

Getting Around

From Abaya outside the bus station, trams 1, 2, 3 and 4 (35T) run to Ordzhonikidze and Kazakhstan on the east side of the Ulba; bus 6 (40T) will take you to Auezova for the Hotel Irtysh. Bus 1 and tram 3 link Zashchita station with the city centre.

ALTAY MOUNTAINS АЛТАЙ

In the far eastern corner of Kazakhstan the magnificent Altay Mountains spread across the borders to Russia, China and, 50km away,

Mongolia. To visit this area you need to plan well ahead to obtain a border-zone permit, which is required if you go beyond the village of Uryl (Orel).

The hassle of getting to this sparsely populated region is certainly well worth it. Rolling meadows, snow-covered peaks, forested hillsides, glaciers, pristine lakes and rivers, archaeological sites and rustic villages with Kazakh horsemen riding by make for scenery of epic proportions. Twin-headed Mt Belukha, a 4506m peak on the Kazakh–Russian border, has many mystical associations and Asian legends refer to it as the location of the paradisal Buddhist realm of Shambhala.

The season of easiest movement and decent weather is short in the Altay – mid-June to the end of September. If you visit the area with the help of a good travel firm such as Altai Expeditions (p188), Rakhmanovskie Klyuchi (p189) or Imperia Turizma (p188), they can obtain the border-zone permit in 30 to 60 days, for around 5000T or 6000T. Imperia Turizma offers 12-day horse treks (103,000T per person) and foot treks (38,000T per person) in the Belukha foothills, with transport and border-zone permit included. Rakhmanovskie Klyuchi may be able to provide speedier permit processing for up to 12,000T.

Near **Berel** you can visit the excavations of a famous group of Scythian burial mounds, where in 1997 archaeologists discovered the amazingly preserved body of a 4th-century BC prince, buried with several horses and carriages.

Rakhmanovskie Klyuchi

The health resort of Rakhmanovskie Klyuchi (Rakhmanov's Springs; ☎ 7232-26 37 44; www.altaytravel.ru; office Protozanova 25/1, Ust-Kamenogorsk; per person incl meals 11,600-18,300T) is 30km up a mountain track from the village of Berel and 400km from Ust-Kamenogorsk (about a 12-hour drive; 10,000T there and back in one of the resort's minibuses or buses). You'll find wooden cottages, some with kitchen, linked by boardwalks through pine forests, nestling in a mountain valley. This is a perfect base for exploring the Altay valleys, mountains, rivers, lakes and passes. Mt Belukha can be seen from the Radostny Pass, a one-hour walk up from the resort. From July to September the resort offers a variety of one- to two-week group horse and foot treks and Belukha ascents, costing from 40,000T to 70,000T per person. Shorter rides, hikes, excursions, fishing and rafting are available too. Packages for 12- or 24-day stays including transport are available.

It's also possible to camp or rent rooms in the nearby village.

SEMEY (SEMIPALATINSK)
СЕМЕЙ (СЕМИПАЛАТИНСК)
☎ 7222 / pop 314,000 / elev 200m

Semey, 200km down the Irtysh from Ust-Kamenogorsk, is sadly better known to the world by its old (Russian) name, Semipalatinsk. Between 1949 and 1989 the Soviet military exploded some 460 nuclear bombs in the Semipalatinsk Polygon, an area of steppe west of the city. An unprecedented wave of popular protest, the Nevada-Semipalatinsk Movement, was largely instrumental in halting the tests in 1989, but radiation has taken a severe toll on the health of many thousands of people in Semey and beyond (see p124).

Despite its Soviet-generated troubles, Semey has a rich cultural heritage. Founded in 1718 as a Russian fortification against the Zhungars, it lies in the territory of the Kazakh Middle Horde, noted for their eloquence and intellect. The area has produced several major Kazakh writers and teachers, notably the national poet Abay Kunanbaev (1845–1904), and Semey was a home in exile to Fyodor Dostoevsky.

Ironically the departure of a large-scale Soviet military establishment when nuclear testing ended only deepened the post-Soviet economic depression here. Semey is only now starting to see the kind of regeneration that has brightened other cities in Kazakhstan. A multi-million-dollar suspension bridge across the Irtysh at least gives the city a modern skyline.

Orientation

Nearly everything of interest is on the north side of the Irtysh River. The main streets, slicing across town from southwest to northeast, are Shakarima and Internatsionalnaya. The main bus station is on Valikhanova, three blocks northwest of Shakarima, next to the busy bazaar. The train station is just off the north end of Shakarima.

Information

Internet Tsentr (Momyshuly 4; internet per hr 120T; ⊙ 9am-6pm) Central internet access.
Semey (www.visitsemey.org) English- and Russian-language website with useful information for visitors, put together by local government, companies and NGOs.

Sights
MUSEUMS

The big, domed **Abay Museum** (☎ 52 17 21; Lenin 12; admission free; ⊙ 10am-1pm & 2-6pm Wed-Sun) is dedicated to the 19th-century humanist poet Abay Kunanbaev (see boxed text, p191). Along with displays about Abay's life and work, the museum has sections on the Kazakh nomadic tradition and Abay's literary successors, including his nephew Shakarim Kudayberdiev (1858–1931) and Mukhtar Auezov (1897–1968), author of the epic novel *Abay Zholy* (The Path of Abay). Free guided tours are

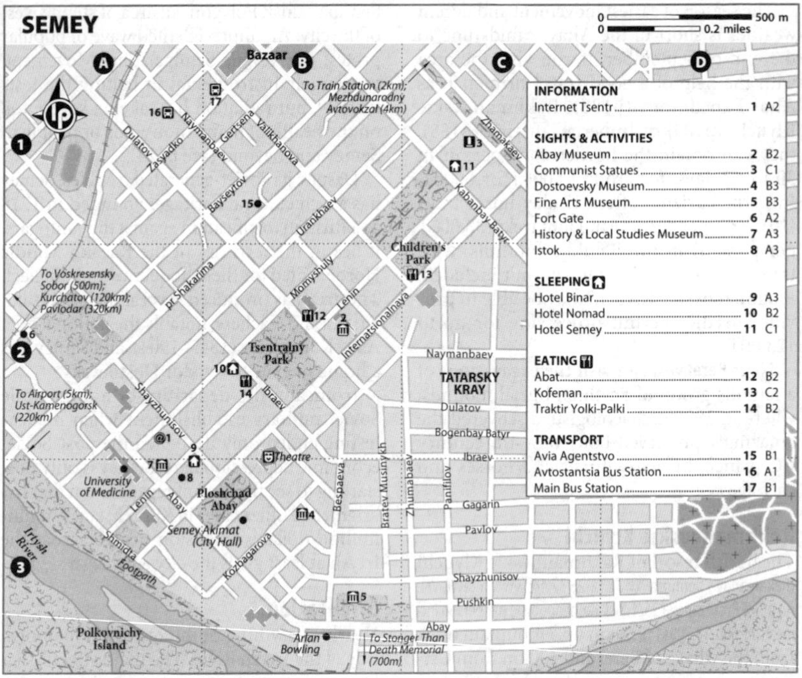

available in Russian or Kazakh only. In the grounds stands the wooden medressa where Abay studied as a boy, brought here from its original site elsewhere in Semey.

The well laid-out **Dostoevsky Museum** (☎ 52 19 42; Dostoevskogo 118; admission 200T; 9am-6pm Mon-Sat) incorporates the wooden house where the exiled writer lived from 1857 to 1859 with his wife and baby. It was in Semey that Dostoevsky began one of his most famous novels, *The Brothers Karamazov*, and made friends with the extraordinary Shokan Ualikhanov (Chokan Valikhanov), a prince of the Kazakh Middle Horde, explorer, intellectual, and spy in the Russian army. A statue of both men stands outside the museum. The museum displays Dostoevsky's life and works, including his five years in jail at Omsk and five years of enforced military service at Semey. His rooms have been maintained in the style of his day, and the vast number of images of Dostoevsky alone make it worth a visit. Tours, in Russian or Kazakh, cost 300T.

The **History & Local Studies Museum** (☎ 52 07 32; Lenin 5; admission 200T; 9am-5pm Mon-Sat) has a small display on nuclear testing and the Nevada-Semipalatinsk Movement, material on regional history, and a collection of traditional Kazakh artefacts. Founded by Russian exiles in 1883, this claims to be the oldest museum in Kazakhstan.

The large **Fine Arts Museum** (☎ 52 31 84; Pushkin 108; admission 200T; 10am-5.30pm Tue-Sat) has some good works by Kazakh, Russian and Western European painters from the 16th century onwards, including a not-to-be-missed Rembrandt etching.

OTHER SIGHTS

A curious collection of 15 **communist statues**, mostly Lenins, stands in a small park behind Hotel Semey, as if no one quite dared do away with them entirely.

Looking somewhat forlorn on a concrete island beside Abay is one of the **fort gates** built in 1776, flanked by a couple of cannons. The blue-and-gold-domed Russian Orthodox **Voskresensky Sobor** (Resurrection Cathedral) stands 500m further along the street.

Rural **Polkovnichy Island** is across a long bridge over the Irtysh. On the left, 600m past the end of the bridge, is the sombre and impressive **Stronger than Death memorial** erected in 2002 for victims of the nuclear tests. Above the marble centrepiece of a mother covering her child billows a Polygon mushroom cloud etched into a 30m-high black tombstone.

Tours

Local environmental NGO **Istok** (☎ /fax 52 48 99, 777-368 5554; vcistok@yandex.ru; Office 8, Lenin 4) can take you horse riding, to local festivals, or on one-day tours of the Shyngystau hills south of Semey, homeland of writers Abay Kunanbaev, Mukhtar Auezov and Shakarim Kudayberdiev. Prices are reasonable and English-speakers may be available.

Sleeping

Hotel Semey (☎ 56 36 04; www.semey.semstar.com; Kabanbay Batyr 26; s/d with shared bathroom 1500/2000T, with private bathroom from 4000/5400T; P ▣) Hotel Semey has that unmistakable Soviet aura but most rooms have been modernised and staff are helpful. Breakfast is included in the rate for rooms with private bathrooms.

Hotel Binar (☎ 52 36 39; binar2006@yandex.ru; Lenin 6; s/d from 7500/9500T; P ✕) This low-key, two-storey place is great value, with a comfortable European feel. The spacious rooms are cosy and carpeted, and the Jacuzzi-style showers will spray you from any angle you choose. Breakfast is included.

Hotel Nomad (☎ 52 04 44; www.hotelnomad.kz; Ibraev 149; s/d 10,000/15,000T; P ✕ ▣ ☜) The best hotel in town, new in 2007, overlooks the central park. For a place of this quality the prices are excellent. Rooms are unfussy but tasteful and well equipped, desk staff speak English, the in-house Restoran Dastur (mains 700T to 1500T; English-language menu available) is good and quiet, and room rates include a proper breakfast.

Eating

Kofeman (☎ 56 55 38; Internatsionalnaya 43; dishes 200-800T; ☾ 10am-1am; ☜) Semey's fashionable coffee lounge, also doing English and Mexican breakfasts, pasta, burgers and *bliny*. The latte is such a work of art it's a shame to drink it!

Abat (☎ 56 85 33; Dulatov; mains 300-700T; ☾ 11am-1am) The outdoor terrace cafe here is *the* place to eat in summer. It has a fun atmosphere and serves reasonable *laghman*, *manty*, shashlyk and salads. The indoor cafeteria (dishes 150T to 300T, open from 9am to 10pm) is cheap but run-of-the-mill. Located between Lenin and Momyshuly.

Traktir Yolki-Palki (☎ 52 57 47; Ibraev 147; mains 400-1000T; ☾ 9am-1am) Behind the heavy wooden street door are two tavernlike rooms where you can enjoy good traditional Russian cooking (including breakfasts) as well as a big variety of drinks.

Getting There & Away

From the **airport** (☎ 33 53 77), 5km south of the centre, there are daily flights to Almaty (23,000T), four a week to Astana (15,000T) and three to Ust-Kamenogorsk (2000T). **Avia Agentstvo** (☎ 56 57 69; pr Shakarima 37; ☾ 9am-6pm) sells air and train tickets.

From the **main bus station** (☎ 52 09 25; Valikhanova 167), four daily buses run to Ust-Kamenogorsk (700T to 1150T, four hours), five to Pavlodar (1350T, six hours), three to Astana (3400T, 14 hours) and one to Almaty (3900T, 20 hours). There's a bus every two days to Novosibirsk (3500T, 12 hours). Shared taxis to Ust-Kamenogorsk (2000T) gather here too. Daily buses to Barnaul, Tomsk and Omsk, and a couple a week to Ürümqi (China), go from the **Mezhdunarodny Avtovokzal** (International Bus Station; ☎ 51 47 97; Karzhaubayuly 249).

The **train station** (☎ 38 12 32; Privokzalnaya 1) has two or more daily departures to Almaty (3400T to 3700T, 19 to 22 hours), one daily to Barnaul, Novosibirsk and Pavlodar, and one every two days to Astana.

Getting Around

Buses 3, 11 and 13 (35T) run from the train station to the centre along pr Shakarima. Bus 33 runs from the train station to the main bazaar (near the main bus station) then along Kabanbay Batyra and Internatsionalnaya to ploshchad Abay. Buses 35 and 41 also run between ploshchad Abay and the bazaar. Taxis cost 200T to 300T in town, and 2000T to or from the airport.

AROUND SEMEY

Kurchatov & the Polygon

Kurchatov, 120km west of Semey, was the command centre for the Semipalatinsk Polygon. The nuclear testing zone itself stretched some 100km to 120km south and west from Kurchatov. Today, the semideserted town is home to Kazakhstan's **National Nuclear Centre** (Natsionalny Yaderny Tsentr; ☎ 72251-2 33 33; www.nnc.kz; Lenina 6), which, among other things, works on the development of nuclear power in Kazakhstan. The gruesome **museum** (admission free; 9am-6pm Mon-Fri) has a model of the first test site, where aircraft, buildings, metro tunnels and live animals were placed close to the explosion to test its effects. Animal parts are pickled in formaldehyde. To organise a visit to Kurchatov, email a request to the Director-General of the National Nuclear Centre at nnc@nnc.kz about a week in advance. It's OK to do this in English. The centre can provide accommodation at US$50 per room and meals for US$10, and can also arrange car transport from Semey. There are also four buses a day to Kurchatov from Semey's **Avtostantsia bus station** (Naymanbaev 152).

Though only parts of the Polygon itself are officially restricted, and some areas of it can be visited safely, no one should wander in without an expert guide. Karaganda-based Nomadic Travel Kazakhstan (p184) offers trips in conjunction with the National Nuclear Centre that can take you (with safety equipment) to 'Ground Zero', where above-ground nuclear explosions happened, and the Degelen mountains, where bombs were exploded in tunnels cut into hillsides.

PAVLODAR ПАВЛОДАР

☎ 7182 / pop 358,000

A further 320km down the Irtysh Valley from Semey, Pavlodar is dominated by massive, rabbit-hole-style apartment blocks, but the old streets near the Irtysh south of the centre have pre-Soviet character. The sight not to be missed is the **Mashhur Zhusip Mosque** (cnr Kutuzova & Krivenko), the biggest mosque in Kazakhstan, built in 2001. It rises out of the city with rocketlike 68m-high minarets and a green dome shaped like Darth Vader's helmet. The attendants are welcoming and will show you the expansive main prayer hall (women must view this from the upper gallery).

It's hard to miss the 11-storey tower near the Irtysh that houses the **Hotel Pavlodar** (☎ 32 23 00; Krivenko 23; s/d from 4000/7000T;). An effort has been made to give the rooms a modern look but they retain that unmistakable Soviet flavour. Still, they're fairly well kept and reasonably sized. Breakfast is included.

Air Astana flies to Almaty and Astana. Buses and trains run daily to Astana, Barnaul, Omsk, Novosibirsk and Semey. Minibuses outside the train station offer quicker rides to Astana for 2000T.

KAZAKHSTAN DIRECTORY

ACCOMMODATION

All Kazakh cities have a broad range of accommodation, from cheap Soviet survivors to comfortable modern hotels. Most of the older places, even some of the basic hotels or dorms in train and bus stations, have been renovated and offer clean accommodation. Prices have gone up: you'll rarely get a double room with private bathroom for under 5000T (US$33), or much comfort or style for less than 10,000T (double that in Almaty or Astana). But a dorm bed or basic room with shared bathroom can still be found for 1000T to 2000T per person in most places. Two people with 15,000T to spend on a room can indulge in considerable comfort in most of the country.

In many attractive areas outside the cities, there are now homestay options at around 3500T to 5000T per person with meals included. You can make bookings for many of these at the EIRC in Almaty (p130).

Many hotels offer discounts of up to 50% if you occupy the room for not more than 12 hours, a period known as a *pol-sutki*. But bizarrely, some hotels actually charge you for making an advance reservation.

Another economical, often free, option is accommodation in local homes through networks like **CouchSurfing** (www.couchsurfing.com), which is well represented in Kazakhstan. This is often a good way to meet locals and to get an inside perspective on a place.

ACTIVITIES

Southeast and East Kazakhstan, with their high mountains along the Kyrgyz, Chinese and Russian borders, offer the greatest outdoor excitement. There's good hiking and some horse riding in the Zailiysky Alatau near Almaty (p142 and p146), and at Aksu-Zhabagyly Nature Reserve (p155) and Sayram-Ugam National Park (p156). The northeastern city of Ust-Kamenogorsk is the gateway to a mountainous area full of adventurous possibilities (see p188), culminating in the gorgeously beautiful Altay Mountains (p188). Exciting biking, hiking and riding in the little-visited steppes and hills of central Kazakhstan are offered by Karaganda-based Nomadic Travel Kazakhstan (p184).

Ascents of Belukha in the Altay, and Khan Tengri and other peaks in the central Tian Shan, are superb challenges for climbers in July and August. In winter skiers and snowboarders enjoy Central Asia's best facilities in the mountains near Almaty, especially at the modern Chimbulak resort (p143), with the famous giant outdoor ice-skating rink at Medeu nearby. Amazing summer heli-skiing is possible on the glaciers of the central Tian Shan (p148).

Rafters can tackle the Chilik River east of Almaty (p130) and several rivers out of Ust-Kamenogorsk (p188).

Birdwatchers should make especially for the Aksu-Zhabagyly (p155) and Korgalzhyn (p179) nature reserves. The latter is the world's most northerly flamingo habitat. See www.kazakhstanbirdtours.com for good bird background.

PRACTICALITIES

- Local broadcasting and press are in Russian and Kazakh, but TVs in better hotels often receive international channels such as CNN and BBC World.
- A few top-end hotel bookshops and newsstands in Almaty and Astana erratically sell a few Western news magazines and newspapers, plus the worthwhile, Bishkek-published *Times of Central Asia*.

CITY & STREET NAMES

Kazakh names replaced the Soviet-era Russian names of most Kazakhstan cities in the 1990s. In a few cases, mostly in the heavily ethnic-Russian north, the old names are still more commonly used: more people still talk of Uralsk rather than Oral, and of Ust-Kamenogorsk than Oskemen.

Most city streets also have Kazakh names. In some cities you may see Kazakh and Russian street names side by side, and in the north you may see Russian only. The Kazakh for street (Russian: 'ulitsa') is 'koshesi'; for avenue ('prospekt') 'dangyly', and for square ('ploshchad') 'alangy'. Meanwhile, many local people continue to use some still-familiar Soviet street names.

In this chapter we use the names that are most commonly used.

Almaty agencies specialising in active tourism are listed on p130. The EIRC (p130) is another good source of assistance in Almaty.

CUSTOMS

Customs declaration forms don't need to be filled in on entering the country unless you are carrying goods above normal duty-free limits. Up to US$3000 cash in any currencies can be taken into or out of the country without a written declaration.

DANGERS & ANNOYANCES

Kazakhstan is a safe country to travel in, provided that you maintain normal safety precautions (p500).

Try to avoid the police, who are often only interested in foreigners as possible sources of bribes for minor 'infringements'. Though police harassment is less common these days, it can still happen. It's best not to carry much cash around, and you wouldn't want to let your wallet into police hands. If you are stopped on the street, show only a photocopy of your passport and visa. Writing down a name and badge number helps to keep police honest (and may unmask impostors).

EMBASSIES & CONSULATES
Kazakhstan Embassies in Central Asia

Kazakhstan has embassies in Tashkent (Uzbekistan; p282), Bishkek (Kyrgyzstan; p366), Ashgabat (Turkmenistan; p462),

Dushanbe (Tajikistan; p417) and Kabul (Afghanistan; p491).

Kazakhstan Embassies & Consulates in Other Countries

Kazakhstan's diplomatic missions abroad include the following (see www.mfa.kz for details of all Kazakh embassies). Main missions are given first.

Azerbaijan (☎ 012-465 6247; embassyk@azdata.net; Dom 8,10, H Aliyeva proezd 15, Baku)

Canada (☎ 613-788 3704; www.kazembassy.ca; 56 Hawthorne Ave, Ottawa, K1S 0B1)

China Beijing (☎ 010-6532 4779; www.kazembchina.org; 9 Dong 6 Jie, San Li Tun, Chaoyang District, 100600); Hong Kong consulate (☎ 2548 3841; www.consul-kazakhstan. org.hk; Unit 3106, 31 fl, West Tower, Shun Tak Centre, 200 Connaught Rd Central, Sheung-Wan); Shanghai consulate (☎ 021-6275 2838; www.kazembchina.org; Room 1005/1006, Orient International Plaza, 85 Loushanguan Rd 200336); Visa & Passport office in Ürümqi (☎ 0991-381 5857; pvs_mid@yahoo.cn; Kunming Lu 216)

France (☎ 1-4561 5206; www.amb-kazakhstan.fr; 59 rue Pierre Charron, 75008 Paris)

Georgia (☎ 22-997684; kazembge@gmail.com; Shat-berashvili 23, Tbilisi 0179)

Germany (☎ 030-4700 7111; www.botschaft-kaz.de; Nordendstrasse 14-17, 13156 Berlin) Consulates in Bonn, Frankfurt, Hanover and Munich.

Iran (☎ 021-2256 5933; www.kazembassyiran.com; 4 North Hedayat St, cnr Masjed Alley, Darrus, Tehran)

Japan (☎ 03-3791 5273; www.embkazjp.org; 5-9-8, Himonya, Meguro-ku, Tokyo 152-0003)

Mongolia (☎ 011-34 54 08; info@kazembassy.mn; Zaisan 31/6, 1 khoroo, Khan-Uul district, 'Twin' town, Ulaanbaatar)

Pakistan (☎ 051-226 29 25; embkaz@isb.comsats.net. pk; House 11, Street 45, Sector F-8/1, Islamabad)

Russia Moscow (☎ 495-608 40 80; www.kazembassy. ru; Chistoprudny bulvar 3A, 101000); Astrakhan consulate (☎ 8512-25 18 85; www.kazembassy.ru; Akvarelnaya 2B, 414056); Omsk consulate (☎ 3812-32 52 13; www. kz-omsk.ru; Valikhanova 9); St Petersburg consulate ☎ 812-335 25 46; www.kazembassy.ru; Vilensky pereulok 15)

UK London (☎ 020-7581 4646; www.kazembassy.org. uk; 33 Thurloe Sq, London SW7 2SD); Aberdeen consulate (☎ 01224-611 923; kazcon@btconnect.com; 10 N Silver St, AB10 1RL)

USA (☎ 202-232 5488; www.kazakhembus.com; 1401 16th St NW, Washington, DC 20036)

Embassies & Consulates in Kazakhstan

Most embassies have moved to Astana, although a few remain in Almaty. Many of those that have moved to Astana have consulates or representative offices in Almaty. In the following listings the main missions are given first.

Afghanistan Astana (Map p174; ☎ 7172-57 14 42; www.afghanembassy.kz; 3 Mikrorayon Karaotkel-2); Almaty consulate (☎ 727-227 23 90; af_embassyalmaty@ yahoo.com; Mikrorayon Shkolny 2-238)

Azerbaijan Astana (Map p174; ☎ 7172-24 15 81; www. azembassy.kz; Diplomatichesky Gorodok V-6); Aktau consulate (☎ 7292-33 67 07; Dom 12, Mikrorayon 4)

Canada (Map p128; ☎ 727-250 11 51/52; www.canada international.gc.ca/kazakhstan; Karasay Batyr 34, Almaty)

China Astana (Map p174; ☎ 7172-79 35 83; http:// kz.china-embassy.org, in Russian; Block 5, Kabanbay Batyr 37); Almaty consulate (Map p128; ☎ 727-270 02 21, visa inquiries 270 02 11; Baytasov 12)

France Astana (Map p174; ☎ 7172-79 51 00; www. ambafrance-kz.kz; Kosmonavtov 62); Almaty office (Map p128; ☎ 727-396 98 00; Furmanov 99)

Georgia (Map p174; ☎ 7172-24 32 58; astana.emb.@ mfa.gov.ge; Diplomatichesky Gorodok C-4, Astana)

Germany Astana (Map p174; ☎ 7172-79 12 00; www. astana.diplo.de; Kosmonavtov 62); Almaty consulate (Map p128; ☎ 727-262 83 41/46; www.almaty.diplo.de; Ivanilova 2)

Iran Astana (Map p174; ☎ 7172-24 25 11; www.mfa.gov. ir; Diplomatichesky Gorodok V-7); Almaty office (off Map p128; ☎ 727-261 96 46; iranembassy@itte.kz; Radlova 5A)

Japan Astana (Map p174; ☎ 7172-97 78 43; www. kz.emb-japan.go.jp/jp; 5th fl, Kosmonavtov 62); Almaty office (Map p128; ☎ 727-298 06 00; 3rd fl, Kazybek Bi 41)

Kyrgyzstan Astana (Map p174; ☎ 7172-24 20 24; kz@ mail.online.kz; Diplomatichesky Gorodok V-5); Almaty consulate (Map p128; ☎ 727-291 66 10; www.consulkg. kz; Lugansky 30A)

Mongolia (Map p128; ☎ 727-229 37 90; www.mongemb .kz; Musabaev 1, Almaty)

Pakistan (Map p128; ☎ 727-273 15 02; parepalmaty@ yahoo.com; Tolebaev 25, Almaty)

Russia Astana (Map p174; ☎ 7172-22 24 83; www. rfembassy.kz; Baraeva 4); Uralsk consulate (☎ 7112-51 16 26; Mukhita 78); Almaty consulate (Map p128; ☎ 727-274 61 22; gcrusalmaata@gmail.com; Zhandosov 4)

Tajikistan Astana (Map p174; ☎ 7172-24 09 29; embassy_tajic@mbox.kz; Marsovaya 15); Almaty office (Map p128; ☎ /fax 727-269 70 59; tajemb_almaty@ ok.kz; Sanatornaya 16, Mikrorayon Baganashyl) The Almaty office is in the south of the city: take bus 63 south from Furmanov as far as the Pediatria Instituty stop on Al-Farabi. Walk 100m further and continue straight over where Al-Farabi bends right at the traffic lights. The consular section entrance is on the left, 200m up this road, Syrgabekov: look for the flag.

Turkmenistan Astana (Map p174; ☎ /fax 7172-21 08 82; tm_emb@astanatelecom.kz; Otyrar 8/1); Almaty consulate (Map p128; ☎ /fax 727-272 69 44; Furmanov 137)

UK Astana (Map p174; ☎ 7172-55 62 00; http://ukinkz.fco.gov.uk; 6th fl, Kosmonavtov 62); Almaty office (Map p128; ☎ 727-250 61 91; http://ukinkz.fco.gov.uk; Block A2, Samal Towers, Zholdasbekov 97, Mikrorayon Samal-2)
USA Astana (Map p174; ☎ 7172-70 21 00; http://kazakhstan.usembassy.gov; Bldg 3, 23-22 ulitsa, Mikrorayon Ak Bulak 4); Almaty consulate (Map p128; ☎ 727-250 76 12; http://kazakhstan.usembassy.gov; Zholdasbekov 97, Mikrorayon Samal-2)
Uzbekistan (Map p128; ☎ 727-291 02 35; fax 727-291 10 55; Baribaev 36, Almaty)

Visas for Onward Travel

Afghanistan One-month visas (US$30) processed in three or four working days in Almaty: documents are accepted from 9am to noon, Monday to Friday. Agents will charge double. You may be asked for a letter from a sponsor or employer showing that you have sufficient funds.
Azerbaijan Thirty-day single-entry tourist visas are issued without a letter of invitation (LOI) on arrival at Baku airport to most Western nationalities for US$90 to US$130 cash. Visas from the Astana embassy or the Aktau consulate at the time of writing are available for US$20 if you have an LOI and the tourist vouchers that are commonly issued with the LOI. LOIs with tourist vouchers currently cost US$50 from agencies such as Azerbaijan24 (www.azerbaijan24.com) and Stantours (www.stantours.com), but the price can fluctuate wildly. Without tourist vouchers, visas with LOI cost US$40 to US$130 depending on your nationality. The Aktau consulate was issuing same-day visas at the time of research; it's open from 9am to 1pm Monday to Friday.
China Visa policy at Chinese representations in Kazakhstan changes frequently; at time of writing, visas were not being issued in Almaty. When they are being issued, one-month, single-entry visas cost US$30 and take about five working days. An LOI or even proof of residence in Kazakhstan may be required. The office opens for visa matters from 9am to noon, Monday, Wednesday and Friday: be prepared for long queues. For urgent processing (US$60) apply on Monday. Using an agent is easier, but it's much better to get your visa before leaving home or, failing that, try in Tashkent.
Kyrgyzstan Procedures at the time of writing are time-consuming and costly. The Almaty consulate accepts applications from 10am to 1pm Monday to Thursday (get there at 9.30am to minimise queuing time). Take your passport and one photo. Normal processing time (US$55 to US$80 for most types of visa) is up to 10 days; three-day 'urgent' processing costs US$100 to US$150. In either case you have to make three visits: one to put in the application, one to come back with the bank receipt for payment, and one to pick up the visa. The Kyrgyz consulates in Tashkent, Dushanbe and Novosibirsk are much more straightforward.
Russia It's best to get your Russian visa before you leave home. The Almaty consulate is a headache for tourist visas,

although travellers have obtained transit visas in a couple of days without LOIs or even onward tickets. Applications are accepted from 9.30am to 12.30pm Monday, Tuesday and Friday. For a tourist visa you need to work through a specialised agency such as Transavia (p130), and total costs will add up to at least US$250 including an LOI. The Astana embassy is reportedly less difficult, but the only Russian embassy in Central Asia regularly issuing tourist visas to outsiders who apply directly is at Tashkent.
Tajikistan Tourist visas are issued in Almaty without LOIs. For a one-month tourist visa (US$100 for same-day processing), provide photocopies of your passport and Kazakh visa and a written request to the ambassador. The office is open Monday to Friday, from 10am to 1pm for receiving documents and 3pm to 6pm for issuing them. Cheaper processing takes about two weeks. This office does not issue the GBAO permit for travel in the Pamirs.
Turkmenistan To get a Turkmen visa here you either need to book a tour through a travel agency, or have visas for the bordering countries from which you will enter Turkmenistan and go to from Turkmenistan (these can include Azerbaijan), enabling you to get a transit visa. Transit visas are also available if you fly in or fly out (but not normally both). You have to go in person with your passport to the embassy or consulate. Procedures and acceptance are easier in Astana, Tashkent and Dushanbe, where the embassies are more used to travellers, than in Almaty.
Uzbekistan Some Almaty travel agents can provide Uzbek LOIs hassle free if given enough time (US$35 for about two weeks' processing at Stantours). The embassy issues visas on the spot with an LOI. It opens for applications from 2.30pm to 5pm Monday, Tuesday, Wednesday and Friday. Go before 2pm, put your name on a list and you'll probably get in before the door closes. In the peak summer travel season you may need to get there in the morning. All applicants should take their passport, a photocopy of it, their Kazakh visa and registration, one photo, an LOI and a completed application form (normally supplied with an LOI). Tourist visas cost US$55/65/75 for seven/15/30 days, US$95 for three months: for more than one entry, add US$10 per entry. US citizens pay US$130 for any visa. Payments must be in US dollars.

FESTIVALS & EVENTS

The biggest festivities around the country are for Nauryz, the Muslim spring equinox festival on 22 March, with traditional sports, music festivals and family get-togethers. Shymkent is a particularly good place to be for Nauryz (see p153). Major religious festivals – the Muslim Qurban Ait (Eid al-Azha) and Eid al-Fitr (p503), and Russian Orthodox Christmas (7 January) – are widely celebrated though they are not official holidays.

HOLIDAYS

New Year 1 & 2 January
International Women's Day 8 March
Nauryz 21–23 March (see p503)
Kazakhstan Peoples Solidarity Day 1 May
Victory Day 9 May
Capital City Day 6 July
Constitution Day 30 August
Independence Day 16 December

INTERNET ACCESS

Public internet facilities are abundant, and generally charge 200T to 300T per hour. Nearly all midrange and top-end hotels, and some budget accommodation and cafes and restaurants, have wi-fi (sometimes free, sometimes not).

INTERNET RESOURCES

Kazakhstan Embassy in Washington (www.kazakh
embus.com) This embassy has assorted information on the
country and some helpful links, as do the sites of several
other Kazakh embassies and foreign embassies in Kazakhstan (see p194).
Kazworld.info (http://kazworld.info) Good news site,
including cultural news.
Ministry of Foreign Affairs (www.mfa.kz) Includes
visa, registration and customs regulations, but the English
is not always very clear.
Official Language Portal (http://til.gov.kz) Includes a
useful Kazakh–English–Russian translation tool.
Visit Kazakhstan (www.visitkazakhstan.kz) Helpful site
of the Ministry of Tourism & Sport.

MAPS

Kasachstan, published by **Reise Know How** (www.
reise-know-how.de) is an excellent map for travellers, printed on waterproof, rip-resistant
paper. The best source of topographical maps
of Kazakhstan's regions is GEO in Almaty
(p127).

MONEY

Prices in this chapter are given in the currency
they are normally quoted in – usually the national currency, tenge (T), but occasionally
US dollars or euros.

ATMs abound at banks, shopping centres,
supermarkets, hotels, some train stations
and elsewhere. Look for 'Bankomat' signs.
Most accept at least Maestro, Cirrus, Visa and
MasterCard.

You can make purchases with credit cards
(Visa and MasterCard preferred) at a fair
number of shops, restaurants, hotels and

travel agencies. There is often a surcharge
for doing so.

Bring a little cash (euros or US dollars)
to start out and as a fallback if you run out
of tenge. Exchange offices (marked 'Obmen
Valyuty') are common on city streets.

You can change US-dollar or euro travellers
cheques at many banks but it's time-consuming
and there's usually a 2% fee. Amex is the most
widely accepted brand.

At the time of research, exchange rates were
as follows:

Country	Unit	Tenge
Australia	A$1	133T
Canada	C$1	143T
China	Y1	21T
Euro zone	€1	200T
Japan	Ÿ10	16T
Kyrgyzstan	10som	33T
New Zealand	NZ$1	102T
Russia	R10	50T
UK	UK£1	221T
USA	US$1	145T
Uzbekistan	100S	10T

POST

Airmail letters under 20g to anywhere outside
the CIS cost 250T. If you have anything of
importance to post it's generally safer and
quicker to use an international courier firm.
DHL (www.dhl.kz) has a particularly wide network
of drop-off centres around the country.

REGISTRATION

For nationalities on the 'economically developed and politically stable' list (see p198),
registration may be carried out when visas
are issued at a Kazakhstan embassy or consulate. If it doesn't happen there, it happens
automatically on arrival at the country's international airports. Two entry stamps (one
is not enough) on your migration card are the
indication that registration has taken place
and is valid for 90 days.

Travellers entering by land or sea, or who
for any reason don't get registered on airport
arrival, have to register with the migration
police (Migratsionnaya Politsia, Koshi-Kon
Politsiyasi, OVIR) no later than day five of
their stay in the country if they are staying
in Kazakhstan beyond that day (counting
the arrival date as day one). Many hotels
and travel agencies can handle your registra-

tion for a fee of 2000T to 5000T, or you can spend time going to the migration police in Almaty, Astana or one of Kazakhstan's 14 regional capitals, where registration can cost from nothing to 1000T. Migration police offices are generally open for limited hours, on Monday, Tuesday, Wednesday and Friday only, and also close on public holidays and often on Mondays following public holidays that fall on a weekend. Take your passport, your migration card and the address of your hotel (don't give a private address). Addresses of regional migration police offices are given at http://e.gov.kz under Citizenry/Migration/List of Migration Police's Regional Units: click a region and the local headquarters will be at the top of the next page.

Note that if you have a double-entry visa, you must obtain registration again on your second entry (unless you are leaving Kazakhstan again within five days).

The registration rules change from time to time and may be interpreted differently in different places: check the situation when you get your visa and again when you reach Kazakhstan. The official fine for registering late is around US$100.

If your visa was obtained with a letter of invitation (LOI) and you are registering at a migration police office, you should have the LOI issuer help you out. If they can't (for example if they are in Almaty and you are on the other side of the country), provincial migration police will often only register you for five days and you will need to show them your LOI. You can get registration for the duration of your visa once you hook up with your LOI issuer.

TELEPHONE

Almost everyone in Kazakhstan has a mobile (cell) phone and it's easy to get a local SIM card for your phone if you have a 900-frequency phone (most European mobiles have this; most North American ones don't). Shops and kiosks selling SIM cards with call credit for a few hundred tenge are everywhere. Take your passport when you go to buy. The same outlets often sell inexpensive phones too, and will top up your credit for cash or with PIN cards. Activ, KCell and Beeline are the best networks for nationwide coverage. Typically 1000T credit gives you about an hour of talking to a combination of mobile and landline numbers.

Mobile numbers have 10 digits. Landlines have a three-, four- or five-digit area code followed by a local number: the area code plus the local number always totals 10 digits. The Kazakhstan country code is ☎ 7.

You can make phone calls for cash from some Kazaktelekom offices, from call offices signed 'Peregovorny Punkt', and from some shops and kiosks with phones for public use. Local calls are generally free, while other calls within Kazakhstan cost around 10T per minute, calls to Kazakhstan mobile numbers and other ex-Soviet states cost around 30T per minute,

HOW TO DIAL

From	To	Dial
Kazakhstan landline or mobile	mobile in Kazakhstan or Russia	☎ 8-mobile number
Kazakhstan landline	Other countries except Russia	☎ 8-10-country code-area code-local number
Kazakhstan landline	landline in other Kazakh city or Russia	☎ 8-area code-local number
Kazakhstan landline	landline in same city	local number only
Kazakhstan mobile	landline in Kazakhstan or Russia	☎ 8-area code-local number
Kazakhstan mobile	Other countries except Russia	☎ country code-area code-local number
Other countries	Kazakhstan landline	☎ international access code-7-area code-local number
Other countries	Kazakhstan mobile	☎ international access code-7-mobile number

and other international calls cost around 100T to 200T per minute. Calls from hotel rooms are typically double the call-office rate.

You can cut costs for some international calls by using a Nursat i-Card or an Emax card, sold at mobile-phone shops and kiosks. Get a Russian-speaker to show you how to use them. Basically, you scratch off a PIN then dial a local access number given on the card. Calling instructions are then available in English. Nursat i-Card calls cost around 20T per minute to any phone in the USA, Canada, Russia or China, and about 30T per minute to other Central Asian countries and landlines in Britain, Germany, Italy or France.

TRAVEL PERMITS

A special permit (sometimes called a *propusk*) is needed for travel to sensitive areas close to the Chinese border, notably the Altay Mountains and Mt Khan Tengri. Tour firms taking you to these areas can arrange such permits, but processing can take up to 45 days.

A permit is also officially required for areas near the Kyrgyz border in the mountains south of Almaty. Local guides know the score.

Baykonur Cosmodrome (p159) can only be visited on tours organised through agencies and you need to start the paperwork process about two months ahead.

Entry to nature reserves usually requires a permit, normally arranged quickly through the local reserve office, for a fee of anything up to 2000T.

VISAS

One-month, single-entry tourist and business visas, and two-month double-entry tourist visas, can usually be obtained at Kazakh consulates or embassies *without* a letter of invitation (LOI) if you are from any of a list of countries that Kazakhstan officially considers 'economically developed and politically stable'. These include the 27 EU states, Australia, Canada, Israel, Japan, New Zealand, Norway, South Korea, Switzerland and the USA. Required documentation usually includes your passport, a letter from you explaining the purpose of your visit, a photo and an application form, which is available at www.mfa.kz ('Consular Information') and often on embassy websites. Some Kazakh consulates, however, mainly in non-Western countries, won't issue double-entry tourist visas without a LOI.

For other visas, or if you are not from one of the 'economically developed and politically stable' states, you must obtain 'visa support' in the form of a LOI. This is available, usually by email, through many travel agencies in Kazakhstan (see p130), Central Asia travel specialists in other countries, or Kazakh businesses. Agents' fees for obtaining LOIs normally range from around US$30 to US$70 depending on the visa required (more for urgent processing). In your application to the embassy or consulate you need to submit your LOI's official reference number, and often a copy of the LOI itself (fax or email copies are fine). Allow one to two weeks to obtain the LOI before you apply for the visa itself, but note that LOIs cannot normally be issued more than a month before your arrival in Kazakhstan. The maximum length of a tourist visa is two months; for longer periods you can get a business visa.

Fees for the visa itself depend on the type of visa. A single-entry, one-month tourist visa is normally around US$40. Urgent processing is usually available at extra cost.

Single-entry, one-month visas are also available with a LOI on arrival at Almaty, Astana, Atyrau and Uralsk airports. Fees (US$45/75 for a tourist/business visa) must be paid in cash US dollars (issued after 1996 and not worn or torn!), at the airport's consular section. You must provide a photograph and complete a form that, among other things, asks for dates of any previous visits to Kazakhstan. When you request a LOI from a travel agency for this purpose, tell them why: not all agencies can provide LOIs suitable for visas on arrival.

Some consulates, including those in London and Washington, DC, will deal with visa applications by mail; others require you to apply for and collect your visa in person. Processing time at consulates in the West is normally three to five working days.

Kazakhstan's visa rules are modified from time to time. Recommended travel agents and the websites of Kazakh embassies usually have up-to-date information.

If you are in a country without a Kazakh embassy or consulate (such as Australia, Ireland, New Zealand or Sweden), you can apply to Kazakh missions in other countries – London and Washington, DC, are usually the best bets. Visa agents will do the legwork for fees of around US$50 to US$70 per visa plus courier charges and the visa-processing costs. To save money, consider getting visas in countries en route to Kazakhstan. Visa processing at Kazakh consulates in Central Asia is officially three working days, but most (except Bishkek at the time of writing) will issue visas the same day if asked nicely. For further information see 'Visas for Onward Travel' in other countries' Directory sections in this book.

In Baku (Azerbaijan), one-month, single-entry tourist visas are normally issued in one or two working days. In Beijing the Kazakh embassy is open for visa applications from 9am to 1pm, Monday, Wednesday, Thursday and Friday, with processing normally taking five working days (three working days for urgent processing). Processing times at the often crowded and chaotic Kazakh visa office in Ürümqi are erratic. At the time of writing Western travellers could usually obtain visas in three or four days, though there have been cases where it took two weeks. In addition, the office's location and opening hours (9.30am to 12.30pm for applications at time of writing) have a habit of changing. The Kazakh consulates in Shanghai and Hong Kong may insist on a LOI or proof of hotel bookings for your whole stay for any visa. See also Registration, p196.

For details on getting visas for neighbouring countries in Kazakhstan see p195.

Copies

You are supposed to carry your passport with you with your visa in it, and your migration card, at all times to show to police or military on demand. In practice, photocopies are almost always acceptable unless you're travelling outside the city where you are staying.

Extensions

Extending a Kazakh tourist visa is only possible with a medical certificate saying that you are unable to travel. Business visas can be extended through many travel agencies: fees start at around US$50.

VOLUNTEERING

WWOOF (World Wide Opportunities on Organic Farms; www.wwoofkazakhstan.org) recently started up in Kazakhstan and look for pioneering volunteers who are willing to work on organic properties for a few days or more, in exchange for food and accommodation. **Komanda SOS/**

Seimar Social Fund (www.volunteer.kz) coordinates short-term volunteer projects, mainly based in Almaty. Projects include work with orphanages, disabled children, and the environment. **Volunteer Club DAR** (aktobeinvalids@gmail.com) manages volunteer projects in Aktobe, working primarily with disabled children. **United Nations Volunteers** (www.unv.org) also operates in Kazakhstan.

TRANSPORT IN KAZAKHSTAN

GETTING THERE & AWAY
Entering Kazakhstan

As long as you have your visa organised, you should have no problems getting into Kazakhstan. Keep the migration card you receive in your passport: you have to hand it in when you leave the country. What you must pay special attention to is registration (see p196).

Air

Kazakhstan has good air connections with the outside world, through numerous carriers including the national airline, **Air Astana** (www.air-astana.com), which is a good international-class carrier. See p518 for some fare information. Most airlines flying in and out of Kazakhstan offer online booking and e-tickets: the main exceptions are Tajik Air and Turkmenistan Airlines.

The biggest and busiest airports are at **Almaty** (ALA; ☎ 727-270 33 33; www.almatyairport.com) and **Astana** (TSE; ☎ 7172-70 29 99; www.astanaairport.kz). Almaty's international connections are as follows:

Abu Dhabi Etihad Airways three or four weekly.
Amsterdam Air Astana and KLM four weekly.
Ashgabat Turkmenistan Airlines three weekly.
Baku Air Astana two weekly.
Bangkok Air Astana three weekly.
Beijing Air Astana five weekly.
Bishkek Air Astana four weekly.
Cairo EgyptAir two weekly.
Delhi Air Astana three weekly.
Dubai Air Astana daily.
Dushanbe Tajik Air three weekly.
Frankfurt Lufthansa daily, Air Astana six weekly.
İstanbul Turkish Airlines daily, Air Astana six weekly.
Kabul Kam Air one weekly.
Kiev Ukraine International Airlines two weekly.

Kuala Lumpur Air Astana one weekly.
London BMI three weekly, Air Astana two weekly.
Moscow Air Astana and Transaero two daily.
Novosibirsk S7 one weekly.
Prague Czech Airlines two or three weekly.
Riga Air Baltic two weekly June to October.
Seoul Air Astana and Asiana Airlines two weekly.
Sharjah Air Arabia five or six weekly.
St Petersburg Rossiya two weekly.
Tashkent Uzbekistan Airways five weekly; SCAT two.
Ürümqi China Southern Airlines daily.

See p140 for airline details in Almaty.
  Astana's direct international flights:
Abu Dhabi Etihad Airways one weekly.
Dubai Air Astana three weekly.
Frankfurt Air Astana daily, Lufthansa three weekly.
İstanbul Air Astana and Turkish Airlines each two weekly.
Moscow Transaero daily, Air Astana five weekly.
Novosibirsk Air Astana three weekly.
Tashkent Uzbekistan Airways two weekly.
Ürümqi Air Astana two weekly.
Vienna Austrian Airlines three weekly.

See p179 for airline details in Astana.

Atyrau and Uralsk also have flights to/from Amsterdam, and Atyrau has flights to/from İstanbul. Aktau is a hub for trans-Caspian flights, with direct services to/from Baku, Tbilisi, Yerevan and five cities in southern Russia. Ust-Kamenogorsk has weekly flights to/from Bayan-Ölgii (Mongolia) and Novosibirsk. Several cities around the country have direct Moscow flights. See city sections for further detail.

DEPARTURE TAX

There is no departure tax when leaving Kazakhstan.

Land
BORDER CROSSINGS
To/From China

From Almaty's Sayran bus station, sleeper buses are scheduled to Ürümqi (7800T, 24 hours), via the border at Khorgos, at 7am daily except Sunday. Saturday departures are not always reliable. Buses to Yining (4800T, 12 hours), about 100km from Khorgos, go at 7am Wednesday and Saturday. Sayran's international ticket window opens from 8am to 6pm: Ürümqi tickets go on sale 10 days ahead. Be ready to show your Chinese visa.

Same-day tickets are sold from 6.30am to 7am but in summer book as far ahead as you can. An alternative is to take a bus or minibus to Zharkent, 40km before Khorgos, then a taxi (about 600T) or minibus to the border, and a bus, taxi or train from there to Ürümqi. The crossing is usually crammed with Kazakh and Uyghur families and traders with vast amounts of baggage. Buses from Ürümqi to Almaty depart at 7pm, daily except Saturday, from **Nianzigan bus station international section** (☎ 0991-587 8639; Heilongjiang Rd 370). Tickets are sold there and at **Room 2121, Bian Jiang Hotel** (☎ 0991-2562981-2121; Yingbin Rd 32), from 11am to 7pm.

The Zhibek Zholy (Silk Road) train departs Almaty-II station for Ürümqi at 11.58pm Saturday (a Kazakh train) and Monday (a Chinese train). It's scheduled to take 31 hours, crossing the border at Dostyk (Druzhba). *Kupeyny* (2nd-class couchette) tickets cost 16,200T. The return train departs Ürümqi at the same time on the same days. The trains have restaurant cars but the food is poor and overpriced. At Dostyk, you have to wait several hours while the train bogies are changed and customs checks take place. The train toilets are locked during this time except for the 20-minute dash between the Kazakhstan and China border posts: get in line early for this!

The international ticket office at Almaty-II is open from 8am to 1pm and 2pm to 8pm. Be ready to show a Chinese visa when buying a ticket. The trains can get fully booked two weeks in advance, especially the Monday train from Almaty. You can save trouble by booking ahead through an agent such as Stantours (p130) or Valentina Guesthouse (p130), which charge US$10 to US$15 for train ticket bookings.

In Ürümqi, the **ticket office** (⊙ 10am-1pm, 3-7pm & 9-11pm Mon, Thu & Sat) for Almaty trains is in Yaou Hotel next to the station.

There is also a weekly train between Astana and Ürümqi, and buses connect Ust-Kamenogorsk and Semey with Ürümqi, and Ust-Kamenogorsk with Altay, China (see city sections).

To/From Kyrgyzstan
Official Kazakh–Kyrgyz border crossings are largely hassle free. They remained open to foreigners even when closed to Kazakhstan and Kyrgyzstan citizens after the April 2010

uprising in Kyrgyzstan. The 'green border' – foot or horse routes through the mountains, without border posts – is now closed: Kazakh border guards patrol these routes and turn back anyone trying to cross that way.

Plenty of minibuses (1000T) and shared taxis (2000T) make the four- to five-hour run to Bishkek from Almaty's Sayran bus station, crossing the border at Korday. A whole cab is 8000T (you may need to haggle a bit).

From Taraz bus station, minibuses (900T, five to six hours) and shared taxis (1500T, five hours) leave for Bishkek when full, between about 9am and 5pm. From Shymkent's Samal bus station, there's a bus to Bishkek (1500T, eight hours) at 7pm.

No public transport makes the Karkara valley crossing, south of Kegen, Kazakhstan, and east of Tüp and Ken-Suu, Kyrgyzstan, but from about April to October you can get through by a combination of hitching, taxi and patience – or a vehicle transfer all the way between Almaty and Karakol (see p147).

To/From Russia

All main Kazakhstan cities have train service to and from Moscow, daily or every two days. 'Fast' train No 7/8 takes 80 hours between Moscow's Paveletsky station and Almaty (about US$200 in *kupeyny*), running every two days via Saratov, Aktobe, Aralsk, Turkistan, Shymkent and Taraz. Many Kazakh cities also have trains to and from Siberian cities. Train No 325/326, every two days, takes 40 hours along the 'Turksib' line between Novosibirsk and Almaty, via Semey, for US$110. Several other lines enter northern Kazakhstan from Russia and meet at Astana. Daily trains from Moscow's Kazansky station to Astana take 55 to 58 hours for US$180.

There are many road crossings between Kazakhstan and Russia. Bus services, and in some cases shared taxis, link cities within striking distance of the border.

See p522 and city sections in this chapter for further detail.

To/From Turkmenistan

The remote Temirbaba border point is 165km south of Zhanaozen (p170), which is 150km east of Aktau (p170). Turkmen 4WDs carrying about seven passengers leave Zhanaozen bus station in the morning for Turkmenbashi (US$50 per person, about seven hours). The border crossing is normally straightforward if you have

the right documents. The road is unpaved for the last 70km to the border and then to Karabogas, 30km south of it.

To/From Uzbekistan

There are occasional tales of Kazakhstan officials on the Uzbek border attempting to extract bribes, but if all your papers are 100% in order you shouldn't have any problems.

The main road border between Shymkent and Tashkent, at Chernyaevka (Zhibek Zholy/Gisht Koprik), was closed for reconstruction at research time but expected to reopen in 2011. When open, it's reached by fairly frequent marshrutkas (400T, two hours) from Shymkent's Samal bus station and one overnight bus from Almaty's Sayran bus station (2500T, 16 hours). Meantime, foreigners have to use the Yallama crossing, about 60km southwest of Tashkent. Shymkent to Yallama by public transport requires a marshrutka from Samal bus station to Abay (500T), another marshrutka to Kyzylasker (200T), then a taxi for the last 25km to the border (800T) – about five hours all up. You might get a taxi the whole way for around 5000T. Coming from the border to Shymkent you may also have to change marshrutkas at Saryagash, between Abay and Shymkent. See p287 for information on transport between both border points and Tashkent.

The railway border at Saryagash, a few kilometres north of Tashkent, is crossed by nine trains each way per week. Seven of these head to Tashkent from Russia via Aktobe, Aralsk and Turkistan. Train No 321 from Almaty to Nukus, via Taraz, Shymkent, Tashkent and Samarkand, runs once a week, starting out on Sunday.

Another road and rail crossing exists between Beyneu, western Kazakhstan, and Kungrad, Uzbekistan. From Beyneu to about 130km before Kungrad, the road is little used, unpaved, and almost nonexistent in parts, but the crossing is hassle free. Daily trains run from Beyneu to Kungrad (10 hours; immigration is done on the train); many of them come from Atyrau having started in Russia, and continue to Urgench, Samarkand or Tashkent.

Sea

To/From Azerbaijan

A very irregular ferry sails between Aktau and Baku – see p169 for more details.

GETTING AROUND

Air

A good network of domestic flights links cities all round Kazakhstan and fares are reasonable (see the chart, Map p525). The main airlines are **Air Astana** (KC; www.airastana.com; ☎ 24hr call centre 727-244 44 77), an international-standard, Kazakh–British joint venture, and **SCAT** (DV; www.scat.kz, in Russian), which flies mainly prop-driven Russian planes. Air Astana offers various fare levels on each flight and the cheapest can sell out well before departure.

With the honourable exception of Air Astana, all Kazakh airlines including SCAT have been banned from flying to EU countries because they do not meet internationally accepted safety requirements.

See city sections in this chapter for details on flights. Tickets are sold by abundant travel agencies and *aviakassy* (air-ticket offices) in cities. Air Astana also issues e-tickets online – easily obtained if you have a Visa, MasterCard or Amex card.

Bus

Bus services are reasonably good. Many inter-city buses are second-hand European coaches still in their original livery. Though they're slow compared to other road traffic, buses are generally a little faster than trains, and usually more frequent. Fares are typically 150T to 250T per hour (50km to 60km), somewhere between the *platskartny* (3rd-class) and *kupeyny* (2nd-class) fares for the equivalent train ride. For trips of more than five or six hours trains are usually more comfortable.

Car & Motorcycle

Traffic police and bad roads (in that order) are the main hazards of driving in Kazakhstan. Main intercity roads are mostly in good condition but often have bad, potholed stretches. Traffic police can stop motorists just to check their papers. Go very slowly past any parked police vehicle or police observation post.

Hertz (www.hertz.kz) has rental offices in Almaty, Astana, Aktau and Atyrau. **Europcar** (www.europcar.com) has an office in Astana. You can also rent cars through local rental agencies or travel agencies. Self-drive rates at reputable agencies start at around US$50 per day for short-term rental. Be very certain about what the rental agreement involves: some companies don't allow vehicles to be taken out of the local *oblast* (region), or they impose surcharges for more than a fixed number of kilometres, or require the car to be washed before return.

Marshrutka, Minibus & Taxi

For many trips of up to four or five hours, assorted marshrutkas, minibuses and shared taxis offer a faster alternative to buses. They're generally found waiting outside bus and train stations. Marshrutkas and minibuses (often the same thing these days) usually cost a little more than buses; shared taxis are double or triple. If other passengers fail to materialise for a shared taxi, you may be invited to pay for the whole vehicle yourself. The full fare is normally four times the per-person fare, but you may be able to bargain that down.

Train

Trains serve all cities and many smaller places. They're a good way to meet people and get a feel for the country's terrain and vast size: it takes more than two days to cross the country from Almaty to Aktobe. Except for small local trains, tickets are best bought in advance. Station ticket queues can be slow: all cities also have downtown train-booking offices, called Zheleznodorozhnaya Kassa (Russian) or Temir Zhol Kassasy (Kazakh), where you can buy tickets at a small commission without having to schlep to the station. Take your passport when buying tickets.

All train fares in this chapter are *kupeyny* (2nd-class; four-berth sleeper compartments) unless stated. Timetables in English are available at www.poezda.net.

Uzbekistan
Узбекистан

No country in Central Asia seems to have it so good, yet at the same time have it so bad, as Uzbekistan. The region's cradle of culture for more than two millennia, it is the proud home to a spellbinding arsenal of architecture and artefacts, all deeply infused with the raw, fascinating history of the country. But as students of that history know, it's also sprung a few bad apples over the years. Tyrants enamoured of the country's physical bounty have run the territory we now call Uzbekistan since time immemorial.

Concentrating on the good, if there was a Hall of Fame for Central Asian cities, Uzbekistan would own the top three entries: Samarkand, Bukhara and Khiva. The names practically epitomise the region, conjuring up images of knife-twirling dervishes, serpentine desert caravans and architecture that blends with the sand.

Seen in person, the Big Three do not disappoint (the occasional overzealous restorative effort notwithstanding). Alas, they sometimes overshadow the country's other attractions, which include dazzling bazaars, ancient desert fortresses and an impressive array of largely unsung natural attractions.

All of that is enough to eclipse the bad memories evoked by names such as Chinggis (Genghis) Khan, Timur, Nasrullah Khan and Stalin. The country's long-serving current leader, Islam Karimov, is no saint either. Despite it all, the Uzbek people remain good-spirited and genuinely hospitable – yet another prime attraction in this oddly endearing country.

UZBEKISTAN

FAST FACTS

- **Area** 447,400 sq km
- **Capital** Tashkent
- **Country Code** ☎ 998
- **Famous for** *plov*, tasty pomegranates, Samarkand, Timur (Tamerlane), President Karimov's socialite/singer daughter Gulnara ('Googoosha')
- **Languages** Uzbek, Russian, Tajik, Karakalpak
- **Money** Uzbek som (S); US$1 = 2300S; €1 = 2900S (black market, and sliding fast; see the boxed text on p284 for more)
- **Off the Map** Boysun, Surkhandarya province (p254)
- **Phrases** *asalam aleykum* (hello); *rakhmat* (thank you)
- **Population** 27.8 million

UZBEKISTAN

HIGHLIGHTS

- **Samarkand** (p240) The breathtaking Registan leads a formidable cast of larger-than-life Timurid architectural gems.
- **Bukhara** (p257) Exquisitely preserved holy city boasting stunning 15th-century medressas, awesome B&Bs and fascinating history.
- **Quirky Cultural Gems** *Carmen* for a dollar at Tashkent's Alisher Navoi Opera & Ballet Theatre (p225) and Central Asia's greatest art collection in Nukus' Savitsky Karakalpakstan Art Museum (p278).
- **Khiva** (p270) The last independent khanate frozen in time amid the desert.
- **Crafty Uzbekistan** Silk in Margilon (p238), ceramics in Rishton (p239), and everything under the sun in Bukhara (p266).

ITINERARIES

- **Three days** Start in Bukhara (p257), either with a domestic flight from Tashkent or overland from Turkmenistan. Wander around Lyabi-Hauz (p259), tour the Ark (p261), and gape at the 47m Kalon Minaret (p261) and the stunning medressa (Islamic academy or seminary) ensembles. Pamper yourself in a bodacious B&B, then zip to Samarkand (p240) the next morning to explore the four pearls of Timurid-era architecture: the Registan (p243), Bibi-Khanym Mosque (p244), Shah-i-Zinda (p244) and Gur-e-Amir Mausoleum (p244). On day three exit to Tajikistan, taking a detour on the way to Shakhrisabz (p251) or the Urgut bazaar (p250).
- **One week** Fly to Urgench (p268), from where it's a short shared-taxi ride to the 'museum city' of Khiva (p270). Spend a day wandering around the walled old city, Ichon-Qala (p272). The next day travel by shared taxi to Bukhara and Samarkand, giving each place an extra day. On your last day in Tashkent (p212) catch an opera and a museum or two.
- **Two weeks** Fly west to Nukus (p276) and spend a half-day appreciating Central Asia's greatest art collection in the Savitsky Karakalpakstan Art Museum (p278). Head south to Khiva via the ancient ruined fortresses of Elliq-Qala (p270). Around Bukhara, take a time-out from architecture with a yurtstay near Lake Aidarkul (p256). After three days cover-

HOW MUCH?

- **Snickers bar** US$0.50
- **100km bus ride** US$1
- **One-minute phone call to the US/UK** US$0.60
- **Internet per hour** US$0.40-0.60
- **Uzbek skull cap** US$3
- **1L petrol** US$0.55
- **1L bottled water** US$0.40
- **Domestic beer (bar)** US$0.75-2
- **Domestic beer (store)** US$0.50
- **Shashlyk** US$0.50-$1.50

ing Samarkand and vicinity, history buffs should head south to the archaeological oasis of Termiz (p253) before flying back to Tashkent for some museum hopping, good food and a night or two on the town. Bazaar lovers should consider the Fergana Valley (p232) instead of Termiz.
- **One month** All of the above sights can be seen in a month at a more relaxed pace. You can hit both Termiz and the Fergana Valley and devote more time to exploring Uzbekistan's natural wonders, including hiking, rafting or skiing in Ugam-Chatkal National Park (p230), and camel trekking, hiking and community-based tourism near Lake Aidarkul and the Nuratau Mountains (p257).

CLIMATE & WHEN TO GO

Large areas of Uzbekistan are desert. Summer is long, hot and dry; spring is mild and rainy; autumn has light frosts and rains; and winter, although short, is unstable with snow and temperatures below freezing.

From June to August average afternoon temperatures hit 32°C or higher. The average annual maximum temperature is 40°C in June. Most rain falls in March and April.

The summer furnace of 35°C days lasts from mid-July to the end of August. The worst of winter lasts from Christmas to mid-February; see also Climate Charts on p499.

In this chapter, the high season is spring (mid-March to the end of May) and autumn (September to the beginning of November). Summer is from June to August, and winter is from December to February.

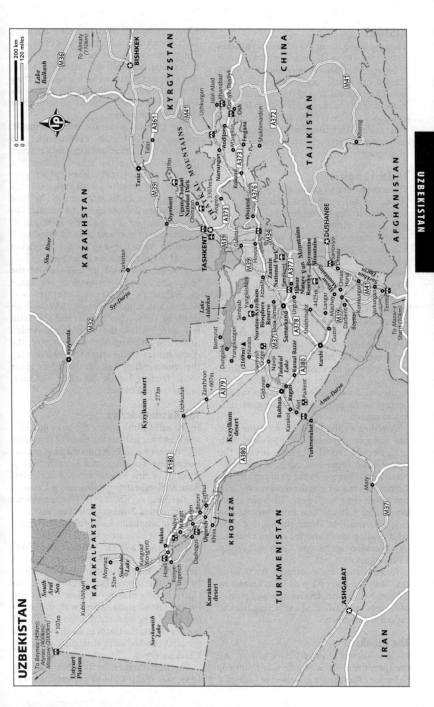

UZBEKISTAN

HISTORY

The land along the upper Amu-Darya (Oxus River), Syr-Darya (Jaxartes River) and their tributaries has always been different from the rest of Central Asia – more settled than nomadic, with patterns of land use and communality that has changed little from the time of the Achaemenids (6th century BC) to the present day. An attitude of permanence and proprietorship still sets the people of this region apart.

Ancient Empires

The region was part of some very old Persian states, including Bactria, Khorezm and Sogdiana. In the 4th century BC Alexander the Great entered Cyrus the Great's Achaemenid empire. He stopped near Marakanda (Samarkand) and then, having conquered the Sogdians in their homeland mountains, married Roxana, the daughter of a local chieftain (see p35).

Out of the northern steppes in the 6th century AD came the Western Turks – the western branch of the empire of the so-called Kök (Blue) Turks. They soon grew attached to life here and abandoned their wandering ways, eventually taking on a significant role in maintaining the existence of the Silk Road (see p36). The Arabs brought Islam and a written alphabet to Central Asia in the 8th century but found the region too big and restless to govern.

A return to the Persian fold came with the Samanid dynasty in the 9th and 10th centuries. Its capital, Bukhara, became the centre of an intellectual, religious and commercial renaissance. In the 11th century the Ghaznavids moved into the southern regions. For some time the Turkic Khorezmshahs dominated Central Asia from present-day Konye-Urgench in Turkmenistan, but their reign was cut short and the region's elegant oases ravaged by Chinggis Khan in the early 13th century.

Central Asia again became truly 'central' with the rise of Timur (also known as Tamerlane), the ruthless warrior and patron of the arts who fashioned a glittering Islamic capital at Samarkand.

The Uzbeks

Little is known of early Uzbek history. At the time the Golden Horde was founded, Shibaqan (Shayban), a grandson of Chinggis Khan, inherited what is today northern Kazakhstan and adjacent parts of Russia. The greatest khan of these Mongol Shaybani tribes (and probably the one under whom they swapped paganism for Islam) was Özbeg (Uzbek, ruled 1313–40). By the end of the 14th century these tribes had begun to name themselves after him.

The Uzbeks began to move southeast, mixing with sedentary Turkic tribes and adopting the Turkic language; they reached the Syr-Darya in the mid-15th century. Following an internal schism (which gave birth to the proto-Kazakhs; see p47), the Uzbeks rallied under Mohammed Shaybani and thundered down upon the remnants of Timur's empire. By the early 1500s, all of Transoxiana ('the land beyond the Oxus') from the Amu-Darya to the Syr-Darya belonged to the Uzbeks, as it has since.

The greatest (and indeed last) of the Shaybanid khans, responsible for some of Bukhara's finest architecture, was Abdullah II, who ruled from 1538 until his death in 1598. After this, as the Silk Road fell into disuse, the empire unravelled under the Shaybanids' distant cousins, the Astrakhanids. By the start of the 19th century the entire region was dominated by three weak, feuding Uzbek city-states – Khiva, Bukhara and Kokand.

The Russians Arrive

In the early 18th century the khan of Khiva made an offer to Peter the Great of Russia (to become his vassal in return for help against marauding Turkmen and Kazakh tribes), stirring the first Russian interest in Central Asia. But by the time the Russians got around to marching on Khiva in 1717, the khan no longer wanted Russian protection, and after a show of hospitality he had almost the entire 4000-strong force slaughtered.

The slave market in Bukhara and Khiva was an excuse for further Russian visits to free a few Russian settlers and travellers. In 1801 the insane Tsar Paul sent 22,000 Cossacks on a madcap mission to drive the British out of India, along with orders to free the slaves en route. Fortunately for all but the slaves, the tsar was assassinated and the army recalled while struggling across the Kazakh steppes.

The next attempt, by Tsar Nicholas I in 1839, was really a bid to pre-empt expansion into Central Asia by Britain, which had just taken Afghanistan, although Khiva's Russian slaves were the pretext on which General Perovsky's 5200 men and 10,000 camels set out from Orenburg. In January 1840, a British officer, Captain James Abbott, arrived in Khiva (having travelled from Herat in Afghan disguise) offering to negotiate the slaves' release on the khan's behalf, thus nullifying the Russians' excuse for coming.

Unknown to the khan, the Russian force had already turned back, in the face of a devastating winter on the steppes. He agreed to send Abbott to the tsar with an offer to release the slaves in return for an end to Russian military expeditions against Khiva. Incredibly, Abbott made it to St Petersburg.

In search of news of Abbott, Lieutenant Richmond Shakespear reached Khiva the following June and convinced the khan to unilaterally release all Russian slaves in Khiva and even give them an armed escort to the nearest Russian outpost, located on the eastern Caspian Sea. Russian gratitude was doubtlessly mingled with fury over one of the Great Game's (p50) boldest propaganda coups.

When the Russians finally rallied 25 years later, the khanates' towns fell like dominoes – Tashkent in 1865 to General Mikhail Grigorevich Chernyaev, Samarkand and Bukhara in 1868, Khiva in 1873, and Kokand in 1875 to General Konstantin Kaufman.

Soviet Daze

Even into the 20th century, most Central Asians identified themselves ethnically as Turks or Persians. The connection between 'Uzbek' and 'Uzbekistan' is very much a Soviet matter. Following the outbreak of the Russian Revolution in 1917 and the infamous sacking of Kokand in 1918, the Bolsheviks proclaimed the Autonomous Soviet Socialist Republic of Turkestan. Temporarily forced out by counter-revolutionary troops and *basmachi* (Muslim guerrilla fighters), they returned two years later and the Khiva and Bukhara khanates were forcibly replaced with 'People's Republics'.

Then in October 1924 the whole map was redrawn on ethnic grounds, and the Uzbeks suddenly had a 'homeland', an official identity and a literary language. The Uzbek Soviet Socialist Republic (SSR) changed shape and composition over the years as

it suited Moscow, hiving off Tajikistan in 1929, acquiring Karakalpakstan from Russia in 1936, taking parts of the Hungry Steppe (the Russian nickname for the dry landscape between Tashkent and Jizzakh) from Kazakhstan in 1956 and 1963, then losing some in 1971.

For rural Uzbeks, the main impacts of Soviet rule were the forced and often bloody collectivisation of the republic's mainstay (agriculture) and the massive shift to cotton cultivation. The Uzbek intelligentsia and much of the republic's political leadership was decimated by Stalin's purges. This and the traditional Central Asian respect for authority meant that by the 1980s *glasnost* (openness) and *perestroika* (restructuring) would hardly trickle down here; few significant reforms took place.

Independence

Uzbekistan's first serious noncommunist popular movement, Birlik (Unity), was formed by Tashkent intellectuals in 1989 over issues that included Uzbek as an official language and the effects of the cotton monoculture. Despite popular support, it was barred from contesting the election in February 1990 for the Uzbek Supreme Soviet (legislature) by the Communist Party. The resulting communist-dominated body elected Islam Karimov, the first secretary of the Communist Party of Uzbekistan (CPUz), to the new post of executive president.

Following the abortive coup in Moscow in August 1991, Karimov declared Uzbekistan independent. Soon afterward the CPUz reinvented itself as the People's Democratic Party of Uzbekistan, inheriting all of its predecessor's property and control apparatus, most of its ideology, and of course its leader, Karimov.

In December 1991, Uzbekistan held its first direct presidential elections, which Karimov won with 86% of the vote. His only rival was a poet named Muhammad Solih, running for the small, figurehead opposition party Erk (Will or Freedom), who got 12% and was soon driven into exile (where he remains to this day). The real opposition groups, Birlik and the Islamic Renaissance Party (IRP), and all other parties with a religious platform, had been forbidden to take part.

A new constitution unveiled in 1992 declared Uzbekistan 'a secular, democratic presidential republic'. Under Karimov, Uzbekistan would remain secular almost to a fault. But it would remain far from 'democratic'.

Onward to Andijon

The years after independence saw Karimov consolidate his grip on power. He remained firmly in charge of everything from municipal gardeners' salaries to gold production quotas – as he was, under a different title, even before independence. Dissent shrivelled thanks to control of the media, police harassment and imprisonment of activists. Through it all, the economy stagnated and the devastating cotton monoculture continued.

A new threat emerged in February 1999 when a series of devastating bomb attacks hit Tashkent. This led to a crackdown on radical Islamic fundamentalists – *wahabis* in the local parlance – that extended to a broad spectrum of opponents. Hundreds of alleged Islamic extremists were arrested. The IRP, with support in the Fergana Valley, was forced underground and Erk was declared illegal.

After extending his first term by referendum, Karimov won a second term as president in January 2000, garnering 92% of the votes. Foreign observers deemed the election a farce and international condemnation was widespread. But the 9/11 attacks on the United States gave Karimov a reprieve. The Uzbek president opened up bases in Termiz and Karshi to the US and NATO for use in the war in Afghanistan, then sat back and watched the US aid money – US$500 million in 2002 alone – start flowing in.

As an added bonus for Karimov, solidarity with the US in the 'War on Terror' effectively gave him a licence to ratchet up his campaign against the *wahabis*. According to human rights groups, Karimov used this license to brand anyone he wanted to silence a 'terrorist'. Another rigged election in 2004, this one parliamentary, drew only modest international criticism.

Such was the situation on 13 May 2005 when events in the eastern city of Andijon rocked the country and instantly demolished Uzbekistan's cosy relationship with the United States. The Andijon Massacre, as it was later dubbed, was touched off when two dozen powerful local businessmen were jailed for being members of Akramiya, an allegedly extremist Islamic movement banned by the Uzbek government. A group of their allies stormed the prison where they were being held, touching off a massive but largely peaceful demonstration in Andijon's main square. The authorities overreacted, and somewhere between 155 and 1000 civilians were killed by government troops in the ensuing melee.

International condemnation of Andijon was swift in coming. After Uzbekistan refused to allow an independent international investigation, the US withdrew most of its aid and the EU hit the country with sanctions and an arms embargo. Karimov evicted American forces from the strategically important Karshi-Khanabad (K2) airbase near Karshi (the less-critical Germans were allowed to remain at their base in Termiz). The post-9/11 thaw in Uzbekistan's relations with the West was over.

CURRENT EVENTS

Indignant in the face of Western criticism over Andijon, Karimov's response was to eject most Western-funded NGOs from the country. The US Peace Corps and high-profile NGOs such as Freedom House, the Open Society Institute and UNHCR were forced to leave in the face of registration problems or similar technicalities.

Domestically, Karimov has used the Andijon events to launch what Human Rights Watch has called an 'unprecedented' crackdown against opposition political activists and independent journalists. Nor have international journalists been immune to the onslaught. The BBC was harassed out of Tashkent in 2005; Reuters and the Associated Press managed to hold out until 2008 before getting the boot. It remains next to impossible for a Western journalist to get a visa to Uzbekistan.

Uzbekistan has yet to meet Western demands for an independent investigation of Andijon, yet it appears that time heals old wounds, as relations with the West have gradually improved. The EU eased its sanctions in 2008 and lifted the arms embargo in 2009.

The US has taken a more cautious approach, but all signs point to a *rapprochement*. In 2009 Uzbekistan granted the US permission to use Uzbek territory to transport supplies to Afghanistan. In a separate agreement, Karimov granted the US limited use of a non-military supply base in Navoi.

COTTON PICKIN' MAD

For better or for worse, the Uzbek economy hums to the tune of the 'White Gold'. Truth be told, cotton is and always was a poor match for much of Uzbekistan – a thirsty crop in a parched land. Decades of monoculture and the drying up of the Aral Sea, which has saturated the land with salt, has done little to help the fecundity of the soil. Poor yields and low government-controlled prices leave farmers too poor to pay for machinery or labour. Yet the government won't let them rotate their crops or convert to fruit. It's all cotton, all the time.

The whole system would collapse entirely but for the country's policy of sending students and adults into the fields every autumn to harvest cotton. The practice has drawn international condemnation and boycotts of products made with Uzbek cotton by Wal-Mart and other juggernauts of the Western apparel industry.

The Uzbek government, which has always denied all accusations, finally passed a law in 2009 banning the forced labour of kids under 16 (it paid little attention to forced adult labour, but then again neither do the critics). Did it curb the practice? Not one bit, according to the Environmental Justice Foundation and Anti-Slavery International, which found evidence of continued widespread child 'slave labour' in 2009.

Ordinary Uzbeks in the cotton fields are mostly unaware there's such a fuss about it. They pick because, well, that's what they do every autumn. It's certainly true that, as slave labour goes, it's hardly the Gulag. You can draw your own conclusions if you travel around Uzbekistan in October or November, when the cotton pickers are out in force. Some of them are indeed youngish looking. They are also approachable and, surprisingly, not at all camera shy.

A string of high-profile diplomatic visits followed, leading some to speculate that the US may once again be granted full-fledged use of the K2 airbase.

Meanwhile, flouting a constitutional two-term limit, Karimov quietly won a third successive term in 2007, running practically unopposed, while another parliamentary election in 2009 resulted in another sweep for Karimov's People's Democratic Party. At 72 years old at the time of writing, the Uzbek president was showing few signs of relinquishing his grip on power any time soon.

PEOPLE

Centuries of tradition as settled people left the Uzbeks in a better position than their nomadic neighbours to fend off Soviet attempts to modify their culture. Traditions of the Silk Road still linger as Uzbeks consider themselves good traders, hospitable hosts and tied to the land. For more on Uzbek ethnicity see p66.

While Uzbek men toil to make ends meet, women struggle for equality. Considered second-class citizens in the workplace and in the home, women are not given the same rights as their Western counterparts, or even their Kyrgyz and Kazakh neighbours for that matter. Although the Soviets did much to bring women into the mainstream of society, no amount of propaganda could entirely defeat sexist attitudes. There are some signs of change – dress codes continue to liberalise, for example, but old habits die hard and women in conservative families are expected to be subservient to their husbands. Marriages in Uzbek society are traditionally arranged.

Population

Tashkent is Uzbekistan's biggest city and the Fergana Valley is home to Uzbekistan's largest concentration of people, a quarter of the population. About three-quarters of the population are ethnic Uzbek. Samarkand, the second city, is Tajik-speaking, as are many of the communities surrounding it, including Bukhara and Karshi. The further west you travel the more sparsely populated the land becomes. Karakalpakstan, home to Kazakhs, Karakalpaks and Khorezmians, has seen its population dwindle as a result of the Aral Sea disaster (p100). Around 37% of Uzbeks live in cities, with the rest in rural farming towns and villages.

Independent Uzbekistan has never done a census (although one is scheduled for 2010), so updated demographic information is certainly hard to come by. The population growth rate, which was 2.2% at the time of independence, had declined to 0.94% in 2009 according to the CIA World Factbook. The emigration of tens of thousands of mostly Russian Slavs has something to do with that. Ethnic Russians comprised almost 10% of the population in the late 1980s; by 1996 that number was down to 5.5%, and today it could be as low as 2%. About 28% of the population is under 15 years of age. A number of minority groups make up a tiny portion of the population, most notably Koreans and Russians in Tashkent. There is still a miniscule Jewish population in Bukhara (see the boxed text on p262) and an even smaller one in Samarkand.

RELIGION

Close to 90% of Uzbeks claim to be Muslim, although the vast majority are not practising. Most are the moderate Hanafi Sunni variety, with Sufism (see p72) also popular. About 10% of the population is Christian (mostly Eastern Orthodox), according to the CIA Factbook. The Fergana Valley maintains the greatest Islamic conservative base. Since the 1999 bomb attacks in Tashkent, mosques have been banned from broadcasting the azan (call to prayer), and mullahs have been pressured to praise the government in their sermons. Attendance at mosques, already on the decline, fell drastically in the wake of the 2005 Andijon incident (see p208).

ARTS

Traditional art, music and architecture – evolving over centuries – were placed in a neat little box for preservation following the Soviet creation of the Uzbek SSR. But somehow, in the years to follow, two major centres of progressive art were still allowed to develop: Igor Savitsky's collection of lost art from the 1930s, stashed away in Nukus' Savitsky Karakalpakstan Art Museum (p278), and the life stories told inside the late Mark Weil's legendary Ilkhom Theatre (p225) in Tashkent.

Contemporary art is, like the media, tightly controlled by the state. Renegade artists who push buttons, such as Weil and photographer Umida Ahmedova, find themselves in trouble. Ahmedova, whose work captures the lives and traditions of ordinary Uzbeks, drew international attention in 2009 when she was arrested and convicted of 'slandering the Uzbek nation' for a series that eventually ran on the BBC website.

While Karimov pardoned her, a glance at the seemingly harmless photos reveals much about the president's artistic ideal. Uzbekistan should be portrayed as clean, orderly, prosperous and modern. This ideal has also had an impact on urban planning – witness the makeover of Samarkand, where planners have cordoned off the old town from tourists' view (see the boxed text on p247), and the demolition of Amir Timur maydoni (p220) in Tashkent.

The Amir Timur Museum in Tashkent is one of the best examples of state-supported art, with its mock Timurid dome and interior murals filled with scenes of epic nation-building. Colossal edifices such as the Senate building (p220) and the new Dom Forum (p220) in Tashkent speak to the Uzbek leader's predilection for monumentalism.

Moving to music, Uzbeks love Turkish pop, and their own music reflects that. The country's most famous singer is President Karimov's politician/socialite/business mogul/Harvard alumni/pop star daughter Gulnara, better known to some by her stage name, Googoosha. Lamentably, Googoosha steals some of the thunder from more accomplished artists, such as classical Uzbek pop artist Dado, the ever-changing girl band Setanho (erstwhile Setora) and grizzled '90s rockers Bolalar.

ENVIRONMENT

Uzbekistan spans several ecosystems, and topographic and geographic shifts. Its eastern fringes tilt upwards in a knot of rugged mountains – Tashkent's Chatkal and Pskem Mountains run into the western Tian Shan range, and Samarkand's Zarafshon Mountains and a mass of ranges in the southeast flow into the Pamir Alay. This isolated, rocky and forested terrain makes up an important habitat for the bear, lynx, bustard, mountain goat and even the elusive snow leopard.

To the west of the well-watered mountains are vast plains of desert or steppe. The Amu-Darya (Oxus) river drops out of Tajikistan and winds its way westward along the Turkmen border for more than 2000km before petering out short of Moynaq, cleaving the landscape into two halves: the Karakum (White Sands) desert and the Ustyurt Plateau (see the boxed text on p277) to the west; and the Kyzylkum (Red Sands) desert to the east.

Despite its bleakness, this land is far from dead; the desert is home to the gazelle, various raptors and other critters you'd expect to find – monitors, scorpions and venomous snakes.

There are some 15 *zapovednik* (nature reserves) in Uzbekistan, the largest of which is the Hissar Nature Reserve (750 sq km), due east of Shakhrisabz. This remote region of pine and juniper forests is home to the country's highest peaks – 4425m Khojapiryokh and a 4643m peak on the Tajik border still known by its wonderful Soviet sobriquet, 22nd Party Congress Peak.

Environmental Issues

Much of this protected territory is threatened by Uzbekistan's lacklustre environmental protection laws and the deterioration of its national park system, which lacks the funds to prevent illegal logging and poaching.

The faltering of the reserves, however, pales in comparison to the Aral Sea disaster (see p100). In addition to the existing tragedy of the Aral, there's the issue of notorious Vozrozhdenie Ostrov (Rebirth Island, or 'Voz Island'), which the Soviets once used to test chemical weapons. In 2002 the island became a peninsula, sparking fears that contamination would migrate southward to the mainland. United States government contractors were brought in to destroy the toxic elements, and today it is safe to visit.

FOOD & DRINK

Plov (see the boxed text, p223), a Central Asian pilaf consisting of rice and fried vegetables, is the national staple and every region prepares its own distinct version. Every region also has its own variation of *non* bread, commonly known by its Russian name, *lepyoshka;* the raised rim of Kokand's speciality makes it a particularly fine shashlyk plate. Samarkand's *non* resembles a giant bagel without the hole.

Regional staples such as *laghman* (long, flat noodles), *beshbarmak* (noodles with horse meat and broth), *halim* (porridge of boiled meat and wheat) and *naryn* (horse meat sausage with cold noodles) are all popular. *Moshkichiri* and *moshhurda* are meat and mung-bean gruels, respectively. *Dimlama* (also called *bosma*) is meat, potatoes, onions and vegetables braised slowly in a little fat and their own juices; the meatless version is *sabzavotli dimlama. Buglama kovok* (steamed pumpkin) is a light treat. Uzbeks love their ubiquitous *kurut* (small balls of tart, dried yoghurt) and their *noz* (finely crushed chewing tobacco).

Apricot pits are a local favourite; they're cooked in ash and the shells are cracked by the vendor before they reach the market.

Besides green tea, nonalcoholic drinks include *katyk,* a thin yoghurt that comes plain but can be sweetened if you have some sugar or jam handy. See the Food & Drink chapter for more information (p85).

RECOMMENDED READING

Something about Uzbekistan inspires many expatriates who live there to write a book about their experiences. A few are listed below.

A Carpet Ride to Khiva (2010), by Christopher Aslan Alexander, is practically a must read for anybody looking to understand the culture, traditions, superstitions and quirks of the Uzbek people. The author spent seven years in Khiva launching the Unesco carpet workshop.

Taxi to Tashkent (2007), by Tom Fleming, is the memoir of a 40-year-old Peace Corps volunteer's time in Uzbekistan in the years before the US government's flagship volunteer program was kicked out of the country after the Andijon massacre.

Chasing the Sea: Lost Among the Ghosts of Empire in Central Asia, by Tom Bissell, is a sort of travelogue-cum-history-lesson about Uzbekistan written by another former Peace Corps volunteer who returns to investigate the disappearing Aral Sea. It is quick-witted and insightful.

Murder in Samarkand (2007), by Craig Murray, is a damning account of alleged atrocities committed by the Karimov administration, penned by a maverick former British ambassador to Uzbekistan. Equally damning is Murray's account of his own government's efforts to discredit him in the context of the 'War on Terror'.

The Opportunists (2009), by Yohann de Silva, is a suspense thriller about the exploits of a Russian American who flees to Uzbekistan to escape his debts to a Brighton Beach (New York) crime boss. The author spent two years in Tashkent as a US State Department foreign service officer.

TASHKENT
ТАШКЕНТ

☎ 71 / pop 2.2 million / elev 478m

Sprawling Tashkent, Central Asia's hub, is an eccentric kind of place. In one part of the city Russian-speaking cabbies scream down broad Soviet-built avenues. Across town, old men wearing long, open-fronted *chapan* (quilted coats) cart nuts through a maze of mud-walled houses towards a crackling bazaar. In a third part of town hundreds gather amid steaming cauldrons for their daily repast of *plov*.

In the middle of it all roosts the president, his loyal Senate nearby in a newly built hulk of white glory on Mustaqillik maydoni (Independence square). This is meant to be the new centre of the formerly centreless capital. The behaviour of the centre, of course, dictates the mood in the outskirts – a mood that actually seems pretty good considering you're in a supposed police state.

Like most places that travellers use mainly to get somewhere else, Tashkent is no instant charmer. But peel under its skin and suddenly you're thinking, hey, maybe it's not all that bad. Many expats truly love living in Tashkent, and many visa-foraging travellers find themselves wishing they could stay a few more days.

And it's not just Tashkent's Jekyll-and-Hyde, Muslim-and-Soviet oddness that gets people's attention. There's a cosmopolitan populace enjoying real, live culture, a rapidly improving restaurant scene and the best nightlife in the Muslim world east of Beirut (or at least Baku). There's also plenty of green space, a clutch of interesting museums and, within a 1½-hour drive, great hiking, rafting and skiing in Ugam-Chatkal National Park.

HISTORY

Tashkent's earliest incarnation might have been as the settlement of Ming-Uruk (Thousand Apricot Trees) in the 2nd or 1st century BC. By the time the Arabs took it in AD 751 it was a major caravan crossroads. It was given the name Toshkent (Tashkent, 'City of Stone' in Turkic) in about the 11th century.

The Khorezmshahs and Chinggis Khan stubbed out Tashkent in the early 13th cen-

---

TASHKENT MUST-SEES

Chorsu Bazaar (p218) Haggle till you drop in this vast goods emporium.

History Museum of the People of Uzbekistan (p219) The great repository of Uzbek history.

Central Asian Plov Centre (p223) & **National Food** (p223) Sample the Central Asian ambrosia and other Uzbek faves.

Khast Imom (p218) An ancient Quran lies hidden behind this Leviathan new mosque.

Ilkhom Theatre (p225) Progressive theatre with English subtitles.

---

tury, although it slowly recovered under the Mongols and then under Timur and grew more prosperous under the Shaybanids in the late 15th and 16th centuries.

The khan of Kokand annexed Tashkent in 1809. In 1865, as the Emir of Bukhara was preparing to snatch it away, the Russians under General Mikhail Grigorevich Chernyaev beat him to it, against the orders of the tsar and despite being outnumbered 15 to one. They found a proud town, enclosed by a 25km-long wall with 11 gates (of which not a trace remains today).

The newly installed Governor General Konstantin Kaufman was to gradually widen the imperial net around the other Central Asian khanates. Tashkent also became the tsarists' (and later the Soviets') main centre for espionage in Asia, during the protracted imperial rivalry with Britain known as the Great Game (p50).

Tashkent became the capital of the Turkestan Autonomous SSR, declared in 1918. When this was further split, the capital of the new Uzbek Autonomous SSR became Samarkand. In 1930 this status was restored to Tashkent.

Physically, Tashkent was changed forever on 25 April 1966, when a massive earthquake levelled vast areas of the town and left 300,000 people homeless (see the Earthquake Memorial, p220).

Security in the city, particularly in the metro stations, has been high since February 1999, when six car bombs killed 16 and injured more than 120. The blasts were attributed by the government to Islamic extremists, but it will probably never be known who was responsible.

ORIENTATION

Before the 1966 earthquake, the Anhor Canal separated old (Uzbek) and new (Russian) Tashkent, the former a tangle of alleys around the Chorsu Bazaar, the latter with shady avenues radiating from what is now Amir Timur maydoni (square). The city has since grown out of all proportion and sprawls over a vast plain. Covering it on foot requires long walks and it's best to use public transport.

Uzbeks perhaps still consider Chorsu their 'centre'. The Soviet centre was Mustaqillik maydoni, which has attained prominence anew thanks to its huge Senate building. Amir Timur maydoni is a useful reference point, with Broadway leading off to the west.

Tashkent's main (north) train station is 2.5km south of Amir Timur maydoni; the airport is 6km south of Amir Timur maydoni; and the main bus departure points are about 15km southwest of Amir Timur maydoni, at Sobir Rahimov metro and Ippodrom Bazaar.

Maps

Most bookshops and hotels sell several serviceable maps of Tashkent in Latinised Uzbek, English or Russian. The best selection is at Sharq Ziyokori (p213).

INFORMATION
Bookshops

Other than slim paperbacks of Karimov's political philosophies, bookshops have little more than school textbooks in Russian or Uzbek. All four-star hotels have bookstands with touristy books about Uzbekistan. You can browse old Russian books and find an English title or two in the street stalls that line the pavement just south of TsUM department store.

Knizhny Mir (Book World; Toytepa 1; 9am-7pm Mon-Sat) Has a decent map selection along with a smattering of English-language classics.

Sharq Ziyokori (Bukhara 26; 9am-6pm) Has maps of Tashkent, Uzbekistan and most provincial centres, plus excellent 1:450,000 maps of most provinces published by Ozbekiston Viloyatlari.

Cultural Centres

British Council (140 06 60; www.britishcouncil. org/uzbekistan; Mirobod 11; 10am-6pm Mon-Thu) Tourists are welcome to browse the wealth of English-language books and videos without a membership.

Goethe Institut (234 23 90; www.goethe.de/ taschkent; Amir Timur 42; 9am-5pm Mon-Fri) Tourists don't require a membership to browse the full complement of German periodicals and take advantage of free internet surfing (.de domain only).

Institut Francais D'Etudes Sur L'Asie Centrale (IFEAC; 239 47 03; www.ifeac.org; Rakatboshi 18A; 9am-6pm Mon-Fri) Diverse collection of books in French.

Tashkent English Library (Navoi 48, opposite Hotel Chorsu; noon-6pm Mon-Fri, 10am-3pm Sat) A wonderful student-orientated library with English-language literature, textbooks and DVDs. Movies are shown daily at 2pm and conversation hour starts at 4pm. Membership is 1000S per visit or 30,000S for six months.

Emergency

See also Medical Services (p216).

Ambulance (03)
English-speaking doctor (185 84 81)
Fire service (01)
Police (02)

Internet Access

The following all have fast connections, few or no gamers and/or keep late hours. Additional net cafes are at the Central Telephone & Telegraph office (Navoi 28) and at most post offices.

Internet Center (Usmon Nosir 13; per hr 1000S; 24hr) Convenient to hotel-heavy Mirobodsky District.

Internet Premium (Amir Timur Ц4; per hr 1000S; 9am-11pm) No gamers here.

Prime Time (Mirobod12; per hr 1000S; 24hr) Fast connection, and hot dogs are sold at the kiosk out front.

Stud.net.cafe (Yusuf Khos Khodjib 72; per hr 1000S; 9am-11.30pm) Across from the Pedagogic University, it has a cafe downstairs teeming with student life.

Theatre Internet (Navoi 34; per hr 1000S; 8am-9pm) More gamer-free internet.

Internet Resources

The website www.goldenpages.uz is the best source of general listings in English, followed by the somewhat less comprehensive http://en.yellowpages.uz.

WI-FI ACCESS

Wi-fi is becoming increasingly popular in Tashkent. All hotels and restaurants listed with the icon have it, and it's usually free. The best hotspot, convenient to the hotels in Mirobodsky District, is in the cosy lobby of the four-star **Grand Mir Hotel** (140 20 00; Mirobod 2). Ordering a coffee earns you free wi-fi for the day.

UZBEKISTAN

UZBEKISTAN

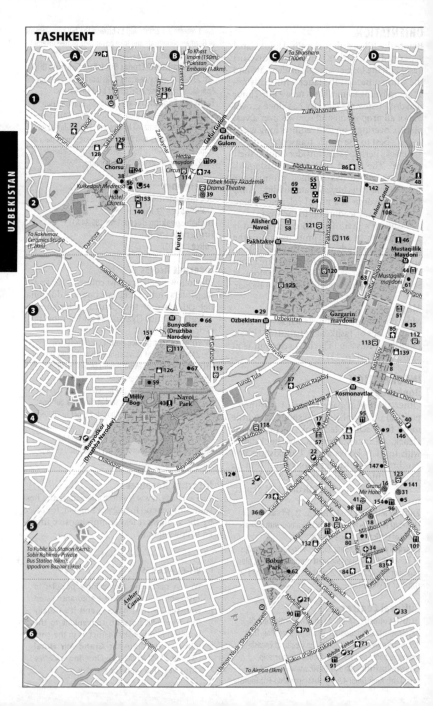

TASHKENT

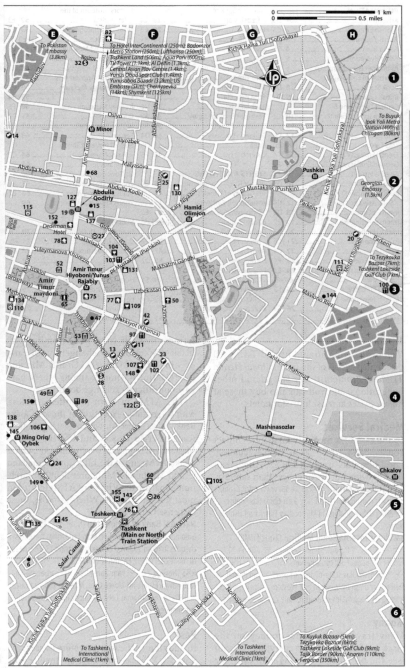

UZBEKISTAN

UZBEKISTAN

Media

Vendors hanging around behind TsUM sell discounted copies of the *International Herald Tribune, Economist, Der Spiegel* and other publications, and you can also buy these at higher prices at most four-star hotels.

Medical Services

In the case of a medical emergency contact your embassy, which can assist in evacuation. Local hospitals are a lot less expensive than the following but are often less than sanitary.

Safo Tibbiyot Clinic (☎ 255 31 36; www.safouz.com; Ivliev 21; consultation US$8; ⏲ 9am-6pm) Has English-speaking Uzbek doctors. In Mirobodsky District off Usman Nosir.

Tashkent International Medical Clinic (TIMC; ☎ 291 01 42, 24hr emergency hotlines ☎ 704 13 20, 185 84 81; Sarikul 38; consultation US$65, after hr US$150; ⏲ 8am-5pm) Has state-of-the-art medical and dental facilities and run by Western and Western-trained doctors who speak English. It's difficult to find; call for directions.

Money

Many travellers exchange money on the black market and pay for everything in som (see the boxed text on p284). All open-air farmers markets (p227) are teeming with black-market money changers until early evening. The Markaziy, Grand Mir and InterContinental hotels, among others, have 24-hour official exchange booths.

The ATMs in town are often cashless, with the notable exception of those of **Asaka Bank** (Abdulla Kahhor 73), which issue unlimited wads of crisp US$50 and US$100 bills to MasterCard holders at 0% commission. Other Asaka ATMs are at the InterContinental and Grand Mir hotels. More prevalent but rarely functional are the Visa-card ATMs located in most four-star hotels. When working, these dispense Uzbek som.

National Bank of Uzbekistan (NBU; ☎ 233 34 49; Gulomov 95; ⏲ 8.30am-4pm Mon-Fri) Cashes travellers cheques in room 213. For Visa cash advances (3.5%), head to room 212, where English is spoken.

RBS (Nosirov 77; ⏲ 9am-2pm Mon-Fri) Charges 4% for cash advances against MasterCard, Maestro and Visa cards, and 3% to cash Thomas Cook or American Express travellers cheques.

Post

In addition to the **main post office** (pochta bulimi; Shakhrisabz 7; ⏲ 9am-8pm), there are smaller post offices scattered around town, including a **branch** (Farabi 5; ☽ 9am-5pm) near Chorsu Bazaar.

DHL (☽ 9am-6pm Mon-Sat; main office ☎ 120 55 25; tassn@dhl.com; Bobur 6; train station ☎ 232 19 15) charges US$62 for a letter and US$82 for a 1kg package to the US. There are several much cheaper international mail services next to DHL's train station branch at the **Main International Post Office** (Turkestan 4; ☽ 9am-6pm Mon-Sat), including **EMS Falcon** (☎ 232 27 20; www.ems.uz).

Registration

For information on registration requirements in Uzbekistan, see p285.
OVIR Central Office (☎ 132 65 70; Uzbekistan 49A)

Telephone

Central Telephone & Telegraph Office (Navoi 28; ☽ 24hr)

Travel Agencies

Contrary to what the government would have you believe, it's easy to go it alone in Uzbekistan. Still, if you can afford them, travel agencies are useful for planning hassle-free excursions, prearranging domestic air tickets and securing qualified guides for out-

door activities such as trekking, rafting and heli-skiing. And unless you have friends in Uzbekistan they are essential for visa support.
Advantour (☎ 120 30 20; tashkent@advantour.com, www.advantour.com; 47A Mirobod lane I) Advantour draws raves for its service and can customise tours for both groups and individuals in Uzbekistan and across Central Asia. The personable and knowledgeable owners speak perfect English.
Arostr Tourism (☎ 8390-186 8648; arostr@mail.ru, www.arostr.uz; Afrosiab 13) Operated by the attentive Airat Yuldashev, Arostr is a solid choice for individual travellers. Airat also arranges obligation-free visas, and is a good source of general visa advice.
Asia Adventures (☎ 252 72 87; info@asad.uz, www.asad.uz; Mirobod 27/10) This adventure-travel specialist's eye-catching glossy brochure outlines a range of exciting mountaineering and other trips across Central Asia. Also the exclusive operator of heli-skiing tours in Chimgan (see p230 and p115).
Asian Specialized Tours (AST; ☎ 255 91 23; hiking-club@ bk.ru, www.ast.uz; Azimov 63, Apt No 1) Few people know the local mountains like agency lead guide Boris Karpov, who also leads the twice-per-month excursions of the Tashkent Hiking Club (p221). This company also runs one- to three-day easy rafting trips on the Syr-Darya around Bekobod, plus the full gamut of standard tours.

Stantours (www.stantours.com) Based in Kazakhstan, it nonetheless arranges obligation-free Uzbek visas and doles out informed advice on securing Central Asian visas in Tashkent.

Visa Extensions
One-week visa extensions are relatively easy to obtain at the airport (see p286).

DANGERS & ANNOYANCES
Tashkent is generally a safe place. Unlike in years gone by, the legions of *militsia* (police) around won't bother you too much, although travellers continue to report being shaken down for bribes in Tashkent's heavily policed metro stations. Have your passport and valid registration slips on you when riding the metro.

Tashkent's airport is a generally annoying place. Queues at both immigration and customs are long and disorganised and the whole process can last two or three hours. If you are offered 'help' with your forms or luggage when going through customs, you should politely decline, as you'll be expected to pay a premium for this service. Ask for two customs forms in English and fill them out on your own.

SIGHTS
Modern Tashkent is a big, sprawling city that's best appreciated for its whole rather than its parts. If you're short on time, pick your spots and hone in on them by car. At minimum check out Khast Imom, Chorsu Bazaar and a few museums. If you have a few more days cover as much as you can on foot – you'll catch random glimpses of city life that are often more rewarding than the sights themselves. Old Town makes for the best wandering.

Old Town
The Old Town (Uzbek: *eski shahar,* Russian: *stary gorod*) starts beside Chorsu Bazaar and Hotel Chorsu. A maze of narrow dirt streets is lined with low mudbrick houses and dotted with mosques and old medressas.

Taxi drivers get lost easily here. On foot, you could easily get lost too, but that's part of the fun. Wandering around you'll often be invited into someone's home, where you'll discover that the blank outer walls of traditional homes conceal cool, peaceful garden courtyards.

CHORSU BAZAAR & AROUND
Tashkent's most famous farmers market, topped by a giant green dome, is a delightful slice of city life spilling into the streets off Old Town's southern edge. If it grows and it's edible, it's here. There are acres of spices arranged in brightly coloured mountains; Volkswagen-sized sacks of grain; entire sheds dedicated to candy, dairy products and bread; interminable rows of freshly slaughtered livestock; and – of course – scores of pomegranates, melons, persimmons, huge mutant tomatoes and whatever fruits are in season. Souvenir hunters will find *kurpacha* (colourful sitting mattresses), skull caps, *chapan* (traditional cloaks) and knives here.

The grand **Kulkedash medressa** (admission US$0.75) sits beside Tashkent's principal **Juma (Friday) mosque** on a hill overlooking Chorsu Bazaar. The mosque was built in the 1990s on the site of a 16th-century mosque destroyed by the Soviets. On warm Friday mornings the plaza in front overflows with worshippers.

KHAST IMOM
The official religious centre of the republic, located 2km north of the Circus, was the focus of a massive reconstruction project completed in 2010.

The primary attraction here remains the **Moyie Mubarek Library Museum** (admission US$1.50; ⏰ 9am-1pm & 2-4pm Mon-Fri, 9am-noon Sat), which houses the 7th-century Osman Quran (Uthman Quran), said to be the world's oldest. This enormous deerskin tome was brought to Samarkand by Timur, then taken to Moscow by the Russians in 1868 before being returned to Tashkent by Lenin in 1924 as an act of goodwill towards Turkestan's Muslims. It is Tashkent's most impressive and important sight. The museum also contains 30 or 40 rare 13th-century books among its collection. The library is next to the spartan **Telyashayakh Mosque**.

The Leviathan **Hazroti Imom Friday mosque** (Karasaray), flanked by two 54m minarets, is a brand new construction, as is sprawling **Khast Imom Square** behind it. The Muslim Board of Uzbekistan, whose grand mufti is roughly the Islamic equivalent of an archbishop, occupies a new building to the north of the mosque.

On the west side of the square, close to the museum, souvenir shops occupy the student rooms of the 16th-century **Barak Khan Medressa**. Northwest of the square is the little 16th-century **mausoleum of Abu Bakr Kaffal Shoshi**, an Islamic scholar and poet of the Shaybanid period. The front room contains his large tomb and five smaller ones. Larger tombs of three more sheikhs are at the back.

Yunus Khan Mausoleum

Across Navoi from the Navoi Literary Museum are three 15th-century mausoleums. The biggest, on the grounds of the Tashkent Islamic University, bears the name of Yunus Khan, grandfather of the Mughal emperor and Andijon native Babur. The mausoleum itself sits locked and idle, but you can check out its attractive Timurid-style *pishtak* (entrance portal). Access is from Abdulla Kodiri. Two smaller mausoleums are east of the university grounds, accessible via a small side street running north from Navoi – the pointy-roofed **Kaldirgochbiy** and the twin-domed **Shaykh Hovendi Tahur**. Next to the latter is a mosque with beautifully carved wooden doors and attractive tilework.

Museums & Galleries

The **History Museum of the People of Uzbekistan** (☎ 239 48 39; Rashidov 30; admission US$1.50, camera US$3.50, guided tour in English US$1; ☽ 10am-5pm Tue-Sun) is a must-stop for anyone looking for a primer on the history of Turkestan from ancient times to the present. The 2nd floor has Zoroastrian and Buddhist artefacts, including several 1st- to 4th-century Buddhas and Buddha fragments from the Fayoz-Tepe area near Termiz. On the 3rd floor English placards walk you through the Russian conquests of the khanates and emirates, and there are some foreboding newspaper clippings of revolts in Andijon and elsewhere being brutally suppressed by the Russians around the turn of the 20th century. On the 3rd floor you'll also find the requisite shrine to Karimov, including placards bearing choice quotes.

The four floors of the **Fine Arts Museum of Uzbekistan** (☎ 236 47 73; Amir Timur 16; admission US$2, camera US$4; ☽ 10am-5pm Wed-Sun, to 2pm Mon) walk you through 1500 years of art in Uzbekistan, from 7th-century Buddhist relics, to the art of pre-Russian Turkestan, to Soviet realism, to contemporary works. There are displays of East Asian and South Asian art and even a few 19th-century paintings of second-tier Russian and European artists hanging about. Nineteenth- and 20th-century Central Asian masters are well represented, and there's an impressive section on Uzbek applied art –

notably some brilliant old plaster carvings *(ghanch)* and the silk-on-cotton embroidered hangings called *suzani*.

The **Museum of Applied Arts** (☎ 256 39 43; Rakatboshi 15; admission US$1.75, camera US$2; ☽ 9am-6pm) occupies an exquisite house full of bright *ghanch* and carved wood. It was built in the 1930s, at the height of the Soviet period, but nonetheless serves as a sneak preview of the older architectural highlights lurking in Bukhara and Samarkand. The ceramic and textile exhibits here, with English descriptions, are a fine way to bone up on the regional decorative styles of Uzbekistan, and there's a pricey gift shop to trap impulse buyers.

The richly decorated **History Museum of the Timurids** (☎ 232 02 11; Amir Timur 1; admission US$1.50, camera US$1.75; ☽ 10am-5pm Tue-Sun) is a must for aficionados of kitsch and cult-making. Murals show Timur commissioning public projects and praising his labourers, yet conspicuously overlooking his bloody, skull-stacking military campaigns.

The **Art Gallery of Uzbekistan** (☎ 233 56 74; Buyuk Turon 2; admission US$0.25, guided tour US$1; ☽ 11am-5pm Tue-Sat) and the **House of Photography** (Istikbol 4; admission US$1.50; ☽ 10am-5pm Tue-Sun) are in a similar vein, with rotating exhibits of Uzbekistan's top contemporary artists and photographers.

Besides memorabilia of 15th-century poet Alisher Navoi and other Central Asian literati, the **Navoi Literary Museum** (☎ 244 12 68; Navoi 69; admission US$1.50; ☽ 9am-5pm Mon-Fri, to 2pm Sat) has replica manuscripts, Persian calligraphy, and old miniatures that offer a glimpse of life in the 15th and 16th centuries.

The magnificent collection of 1930s to 1950s Soviet locomotives at the open-air **Railway Museum** (☎ 299 70 40; Amir Timur 1; admission US$0.50; ☽ 9am-5pm) will thrill train buffs and is worth visiting even if you aren't one. You have license to clamber all over any train with an open door.

Navoi Park

Downtown Tashkent's largest park, sprawling southward from Bunyodkor metro, is a haven for joggers, Sunday strollers, and appreciators of Uzbek eccentricity. Soviet architects had a field day here, erecting a pod of spectacularly hideous concrete monstrosities, such as the **Istiklol Palace** (Furqat 3), formerly the People's Friendship Palace, which appears like a moon-landing station from a 1950s film set, and the chunky **Wedding Palace**.

The tightly guarded building southwest of Istiklol Palace is the **Oliy Majlis** (lower house of parliament). It currently functions as a giant rubber stamp in its infrequent sessions. Nearby are a vast promenade and a post-Soviet **Alisher Navoi monument**.

Continuing south you'll find some amusement park rides and a large manmade lake, which you can traverse in hired peddle boats in the warm months.

Other Sights

Tashkent's main streets radiate from **Amir Timur maydoni**, emasculated by Karimov without warning in 2010 as part of his grand plan to 'beautify' the city. The dozens of century-old chinar (plane) trees that provided shade for the legions of chess players and strollers who once populated the park were all cut down. With the chess players now gone, the **statue of Timur** on horseback in the middle of the square cuts a lonely figure. A glance under the statue reveals that the stallion has been divested of a certain reproductive appendage. Just who stole it is one of Tashkent's great mysteries. Fortunately the horse's formidable family jewels remain intact.

Nobody is quite sure why Karimov cut down the chinar trees but conventional wisdom holds that he wanted to allow unobstructed views of the new, preposterously large **Dom Forum** (Amir Timur maydoni). It's usually closed but occasionally hosts state-sponsored events for honoured guests. You may recognise the tigers on the facade from the Sher Dor Medressa at the Registan in Samarkand.

Further west, good-luck pelicans guard the gates to **Mustaqillik maydoni** (Independence square), where crowds gather to watch parades on Independence day and whenever else Karimov wants to stir up a bit of nationalistic spirit. The shiny white edifice on the west side of the square is the relatively new **Senate** building. East of the square across Rashidov, the animal-festooned facade of the Tsarist-era **Romanov Palace** faces the Art Gallery of Uzbekistan, and is now closed to the public.

North of Mustaqillik maydoni is the **Crying Mother Monument**. Fronted by an eternal flame, it was constructed in 1999 to honour the 400,000 Uzbek soldiers who died in WWII. The niches along its two corridors house their names. Karimov has built a nearly identical monument near the centre of most major Uzbek cities. Hey, at least he's not building Turkmenbashi-style monuments to himself.

The New Soviet men and women who rebuilt Tashkent after the 1966 earthquake are remembered in stone at the **Earthquake Memorial**. Soviet propagandists made much of the battalions of these 'fraternal peoples' and eager urban planners who came from around the Soviet Union to help with reconstruction. But when Moscow later announced it would give 20% of the newly built apartments to these (mainly Russian) volunteers and invite them to stay, local resentment boiled over in street brawls between Uzbeks and Russians in the so-called Pakhtakor Incident of May 1969.

The **TV Tower** (☎ 150 90 24; Amir Timur 109; admission US$1; ☼ 10am-8pm, restaurant 10am-11pm Tue-Sun), a 375m three-legged monster, the epitome of Soviet design, stands north of the Hotel InterContinental. The price of admission gets you up to the 100m viewing platform. You'll need your passport to buy a ticket. To go up to the next level (about 220m) you'll have to grease the guard's palm – US$2 should do the trick. At 110m there's a revolving restaurant that serves a decidedly mediocre set Russian meal (5600S).

At the other end of town, Bobur Park is home to the poignant **Seattle Peace Park**, a collection of small tiles that recall the Cold War era with messages of peace designed by Tashkent- and Seattle-based schoolchildren in the 1980s. A few to search for: 'You can't hug your child with nuclear arms'; 'USA–USSR: Understanding Fish'; 'Make Love Not War'; 'Led Zeppelin'; and 'All Water Flows'.

Near Mirobod Bazaar is one of Tashkent's four Orthodox churches, the **Assumption Cathedral** (Uspensky Sobor), built in 1958, with several onion domes and a brand-new 50m belltower. A **German Protestant Church** (Azimov), once used as a recital hall, is now holding Lutheran services again.

It's worth taking the metro to reach some of these sites, if only to visit some of the lavishly decorated stations. A must is the Kosmonavtlar station, with its unearthly images of Amir Timur's astronomer grandson, Ulugbek, and Soviet cosmonaut Yuri Gagarin, among others.

ACTIVITIES

Thanks to President Karimov's personal affinity for the game, tennis courts have sprung up across the country. You can rent equipment and play at **Yunus Obad Sport Club** (☎ 234 77 60;

Iftihor 1; per hr 5000-7000S) in the shadow of the TV Tower. The club also boasts an ocean-sized Olympic **pool** (☎ 234 23 85; per hr 6000S).

There are a couple of places to go bowling, including **Yulduz Bowling Alley** (☎ 232 20 02; Amir Timur 60; per person per game 3500-4500S; ☒ 10am-midnight) and **Uz Bowling** (☎ 140 03 00; Uzbekistan 8/1; per person per game 3500-4500S; ☒ noon-midnight).

Runners and walkers can join the local branch of the Hash House Harriers as they cruise the streets of Tashkent every Sunday before repairing to the nearest watering hole. Hashers meet at the Hotel Uzbekistan (5pm summer, 4pm spring and autumn, and 3pm winter). Call or email organiser **Charles Rudd** (☎ 897-156 1936; ruddcl@interconcepts.com) to confirm times.

The **Tashkent Hiking Club** (hiking-club@bk.ru) goes hiking around Chimgan every other Sunday and takes occasional weekend excursions further afield.

The Korean-designed **Tashkent Lakeside Golf Club** (☎ 295 69 90/1; uzgolf@tlgt.uz; Bektemir District 1; 1 round weekdays/weekends US$80/100) is at Lake Rokhat, on the southeast edge of the city.

Just north of the InterContinental, Uzbekistan's largest amusement park, **Tashkent Land** (Amir Timur; adult/child US$4/3; ☒ 10am-7pm Apr-Oct, closed Mon), has a handful of creaky Soviet rides. It's an amusing diversion, just don't expect Walt Disney World. More worthwhile in the warm months is the **Aqua Park** (Amir Timur; adult/child US$7/5; ☒ 9am-8pm May-Sep) just north of Tashkent Land.

TOURS

There aren't any organised city tours per se, but most hotels and travel agencies can scare up a guide for no more than US$5 per hour, or US$30 per day.

SLEEPING

Tashkent has a dearth of centrally located budget and midrange accommodation, so book ahead during the peak months. Most midrange accommodation is in or around the Mirobodsky District south of Usmon Nosir (Shota Rustaveli) kochasi, convenient to the airport, the train station and many restaurants.

The foreign operators of several of Tashkent's fancier hotels pulled out of Uzbekistan in the wake of the 2005 Andijon incident, turning management over to the state. These hotels, including the Markaziy

(formerly the Sheraton), Le Grande Plaza (formerly the Tata) and Tashkent Palace (formerly Le Meridien), have seen service standards decline but their four-star facilities remain and they'll usually give small discounts if you ask, especially on weekends.

Travellers have been known to save wads of money by paying in Uzbek som bought on the black market (see the boxed text on p284). This trick doesn't work at budget guesthouses like Gulnara and Mirzo, however.

Budget

Hotel Hadra (☎ 244 27 13; Gafur Gulom 53A; d without/with bathroom US$6.50/10) The darkest hole in all of Central Asia has been spruced up a bit and even borders on liveable these days, although it still draws plenty of shady characters. It's in a dank apartment block above Cafe Hadra opposite the Circus. Breakfast not included.

Komnata Otdikha (outside train station ☎ 299 76 49; dm/d without breakfast US$6.50/29; ☒ ; inside train station ☎ 299 72 29; r/lux US$25/40; ☒) Known as Dam Olish Honasi ('resting rooms') in Uzbek, there are two versions of Tashkent's train station hotel. Unfortunately, both lost their license to admit foreigners in mid-2010, so check to see whether they are once again accepting foreigners before bunking here.

Gulnara Guesthouse (☎ 240 28 16; gulnara@globalnet.uz; Ozod 40; dm US$13, s without/with bathroom US$15/25, d US$30/40; ☒ ☐) Cheap prices, filling breakfasts, well-maintained rooms and an Old Town location make this friendly, family-run B&B a hit with backpackers.

Mirzo Guesthouse (☎ 240 37 64; turkturizm@mail.ru; Sagban 95; r with shared bathroom per person US$15) It's of a similar ilk to Gulnara, without the sumptuous breakfast and bathrooms (think squat toilets). Eccentric historian host Mirzo plays the *dutar* (two-stringed guitar).

Midrange

Sam Buh Hotel (☎ 120 88 26; www.sambuh-hotel.com; Tsekhovaya 1; s/d US$40/50; ☒ ☐) Sam Buh's rooms trump those of the nearby (and pricier) Orzu Hotel in terms of space, although couples will have to make do with twin beds.

Rovshan Hotel (☎ 120 77 47; www.rovshanhotel.com; Katta Mirobod 118; s/d/tr US$40/50/55; ☒ ☐ ☎) Not thrilling but a solid midrange option in quiet Mirobodsky District. The twin beds are more comfy than in other hotels of this ilk, and a lux with king-sized bed is just a small step up in price.

UZBEKISTAN

Grand Tashkent (☎ 255 05 99; www.grand-tashkent. com; Abdulla Kahhor Lane VI; s/d US$40/50; 🖭 🛜) It's a virtual clone of the Rovshan, only newer and with a gaudier restaurant and a slightly worse location next to the Tajik embassy.

Raddus JSS (☎ 120 77 48; Suleymanov 39/41; s/d US$50/70; 🖭 💻) A much-needed renovation has brought it up to the standards of its mid-range brethren in Mirobodsky District. The cover over the courtyard out back is a questionable call, but the rooms look brand new and some have king-sized beds for couples.

our pick Hotel Bek (☎ 215 58 88; www.bek-hotel. uz; Yusuf Khos Khodjib; s/d from US$70/80; 🖭 💻 🛜 🖭) Rooms here match or exceed the rooms at many of Tashkent's four-star hotels. California king beds big enough to host a sumo wrestling match and attractively swathed in cotton comforters hog space in the smartly designed rooms. A generous helping of creature comforts woos guests, including fluffy bathrobes, wall-to-wall wi-fi and free tea in every room along with generous sitting areas in which to enjoy it.

Arostr Tourism (p217) rents out a villa on the outskirts of town and can arrange apartment rentals in the city centre for US$20 to US$50 (three nights minimum stay). You can also rent apartments through www.orexca.com.

Also recommended:

Turkestan Hotel (☎ 239 18 21; Yunus Rajabi 4; s US$30-40; d from US$45; 🖭) Musty old classic is a bit out of the way but quiet and reasonable value.

Orzu Hotel (☎ 120 88 22; www.orzu-hotels.com; Ivliev 14; s/d/tr US$50/60/70; 🖭) Little to distinguish it from less expensive neighbours Rovshan and Sam Buh.

Grand Orzu Hotel (☎ 120 88 77; www.orzu-hotels. com; Tarobi 27; s/d from US$65/75; 🖭 💻 🛜 🖭) Similar to its sister, Orzu, but with a pool.

Top End

Hotel Uzbekistan (☎ 131 11 11; www.hoteluzbekistan. uz; Tarakkiyot 45; s/d from US$100/130; 🅿 🖭 💻 🛜 🖭) This old dinosaur towering over central Amir Timur maydoni has reinvented itself as Tashkent's best-value top-end hotel. Where there were once scowling *babushkas* there are now smiling and helpful receptionists. Where there were once musty shoeboxes there are now sleek, modern, fully wired rooms with flat-screen TVs, cushy white comforters and shiny bathrooms.

Markaziy Hotel (☎ 238 30 00; markaziy.hotel@gmail. com; Amir Timur 15; s/d from US$160/180; 🅿 🖭 💻 🛜 🖭) Most of the glorious vestiges of the Markaziy's four-star past remain, including two pools, inviting king-sized beds with fine linens, smart art and, most importantly, rooms with space enough to jump around.

our pick The Park Turon (☎ 140 60 00; www. theparkturon.com; Abdulla Kodiri 1; s US$200-300, d US$230-380; 🅿 ⊗ 🖭 💻 🛜 🖭) The initial article in the name is a bit pretentious, but this newly opened gem's bravado is entirely justified. The tidy, bright standard rooms aren't huge but they are loaded with every extra imaginable, including flat-screen TVs and the fluffiest towels in Tashkent. The impeccable Indian-trained service actually makes you feel wanted. Only the hulking exterior betrays its past as the Soviet Leningrad Hotel.

Also recommended:

Le Grande Plaza (☎ 120 66 00; www.legrandeplaza .com; Uzbekistan Ovozi 2; s/d from US$160/180; 🅿 🖭 💻 🛜 🖭) All rooms are sleek and nicely maintained here.

Tashkent Palace (☎ 120 58 00; www.tashkent-palace .com; Buyuk Turon 56; s/d from US$160/180; 🅿 🖭 💻 🛜 🖭) Can't beat the location facing the opera house.

Radisson SAS (☎ 120 49 00; www.radissonsas.com; Amir Timur 88; s/d from US$180/230; 🅿 ⊗ 🖭 💻 🛜 🖭) All hairs in place at this cosy four-star standby.

Hotel InterContinental (☎ 120 70 00; www.intercon tinental.com, tashkent@interconti.com; Amir Timur 107A; s/d from US$290/310; 🅿 ⊗ 🖭 💻 🛜 🖭) The 'Intercon' has unmatched service but standard rooms could use a freshen-up.

EATING

National, European, Middle Eastern and of course Russian cuisine are all well represented in Tashkent, although passable Southeast and South Asian food is hard to come by. For lunch on Tuesday and Friday try the 7000S Indonesian smorgasbord served up at the **Indonesian embassy** (Gulomov 73; ⏲ noon-2pm Tue & Fri).

Cafes, Chaikhanas & Fast Food

For cheap eats and beer there are hundreds of street-side cafes, Korean noodle outfits and shashlyk stands to choose from; one cluster is on Mirobod roughly across from Mirobod Bazaar, where you'll find draft beer for 1500S and shashlyk for 3000S. Another cluster is on the walking street between Kulkedash Medressa and Chorsu Bazaar in the Old Town, where you'll find 1500S shawarmas, kebabs, hamburgers and hot dogs.

PLOV GLORIOUS PLOV

Few things excite the Uzbek palate like *plov*, that delicious conglomeration of rice, vegetables and meat bits swimming in lamb fat and oil. This Central Asian staple has been elevated to the status of religion in Uzbekistan, the country with which it is most closely associated. Each province has its own style, which locals loudly and proudly proclaim is the best in Uzbekistan – and by default the world. That *plov* is an aphrodisiac goes without saying. Uzbeks joke that the word for 'foreplay' in Uzbek is '*plov*'. Men put the best cuts of meat in the *plov* on Thursday; not coincidentally, Thursday's when most Uzbek babies are conceived. Drinking the oil at the bottom of the *kazan* (large *plov* cauldron) is said to add particular spark to a man's libido.

To sample the city's best *plov* – and drink the oil if you dare – head to the celebration of *plov* that is the **Central Asian Plov Centre** (cnr Amir Timur & Iftihor 1; plov 4000S; ☽ lunch). Walk past the mob of people crowding around steaming *kazans* and take a seat inside, where a waitress will eventually come and serve you. Your group's order will arrive Uzbek-style on a single plate from which everybody will eat. The best day to come? Why Thursday, of course! Other worthy *plov* options include a lunch-time restaurant just north of the Chorsu Bazaar atrium, and National Food opposite the Circus on Gafur Gulom (p223).

Mir Burger (Ataturk 1; burgers 3000S; ☽ 8am-11pm) Well-heeled teenagers gather to preen in this Western-style fast-food court, with pasta, burgers, sandwiches and kebabs on offer. A coffee shop on the top floor of the mall serves a decent cup of coffee and has slow wi-fi.

ourpick National Food (Milliy Taomlar; Gafur Gulom 1; dishes 3000-5000S; ☽ 6am-10pm) You'll be hard pressed to find a restaurant with more local colour than this bustling eatery opposite the Circus. Walk through the entrance, overhung with goat parts, and be greeted by giant *kazan* (cauldrons) filled with various national specialities. In addition to the requisite *plov*, and *laghman*, you can sample *beshbarmak*, *dimlama*, *halim* and *naryn*, the latter prepared in the main dining room by an animated assembly line of middle-aged women.

Il Perfetto (Mirobod 9A; sandwiches 4000-6000S, pizzas 9000-14,000S; ☒ ☎ Ⓥ Ⓔ) A popular meeting spot in a great location, it's best known for coffee and tuna sandwiches, but also serves middling Italian fare and US$1.50 draft beer. Wi-fi only available from 10am to 12.30pm and from 3pm to 6pm.

Turkuaz Hypermart (see p227) has two fast-food eateries on the ground floor that are worthy of your som. To the left as you enter, **Troy** (mains 2500-8500S; ☽ 9am-10pm; ☒ ☎) has a generous picture menu of Western fare plus *lide* (pizzas), doner kebabs and other Turkish specialities. Towards the right the **Waffle House Cafe** (waffles 3500-6000S; ☽ 9am-8pm; ☒) does a surprisingly faithful rendition of a Belgian waffle.

Restaurants

The following add on a 15% to 20% service charge unless otherwise noted.

Efendi (☎ 233 15 02; Azimov 79A; kebabs 5000-8000S; ☒ Ⓥ) This non-alcoholic Turkish resto has a menu, but don't bother – just saunter inside and pick out a kebab and a mouth-watering salad from the refrigerated display case. The mixed grill (*assorti*) is a good bet for small groups.

Sharshara (☎ 240 67 77; Bobojonov 10; mains 5000-10,000S; ☒ Ⓥ) Restaurant real estate comes no riper than the canalside patch occupied by this popular Old Town standby. The sprawling patio is cooled by gentle mist from the rumbling manmade waterfall on the premises, making it an almost perfect warm-weather spot for a shashlyk and a cold beer.

Sunduk (☎ 232 11 46; Azimov 63; mains 5000-10,000S; ☽ 9.30am-midnight; ☒ ☎ Ⓥ Ⓔ) The comfort food at this diminutive eatery, kitted out like a French kitchen, is as perfect as the handwriting on the menus – on homemade paper, no less. The 8000S business lunch is popular with the diplomatic set, many of whom work nearby.

Manas Art Cafe (☎ 252 38 11; Mirakilov; mains 5000-13,000S; ☒ ☎ Ⓥ Ⓔ) To dine in a yurt without schlepping over the desert on a camel, head here. There are a few yurts decorated in traditional style, with chill-out tunes and *shisha* (hookah) smoke wafting through the air. It specialises in Kyrgyz cuisine such as *beshbarmak*. Reservations recommended.

ourpick Al Delfin (☎ 372 18 96; Bogishamol & Bodomzor Yuli; appetisers 4000-5000S, mains 8000-10,000S; Ⓥ Ⓔ) At this colourful Syrian restaurant, you can load up on appetisers such as *baba ganush* (eggplant purée), hummus, falafel, *samsa* (samosa) and tabbouleh, all redolent with ancient spices and bathing in exotic oils. If you still have room, dive right into the equally scrumptious mains – try the *mosakan* (chicken cooked with sumac and olive oil). Once you're finished, lie back on your *tapchan* (bedlike sitting platform) and send wisps of heavenly *shisha* smoke into the air.

Bistro (☎ 252 11 12; Amir Timur 33; pasta dishes 8000-15,000S; 🕙 lunch & dinner; ✗ 🆅 🅴) This delicious Italian eatery serves up large portions of pasta, pizza and grilled meats along with bottles of Uzbek or Georgian wines. The Roquefort salad is to die for. It's in a candlelit, courtyard setting, with live music.

Caravan One (☎ 255 11 99; 69 Abdulla Kahhor Lane VI; mains 8000-20,000S; ✗ ✗ 🛜 🆅 🅴) Caravan's newly opened sister also has lovely local art on the walls and an excellent crafts store. But the ambience is more understated, the service better and the Westernised Uzbek food even better here – try the lamb in pomegranate sauce. There's no service charge.

Han Kuk Kwan (☎ 252 33 22; Yusuf Khos Khodjib 1; mains 10,000-15,000S; ✗ 🆅 🅴) Tashkent's large population of ethnic Koreans is what drives demand for all those Korean restaurants around town. Popular Han Kuk Kwan is one of the best. It fries up pork and national dishes like *bi-bim-bab* (rice, egg and chopped meat) right at your table.

Amaretto (☎ 215 55 57; Usmon Nosir 28; mains 10,000-20,000S; ✗ 🆅 🅴) The mouth-watering Italian food, professional English-speaking service and subdued, candlelit ambience combine to make this the obvious choice for a romantic dinner. The pasta dishes, perfectly al dente and enriched by a choice of four sauces, are the highlight.

City Grill (☎ 241 52 02; Shayhontohur 1; mains 10,000-25,000S; ✗ 🅴) This steak house has an understated, refined interior and some of the best beef in the city, plus pasta dishes and a lengthy wine list heavy on French vintages.

Caravan (☎ 150 66 06; Abdulla Kahhor 22; mains €3-12; ✗ ✗ 🛜 🆅 🅴) Tashkent's quintessential theme restaurant is tarted up like a made-for-Hollywood Uzbek home. The original menu is heavy on arcane but well-prepared Uzbek dishes. The walls are festooned with purchasable paintings by local artists, and the attached store, filled with high-quality crafts from all over the country, is open late, making

Caravan a great place for a last-minute gift-buying spree. No service charge.

Also recommended:

Yolki Palki (☎ 233 22 59; Shakhrisabz 5; mains 5000-16,000S; ✗ 🆅 🅴) Sprawling Russian chain famous for all-you-can-eat hot and cold salad bars with every Ukrainian and Russian speciality imaginable. No service charge.

Peggy's Bar & Grill (☎ 890-977 32 23; Mashhadi; mains 6000-15,000S; ✗ 🆅 🅴) Intriguing Uzbek version of American Tex-Mex resto grills mouth-watering T-bone steaks and more-than-passable Mexican food.

Self-Catering

Western-style supermarkets and minimarkets (p227) are now abundant, but for fresh produce you are much better off at a farmers market (p227).

DRINKING

VM (Shakhrisabz 33a; 🕙 7pm-late) For flat-out debauchery, it's hard to beat this little student venue. Ostensibly a warm-up – or warm-down – bar for club-goers, its small dance floor often takes on a life of its own, obviating the need to go elsewhere. Snowboards on the wall suggest an extreme-sports bent, but the clientele is more biker than X-gamer.

Gasthaus (Fargona Yuli 7; 0.5L beer 3000-5000S; ✗ 🛜 🅴) Spry waitresses in German country outfits serve up foaming litre steins of homemade brew and Teutonic sausages to the strains of oompah music in this *biergarten* by a bridge. It's difficult to find but worth a visit.

Traktir Sam Prishyol (Navoi 2; beer 3500S, mains 12,000-16,000S; ✗ 🅴) Occupying a prime, shady nook right on Anhor Canal, this is Tashkent's swankiest brewpub-restaurant. There's live music by night and an equally cacophonic chorus of birdsong by day.

Irish Pub (Shevchenko 30; beer from 4000S; ✗ 🆅 🅴) There's more homebrew here, along with overpriced food and usually at least a smattering of expats – they gather here for happy hour on Fridays.

Brauhaus (Shakhrisabz 5; beer 5000S; 🕙 11am-midnight; ✗ 🛜 🅴) Sports fans flock here to watch big football matches on one of several screens in the cavernous basement. Upstairs features live music, German sausages and other beer-hall classics, which you can wash down with any of 12 varieties of homebrew, including a *weisbier*. No service charge.

Studio Cafe (Toytepa 1; beer from 5000S; 🕙 11am-midnight; ✗ 🛜 🆅 🅴) This hip bar-cafe has a sweet street-side patio and a Hollywood-themed interior where bartenders adeptly shake up a dizzying array of cocktails to the beat of crisp-sounding Russian and Western pop. Wi-fi is paid.

ENTERTAINMENT

Opera, theatre and ballet options are readily available, most catering to an older crowd with the exception of the Ilkhom Theatre. To get their groove on, Uzbeks gravitate to 'dance bars'. These quintessential Central Asian nightclubs are basically restaurants that morph into rollicking dance parties once dinner's over. Lengthy floor shows are *de rigueur* at such places, and the shenanigans can last until 2am or later. Regular nightclubs stay open until 4am but many are closed on weekdays.

For listings, check out www.tashkent-events.info for expatriate-oriented events news, and www.afisha.uz (in Russian) for general entertainment listings.

Cinemas

Panorama (☎ 244 51 60; Navoi 15; tickets 2500S) Tashkent's biggest movie theatre, although films are dubbed into Russian.

Premier Cinema Hall (☎ 252 16 25; www.premier.uz; Mirobod 25; private screenings US$25) Screens DVDs of your choice in English in its 12-seat 'VIP Hall'. Big screens show films dubbed into Russian.

Nightclubs

Sky Club (☎ 120 66 00; Uzbekistan Ovozi 2; cover 3000S, women admitted free except Sat) As other clubs have come and gone like so many Tashkent NGOs, Sky Club, now incongruously in the basement of Le Grande Plaza hotel, remains popular year-in, year-out.

K.T. Komba (Catacoomba; Rakatboshi 23; admission 20,000S, drinks 9000-16,000S; ☺ Fri & Sat) This pricey party palace is the premier weekend playground for the Uzbek *nouveau riche*. The music is a bit homogenous, but it's better than anything else Tashkent has to offer, and occasionally a big name from Moscow will drop in. It gets hopping after midnight and usually doesn't stop until the sun is up.

Krik (☎ 281 59 22; Usmon Nosir 22a; karaoke rooms 15,000-20,000S) If it's karaoke you crave, this little dive behind Salvador Dali is a fine place to belt out drunken lyrics late at night.

Diplomat-S (Navoi; admission free) The disco has a slutty, nutty streak that belies its serious name.

Probably the only place where you can still be making poor lifestyle decisions at 3am on a Tuesday night.

The president's daughter Gulnara controls much of the club scene, including K.T. Komba and two additional swanky and popular outfits: **Barhan** (☎ 338 10 55; Rashidov 40; admission 15,000-30,000S; ☺ Fri, Sat & Wed), which caters to the uber-rich set, and slightly less velvet-ropey **People** (Istikbol; ☺ 8pm-5am), which is more of a lounge and doesn't charge a cover.

Check out Uzbeks in their element at two of the best dance bars in town: **Alis** (☎ 490 30 30; Mashhadi 21; admission 3000S) and the funky, more upmarket **Salvador Dali** (☎ 281 58 09; Usmon Nosir 22A; weekday/weekend free/5000S). Reserve a table ahead of time on weekends because you need a seat to get in.

Sport

Soccer matches are held at the **Pakhtakor Stadium** (Cotton Picker stadium), in the central park between Uzbekistan and Navoi. Tickets (local matches 2000S to 4000S, international matches 3000S to 12,000S) can be bought directly from the stadium box office.

Theatres & Concert Halls

Tashkent has a full cultural life, some of it, such as drama, of interest mainly to Uzbek and Russian speakers.

Alisher Navoi Opera & Ballet Theatre (☎ 233 90 81; Ataturk 28; admission 2000-5000S; ☺ box office 10am-7pm show days, performances 6pm Tue-Fri, 5pm Sat & Sun, noon matinees most Sun, closed late Jun-Aug) Where else can you enjoy quality classical Western opera and ballet for less than a buck? Shows change daily – in just a week you can see *Swan Lake, Carmen, Rigoletto* and the Uzbek opera *Timur the Great*. The interior harbours various regional artistic styles – a different one in each room – executed by the best artisans of the day, and under the direction of the architect of Lenin's tomb in Moscow. Japanese prisoners of war constructed the building itself in 1947. It's one of Central Asia's best cultural bargains and a highlight for all visitors to Tashkent.

Ilkhom Theatre (Inspiration Theatre; ☎ 241 22 41; www.ilkhom.com; Pakhtakor 5; tickets 8000-13,000S; ☺ box office 11am-6.30pm, shows 6.30pm Tue-Sun) Tashkent's other main cultural highlight is this progressive theatre, which stages productions in Russian but often with English subtitles.

Known for bucking trends, its productions often touch on gay themes and racial subjects, putting off more conservative elements of Uzbek society. The Ilkhom's director, Mark Weil, who founded the theatre in 1976, was tragically stabbed to death in 2007, allegedly for blaspheming the Prophet Mohammed in his Pushkin-inspired play *Imitations of the Koran*. But the theatre continues to thrive and produce cutting-edge plays as well as occasional jazz concerts and art exhibitions in its lobby. *Imitations of the Koran* remained in the repertoire as of 2010.

Other theatres of interest:

Circus (☎ 244 37 31; Gafur Gulom 1; tickets 2000-5000S; ☺ 3pm Sat, noon & 3pm Sun, closed Jun-Aug) This popular kiddie diversion sells out quickly.

Academic Russian Drama Theatre (☎ 238 81 65; Ataturk 24; tickets 3000-4500S; ☺ shows 6.30pm Tue, Thu & Fri, 5pm Sat & Sun) Classical Western drama in Russian.

Muqimi Musical Theatre (☎ 245 16 33; M Gafurov 187; tickets 3000S; ☺ shows 6pm) Best bet for traditional Uzbek folk singing, dancing and operettas.

Istiklol Palace (formerly People's Friendship Palace; ☎ 245 92 51; Furqat 3) Big events are staged here, including pop concerts.

Tashkent State Conservatory (☎ 241 53 20; Abai 1) Chamber concerts, Uzbek and Western vocal and instrumental recitals in an impressive new edifice. Entrance is around the back.

SHOPPING
Handicrafts & Art

Ask around about private sellers who peddle high-quality Turkmen carpets and *suzani* from their apartments at reasonable prices. It's recommended that you certify antique purchases with the vendor or with the **Culture Ministry Antiques Certification Office** (☎ 237 07 38; Lashkarbegi 19), which is roughly opposite the Latvian embassy. See p500 for more information on exporting antiques.

Abulkasim Medressa (Navoi Park; ☺ 9am-6pm) Close to the Oliy Majlis in Navoi Park, this medresse has been turned into an artisans' school and workshop where local wood carvers, lacquerware makers, metal workers and miniature painters ply and teach their craft. It's a great place to buy the fruits of their labour, plus souvenirs such as *suzani, rospic* (lacquer boxes) and ceramics. Andijon native Madraimov Abdumalik Abduraimovich fashions fine traditional Uzbek musical instruments and can wax eloquent in English

about the nuances of the *dutar, tambur* (long-necked lutes) and *rabab* (six-stringed mandolin).

Chorsu Antiques (Sakichmon; ☺ 10am-5pm) It's not one but rather several antique shops nestled amid a row of hardware and trinket shops behind Chorsu Bazaar. There are some *suzani* of exceptional quality here, but you'll want to haggle hard.

Human House (☎ 255 44 11; www.humanhuman.net; Usmon Nosir 30/9; ☺ 10am-7pm Mon-Sat) This shop not only has carpets, skull caps, *suzani* and textiles from various Uzbek provinces, but it also doubles as one of Tashkent's most fashionable boutiques, featuring modern clothing infused with Uzbek styles and designs. Human House's Unesco-supported latest project, dubbed Human Made, is a small factory on the outskirts of town that specialises in traditional folk-printing on scarves and other items of clothing. Tours of the factory are available by appointment.

National Art Centre (☎ 150 40 12; Zarkaynar 1; ☺ 9am-7pm) Several stores, specialising in anything from paintings to national costumes to carpets, occupy the top floor of this newly opened exhibition centre, which also stages periodic fashion shows.

Rakhimov Ceramics Studio (☎ 249 04 35; www.ceramic.uz; Kukcha Darbaza 15; ☺ by appointment) As much a museum as a ceramics shop (see the boxed text on p249).

The sister restaurants of Caravan and Caravan One (see p223) double as art galleries and have on-site handicraft shops. The prices are competitive with shops across the country, making them reasonable places to stock up on items you might have missed while travelling. The ceramics of Rustam Usmanov and other Rishton masters are sold here (see p239).

Most museums and top-end hotels have overpriced souvenir shops, including the Museum of Applied Arts (p219) and the Fine Arts Museum of Uzbekistan (p219).

Open-Air Bazaars

The local, vast 'flea market' of **Tezykovka Bazaar** (Tolarik 1; ☺ Sun) is also known as Yangiobod Market. This sombre sea of junk – 'everything from hedgehogs to jackets' as one resident put it – is located in the Khamza District, and reached by bus 30 from the Mustaqillik Maydoni metro. Keep a close watch on your purse or wallet in this or any bazaar.

FARMERS MARKETS

Tashkent has at least 16 open-air farmers markets or bazaars (Uzbek: *dekhon bozori*, Russian: *kolkhozny rynok or bazar*). The following are the most interesting to visit:

Chorsu Bazaar See p218.

Mirobod Bazaar (Gospitalny Bazaar; Mirabod kochasi) A fiesta of fruit bathing in the teal-green glow of its giant, octagonal flying saucer of a roof.

Oloy Bazaar (Alaysky Bazaar; Amir Timur kochasi) Lacks the character of Chorsu, but locals say it has the best, if priciest, produce.

Supermarkets

Tashkent has plenty of supermarkets and up-market minimarkets that stock Western food and pharmaceutical products, including the following:

Mir supermarket (Ataturk 1; ⏰ 9am-9.30pm) Large supermarket convenient to Broadway.

Ardus (Amir Timur 3; ⏰ 8am-10pm) This minimarket is the best choice along busy Amir Timur.

Dunyo supermarket (Shakhrisabz Ц1; ⏰ 9am-9pm) Large supermarket.

Korzinka.uz supermarket (Yusuf Khos Khodjib 1A; ⏰ 8am-11pm) Near Kosmonavtlar metro.

Ozbegim (Afrosiab 41; ⏰ 9am-10pm) Well-stocked minimarket near Oybek metro.

Turkuaz Hypermart (formerly GUM; pr Navoi; ⏰ 9am-9pm) Across the street from the mothballed Hotel Chorsu, this is Tashkent's biggest and best supermarket. The department store upstairs is your best bet for Western brand-name clothing and travel accessories such as money belts and rucksacks.

Silk

It doesn't have the atmosphere of the bazaars, but for the best prices and a surprisingly good selection of silk by the metre, try the old Soviet-style department store (*univermag*) **TsUM** (cnr Uzbekistan & Rashidov).

GETTING THERE & AWAY

Air

Domestic flights leave from the domestic terminal, about 150m from the international terminal, 6km south of the centre. Pay for flights in som only (see the boxed text on p284).

From Tashkent, Uzbekistan Airways flies to Andijon (one way €30, four weekly), Bukhara (€33, at least daily except Sunday), Fergana (€28, daily except Monday), Karshi (€35, two daily), Navoi (€31, daily); Nukus (€47, two daily), Termiz (€37, three daily), Samarkand (€30, six weekly) and Urgench (€51, at least two daily).

Most of the above routes are serviced by a mix of Boeings and Russian planes such as Tupolevs and Yaks. If you are leery of the latter, pick up a timetable at the Uzbekistan Airways office to see what is flying where.

AIRLINE OFFICES

Additional Russian and Ukrainian carriers serving Tashkent from Kyiv, Rostov-on-Don, Novosibirsk and other regional hubs include S7, Kuban Air and UM Airlines. Prices listed are one-way unless otherwise noted. Save money by paying in local currency instead of credit card.

AC Kyrgyzstan (☎ 252 16 45; Mirobod 27) Bishkek flights are US$190.

Aeroflot (☎ 120 05 55; Abdulla Kodiri 1A; ⏰ 9am-6pm Mon-Fri, 10am-3pm Sat) Moscow for US$425.

Air Baltic (☎ 120 88 99; BCD Travel office, Turkestan 8) Riga tickets are US$235.

Asiana Airlines (☎ 140 09 00/01; Afrosiab 16) Tickets to Seoul are US$650.

China Southern (☎ 252 16 04; Afrosiab 2) Tickets to Ürümqi for €200.

Czech Airlines (☎ 120 89 89; Air Travel Systems office, Mirobod 12/19) Prague flights for US$550.

Iran Air (☎ 233 81 63; Toytepa 1) Flies to Tehran for US$620 on Mondays.

Korean Air (☎ 129 2001; Oybek 28/14) Seoul for US$560.

Lufthansa (☎ 120 74 01/02; tasgulh@dlh.de; Hotel InterContinental, Amir Timur 107A) Munich return US$957; also services most major world cities via Uzbekistan Airways planes to Frankfurt (Frankfurt cannot be the final destination).

SCAT (☎ 898-300 115; Shevchenko 24, apt 7) Almaty flights are US$180, twice-weekly.

Transaero (☎ 227 09 19; Bunyodkor 6A) Flights to Moscow are €223.

Turkish Airlines (☎ 236 79 89; Navoi 11A) Istanbul flights for US$420; five weekly.

BUYING TICKETS

International tickets are best bought at the airline office but can also be bought at any of the ubiquitous *aviakassa* (private travel agents) around town. Domestic tickets *must* be bought at the main **Uzbekistan Airways booking office** (☎ 140 02 00; www.uzairways.com; Shota Rustaveli 9; ⏰ 8am-7pm) or at its **airport office** (☎ 140 28 01/2). An information desk in the centre of the main booking office will direct you towards an English-speaking agent. For more tips, see p287.

UZBEKISTAN

Bus & Shared Taxi

Private buses, marshrutkas and shared taxis to Samarkand, Bukhara and Urgench leave from two locations: from the Sobir Rahimov private bus station (not to be confused with the public bus station) on prospekt Bunyodkor (Druzhba Narodev), about 7km southwest of Navoi Park, near Sobir Rahimov metro; and from the huge private bus yard behind the Ippodrom Bazaar, 3km beyond Sobir Rahimov metro on pr Bunyodkor. Rides to Termiz, Denau and Karshi leave exclusively from the latter.

The **public bus station** (Tashkent Avtovokzal; pr Bunyodkor), across the street from Sobir Rahimov metro, has a smattering of scheduled trips to most major cities.

The main departure point for shared taxis and marshrutkas to the Fergana Valley is near Kuyluk Bazaar, about 20 minutes east of the centre on the Fergana Hwy. Take bus 68 eastbound along Navoi from the Turkuaz stop, or tram 9 from Usmon Nosir kochasi or the train station.

For Chimgan, see p232. For information on getting to the Tajikistan and Kazakhstan borders, see p287.

There aren't any schedules, but there are dozens of vehicles heading to all of the above destinations throughout the day. As long as you don't arrive too late in the afternoon, you'll have no problem finding a ride and should be on your way within an hour. For more land travel hints, see p289.

Sample routes and fares for shared taxis, marshrutkas and buses are outlined in the table.

Train

The most comfortable if not the most flexible way to travel westward from Tashkent is via train out of Tashkent's **train station** (zheleznodorozhny vokzal; ☎ 005), next to the Tashkent metro station.

Express (*skorostnoy* or 'high-speed') trains with airplane-style seating run to Samarkand ('Registan'; US$7.50, 3½ hours, five weekly at 7am), Bukhara ('Sharq'; US$12, seven hours, daily at 8.15am) and Karshi ('Nasaf'; US$12, seven hours, six weekly at 7.35am). The latter two both stop in Samarkand.

Slower Soviet-style passenger night trains trundle to those and other cities. The following prices are for *platskartny* (hard sleeper) carriages: Bukhara (US$13.50, 11 hours, nightly), Nukus (US$18, 22 hours, six weekly), Samarkand (US$8, 6½ hours, frequent), Termiz (US$15, 14 hours, even days) and Urgench (US$15, 22 hours, four weekly).

BUYING TICKETS

The main ticket booth is to the right as you enter the train station; the ticket booth for slow local (*prigorodny*, or 'suburban') trains is on the left. If the lines are long there's another ticket booth in a separate building around the back and to the right with a desk for foreign-passport holders. You'll need your passport to purchase train tickets (a photocopy won't do).

GETTING AROUND
To/From the Airport

Buses are the cheapest way to/from the airport. Coming from the airport, they're also an alternative to the greedy, sometimes crooked, taxi drivers. Unfortunately they stop running at 10.30pm despite the fact that many flights arrive in the middle of the night. The bus stop is in front of the domestic terminal; exit the international terminal and walk right.

BUS, SHARED TAXI & MARSHRUTKA TIMETABLE

Destination	Shared taxi (cost/duration)	Marshrutka (cost/duration)	Bus (cost/duration)
Andijon	US$12/5hr	US$7/7hr	-
Bukhara	US$20/6½hr	US$10/8hr	US$6/8-10hr
Fergana	US$10/4hr	US$6/5½hr	-
Kokand	US$9/3hr	US$5/4hr	-
Samarkand	US$10/3½hr	US$6/4½hr	US$3.50/6hr
Termiz	US$20/9hr	US$10/12hr	US$7.50/13hr
Urgench/Khiva	US$25/12hr	US$13/13hr	US$10/20hr

TAXI TIPS

Every car is a potential taxi in Tashkent, but essentially there are two forms: licensed cabs and 'independent' cabs. The former have little roof-mounted 'taxi' signs. The latter are just average cars driven by average dudes.

Independent taxis generally leave it up to you to pick the price, which is fine. As long as you don't insult them with your offer, they will usually accept it. Give the som black-market equivalent of US$0.50 for short trips (less than 2km), US$1 for midrange, US$1.50 for cross-town and US$2 to the city's outskirts (eg Ippodrom or Kuyluk Bazaar).

Licensed cabs – especially those waiting outside bars and hotels – are a different beast. Do not go anywhere in a licensed cab without agreeing to a price first. Use the same rate guidelines as above, but be ready to pay slightly more – these are professionals after all (professionals who will demand quadruple the going rate if you don't agree on a price up front).

If you don't care for nickel-and-dime haggling and just want to book a damn taxi, you'll pay only slightly higher rates – about US$1 for up to 5km, and US$0.20 per additional kilometre – by dialling **Premier Taxi** (☎ 244 11 11) or **Millennium Taxi** (☎ 129 55 55).

Cab drivers tend not to know street names, so use landmarks – big hotels and metro stations work best – to direct your driver to your destination.

Bus 67 travels from the airport to the Intercon via Usmon Nosir, Shakhrisabz and Amir Timur, a 35-minute journey. Marshrutka 62 follows the same route. Buses 11 and 76 go from the airport to Chorsu Bazaar via Bobur and Furqat streets.

The 7km, 20-minute taxi ride to/from Hotel Uzbekistan should cost no more than US$2, but an unofficial airport cartel won't accept less than about US$10 from foreigners; you're doing well if you get them down to US$5.

To elude the airport taxis, simply walk three minutes out to the main road to hail a cab, or take a bus to the centre and flag down a cheaper taxi there.

If you do end up taking an airport taxi, make sure to agree on a firm price beforehand.

Car

Any hotel or travel agency can arrange a comfortable private car and driver from about US$10 per hour. You'll pay less – US$5 to US$8 per hour, depending on your negotiating skills – on the street (see the boxed text, above, for more tips).

Public Transport

Buses, trolleybuses and trams cost 400S to 500S, payable on board to the conductor or driver. Most of them are marked in Latinised Uzbek and given a number (older buses are still marked in Cyrillic).

The destination of public buses, trams, trolleybuses and marshrutkas is written clearly in the window. Useful stops for tourists include the Chorsu Bazaar and Turkuaz/GUM stops, on opposite sides of Navoi near Hotel Chorsu; the train station ('Vokzal') stop on Shevchenko opposite the train station; the Grand Mir (Rossiya) hotel on Shuta Rustaveli; and TsUM.

From the Turkuaz stop, bus 91 goes to the Intercon via Navoi, while tram 8 rumbles to the train station. From the train station, take bus 60 to the Intercon via Amir Timur kochasi, or take marshrutka 11 to TsUM, and bus 3 to the Grand Mir. From TsUM, bus 97 takes you to Yunusobod Bazaar via the Intercon.

Metro

Tashkent's **metro** (per trip 400S; ⏲ 5am-midnight) is the easiest way to get around – see p231 for a metro map. During the day you'll never wait more than five minutes for a train, and the stations are clean and safe. You'll need to buy a token (zhyton) for each trip. The metro was designed as a nuclear shelter and taking photos inside is strictly forbidden – a pity given its often striking design.

Despite the use of Uzbek for signs and announcements, the system is easy to use, and well enough signposted that you hardly need a map. If you listen as the train doors are about to close, you'll hear the name of the next station at the end of the announcement: 'Ekhtiyot buling, eshiklar yopiladi; keyingi bekat…' ('Be careful, the doors are closing; the next station is…').

UZBEKISTAN

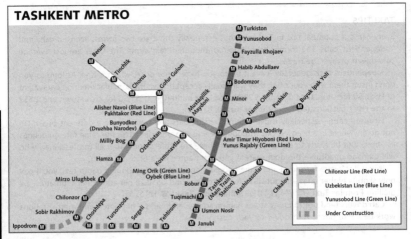

AROUND TASHKENT
Chimgan & Around
Just over an hour northeast of Tashkent by car lies **Ugam-Chatkal National Park**, an outdoor haven loaded with hiking and adventure-sport opportunities as well as more relaxing pursuits. The mountains here are not quite as extreme or scenic as the higher peaks around Almaty and Bishkek, but certain activities (heli-skiing, trekking and rafting come to mind) are more accessible and at least as challenging.

You don't have to be an X-gamer to enjoy Chimgan. A major sanatoria centre in Soviet times, today it has hatched a few newer resorts and retreats to complement the usual diet of decrepit yet still-functioning concrete Soviet hulks. And the Chorvok Reservoir offers more mellow outdoor pursuits such as fishing, swimming and canoeing – ask about these at the Chorvok Oromgohi hotel.

This entire area is known locally as Chimgan, a reference to both its biggest town and its central peak, Bolshoy (Big) Chimgan (3309m).

ACTIVITIES
Trekking
Ugam-Chatkal National Park covers the mountainous area west and southwest of the Kyrgyzstan border, from the city of Angren in the south all the way up to the Pskem Mountains in the fingerlike, glacier-infested wedge of land jutting into Kyrgyzstan northeast of Chimgan town. The Pskem top out at 4319m but are off limits to all but well-heeled heli-skiers because of their location in a sensitive border zone. Should the situation change, this will become prime virgin trekking territory.

For now, all of the national park's accessible terrain lies in the Chatkal Mountains, which stretch into Kyrgyzstan. Lacking the stratospheric height of the big Kyrgyz and Tajik peaks, the appeal of the Chatkals is their accessibility. Escaping civilisation involves walking just a short way out of the Chimgan or Beldersoy ski areas.

Hook up with the Tashkent Hiking Club (p221) or talk to Boris at AST (p217) to get the scoop on day and overnight hiking possibilities around here.

A guide is highly recommended for all hikes as the routes are not marked and topographical maps are about as common as Caspian Tigers (which died out from these parts in the 1970s). Guides are mandatory for multiday hikes to secure the necessary border-zone permits and ensure that you don't inadvertently walk into Kyrgyzstan (highly possible given the jigsaw borders).

Skiing & Heli-skiing
In the winter months, **downhill skiing** is possible at the Beldersoy and Chimgan ski areas. They encompass both the best and the worst of Soviet-style ski resorts. The best: limited grooming, excellent free-riding, some unexpectedly steep terrain, rock-bottom prices and plenty of hot wine and shashlyk. The worst: crummy lifts, limited total acreage and no snow-making to speak of.

The best terrain is way up above the tree line at Beldersoy, accessible by a lone T-bar. From the base, a long, slow double chairlift leads up to the T-bar. With just one chairlift and two trails, Chimgan is more for beginners, but also has challenging free-riding off-piste. A full-day lift pass at either 'resort' costs US$10, or you can pay by the ride (T-bar/chairlift US$0.50/2). Beldersoy has surprisingly passable equipment available for hire.

While the resorts are not worth a special trip to Uzbekistan, the **helicopter skiing** most definitely is, as the Chatkal and Pskem Mountains are reputed to get some of the driest, fluffiest powder you'll find anywhere. Figure on paying US$500 per day for heli-skiing – a bargain by international standards. Book through Asia Adventures (p217).

Rafting
In the warmer months, **white-water rafting** trips are possible on the raging gazpacho of the Pskem, Ugam and Chatkal rivers. Talk to **Asia Raft** (Map p214; ☎ in Tashkent 71-267 09 18; www.asiaraft. uz; Mavlono Riezi 77) in Tashkent.

SLEEPING
Hotel Chimgan (☎ 8390-105 5002; Chimgan; r per person US$7.50) Well, here's your chance to experience one of those (barely) still-standing Soviet relics. With a mix of threadbare but clean doubles and quads, it's *the* place to stay for skiers and hikers on a budget. Three square meals per day costs 10,000S.

Chorvok Oromgohi (☎ 8390-188 0553; Posyolok Bokachul; s/d from €30/40) This huge pyramid on the shore of the Chorvok Reservoir will certainly catch your eye, for better or for worse. Standard rooms are pretty basic fare; you're paying for the balconies with mountain or lake views.

Arostr-Chimgan (☎ 8390-997 4497; Chimgan; d US$90, 6-person cabin US$200) The six-person cabins here have simple bedrooms and cosy common areas with fireplaces and satellite TV. *The* place to ride out a blizzard with good company and a few handles of vodka.

Beldersoy Hotel (☎ 8390-176 3826, in Tashkent 71-232 17 90; r from US$110; ❄ 🏊) This swanky four-season mountain lodge belonging to Beldersoy ski area is the best bet for well-heeled skiers and hikers.

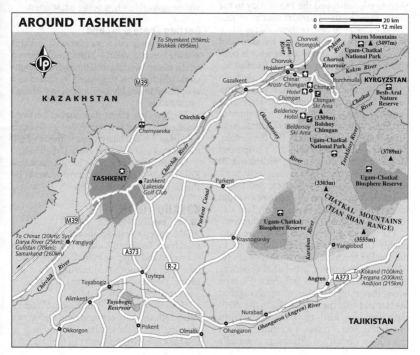

AROUND TASHKENT

GETTING THERE & AWAY

To get to Chimgan from Tashkent, take a marshrutka (US$1) or shared taxi (US$2) from Buyuk Ipak Yoli metro to Gazalkent (50 minutes) and transfer to a shared taxi to Chimgan (US$1.50, 40 minutes). A private taxi direct to Chimgan from Tashkent from the metro costs about US$30.

A local train connects Tashkent with Chinar (US$0.50, two hours, four daily), just a 10-minute taxi ride from the action on the Chorvok Reservoir. Chinar, near Hojakent, is known for its outdoor shashlyk eateries near the Chorvok dam.

FERGANA VALLEY
ФЕРГАНСКАЯ ДОЛИНА

The first thought many visitors have on arrival in the Fergana Valley is, 'Where's the valley?' From this broad (22,000 sq km), flat bowl, the surrounding mountain ranges (Tian Shan to the north and the Pamir Alay to the south) seem to stand back at enormous distances – when you can see them, that is. More often these spectacular peaks are shrouded in a layer of smog, produced by what is both Uzbekistan's most populous and its most industrial region.

It's also the country's fruit and cotton basket. Drained by the upper Syr-Darya, the Fergana Valley is one big oasis, with some of the finest soil and climate in Central Asia. Already by the 2nd century BC the Greeks, Persians and Chinese found a prosperous kingdom based on farming, with some 70 towns and villages. The Russians were quick to realise the valley's fecundity, and Soviet rulers enslaved it to an obsessive raw-cotton monoculture that still exists today. It is also the centre of Central Asian silk production.

The valley's eight million people are thoroughly Uzbek – 90% overall and higher in the smaller towns. The province has always wielded a large share of Uzbekistan's political, economic and religious influence. Fergana was at the centre of numerous revolts against the tsar and later the Bolsheviks. In the 1990s the valley gave birth to Islamic extremism in Central Asia. President Karimov's brutal crackdown on alleged extremists eventually

came to a head in the form of the Andijon Massacre in 2005 (see p208).

The post-Andijon crackdown has increased the police presence in the valley, but it's not something that's likely to affect most tourists as long as they keep a low profile. The valley's people remain among the most hospitable and friendly in the country. Other attractions are exceptional crafts and several kaleidoscopic bazaars.

Dangers & Annoyances

Standards of dress are a potential source of misunderstanding in the valley. Except perhaps in the centre of Russified Fergana town, too much tourist flesh will be frowned upon, so dress modestly (ie no shorts or tight-fitting clothes). Women travellers have reported being harassed when walking alone in cities such as Andijon, especially at night.

Security is tight compared with other parts of the country and all foreigners entering the Fergana Valley must register at a major roadblock west of the tunnels separating the valley from Tashkent. The police are friendly enough, just keep your passport at the ready and be agreeable when being questioned.

Getting There & Around

There is no public bus service between Tashkent and the Fergana Valley – buses aren't allowed on the scenic, winding road through the mountains, which is best negotiated by shared taxi as opposed to wobbly looking Daewoo Damas marshrutkas.

The few slow trains that lumber between Tashkent and the Fergana Valley go through Tajikistan. Do not board these without a Tajik transit visa and a double-entry Uzbek visa.

Within the valley, slow local trains link Kokand and Andijon, but most travel is by shared taxi, marshrutka or bus.

KOKAND   КОКАНД
☎ 73 / pop 200,000

As the valley's first significant town on the road from Tashkent, Kokand is a gateway to the region and stopping point for many travellers. With a historically interesting palace and several medressas and mosques, it makes for a worthwhile half-day visit.

This was the capital of the Kokand khanate in the 18th and 19th centuries and the valley's true 'hotbed' in those days – second only to Bukhara as a religious centre in Central Asia, with at least 35 medressas and hundreds of mosques. But if you walk the streets today, you will find only a polite, subdued Uzbek town, its old centre hedged by colonial avenues, bearing little resemblance to Bukhara.

Nationalists fed up with empty revolutionary promises met here in January 1918 and declared a rival administration, the 'Muslim Provincial Government of Autonomous Turkestan' led by Mustafa Chokaev. The Tashkent Soviet immediately had the town sacked, most of its holy buildings desecrated or destroyed and 14,000 Kokandis slaughtered.

Traditionally conservative Kokand is changing fast as money flocks in from somewhere. A few high-end boutiques have sprouted on the spruced-up main street, Istiklol, and all central squares and parks were getting massive makeovers when we visited. The town still shuts down by about 9pm, however.

Orientation

The Khan's Palace stands in the central Muqimi Park. Most restaurants and shops of interest are on or just off the 1km stretch of Istiklol running east–west between Muqimi Park and Abdulla Nabiev maydoni. The mosque-sprinkled old-town lanes squeezed between Khamza, Akbar Islamov and Furqat make for good wandering.

Information

Black market money changers hang out at Dekhon Bazaar (the main farmer's market), near the bus station. OVIR's Kokand office does not handle foreigner registrations; register in Fergana, if necessary.

Asaka Bank (Istiklol) Advances cash on MasterCard.

Internet Centre (Istanbul 8; per hr 1200S; ☽ 24hr) If it's full there's another net cafe next door; both have state-of-the-art facilities.

Internet Club (Navoi 1; per hr 1000S; ☽ 8am-midnight)

Sights
KHAN'S PALACE

The **Khan's Palace** (☎ 553 60 46; http://museum.dino soft.uz; Istiklol 2; admission US$1, guided tours US$2.50; ☽ 9am-5pm), with seven courtyards and 114 rooms, was built in 1873 – just three years before the tsar's troops arrived, blew up its fortifications and abolished the khan's job.

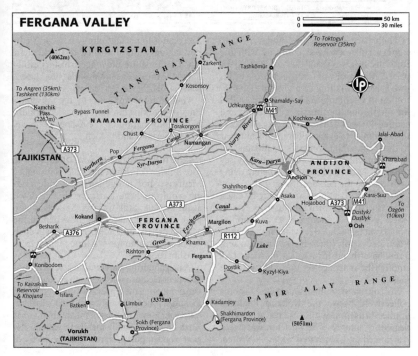

FERGANA VALLEY

UZBEKISTAN

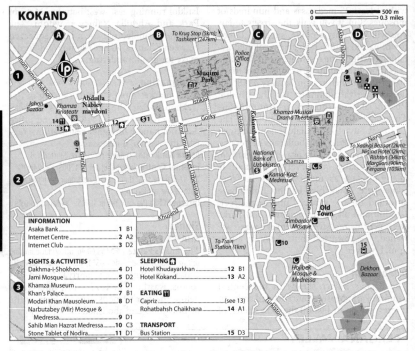

KOKAND

0 — 500 m
0 — 0.3 miles

To Krug Stop (5km);
Tashkent (247km)

Police Office

Muqimi Park

Imom Ismoil Bukhori

Jahon Bazaar

Khamza Kinoteatr

Abdulla Nabiev maydoni

Istiklol

Istiklol

Gorky

Turkiston

Kokandsoy

Khamza Musical Drama Theatre

National Bank of Uzbekistan

Khamza

Kamal-Kazi Medressa

Navol

To Yaangi Bazaar (2km);
Nigina Hotel (2km);
Rishton (34km);
Margilan (90km);
Fergana (103km)

Amir Timur (4) ul Uzbekistan

Istanbul

Khujand

To Train Station (1km)

Zimbardor Mosque

Old Town

Turkiston

Hojibek Mosque & Medressa

Dekhon Bazaar

Fergana

Muqimi

Anut Umakhoram

INFORMATION
Asaka Bank	1	B1
Internet Centre	2	A2
Internet Club	3	D2

SIGHTS & ACTIVITIES
Dakhma-i-Shokhon	4	D1
Jami Mosque	5	D2
Khamza Museum	6	D1
Khan's Palace	7	B1
Modari Khan Mausoleum	8	D1
Narbutabey (Mir) Mosque & Medressa	9	D1
Sahib Mian Hazrat Medressa	10	C3
Stone Tablet of Nodira	11	D1

SLEEPING
Hotel Khudayarkhan	12	B1
Hotel Kokand	13	A2

EATING
Capriz	(see 13)	
Rohatbahsh Chaikhana	14	A1

TRANSPORT
Bus Station	15	D3

The palace was built by Khudayar Khan, a mean ruler who was chummy with the Russians. Just two years after completing the palace, Khudayar was forced into exile by his own subjects, winding up under Russian protection in Orenburg. As his heirs quarrelled for the throne, the Russians moved in and snuffed out the khanate, in the process breaking a promise to eventually return Khudayar to the throne. The homesick khan later fled Orenburg and embarked on an epic odyssey through Central and South Asia before dying of disease on the lam near Herat.

Roughly half of the palace used to be taken up by the harem, which the Russians demolished in 1919. Khudayar's 43 concubines would wait to be chosen as wife for the night – Islam allows only four wives so the khan kept a mullah at hand for a quick marriage ceremony (the marriage set up to last just one night).

Six courtyards remain and their 27 rooms collectively house the Kokand Regional Studies Museum, with displays of varying degrees of interest. The museum was being rearranged and renovated when we visited.

The plan is to make it more khan-centric by moving anything unrelated to the khanate (such as the nature and modern history exhibits) to the musty **Khamza Museum** (Akbar Islamov 2; admission US$1; 9am-5pm Tue-Sun).

Guided tours are given by the museum's English-speaking director, who is also a fountain of information on the region. Tours are also in German and French.

NARBUTABEY MOSQUE & MEDRESSA
The Bolsheviks closed the 1799 Narbutabey Medressa, but it opened after independence only to have Karimov shut it down again in 2008. Still, tourists are welcome to poke around the **medressa** (now named the Mir Medressa) and adjacent **mosque**, which Stalin reopened to win wartime support from Muslim subjects.

A neighbouring **graveyard** has several prominent mausoleums associated with another khan, Umar. Entering the graveyard's north gate from the street, proceed straight to the 1830s **Dakhma-i-Shokhon** (Grave of Kings), the tomb of Umar Khan and other family members, with an elegant wooden portal carved with the poetry of

Umar's wife, Nodira (see the boxed text). To the west of here, the unrestored **Modari Khan Mausoleum**, built in 1825 for Umar's mother, lies under a bright, sky-blue cupola.

Originally buried behind Modari Khan, Nodira was adopted by the Soviets as a model Uzbek woman and moved to a prominent place beneath a white **stone tablet**, beyond Dakhma-i-Shokhon near the graveyard's south gate.

SAHIB MIAN HAZRAT MEDRESSA

From the uninteresting Kamal-Kazi Medressa on Khamza, walk five minutes down Muqimi to the truncated remnants of the large 19th-century Sahib Mian Hazrat Medressa, where the great Uzbek poet and 'democrat' Mohammedamin Muqimi (1850–1903) lived and studied for the last 33 years of his life. There is a small **museum** (admission US$0.50) in Muqimi's old room, which contains a few of his personal belongings, plus Arabic calligraphy by Muqimi himself.

JAMI MOSQUE

Kokand's most impressive mosque, built by Umar Khan in 1812, is centred on a 22m minaret and includes a colourful 100m-long *aivan* (portico) supported by 98 red-wood columns brought from India. The entire complex has reverted to its former Soviet guise as a **museum** (Khamza 5; admission US$1; ⏰ 9am-5pm), with one room housing a collection of *suzani* and ceramics from the region. The large wall separating the courtyard from the street was being torn down when we visited, heralding a possible new look for the complex.

Sleeping & Eating

For budget accommodation you are better off continuing on to Fergana. The hotels listed here convert dollars to som at black-market rates.

Nigina Hotel (☎ 552 85 33; Usta Bozor; shared d with bathroom US$12.50, d/tr US$25/37.50; ❄) Its location out by Yaangi Bazaar is a minus, but it's clean and less expensive than anything in the centre. If you're travelling solo and nobody else turns up, you'll have the shared double to yourself.

Hotel Khudayarkhan (☎ 727 82 32; Istiklol 31; s/d US$30/60; ❄ 🖵) Finally, a hotel in Kokand with a little panache. Little extras such as felt slippers, free bottled water and flat-screen TVs (albeit with Russian channels only) make all the difference. Request a room at the quieter back side.

Hotel Kokand (☎ 552 64 03; Imom Ismoil Bukhori 1) This notoriously dingy hotel was finally being upgraded and was closed to foreigners when we visited. Expect it to reopen with room prices in the US$50 range.

Rohatbahsh Chaikhana (Imom Ismoil Bukhori 1; shashlyk 1200S; ⏰ 8am-8pm) This popular chaikhana, also known as Jahon Chaikhana, tends to close earlier than advertised, but during daylight hours it's the best place in town.

Capriz (Imom Ismoil Bukhori 1; mains 2000-4000S; ⏰ 9am-10pm) Clean premises and a menu of Russian staples makes this Kokand's safest all-around eating option.

Vegetarians and self-caterers can go to Dekhon Bazaar by the bus station, or to Jahon Bazaar near Hotel Kokand.

NODIRA

Of the pastiche of colourful characters to have emerged from Fergana Valley lore over the years, perhaps the most beloved was the beautiful poetess Nodira (1792–1842), wife of Umar Khan of Kokand. When Umar died in 1822, his son and successor, Mohammed Ali (Madali Khan), was only 12 years old. The popular Nodira took over as de facto ruler of the khanate for the better part of a decade, turning Kokand into an artistic hotbed and oasis of liberalism in a region accustomed to sadistic despots.

Unfortunately, little of this liberal spirit rubbed off on Madali, who developed a reputation for ruthlessness during a successful campaign to expand the khanate's borders. His territorial ambitions drew the ire of the notorious Emir Nasrullah Khan of Bukhara. Nasrullah would eventually get the upper hand in this battle, and in 1842 he seized Kokand and executed Madali, his brother and, when he refused to marry him (or so the story goes), Nodira. Within three months the Emir's troops would be forced out of Kokand, touching off a battle for succession that would ultimately result in the rise to power of Khudayar Khan, a distant cousin of Madali.

Best known for her poetry (in both Uzbek and Tajik), Nodira remains as popular as ever today, as evidenced by the preponderance of Uzbek women named Nodira.

Getting There & Around

Transport to points within the Fergana Valley leave from the bus station by Dekhon Bazaar on Furqat. Shared taxis head to Rishton (US$1.25, 45 minutes), Fergana (US$1.25, 1¼ hours) and Andijon (US$3, two hours). Marshrutkas cover the same routes, while buses leave every 15 minutes until 6.30pm to Fergana (US$0.75, two hours) and every 45 minutes until 3pm to Andijon (US$1.25, four hours).

Shared taxis to Tashkent congregate at the 'Krug' ('Circle') stop about 5km north of town (US$9, three hours).

From the **train station** (Amir Timur 40), there is a 5am train to Andijon via Namangan, and a 2.30pm train to Andijon via Margilon (both US$1, five hours).

Useful public transport options include marshrutka 2 or 4 from Dekhon Bazaar to the Hotel Kokand area, and marshrutka 15, 28 or 40 north from the bazaar to the Jami Mosque.

FERGANA ФЕРГАНА

☎ 73 / pop 216,000

Tree-lined avenues and pastel-plastered tsarist buildings give Fergana the feel of a mini-Tashkent. Throw in the best services and accommodation in the region, plus a central location, and you have the most obvious base from which to explore the rest of the valley.

Fergana is the valley's least ancient and least Uzbek city. It began in 1877 as Novy Margelan (New Margilon), a colonial annexe to nearby Margilon. It became Fergana in the 1920s. It's a nice enough place to hang out, and somewhat cosmopolitan with its relatively high proportion of Russian and Korean citizens.

Orientation

The streets radiate out from what's left of the old tsarist fort, 10m of mudbrick wall within an army compound (off-limits to visitors) behind the city and provincial administration buildings. The centre of the city is around the Hotel Ziyorat, within walking distance of central Al-Farghoni Park and the bazaar. The airport is 5km south of town.

Information

Black-market money changers are at the bazaar. The Asia Hotel has a 24-hour official currency exchange.

Asaka Bank (cnr Navoi & Kuvasoy) You can get cash out on your MasterCard here.

Infinity Internet Cafe (Navoi 18-23; per hr 800S; ☉ 9am-10pm) Convenient near Asia Hotel and Valentina's Guesthouse.

Lion Net (Kambarov 47; per hr 800S; ☉ 24hr) Internet access.

National Bank of Uzbekistan (Al-Farghoni 35) Cash-advance office for Visa cardholders is on the 3rd floor.

OVIR (Ahunbabaev 36)

Post office (Mustaqillik 35; ☉ 7am-7pm)

Uzbektourism (☎ 224 77 40; Hotel Ziyorat; ☉ 8am-5pm Mon-Fri) Organises multilingual tours to just about anything worth seeing in the Fergana Valley. Guides per day are US$25 plus transport. It was closed when we visited as Hotel Ziyorat went under the knife, but should reopen in this location.

Sights

Fergana's most appealing attraction is the **bazaar**, filled with good-natured Uzbek traders, leavened with Korean and Russian vendors selling homemade specialities. It sprawls over several blocks north of the centre, posing a considerable obstacle to the flow of traffic.

The sparse **Museum of Regional Studies** (☎ 224 31 91; Murabbiylar 26; admission US$1; ☉ 9am-5pm Wed-Sun, to 1pm Mon) covers the Fergana region, including Kokand and Margilon. Visitors can inspect satellite photos of a green, lush Fergana Valley nestled amid snow-capped peaks. Other displays include a Stone Age diorama with some excessively hairy Cro-Magnons, and a Great Patriotic War section unchanged from Soviet times.

Sleeping

Asia Hotel and Club Hotel 777 accept som converted at official rates; the rest convert at black-market rates. Homestays and B&Bs listed register you only if you are staying for at least three nights.

Sonya's B&B (☎ 224 64 31; Ahunbabaev 49; r per person US$10; ☒) Markets itself as a B&B but essentially it's a homestay. The host family is friendly and polite, and can cook you a serious Uzbek repast. The location near the bazaar makes it probably the best of the homestay lot.

Golden Valley Homestay (☎ 215 07 33; ijod@inbox. ru; Shakirovoy 10; r per person US$10; ☒ ☐) Golden Valley has three ship-shape apartments that you can have to yourself. Walk east from Hotel Ziyorat for 1km on Kurbunjon Dodhoh, go left on Shakirovoy, and immediately turn right. Or call for a pick-up.

Valentina's Guesthouse (☎ 224 89 05; daniol26@ yandex.ru; Al-Farghoni 11; r per person US$15; ☒ ☐) This

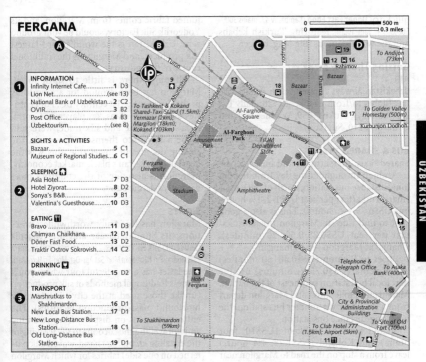

FERGANA

0 — 500 m
0 — 0.3 miles

UZBEKISTAN

very Russian homestay has four big, comfortable rooms with king-sized beds in two neighbouring Soviet apartments. The hulking apartment block, topped by a huge antenna, sticks out like a sore thumb; take the left-hand entrance. Valentina speaks Russian.

Club Hotel 777 (☎ 224 37 77; www.hotel777.uz; Pushkin 7A; s/d from US$45/65; ✷ ❡) With a few bungalows and a festive poolside bar, this sprawling number just south of the centre is about as close as you're liable to come to Club Med in double-land-locked Uzbekistan. 'Three Sevens' trounces similarly tour group–oriented Asia Hotel in all facets save location.

Also recommended:

Asia Hotel (☎ 224 52 21; www.asiahotels.uz; Navoi 26; s/d from US$55/86; ✷ ❡) Overpriced option associated with uberpowerful Marco Polo travel agency.

Hotel Ziyorat (☎ 224 77 42; Dekhon 2A) Was undergoing renovations when we visited. Expect a step up in price and quality from its former cheap, unrenovated, unabashedly Soviet self.

Eating & Drinking

our pick **Bravo** (Khojand 12; mains 3000-5000S; ❡ 9am-11pm; ✷ ❡ ❡) Nowhere is Fergana's liberal bent more evident than in this bohemian little cafe. The shabby-chic interior is plastered with the products of local artists and awash with the strains of live jazz. In the warm months the action moves outside to the patio. Expect a fair share of artists, musicians and drunks enjoying life until well into the evening. The next morning they'll be back for espresso. Hell, this place would be hip in Paris.

Bavaria (Kuvasoy 89; mains 3000-5000S; ✷ ❡ ❡) Bavarian sausages are the speciality here. Summer sees shashlyk cooked on the patio out front. It morphs into a half-decent bar by night.

Traktir Ostrov Sokrovish (Treasure Island Tavern; Marifat 45; mains 4000-9000S; ✷ ❡ ❡ ❡) The music at this island-themed restaurant-bar is too loud and the Russian food only OK, but it's certainly the cleanest, most modern restaurant in Fergana.

Near the bazaar you'll find several chaikhanas, including **Chimyan** (cnr Rahimov & Khamza; laghman US$1). Shashlyk stands occupy Al-Farghoni Park in the warm months; a cluster of them are along pedestrian Mustaqillik near the TsUM department store. For something quick try **Döner Fast Food** (Kambarov 47; mains 3000-5000S; ⊙ 9am-10pm), featuring Turkish kebabs and the world-famous 'Big Mag' burger.

Getting There & Away
AIR
Uzbekistan Airways (Fergana Airport; ⊙ 8am-5pm) has flights to/from Tashkent (€28, daily except Sunday), Nukus (€59, Wednesday) and Ürümqi (€210, Sunday).

BUS & SHARED TAXI
Shared taxis, marshrutkas and buses depart to Andijon throughout the day from the old long-distance bus station, north of the bazaar (marshrutka/taxi per seat US$1/2, 1¼ hours; bus US$0.75, two hours). This is also a good spot to find rides to Margilon (marshrutka/taxi per seat US$0.25/0.50, 20 minutes). Change in Margilon for Namangan.

Buses to Rishton (US$0.50, 50 minutes) and Kokand (US$0.75, two hours) use the new local bus station southeast of the bazaar. Marshrutkas to Rishton and Margilon depart from a stop near yet another bus station, the new long-distance bus station.

Shared taxis to Tashkent (US$10, four hours) and Kokand (US$1.25, 1¼ hours) leave from a stop on the road to Margilon near Yermazar Bazaar, 2km northwest of the centre.

Foreigners are technically not allowed across the Kyrgyz border to the Uzbek enclave of Shakhimardon, but touts at the old Fergana bus station claim they can sneak foreigners over in a public marshrutka. The asking price starts at US$15 for the 1¼-hour trip. As this can cause big-time headaches if you get caught, we cannot recommend it. The only legal way to enter Shakhimardon is to cross into Kyrgyzstan near Osh and proceed to Shakhimardon from there. For that you'll need multiple-entry Kyrgyz and Uzbek visas.

Getting Around
The airport is a 25-minute trip on marshrutka 6 to/from the new local bus station. Going to the airport you can flag it down in front of Asia Hotel, but check with the driver to make sure he's going all the way to the *aeroport*.

AROUND FERGANA
Margilon Маргилан
☎ 73 / pop 145,000
If you've been travelling along the Silk Road seeking answers to where in fact this highly touted fabric comes from, Margilon, and its Yodgorlik Silk Factory, should be your ground zero. Uzbekistan is the world's third-largest silk producer, and Margilon is the traditional centre of the industry.

Although there is little to show for it, Margilon has been around for a long time, probably since the 1st century BC. For centuries its merchant clans, key players in Central Asia's commerce and silk trade, were said to be a law unto themselves; even in the closing decades of Soviet rule, this was the heart of Uzbekistan's black-market economy. Margilon is also one of the country's most devoutly Islamic cities.

SIGHTS
Margilon has two truly worthwhile attractions: its Sunday bazaar and the **Yodgorlik (Souvenir) Silk Factory** (☎ 233 88 24; silk@mail.ru; Imam Zakhriddin; ⊙ 8am-5pm Mon-Sat Apr-Oct, Mon-Fri Nov-Mar). The latter has a wonderful tour where you'll witness traditional methods of silk production (unlike those used at the city's increasingly moribund mass-production factories). The entire process is on display, from steaming and unravelling the cocoons to the weaving of the dazzling *khanatlas* (hand-woven silk patterned on one side) fabrics for which Margilon is famous. Amazingly, it's almost all done sans electricity, just as it was 1500 years ago. After the tour (available in English, French, Russian or German), you can buy silk by the metre: US$4 for *khanatlas*, US$7.50 for *adras* (half-cotton, half-silk) and US$9 for *shoyi* (pure silk). There is also premade clothing, carpets and embroidered items for sale. The US$5 tour fee can go towards purchases in the shop.

A much less sanitised experience is Margilon's fantastic Sunday **Kumtepa Bazaar**, 5km west of the centre. It's a time capsule full of weathered Uzbek men in traditional clothing exchanging solemn greetings and gossiping over endless pots of tea, with hardly a Russian or a tourist in sight. Margilon's conservative streak, extreme even by Fergana Valley standards, is in full view here, with Uzbek matrons dressed almost exclusively in the locally produced *khanatlas* dresses and head scarves and men in skull caps and *chapan*. Rows of handmade *khanatlas* and *adras* silk, available for just 4000S to 5000S per metre, are both the shopping highlight and the visual highlight – have your camera ready. It's probably the most interesting bazaar in the country. Kumtepa

Bazaar also happens on Thursdays; on other days you might check out Margilon's newly reconstructed central **farmers market**.

A good tour guide (ask at Uzbektourism in Fergana) should be able to get keen silk connoisseurs into the private homes of weavers whose silk is for sale at Kumtepa Bazaar. They should also be able to organise tours to one of Margilon's larger commercial silk factories.

If you want to stay the night, your choices are the new **Hotel Atlas** (☎ 279 00 75; hoteladras@gmail.com; B Margiloni 32; s/d US$25/50; 🖳) and the dingy **Hotel Margilon** (☎ 233 46 42; B Margiloni & Mustaqillik; r US$10), which has electricity and running water but few other comforts. Yodgorlik Silk Factory can arrange a homestay.

GETTING THERE & AWAY
See p232 for transport from Fergana. Marshrutkas and taxis drop you off near the town's main intersection, kitty-corner from the central bazaar.

Rishton   Риштан
☎ 73 / pop 22,000

This town just north of the Kyrgyzstan border is famous for the ubiquitous cobalt and green pottery fashioned from its fine clay. About 90% of the ceramics you see in souvenir stores across Uzbekistan originates here – most of it handmade.

Some 1000 potters make a living from the legendary local loam, which is so pure that it requires no additives (besides water) before being chucked on the wheel.

Of those 1000 potters only a handful are considered true masters who still use traditional techniques. Among them is Rustam Usmanov, erstwhile art director of the defunct local collectivised ceramics factory. He runs the **Rishton Ceramic Museum** (☎ 452 15 85, 271 18 65; Ar-Roshidony 230) out of his home 1km west of the centre on the main road to Kokand. Of Tatar heritage, Usmanov gives free tours of his workshop as well as lunch (US$8) and vodka shots to travellers who call ahead (as many tour groups do).

Usmanov says that Rishton potters are facing a potential crisis, as the purest clay is becoming scarce. Taking no chances, Usmanov bought 120 tonnes of it in 2006 – 'enough to last 20 years!'

Alisher Nazirov (☎ 452 33 43, 8390-302 1319; Ferganskaya 152) is another master who not only gives tours and serves lunch but also offers travellers an informal training course in traditional Rishton ceramic making. It costs US$35 per day for full room and board (three-day minimum stay; registration done in Fergana) plus US$5 per day for training. To find it, turn right (south) off the main road to Fergana just south of the centre; from the turnoff it's about 600m down on the left.

Rishton is best visited as a stop on the way to Fergana from Kokand (or vice-versa). It's about a 45-minute shared taxi ride from either (US$1.25), or take a slower bus (US$0.50).

ANDIJON   АНДИЖАН
☎ 74 / pop 350,000

Andijon – the Fergana Valley's largest city and its spiritual mecca – will forever be linked with the bloodshed of 13 May 2005 (p208). The very word 'Andijon' is a hot potato in Uzbekistan; just mentioning it is enough to stop any conversation in its tracks.

That's a shame because both culturally and linguistically Andijon is probably the country's purest Uzbek city, and the best place to observe Uzbeks in their element. Architecturally there's not much to see here – an earthquake in 1902 took care of that. Rather, it's Andijon's bazaars and chaikhanas, brimming with colour and life, that make a trip worthwhile. Andijonians are warm and friendly, and whatever concerns they have about their government appear not to have negatively affected their demeanour.

Most travellers who pass through Andijon are on their way to or from Kyrgyzstan and don't linger long because of security concerns. Make no mistake: the local police are on their guard here. Have your papers in order and take the normal precautions, but don't let all the hype that Andijon is 'dangerous' prevent you from coming.

Orientation
Museums, medressa, shops and the post office are clustered in the old town around the central farmers market, known as Eski (Old) Bazaar. Just southeast of the old town is Navoi Sq (formerly Bobur Sq), where the violence took place in 2005. The neighbouring bus and train stations and a few hotels are near Yaangi Bazaar in the new town, 3km to the south. Broad, busy Navoi kochasi links Navoi Sq and the new town.

Information
Black market money changers can be found outside Eski Bazaar. Head to **Asaka Bank**

(Rashidov 1) for MasterCard cash advances, while the **National Bank of Uzbekistan** (opposite Navoi 32) takes care of Visa cash advances. **Jahon Internet Cafe** (Rashidov 18; per hr 1000S; ☻ 9am-10pm) is around the corner from Villa Elegant Hotel.

Sights

Andijon's **Jahon Bazaar** is the biggest bazaar on the Uzbek side of the Fergana Valley. On Sunday and Thursday it is teeming with people, and there are also silk stalls here in case you miss Kumtepa Bazaar in Margilon. From Kolkhoz Bazaar, it's 4km northeast on marshrutka 6, 10 or anything saying Жахон бозор.

When Jahon Bazaar isn't happening, bazaar lovers can check out **Eski Bazaar**, which spills into the streets of the old town.

Across from Eski Bazaar on Oltinkul is the handsome 19th-century **Jome Mosque & Medressa**, said to be the only building to survive the 1902 earthquake. It reopened as a working medressa in the 1990s but was turned into a **museum of local ethnography** (admission US$1; ☻ 9am-4pm Tue-Sun) after a police crackdown on suspected Islamic militants. The museum's highlight is its collection of folk instruments. Next door is a dusty **Regional Studies Museum** (admission US$0.75; ☻ 9am-5pm), with the usual chipped ceramics and stuffed animals.

The marginally more interesting **Babur Literary Museum** (admission $0.75; ☻ 9am-6pm), on a small lane west of Eski Bazaar, occupies the site of the royal apartments where Zahiruddin Babur (Uzbek: Bobur) lived and studied as a boy within Ark-Ichy, the town's long-gone citadel. Born in 1483 in Andijon to Fergana's ruler, Umar Sheikh Mirzo (a descendant of Timur), Babur inherited his father's kingdom before he was even a teenager. The young king took Samarkand at the tender age of 14, but subsequently lost both Samarkand and Fergana and was driven into Afghanistan by the Uzbek Shaybanids before ultimately going on to found the Mughal Empire in India (see p47). On display are various miniatures depicting Babur's life.

Sleeping & Eating

Hotel Andijon (☎ 225 53 00; Fitrat 241; d without/with bathroom US$8/13, half-lux US$23) This no-frills Soviet-style hotel across from Navoi Sq sports a typical mix of tatty unrenovated rooms and somewhat renovated half-*lux* rooms. The shared bathroom is appalling – opt for a private bathroom.

Villa Elegant Hotel (☎ 261 61 61; Bobur 40; s/d in old hotel US$23/35, in new hotel US$25/40; ☒ ☎) Consisting of an old and new building on opposite sides of Bobur near the train station, this is Andijon's most comfortable option. Rooms in the preferred new building come with complementary toothpaste and toothbrushes, not to mention huge bathtubs.

There are two old Intourist cinder blocks near each other in a huge park 2km southeast of Villa Elegant. **Oltyn Vody** (☎ 226 69 93; Mashrab 19; s/d US$11/20) is by far the better choice over the grossly overpriced **Sport Hotel** (☎ 226 10 78; Mashrab 21; s/d from US$24/32).

Chaikhanas abound near the bazaars and just about everywhere else. For something fancier, try **Bosco** (Istiklol 8; mains 7000-11,000S), just north of Villa Elegant's new hotel, with good soups and a standard menu of Russian classics.

Getting There & Around

Uzbekistan Airways (airport) has four weekly flights to/from Tashkent (€30). The airport is 3km southwest of the train station.

All vehicular transport roosts near the bus station. There are plenty of rides to Fergana (marshrutka/shared taxi per seat US$1/2, 1¼ hours; bus US$0.75, two hours) and Tashkent (shared taxi US$12, five hours).

Daily trains trundle to Kokand (1200S, five hours) via Margilon (5.05am) or Namangan (1.40pm).

Marshrutka 33 travels from Eski Bazaar in the old town past Navoi Sq, Villa Elegant Hotel and Hotel Oltyn Vody before passing near the airport. Any marshrutka signboarded 'Ескй Шахар' ('Eski Shahar' or Old Town) goes to Eski Bazaar.

For information on transport to Kyrgyzstan, see p287.

CENTRAL UZBEKISTAN

SAMARKAND САМАРКАНД
☎ 66 / pop 405,000 / elev 710m

We travel not for trafficking alone,
By hotter winds our fiery hearts are fanned.
For lust of knowing what should not be known
We take the Golden Road to Samarkand.

These final lines of James Elroy Flecker's 1913 poem *The Golden Journey to Samarkand* evoke the romance of Uzbekistan's most glorious city. No name is so evocative of the Silk Road as Samarkand. For most people it has the mythical resonance of Atlantis, fixed in the Western popular imagination by poets and playwrights of bygone eras, few of whom saw the city in the flesh.

From the air your eye locks onto the domes and minarets, and on the ground the sublime, larger-than-life monuments of Timur, the technicolour bazaar and the city's long, rich history indeed work some kind of magic. Surrounding these islands of majesty, modern Samarkand sprawls across acres of Soviet-built buildings, parks and broad avenues used by buzzing Daewoo taxis.

You can visit most of Samarkand's high-profile attractions in two or three days. If you're short on time, at least see the Registan, Gur-e-Amir, Bibi-Khanym Mosque and Shah-i-Zinda.

Note that the people of Samarkand, Bukhara and southeastern Uzbekistan don't speak Uzbek but an Uzbek-laced Tajik (Farsi). Some members of the ethnic Tajik minority wish Stalin had made the area part of Tajikistan, but the issue is complicated by ethnic Uzbek city folk who speak Tajik.

History

Samarkand (Marakanda to the Greeks), one of Central Asia's oldest settlements, was probably founded in the 5th century BC. It was already the cosmopolitan, walled capital of the Sogdian empire when it was taken in 329 BC by Alexander the Great, who said, 'Everything I have heard about Marakanda is true, except that it's more beautiful than I ever imagined.'

A key Silk Road city, it sat on the crossroads leading to China, India and Persia, bringing in trade and artisans. From the 6th to the 13th century it grew into a city more populous than it is today, changing hands every couple of centuries – Western Turks, Arabs, Persian Samanids, Karakhanids, Seljuq Turks, Mongolian Karakitay and Khorezmshah have all ruled here – before being obliterated by Chinggis Khan in 1220.

This might have been the end of the story, but in 1370 Timur decided to make Samarkand his capital, and over the next 35 years forged a new, almost-mythical city – Central Asia's economic and cultural epicentre. His grandson Ulugbek ruled until 1449 and made it an intellectual centre as well.

When the Uzbek Shaybanids came in the 16th century and moved their capital to Bukhara, Samarkand went into decline. For several decades in the 18th century, after a series of earthquakes, it was essentially uninhabited. The emir of Bukhara forcibly repopulated the town towards the end of the century, but it was only truly resuscitated by the Russians, who forced its surrender in May 1868 and linked it to the Russian Empire by the Trans-Caspian railway 20 years later.

Samarkand was declared capital of the new Uzbek SSR in 1924, but lost the honour to Tashkent six years later.

Orientation

A map of Samarkand's centre shows the city's Russian-Asian schizophrenia. Eastward are the tangled alleys of the old town, whose axis is pedestrian Tashkent kochasi. Across town, shady 19th-century Russian avenues radiate westward from Mustaqillik maydoni, the administrative centre of the new city and province.

Most sights are within a couple of kilometres west and north of the Registan. The newer downtown area is also centred on a pedestrian thoroughfare, Navoi. A useful tourist landmark, roughly betwixt the city's two halves, is mothballed Hotel Samarkand on parklike Universitet bulvar (known simply as 'Bulvar' by locals).

MAPS

A detailed, accurate 2004 map called *Guide of Samarkand* (scale 1:13,000) includes a full list of sights and facilities. Buy it at the small **map store** (Registan; ☼ 7am-8pm) opposite the Registan for 2000S.

Information

CULTURAL CENTRES

Victor Hugo French Cultural Centre (☎ 233 66 27; dilallia@yahoo.fr; Baraka 26; ☼ 2-6pm Mon-Fri) French papers and magazines, plus a handful of French TV channels. Manager Dila also doles out travel tips.

INTERNET ACCESS

Wi-fi can be found at a few hotels and at Venezia and Platan restaurants.

Foreign Language Institute (Ahunbabaev 23; per hr 800S; ☼ 8am-8pm) Internet was slow when we visited, but this place is well-located.

International telephone office (Pochta 9; per hr 900S; ☼ 8am-7pm) Big monitors and no gamers here.

SAMARKAND

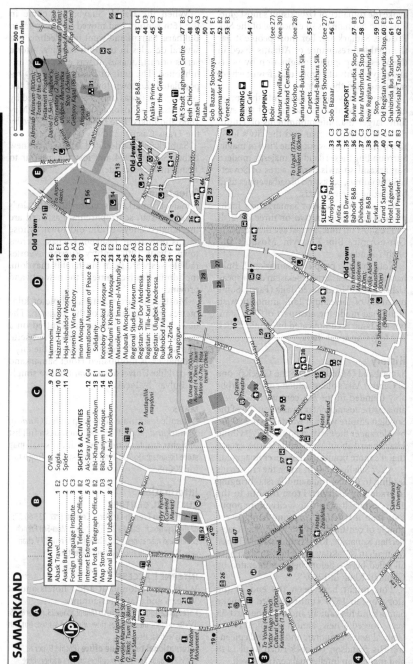

INFORMATION
Abask Travel	1 E2
Asaka Bank	2 C2
Foreign Language Institute	3 C3
International Telephone Office	4 B2
Internet Extreme	5 A3
Main Post & Telegraph Office	6 B2
Map Store	7 D3
National Bank of Uzbekistan	8 A3
OVIR	9 A2
Sogda	10 D3
Spider	11 A3

SIGHTS & ACTIVITIES
Ak-Saray Mausoleum	12 C4
Bibi-Khanym Mausoleum	13 E1
Bibi-Khanym Mosque	14 E1
Gur-e-Amir Mausoleum	15 C4
Hammom	16 E2
Hazrat-Hizr Mosque	17 E2
Hoja-Nisbatdor Mosque	18 D4
Hovrenko Wine Factory	19 A2
Imon Mosque	20 D3
International Museum of Peace & Solidarity	21 A2
Koroboy Oksokol Mosque	22 E2
Makhdumi Khorezm Mosque	23 E2
Mausoleum of Imam-al-Matrudy	24 E3
Mubarak Mosque	25 E2
Regional Studies Museum	26 A3
Registan: Sher Dor Medressa	27 D2
Registan: Tilla-Kari Medressa	28 D2
Registan: Ulugbek Medressa	29 D3
Rukhobod Mausoleum	30 C3
Shah-i-Zinda	31 F1
Synagogue	32 C4

SLEEPING
Afrosiyob Palace	33 C3
Antica	34 C2
B&B Davr	35 D4
Bahodir B&B	36 E2
Dilshoda	37 C3
Emir B&B	38 C3
Furkat	39 E2
Grand Samarkand	40 A2
Hotel Légende	41 F1
Hotel President	42 B3
Jahongir B&B	43 D4
Joni	44 D3
Malika Prime	45 C3
Timur the Great	46 E2

EATING
Alt Stadt Laghman Centre	47 B3
Besh Chinor	48 C2
Fratelli	49 A3
Platan	50 A2
Siob Bazaar Stolovaya	51 E1
Supermarket Aziz	52 B2
Venezia	53 B3

DRINKING
Blues Cafe	54 A3

SHOPPING
Bobir	(see 27)
Mansur Nurillaev	(see 30)
Samarkand Ceramics Workshop	(see 28)
Samarkand-Bukhara Silk Carpets	55 F1
Samarkand-Bukhara Silk Carpets Showroom	(see 27)
Siob Bazaar	56 E1

TRANSPORT
Bulvar Marshrutka Stop I	57 B3
Bulvar Marshrutka Stop II	58 C3
New Registan Marshrutka Stop	59 D3
Old Registan Marshrutka Stop	60 E3
Shahrisinda Bus Station	61 F1
Shakhrisabz Taxi Stand	62 D3

Old Town

Old Jewish Quarter

Afrosiab Site

0   500 m
0   0.3 miles

Internet Extreme (Abdurahmon Jomi 92; per hr 800S; 8am-11pm) Sometimes stays open past midnight.

Spider (Amir Timur 44; per hr 800S; 24hr) Fast connection (usually), Skype, webcams and a range of computing services.

MONEY
Black-market moneychangers hang out around Siob Bazaar. Hotel President and Afrosiyob Palace have exchange offices that sometimes can advance cash on Visa.

Asaka Bank (Mustaqillik maydoni) Advances cash on MasterCard.

National Bank of Uzbekistan (Firdavsi 7) Cashes travellers cheques and handles Visa card cash advances.

POST & COMMUNICATIONS
International telephone office (Pochta 9; 24hr) Standard Uztelekom rates apply (see p285).

Main post & telegraph office (Pochta 5; 8am-5pm)

REGISTRATION
OVIR (233 69 34; cnr Mahmud Kashgari & Ulugbek)

TRAVEL AGENCIES
Most of the B&Bs listed under Sleeping double as travel agencies and/or can organise cars, guides, camel trekking and yurtstays around Lake Aidarkul (see p256), and homestays in the Nuratau-Kyzylkum Biosphere Reserve (see the boxed text on p257). Antica and Hotel Légende are particularly resourceful.

Tour guides Denis Vikulov and Farruh Bahronov (see p246) are also good fixers. Denis has a car and will travel, and is fixing up a 19th-century Jewish Quarter building to serve meals to tourists. Farruh runs **Abask Travel** (www.abasktravel.info; Tashkent 41) out of his souvenir store – look for the store with the woodworking workshop inside. **Sogda Tour** (235 29 85; www.sogda-tour.com; Registan 38), located behind Mojiza restaurant, has refreshing ideas for touring the region, including excursions to the caves and mountains around Darbent and Boysun.

Sights
You can enter the courtyards of some of the main sights outside working hours for free or by 'tipping' the guard on duty; the Registan and Bibi-Khanym are spectacular in the early morning light; Gur-e-Amir is sublime by night. Camera charges are US$0.75 at all main sights unless otherwise indicated.

THE REGISTAN
This ensemble of majestic, tilting medressas – a near-overload of majolica, azure mosaics and vast, well-proportioned spaces – is the centrepiece of the city, and one of the most awesome single sights in Central Asia. The **Registan** (cnr Registan & Tashkent; admission US$3.50, camera US$1.50; 8am-7pm Apr-Oct, 9am-5pm Nov-Mar), which translates to 'Sandy Place' in Tajik, was medieval Samarkand's commercial centre and the plaza was probably a wall-to-wall bazaar.

The three grand edifices here are among the world's oldest preserved medressas, anything older having been destroyed by Chinggis Khan. They have taken their knocks over the years courtesy of the frequent earthquakes that buffet the region; that they are still standing is a testament to the incredible craftsmanship of their builders. The Soviets, to their credit, worked feverishly to protect and restore these beleaguered treasures, but they also took some questionable liberties, such as the capricious addition of a blue outer dome to the Tilla-Kari Medressa.

Ulugbek Medressa, on the west side, is the original medressa, finished in 1420 under Ulugbek (who is said to have taught mathematics here; other subjects included theology, astronomy and philosophy). Beneath the little corner domes were lecture halls, and at the rear a large mosque with a beautiful interior and an austere teaching room to one side.

The other buildings are rough imitations by the Shaybanid Emir Yalangtush. The entrance portal of the **Sher Dor (Lion) Medressa**, opposite Ulugbek's and finished in 1636, is decorated with roaring felines that look like tigers but are meant to be lions, flouting Islamic prohibitions against the depiction of live animals. It took 17 years to build but hasn't held up as well as the Ulugbek Medressa, built in just three years.

In between is the **Tilla-Kari (Gold-Covered) Medressa**, completed in 1660, with a pleasant, gardenlike courtyard. The highlight here is the mosque, intricately decorated with gold to symbolise Samarkand's wealth at the time it was built. The mosque's delicate ceiling, oozing gold leaf, is flat but its tapered design makes it look domed from the inside. Inside the mosque is a magnificent picture gallery featuring blown-up black-and-white photos of old Samarkand.

Another interesting picture gallery is the Ulugbek Medressa's mosque. Many of the medressas' former dormitory rooms are now art and souvenir shops. In the high season mock weddings are put on for tourists in the Sher Dor courtyard, while tacky sound-and-light shows take place in the square.

From dawn until opening time police guards offer to clandestinely escort visitors to the top of a minaret for 10,000S or more, but this is negotiable.

BIBI-KHANYM MOSQUE

The enormous congregational **Bibi-Khanym Mosque** (Tashkent kochasi; admission US$1.50; ☽ 8am-7pm Apr-Oct, 9am-5pm Nov-Mar), northeast of the Registan, was finished shortly before Timur's death and must have been the jewel of his empire. Once one of the Islamic world's biggest mosques (the cupola of the main mosque is 41m high and the *pishtak* 38m), it pushed construction techniques to the limit. Slowly crumbling over the years, it partially collapsed in an earthquake in 1897 before being rebuilt in the 1970s.

Legend says that Bibi-Khanym, Timur's Chinese wife, ordered the mosque built as a surprise while he was away. The architect fell madly in love with her and refused to finish the job unless he could give her a kiss. The smooch left a mark and Timur, on seeing it, executed the architect and decreed that women should henceforth wear veils so as not to tempt other men.

The interior courtyard contains an enormous marble Quran stand that lends some scale to the place. Local lore has it that any woman who crawls under the stand will have lots of children. The courtyard also contains two smaller mosques. The one on the left as you enter through the enormous main gate has an impressive unrestored interior festooned with Arabic calligraphy.

Across Tashkent kochasi is Bibi-Khanym's own compact 14th-century **mausoleum** (admission US$1.50; ☽ 8am-6pm), brightly restored in 2007.

SHAH-I-ZINDA

Samarkand's most moving and beloved site is this stunning **avenue of mausoleums** (admission US$1.50; ☽ 8am-7pm Apr-Oct, 9am-5pm Nov-Mar), which contains some of the richest tilework in the Muslim world. The name, which means 'Tomb of the Living King', refers to its original, innermost and holiest shrine – a complex of cool, quiet rooms around what is probably the grave of Qusam ibn-Abbas, a cousin of

the Prophet Mohammed who is said to have brought Islam to this area in the 7th century.

A shrine to Qusam existed here on the edge of Afrosiab long before the Mongols ransacked it in the 13th century. Shah-i-Zinda began to assume its current form in the 14th century as Timur and later Ulugbek buried their family and favourites near the Living King.

After remarkably surviving more than seven centuries with only minor touch-up work, many of the tombs were aggressively and controversially restored in 2005. As a result, much of brilliant mosaic, majolica and terracotta work you see today is not original.

The most beautiful tomb is the Shodi Mulk Oko Mausoleum (1372), resting place of a sister and niece of Timur, second on the left after the entry stairs. The exquisite majolica and terracotta work here – notice the miniscule amount of space between the tiles – was of such exceptional quality that it merited almost no restoration.

Shah-i-Zinda is an important place of pilgrimage, so enter with respect and dress conservatively.

GUR-E-AMIR MAUSOLEUM & AROUND

Timur, two sons and two grandsons, including Ulugbek, lie beneath the surprisingly modest **Gur-e-Amir Mausoleum** (Oksaroy; admission US$2; ☽ 8am-7pm Apr-Oct, 9am-5pm Nov-Mar) and its trademark fluted azure dome.

Timur had built a simple crypt for himself at Shakhrisabz, and had this one built in 1404 for his grandson and proposed heir, Mohammed Sultan, who had died the previous year. But the story goes that when Timur died unexpectedly of pneumonia in Kazakhstan (in the course of planning an expedition against the Chinese) in the winter of 1405, the passes back to Shakhrisabz were snowed in and he was interred here instead.

As with other Muslim mausoleums, the stones are just markers; the actual crypts are in a chamber beneath. In the centre is Timur's stone, once a single block of dark-green jade. In 1740 the warlord Nadir Shah carried it off to Persia, where it was accidentally broken in two – from which time Nadir Shah is said to have had a run of very bad luck, including the near-death of his son. At the urging of his religious advisers he returned the stone to Samarkand, and of course his son recovered.

The plain marble marker to the left of Timur's is that of Ulugbek; to the right is that of Mersaid Baraka, one of Timur's teachers. In front lies Mohammed Sultan. The stones behind Timur's mark the graves of his sons Shah Rukh (the father of Ulugbek) and Miran Shah. Behind these lies Sheikh Seyid Umar, the most revered of Timur's teachers, said to be a descendent of the Prophet Mohammed. Timur ordered Gur-e-Amir built around Umar's tomb.

The Soviet anthropologist Mikhail Gerasimov opened the crypts in 1941 and, among other things, confirmed that Timur was tall (1.7m) and lame in the right leg and right arm (from injuries suffered when he was 25) – and that Ulugbek died from being beheaded. According to every tour guide's favourite anecdote, he found on Timur's grave an inscription to the effect that 'whoever opens this will be defeated by an enemy more fearsome than I'. The next day, 22 June, Hitler attacked the Soviet Union.

Behind the ugly new wall surrounding Gur-e-Amir is little **Ak-Saray Mausoleum** (Oksaroy; admission US$0.50; 9am-6pm), with some bright frescoes and majolica tilework inside. The frescoes were barely visible before being restored in 2008.

Between Gur-e-Amir and the main road is **Rukhobod Mausoleum**, dated 1380 and possibly the city's oldest surviving monument. It now serves as a souvenir and craft shop.

ANCIENT SAMARKAND (AFROSIAB)
At a 2.2-sq-km site called Afrosiab, northeast of Siob Bazaar, are excavations of Marakanda (early Samarkand) more or less abandoned to the elements.

The **Afrosiab Museum** (235 53 36; Tashkent kochasi; admission US$2; 8.30am-6pm Apr-Oct, 9am-5pm Nov-Mar) was built around one of Samarkand's more important archaeological finds, a chipped 7th-century fresco of the Sogdian King Varkhouman receiving ranks of foreign dignitaries astride ranks of elephants, camels and horses. You'll see reproductions of this iconic fresco throughout the country. It was only discovered in 1965 during the construction of Tashkent kochasi. The 2nd floor of the museum leads the visitor on a chronological tour of the 11 layers of civilisation that is Afrosiab.

Nearby, the restored **Tomb of the Old Testament Prophet Daniel** (admission US$1.50; 9am-8.30pm Apr-Oct, to 5pm Nov-Mar) lies on the banks of the Siob River (turn left off Tashkent kochasi 400m northeast of the museum). The building is a long, low structure topped with five domes, containing an 18m sarcophagus – legend has it that Daniel's body grows by half an inch a year and thus the sarcophagus has to be enlarged. His remains, which date to at least the 5th century BC, were brought here for good luck by Timur from Susa, Iran (suspiciously, an alleged tomb of Daniel can also be found in Susa).

Continuing north you'll encounter the remains of **Ulugbek's Observatory** (admission US$2; 8am-7pm Apr-Oct, 9am-5pm Nov-Mar), one of the great archaeological finds of the 20th century. Ulugbek was probably more famous as an astronomer than as a ruler. His 30m astrolab, designed to observe star positions, was part of a three-storey observatory he built in the 1420s. All that remains now is the instrument's curved track, unearthed in 1908. The small on-site **museum** has some miniatures depicting Ulugbek and a few old ceramics and other artefacts unearthed in Afrosiab.

The best way to reach Afrosiab is on foot. Cross the intersection north of Bibi-Khanym and follow pedestrian Tashkent kochasi for about 1km to the Afrosiab Museum; Ulugbek's Observatory is 1.5km beyond that, or take bus 70 to the Ulugbek marshrutka stop from Usto Umar kochasi opposite Shah-i-Zinda, or any bus signposted Bulungur or Jambay from the new Shahizinda bus station, 200m east of Shah-i-Zinda.

STATE ART MUSEUM
Samarkand's most important museum once occupied the square east of the Registan, but was bulldozed in late 2009 as part of Samarkand's makeover. The collection, including one of the world's largest Qurans (1m by 1.5m), was locked away in storage when we visited, but reportedly will be moved to a new facility near **Tsum** (Beruni 32) by 2011.

NAVOI KOCHASI & PARK
Samarkand's Russified downtown area tends to escape tourists' radar, which is unfortunate because it's quite un-Sovietised and charming. Gussied-up locals stroll along Navoi (formerly Leninskaya), a sight that would have Lenin rolling in his coffin.

The quirky **International Museum of Peace & Solidarity** (☎ 233 17 53; http://peace.museum.com; Abdurahmon Jomi 56; ☻ by appointment only) tends to move around a lot so check the website for the latest location. Curator Anatoly Ionesov speaks fluent Esperanto and has a remarkable collection of disarmament and environmental memorabilia. He has collected thousands of signatures, including some very famous ones, in the name of peace.

The **Regional Studies Museum** (Abdurahmon Jomi 51; admission US$2; ☻ 9am-5pm) occupies an old Jewish merchant's house, and has a lavish wing devoted to Jewish history, with old photos of Samarkand's once-prominent population of both European and Bukhara Jews. The rest of the museum contains the standard line-up of old ceramics, stuffed animals and historical displays.

OTHER SIGHTS

Across the intersection from the Siob Bazaar, the **Hazrat-Hizr Mosque** (Tashkent kochasi; admission US$0.50, minaret US$0.50; ☻ 8am-6pm) occupies a hill on the fringes of Afrosiab. The 8th-century mosque that once stood here was burnt to the ground by Chinggis Khan in the 13th century and was not rebuilt until 1854. In the 1990s it was lovingly restored by a wealthy Bukharan and today it's Samarkand's most beautiful mosque, with a fine domed interior and views of Bibi-Khanym, Shah-i-Zinda and Afrosiab from the minaret. The ribbed *aivan* ceiling drips colour.

If you prefer your ruins really ruined, it's worth the slog out to the *Tomb Raider*–style, 15th-century **Ishratkhana Mausoleum** (Sadriddin Ayni), newly topped by a tin roof. With a preponderance of pigeons and an eerie crypt in the basement, this is the place to film your horror movie. Across the street is the **Hodja Abdi Darun Mausoleum** (Sadriddin Ayni), which shares a tranquil, shady courtyard with a mosque and a *hauz* (artificial stone pool).

South of the Registan on Suzangaran are two lovely mosques: the small, 19th-century **Imon Mosque**, with an open porch, tall carved columns and a brightly restored ceiling. Further along, the **Hoja-Nisbatdor Mosque** has a large *aivan* embraced by walls inlaid with beautifully restored *ghanch* (carved alabaster).

Wine tasting tours are possible at the **Hovrenko Wine Factory** (☎ 939 13 13; Mahmud Kashgari; ☻ 2-7pm Apr-Oct) in a converted 19th-century Jewish industrialist's house.

Tours

For guides, go through your hotel. Recommended guides are listed below.
Denis Vikulov (☻ 227 93 40; denis-guide@rambler.ru) English.
Farruh Bahronov (☎ 241 01 02; faruhb@yahoo.com) English and French.
Firuza Fazilova (☎ 260 14 25) German.
Natalya Tyan (☎ 241 29 87; jam-naty@mail.ru) French.
Valentina Belova (☎ 241 88 07) The grand dame of Samarkand's guides. Speaks English.

The going rate for trained guides is US$25 to US$30 per day. Students often cost less, and can be found through Dila at the Victor Hugo French Cultural Centre (p241), or try the **Foreign Language Institute** (Ahunbabaev 93).

Festivals & Events

Most of the action during Samarkand's **Navrus Festival** (see p283) takes place in Navoi Park. Ask travel agencies or tour guides about the annual Navrus *kupkari* (Tajik: *buzkashi*; traditional polo-like game played with a headless goat carcass) match in Urgut or Koshrabot.

The city is also home to the **Sharq Taronalari** (Melodies of the East) classical Oriental music festival, held every other year (next in August 2011 and 2013) at Registan Sq.

Sleeping

Samarkand's B&Bs aren't quite up to Bukhara's lofty standards but are preferable to the tour group–laden hotels. Pay in Uzbek som at top-end hotels for big savings (see the boxed text on p284).

BUDGET

Bahodir B&B (☎ 220 30 93; Mulokandov 132; dm from US$6, s/d US$10/16) Opinion is divided on this popular backpacker standby. Some love it because it's cheap, prices are negotiable, the breakfast is generous, the dorm room is passable, and the notebook filled with backpacker advice is useful. Others complain about the dank, steamy common bathroom and the dilapidated en suite rooms. Ask to see several rooms, as some aren't too bad. Dinner costs US$2.

Timur the Great (☎ 235 03 38; Buhoro 84; s/d US$15/20; ☒) Was closed for renovations when we visited but readers recommend it.

B&B Davr (☎ 235 47 48; www.davrhotel.uz; Ali Kushchi 43; s/d US$15/30; ☒) It's a tad out of the way but the price is right considering what it offers –

WHERE'S THE OLD TOWN?

Over the last few years, city planners have completely redesigned Samarkand to seal off older sections of town from tourists' view. Roads have been rerouted, and statues of Navoi, Gorky, Gagarin and others have disappeared or been relocated. Hideous walls have been erected around Gur-e-Amir and behind the Registan, and virtually all access points between the old town and touristy Tashkent and Registan streets have been closed off.

Plucky travellers who do manage to find their way into the old town will be rewarded with an authentic slice of *mahalla* (neighbourhood) life. The most interesting neighbourhood is the old Jewish Quarter, accessible by a gate off Tashkent kochasi. From the gate, walk east along the main lane, Abu Laiz Samarkandi, and find the gloriously faded **Koroboy Oksokol Mosque** down an alley on your right. Continuing along Abu Laiz Samarkandi, pass the diminutive **Mubarak Mosque** on your left and proceed to the neighbourhood **Hammomi** (Baths; admission 5000S, massage 12,000S; 4am-10pm Mon-Wed for women & Thu-Sun for men). Take a left on unmarked Denau kochasi opposite the *hammomi* and look for a working 19th-century **synagogue** a few houses down on the left.

Wander through the lanes south of the *hammomi* until you locate the tidy new **Mausoleum of Imam-al-Matrudiy** (Buhoro). Just west of here is the more interesting **Makhdumi Khorezm Mosque** (Buhoro), with a colourful ceiling under its *aivan* and some fine interior tilework.

Other neighbourhoods worth wandering are west-southwest of Bibi-Khanym and behind Gur-e-Amir.

---

satellite TV, a well-groomed courtyard for hanging out and a decent breakfast.

Emir B&B (☎ 233 01 97; muhandis2005@mail.ru; Oksaroy 142; s/d/tr US$20/30/45;) Rooms here are clean and cosy, but are set around a glass-roofed interior courtyard that leaves some feeling a bit claustrophobic. On the other hand the greenhouse effect makes it a great cold-weather choice.

MIDRANGE

Furkat (☎ 235 62 99; hotelfurkat@mail.ru; Mulokandov 105; dm US$8-12; s without/with bathroom US$15/40, d US$40-60;) Samarkand's original B&B has a dizzying variety of rooms in a sprawling three-storey, old-town edifice. Top-floor rooms have splendid views of the Registan and the snowcapped mountains surrounding Samarkand. Surly staff bolt the front door annoyingly early here; night owls should consider Furkat's two annexes.

Dilshoda (☎ 235 03 87; www.dilshoda.by.ru; Oksaroy 150; s/d/tr US$25/40/50;) Set in the shadow of Gur-e-Amir, this B&B serves up warm if basic rooms with attractive carpets, narrow beds and small bathrooms. The chipper host family serves up mouthwatering three-course dinners (US$7) upon request.

our pick Antica (☎ 235 20 92, 937 00 92; antica samarkand@hotmail.com; Iskandarov 58; s/d without bathroom US$30/40, s/d/tr with bathroom from US$35/50/65;) You can capture the vibe of living in a traditional home in this boutique B&B. The 19th-century

annexe has four rooms generously furnished with antique carpets, *suzani* and trinkets. The newer main house is set around a lush garden courtyard shaded by pomegranate, persimmon and fig trees. Rooms here have hand-carved walnut-wood doors and ribbed, brightly painted ceilings. If it's full you can roll out sleeping bags on a terrace overlooking the courtyard for US$12. Dinners (US$8) and breakfasts are equally scrumptious.

Hotel Légende (☎ 233 74 81; www.legendm7.com; Tolmosov 60; s US$30-45, d US$40-50;) Tucked away in a 170-year-old house deep in the Jewish Quarter, the Légende has character that few can match. Rooms surround a lush courtyard, have gorgeous high ceilings and are awash in old carpets and textiles. As the name implies, it caters to a French crowd.

Also recommended:

Joni (☎ 235 69 41; www.joni-hotel.net; Penjikent 9; s/d US$25/40;) Pluses: comfy renovated rooms. Fusses: drab exterior complying with Samarkand's zoning laws, claustrophobia-inducing glass cover over interior courtyard.

Jahongir B&B (☎ 391 92 44; www.jahongirbandb. com; Chirokchi 4; s/d US$30/45;) Lacks old-school character but concrete quarters are tastefully decorated. Wi-fi is paid.

TOP END

Grand Samarkand (☎ 233 28 80; www.grand-samarqand. com; Yalantush 38; s/d/lux US$55/75/90;) This midsized offering is ugly on the outside but swanky on the inside, with extra-wide twin beds, fine towels and linens and tasteful miniatures on the walls. The restaurant is a tad garish but you can eat outside in the warm months. Wi-fi is paid.

Malika Prime (☎ 233 01 97; www.malika-samarkand. com; Universitet bul 1/4; s/d US$55/80; ✉ 🖳 🛜) The newest and nicest of the Malika chain's hotels is well situated between the old and new towns. The highlight is the roof-deck terrace overlooking Gur-e-Amir. The 22 rooms are big and clean with lots of blonde wood, and are often occupied by tour groups.

High rollers who prefer full-service highrises to B&Bs can choose from **Hotel President** (☎ 233 24 75; www.uzhotelpresident.com; Shohruh 53; s/d/ ste US$105/165/300; 🅿 ✉ 🖳 🛜) and **Afrosiyob Palace** (☎ 231 11 95; www.afrosiyobpalace.com; Registan 2; s/d from €60/80; 🅿 ✖ ✉ 🖳 🛜 🛜). The President has bigger, better-looking rooms; the Palace boasts friendlier service, has an outdoor pool and is a shorter walk to the sights.

Eating

Most restaurants are in the newer Russian part of town, far removed from the touristy Registan area. Expect to pay 10% to 15% for service at restaurants.

CHAIKHANAS & LOCAL RESTAURANTS

Siob Bazaar Stolovaya (Bibikhanym; plov 2000S; ⊙ lunch) Among several makeshift eateries and shashlyk stands behind Siob Bazaar, this one fires up a fresh daily batch of *plov* in a giant *kazan*. Look for the 'Milliy Taomlar' ('National Food') sign.

Siob (mains 2000-3000S; ⊙ late Mar-Oct) This dreamy chaikhana lays out *tapchan* on the banks of the babbling Siab (Siob) River. From the Shahizinda bus station, take the new Shahizinda kochasi for 1.1km, turn right and follow the left fork 300m.

Alt Stadt Laghman Centre (Navoi 49; laghman 2500-3000S; beer 1000S) Wash down *laghman* and other Uighur specialities with affordable unfiltered homebrew on a pleasant people-watching terrace behind Cinema Samarkand.

Besh Chinor (Temerchilar; plov 5000S; ⊙ 9am-10pm) A lunchtime *plov* option, it's pricier and less atmospheric than Siob Bazaar Stolovaya, but probably easier on Western stomachs.

You can wash *plov* down with vodka at one of several home restaurants behind Ulugbek's Observatory. Ask to be pointed in the right direction.

RESTAURANTS

Karimbek (☎ 221 27 56; Gagarin 194; mains 2500-5000S; ⊙ 8am-11pm) This Uzbek theme restaurant trounces touristy Oasis restaurant in Navoi Park. The national- and Russian-influenced cuisine can be enjoyed in a variety of settings, from private country hut to airy streetside patio. A nightly belly-dancing show jiggles to life around 8pm.

Venezia (☎ 233 43 22; durahmon Jomi 96; pasta 3300-4000S, mains 2500-7500S; ✖ 🛜 Ⓥ Ⓔ) This Italian-themed eatery turns out thin-crust pizza, a random assortment of salads and reasonably priced pasta dishes.

Platan (☎ 233 80 49; Pushkin 2; mains 4000-6000S; ✖ 🛜 Ⓥ Ⓔ) The main dining facility – a sort of tropical-style, thatched-roof yurt – counts as one of Samarkand's stranger structures. The menu, which includes Arabian-, Thai- and Egyptian-style meat dishes, is no less charismatic, but all dishes are cooked-to-order and tasty.

Fratelli (☎ 231 19 91; Amir Timur 31; veggie wraps 4300S, mains 4500-11,000S; ✖) This big, bright, bustling bistro, popular with students, is a perfect place for coffee or a light lunch.

SELF-CATERING

Supermarket Aziz (Pochta 6; ⊙ 8am-8pm) is Samarkand's closest approximation of a Western-style supermarket.

Drinking & Entertainment

The Registan area shuts down around 9pm, but there's action downtown if you look hard enough.

Blues Cafe (Amir Timur 66; ⊙ noon-11.30pm) The nightly live jazz at this snug cocktail lounge usually takes the form of Eddie the solo piano player, but occasionally a larger ensemble materialises. The creative snack menu includes *khachapuri* (cheese-filled Georgian *samsa*).

Rayskiy Ugolok (☎ 221 19 85; Busygina 32; table fee 20,000S) Outside of Tashkent it's taboo for women to attend nightclubs. This dance bar solves that problem by hiring women to boogie with the mostly male clients – for a small tip, of course. If nothing else it's a fascinating study of provincial Uzbek culture.

Your best late-night option is the basement nightclub at the Afrosiyob Palace, which is usually moribund but has its moments at weekends. The new town also has a few nightclubs, including **Volna** (Wave; Isaev 10).

RESPONSIBLE SHOPPING

Besides being blessed with former Soviet Central Asia's most splendid architecture, Uzbekistan boasts a rich textile industry – as evidenced by the sometimes baffling array of fabrics spilling out of tourist attractions from Tashkent to Khiva.

If you're the sort who can't tell the difference between a 19th-century Nuratinsky *suzani* (silk-embroidered tapestry) and some farmer's dirty old handkerchief, the least you can do is buy responsibly. Uzbekistan is hardly known for being small-business friendly, but a growing number of individual artisans and merchants have set up small-scale, tourist-focused enterprises that are turning profits while also contributing to the cultural and economic revival of local communities. The following fit the bill:

Rakhimov Ceramics Studio In Tashkent (p226); working to revive extinct or nearly extinct schools of Uzbek ceramic-making. A great place to witness and/or buy some fine pieces of pottery and learn about Uzbekistan's many ceramic styles.

Samarkand-Bukhara Silk Carpets (Map p242; ☎ 235 22 73; www.silkcarpets.net; A Hojom 12; ⏰ by appointment) This natural-dye silk carpet factory sees benefits in offering employees benefits – rare for Uzbekistan. Carpets from US$1200.

'Unesco' carpet workshops More lovely but expensive silk carpets woven with natural dyes under favourable working conditions. Workshops in Bukhara (p266) and Khiva (p276).

Embroidery Group (Map p251; ☎ 529 39 67; yulduz1967@mail.ru; Ipak Yoli) Yulduz Mamadiyorova runs this weaving project in Shakhrisabz, which employs more than 300 local women stitching in the local style. Look for her bags and items of clothing at Human House (p226) in Tashkent.

Shopping

There are souvenir shops and craft workshops of varying quality at all the big sights, in particular at the Rukhobod Mausoleum and the Registan. At the Registan look out for the **Samarkand Ceramics Workshop** (Tilla-Kari Medressa), one of the few places still practising the Samarkand school of ceramic-making. There are also several noteworthy antique shops in Tilla-Kari Medressa and one in Sher Dor Medressa, but textile and *suzani* buffs are better off going to Urgut (p250).

Samarkand-Bukhara Silk Carpets (see the boxed text) also has a Registan-based **showroom** (Sher Dor Medressa). Multilingual Bobir has a traditional musical instrument shop in Sher Dor Medressa and gives spontaneous concerts. Accomplished miniaturist Mansur Nurillaev is at the Rukhobod Mausoleum.

Around and behind Bibi-Khanym, the frenetic, colourful main market **Siob Bazaar** is a great place for vegetarians and photographers, and may reward silk and souvenir hunters as well.

Getting There & Away

AIR

Uzbekistan Airways (☎ 230 86 59) flies between Samarkand and Tashkent daily except Friday for €30. Buy domestic tickets at the airport office.

LAND

Tashkent is four hours away by car across a flat, dry landscape that tsarist Russians nicknamed the Hungry Steppe. The main departure point to Tashkent for private buses and shared taxis is the Ulugbek marshrutka stop, about 200m east of the observatory (bus/shared taxi per seat US$3.50/10, six/3½ hours).

Shared taxis to Termiz (US$15, five hours) and Denau (US$15, five hours) gather at 'Grebnoy Kanal' on the city's outskirts about 6km east of the Ulugbek stop. Infrequent Tashkent–Termiz buses pass by Grebnoy Kanal, but don't count on them having seats.

Buses to Bukhara originate in Tashkent and pass by the highway opposite the Ulugbek stop (US$4, 4½ hours). Buses pass at least every hour, and traffic is heaviest around 4.30pm. Departures peter out around 5pm because of the nationally imposed 10pm curfew on bus traffic. There are two daily buses to Urgench (US$6, 12 hours).

Shared taxis to Bukhara involve a transfer in Navoi. The main departure point to Navoi (US$6, two hours) is the Povorot marshrutka stop about 2.5km west of the Crying Mother monument on Ulugbek kochasi. Take any marshrutkas signposted 'Поворот'. Shared taxis from Navoi to Bukhara take an hour and cost US$4.

For Shakhrisabz, shared taxis congregate on Suzangaran, about 25m south of the old 'Registan' marshrutka stop (US$3, 1½ hours). They go only as far as Kitab, where you pick up a marshrutka for the last 10km. For Penjikent, see p288.

Train

The speedy 'Registan' train, with airplane-style seating, departs five times a week to Tashkent at 5pm (US$7.50, 3½ hours). The equally priced and equally speedy Bukhara–Tashkent express 'Sharq' train rolls through Samarkand daily at 11:10am, while the Tashkent-bound 'Nasaf' hits Samarkand six times weekly at 5:45pm, en route from Karshi.

There are several slower regular passenger trains daily to Tashkent (*platskartny/kupeyny* US$8/12; six hours), including a night train originating in Samarkand.

For Bukhara you can pick up the Sharq heading west at about noon (2nd class US$6, 2¾ hours). The daily Tashkent–Bukhara passenger train rumbles through Samarkand at 1.20pm (*platskartny/kupeyny* US$9/15, 6½ hours) and several late-night variants also exist. The cheapest option to Bukhara is the daily local train (US$1.30; six hours) at 4pm. Local trains also trundle to Karshi (US$0.70, four hours) and Jizzakh (US$0.25, two hours).

The trains from Tashkent to Urgench, Termiz and Kungrad via Nukus go via Samarkand (see p228).

The **train station** (☎ 229 15 32; Rudaki) is 5km northwest of Navoi Park. Take any bus or marshrutka that says 'Вокзал', such as bus 22 or marshrutkas 3, 27, 35 or 72, from the Registan or Bulvar stops.

Getting Around
TO/FROM THE AIRPORT

Marshrutka 56 goes from the airport to the Registan marshrutka stop, while marshrutkas 10 and 60 and bus 45 go to the Bulvar (Бульвар) stop near Hotel Samarkand. A taxi from the airport to the Registan will cost about 5000S, or walk 500m out to the main road and pay 3000S.

PUBLIC TRANSPORT

Marshrutkas (400S) and buses (300S) run from about 6am until 8pm or 9pm. To get between the Registan stop and Navoi in the heart of the downtown area take any vehicle marked ГУМ (GUM), such as bus 3, 22 or

32, or marshrutka 6 or 35. A taxi between the old town and new town should cost less than US$1.

At the time of research, the 'Registan' marshrutka stop had moved from its traditional location east of the Registan to a new location south of Registan kochasi near Gur-e-Amir. It was unclear if the move was permanent.

AROUND SAMARKAND
Hoja Ismail

In Hoja Ismail, a village 20km north of Samarkand, is one of Islam's holier spots, the modest **Mausoleum of Ismail al-Bukhari** (admission US$2, guided tour in English US$0.50; ☺ 7am-8pm). Al-Bukhari (AD 810–872) was one of the greatest Muslim scholars of the *Hadith* – the collected acts and sayings of the Prophet Mohammed. His work is regarded by Sunni Muslims as second only to the Quran as a source of religious law. Following his refusal to give special tutoring to Bukhara's governor and his children, he was forced into exile here.

This peaceful place of pilgrimage contains a mosque, a small museum and two courtyards, the main one containing Ismail al-Bukhari's gorgeous tomb, made of yellow marble and inlaid with majolica. It's surrounded by an *aivan,* under which an imam usually sits, chanting prayers. The *aivan's* brightly painted ceiling uncharacteristically lacks red – supposedly on the orders of President Karimov, who wanted to avoid communist associations.

It's essential to dress conservatively here, respect the calm and reverent atmosphere, and ask before you take photos.

Hoja Ismail village is 4km off the road to Chelek. From Samarkand, take a marshrutka straight there from the Shahizinda bus station or a shared taxi from outside Umar Bank on Dahbet. Marshrutkas 35 and 11 pass Umar Bank from the Hotel Samarkand.

Urgut

This town's **bazaar** is one of the best places in the country to buy jewellery, *suzani* and antique clothing. Prices are lower and the quality on par with anything sold in Samarkand and Bukhara, but you'll have to negotiate hard. It overflows with tourists in the high season – go in the low season when tourists are scarce and prices drop even further. Arrive at the crack of dawn for the best selection.

While the bazaar is open every day, the textile and jewellery section, located at the back of the main bazaar, only happens on Sunday and Wednesday, and to a lesser extent on Saturday too. To get here from Samarkand, take a shared taxi (US$1.50) or marshrutka (US$1) from the Registan stop (45 minutes).

SHAKHRISABZ ШАХРИСАБЗ

☎ 75 / pop 75,000

Shakhrisabz is a small, un-Russified town south of Samarkand, across the hills in the Kashkadarya province. The town is a pleasant Uzbek backwater and seems to be nothing special – until you start bumping into the ruins dotted around its backstreets, and the megalomaniac ghosts of a wholly different place materialise. This is Timur's hometown, and once upon a time it probably put Samarkand itself in the shade. It's worth a visit just to check out the great man's roots.

Timur was born on 9 April 1336 into the Barlas clan of local aristocrats, at the village of Hoja Ilghar, 13km to the south. Ancient even then, Shakhrisabz (called Kesh at the time) was a kind of family seat. As he rose to power, Timur gave it its present name (Tajik for 'Green Town') and turned it into an extended family monument. Most of its current attractions were built here by Timur (including a tomb intended for himself) or his grandson Ulugbek.

You can easily see all of Shakhrisabz as a day trip from Samarkand. There are a couple of sleeping options for those who want to linger and absorb the city's easy-going provincial vibe.

Orientation

Almost everything of interest in Shakhrisabz happens along a 2km stretch of the town's main road, Ipak Yoli (Uzbek for 'Silk Road'). The long-distance (new) bus station is south of town, about 3.5km beyond the Kok-Gumbaz Mosque.

Information

The Orient Star hotel can summon English-, German- and French-speaking guides for city tours.

Marinet Internet Cafe (Ipak Yoli; per megabyte 200S; ☯ 9am-5pm) It's in the building between Aquarium cafe and Orient Star.

National Bank of Uzbekistan (Firdavsi)

Sights

AK-SARAY PALACE

Just north of the centre, **Timur's summer palace** (White Palace; admission free, access to staircase US$1; ☯ 9am-6pm) has as much grandeur per square centimetre as anything in Samarkand. There's actually nothing left of it except bits of the gigantic, 40m-high *pishtak*, covered with

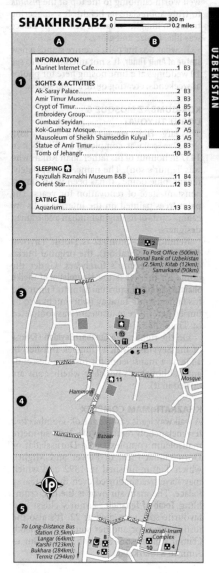

SHAKHRISABZ   0 ——— 300 m
0 ——— 0.2 miles

INFORMATION
Marinet Internet Cafe.................................1 B3

SIGHTS & ACTIVITIES
Ak-Saray Palace..2 B3
Amir Timur Museum....................................3 B3
Crypt of Timur..4 B5
Embroidery Group.......................................5 B4
Gumbazi Seyidan..6 A5
Kok-Gumbaz Mosque..................................7 A5
Mausoleum of Sheikh Shamseddin Kulyal 8 A5
Statue of Amir Timur...................................9 B3
Tomb of Jehangir......................................10 B5

SLEEPING
Fayzullah Ravnakhi Museum B&B...............11 B4
Orient Star..12 B3

EATING
Aquarium..13 B3

To Post Office (500m);
National Bank of Uzbekistan
(2.5km); Kitab (12km);
Samarkand (90km)

Gagarin

Pushkin

Abay

Ravnakhi   Mosque

Hammom

Pak Yoli

Namatmon   Bazaar

Shamsiddin Kulol

To Long-Distance Bus
Station (3.5km);
Langar (64km);
Karshi (123km);
Bukhara (284km);
Termiz (294km)

Khazrati-Imam
Complex

gorgeous, unrestored filigree-like mosaics. This crumbling relic blending seamlessly with everyday life will thrill critics of Samarkand's zealous restoration efforts.

Ak-Saray was probably Timur's most ambitious project, 24 years in the making, following a successful campaign in Khorezm and the 'import' of many of its finest artisans. It's well worth climbing to the top of the *pishtak* to truly appreciate its height. It's staggering trying to imagine what the rest of the palace was like, in size and glory.

In what was the palace centre stands a new **statue of Amir Timur**. It's not uncommon to see 10 weddings at a time posing here for photos at weekends, creating quite a mob scene.

KOK-GUMBAZ MOSQUE & DORUT TILYOVAT

This large **Friday mosque** (Ipak Yoli; admission US$1; 8.30am-6pm) was completed by Ulugbek in 1437 in honour of his father Shah Rukh (who was Timur's son). The name, appropriately, means 'blue dome'. It has been in an almost constant state of renovation for years. The palm trees painted on the interior walls are calling cards of its original Indian and Iranian designers.

Behind Kok-Gumbaz is Dorut Tilyovat (House of Meditation), the original burial complex of Timur's forebears. Under the dome on the left is the **Mausoleum of Sheikh Shamseddin Kulyal**, spiritual tutor to Timur and his father, Amir Taragay (who might also be buried here). The mausoleum was completed by Timur in 1374.

On the right is the **Gumbazi Seyidan** (Dome of the Seyyids), which Ulugbek finished in 1438 as a mausoleum for his own descendants (although it's not clear whether any are buried in it).

KHAZRATI-IMAM COMPLEX

A walkway leads east from Kok-Gumbaz to a few melancholy remnants of a 3500-sq-metre mausoleum complex called Dorussiadat or Dorussaodat (Seat of Power and Might), which Timur finished in 1392 and which may have overshadowed even the Ak-Saray Palace. The main survivor is the tall, crumbling **Tomb of Jehangir**, Timur's eldest and favourite son, who died at 22. It's also the resting place for another son, Umar Sheikh (Timur's other sons are with him at Gur-e-Amir in Samarkand).

In an alley behind the mausoleum (and within the perimeter of the long-gone Dorussiadat) is a bunker with a wooden door leading to an underground room, the **Crypt of Timur**. The room, plain except for Quranic quotations on the arches, is nearly filled by a single stone casket. On the casket are biographical inscriptions about Timur, from which it was inferred (when the room was discovered in 1963) that this crypt was intended for him. Inside are two unidentified corpses.

AMIR TIMUR MUSEUM

Housed inside the renovated Chubin Medressa is this simple **museum** (Ipak Yoli; admission US$1; 9am-5pm). Its highlight is a model depicting Timur's entire kingdom, from Egypt to Kashgar. Beyond the boundaries of the kingdom, a yellow line illustrates his 'protectorates', including Kiev and Moscow. If that doesn't interest you, the museum is probably not worth the price of admission, although there are some old Buddhist and Zoroastrian artefacts here that predate Timur by many centuries.

Sleeping & Eating

Fayzullah Ravnakhi Museum B&B (521 02 77; Ravnakhi 55; r per person US$15) This homey spot has two unique quads and one cosy double. The quads are basically open spaces with patchwork carpeting, two basic beds and not much else. Staff will throw a couple of *kurpacha* on the floor to accommodate bigger groups. The owner has refreshing tour ideas – see the boxed text, p254. To find it, look for the Shakhrisabz Tours & Travel sign.

Orient Star (522 06 38; www.tour-orient.com; Ipak Yoli 26; s/d US$30/50;) This is the only real hotel in town and it's often occupied by tour groups, so book ahead in the high season. It's typical fare for the Orient chain – a few bells and whistles but not much character.

Aquarium (Ipak Yoli 22) This bustling cafe is in view of Ak-Saray and serves up the usual shashlyk, *laghman* and vodka shots.

Along Ipak Yoli are a strip of chaikhanas whose fortunes ebb and flow like the surrounding desert sands. Popularity generally suggests quality. The bazaar has *samsa*, fruit and what not.

Getting There & Around

Shakhrisabz is about 90km from Samarkand, over the 1788m Takhtakaracha (Amankutan)

Pass. The pass is occasionally closed by snow from January to March, forcing a three-hour detour around the mountains. For details on getting here from Samarkand, see p249.

Buses and shared taxis to a handful of other destinations leave from the long-distance (new) bus station, south of town. To Tashkent's Ippodrom station there are about six daily buses (US$4, eight hours) and regular shared taxis (US$15, five hours). To get to Bukhara take a shared taxi to Karshi (US$3.50, 1½ hours) and change there.

TERMIZ TEPME3
☎ 76 / pop 130,000 / elev 380m

Modern-day Termiz bears few traces of its colourful cosmopolitan history. However, set in attractive landscapes on the fringes of town are some ancient monuments and sites attesting to more glorious times.

The expat aid workers and German soldiers who once populated Termiz' bars and restaurants have moved on, but Termiz has retained an edgy, Wild West border-town feel. A steady flow of contraband from Afghanistan crosses the Amu-Darya here on its way to Europe, as well as contraband alcohol headed into Afghanistan.

Orientation & Information
The main road is Al-Termizi, with the train station at its northern end. The clock tower on the corner of Al-Termizi and Navoi marks the central axis of town. The bus station is 2km west of this.

Asaka Bank (Navoi 45) Currency exchange and cash advances for MasterCard holders.

Internet Cafe (Al-Termizi; per hr 800S; ☀ 8am-8.30pm) Located opposite the clock tower.

Sights
The **Termiz Archaeological Museum** (☎ 227 58 29; Al-Termizi 29; admission US$1.50, camera US$1; ☀ 9am-6pm) is reason enough to visit Termiz. Unveiled in 2001, the museum is a treasure trove of artefacts collected from the many ravaged civilisations that pepper the Surkhandarya province of which Termiz is the main city. The highlight would be to be the collection of 3rd- to 4th-century Buddhist artefacts. The museum also has an excellent model of Surkhandarya that depicts the area's most

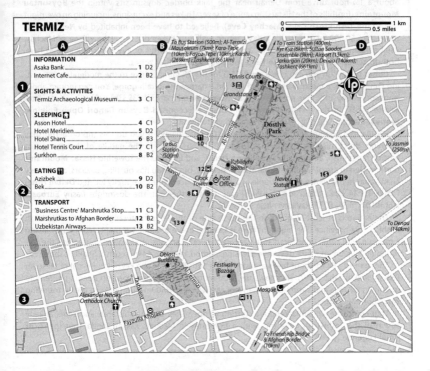

important archaeological sights. Serious archaeological buffs can use this map to plot their course to a wealth of caves, petroglyphs and excavations in the north of Surkhandarya province.

There are several sights around Termiz that can be visited in a half-day. Figure on paying a driver US$4 to US$5 per hour, or about US$15 for a half-day tour.

The main sights lurk northwest of the city on the road to Karshi. Driving out here you'll notice various piles of rubble in the cotton fields of what used to be Termiz (and is now known as Old Termiz). These are Buddhist ruins, levelled by Chinggis Khan along with the rest of Old Termiz in 1220.

Today archaeologists are busy trying to reverse some of the damage at **Fayoz-Tepe**, a

---

OFF THE BEATEN TRACK IN SOUTHERN UZBEKISTAN

North of Termiz, the baked landscape twists and contorts itself into a mesmerising collage of canyons, cliffs, grottoes, buttes, mesas, peaks and rubble, all rendered in the tawny, inimitable hues of the desert. This is Surkhandarya, Uzbekistan's southernmost province. The region's caves provided shelter for primitive humans some 50,000 years ago, and the area that would become known as the Surkhan Oasis in the Bronze Age continued for a millennium to function as an important prehistoric hub of human civilisation.

Today, sparsely populated Surkhandarya feels a world apart from the rest of Uzbekistan. Off the highway, transport is more likely to be by donkey than by vehicle, and long mountain walks might lead you through villages that have little contact with the outside world. Temporary bazaars erupt seemingly out of nowhere, blanketing the desert in a pulsating quilt of colour before disappearing. Houses blend seamlessly with the earth from which they were fashioned.

A popular tourist destination for outdoorsy types in Soviet times, Surkhandarya looks set for a revival after a new train line traversing the province opened in 2009. Hone in on **Boysun** (Бойсун), about a 1½-hour drive from Denau near the Tajik border. Boysun sits within the **Boysuntau Mountains** (foothills of the Hissars), in range of several hikes and excursions, including an overnight trek to the **Teshiktosh Cave (Machay Cave)**, believed to have been inhabited by Neanderthals more than 50,000 years ago. It's a day's return walk or donkey ride from the village of Machay, itself a 45km drive north of Darbent. You'll need a guide for this or any other trek around here, both to set up homestays and to keep you away from border zones.

Closer to Boysun you can hire a car (US$5) for the 25-minute drive to the moderately interesting **Oman Hona**, a mosque and cave shrine on a narrow mountain gorge. You can inquire about transport at Boysun's lone hotel, the grotty **Nomat Hotel** (☎ 8371-335 3380, 8392-503 8726; d without bathroom US$8) in the middle of town. The Unesco-recognised **Boysun Bahori Open Folklore Festival**, held in late May, is a good time to visit Boysun.

Regular public transport links Boysun with **Denau** (Денов). If you do this trip on a Thursday morning, don't miss the bazaar that suddenly springs to life in the middle of the desert just east of Tangimush, about halfway between Denau and Boysun. The towering **Hissar Mountains** north of Denau are off-limits without special permits, but Denau has bustling bazaars, a few lively chaikhanas in the centre, and a couple of attractively priced hotels: centrally located **Denau Hotel** (☎ 76-412 14 90; Rashidov; s/d from US$4/8) and, a bit further out, the downright flashy **Euroasia Hotel** (☎ 76-542 00 38; Rashidov; r from US$15; ✷).

The action is at least as good on the north side of the Boysuntau range near Shakhrisabz in Kashkadarya province. The highlight here is **Langar**, home to a famous mausoleum on a hill and a mosque with some unrestored 16th-century tilework. Langar's mud-walled houses, like the surrounding hills, are shaded a deep, eye-pleasing maroon. Langar is 64km south of Shakhrisabz by car.

The man to talk to about hikes around here is Lutfullohon at the Fayzullah Ravnakhi Museum B&B in Shakhrisabz (p252). He knows the local routes well and can have you sleeping in remote mountain villages and sitting atop relatively easy-to-climb 3500m-plus peaks in the surrounding Zarafshon Mountains.

Tour companies in Samarkand are starting to open their eyes to this area, and some already advertise the Teshiktosh Cave trip, with a homestay in Machay. Ask at Sogda Tour (p243) or Hotel Légende (p247).

3rd-century-AD Buddhist monastery complex 9km west of the bus station. Discovered only in 1968, in recent years it has been restored and a teapot dome put over the monastery's original stupa, visible through a glass window. Looking southwest from here, the remains of **Kara-Tepe**, a Buddhist cave monastery, are visible on the banks of the Amu-Darya, opposite the Afghan border. You need special permission to visit Kara-Tepe – ask at the Archaeological Museum.

Closer to town is a slightly younger but still quite sacred edifice, the **Mausoleum of Al-Hakim al-Termizi**. Its namesake was a 9th-century Sufi philosopher, known locally as Al-Hakim, the city's patron saint. In a triumph for preservationists, the interior's cheap plaster *ghanch*-work, spuriously installed as part of the government's general monument beautification drive, is being gradually removed to expose the original 15th-century brick. The mausoleum gets packed to the gills on Wednesday, when the faithful are served lunch. The Amu-Darya and Afghanistan are once again in sight here; photographing the border is forbidden. To get out here catch marshrutka 15 heading north on Al-Termizi from Yubileyny Bazaar (500S, 20 minutes), just north of the clock tower.

Termiz' other main sights are clustered northeast of town off the airport road. The restored Timurid-style **Sultan Saodat Ensemble** of mausoleums probably won't impress you if you've been to Samarkand. Buried here are members of the Sayyid dynasty, which ruled Termiz from the 11th to 15th centuries. About 5km closer to town is a real ruin, the mud-walled **Kyr Kyz** (Forty Girls) fortress. Legend has it that 40 young women lived here in the 11th century after their nobleman-husband was slain, successfully fighting off sex-crazed nomads before eventually succumbing to their own ambition to avenge their husband's murder.

Tours
Gulya (☎ 222 71 25; gul_1982@rambler.ru) is a friendly guide who works part-time at the archaeological museum. **Alisher Choriev** (☎ 8391-580 8090) is another capable English-speaking guide.

Sleeping
Termiz has some great-value accommodation. Breakfast is not included at the following places.

Hotel Tennis Court (Al-Termizi 29B; dm from US$5) The rote basic rooms at this central sports complex are a budget option if you can find the caretaker to let you in. It's opposite the archaeology museum.

Surkhon (☎ 222 75 99; cnr Al-Termizi & Navoi; s/d from US$10/15; ✴) The smartly renovated Soviet rooms here are an incredible deal, with big, clean bathrooms and white cotton bedspreads. It's well located kitty-corner from the clock tower.

Hotel Sharq (☎ 223 46 13; sharqhotel@yandex.ru; Fayzulla Khojaev 15; s/d US$10/20; ✴) Another great renovated Soviet deal in the mould of Surkhon. The rooms here have ample space, big beds and TVs. Only drawback is the location 1km south of the clock tower.

Asson Hotel (☎ 227 58 76; cnr Al-Termizi & Jurabaev; s/d US$20/30; ✴) It's at best a slight upgrade on Sharq and Surkhon, but the location next to the archaeological museum is perfect.

Hotel Meridien (☎ 227 26 74; Alpomysh 23; s/d US$60/80; ✴) This modern high-rise has large rooms in pastel colours and a decent restaurant that's open well into the evening, but there's much better value to be had elsewhere.

Eating & Drinking
Azizbek (☎ 390 06 72; Navoi; mains 2000-3000S, disco admission US$0.50) There's a little bit of everything at this complex near Hotel Meridien, including plenty of grilled meat and beer served on a vast outdoor patio, and a smoky upstairs discotheque.

Bek (☎ 227 34 43; off Al-Termizi; mains 3000-5000S; ⏲ 7am-midnight; ✴ Ⓥ) Located on a little side street just south of Asson Hotel, Bek has melt-in-your-mouth ground-meat Gijduvan shashlyk, a large salad selection and cheap beer (1500S).

Jasmin (Navoi, Fifth Rayon; mains 4000-6000S) A vintage local eatery, Jasmin is the place to sample *chopancha*, a Surkhandarya meat-and-potatoes dish. It's on the outskirts of town about 1.5km north of the Hotel Meridien.

Getting There & Around
Uzbekistan Airways (☎ 222 85 77; Al-Termizi) has three flights a day to/from Tashkent (€37). The office is 300m south of the clock tower on the right (west) side of the street. The airport is 15km north of town. Take marshrutka 11 from Yubileyny Bazaar.

Shared taxi is the way to go to/from Boysun (US$3.50, 1½ hours), Denau (US$4,

1½ hours), Samarkand (US$15, five hours) and Karshi (US$7.50, 3½ hours). Transfer in Karshi for Bukhara. There's also a 6am bus to Samarkand (US$5, 8½ hours). There are a couple of morning buses to Tashkent (US$7.50, 13 hours) via Samarkand or take a shared taxi (US$20, nine hours). Marshrutkas are cheaper options to Denau (US$1.75) and Boysun (US$2.50).

All of the above leave from the bus station, a straight shot west on either Jurabaev (marshrutkas 18 and 20) or Navoi (marshrutkas 6, 7 and 8).

Trains to Termiz from Tashkent/Samarkand no longer go through Turkmenistan thanks to a brand-new track opened in 2009 that links Guzor and Termiz via Boysun and Jarkurgan. Train 379 departs on odd days at 4pm to Tashkent (platskartny/kupeyny US$15/22, 14 hours) with stops in Boysun, Karshi and Samarkand. The return trip departs Tashkent even days at 9.20pm.

Local trains depart thrice daily to Denau (US$0.50; three hours), and continue another hour to Sariosiyo at the Tajik border. For more information on getting to Tajikistan see p288.

NURATA
☎ 436 or 79 / pop 30,000

To the north of the featureless Samarkand–Bukhara 'Royal Road', the Pamir-Alay Mountains produce one final blip on the map before fading unceremoniously into desertified insignificance. The Nuratau Mountains, which top out at 2169m, are rapidly becoming the centre of Uzbekistan's growing ecotourism movement (see the boxed text). Modest Nurata town makes a logical base for jumping off to the mountains or to one of several nearby yurt camps.

Nurata is most famous for its old, circle-patterned suzani, which can sell for thousands of dollars at international auctions, but it also has a few quirky tourist attractions, most notably an old **fortress of Alexander the Great**. You can make like Alexander – go ahead, even throw on your suit of armour – and clamber all over the fortress, which looms over the town like a giant sandcastle. Behind the fortress, a path leads 4km to the **Zukarnay Petroglyphs**, which date to the Bronze Age. Ask the curator at the museum how to find the trail. If it's too hot to walk, there are sometimes guys with motorcycles hanging out near the museum who will whisk you out there for a couple of

thousand som. (If you miss these, there are many more petroglyphs at Sarmysh Gorge, accessible by car 40km northeast of Navoi.)

Beneath Alexander's fortress you'll encounter the anomaly of several hundred trout occupying a pool and well next to a 16th-century mosque and a 9th-century mausoleum. This is the **Chashma Spring** (admission US$1), formed, it is said, where the Prophet Mohammed's son-in-law Hazrat Ali drove his staff into the ground. The 'holy' fish live off the mineral-laden waters of the spring and canals that feed it. Also on the grounds here is a small **museum** (admission US$0.25; ⏱ 7am-5pm Tue-Sun) with some old suzani and other trinkets. Curator Shavat is Nurata's best source of regional information; he speaks Russian and some French.

The passable **Hotel Nur** (☎ 323 00 16; s/d without bathroom US$5/10), 500m from Chashma Spring on the road to the centre, is the only hotel in town and has a ground-floor restaurant. Close to the centre, **Mr Nemat** (☎ 523 18 74, 8393-316 1444) runs a pleasant homestay with a hammoni, and can prepare meals and organise excursions. Navoi has better hotels, such as the **Yoshlik Hotel** (☎ 436-224 40 21; Halklar Dustligi 138; r without/with bathroom US$25/40; ❄).

LAKE AIDARKUL & YURT CAMPS
After briefly taking in Nurata's sights, you'll want to hightail it to the yurt camps to the north of Nurata. There are four within shooting distance. Two are about 60km due north of Nurata in Yangikazgan; two others are further east in Dungalok near the shores of manmade Lake Aidarkul, formed from the diverted waters of the Syr-Darya in 1969.

All yurt camps include short **camel trekking** rides in their rates; the ones in Dungalok offer fishing. Longer treks, including multiple-day excursions, are also possible for an extra charge.

The comfortable camel-hair yurts, most of them tastefully decorated with carpets and suzani, sleep six to eight people. Prices vary from camp to camp according to the level of comfort. Rates listed include three meals a day. Camps close from November to mid-March, and sometimes during July and August. Showing up unannounced may work, but as they are often booked by tour groups you're best off calling ahead.

Yangikazgan
Sputnik Camel Camp (☎ 436-223 8081, 8379-221 6660; sputnik-navoi@yandex.ru; per person US$45) The

---

GOING LOCAL IN THE NURATAU MOUNTAINS

South of Lake Aidarkul, there is great hiking and birdwatching in the mountains of the **Nuratau-Kyzylkum Biosphere Reserve**, which is also the site of a wonderful **community-based tourism project** (www.nuratau.com) – the only one of its kind in Uzbekistan. Under this UN Development Programme–sponsored 'cultural tourism' project, families in several villages have converted their homes into rustic guesthouses. The families offer hiking, horse- and donkey-riding, traditional cooking, weaving and craft-making lessons, and the opportunity to breathe in mountain air and sleep on *tapchan* (tea beds) under the stars. During winter weekends you can observe authentic *kupkari* (traditional polo-like game played with a headless goat carcass) matches.

This is a great opportunity to interact with the local ethnic Tajiks in their element – and a great way to ward off architecture burnout if you've seen one too many medressas. The program's website has information on getting to the various villages. To save money take public transport to Nurata or to the project **field office** (☎ 72-452 17 68/7, 72-261 27 97, Russian only; nature-of-farish@mail.ru) in Yangikishlok, a small town 80km west of Jizzakh, and proceed from there.

Alternatively, you can arrange everything through a guesthouse or tour company in Samarkand, Bukhara or Tashkent. Tour companies refer to the program as 'Sentyab' after one of the host villages. Registration should be possible by 2011.

---

first and probably the fanciest of the lot, run by the mischievous, tough-as-nails Radik. Has attractive dining yurt and lots of creature comforts.

Yangikazgan Yurt Camp (☎ 436-225 1419, 8379-373 1953; murat2005@bk.ru; per person US$35) Also has electricity and creature comforts, but dining is in a cement building. It's quite close to Sputnik, in the middle of the desert 6km north of Yangikazgan.

Dungalok

Aidar Yurt Camp (☎ 436-223 9546, 436-222 5618; per person US$40) Closest camp to the lake, also has electricity and hot water. Reserve through English-speaking Gulzal.

Safari Camp (☎ 8379-532 3938; 8379-320 0444; navoi-tur@mail.ru; Halklar Dustigli 73, Navoi; per person US$40) Associated with the provincial tourism office in Navoi.

GETTING THERE & AWAY

To get to Nurata, make your way from Bukhara or Samarkand to Navoi, then take a shared taxi (US$1.75, one hour) or marshrutka (US$1.25). In Nurata sporadic marshrutkas run to Dungalok and Yangikazgan, but you'll likely have to hire a private car. Negotiations start at US$15 one-way to the yurt camps.

BUKHARA БУХАРА
☎ 65 / pop 263,000

Central Asia's holiest city, Bukhara has buildings spanning a thousand years of history, and a thoroughly lived-in old centre that probably hasn't changed much in two centuries. It is one of the best places in Central Asia for a glimpse of pre-Russian Turkestan.

Most of the centre is an architectural preserve, full of medressas, minarets, a massive royal fortress and the remnants of a once-vast market complex. Government restoration efforts have been more subtle and less indiscriminate than in flashier Samarkand, and the city's accommodation options go from strength to strength.

Until a century ago Bukhara was watered by a network of canals and some 200 stone pools where people gathered and gossiped, drank and washed. As the water wasn't changed often, Bukhara was famous for plagues; the average 19th-century Bukharan is said to have died by the age of 32. The Bolsheviks modernised the system and drained the pools.

You'll need at least two days to look around. Try to allow time to lose yourself in the old town; it's easy to overdose on the 140-odd protected buildings and miss the whole for its many parts.

History

It was as capital of the Samanid state in the 9th and 10th centuries that Bukhara – Bukhoro-i-sharif (Noble Bukhara), the 'Pillar of Islam' – blossomed as Central Asia's religious and cultural heart. Among those nurtured here were the philosopher-scientist Ibn Sina and the poets Firdausi and Rudaki – figures with stature in the Persian Islamic world that, for example, Newton or Shakespeare enjoyed in the West.

After two centuries under the smaller Karakhanid and Karakitay dynasties, Bukhara succumbed in 1220 to Chinggis Khan, and in 1370 fell under the shadow of Timur's Samarkand.

A second lease of life came in the 16th century when the Uzbek Shaybanids made it the capital of what came to be known as the Bukhara khanate. The centre of Shaybanid Bukhara was a vast marketplace with dozens of specialist bazaars and caravanserais, more than 100 medressas (with 10,000 students) and more than 300 mosques.

In 1753 Mohammed Rahim, the local deputy of a Persian ruler, proclaimed himself emir, founding the Mangit dynasty that was to rule until the Bolsheviks came. Several depraved rulers filled Rahim's shoes; the worst was probably Nasrullah Khan (also called 'the Butcher' behind his back), who ascended the throne in 1826 by killing off his brothers and 28 other relatives. He made himself a household name in Victorian England after he executed two British officers (see the boxed text, p264).

In 1868, Russian troops under General Kaufman occupied Samarkand (which at the time was within Emir Muzaffar Khan's domains). Soon afterward Bukhara surrendered, and was made a protectorate of the tsar, with the emirs still nominally in charge.

In 1918 a party of emissaries arrived from Tashkent (by then under Bolshevik control) to persuade Emir Alim Khan to surrender peacefully. The wily despot stalled long enough to allow his agents to stir up an anti-Russian mob that slaughtered nearly the whole delegation, and the emir's own army sent a larger Russian detachment packing, back towards Tashkent.

But the humiliated Bolsheviks had their revenge. Following an orchestrated 'uprising' in Charjou (now Turkmenabat) by local revolutionaries calling themselves the Young Bukharans, and an equally premeditated request for help, Red Army troops from Khiva and Tashkent under General Mikhail Frunze stormed the Ark (citadel) and captured Bukhara.

Bukhara won a short 'independence' as the Bukhara People's Republic, but after showing rather too much interest in Pan-Turkism it was absorbed in 1924 into the newly created Uzbek SSR.

Orientation

An oasis in the enveloping Kyzylkum desert, Bukhara sits 250km downstream

of Samarkand on the Zarafshon River. The heart of the *shahristan* (old town) is the pool and square called Lyabi-Hauz; the landmark Kalon Minaret is five minutes further, the Ark five more. Further west are Samani Park and the main farmers market, Kolkhoz (Dekhon, Markazi) Bazaar. The bulk of the modern town lies southeast of the historical centre.

Information

BOOKSHOPS

Yog' Du Bookshop (Bakhautdin Naqshband 88; ⊗ 8am-8pm) Sells picture books and maps of Bukhara and Uzbekistan.

INTERNET ACCESS

Wi-fi remained limited to a select few hotels when we visited, but appeared ready to take off.
Internet Klub (Bakhautdin Naqshband 88; per hr 1000S; ⊗ 9am-11pm) Slow but central.
Net Club (Muminov; per hr 800S; ⊗ 10am-11pm) The best of several internet cafes located between S Ayni and M Ikbola.

MONEY

Most vendors around Taki-Sarrafon (Bakhautdin Naqshband) and elsewhere exchange money at fair black-market rates. Official exchange booths are at Taki-Sarrafon and **Asia Hotel** (☎ 224 64 31; Mehtar Ambar). The latter also advances cash for Visa cardholders, as does **Hotel Bukhara Palace** (☎ 223 50 04; Navoi 8) and the **National Bank of Uzbekistan** (M Ikbola 3). **Asaka Bank** (Bakhautdin Naqshband 168) does MasterCard cash advances.

REGISTRATION

OVIR (☎ 223 88 68; Murtazaev 10/3)

TELEPHONE & FAX

Telephone & telegraph office (Muminov 8; ⊗ 24hr) International calls for standard Uztelekom rates (see p285).

TOURIST INFORMATION

Bukhara's excellent tourist information centre has closed, but B&Bs have stepped in to fill the void. All of those listed under Sleeping can sort you out with just about anything you need.
Uzbektourism (☎ 770 10 33; info@bukharatourist.com; Grand Bukhara Hotel, Muminov 8) is useful mainly for its stable of multilingual guides (per hour US$5).

TRAVEL AGENCIES

Several B&Bs have attached travel agencies. The best are Emir, K Komil, Salom and

Sarrafon. Besides yurtstays near Nurata and homestays near Yangikishlok (which just about any hotel can arrange), area attractions include endangered Persian gazelles north of Karaul Bazaar, swimming in Tudakul Lake and the excavated remains of the pre-Islamic era city of Paikent, 60km southwest of Bukhara.

East Line Tour (☎ 224 22 69; www.eastlinetour.com; Bakhautdin Naqshband 98) runs the full gamut of tours, but specialises in birdwatching tours around Tudakul Lake and further afield.

Sights
LYABI-HAUZ
Lyabi-Hauz, a plaza built around a pool in 1620 (the name is Tajik for 'around the pool'), is the most peaceful and interesting spot in town – shaded by mulberry trees as old as the pool. The old tea-sipping, chessboard-clutching Uzbek men who once inhabited this corner of town have been moved on by local entrepreneurs bent on cashing in on the tourist trade. Still, the plaza maintains its old-world style and has managed to fend off the glitz to which Samarkand's Registan has succumbed.

On the east side is a statue of **Hoja Nasruddin**, a semimythical 'wise fool' who appears in Sufi teaching-tales around the world.

Further east, the **Nadir Divanbegi Medressa** was built as a caravanserai, but the khan thought it was a medressa and it became one in 1622. On the west side of the square, and built at the same time, is the **Nadir Divanbegi Khanaka**. Both are named for Abdul Aziz Khan's treasury minister, who financed them in the 17th century.

North across the street, the **Kukeldash Medressa** (1569), built by Abdullah II, was at the time the biggest Islamic school in Central Asia.

COVERED BAZAARS
From Shaybanid times, the area west and north from Lyabi-Hauz was a vast warren of market lanes, arcades and crossroad mini-bazaars, whose multidomed roofs were designed to draw in cool air. Three remaining domed bazaars, heavily renovated in Soviet times, were among dozens of specialised bazaars in the town – Taki-Sarrafon (money-changers), Taki-Telpak Furushon (cap makers) and Taki-Zargaron (jewellers). Now given over to tourist shops, they remain only loosely faithful to those designations today.

Taki-Sarrafon & Taki-Telpak Furushon Area
Between these two covered bazaars, in what was the old herb-and-spice bazaar, is Central Asia's oldest surviving mosque, the **Maghoki-Attar** (Pit of the herbalists), a lovely mishmash of 9th-century facade and 16th-century reconstruction. This is probably also the town's holiest spot: under it in the 1930s archaeologists found bits of a 5th-century Zoroastrian temple ruined by the Arabs and an earlier Buddhist temple. Until the 16th century, Bukhara's Jews are said to have used the mosque in the evenings as a synagogue.

Only the top of the mosque was visible when the digging began; the present plaza surrounding it is the 12th-century level of the town. A section of the excavations has been left deliberately exposed inside. Also here is a **museum** (admission US$1; 9am-5pm) exhibiting beautiful Bukhara carpets and prayer mats.

Taki-Zargaron Area
A few steps east of the Taki-Zargaron Bazaar, on the north side of Hoja Nurabad, is Central Asia's oldest medressa, and a model for many others – the unrestored, blue-tiled **Ulugbek Medressa** (1417), one of three built by Ulugbek (the others are at Gijduvan, 45km away on the road to Samarkand, and in Samarkand's Registan complex). Today it's occupied by pigeons and a small **museum** (admission US$0.50; 9am-4.30pm) with some great old photos, including one of the Kalon Minaret looking the worse for wear after the Soviets bombed it in the 1920s. Peeking into the cool, abandoned student rooms here is a real treat.

By contrast, the student rooms across the way at the 16th-century **Abdul Aziz Khan Medressa** are occupied, rather typically, by souvenir shops. This is another unrestored gem, built by its namesake to outdo the Ulugbek Medressa. The highlight is the prayer room, now a **museum of wood carvings** (admission US$0.50; 9am-5pm), with jaw-dropping *ghanch* stalactites dripping from the ceiling. It is said that Abdul Aziz had the image of his face covertly embedded in the prayer room's mihrab (Mecca-facing niche) to get around the Sunni Muslim prohibition against depicting living beings (Abdul Aziz Khan was a Shiite). The only other medressa in town that depicts living beings is the Nadir Divanbegi Medressa.

UZBEKISTAN

BUKHARA

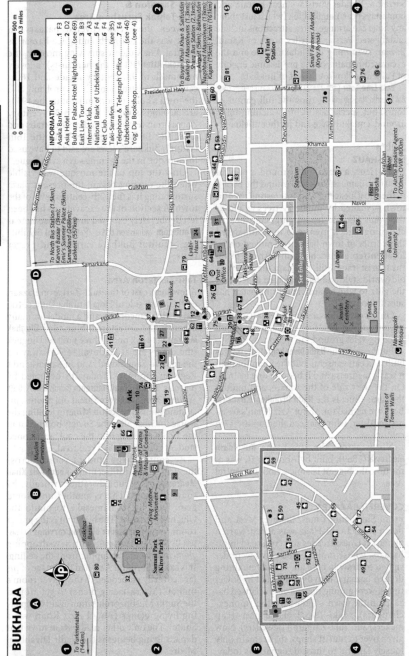

0 500 m
0 0.3 miles

INFORMATION
Asaka Bank	.1 F3
Asia Hotel	.2 D2
Bukhara Palace Hotel Nightclub	(see 69)
East Line Tour	.3 B3
Internet Klub	.4 A3
National Bank of Uzbekistan	.5 F4
Net Club	.6 F4
Taki-Sarrafon	(see 35)
Telephone & Telegraph Office	.7 E4
Uzbektourism	(see 46)
Yog' Du Bookshop	(see 4)

To Turkmenabat (146km);

To North Bus Station (1.5km);
Karvon Bazaar (3km);
Emir's Summer Palace (5km);
Samarkand (268km);
Tashkent (557km)

To Buyan Khuli khan & Saifuddin
Bukhan Mausoleums (1.3km);
Fazl Mausoleums (2km);
Sharq Bus Station (2.1km);
Airport (5km); Bakhautdin
Naqshband Mausoleum (13km);
Kagan (15km); Bakhautdin
Kagan (15km); Karshi (161km)

Presidential Hwy

Old Train Station

Small Farmers Market (Kryty Rynok)

To Airline Booking Agents
(700m); OVIR (800m)

UZBEKISTAN

SIGHTS & ACTIVITIES
Abdul Aziz Khan Medressa	8 D2
Abdulla Khan Medressa	9 B2
Ark	10 C2
Bolo-Hauz Mosque	11 B2
Bozori Kord	12 D2
Char Minar	13 E2
Chashma-Ayub 'Mausoleum'	14 B2
Fayzulla Khojaev House	15 C3
Gaukushan Medressa	16 C3
Hammom Kunjak	17 C2
Hoja Nasruddin Statue	18 D3
Hoja Zaynıddin Mosque	19 C2
Ismail Samani Mausoleum	20 B2
Jewish Community Centre &	
Synagogue	21 A3
Kalon Minaret	22 C2
Kalon Mosque	23 C2
Kukeldash Medressa	24 D2
Lyabi-Hauz	25 D3
Maghoki-Attar Mosque	26 D3
Miri-Arab Medressa	27 C2
Modari Khan Medressa	28 B2
Museum of Art	29 D3
Nadir Divanbegi Khanaka	30 D3
Nadir Divanbegi Medressa	31 D3
Old Town Walls	32 A2
Photo Gallery	33 D3
Synagogue	34 C3
Taki-Sarrafon Bazaar	35 A3
Taki-Telpak Furushon	
Bazaar	36 D2
Taki-Zargaron Bazaar	37 D2
Turki Jandi Mausoleum	38 D3
Ulugbek Medressa	39 D2
Water Tower	40 C2
Zindon	41 C2

SLEEPING
Akbhar House	42 B3
Amelia Boutique Hotel	43 E3
Amulet	44 E3
Emir B&B	45 B3
Grand Bukhoro Hotel	46 D4
Hotel Atlas	47 D2
Hovli Poyon B&B	48 C3
K Komil Hotel	49 A4
Lyabi House Hotel	50 B3

Madina & Ilyos	51 C3
Malikjon B&B House	52 A4
Mehtar Ambar	53 E3
Minzifa	54 B4
Mubinjon's Bukhara	
House	55 B4
Nasruddin Navruz	56 B4
Salom Inn	57 B3
Sarrafon B&B	58 A3
Sasha & Son B&B	59 B3

EATING
Bella Italia	60 F3
Chashmai Mirob	61 C2
Dolon	62 D2
Hammomi Sarrafon	63 A3
Lyabi-Hauz	64 D3
Minzifa	65 B3

DRINKING
Bolo Hauz Chaikhana	66 C2
Nughay Caravanserai Wine	
Tasting	67 D3
Silk Road Spices	68 C2

ENTERTAINMENT
Bukhara Palace Hotel Nightclub	69 D4
Folklore & Fashion Show	(see 31)
Puppet Theatre	(see 30)

SHOPPING
Bukhara Artisan Development	
Center	70 A3
Tim Abdulla Khan	71 D2
Unesco Carpet Weaving Shop	72 B4

TRANSPORT
Air & Rail Ticketing Agents	73 F4
Ark Marshrutka Stop	74 C2
Bike Shop	75 D3
East Line Tour	76 F4
Gorgaz Bus Stop	77 B3
Kryty Rynok Bus Stop	78 E3
Primary Lyabi-Hauz Marshrutka Stop	78 E3
Secondary Lyabi-Hauz	
Marshrutka Stop	79 D2
Shared taxis to Karakol & Olot	
(Turkmen border)	80 A1
Vokzal Bus Stop	81 F3

KALON MINARET & AROUND

When it was built by the Karakhanid ruler Arslan Khan in 1127, the **Kalon Minaret** was probably the tallest building in Central Asia – *kalon* means 'great' in Tajik. It's an incredible piece of work, 47m tall with 10m-deep foundations (including reeds stacked underneath in an early form of earthquake-proofing), and has stood for 880 years. Chinggis Khan was so dumbfounded by it that he ordered it spared.

Its 14 ornamental bands, all different, include the first use of the glazed blue tiles that were to saturate Central Asia under Timur. Up and down the south and east sides are faintly lighter patches, marking the restoration of damage caused by Frunze's artillery in 1920. Its 105 inner stairs, accessible from the Kalon Mosque, have been closed off to tourists for several years but may reopen.

A legend says that Arslan Khan killed an imam after a quarrel. That night in a dream the imam told him, 'You have killed me; now oblige me by laying my head on a spot where nobody can tread', and the tower was built over his grave.

At the foot of the minaret, on the site of an earlier mosque destroyed by Chinggis Khan, is the 16th-century congregational **Kalon Mosque**, big enough for 10,000 people. Used in Soviet times as a warehouse, it was reopened as a place of worship in 1991.

Opposite the mosque, its luminous blue domes in sharp contrast to the surrounding brown, is the working **Mir-i-Arab Medressa**. Especially at sunset, it's among Uzbekistan's most striking medressas. Mir-i-Arab was a 16th-century Naqshbandi sheikh from Yemen who had a strong influence on the Shaybanid ruler Ubaidullah Khan. Tourists can technically only go as far as the foyer. However, if you ask permission you may be allowed to view the tombs of Mir-i-Arab and Ubaidullah Khan in a room under the northern dome. From there you get a decent view of the courtyard, where you might see students playing ping-pong.

THE ARK & AROUND

The **Ark** (☎ 224 38 53; Registan Sq; admission US$1, incl museums US$2, guide US$2; ⏰ courtyards 9am-6pm, museums ⏰ 9am-4.30pm Wed-Sun, to 2pm Tue), a royal town-within-a-town, is Bukhara's oldest structure, occupied from the 5th century right up until 1920, when it was bombed by the Red

Army. It's about 80% ruins inside now, except for some remaining royal quarters, now housing several **museums**.

At the top of the entrance ramp is the 17th-century **Juma (Friday) Mosque**. Turn right into a corridor with courtyards off both sides. First on the left are the former living quarters of the emir's *kushbegi* (prime minister), now housing an archaeological museum and a nature museum where you can see what healthy cotton looks like (in contrast to the forlorn, stunted variety you'll see growing in central Uzbekistan).

Second on the left is the oldest surviving part of the Ark, the vast **Reception & Coronation Court**, whose roof fell in during the 1920 bombardment. The last coronation to take place here was Alim Khan's in 1910. The submerged chamber on the right wall was the treasury, and behind this room was the harem.

To the right of the corridor were the open-air royal stables and the *noghorahona* (a room for drums and musical instruments used during public spectacles in the square below).

Around the Salamhona (Protocol Court) at the end of the corridor are what remain of the royal apartments. These apparently fell into such disrepair that the last two emirs preferred full-time residence at the summer palace (p268). Now there are several museums here, the most interesting of which covers Bukhara's history from the Shaybanids to the tsars. Displays include items imported to Bukhara, including an enormous *samovar* made in Tula, Russia. Another room contains the emir's throne.

Outside, in front of the fortress, is medieval Bukhara's main square, the **Registan**, a favourite venue for executions, including those of the British officers Stoddart and Conolly (see the boxed text, p264).

Behind the Ark is the **Zindon** (admission US$1, guide US$1; 9am-5pm Wed-Mon), or jail, now a museum. Cheerful attractions include a torture chamber and several dungeons, including the gruesome 'bug pit' where Stoddart and Conolly languished in a dark chamber filled with lice, scorpions and other vermin.

Beside a pool opposite the Ark's gate is the **Bolo-Hauz Mosque**, the emirs' official place of worship, built in 1718. Beside it is a now-disused 33m **water tower**, built by the Russians in 1927. If you are going to climb this (as the author did), you best not be afraid of heights (as the author is) or rickety-looking Soviet structures. The views of the Ark and beyond are worth the 1000S demanded by the local shepherd or whoever else is around.

ISMAIL SAMANI MAUSOLEUM & AROUND

This **mausoleum** in Samani Park, completed in 905, is the town's oldest Muslim monument and probably its sturdiest architecturally. Built for Ismail Samani (the Samanid dynasty's founder), his father and grandson, its intricate baked-terracotta brickwork – which gradually changes 'personality' through the day as the shadows shift – disguises walls almost 2m thick, helping it survive without restoration (except of the spiked dome) for 11 centuries.

Behind the park is a partially restored section (a total of 2km out of an original 12km) of the Shaybanid **town walls**; another big section is about 500m west of the Namozgokh Mosque.

Nearby is the peculiar **Chashma Ayub 'mausoleum'** (admission US$0.50; 9am-4pm Tue-Sun), built from the 12th to 16th centuries over a spring.

BUKHARA'S JEWS

South of Lyabi-Hauz is what's left of the old town's unique **Jewish Quarter**. There have been Jews in Bukhara since perhaps the 12th or 13th century, evolving into a unique culture with its own language – Bukhori, which is related to Persian but uses the Hebrew alphabet. Bukhara's Jews still speak it as do about 10,000 Bukhara Jews who now live elsewhere (mainly Israel).

They managed to become major players in Bukharan commerce in spite of deep-rooted, institutionalised discrimination. Bukhara Jews made up 7% of Bukhara's population at the time of the Soviet Union's collapse, but today only a few hundred remain.

The **Jewish community centre & synagogue** (65-224 23 80; Sarrafon 20), roughly across from Salom Inn, holds regular services and also sponsors a functioning Jewish school just around the corner. A century ago there were at least seven synagogues here, reduced after 1920 to two. The second synagogue is located south of Kukluk Bazaar – walk through the bazaar's rear entrance, proceed about 250m straight ahead, and look for it on your right.

The name means 'Spring of Job'; legend says Job struck his staff on the ground here and a spring appeared. Inside is a small water museum where you can drink from the spring. Next door is a glistening glass-walled memorial to Imam Ismail al-Bukhari.

FAYZULLA KHOJAEV HOUSE

The **Fayzulla Khojaev House** (☎ 224 41 88; Tukaev; admission US$2.50, camera US$1; ☽ 9am-5pm Mon-Sat, by appointment Sun) was once home to one of Bukhara's many infamous personalities, the man who plotted with the Bolsheviks to dump Emir Alim Khan. Fayzulla Khojaev was rewarded with the presidency of the Bukhara People's Republic, chairmanship of the Council of People's Commissars of the Uzbek SSR, and finally liquidation by Stalin.

The house was built in 1891 by his father, Ubaidullah, a wealthy merchant. Fayzulla lived here until 1925, when the Soviets converted it into a school. Meticulous restoration of the elegant frescoes, *ghanch*, latticework and Bukhara-style ceiling beams (carved, unpainted elm) has returned it to its former glory. If there's a tour group present you may be treated to a fashion show.

OTHER SIGHTS

Deep in the old town is the tiny, decrepit **Turki Jandi mausoleum** (Namozgokh) favoured for getting one's prayers answered. Its importance is signalled by the hundreds of other graves around it – allegedly in stacks 30m deep! Turki Jandi's tomb is through the mosque under the taller, second cupola. A well inside the mosque contains holy water that locals drink from a cooler near the complex entrance. Have the chatty mullah show you the sections of original 10th-century Arabic script on the mosque's doors, allegedly inscribed by Turki Jandi himself.

Photogenic little **Char Minar**, in a maze of alleys between Pushkin and Hoja Nurabad, bears more relation to Indian styles than to anything Bukharan. This was the gatehouse of a long-gone medressa built in 1807. The name means 'Four Minarets' in Tajik, although they aren't strictly minarets but simply decorative towers.

West of Taki-Sarrafon is the interesting 16th-century **Gaukushan Medressa** with chipped majolica on its unrestored facade. Nearby, the **Museum of Art** (admission US$0.50; ☽ 9am-4.30pm Wed-Mon) has a worthy collection of mostly 20th-

century paintings by Bukharan artists. It's in the former headquarters of the Russian Central Asian Bank (1912). Look out for works by Zelim Saidjuddin, the Bukharan artist featured in Colin Thubron's *Lost Heart of Asia* and *Shadow of the Silk Road*. Also nearby is a **Photo Gallery** (admission free; ☽ 9am-7.30pm) containing mesmerising photos of Bukhara Jews, gypsies and city life shot by Bukhara Iranian photographer Shavkat Boltaev.

Across from the Ark on Hoja Nurabad, the interior of the 16th-century **Hoja Zayniddin Mosque** has a tremendous *aivan* and some of the best original mosaic and *ghanch*-work you're going to see anywhere.

Southeast of Samani Park are two massive medressas, one named for the great Shaybanid ruler **Abdulla Khan**, and one for his mother called **Modari Khan** ('Mother of the Khan'). The former is locked, the latter contains yet more craft shops.

Two kilometres east of the centre on Bakhautdin Naqshband, the mammary-like twin domes of the **Saifuddin Bukharzi Mausoleum** tower over the delicate little **Buyan Khuli Khan Mausoleum**. With sheep grazing in the foreground and a massive flour factory looming in the background, this spot might as well be a metaphor for Central Asia. Taxi drivers know this place as 'Rayon Fatobod Bogi'. The architectural highlight here is the chipped 14th-century mosaic and terracotta on the smaller mausoleum, the resting place of a Mongol khan.

Activities

Readers rave about Bukhara's famed *hammomi* (baths), most notably the **Bozori Kord** (Taki-Telpak Furushon; admission 10,000S; ☽ 6am-4pm Wed-Mon). It's technically a men's bathhouse, but groups of tourists can reserve it after-hours for mixed use. Massages cost extra.

Hammom Kunjak (Ibodov 4; 2hr private session incl massage 30,000S; ☽ 7am-6pm) is a women's bathhouse behind Kalon Minaret. It's also available for private group rental after-hours.

Tours

Most hotels and B&Bs can also arrange guides, as can Uzbektourism. Our recommendations include the following:

Gulya Khamidova (☎ 8390-718 5889) English.
Ilkhom (☎ 191 01 13) From Emir Travel; German.
Nellia (☎ 592 84 56; lumiere-nelly@mail.ru) From Salom Travel; French.

UZBEKISTAN

STODDART & CONOLLY

On 24 June 1842 Colonel Charles Stoddart and Captain Arthur Conolly were marched out from a dungeon cell before a huge crowd in front of the Ark, the emir's fortified citadel, made to dig their own graves and, to the sound of drums and reed pipes from atop the fortress walls, were beheaded.

Colonel Stoddart had arrived three years earlier on a mission to reassure Emir Nasrullah Khan about Britain's invasion of Afghanistan. But his superiors, underestimating the emir's vanity and megalomania, had sent him with no gifts, and with a letter not from Queen Victoria (whom Nasrullah regarded as an equal sovereign), but from the governor-general of India. To compound matters Stoddart violated local protocol by riding, rather than walking, up to the Ark. The piqued Nasrullah had him thrown into jail, where he was to spend much of his time at the bottom of the so-called 'bug pit', in the company of assorted rodents and scaly creatures.

Captain Conolly arrived in 1841 to try to secure Stoddart's release. But the emir, believing him to be part of a British plot with the khans of Khiva and Kokand, tossed Conolly in jail too. After the disastrous British retreat from Kabul, the emir, convinced that Britain was a second-rate power and having received no reply to an earlier letter to Queen Victoria, had both men executed.

Despite public outrage back in England, the British government chose to let the matter drop. Furious friends and relatives raised enough money to send their own emissary, an oddball clergyman named Joseph Wolff, to Bukhara to verify the news. According to Peter Hopkirk in *The Great Game*, Wolff himself only escaped death because the emir thought him hilarious, dressed up in his full clerical regalia.

Noila Kazidzanova (☎ 8390-718 2012; barocco@yandex.ru) English.

Zinnat Ashurova (☎ 190 71 27) English.

Maksuma, a guide at the Ark (p261), is an archaeological specialist who can recommend excursions to excavations and petroglyphs in the desert north of Bukhara.

Festivals

The four-day **Silk & Spices Festival** in early May is a celebration of local folk art as well as silk and spices, with lots of music and dancing in the streets.

Sleeping

Bukhara's wonderful, largely traditional-style B&Bs set the standard for accommodation in Central Asia. Bukhara B&Bs convert prices to som at the black-market rate so you might as well pay in dollars (see the boxed text on p284). The Grand Bukhara is an exception to that rule.

BUDGET

Mubinjon's Bukhara House (☎ 224 20 05; Sarrafon 4; dm US$5-6) Bukhara's pioneer B&B is housed in a home dating from 1766. Traditional *kurpacha* are spread on the floor and the bathrooms are basic but the legendary Mubinjon – a true Bukharan eccentric – can direct you to traditional baths. Mubinjon doesn't speak much

English but makes himself understood. To find it, look for the Olympic symbols painted on the garage door.

Madina & Ilyos (☎ 224 61 62, 8390-512 5820; Mehtar Ambar 18; dm US$7-8, d per person from US$10) This perennial backpacker fave is famous for being great value and for being hard to find. Walk past No 18, hang a left and look for a blue wooden door, also marked No 18. Madina now has an annexe with 10 rooms at Mehtar Ambar 15.

Sarrafon B&B (☎ 223 64 63; www.sarrafon-travel.uz; Sarrafon 4; dm US$8-9, s/d US$15/25; ✶) A relatively new addition to the scene, Sarrafon has quickly forged a reputation as great value due to its ideal location, friendly host family and toothsome breakfasts.

Also recommended:

Malikjon B&B House (☎ 224 50 50; malikjon_house@mail.ru; Sarrafon 9; s/d US$10/20) Readers rave about its location and food.

Nasruddin Navruz (☎ 224 34 57; www.nasriddinhotel.com; Babahanov 37; s/d/tr US$15/30/40; ✶) Negotiable prices make this simple but effective guesthouse attractive for the backpacker set.

MIDRANGE & TOP-END

our pick Amelia Boutique Hotel (☎ 224 12 63; www.hotelamelia.com; Bozor Hoja 1; s/d from US$30/50; ✶ 🖵) All details get attention at this cosy, casual boutique. Pinewood furniture gives it a foresty feel, but niched walls and a stunning 18th-century breakfast room bring you back to Bukhara. The well-appointed rooms range from exquisite to, well, creative. The mud-walled suite downstairs is a pearl. Across the street in a new annexe, the 'Afrosiab' room recreates the famous Sogdian fresco from the Afrosiab Museum in Samarkand (see p245). Another room has Ismail Samani Mausoleum bedside lights.

K Komil Hotel (☎ 223 87 80; www.komiltravel.com; Barakiyon 40; s/d from US$30/50; ✖ ▣) This friendly B&B has stunning *ghanch*-work and a young, laid-back proprietor who speaks fluent English. Komil recently opened an annexe with contemporary rooms to complement pre-existing digs in an authentic 19th-century rich person's home. Good vegetarian food is an added bonus.

Salom Inn (☎ 224 37 33; www.salomtravel.com; Sarrafon 3; s/d/tr US$35/50/65; ✖ ▣ ▣) This long-running establishment has small but classy wood-furnished rooms with traditional interior decorations, including antiques and colourful wall hangings. Rooms lack TVs.

Hovli Poyon B&B (☎ 224 18 65; hovli-poyon@mail. ru; Usmon Khojaev 13; s/d US$35/50; ✖) Few Bukhara B&Bs are more memorable than this one, set in a 19th-century house dripping with both character and history. It was a gift for Emir Ahad Khan, and the grand *aivan* and huge courtyard festooned with fruit trees are certainly emir-worthy. If it were not a hotel it could easily be a museum. The rooms, of various sizes, are simple with traditional touches.

Emir B&B (☎ 224 49 65; www.emirtravel.com; Husainov 17; s/d/tr US$35/50/65; ✖ ▣) This place consists of two buildings set around twin courtyards in the heart of the old Jewish Quarter, run by the friendly and knowledgeable Milla, who also runs a travel agency. One has traditional-style rooms filled with *ghanch* and trinket-laden niches, the other is all new and shiny.

Minzifa (☎ 224 56 28; minzifa_inn@mail.ru; Eshoni Pir 63; s/d US$40/60; ✖ ▣) The ubiquitous local style is faithfully on display here, although the decor is toned down by softer than usual colour schemes. It has some of the friendliest service in town, ultracomfy oversized twin beds and 12 uniquely decorated rooms, each with a TV and giant bathtub.

Lyabi House Hotel (☎ 224 24 84; www.lyabihouse. com; Husainov 7; s/d/tr US$40/60/80; ✖) No place in town better combines authentic old-Bukhara

design with modern amenities. Highlights are the eclectic range of rooms and the dignified *aivan* with carved wooden columns, where breakfast is served. Request a room away from the noisy reception area.

Sasha & Son B&B (☎ 224 49 66; www.sashasonho tels.com; Eshoni Pir 3; s/d US$50/70; ✖ ▣ ≈) Behind a beautifully carved wooden front door is a maze connecting several small edifices with new rooms elaborately done up in old style. All rooms have satellite TV and snazzy bathrooms with fine tilework. The staff is more professional than friendly here.

Grand Bukhara Hotel (☎ 223 13 26; info@bukhara tourist.com; Muminov 8; s/d from US$57/112; ▣ ✖ ▣) If you've had enough of the local flavour and are looking for Western-style luxury, this high-rise in the new part of town has been transformed from dusty monstrosity into a pillar of poshness, with slick white duvet covers and a bevy of amenities. It beats similarly reconstructed Bukhara Palace next door.

A brace of neighbouring medressa B&Bs just east of Lyabi Hauz offers a change of pace from all those old classic Bukhara homes. The swankier one is **Amulet** (☎ 224 53 42; www.amulet -hotel.com; Bakhautdin Naqshband 73; s/d/tr US$40/60/80; ✖ ≈), where amenities such as satellite TV and wi-fi mean you'll hardly be living like a student. Individuals should request a plush corner single room. Out back is a fabulous, decaying 18th-century mosque. By contrast, **Mehtar Ambar** (☎ 8393-960 0085; mekhtarambar@ inbox.ru; Bakhautdin Naqshband 91; s/d/tr US$25/50/60; ✖) is more austere – which those looking for an authentic medressa experience may prefer. The 2nd-floor rooms are brighter than ground-floor rooms. The breakfast room is a *ghanch*-laden gem.

Also recommended:

Akhbar House (☎ 224 21 12; akhbarhouseantiques@ yahoo.com; Eshoni Pir 22; s/d US$30/50; ✖) A 19th-century beauty better known for its museum-quality decor than for its service. Doors are locked early and may stay that way – night owls beware!

Hotel Atlas (☎ 224 62 10; atlas_hotel@mail.ru; Taki Telpak Furushon; US$35/50; ✖ ▣) While the faux-mud facade looks like any other main-drag Bukhara hotel, friendly staff and well-appointed rooms set it apart.

Eating

You don't go to Bukhara for the food, that's for sure. Some villagers invite tourists into their houses for US$5 meals. Be warned that those hanging out near Ulugbek Medressa often try to sell you worthless stuff at inflated prices once they have you trapped.

Lyabi-Hauz (Lyabi-Hauz; mains 3000S) Dining alfresco around the venerable pool with greybeards, local families and plenty of other tourists is the quintessential Bukhara experience. There are two chaikhanas here, both serving shashlyk, *plov*, *kovurma laghman* (with meat and tomato sauce) and cold beer.

Dolon (☎ 224 33 54; Hakikat 27; mains 3500-7000S; 🛇 🚾 🅔) This Uzbek eatery is popular with tour groups but if you can hit it at a quiet time it has a pleasant atmosphere and food as good as anywhere in Bukhara (which isn't saying much). Ascend to the roof for a great panorama.

Chashmai Mirob (☎ 225 63 68; Bakhautdin Naqshband; mains 4000-6000S; 🕙 closed winter; 🅔) It's known more for its artist's view of Mir-i-Arab than for its food. The menu is heavy on Russian classics and you can pre-order *plov*.

Minzifa (Bakhautdin Naqshband; mains 4000-6000S; 🛇 🚾 🅔) This once-delightful eatery is not what it was in terms of food or service, but there's always hope that it will return to its heyday. Its location and rooftop terrace are strong assets.

Bella Italia (☎ 224 33 46; Bakhautdin Naqshband; pasta 6000-7000S, homemade wine per glass 2000S; 🛇 🚾 🅔) It's not the world's best Italian food, but nor is it the worst and by this point in your trip you're undoubtedly ready for some pasta.

Hammomi Sarrafon (Bakhautdin Naqshband; meals US$10; 🕙 Apr-Oct) It has probably the best food in Bukhara, but it caters to tour groups (piggybackers welcome) and requires advance booking.

For self-caterers there are farmers markets, including Kolkhoz Bazaar and the morning-only Kukluk Bazaar, buried deep in the Jewish Quarter.

Drinking

Bolo Hauz Chaikhana (Afrosiab; beer 1000S) This large chaikhana in the park opposite the Ark is an ideal place for a fine-priced, frosty draft beer post-sightseeing.

Silk Road Spices (Halim Ibodov 5; unlimited tea & sweets US$5; 🕙 8am-8pm) This boutique teahouse offers a delightful diversion from all that sightseeing. It has exactly six spicy varieties of tea and coffee, served with rich local sweets such as halva and *nabat* (crystal sugar).

Nughay Caravanserai wine tasting (Bakhautdin Naqshband 78; per 8 large samples 10,000-15,000S; 🕙 10am-10pm) Djamal Akhrarov has an informal wine shop and tasting room in this 18th-century caravanserai. The local wines are surprisingly good, in particular the Cabernets.

Entertainment

Bukhara's old town is eerily silent by night, which is part of its charm, but there are several early-evening entertainment options.

Puppet performance (admission US$4; 🕙 5pm & 6pm Apr-May & Sep-Oct, by appointment Jun-Aug) Held at a theatre on the western end of Lyabi-Hauz, this is the consensus reader favourite entertainment option. The three-part amateur performance, with a traditional wedding ceremony as the usual theme, is held in Tajik, Uzbek and English.

Folklore & fashion show (admission €5, incl dinner €10; 🕙 7pm & 8.30pm Apr-May & Sep-Oct, 7.30pm Jun-Aug, by appointment after hr) Across Lyabi-Hauz in the Nadir Divanbegi Medressa, this nightly show features traditional musical performances and decidedly nontraditional exotic (borderline erotic) dancing.

Both of the above shows are staged mainly for the tour-bus crowd but individuals can piggyback. Shows are often cancelled if there are no tour groups in town.

For anything rowdier than puppets you must head southeast of the centre into the newer part of town, but the nightclubs here are decidedly provincial (read: mostly male). The basement **nightclub** (Navoi 8; admission 4000S) in the Hotel Bukhara Palace occasionally shows a pulse at weekends.

Shopping

With many tourist sights overflowing with vendors, it's not hard to find a souvenir in Bukhara. They are, of course, of varying quality.

Tim Abdulla Khan (Hakikat; 🕙 9am-6pm) For carpets, you couldn't ask for a better shopping atmosphere than at the silk-weaving centre in this late-16th-century building, located near Taki-Telpak Furushon Bazaar (a *tim* was a general market). Vendors are not pushy and will openly inform you on what's handmade and what's machine-made. You can watch silk-clothing makers in action here.

Unesco Carpet Weaving Shop (☎ 223 66 13; Eshoni Pir 57; 🕙 9am-5pm Mon-Sat) This no longer has anything to do with Unesco (which helped them launch in 2001), but you can still observe weavers here handmaking pricey silk carpets and *suzani* with unique Bukhara designs.

Bukhara Artisan Development Centre (Bakhautdin Naqshband) Here you can watch artisans at work on a variety of handicrafts including *suzani,* miniature paintings, jewellery boxes and chess sets.

Serious *suzani* and textile collectors should head to Akhbar House (p265) for a glimpse of owner Akhbar's fantastic collection. Much of it isn't for sale but he may be willing to part with gems from his personal collection for the right price.

Getting There & Away
AIR
Uzbekistan Airways (☎ 225 39 46; Airport; ☽ 8am-9pm Mon-Fri, to 6pm Sat & Sun) has flights from Bukhara to Tashkent (€33, at least daily), plus a handful of flights to Urgench in the high season. You can also use one of several private booking agents located at Navoi 15, about 1km south of the Grand Bukhara Hotel.

LAND
All eastbound vehicular transport leaves from the North Bus Station, about 3km north of the centre. Here you'll find plenty of private buses (Navoi US$1, 2½ hours; Samarkand US$4, 4½ hours; Tashkent US$6, eight to 10 hours) and shared Nexias (Navoi US$4, one hour; Tashkent US$20, 6½ hours), plus a few marshrutkas. Shared taxis to Samarkand (US$10, three hours) involve a change in Navoi.

About 1.5km north of here is Karvon Bazaar, departure point for Urgench/Khiva. Shared taxis congregate in a lot on the less-crowded south end of the market. The going rate is US$13 per seat for Urgench (4½ hours). Drivers demand a few dollars extra for Khiva; you're better off transferring in Urgench. For buses to Urgench (US$4, eight hours) you have to wait out on the main road in front of the taxi stand and flag buses originating in Tashkent, which come through sporadically in the morning.

To get to the North Bus Station and Karvon Bazaar take marshrutka 61 from the secondary Lyabi-Hauz marshrutka stop (near Asia Hotel), or take public bus 7 or marshrutka 67 or 73 from the 'Vokzal' stop (site of the old train station, 1km east of Lyabi-Hauz).

The 'Sharq' bus station east of the centre no longer functions. However, shared taxis depart from across the street to Karshi (US$7.50,

two hours), Shakhrisabz (US$12, four hours), and Denau on the Tajik border (US$17, 5½ hours). Change in Karshi for Termiz (from Karshi US$7.50, 3½ hours).

See p288 for information on getting to Turkmenabat.

Train
The **train station** (☎ 524 73 32) is 9km southeast of Bukhara in Kagan. The 'Sharq' express train zips from Kagan to Tashkent every morning at 8:05am (US$12, seven hours) via Samarkand (US$6, 2¾ hours).

A slower passenger train rumbles to Tashkent nightly at 7.15pm (*platskartny/kupeyny* US$13.50/19, 11 hours). It also stops in Samarkand (*platskartny/kupeyny* US$9/15, 6½ hours). A final option to Samarkand is a nightly local train (sans sleeper cars) at 11:55pm (US$1.30, six hours). There are also local trains to Karshi (US$1, four hours, daily at 1:55pm) and Olot (US$0.50, two hours, two daily) near the Turkmen border.

Westbound trains from Tashkent to Nukus, Kungrad, Urgench and Russia go via Navoi, not Bukhara (see p228).

To get to Kagan take marshrutka 68 from the Lyabi-Hauz stop (500S, 25 minutes). There are several air and rail ticketing offices on Mustaqillik around Kryty Rynok.

Getting Around
TO/FROM THE AIRPORT
The airport is 6km east of town. Figure on US$1.50 to US$2 for a 10-minute taxi trip between the centre and the airport. Marshrutka 100 or bus 10 to/from the Vokzal, Kryty Rynok or Gorgaz stops takes 15 to 20 minutes.

BIKE RENTAL
In a town that's perfect for exploring on bike, **East Line Tour** (☎ 224 22 69; www.eastlinetour.com; Bakhautdin Naqshband 98) is the only agency that rents quality ones (per day US$10). A small bike shop on Hakikat rents older models (per day US$5).

PUBLIC TRANSPORT & TAXI
From the primary Lyabi-Hauz stop, marshrutka 52 goes to the new part of town via Mustaqillik, while both 52 and 68 pass by the useful Vokzal stop, where you can pick up transport going just about anywhere. Useful destinations are Kolkhoz (Dekhon) Bazaar, the Ark stop and Karvon Bazaar.

UZBEKISTAN

You should be able to get anywhere in town in a taxi for about US$1, as long as you avoid the cheats who hang out at the Lyabi-Hauz stop. From the centre a one-way taxi should cost about US$3 to Bakhautdin Naqshband Mausoleum and Kagan; less to Emir's Summer Palace and Chor-Bakr.

AROUND BUKHARA
Emir's Summer Palace
For a look at the kitsch lifestyle of the last emir, Alim Khan, go out to his summer palace, Sitorai Mohi Hosa (Star-and-Moon Garden), now a **museum** (☎ 228 50 47; admission US$4; ◷ 9am-7pm Apr-Oct, to 5pm Nov-Mar), 6km north of Bukhara.

The three-building compound was a joint effort for Alim Khan by Russian architects (outside) and local artisans (inside), and no punches were pulled in showing off both the finest and the gaudiest aspects of both styles. A 50-watt Russian generator provided the first electricity the emirate had ever seen. In front of the harem is a pool where the women frolicked, overlooked by a wooden pavilion from which – says every tour guide – the emir tossed an apple to his chosen bedmate.

To get here from Bukhara take bus 7 or marshrutka 70 from the Vokzal stop. The palace is at the end of the line.

Bakhautdin Naqshband Mausoleum
Northeast of Bukhara in the village of Kasri Orifon is one of Sufism's more important **shrines** (admission free; ◷ 8am-7pm), the birthplace and the tomb of Bakhautdin (or Baha-ud-Din) Naqshband (1318–89), the founder of the most influential of many ancient Sufi orders in Central Asia, and Bukhara's unofficial 'patron saint'. For more information on Sufism, see p72.

Entering the complex through the main, east entrance, you'll walk towards a 16th-century *khanaka* covered by a huge dome, now a Juma (Friday) mosque. In front of it is a precariously leaning minaret. Two more mosques surround Bakhautdin's tomb in the courtyard to the left. The lovingly restored *aivan* here is one of the country's most beautiful. The tomb itself is a simple 2m-high block, protected by a horse-mane talisman hanging from a post. Tradition says that it is auspicious to complete three anticlockwise circumambulations of the tomb.

Back in the main courtyard you'll spot more locals walking anticlockwise around a petrified tree. Legend has it that this tree sprouted where Bakhautdin stuck his staff, upon returning from a pilgrimage to Mecca. He then added drops of holy water from Mecca to a nearby well. Faucets near the minaret continue to supply this well's water to pilgrims, who splash their faces with it and bring it home by the jugful for good luck.

North of the complex a long path leads to the tomb of Bakhautdin's mother, also a place of pilgrimage.

Marshrutkas 125 and 60 go to the compound from the Vokzal stop in Bukhara (400S, 25 minutes).

KHOREZM ХОРЕЗМ

URGENCH УРГЕНЧ
☎ 62 / pop 140,000
Urgench, the capital of Khorezm province, is a standard-issue Soviet grid of broad streets and empty squares, 450km northwest of Bukhara across the Kyzylkum desert. When the Amu-Darya changed course in the 16th century, the people of Konye-Urgench (then called Urgench), 150km downriver in present-day Turkmenistan, were left without water and started a new town here. Today travellers use Urgench mainly as a transport hub for Khiva, 35km southwest. It's also the jumping-off point for the 'Golden Ring' of ancient fortresses in southern Karakalpakstan.

Orientation
The town's axis is Al-Khorezmi, with the post office at its intersection with Al-Beruni marking the centre of things. The train station is 600m south of the centre down Al-Khorezmi, the airport is 3km north, and the main bazaar 500m west.

Information
Bahadir & Bakhtiyar Rakhamov (☎ Bahadir 352 41 06, 512 12 41, Bakhtiyar 517 51 33) English-speaking father-and-son driving tandem offer excursions to the *qalas* (fortresses; US$60 per carload, including unlimited stops).
Delia Madrashimova (☎ 290 96 36; per day US$25) This English-speaking guide is your best bet for excursions to the *qalas* or Khiva.
Internet Cafe (Al-Khorezmi 1; per hr 600S; ◷ 9am-9pm)
Post, telephone & telegraph office (Al-Khorezmi 1)

Sleeping & Eating

Komnata Otdikha (☎ 220 31 66; Train Station; 2-bed dm US$2.50) The dirt-cheap train station hotel isn't too terrible and at least they'll register you too.

Hotel Urgench (☎ 226 20 24; Al-Khorezmi 35/1; d/lux US$20/50) This formerly notorious hotel has been renovated and now displays perfectly acceptable, clean, Soviet-style rooms. Try bargaining.

Khorezm Palace (☎ 224 99 99; www.khorezmpalace .uz; Al-Beruni 2; s/d/ste €40/60/150; P ⊠ □ ⊠) Urgench's fancier sleeping option has all the amenities you would expect at these prices.

Chaikhana Urgench (Al-Khorezmi 35/1; mains 1000-3000S; ☺ 8am-10pm) Located right next to the Hotel Urgench is this cafe serving shashlyk, *laghman* and *plov*.

Shashlyk stands are along pedestrian Uzbekistan kochasi. Go one short block north from the Hotel Urgench and take a left.

Getting There & Away

AIR

Uzbekistan Airways (☎ 226 88 60; Al-Khorezmi 1; ☺ 8am-7pm) has two or three flights daily to Tashkent (€51) and weekly flights to St Petersburg and Moscow. Three or four Tashkent-bound flights per week stop in Bukhara in the high season.

LAND

Shared taxi is the favoured way across the Kyzylkum desert to Bukhara and beyond. Regular shared taxis leave from a stand near the bus station (US$13, 4½ hours). Less frequent are shared taxis (US$25) and vans (US$14) to Tashkent (12 hours), but you can always transfer in Bukhara – also the preferred method for getting to Samarkand.

The **bus station** (Al-Khorezmi), just north of the train station, has a midday bus to Bukhara (US$4, eight hours), two daily buses to Samarkand (US$6, 12 hours) and a few buses to Tashkent (US$10, 20 hours) via Bukhara and Samarkand.

Shared taxis (US$5, 1½ hours) to Nukus congregate at Olympic (Olympiysky) Stadium, about 2km north of the centre. Traffic is heaviest in the morning. If nothing's going to Nukus, go to Beruni and change there. There's also a 10am bus to Nukus that departs from Raytsentr Bazaar (US$2, three hours).

The trolleybus to Khiva (400S, 1½ hours) waits on Al-Beruni one block west of the post

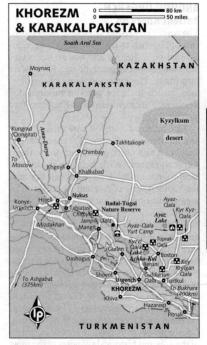

office. The stand for shared taxis to Khiva (US$0.75, 30 minutes) is south of the bazaar on Al-Beruni, about 250m west of the trolleybus stop. Shared taxis to Beruni and Boston hang out roughly opposite the Khiva taxi stand on Al-Beruni.

For instructions on getting to Dashogus, Turkmenistan, see p288.

Train

From the **train station** (Al-Khorezmi), train 55 departs for Tashkent every Tuesday, Wednesday and Saturday at 2.54pm (*platskartny/kupeyny* US$15/23, 22 hours) via Zarafshon, Navoi and Samarkand. The Saratov–Urgench–Tashkent train (No 333) passes through every Sunday evening. Other transit trains, such as the Kungrad–Tashkent, St Petersburg–Tashkent and Saratov–Tashkent (No 331) trains, pass through Turtkul.

Getting Around

Marshrutka 19 runs from the train station to the post office via the bazaar. Marshrutka 3 and 13 go from the south side of the bazaar to the airport via Al-Khorezmi.

AROUND URGENCH
Ancient Khorezm

The Amu-Darya delta, stretching from south-east of Urgench to the Aral Sea, has been in-habited for millennia and was an important oasis long before Urgench or even Khiva were important. The historical name of the delta area, which includes parts of modern-day northern Turkmenistan, was Khorezm (see also p457).

The ruins of many Khorezmian towns and forts, some well over 2000 years old, still stand east and north of Urgench in southern Karakalpakstan. With help from Unesco, local tourism officials have dubbed this area the 'Golden Ring of Ancient Khorezm'. The area's traditional name is Elliq-Qala (Fifty Fortresses).

For fans of old castles in the sand, this is an area not to be missed. Outdoor and na-ture enthusiasts will also find plenty to do here, from scrambling among the *qala* ruins, to camel trekking near Ayaz-Qala, to hiking in **Badai-Tugai Nature Reserve** (admission per person US$6), a *tugai* (trees, shrubs and salt-resistant plants unique to Central Asia) forest just off the main road about 60km north of Urgench. Unesco produced a brochure containing a map of the area and historical synopses of the most prominent *qalas*, but these days it's hard to find; ask the Khiva tourist information office.

ELLIQ-QALA

There are about 20 forts that you can explore here today, and who knows how many that have yet to be discovered (the 'Fifty Fortresses' moniker is an approximation). The most well-known *qala* is impressive, mud-walled **Ayaz-Qala**, which is actually a complex of three forts about 23km north of Boston (Bustan). Its heyday was the 6th and 7th centuries. In its shadow is **Ayaz-Qala Yurt Camp** (☎ 61-532 43 61, 8361-350 5909; per person US$25, meals US$10), with several yurts big enough to hold five to eight people, and **camel trekking** (per hr US$10) avail-able. You can also hike down to tiny Ayaz *kol* (lake), which is ringed by salt and appears to be evaporating. A fulltime chef and a solar panel generator installed by Unesco ensure that you won't really be roughing it out here. Call ahead to reserve yurts and camels, and to discuss transport options. Tour groups often book out Ayaz-Qala, especially for lunch. At other times you're practically at one with the desert.

The oldest, most unique, and most difficult-to-pronounce fort is circular **Koy Krylgan Qala**, which archaeologists believe doubled as a pagan temple and an observatory complex. It was in use as early as the 4th century BC. Drivers will be reluctant to take you here via the poor road from Beruni; instead, drive south towards Turtkul and turn north on a paved road towards the mammoth **Guldursun Qala**, built as early as the 1st century but in use until the Middle Ages. Koy Krylgan Qala is 18km east of Guldursun Qala.

Two other not-to-be-missed *qalas* are **Toprak Qala** and **Kyzyl Qala**, on opposite sides of the road about 10km west of Boston. The former was the main temple complex of Khorezm kings that ruled this area in the 3rd and 4th centu-ries. Near the latter you'll see students working the cotton fields in the autumn.

Another interesting old ruin is **Chilpyk**, a Zoroastrian *dahma* (tower of silence) that looms over the Amu-Darya plain just west of the highway about 30km south of Nukus. Fire-worshiping Zoroastrians would deposit their dead here to have their bones picked clean by vultures. The long slog up to the tower is worth it for the views.

Getting There & Away

The only way to explore Elliq-Qala is with private transport. Make absolutely sure your driver knows this area well and negotiate hard. Most drivers in Urgench and Khiva charge US$45 to US$70 for an all-day excursion with unlimited stops, or slightly less for an abbrevi-ated tour of two or three forts. Nukus driv-ers charge more. The best strategy is to visit Guldursun Qala first and go anticlockwise, but you may have to insist on this! You can save money by travelling to Beruni or Boston by public transport and hiring a taxi there. A one-way taxi from Boston to Ayaz-Qala costs US$4.

KHIVA ХИВА
☎ 62 / pop 50,000

Khiva's name, redolent of slave caravans, barbaric cruelty and terrible journeys across deserts and steppes infested with wild tribes-men, struck fear into all but the boldest 19th-century hearts. Nowadays it's a mere 35km southwest of Urgench, past cotton bushes and fruit trees.

The historic heart of Khiva has been so well preserved that it's often criticised as lifeless – a 'museum city'. Even if you subscribe to that theory, you'll have to admit that it's one helluva museum. To walk through the walls and catch that first glimpse of the fabled Ichon-Qala (inner walled city) in all its monotoned, mud-walled glory is like stepping into another era. History is just a sniff away here.

You can see it all in a day trip from Urgench, but you'll take it in better by staying longer. Khiva is at its best at dawn and by night, when the moonlit silhouettes of the tilting columns and medressas, viewed from twisting alleyways, work their magic.

History
Legend has it that Khiva was founded when Shem, son of Noah, discovered a well here; his people called it Kheivak, from which the name Khiva is said to be derived. The original well is in the courtyard of an 18th-century house in the northwest of the old town (look for a small white door in a mud wall).

Khiva certainly existed by the 8th century as a minor fort and trading post on a side branch of the Silk Road, but while Khorezm prospered on and off from the 10th to the 14th centuries, its capital was at Old Urgench (present-day Konye-Urgench in Turkmenistan), and Khiva remained a bit player. See opposite for more on Ancient Khorezm.

It wasn't until well after Konye-Urgench had been finished off by Timur that Khiva's time came. When the Uzbek Shaybanids moved into the decaying Timurid empire in the early 16th century, one branch founded a state in Khorezm and made Khiva their capital in 1592.

The town ran a busy slave market that was to shape the destiny of the khanate, as the Khiva state was known, for more than three centuries. Most slaves were brought by Turkmen tribesmen from the Karakum desert or Kazakh tribes of the steppes, who raided those unlucky enough to live or travel nearby.

RUSSIAN INTEREST AWAKENS
Khiva had earlier offered to submit to Peter the Great of Russia in return for help against marauding tribes. In a belated response, a force of about 4000, led by Prince Alexandr Bekovich, arrived in Khiva in 1717.

Unfortunately, the khan at the time, Shergazi Khan, had lost interest in being a vassal of the tsar. He came out to meet them, suggesting they disperse to outlying villages where they could be more comfortably accommodated. This done, the Khivans annihilated the invaders, leaving just a handful to make their way back with the news. Shergazi Khan sent Bekovich's head to his Central Asian rival, the Emir of Bukhara, and kept the rest of him on display.

In 1740, Khiva was wrecked by a less gullible invader, Nadir Shah of Persia, and Khorezm became for a while a northern outpost of the Persian empire. By the end of the 18th century it was rebuilt and began taking a small share in the growing trade between Russia and the Bukhara and Kokand khanates. Its slave market, the biggest in Central Asia, continued unabated, augmented by Russians captured as they pushed their borders southwards and eastwards. See p206 for details on Khiva's role in the Great Game.

RUSSIAN CONQUEST
When the Russians finally sent a properly organised expedition against Khiva, it was no contest. In 1873 General Konstantin Kaufman's 13,000-strong forces advanced on Khiva from the north, west and east. After some initial guerrilla resistance, mainly by Yomud Turkmen tribesmen, Mohammed Rakhim II Khan surrendered unconditionally. Kaufman then indulged in a massacre of the Yomud. The khan became a vassal of the tsar and his silver throne was packed off to Russia.

The enfeebled khanate of Khiva struggled on until 1920 when the Bolshevik general Mikhail Frunze installed the Khorezm People's Republic in its place. This, like the similar republic in Bukhara, was theoretically independent of the USSR. But its leaders swung away from socialism towards Pan-Turkism, and in 1924 their republic was absorbed into the new Uzbek SSR.

Orientation
There's not much reason to stray too far from the compact and user-friendly Ichon-Qala. Most sights are around its main axis, Pahlavon Mahmud, running between the West and East Gates. Walking through Ichon-Qala's North Gate brings you into the new town, where banking and postal facilities are located.

Information
The Malika Kheivak hotel's restaurant was the only wi-fi hotspot when we visited. There

are plenty of black-market money changers around; ask at the Tourist Information Office.

Asia Hotel (☎ 375 81 98; Yakubov) Has a (usually) working Asaka Bank ATM machine for MasterCard holders.

Internet Cafe (Pahlavon Mahmud 1; per hr 3000S; ◷ 9am-8.30pm) Expensive internet in front of Orient Star Hotel.

Post & telephone office (Amir Timur 23) Located 650m north of the North Gate.

Tourist information office (☎ 375 69 28; ◷ 9am-7pm) Quasi-independent tourist centre has internet access (2000S per hour), changes money, organises tours and guides for both Khiva and Elliq-Qala (US$6 per hour or US$25 per day) and sells maps and information booklets. There's another tourist information centre with sporadic hours in the Allakuli Khan Medressa.

Sights

Shutterbugs should head out in the late afternoon for shots of Khiva's mostly west-facing facades bathed in the orange glow of the setting sun. The top of the West wall, the watchtower at the Kuhna Ark, and the Ferris wheel outside the Ichon-Qala's North Gate offer the best viewpoints.

ICHON-QALA GATES & WALLS

The main entrance to the **Ichon-Qala** (2-day adult/student US$7.50/5, camera US$2.50; ◷ ticket booth & sights 9am-6pm) is the twin-turreted brick West Gate (Ota-Darvoza, literally 'Father Gate'), a 1970s reconstruction – the original was wrecked in 1920. The two-day ticket gives you access to all the sights and museums in the Ichon-

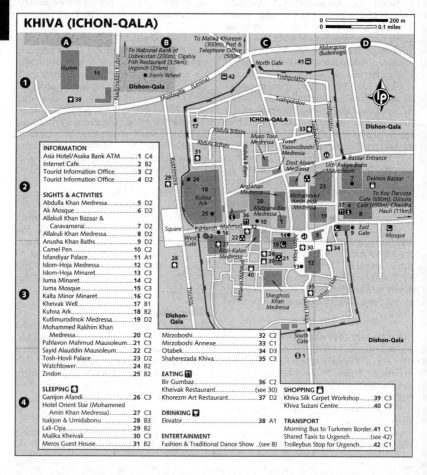

KHIVA (ICHON-QALA)

Qala besides the various viewpoints and the Pahlavon Mahmud Mausoleum.

You are free to walk around the Ichon-Qala without a ticket, you just won't be able to access (or, technically, to photograph) any sights. The North, East and South Gates are known as, respectively, the Bogcha-Darvoza (Garden Gate), Polvon-Darvoza (Strongman's Gate) and Tosh-Darvoza (Stone Gate).

One highlight for which no ticket is needed is the **walk** along the northwestern section of the wall. The stairs are at the North Gate. The 2.5km-long mud walls date from the 18th century, rebuilt after being destroyed by the Persians.

KUHNA ARK

To your left after you enter the West Gate stands the Kuhna Ark – the Khiva rulers' own fortress and residence, first built in the 12th century by one Ok Shihbobo, then expanded by the khans in the 17th century. The khans' harem, mint, stables, arsenal, barracks, mosque and jail were all here.

The squat protuberance by the entrance, on the east side of the building, is the **Zindon** (Khans' Jail), with a display of chains, manacles and weapons, and pictures of people being chucked off minarets, stuffed into sacks full of wild cats etc.

Inside the Ark, the first passage to the right takes you into the 19th-century **Summer Mosque**, open-air and beautiful with superb blue-and-white plant-motif tiling and a red, orange and gold roof. Beside it is the old **mint**, now a museum that exhibits things such as money printed on silk.

Straight ahead from the Ark entrance is the restored, open-air **throne room**, where khans dispensed judgement (if not justice). The circular area on the ground was for the royal yurt, which the no-longer-nomadic khans still liked to use.

At the back right corner of the throne room, a door in the wall leads to a flight of steps up to the **watchtower** (admission US$1), the original part of the Kuhna Ark, set right against the Ichon-Qala's massive west wall.

MOHAMMED RAKHIM KHAN MEDRESSA

East of the Kuhna Ark, across an open space that was once a busy palace square (and place of execution), the 19th-century Mohammed Rakhim Khan Medressa is named after the khan who surrendered to Russia in 1873

(although he had, at least, kept Khiva independent a few years longer than Bukhara). A hotchpotch of a museum within is partly dedicated to this khan and his son, Isfandiyar. Mohammed Rakhim Khan was also a poet under the pen name Feruz.

Khiva's token camel, Katya, waits for tourists to pose with her outside the medressa's south wall.

KALTA MINOR MINARET

Just south of the Kuhna Ark stands the fat, turquoise-tiled **Kalta Minor Minaret**. This unfinished minaret was begun in 1851 by Mohammed Amin Khan, who according to legend wanted to build a minaret so high he could see all the way to Bukhara. Unfortunately, the khan dropped dead in 1855 and it was never finished.

East of the minaret, beside the medressa housing Restoran Khiva, is the small, plain **Sayid Alauddin Mausoleum**, dating to 1310 when Khiva was under the Golden Horde of the Mongol empire. You might find people praying in front of the 19th-century tiled sarcophagus.

JUMA MOSQUE

Continuing east from the Sayid Alauddin Mausoleum, the large Juma Mosque is interesting for the 218 wooden columns supporting its roof – a concept thought to be derived from ancient Arabian mosques. Six or seven of the columns date the original 10th-century mosque (see if you can spot them), though the present building dates from the 18th century. From inside, you can climb the very dark stairway up to the pigeon-poop-splattered gallery of the 47m **Juma Minaret** (1000S).

ALLAKULI KHAN MEDRESSA & AROUND

Just east of the Juma Mosque, a lane leading north from Pahlavon Mahmud St contains some of Khiva's most interesting buildings, most of them created by Allakuli Khan – known as the 'builder khan' – in the 1830s and '40s. First come the tall **Allakuli Khan Medressa** (1835) and the earlier **Kutlimurodinok Medressa** (1804–12), facing each other across the street, with nearly matching facades.

North of the Allakuli Khan Medressa are the **Allakuli Khan Bazaar & Caravanserai**. The entrance to both is through tall wooden gates beside the medressa. The bazaar is a domed market arcade, still catering to traders, which opens onto

Khiva's modern **Dekhon Bazaar** at its east end. Both bazaars and the caravanserai were closed for extensive renovations when we visited.

Opposite the Allakuli Khan Medressa to the south are the 1855 **Abdulla Khan Medressa**, which holds a tiny nature museum, and little **Ak Mosque** (1657). The latter contains the **Anusha Khan Baths** (Anushahon Hammomi; admission US$1.50).

The **East Gate**, a long, vaulted 19th-century passage with several sets of immense carved doors, bridges the baths and the bazaar area. The slave market was held here, and niches in the passage walls once held slaves for sale. Just outside the gate is a working mosque that overflows with wizened old men on Fridays.

TOSH-HOVLI PALACE

This palace, which means 'Stone House', contains Khiva's most sumptuous interior decoration, including ceramic tiles, carved stone and wood, and *ghanch*. Built by Allakuli Khan between 1832 and 1841 as a more splendid alternative to the Kuhna Ark, it's said to have more than 150 rooms off nine courtyards, with high ceilings designed to catch any breeze. Allakuli was a man in a hurry – the Tosh-Hovli's first architect was executed for failing to complete the job in two years.

Two separate entrances take you into two separate wings of the palace. Don't miss the harder-to-spot south wing, where the throne room and a sumptuous *aivan* are located.

ISLOM-HOJA MEDRESSA

Walk south from the Abdulla Khan Medressa to the Islom-Hoja Medressa and minaret – Khiva's newest Islamic monuments, both built in 1910. You can climb the **minaret** (admission US$1). With bands of turquoise and red tiling, it looks rather like an uncommonly lovely lighthouse. At 57m tall, it's Uzbekistan's highest.

The medressa holds Khiva's best museum, the **Museum of Applied Arts**. It exhibits Khorezm handicrafts through the ages – fine woodcarving; metalwork; Uzbek and Turkmen carpets; stone carved with Arabic script (which was in use in Khorezm from the 8th to the 20th centuries); and large pots called *hum* for storing food underground.

Islom Hoja himself was an early-20th-century grand vizier and a liberal (by Khivan standards): he founded a European-style school, brought long-distance telegraph to the city and built a hospital. For his popularity, the khan and clergy had him assassinated.

PAHLAVON MAHMUD MAUSOLEUM

This revered **mausoleum** (Islom Hoja; admission US$1), with its sublime courtyard and stately tilework, is one of the town's most beautiful spots. Pahlavon Mahmud was a poet, philosopher and legendary wrestler who became Khiva's patron saint. His 1326 tomb was rebuilt in the 19th century and then requisitioned in 1913 by the khan of the day as the family mausoleum.

The beautiful Persian-style chamber under the turquoise dome at the north end of the courtyard holds the tomb of Mohammed Rakhim Khan. Pahlavon Mahmud's tomb, to the left off the first chamber, has some of Khiva's loveliest tiling on the sarcophagus and the walls. Tombs of other khans stand unmarked east and west of the main building, outside the courtyard.

DISHON-QALA

The Dishon-Qala was old Khiva's outer town, yet another creation of the 'builder khan' Allakuli, and surrounded by its own 6km wall. Most of it is buried beneath the modern town now, but part of the Dishon-Qala's wall remains, 300m south of the South Gate.

The **Isfandiyar Palace** (Mustaqillik; admission US$0.50, camera US$0.50; 9am-6pm) was built between 1906 and 1912, and like the Emir's Summer Palace in Bukhara displays some fascinatingly overdone decorations in a messy collision of East and West. The rooms are largely bare, allowing one to fully appreciate the gold-embroidered ceilings and lavish touches such as 4m-high mirrors and a 50kg chandelier. The harem, in case you're wondering, was behind the huge wall to the west of the palace. It's undergoing renovation and may open some day.

Tours

Our recommended guides are listed below.
Amon (225 42 45, 719 80 50) French.
Elena Alayarova (229 46 22, 517 78 32; marina _allayarova@yahoo.com) German.
Jonibek Roziev (8397-789 7111; joni.uz@gmail. com) English.
Muhammad Yunusov (297 77 64; muhammad-987@ inbox.ru) English.

Sleeping

Negotiating often bears fruit at Khiva hotels. You'll save money paying in som at the Orient Star and Malika hotels; at the others listed below, it won't matter. Only the Malika hotels,

Asia Hotel and a few others stay open from December to February.

BUDGET

Lali-Opa (☎ 375 44 49; laliopa@mail.ru; Rahmonov 11A; dm/s/d US$7/10/20; ✖) This cosy little guesthouse, located just a few steps outside the West Gate, boasts the cheapest en suite rooms in town. What it lacks in character it makes up for in friendly service.

Ganijon Afandi (☎ 375 95 69; ganifjon_afandi_@ inbox.ru; Pahlavon Mahmud; d without bathroom per person US$10; ✖) Backpackers are drawn to the simple but effective rooms, chill courtyard, yummy meals (US$4) and communal vibe. Negotiable prices sweeten the deal.

Otabek (☎ 375 61 77; Islom Hoja 68; dm US$10; ✖) The two triples and one double at this family-run B&B have cosy beds and warm carpeting. You can self-cater and store your stuff in the owners' fridge, or pay US$5 for dinner – often *plov*, soup and salad.

Mirzoboshi (☎ 375 27 53; mirzaboshi@inbox.ru; Pahlavon Mahmud 1; dm US$10) This mud- and brick-walled B&B is located right in the heart of the Ichon-Qala across from Katya the camel's lair; the entrance is around the back. You essentially move in with the family by occupying one of the two dorm rooms (a double and a quad). For more privacy opt for their clean **annexe** (☎ 375 91 88; Toshpolatov 24; s/d US$15/30; ✖ 💻).

Islambek (☎ 375 30 23; www.islambekhotel.uz; Toshpolatov 60; s/d/lux US$15/25/30; ✖ 💻) The 20 bright rooms here are a tad overdone but represent good value, with enough aged furniture for an afternoon tea session in most rooms. Then again you're probably better off taking tea on the roof, where the view's much better.

MIDRANGE

Meros Guest House (☎ 375 76 42; meros_bnb@mail.ru; Abdulla Boltaev 57; s/d US$15/30; ✖) The six simple rooms with nice twin beds and bedside tables are beyond what you'd expect for this price. The breakfast is excellent and can be taken on the upstairs patio or in the beautiful dining room, with an *aivan*-style painted ceiling installed by the owner, a restoration master.

Isakjon & Umidabonu (☎ 375 92 83; isaqjan02@ mail.ru; Rahmonov 70; s/d US$25/35; ✖) A solid value option located just outside the West Gate. Rooms lack character and the wall-to-wall carpeting is ageing, but you could swing a camel in what are certainly Khiva's largest rooms.

ourpick Shaherezada Khiva (☎ 375 95 65; www. khivashaherezada.uz; Islom Hoja 35; s/d/tr US$45/60/75; ✖) Finally, a classy, midrange B&B that truly distinguishes itself from the unimaginative Khivan pack. With beautiful wooden beds and furniture, *tapchan* dining in a remarkable dining room, and large rooms strewn with beautiful carpets and porcelain, the Shaherezada would stand out in B&B-rich Bukhara. Every exquisite piece of wood here – including the memorable front door – was hand-carved in the workshop of the owner.

Hotel Orient Star (☎ 375 49 45; orient-s-khiva@ mail.ru; Pahlavon Mahmud 1; s/d US$45/72; ✖) This recently privatised hotel is in fact the 19th-century Mohammed Amin Khan Medressa. Accommodation in former *hujra* (study cells) is somewhat austere, but with satellite TVs and fancy bathrooms in place you need not live a completely hermit-like existence.

Malika Kheivak (☎ 375 77 87; www.malikahotels. com; Islom Hoja; s/d US$60/80; ✖ 🛜) It's the Ichon-Qala's most modern, amenity-laden hotel, but better value is available elsewhere. The Malika chain has two additional upmarket offerings just outside the North and West gates.

Eating & Drinking

The choices are limited but growing. The chaikhanas in the Ichon-Qala are OK but gouge you a bit on food and especially beer. Leave the Ichon-Qala and prices suddenly halve.

ICHON-QALA

ourpick Khorezm Art Restaurant (mains 3000-5000S; ✖ Ⓥ Ⓔ) Its opening in 2009 was a godsend for restaurant-starved Khiva. Choose between the outdoor patio in the shadow of the Allakuli Khan Medressa and the tasteful dining room done up in traditional Khorezm style. The menu changes nightly and features both Khorezm specialities and safe eats like pumpkin cream soup.

Bir Gumbaz (Pahlavon Mahmud; mains 4000-6000S) A diminutive chaikhana, it's known for tasty soups and its artist's view of Kalta Minor.

Kheivak Restaurant (Islom Hoja; mains 4000-10,000S; 🛜 Ⓥ Ⓔ) The Malika Kheivak hotel wisely lays *tapchan* and tables in its vast garden. The food is among the best in town and it seems to stay open later than anything else.

DISHON-QALA

Dilnura Cafe (opposite Koy-Darvoza; mains 2000-3500S) Well worth the short walk out the east gate to enjoy unique Khiva specialities like *fityi* (small meat pies with Uzbek spices), *turkhum barak* (dough with egg), *shurva* (meat soup) and *shivit oshi* (meat over noodles embedded with dill).

Ogahiy Fish Restaurant (☎ 297 36 64; fish per kg US$5) This relaxing restaurant wraps around a pond among vineyards in a bucolic spot 3.5km northwest of Isfandiyar Palace. Take marshrutka 2 from the trolleybus stop.

Ekvator (Mustaqillik) This bar would have the builders of the 1912 Nurullaboy Medressa that it occupies rolling in their graves. It has a cavernous interior and a dance floor that occasionally comes to life on weekends.

Entertainment

The **Fashion & traditional dance show** (admission €5; ☯ first show5pm) takes place in the Allakuli Khan Medressa at least twice nightly in the high season. Book tickets through the tourist information office or at the gate, and be sure to ask for a discount, which is often granted to individual tourists. There's a shorter (30-minute) traditional show at Tosh-Hovli on most nights for a negotiable 3000S.

Shopping

Souvenir and craft shops line the streets of the Ichon-Qala and are wedged into many attractions. The best quality is to be found in the Kutlimurodinok Medressa, which contains several handicraft workshops as well.

Khiva Silk Carpet Workshop (☎ 375 72 64; www.khiva.info/khivasilk; Pahlavon Mahmud; ☯ 9am-6pm Mon-Fri) Apprentice carpet makers hand-weave silk rugs patterned after Khiva-style majolica tiles, doors and miniature paintings. There's lots of natural-dyed silk hanging around and you can watch women work the looms. The book *A Carpet Ride to Khiva* (see the boxed text, p211) is about its Unesco-sponsored launch. Ask manager Madrim for a tour.

Khiva Suzani Centre (Pahlavon Mahmud) The British Council and Operation Mercy helped this centre get its wings in 2004. The now-independent centre churns out marvellous handmade silk and *adras* creations.

Getting There & Away

The way between Urgench and Khiva is by shared taxi (US$0.75, 30 minutes) from the stand by the trolleybus stop, just outside the North Gate. The interminable trolleybus (400S, 1½ hours) is another option.

If you are heading east to Bukhara your best bet is a shared taxi from Urgench (see p269). The Tourist Information Office may be able to match you with other travellers for this trip.

A couple of late-morning and early-afternoon private buses per day depart when full to Tashkent (US$10, 21 hours) via Samarkand and Bukhara from the Koy-Darvoza Gate, east of the Ichon-Qala. There's also a Saturday bus that goes all the way to Almaty from here.

KARAKALPAKSTAN

If you're attracted to desolation, you'll love the Republic of Karakalpakstan. The Karakalpaks, who today number only about 400,000 of the republic's 1.2 million population (there are almost as many Kazakhs), are a formerly nomadic and fishing people who are struggling to recapture a national identity after being collectivised or urbanised in Soviet times. Karakalpak, the official language of the republic, is Turkic, close to Kazakh and less so to Uzbek.

The destruction of the Aral Sea has rendered Karakalpakstan one of Uzbekistan's most depressed regions. The capital, Nukus, feels half deserted, and a drive into outlying areas reveals a region of dying towns and blighted landscapes. In a cruel irony, Karakalpaks have been forced to embrace the devil in the sense that cotton – the very crop that devastated the Aral Sea in the first place – is now one of the region's main industries. The long-running government practice of forcing state workers and school children into the cotton fields is alive and well here, as any autumn jaunt into the Karakalpak countryside will prove (see the boxed text, p209).

For all the indignities it has suffered, the Aral has been generous in defeat, yielding vast oil and gas reserves in its dried-up seabed. Unfortunately, the spoils so far have been divided between Chinese investors and their Tashkent-based patrons, with little trickling down to the people of Karakalpakstan.

NUKUS НУКУС
☎ 61 / pop 230,000
The isolated Karakalpak capital lies 166km northwest of Urgench, well beyond the reach of most tourist buses. Nukus, a lifeless city of tree-lined avenues and nondescript Soviet architecture, is the gateway to the fast-disappearing Aral Sea and home to a remark-

able art museum that for some travellers is worth the hardship of getting here.

Orientation

The main street is Turan (Lenina), which intersects with the bazaar at its western end and with busy Dosnazarov at its eastern end. The bus station and the train station are relatively near each other about 5km south of the bazaar. The airport is 3km north of the centre.

Information

There are plenty of black market money changers near the entrance to the bazaar. Check www.karakalpakstan.org or www.karakalpak.com for general information about Karakalpakstan and ideas for tours in the region.

Asaka Bank (Turtkul Bazare 1A) MasterCard cash advances. It's out past the train station.

Internet (Lumumba 4; per hr 800S; ☯ 9am-midnight) Located in the basement of Hotel Nukus.

National Bank of Uzbekistan (Gharezsizlik 52) Cash advances for Visa cardholders on the 2nd floor.

Post & telephone office (Karakalpakstan 7; ☯ post 7am-7pm, telephone 24hr)

Savitsky Museum (☎ 222 88 83; Rzaev 127) The best art museum in Central Asia doubles as Nukus' de facto tourist information centre. The multilingual staff know the region well and can organise homestays and tours to Mizdakhan, Moynaq and the Elliq-Qala region.

UZBEKISTAN

A VISIT TO THE ARAL SEA Greg Bloom

Catching a glimpse of the notorious Aral Sea's new southern shoreline holds no small amount of appeal for adventurous travellers. The favoured route these days is straight north from Moynaq. It's essential to go with an experienced driver with intimate knowledge of the tracks heading north from Moynaq and Kungrad. See p278 for recommended operators.

I did the trip in October 2009 with a group in Russian UAZ jeeps. We drove west for awhile along the sea's former bank and then set out across the dried-up sea bed, where oil refineries belched fire and black smoke in an eerie scene reminiscent of a *Mad Max* movie. After a half-hour we left the smokestacks behind and entered the heart of the Aral Sea bed. The part we were traversing had been dry for so long that already a forest of sage brush had spouted. Then the foliage petered out, and we entered a land of interminable salt flats receding into mirages in every direction.

In front of us loomed the Ustyurt Plateau, stretching into Kazakhstan to the north and all the way to the Caspian Sea to the west. We had a picnic lunch in the shadow of cliffs that once abutted the western border of the Aral Sea, before ascending to the top of the plateau. There wasn't much up there, although it's said to be prime grounds for hunting boar, fowl and rare Saiga antelope. Our drivers picked out their route then sped across the top of the plateau, often at breakneck speeds. After about 45 minutes an intensely blue slick appeared on the horizon. It was our first sighting of the Aral Sea. Against the barren backdrop of the dried-up sea bed and the rocky Ustyurt Plateau it looked profoundly beautiful, all the more so for what it represented – the futility of man's attempts to subjugate nature.

An hour later we drew level with the water's edge. Here, recently exposed bits of sea bed were rendered in various shades of grey. The bits closest to the water were the darkest. They still glistened, like mudflats exposed by low tide, only in this case the low tide was eternal. The mud would soon dry up and crack. In a few years it might sprout sage brush and draw oil prospectors. Thus was the future of the South Aral Sea.

Watching the Aral Sea recede before our eyes was moving and depressing. We rode in silence for another 45 minutes before descending to our campsite near the water's edge. It had taken us about five hours to get out here from Moynaq (including many stops), and it was already getting chilly. Only two of us remained committed to swimming. To do so required wading through 50 metres of knee-deep muck before the water became deep enough to submerge. It proved worth the slog. The water was salty enough to suspend a brick. We lay flat on our backs without moving a muscle, buoyant as corks.

That night we were treated to a stunning harvest-moonrise over the Aral. Conversation, vodka, a huge meal, and a cold, restless night of sleep in a camouflaged tent followed. The next morning I departed about as satisfied as one could be with an organised tour, armed with the following painfully obvious advice: see it while you still can.

Sights

SAVITSKY KARAKALPAKSTAN ART MUSEUM

The **Savitsky Museum** (☎ 222 25 56; www.savitsky collection.org; Rzaev 127; adult/student US$3.50/2, camera US$15, guide US$1.50; ⌚ 9am-5pm Mon-Fri, 10am-4pm Sat & Sun) houses one of the most remarkable art collections in the former Soviet Union. The museum owns some 90,000 artefacts and pieces of art – including more than 15,000 paintings – only a fraction of which are actually on display. About half of the paintings were brought here in Soviet times by renegade artist and ethnographer Igor Savitsky. Many of the early-20th-century Russian paintings did not conform to Soviet Realism, but found protection in these isolated backwaters. See the boxed text, opposite, for more on how this nonconformist museum survived during the Soviet era.

The museum has impressive archaeological and folk art collections to match its collection of paintings. The huge collection is rotated every few months, so you could visit many times and continue to see new works.

If you crave more, the Savitsky Museum has an **extension** (☎ 222 73 81; camera US$15; ⌚ 9am-5pm Mon-Sat) on the 2nd floor of the Regional Studies Museum. It actually has more paintings on display than the main museum.

The Savitsky Museum's warehouse of stored works, many in the process of restoration, is also open for viewing. It costs US$40 for small groups.

REGIONAL STUDIES MUSEUM

This **museum** (☎ 222 73 89; Karakalpakstan; admission US$2, per photo US$1; ⌚ 9am-1pm & 2-5pm Mon-Fri, 10am-4pm Sat) is minor league compared to the Savitsky, but still contains a strong exhibition of fauna and flora of the Karakalpakstan region, plus various ethnographic exhibits. The very last Turan (Caspian) tiger, killed in 1972, stands stuffed and mounted in a corner.

Tours

The mother of all Uzbek excursions is the trip out to the South Aral Sea – which might not outlast the life of this book. The only Aral Sea operator with any sort of marketing strategy is **Bes Qala Nukus** (☎ 224 51 69; www.kr.uz/besqala, bqntravel2006@rambler.ru), run by Tazabay Uteuliev. The overnight trips cost US$400 to US$440 for the car, plus US$30 per person for food and a bit more for extras like sleeping bags and tents. Others doing the tours are **Omirbay Sarsenbayev** (☎ 504 77 87; omish_87@mail.ru), **Ayap Ismayilov** (☎ 505 07 75) and **Oktyabr Dospanov** (☎ 351 13 65, 222 67 57; oktyabrd@gmail.com). Ayap does cut-rate Aral Sea tours in a Lada! Oktyabr can also organise homestays around Karakalpakstan. All guides speak English except Ayap.

Festivals & Events

The annual **Pakhta-Bairam** festival takes place on the first Sunday after Karakalpakstan meets its cotton-picking quota, usually in late November or early December. Competitions are held in traditional sports such as wrestling, ram-fighting and cock-fighting.

NUKUS

0 — 500 m
0 — 0.3 miles

INFORMATION
Internet..(see 6)
National Bank of Uzbekistan..............**1** B3
Post & Telephone Office......................**2** B4
Savitsky Museum..................................(see 5)

SIGHTS & ACTIVITIES
Jipek Joli..**3** A3
Regional Studies Museum...................**4** B4
Savitsky Karakalpakstan Art Museum...**5** A3
Savitsky Museum Extension................(see 4)

SLEEPING 🏨
Hotel Nukus...**6** B4
Hotel Tashkent......................................**7** A4

EATING 🍴
BBQ & Beer Stands...............................**8** A4
Mona Lisa..**9** A4
Neo...**10** A4
Sheraton Cafe.....................................**11** B4

TRANSPORT
Airline Booking Office........................**12** B3
Bazaar Bus Stop..................................**13** A3
Buses to Airport..................................**14** B3
Buses to Train Station.......................**15** B3

To Airport (2km);
To Amu Darya (3km); Hojeli (10km); Mizdakhan (13km); Gyaur-Qala (13.5km); Turkmen border (18km); Kungrad (120km); Moynaq (210km)
To South Bus Station (5km); Train Station (5km); Urgench (166km)
To Train Station (5km); Asaka Bank (5.5km)

Sleeping & Eating

Tazabay of Bes Qala Nukus arranges apartment rentals with registration. The Rahnamo – a fancy, pricey, newly opened hotel next to the Hotel Nukus – should be licensed to accept foreigners by early 2011.

Jipek Joli (☎ 222 11 00; www.ayimtour.com; Rzaev 4; s/d from US$20/30; ❀) This recently expanded B&B a block north of the Savitsky Museum is easily Nukus' best all-around choice. The only problem is getting a room in the high season – book ahead.

Hotel Tashkent (☎ 224 18 28; Berdakh 59; s/d/lux US$25/30/50; ❀) This decrepit high-rise at the western end of Karakalpakstan offers spacious, if run-down, rooms that are poor value at the asking price, but you can usually bargain them down substantially. Only the spruced up lux rooms have air-con.

Hotel Nukus (☎ 222 89 41; Lumumba 4; d/tr from US$26/30; ❀) Conveniently located in the heart of town, this old hotel has been spruced up but poor service makes it a less-than-pleasant place to stay. The renovated 1st-floor rooms, at US$36, are reserved for 'tourists'. Cheaper rooms are upstairs.

Eating

Sheraton Cafe (☎ 222 87 81; Gharezsizlik 53; mains 6000-7000S; Ⓔ) It may not live up to its international hotel namesake, but the Sheraton's menu of European dishes with Russian and

---

MARINIKA BABANAZAROVA

We chatted with the engaging director of the Savitsky Karakalpakstan Art Museum about the life and loves of the man who founded the museum in 1966.

Who was Igor Savitsky? Savitsky was an artist from Moscow who first came to Karakalpakstan in 1950 with an archaeological expedition. He became fascinated with the local culture, nature and history, fell in love with the land, and in 1957 moved to Nukus. He believed that the Russian Avant Garde artists of the early 20th century were very special. And he started to collect this art, which was not recognised by the Soviet regime, first from cities of Uzbekistan, then from Moscow, St Petersburg and other Russian cities. No one cared about most of these painters because they were either forbidden – many of the artists were repressed – or just forgotten.

How did the Soviet regime view him? He started in the late '60s, early '70s when the regime was not as tough as in Stalin's time. It was already Brezhnev's time, the so-called period of stagnation. Some people knew, some people didn't care; they were letting him do this because it was so far from anything… A special network of people in Moscow were helping Savitsky because he was the only director of an official museum who was openly buying art not recognised by the regime. Only Savitsky was brave enough to do this. … And he bought thousands of items. He was a saviour for the arts because otherwise those paintings would have just disappeared.

How did he obtain so many paintings? Many paintings were lying in attics or basements in the houses of poor widows [of artists]. Savitsky recognised the artistic value of this art and collected it for the Nukus museum. Sometimes he paid some money, but usually he took the paintings with IOU letters, promising to pay out within 10 or 15 years. He was hunting for money all his life and we were paying off his debts for eight years after he died.

What kind of person was Savitsky? Of course he was very special, very extraordinary in all senses. He was obsessed with art. He didn't think about anything else. No personal life, only the museum and everything for the sake of the museum. And he was persuasive. He could persuade some people who were owners of some objects that were very special, like [Lyubov] Popova and some other great names. They would give what they had in their house sometimes even without any money.

Was the museum well known in Soviet times? What we called the intelligentsia knew about this museum, and the museum had a kind of unofficial fame. But official recognition came much later, after Savitsky died. He didn't live up to that time but he believed – I always cite this phrase that he used to say – 'one day people from Paris will be coming to Nukus to see our museum'. We were very sceptical about his words, of course, but he was right.

Marinika Babanazarova has been the director of the Savitsky Karakalpakstan Art Museum since Igor Savitsky's death in 1984. For the full interview transcript, visit the author's website (mytripjournal.com/bloomblogs).

Uzbek influences is cause for celebration in Nukus.

Neo (Gharezsizlik; mains 6000-7000S; [icons] [E]) Co-owned with Sheraton Cafe, it consists of a giant upstairs banquet hall next to an ill-lit street-side eatery and serves an assortment of safe Russian and 'European' food.

Gharezsizlik qualifies as a restaurant row in Nukus. There are BBQ and beer stands around the corner from Neo, and towards the western end of the street is a row of cafes, the best of which is **Mona Lisa** ([phone] 224 06 32; Gharezsizlik 107; 6000-8000S; [E]), specialising in *fidzhin* (Ossetian meat pies), Georgian stews and other Caucasian fare.

Getting There & Away
AIR
Uzbekistan Airways has flights to Tashkent (€47, two daily), Fergana (€59, weekly) and Moscow (three weekly). Book tickets at the **airline booking office** ([phone] 222 79 95; Pushkin 43; [time] 9am-7pm).

LAND
Shared taxis to Urgench (US$5, 1½ hours), Beruni (US$4, one hour) and Boston (US$4, one hour) depart from the **South (New) Bus Station** (Yuzhny Avtovokzal; [phone] 223 22 93), 6km south of town. Cheaper marshrutkas also serve these destinations. You may have to transfer in Beruni for Urgench.

Buses from the South Bus Station lumber to Urgench (US$2, three hours, daily) and Samarkand (US$8, 13 hours, daily) via Bukhara (US$6).

For buses to Tashkent, try the private-bus lot in front of the Hotel Nukus. There are two buses to Tashkent per day from there (US$11, 22 hours) via Samarkand and Bukhara.

For information on getting to Moynaq, see opposite. For the Turkmen border, see p288.

Train
Twice-weekly train 54 from Kungrad (120km northwest of Nukus) to Tashkent (*platskartny/ kupeyny* US$18/26, 22 hours) comes through Nukus, with stops in Turtkul, Navoi and Samarkand. Train 322 to Almaty (two days) and several passing trains from Russia provide additional options to Tashkent.

Getting Around
Bus 15 goes between the airport and train station along Dosnazarov; a handy stop is at

the corner of Pushkin. From the bazaar, take bus 1 to the train station and bus 34 to the bus station. A taxi from the airport, train or bus station to the centre costs about US$1.50.

AROUND NUKUS
Mizdakhan
On a hill 13km west of Nukus, near Hojeli, are the remains of ancient Mizdakhan, once the second-largest city in Khorezm. Inhabited from the 4th century BC until the 14th century AD, Mizdakhan remained a sacred place even after Timur destroyed it; tombs and mosques continued to be built here right up to the 20th century.

Today the main attraction is a hill littered with those mosques and mausoleums, some ruined, some intact. The most impressive is the restored **Mausoleum of Mazlum Khan Slu**, dating from the 12th to 14th centuries.

On the neighbouring hill towards the Turkmen border are the remains of a 4th-to 3rd-century BC fortress called **Gyaur-Qala**, which is worth checking out if you missed the forts of Elliq-Qala (p270).

To get here from Nukus, take a shared taxi from the Nukus bazaar to Hojeli (US$0.50, 20 minutes), then get in a shared taxi bound for the Turkmen border and get off after 3km in Mizdakhan. A private taxi from Nukus costs US$10 return with wait time.

MOYNAQ МУЙНАК
[phone] 61 / pop 12,000
Moynaq, 210km north of Nukus, encapsulates more visibly than anywhere the absurd tragedy of the Aral Sea. Once one of the sea's two major fishing ports, it now stands some 180km from the water. What remains of Moynaq's fishing fleet lies rusting on the sand in the former seabed.

The mostly Kazakh residents have moved away in droves, and Moynaq today is a virtual ghost town populated by livestock herders and the elderly looking after grandchildren whose parents have left to find work elsewhere. The few who remain suffer the full force of the Aral Sea disaster, with hotter summers, colder winters, debilitating sand-salt-dust storms, and a gamut of health problems (see p100).

Moynaq used to be on an isthmus connecting the Ush Say (Tiger's Tail) peninsula to the shore. You can appreciate this on the approach to the town, where the road is raised above the surrounding land. The town itself consists of one seemingly endless main street linking the bus station at its southeast end with the Oybek Hotel and the ships graveyard to the northwest.

Sights

Poignant reminders of Moynaq's tragedy are everywhere: the sign at the entrance to the town has a fish on it; a fishing boat stands as a kind of monument on a makeshift pedestal near Government House. The local **museum** (Main Rd; admission US$1, camera US$1) in the city hall has some interesting photos and paintings of the area prospering before the disaster.

The **beached ships** are a five-minute walk from the Oybek Hotel, across the main road and beyond the collection of homes. Once difficult to find, most ships have now been moved to a centralised location beneath the **Aral Sea memorial**, which occupies a bluff that was once the Aral Sea's bank.

From the memorial you can spot a lake southeast of town, created in an attempt to restore the formerly mild local climate. It didn't quite work, but it's at least given the locals a source of recreation. The lake was filled to the brim in 2009, as a dam in Tajikistan came close to bursting, prompting a massive release of water, some of which made it all the way to Moynaq via canals linked to the Amu-Darya. The Amu-Darya itself peters out in the desert southeast of Moynaq.

Sleeping

Oybek Hotel (☎ 220 41 13; r without bathroom US$8) A once-notorious dive, the Oybek has transformed into an adequate budget living space. The rooms are simple but spacious and they now have electricity and even running hot water in the common bathroom.

Your other choice is a homestay. **Makhmudjan Sagitjan** (☎ 221 30 90; Amir Timur 2; per person US$20) is an easy walk from the bus station and his family cooks *plov* dinners for US$5. There's no central plumbing but there's a tap and shower outside. If you can't get hold of him, try his brother Aitjanov (☎ 351 72 12; aitsagit@rambler.rup) in Nukus.

There are basic lunch options near the bus station but dinner is problematic. See what the Oybek Hotel can whip up, or bring some food along with you.

Getting There & Away

Several buses make the trip from Nukus (US$2, four hours) via Kungrad (Kongirot).

New private buses depart from Nukus' bazaar at roughly 1pm, 3pm and 4.30pm, while two decrepit public buses leave the South Bus Station at 8.45am and 2.45pm, passing by the Hotel Tashkent about five minutes later. Most return buses from Moynaq depart in the morning. All buses to Moynaq are standing-room-only; board early if you want a seat.

It's swifter to take a shared taxi or marshrutka to Kungrad from a stop opposite the train station, and transfer at Kungrad's train station to a marshrutka or another shared taxi. This will cost about US$6 in total and save you two hours of driving time. Get to Kungrad by mid-afternoon to ensure an onward ride.

A day trip from Nukus in an ordinary taxi costs US$60 to US$70 (less from the Kungrad shared taxi lot).

UZBEKISTAN DIRECTORY

ACCOMMODATION

The B&B scene in Uzbekistan has taken off more than in any other Central Asian republic. The best are in Bukhara, with Samarkand and Khiva gradually catching up.

Uzbekistan's first community-based tourism program is going strong in the Nuratau Mountains (p257). Yurtstays are possible too (see p256 and p270).

Accommodation rates listed in this chapter are for rooms with private bathroom and include breakfast unless otherwise stated.

Homestayers and especially campers face a range of potential problems related to registration – see p285.

ACTIVITIES

Camel trekking, usually combined with a yurtstay, is the most intriguing activity, though most trips are relatively short jaunts around one of the yurt camps mentioned on p256 and p270. East Line Tour in Bukhara (p258) is the authority on **birdwatching** (www.birdwatching-uzbekistan.com), of which Uzbekistan is meant to offer the best in Central Asia.

Other popular outdoor activities are **rafting**, **skiing** and **trekking**, all remarkably accessible from Tashkent (see p104 and p230). Other good places for a walk include the Nuratau Mountains (p257) and the mountains

around Boysun and Shakhrisabz in southern
Uzbekistan (see the boxed text on p254).

DANGERS & ANNOYANCES

As in many police states, the main danger is
the overzealous police. That said, the *militsia*
(police) have become much less of a nuisance
in recent years. Worried about Uzbekistan's
international image, President Karimov has
curbed the police habit of shaking down travellers for bribes at roadside checkpoints in
the provinces. Indeed, taxi drivers now *prefer*
having tourists in the car, as foreigners supposedly provide 'protection' against spurious
roadside checks.

You may still be stopped, particularly on
Tashkent's metro, in the sensitive Fergana
Valley and in border towns like Termiz. See
Crooked Officials (p501) for tips on dealing with the *militsia*. With all of those police
around, petty crime and armed robbery are
relatively rare.

The main annoyance in Uzbekistan is the
need to obsessively collect flimsy registration
slips (see p285).

EMBASSIES & CONSULATES
Uzbek Embassies in Central Asia

Uzbekistan has embassies in Afghanistan
(p491), Kazakhstan (p194), Kyrgyzstan (p366),
Tajikistan (p417) and Turkmenistan (p462).

Uzbek Embassies & Consulates

For more Uzbek missions abroad see the web-
site of the **Ministry of Foreign Affairs** (www.mfa.uz).
China (☎ 86-10-6532 6305/2551; www.uzbekistan.cn;
Beijing 100600, Sanlitun, Beixiao gie 11)
France (☎ 331-5330 0353; www.ouzbekistan.fr; 22 rue
d'Aguesseau, 75008, Paris)

PRACTICALITIES

Any independent media dealing with
Uzbekistan is online and offshore. The government blocks politically sensitive Uzbek-
language websites, but you can access most
English-language sites, regardless of political bent, from within the country. For useful
internet resources, see p283.

Cable and satellite TV are common in all
but the cheapest hotels. Satellites receive
thousands of channels but usually only a few
in English – BBC, CNN, that's about it. Cable
networks offer mostly Russian channels.

Germany (☎ 49-30-394 09 80; www.uzbekistan.de;
Perleberger Strasse 62, Berlin 10559) Consulate in Frankfurt.
Russia (consulate; ☎ 7-499-230 00 54; www.uzembassy
.ru; 2 Kazachy pereulok II, Moscow, 119017)
UK (☎ 44-020-7229 7679; www.uzbekembassy.org;
Consular Section, 41 Holland Park W11 3RP, London)
USA (☎ 1-202-887 5300; www.uzbekistan.org; 1746
Massachusetts Ave NW, Washington DC 20036) Consulate-
General in New York (www.uzbekconsulny.org).

Embassies & Consulates in Uzbekistan

The following are all located in Tashkent
(☎ 71; see Map p214). For additional em-
bassy listings see www.goldenpages.uz. Hours
of operation listed below are for visa applica-
tions only.
Afghanistan (☎ 140 41 31/4; fax 140 41 33; 47
Bogtepa lane V; ⏲ 9am-3pm Mon-Fri)
Azerbaijan (☎ 273 61 67; Shark Tongi 25; ⏲ 10am-
noon & 3-4pm Mon-Fri)
China (☎ 233 47 28; www.uzbekistan.cn; Gulomov 79;
⏲ 9am-noon Mon, Wed & Fri)
France (☎ 233 53 82/4; www.ambafrance-uz.org;
Istikbol 25)
Georgia (☎ 262 62 43; http://uzbekistan.mfa.gov.ge;
Ziyolilar str, 6)
Germany (☎ main 120 84 40, 24hr citizen's services 181
54 06; www.taschkent.diplo.de; Rashidov 15)
India (☎ 140 09 83; www.indembassy.uz; Kara-Bulak
15-16; ⏲ 9.30am-12.30pm Mon-Fri, pick-up 4-5pm)
Indonesia (☎ 232 02 36; http://indonesia.embassy.uz;
Gulomov 73)
Iran (☎ 268 38 77; Parkent 20; ⏲ 9am-noon Mon-Thu)
Israel (☎ 120 58 08; http://tashkent.mfa.gov.il; Abdulla
Kahhor 3)
Italy (☎ 252 11 19; Yusuf Khos Khodjib 40)
Japan (☎ 120 80 60; www.uz.emb-japan.go.jp; 28
Azimov lane I)
Kazakhstan (☎ 252 16 54; Chekhov 23; ⏲ 9am-noon
Mon-Fri, pick-up 4-5pm)
Kyrgyzstan (☎ 239 86 13; Samatov 30; ⏲ 10-
11.30am & 2.30-4pm Mon-Fri, closed Tue morning & Thu)
Pakistan (☎ 248 25 60; pakemb2@yahoo.com; Kichik
Halka Yuli [Sofiyskaya] 15; ⏲ applications 9am-5pm
Mon-Fri, interviews 3pm Mon, pick-up 3pm Thu)
Russia (☎ 120 35 19; www.russia.ua; Nukus 83;
⏲ 10am-1pm Mon-Fri)
South Korea (☎ 252 31 51/52; Afrosiab 7)
Tajikistan (☎ 254 84 13; Abdulla Kahhor Lane VI 61;
⏲ 9am-noon Mon-Fri)
Turkmenistan (☎ 256 94 06; Afrosiab 19; ⏲ 11am-
1pm Mon-Fri)
UK (☎ 120 15 00; ukinuzbekistan.fco.gov.uk; Gulomov 67)
USA (☎ 120 54 50; www.usembassy.uz; 3 Moykorgon
lane V) Take bus 51 from Amir Timur kochasi.

VISAS FOR ONWARD TRAVEL

Contact David at Stantours (p218) for up-dated information and honest advice. If you can avoid purchasing letter of invitation (LOI) support, Stantours will tell you. Most embassies require you to show an onward ticket if you are applying for a transit visa.

Afghanistan A 30-day visa costing US$31 to US$60 for most Europeans, US$90 for Americans, and US$105 for British citizens is issued same-day or next-day.

Azerbaijan A 30-day visa costs US$131 for Americans, US$101 for British citizens and about US$70 for most other European citizens (less with a tourist voucher). An LOI or letter of recommendation from your embassy is sometimes needed. US$25 five-day transit visas are also available.

China The best you can do here is a 20-day tourist visa. Five-day processing costs US$100 to US$130; same-day processing costs US$120 to US$170. You'll need a copy of your passport and Uzbek visa on a single page, plus copies of hotel and airline bookings.

Iran First you must apply for an authorisation through an Iranian agent. This costs €30 and takes one to two weeks to arrive, after which you can apply for a 30-day tourist visa (valid for entry within three months) costing €40 to €90 for seven-day processing. Add €50 for two-day processing.

Kazakhstan A 30-day visa (US$30) takes two days to process. An LOI is needed for double entry or for visas longer than 30 days. Transit visas cost US$20 for one- or two-day processing and do not require an LOI.

Kyrgyzstan A 30-day visa costs US$70 for four- to six-day processing, or US$110 for same-day rush processing. No LOI needed for US, Commonwealth and most EU citizens.

Pakistan A 30-day visa costs about US$72 for UK citizens, US$120 for Americans and US$24 to US$36 for most others. Hotel booking, four photos on a blue background and supporting letter required. To get here take bus 42 or 43 from the Turkuaz/GUM bus stop, get off at Kichik Halka Yuli kochasi, and walk 400m west.

Russia Tourist voucher and booking confirmation is needed to apply for a 30-day tourist visa. The price for standard four-day processing is US$50 to US$65. Pay about US$50 extra for same-day rush. Americans pay US$131 for 10- to 14-day processing (no rush available). This is the only Russian embassy in Central Asia that regularly issues tourist visas.

Tajikistan A single-/double-entry 30-day tourist visa costs US$100/120 for same-day processing. Drop off before noon, pick up at 4pm. All nationalities require an LOI.

Turkmenistan Five-day transit visas issued without an LOI for US$31. Arrive two hours early or the afternoon before to put your name on a waiting list. Allow 10 to 15 days for visa authorisation, plus another two days for visa processing. Ask about possible urgent rush processing. Tourist visas require expensive tour arrangements through

a specialised agent and cost US$30 to US$115, with one- to three-day processing (see p465).

FESTIVALS & EVENTS

There are colourful celebrations throughout the country during the vernal equinox festival of **Navrus** (celebrated on 21 March). Festivities typically involve parades, fairs, music, dancing in the streets, plenty of food and in some places a rogue game of *kupkari*. Samarkand has a good one (p246), although the best place to enjoy Navrus is in the countryside.

HOLIDAYS

January 1 New Year's Day
March 8 International Women's Day
March 21 Navrus
May 9 Day of Memory and Honour (formerly Victory Day)
September 1 Independence Day
October 1 Teachers' Day
December 8 Constitution Day

For information on Islamic holidays observed in Central Asia, see p502.

INTERNET ACCESS

Internet cafes are found in most places travellers go, although access is annoyingly slow outside a handful of spots in Tashkent. Wi-fi is common in Tashkent hotels and restaurants and is slowly gaining popularity in Samarkand, Bukhara and Khiva, but remains practically nonexistent elsewhere.

INTERNET RESOURCES

The travel agencies on p217 have great websites packed with tourist information and background on Uzbek culture and history. The Advantour (www.advantour.com) and Arostr Tourism (www.arostr.uz) websites are particularly informative. A good source of political and hard news on Uzbekistan is www.uznews.net, and www.crisisgroup.org has analysis and lengthy reports on the latest political developments.

MONEY

Few currencies burn a hole in your pocket like the Uzbek som. The highest Uzbek note (1000S) is worth less than US$0.50 on the black market. One US$100 bill turns into a satchel full of ragged bills, usually tied together with a rubber band.

The black market is king in Uzbekistan; exchanging money at official exchange points is generally avoided by many travellers. See below, for a full explanation of the black market and of prices used in this book.

A select few ATMs can be found in Tashkent (see p216). In the provinces, cash advances are usually possible at Asaka Bank for MasterCard holders and at the **National**

Bank of Uzbekistan (NBU; full branch list at http://eng.nbu.com/branches) for Visa cardholders. Commission is 1% on MasterCard advances and 1% to 4% on Visa card advances. The NBU is also usually the best bet for cashing travellers cheques. The US dollar is king in Uzbekistan, with the euro catching up. Pounds warrant poorer

THE BLACK MARKET

At the time of writing, the Uzbek som was in rapid decline and the spread between the black-market rate and the National Bank of Uzbekistan official rate was about 30%. This means that travellers will generally achieve 30% savings by paying for everything – including items priced in dollars – with Uzbek som bought on the black market, rather than with US dollars or by credit card.

At press time, there was little to no risk in exchanging money on the black market. However, this could always change so check the situation on the ground to make sure there hasn't been a police crackdown on the technically illegal black currency trade.

The de facto black-market money exchange headquarters in any given city is the central bazaar, but almost anybody and everybody – including policemen, airline ticketing agents, and tourist offices – are eager to exchange dollars at black-market rates. Ask a cab driver for assistance if you are having trouble.

This book applies the following pricing conventions:

Hotels & Travel Agencies

In this chapter we follow local convention by listing prices of hotels and travel-agency services in dollars. However, the following caveats apply:

■ Hotels in Tashkent and state-owned hotels outside of Tashkent list prices in dollars, but convert their room prices to som *at the official exchange rate*. This means that travellers will save 30% (at the time of research) by paying with som instead of with dollars or a credit card, if they buy their som on the black market.

■ Most travel agencies and private hotels outside of Tashkent – such as the B&Bs of Bukhara, Samarkand and Khiva – also list prices in dollars. However, they convert their room prices to som *at the black-market rate*. At these places you will not realise any savings by paying in som.

Airfares

We follow local convention and list prices in dollars or euros. However, like state-run hotels, airlines do accept local currency, and they convert their fares to som at the official exchange rate, allowing for big savings for those who pay in som.

Sights & Train Tickets

Sight admission prices and train ticket prices in Uzbekistan are listed in som, but are pegged to the US dollar. To ensure price stability and reflect the real price of sights and train tickets, we go against local convention and list these prices in US dollars converted *at the black-market rate*.

Shared Taxis & Long-Distance Buses

These are listed in som and tied loosely to the US dollar. To ensure price stability and reflect the real price of public transport, we go against local convention and list shared taxi and bus prices in US dollars converted *at the black-market rate*.

Restaurants & Other Items

For most other items in this book – including restaurant prices and local public transport – we follow local convention and list prices in som, unless the listed establishment itself lists prices in euros.

rates and are more difficult to exchange outside of major cities.

POST

An airmail postcard costs 1200S and a 20g airmail letter costs 1300S. The postal service is not renowned for speed or reliability in delivering letters or parcels; send your friends two postcards and hope they will receive at least one. International couriers are listed under Post in the Tashkent section (p216).

REGISTRATION

Registration rules (p507) are stricter in Uzbekistan than in most former Soviet countries. The law states clearly that you must register somewhere within three days of arriving in Uzbekistan.

Beyond that, the rules get hazy. Officially you don't need to register if you are staying in a given town for less than three nights. But like everything else in Uzbekistan this rule is open to interpretation. If the authorities decide you need to be registered for shorter stays, well then you need to be registered. Failure to comply with the 'law' can result in anything from a small bribe being demanded, to a fine of up to a couple of thousand US dollars and deportation.

Such harsh fines are unlikely, but if you go several consecutive days without registering you are asking for trouble – even if technically you have not stayed in any one place for more than two nights. Bottom line: the authorities like to see at least some registration slips in your passport. The more you have, the better, and the only way to be completely safe is to ensure that every night of your stay is accounted for by a registration slip or overnight train ticket.

Checking into a hotel licensed to take foreigners means automatic registration. If you spend a night in a private home you are supposed to register with the local Office of Visas & Registration (OVIR), but this can create more problems than it solves for you and your hosts. Asking the next hotel you stay at to supply missing registration slips is a possibility (they may demand a fee for this service or refuse your request outright).

When you leave the country, border officials may thoroughly scrutinise your registration slips or they may not look at them at all. Authorities may also check your registration slips when you are in the country, especially if they catch you staying at a hotel that isn't licensed to take foreigners. Certain hotels, especially in Tashkent, may also refuse to admit you if you can't produce a registration slip for all previous days spent in Uzbekistan.

This system creates obvious problems for campers and (less problematically) for homestayers. If you plan to camp your way around Uzbekistan, resign yourself to staying in hotels from time to time to accumulate some registration slips. If you are missing only a few registration slips upon departure from the country, you should be in the clear – in theory. In practice, police often hassle departing tourists over just one or two missing registration slips. If this happens, stand your ground and argue forcefully that you were in some towns for less than three nights, and were not required to register for nights.

TELEPHONE

You can pick up local prepaid SIM cards for US$1.50 (including some prepaid credit) at any office of mobile phone operators Ucell (national codes ☎ 93/94), Beeline (national codes ☎ 90/91) or MTS (Tashkent codes ☎ 92/97). You need your passport and valid registration slips to subscribe. The main office of **Ucell** (Map p214; ☎ 120 72 65; www.ucell.uz; Vokhidov 38, Tashkent; ☺ 9am-6pm Mon-Sat) has English-speaking staff that will change your phone settings to English. Domestic calls with Ucell or Beeline cost a minuscule US$0.005 to US$0.02 per minute. International text messages cost US$0.12 per message.

Uzbekistan's antiquated fixed-line system is creaky but functional. Local calls cost almost nothing and domestic long-distance calls are cheap. International calls from landlines or central telephone offices cost 1150S per minute to the UK, 1265S to the USA and 1725S to Australia. Post offices and minimarts sell a range of cards good for discounted long-distance calls out of Uzbekistan. Most internet cafes listed in this book offer Skype.

To place a call to a mobile phone, dial ☎ 83 (from a land line) or ☎ +998 (from another mobile phone), followed by the two-digit code and the seven-digit number.

To place a call to a land line, dial ☎ 83 (from either a land line or a mobile phone) followed by the two-digit city code and the seven-digit number. If the city code is three digits, drop the ☎ 3 and just dial ☎ 8.

If dialling from any Tashkent number (mobile or fixed) to any other Tashkent number,

---

INCOMING AREA CODES

When calling from outside Uzbekistan, dial ☎ +998, the two-digit area code marked in the individual sections (without the ☎ 3), and the seven-digit number.

---

regardless of carrier, just dial the seven-digit number (no code).

To place an international call from a land line, dial ☎ 8, wait for a tone, then dial ☎ 10.

In this chapter, mobile phone numbers are preceded by ☎ 83.

TRAVEL PERMITS

Border permits are required for all mountain areas near the Tajik and Kyrgyz borders, including most of Ugam-Chatkal National Park (p230), the Zarafshon and Hissar Mountains (p254), and Zaamin National Park (not covered in this book). Secure these with the help of any travel agency that arranges tours in these regions.

VISAS

Uzbek visa rules depend entirely on the state of Uzbekistan's relations with your country's government. At the time of writing, citizens of the following countries were technically exempt from LOIs: Austria, Belgium, France, Germany, Italy, Japan, Spain, Switzerland, the UK and the US. Everybody else needs LOIs, as do (sometimes) citizens of the above countries who are applying for visas outside their country of citizenship. No matter what your citizenship, it will be easier and quicker to obtain an Uzbek visa with an LOI.

If there is no Uzbek embassy in your country, you should be eligible for 'visa-on-arrival' at Tashkent International Airport if you arrange special LOI support for this several weeks in advance through a travel agency or inviting business.

Any Uzbek travel agency can arrange LOI support, but most demand that you also purchase a minimum level of services – usually hotel bookings for at least three nights. A few agencies still provide LOI support with no strings attached, including Arostr Tourism and Stantours (p217). They charge US$35 for an LOI for a single-entry 30-day tourist visa. Tack on US$10 per entry for multiple-entry visas, and another US$10 per entry for visa-on-arrival support. Allow five to 10 business days for LOI processing, or pay double for four- to five-day 'rush' processing.

The standard tourist visa is a 30-day, single-entry visa. They cost US$70 to US$80 for most passports and at least US$131 for US citizens. Additional entries cost US$10 per entry. Single-entry tourist visas lasting more than 30 days are difficult to obtain. Three-day transit visas are possible without an LOI. They cost about US$30 and require a visa for an onward country (eg Tajikistan).

Most embassies can issue same-day visas when you present an LOI. Visa processing without an LOI usually takes three to 10 days, depending on the embassy. For lots more information on LOIs and obtaining visas, see p510.

Application forms are available online at http://evisa.mfa.uz/Registration.aspx. For updated visa information and advice on specific application requirements, see the website of the travel agency **Advantour** (www.advantour.com) or www.mytripjournal.com/bloomblogs.

Visa Extensions

A one-week 'exit visa' (essentially an extension) costing about US$40 is available from an OVIR booth at Tashkent International Airport. Longer extensions are time-consuming, expensive and involve much red tape. Many frustrated travellers give up and go to neighbouring Kazakhstan or Kyrgyzstan and buy a new visa. If you insist on trying, seek support from a Tashkent-based travel agency (see p217 for details).

TRANSPORT IN UZBEKISTAN

GETTING THERE & AWAY
Entering Uzbekistan

As long as your papers are in order, entering Uzbekistan should be relatively easy, long lines at the airport notwithstanding. You will be asked to fill out two identical customs declarations forms, one to turn in and one to keep (which must be handed in upon departure). The customs form is necessary for changing travellers cheques and will smooth your departure, so don't lose it. Declare every cent of every type of money you bring in on your customs form; travellers have reported being hassled and/or having large sums of money confiscated for the most minor discrepancies. See Dangers & Annoyances in the Tashkent section (p218) for airport concerns.

Air

If arriving by air, your grand entrance into Uzbekistan will most likely occur at **Tashkent International Airport** (☎ 71-140 28 01/04). A few flights from Russia arrive in regional hubs such as Samarkand, Bukhara and Urgench.

The numerous *aviakassa* (private ticket kiosks) scattered around major cities can help book international tickets on national carrier **Uzbekistan Airways** (www.uzairways.com) and other airlines. For a full list of airlines flying to/from Tashkent, see p227.

Uzbekistan Airways has convenient booking offices in Tashkent (p227) and all regional hubs. Pay for airline tickets in Uzbek som only (see the boxed text on p284).

Sample one-way fares (including taxes) on Uzbekistan Airways from Tashkent (you'll likely pay more flying to Tashkent) at the time of research were Almaty €136, five weekly; Ashgabat €190, Wednesdays; Astana €167, two weekly; Baku €214, two weekly; Bangkok €369, three weekly; Bishkek €134, four weekly; Delhi €212, two weekly; Frankfurt/London/Paris €339, two weekly; Moscow €230, two daily; and New York €818, Tuesdays. Other destinations include Athens, Beijing, İstanbul, Kyiv, Milan, Rome, Seoul, Tel Aviv, Tokyo and a host of Russian cities from Tashkent, and Ürümqi from Tashkent and Fergana.

Land

BORDER CROSSINGS

To/From Afghanistan

The Friendship Bridge linking Termiz with northern Afghanistan has been opened to tourist traffic since 2005. While Afghan officials seem happy with this arrangement, the Uzbeks have been known to close their side of the border for security or other concerns. Contact a reliable travel agency in Tashkent to make sure it's open before setting out.

To get to the *tamozhnya* (border, or 'customs house') from Termiz, take marshrutka 21 from opposite Yubileyny Bazaar (US$0.25, 20 minutes). The bridge is 10km south of town. There's a fair bit of walking involved to get between the various checkpoints on the Uzbek side, and then across the bridge. From the Afghan side you're looking at about a 30-minute, US$10 taxi ride to Mazar-e-Sharif.

To/From Kazakhstan

Despite their very long common border there are just two main places to cross. The more common is the Chernyaevka (Gisht Koprik/Zhibek Zholy) crossing between Tashkent and Shymkent. However, this border was closed for renovations at the time of writing. Until it reopens, foreign travellers must use a temporary crossing at Yallama, near the town of Chinaz, about 60km southwest of Tashkent. Frequent local trains from Tashkent to Syrdarya, Gulistan and Havast stop in Chinaz (US$0.30, 1½ hours), or take a shared taxi from Sobir Rahimov metro (50 minutes).

Chernyaevka should reopen in 2011, and will hopefully be smoother than it was. Waits of up to six hours were common, and there were widespread reports of corruption, especially on the Kazakh side. It's a US$6 cab ride to Chernyaevka from central Tashkent, or you can take a shared taxi (US$0.50, 20 minutes) or marshrutka from Yunusobod Bazaar.

For details on onward travel on the Kazakh side from both Yallama and Chernyaevka, see p201.

There is a Wednesday Tashkent–Almaty train (*platskartny/kupeyny* US$39/54, 25 hours, 9.55am) that originates in Nukus. Or take a Russia-bound train such as No 381 (Tashkent–Ufa) or No 5 (Tashkent–Moscow) to Arys, Kazakhstan, and connect to Almaty there.

The other crossing is by train or road between Karakalpakstan and Beyneu in western Kazakhstan. Train 917 departs daily from Kungrad, about 225km southeast of the border, to Beyneu at 9.20am (10 hours). Other trains crossing this border include Tashkent–St Petersburg (weekly), Tashkent–Saratov (twice weekly) and Moscow–Dushanbe (three weekly).

To/From Kyrgyzstan

The only border crossings into Kyrgyzstan that are open to foreigners are at Uchkurgon/Shamaldy-Say (northeast of Namangan) and Dustlyk (Dostyk), between Andijon and Osh. They are generally hassle-free, although long lines do occur.

Most travellers use the Osh crossing. In Andijon, frequent shared taxis to the *tamozhnya* at Dustlyk depart from a stop on Babur St about 400m southeast of the train station (US$2, 40 minutes). Walk across the border and pick up public transport on the other side for the short trip to Osh.

Shared taxis and minibuses are plentiful on both the Kyrgyz and Uzbek sides of the Uchkurgon crossing.

Summer-only Tashkent–Bishkek trains pass through a long section of Kazakhstan, as do twice-daily buses to Bishkek from the Chernyaevka border crossing between Kazakhstan and Uzbekistan. You'll need a transit visa for either. Note that the Chernyaevka border is closed until at least 2011 – see p287). Until it reopens, foreigners are advised to make their way to Shymkent, Kazakhstan, and continue to Bishkek from there.

To/From Russia

From Moscow, train 382 departs at 11.35pm, arriving in Tashkent about 66 hours later (*platskartny/kupeyny* US$162/275). The return train leaves Tashkent at 7.35pm.

There are also trains between Tashkent and Chelyabinsk, Kharkiv (Ukraine), Saratov, St Petersburg, Yekaterinburg (all weekly) and Ufa (thrice weekly).

To/From Tajikistan

Most travellers making a beeline from Tashkent to Dushanbe drive to Khojand via the pain-free Oybek border crossing and then take a Tajik domestic flight. To get to this border from Tashkent take a marshrutka or shared taxi from Kuyluk Bazaar to Bekobod and get off at Oybek (marshrutka/taxi per seat US$2/4, 1½ hours), about 35km shy of Bekobod, near Chanak village. An ordinary taxi between Tashkent and Oybek costs about US$30. Once across the border take a taxi to Khojand (US$15) or a taxi to nearby Bostan (US$1) and then a minibus to Khojand.

The other main border crossings are Samarkand/Penjikent and Denau/Tursanzade. Long lines and other hassles are reportedly common on the Uzbek side at both of these crossings.

Marshrutkas to the Penjikent *tamozhnya* depart regularly from the Registan stop in Samarkand (US$1, 40 minutes). Walk across the border and pick up a shared taxi (US$2) for the 22km ride to Penjikent.

Denau is a 1½-hour drive from Termiz, a five-hour drive from Samarkand, or a 5½-hour drive from Bukhara. Shared taxis go to Samarkand (US$15) and Bukhara (US$16), as do a few morning marshrutkas. From Termiz, regular shared taxis (US$4.50) and marshrutkas (US$1.75) signboarded Денов depart to Denau from the bus station, and there are also three daily local trains directly to the border town of Sariosiyo (US$0.75, four hours), 15km north of Denau.

From Denau, take the train or a marshrutka to Sariosiyo, cross the border and proceed by taxi from Tursanzade to Dushanbe (US$10, 45 minutes).

For info on getting to Khojand via Kanibadam, see p422.

To/From Turkmenistan

The three main border points are reached from Bukhara, Khiva/Urgench and Nukus. You have to pay US$12 to enter Turkmenistan. Each crossing requires a potentially sweltering walk of 10 to 20 minutes across no-man's-land. Shared taxis or buses are sometimes available to ferry travellers across.

From Bukhara a taxi should cost US$25 to the border. Shared taxis (US$2, 40 minutes) make the trip from Kolkhoz Bazaar to Karakol (or Olot), about 10km short of the border. From Karakol a taxi to the border costs US$2.50. You can also take a slow local train to Olot from Kagan (US$0.75, two hours, two daily). Once over the border, take a shared taxi to Turkmenabat (US$1.50, 40 minutes).

From Khiva or Urgench it costs about US$10 to hire a car to the border, from where it's a short, US$1.75 taxi ride to Dashogus. Alternatively, you can take a bus to the border from Khiva (US$0.50, one hour). There's an early morning departure from a lot outside the North Gate, and two later departures from Dekhon Bazaar. In Urgench, regular shared taxis to the *tamohzhnya* leave from a stand kitty corner from Halk Bank, 700m northeast of the bazaar (US$2.50, 40 minutes).

From Nukus it's about a US$10, 20km ride to the Konye-Urgench *tamozhnya*. Alternatively, take public transport to Hojeli (see p280) and take a shared taxi from Hojeli to the border (US$0.75). Once you've walked across the border you can pick up a shared taxi to Konye-Urgench (US$2).

For information on exiting Turkmenistan, see p467.

GETTING AROUND
Air

Most routes along the tourist trail are well-served by domestic flights to/from Tashkent, if not to each other (see p227). If you book fewer than three days in advance, Uzbekistan Airways will often say the plane is full. In that case, paying a 'finder's fee' (to the ticket agent or touts on the street) of US$5 to US$20 should free up a blocked seat. Buying a ticket for a later date and flying standby often works too.

Bus & Marshrutka

Clapped-out state buses are fast disappearing from Uzbek roads, undercut by a boom in private buses that do not keep schedules and leave when full. They are newer and more comfortable, but can be slow as drivers and touts are preoccupied with overselling seats and transporting cargo and contraband.

Marshrutkas usually take the form of 11- to 14-seat Russian-made 'Gazelle' vans, or seven-seat Daewoo Damas minivans. For simplicity's sake, we do not distinguish between the two types in this chapter.

Car

Driving your own car is possible, provided you have insurance from your home country and a valid international driving licence. Be prepared for the same kind of hassles you'll experience anywhere in the former Soviet Union: lots of random stops and traffic cops fishing for bribes. There are no car-rental agencies. In Uzbekistan, motorists drive on the right and seat belts are not required at all.

Shared & Ordinary Taxi

Shared taxis save tons of time but are of course more costly than buses. They ply all the main intercity routes and also congregate at most border points. They leave when full from set locations – usually from near bus stations – and run all day and often through the night. Prices fluctuate throughout the day/week/month/year, increasing towards the evening, on weekends and on holidays. See p527 for more on shared taxis. Ordinary taxis give you

---

> **FUSSY BUSES**
>
> Don't be surprised if you can't catch a bus during cotton-picking season (October to November), when the state requisitions many marshrutkas and buses to do duty in the cotton fields. It affects mainly public local transport, but long-distance transport can be affected too. With less competition to deal with, shared taxis raise their prices during these times.
>
> Meanwhile, a horrific bus crash in May 2009 led the government to put a curfew on all bus travel between the hours of 10pm and 4am. This rule, which may or may not last, effectively adds six hours to any long-distance bus trip that can't be completed in a day, such as the Urgench–Tashkent bus. On shorter routes, buses have adjusted their schedules to ensure arrival well before 10pm.

---

the freedom to stop and explore but obviously cost more money.

Train

Trains are perhaps the most comfortable and safest, if hardly the fastest, method of intercity transport. That said, the express (*skorostnoy*, or 'high-speed') trains between Tashkent, Samarkand and Bukhara, with airplane-style seating, are not much slower than a shared taxi and a *lot* more comfortable. Book a couple of days in advance – they're popular. These have 2nd-class, 1st-class and deluxe 'SV' class (private compartment) seating. First class is not noticeably more comfortable than 2nd class. This chapter lists 2nd-class prices for express trains.

Other long-haul trains are of the deliberate but comfortable Soviet variety, with *platskartny* (hard sleeper) and *kupeyny* (soft sleeper) compartments available. Slow, dirt-cheap local *prigorodny* trains, with bench-style seating, cover middle-distance routes such as Samarkand–Bukhara.

Kyrgyzstan
Кыргызстан

Kyrgyzstan is a nation defined by its topography. Like some kind of Central Asian Shangri-La, the soaring peaks and rugged ranges of this small country form both barriers and borders. And like James Hilton's mythical landscape, once entered it can be difficult to leave.

The Kyrgyz themselves probably thought as much when they arrived some 400 years ago. To a nomadic people from Siberia, the cool mountains and glorious pastures must have seemed like the perfect place to fatten their animals while securing the high ground against invaders. Despite 21st century encroachment the Kyrgyz maintain a semi-nomadic existence, as shepherd families move from village to *jailoos* (summer pastures) with the coming of summer.

While Kyrgyz shepherds cling to their centuries-old way of life, their urban cousins are forging a new direction for the country. Periodic revolutions notwithstanding, Kyrgyzstan has built a foundation of solid democratic institutions and is oft-cited as the freest republic in Central Asia.

The market economy has been allowed to run its course and tourism has emerged as an important income generator. Communities across the country have established 'tourism co-ops', making independent travel simple. After conquering a mountain range or two, go for some R&R on the tranquil shores of Lake Issyk-Köl, or haggle for a handmade felt rug. Adrenalin junkies can scale 7000m peaks, trek over glaciers, ski in winter or kayak in summer.

Despite its small size Kyrgyzstan offers a tremendous variety of travel opportunities and is regarded as a priority destination for Central Asia explorers. Once you've had your fill of deserts and domes, get back to your nomadic roots and see what this small but spectacular republic has to offer.

FAST FACTS

- **Area** 198,500 sq km
- **Capital** Bishkek
- **Country code** ☎ 996
- **Famous for** Towering mountains, eagle hunting, nomadic yurts
- **Languages** Kyrgyz, Russian
- **Money** Kyrgyz som: US$1 = 46.53som, €1 = 58.31
- **Off the map** Kyzyl-Oi, Inylchek Glacier, Achik Tash
- **Phrases** *salam* (hello); *rahmat* (thank you); *jaqshi* (good)
- **Population** 5.2 million (2008 estimate)

HOW MUCH?

- Snickers bar US$0.50
- 100km bus ride US$2.50
- One-minute phone call to the US US$0.25
- Internet per hour US$0.80
- Kyrgyz hat US$3-6
- 1L of petrol US$0.80
- 1L of bottled water US$0.35
- Bottle of beer US$0.80-1.20
- Shashlyk US$1.20-2

HIGHLIGHTS

- **Horse treks** (p364) A chance to see the Kyrgyz countryside at its best, with rides high into the mountains and across summer pastures.
- **Lake Issyk-Köl** (p315) Hemmed in by mountains, this bizarrely un-freezable lake is the country's premier attraction.
- **Altyn Arashan** (p326) Breathtaking scenery, steaming hot pools and the first glimpse of the secret Ala-Köl lake make for great trekking.
- **Osh** (p356) For centuries Silk Road traders have haggled their way from one stall to the next in a bazaar that locals claim is older than Rome – join them.
- **Arslanbob** (p352) The world's largest walnut forest on a network of blossoming woodland treks.

ITINERARIES

- **Three days** Spend a day in Bishkek (p298), wandering its parks, museums and booming markets then go trekking in the Ala-Archa Valley (p311).
- **One week** After Bishkek head east to Karakol (p320) on the shores of Lake Issyk-Köl and spend a few days hiking, horse riding or visiting local eagle hunters.
- **Two weeks** Add on Kochkor (p335), a horse trek to Song-Köl (p339) and a visit to Tash Rabat caravanserai (p346).
- **One month** Conquer the above mentioned areas then head west via either Kyzyl-Oi or Kazarman to Arslanbob (p352) and/or Lake Sary-Chelek (p351). Finally, push south to Osh (p356) and spend a day or two exploring this quintessential Central Asian city. From Osh head overland and out of the country to China, Tajikistan or Uzbekistan.

CLIMATE & WHEN TO GO

Siberian winds bring freezing temperatures and snow from November to February, with ferocious cold in the mountains. The average winter minimum is -24°C.

Throughout the country springtime buds appear in April and May, though nights can still be below freezing. Mid-May to mid-June is pleasant, though many mountain passes will still be snowed in. From the end of June through to mid-August most afternoons will reach 32°C or higher, with a maximum of 40°C in Fergana Valley towns such as Jalal-Abad; mountain valleys are considerably cooler.

Of course in the mountains the 'warm' season is shorter. The best time to visit is July to September, although camping and trekking are pleasant from early June through mid-October. Avalanche danger is greatest during March and April and from September to mid-October.

Overall, the republic is best for scenery and weather in September, with occasional freezing nights in October. See the climate charts, p499, for more details.

HISTORY
Early Civilizations

The earliest recorded residents of what is now Kyrgyzstan were warrior clans of Saka (also known as Scythians), from about the 6th century BC to the 5th century AD. Rich bronze and gold relics have been recovered from Scythian burial mounds at Lake Issyk-Köl and in southern Kazakhstan.

The region was under the control of various Turkic alliances from the 6th to 10th centuries. A sizeable population lived on the shores of Lake Issyk-Köl. The Talas Valley in southern Kazakhstan and northwest Kyrgyzstan was the scene of a pivotal battle in 751, when the Turks and their Arab and Tibetan allies drove a large Tang Chinese army out of Central Asia (see the boxed text, p41).

The cultured Turkic Karakhanids (who finally brought Islam to Central Asia for good) ruled here in the 10th to 12th centuries. One of their multiple capitals was at Balasagun (now Burana, east of Bishkek; see p314). Another major Karakhanid centre was at

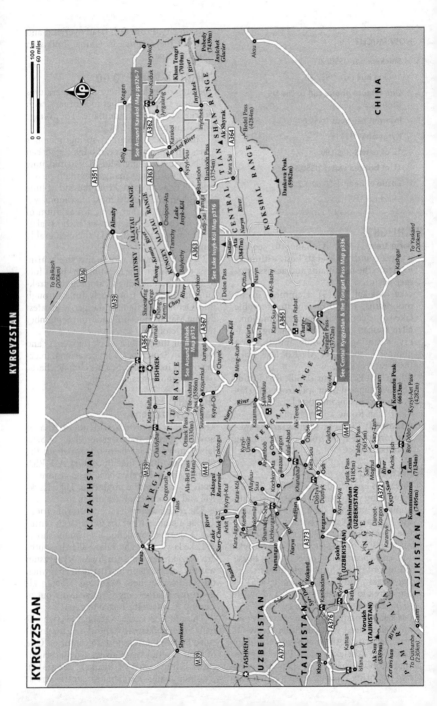

KYRGYZSTAN

CHINA

KAZAKHSTAN

UZBEKISTAN

TAJIKISTAN

0 100 km
0 60 miles

Aksu

To Balkash (200km)

Pobedy (7439m)
Inylchek Glacier

Khan Tengri (7010m)

Inylchek River

Char-Kuduk Narynkol

Jyrgalang

Kegen

CENTRAL TIAN SHAN RANGE

Ak-Shyrak

Bedel Pass (4284m)

See Around Karakol Map pp326-7

A362

Inylchek

ZAILYSKY ALATAU RANGE

Satty

A363

Karakol River

Karakol

Dunkova Peak (5982m)

Barskoön Pass (3754m)

KOKSHAL RANGE

Kyzyl-Suu

Barskoön

A364

Kara Sai

Almaty

Chong-Kemin River

Kadji-Sai Tamga

KÜNGEY ALATAU RANGE

Cholpon-Ata

Lake Issyk-Köl

A363

Tamchy

Naryn River

To Yarkand (200km)

Tastar-Ata (3847m)

Kashgar

See Lake Issyk-Köl Map p316

M36

Shisee A
Gorge

Chong-Kemin

Balykchy

Kochkor

Dolon Pass

Ottuk

Naryn

At-Bashy

See Central Kyrgyzstan & the Torugart Pass Map p336

M39

To Balkash (200km)

Chuy River

A367

Kara-Suu

A365

Tash Rabat

Chatyr-Köl

Toktok

BISHKEK

See Around Bishkek Map p312

A365

Kara-Balta

Shamaldy-Say

A L A T A U   R A N G E

Kojumkul

Jumgal

Chayek

Ming-Kush

Song-Köl

Kurta

Ak-Tal

Kara-Suu

A365

Torugart Pass (3752m)

Korumdu Peak (6613m)

Ozgorush

Tör-Ashuu Pass (3586m)

Suusamyr

Kyzyl-Oi

Naryn River

Sülmaluu Talaa

F E R G A N A

Kök-Art

A370

Irkeshtam

Kyzyl-Art Pass (4282m)

Talas

Ottuk Pass (3330m)

Kazarman

Ak-Terek

Bor-Döbö

Taraz

Ala-Bel Pass (3184m)

K Y R G Y Z   A L A T A U   R A N G E

M41

Toktogul Reservoir

Toktogul

Kyzyl-Köl

Kara-Köl

Kochkor-Ata

Aylanbob

Bazaar Korgon

Jalal-Abad

Osh

Kara-Suu

Gulcha

M41

Sary-Tash

Achik-Tash

R A N G E

Lenin (7134m)

Kommunizma (7495m)

Shymkent

M39

Sary-Chelek

Akit

Kerben

Tashkömür

Kyzyl-Köl

Maylu-Suu

R A N G E

Daroot-Korgon

Karamyk

Lake River

Kara-Jigach

Chatkal

Uchkurgan

Shamaldy-Say

Addhan

Namangan

Fergana

Kochkor-Ata

Ortun

Dostyk

Dustlyk

Shakhimardan (UZBEKISTAN)

Kyzyl-Kiya

Jiptik Pass (4185m)

Sary Moghul

A372

Kyzyl-Suu

Taldyk Pass (3615m)

P A M I R

Zeravshan River

TASHKENT

A373

Syr Darya

Kokand

Sokh (UZBEKISTAN)

Sary Tash (UZBEKISTAN)

Kanibadam

A376

Batken

Vorukh (TAJIKISTAN)

Ak-Suu (5539m)

Khojand

Istana

Zeravshan River

Garm

To Dushanbe (230km)

To Dushanbe (210km)

THE KIDNAPPED BRIDE

Kyrgyz men have a way of sweeping a woman off her feet – off her feet and into a waiting car or taxi, that is. Kidnapping is the traditional way young men find themselves a wife. Although the practice has been illegal since 1991 the custom is once again on the upswing. Some say it's a reassertion of national identity, although many point to the rising cost of wedding celebrations and brides (Kyrgyz women command a 'bride price') – as a well-executed abduction can dramatically slash wedding costs.

An old Kyrgyz adage foretells that tears on the wedding day bodes for a happy marriage, and in some cases it's true – many marriages that begin this way are successful and long lasting. Perhaps this explains why parents of kidnapped daughters consent to the forced marriage when consulted as part of the kidnapping process. Certainly, many of these marriages are also doomed to fail. If the girl is to escape, and some do, it takes a lot of determination and courage to withstand the tremendous amount of pressure that is brought to bear.

For further information and video interviews, check out journalist Petr Lom's excellent report at www.pbs.org/frontlineworld/stories/kyrgyzstan.

Özgön (Uzgen) at the edge of the Fergana Valley.

Ancestors of today's Kyrgyz people probably lived in Siberia's upper Yenisey Basin until at least the 10th century, when, under the influence of Mongol incursions, they began migrating south into the Tian Shan – more urgently with the rise of Chinggis (Genghis) Khan in the 13th century. Present-day Kyrgyzstan was part of the inheritance of Chinggis' second son, Chaghatai.

Peace was shattered in 1685 by the arrival of the ruthless Mongol Oyrats of the Zhungarian empire, who drove vast numbers of Kyrgyz south into the Fergana and Pamir Alay regions and on into present-day Tajikistan. The Manchu (Qing) defeat of the Oyrats in 1758 left the Kyrgyz as de facto subjects of the Chinese, who mainly left the locals to their nomadic ways.

The Russian Occupation

As the Russians moved closer during the 19th century, various Kyrgyz clan leaders made their own peace with either Russia or the neighbouring khanate of Kokand. Bishkek – then comprising only the Pishpek fort – fell in 1862 to a combined Russian-Kyrgyz force and the Kyrgyz were gradually eased into the tsar's provinces of Fergana and Semireche.

The new masters then began to hand land over to Russian settlers, and the Kyrgyz put up with it until a revolt in 1916, centred on Tokmok and heavily put down by the Russian army. Out of a total of 768,000 Kyrgyz, 120,000 were killed in the ensuing massacres and another 120,000 fled to China. Kyrgyz lands

became part of the Turkestan Autonomous Soviet Socialist Republic (Turkestan ASSR) within the Russian Federation in 1918, then a separate Kara-Kyrgyz Autonomous Oblast (an *oblast* is a province or region) in 1924.

Finally, after the Russians had decided Kyrgyz and Kazakhs were separate nationalities (they had until then called the Kyrgyz 'Kara-Kyrgyz' or Black Kyrgyz, to distinguish them from the Kazakhs, whom they called 'Kyrgyz' to avoid confusion with the Cossacks), a Kyrgyz ASSR was formed in February 1926. It became a full Soviet Socialist Republic (SSR) in December 1936, when the region was known as Soviet Kirghizia.

Many nomads were settled in the course of land reforms in the 1920s, and more were forcibly settled during the cruel collectivisation campaign in the 1930s, giving rise to a reinvigorated rebellion by the *basmachi,* Muslim guerrilla fighters, for a time. Vast swathes of the new Kyrgyz elite died in the course of Stalin's purges (see the boxed text, p294).

Remote Kyrgyzstan was a perfect place for secret Soviet uranium mining (at Mayluu-Suu above the Fergana Valley, Ming-Kush in the interior and Kadji-Sai at Lake Issyk-Köl), and also naval weapons development (at the eastern end of Issyk-Köl). Kyrgyzstan is still dealing with the environmental problems the Soviets created, see p297.

Kyrgyz Independence

Elections were held in traditional Soviet rubber-stamp style to the Kyrgyz Supreme Soviet (legislature) in February 1990, with the Kyrgyz Communist Party (KCP) walking away with nearly all the seats. After multiple ballots a compromise candidate, Askar Akaev, a physicist and president of the Kyrgyz Academy of Sciences, was elected as leader. On 31 August 1991, the Kyrgyz Supreme Soviet reluctantly voted to declare Kyrgyzstan's independence, the first Central Asian republic to do so. Six weeks later Akaev was re-elected as president, running unopposed.

In the meantime, land and housing were at the root of Central Asia's most infamous 'ethnic' violence between Kyrgyz and Uzbeks in 1990 around Osh and Özgön, a majority-Uzbek area stuck onto Kyrgyzstan in the 1930s (p355), during which at least 300 people were killed.

Akaev initially established himself as a persistent reformer, restructuring the executive apparatus to suit his liberal political and economic attitudes, and instituting reforms considered the most radical in the Central Asian republics.

In the late 1990s the country faced a new threat – Islamic radicals and terrorism. In 1999 and 2000 militants from the Islamic Movement of Uzbekistan (IMU; based in Tajikistan) staged a series of brazen kidnappings of foreign workers and climbers in the province of Batken. Kyrgyz security forces largely contained the threat while IMU leadership fell to US bombs in Afghanistan.

The Tulip Revolution

By the early 2000s, Kyrgyzstan's democratic credentials were once again backsliding in the face of growing corruption, nepotism and civil unrest. The 2005 parliamentary elections were plagued by accusations of harassment and government censure. Demonstrators stormed governmental buildings in Jalal-Abad and civil unrest soon spread to Osh and Bishkek. On 24 March the relatively peaceful Tulip Revolution effectively overthrew the government amid bouts of looting and vandalism. President Akaev fled by helicopter to Kazakhstan and on to Moscow – subsequently resigning and becoming a university lecturer. New presidential elections were held in July 2005; the opposition leader and former prime minister, Kurmanbek Bakiev, swept to victory.

The Bakiev Era

Bakiev's first term in office was hardly a bed of tulips. The one-time opposition leader soon faced the same criticisms levelled at his predecessor – corruption and abuse of power. Wide-scale street demonstrations in 2006 and 2007 forced him into concessions that curbed his presidential power. Bakiev's promises of peace and security were also derailed by a spate of high-profile political assassinations – three members of parliament were murdered in the late 2000s.

Bakiev was re-elected in July 2009 amid widespread accusations of ballot rigging and media censure. Voters, unable to unseat Bakiev with the ballot, reverted to a tried and true method of overthrowing Kyrgyz leaders – revolution. On 6 and 7 April 2010, opposition crowds massed in Talas and Bishkek. In what was intended to be a demonstration against the government turned into a riot in both cities. Security forces were overwhelmed and the protestors stormed the halls of government. By the end of the day some 88 people had been killed and more than 500 injured in the fighting.

Bakiev fled, first to southern Kyrgyzstan, then Kazakhstan and finally to Belarus. The Kyrgyz opposition set up an interim government with Roza Otombayeva as its new leader. Maintaining order became a major priority for

---

SOVIET SECRETS

The town of Chong-Tash, 10km from Kashka-Suu village, holds a dark secret. On one night in 1937, the entire Soviet Kyrgyz government – nearly 140 people in all – were rounded up, brought here and shot dead, and their bodies dumped in a disused brick kiln on the site. Apparently almost no one alive by the 1980s knew of this, by which time the site had been converted to a ski resort. But a watchman at the time of the murders, sworn to secrecy, told his daughter on his deathbed, and she waited until *perestroika* to tell police.

In 1991 the bodies were moved to a mass grave across the road, with a simple memorial, apparently paid for by the Kyrgyz author Chinghiz Aitmatov (whose father may have been one of the victims). The remains of the kiln are inside a fence nearby.

Minibuses 365 runs daily to Chong-Tash from the Osh Bazaar bus stands in Bishkek.

OSH RIOTS

The ethnic tensions that simmer underneath the streets of Osh – dormant since the bloody Özgön riots of 1990 – boiled over once again on 9 June, 2010. Precisely how the fighting got underway is a matter of contention but no one debates the speed at which the violence progressed. Within a day Osh was burning and scores of bodies lay in the streets. The violence soon spread to Jalal-Abad. Five days of rioting left nearly 200 people dead and some 200,000 others displaced, mainly women, children and the elderly. Uzbekistan allowed half of these refugees across the border before closing the gates. The interim government in Bishkek, which had come to power in a bloody coup just months earlier, lost control of Osh and pleaded with the international community to send peacekeeping troops. As it went, the violence was quelled on its own accord, the rioters simply too exhausted to continue. As we went to press the situation remained tense, with thousands of refugees still seeking safety at the border. Southern Kyrgyzstan will likely remain a tinderbox for some time – check the situation before heading this way.

---

the new government. On 19 May 2010 tensions flared at a private university in Jalabad where communal violence between Uzbeks and Kyrgyz led to two deaths and scores of injuries.

Where Bakiev goes from here remains unclear. Certainly he won't be returning to Kyrgyzstan any time soon, unless he is extradited and put on trial over the deaths of the April 2010 riots. In the meantime the former president watches his country from afar in Minsk.

CURRENT EVENTS

Despite the controversy surrounding Bakiev's domestic policies, he is credited with successfully navigating a geopolitical tightrope between China, Russia and the US. At the heart of the matter is the controversial rental of Manas airport by the United States Air Force. It is from here that the US conducts sorties to Afghanistan, supplying both cargo and fuel.

The US lease on the airstrip expired in 2009 and at the behest of Moscow was not immediately renewed. The US managed to keep its foothold in Central Asia but only after agreeing to a new rental price of US$63 million (up from US$17.4 million). Not to be outdone, Russia also operates an air base at Kant, 20km east of Bishkek.

Kyrgyzstan maintains good relations with its neighbour to the east, China, evinced by heavy trade that plies over the Torugart Pass (China is Kyrgyzstan's biggest trading partner). To the north, Kazakhstan is both figurative and literal big brother to Kyrgyzstan. Cultural and political links are strong between the countries and the two economies are joined at the hip – Kazakhstan owns 40% of the banks in Kyrgyzstan. Only Uzbekistan

remains something of a loose end, with an on-going war of words over water and energy usage.

The global economic downturn caused hardship for thousands of traders in Bishkek's Dordoy bazaar but the national economy has managed to limp along, thanks in part to rising gold prices. The Canadian-owned Kumtor mine, one of the world's largest, pumps out 20 tonnes of gold a year.

Simmering beneath the surface of all this is a palpable sense of ethnic tension. Kyrgyzstan's mountains effectively isolate the country's northern and southern population centres from one another, especially in winter. The geographically isolated southern provinces of Osh and Jalal-Abad have more in common with the conservative, Islamised Fergana Valley than with the industrialised, Russified north. Ancient but still-important clan affiliations reinforce these regional differences and surveys show that a majority of Kyrgyz people believe the north–south cultural divisions are the main destabilising factor within society.

PEOPLE

There are approximately 80 ethnic groups in Kyrgyzstan; the principle ethnicities being Kyrgyz (66%), Uzbek (14%) and Russian (10%). Notable minorities include the Dungan, Ukrainian and Uyghur peoples. The Kyrgyz are outnumbered almost two to one by their livestock and about two-thirds of the population lives in rural areas.

Since 1989 there has been a major exodus of Slavs and Germans – with tens of thousands returning to their countries of ancestry. Most cite the dearth of job prospects and continued economic hardship as the main reason for leaving. Many fear that the steady stream of departing skilled workers and educated professionals will have dire effects on the economy.

Kyrgyz (with Kazakhs) in general, while probably the most Russified of Central Asian people, are adapting to 21st-century trends. While Russian is still the lingua franca, young people are increasingly learning European languages, English and Mandarin. About one fifth of working adults are overseas, sending home remittances from Russia and elsewhere.

For more on the Kyrgyz people refer to p63.

RELIGION

Like the Kazakhs, the Kyrgyz adopted Islam relatively late and limited it to what could fit in their saddlebags. Northern Kyrgyz are more Russified and less observant of Muslim doctrine than their cousins in the south (in Jalal-Abad and Osh provinces). One consequence of this is the high number of young women in hip-hugging jeans on the streets of Bishkek with nary a headscarf between them.

Dwindling communities of Russian Orthodox Christians are still visible, particularly in Bishkek and Karakol, both of which have Orthodox cathedrals.

ARTS
Literature

Central Asian literature has traditionally been popularised in the form of songs, poems and stories by itinerant minstrels or bards, called *akyn* in Kyrgyz. Among better-known 20th-century Kyrgyz *akyns* are Togolok Moldo (whose real name is Bayymbet Abdyrakhmanov), Sayakbay Karalayev and Sagymbay Orozbakov.

Kyrgyzstan's best-known author is Chinghiz Aitmatov (1928–2008), whose works have been translated into English, German and French. Among his novels, which are also revealing looks at Kyrgyz life and culture, are *Djamila* (1967), *The White Steamship* (1970), *Early Cranes* (1975) and *Piebald Dog Running Along the Shore* (1978), the latter was made into a prize-winning Russian film in 1990.

MANAS

The *Manas* epic is a cycle of oral legends, 20 times longer than the *Odyssey*, which tells of the formation of the Kyrgyz people through the exploits of a hero-of-heroes called Manas.

Acclaimed as one of the finest epic traditions, this '*Iliad* of the steppes' is the high point of a widespread Central Asian oral culture.

The *Manas* narrative revolves around Manas, the khan, or *batyr* (heroic warrior), and his exploits in carving out a homeland for his people in the face of hostile hordes. Subsequent stories deal with the exploits of his son Semety and grandson Seitek.

Manas actually predates the Kyrgyz in the same sense that Achilles or Agamemnon predate the Greeks. The stories are part of a wider, older tradition that have come to be associated with the Kyrgyz people and culture. The epic was first written down in the mid-19th century by Kazakh ethnographer Chokan Valikhanov.

Akyns who can recite or improvise from the epics are in a class by themselves, called *manaschi*. According to tradition, bona fide *manaschi* find their role in life after a long illness or life-changing dream. Since independence, the *Manas* epic has become a cultural rallying point for the Kyrgyz. Legend has even assigned Manas a tomb, located near Talas and supposedly built by his wife Kanykey, where Muslim pilgrims come to pray.

Other Arts

Kyrgyzstan's Aktan Abdykalykov is one of Central Asia's most accomplished filmmakers. His 1998 bittersweet coming-of-age *Beshkempir* (The Adopted Son) was released to critical acclaim and *Maimil* (The Chimp) received an honourable mention at Cannes in 2001. Both are well worth viewing.

Tengri: Blue Heavens (2008) is a French-made film that follows the romantic pairing of a down-on-his-luck Kazakh fisherman with a Kyrgyz widow, set and shot in Kyrgyzstan.

Kyrgyz traditional music is played on a mixture of two-stringed *komuz* guitars, a vertical violin known as a *kyl kyayk,* flutes, drums, mouth harps (*temir komuz,* or *jygach ooz* with a string) and long horns.

Pop and rap music sung in both Russian and Kyrgyz are popular among young urbanites. Look out for CDs by pop singers Aya Sadykova and Sezdbek Iskenaliev and rapper Tata Ulan, all of whom mix traditional lyrics about their homeland with 21st-century beats.

ENVIRONMENT
The Land

Kyrgyzstan is a bit larger than Austria plus Hungary; 94% of the country is mountain-

COMMUNITY BASED TOURISM

Thanks to several innovative Kyrgyz grassroots organisations, it is seriously easy for travellers to scramble over the cultural divide and rub shoulders with the locals.

Shepherd's Life and Community Based Tourism (CBT) are the two programs you'll hear being bandied about most often and there is considerable overlap in the services they provide. In a nutshell, both connect tourists with a wider network of guides, drivers and families willing to take in guests, either in villages or *jailoos* (summer pastures), across the country. You can use the network of information offices to organise anything from a comfortable homestay to a fully supported horse trek. Because each office is independently run, the level of service varies but standout CBT offices can be found in Arslanbob (p353), Karakol (p320), Kochkor (p336) and Naryn (p340).

Other CBT offices include Tamchy (p316), Bokonbayevo (p332), Kazarman (p344), Osh (p358), Talas (p350) and Sary Moghul (p362) – see those entries for more details.

Homestays are ranked from one to three edelweiss and generally cost around 350som to 500som per day for bed and breakfast and 100som per additional meal. Depending on the quality and availability of local restaurants, it is often cheaper to eat out. Horse hire is 400som to 500som per day and guides range from 400som to 1000som per day. A car and driver costs 9som to 11som per kilometre, though this is dependent on the price of fuel. It's worth picking up a copy of the *CBT Guidebook* (170som, or download it for free from www.cbtkyrgyzstan.kg) that lists each office's services, a description of local trips and useful town maps.

Shepherd's Life is cheaper than CBT, slightly less organised and has five coordinators, in Kochkor (p337), Jumgal (p339), Naryn (p341), At-Bashy (p345) and Kurtka (near Ak-Tal; p343).

For an overview of these organisations' aims and objectives, see p106.

ous. The country's average elevation is 2750m with 40% over 3000m high and three-quarters of that under permanent snow and glaciers.

The dominant feature is the Tian Shan range in the southeast. Its crest, the dramatic Kokshal-Tau, forms a stunning natural border with China, culminating at Pik Pobedy (7439m), Kyrgyzstan's highest point and the second-highest peak in the former USSR. The Fergana range across the middle of the country and the Pamir Alay in the south hold the Fergana Valley in a scissor-grip.

In a vast indentation on the fringes of the Tian Shan, Lake Issyk-Köl, almost 700m deep, never freezes due to its high salinity. Kyrgyzstan's only significant lowland features are the Chuy and Talas Valleys.

Its main rivers are the Naryn, flowing almost the full length of the country into the Syr-Darya in the Fergana Valley, and the Chuy along the Kazakhstan border.

Wildlife

Kyrgyzstan offers an annual refuge for thousands of migrating birds, including rare cranes and geese. The country is believed to have had the world's second-largest snow leopard population, although numbers are declining rapidly. Issyk-Köl and Sary-Chelek lakes are Unesco-affiliated biosphere reserves.

Environmental Issues

At the end of the Soviet era there were an estimated 14 million sheep in Kyrgyzstan. Since then flock numbers have been privatised and divided. Economic hardship, a loss of effective management and a lack of governmental infrastructure have seen flocks numbers dwindle to about six million.

Individuals lack the means for covering shepherds' wages, meeting transport costs or maintaining infrastructure (eg bridges) that would allow these small flocks to travel to traditional *jailoos*. This in turn has resulted in serious undergrazing of mountain pastures leading to a succession of foreign plant invasions. Meanwhile pastures near villages are ironically overgrazed, leading to degraded fields prone to soil erosion.

Uranium for the Soviet nuclear military machine was mined in Kyrgyzstan (the Kyrgyz SSR's uranium sector earned the sobriquet 'Atomic Fortress of the Tian Shan'), and a number of abandoned mine sites threaten to leak their radioactive contents into rivers and groundwater. Independent Kyrgyzstan has closed most of the mines and institutes and begun to grapple with the environmental problems they created.

Kyrgyzstan's faced its biggest environmental disaster in 1998 when almost 2 tonnes of cyanide and sodium hydrochloride destined for the Kumtor gold mine spilled into the Barskoön River and thence Issyk-Köl. Several people reportedly died, hundreds sought medical treatment, and thousands were evacuated.

The country's reserves of fresh water, locked up in the form of glaciers, remain its greatest natural resource. But these are shrinking and a UN climate study predicts that at the current pace of retreat, the number of glaciers will fall from 8200 to just 150 in 40 years. The loss of Kyrgyzstan's glaciers could result in drought, desertification and crop failure here and also in neighbouring countries.

FOOD & DRINK

Spicy *laghman* (noodle) dishes reign supreme, partly the result of Dungan (Muslim Chinese) influence. Apart from standard Central Asian dishes (p85), *beshbarmak* (literally 'five fingers', since it is traditionally eaten by hand) is a special holiday dish consisting of large flat noodles topped with lamb and/or horsemeat cooked in vegetable broth. *Kesme* is a thick noodle soup with small bits of potato, vegetable and meat. *Jurkop* is a braised meat and vegetable dish with noodles.

Hoshan are fried and steamed dumplings, similar to *manty* (stuffed dumplings), best right off the fire from markets. Horsemeat sausages known as *kazy, karta* or *chuchuk* are a popular vodka chaser, as in Kazakhstan.

In Dungan areas (eg Karakol or certain suburbs of Bishkek), ask for *ashlyanfu*, made with cold noodles, jelly, vinegar and eggs. Also try their steamed buns made with *jusai*, a mountain grass of the onion family, and *fyntyozi*, spicy cold rice noodles. *Gyanfan* is rice with a meat and vegetable sauce.

Kymys (fermented mare's milk), available in spring and early summer, is the national drink. *Bozo* is a thick fizzy drink made from boiled fermented millet or other grains. *Jarma* and *maksym* are fermented barley drinks, made with yeast and yoghurt. Shoro is the brand name of a similar drink, available at most street corners in Bishkek. All four, and tea, are washed down with *boorsok* (fried bits of dough). *Kurut* (small balls of tart, dried yoghurt) are a favourite snack.

Tea is traditionally made very strong in a pot and mixed with boiling water and milk in a bowl before serving.

BISHKEK БИШКЕК

☎ 312 / pop 900,000 / elev 800m

The green, quiet and laid-back Kyrgyz capital seems to be the perfect introduction to the mountain republic. The entire downtown feels like one big park, with trees sprouting from every crack in the concrete. The Kyrgyz Ala-Too range creates a magnificent backdrop and their glacial melt pours through the city centre in gurgling troughs. The low-rise Soviet-era buildings and odd Lenin or Frunze statue lend a time warp ambience that is quaint, if not a little drab.

Daytime commerce is brisk across Bishkek and you'll find modern shopping malls, heaving bazaars and fast-flowing traffic. It's a great place for walking, but apart from a couple of museums there are few headline attractions. Nightlife is fairly tame, especially if you've just arrived from Almaty, with the only real action a PG-rated water fountain sound-and-light show in Ala-Too Square. For the traveller, Bishkek is more than anything a place to unwind after a long trek, dine in some good restaurants and pick up a visa or two.

Despite its mellow exterior, Bishkek does have an underlying edge that occasionally flares up. Residents are highly politicised and violent demonstrations seem to flare up every few years. The edgy atmosphere is reflected in the numerous NGOs that have set up shop here, using Bishkek as a listening post for the rest of Central Asia. Throw in the US servicemen at nearby Manas airport and you've got plenty to gab about with the locals.

Bishkek may not thrill at first glance, but the main sites – its parks and the national museum – are easily visited in a day or two, making this is a good place to start or end the Kyrgyz leg of your Central Asian odyssey.

HISTORY

In 1825, by a Silk Road settlement on a tributary of the Chuy River, the Uzbek khan of Kokand built a little clay fort, one of several along caravan routes through the Tian Shan mountains. In 1862 the Russians captured and wrecked it, and set up a garrison of their own. The town of Pishpek was founded 16 years later, swelled by Russian peasants lured by land grants and the Chuy Valley's fertile black earth.

In 1926 the town, rebaptised Frunze, became capital of the new Kyrgyz ASSR. The name never sat well; Mikhail Frunze (who was born here) was the Russian Civil War commander who helped keep tsarist Central Asia in Bolshevik hands and hounded the *basmachi* rebellion into the mountains.

In 1991 the city became Bishkek, the Kyrgyz form of its old Kazakh name. A *pishpek* or *bishkek* is a churn for *kymys*. Numerous legends (some quaint, some rude) explain how it came to be named for a wooden plunger. Others conclude disappointingly that this was simply the closest familiar sound to its old Sogdian name, Peshagakh, meaning 'place below the mountains'. With the 4800m, permanently snow-capped rampart of the Kyrgyz Ala-Too range looming over it, the Sogdian name still fits.

ORIENTATION
Bishkek sits on the northern hem of the Kyrgyz Ala-Too mountains, an arm of the Tian Shan. Nineteenth-century military planners laid out an orderly, compass-oriented town and getting around is quite easy.

East–west Jibek Jolu prospektesi (Silk Road Ave), just north of the centre, was old Pishpek's main street. Now the municipal axes are Chuy and parklike north–south Erkindik. The busiest commercial streets are Kiev and Soviet (Abdurakhmanov). At the centre yawns Ala-Too Sq, flanked by Panfilov and Dubovy (Oak) Parks. Street numbers increase as you head north or west.

Most street signs now indicate the new Kyrgyz names but many locals may still use the old Soviet-era names. Confusion reigns supreme and the only thing you can do is try to bear in mind both names when looking for an address or getting directions.

Maps
Geoid (☎ 61 38 69; geoid@land.ru; Kiev 107; ☷ 8am-5pm Mon-Fri, 9am-3pm Sat-Sun) sells Bishkek city maps in Cyrillic, as well as trekking and 1:200,000 topo maps (from 140som). For more on maps see p368. The entrance to the shop is around the west side of this oddly shaped building.

INFORMATION
Bookshops
Raritet (☎ 66 72 21; Pushkin 78) It has a limited selection of English-language titles (including the *Manas* epic), plus maps and guidebooks. Located in the basement of the Dom Druzhby, enter from the west side of the building.

Emergency
Ambulance (☎ 103)
Fire (☎ 101)
Police (☎ 102)

Internet Access
Internet cafes are fairly common in Bishkek but connections tend to be slow. Expect to be charged for both minutes and megabytes. **In-tel Internet** (☎ 66 05 56; Kiev 92; per hr 40som; ☷ 8am-11pm) Also offers cheap internet phone calls. **Skynet** (Manas 59; per hr 40som; ☷ 7am-midnight) One of several internet cafes along this strip.

Laundry
Most hotels offer laundry service at reasonable rates; if not try the following option. **Novosti Laundry** (☎ 43 36 25; Moskva 2; ☷ 8am-6pm Mon-Sat, 9am-1pm un) Washes clothes for 60som per kg. Pick up the next day or add 50som for same day service.

Medical Services
Pharmacies are marked *darykhana* (Kyrgyz) or *apteka* (Russian) and there is a 24-hour one on the north side of the Hyatt; the **Metro-pol** (☎ 68 10 05; Soviet 340; ☷ 24hr). **Kyrgyz Republic Hospital** (☎ outpatients 22 89 60, 24hr emergencies & hospital ambulance 26 69 16; Kiev 110) Also known as State Clinic No 2, this is probably the best bet for medical attention. Bring an interpreter. **Tsadmir** (☎ 65 95 77, 0555-651 814; Moskva 225) Clinic; go here if you need a rabies shot.

KYRGYZSTAN

BISHKEK

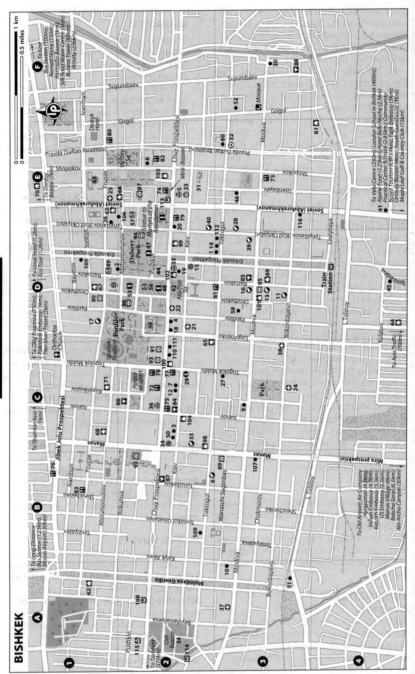

Meerim (☎ 66 40 69; Bokonbayev 144A) Recommended dentist.

Kyrgyz-German Medical Centre (☎ 90 00 20; Chuy 122; ☺ 9am-6pm Mon-Fri, 9am-3pm Sat) General medical services in a central location.

Money

There are exchange desks all over Bishkek, including most hotels. ATMs are found at most banks and some shopping centres including Beta Stores.

Kazkommertsbank (☎ 69 03 83; Soviet 136; ☺ 9am-6pm Mon-Fri, 9am-3pm Sat) Has two ATMs outside and another by the left (west) exit of TsUM department store and outside Central Asia Tourism Corporation. All accept foreign cards with a 2% commission. This bank handles payments for the Kazakh visa in US dollars.

Post

American Resources International (ARI; ☎ 66 00 77; bishkek@aricargo.com; Erkindik 35) Ships large items if you are moving to/from Bishkek.

KYRGYZSTAN

DHL (☎ 61 11 11; www.dhl.com; Kiev 107)
FedEx (☎ 65 00 12; www.fedex.com; Moskva 217)
Main post office (Soviet; ☷ 7am-8pm Mon-Sat, 8am-7pm Sun) There is a separate mailroom for EMS (Express Mail Service), between the post and telecom offices.

Registration & Visas

A couple of different offices handle visa registration and extensions.

Ministry of Foreign Affairs (☎ 66 32 70; Togolok Moldo 10A; ☷ 9-11am, 4-4.30pm Mon-Tue & Thu-Fri) If you are working or studying in Kyrgyzstan this is the place to come for visa extensions. An extension costs US$50 plus a US$10 processing fee for a total of US$60. It takes 10 days to process a visa. The extension begins at the end of your current visa (not from the day you apply).

Office of Visas & Registrations (OVIR; Kiev 58; ☷ 9.30am-12.30pm & 2-5pm Mon-Fri) Most Western nationals do not require registration, but if you do need to register, inquire at this office or ask your hotel, as your place of residency determines where you need to register.

Police Department (☎ 48 64 28; cnr Sultan Ibraimov & Toktogul; ☷ 8.30am-noon & 1.30-5pm Mon-Fri) Handles visa extensions for most travellers. Bring a copy of your passport and 1085som. One-month extensions are given in one day. The extension starts from the day you apply.

Telephone & Fax

Central telecom office (cnr Soviet & Chuy; ☷ 7am-10pm) Also provides international fax service. There are smaller telephone offices on the corners of Chuy and Erkindik, and Chuy and Isanov.

TRAFFIC JAM

Some internet cafes and hotels in Bishkek and elsewhere in the country charge a 'traffic' fee on top of your per hour use fee. This is a charge for each megabyte you use while surfing the web.

The charge is reasonable if you are just checking email but rises steeply if you start surfing around different websites, upload photos or watch videos. You never really know what you are going to pay until you get the bill.

If you need to do a lot of uploading and downloading of content, shop around for an internet cafe that charges a flat per hour fee. If you are using your own laptop make sure to quit any programs (such as iTunes) that might download content while you happily check your email.

Tourist Information

Community Based Tourism (CBT; ☎ 54 00 69, 44 33 31; www.cbtkyrgyzstan.kg; Gorky 58; ☷ 9am-6pm Mon-Fri) Gives information on CBT groups across the country (see p106) and sells the *CBT Guidebook* (170som), which outlines services available at each office. The office is just past the Tash Rabat shopping mall, on the opposite side of the street.
NoviNomad (☎ 62 23 81; www.novinomad.com; Togolok Moldo 28) Has a noticeboard for contacting other travellers and is an invaluable source of regional information. Recommended.

Travel Agencies

The following agencies can book flights, arrange transport and help with the logistics of getting around the country.

Carlson Wagonlit (☎ 66 61 02; Toktogul 93) Sells air tickets and offers visa support for Kazakhstan.
Central Asia Tourism Corporation (CAT; ☎ 66 36 64; www.cat.kg; Chuy 124) Visa support, rental cars, air tickets, accommodation and inclusive tours.
Glavtour (☎ 66 32 32; www.glavtour.kg; Toktogul 93) Books flights; the website lists airfares from Bishkek. Visa cards accepted.
Kyrgyz Concept (☎ 66 60 06, 903 202; www.concept.kg; Chuy 126) Kyrgyz Concept has several offices; this is the one to go to for booking flights and transport. It also runs a daily bus to Almaty airport. Book ahead.

DANGERS & ANNOYANCES

Bishkek smiles during the day but is neither safe nor well lit after dark. At this time, all the normal Central Asian security rules apply (p500). If you're out after dark, stick to main streets, avoid the parks and steer clear of the area around the train station.

Crooked plain-clothed policemen are a problem in Bishkek, particularly at Osh Bazaar. We've heard reports of some demanding your passport and trying to look in your bag and searching your money. Legally you are required to carry your passport at all times but it's always worth trying to give them only a copy. If your passport is at an embassy, then get the embassy to write this on a photocopy of your passport.

SIGHTS
Ala-Too Square

This sea of concrete ceased to be called Lenin Square in 1991. Lenin enjoyed centre stage on his plinth until 2003, when he was relegated to the square behind the museum and replaced by (yet) another statue of Erkindik (Freedom). During the hot summer afternoons the fountains in the square attract locals hoping to soak in the cool mist. Every evening at 9pm (winter 8pm) throngs of people gather here to watch the fountains dance to a coordinated sound and light show.

The **State Historical Museum** (adult/student 150/75som; �9am-1pm & 2-7pm Tue-Sun) is an archaic and creaky repository of yurts, carpets, embroidery and open-air *balbals* (Turkic totemlike gravestones). The star attraction, however, is the mural-cum-shrine to Lenin and the Revolution upstairs. This over-the-top installation features some impressive faux-bronze sculptures charting the Bolshevik uprising scene-by-scene. On the top floor, the charming permanent photo-exhibition of life on the steppe is a great intro to the countryside.

The unmarked marble palace full of chan-deliered offices just west of the square, the **'White House'**, is the seat of the Kyrgyzstan government and the president's office. Behind this is **Panfilov Park**, full of rusting rides and arcades.

The conspicuously older structure north-east of Ala-Too Sq at Pushkin 68 was the headquarters of the Central Committee of the Kyrgyz ASSR, declared in 1926. It's now home to the **Dom Druzhby** community centre for advocacy and self-help groups.

Beyond this is **Dubovy (Oak) Park**, full of strollers on warm Sundays, a few open-air cafes, some neglected modern sculpture and, funnily enough, century-old oaks. Where **Erkindik prospektesi** (Freedom Ave) enters the park, there is an open-air art gallery. Nearby is the Erkindik (Freedom) Statue, formerly a statue of Felix Dzerzhinsky, founder of the Soviet secret police.

State Museum of Fine Arts

This **museum** (☎ 66 15 44; Soviet 196; adult/student 50/25som; �9am-5pm), also called the Gapar Aitiev Museum of Applied Art, features Kyrgyz embroidery, jewellery, utensils, eye-popping felt rugs, works by local artists, and a startling collection of reproduction Egyptian and classical statues.

Frunze House-Museum

Mikhail Vasilievich Frunze (1885–1925) was born in what was then Pishpek and later moved onto Moscow where he commanded the Red Guards during the 1917 Revolution. He then led the Bolshevik forces that seized

Khiva and Bukhara in 1920. This modest **museum** (☎ 66 06 07; Frunze 364; admission 40som; ☀10am-5.30pm Wed-Mon) contains the thatched hut in which he was allegedly born. The hut is most likely a recreation but it does give you an idea of pastoral life in Tsarist Russia.

Victory Square

This sun-bleached plaza with an immense yurt-shaped **WWII monument**, erected on the 40th anniversary of the end of the war, sprawls across an entire city block. On cold evenings you might see a knot of young men passing the bottle and warming themselves at its eternal flame. On weekends it's yet another destination for the endless stream of happy wedding parties.

The nearby Circus on Frunze, that once played to packed houses in Soviet times, looks like a 1950s UFO that crash landed and never had the impetus to move again.

Manas Village

In the south of town, the **Manas Village** (Mira; per person 10som; ☀10am-6pm) was built in 1995 in honour of the 1000th anniversary of the epic Manas tale. Today it's a weedy park of concrete monuments that depict Kyrgyz symbols (hats, horses etc) in contemporary fashion. Climb the tower for nice views of the city and mountains. It's fairly desolate on weekdays so time your visit for a weekend when the wedding parties roll through for a photo shoot. Note that most locals mistakenly call it 'Manas Ordo' although the real Manas Ordo is near Talas (p350). It's located behind the Issyk-Kul Hotel.

Markets

The city has three daily farmers markets, all fairly distant from the centre. **Osh Bazaar**, 3km to the west on Chuy, though not very colourful, offers a glimpse of Kyrgyz and Uzbeks from the more conservative south of the republic. Produce is sold inside the main bazaar and all around the outside of the complex. There is a separate clothes market south of the main produce bazaar. To get there take trolleybus 14 on Chuy, bus 20 or 24 on Kiev, or 42 from Soviet.

Smaller markets include the **Alamedin Bazaar**, 2.5km to the northeast (trolleybus 7 or 9 from TsUM, return by bus 20 or 38), and **Ortosay Bazaar**, 6km to the south (trolleybus 12 on Soviet). All are open daily but are biggest on weekends.

Dordoy Bazaar is Central Asia's biggest market of imported goods (mostly from China), that are sold off and shipped around the region. It's open daily and busiest on Sundays. The market is about 7km north of the centre; buses 185, 132, 25 and 200 go here from the northern corner of Soviet and Chuy.

ACTIVITIES
Baths
Buy tickets for the **Zhirgal Banya** (cnr Sultan Ibraimov & Toktogul; bath 80som; ☻8am-9pm) from the *kassa* (ticket office) around the side. Start with the sauna, then jump into an ice-cold pool. For an extra 200som an attendant will lather you up, scrub you down and hose you off, which is about at kinky as things get in Central Asia. Birch branches are available free of charge for those into a bit of self-flogging.

Swimming & Fitness
Karven Club (☎ 68 12 18; Toktogul 77; ☻7am-9.30pm) The outdoor swimming pool is a godsend on the blazingly hot days of August. It has a modern fitness centre too. One hour of use costs 400som or it's 500som all day.

Other Activities
Just to the south of the city, you can ski, hike, mountain bike or picnic in the mountains. For the low-down on skiing see p313 or for white-water rafting options see p314. Contact a tour operator (p304) or trekking company to help with logistics. Some of the Bishkek trekking companies (p304) also organise these activities.

COURSES
LANGUAGE
The **London School in Bishkek** (☎ 54 52 62; www.tlsbi.com; Soviet 39) offers Kyrgyz and Russian language classes (per hour 140som). Schedules are flexible.

The **Practical Center Bishkek** (☎ 595 180, 0555-550 557; www.centerpcb.com; Bldg 4, Ahunbaev 129) has one-month language classes (Russian, Kyrgyz, Chinese, among others) for 1600som.

TOURS
Myriad tour operators can whisk you out of the capital and into Kyrgyzstan's furthest hinterlands. Try the following.
Celestial Mountains (☎ 31 18 14; www.celestial.com.kg; Kiev 131-4) British-run agency that runs excellent cultural tours and overland trips. Experienced in handling

the run over Torugart Pass and can offer visa support for China and Central Asian countries. Runs a hotel in Naryn. Contact Ian Claytor.
Ecotour (☎ 46 08 03, 0772-802 805; www.ecotour.kg; Donskoy 46A) Ecofriendly and flexible with budget demands. Stay in traditional yurts with solar-heated water and small hydroelectric turbines at Temir Kanat, Ak-Sai, Song-Köl, Tuura-Su and Jeti-Öghuz for €35 per night (includes three meals and horse riding). Contact English-speaking Elmira or German-speaking Zamira.
Kyrgyz Concept (☎ 90 08 66; www.concept.kg; Tynystanov 231) Kyrgyzstan's biggest tour operator offers cultural tours, visa support, horse treks and homestays, and is flexible with budget demands. It has several offices (including one on Kiev) but this one focuses on tours.
London School in Bishkek (☎ 54 52 62; bishkeksch ool@gmail.com; Sovietskaya 39) Offers short excursions (two days to a week) around the country with horse riding and yurtstays. Trips start from 2500som. Contact Kendje.
Maison du Voyageurs (☎ 66 63 30; Moskva 122) Organises flexible, general-interest trips throughout Kyrgyzstan and neighbouring countries for small groups. French-speaking guides available. Located on the corner of Orozbekov.
NoviNomad (☎ 62 23 81; www.novinomad.com; Togolok Moldo 28) An excellent operator for cultural tours, Torugart trips and trekking and translating services. Can book CBT and yurt-camp accommodation across the country.

TREKKING & MOUNTAINEERING
Other tour operators specialise in trekking, mountaineering, biking, rafting and other adventure sports. Check the following options.
Ak Sai (☎ 59 17 59; www.ak-sai.com; Soviet 65) Operates base camps at Inylchek, Achik Tash and Karavshin, and the Red Fox camping store (p309).
Alpine Fund (☎ 47 16 35, 0555-722 817; www.alpinefund.org; room 502, Ahunbaev 119A) This non-profit organisation, established to assist Kyrgyz youth, runs weekend hikes and climbs in Ala-Archa National Park, including overnight summit attempts on Peak Uchityel (4572m). It also rents trekking gear. Located on the corner of Tynystanov.
Asia Mountains (☎ 69 02 35; www.asiamountains.net; Lineynaya 1A) A well-organised agency charging US$25 to US$55 per person per day, depending on the program. Can get border permits for the Central Tian Shan, even if you're not trekking with them. Runs a base camp at Achik Tash (US$30 including three meals) and a guesthouse in Bishkek (p306).
Dostuck Trekking (☎ 54 54 55, 50 38 02; www.dostuck.com.kg; Igemberdieva 42-1) Offers ascents to peaks, including Khan Tengri, Pobedy and Lenin, as well as less specialised, fixed date treks including yurt camps in

the Suusamyr Valley and Tash Rabat' to Kyrgyzstan. Can arrange helicopter transport and border permits. To find the office from Soviet St, walk 450m west on Gorky, turn right on Aktubinsky Lane (at School 29), the road curves to the left and then take the first left; look for the orange gate.

Edelweiss (☎ 43 20 04; www.edelweiss.elcat.kg; Usenbayev 68/9) Trekking, mountaineering, heli-skiing, horse tours, ski trips and visa support. Contact Slava Alexandrov.

International Mountaineering Camp Pamir (IMC Pamir; ☎ 31 14 72; www.imcpamir.com; Apt 30, Kiev 133) Operates the Achik Tash base camp at the foot of Peak Lenin. Contact Bekbolot Koshoev.

ITMC Tien-Shan (☎ 65 14 04; www.itmc.centralasia.kg; Molodaya Gvardia 1A) Adventure-travel operator with base camps at Khan Tengri, Achik Tash (Pik Lenin) and Koh-i-Samani (Kommunizma); trekking; heli-skiing; mountain biking; and crossing the Torugart. Not to be confused with its former partner at Tien-Shan Travel.

Tien Shan Travel (☎ 46 60 34; www.tien-shan.com; Sherbekov 127) Experienced mountaineering and trekking company with a raft of tour options, but unaccustomed to walk-in clients. Contact Vladimir Birukov.

Top Asia (☎ /fax 66 62 18; www.topasia.kg; Panfilov 183) Trekking outfit with a yurt camp at Tash Rabat. The office is tricky to find because it's not really on Panfilov (it's closer to Orozbekov). From the corner of Moskva and Orozbekov, walk north and then turn left behind Orozbekov 44 – it's the brown building down the alley.

RAFTING

Silk Road Water Centre (☎ 60 96 19, 0515-750 972; www.rafting.com.kg; Musa Jalil 104, Bishkek 720051) Specialists in white-water rafting, kayaking and fishing trips on the Chuy, Chong-Kemin, Kokomoron and Naryn rivers. The charge is 1400som per person for two hours of rafting. Contact Alexander Kandaurov.

FESTIVALS & EVENTS

Once upon a time, on summer Sundays, you might have seen traditional Kyrgyz horse-back games at the Hippodrome, southwest of the centre. Lately the best you can expect around Bishkek are exhibition games during the **Nooruz festival** (Navrus; 21 March; p368) and on **Kyrgyz Independence Day** (31 August).

SLEEPING
Budget

Nomad Home (☎ 48 21 38, 077-249 0608; http://nomadshome.googlepages.com; Drevesnaya 10; tent/dm/d 130/200/500som) This popular backpacker haunt offers lodging in a dim, scruffy dorm room or a spot inside a yurt. There are also one or two coveted rooms inside the house. Travellers with a tent can camp on the lawn. It's the

fourth house on the left as you walk north of the old bus station (eastern bus terminal). To get here from the *avtovaksal* (western bus station) take minibus 114.

South Guesthouse (☎ 57 26 23, 95 87 30; 4th fl, Aaly Tokombaev 31V; dm 150som) This apartment-style guesthouse is located in the extreme southern suburbs (8th *mikrorayon*). It's popular with Japanese backpackers and the surrounding neighbourhood offers a slice of Kyrgyz suburban life. Call in advance to make sure there's space before trekking all the way down here. Take minibus 232, 252 or 150 and get off when the bus turns off Soviet. From the bus stop, cross the road, go into the first gap between apartment blocks, turn left and go in the second door on the left. The door code is 135. A taxi to/from the centre costs 80som.

Bishkek Guesthouse (☎ 64 23 66, 0552-152 207; www.bishkekhouse.ucoz.com; apt 26, Molodaya Gvardia 72; dm 190som; 🖳) This apartment-guesthouse consists of three small dorm rooms, a kitchen and a common area. The showers are usually hot. It has a fairly central location and the friendly owner Davron speaks English. Try to call before turning up or he may not be there. To get here from Chuy, walk north on Molodaya Gvardia and go to the last apartment block on the left before Frunze. Look for the passage under the apartment to a courtyard (if you pass two stone dragons you've gone about 40m to far). After the passage it's the first door on the left and up to the 7th floor – the door is on the right.

Sakura Guesthouse (☎ 38 02 09; kobuhei-hikita@hotmail.com; Michurina 38; dm/s/d 300/500/800som) The busy Sakura Guesthouse offers cheap and friendly accommodation near the downtown area. In a newly built block, it contains spotless rooms and hot showers, but is lacking in character. The area around the guesthouse is fine in daylight but a little dicey at night – some travellers have been assaulted so take care. To find the place, go to the corner of Jibek Jolu and Soviet, then head north for about 100m and turn right down an alley (look for the sign: Магазин Жаркынай). After another 50m take a right down a short alley to the guesthouse.

London School in Bishkek (☎ 54 52 62; bishkekschool@gmail.com; Soviet 39; s without bathroom 300-350som) This language school has a few dishevelled rooms available to travellers and long-term students and teachers. Rooms are basic – what you'd expect from student accommodation –

but it's clean and quiet and there are opportunities to connect with Kyrgyz students at the school. It's a DIY sort of place so don't expect much assistance from the management.

Sabyrbek's B&B (☎ 30 07 10, 0550-715 153; alymk an@yandex.ru; Razzakov 21; per person dm 360-450som, r 600som; **P**) This character-filled place makes an interesting first impression. It's basically a big house with the host family living upstairs. Downstairs rooms have been converted to dorms and closet-sized private rooms that are divided by old curtains. Private rooms upstairs are spacious. Visitors hang out in the communal kitchen or in the garden out back. Sabrybek and his family are extremely cordial and staying with them provides an excellent glimpse into the life of a Kyrgyz family. On the downside, there is only one bathroom and only cold showers are available. To find it, look for an unmarked gate opposite the German embassy, next to a kiosk.

Hotel Bella Noche (☎ 54 74 62; Ahunbaev 98; r without/with shower 750/1500som) A hotel rather than a backpacker guesthouse, this is a good choice for budget travellers wanting some privacy. It's about 3km south of the centre but relatively easy to find. Take Blue Bus 29 from anywhere along Soviet, get off at the second stop after it turns onto Ahunbaev. Or take marshrutka 215 from the corner of Manas and Chuy.

There are a few homestay options in Bishkek. The London School in Bishkek (p304) can put you up with a host family for 2520som per week or 11,160som per month. The price includes breakfast and a homemade dinner. The national CBT office (p302) can also arrange homestays.

Midrange

Shumkar Asia (☎ 37 30 09; Osipenko 34; s/d cottage 1130/2260som, s/d main bldg 1700/2830som; ▣ ▣ ▣) Located in a quiet neighbourhood north of the centre, this is a peaceful getaway with a garden and small pool. The staff speaks English and rooms are spacious and simply furnished. To get there, go north on Isanov, then, after crossing Leningrad (Bayalinov), take the first left onto Osipenko.

Hotel Alpinist (☎ 59 56 47, 69 96 21; www.alpinist.cen tralasia.kg; Panfilov 113; s/d 1700/2300som; ▣) Looking like a misplaced prop from *The Sound of Music* this alpine-themed hotel is about 30 minutes by foot from the city centre. Facilities include a restaurant, climbing wall, conference room and transport to local ski fields.

Hotel Semetei (☎ 61 39 09; Toktogul 125; s/d 2000/2300som, q 2500som) This old Soviet dinosaur was recently renovated with fresh wallpaper, new furniture and horrid pink-tile bathrooms. You'll need binoculars to see the miniature TVs. It's worth considering for its central location.

Radison Guesthouse (☎ 32 31 81, 93 50 25; www. radisonhouse.com; Abdumomunov 259; s/d incl breakfast US$40/50; **P** ▣) This unsigned guesthouse (behind a green gate) is run by a motherly manager and her son. The twin rooms are clean with a small en suite but water pressure in the shower is pretty weak. You can eat breakfast (dried fruit, nuts, an egg and bread) on the outdoor patio. It has a good, central location.

Asia Mountains Guest House (☎ 69 02 35; www. asiamountains.net; Lineynaja 1A; s/d US$50/70; ▣) Trekking groups love this clean, fresh lodge, and with good reason. Guests have access to a kitchen and a nice communal seating area ideal for swapping climbing stories. The travel agency of the same name is in the basement. The guesthouse is on the outskirts, tucked down an alley by the railway line. Breakfast is included.

Umai Hotel (☎ 46 08 03, 077-280 2805; www.umai -hotel-kg.com; Donskoy Pereulok 46A; s/d/tr incl breakfast €30/45/60) This newly built boutique-style hotel has friendly, English-speaking management but slightly bland rooms. From the corner of Jibek Jolu and Orozbekov, go north to Bayalinov, take a left and then a quick right on to Donskoy Pereulok.

Top End

Holiday Hotel (☎ 90 29 00; www.holiday.kg; Soviet 204A; s/d/lux €90/105/115; ▣) This 18-room hotel is newly built and clean but the rooms are oddly shaped and some have poor views. Many guests stay for the location – it's just opposite the Hyatt Regency. The hotel allows you to use its bicycles at no charge.

Silk Road Lodge (☎ 32 48 89; www.silkroadlodge .kg; Abdumomunov 229; s/tw/lux/ste incl breakfast €105/115/125/140; ▣ ▣) Run by the Celestial Mountains travel agency, the 28 rooms are equipped with everything (iron, fridge, hairdryer, kettle and satellite TV) but style. Nonetheless it's a good option. There's a small heated plunge pool and live music on the weekends. Travellers cheques and credit cards accepted.

Park Hotel (☎ 66 55 18; www.parkhotel.kg; Orozbekov 87; s/d/lux US$127/147/200; ▣ ▣) This 34-room hotel has small, stylish rooms fitted with flat-panel TVs, minibar and safety box. It's a friendly place with a business centre, European restaurant and nice views over a quiet side street. The location is ideal and breakfast is included.

Hyatt Regency (☎ 66 12 34; www.bishkek.regency. hyatt.com; Soviet 191; s/d incl tax US$311/359; ✖ ▢ ▨) Bishkek's best hotel includes a couple of restaurants, an outdoor pool (nonguests 900som), fitness club and the obligatory casino. Breakfast is a cheeky US$25 extra.

EATING

Most restaurants add a 10% service charge and a few cheeky blighters even exhort extra for background music.

Cafes

Coffee (☎ 62 61 25; Togolok Moldo 40/1; coffee from 150som; ⏲ 9am-8pm; 🛜 E) The name says it all. Besides coffee it has teas and snacks. Wi-fi is available if you have a card (purchasable at Vefa Centre).

Chaikhanas

our pick **Café Faiza** (☎ 32 33 58; Jibek Jolu; mains 30-100som; ⏲ 9am-9pm; E) A wildly popular Kyrgyz restaurant in the north of town that offers high-quality local dishes at reasonable prices. You won't get near the place at lunch.

Bakai (Chuy; mains 30-180som; ⏲ 10am-11pm) Cheap eats and cheap beer can be found next door to TsUM at this open-air cafe serving Central Asian dishes such as Kazakh-style ribs and *beshbarmak* (flat noodles with a meat broth).

Chaikhana Jalal-Abad (☎ 61 00 83; cnr Kiev & Togolok Moldo; mains 35-85som; ⏲ 8am-midnight; E) Has pleasant bamboo huts, cordial staff and, as the name suggests, serves up southern specialities such as *larzuro* (fried beef and vegetables), salads and shashlyk.

Bishkek has Central Asia's best *samsas* (samosas), sold hot out of miniovens all around town for around 10som each. The chicken *samsas* are generally the best.

Restaurants

Fatboys (☎ 62 31 28; Chuy 104; mains 190-300som; ⏲ 8am-10pm Sun-Thu, 8am-midnight Fri-Sat; E) A prime foreigners' hang-out – especially at breakfast, where you'll find fresh juices, fruit teas, hash browns, bacon, eggs, yoghurt, muesli and pancakes. It's got a central loca-

tion and in summer the sidewalk tables make for great alfresco dining.

Beta Stores Restaurant (☎ 61 10 76; Chuy 150; salads 70-100som, mains 170-250som; ⏲ 8am-11pm; E) Don't be put off by the mall location – this place serves some of the best-value food in town. It specialises in Turkish and Central Asian dishes; the Iskender plate was so good we came back for more.

our pick **Watari** (☎ 69 48 01; Frunze 557; mains 130-250som; ⏲ 11am-9.30pm; E) Some of the best udon (noodles) we've ever tasted were served at this Bishkek newcomer. The slew of Japanese expats found here is testament to the quality curries and soups. The 'hot soba with tempura' and the green tea ice cream are both recommended.

Adriatico Paradise (☎ 61 46 09; Chuy 219; mains 200-300som; ⏲ 11am-midnight; E) The excellent Italian food here is prepared by a genuine Italian chef, with imported ingredients and Chianti wines. A 30cm pizza costs 250som and pasta dishes run at around 275som. Lunch deals (pasta and salad) cost 185som.

L'Azzuro (☎ 43 20 00; Ibraimov 105; mains 200-250som; ⏲ noon-1am; E) The Lebanese chef here goes all out to prepare some of the best Middle Eastern food this side of Beirut. Try the excellent *shish taouk* (grilled meat) or a mezze platter. It's an upscale kind of place, where you're expected to at least tuck in your shirt.

Parsi (☎ 62 48 19; Toktogul 103; mains 200-250som; ⏲ 9.30am-11.30pm; E) Mouth-watering Persian cuisine is served hot and is delicately spiced at Parsi. It has nice outdoor seating and occasional dancing inside. Service, however, can be slow.

Side by side on the south side of Victory Sq, are a couple of decent Chinese restaurants: the popular **Shanghai** (☎ 68 14 12; Ogonbayev; mains 140som; ⏲ noon-10pm) and the more upscale **Kontinental** (☎ 43 98 98; Ogonbayev; mains 150-200som; ⏲ noon-11pm; E).

Self-Catering

Ak Emir Bazaar (cnr Moskva & Shopokov) A great place for do-it-yourselfers, with samosas, roast chicken, pickled Korean salads, honey, buckets of blackcurrants and *piroshki* (Russian-style pies) – plus fruit and vegetables.

Beta Stores (Chuy 150) You can get everything from baklava to bottled *kymys* (25som) in the most popular supermarket in town. Trekkers will find the soup mixes useful.

KYRGYZSTAN

DRINKING

Remember, in Bishkek you are never far from a shot of vodka. For those too busy to actually go inside a bar, most street stalls sell 'kiosk shots' (also known as juice grams) of vodka or cognac for 5som a nip.

The following places also serve excellent food.

Metro (☎ 61 44 24; Chuy 168A; beer 50-70som; ☽ 10.30am-2am; **E**) This place is popular with expats capping off the day with a pizza and a pint or two of beer. The TVs are usually tuned to international sports, possibly to distract you from the spotty service.

2X2 (☎ 61 54 19; Isanov 89; beer 60som, cocktails 70-400som; ☽ noon-5am; **E**) This chic Italian-run pastel-and-chrome bar attracts a variety of creatures, from local mafiosos and working girls to NGO workers and US servicemen stationed at Manas airport.

Derevyashka (☎ 32 35 74; Riskulova 1; beer 65som; ☽ noon-3am) This large beer hall has an indoor area and an outdoor garden with big TVs flashing soccer matches. It's a great place to down pints with a few friends, but less inviting for solo travellers.

Bar Navigator (☎ 66 51 51; Moskva 103; 1L beer 200som; ☽ 8am-midnight; **E**) A stylish spot frequented by embassy staff working in the neighbourhood. It also serves great appetisers and vegetarian meals. Pay wi-fi is available (200som per hour).

Steinbräu (☎ 43 21 44; Gertse 5; 0.4L draught beer 40-52som; **E**) The German-style pilsner and recommended dark beer (Salvator) is brewed on-site here and is the main draw. Georgian wines and a full menu of German food (mains 200som), from sausages to pretzels, adds to the Munich beer-hall vibe.

ENTERTAINMENT
Theatres & Concert Halls

Philharmonia (☎ 21 22 35; Chuy 210) Features Western and Kyrgyz orchestral works and the occasional Kyrgyz song-and-dance troupe, but you may need a local person to identify these from the playbills. In front of the Philharmonia is a statue of the legendary hero Manas slaying a dragon, flanked by his wife, Kanykey, and his old adviser, Bakayn. The *kassa* is on the west side. Located by Belinsky.

State Opera & Ballet Theatre (☎ 66 15 48; Soviet 167) Opposite the State Museum of Fine Arts, classical Western and local productions play in this elegant building to half-empty halls.

Check the billboards outside for current productions.

State Academic Drama Theatre (☎ 66 58 02; Panfilov 273) On the east side of Panfilov Park, this is the place for popular Kyrgyz-language works, more often than not written by Chinghiz Aitmatov, Kyrgyzstan's premier man of words.

Russian Drama Theatre (☎ 66 20 32; Tynystanov, Dubovy Park) For classics in Russian.

The Jetigen and Samaa ensembles and Ordo Sakhna folk troupe are also good to see. Ask NoviNomad (p304) about upcoming concerts.

Nightclubs

Bishkek nightclubs seem to attract a middle-aged, mainly male clientele who are in town for '*biznez*' and a good time.

Apple (☎ 31 29 19; Manas 28; cover women/men 150/300som; ☽ 10pm-late) This is one of the more popular dance places in town, with a big dance floor and blaring techno music. It sometimes attracts the local hooligan crowd – which may or may not end up being a problem.

Gloss Nightclub (☎ 54 15 62; Mira 24; cover weeknight/weekend 300/700som; ☽ 10pm-5am) Nightclubs come and go but at the time of research this was one of the most popular places in town. It's big, loud and filled with Bishkek's young elite. Weekend cover is exorbitant.

Golden Bull (☎ 62 01 31; Chuy 209; foreigners/Kyrgyz men free/200som, beer 100som; ☽ 10pm-5am) The place attempts to please everyone with its blend of American, Russian, Kyrgyz and Turkish mix of pop and R&B. Strip shows bring in the punters on weekends.

Sky Bar (☎ 90 93 97; 12th fl, Moskva 118; admission 200som; ☽ noon-4am) This exclusive bar/nightclub/restaurant combo is located on the top floor of downtown high-rise. The views from the outdoor terrace are great and you can enjoy it while sitting on comfortable sofas. The food is expertly made and there is a long list of cocktails and wines available. The dance floor gets going quite late in the evening.

Movies

Rossiya Movie Theatre (☎ 66 09 60; cnr Chuy & Togolok Moldo, movie ticket 200-250som; bowling 200-240som; ☽ 11am-midnight) This modern theatre is something of a nightlife hub in Bishkek. It has a bowling alley in the basement.

Vefa Centre Theatre (☎ 59 66 88; 3rd fl, cnr Soviet & Gorky; admission 100-200som) Shows Hollywood blockbusters. Sometimes in original language, sometimes dubbed in Russian.

Other Entertainment

You can play pool for 150som an hour in the **billiards club** (☎ 62 17 17; cnr Orozbekov & Frunze), underneath the Consul Restaurant.

Maple Leaf Golf & Country Club (☎ 051-579 0877; green fee 800som) is Kyrgyzstan's first nine-hole golf course, southeast of Bishkek near the village of Kara-Jigach.

SHOPPING

Bishkek has the country's best collection of souvenirs and handicrafts, though you can often find individual items cheaper at their source (eg *shyrdaks* – felt carpets – in Kochkor, hats in Osh). For details on markets, see p303.

TsUM (☎ 29 27 94; Chuy 155) This state-run department store is surprisingly well stocked with all manner of imported products. Kyrgyz souvenirs are found on the 3rd floor. The 4th floor has electronics.

There is also a cluster of camera shops on Chuy prospektesi around Ala-Too Sq including **Pro Photo** (Chuy) that develops digital photos (7som per print).

The **Vefa Centre** (cnr Soviet & Gorky) will transport you to an American-style, air-conditioned mall, stocking Western brands at Western prices. There is a Columbia clothing store on the 2nd floor.

Artwork

Asia Gallery (☎ 62 45 05; Chuy 108; ☖ 11am-6pm Mon-Fri, 11am-4pm Sat) Features modern Kyrgyz art, with some artists' workshops in the yard out the back.

Stroll along the covered gallery in Dubovy Park to see local artists selling woodcarvings, oil paintings and charcoal portraits most afternoons.

Carpets

Aziya (☎ 66 07 34; Chuy 134) Not necessarily the cheapest store in town but the carpets, gilims and *shyrdaks* here are beautiful, top-quality pieces – those nomads sure do know how to cut a rug! Expect to pay around 1200som for a piece the size of a bathmat.

Another place to look for *shyrdaks* is in the souvenir shops in the State Historical Museum.

Handicrafts

You can find Kyrgyz men's hats – the familiar white felt *ak kalpak* or the fur-trimmed *teb-*

betey – for sale in TsUM or, much cheaper, in the north building at Osh Bazaar.

There are some gimmicky souvenirs in the cabins in front of Beta Stores, also near Ala-Too Sq and opposite Panfilov Park on Chuy. All sell jewellery, wooden soldiers (Manas and company), Kyrgyz handicrafts and the odd *shyrdak*.

Antique Shop (☎ 31 25 85; alwian@mail.ru; Manas 47; ☖ 10am-1pm & 2-5.30pm Mon-Fri, to 3.30pm Sat) An Aladdin's cave of Soviet, Kyrgyz and Russian antiques, strong on coins and memorabilia. Visa cards accepted.

Maison du Voyageurs (☎ 66 63 30; www.lamaisondu voyageur.com; Moskva 122) A wide selection of crafts from all over Kyrgyzstan, all marked with prices, the artist and the region they come from. On the corner of Orozbekov.

Tumar Art Salon (☎ 31 13 23; www.tumar.com; Kiev 152) Sells high-quality, high-priced embroidery. Credit cards accepted.

Academy of Gifts (☎ 62 61 25; Togolok Moldo 40/1) Stocks a variety of crafts including handmade toys and caps.

Outdoor Supplies & Cycle Parts

Red Fox (☎ 59 17 55; Soviet 65) Sells mountain bikes, camping supplies, mountaineering equipment and cycle parts.

Does your bike require physical therapy? Contact local cycle specialist **Oleg Yuganov** (☎ 67 09 74, 055-545 1265; oleg-yuganov@mail.ru; Serova 14A), who repairs bikes and sells spare parts. He works irregular hours from his home, north of the centre (250m south of the Pakistani Embassy). Phone first.

Outdoor clothing can be bought at the North Face store, 2nd floor of Beta Stores (p307).

GETTING THERE & AWAY
Air

Kyrgyzstan has three domestic carriers: Air Company Kyrgyzstan, Esen Air and Avia Traffic Company – all three have both domestic and international routes. On most flights out of the country you are allowed to check in 20kg and on domestic flights you can check 15kg. You're allowed 5kg of carry-on luggage. If flying domestic you'll likely ride in a vintage Antonov 24.

Air Company Kyrgyzstan main office (AC Kyrgyzstan; ☎ 31 30 03; www.air.kg; Manas 12a); branch office (☎ 66 66 99; Abdumomunov 195) Flies daily to Osh (2500som). Also flies several times a week to Jalal-Abad (2500som).

Avia Traffic (☎ 54 47 88; Panfilov 26) Flies daily to Osh and once weekly to Dushanbe (US$184) and Novosibirsk (US$188).

Esen Air (☎ 62 84 05; Chuy 130) Flies Monday, Wednesday, Friday and Sunday to Ürümqi, China (US$264) via Osh (2250som). It also flies weekly to Batken (2250som).

Itek Air (☎ 66 37 98; Chuy 128/10) Flies to Ürümqi, China (US$205) on Saturday.

AIRLINE OFFICES

Aeroflot (☎ 66 73 00; Erkindik 64/1)
BMI (☎ 66 60 15; Hyatt Regency Hotel, Soviet 191 rm 101)
China Southern (formerly Xinjiang Airlines; ☎ 66 46 68; Chuy128/3) Can book Ürümqi-Kashgar tickets.
KLM – Royal Dutch Airlines (☎ 66 15 00; fax 66 34 50; Toktogul 93) Books tickets for KLM flights from Almaty.
Lufthansa (☎ 66 66 06; Chuy 126) This agent handles Lufthansa flights departing from Almaty.
Turkish Airlines (☎ 30 18 00; Soviet 136) On corner of Bokonbayev.
Uzbekistan Airlines (☎ 90 03 21; uzb-air@muza.com.kg; Kiev 107) Flies to Tashkent (US$176) four days a week.

For details of international flights and fares see p370. For booking airline tickets see Travel Agencies, p302.

Bus & Shared Taxi

The west (zapadny) or **long-distance bus station** (☎ 65 65 75) is the place for catching long-distance buses and shared taxis; get there via bus 7 on Kiev, bus 35 or 48 or minibus 113 or 114 from Jibek Jolu, or trolleybus 5 on Manas.

The station is divided up into a few different parts, so you may need to wander for a bit to find what you are looking for. In the car park around the bus station you'll find share taxis going to points across the country. Just state your destination and the touts will whisk you to the appropriate share taxi. Some taxis will have their destinations posted on the windshield.

On the north side of the station is a separate lot for (marshrutkas) minivans. Like taxis, minivans go to just about every corner of the country, but they tend to be slower and less comfortable.

The bus station itself is nearly deserted as there are only a handful of daily departures and most of these leave late in the evening. On the bus station's upper floor are 21 ticket booths, all closed bar one. There is an information office next to counter number 7 and a 24-hour exchange here too. Don't trust the schedule board.

BUSES

Morning buses depart to Karakol (260som, 8½ hours) once per hour between 7.30am and 2.30pm and night buses depart hourly from 7pm to 11pm; these stop at Cholpon-Ata (160som) and most places in between. There are night buses to Naryn (230som, eight hours) and At-Bashy (260som, nine hours) at 8pm, 9pm, 10pm and 11pm.

Night buses to Talas (280som, nine hours) depart at 9pm, 10pm and 11pm. The bus to Uzbekistan only goes to the border at Chernaevka (but this border will remain closed until 2011). Both these journeys require a Kazakh visa.

MINIVANS & TAXIS

The private minivans offer better value than buses or, to ride in comfort, wedge yourself into a shared taxi. To hire the whole car, offer to pay for all four seats.

You'll find prices fluctuate with petrol costs and seasonal variations. The per seat fares for minibuses/shared taxis include Karakol (250/300som, seven hours), Cholpon-Ata (200/300som, four hours), Kochkor (200/250som, three hours), Naryn (350/400som, six hours), At-Bashy (400/500som, seven hours), Bokonbayevo (200/250som, five hours), Tamchy (150/250som, five hours), Balykchy (150/200som, 2½ hours), Talas (250/300som, five hours), Isfana (1800/2000som, 15 hours), meanwhile a seat to Almaty in a minivan is 300som.

Minibuses (800som) and private cars (1000som to 1200som) make the run to Osh in around 10 hours depending on the road and vehicle.

OTHER BUS STANDS

For Osh you can also catch rides from Osh Bazaar, which has two separate bus stands, a north and west stand. Most vehicles wait on the west side.

The Osh Bazaar bus stand also has local buses to destinations west including Sokuluk, Tash-Bulak, Kashka-Suu and Chong-Tash. Buses 160, 169 and 177 leave several times a day for Kashka-Suu, for Ala-Archa National Park.

The east (vastotshny avtovaksal) bus station is for regional points east such as Kant, Tokmok, Chong-Kemin, Kemin, Kegeti and Issyk-Ata.

Train

From the **train station** (☎ 30 02 09) trains 17 and 27 run on Monday and Thursday from Bishkek to Moscow (*platskartny/kupeyny* 7350/12,500som) via Almaty. Train 305 from Bishkek to Novosibirsk (*platskartny/kupeyny* 4100/6510som) runs on even days. It is also possible to travel to Tashkent on Wednesday (*kupeyny* 2600som) but the train passes through Kazakhstan.

The train to Balykchy departs daily at 6.42am and arrives at 11.30am (about twice as long as a minivan). The fare is 70som.

GETTING AROUND
To/From the Airport

Manas airport (☎ 69 37 98, 69 31 09), 30km northwest of the centre, doesn't quite live up to its poetic namesake, and now doubles as an American air-force base. The airport bus 380 (30som) picks up and drops off passengers on Chuy just west of Molodaya Gvardia, about three times per hour, between 6am and 8.30pm.

A taxi between the airport and the centre costs around 350som. Ekspress Taxis at the airport can arrange a reliable taxi. Most flights arrive in the middle of the night playing nicely into the hands of the taxi touts. Haggle.

Bicycle

Drive (☎ 65 55 51; Toktogul 213) sells Giant bicycles and **Free Bike** (☎ 0555-975 048) Rents mountain bikes for $15 a day. At the time of research there was no fixed address; call for info.

Bus

Municipal trolleybuses cost 3som, payable as you disembark at the front or to the conductor. At rush hour these are so crammed that you must plan your escape several stops ahead. Mercedes minibuses (8som) are generally better, as they are faster and less crowded.

Some useful minibus routes:

No 7 Handy for getting from Philarmonia to the Aftovaksal.

No 110 From Osh Bazaar, along Moskva to Soviet and then south.

Nos 113, 114 From the west (long-distance) bus station, down Jibek Jolu to Alamedin Bazaar.

Nos 125, 126 From Soviet (opposite the Orient International restaurant) south down Mira prospektesi to the old airport, US embassy and Hotel Issyk-Köl.

Trolleybus 4 From Osh Bazaar, along Moskva, left on Soviet and then north to Jibek Jolu.

Car & Taxi

Most travel agencies (p302) can arrange a car and driver but you are better off just hiring a taxi for the day at what will be a fraction of the price.

Essentially anyone with a car is a taxi. Official taxis, marked by the checkerboard symbol, are most reliable. The best-quality taxis are **Super Taxi** (☎ 152) or **Salam Taxi** (☎ 188). A short ride in the city costs around 70som, more at night.

You can book a taxi 24 hours a day on ☎ 182 for a small surcharge.

AROUND BISHKEK

Rolling out of the Kyrgyz Ala-Too, the Ala-Archa, Alamedin and dozens of parallel streams have created a phalanx of high canyons, good for everything from picnics to trekking and skiing to mountaineering.

Trekking & Spas

There are many possible do-it-yourself summer treks, but bring your own food and gear and be prepared for cold weather and storms, even in summer. There is limited public transport and you are best off hiring a taxi to drop you at the trailheads, though Bishkek tour operators and trekking companies (p304) can provide transport and arrange guided trips.

ALA-ARCHA CANYON

In this very grand, rugged but accessible gorge south of Bishkek, you can sit by a waterfall all day, hike to a glacier (and ski on it, even in summer) or trek on to the region's highest peaks. Most of the canyon is part of a state nature park, and foreigners must pay an entrance fee of 60som if you come on foot or 120som if you're in a car. For some hiking routes, see p313.

The park gate is 30km from Bishkek. Some 12km beyond the gate, at 2150m, the sealed road ends at the *alplager* (base camp), home to a weather station, an A-frame lodge and a basic hotel. In summer it has recreational facilities, baths and a sauna. Beyond this point the only transport is by foot or 4WD.

Sleeping & Eating

The best way to enjoy Ala-Archa is by bringing your own tent and sleeping bag. The only year-round accommodation is a wooden **hotel** (d 460som) in the *alplager*, with a dozen spartan

KYRGYZSTAN

KYRGYZSTAN

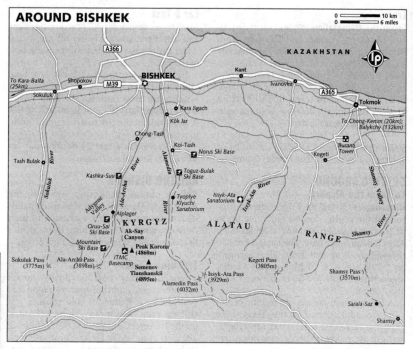

AROUND BISHKEK

doubles, a common toilet and no running water. A passable breakfast of sausages, eggs, bread and chai costs 80som, *laghman* is 90som. A better option is the nearby A-frame, alpine-style **lodge** (☎ 0543-91 60 48; s/tw/tr 1800/2400/3000som). Try to avoid visiting on Saturday or Sunday, when *'biznezmen'* turn up by the BMW-load to drink vodka and eat salami.

Getting There & Away
Bishkek travel agencies can arrange pricey day and longer trips including guides and gear. The best budget alternative would be to hire a taxi or hitch (though you'll still end up paying for the ride).

From the Osh Bazaar bus stand in Bishkek, bus 265 runs five times a day to the gate (21som). Ask *vorota zapovednika?* (nature park gate?) when you board. You may even find minibuses running as far as the *alplager*. If these aren't running (this is likely outside of summer weekends), take a minibus from the Osh Bazaar bus stand as far as Kashka-Suu village, 7km from the park gate (itself 12km from the *alplager*), and hitch or hike from there.

Also from Bishkek, on Moskva, west-bound bus 11, and on Soviet, west-bound bus 26, go about 12km south to the end of the line near the city limits, from where you can hire a taxi or hitch (ask for *alplager*, not just 'Ala-Archa').

A taxi from Osh Bazaar costs around 150som one way to the gate, or 400som to the *alplager*. If you are planning to return the same day negotiate a rate for the day, otherwise you face a long hike back to the gate or leave yourself to the mercy of the taxi sharks at the *alplager*.

OTHER CANYONS
Several valleys east of Ala-Archa have good walks and fewer visitors. In next-door **Alamedin Canyon**, 40km south of Bishkek, the main destination for local people is an old sanatorium called **Tyoplye Klyuchi** (hot springs/mud bath 80/800som) run by the Ministry of Power, with cheap accommodation and food. Although not protected by a national park, the scenery above and beyond here is as grand and walkable as that of Ala-Archa Canyon.

TREKKING IN ALA-ARCHA

There are dozens of trekking and climbing possibilities here, but three main options. The gentlest walk runs 300m down-valley from the *alplager* (base camp), then across a footbridge and southwest up the **Adygene Valley**. Along this way is a climbers' cemetery in a larch grove, a pretty and poignant scene. The track continues for about 7km to 3300m, below Adygene Glacier.

The most popular trek goes straight up the main canyon on a disused 4WD track about 22km, to the abandoned Upper Ala-Archa **Mountain Ski Base**. There's a run-down ski chalet here, where trekkers can stay if it's not full. This is a long and tiring walk (six to seven hours) so start early in order to reach the ski chalet before nightfall. You may find it difficult getting there – early in the season there may be too much snow, late in the season the river may be too high to cross.

Most demanding and dramatic is **Ak-Say Canyon**, with access via Ak-Say Glacier to the area's highest peaks. A trail climbs steeply to the east immediately above the *alplager*, continuing high above the stream. A strenuous four to five hours brings you to the Ratsek Hut at the base of the icefall at 3370m (with a backpackers' tent city in summer). The hut is managed by ITMC (p305) and has dorm beds for 300som to 500som. Bring all your own food.

Another hour or two's hike brings you to the beautiful glacial valley. Beyond here, climbers use a steel hut beside the glacier at 4150m (accessible only with some glacier walking). Climbing routes continue up to the peaks of Korona (4860m) and Uchityel (4572m). Semenov Tianshanskii (4895m), the highest peak in the Kyrgyz Ala-Too, is nearby.

You should be particularly careful about altitude sickness on this route. Try to do at least one day hike before tackling this route and don't sleep any higher than the icefall on the first night. See p535 for more info.

The trekking season around Ala-Archa is May to September or October, though the trail to the Ak-Say Glacier can be covered in snow even in August. Geoid in Bishkek (p299) sells a good 1:50,000 topographic map of the entire park, called *Prirodnyy Park Ala-Archa*.

Take bus 145 from Alamedin Bazaar in Bishkek, get off at Koy-Tash village and hitch the 14km to the gate. Buses are said to depart frequently throughout the day in summer.

Another thermal-spring complex *(kurort)* and guesthouse is about 45km southeast of Bishkek in **Issyk-Ata Canyon** (hot-spring in public/private pool 50/200som). A guesthouse here has foreigners' rooms for US$40, or a spartan hostel for around 500som. There are five or six buses a day to the complex (193 and 307) from Bishkek's east bus station.

Skiing

So many mountains, so few chair lifts. By international standards the ski fields in the Ala-Archa and Alamedin Valleys, 30km and 40km south of Bishkek, are undeveloped. If you have realistic expectations or prefer your piste uncrowded, strap on your sticks for there's plenty of powder. Kyrgyz Concept (p302) and Edelweiss (p305) arrange ski tours and jeeps, although it is possible to get there by 4WD taxi (400som), depending on road conditions. ITMC Tien Shan (p305) rents skis and boards.

Tourist Center Kashka-Suu (☎ 077-222 2443, 055-010 7522; www.kashka-suu.on.kg; tw/tr/q 1400/2100/2800som; lift pass adult/child 500/300som, ski rental 300-500som) operates a rope tow and one 1.5km long chairlift (provided there is electricity) in a picturesque gorge on the northern slope of Kyrgyz Ridge in the Ala-Archa Valley. The hotel sleeps 65, is rather pleasant and includes a sauna, restaurant and ice-skating (admission 100som, skate rental 100som).

Oruu-Sai Ski Base (☎ 312-592 245, 055-000 8198; tw/tr/lux US$25/40/54, rope tow pass 400som, ski rental 250-400som) has two tow ropes. This complex has a sauna and cafe; located in the Adygene Valley.

Norus Ski Base (☎ 66 11 11; s/tr/tr US$50/60/70; lift pass adult/child US$6/4, snowboard/ski rental US$10/15) in the Alamedin Valley has three chairlifts. There is accommodation in an A-frame hotel.

Toguz-Bulak Ski Base (☎ 0312-936 479, 055-041 4313; www.toguz-bulak.webou.net; r 500som, cottage US$80-$100; lift pass adult/child 500/400som) has one 1800m long chairlift. It's in Toguz-Bulak gorge 40km from Bishkek.

KYRGYZSTAN

HELI-SKIING

Despite mountains of snow, the Terskey Alatau range has little in the way of ski-field development and many side valleys, ridges and glaciers are seldom, if ever, skied. Several companies such as Bishkek's Ak Sai Travel (p304) and Karakol's Turkestan (p321) can arrange heli-skiing – Kyrgyzstan's answer to the chairlift shortage.

MI-8-MTB helicopters ferry groups of up to 15 skiers and boarders plus guides and pilots to terrain within a zone selected according to snowfall, the weather and your group's ability. It is possible to get as many as six different adrenalin-inducing descents within a day's skiing. Cost is approximately US$200 per day. It's worth checking that the guides carry an emergency radio to contact either the helicopter or mountain rescue in case of emergency.

White-Water Rafting

It is also possible to raft some of the rivers spilling from the mountains. The most commonly rafted river is a 25km stretch of the Chuy between Tokmok and Balykchy (Class II to IV, group of four to seven US$40 per person, two hours) although some people extend this by continuing on the calm section of the river for a further two hours. See the Silk Road Water Centre (p305) to arrange trips.

Burana Tower

East of Kegeti at the mouth of the Shamsy Valley, 80km from Bishkek, is a 1950s Soviet restoration of the so-called Burana Tower, an 11th-century monument that looks like the stump of a huge minaret. A mound to the northwest is all that's left of the ancient citadel of Balasagun, founded by the Sogdians and later, in the 11th century, a capital of the Karakhanids, which was excavated in the 1970s by Russian archaeologists. The Shamsy Valley itself has yielded a rich hoard of Scythian treasure, including a heavy gold burial mask, all either spirited away to St Petersburg or in storage in Bishkek's State Historical Museum.

You can climb the 24m-high octagonal minaret (40som) to get an overview of the old city walls. On the other side of the citadel

mound is an interesting collection of 6th- to 10th-century *balbals* (Turkic totem-like stone markers). The small **museum** (admission 60som, guided tour 10som; ☉ 9am-6pm summer, until 5pm in winter) has 11th-century Christian carvings, Buddhist remains and Chinese coins, as well as info on local literary hero Haji Balasagun and his masterwork, the *Kutudhu Bilik*. Next door are the foundations of several mausoleums.

The director of the museum, Anita Shamenova (☎ 0313-87 72 97, 0772-800 588) runs a guesthouse about 2km from Burana Tower. She offers hearty dinner for 300som or a room with full board for 1000som. Contact Anita at the tower before going to the guesthouse.

To get to Burana on your own, take the frequent 353 minibus from Bishkek's east bus station to Tokmok (40som, 45 minutes), from where it's about a 24km (300som) round trip by taxi. The minaret could easily be visited en route to or from Issyk-Köl.

To the north, **Tokmok** has a large Sunday animal bazaar on the outskirts of town. Buses run frequently from the east bus station.

Chong-Kemin Valley

The 80km-long Chong-Kemin Valley and National Park lies about 140km east of Bishkek, along the Kazakh border. The valley is famous locally as the birthplace of deposed president Akaev, but more importantly for travellers, it provides another great opportunity to roll up your sleeping bag and trek into the hills.

A six-day trekking route leads up the valley to Jasy-Köl (Green Lake) and the Ak-Suu Pass (4062m) and then onto Grigorievka on the northern shores of Issyk-Köl. There is also a route over the Ozyorny Pass (3609m) to Kazakhstan's Bolshoe Almatinskoe region but contact a tour operator first to inquire about whether or not you can cross the border on foot.

There's no formal accommodation in the valley but travellers recommend contacting Temirlan Daniyarov in Kaindy, the last hamlet in the valley, who can arrange a place to stay and horse treks. There are two buses a day to Kaindy (80som, 2½ hours) from Bishkek's east bus station. Otherwise take a more frequent 352 bus to Kemin (50som, one hour) and then hitch or take a shared taxi to Kaindy.

LAKE ISSYK-KÖL & THE CENTRAL TIAN SHAN
ОЗЕРО ИССЫК-КУЛЬ И ЦЕНТРАЛЬНЫЙ ТЯНЬ ШАНЬ

Lake Issyk-Köl (also Ysyk-Köl) is basically a huge dent, filled with water, between the Küngey (Sunny) Ala-Too to the north and the Terskey (Dark) Ala-Too to the south, which together form the northern arm of the Tian Shan. The name means 'hot lake'. A combination of extreme depth, thermal activity and mild salinity ensures the lake never freezes; its moderating effect on the climate, plus abundant rainfall, have made it something of an oasis through the centuries.

Scores of streams pour into the lake but none escape her. Over 170km long, 70km across and the second-largest alpine lake in the world (after Lake Titicaca in South America), Issyk-Köl is a force of nature and she knows it.

Some people say the lake level has periodically risen and fallen over the centuries, inundating ancient shoreline settlements. Artefacts have been recovered from what is called the submerged city of Chigu, dating from the 2nd century BC, at the east end. Mikhaylovka inlet, created by an earthquake near Karakol, reveals the remains of a partly submerged village. Despite recent fluctuations, geological evidence points to a long-term drop – some 2m in the last 500 years.

After tsarist military officers and explorers put the lake on Russian maps, immigrants flooded in to found low-rise, laid-back, rough-and-ready towns. Health spas lined its shores in Soviet days, with guests from all over the USSR, but spa tourism crashed along with the Soviet Union, only reviving in the last few years thanks to an influx of moneyed Kazakh tourists.

The part of the central Tian Shan range accessible from the lake comprises perhaps the finest trekking territory in Central Asia. The most popular treks hop between valleys south of Karakol.

History

The Kyrgyz people migrated in the 10th to 15th centuries from the Yenisey river basin in Siberia, and in all probability arrived by way of Issyk-Köl. This high basin would be a natural stopover for any caravan or conquering army as well. It appears to have been a centre of Saka (Scythian) civilisation and legend has it that Timur (Tamerlane) used it for a summer headquarters (p319). There are at least 10 documented settlements currently under the waters of the lake and treasure hunters have long scoured the lake for flooded trinkets attributed to everyone from Christian monks to Chinggis (Genghis) Khan.

The first Russian, Ukrainian and Belarussian settlers came to the east end of the lake in 1868. Karakol town was founded the next year, followed in the 1870s by Tüp, Teploklyuchenka (Ak-Suu), Ananyevo, Pokrovka (now Kyzyl-Suu) and a string of others, many of whose Cossack names have stuck. Large numbers of Dungans and Uyghurs arrived in the 1870s and '80s following the suppression of Muslim uprisings in China's Shaanxi, Gansu and Xinjiang provinces. At that time local Kyrgyz and Kazakhs were still mostly nomadic.

The Issyk-Köl region (and in fact most of Kyrgyzstan beyond Bishkek) was off limits to foreigners in Soviet times. Locals mention officially sanctioned plantations of opium poppies and cannabis around the lake, though most of these had disappeared under international pressure by the early 1970s.

More importantly, Issyk-Köl was used by the Soviet navy to test high-precision torpedoes, far from prying Western eyes. An entire polygon or military-research complex grew around Koy-Sary, on the Mikhaylovka inlet near Karakol. In 1991 Russian President Boris Yeltsin asked that it be continued but Kyrgyz President Askar Akaev shut down the whole thing, ordering it to be converted to peaceful pursuits. These days the most secretive thing in the lake is the mysterious *jekai*, a Kyrgyz version of the Loch Ness monster.

Jokes about the 'Kyrgyz navy' refer to a fleet of some 40 ageing naval cutters, now mothballed at Koy-Sary or decommissioned and hauling goods and tourists up and down the lake.

Getting There & Away

The western road access to Issyk-Köl is a 40km-long, landslide-prone, slightly sinister

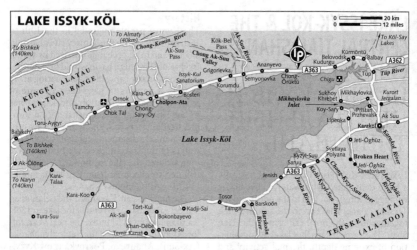

canyon called Shoestring Gorge (Boömskoe ushchelie), which climbs into the Ala-Too east of Tokmok, with a howling wind funnelling up it most of the time.

From the north, a rough jeep road (4WD only) from Almaty's Bolshoe Almatinskoe Lake leads over the Ozerny Pass, through the Chong-Kemin Valley and then the Kok Ayryk Pass to Chong-Sary-Oy near Cholpon-Ata. There's no public transport along the route, the bridges often get washed out and there's no immigration post, making it a particularly tricky option for foreigners. It might make an interesting mountain-bike trip if you can sort out the visa situation.

TAMCHY ТАМЧЫ
☎ 3943

This small lakeshore village, 35km from Cholpon-Ata, has a decent beach and offers a quieter alternative to larger, bustling Cholpon-Ata. Out of season, you'll likely see more donkeys than tourists on the beach. The town boasts one small supermarket, near the mosque on the main road (Manas), which is big on vodka and light on everything else. By the end of September you'll find more life in a morgue.

If you are on public transport, remind the driver you want to get out, they usually speed right through town en route to Cholpon-Ata. If you ask to be dropped off at the mosque you'll be near the centre of town.

The local CBT (☎ 2 12 72, 077-335 5611; Manas 55) coordinator, Sati Baktagula-Sanaleyav, can help you organise, vehicles, horse trips and homestays.

Tamchy Guesthouse (☎ 2 11 12, 055-044 5115; Chyngyshbaev 24; per bed 300som) is an eccentric old home run by the friendly, English-speaking Iskender Osmaev, who keeps a signed photo of Tom Cruise in the outhouse. There are a few colourful, comfortable rooms and breakfast is available for an additional 150som. It's across the road from a weird, half-built castle-like hotel, and is on the corner of Batikov.

During the summer months many locals rent rooms to Kazakh holidaymakers and, once over their disbelief that a foreigner wants to stay, are happy to take in guests. Ask around.

There's lots of minibus traffic through to Bishkek (200som, 3½ hour) and Cholpon-Ata (80som, 40 minutes) and Balykchy (50som, 25 minutes). Flag down anything with wheels going your way on the main road.

CHOLPON-ATA ЧОЛПОН АТА
☎ 3943

Cholpon-Ata is about as close as you can get to Cancun and still be in Central Asia. By day it's a scene of tan bods, zipping jet skis and ice cream licking tots. By night it's open-air cafes, thumping discos and young lovers breaking social mores. Most of the visitors are wealthy Kazakhs and Russians from north of the border but outside high season (mid-July to August) you may have the place to yourself.

Sports teams from other Central Asian republics and Russia compete here in early

September in track and field events and soccer tournaments. Besides the beach, the ancient rock inscriptions on the outskirts of town are the village's main attraction. The sanatorium, formerly a retreat for the Communist Party elite, has fallen into disrepair, although it's still operational.

Orientation & Information

The town has two reference points: the El Nuur Bazaar and, 1km west, the cluster of shops around the post office. Both are on the main road.

There is an overpriced **Internet Cafe** (Soviet 74; per 10min 50som; ☉ 9am-10pm) and lots of exchange booths around town.

Investbank (☉ 8am-5pm Mon-Fri, 9am-3pm Sat) gives advances on Visa and MasterCard for 3% commission and has an ATM. The bank is set off the road, within the newly revamped children's park.

At the time of writing there was no CBT or tourist office in town. The most reliable tourist information is from Tatiana at the Pegasus Guest House (see p318).

An **Ecocentre** (☎ 4 22 76; Soviet 61; ☉ 9am-5pm Mon-Fri) has a small exhibit of local flora and fauna, but a planned information centre for the place seems to have faltered.

Sights & Activities

BEACHES & BOATS

A pleasant public beach lies 1km south of the main road, in the western part of town. Walk south from the large concrete overhang (a nightclub) to the chalets of the Gost Residenza and then head east, across a bridge over a lagoon to the beach. In true Soviet style, the Speedo-sporting, pot-bellied men here like to sunbathe standing up. The presidential beach house is nearby; when the president is in town the police are out in force. Keep your passport at the ready and an eye out for the presidents' luxury yacht. There is another larger beach called Alytn-Köl, 4km east of Cholpon-Ata.

The Manas Cultural Park on the lakeshore has a small sculpture garden.

The **Kruiz Yacht Club** (☎ 4 43 73) has a handful of sailboats (US$25 per hour for up to six people) and even an overpriced scuba-diving centre.

PETROGLYPHS

Above the town is a huge field of glacial boulders, many with pictures scratched or picked into their surfaces. Some of these **petroglyphs** (adult/student 30/5som, guides per person 25som; ☉ daylight) date from the later Bronze Age (about 1500 BC) but most are Saka-Usun (8th century BC to 1st century AD), predating the arrival of the Kyrgyz in the area. The Saka priests used this sacred site for sacrifices and other rites to the sun god and they lived in the settlements that are currently underwater in the Cholpon-Ata bay. Later engravings date from the Turkic era (5th to 10th century). Most are of long-horned ibex, along with some wolves, deer and hunters, and some rocks appear to be arranged in sacred circles. Late afternoon is a good time to view the stones, which all face south.

KYRGYZSTAN

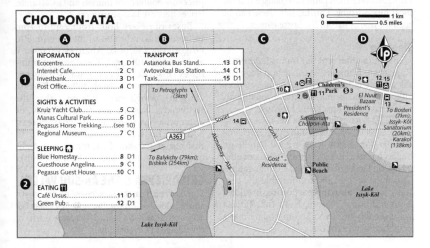

CHOLPON-ATA

0 — 1 km
0 — 0.5 miles

INFORMATION
Ecocentre...................................1 D1
Internet Cafe.............................2 C1
Investbank.................................3 D1
Post Office.................................4 C1

SIGHTS & ACTIVITIES
Kruiz Yacht Club........................5 C2
Manas Cultural Park..................6 D1
Pegasus Horse Trekking.......(see 10)
Regional Museum......................7 C1

SLEEPING
Blue Homestay...........................8 D1
Guesthouse Angelina................9 C1
Pegasus Guest House..............10 C1

EATING
Café Ursus.................................11 D1
Green Pub.................................12 D1

TRANSPORT
Astanorka Bus Stand...............13 D1
Avtovokzal Bus Station............14 C1
Taxis...15 D1

To Petroglyphs (3km)

Children's Park

El Nuur Bazaar

President's Residence

Sanatorium Cholpon-Ata

To Bosteri (7km); Issyk-Köl Sanatorium (20km); Karakol (138km)

A363

Soviet

Almaty Ave

Gorki

To Balykchy (79km); Bishkek (254km)

Gost Residenza

Public Beach

Lake Issyk-Köl

Lake Issyk-Köl

Take the signed road opposite the boatyard turn-off north for 2.2km, bearing left to a section of black iron fence. The stones are behind this. There's a nice view of Issyk-Köl below. Guided tours of the petroglyphs can be arranged at the regional museum and help pinpoint the field's more impressive inscriptions.

There are more petroglyphs in the region, at Kara-Oi, a 2km walk from the site, and near Ornok (4km up the new jeep road to Kazakhstan).

REGIONAL MUSEUM

This small **Issyk-Köl museum** (☎ 4 21 48; Soviet 69; adult 40som, camera 250som; ⊙ 9am-6pm) is worth a quick visit. The emphasis is on archaeology, with displays of local Scythian (Saka) gold jewellery, *balbal* gravestones and a fine set of mouth harps. Other rooms are devoted to ethnography, Kyrgyz bards, music and costume.

TREKKING & HORSE RIDING

Ornok forest, north of the petroglyph park, is popular with locals who collect mushrooms here during August. Follow the old logging road on the left side of the valley, keep the river on the right.

Pegasus Horse Trekking (☎ 4 24 50; pegaso@mail.ru; Soviet 81) is run by the same lady who operates the Pegasus Guest House. She organises horse treks to Ornok Valley and along the lakeshore, offers expert instruction for less-confident riders and can arrange multiday excursions to Grigorievka (p318) and beyond. With a few days notice she will also organise a display of nomadic equestrian games (20,000som) at the local hippodrome. During July these can be seen for free as part of the horse games.

Sleeping

Plenty of families rent out rooms (*komnat* in Russian) in Cholpon-Ata. The best people to ask are the elderly ladies at the bus station, although someone may approach you directly if you have a backpack and look lost.

ourpick Pegasus Guest House (☎ 4 24 50; pegaso@ mail.ru; Soviet 81; dm 300som) Tatiana Kemelevna and her son, Bukit, have a good handle on budget backpacker requirements and can offer advice on local activities and all things equine. The house is clean and comfortable and centrally located near the post office. Breakfast is an additional 100som. If it's full, Tatiana will probably offer you accommodation at a neighbours' guesthouse.

Guesthouse Angelina (☎ 4 29 04, 055-013 8750; Kurorshnaya 21; r without bathroom 350-500som, r with bathroom 500-800som; ⊠) This comfortable and friendly guesthouse has a number of rooms of varying size and quality. The en suite rooms are good value when available.

Blue Homestay (☎ 4 23 02; Soviet 39; s/d 350/600som) Unsigned but unmistakably painted dark blue, this place has a communal kitchen, dining area, large garden and a shared bathroom. Some rooms are small and claustrophobic. The houses nearby are also homestays and also unsigned. Ask for '*Gastinochnyi Dom*' when you ring the doorbell, or just look lost.

Eating & Drinking

Most cafes close between October and May. In addition to the following, you'll find lots of cafes strung along Gorki on the way to the beach.

Café Ursus (Soviet 68; mains 60-100som; ⊙ 8am-11pm; Ⓔ) Nestled among a string of cafes, it serves decent food at reasonable prices.

Green Pub (☎ 4 29 76; Soviet 11; mains 100-180som, tap beer 45som; ⊙ 10am-11pm, summer only; Ⓔ) This Russian-operated restaurant gives *shashlyk* (100som) a new twist by threading vegetables between the meat chucks. The barbecue fish (160som) is also recommended.

Getting There & Away

Cholpon-Ata, being the premier resort town for nearby and comparatively wealthy Kazakhs, is particularly prone to fluctuating transport costs. During summer, shared-taxi prices are doubled for tourists and locals alike. Prices here are low-season rates.

Buses run every hour from 7am to 7pm to/from Bishkek (160som) and continue to Grigorievka (50som), Ananyevo (60som), and Karakol (100som). There are also minibuses (Bishkek 200som; Karakol 150som) and shared taxis (Bishkek 300som; Karakol 180som), which depart from either the Avtovokzal bus station (west bound) or Astanorka bus stand near the bazaar (east bound). Taxis costs around 1000som to Bishkek or Karakol. In summer, overnight buses run to Almaty around 8am (600som).

GRIGORIEVKA & THE AK-SUU VALLEY

Some of the best alpine scenery on the north shore is located up the **Chong Ak-Suu Valley** (admission per person 20som, per car 50som), due north of the village of Grigorievka.

Cut by a raging river, the valley runs 22km from Grigorievka to a trio of small alpine lakes. It's possible to hike the whole way, but you could also hitch a lift or take your own vehicle. In summer there are plenty of yurt-stays and roadside restaurants, plus another yurtstay at the first lake. Local boys inevitably appear to offer horses for rent (300som to 500som per hour), plus a few falconers who will charge you for the thrill of holding an eagle on your arm.

Pegasus Horse Trekking (p318) organ-ises horse treks between Grigorievka and Semyenovka gorges overnighting in either tents or yurts.

The nearby village of Semyenovka offers access to the Kichi (Little) Ak-Suu Valley, which has the Kyrchyn Gorge, a winter sports centre and one yurtstay called **Yurta Kubat Sidikov** (☎ 055-034 2939; bed & breakfast 400som) with two cosy guest yurts, located 2.5km past the ranger gate.

KARKARA VALLEY
КАРКАРАНСКАЯ ДОЛИНА

The eastern gateway to the Issyk-Köl Basin is an immense, silent valley called Karkara, straddling the Kyrgyzstan–Kazakhstan bor-der. On the Kyrgyzstan side it begins about 60km northeast of Karakol and widens out to 40km or more, shoulder-deep in good pasture during summer. Every herder in the Karakol region (and in the Kegen region on the Kazakhstan side) brings animals up here in summer to fatten, and the warm-weather population is an easy-going mix of Kyrgyz and Kazakh *chabana* (cowboys), their families and their yurts.

The name Karkara means Black Crane, after the graceful migratory birds that stop here in June and again in August to September, en route between South Africa and Siberia.

Summer's end brings the **Shepherds' Festival**, an annual gathering of cowboys and herders at the end of August. Horseback games and eagle hunting are held at the yurt camps near Char-Kuduk village.

In his *A Day Lasts Longer Than a Century* the Kyrgyz writer Chinghiz Aitmatov has the ancient Kyrgyz peoples arriving here from the Yenisey region of Siberia.

Some people suggest that Timur (Tamerlane) made Karkara his summer headquarters for several years, and point to a house-size pile of round stones in the south-west part of the valley. These, they say, were Timur's way of estimating his losses in east-ern campaigns – each departing soldier put a rock on the pile, each returnee removed one, and the stones that remained represented the dead. The name of the site, **San-Tash**, means 'Counting Stones'.

Sceptics and amateur historians point to an adjacent, stone-lined pit that appears to be the remnant of a burial chamber, and suggest that the football-size stones were just used to cover the chamber, and were removed by archaeologists or grave-robbers. Either way, the site has a dreamy, magical feel.

Sleeping

Issyk Kul Travel (☎ in Karakol 077-384 4954; per person incl breakfast US$20) Has a yurt camp 40km south east of San-Tash, near Char Kuduk village, close to the Alpinist's and the Kazakh com-pany Kan Tengri's base camps, just across the river in Kazakhstan.

Getting There & Away

The Karkara Valley is about 50km east of Tüp or 80 much prettier but rougher kilometres from Karakol (p199) via Novovoznesenovka. On the Tüp route a round trip by taxi from Karakol is about 1800som return. Ask for *pamyatnik San-Tash* (San-Tash Monument), located 1km from San Tash village, 19km from the Kazakhstan border.

A derelict bus runs from Karakol's Ak-Tilek Bazaar to San-Tash (80som) via Tüp at 1.30pm. It returns the following morning.

There are daily buses to Kyzyl Jar (former Sovietskoe) or on to the mining town of Jyrgalang (Russians call it Jergalan *shakhta,* which means 'mine'); you might try hitching from Kyzyl Jar.

The Karkara (Karkyra) River forms the modern Kyrgyzstan–Kazakhstan border through part of the valley and this makes an interesting route to or from Kazakhstan. If you are headed to Kazakhstan make sure you get a border stamp, even if it means waiting some time. You will of course need valid visas for both republics. There's no cross-border public transport.

Coming from the Kazakhstan side, you can get a Kegen, Saryzhaz or Narynkol bus from Almaty and get off at Kegen, from where it's a difficult 28km hitch south to the border itself. A taxi from Karakol to Almaty via Kegen takes about seven hours and costs around US$150, including car customs fees.

KARAKOL КАРАКОЛ
☎ 3922 / pop 75,000
Karakol is a peaceful, low-rise town with backstreets full of Russian gingerbread cottages, shaded by rows of huge white poplars. Around the town are apple orchards, for which the area is famous. This is the administrative centre of Issyk-Köl province, and the best base for exploring the lakeshore, the Terskey Ala-Too and the central Tian Shan. It also has a very good Sunday market. In fact, try to time your visit to include a Sunday, when the animal bazaar and Russian cathedral are at their most active.

It's not quite paradise for those who live here – the economic stresses since independence and the decline in spa tourism have led to considerable hardship, thinned out available goods and services, and returned a kind of frontier atmosphere to this old boundary post. It is extremely dark at night and some travellers have reported being hassled, so be vigilant and carry a torch (flashlight).

The town name means something like 'black hand/wrist', possibly a reference to the hands of immigrant Russian peasants, black from the valley's rich soil.

History
After a military garrison was established at nearby Teploklyuchenka (Ak-Suu) in 1864, and it dawned on everybody that the area near the lake was a fine spot – mild climate, rich soil, a lake full of fish, and mountains full of hot springs – the garrison commander was told to scout out a place for a full-sized town. Karakol was founded on 1 July 1869, with streets laid out in a European-style checkerboard, and the garrison was relocated here. The town's early population had a high proportion of military officers, merchants, professionals and explorers.

It was called Przewalski in Soviet times, after the explorer Nikolai Przewalski, whose last expedition ended here, and who is buried on the lakeshore nearby (p325). The town didn't escape a trashing by the Bolsheviks. Its elegant Orthodox church lost its domes and became a club; only one small church on the outskirts was allowed to remain open. Of nine mosques (founded by Tatars, Dungans and various Kyrgyz clans), all bar the Dungan's were wrecked.

Orientation
Karakol has a central square, but the commercial hubs are the Makish Bazaar (nicknamed *gostinny dvor* – the Russian equivalent of a caravanserai or merchants' inn, after its namesake in St Petersburg) and also Ak-Tilek Bazaar (good wishes). The long-distance bus station is about 2km to the north and the 'better' part of the town is considered to be west of the river.

Information

INTERNET ACCESS
Vista Internet (☎ 2 51 95; Tynystanova 23; per hr 40som; ☺ 9am-11pm) This internet cafe has several computers running at a fairly slow speed. At the time of research the cafe were setting up a wi-fi connection, so if you have a laptop it might be worth checking out.

MEDICAL SERVICES
Karakol Medical Clinic (☎ 5 13 23; Jusup Abdrakhmanov; ☺ 8am-5pm) This building is directly opposite the Tourist Information Centre (TIC) whose staff are happy to help translate in an emergency. Doctors keep individual hours and there is a pharmacy on the ground floor.

MONEY
Moneychangers everywhere will change crisp, near-new US dollars into som.
AKB Bank (☎ 5 37 45; Toktogul; ☺ 8.30am-noon & 1-3pm Mon-Fri) Changes US-dollar travellers cheques into som for a 3% commission (minimum US$5) and gives cash advances on Visa and MasterCard for 2.5% commission. Go in the main building, turn left and head upstairs; look for the Western Union sign. The bank is also known as RSK.
ATF Bank (cnr Lenina & Toktogul) Has an ATM that accepts visa and MasterCard.

REGISTRATION & VISAS
OVIR (☎ 5 13 10; room 114, Kushtobaev; ☺ 9am-6pm) Thirty-day visa extensions are available. Bring two passport photos, copy of relevant passport pages and a receipt for 1000som deposited at RSK Bank. You'll have to fill out two application forms. Processing takes one to two days. The office is around the side of the militsia (police) office.

TOURIST INFORMATION
CBT (☎ 5 50 00, after hr 077-220 3087; cbtkarakol@ rambler.ru; Jusup Abdrakhmanov 123/20; ☺ 9am-5pm daily summer, 10am-3pm Mon-Fri winter) Offers homestays options in town and yurtstays at Jeti-Öghüz, the Bel Tam *jailoo* and Karkara. Staff also arrange local excursions, help with onward transport, arrange guides (1000som to 1200som per day) and advise on trekking permits.
Tourist Information Centre (TIC; ☎ 5 23 41; tourinfo centre@gmail.com; Jusup Abdrakhmanov 130; ☺ 9am-

5pm Mon-Sat) Make this excellent resource your first stop. Arranges homestays and transport. It also sells 1:100,000 topo maps (250som) of southeast Issyk-Köl trekking routes.

TRAVEL AGENCIES

Issyk-Kul Travel (☎ 077-384 4954; santash@rambler. ru; cnr Lenina & Toktogul) Specialises in trips to the Karkara Valley. At the time of research it was under the ATF

Bank but could move so it's best to call first. Contact Tolon Jumanaliev.

Kyrgyz Tours (☎ 5 29 29; www.kyrgyz-tours.info; Lenina 130/1) This cooperative of young guides can arrange treks with English, French or German interpreters. Also leads five-day mountain-biking trips to Barskoön via Saruu, Juuku Pass and Ara-Bel Valley (you must bring your own bike).

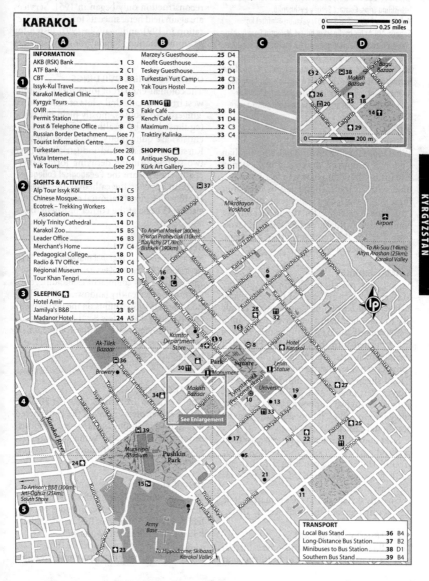

KARAKOL

0   500 m
0   0.25 miles

INFORMATION
AKB (RSK) Bank	**1** C3
ATF Bank	**2** C1
CBT	**3** B3
Issyk-Kul Travel	(see 2)
Karakol Medical Clinic	**4** B3
Kyrgyz Tours	**5** C4
OVIR	**6** C3
Permit Station	**7** B5
Post & Telephone Office	**8** C3
Russian Border Detachment	(see 7)
Tourist Information Centre	**9** C3
Turkestan	(see 28)
Vista Internet	**10** C4
Yak Tours	(see 29)

SIGHTS & ACTIVITIES
Alp Tour Issyk Köl	**11** C5
Chinese Mosque	**12** B3
Ecotrek – Trekking Workers Association	**13** C4
Holy Trinity Cathedral	**14** D1
Karakol Zoo	**15** B5
Leader Office	**16** B3
Merchant's Home	**17** C4
Pedagogical College	**18** D1
Radio & TV Office	**19** C4
Regional Museum	**20** D1
Tour Khan Tengri	**21** C5

SLEEPING
Hotel Amir	**22** C4
Jamilya's B&B	**23** B5
Madanor Hotel	**24** A5
Marzey's Guesthouse	**25** D4
Neofit Guesthouse	**26** C1
Teskey Guesthouse	**27** D4
Turkestan Yurt Camp	**28** C3
Yak Tours Hostel	**29** D1

EATING
Fakir Café	**30** B4
Kench Café	**31** D4
Maximum	**32** C3
Traktiry Kalinka	**33** C4

SHOPPING
Antique Shop	**34** B4
Kürk Art Gallery	**35** D1

TRANSPORT
Local Bus Stand	**36** B4
Long-Distance Bus Station	**37** B2
Minibuses to Bus Station	**38** D1
Southern Bus Stand	**39** B4

KYRGYZSTAN

Turkestan (☎ 2 64 89; www.turkestan.biz; Toktogul 273) Turkestan specialises in group trekking and is pricier, but much more professional, than Yak Tours. It can arrange trekking and mountaineering trips to Khan Tengri, horse treks into the Küngey Ala-Too mountains north of Issyk-Köl, and visits to eagle hunters, as well as no-strings-attached visa support, plus an awesome helicopter trip to Inylchek (€200 one way, €400 return). In winter it operates heli-skiing trips. Contact Sergey Pyshnenko.

Yak Tours (☎ office 5 69 01; yaktours@infotel.kg; Gagarin 10) At his backpacker hostel, Valentin Derevyanko makes on-the-spot arrangements for individuals, including trekking and horse trips. He puts his 50-year-old jeep – which is in a constant state of running repair – to good use ferrying backpackers to his Altyn Arashan accommodation. It's important you make it clear exactly what kind of arrangements you want at the outset and pin down a price.

Sights

CHINESE MOSQUE

What looks for all the world like a Mongolian Buddhist temple on the corner of Bektenov and Jusup Abdrakhmanov is in fact a mosque, built without nails, completed in 1910 after three years' work by a Chinese architect and 20 Chinese artisans, for the local Dungan community. It was closed by the Bolsheviks from 1933 to 1943, but since then has again become a place of worship.

ANIMAL MARKET

This is no match for Kashgar's Sunday Market, but it is still one of the best **animal markets** *(mal bazari)* in Central Asia. Locals like to load their Ladas with livestock – quite a spectacle if the beast in question refuses to be pushed into the back seat. Fat-tailed sheep, worth their weight in *shashlyk*, don't come cheap. Depending on its age, sex and size, a sheep can cost as much as US$120. Horses start at around US$300. The market is divided into two compounds, one for sheep and goats; the other, for horses, cattle and the occasional camel.

Next door is another area reserved for used cars and parts. A rock-bottom Lada goes for around US$300 but you'll have to bargain hard. The men here (and it is only men) set their prices high.

Go early if you want to see the market at its best: it starts at 5am and is all over by 10am.

HOLY TRINITY CATHEDRAL

The yellow domes of this handsome cathedral have risen from the rubble of Bolshevism at the corner of Lenina and Gagarin. Karakol's first church services were held in a yurt on this site after the town was founded. A later stone church fell down in an earthquake in 1890 (its granite foundations are still visible). A fine wooden cathedral was completed in 1895 but the Bolsheviks destroyed its five onion-domes and turned it into a club in the 1930s. Serious reconstruction only began in 1961. Services are again held here, since its formal reconsecration in 1991 and again in 1997. Listen for its chimes marking Sunday morning services (7am to 11am).

OTHER COLONIAL BUILDINGS

The colonial-era part of town sprawls southwest from the cathedral – lots of single-storey 'gingerbread' houses, mostly plain but some (eg those built by wealthier officers and scientists) are quite pretty, and a few (those of Russian merchants and industrialists) have two storeys. Among decaying former merchants' houses are the **Pedagogical College** on Gagarin opposite the cathedral, the **radio and TV office** on Gebze (Kalinina) and another old **merchant's home** at the corner of Koenközova and Lenina.

REGIONAL MUSEUM

Karakol's modest **regional museum** (☎ 2 18 68; Jamansariev 164; admission 50som, camera 10som; ⌚ 9am-5pm) is in a sturdy colonial brick building, once the home of a wealthy landowner. It's of limited interest, with exhibits on the petroglyphs around Issyk-Köl, a few Scythian bronze artefacts, a Soviet history of the Kyrgyz union with Russia, some Kyrgyz applied art and photographs of old Karakol – all of it better with a guide.

KARAKOL ZOO

The local **zoo** (☎ 2 55 18; adult/child 25/15som; ⌚ 9am-6pm) protects many of the endangered local fauna, including bears, wolves, bobcats, mongoose, eagles and some ill-tempered ducks. It's a shady spot and nice to visit on warm day.

OTHER SIGHTS

The leafy **Pushkin Park** by the stadium, four blocks south of the centre, includes the collective grave of a squad of Red Army soldiers killed in the pursuit of *basmachi*.

About 3km south of the centre (take bus 1) is Central Asia's very first **hippodrome**. Headless goats are still passionately fought over by mounted horsemen during **Independence Day (31 August)** celebrations. If you are in town at this time, the games are well worth checking out.

Activities

Karakol's travel agencies (p321) organise activities such as horse riding, skiing, mountaineering and mountain biking.

TREKKING

Karakol is one of the best places in the country to launch yourself into the hills and mountains of the Tian Shan. With so many trekking opportunities and a concentration of well-informed travel agencies (p321) there is no good reason not to. See the boxed text, p328 for a sample of the possible routes.

Alp Tour Issyk Köl (☎ 2 05 48; khanin@infotel.kg; Telmona 158) This professional company offers a range of treks around Karakol and further afield, including Kazakhstan and Khan Tengri base camp. It can arrange border permits in a day, supply guide/cooks (€25/35 per day), porters (€20) and climbing guides for Khan Tengri (€40). The staff will also resupply your own long-distance treks and arrange daily transport on request to the Karakol ski base in winter. Contact Igor.

Ecotrek – Trekking Workers Association (☎ 5 11 15; karakol@rambler.ru; Jusup Abdrakhmanov 116) The staff can arrange guided treks (guides, cooks and porters) and guided horse treks in the surrounding valleys, including a five-day trek from its yurt camp in the Valley of the Flowers, and Jeti-Öghüz to Altyn Arashan.

Leader (☎ 4 22 25; leader_kg@mail.ru; Jantosheva 18A) This NGO rents out trekking equipment to fund its youth development programs. The office and guesthouse is located close to the Issyk-Kul Hotel (coming from the town centre the hotel will be on your left, look for the signs to Leader on your right).

Tour Khan Tengri (☎ 5 25 43, 055-047 6606; www. tour-khantengri.com; Lenina 114) This experienced outfitter has a well-established camp located in the Inylchek Valley, see p334 for details.

CAMPING GEAR HIRE & PURCHASE

It's possible to hire camping equipment to outfit your trek but supplies are often limited and quality may be poor. Check the following places:

Alp Tour Issyk Köl (p323) One of the best places to rent sporting equipment, including skis, snowboards, climbing gear, tents and sleeping bags.

CBT office (p320) Rents trekking gear and sells Kovea gas canisters.

Ecotrek – Trekking Workers Association (p323) Rents trekking equipment including sleeping bags (80som to 100som), two-/three-person tents (160som), primus stoves (40som to 120som) and sells gas canisters (300som). Bikes can be rented for €10 per day.

Leader Equipment includes backpacks (50som per day), tents (100som to 150som), sleeping bags (50som), sleeping mats and stoves (20som each).

Kyrgyz Tours (p321) Rents tents (100som to 180som), sleeping bags (50som), sleeping mats (30som) and gas stoves (130som).

Sleeping

Karakol has more homestays than you can shake a sleeping bag at and both CBT and TIC (p320) can put you in touch with the local homestays. Generally prices range from 350som to 500som per person including breakfast and most can provide dinner for an additional 120som to 150som, although (depending what you are served) this is not always the best value; local restaurants are often cheaper.

Yak Tours Hostel (☎ 5 69 01; yaktours@infotel.kg; Gagarin 10; tent 100som, r 200som; ☐) This was the first backpacker-style hostel in Central Asia. It's a little neglected these days as owner Valentin is usually up at Altan Arashan camp. The caretaker who stands in for him will show you a room and take your money but that's about it. The rooms are generally clean but dark and a bit musty. The solitary bathroom is another downside. However, the prices are some of the cheapest around, making it popular with travellers on a shoestring budget.

Turkestan Yurt Camp (☎ 5 64 89; Toktogul 273; tent/yurt 100/250som, r 300-400som; ☐) The slightly muttony-smelling yurt dorms here have a base-camp feel as trekking expeditions bustle in and out in the Russian Zil trucks. Breakfast is not included in the price but you can add this option for 100som. Rooms are also available, the slightly better ones have en suite shower and toilet.

Neofit Guesthouse (☎ 2 06 50; neofit@issyk-kul.kg; Jamansariev 166; dm/s/d 360/700/1400som; ☐) A central, clean option, popular with trekkers who swap stories over a beer in the sociable courtyard. There's a wide range of old-fashioned but comfortable rooms with a private bathroom (but common shower), plus parking and a bizarre dungeon restaurant (summer only).

Artisan's B&B (☎ 7 01 71; Murmansk 114; dm 500som) This appropriately named B&B is run by a

KYRGYZSTAN

family of artisans who built everything by hand themselves; from the house itself to the painted Chinese horoscope on the ceiling.

our pick **Teskey Guesthouse** (☎ 2 62 68, 0772-801 411; www.teskey.narod.ru; Asanalieva 44; dm 500som) It has Western-style bathrooms, a Russian-style sauna, excellent food and a laundry service. The son, Taalai, speaks good English; his mother is a wonderful host and his father owns a Subaru which he uses to take guests on days trips to local sights such as Jeti-Öghüz. They also have two Giant bicycles for rent.

Jamilya's B&B (☎ 5 30 19, 054-398 0981; kemelov@ hotmail.com; Shopokova 34B; s/d 600/1200som) The mother-and-son team both speak excellent English and offer rooms with a hue – lime, purple, yellow or blue. It has spotless bathrooms, hot showers and a pleasant balcony overlooking the yard. Look for the white gate near the river.

Marzey's Guesthouse (☎ 5 55 55; marzeysguest house@yahoo.com; Korolkova 86; s/d with bathroom 700/1400som) This little-known guesthouse has clean and spacious rooms, a piano in the foyer and a beautiful lawn with flowers and mountain views.

Madanor Hotel (☎ 5 24 90; Toktogul 201; r with breakfast 800som; P ⌨) This new place has medium-sized rooms, an English-speaking manager and free internet access. A good pick at this price point.

Hotel Amir (☎ 5 13 15; info@hotelamir.kg; Ayni 78; baby's cot/child's bed €15, s/d €33/47; ⌨) This newish hotel fills a void in the midpriced market, offering simple but bright and cheerful rooms with *ala-kiyiz* wall hangings and queen-sized beds. It has its own power generator and a rather plain cafe. Breakfast is included.

Eating

Traktiry Kalinka (☎ 5 88 88; Jusup Abdrakhmanov 99; dishes 30som; ⏰ 10am-10pm; E) This wood-panelled place has Russian cuisine and a Tsarist-era atmosphere, so long as you ignore the Russian pop soundtrack. Some menu items take 30 to 40 minutes to prepare so bring some reading material. Look for the pretty Russian facade.

Fakir Café (☎ 5 10 88; cnr Gorkogo & Kushtobaev; mains 60som; ⏰ 9am-10pm; E) Offers a wide selection of dishes from Uyghur to Georgian, inside and outside seating, English menus, friendly staff and decent portions.

Maximum (126 Toktogul; mains 70som; ⏰ 10am-11pm) At the recommendation of some local

Peace Corps volunteers we gave this place a go and thought it one of the better spots in town. It has good *azu* (a Tartar dish of fried beef and fried potatoes with pickles and onions) and *laghman*, along with pink frilly drapery and the requisite Stevie Wonder soundtrack.

Kench Café (☎ 2 07 07; cnr Telmona & Gebze; meal 150som; ⏰ 11am-11.30pm; E) One of the better restaurants in town, located in the southern outskirts and with an English menu. The chicken with mushroom sauce is recommended.

You'll also find Dungan snacks such as *ashlyanfu* (meatless, cold, gelatine noodles in a vinegary sauce) in the Ak-Tilek Bazaar for only a few som. It can be quite spicy so watch the red stuff.

Entertainment

The nightclub located on the second floor of the **Fakir Café** (p324) is probably the best spot in town for a late night drink and a dose of Russian pop. Admission is 20som.

Shopping

Kürk Art Gallery (Makish Bazaar) Has some nice, neutral-coloured *shyrdaks* and an interesting collection of *voilochnaya shapka* – felt hats worn in *banyas* to bring the sweat out.

Antique Shop (☎ 0772-102 727; Toktogul 249; ⏰ 10am-5pm) Soviet-era antiques including pins, buttons, posters and lots o' Lenin busts.

Getting There & Away

Karakol's **long-distance bus station** (☎ 2 29 11; Przhevalskogo) has buses to Bishkek (per seat 260som, per bag 60som, eight hours) hourly between 7.30am and 1.40pm, and at night between 7pm and 11pm. These stop in Cholpon-Ata (90som) and Balykchy (140som) following the northern shore route. Only the 7.30am bus goes along the southern road.

Out in front of the long-distance bus station are minibuses and taxis that leave when full to Bishkek (minibus/taxi 300/500som) and Cholpon-Ata (minibus/taxi 120/200som). There is one bus a day in summer to Almaty (610som) but note that this runs via Bishkek not the Karkara Valley.

To get to the bus station, take local bus 105 or 109.

If you are looking for transport along the southern shore of the lake, its best to catch a *marshrutka* from the **southern bus stand** (☎ 5

13 53; Toktogul). There are departures hourly to Balykchy (180som) between 8am and 3pm, hourly to Barskoön (75som) between 8am and 5pm and hourly to Bokonbayevo (105som) between 7am and 6pm. A drop off in Tamga will cost 85som. For Naryn and Kochkor, change at Balykchy.

Most local buses (eg to Ak-Suu, Jeti-Öghüz and Barskoön) go from the local bus stand in the centre of town, at the Ak-Tilek Bazaar. You will also find taxis here for local hire around the region, but agree on a price and waiting time beforehand.

Getting Around

Marshrutka minibuses trundle back and forth between the bus station and the centre. Taxis are fairly plentiful and cost around 50som in town, 60som at night. You can book a taxi at **Econom Taxis** (☎ 166) or **Issyk-Kul Taxis** (☎ 161).

Minibus 103 runs a loop through the centre and around town.

AROUND KARAKOL
Przewalski Memorial & Pristan Prahevalsk

Thanks perhaps to the efforts of Soviet historiographers, and to the fact that he died here, the Russian explorer Nikolai Przewalski (p325) is something of a local icon, an increasingly poignant reminder of what the Russians accomplished in this part of the world. His grave and memorial museum are 12km north of Karakol on the Mikhaylovka Inlet. A visit with a Russian guide still has the flavour of a pilgrimage.

The **museum** (Muzey Prezhezhwalskovo; admission 50som, guided tour 30som, photos/video 10/20som; ⏰ 9am-5pm) features a huge map of Przewalski's explorations in Central Asia and a gallery of exhibits on his life and travels, plus a roll call of other Russian explorers. Captions are in Russian. English-speaking guides are sometimes available but the tour is a little heavy on statistics – ask them to tell you some of the legends. Your guide will surely point out the murals that change perspective from different angles.

The grave and monument overlook the Mikhaylovka Inlet and a clutter of cranes, docks and warehouses – all once part of the old Soviet top-secret 'polygon' for torpedo research. **Pristan** (Russian for pier) is a nearby strip of lakeshore several kilometres long that includes a sea of *dachas* (holiday bungalows) to the northeast and a popular beach to the west. The old military zone villages of Mikhaylovka, Lipenka and certain parts of Pristan Prahevalsk are off limits to foreigners.

KYRGYZSTAN

GREAT GAMER

The golden age of Central Asian exploration was presided over by Nikolai Mikhailovich Przewalski. Born in Smolensk on 12 April 1839, his passion from an early age was travel. His father was an army officer and young Nikolai, under heavy pressure to be one too, apparently decided that an army career would give him the best chance to hit the road, although he never enjoyed the military life.

To prove to both the Russian Geographical Society and his senior officers that he would be a good explorer, he persuaded the society to sponsor his first expedition, to the Ussuri River region in the Russian Far East from 1867 to 1869. Limited funding forced him to try his hand at cards and he was able to raise 12,000 roubles in a poker match (which embarrassed him to the point where he threw away his playing cards).

The results of the expedition impressed everyone, the society agreed to help finance future trips, and the army gave him the time he needed, insisting only that on his return from each trip he be debriefed first before saying anything to the society.

Przewalski's Faustian bargain got him his freedom to travel in return for being, in effect, an army agent. He never married, going on instead to become a major general and the most honoured of all the tsarist explorers. He focused on Central Asia, launching four major expeditions in 15 years, mainly to Mongolia, Xinjiang and Tibet. On one of his journeys he discovered the tiny steppe-land horse that now bears his name – Przewalski's horse.

On the last of these trips he arrived via the Bedel Pass at Karakol. In 1888 he was at Bishkek (then Pishpek) outfitting for his next, grandest, expedition. While hunting tiger by the Chuy River he unwisely drank the water, came down with typhus and was bundled off to Lake Issyk-Köl for rest and treatment. From here he wrote to the tsar asking to be buried beside the lake, dressed in his explorer's clothes. He died at the military hospital on 20 October 1888.

To get here on your own, take a public bus (15som) or a shared taxi (25som) marked Дачи (Dachi) or Пляж Plaj (Beach) from Karakol just north of the local bus stand, departing every hour or so. A taxi to the museum costs 100som one way.

Altyn Arashan

Probably the most popular destination from Karakol is a spartan hot spring development called Altyn Arashan (Golden Spa), set in a postcard-perfect alpine valley at 3000m, with 4260m Pik Palatka looming at its southern end.

Much of the area is a botanical research area called the Arashan State Nature Reserve and is home to about 20 snow leopards and a handful of bears, although the only animals you're likely to see are the horses and sheep belonging to local families.

During Soviet times it is rumoured that 25 snow leopards were trapped here and shipped to zoos around the world until Moscow cancelled all collecting and hunting permits in 1975.

Altyn Arashan has several small **hot-spring developments** (admission 200som). Natural hot water flows into a series of concrete pools enclosed by wooden sheds. The pools reek of sulphur but there is a translated certificate pinned to the door extolling the curative properties of these waters and listing, in exhaustive detail, the diseases they will cure.

Each shed is lockable and you can get the key from the house closest to whichever shed

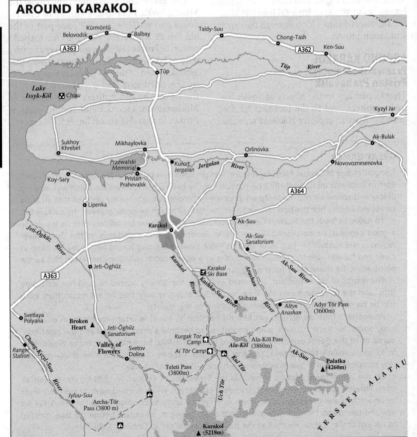

AROUND KARAKOL

you select. It is a great way to relax and it's almost mandatory to run, screaming, into the icy river afterwards.

From the springs it's about a five-hour walk on foot to the snout of the Palatka Glacier, wrapped around Pik Palatka.

SLEEPING & EATING

Yak Tours Camp (dm 250som, with 3 meals 600som) The first place you come to is run by Karakol's Yak Tours. The communal lounge has an atmospheric open fire but the bedding upstairs is usually dirty. On nights when the guide, Valentin, stays the food is excellent, at other times, less so and occasionally meals are dispensed with altogether. There are no hot springs here.

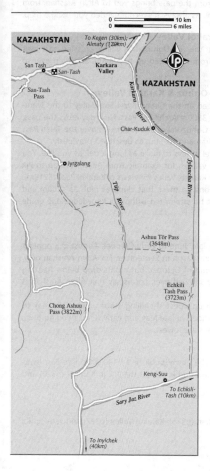

Arashan Travel Hotel (dm 400som incl hot pool usage) The next along from Yak Tours and a small step up in cleanliness; the beds are, however, in large dorms. Staff can also organise guides and horses and run a small shop selling essentials (Snickers bars, Coke and toilet paper). Meals are 80som to 200som and the hot pools cost 50som.

There are a half dozen families in the area that take guests. If one place is full, they will refer you to the next.

By far your best option is to take a tent and camp somewhere undisturbed. Pitching your tent near one of the camps usually carries a 100som charge. You can buy a few things here in summer but it's better to bring your own food (and purifying tablets for the water), plus a bit of tea, salt, sugar or coffee for the caretaker.

GETTING THERE & AWAY

An avalanche-prone road, strewn with rocks and winter debris, makes for a slow crawl up to the springs by 4WD. A taxi (250som) or minibus 350 (20som per person, 20som per rucksack) can drop you at the turn-off to Ak-Suu Sanatorium. From here it's a steep, five- to six-hour (14km) climb south on the 4WD track beside the Arashan River, through a piney canyon full of hidden hot and cold springs.

Valentin of Yak Tours will bring you up to Altyn Arashan from Karakol in his jeep for about US$25 per 4WD. The TIC or CBT in Karakol can arrange transport for a similar fee. There's little traffic so hitching is hit and miss. You can hike in as the climax of several possible treks to/from the Karakol Valley (see p327).

Karakol Valley

Due south of Karakol lies the beautiful Karakol Valley. The valley is a national park, which means there's a 250som entry fee collected at the gate.

TREKKING

The valley offers some fine hikes (see p328), although you really need to invest in a tent, stove and a day's hiking before the valley reveals its charm. Further up the main valley, at the junction of several valleys and trekking routes is the Ai Tör camp, run by Alp Tour Issyk Köl (p323), with shower, *banya* (US$3), tent sites (100som), mountain rescue, radio service and park permit check.

TREKKING AROUND KARAKOL

The Terskey Ala-Too range that rises behind Karakol offers a fine taste of the Tian Shan. Of numerous possible routes that climb to passes below 4000m, the best of them take in the alpine lake Ala-Köl above Karakol and the Altyn Arashan (p326) hot springs above Ak-Suu (Teploklyuchenka).

Ak-Suu village to Altyn Arashan & Back

Minimum one or two nights. Hike about 3½ to four hours up the Arashan Valley, climbing from 1800m to 3000m. Tell the driver you want to go to Arashan Valley. A day-hike extension could take you 4½ hours further up the valley, branching east and then south for views of Palatka (4260m).

Karakol Valley to Arashan Valley, via Ala-Köl

Minimum two nights. Hike up from the end of the bus 101 route for about six hours to where the Ala-Köl Valley branches to the left. Two hours up takes you to the carved wooden Kurgak Tor camp; another five hours takes you past waterfalls to the high-altitude and barren Ala-Köl lake. A 30-minute walk along the north shore offers camping at the base of the pass. The trail to the 3860m Ala-Köl Pass is indistinct and the crossing can be tricky at the end of the season, so consider a guide from September onwards. Five hours downhill from the pass brings you to Altyn Arashan, from where you can hike down to Ak-Suu the next day. As always, it's recommended you bring a map.

Jeti-Öghüz to Altyn Arashan, via the Karakol Valley

Minimum four or five nights. The trail heads up the Jeti-Öghüz river valley, crossing east over the 3800m Teleti Pass into the Karakol Valley. From here head up to Ala-Köl, and then over to Altyn Arashan and Ak-Suu.

Kyzyl-Suu to Altyn Arashan, via the Jeti-Öghüz & Karakol Valleys

Minimum six to eight nights. From Kyzyl-Suu head up the Chong-Kyzyl-Suu Valley to the Jyluu-Suu hot springs or on to a camp site below the 3800m Archa-Tör Pass. Next day cross the pass, head down the Asan Tukum Gorge into the Jeti-Öghüz Valley. From here it's over the Teleti Pass to the Karakol Valley and to Ala-Köl, Altyn Arashan and Ak-Suu, as described previously.

You can combine any number of these parallel valleys to make as long a trek as you like. You can also add on wonderful radial hikes up the valleys, for example from Altyn Arashan to Pik Palatka or up the Kul Tör Valley at the head of the Karakol Valley for views of Karakol Peak (5218m).

There are also longer, more technical variations on these that climb as high as 4200m and cross some small glaciers, but these should not be attempted without a knowledgeable guide and some experience with glacier walking.

When to Go

The season for the treks noted here is normally late June to early October. August is a popular time for picking mushrooms; blackcurrants are in season in September. For Altyn Arashan only, you could go as early as May or as late as the end of October, but nights drop below freezing then and the surrounding mountain passes are snowed over. Locals say that Altyn Arashan is loveliest in June and in September.

Weather is the region's biggest danger, with unexpected chilling storms, especially May to June, and September to October. Streams are in flood in late May and early June; if you go then, plan your crossings for early morning when levels are lowest.

Maps

These routes are indicated on the map (p326). The newly published 1:100,000 *South-East Issyk-Köl Lake Coast Trekking Map* shows all these routes and is sold at the TIC in Karakol (p320) and Geoid in Bishkek (p299) for 250som.

Getting to the Trailheads

For access to trailheads, refer to the Altyn Arashan (p326), Karakol Valley (p327) and Jeti-Öghüz (p329) sections of this chapter.

From May to mid-October you can make a strenuous day hike (or better an overnight camping trip) to a crystal-clear lake called Ala-Köl (3530m). You can also reach this lake in four hours over the ridge from Altyn Arashan; in fact this is on several alternative trek routes to/from Altyn Arashan (see the boxed text, p328).

A taxi from Karakol to the park gate is 80som. Bus 101 will take you part of the way, from where you can start hiking or hitching.

SKIING

About 17km south of Karakol, the Kashka-Suu Valley becomes the area's winter playland of snow and ice. The season kicks off at the end of November and runs to March although canny locals sometimes get an additional two weeks worth of skiing in May when avalanches create temporary ski fields.

Karakol Ski Base (☎ 5 14 94, 077-253 4081; www.karakol-ski.kg; lift pass adult/child 700/500som, ski kit/snowboard rental 400-600som) operates three chairlifts to a height of 3040m and one sledge drag. Together they access over 20km of trails. Most trails run through coniferous fir woodlands and the guided, winter forest ski tours are a magical experience. The ski rental equipment is relatively new.

Karakol Ski Resort (d/tr 3000/3500som) operates the Karakol Ski Base and the only accommodation on the mountain itself. There are a total of six doubles, four triples and two apartments (each with two bedrooms) and the hotel and two A-frame chalets that each sleep eight to 10 people. The rooms are basic but comfortable, all with TV and en suite. There is also an attached restaurant (three meals US$10).

The other option is to stay in Karakol town and hire a 4WD to take you up to the ski base. The TIC (p320) and many of the trekking companies (p323) can arrange this, but be sure to negotiate waiting time if you want a lift down. For heli-skiing see the boxed text, p314.

Jeti-Öghüz

About 25km west of Karakol, at the mouth of the Jeti-Öghüz Canyon, is an extraordinary formation of red sandstone cliffs that has become a kind of tourism trademark for Lake Issyk-Köl.

Jeti-Öghüz village is just off the main around-the-lake road. South of the village

the earth erupts in red patches, and soon there appears a great splintered hill called Razbitoye Serdtse or **Broken Heart**. Legend says two suitors spilled their blood in a fight for a beautiful woman; both died, and this rock is her broken heart.

The other side of the hill forms the massive wall of Jeti-Öghüz. The name means **Seven Bulls** (named after the seven main bluffs), and of course there is a story here too – of seven calves growing big and strong in the valley's rich pastures. Erosion has meant that the bulls have multiplied. They are best viewed from a ridge to the east above the road. From that same ridge you can look east into Ushchelie Drakonov, the Valley of Dragons.

Below the wall of Seven Bulls is one of Issyk-Köl's surviving spas, the ageing **Jeti-Öghüz Sanatorium** (☎ 03946-97711; s incl breakfast & massage 865som, massage 150som; ☼ summer only), built in 1932 with a complex of several plain hotels, a half-empty, semiheated pool, a restaurant (with meals for 100som) and some woodland walks. Former Russian president Boris Yeltsin and former Kyrgyzstan president Askar Akaev had their first meeting here in 1991 – and it has been downhill ever since.

From here you can walk up the parklike lower canyon of the Jeti-Öghüz River to popular summer picnic spots. Some 5km up, the valley opens out almost flat at **Svetov Dolina**, the Valley of Flowers (Kok Jayik in Kyrgyz); it's a kaleidoscope of colours in May when the poppies bloom. From here it's possible to hike to the Kok Jayik waterfall on the west side of the valley.

The **Festival of National Cuisine & Folklore** is held in the yurt camp in the Jeti-Öghüz gorge on the last Sunday in July. It is a good opportunity to sample Kyrgyz, Tartar, Russian and Dungan specialities.

Several yurt camps appear in the Valley of Flowers in summer. Just after the fourth bridge you'll spot the small **Jenish Gol Yurt Camp** (per person 200som, per meal 140som) with a nice location by the stream. This camp and the others in the area are normally accessible by car and offer a taste of the mountains if you are short of time, and a good base for day hikes if you have a couple of days.

Jeti-Öghüz canyon is one of several alternatives for treks to/from Altyn Arashan and Ala-Köl (see the boxed text, p328).

KYRGYZSTAN

GETTING THERE & AWAY

There are regular minivans going from Ak-Tilek Bazaar in Karakol to Jeti-Öghüz village (30som, hourly) *but* the village is actually 11km short of the sanatorium. It's not too hard to hitch from the village to the sanatorium or further up the valley, otherwise, share taxis sometimes go there for 30som per seat. One minibus per day (departing at noon) does go all the way to the sanatorium (60som), but check first as schedules are bound to change. To return from the sanatorium, stand by the main road and wave down the first car heading back to town; most drivers happily act as impromptu shared taxis.

A taxi from Karakol costs 300som to the spa and 900som to the Valley of Flowers.

BARSKOÖN & TAMGA
БАРСКООН & ТАМГА
☎ 3946

Barskoön village was an army staging point in the days of Soviet–Chinese border skirmishes, and the small adjacent settlement of Tamga is built around a former military sanatorium, now open year-round to all. Today Barskoön is all Kyrgyz, with more horses than cars; Tamga is mainly Russian.

The area's most illustrious resident was the 11th-century Mahmud al-Kashgari, the author of the first-ever comparative dictionary of Turkic languages, *Divan Lughat at-Turk* (A Glossary of Turkish Dialects), written in Baghdad during 1072–74.

The excellent horse trekking and hiking routes in the mountains behind Barskoön are the main reason to visit the area today. While the nearby villages of Tamga and Tosor are worthwhile for their serene beachfront property.

Sights & Activities

Shepherds Way Trekking (☎ 2 62 33, 07-721 24144; www.kyrgyztrek.com) is a very professional local company that runs horse treks into the mountains behind Barskoön. It's run by local brothers Ishen and Raiymbek Obelbekov and Ishen's wife, Gulmira.

Shepherds Way Trekking also helps to organise the annual **At Chabysh (Horse Racing) Festival** (Kyrgyz Ate Foundation; ☎ 077-251 8315, in Bishkek 031-243 4532; www.atchabysh.com) held in early November. By hosting a series of horse games and races the festival aims to promote the breeding of the Kyrgyz horse, which along with its associated nomadic traditions is now faced with extinction. The feature event is raced over a gruelling 47km course between Barskoön and Tosor villages.

In Barskoön you can see yurts in production at the **Ak Orgo yurt workshop** (☎ 077-306 4137; Lenin 93), including machines that make felt and devices that bend the wood and reeds for the curved yurts. It takes the 27 employees two months to make a yurt, which retail here at around US$4500. The workshop is on the right as you drive into Barskoön from the east. There is no sign so you'll need to ask some of the locals to point the way. Contact Mekenbek Osmonaliev.

Locals pack picnics and head 20km up the huge Barskoön Valley to the **Barskoön Waterfall**, where *kymys* is sold from summertime yurts near a defaced inscription by Russian cosmonaut Yuri Gagarin. It's possible to climb 1½ hours up to closer views of the falls. Shared taxis (160som return) run from Barskoön sanatorium to the falls along the well-maintained road that leads to the Kumtor gold mine.

The Canadian gold-mining company Centarra Gold operates the **Kumtor Gold Mine**, the eighth-largest gold field in the world, located in the mountains behind Barskoön. There are no tours of the operations, presumably as result of environmental concerns (p330) and you'll need a special invitation to get past the various checkpoints. The gold mine is at 4200m and even in summer it snows regularly.

Trekking is also possible in the valleys behind Tamga. About 6km from the village is a Tibetan inscription known as **Tamga Tash** but you'll need local help to find it.

The Tamga Guesthouse arranges one- to three-day treks or horse trips up to the Tamga Gorges or Ochincheck Lake, or a four-day trip to Chakury Köl at a lofty 3800m.

Sleeping & Eating

Altyn Kum Yurt Camp (☎ 077-271 6663; cholponordo baeva@rambler.ru; Tosor, per person incl breakfast 400som, full board 800som) Located on an exposed stretch of sandy beach, this basic camp is a great place to get away from it all. It's just a few steps from the lake and there is little to do except go for a swim and work on your tan. Food is available but you may want to bring your own beer.

Askar & Tamara Guesthouse (☎ 2 53 61, 077-398 8449; Issyk-Kulskaya St 4, Tamga; per person incl breakfast

---

EAGLE HUNTING: A REFLECTION

Alymkul Obolbekov, 80, is an eagle hunter. That is not to say that he hunts *for* eagles but rather *with* an eagle. For over 65 years Alymkul has been training these powerful raptors to hunt for game, including rabbits, fox, wolves, pheasants and badgers. He spoke with us at his home in Barskoön.

Alkymkul recalls catching his first eagle when he was 13 and trained it with the help of his father. 'The knowledge of this trade has been passed down from father to son for hundreds of years. I am only one link in the long line of history,' he said.

Alkymkul placed the eagle on a perch and swayed it while his father sang ballad after ballad. The sound of his voice became imprinted upon the bird and formed a union between master and servant. Later Alkymkul did the same with the many birds he caught.

In the next stage of training, Alkymkul attached animal skins to a rope and dragged them behind his galloping horse. His father released the eagle, giving it a chance to chase after the skins. When the eagle was ready for the real thing, they headed for the hills.

'Hunting is a team effort,' said Alkymkul. 'My dad would take the eagle to the top of the hills and I would stay below to scare up game.'

Their team effort paid dividends, as the fox and rabbit pelts added up. But Alkymkul recalls catching a wolf as his single best memory. With one talon the eagle grabbed the wolf's back and with the other talon she clenched onto its snout. Using a club, Alkymkul's father put the wolf out of its misery.

Alkymkul emphasized that raising eagles is a labour of love and real *berkutchi* (hunters) do not seek a profit from it. 'We loved our eagles like members of the family, but we know that they had their own home in the mountains. After a year or two we released them back to the wild to free their spirit.'

For travellers, the best time to see eagles in action is after their summer moult between October and February.

500som) Run by a chatterbox granny and her quiet husband, this place offers a couple of clean rooms that look over a leafy garden. It's the brick home on the left as you approach the front gate of the sanatorium.

Tamga Guesthouse (☎ 2 53 33; tamgahouse@gmail. com; Ozyornaya 3, Tamga; per person incl breakfast 700som) The slightly better Tamga Guesthouse is run by a friendly Russian couple and has a lovely fruit garden and sauna (500som per person). It's the first road on the right as you pull into town. Contact Denikin Alexandr.

Shepherds Way Guesthouse (☎ 2 61 33, 077-212 4144; Ozyornaya 3, Barskoön; per person incl breakfast 750som, full board 1200som) The trekking company of the same name offers accommodation at a cosy lodge, which has a large yard, dining yurt, hot showers, sauna and English-speaking staff. The guesthouse is near the top of the village but difficult to find on your own and they are not used to walk-in clients (most guests come with the trekking company). Call first.

Getting There & Away

Barskoön is about 90km west of Karakol, with daily buses to/from Karakol (75som) and Balykchy. Minibuses from Karakol to Barskoön leave at 9.20am, noon, 2pm, 3pm, 4pm and 5pm from the southern bus stand. Barskoön is a couple of kilometres off the main road. Buses to Tamga, a few kilometres further west, leave less frequently. There is little public transport between Barskoön and Tamga but taxis are available for 100som.

Tosor is another 6km west of Tamga and it's fairly easy to hitch here as it's right on the main road. A private taxi to Karakol costs 1000som and to Kadji-Sai 350som.

KADJI-SAI КАДЖИ-САИ
☎ 0394 / pop 4500

Surrounded by low, wind-and-water-carved canyons, Kadji-Sai makes for a convenient midway point between Bishkek and Karakol. In 1947 Kadji-Sai became somewhat of a 'Soviet secret' when uranium was mined here by Soviet Russia; at that time the town had no official name but was simply referred to as Frunze (after the capital) 10. The uranium, however, was of poor quality and the mine closed three years later.

The town is set 3km back from the main road that runs the length of Issyk-Köl. Minibuses will drop you near the petrol station, cafes and a boarded-up Tourist Information Centre; from here it is a 10som taxi ride up to the village.

Sights

There are no must-sees in Kadji-Sai although it's possible to take short treks to local geological formations including the **Kydyrmadjar Gorge** and **Skazka Rocks** – pillars of rock sculptured by the elements. The 14km taxi ride here will cost 700som including waiting time and swimming stops along the way.

The local **eagle hunter** (☎ 9 21 37; Sportivnaya 6), Ishenbek, in additional to running Zina's B&B, guides horseback hunting trips (8000som per group; plus horse hire, 300som per person) into the surrounding hillside in search of wild rabbits and foxes. Ishenbek will also put on hunting demonstrations using domesticated rabbits reared for food (2000som per group) but be warned, it's not pretty for the bunny.

Sleeping

Kut B&B (☎ 9 26 63, 077-354 2114; Sportivnaya 9; dm incl breakfast 400som) A comfortable guesthouse with three clean rooms. The talented owner, Serkebaev Akelbek, can play 13 different musical instruments and is part of a local music ensemble (to which his wife also belongs). They can organise a music concert for 500som. The house is located 650m from the main road. There is no sign so it's best to call first or to get a local to show you the way.

Zina's B&B (☎ 9 21 37; Sportivnaya 6; dm with 2 meals 600som) This is the house just behind Kut B&B. It has hot showers and a sunny room in the attic. Local eagle hunter Ishenbek runs the homestay and he is happy to explain the rearing and training of eagles. Three meals cost an additional 200som.

Getting There & Away

Minibuses, buses and shared taxis will stop at the intersection of the main road between Balykchy (minibus 95som) and Karakol (minibus 70som) and the road that leads to town. Taxis also wait here to ferry passengers the 3km to town.

BOKONBAYEVO БОКОНБАЕВО
☎ 3947 / pop 12,500

Bokonbayevo is the largest administrative centre on the southern part of the lake. The light industry that existed during Soviet times

is a distant memory and this is one of the poorer towns in the region. There is little to see in the town itself but the local CBT can arrange trips into the nearby mountains or a visit to a local eagle hunter – there are at least five around town.

Most of the town's activity is centred along Bolot Mambetov, from where the local minibuses and shared taxis arrive and depart. There is a string of shops, a small bazaar, a smaller police office, CBT and a mosque all within this block. If you are not eating at your homestay, the cafe, 100m from CBT, serves up a fine *laghman* (50som) along with other Kyrgyz staples.

Information

CBT (☎ office 9 31 66, 0543-144 166; reservation@ cbtkyrgyzstan.kg; Bolot Mambetov; ☼ 9am-5pm) This CBT can arrange homestays, horse treks and eagle hunting demonstrations. Contact Marym Atambaeva.

Sights & Activities

The local **museum** (☎ 9 31 21; admission 10som; ☼ 9am-5pm) is primarily a gallery for local artists. The curator will proudly show off landscapes creatively painted onto oddly shaped stones. Bokonbayevo is also home to a couple of craft cooperatives that make *shyrdaks* and other felt products. Contact CBT to arrange a visit.

The local **eagle hunter** (1-3 people 2500som), Talgar, and his eagle, Tumara, put on a deadly demonstration in a field on the outskirts of town. A sacrificial rabbit is used, rather than a piece of meat tied to a string. Organise demonstrations through CBT.

The **Birds of Prey Festival** (admission 600som) is worth a visit if you are in the area in August, when falconers from around Issyk-Köl compete here with their eagles, hawks and falcons. Contact CBT for exact dates.

Sleeping

Asanakunova Jyldyz Homestay (☎ 9 14 12, 077-734 7419; Osmoev 35; dm 500som) It's a 15-minute walk from the town centre and run by a large but quiet extended family who will mainly leave you to your own devices. Colourful *shyrdaks* brighten the entire home. Breakfast is included, additional meals are 200som. To get there from the CBT, walk along the main road (towards Bishkek), turn left after 700m on Osmoev, it's 250m up on the right.

Hotel Rakhat (☎ 0555-962 966; cnr Turusbekov & Atakan; r without/with bathroom 700/1000som) This place has a half dozen unexciting rooms cluttered with old furniture. It's a little threadbare for the price. Bargain.

Getting There & Away
Minibuses run to Tamga (50som), Balykchy (90som) and Karakol (105som) from opposite the CBT (east bound) and to the left of it (west bound). Shared taxis charge 200som to Karakol and 300som to Bishkek.

AROUND BOKONBAYEVO & KADJI-SAI
There are several trekking opportunities in the nearby Terskey Ala-Too mountains and Konur Ölön Valley. Community Based Tourism can advise on trails and arrange yurtstays. For the adventurous it is possible to trek to Naryn from here.

Amateur archaeologists might want to check out the scant remains of **Khan Débë**, an 8th-century pre-Kyrgyz settlement located near Tura-Suu (8km south of Bokonbayevo). A taxi will cost you around 300som round trip.

For a Dead Sea–like swimming experience try the buoyant but eye-stinging salty waters of **Kara-Köl**, (aka Shor-Köl, salty lake), 40km west of Bokonbayevo. It's best reached by taxi (which costs 1200som return from Bokonbayevo).

If you find yourself still lacking in spirit and health, locals suggest climbing to the sacred summit of Tastar-Ata (3847m) to drink from the large **Stone Pot** you'll find there. According to local folklore the pot was used by Manas himself while in residence and the stone pillars found in the area are referred to as the **Forty Soldiers of Manas**. The grassy south side makes an easier accent than the forested north side. The mountain is 20km south of Bokonbayevo.

Yurtstays
Community Based Tourism Bokonbayevo (p332) operates a yurtstay at **Bel Tam** (☎ 0502-705 198; beltam2003@mail.ru), 17km from Bokonbayevo, beyond Tuura-Su.

Ecotour (p304) has full-service yurts at neighbouring Temir Kanat and at Tuura-Su village at the west end of the Kongur Ölön Valley. These well-maintained camps offer solar-heated showers, guided horse treks and cultural activities.

THE CENTRAL TIAN SHAN
ЦЕНТРАЛЬНЫЙ ТЯНЬ ШАНЬ
This highest and mightiest part of the Tian Shan system – the name means Celestial Mountains in Chinese – is at the eastern end of Kyrgyzstan, along its borders with China and the very southeast tip of Kazakhstan. It's an immense knot of ranges, with dozens of summits over 5000m, culminating in Pik Pobedy (Victory Peak, 7439m, second-highest in the former USSR) on the Kyrgyzstan–China border, and Khan Tengri (Prince of Spirits or Ruler of the Sky, 7010m), possibly the most beautiful and demanding peak in the Tian Shan, on the Kazakhstan–Kyrgyzstan border. Locals call the latter peak 'Blood Mountain', as the pyramid-shaped peak glows crimson at sunset.

The first foreigner to bring back information about the Central Tian Shan was the Chinese explorer Xuan Zang (602–64), who crossed the Bedel Pass in the 7th century, early in his 16-year odyssey to India and back. His journey nearly ended here; in the seven days it took to cross the pass half of his 14-person party froze to death.

The first European to penetrate this high region was the Russian explorer Pyotr Semenov in 1856 (for his efforts the tsar awarded him the honorary name Tian-Shansky). In 1902–03 the Austrian explorer Gottfried Merzbacher first approached the foot of the elegant, Matterhorn-like Khan Tengri, but it was only climbed in 1931, by a Ukrainian team.

Of the Tian Shan's thousands of glaciers, the grandest is 60km-long Inylchek (Engilchek), rumbling westward from both sides of Khan Tengri, embracing an entire rampart of giant peaks and tributary glaciers. Across the glacier's northern arm, where it joins the southern arm, a huge, iceberg-filled lake – Merzbacher Lake – forms at 3300m every summer. Some time in early August, the lake bursts its ice-banks and explodes into the Inylchek River below.

Along with the eastern Pamir, the central Tian Shan is Central Asia's premier territory for serious trekking and mountaineering. Several Central Asian adventure-travel firms will bring you here by helicopter, 4WD and/or foot right up to these peaks. Even intrepid, fit, do-it-yourselfers can get a look at Inylchek Glacier (see the boxed text, p334).

TREKKING TO THE INYLCHEK GLACIER

The most common trekking route to the Inylchek Glacier is the remote and wild seven- or eight-day trek from Jyrgalang, 70km east of Karakol. Most trekkers will need support for this trek, not least because you will need a military permit from Karakol to head up the Sary Jaz Valley. There's one daily bus from Karakol to Jyrgalang.

Stage one From Jyrgalang the trail heads south up the valley, before cutting east over a 2800m pass into the Tüp Valley (seven to eight hours).

Stage two Over the 3648m Ashuu Tör Pass into the Janalach Valley (six hours).

Stage three Head south over the 3723m Echkili-Tash Pass into the Sary Jaz Valley.

Stage four Seven hours hike up the Tüz Valley to camp at the junction of the Achik Tash River.

Stage five Cross the river and head up four hours to the tricky Tüz Pass (4001m), from where there are stunning views of the Inylchek Glacier and Nansen Peak. From here it's a long descent to the Chong-Tash site at the snout of the Inylchek Glacier.

It is possible to hire a 4WD (costing 7000som; hire from the CBT in Karakol) to the yak farm in Echkili-Tash and join the trek there, leaving only two or three days to reach Chong-Tash. From Chong-Tash you'll face a one- or two-day hike back west to Ak-Jailoo or Maida Adyr camp and Inylchek town.

To continue from Chong-Tash on to the Inylchek Glacier you definitely need the support of a trekking agency to guide you over the glacier, keep you in supplies and let you stay in its base camps. With an experienced guide it's possible to continue from Chong-Tash over the glacier for one long day to Merzbacher Lake and to continue the next day to the camps. A popular excursion for trekking groups based here is to make a trekking ascent of Mt Diky (4832m) or Pesni Abaji (4901m), or to hike up the Zvozdochka Glacier to the foot of Pik Pobedy (7439m). Most groups take in a stunning helicopter route around the valley and out to Inylchek town and you might be able to buy a ride back up to Inylchek for US$200 to US$250.

The best time for trekking in this region is July and August. See p334 for information on permits, maps and agencies.

Information

Mid-July to August is the only feasible season to visit as at these elevations winter temperatures around the glacier are -15°C during the day and -25°C at night.

The best book to take along is Frith Maier's comprehensive *Trekking in Russia & Central Asia*, which has several maps and basic route descriptions for this region.

PERMITS

To go into the sensitive border zone past Inylchek town or anywhere in the upper Sary Jaz Valley you need a military border permit *(propusk)* from the permit station of the Russian border detachment stationed at the army base of Karakol's original garrison. Trekking agencies normally need at least two days to arrange this (€30).

You must have a letter with the stamp of a recognised travel agency in Karakol, Bishkek or Almaty, a list of everyone in your party and your itinerary. To climb in the region you'll need a mountaineering permit, which trekking companies can get you for US$105.

Dangers & Annoyances

This is not a place to pop into for a few days with your summer sleeping bag. You need to be properly equipped against the cold, which is severe at night, even in summer, and give yourself plenty of time to acclimatise to the altitude.

Sleeping & Eating

There are several base camps in the Inylchek Valley: en route at scruffy Maida Adyr and the newer, nicer Gribkov Camp at At-Jailoo, 20km nearer the glacier; as well as at several locations up on the glacier in tent-towns owned and run by ITMC Tien-Shan, Ak-Sai Travel and Dostuck Trekking (see p304) in Bishkek and Kan Tengri in Almaty, among others. The At-Jailoo camp is run by **Tour Khan Tengri** (☎ in Karakol 3922-5 25 43; www.tour-khantengri. com; Lenina 114) and has wooden buildings (per person €20), yurts (€7) and camp space (€3), plus meals (€5 to €8) and sauna €10. From the camp it's a 30km trek to Merzbacher Lake (10 hours on horseback). ITMC's camp costs around US$5 per night in a tent, or US$10 in huts and there's a sauna and bar. You can camp here and just pay for meals, although food is pricey.

Kan Tengri maintains the only camp on the north side of the glacier and also a yurt camp at 2200m at the edge of the Karkara Valley. All these are intended for trekkers and climbers, but anybody with the urge to see this cathedral of peaks can make arrangements with those firms, and pay a visit.

Getting There & Away

Bishkek trekking agencies (p304) organising climbs and treks in the central Tian Shan include Dostuck Trekking, Edelweiss, ITMC Tien-Shan, Ak-Sai and Tien-Shan Travel in Bishkek; Turkestan (p321) and Alp Tour Issyk-Köl (p323) in Karakol; and Kan Tengri in Almaty (p130).

Access to the region surrounding Khan Tengri is by road, air or on foot. It's a four-hour (150km) trip on a roller-coaster, all-weather road from Karakol via Inylchek town, a mining centre at about 2500m and 50km west of the snout of the Inylchek Glacier. Do-it-yourselfers could hire a UAZ Jeep from CBT Karakol, for around 7000som or a 4WD 15-seater from Alp Tour Issyk-Kul for US$230. Even though maps show a road between Ak Shyrak and Inylchek, the last part of this road is no longer passable and access via this approach is by foot only. The new road to At-Jailoo has a US$10 toll for jeeps, or US$20 for trucks.

If you have the cash, take a mind-boggling helicopter flight over the Tian Shan to Khan Tengri base camp with Kan Tengri from its Karkara Valley base camp, or with other agencies from Gribov Camp. It is possible to hitch a lift on a helicopter from Maida Adyr to the base camps for US$150 to US$200 (plus US$1 per kilo if you have more than 30kg of luggage). These trips run every two days in August.

You can trek to Khan Tengri's north face from Narynkol (Kazakhstan), Jyrgalang (Kyrgyzstan) or, less interestingly, from the Ak-Jailoo road head.

CENTRAL KYRGYZSTAN

The mountainous heart of Kyrgyzstan offers travellers unrivalled opportunities to explore *jailoos* on foot, horseback or by 4WD. At every turn you will find a family offering to put you up for the night or a group of herdsmen who will eagerly invite you into their yurt for a cup of tea and a bowl of fresh yoghurt. Add this to some of the world's most glorious alpine lakes and it is easy to see why central Kyrgyzstan now rivals Lake Issyk-Köl in the hearts and minds of travellers.

BISHKEK TO NARYN

The route begins as you would for Lake Issyk-Köl, winding up the **Shoestring Gorge** towards Balykchy before a short cut (by taxi) heads over a small pass and past the azure **Orto-Tokoy Reservoir**, effectively nipping off the Balykchy corner.

Three hours (185km) from Bishkek is the town of Kochkor (p335) and 38km past that, tiny **Sary-Bulak**, where you can buy *laghman* and snacks by the roadside. It's another 11km on to the 3038m summit of the **Dolon Pass**, the highest point on the Bishkek–Naryn road, and a further 16km to **Ottuk**, a tidy Kyrgyz settlement. A further 24km brings you to a fork in the road – both branches of which take you the final 10km into Naryn.

KARAKOL TO NARYN

This route follows the southern shores of Lake Issyk-Köl to Balykchy, winding between the barren, low rock escarpments that characterise this side of the lake.

From Bokonbayevo the road heads inland passing the picturesque village of **Ak-Sai** with its haystacks, apple orchards and cemetery, whose graves sprout a multitude of Islamic stars and crescents, to **Balykchy**. Here you'll almost certainly need to switch minibuses to head south towards Kochkor. Ask to be dropped off at the southern bus stand on the outskirts of Balykchy to catch a waiting south-bound shared taxi (70som to 150som) to Kochkor.

An alternative road that cuts between Tamga and Naryn is seldom used, requiring your own 4WD transport.

KOCHKOR КОЧКОР

☎ 3535 / pop 16,000 / elev 1800m

The little alpine, tree-lined town of Kochkor (Kochkorka in Russian) is the kind of place where everyone seems to know everyone else. People and vehicles congregate around the roadside bazaar on Orozbakova. One side of the road has colourful vegetable stalls, the

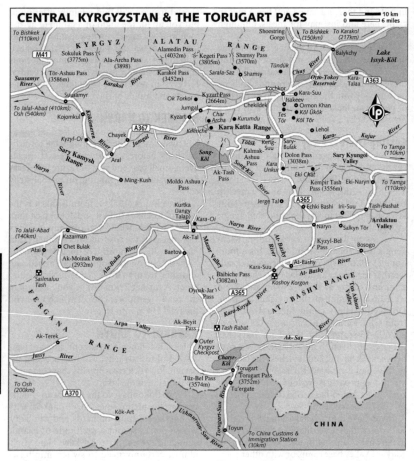

CENTRAL KYRGYZSTAN & THE TORUGART PASS

KYRGYZSTAN

other side a clothes market. Mountains loom in the distance, a reddish light playing off their snow-capped peaks at dusk.

Kochkor is home to CBT and Shepherd's Life projects, and as such is a fine base from which to make trips to Song-Köl or the surrounding countryside and experience traditional life in the Kyrgyz *jailoos*.

Information

There's internet access in the **telephone office** (Orozbakova; per hr 30som; ☺ 8am-noon & 1-10pm Mon-Fri, 9am-2pm Sat & Sun) and at **Aildagy Internet** (Isakeev 31; per min 0.5som; ☺ 9am-7pm Mon-Sat), from where you can also send faxes.

CBT (☎ 2 23 55, 077-771 8334; cbt_kochkor@rambler.ru; Pioneerskaya 22A; ☺ 9am-6pm) Arranges transport for

11som per kilometre, horses for 400som per day, guides for 800som (with their own horse) and B&B yurtstays in *jailoos* for 350som (or 450som for full board). A horse trek for two with one guide staying in yurts works out at around US$30 per day. CBT can put you in touch with the folkloric musical group Min Kyal (1500som to 2000som). Contact Myrza Ozubekov.

CBT Plus Eco (☎ 2 19 90, 0543-236 095, Orozbakova) This tour operator has copied the CBT name in hopes of luring newly arrived tourists. In fact they have nothing to do with CBT (although they do offer the usual range of travel services). If you are looking for the official CBT, it's across the road, just past the milk sellers.

Jailoo Tourist Community (Jailoo; ☎ 2 11 16, 0555-494 203; Orozbakova 125/3; ☺ 9am-8pm) The former CBT coordinator and English teacher, Asipa Jumabaeva, has set up her own business, offering similar services to

CBT at similar prices. She is able to arrange homestays (600som per person including three meals), horses, guides and transport (Song-Köl 1800som, waiting 100som per day) and give directions to any of 10 *jailoos* in the surrounding valleys. The office has a good showroom for local *shyrdaks;* local producers fix the prices and Jailoo takes a 15% commission.

Kredobank (☎ 2 21 38; Orozbakova 133; ☺ 8am-noon, 1-5pm Mon-Fri) Will change cash US dollars and euro (when it has enough money!).

Shepherd's Life (☎ 2 13 67, 0556-707 707) This outfit offers similar services to CBT at similar prices but with slightly ropier arrangements. Cars rent for 11som per kilometre and a yurt B&B is 250som (with meals an additional 150som). Like the other agencies, horse riding, luggage storage and guiding services can all be arranged here. It's located in the small shack at the back of the bus stand.

Sights & Activities

There's not much to do in the town except visit the small **regional museum** (admission 50som; ☺ 9am-noon & 1-5pm Mon-Fri). A fine yurt is on display along with a collection of local Kyrgyz crafts, plus displays on all the usual Soviet-era local heroes such as the local scientist Bayaly Isakeev. More Soviet heroes are celebrated in the busts to the east of the museum.

There is also an excellent **animal bazaar** in town on Saturday morning. It runs from 8am to 12.30pm.

Kochkor makes a good base for horse treks and yurtstays in the region.

Sleeping

There are more than 20 homestays in Kochkor, most costing 300som to 350som with breakfast. Each one is affiliated with CBT, Shepherd's Life or Jailoo. The B&Bs listed here are mentioned in case you arrive in town late and cannot contact these agencies. Check each agency to compare prices (we found Jailoo to be slightly cheaper). All include breakfast and serve home-cooked meals for an additional 100som.

Hotel (dm 100som) The only hotel in town is a grim hovel. But it remains the cheapest place in town.

Jumagul's B&B (☎ 2 24 53; Kuttuseyit uulu Shamen 58; dm 300som) Hosts Jumagul Akhmadova and her husband do a good job here. The B&B offers two large twin rooms, has a Russian sauna and a clean squat toilet in the garden.

Shepherd's Life B&B (☎ 0555-434 347; Kuttuseyit uulu Shamen 91; dm 300som) Considering this is run by Shepherd's Life, the farmyard vibe is entirely appropriate. An orchard and stable separate the two main buildings – each have a selection of rooms; some with beds, others with *shyrdaks.*

Tulekyev B&B (☎ 2 18 03; Sultan Kulovo 19; B&B 350som) A Jailoo-affiliated guesthouse in a two-storey house with hot shower and curious decor (wolf pelts, lion murals). From the main road walk east from the bus stand, take a left at the petrol station and then a right at the end of the alley. Look for the blue balcony.

HOME SWEET YURT

For the nomad, modern day or otherwise, there's no better home than a yurt. These easily collapsible felt homes are light, portable, spacious and well suited to the harsh and changeable climate conditions of Central Asia.

Yurts (*bosuy* in Kyrgyz, *kiiz-uy* in Kazakh) are made of multilayered felt (*kiyiz* or *kiiz*) and stretched around a collapsible wooden frame (*kerege*). The outer felt layer is coated in waterproof sheep fat, the innermost layer is lined with woven mats from the tall grass called *chiy* to block the wind. Looking up, you'll see the *tunduk,* a wheel that supports the roof (and which is depicted on Kyrgyzstan's national flag). Long woven woollen strips of varying widths, called *tizgych* and *chalgych,* secure the walls and poles.

The interior is richly decorated with textiles, wall coverings, quilts, cushions, camel and horse bags, and ornately worked caskets. Floors are lined with thick felt (*koshma*) and covered with bright carpets (*shyrdaks* or *ala-kiyiz*), and sometimes yak (like cows but with bad hair) skin. The more elaborate the decoration, the higher the social standing of the yurt's owners.

Spending a night in a yurt is easy – Community Based Tourism (CBT; p302) can arrange authentic yurtstays, particularly in central Kyrgyzstan, from Suusamyr to Naryn. Nothing gets the nomadic blood racing through your veins like lying awake at night under a heavy pile of blankets, staring at the stars through the *shanrak* (the hole in the roof that allows air and light to enter and smoke from the fire to escape), wondering if wolves will come and eat your horse.

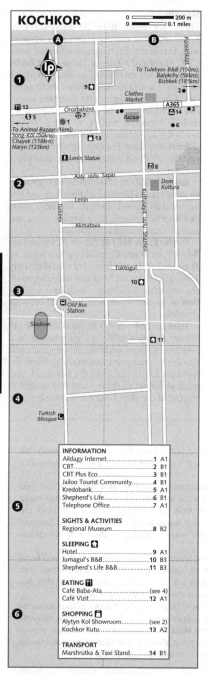

Eating & Drinking

Café Baba-Ata (☎ 077-315 3144; Orozbakova 125; mains 60-100som; ⏰ 8am-11pm) Thanks to its central location, outside summer seating and DJ, this cafe is popular with travellers, although the menu is limited and the food only passable. At night the attic thumps with Russian pop music as it transforms into a bar and mini-disco. The gold-toothed bartender pours strong drinks.

our pick **Café Vizit** (☎ 2 17 60; Orozbakova; mains 70-120som; ⏰ 9am-11pm Mon-Sat, 9am-5pm Sun; **E**)) This place offers the best food in town, dishing up delicious, no-fuss meals with no-fuss names. The unappealingly christened 'Chinese meat' (90som) is a delicious, diced-beef stir-fry. The goulash is another tasty dish.

Shopping

Kochkor is one of the best places to buy *shyrdaks*.

Altyn Kol (Golden Hands; ⏰ 077-762 2901; www.altyn -kol.com; Pioneerskaya 92) This local women's collective has a *shyrdak* showroom next to the CBT office. A good-quality 1.6m by 2.25m rug will set you back 5000som. It can arrange airmail postage (8000som for this size) or delivery to either Osh or Bishkek.

our pick **Kochkor Kutu** (☎ 2 24 22; kanay_zina@mail. ru; Abubakir 15) Another excellent place to shop, this place has the best variety of items in town (and probably the best outside of Bishkek). *Shyrdaks* are available, as well as carpets, woven bands (*örmök*), grass mats (*chiy*) and all manner of souvenirs and antiques. There is no sign outside so look for the blue gate.

Good-quality *shyrdaks* are also for sale at Jumagul's B&B and at Jailoo, which has a large selection of naturally dyed felt products using barberry, walnut, juniper, immortal and wormwood. *Shyrdak* prices range from US$30 to US$40 per square metre. The highly decorative, 10m-long *örmöks* that are wrapped around the insides of yurts (US$30 per metre) are also sold here.

Getting There & Away

Most people take a seat in a shared taxi from opposite the bazaar to Bishkek (250som), Balykchy (100som, 40 minutes) and Naryn (150som to 200som, 2 to 2½ hours). Infrequent afternoon buses and minibuses pass through to Chayek (150som, two hours) and Ming-Kush via Jumgal, picking up passengers by the bazaar at Orozbakova.

CRAFTY CARPETS

No craft smacks more of Kyrgyzstan than the quintessential nomadic felt rug called a *shyrdak*. *Shyrdaks* are pieced together from cut pieces of sheep's wool after weeks of washing, drying, dyeing and treatment against woodworm. The appliqué patterns are usually of a *kochkor mujuz* (plant motif), *teke mujuz* (ibex horn motif) or *kyal* (fancy scrollwork) bordered in a style particular to the region. Brightly coloured designs were introduced after synthetic dye became readily available in the 1960s, although natural dyes (made from pear and raspberry leaves, dahlia and birch root, among others) are making a comeback.

The 'blurred' design of the *ala-kiyiz* (rug with coloured panels pressed on) is made from dyed fleece, which is laid out in the desired pattern on a *chiy* (reed) mat. The felt is made by sprinkling hot water over the wool, which is then rolled up and rolled around until the wool compacts.

Before you purchase a *shyrdak*, ensure that it's handmade by checking for irregular stitching on the back and tight, even stitching around the panels. Also check the colour will not run (lick your finger and run it lightly over the colours to see that they do not bleed). There are women's *shyrdak* cooperatives in Bishkek and Kochkor and Community Based Tourism (CBT) coordinators can often put you in touch with *shyrdak* makers.

AROUND KOCHKOR

The following trips can all be arranged by CBT, Jailoo or Shepherd's Life. By yourself, you'll have difficulties finding yurtstay accommodation.

One of the most popular trips is to **Sarala-Saz** (53km northwest), a wide open *jailoo* with fine views, from where you can take day trips on horseback to petroglyphs (three hours by horse). Community Based Tourism organises **horse games** here in August. For dates, ask at the CBT in Kochkor or Bishkek. An adventurous two- or three-day horse trek leads from Sarala-Saz over the 3570m Shamsy Pass and down the Shamsy River valley to Tokmok.

Köl Ükök (Treasure Chest) is a beautiful mountain lake above Tes Tör *jailoo*, south of Kochkor and is a recommended overnight or three-day trip. Take a taxi 6km to Isakeev and then trek by horse or on foot half a day to the *jailoos*. Before June it's better to stay at Tes Tör (four hours from Isakeev by horse); after June you can stay up by the lake (six hours from Isakeev). Day excursions from the lake include the **Köl Tör** glacial lake, a couple of hours further up into the mountains. For a slightly longer alternative trip take a taxi 15km to Kara-Suu village and then go first to Kashang Bel or Bel Tepshay (Bel means pass), for views of Issyk-Köl, and then ride or hike the next day to Köl Ükök (seven hours).

If you really want to get off the beaten track, the **Shepherd's Life coordinator** (☎ 0553-720 909; Jetigenov Akun 16) in **Jumgal**, history teacher Stalbek Kaparbekov, can arrange horses to, and accommodation at, the nearby *jailoos* of Ok Torkoi and Kilenche. Jumgal is the first village after the Kyzart Pass, and is sometimes referred to as Dos Kulu. Stalbek's house is on the main road through town and has a prominent sign outside. He offers B&B accommodation for 350som per night.

There are also Shepherd's Life coordinators further west in **Kyzart** (☎ 077-335 4586), contact Abdykazar Talgar, and **Chayek** (☎ 3536-2 24 69; Moldaliev 4), contact Guljan Mykyeva. The Kochkor office has further details.

LAKE SONG-KÖL
ОЗЕРО СОН-КОЛ

Alpine lake Song-Köl (Son-Kul), at 3016m, is one of the loveliest spots in central Kyrgyzstan. All around it are lush pastures favoured by herders from the Kochkor Valley and beyond, who spend June to August here with their animals. Visitors are welcome, and this is a sublime place to camp and watch the sun come up. The cold, crystal-clear air, far away from light pollution and smog, guarantees a starry night sky so grand it is able to dwarf even this open landscape. The lake is jumping with fish, and you might be able to trade tea, salt, sugar, cigarettes or vodka with the herders for milk, *kurut* or full-bodied *kymys*. In any case bring plenty of food and water.

Naryn and Kochkor CBT and Shepherd's Life projects offer more than a dozen **yurtstays** (per person full board 650som) around the lake, where you can also ride horses. There is no real need to arrange horses prior to arrival, unless you are planning an extensive excursion, as horses are easily rented directly from

KYRGYZSTAN

the locals. Bishkek-based travel companies such as NoviNomad (north shore) and ITMC Tien-Shan (south shore) operate tourist yurt camps in summer, where you can stay if there are no groups.

The lake and shore are part of the Song-Köl Zoological Reserve. Among animals under its protection are a diminishing number of wolves and lots of waterfowl, including the Indian mountain goose. The weather is unpredictable and snow can fall at any time so dress and plan accordingly. July to mid-September is the best season. Tourist organisations arrange **horse games** at the lake in July and August (check with CBT in Kochkor). The lake is frozen from November to May.

It is possible to trek to Ak-Tal (see p343), a tiny village south of Song-Köl on the Naryn–Kazarman road.

Getting There & Away

It's 60km from the Bishkek–Naryn road to the lake: 6km to Keng-Suu (Tölök) village, 21km to the end of the narrow valley of the Tölök River, and then a slow 23km (1½ hours) up and over the Kalmak-Ashuu Pass into the basin. This upper road is normally open only from late May to late October. The valley has little traffic and no regular buses.

A car hired from Kochkor through CBT or Shepherd's Life is the easiest option to get here. Prices depend upon the price of petrol; rates are currently 11som per kilometre. Generally a car costs around 2200som for the return trip. You may find something cheaper in the bazaar.

There are at least three other unpaved 4WD tracks to the lake: from west of the lake at Chayek, to the south from Ak-Tal (p343) on the Naryn–Kazarman road, and a winter road from the southeast corner of the lake to the Bishkek–Naryn road. It's therefore possible to drive in from Kochkor and out to Naryn or Chayek, making a nice, although expensive (as you will have to pay the return price of both cars) loop route. Hitching is possible but only if you have lots of time and your own supplies.

It's also possible to trek in to the lake on foot or horseback from Kyzart, near Jumgal, in one or two days, staying in shepherds' yurts in the Char Archa and Kilenche *jailoos*, although check with Kochkor travel agencies to ensure the current location of yurts en route. This approach has the merit of avoiding the expensive transport to Song-Köl as there are

daily marshrutkas from Bishkek to Kyzart via Kochkor.

The CBT and Shepherd's Life representatives in Kochkor or Shepherd's Life in Jumgal (p341) can arrange accommodation, horses and a guide for around 1400som per day, plus food. Without a tent you really need a guide as it's impossible to find the yurtstays by yourself.

NARYN НАРЫН

☎ 3522 / pop 38,000 / elev 2030m

Naryn makes a convenient base for visits to both Song-Köl and the Tash Rabat caravanserai and from here it is possible to strike westward to Jalal-Abad via Kazarman. Naryn is derived from the Mongolian for 'sunny' – a rare moment of Mongol irony. The region's one real claim to fame is that the best quality *shyrdaks* are said to be made here.

Orientation

Dusty brown Naryn is strung along the milky-blue Naryn River for 15km. The road from Bishkek forks north of the town, each branch of the fork leading to one end of town. A trolleybus (3som) and minibuses (5som) run along the main street, Lenina.

The *hakimyat* (municipal administration) on Lenina is the designated centre of town. Other landmarks are the small bazaar on Orozbaka, and the bus station, 800m east of the *hakimyat* on Lenina.

Information

In an emergency it's possible to extend your visa at the **OVIR office** (Togolok Moldo 11; ☺ 9am-noon & 2-5pm Mon-Fri, 9am-noon Sat).

Naryn is the last place to change money before the Chinese border. The **telephone office** has an ATM that accepts Visa.

AKB Bank (1st fl, Kulumbayerva 23; ☺ 8.30am-noon & 1-5pm Mon-Fri) Can change clean US dollars (and occasionally euros), as can CBT.

CBT (☎ 5 08 95, 5 08 65, 077-268 9262; kubat-tour@ mail.ru; Lenina 8) Contact Kubat Abdyldaev, a fount of information and can arrange regional yurtstays (400som), transport and horse treks. Per day charges include 1100som for a guide, 550som for a horse. In addition to arranging trips to Song-Köl and Tash Rabat CBT burns digital photos to CD (50som). A car to Kashgar via the Torugart Pass costs US$340 to US$360 and it takes one day to organise the Chinese permit.

Khimchistka Prachechnaya (Kulumbayerva) Does laundry for 40som per kilogram (takes two days).

Sez Naryn (Lenina) Exchange booth 500m east of the *hakimyat*.

Zagruzka (☎ 5 01 20; Lenina; per hr 35som ⏰ 9am-9pm) Internet access.

Sights & Activities

The **regional museum** (Moscovskaya; admission 50som; ⏰ 9am-noon & 1-5pm Mon-Fri) has an interesting ethnological room featuring a dissected yurt and every accessory a nomad could ever need. Soviet Kyrgyz legends such as Jukeev Tabaldy Pudovkin, a local Bolshevik hero, are also featured.

There's little else to see except the town's garish but striking **mosque**, 2.5km west of the centre – completed with Saudi money in 1993.

The CBT organises horse treks and has maps and photos of hikes in the hills south of Naryn. The treks range between two and seven hours, and offer views over Naryn, the At-Bashy range and local farmland. Herds of yak graze these parts so watch your step.

Sleeping

The CBT has 18 excellent guesthouses in Naryn (B&B 350som per person, meals 120som), either in central apartment blocks or suburban houses; many in the eastern Moscovskaya suburb. Try the CBT first to see what is available.

Hotel Ala-Too (☎ 5 21 89; Lenina; tw without/with bathroom 150/300som, tr with bathroom 900som, lux 1000-1200som) Some rooms here have seen recent renovations but overall this place is pretty dilapidated. Beds are lumpy, lamps flicker and toilets gurgle non-stop no matter how many times you jiggle the lever. The lux rooms are clean and spacious, have hot water and balconies. Don't bother going to the restaurant, it looks like it was abandoned sometime in the 1960s – its windows are smashed, various pieces are falling off and trees are growing out the roof.

Satar Inn (☎ 5 03 22, 077-274 3372; Checkeybaeva; yurtstay 300som, r 350som) Has two tourist yurts, each with five beds. Facilities include Western toilets, a shower and a small restaurant (meals 70som to 100som). The twin and double rooms are modest but clean.

Shepherd's Life (☎ 5 43 47, 077-718 2974; a.marima2009@gmail.com; Kalykova 14; B&B 350som) The coordinator Marima Amankulova's house

KYRGYZSTAN

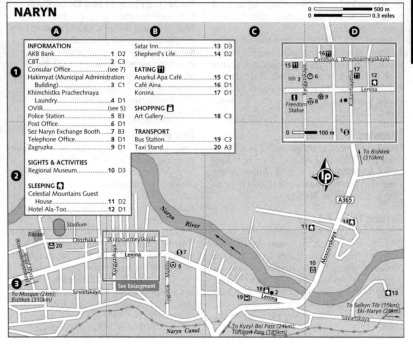

NARYN

0 _____ 500 m
0 _____ 0.3 miles

INFORMATION	
AKB Bank................................1 D2	
CBT...2 C3	
Consular Office....................(see 7)	
Hakimyat (Municipal Administration Building)..........................3 C1	
Khimchistka Prachechnaya Laundry................................4 D1	
OVIR.....................................(see 5)	
Police Station...........................5 B3	
Post Office...............................6 D1	
Sez Naryn Exchange Booth......7 B3	
Telephone Office.....................8 D1	
Zagruzka..................................9 D1	

SIGHTS & ACTIVITIES
Regional Museum...................10 D3

SLEEPING 🏠
Celestial Mountains Guest House......................................11 D2
Hotel Ala-Too..........................12 D1

Satar Inn.................................13 D3
Shepherd's Life.......................14 D2

EATING 🍴
Anarkul Apa Café....................15 C1
Café Aina................................16 D1
Korona....................................17 D1

SHOPPING 🛍
Art Gallery..............................18 C3

TRANSPORT
Bus Station.............................19 C3
Taxi Stand..............................20 A3

Orozbaka (Krasnoarmeyskaya)
Kyrgyzskaya
Kumbayeva
Lenina
Freedom Statue
0 ___ 100 m

To Bishkek (310km)
A365
Naryn River
To Mosque (2km); Bishkek (310km)
Stadium
Bazaar
Orozbaka (Krasnoarmeyskaya)
Kyrgyzskaya
Lenina
Togolok Moldo
Sovietskaya
See Enlargment
Moscovskaya
Lenina
Sovietskaya
To Salkyn Tör (15km); Eki-Naryn (28km)
Naryn Canal
To Kyzyl-Bel Pass (24km); Torugart Pass (185km)

and homestay (meals 100som), in the eastern Moscovskaya suburb, are one and the same and one of the cheapest in town (because there is no shower). A 20som taxi or 5som minibus ride will save you the 15-minute walk from the bus station.

Celestial Mountains Guest House (☎ /fax 5 04 12; www.celestial.com.kg; Moscovskaya 42; 3-bed yurt per person 800som, tw/tr without bathroom 2000/2400som, ste 2500som ; 🖳) This hospitable hotel is the best option in town in the mid to upper range category. It's operated by the Bishkek travel agency of the same name (p304). To escape the rigours of the road, unwind with free videos from its library. The suite, with en suite, offers the best value. Two meals are included in the price of the yurtstay.

Eating

Anarkul Apa Café (☎ 5 13 17; Orozbaka; mains 50-90som; 🕒 8.30am-9pm Mon-Sat; 🇪) The best place in town for a meal. It has a varied menu that includes a tasty baked pelmeni (dumplings) with cheese, Chinese stir-fry and *dapanzhi* (a large platter of spiced chicken and potatoes).

Café Aina (☎ 2 47 78; Orozbaka; mains 60-70som; 🕒 9am-9pm) Tries its hand at most things, from pizza and pancakes to Chinese the usual Kyrgyz favourites. Unlike most others, it stays open on Sunday.

Korona (☎ 5 02 94; Kulumbayerva; mains 90-140som; 🕒 10am-11pm) This place looks like the reception hall for weddings and indeed it probably is on weekends. It serves salads and a decent *kurdak* (a dish of fried meat and potatoes). In the late evening it morphs into the town nightclub.

Shopping

Locally produced *shyrdaks* can be purchased from the CBT office or next door at a shop called **Art Gallery** (Lenin 8, apt 59). Supplies are somewhat limited; you may be better off shopping in Kochkor or Bishkek.

Getting There & Away

Minibuses depart between 8am and 10am from the bus station on Lenina for Bishkek (250som, six hours). Buses to Kazarman (600som, seven hours) depart at 8am on Tuesday and Friday. The daily bus to Kurtka (Jangy Talap) leaves between 2pm and 3pm (80som, 2½ hours) and in winter at 1pm. Buses also go to At-Bashy (40som) to the south.

Shared taxis are a good alternative but the sharklike taxi drivers outside the bus station go into a feeding frenzy at the sight of a foreigner. A seat in a shared taxi will cost 45som to At-Bashy, 150som to Jangy Talap, 150som to 200som to Kochkor and 300som to 350som to Bishkek. To hire your own taxi costs 1400som to 1700som to Bishkek, 2500som to 2700som to Tash Rabat, 1000som to 1200som to Eki-Naryn and 4500som to Kazarman.

For Kurtka (Jangy Talap) you can also catch a daily 1pm bus (120som) from the bazaar.

AROUND NARYN
Activities

CBT (p340) can give the low-down on a range of trips around Naryn, including yurtstays in the Ardaktuu Valley and Tyor Jailoo in the Eki-Naryn Valley. Given a one-day warning, it can organise the following multi-day horse treks. Most horse trips start from Kurtka (Jangy Talap) or Eki-Naryn. Ask CBT about visits to the Tian Shan deer nursery at Irii-Suu (great for kids) and day trips up the Ak-Tam Valley to see petroglyphs.

Eki-Naryn to Bokonbayevo (six days by horse) Via Jiluu Suu.

Kurtka (Jangy Talap) to Song-Köl (two days by horse, three days by foot) Starting from Kurtka (Jangy Talap) village, west of Naryn to Song-Köl's southern shore, overnighting in yurts (July and August) or tents.

Naryn State Reserve (2½ days by horse, 4½ days by foot) Transport by car to the state reserve then you follow the Big Naryn River to Karakalka village overnighting with the ranger or staying in tents. It is possible to arrange transport or trek independently to Barskoön from Karakalka.

East of Naryn

The scenic Kichi (Little) Naryn Valley stretches to the northeast of Naryn and offers plenty of opportunities for exploration. About 12km along the road is Salkyn Tör, a scenic canyon that makes a great picnic spot and popular weekend hang-out for people from Naryn.

Further along the road is the hamlet of Tash-Bashat. Close to the village is a fascinating **swastika-shaped forest**. The origin of the forest is hotly debated. For years it was believed the German POWs had planted the seedlings as a sort of practical joke on their Soviet captors. But competing theories have popped up in recent years. One states that it was planted before WWII when Stalin and Nazi Germany were on good terms and the forest was his way of promoting solidarity. According to another theory, Kyrgyz workers planted the forest at the behest of a sympathetic German agronomist. Everyone in Tash-Bashat seems to have his own theory. The swastika can be seen from the river crossing, in the hills to the southeast of town; but unless you are obsessed with hunting out bizarre quirks of history, this is a long way to come for very little.

About 42km out of Naryn is the town of **Eki-Naryn**, close to where the Kichi Naryn River meets the Naryn. The town is in a lovely setting, with red cliffs all around and plenty of hiking opportunities. With your own transport it's possible to continue northeast and then swing west to follow the Kara-Kujur Valley back to Sary-Bulak and the main Naryn–Kochkor road.

If you don't wish to camp in the valley, check with CBT and Shepherd's Life in Naryn for service providers in the area. Community Based Tourism arranges homestays at Lehol, and Shepherd's Life has a summer yurtstay at Ardakty Jailoo.

NARYN TO JALAL-ABAD

The high road between Naryn and the Fergana Valley makes for an adventurous overland route across one of the most remote parts of the country. The route (along with the Suusamyr Valley road, see p348) is a good way to connect the western and eastern halves of Kyrgyzstan, without having to double back through Bishkek. The road passes through Kazarman (220km from Naryn), a rough-and-ready gold-mining town in the middle of nowhere. The mountain pass to the Fergana Valley is closed from November to late May or early June.

Naryn to Kazarman

From Naryn there are two ways to reach Kazarman and the one you'll end up taking largely depends on the transport you end up catching. The shorter route (five to six hours, excluding running repairs), favoured by shared taxis, starts with a fairly monotonous drive along straight and mostly flat roads, as far as Ak-Tal (or Ak-Talaa – White Fields), 75km west of Naryn.

The road turns right here, crosses the Naryn River and starts to wind through John Ford-esque landscape of desert bluffs and bad lands along a road blasted in 1903 by

the Russian military. Statues of camels that look more like llamas on the left-hand side signal the top of the pass, after which there is another series of hairpin bends and jaw-dropping views as the road winds down to Kazarman.

The second route, favoured by buses (six to eight hours), is the same as far as Ak-Tal but instead of crossing the river the road heads west and then swings south to Baetov, a forgotten rayon capital 40km southwest of Ak-Tal. About 35km past Baetov the dirt heads down a 3km long canyon with brown, eroded hills that look like melting ice cream. Some 5km past the canyon, on the right, are some small-scale ruins of a fort (near the 43km marker). After another 5km, look out for the small but impressive Shirdak Bek Mausoleum, by the roadside. Some 100km past Baetov you finally start to climb towards the 2932m Ak-Moinak Pass that leads to Kazarman. Around 42km before Kazarman the road improves and a series of switchbacks finally brings you into town.

Note that the Ak-Tal junction is also the point where you can catch the lonely 4WD track that leads up to the southern shore of Song-Köl (65km), via 33 switchbacks and the Moldo Ashuu Pass.

In **Ak-Tal** there is basic accommodation at **Konurchok Hotel** (☎ 3537-9 15 50; Zina Oshyrbaeva; r 100-150som), contact Busara Sagyndykova. Another option is to veer 7km off the main road to Kurtka (Jangy Talap) across the river, where you can stay with the **Shepherd's Life coordinators** (☎ 077-211 2324, 077-211 2324; Yntymak 45; per bed 350-400som), ask for Monsur Isakov or Sveta Jusupanova. For cyclists, the route that goes via Baetov is longer but involves fewer mountains to climb.

There are irregular shared taxis (100som per seat) to Ak-Tal and Kurtka (Jangy Talap). If you have time, try to track down the photogenic **Taylik Batyr Mausoleum**, near Kara-Oi village, around 8km from Kurtka.

Kazarman
☎ 3738 / pop 15,000 / elev 1230m
Kazarman is the kind of town that begs to be bypassed. Even the main road (Kadykulov) from Naryn to Jalal-Abad sweeps by on the southern outskirts of town. However it's not all bad; raw, untamed Kazarman's redemption lies in the nearby petroglyphs of Sailmaluu Tash.

The town exists to serve the open-cast Makhmal gold mine about an hour to the east, and the nearby ore-processing plant, but not much of the wealth has trickled down into local hands.

Buses and taxis turn off the Naryn–Jalal-Abad through road and drop you five blocks north on the town's main drag, Jeenaliev (also called Mira). From west to east on Jeenaliev you'll find the Sailmaluu Tash park office, the Dom Kultura building, bus station and cafes. One block north of the cafes is a tiny bazaar.

Be aware that access to the town may be impossible in the winter months when snow blocks the passes from both Jalal-Abad and Naryn. Check the road situation before setting off if you are travelling any time from September to May.

INFORMATION

CBT (☎ 4 12 53; Bekten 36) At the time of research CBT had no office. Contact coordinator Bujumal Arykmoldoeva at her home/B&B.

Sailmaluu Tash park office (☎ 4 16 76; Jeenaliev) Located next to the Dom Kulturi. Responsible for maintaining the park and selling admission tickets but might also run transport to the site. Before signing up for a trip with CBT, check here and see if the prices are competitive.

SLEEPING & EATING

Now that the sole hotel in Kazarman has closed, homestays are the only accommodation option. Common practice is for CBT coordinators to rotate the homestays so that each home gets an equal share of tourists. At last check this was not happening in Kazarman and we received several reports of travellers getting bottlenecked at one homestay (that of the CBT coordinator). To avoid this snafu insist on staying with a family that has not hosted lately.

CBT **homestays** (B&B 450som, meals 90som) include that of English-speaking **Bakhtygul Chorobaeva** (☎ 5 03 43, 077-768 8803; Kadyrkulova 35), who offers three comfortable rooms and hot showers. Right across the street from Bakhtygul is the homestay of **Shirinkan Karmyshova** (☎ 5 01 01, 077-361 4547; Kadyrkulova 36) who speaks German and offers an outdoor shower. Bakhtygul's homestay is located behind the bank, about five blocks south of Jeenaliev. Another landmark is the green-coloured petrol station called Bakit (Бакыт) on Orokov Baki St. From the petrol station go south to the next corner (Kadyrkulova St) and turn left. The

CBT coordinator also hosts travellers in her **homestay** (Bekten 36). However, this one can get very crowded while others remain empty.

There is a handful of cafes on Jeenaliev that serve basic but filling food (when available). Try **Café Ervol** (Jeenaliev), opposite the post office, which has *laghman* (35som).

GETTING THERE & AWAY

Buses depart Kazarman for Naryn (600som) on Wednesday and Saturday at around 8am (eight hours). At other times shared taxis and 4WDs congregate next to the bus parking lot on Jeenaliev and leave if and when they fill up. A seat in a shared taxi to Naryn costs 800som (5½ hours), Bishkek 1200som, and 600som per seat in 4WDs bound for Jalal-Abad (four to six hours). Occasional minibuses also depart from here to Bishkek (800som).

Because of the very real possibility that there will be no one to share your taxi, budget for the worst-case scenario – having to fork out for all four seats.

Sailmaluu Tash

The several thousand 'embroidered stones' of **Sailmaluu Tash** (admission 200som) are Central Asia's most dramatic petroglyphs. Over the millennia Aryan, Scythian and Turkic peoples have added to the earliest Bronze Age carvings. The carvings are spread over two slopes and depict hunting, shamanistic rites and battle scenes, some dating back more than 4000 years.

The petroglyphs are difficult to reach and are for the committed and adventurous. From Kazarman there are two route options, via Atai, 45km west along the road to Jalal-Abad, and the second via Chet Bulak south of Kazarman (so you can take one up and another one back). Both trips involve a car trip of about two hours, followed by a half-day hike or horse trip (three hours each way). The petroglyph gallery is only accessible from June to mid-September. It's best to spend the night at yurts near the site and explore the stones for a few hours early the next morning, although a rushed day trip is also possible.

At the time of writing CBT was not offering overnight trips to Saimaluu Tash. They were offering very long and tiring day trips, which included 2500som (per vehicle) for 4WD transport to the yurts, 450som (per person incl breakfast) for a horse to the petroglyphs and 200som (per person) for lunch. Horses, however, are not always available. You may also have to pay a parking fee for your vehicle (50som) and an admission ticket for your driver (50som). CBT can offer a guide but don't expect more than the most basic information.

If you want to spend the night at the yurts (recommended) you may need to source your own transport as CBT insists on the day trip only policy. In any case, bring your own food and a tent if you have one.

You might be able to get a better deal (and more flexible options) at the park office (*monpekettik zharalypish parky*) on Kazarman's main street. Ask the staff if they can organise guides and yurt accommodation; rates might be better than CBT.

It is also possible to approach Sailmaluu Tash on a longer route from the Fergana Valley, from Kalmak-Kyrchyn up the Kök Art Valley. The CBT in Jalal-Abad (p355) used to arrange such a trip but was not doing it the last time we checked. Check and see if the situation has changed.

Kazarman to Jalal-Abad

There are no scheduled buses to Jalal-Abad, only when and if they fill up will Nivas and Russian 4WDs depart (500som per person).

The road begins benignly enough, but the asphalt soon splutters out leaving a degraded dirt road, long overdue for some serious attention. Parts have been gouged away by rainwater run-off and the views down into the ravines from the crumbling track will have you reaching for your nonexistent seat belt. The road finally crests a 3100m summit at a spot commemorated by a statue of an eagle and a row of ugly pylons. From the scenery on the Fergana side you can see why the area is referred to as Central Asia's breadbasket. All going well the trip finishes sometime between four and six hours later at Jalal-Abad bazaar.

NARYN TO TORUGART
At-Bashy

At-Bashy is off the Naryn–Torugart road, 6km by an easterly access road, 4km by a westerly one, and truly the far end of populated Kyrgyzstan. Sandwiched between the At-Bashy and Naryn Tau ranges, the town has a great location and can be used as a springboard for visits to Tash Rabat, Koshoy Korgon and the Torugart Pass. Through the Shepherd's Life program you could also arrange visits to the surrounding villages of Tus

Bogoshtu (6km), Kök Köl (40km), or further afield to Bosogo Jailoo – a forested region ideal for trekking and, during September, blackcurrant picking. The lively animal bazaar happens on Sundays from 8am to 1pm.

ORIENTATION

From the bus station at the east end of town head 1.5km west past the new mosque to the cinema and city administration building. Turn right at this building and head north on Atty Suleimanov towards the low hill that marks the canal 1km in the distance. Continue four blocks and turn left down a dirt road, Arpa, for 250m to get to Tursan's homestay. A taxi will cost 30som.

SLEEPING & EATING

Homestay of Tursan Akieva (☎ 3534-219 44, 077-310 5774; Arpa 25; dm 300som) Tursan is the local coordinator of Shepherd's Life and offers a family atmosphere (breakfast included, meals 200som) in a home resplendent with *shyrdaks* and carpets. Tursan also arranges transport to Tash Rabat and Torugart, dispenses info on local *shyrdak* cooperatives and puts travellers in touch with several yurtstays in the surrounding mountains.

There are a couple of grotty cafes at the bus station and on Lenin, plus a small bazaar about 600m west of the bus station.

GETTING THERE & AWAY

There are daily buses in the morning to Naryn (40som, 1½ hours), a 6.30pm night bus to Bishkek (200som, eight hours) and Kara-Suu (35som, 30 minutes). A seat in a shared taxi to Bishkek costs 500som, or 80som to Naryn.

Taxis ask 1200som (negotiate waiting time) return to Tash Rabat. Tursan at the Shepherd's Life program can arrange a taxi for 11som per kilometre. **Zuu Stamakunav** (☎ 0555-708 556) is a local driver who charges honest prices and (for once) respects the rules of the road.

Koshoy Korgon

In a field behind the village of Kara-Suu are the eroded ruins of a large citadel, occupied during the 10th to 12th (or early 13th centuries), and probably Karakhanid. An appealing local legend tells that the Kyrgyz hero Manas built the citadel and a mausoleum here for his fallen friend Koshoy.

A new **museum** (☎ 077-771 2231; admission 50som; ⊗ 9am-1pm & 2-6pm) near the entrance to the ruins displays some of the bits and pieces plucked from the site, such as pottery shards and arrowheads.

A private taxi (four seats) from At-Bashy to the site costs about 400som for a return visit. About 14.5km west of the western access road to At-Bashy, by a petrol station on the Naryn–Torugart road, turn south (signposted) to Kara-Suu village. Take the first left turn in the village after the mosque and silver war memorial, continue past all the houses and then take a right and then another right to the ruins, 3km from the main road.

Near to the ruins, Shepherd's Life has a **homestay** (☎ 077-357 7166; 300som), which could be a good base for hikes in the At-Bashy range.

Tash Rabat

About 60km from At-Bashy, a dirt track heads into a hidden, surprisingly level valley, surrounded by lush corduroy hillsides that for centuries have been offering shelter to well-to-do travellers in a fortified **caravanserai** (admission 50som; ☺ 9am-5pm mid-May–mid-Oct), which looks like a mausoleum, sunk into the hillside.

Local sources say it dates from the 15th century, although some sources say the site dates from the 10th century, when it was a Christian monastery. Either way historians agree that at one time Tash Rabat (Kyrgyz for stone fortress) must have had significant Silk Road political and trade importance to justify the investment of the labour required for its construction.

It's irregular shape and improbable location has fuelled a number of local legends. One relates how a ruling khan devised a test for his two sons to see who was worthy to inherit his throne. One son, determined to prove that he could provide for his people, pursued the development of education, agriculture and industry. The other son amassed armies and built fortresses. Tash Rabat stands as a silent reminder of a war-mongering man who lost a khanate to his philanthropic brother.

A clumsy Soviet restoration was completed in 1984. A few fragments of the original central mosque are visible in the main chamber; leading off this are many other chambers, including a well (some say a treasury) in the far left corner and a dungeon (in the central right chamber). An opening in the far right corner leads to what the caretakers say is a tunnel, explored generations ago for as far as

about 200m, and perhaps once leading to a lookout point to the south.

Community Based Tourism Naryn (p340) sells a photocopied pamphlet, *A Self-Guided Tour of Tash Rabat*, which helps fill in some of the gaps.

From Tash Rabat a six-hour horse ride or hike will take you to a broad ridge overlooking **Chatyr-Köl**; if you continue for a couple of hours you can stay the night in a yurt at Chatyr-Köl before returning to Tash Rabat the next day. Remember that you are about 3500m high here, so even a short walk could set your head pounding. Neither Tash Rabat nor Chatyr-Köl are in a restricted border zone. The caretakers at Tash Rabat can arrange the trip and rent horses for 550som per day and a trekking guide for 550som per day or a mounted guide for 650som per day, making this a great place to spend a day or two exploring.

You can stay at the **yurts** (400som) of **Shepherd's Life** (☎ 077-388 9098; meals 200som) or the caretaker's yurts across from the caravanserai. There are two more yurtstays located 1km back downstream.

There's no public transport here and because of snow the road is closed from mid-October to mid-May. A day trip by taxi from Naryn to Tash Rabat (two hours) costs around 2250som; otherwise drivers charge an additional 700som per day for food and lodging. For a further 70som you can visit Koshoy Korgon (p345) on the same day. Alternatively, it is also possible (and recommended) to include Tash Rabat as a side trip en route to the Torugart Pass, although this involves setting out an hour and a half earlier and an additional US$10 to cover the extra kilometres.

TORUGART PASS
ПЕРЕВАЈ ТОРУГАРТ

Torugart is one of Asia's most unpredictable border posts. Even the most painstaking arrangements can be thwarted by logistical gridlock on the Chinese side or by unpredictable border closures (eg for holidays, snow or heaven knows what else).

From the Kyrgyzstan customs and immigration station it is 6.8km to the summit. Below this, about 5km away, is a checkpoint, though the main Chinese customs and immigration post is another 70km away.

The Torugart Pass is normally snow-free from late May through to September. The crossing is theoretically kept open all year, but is icy and dangerous in winter. The **customs and immigration facilities** are open from 10am to 5pm Monday to Friday, but in reality you must cross between 9am and noon. There is a spartan state 'hotel' here, though most people who stay do so in basic caravans 1km before the customs area.

Red Tape

Essentially many of the difficulties crossing the pass boil down to Torugart being classified by the Chinese as a 'Class 2' border crossing, for local traffic only, and so special regulations are in force for foreigners, many of which seem deliberately set up to milk foreigners of some hard currency. For example, foreigners aren't allowed to take the weekly bus that runs between Kashgar and Kyrgyzstan. The bottom line is that you must have onward Chinese transport arranged and waiting for you on the Chinese side to be allowed past the Kyrgyz border post.

Kyrgyz border officials are insistent on written confirmation of this onward transport into China, and detain visitors until their transport arrives at the summit from Kashgar. The best thing to have is a fax from an accredited Chinese tour agency, who will come and meet you. No special endorsement is required on your Chinese visa.

The three-point border – two border controls 12km apart and a security station in between – makes for further confusion. You are not allowed to walk or cycle on the Chinese side of the border in no-man's-land. It is therefore *essential* that your Kyrgyz transport continues past the custom post to the actual border to meet your prearranged Chinese onward transport. Only drivers with a Kyrgyz Foreign Ministry special permit can go this far. Normally the Chinese guards at the arch radio to Kyrgyz immigration when your transport arrives and only then are you allowed to leave the Kyrgyz border post. See p347 for further advice and p370 for general advice.

Travel Agencies

Travel agencies can arrange all manner of trips over the pass and prices vary depending on what options you take. It can sometimes work out cheaper if you make your own way to Naryn and start the program from there, rather than starting from Bishkek. Sharing the costs among other travellers will also

kick the costs down; with some planning you might be able to tag onto a group. The best companies to contact include NoviNomad, Celestial Mountains and Kyrgyz Concept (p304). Program options can include a side trip to Tash Rabat, horse riding, border permits and hotel accommodation.

Community Based Tourism Naryn (p340) arranges reliable transport to Kashgar from Naryn for US$340 per vehicle (US$140 for Kyrgyz transport, US$200 for Chinese transport) in a car capable of seating four. Allow one full day to organise.

Most agents can make arrangements with a cooperating Chinese agency for onward transport. The charge for this is set by the Chinese agency and normally paid in US dollars to the Chinese driver once in China. If this is the case, get a printed confirmation of the price from your Kyrgyz agent to avoid any dispute later. You could deal directly with a Chinese travel agency from abroad but it's generally easier to let the agency make the arrangements.

If you do wish to contact Chinese agencies directly, you could start with **John's Information Café** (☎ 86-998-255 1186; www.johncafe. com) in Kashgar.

Cycling

It is possible to cycle from Naryn to the border (or in the reverse direction) but once you cross into China you'll have to load your bike onto pre-arranged transport for the last leg to Kashgar.

Community Based Tourism Naryn (p340) can arrange the Chinese transport (US$200 per car) and provide a covering letter (US$50) that states a Chinese representative is waiting on the Chinese side for you and your bike. The covering letter will also explain that you have been informed not to leave the main road past the Korgon Tash checkpoint, and will only camp by the roadside.

Crossing the Pass
KYRGYZSTAN

When both sides of the border finally open, you and your driver show confirmation of onward transport and then wait until the radio call comes from the Chinese side that your onward transport has arrived. After this you'll go through customs and immigration while your vehicle is being strip-searched in a garage next door.

After inspection you jump back into your vehicle and continue 7km to the border. If you don't have transport for this section, this is where your headache begins, as you'll have to negotiate with a driver to give you a lift and with the officials to let you pass.

In the border zone, roughly halfway between the two customs and immigration stations, permitted vehicles are allowed, but apparently no pedestrians. At the summit, your new driver and some Chinese soldiers will be waiting for the transfer. Big handshakes all around. Don't forget to take a look at the beautiful pass, which you just fought so hard to cross.

CHINA

Another 5km later you will arrive at the original Chinese border post where your luggage will be inspected and passport checked.

It's surprising how the climate and landscape change when you cross the pass. The Chinese side is abruptly drier, more desolate and treeless, with little physical development other than adobe Kyrgyz settlements.

The 100km of road closest to the border is a miserable washboard surface, spine-shattering to travel along and choked with dust. At the junction of the Torugart and Irkeshtam roads is the spanking new Chinese customs and immigration station.

Chinese immigration is open from 1pm to 5pm Beijing time but officers will wait for you if you are late. Here you fill out entry forms and get your passport stamped, both relatively painless. The post has a Bank of China branch, a couple of simple noodle shops and a small guesthouse, though travellers in either direction are discouraged from staying. From here to Kashgar it's 60km of paved road.

The whole Torugart to Kashgar trip is 160km, a 3½- to four-hour 4WD trip.

BISHKEK TO OSH & THE KYRGYZ FERGANA VALLEY

From the standpoint of landscape, the Bishkek–Osh road is a sequence of superlatives, taking the traveller over two 3000m-plus passes, through the yawning Suusamyr Valley, around the immense Toktogul reser-

voir, down the deep Naryn River gorge and into the broad Fergana Valley.

The road has improved dramatically recently as the government tries to solder the two halves of the country together using better transport and communication links. The Bishkek to Toktogul stretch is still blocked occasionally by rock falls and avalanches. Snow fills the passes from late October until March; the road is kept open but is dangerous. Scheduled transport thins out by October, although cars continue to push through.

BISHKEK TO TASHKÖMÜR
Bishkek to Suusamyr Valley

Even before you climb out of the Chuy Valley from Kara-Balta, the craggy Kyrgyz Ala-Too range rises like a wall. The road climbs through a crumbling canyon towards the highest point of the journey, the 3586m **Tör-Ashuu Pass** at the suture between the Talas Ala-Too and Kyrgyz Ala-Too ranges. Instead of climbing over, the road burrows through, in a series of dripping tunnels (built by the same team that constructed the metros in Leningrad and Moscow) that open to a grand, eagle's-eye view of the Suusamyr Basin.

There is a 45som toll collected (or checked) at each end of the Tör-Ashuu Pass.

In 2001 the longest tunnel (2.6km) was the scene of a freak accident when a car broke down midway through causing a traffic-jam. By the time the truck drivers turned off their engines four people had died from carbon monoxide poisoning. Cyclists should consider hitching a lift through the tunnel, particularly in the southern direction as there is a slightly uphill grade this way.

About 4½ hours out of Bishkek a side road shoots across the basin towards Suusamyr, Chayek and eventually the Bishkek–Naryn road (p335). This is classic Kyrgyz yurt country, with plenty of summer roadside stands, offering fresh *kymys* (1L 50som) and other dairy products.

After another 1¼ hours another road branches right, this one over the 3330m Otmek Pass, 106km towards Talas, and Taraz in Kazakhstan.

Suusamyr Valley

This rarely visited valley offers quaint villages, mountain *jailoos,* rushing rivers and great off-the-beaten-path adventures. It's popular with overland cyclists, who use the route as a handy way to connect Kochkor (see p335) and southern Kyrgyzstan, without having to backtrack through Bishkek.

If you don't have bike, you'll need to hire a vehicle to get you through here, or try your luck hitching. Public marshrutkas (originating in Bishkek) can only get you as far as Chayek (via Kochkor) or to Kyzyl-Oi (via Kara-Balta). The stretch between Chayek and Kyzyl-Oi is something of a black hole. Hitchhikers will need patience to get through but can take comfort in travelling through some gorgeous scenery.

Adventurous trekkers can visit the valley as part of a trek to/from Bishkek over the Kyrgyz Ala-Too via the Sokuluk (3775m), Ala-Archa (3898m) or Alamedin (4032m) passes.

To reach **Suusamyr** village, take the Bishkek–Toktogul road and turn off at the bottom of the hill beyond the Tör-Ashuu pass. It's a 13km gravel road down to the village from the turn-off. Once in the village it's possible to stay at the **Kubanychbek Amankulov** (☎ 0777-443 275; B&B 350som; Nasirjan 7), look for the tourist info sign on the main road.

Kubanychbek (aka Nayaber) can also arrange transport and yurtstays in *jailoos* east at Joo Jurok (30km from Suusamyr; contact Negizbek Imankulov), 20km north at Boirok (contact Eshbolot Cheinekeev) and 13km southeast at Sandyk (contact Kubat Amankulov). Little English is spoken at any of these. A round trip taxi ride to Sandyk, including overnight stay, will cost 500som.

Continuing east from Suusamyr the gravel road winds another 13km to **Kojumkul**. The village is named after a local hero who stood 2.3m tall and weighed 165 kilos. Kojumkul (1889–1955) remains a legend in these parts and a museum in the town is dedicated to his exploits (the huge stones outside are reportedly the same ones he used to lift for fun). The museum, under renovation at the time of research, is on the main road through town; look for the red roof.

Beyond Kojumkul the road enters a foreboding steep-sided valley cut by the fast-flowing Kokomoron River. A break in the gorge has left just enough space for the hamlet of **Kyzyl-Oi**, one of the most picturesque settings in Kyrgyzstan. The stunning mountains that hover over the town are just begging to be explored. A CBT office here can help get you on your way, ask for the coordinator Artyk Kulubaev at the shop 'Aksar'.

Recommended horse treks include the five-hour ride up the Char Valley and over the Kumbel Pass to Balik Köl lake, where shepherds graze their flocks in summer. It may be possible to overnight in a yurt en route (inquire at the CBT). You'll also encounter shepherds at *jailoos* in the Sary Kamysh range to the south of town.

There are around 10 homestays in the village and the CBT office can direct you do one of them (a board on the wall of the CBT office displays photos of each host). Nurzada Tajebekova runs a recommended B&B. The CBT office also has a wall map of the area so that you can orient yourself.

From Kyzyl-Oi it's about 23km to the roadside hamlet of Aral and then another 17km to Chayek. Transport in this direction is a rare commodity so hop in whatever rolls past.

Chayek is a little rough-around-the-edges and somewhat anti-climatic after the stunning gorge you've just passed through, but for cyclists it's a good place to break for lunch. Try the decent **Daam Cafe** (Matieva 84; ✉ 8am-8pm) on the main road 100m west of the bus stand. Chayek also has the basic **Masimkul Hotel** (per night 200som; Matieva 121) and a couple of home-stays. The **Jamantaeva Begimkan B&B** (☎ 3536-2 14 42, 077-267 5508; Muratbek Riskulova 82; dm incl breakfast 300som) is a large house run by a religious family. It's located uphill, behind some small shops that are opposite the bus station. Call ahead and they will meet you.

Chayek also has a Shepherd's Life coordinator (see p339).

From Chayek you can get a shared taxi to Kochkor (250som) or Bishkek (450som). However, most cars are going all the way to Bishkek so you may have to pay the full fare even if you are just headed to Kochkor. Hitching or private taxi is another option, especially if you are just headed for the Shepherd's Life coordinator in Jumgal (45km beyond Chayek).

Talas
☎ 3422 / pop 30,000

Wind-raked Talas, isolated from the rest of Kyrgyzstan by a wall of mountains, sees little visitors. Most locals (and even the Peace Corps volunteers) do their shopping in Taraz (Kazakhstan) rather than make the trek over to Bishkek. While there is little to see in town, Talas does get a trickle of visitors who come to visit the nearby Manas Ordu, claimed to be the 14th-century tomb of Manas, the Kyrgyz tour-de-force that inspired so many legends.

INFORMATION

CBT Talas (☎ 5 29 19, 0772-643 466; cbt_talas@list.ru; Kayimov Yuzhnaya 76) Offers accommodation (250som to 420som) around town and at Ozgorush, 50km northeast of town. Contact Turdubek Aiyilchiev.

Internet Cafe (☎ 5 53 13; per hour 30som; Batyr Berdike; 🕙 9am-10pm) Internet access on the 2nd floor of the Telecom office.

SIGHTS & ACTIVITIES

The main draw in Talas is **Manas Ordu** (admission 400som; 🕙 9am-7pm), the legendary last resting place of Manas (see p296). The site is largely symbolic, as no one knows for sure where Manas was buried (or even if such a person actually existed). The *gumbez* (tomb) has been dated to 1334, which does not bode well for traditionalists as Manas is said to have died in the 10th century. Whatever the reality, there is much legend attached to this place. It is said that Manas' wife Kanykey ordered the construction of the *gumbez* but to prevent it from being looted she ordered the engraver to include an inscription saying it is the mausoleum of a young girl. The well-tended gardens around the complex are a fine place to sit and contemplate it all. To reach the site, travel 10km east of Talas on the road to Bishkek. The 4km access road to the complex is well signed from the highway. A taxi will cost 300som to 400som.

Besh-Tash (Five Stones) National Park (admission 80som, vehicle 45som), 15km south of Talas, offers cool rushing rivers, hot springs and stunning alpine scenery. As legend has it, the name is derived from a tale about five brigands turned to stone by a good witch. CBT in Talas organises day and overnight trips, horse riding (per hour 100som, per day 400som) and yurt stays (400som). The first yurt is 38km from town.

SLEEPING & EATING

There are four **guesthouses** (B&B 400-500som) in Talas, including the home of the CBT coordinator, Turdubek Aiyilchiev. His spacious home is a 20-minute walk from town but if you call he will pick you up.

Talant Hotel (☎ 5 27 42; cnr Berdike Batyr & Panfilova; r/lux incl breakfast 800/1200som) The rooms at this place are nothing special, but it's probably the best that Talas can muster. It's located 300m west of the Telecom office, on the opposite

side of the street. There is no sign and the entrance is on the side of the building.

Erlan Hotel (☎ 5 24 97; Sarygulova; r 500som) Slightly run down but habitable and easy to find; it's located 100m south of the *Hakimyat* (Municipal Building).

Kanat Ata restaurant (☎ 0543-112 030; Sarygulova; 🕙 9am-midnight) This place has gone a bit heavy on the drapery and strobe lights but the pizza and *shashlyk* are very good. It's opposite the post office.

GETTING THERE & AWAY

Minibuses run over the Otmek Pass between Talas and Bishkek's Osh Bazaar (marshrutka/share taxi 350/450som) at least once a day. The road through the Talas Valley goes as far as Taraz in Kazakhstan and makes an interesting alternative route to Kazakhstan. If you are hitching, try to get a ride to the Otmek junction (90 minutes), where you can thumb a lift to Toktogul and points south. From Talas to the junction should cost around 150som.

Suusamyr Valley to Tashkömür

A further 30 minutes' drive after the turn-off to Talas the road climbs again, up to the 3184m summit of the **Ala-Bel Pass** over the Suusamyr-Tau mountains. Lower, broader and longer than the Tör-Ashuu Pass, it is nevertheless colder, and said to be the bigger wintertime spoiler. The beautiful valley down the south side of the pass is part of the **Chychkan state zoological reserve** (*chychkan* means mouse).

The flash **Ak Ilbirs Hotel** (☎ 0312-689 600; s/d/tw/tr 850/1650/2200/3300som), by the roadside, is recognisable by a line of flags and its suitably alpine architecture. The standard rooms have more reliable hot water than the *lux*. Meals are 40som to 100som.

The town of **Toktogul** (population 70,000) and the reservoir it sits next to are named after a well-known Kyrgyz *akyn*, Toktogul Satilganov (1884–1933), who was born there. The **Ak-Jibek Hotel** (☎ 077-629 9991; per person 300som), next to the bus station, has decent rooms if you need to be put up for the night.

It takes over an hour to detour around the vast Toktogul Reservoir. Several roadside stalls on the south side of the lake serve delicious fried *farel* (trout).

The town of **Kara-Köl** (population 22,000) is of note only for its dam, part of the Nizhnenarynskiy Kaskad, a series of five dams down the lower gorge of the Naryn River. This *kaskad* (dam), topmost in the series, was completed in 1976 after 14 years' work and is a pretty awesome feat of Soviet engineering: 210m high, 150m wide at the top, and holding back a 19-billion-cubic-metre lake. Just about everybody in town works for the hydroelectric station Toktogulsky Gidroelektrostantsia (GES). Kara-Köl is not to be confused with the much pleasanter town of Karakol on Lake Issyk-Köl. The dam isn't visible from the road and a visit needs special permission.

South of Kara-Köl the gorge of the **lower Naryn River** is an impressive passage, with sheer walls and towering pillars of red sandstone, and a little road clinging to the side. Looking down you will see that there is no longer any river at all, just a depressing series of narrow, utterly still lakes behind the dams of the Nizhnenarynskiy Kaskad.

Tashkömür
☎ 3745

About 5½ hours' drive from Toktogul is the coal-mining town of Tashkömür, strung for miles along the west side of the river below one of the dams. The deserted slag heaps outside the town are silent testament to the collapse of Kyrgyzstan's coal industry since independence. The town itself is one of the lowlights of Kyrgyzstan, but it is one of the main starting points to beautiful Lake Sary-Chelek, 70km west.

The town **gostinitsa** (hotel; ☎ 077-221 7497; r per person 70som), next to the bus station, has ratty rooms without bathrooms. A better bet is the blue-tiled **Tash Kömür Hotel** (☎ 077-346 7729; Lenina; r per person 200som), which is better than the smashed windows and deserted foyer might suggest. Go out of the bus station, turn right, veer right at the fork, turn right at the end of the road and take the first left to the end of this lane.

There are a few cheap cafes serving lukewarm *laghman* at lunchtime near the bus station, along with what may well be Central Asia's most pitiful bazaar.

From the bus station in the centre of town a minibus leaves at 5.40am for Osh (180som); 5.40am, 6.40am, 7.20am, 10.15am and 12.20pm for Jalal-Abad (110som); 9.50am for Kerben (60som); and at 12.40pm and 1.20pm for Kara-Jigach (60som). To get a shared taxi, head 3km from town to the Naryn River bridge, where there is a collection of kiosks and food stalls and a telephone office. A seat in a shared taxi costs 300som to Osh, 150som to Jalal-Abad and 600som to Bishkek.

LAKE SARY-CHELEK
ОЗЕРО САРЫ-ЧЕЛЕК
☎ 3742 / elev 1878m

This beautiful 7km-long alpine lake, nature reserve and biosphere lies hidden in the northern flanks of the Fergana Valley amid groves of wild pistachios, walnuts and fruit trees. The lake is thought to have been created by an earthquake that caused a giant landslide about 800 years ago, and reaches a depth of 234m.

There is a park entry fee of 500som (50som for locals), plus 60som per car. The park is part of Unesco's Western Tian Shan Biodiversity project and lynx, bears and maral deer live in the surroundings.

The base for visits to the lake is the small village of Arkit, actually inside the park, where you'll find the **park office** (☎ 2 22 84), a nearby **nature museum** (⌚ 8am-noon & 1-5pm) and a couple of homestays. The lake is 15km from here, accessible by car.

At the time of research there was no CBT coordinator in Arkit. There is, however, a CBT coordinator in Kyzyl-Kul village in the Kara-Suu Valley, one valley over from Arkit. It is possible to walk to Lake Sary-Chelek from Kyzyl-Kul (via the Kemerty Pass) but there is no vehicle access so it's only worth coming here if you feel like trekking to the lake. The coordinator, **Baban Zhooshbaev** (☎ 3125-5 93 31; reservation@cbtkyrgyzstan.kg) can organise treks and has tents and sleeping bags for hire.

Trekking
Once you get to the lake there's not much else to do except go for a walk. Unfortunately, the hiking trails are not well maintained and quite overgrown. If you don't mind bush-whacking a bit, follow the faint path east uphill behind the lakeshore caretaker's house for fine views of the lake. To go west along the shore you first need to follow the road back downhill (towards Arkit) then take the first right uphill to a lodge that overlooks the lake. A short path downhill leads to a dock that makes a great springboard into the lake. Tempting as it may look to hike around the lake, there simply is no trail.

It's possible to make a six-day trek in to Sary-Chelek from Leninopol (catch a daily

KYRGYZSTAN

bus from Talas). An easier trek starts from Kyzyl-Kul in the next-door valley. From here it's a long day's walk up the valley to Kara-Suu Lake, where you can stay in a CBT-arranged yurt. The next day is a hard slog over the 2446m Kemerty Pass and then down to Sary-Chelek, either directly or via Iyri Köl lake.

Both routes are marked on the 1:120,000 *Cherez Talasskii Khrebet k Ozeru Sary-Chelek*, available at Geoid in Bishkek (p299).

Sleeping

Arkit's homestays are generally more basic than those of CBT or Shepherd's Life. It's a pretty informal place and villagers may offer you a bed for the night at a standard rate of 150som. Food is available in the homestays.

Attakur Omurbekov's Guesthouse (☎ 9 21 41, 077-042 0773; dm 150som) Another 250m up the main road from the Saberia on the opposite side of the street is another friendly option. All the household action takes place around the kitchen (meals 50som) in a garden shed. Omurbekov will take you up to Sary-Chelek in his car for 1000som. It's located behind a shop and electrical transformer.

Saberia Guesthouse (☎ 077-349 3811; dm 200som) About 1km from the first gates, and recognisable by its sign, the Saberia is run by the town's eccentric but charming English teacher and her husband, an ornithologist. Guests wash in the river although water can be heated. The hosts can also help arrange horses for trekking. The price includes breakfast and dinner.

Makmal Hotel (☎ 0777-714 719; r 350som) Located opposite the museum (in the lower part of town, 500m from the first gate), this small hotel has basic rooms and a friendly staff. You'll get more privacy here compared to the homestays.

Getting There & Away

The lake's remote location makes it a real pain to reach by public transport; consider hiring a taxi here if nowhere else in the country.

By public transport you need to catch the 12.30pm bus from Tashkömür to Kara-Jigach (60som, 90 minutes) and then hitch or wait for the afternoon buses from Kerben (Karavan) to pass through en route to Arkit (35som to 50som) around 5pm. A bus from Osh sometimes comes this way, passing through around 2.30pm.

The route to Kara-Jigach passes neglected coal mines and weird eroded *hoodoos* (rock columns). The decrepit local snub-nosed buses are packed, hot, uncomfortable and mind-numbingly slow. From Arkit you'll need to hire a car (800som to 1000som return) or hike (four hours, but little traffic) to the lake.

Heading back, there is a bus from Arkit to Kara-Jigach at 6am and 7.30am (the 6am bus continues to Osh while the 7.30am bus continues to Kerben), from where you can get a shared taxi to Tashkömür from the junction.

If you are headed for Kyzyl-Kul, the 4.20pm bus from Kerben to Kyzyl-Suu also passes through Kara-Jigach between 6pm and 7pm, returning the next day at 7am.

A taxi from Tashkömür will cost around 2000som to Arkit or 500som per seat if you are lucky enough to find a shared one.

ARSLANBOB АРСЛАНБОБ
☎ 3722 / elev 1600m

Arslanbob is an elevated oasis, a vast tract of blossoming woodland and home to the largest walnut grove on earth (11,000 hectares) and part of the even larger (60,000 hectare) walnut forest that extends between the spurs of the Fergana and Chatkal ranges.

Whether you've come by bus or taxi, you'll probably be dropped off at the main square by the lion statue; the CBT office is about 200m uphill. The little-used bus station is downhill from the square. From the statue the road continues uphill, branching left to the *turbaza* (former Soviet holiday camp) and right to the upper waterfall. Behind the town are the wall-like Babash-Ata Mountains and a raft of trekking opportunities.

On the other side of the square is a bridge spanning a rocky stream. Over the bridge are the town's cafes, a (summer only) bazaar and the local mosque. This is a fairly conservative village; so don't walk around in shorts and tank tops.

From mid-September the town undergoes a mass exodus when locals move into the forest and go nuts. Each year 1500 tonnes of walnuts (and 5000 tonnes of apples, pistachios and cherry plums) are harvested in the Arslanbob Valley and by all accounts gathering nuts is fun. Tradition dictates that during the harvest each family kill a sheep and share the meat with their neighbours. The fire-lit autumn nights are a time to sing songs, retell stories and eat way too much greasy mutton.

History

The nuts of Arslanbob are somewhat of a misnomer. While native to Central Asia they originated in Malaysia and somehow, many thousands of years ago, spread to this isolated valley. Locals will tell you this was the work of a modest gardener, charged by the Prophet Mohammed with finding paradise on earth. He travelled through many lands until he stumbled upon a picturesque valley, framed by mountains, watered by mountain rivers but lacking in trees. Delighted with this discovery, the Prophet sent him a bag of fruit and nut seeds which the hero scattered from a mountaintop.

By the time Alexander the Great led his troops to these parts the forests were already locally famous as hunting grounds. On his return to Greece he took with him the humble Kyrgyz walnut, from which European plantations were founded; hence the walnut is commonly, but mistakenly, referred to as the 'Greek nut'.

Information

There is no internet in the village. There are no formal money exchange offices so change all money before coming here.

CBT (☎ 077-334 2476, 077-745 0266; arslanbob_2003@ rambler.ru) Has an excellent branch, which can help with everything from homestays and transport to horse treks. Contact Hayat Tarikov.

Sights & Activities

There are several day-hike options, though the most popular is the three-hour return hike to a holy 80m-high **waterfall**. The last half hour is an uphill grind over a slippery scree slope – wear good shoes as the return leg is like walking down a slope of marbles. Horses are available but aren't all that useful as you still have to slog up the last hill yourself. The fence in front of the falls is covered in votive rags, harking back to a pre-Islamic animism.

An easier walk leads about 30 minutes to a smaller **twin waterfall** (23m) to the east, from where you can continue to a **walnut forest** and the **shrine of Ibn Abbas**. To get to the forest, follow the path back up the hill from the waterfall, then turn right and walk over the small stream (above the falls) and follow the path along the ridge. In a similar direction is

Panorama, a viewpoint that looks back towards town. To get there, follow the road from the waterfall past the souvenir stands and take the second left, follow the path as it goes downhill, over a wood bridge and then up towards the view point.

It is also possible to walk to the **Dashman walnut forest** via Gumhana village and Jaradar in a long day.

Back at the village square, check out the riverside **mazar** (tomb) of Arslan Bab-Ata, after whom the town and mountains are named.

If you're travelling in the winter months, try to time your visit for a weekend as you may be able to catch the locals playing horse games.

TREKKING

Community Based Tourism can arrange a couple of trekking options to the holy lakes of Köl Kupan (marked Kulan on maps), Paino Köl, Kabyr Köl and Ainek Köl (Mirror Lake), collectively referred to as the Köl Mazar. This makes for a fine three- or four-day trek or horse trek, stopping at a cube-shaped holy rock en route.

Instead of retracing your steps you can continue over the Kerets Pass and east along the Kerets Valley, with the Nurbuu-Tau Mountains to the north, until you swing south down the Kara-Ünkür Valley. You can then continue down to Kyzyl Ünkür or head back to Arslanbob via the Kara-Bulak Valley for an excellent five- or six-day trek.

A CBT-organised trek with a guide, cook and three meals costs around US$27 per person per day on foot or US$50 per day on horseback, assuming there are two people. A horse costs 450som to 600som per day; donkeys are cheaper. Community Based Tourism has tents (per night 200som), sleeping bags (per night 100som), and sleeping pads (70som), but it's best to bring your own gear in case they run short.

The adjacent **Kyzyl Ünkür** (Red Cavern) Valley has a network of hiking and fishing routes equal to, if not grander than, those around Arslanbob. If it's open you might be able to stay at the *turbaza* in the valley, ask at CBT first. If it's closed bring a tent and supplies. Travellers recommend the trek north from Kyzyl Ünkür, up the Kara Ünkür Valley to tiny Kön-Köl (you can do this bit by car) and then northeast over the Kymysh Bel Pass (3754m) to the fish-stocked Kara-Suu Lake. From here you can head down the Kara-Suu

KYRGYZSTAN

Valley to join the main Bishkek–Osh road at Kök Bel, between Kara-Köl and Toktogul, or return on a loop back to Kyzyl Ünkür via Kön-Köl Pass, either way making an intrepid six-day trek.

The most demanding trek leads to the top of Babashata peak (4427m). You don't need to be an expert mountaineer to do this but you should have some mountain experience. CBT organises a four-day trek up the mountain for US$300 per person.

The longest trek offered by CBT is a 14-day slog to Song-Köl (p339).

SKIING

Community Based Tourism is developing the mountain *jailoos* surrounding Arslanbob for cross-country skiing. About 10 pairs of skis and boots are available for hire (per day 200som). Proposed transport to the *jailoos* would be via 4WD and on foot with the aid of snowshoes.

Sleeping

CBT (☎ 077-334 2476, 077-745 0266; arslanbob_2003@rambler.ru; per night incl breakfast 300-350som, lunch/dinner 100som) The best digs in town are the 15 or so CBT-affiliated homestays scattered around the village. These aren't always easy to find or centrally located, so call into the office to check out your options. Each guesthouse is numbered and descriptions are posted on the wall – pick one or let the coordinator choose one for you (they try to rotate the guesthouses so everyone gets a chance). In case CBT is closed you can go directly to a guesthouse. Recommended homestays:

B&B No. 9 (☎ 077-381 4758; Yusupov Sabarjav 35) A pretty homestead with cosy rooms and field of alfalfa and poplar trees.

B&B No. 10 (☎ 077-745 7870; Turpolok 15) A nice two-storey house with a garden and English-speaking hosts.

B&B No. 11 (☎ 077-329 2434; Aral 13) A small home with a gorgeous flower-filled garden.

B&B No. 12 (☎ 077-341 5068; Vadapad 58) Has extraordinary views over the valley.

B&B No. 14 (☎ 077-342 6463; 24 Rakhim Palwan St) A four-room single storey house with a German-speaking owner.

Turbaza Arslanbob (☎ 5 28 40; r without/with bathroom 150/250som) Run down but rustic, this scruffy former Soviet holiday camp has dozens of bungalows scattered around 29 hectares of grounds. Only the best rooms have hot water

and en suite toilets but even these are quite basic. There is an open-air swimming pool, which is popular with locals, as is the disco that keeps most people awake half the night. From here it's a one-hour hike to the big waterfall.

Eating

Most travellers eat at their guesthouse (which will serve at least two meals a day). Trekkers can stock up at the bazaar and there are a couple of place to eat in the town centre.

Atalar Chaikhana (meals 50som; ✆ 8am-6pm) hangs precariously over the river near the bridge. It has traditional *tapchan* (bedlike platform) seating and is popular with Arslanbob's silver-bearded elders. The *laghman* here is good and the views are stunning.

Chaikhana Ashkana (meals 50som; ✆ 8am-8pm) Next to the bazaar, this restaurant has a quiet location in a garden and serves tasty kebabs.

Getting There & Away

To reach Arslanbob, first go to Bazaar Korgon (just off the main Bishkek–Osh highway) and grab a shared taxi (50som to 70som, 50km, 45 minutes), which depart when full.

Leaving Arslanbob, get a taxi from the main square back down to Bazaar Korgon where taxis head to Jalal-Abad, Osh, Tashkömür and Bishkek. Note that Bazaar Korgon is about 3km off the main road, so if possible try to get a direct to/from Arslanbob that avoids this town.

JALAL-ABAD   ДЖАЛАЛ-АБАД
☎ 3722 / pop 74,000

Jalal-Abad (the City of Jalal, named after a 13th century warrior) may be Kyrgyzstan's third-largest city but you wouldn't know it from its laid-back, easy-going feel. Most everything of use to travellers can be found on Lenina between the bazaar in the northwest and Hotel Mölmöl (a 10-minute walk) in the southeast.

In its Soviet heyday the town boasted an upmarket health resort, still alive today but rather run down. On the grounds of the sanatorium is a **natural spring** (✆ 6.30-9am, noon-2pm & 5-8pm) enclosed in a wooden circular building. Locals queue anxiously for the building to open in order to collect the curative, sulphuric waters. The springs and sanatorium are 4km from the town centre; a taxi will cost 250som including waiting time.

Information

Aisnet Internet (Dom Bita Centre, Lenina; per hr 50som; ☉ 9am-9pm) Also downloads flash cards and burns CDs.

CBT (☎ 077-237 6602, 0555-185 170; cbt_ja@rambler.ru; Toktogul 20-3; ☉ 9am-5pm Mon-Fri) Contact Ruhsora Abdullaeva in Russian or Nigora in English. This branch helps with local accommodation and transport. From the bazaar head along Lenina to tree-lined Toktogul, turn right and it's near the second crossroad on the left.

Sleeping & Eating

Hotel Mölmöl (☎ 5 50 59; Lenina 17; dm 186som, r 466-725som, lux 1346som) This spartan, but essentially clean, ex-Soviet survivor offers standard rooms with either communal or private bathrooms. Pricier rooms have hot showers.

Matlyba's homestay (☎ 0557-090 530; Toktogul 33; B&B 500som) If the CBT office is closed, try the house behind mint-green walls, on the opposite side of the street. The enthusiastic Uzbek woman who runs it offers clean rooms and hot showers.

Café Navruz (☎ 2 10 90; Toktogul Park; mains 60-150som; ☉ 10am-10pm; **E**) If Jalal-Abad had much hustle and bustle this would be the place to escape it. It has a great parkside location; just off Lenina and part of the upscale Nauryz Hotel.

The CBT offers 14 comfortable **homestays** (350-450som), all of which are good, although some are a little way from the centre. Meals are 100som.

Getting There & Around

AIR

AC Kyrgyzstan flies six times a week to/from Bishkek (2500som). Buy tickets at the airport or **Sputnik Agency** (☎ 5 07 06; Lenina 17). Marshrutkas 1 and 5 from the centre go to the airport via the bus station. A taxi to the airport costs 50som to 80som.

BUS

Marshrutkas and buses depart regularly from the bus station, 3km west of the centre. Scheduled buses depart for Bazaar Korgon (for Arslanbob) every 20 minutes (50som, 30 minutes) and to Osh every half-hour or so until 5pm (80som).

Shared taxis depart from Lenina near the bazaar. You can catch rides to Osh (180som), Özgön (90som), Bazaar Korgon (50som) and Bishkek (1000som).

For villages neighbouring Jalal-Abad you'll need to head for the local bus stand in the far northern corner of the bazaar past the fresh produce (600m north of the taxi stand). Shared Nivas and 4WDs for the mountain route to Kazarman (400som to 600som per seat) also depart from near here.

Minibus 10 runs along Lenina from the Hotel Mölmöl to bus station (5som).

ÖZGÖN УЗГУН
☎ 3233

Özgön (Uzgen) is located 55km northeast of Osh. It is claimed to be the site of a series of citadels dating back to the 1st century BC; there is also a story that the town began as an encampment for some of Alexander the Great's troops. It was one of the multiple Karakhanid capitals in the 10th and 11th centuries.

Its recent history is somewhat less glorious. Communal violence rocked Özgön in 1990 and for three straight nights local Kyrgyz and Uzbeks attacked each other with crude weapons. Casualty reports range from 300 to 1000. The town is nominally 85% Uzbek; locals say it was about two-thirds Uyghur in pre-Soviet days.

Little of Özgön's ancient history remains intact, apart from a quartet of Karakhanid buildings – three joined 12th-century **mausoleums** (admission 10som, photos 10som) and a stubby 11th-century **minaret** (whose top apparently fell down in an earthquake in the 17th century), faced with very fine ornamental brickwork, carved terracotta and inlays of stone. Each mausoleum is unlike the others, though all are in shades of red-brown clay (there were no glazed tiles at this point in Central Asian history). In the corner of the right-hand side mausoleum a small section has been deliberately left off to reveal older layers of the middle one (the Mausoleum of Nasr ibn Ali, founder of the Karakhanids). You can climb the minaret for 5som.

Apart from the architectural attractions, Özgön's bazaar is an interesting place to wander around, particularly if you haven't seen much of Uzbekistan.

The mausoleums are close to the centre of town, about 600m east of the bazaar. Look for the minaret behind the town square.

Sleeping & Eating

Kurmanjan Datka (☎ 077-245 3558; Manas 74/1; d 1000som) This hotel and cafe has an English-speaking staff, and four rooms decorated with wallpaper that belongs in a museum. It's about 50m west of the Telecom/post office, on the left, behind a green fence.

Malika Cafe (Manas; mains 50-60som; ☧ 7am-9pm) Located on the main road, this open-air *chaikhana* serves *shashlyk, samsa* and *manty*.

Getting There & Away

Shared taxis to Jalal-Abad lurk down a side street, a block east of the bazaar near Restaurant Almaz, and cost 60som a seat. Shared taxis to Osh cost 50som and run all day.

AROUND ÖZGÖN

The village of **Ak-Terek**, about 45km east of Özgön, has five **homestays** (B&B 250som), which can be arranged through village head Jengish Akmataliev. Daily buses run every afternoon to Ak-Terek (40som) from Özgön's old bus station.

From Ak-Terek you can take a horse 35km further into Kara Shoro National Park, where there are yurtstays. An adventurous option is the seven-day horse trek along the Jassy River and over the Fergana range to the Arpa Valley, and from there to Naryn.

OSH ОШ

☎ 3222 / pop 300,000

Osh is Kyrgyzstan's second-biggest city and the administrative centre of the huge, populous province that engulfs the Fergana Valley on the Kyrgyzstan side. It is one of the region's genuinely ancient towns (with a history dating back to at least the 5th century BC) but few souvenirs remain. Although the Soviet legacy of town planning and architecture dominate, a sense of ancient Central Asia still pervades, especially around the bustling bazaar.

Locals maintain that 'Osh is older than Rome'. Legends credit all sorts of people with its founding, from King Solomon (Suleyman) to Alexander the Great. Certainly it must have been a major hub on the Silk Road from its earliest days. The Mongols smashed it in the 13th century but in the following centuries it bounced back, more prosperous than ever. In 1496, Babur, the founder of the Mughal dynasty, passed through on his way to India and commissioned the mosque on top of Suleyman Too. Osh was absorbed into the Kokand Khanate in 1762 and later fell to Russian forces.

Osh suffers a kind of demographic schizophrenia, being a major centre of Kyrgyzstan but with a strong (40%) Uzbek population more in tune with Uzbekistan and the rest of the Fergana Valley but isolated from it by one of the world's more absurd international borders, created by Joseph Stalin. His plan to divide and conquer the region still has consequences – ethnic strife rocked it in 1990 and again in 2010 (see the boxed text, p295). While Osh remains a highlight of Central Asia, it will be some time before the city can get over these fresh wounds.

Orientation

Osh sprawls across the valley of the Ak-Buura (White Camel) River, flowing out of the Pamir Alay mountains. The most prominent landmark is 'Solomon's Throne', a craggy mountain that squeezes up to the river from the west.

Along the west bank run two parallel main roads – one-way south-bound Kurmanjan Datka and one-way north-bound Lenin.

Osh's old bus station *(stary avtovokzal)* is on Alisher Navoi just east of the river, while the new, long-distance one *(novyy avtovokzal)* is about 8km north of the town centre. The airport is about five minutes by bus from the new bus station.

Information

BOOKSHOPS

Raritet (☎ 2 25 55; Kurmanjan Datka 271) Has a handful of English-language books and maps.

CULTURAL CENTRES

American Centre (☎ 2 69 84; Lenin 333; ☧ 9am-5pm Mon-Fri) This small centre has an English-language library and is a good place to meet local students. In a large purple building; walk through the main entrance and turn right.

INTERNET ACCESS

Osh has a fair amount of internet cafes but the connections are slow. There is a good crop around the university buildings on Kurmanjan Datka.

Fox Club (☎ 2 31 29; Gapar Aytiev 7; per hr 35som; ☧ 9am-10pm) Has a relatively fast connection speed.

MEDICAL SERVICES

Polyclinic (health centre; ☎ 2 07 35, 3 46 47; Abdykadyrov; ☧ 24hr)

MONEY

In general it's easiest to change cash (including Uzbek sum and Tajik somani) at the

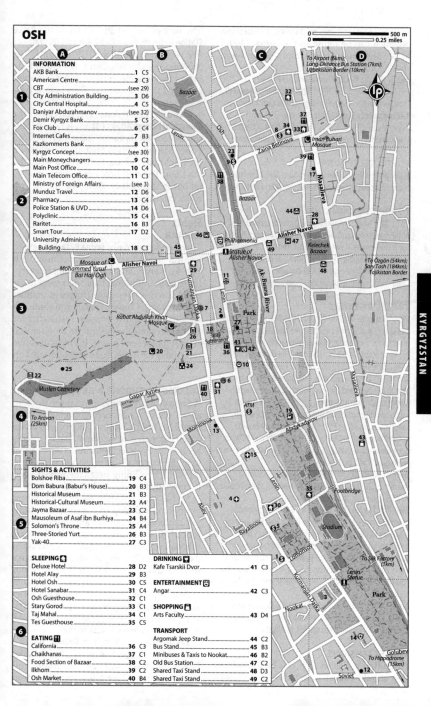

OSH

KYRGYZSTAN

various moneychangers' kiosks, a collection of which can be found in the bazaar (100m before the roundabout). Shop around and check your change.

Demir Kyrgyz Bank (Kurmanjan Datka 180A; ⏰ 8.45am-noon & 1-3.30pm Mon-Thu, until 1.30pm Fri) Changes travellers cheques and gives Visa cash advances.

Kazkommerts Bank (Zaina Betinova; ⏰ 9am-1pm & 2-6pm Mon-Fri) Next door to Taj Mahal Hotel, it has an ATM and cashes travellers cheques for a 3% commission.

POST & TELEPHONE

Main post office (Lenin 320; ⏰ 8am-5pm Mon-Fri)
Main telecom office (Lenin 422; ⏰ 24hr) Fax available.

TOURIST INFORMATION

CBT (☎ 2 02 76; cbtgulcho@mail.ru; 2nd fl, Hotel Alay) At the time of research, the CBT office was at Hotel Alay but it could move. If you can't find it, contact the coordinator Talant Tuksombaev (☎ 0555-077 621 or 0773-871 595; talant_85@yahoo.com). CBT can offer trips to Pik Lenin. Vehicles are available for 12som per kilometre.

TRAVEL AGENCIES

Alptreksport (☎ 7 06 44, 0773-801 081; alptreksport@ bk.ru) Yury and Sasha Lavrushin, two brothers, are veteran mountaineers who offer trekking and caving trips, including some around Achik, Sary Moghul and the Alay Valley. Trips cost around €35 to €38 per day. Yury speaks English and prefers advance bookings. They have no office so it's best to call them and they will meet you at your hotel.

Daniyar Abdurahmanov (☎ 077-237 2311; www. oshguesthouse.hotbox.ru) Daniyar, the operator of Osh Guesthouse, runs trips in the region and can help with onward transport, including Kashgar. He can also help you get a Gorno-Badakhshan (GBAO) permit (US$45, three days to process) if you are headed to Tajikistan.

Kyrgyz Concept (☎ 5 94 50, 0555-749 407; osh@ concept.kg; Hotel Osh, Bayalinov 1) A branch of the reliable Bishkek company, strong on air tickets.

Munduz Travel (☎ 2 66 55, 0777-629 182; munduz_ tourist@hotmail.com; Kurmanjan Datka 104) Can arrange transport to Irkeshtam (overnighting in its yurt camp near Sary Tash, US$23 per person including two meals), Batken, Pik Lenin base camp, Tashkent (Uzbekistan) and Tajikistan. Gorno-Badakhshan (GBAO) permits for Tajikistan cost US$85 and take two days to organise, or US$57 for six days.

Smart Tour (☎ 7 83 52; Masalieva 30/35) Sells airline tickets, strong on Middle East destinations (eg Istanbul, Dubai). Flights depart from Bishkek or Almaty.

VISA EXTENSIONS

Extending a visa in Osh can be a hassle – you should expect to get the run-around.

The first place you should try is the **Police Station** (Lenin; ⏰ 9am-noon & 2-6pm Mon-Fri). The office you want is ОПВК УВД (ask for UVD, pronounced 'Oo-Veh-Deh'). It's around the side of the building in room 2. An extension costs 1023som; come five days before your visa expires.

If you can't get it done here, you can try the **Ministry of Foreign Affairs** (☎ 5 55 46; Lenin; ⏰ 9am-noon & 1-6pm Mon-Fri) about 300m north of the Police Station. This is the building opposite the giant Lenin statue. Go to room 40 on the 4th floor. The staff here can be very unhelpful but in theory they should be able to give a visa extension.

Sights
BAZAAR

The thunderous daily **Jayma Bazaar** is one of Central Asia's best markets, teeming with Uzbeks, Kyrgyz and Tajiks dealing in everything from traditional hats and knives to pirated cassettes, horseshoes (forged at smithies in the bazaar), Chinese tea sets and abundant seasonal fruit and vegetables. It stretches for about 1km along the west side of the river, and crosses it in several places. It's most dynamic on Sunday morning, and almost deserted on Monday.

SOLOMON'S THRONE & AROUND

A jagged, barren rock that seems to loom above the city wherever you go, **Solomon's Throne** has been a Muslim place of pilgrimage of some importance for centuries, supposedly because the Prophet Mohammed once prayed here. From certain perspectives it's said to resemble a reclining pregnant woman, and is especially favoured by hopeful mothers.

In 1497, 14-year-old Zahiruddin Babur, newly crowned king of Fergana, built himself a little shelter and private mosque on the rock's high eastern promontory. In later years this came to be something of an attraction in its own right. It collapsed in an earthquake in 1853 and was rebuilt. Then in the 1960s it was destroyed by a mysterious explosion; most local people are convinced it was a Soviet attempt to halt the persistent pilgrim traffic and put a chill on 'superstition' (ie Islam). After independence it was rebuilt.

Local people call it **Dom Babura**, Babur's House. If you speak Russian, the friendly Uzbek caretaker will tell you more, and offer you a prayer for a few som. The steep

25-minute climb begins at a little gateway behind a futuristic silver dome on Kurmanjan Datka. The promontory offers long views but little to see except for a vast **Muslim cemetery** at the foot of the hill. Dusk is a good time to visit. Admission to the mountain is 3som.

It's worth visiting the nearby **Historical Museum** (☎ 2 71 32; admission 50som, photos 10som each, guides 15som; ☺ 9am-noon & 1-6pm), built during the Osh 3000-year celebrations. It's strong on local archaeology and ethnography but has little info in English. There are some great weapons, displayed as if caught up in a mad whirlwind.

Outside, the giant **three-storied yurt** (admission 40som; ☺ 9am-6pm) has a fairly lacklustre collection of national clothing, traditional textiles and *shyrdaks*.

The **Historical-Cultural Museum** (admission 50som) is located on the southern slope of the mountain. With typical Soviet subtlety, a hole was blasted into the side of this sacred mountain into one of its many caves, and a grotesque sheet-metal front stuck on. Inside is a series of badly lit exhibits of potsherds, old masonry, rocks, bugs and mangy stuffed animals.

Back down at the bottom of the hill is the small **Rabat Abdullah Khan Mosque**, dating from the 17th or 18th century but rebuilt in the 1980s. It's a working mosque (ie male visitors only, and by permission only; shoes off at the entrance).

OTHER SIGHTS

The riverbank **park**, stretching from Alisher Navoi to Abdykadyrov, is great for strolling. A central feature is an old **Yak-40** plane, a one-time video salon, looking poised to leap over the river. There's a *palvankhana* (wrestling hall) here but wrestling bouts are infrequent.

Locals swim in the **Ak-Buura River** during summer or head to the **Bolshoe Riba** (Big Fish Pool; big pool/small pool 60/100som; ☺ 9am-10pm) swimming pool, under the Abdykadyrov Bridge. The smaller pool is cleaner.

Osh **hippodrome**, 16km south of town at Tolüken village (minibus 24), puts on Kyrgyz national sports and eagle-hunting competitions during national holidays.

Sleeping

BUDGET

In theory, CBT has homestays in Osh. In practice these are hard to get because they are not actually offered by the CBT office. Try

contacting the CBT affiliate **Ainura Tajibaeva** (☎ 0772-574 940) to see what she has to offer.

Osh Guesthouse (☎ 2 48 51, 077-237 2311; fax 3 06 29; www.oshguesthouse.hotbox.ru; flat 48, apt 8, Kyrgyzstan; dm/d 200/640som; ▯) A popular backpacker crash pad with the only dorms in town. It's a good place to connect with other travellers but it can get very crowded when full. Hot showers, wi-fi access and laundry service are available and you can cook in the kitchen. The owner, Daniyar Abdurahmanov, is a fount of knowledge. Solo travellers with the view of sharing transport to the Irkeshtam Pass often meet here. To find it, turn down the alley that is lined with kiosks (it's just south of the 'Areopag' sign), take a diagonal right by the silver metal wall and turn left at the second apartment building; it's the third entrance on the left, top floor.

Taj Mahal (☎ 3 96 52; Zaina Betinova; dm 300som, d 800-1000som) Small and bright, this Indian-built hotel has clean and pleasant doubles with hot water and towels. There are only five rooms so try to book ahead.

Hotel Alay (☎ 5 77 33; palvan@yandex.ru; Alisher Navoi; s without/with toilet 310/610som, d without/with toilet 620/1250) The shared bathrooms here are fine and hot showers are available. En suite rooms are also a good deal and they sometimes put solo travellers in double rooms. It occupies a prime central location.

Hotel Sanabar (☎ 2 54 37; Aytiev; d 600som) The Sanabar has tiny rooms with even tinier bathrooms. Compensation is its pleasant location on a quiet street in the centre of town, close to some nice cafes and the museums.

Deluxe Hotel (☎ 7 47 99; Alisher Navoi 35; d 1000som) A clean and reasonably priced option near the old bus station. Rooms are comfortable and a good value if you don't mind the slightly seedy location.

MIDRANGE

Stary Gorod (☎ 2 49 24; Zaina Betinova 18A; 3-person apt 1500som; ▨) These self-contained apartments are a good deal, with air-con, 40-channel TVs, twin bedrooms, separate bathrooms and fully equipped kitchens. The entrance is around the back of the restaurant. Mira, the manager, speaks English.

Hotel Osh (☎ 7 56 14; Bayalinov; d US$50, lux US$70) This old Soviet-era hotel is in dire need of renovation (check out the antique 'made in USSR' phones); you can probably get a better deal elsewhere. Taxi drivers sometimes refer to it as the Intourist hotel or Osh Nuru.

KYRGYZSTAN

Tes Guesthouse (☎ 5 43 43; guesthouse@tes-centre. org; Say Boyu 5; s/d without bathroom €15/30, s/d with bathroom €30/50; 🖳) The pleasant piney rooms of this quaint guesthouse come with locally produced art and spotless bathrooms. There's a coffee machine, TV room, internet access and a washing machine. Prices include breakfast.

Eating & Drinking

California (☎ 2 23 61; Israil Sulaimanov 3/1; meals 70-140som; 🕒 8.30am-10pm; 🇪) For weary travellers craving a taste from home, this American-run place is a godsend. The extensive menu offers up burgers, pizza, fajitas, pastas and a variety of salads each named after a California celebrity (ever dream you'd eat an Arnold Schwarzenegger salad in Osh?). Filling breakfast options include omelettes, muesli and pancakes. Save room in your belly for their delicious homemade brownies and cakes.

Osh Market (Gapar Aytiev 11; 🕒 9am-10pm) This modern supermarket is a handy place for groceries.

Kafe Tsarskii Dvor (Lenin; beer 45-85som; 🕒 noon-midnight) Beer garden that serves cold brew and sizzling *shashlyk*.

The **chaikhanas** along Masalieva near the intersection with Zaina Betinova are everything good teahouses should be; kebab masters lovingly fanning *shashlyk*, tea beds, beer on tap and a lively evening atmosphere. Just south of the intersection **Ilkhom** (Masalieva; 🕒 7am-10pm) has a standard chaikhana menu, as well as blinis for breakfast.

Entertainment

Angar (Lenin St; admission 100som; 🕒 9pm-1am) This open-air nightclub in the centre of town is a great place to mingle with the locals on a hot summer night.

Shopping

By the entrance to the Jayma Bazaar is one of the best and cheapest places in Kyrgyzstan to buy an *ak kalpak* (from 60som to 100som); for an exceptional statement go the full nine yards and get a towering monstrosity with scrollwork (250som). Pottery and clay Central Asian figurines can be bought cheaply in the **Arts Faculty** (Kyrgyzstan 80).

Getting There & Away

AIR

From Osh there is a daily flight to Bishkek (US$40 to US$50), and twice-weekly flights to both Ürümqi, China (US$225) and Moscow (US$240 to US$300).

BUS & CAR

The old bus station and the shared taxis near Jayma Bazaar are Osh's transport hub.

From the old bus station, minibuses leave for Özgön (40som, every 40 minutes), Jalal-Abad (120som, every 20 minutes) and various points in Kyrgyzstan's southern arm – Sary Tash, Kyzyl-Kiya, Aravan, Gulcha and others – though departures for these latter destinations are a little unreliable.

There is a public bus to Batken via Kyzyl-Kiya but it runs through the enclaves and tourists are not allowed to use it (even tourists with multiple entry Uzbek visas have been sent back). It's better to charter a taxi (1000som) that will plot a course around the enclaves.

Shared taxis for all of the above run from here or near here, the locals will soon point you in the right direction (often a stand behind Kelechek Bazaar). Typically a seat in a shared taxi is about 10% to 20% more expensive than a minibus fare. Shared taxis also run to Toktogul, Tashkömür and Kerben when full.

Shared-taxi prices to Bishkek fluctuate dramatically as seasonal labour travels to and from Moscow for work. When demand is high (April to July) you can expect to pay as much as 1200som per seat to Bishkek and only 600som for the same journey in reverse. This trend is reversed when the labour force returns to Osh in winter.

For destinations along the rugged southern border (eg Sary Moghul and Daroot Korgon), see what's available at the Argomak 4WD stand just uphill from the old bus station. The station is somewhat hidden off the main road, you'll need to go down an alley then veer to the right. The alley entrance is opposite the Narodoni market. You can also ask here for a vehicle to Murgab (in Tajikistan).

Another stand west of Hotel Alay has buses to Aravan and Nookat. Minibuses and taxis to Nookat run from just behind the Philharmonia.

Minibuses 107 and 113 run from opposite the old bus station to the Uzbek border (5som, 10km) via the long-distance bus station. Minibuses 136 and 137 travel north on Lenin from Hotel Alay to the Uzbek border.

Getting Around

Marshrutka 102 runs southbound on Kurmanjan Datka from the old bus station to Hotel Osh and Turbaza Ak-Buura; it returns northbound down Lenin. Other southbound minibuses on Kurmanjan Datka include 101A, 134, 135, 125, 138 and 114. Virtually all minibuses pass by Jayma Bazaar at some stage.

Minibus 102A and 107A shuttle between the airport and the Jayma Bazaar in the centre of town (6som).

A taxi around the centre costs between 30som and 50som, 80som to 100som to the airport and 50som to the new bus station.

OSH TO IRKESHTAM

The Irkeshtam border is a popular overland route between China and Kyrgyzstan. It sees more travellers than the Torugart Pass, mainly because it does not incur the red tape one experiences on the Torugart (p347). The route reconnects the Fergana Valley with Kashgar along an ancient branch of the Silk Road.

Sary Tash
☎ 3243

Sary Tash is conveniently situated at the convergence of three roads and makes a good place to break the Murgab (Tajikistan) to Osh or Kashgar (China) to Osh trip. Local rumours abound that the town is also a major stopover for smugglers trafficking opium and hashish from Afghanistan via Tajikistan. Because of the bleak climatic conditions there is little agriculture and most men work at the border or are involved in animal husbandry. There is a small market on Wednesday.

Since the opening of the Irkeshtam border, locals have been quick to open their homes to tourists. The cafes and shops at the intersection can point the way.

The ladies at **Ieda Café & Hotel** (dm 100som) are super friendly and can help arrange transport to the border if you are hitching. In all there are three large lockable rooms and a smaller, less appealing room. Meals are 30som to 50som.

Eliza B&B (☎ 077-384 8811; incl 2 meals 500som) is another reliable option. From the intersection take the road towards Sary Moghul but turn hard right, taking the right fork in the road. The homestay is 50m up a dirt road in a house with blue doors and window frames.

Finally, Sunrise Travel runs a **yurtstay** (☎ 077-255 2200; www.sunrise-osh.com; per person 350som), located just off the main road, 3km north of Sary Tash.

ALAY VALLEY
АЛАЙСКАЯ ДОЛИНА

The far southern arm of Kyrgyzstan is the exclusive turf of trekkers and mountaineers, consisting as it does mostly of the heavily glaciated Pamir Alay range, a jagged, 500km-long seam running from Samarkand to Xinjiang. The range is threaded right up the middle by the muddy Kyzyl-Suu River (known as the Surkhob further downstream in Tajikistan – the two names mean Red Water in Kyrgyz and Tajik respectively) to form the 60km-long Alay Valley, the heart of the Kyrgyz Pamir.

Access from Kyrgyzstan is along the A372 from Osh, via Sary Tash and the 3615m Taldyk Pass. At the time of research the border crossing at Karamyk was closed to third country nationals.

A trip into the Alay region is not a lightweight jaunt. There is little traffic on the main roads and food supplies are limited, even in summer. From October to May the A372 is often closed by snow, and even in summer snow and rainstorms can appear without warning. The best trekking months are July and August.

For information on taking the M41 Pamir Hwy to Gorno-Badakhshan, see p411.

TREKKING

The Pamir Alay is one of the most remote and rugged parts of Central Asia – this is one place where you can't just head off with a 1970s Soviet map and a handful of Snickers bars. ITMC Tien-Shan, IMC Pamir, Dostuck Trekking, Ak-Sai Travel and Top Asia (p304) all organise trekking and mountaineering trips in both the Kyrgyz and Tajik sides of the valley. Munduz Travel and Alptreksport in Osh (p358) can also arrange trekking support; the latter has a lot of experience in the region.

In theory you need a border zone permit to go within 50km of the CIS-Chinese border and the Alay Valley. Permits are rarely checked these days but it's still a good idea to ask your tour operator for the latest developments.

Sary Moghul
☎ 3243

The dusty village of Sary Moghul, 30km west of Sary Tash, offers the valley's best views of Pik Lenin. Up until 2004 the entire village and

KYRGYZSTAN

TO IRKESHTAM & BEYOND

The east-bound road that leaves Osh for China climbs gently into the Alay Range via the Jiptik Pass (4185m) and the village of Gulcha. There is a roadside cafe and a **CBT homestay** (☎ 0555-077 621 or 0773-103 256; Lenin 26; per night 350som) in Gulcha but little reason (other than some hot springs) to overnight. The road, that had initially followed the Taldyk River, now follows the Gülchö as it climbs – this time in earnest – the steeper but lower Taldyk Pass (3615m) to the surprisingly open Alay Valley and Sary Tash. The drive from Osh to Sary Tash takes five hours.

While it is possible to leave Osh at 1am to arrive at Irkeshtam Pass by 9am you'll end up travelling in the dark and miss much of the stunning scenery. Instead consider starting later and overnighting in Sary Tash and then continuing at 5am the following day to the border controls at Irkeshtam.

From Sary Tash the road rapidly deteriorates into a corrugated dirt track that guarantees to rattle your teeth from your skull. To travel the 90km takes between two and three hours depending on how recently it has rained. At the time of research the road was being upgraded and with luck could be paved by 2012.

About 3km before the border is the hamlet of Nur-a, a village that has built up a reputation for drunkenness and theft. You're better off heading straight to the border.

The Border

Crossing the **border** (☽ 9am-noon & 2-4.30pm Mon-Fri) can be a time-consuming affair. Ten kilometres before the border is the first of two checkpoints. Here everyone is required to show their passport so names can be matched to a master list of bus passengers. Assuming nobody had a last-minute name change the bus is allowed to continue to the second checkpoint and luggage inspection. Finally, you can expect to spend between 1½ to 2½ hours at the border itself, depending on how many trucks are waiting before you.

If you are hitching, ask the border-post army officers to put you on a truck to cross the 7km of no-man's-land to Chinese immigration (closed 11am to 2pm Kyrgyz time).

Unlike the Torugart, no permits are required to get through this border point. Note that the border is closed on Kyrgyz and Chinese holidays, on weekends and May 1 to 10.

surrounding 37,000 hectares of arable land was rented by Tajikistan. The newly established **CBT** (☎ contact Umar Tashbekov 077-261 1096) in the village centre near the village administration office (ail okmotu) can arrange homestays/yurtstays (including breakfast 400som) and horse treks to the Pik Lenin base camps.

There is no regular transport to Sary Moghul. In Osh you can ask around at the Argomak 4WD stand where at least one vehicle will leave each day for Sary Moghul, or try your luck hitching from Sary Tash.

Pik Lenin & Achik Tash

Pik Lenin (now officially called Koh-i-Garmo) is known as one of the most accessible 7000-ers in the world. It is the highest summit of the Pamir Alay and lies right on the Kyrgyz–Tajik border. The snow-covered ridges and slopes are not technically difficult to climb, with many ascents passing **Lipkin Rocks**, named after a pilot who crashed here and then calmly walked out.

Altitude sickness and avalanches are a serious problem; in 1991 an earthquake-triggered avalanche obliterated Camp II on the Razdelnaya approach, killing 43 climbers in the process. It remains the world's worst mountaineering disaster.

For details on trekking around Pik Lenin, see Frith Maier's *Trekking in Russia & Central Asia*.

At Achik Tash meadows (3600m), 30km south of Sary Moghul, IMC Pamir and most of the trekking agencies mentioned, p365, operate Pik Lenin base camps and programs in summer. To get there you'll have to fix arrangements in advance.

There are weekly farmers markets in Daroot-Korgon (on Monday), Kashka-Suu (Tuesday) and Sary Moghul (Sunday), where you can buy basic foodstuffs. Several trailer shops offer the usual kiosk fare in Sary Tash. Beyond this bring all your own food.

If you can time your visit, try to be here on the first weekend of August, when CBT organises a festival and horse games.

To Kashgar

On the Chinese side of the border are Uyghur restaurants, a small hotel and moneychangers. Taxi drivers will offer a ride to Kashgar (US$9 to US$15 per person, four hours), but you'll have to bargain hard. Be ruthless. The 270km road from the border to Kashgar is sealed all the way.

Getting There & Away

Arranging the whole trip with a travel agency from Osh to Irkeshtam (275km) currently costs from around 7000som (US$160) per car, which can seat four. Most travel agencies in Osh can organise a car, although people generally use either Osh Guesthouse (p359) or Munduz Travel (p358). Either way it is important to explain exactly what is expected, where you will spend the night and agree on a price beforehand.

There is a direct bus between Osh and Kashgar (US$70 plus 100som) that leaves the Osh long-distance bus station twice weekly (Wednesday and Sunday). Be warned that you may have to overnight on the bus or at the border so be sure to bring enough food and water.

It is also worth asking around at the back far corner of the Argomak 4WD stand in Osh for cars bound for Sary Tash. In the morning locals often look for passengers here to help cover their fuel costs and the trip to Sary Tash can cost as little as 500som.

Hitching from Sary Tash to the border is fairly straightforward as long as you start early enough to catch the Chinese Kamaz trucks as they pass. Expect the driver to ask for around 300som for the lift.

In Reverse

If you are travelling in the reverse direction, it's possible to take a bus (US$75 or 470RMB) from Kashgar to Osh, departing on Monday or Thursday. Departure time is 8am (but it's usually delayed to 10am) and the bus reaches the border around 2.30pm. Chinese border guards do a very thorough check of your luggage and may look at your digital camera and laptop. It takes about 90 minutes to get through the border. The bus arrives in Osh at 6am. For hitchhikers, get across the Kyrgyz border and flag down a Chinese truck for the ride to Sary Tash. From the town's main intersection there is regular transport to Osh.

GETTING THERE & AWAY

You should be able to hire a 4WD from Sary Moghul to Achik Tash (17km) for the cost of US$30 return. A hired 4WD from Osh to Achik Tash can be negotiated down to US$150 if you ask around the Argomak 4WD stand. Trekking-agency vehicles come at about US$160 to US$200 one way. Daniyar Abdurahmanov, Kyrgyz Concept and Munduz Travel (p358) all organise transport to Achik Tash; you may be able to work in with one of their trips to Irkeshtam Pass to help reduce the cost.

SOUTHWESTERN KYRGYZSTAN

The southern wall of the Fergana Valley forms a curious claw of Kyrgyz territory, although access to most of the mountain villages here comes from the Fergana Valley territory of Tajikistan or Uzbekistan. The beautiful valleys of the Turkestan ridge in particular offer superb trekking territory and the beautiful pyramid-shaped **Ak-Suu** peak (5359m), with its sheer 2km-high wall, is one of the world's best extreme rock-climbing destinations.

This is not a particularly easy place to make your first Central Asian trek. You'll need an Uzbek, Kyrgyz and Tajik visa to transit hassle-free through these republics, as well as a spurious trekking permit. Moreover, some of the passes with Tajikistan are said to be mined. For the time being you are better off planning any trek in the region with an established trekking operator in Bishkek (p304).

Batken

Because of the difficulty and added expense of crossing the Tajik and Uzbek enclaves Batken remains largely unexplored and consequently has little tourist development. CBT has made a modest attempt at setting up a homestay network and it's best to contact the Bishkek office (p316) for details on new places to stay in the region. If you prefer more formal lodging, try the no-frills **Batken Hotel** (☎ 077-729 5370; r 250-350som).

Shared taxis to Osh and to Isfana (Uzbekistan) depart every morning from the post office. Buses from Batken to Osh and Isfana leave from the bus station early in the morning. Public transport to Batken passes through the enclaves. Even with multi-entry visas travellers have reported hassles at the borders. The best option is to use minor roads that scoot around the enclaves but, in doing so, you'll be forced to hire a taxi or arrange your own transport. Osh Guesthouse (p359) and Munduz Travel (p358) will arrange a car from Osh for US$130 to US$150.

KYRGYZSTAN DIRECTORY

ACCOMMODATION

Homestays are the bedrock of accommodation in rural Kyrgyzstan, particularly those of the CBT program (p302), and always include breakfast. CBT has ranked most of the homestays, although what you get for each rating seems to differ in each city or town. Generally speaking, we found that a one-edelweiss homestay (no hot shower) was 350som; a two-edelweiss homestay (hot shower) was 450som; and a three-edelweiss homestay (private room or apartment) was 500som.

Different from yurtstays are private tourist yurt camps, mostly used by groups but open to anyone if there's space. Costs here are around US$30 per person with three meals, and often include some horse riding or other activities.

The unravelling of the Soviet Union has left the once swanky sanatoria high and dry, devoid of customers but chock-a-block with nostalgia.

The main cities (Bishkek, Osh, Jalal-Abad and Karakol) all boast midrange hotels that continue to improve in quality. Some may be newly constructed buildings while others are Soviet-era hotels that have been renovated. Hotel accommodation seldom includes breakfast and since most rooms contain two beds the tariff for a single and a double are often the same, effectively doubling the cost for solo travellers.

Top-end accommodation is limited to Bishkek where you can expect a far higher standard (and price) equal to that of their international counterparts.

ACTIVITIES
Four-Wheel-Drive Trips

There are several opportunities for 4WD safaris. One possible road leads from Talas over the Kara Bura Pass into the Chatkal River valley and then loops around to Sary-Chelek. Other tracks lead from Naryn to Barskoön, and Barskoön to Inylchek, through the high Tian Shan.

Horse Riding

Kyrgyzstan is the best place in Central Asia to saddle up and join the other nomads on the high pastures. Community Based Tourism offices throughout the country can organise horse hire for around 70som per hour or 400som per day.

The horses often give the impression they're only a hoof-beat away from reverting to their wild roots and galloping off to a distant mountain pasture but novice riders are seldom given unruly horses if they make their concerns known.

With so many horse-trekking possibilities it is difficult to recommend one over another and it is worth asking other travellers for any new or outstanding routes. Community Based Tourism is opening and closing routes continuously based on the location and availability of its guides in the *jailoos* however, the following are outstanding:

- Horse trek over the 3570m Shamsy Pass from Salaral-Saz Jailoo to Tokmok (p339)
- Two- or three-day horse trips to/from Kyzart or Jumgal to Song-Köl (p340)
- Horse trek from Eki-Naryn to Bokonbayevo (five to six days; p342)

For organised trips, the following companies are recommended:

AsiaRando (☎ 3132-47710/47711, 517-73 97 78; www.asiarando.com; Padgornaya 67, Rot Front, Chuy Oblast) Horse-riding trips to Song-Köl from its base in Rotfront village. Contact Gérard and Dominique Guillerm.

Shepherds Way See p330 for details of trips around Lake Issyk-Köl.

Mountaineering

Kyrgyzstan is the major base for climbing expeditions to Khan Tengri (p333) and Pik Lenin (in Tajikistan but accessed from Kyrgyzstan; p362). There are many unclimbed peaks in the Kokshal range bordering China. Most of the Bishkek trekking agencies (p304) arrange mountaineering expeditions.

The Kyrgyz Alpine Club has a useful web-site (www.kac.centralasia.kg).

Rafting

Rafting is possible on the Kokomoron (Grade IV), Chuy (Grade III), Naryn (Grade IV) and Chong-Kemin Rivers (Grades II to III). The season runs from 25 June until 15 September and wetsuits are essential in the glacial melt water. Contact **Silk Road Water Centre** (p305) to take the plunge.

Skiing

Despite the fact that 94% of the country averages over 2700m, skiing is still in it's infancy. Currently the only 'ski fields' are around Bishkek (p313) and Karakol (p329). The season runs mid-November until mid-March. With the advent of heli-skiing (p314) Russian-built MI-8 helicopters are ferrying adrenalin-junkies to altitudes of over 4500m for descents of up to 5km.

Trekking

Covered in mountains and lakes, Kyrgyzstan offers unrivalled opportunities to take to the hills. Around Bishkek (p311), Karakol (p327), Kochkor (p339), Naryn (p342), Arslanbob (p353) and Sary-Chelek (p351) are the major trekking regions although any CBT office will suggest countless alternatives.

TREKKING PERMITS

Trekking and mountaineering permits were abandoned by the government in 2002 but regional officials may still require them; notably in the Central Tian Shan (Khan Tengri), Ak-Suu and the Karavshin region. For some border areas you need a border permit, notably in the Inylchek glacier area. Permits prices range between US$15 to US$50 per person and prices can change considerably depending on the whims of Kyrgyz offialdom as well as the agency you are dealing with. At the time of writing Dostuck Trekking (p304) was offering the some of the lowest prices for permits.

CUSTOMS REGULATIONS

If you've bought anything that looks remotely antique and didn't get a certificate saying it's not, you can get one from the 1st floor of the Foreign Department of the **Ministry of Education, Science & Culture** (☎ 62 68 17; Room 210, cnr Tynystanov & Frunze, Bishkek).

DANGERS & ANNOYANCES

As a destination for adventure and activities, travellers need to take necessary precautions before setting off into the mountains. Consider changeable weather patterns, extreme mountain terrain and altitude sickness before setting off. Make sure you have the necessary equipment including tent, sleeping bag, layers of clothing, maps, functioning stove etc. Always let someone know where you are going and when you expect to be back.

The combination of mountain highways and maniacal drivers makes travelling hazardous. Check the road readiness of your vehicle before setting off and, if in doubt, hire a car from a reputable tour operator.

Kyrgyz cities are generally safe but travellers have reported theft in places like Bishkek and Karakol. Keep valuables locked in your hotel and stay on your toes when venturing out after dark.

EMBASSIES & CONSULATES

Kyrgyz Embassies in Central Asia

There are Kyrgyz embassies in the Central Asian capitals of Almaty (p194), Ashgabat (p462), Dushanbe (p417) and Tashkent (p282).

Kyrgyz Embassies & Consulates

If there is no Kyrgyz embassy in your country, inquire at the Kazakh embassy if there is one. There are additional embassies in Belarus, Ukraine, India, Malaysia, Switzerland and the UAE.

If you intend to cross into Kyrgyzstan from China over the Torugart Pass or the Irkeshtam border, you will need to secure your Kyrgyz visa in either Beijing or Ürümqi.

KYRGYZSTAN

Austria (☎ 01-535 0378; fax 535 0379; Naglergasse 25/5, 1010, Vienna)

Belgium (☎ 02-640 1868; aitmatov@photohall.skynet. be; 47 Rue de L'Abbaye, 1050, Brussels) Issues visas on the spot for US$50.

China (☎ 010-6532 6458; kyrgyz@public3.bta.net.cn; 2-4-1 Ta Yuan Diplomatic Office Bldg, Liangmahe Naniu 14 hao, Chaoyang District, Beijing; ☷ 3-6pm Mon, Wed & Fri) Walk down San Li Tun Da Jie until it meets the river and turn left. It's a further five minutes along in an imposing building flying many flags. The embassy is on the 7th floor behind a small, unmarked white door next to the stairwell. The Ürümqi consulate (☎ 0991-518 9980, fax 0991-518 9985; ☷ noon to 2pm, Mon, Tue, Thur, Fri) is at the Central Asia Hotel (Yazhong Fandian; 38 North Hetan Beilu). A 30-day visa is available for Y455/733/1225 in five/three/one days.

Germany Berlin (☎ 030-3478 1338; www.botschaft-kir gisien.de; Otto-Suhr-Allee 146, 10585); Bonn (☎ 0228-36 52 30; kirgistan.bonn@t-online.de; 194A Friesdorferstrasse, 53175); Frankfurt (☎ 069-9540 3926; Bronnerstrasse 20) A 30-day visa costs €50.

Iran Mashhad (☎ 051-818444); Tehran (☎ 021-229 8323, 283 0354, krembiri@kanoon.net; Bldg 12, 5th Naranjastan Alley, Pasdaran St)

Russia (☎ 095-237 4601/4882/4571; fax 237 4452; Bolshaya Ordynka ulitsa 64, 109017, Moscow) Also in Ekaterinburg.

Switzerland (☎ 022-707 9220; fax 707 9221; www. kyrgyzmission.net; Rue Maunoir, 1207, Geneva)

Turkey Ankara (☎ 312-446 84 08; kirgiz-o@tr-net. tr; Boyabat Sokak 11, Gaziosmanpasa, 06700); İstanbul (☎ 212-235 6767; genkon@tr.net; 7 Lamartin Caddesi, Taksim)

UK (☎ 020-7935 1462; www.kyrgyz-embassy.org.uk; Ascot House, 119 Crawford St, W1U 6BJ, London; ☷ 9.30am-12.30pm) A one-month tourist visa costs UK£50/60.

USA (☎ 202-449-9822; www.kyrgyzembassy.org; 2360 Massachusetts Ave NW, Washington DC 20008) A one-month tourist visa costs US$100 and is ready in 10 days. Also a consulate in New York.

Embassies & Consulates in Kyrgyzstan

All the following are in Bishkek (area code ☎ 312; see Map p300). For information on visas for onward travel see p366.

For letters of support try travel agencies (p302) such as Kyrgyz Concept and CAT. The nearest Turkmen embassy is in Almaty.

Afghanistan (☎ 312-426372; afghanembi_bishkek@ yahoo.com; cnr Ayni & Toktonalieva) Temporarily closed at the time of research.

China (☎ 61 08 58, 66 20 01; fax 66 30 14; chinaemb _kg@mfa.gov.cn; Toktogul 196; ☷ 9.15am-noon Mon, Wed & Fri)

France (☎ 66 00 53; france.kg@gmail.com; Bokonbayevo 113)

Germany (☎ 90 50 00; fax 66 66 30; www.bischkek. diplo.de; Razzakov 28)

India (☎ 54 92 14; indembas@infotel.kg; 15a Aeroport-inskaya St; ☷ 9am-1pm & 2-5.30pm Mon-Fri)

Iran (☎ 62 12 81; fax 66 02 09; Razzakov 36; ☷ 9am-5pm Mon-Fri)

Japan (☎ 32 53 87; fax 61 18 82; Frunze 503)

Kazakhstan (☎ 69 20 95; kaz_emb@kazemb.elcat.kg; Mira 95A; ☷ 9am-noon Mon-Tue & Thu-Fri)

Netherlands (☎ 69 05 65; fax 66 02 88; Suite 1, Tynystanov 199) Honorary consulate.

Pakistan (☎ 37 39 01; Serov 37; ☷ 10am-2pm Mon-Thu, 10am-noon Fri) May well refer you to a travel agency. Located on the corner of Leningrad.

Russia (☎ 62 47 38; fax 62 18 23; www.kyrgyz.mid. ru; Manas 55) The consular department is around back, reached from Kiev St.

Tajikistan (☎ 51 23 43; fax 51 14 64; tojsaforat@exnet. kg; Kara-Dar'inskaya 36; ☷ 10am-1pm & 2-5.30pm Mon-Fri) The embassy is lost in suburbia. Using the Vefa Centre as your first point of reference, travel west on Gorky for 1.1km, then turn right on Yunusaliev St (former Karla Marx St) and travel south for 900m, then turn left (west) on Suvanberdiev St, the street comes to an end after 500m and the embassy will be in front of you. Trolleybus No 17 will get you close; you can catch it on Soviet and it will follow the above route to Yunusaliev, get off at the third intersection, which is Suvanberdiev.

Turkey (☎ 62 23 54; fax 66 05 19; biskbe@infotel.kg; Moskva 89; ☷ 9am-noon Mon-Fri)

UK (☎ 62 28 25, 0555-584 245; gbhoncon@mail.kg; Tynystanov 231; ☷ 9am-5pm Mon-Fri) This is a consulate with the closest embassy in Almaty. The honorary consul is the owner of Fatboys restaurant (p307) and the consulate is in the basement. The entry is not through Fatboys; you need to go around to the back of the building.

USA (☎ 55 12 41; http://bishkek.usembassy.gov; Mira 171)

Uzbekistan (☎ 66 20 65; fax 66 44 03; Tynystanov 104/38; ☷ Tue-Fri)

Visas for Onward Travel

For contact details of embassies and consulates in Kyrgyzstan, see p366.

Note that a letter of Invitation (LOI) is sometimes required when applying for visas at some Central Asian embassies. If an LOI is not required you may still be asked to fill out a 'written request' (заявление), which you fill out yourself – basically a write-your-own-LOI. Instructions on how to do this are usually printed at the embassy.

China Policy is fairly erratic at this embassy. Some travellers have walked in and received a visa with little hassle while others have been told they first need an LOI from a Xinjiang tourist agency. It's possible that travellers who have been to China (and have an old visa in their passport) stand a better chance of getting fast-tracked. If you do need an invitation, Celestial Mountains (p304) can get one in a week (US$50). Thirty-day visas cost US$130 for US citizens, US$30 for most others and take a week to issue (urgent service: one day US$30, three days US$20).

India Accepts visa applications 10am to 12.30pm Monday to Friday. A standard six-month tourist visa costs 2880som for US citizens, 1920som for other nationalities. Two photos are necessary. Visas take three to four days to issue.

Iran Transit visas of 10 days' duration are issued in one week. Tourist visas can take weeks or months longer to gain clearance. You need a letter of invitation for a tourist visa. Beware: unsuccessful applicants have lost their US$100 deposit.

Kazakhstan Fees for your visa need to be paid at the Kazkommertsbank (p301). For a transit visa you'll need to show an onward ticket out of Kazakhstan (and a copy), the visa for the country being visited next (and copy), one photo, a photocopy of your passport and Kyrgyz visa; takes five/three days (US$20/35). A tourist visa costs US$30/90/100 for single/double/triple entries. You don't need an LOI for a single entry visa but you do need one for double or triple entry visas. Alternatively, you can go to Carlson Wagonlit (p302) and they will do it all for you (for US$55 instead of US$30).

Russia Applications are accepted from 9am till noon and from 2.30 till 4pm Tuesday and Thursday. You'll need a letter of invitation, four passport photos and plenty of patience. Transit visas cost US$90/190 in a week/day and you'll need tickets in and out of Russia. Tourist visas cost US$131 for US citizens and US$90 for most other nationalities. They take a week to process.

Tajikistan Thirty-day visas are available in three working days. Costs vary depending on what visa you ask for; it's US$30 for seven days, US$40 for two weeks and US$50 for a month. Longer visa are also available but you may need an LOI from a Tajik agent. A processing fee of US$1 is required when you drop off the visa. Pay for the actual visa when you pick it up (eg US$40) plus a second processing fee of 50som. Bring photos, a passport and a photocopy of your passport. At the embassy you can write your own LOI. The embassy can provide a free GBAO permit. The experience here is generally easy and hassle free.

Uzbekistan You need to get a Russian speaker to phone the embassy and put your name on the list. Arrive by 10am the next working day (it's closed on Mondays). Bring the application form, which you can fill out and print here www.evisa.mfa.uz. Attach a photo and hand it in with a copy of the passport (they don't take your real passport). The visa will be ready in eight days (four day expedited visas are available at an additional cost). Your translator needs to call again for a pick-up appointment; come in the next day at 10am. This time you bring your actual passport, give it to them and then come back the same day at 3pm for your visa (Insha'Allah). Tourist visas prices vary: for a two-week visa Americans pay US$130, while most Europeans pay US$62. The process can go quicker if you have an LOI, but these can be expensive; the cheapest we found was US$55 from Central Asia Tourism Corporation (p302).

FESTIVALS & EVENTS

Kyrgyzstan offers a number of festivals in summer, though many of them seem to be put on for tourists. The best and most authentic events are the **horse games** at the end of July and August (notably Independence Day, 31 August) at Bishkek, Cholpon-Ata,

---

HORSING AROUND

Nomadic sports are very popular in Kyrgyzstan and have seen a revival in recent years. The most spectacular of these, an all-out mounted brawl over a headless goat, is *kok boru*, also known as *ulak-tartysh* or *buzkashi* (see the boxed text, p64). The Kyrgyz name means 'grey wolf', which reveals the sport's origins as a hunting exercise.

Kyz-kumay (kiss-the-girl) involves a man who furiously chases a woman on horseback in an attempt to kiss her. The woman gets the faster horse and a head start and, if she wins, gets to chase and whip her shamed suitor. Ah, young love. This allegedly began as a formalised alternative to abduction, the traditional nomadic way to take a bride.

Other equestrian activities in Kyrgyzstan include *at chabysh* (p330), a horse race over a distance of 20km to 30km; *jumby atmai*, horseback archery; *tiyin enmei*, where contestants pick up coins off the ground while galloping past; and *udarysh*, horseback wrestling.

Kok boru is often incorporated into Independence Day celebrations and other festivals and Community Based Tourism (CBT; see the boxed text, p302) arranges demonstrations upon request (5500som) if you give a few days' notice.

Karakol and the *jailoos* around Song-Köl and Kochkor. Gruelling horse races are also held during the **At Chabysh festival** (p330) in Barskoön in early November. NoviNomad in Bishkek (p304) and the nearest CBT can offer details.

During the recently revived **Nooruz** (21 March) celebrations there are numerous sporting events, traditional games, music festivals and street fairs particularly around Osh and Jalal-Abad.

The **Birds of Prey Festival** (p332), held early August in Bokonbayevo, offers an excellent opportunity to see eagle hunters and falconers compete.

HOLIDAYS

See p502 for information on the important Muslim public holidays of Ramadan and Eid festivals.

1 January New Year's Day
7 January Russian Orthodox Christmas
23 February Army Day
8 March International Women's Day
21 March Nooruz.
24 March Anniversary of the March Revolution
1 May International Labour Day
5 May Constitution Day
9 May WWII Victory Day
31 August Independence Day
7 November Anniversary of the October Revolution

INTERNET RESOURCES

Celestial Mountains Tour Company (www.celestial.com.kg) An exhaustive resource on all things Kyrgyz.
Community Based Tourism (www.cbtkyrgyzstan.kg) Contact details and prices for its services.
Helvetas (www.helvetas.kg) General info, Altyn Kol handicrafts (and Shepherd's Life).
Kyrgyzstan OrexCA (www.kyrgyzstan.orexca.com) General background and country notes.
Times of Central Asia (www.timesca-europe.com) Current events.

MAPS

Geoid in Bishkek (p299) has a Kyrgyzstan country map (Cyrillic and English), an interesting Silk Road of Kyrgyzstan map, trekking route maps and 1:200,000 Soviet topographic maps of various parts of Kyrgyzstan. Most maps are in Russian. Maps cost between 110som and 140som.

Trekking maps available at the agency:
Ala-Archa (1:50,000) Routes up to Ak-Say Glacier and the ski base, in English.

Kirgizskii Khrebet (1:200,000) Topographical map, covering the Kyrgyzsky Mountains south of Bishkek. There's also a separate 1:150,000 schematic map showing peaks in the same region.
Ozero Issyk-Kul (1:200,000) Topographical map, covering trekking routes to Kazakhstan via the Chong-Kemin Valley.
Sokh (1:200,000) Alay Mountains.
South-East Issyk-Köl Lake Coast (1:100,000) Trekking routes around Karakol, including the Jeti-Öghüz Valley, Altyn Arashan and Ala-Köl.
Tsentralniy Tyan-Shan (1:150,000) Schematic map of Inylchek Glacier and around.

MONEY

The Kyrgyz som is divided into 100 tiyin. Notes come in 5000, 1000, 500, 200, 100, 50, 20, 10, five and one som denominations. Coins come in denominations of 10, five, three and one som. Banks and licensed moneychanger booths (marked *obmen balyot*) exchange US dollars provided the notes are unblemished in near-mint condition and, if possible, post 2003. Trying to get change for a 5000 som note will likely be met with a look of horror, avoid these or change them at a bank for 1000 som notes.

There are ATMs in Bishkek, Jalal-Abad, Karakol, Naryn and Osh that dispense both US dollars and som. Travellers cheques can be cashed in these places (3% commission). Most prices in this chapter are listed in som, apart from higher-priced items which, as is the custom in Kyrgyzstan, are listed in US dollars – although a few businesses in the hospitality industry fix their prices in euros. There is no black market for currency transactions and exchange rates at the time of research were as follows (Uzbek rate not given due to instability):

Country	Unit	Som
Australia	A$1	38.94
Canada	C$1	43.74
China	Y1	6.86
euro zone	€1	58.31
Kazakhstan	10T	3.15
New Zealand	NZ$1	31.94
Russia	R1	1.49
Switzerland	1Sfr	43.86
Tajikistan	1TJS	10.61
UK	£1	70.45
USA	US$1	46.53

If you need to wire money, MoneyGram has services at main post offices and Western Union works through most banks.

POST

An airmail postcard or letter costs 28som to all countries. Parcels are shipped at 1110som per kilogram and airmail is often less expensive than sea freight.

DHL (www.dhl.kg) has offices in Bishkek and Osh and charges US$92 to send 1kg to North America. **FedEx** (www.fedex.com) has an office in Bishkek. A 1kg box to North America costs $80.

REGISTRATION

Foreigners from 45 countries, including the US, UK, Australia, Canada, Israel and most European countries, no longer need to register with OVIR (Office of Visas and Registrations; UPVR in Kyrgyzstan). Other countries (including South Africans, Brazilians and Argentineans) need to register within three days of arriving in Kyrgyzstan.

SHOPPING

Small pottery figurines shaped as bread sellers, musicians, and 'white beards' are for sale everywhere but most are made at the Arts Faculty in Osh. Hats are also for sale everywhere but most are factory-made in Toktogul. The most popular buys are *shyrdaks* (p339).

Other souvenirs include miniature yurts and embroidered bags, chess sets featuring Manas and company, horse whips, *kymys* shakers, leather boxes, felt slippers and musical instruments such as the Kyrgyz mouth harp.

TELEPHONE

International telephone rates are 9som per minute to Central Asia and 5som per minute to other countries. Domestic calls cost about 4som per minute and local calls 1som per minute. Some older telephones require you to dial 3 after the person picks up.

To make an international call, dial ☎ 00 plus the international code of the country you wish to call.

To make an intercity call, dial ☎ 0 plus the city code.

We occasionally list mobile phone numbers in this guide. Mobile numbers are 10 digits while landlines are five or six digits.

Internet phone calls cost as little as 5som per minute to the USA.

To send a fax, Telecom offices charge around 10som a page. Another option is to scan and email it from an internet cafe.

If you have a GSM mobile phone, you can buy a SIM card and scratchcards in units of 200, 400 and 1000.

SIM cards are available from Beeline and MegaCom for 150som. They can be purchased at mobile phone shops, shopping centres and even street kiosks. No registration is required. MegaCom is the more popular brand.

VISAS

Kyrgyzstan is the easiest of the Central Asian republics for which to get a visa. Kyrgyz embassies issue 30-day tourist visas, with fixed dates, to 45 nationalities (see Registration, p369, or visit www.kyrgyzembassy.org) without letters of support. These nationalities can also obtain a single-entry visa (and single-entry only) on arrival at Bishkek's Manas International Airport (US$70) although not at land borders.

Most nationalities from the former Soviet bloc, as well as Japanese, Turks and Kazakhs do not need visas.

If there is no Kyrgyz embassy in your country, go through a Kazakh embassy instead, although a letter of invitation regardless of nationality is then required. Central Asian travel agencies (p511) can provide these for US$20 to US$30.

It's illegal to enter Kyrgyzstan except at a designated border crossing, which makes cross-border treks (eg Almaty to Issyk-Köl) technically illegal. Cross-border trekking has recently become more difficult and many trekkers have been turned back. Contact a travel or trekking agency for the latest details.

For details on getting visas in Bishkek for neighbouring countries see p366.

Travel Permits

Certain sensitive border areas such as the Khan Tengri region and Alay Valley require a military border permit (*propusk pa granzona*; US$10 to US$20), which trekking agencies can arrange in about 10 days.

Visa Extensions

You can get a 30-day visa extension in Bishkek (p302), Karakol (p320), Osh (p358) and Naryn. Bishkek tends to be the easiest place to do this (but is slightly more expensive). Prices range between 1000som and 1085som depending on where you get it. Processing time varies, in theory you can get it done in a day but travellers have reported delays of several days.

TRANSPORT IN KYRGYZSTAN

GETTING THERE & AWAY
Entering Kyrgyzstan

Remote border posts, for example at Bor Döbo and along the Pamir Hwy, from Tajikistan may not stamp your visa with an entry stamp but you should insist that this is done, otherwise you'll have problems. Generally, entering the country presents no difficulties.

Air

Bishkek's Manas airport is the main international hub, although there are also flights to Moscow, Ürümqi and Dushanbe from Osh. The national carrier, Air Company Kyrgyzstan (AC Kyrgyzstan) was formerly Altyn Air.

From Bishkek, Central Asian destinations include Tashkent (US$170, with Uzbekistan Airways, AC Kyrgyzstan), Ürümqi (US$220, China Southern, Itek Air) and Dushanbe (US$192, Avia Traffic Air, AC Kyrgyzstan).

One-way/return airfares for Russia include Yekaterinburg (US$247/547, AC Kyrgyzstan, once weekly), Novosibirsk (US$240/500, AC Kyrgyzstan, twice weekly) and Moscow (US$300/560, Aeroflot, AC Kyrgyzstan, Itek Air, daily).

Other international destinations reached directly from Bishkek are limited to Dubai (US$360/730, AC Kyrgyzstan, once weekly), İstanbul (US$428/560, Turkish Airlines, once weekly), Delhi (US$245/520, AC Kyrgyzstan, once weekly) and London (US$675/852, British Airways, four times weekly).

Between the months of June and September AC Kyrgyzstan also has a weekly flight to Hanover and Frankfurt for US$450/900 one way/return.

Because flight choice is limited, many choose to fly to Tashkent (p287), Almaty (p199) or Ürümqi (China) and connect from there. A transit visa will be required if you plan to leave these airports.

If you are flying out of Almaty you can take the daily airport shuttle from the Hyatt Hotel in Bishkek (it's operated by Kyrgyz Concept, p302). The bus leaves at 7pm but only when a client has booked it, so contact Kyrgyz Concept before turning up. The trip costs 700som. Bizarrely, Lufthansa passengers are charged 1000som for the same journey.

For more details on airline offices in Bishkek, see p310. The US$10 international departure tax and 4% government tax is included in the ticket price.

Land
BORDER CROSSINGS

For more on the complicated jigsaw borders of the Fergana Valley, see p527. One thing to note is that transport along Kyrgyzstan's southern arm from Osh to Batken passes through the Uzbek enclave of Sokh so you'll need to get an Uzbek visa or hire a taxi to

---

TAKING THE HIGH ROAD

The mountain borders of Kyrgyzstan, Tajikistan and China have become destinations within themselves. A cathedral of peaks, head-spinning altitudes and mythically remote roads guarantee that these are not your usual ho-hum, forgettable border posts. To ensure a hassle-free crossing there are some things worth bearing in mind.

■ Avoid crossing a pass on any day that might even conceivably be construed as a holiday on either side, or in Russia, as the border will probably be closed.

■ Attempting to cross on a Friday is tricky – if the border is temporarily closed for snow or some other reason you won't be able to re-try for another three days. Try to arrive at the border as early as possible as things tend to grind to a halt at lunchtime.

■ Be aware of time-zone differences. In summer (roughly April to September) China (ie Beijing) time is two hours later than Kyrgyzstan time, and in winter it's three hours later.

■ Check the weather. Have your paperwork right.

■ For high-altitude passes be aware that at the beginning and end of the season you really need a 4WD not a little Toyota minivan. Also remember that there is little reliable petrol, oil or parts along the way.

take you on a dirt road detour around the enclave.

To/From China

There are two land routes into China, the Torugart Pass (p346) and the Irkeshtam border (p362) and crossing each has its pros and cons.

To cross the Torugart you will need to arrange transport to meet you on the Chinese side (or Kyrgyz transport if you are going in the other way). Travel agencies can handle this but it can get pricey. On the plus side, you can include a side trip to Tash Rabat on the way to the border.

Crossing at Irkeshtam can be cheaper because you don't need pre-arranged transport to meet you at the border. You can also cycle the whole route (which is not possible at Torugart). However, the road getting to the border is longer, rougher and generally a more time-consuming affair.

If you are only visiting Kashgar (and you have a multiple-entry Kyrgyz visa), you can make a nice loop journey, travelling from Osh to Kashgar via Irkeshtam and then back to Kyrgyzstan via the Torugart Pass.

To/From Kazakhstan

Minibuses go directly from Bishkek to Almaty (300som, 4½ hours) every hour or two, as do private cars (350som per seat). There is a passport check at the border by the Chuy River and you will need a Kazakh visa.

A back-door route into Kazakhstan is possible through the Karkara Valley. There's no through transport so you'll have to hire a taxi or hitch part of the way. See p319 for details.

To/From Tajikistan

The main crossing for travellers is at the Bor Döbo checkpoint on the Pamir Hwy, between Murgab district and Sary Tash. To travel on the Pamir Hwy a GBAO permit that says 'Murgab district' is required.

A vehicle from Osh to Murgab costs anywhere between US$200 to US$300 and this can be split between five people (but it can be difficult to find other travellers willing to share the cost). It takes around eight hours to reach the border from Osh (consider breaking the journey in Sary Tash). The border opens at dawn. This is cold and rugged territory so pack warm clothing. Remind the Kyrgyz border guards to stamp your passport – they sometimes forget.

Another remote crossing leads southwest from the Pamir Alay Valley into the Garm Valley and on to Dushanbe, although this is currently closed to foreigners.

From the Fergana Valley it's possible to cross from Batken to Isfara (not Isfana) in Tajikistan. This will be your only chance if you failed to get a GBAO permit for the Murgab route.

To/From Uzbekistan

The situation is in flux. Buses from Bishkek to the Kazakh–Uzbek border at Chernyaevka were on hold at the time of publishing but may resume.

From Jalal-Abad take a taxi or minibus (20som) to Khanabad (formerly Sovietabad) and cross by foot. Note that the Kara-Suu border crossing is not open. For details on getting to the border from Osh, see p360.

It is also possible to travel to/from Tashkent by rail but all pass through Kazakhstan, necessitating a Kazakh visa.

See p523 for more on travelling around the region.

GETTING AROUND

Travelling around Kyrgyzstan is generally quite straightforward. The bus system is just skin and bones so for most trips your best bet is the shared taxis or marshrutka (minibuses), which wait for passengers at most bus stations.

Shared taxis also act as private taxis if you are willing to pay for all four seats and most travel agencies also arrange private cars.

For airlines flying domestic routes between Bishkek, Osh and Jalal-Abad, see p309.

Tajikistan
Точикистон

A Persian-speaking outpost in a predominantly Turkic region, Tajikistan is in many ways the odd one out in ex-Soviet Central Asia. With its roots in ancient Sogdiana and Bactria, the modern country is a fragile patchwork of mountain valleys, clans, languages and identities, forged together by little more than Soviet nation-building and the shared hopes for a peaceful future.

That peace was shattered in the 1990s, when a brutal civil war claimed over 60,000 lives, turning the remote mountainous republic into the bloodiest corner of the former Soviet empire. Though the wounds are still raw and the political situation fragile, over a decade after the war most Tajiks are moving forward with their lives and a mood of guarded optimism has returned.

The good news for travellers is that today Tajikistan is safe, stable and scenically spectacular. The Pamir region – the 'Roof of the World' – is easily the country's highlight, offering breathtaking high-altitude scenery, excellent ecotourism options, humbling mountain hospitality and the awesome Pamir Hwy – one of Asia's greatest road trips.

Once the playing fields of 'Great Game' spies and explorers, Tajikistan is now the playground for cutting-edge adventure travel, from walks and 4WDs through the Wakhan Valley to nights in remote Kyrgyz yurt camps. For fans of big mountain scenery, or anyone who ranks places like northern Pakistan or western Tibet as their favourite travel destinations, Tajikistan will glimmer as the most exciting republic in Central Asia.

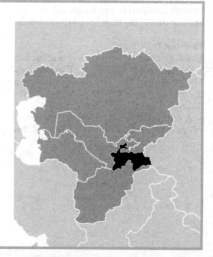

FAST FACTS

- **Area** 143,100 sq km
- **Capital** Dushanbe
- **Country Code** ☎ 992
- **Famous for** Pamir Hwy, trekking, mountain hospitality, drug trafficking
- **Languages** Tajik, Russian, Uzbek and half a dozen Pamiri languages
- **Money** Tajik somani (TJS); US$1=4.42TJS, €1=6.12TJS
- **Off the Map** Pamirs (p399), Istaravshan p393), Yagnob Valley p398), Southern Tajikistan (p384)
- **Phrases in Tajik** khob (OK); mebakhshed (sorry); khair (goodbye)
- **Population** 7.35 million (2009 estimate)

HIGHLIGHTS

- **Pamir Highway** (p411) One of the world's great road trips, offering jaw-dropping high-altitude lakes and fine community-based homestays.
- **Wakhan Valley** (p409) Remote and beautiful valley bordering Afghanistan, with Silk Road forts, Buddhist ruins and spectacular views of the snowbound Hindu Kush.
- **Yurtstays** (p414) Your chance to get up close and personal with Kyrgyz herders, under a spectacular nighttime Pamiri sky.
- **Fan Mountains** (p396) Austere but beautiful trekking destination of turquoise lakes and Tajik shepherds, easily accessible from Penjikent or Samarkand.
- **Iskander-Kul** (p396) Lovely lake at the eastern end of the Fan Mountains and a great place to relax or go hiking.

ITINERARIES

- **Three days** Drive from Samarkand or Khojand (p390) to Dushanbe (p381; with an overnight stop in Iskander-Kul if you hire your own taxi) and then fly out of Dushanbe to Bishkek or Almaty. Alternatively, visit Penjikent (p393) from Samarkand, continue to Khojand via Istaravshan (p393) and then dip back into Uzbekistan.
- **One week** Khojand to Dushanbe with stops in Istaravshan, Iskander-Kul (p396) and Hissar (p389). Or perhaps a short trek in the Fan Mountains (p397).
- **Two weeks** Ten days is really the minimum amount of time required to travel from

Dushanbe to Osh via the Pamir Hwy (p411), especially if you plan to arrange things as you go. Figure in an overnight in the Wakhan Valley (p409) and a yurt-stay in the eastern Pamirs, as the area has much to offer.

- **Three weeks** This will be enough time to get you from Penjikent over the mountains to Dushanbe and then along the Pamir Hwy to Osh (in Kyrgyzstan), with maybe a short trek in the Fan Mountains. Try to add on an overnight trip from Murgab (p412) to somewhere like Jalang (p415), Pshart Valley (p414) or Bulunkul (p411).

CLIMATE & WHEN TO GO

Northern, central and southern Tajikistan sizzle in summer (June to September), with temperatures over 40°C. Unfortunately this is the best time to visit the mountains. Spring (March to May) brings mild temperatures but frequent heavy showers. April is the best time to visit southern Tajikistan in bloom. In winter (November to February) temperatures in Dushanbe hover near freezing, while temperatures in the Pamirs plummet to between -20°C and -45°C.

March, April, September and October are probably the best times to visit. The best time of year for trekking is mid-June to early October, with September perhaps the optimum month. The Pamir region is best visited from July to late September, though the Pamir Hwy technically remains open year-round. During early summer (June and July), melt-water can make river crossings dangerous in mountainous areas.

HISTORY
Tajik Ancestry

Tajik ancestry is a murky area, with roots reaching back to the Bactrians and Sogdians. Tombs from the eastern Pamir show that Saka-Usun tribes were grazing their flocks here from the 5th century BC, when the climate was considerably lusher than today.

In the 1st century BC the Bactrian empire covered most of what is now northern Afghanistan. Their contemporaries, the Sogdians, inhabited the Zerafshan (Zeravshan) Valley in present-day western Tajikistan (where a few traces of this civilisation remain near Penjikent). Alexander the Great battled the Sogdians and besieged

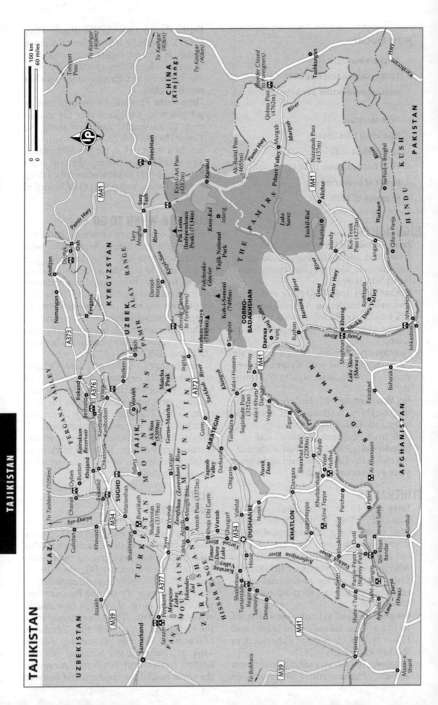

Cyropol (Istaravshan), before founding modern-day Khojand. The Sogdians were displaced in the Arab conquest of Central Asia during the 7th century AD. The Sogdian hero Devastich made a last stand against the Arabs at Mount Mug in the Zerafshan (Zeravshan) Mountains, before he was finally beheaded by the Muslim vanquishers.

Modern Tajikistan traces itself back to the glory days of the Persian Samanid dynasty (AD 819–992), a period of frenzied creative activity which hit its peak during the rule of Ismail Samani (AD 849-907), transliterated in modern Tajik as Ismoili Somoni. Bukhara, the dynastic capital, became the Islamic world's centre of learning – nurturing great talents such as the philosopher-scientist Abu Ali ibn-Sina (known in the West as Avicenna) and the poet Rudaki – both now claimed as sons of Iran, Afghanistan and Tajikistan. Travellers can visit Rudaki's tomb outside Penjikent in northern Tajikistan (see p395).

A Blurring of Identity

Under the Samanids, the great towns of Central Asia were Persian (one reason Tajikistan still claims Samarkand and Bukhara as its own), but at the end of the 10th century a succession of Turkic invaders followed up their battlefield successes with cultural conquest. Despite contrasting cultures, the two peoples cohabited peacefully, unified by religion. The Persian-speaking Tajiks adopted Turkic culture and the numerically superior Turks absorbed the Tajik people. Both weathered conquests by the Mongols and, later, Timur (Tamerlane), though most of the territory of modern Tajikistan remained on the fringes of the Timurid empire.

From the 15th century onwards, the Tajiks were subjects of the emirate of Bukhara, who received 50% of Badakhshan's ruby production as a tax. In the mid-18th century the Afghans moved up to engulf all lands south of the Amu-Darya (Oxus River), along with their resident Tajik population, and later seized parts of Badakhshan (including temporarily the Rushan and Shughnan regions). The Amu-Darya still delineates much of the Afghan–Tajik border today.

The 'Great Game' & the Basmachi

As part of the Russian empire's thrust southwards, St Petersburg made the emir-ate of Bukhara a vassal state in 1868, which gave Russia effective control over what now passes for northern and western Tajikistan. But the Pamirs, which account for the whole of modern-day eastern Tajikistan, remained a no-man's-land, falling outside the established borders of the Bukhara emirate and unclaimed by neighbouring Afghanistan and China. Russia was eager to exploit this anomaly in its push to open up possible routes into British India.

The Pamirs became the arena for the strategic duel between Britain and Russia that British poet and author Rudyard Kipling was to immortalise as the 'Great Game', a game in which Russia's players eventually prevailed, securing the region for the tsar (see p50). It was in the eastern Pamirs, after visiting Murgab, Alichur and Rang-Kul, that Francis Younghusband was thrown out of the upper Wakhan by his Tsarist counterpart, sparking an international crisis. Russia backed up its claims by building a string of forts across the Pamirs, including at Murgab. The Anglo-Russian border treaty of 1895 finally defined Tajikistan's current borders with Afghanistan and China, marking the region's closure to the outside world for the next 100 years.

Following the Russian revolution of 1917, new provisional governments were established in Central Asia and the Tajiks found themselves part of first the Turkestan (1918–24), then the Uzbekistan (1924–29) Soviet Socialist Republics (SSRs), despite pushing for an autonomous Islamic-oriented republic. The next year Muslim *basmachi* guerrillas (literally 'rebels') under the leadership of Enver Pasha began a campaign to free the region from Bolshevik rule. It took four years for the Bolsheviks to crush this resistance, and in the process entire villages were razed. The surviving guerrillas melted away into Afghanistan, from where they continued to make sporadic raids over the border.

Soviet Statehood

In 1924, when the Soviet Border Commission set about redefining Central Asia, the Tajiks got their own Autonomous SSR (ASSR). Although only a satellite of the Uzbek SSR, this was the first official Tajik state. In 1929 it was upgraded to a full union republic, although (possibly in reprisal for the *basmachi* revolt) Samarkand and Bukhara – where over 700,000

TAJIKISTAN

Tajiks still lived – remained in Uzbekistan. As recently as 1989 the government of Tajikistan was still trying to persuade the Soviet leadership to 'return' the area lost in this cultural amputation. Territorial and ethnic tensions with the modern government of Uzbekistan over the two cultural centres remain.

The Bolsheviks never fully trusted the Tajikistan SSR and during the 1930s almost all Tajiks in positions of influence within the government were replaced by stooges from Moscow. The industrialisation of Tajikistan was only undertaken following WWII, after the loss of much of European Russia's manufacturing capacity. But living standards remained low and in the late 1980s Tajikistan endured 25% unemployment, plus the lowest level of education and the highest infant-mortality rate in the Soviet Union.

For most of the Soviet era, Tajikistan was heavily reliant on imports from the rest of the Union – not just food, but fuel and many other standard commodities. When the Soviet trading system started to disintegrate, Tajikistan was left badly equipped to fend for itself, and dangerously unbalanced.

From Civil Unrest...

In the mid-1970s, Tajikistan began to feel the impact of the rise of Islamic forces in neighbouring Afghanistan, particularly in the south around Kurgan-Tyube (Kurgonteppa). This region had been neglected by Dushanbe's ruling communist elite, who were mainly drawn from the prosperous northern city of Leninabad (now Khojand). In 1976 the underground Islamic Renaissance Party (IRP) was founded, gathering popular support as a rallying point for Tajik nationalism. Although in 1979 there had been demonstrations in opposition to the Soviet invasion of Afghanistan, the first serious disturbances were in early 1990 when it was rumoured that Armenian refugees were to be settled in Dushanbe, which was already short on housing. This piece of Soviet social engineering sparked riots, deaths and the imposition of a state of emergency. Further opposition parties emerged as a result of the crackdown.

On 9 September 1991, following the failed coup in Moscow and declarations of independence by other Central Asian states, Tajikistan proclaimed itself an independent republic. Elections were held 10 weeks later and the Socialist Party (formerly the Communist Party of Tajikistan or CPT) candidate, Rakhmon Nabiev, was voted into power. There were charges of election rigging but what really riled the opposition was Nabiev's apparent consolidation of an old-guard, Leninabad-oriented power base that refused to accommodate any other of the various clanfactions that make up the Tajik nation.

Sit-in demonstrations on Dushanbe's central square escalated to violent clashes and, in August 1992, antigovernment demonstrators stormed the presidential palace and took hostages. A coalition government was formed, but sharing power between regional clans, religious leaders and former communists proved impossible and Tajikistan descended into civil war.

...To Civil War

During the Soviet era, Moscow managed to hold the lid on a pressure-cooker of clan-based tensions that had existed long before Russian intervention. Tajikistan's various factions – Leninabadis from the north, Kulyabis from the south and their hostile neighbours from Kurgan-Tyube, Garmis from the east, and Pamiris from the mountainous province of Gorno Badakhshan (Gorno Badakhshan Autonomous Oblast, GBAO, or simply Badakhshan) – had all been kept in line under Soviet rule. When independence came, the lid blew off. Civil war ensued and the clan struggles claimed around 60,000 lives and made refugees of over half a million.

As a way out of the internecine conflict, Emomali Rakhmonov (now known as Rakhmon), the former communist boss of Kulyab district, was chosen to front the government. The Kulyabis fought their way to power with a scorched-earth policy against their Islamic-leaning rivals from the Garm Valley and Kurgan-Tyube.

Rakhmanov was sworn in as president after a disputed election and an all-out push from Kulyab and Leninabad forces to get him into office. Kulyabi forces, led by Sanjak Safarov (who had previously spent 23 years in prison for murder), then embarked on an orgy of ethnic cleansing. Anyone found in Dushanbe with a Badakhshan or Khatlon ID card was shot on the spot.

The November 1992 elections did nothing to resolve the conflict (the opposition in exile refused to take part in the vote) and the Islamic opposition continued the war

THE OPIUM HIGHWAY

Central Asia is a major transit route for the global trade in heroin, most of which comes from neighbouring Afghanistan, the world's largest producer of opium. Somewhere between 100 and 200 tonnes of heroin passes through Tajikistan each year via the 1300km Afghan border. In fact, Tajikistan seizes roughly 90% of all drugs captured in Central Asia and stands third worldwide in seizures of opiates (heroin and raw opium), after Iran and Pakistan.

Warlords and criminal gangs control most of the business, although the army, police, Afghan Taliban and border guards are alleged to have fingers in the opium bowl. Drugs have even turned up in Kazakh diplomatic bags and on Russian military flights. In 2005 a homemade aircraft (a parachute with a motor attached) was shot down flying above the border with Tajikistan with 18kg of heroin. In 2009 Russian police seized 80kg of heroin from smugglers on the Dushanbe–Moscow train, a line well known to antinarcotic police as the 'Heroin Express'. Over the years drug money has financed everything in Tajikistan from weapons for the civil war to the poppy palaces that line the Varzob Valley north of Dushanbe.

In modern Central Asia, camel caravans of silks and spices have been replaced, it seems, by Ladas and train carriages packed with heroin. The Silk Road has become an opium highway.

from bases in the Karategin region and Afghanistan, echoing the *basmachi* campaigns of 70 years earlier. An economic blockade of Badakhshan led to severe famine in the Pamirs during 1992 and '93.

Rakhmanov was propped up by Russian forces, which had been drawn into the conflict as de facto protectors of the Kulyab regime. Russian troops controlled some 50 military posts along the Afghan border. 'Everyone must realise', Boris Yeltsin said in a 1993 pronouncement, 'that this is effectively Russia's border, not Tajikistan's.' Russia's (and later Uzbekistan's) fear was that if Tajikistan fell to Islamic rebels, Uzbekistan would be next.

In late 1994 a second presidential election was held, in which Rakhmanov romped to victory. This surprised no one, as he was the only candidate. Opposition parties had been outlawed.

Precarious Peace

> A bad peace is better than a good war.
> *Khatlon villager*

Pressure on Rakhmanov from Russia (and the faltering loyalty of his own commanders) forced the government to negotiate with the opposition, which was then in exile in Iran. Finally, in December 1996 a ceasefire was declared, followed up by a peace agreement on 27 June 1997. The agreement set up a power-sharing organisation, the National Reconciliation Commission, headed by the opposition leader Sayid Abdullo Nuri, which guaranteed the United Tajik Opposition

(UTO) 30% of the seats in a coalition government in return for a laying down of arms.

When the dust settled, it was clear that independence and civil war had proven catastrophic for Tajikistan, which had always been the poorest of the Soviet republics. During the civil war Tajikistan's GDP per capita shrank 70%, plunging it from part of a global superpower to one of the world's 30 poorest countries within a decade. Two complete harvests were missed and the region suffered major subsequent droughts. Standards of living in the country had been set back by 20 years or more.

Spirits were raised in September 1998 when the Aga Khan, spiritual leader of the Islamic Ismaili sect, visited Gorno-Badakhshan. The Aga Khan Foundation had effectively fed the Pamir region since the start of the civil war and some 80,000 Pamiris came out to hear their spiritual leader tell them to lay down their arms, while another 10,000 Afghan Tajiks strained their ears across the river in Afghanistan.

CURRENT EVENTS

Though the Tajik economy has grown annually at almost 8% in recent years, health and education standards remain low and life in the region remains hard. Over 70% of Tajikistan's people still live on less than US$2 per day. Yet despite the hardship Tajiks are savouring the stability, and prospects for the near future are improving.

A million or so Tajiks work abroad, mostly in the Russian construction industry, sending back around US$800 million a year in remittances, equivalent to half of Tajikistan's GDP. Despite potential in many areas, the annual national budget of Tajikistan remains less than the budget of a major Hollywood movie, and 40% of that is required for the upkeep of the military presence on the Afghan border.

The 2009 global economic downturn had a major effect on remittances (which fell by one-third) as well as on the price of aluminium and cotton, which together constitute 80% of Tajikistan's exports.

Tajikistan's main natural resource is water (glacial reserves amount to 40% of Central Asia's total) and there is a huge potential for hydropower. If it's ever finished, the giant Rogun dam on the Vakhsh River could supply 80% of Tajikistan's badly needed electricity requirements, loosening its dependence on neighbouring Uzbekistan. (In winter the capital is sometimes without electricity and heating for days at a time.) The downstream countries of Uzbekistan and Turkmenistan remain deeply opposed to the project.

Tajikistan has been a parliamentary republic since 1992 but the political landscape remains heavily clan-based. The parliament is fronted by the president, Emomali Rakhmon, who won a third term in 2006 despite a constitution that limits a president to only two terms (the courts decided that the president's first two terms 'didn't count', giving Rakhmon the green light to run for a fourth term in 2013).

Thanks to the very porous 1300km border with Afghanistan, Tajikistan is one of the world's major drug conduits (see the box p377). Up to 50% of Tajikistan's economic activity is thought to be somehow linked to the drug trade. Tajikistan's strategic location bordering Afghanistan has given it an added importance as a logistical supply route to Afghanistan and new road and rail links to the border are planned.

Tajikistan remains a politically fragile state. Uncertainty caused by poor governance, the drug trade and a spill-over in extremism from neighbouring Afghanistan all contribute to the fear that Tajikistan may face increasing instability in the years to come.

PEOPLE

It was only last century that 'Tajik' came to denote a distinct nationality. Despite their predominantly Persian ancestry, there has been so much ethnic blurring that it's often hard to distinguish Tajiks from their Turkic neighbours (Tajik skullcaps closely resemble Uzbek, adding to the confusion). Pure-blooded Tajiks tend to have thin southern European-looking faces, with wide eyes and a Roman nose.

There are some recognisable ethnic subdivisions among the Tajiks. As well as the Pamiris (p401), dwindling numbers of Yagnobis, direct descendants of the ancient Sogdians, survive in the mountain villages of the upper Yagnob Valley (see p398). Sogdian, the lingua franca of the Silk Road and last widely spoken in the 8th century, is still spoken by a few hundred Yagnobis.

About 65% of Tajikistanis are Tajik, 25% are Uzbek, 3.5% are Russian and 6.5% are other groups. Much of the population of the eastern Pamirs are Kyrgyz, who arrived here from the Alay Valley in the 18th and 19th centuries.

For more information on the people of Tajikistan, see p64.

RECOMMENDED READING

The weighty *Odyssey Guide to Tajikistan* (2007), by Robert Middleton and Huw Thomas, is a literate and detailed background guide to Tajikistan, particularly strong on the history of exploration in the Pamirs.

Travel through Tajikistan (2006), by Fozilov Nurullo, is a locally produced guidebook with some useful background information on Tajikistan. It's only available in Dushanbe.

For something more old school, George Curzon's *The Pamirs and the Source of the Oxus* is a classic text delivered to the Royal Geographical Society in 1896 and recently reprinted in paperback by Elibron Classics. It's full of lovely detail on the Pamir region. Elibron have also republished TE Gordon's 1876 *The Roof of the World* and John Wood's 1872 *A Journey to the Source of the River Oxus*.

Land beyond the River: The Untold Story of Central Asia (2003), by Monica Whitlock, pieces together the history of Soviet Central Asia through the lives of half a dozen witnesses, and with a strong focus on modern Tajikistan. Whitlock was formerly the BBC's Central Asia correspondent.

Population

Population figures are only approximate because the demographics of Tajikistan have been fluctuating wildly since the civil war of the 1990s. In addition to the 60,000 or so killed, around 700,000 Tajiks were displaced from their homes during the war, while the majority of the country's 600,000 Russians headed north. Another 60,000 Tajiks fled to Afghanistan, joining the 4.4 million Tajiks who have lived there since the southern region of Badakhshan was annexed by Kabul in the 18th century. One in four families in Tajikistan now has a family member working abroad.

Tajikistan exemplifies the demographic complexity of the Central Asian republics. Its 4.4 million Tajiks constitute only 65% of the country's population, and fewer than half of the world's Tajiks (there are more Tajiks in Afghanistan than Tajikistan, and large groups also live in Uzbekistan, Kazakhstan and China's Xinjiang province). A quarter of Tajikistan's population are Uzbeks, with whom there is considerable ethnic rivalry. Average family sizes remain high, with seven or eight kids the norm. Over 40% of Tajikistan's population is under the age of 14.

RELIGION

About 80% of Tajikistan's people are Sunni Muslim, though most Pamiris are Ismailis and follow the Aga Khan (p401). Between 1990 and 1992, over 1000 new mosques were built in Tajikistan. Central Asia's largest mosque will house 10,000 worshippers when it opens in northwestern Dushanbe in 2014.

In the late 1990s, radical Islamist organisations such as the Islamic Movement of Uzbekistan (IMU) used Tajikistan's Sangvor and Tavildara Valleys as a base for armed raids into Kyrgyzstan and Uzbekistan. These organisations lost relevance following the bombing of Al-Qaeda bases in Afghanistan, though the recent arrests of members of the largely peaceful Hizb-ut-Tahrir movement show the continued support for Islam as a political force.

ARTS

When Tajikistan was hived off from Uzbekistan in 1929, the new nation-state was forced to leave behind all its cultural baggage. The new Soviet order set about providing a replacement pantheon of arts, introducing

modern drama, opera and ballet, and sending stage-struck Tajik aspirants to study in Moscow and Leningrad. The policy paid early dividends and the 1940s are considered a golden era of Tajik theatre. A kind of Soviet fame came to some Tajik novelists and poets, such as Mirzo Tursunzade, Loic Sherali and Sadruddin Ayni, the last now remembered more as a deconstructor of national culture because of his campaign to eliminate all Arabic expressions and references to Islam from the Tajik tongue.

Since independence, ancient figures from the region's Persian past have been revived in an attempt to foster a sense of national identity. The most famous of these figures is Ismail Samani (Ismoil Somoni), but also revered is the 10th-century philosopher-scientist Abu Ali ibn-Sina (980–1037), author of two of the most important books in the history of medicine. He was born in Bukhara when it was the seat of the Persian Samanids, to whom Rudaki (888–941), now celebrated as the father of Persian verse, served as court poet. Tajiks also venerate Firdausi (940–1020), a poet and composer of the *Shah Nama (Book of Kings)*, the Persian national epic, and Omar Khayyam (1048–1123), of *Rubaiyat* fame. Both were born in present-day Iran but at a time when it was part of an empire that also included the territory now known as Tajikistan. Similar veneration goes out to Kamalddin Bekzod (1455–1535), a brilliant miniaturist painter from Herat.

Pamiris have a particular veneration for Nasir Khusraw (1004–1088), an Ismaili philosopher, poet and preacher who worked in Merv and was exiled to Badakhshan, where he wrote his *Safarname,* the account of his extensive seven-year travels throughout the Muslim world.

Tajik Persian poetry is fused with music by *hafiz* (bard musicians). *Falak* is a popular form of melancholic folk music, often sung a cappella. Music and dance is particularly popular among the Pamiri and Kulyabi.

ENVIRONMENT
The Land

At 143,100 sq km, landlocked Tajikistan is Central Asia's smallest republic. More than half of it lies 3000m or more above sea level. The central part encompasses the southern spurs of the Tian Shan and Pamir Alay ranges, while the southeast comprises the Pamir

TAJIKISTAN

plateau. Within these ranges are some of Central Asia's highest peaks, including Koh-i Somoni (former Pik Kommunizma), the highest in the former Soviet Union at 7495m. The Fedchenko Glacier, a 72km-long glacial highway frozen to the side of Koh-i Somoni, is one of the world's longest glaciers and, at 800m thick, allegedly contains more water than the Aral Sea.

The western third of the country is lowland plain, bisected to the north by the Hissar, Zerafshan and Turkestan ranges – western extensions of the Tian Shan that continue into Uzbekistan. The mountain ranges are the source of a fibrous network of fast-flowing streams, many of which empty into Tajikistan's two major rivers – the Syr-Darya (Jaxartes River), rising in the Fergana Valley and flowing through Khojand, and the Amu-Darya, formed from the confluence of two Pamiri rivers, the Vakhsh and the Pyanj.

Together, the Amu-Darya and the Pyanj mark most of the country's 1200km border with Afghanistan. Tajikistan's other borders are much less defined: in the east, 430km of border with China meanders through Pamir valleys, while to the north and west are the seemingly random jigsaw borders with Kyrgyzstan and Uzbekistan.

For administrative purposes the country is divided into three *viloyat* (provinces): Sughd (Khojand), Khatlon (Kurgonteppa) and the 60,000-sq-km autonomous mountain region of Kohistani Badakhshan (Gorno Badakhshan Autonomous Oblast, or GBAO), with much of the central region (including the Garm Valley) ruled directly from Dushanbe.

Tajikistan's territory also includes the strange northern enclave of Vorukh, stranded completely inside Kyrgyzstan.

Wildlife

Tajikistan's impressive megafauna includes snow leopards (perhaps 200 or so), a dozen brown bears, between 5000 and 10,000 Marco Polo sheep and around 12,000 ibex. The best place to see Marco Polo sheep (known as *arkhar* in Kyrgyz) and ibex (*echki* or *kyzyl kyik*) is around Jarty-Gumbaz in the eastern Pamir, particularly after December, when they come to lower altitudes for the rut.

Poaching (largely by border guards) is a major problem. Marco Polo sheep numbers have fallen 300% since independence and down 800% from the 1960s. Marco Polo sheep

meat is sold openly in Murgab bazaar, for less per kilo than mutton. Ironically, the one place where Marco Polo sheep numbers have stabilised and even expanded is areas where strictly controlled hunting has been allowed.

Environmental Issues

The 26,000-sq-km Tajik (Pamir) National Park was founded in 1992 as the largest in Central Asia, covering a whopping 18% of Tajikistan. That's the good news. The bad news is that the park exists only on paper, with only four employees to police and administer it (and none stationed inside the park).

The lack of burnable fuel in the eastern Pamir has led to the disappearance of the slow-growing (and fast-burning) *tersken* bush within a radius of 100km from Murgab, adding to desertification in the treeless region. The population of Murgab is still considered environmentally unsustainable. Several organisations are trying to introduce solar ovens but progress has been slow.

Recent reports indicate that Tajikistan's glaciers have started to retreat as a result of global warming. The area of Fedchenko Glacier, the largest in Central Asia, has shrunk by 10% in recent years.

FOOD & DRINK

For a general rundown of common Central Asian dishes, see p85.

Tajik dishes include *nahud sambusa* (chickpea samosas) or *nahud shavla* (chickpea porridge). Tajiks also prepare many bean and milk soups, while *oshi siyo halav* is a unique herb soup. *Tuhum barak* is a tasty egg-filled ravioli coated with sesame-seed oil. *Chakka* (*yakka* to Tajik speakers around Samarkand and Bukhara) is curd mixed with herbs, and delicious with flat-bread. *Kurtob* is a wonderful rural dish of layered *fatir* bread, yoghurt, onion, parsley and coriander in a creamy sauce, normally served in a wooden bowl.

In Badakhshan you might try *borj* – a meat and grain mix that resembles savoury porridge. In Kyrgyz yurts, expect lots of tea, yoghurt, *barsook* (fried bits of dough) and *kaimak* (cream). If you're lucky you might get *beshbarmak* (noodles and mutton) or *oromo*, a rolled-up steamed pastry flavoured with meat and butter.

Shir chai is a salty, soupy brew of tea with goats' milk, salt and butter that makes a popular breakfast in the Pamirs. It sits somewhere between milk tea and Tibetan butter tea and is guaranteed to put hairs on your chest. Rice pudding (*shir gurch* in Kyrgyz; *shir brench* in Tajik) is another popular Pamiri breakfast choice.

Both Hissar and Dushanbe brew their own beer, though bottled Russian imports like the Baltika range are the most common. Obi Zulol and Pamir are the best brands of fizzy mineral water, bottled in Istaravshan and Khorog.

DUSHANBE
ДУШАНБЕ

☎ 37/pop 600,000 / elev 800m

With a cool backdrop of mountains, lazy tree-lined avenues and pastel-hued neoclassical buildings, Dushanbe is Central Asia's best-looking capital – especially now that the bullet holes have been plastered over. Once scary and more than a little dangerous a decade ago, the Tajik capital is currently blossoming and is one of Central Asia's most pleasant cities, if just a little dull.

HISTORY

Although the remains of a settlement here date to the 5th century BC, modern-day Dushanbe has little history beyond last century. As recently as 80 years ago, Dushanbe was a small, poor village known chiefly for its weekly bazaar (Dushanbe means 'Monday' in Tajik).

In 1920 the last emir of Bukhara took refuge in Dushanbe, fleeing from the advancing Bolsheviks. He was forced to continue his flight early the next year as the Red Army added the Tajik settlement to the expanding Bolshevik empire. The Russian hold was shaken off for a spell when in 1922 Enver Pasha and his *basmachi* fighters liberated Dushanbe as part of their crusade to carve out a pan-Islamic empire, but Bolshevik authority was quickly reasserted following his death in a gun battle in southern Tajikistan.

With the arrival of the railroad in 1929, Dushanbe was made capital of the new Soviet Tajik republic and renamed Stalinabad – a name it bore until the 1950s and the histori-cal reinvention of the Khrushchev era. The region was developed as a cotton- and silk-processing centre and tens of thousands of people were relocated here, turning the rural

> **DUSHANBE MUST-SEES**
>
> **National Museum of Antiquities of Tajikistan** (p382) Eyeball Central Asia's largest surviving Buddha and the tiny ivory portrait of Alexander the Great.
>
> **Hissar** (p389) Get out of the city on a half-day excursion to the fort, museum and medressas here.
>
> **Restaurants** (p386) Savour the big-city comforts of the city's Turkish, Indian and even Ecuadorian restaurants before heading to the survival cuisine of the mountains.
>
> **Rudaki** Stroll leisurely past the pastel-coloured buildings and cool cafes of Dushanbe's tree-lined main drag.

village into a large, urban administrative and industrial centre. The city's numbers were fur-ther swollen by Tajik émigrés from Bukhara and Samarkand, which had been given over to Uzbek rule.

After almost 70 uneventful years of relative peace, if not prosperity, 1990 saw festering nationalistic sentiments explode into riot-ing, triggered by rumoured plans to house Armenian refugees in Dushanbe. Twenty-two people died in clashes with the militia.

There were further demonstrations in the autumn of 1991, organised by opposition fac-tions dissatisfied with the absence of politi-cal change in Tajikistan. The statue of Lenin that stood opposite the parliament building disappeared overnight, and young bearded men and veiled women took to the streets of Dushanbe, calling for an Islamic state.

During the civil war the city remained a capital of chaos. It was kept under a dusk-to-dawn curfew, with armed gangs controlling the roads in and out, and lawless brigands patrolling the streets. Shoot-outs between rival clans were common and most Russians fled the country. Random acts of violence continued through the 1990s but by 2002 the situation had stabilised enough to lift the citywide curfew. These days Dushanbe is sa-vouring its peace.

ORIENTATION

The focus of Dushanbe is the wide, tree-lined prospekt (avenue) Rudaki, which runs roughly north from the train station, past Maydoni Ayni (*maydoni* means 'square'). A walk from north to south along Rudaki offers an excellent introduction to the city.

TAJIKISTAN

Almost everything useful or interesting is within a 15-minute walk of central Maydoni Dusti (Friendship Square). The exception is the main bus station, which is some 3km away on kuchai Ibn Sina in the western part of town. The airport is in the southeastern suburbs of the city, 5km from the centre, along Ahmad Donish.

Dushanbe street signs sport the Tajik terms *kuchai* (street), *khiyeboni* (avenue) and *maydoni*.

INFORMATION

A tourist information office was due to open in 2010 on Ayni, near Hotel Poytaht.

Cultural Centres

Bactria Centre (☎ 227 03 69; www.bactria.net; Mirzo Rizo 22; ♥ 9am-6pm Mon-Fri) Home to occasional art exhibitions and concerts, weekly films and the Tillo Teppe handicraft centre (see p388). If you fancy chatting to Tajik students, come along for English hour every Wednesday at 4pm.

Emergency

Ambulance (☎ 03)
Police (☎ 02)

Internet Access

Klub Plazma (☎ 227 15 15; Rudaki 84; per hr 5TJS; ♥ 24hr) Has Skype and offers drinks.
Vahdat Internet (Rudaki 96; per hr 5TJS; ♥ 8am-10pm) One of a dozen internet cafes around town.

Medical Services

Your embassy will have contact details for recommended doctors, medical services and hospitals.

Prospekt Medical Clinic (☎ 701 90 00, emergency 93-500 0447; www.prospektclinic.com; Sanoi 33, Medgorodok; ♥ 8am-4.30pm Mon-Fri, to 3.30pm Sat & Sun) In the grounds of the Cardiology Hospital.
Eurodent (☎ 95-135 6578, 881 10 07; www.eurodent-tj.com; Rudaki 135) German-trained dentist.
Shifu Clinic (☎ 227 34 59; Lokhuti 3; ♥ 8am-noon & 1-4pm Mon-Fri, 8am-1pm Sat) The best private clinic in town.

Money

Licensed moneychanger booths across the city are the easiest places to change cash US dollars and euros.

You can find ATMs at the airport departure lounge, Hotel Avesto, Hotel Tojikistan, Hotel Dushanbe, TsUM, the main Tajik Air office and the post office. All accept Visa, Cirrus, Maestro and Electron cards.

Orienbank (☎ 221 63 96; www.orienbank.com; Rudaki 95; ♥ 8am-12.30pm & 1.30-5pm Mon-Fri) Exchange booth and ATM. There's another less-useful branch on Shotemur.
Tajprombank (☎ 221 33 15; Rudaki 22; www.tajprombank.tj) Changes cash and has an ATM.

Post

DHL (☎ 221 02 80; Rudaki 105) Enter around the back of the building.
Post office (Maydoni Dusti, Rudaki 57; ♥ 8am-6pm)

Registration

OVIR (☎ 227 67 11; Mirzo Tursunzoda 5; ♥ 8am-noon & 1-5pm Mon-Fri, 8am-noon Sat) If you have to register (see p419), get a travel agency to do it for you (for US$35 to US$45) or do it elsewhere. The process takes as long as three days.

Telephone

Most internet cafes offer Skype, or buy an IP (internet phone; see p419) card at the telephone office.
Central telephone office (Rudaki 55; ♥ 24hr) Next to the post office.

Travel Agencies

See p114 for details of other Dushanbe companies that organise trekking.

Hamsafar Travel (☎ 228 00 93, 93-501 4593; www.hamsafar-travel.com; Pulod Tolis 5/11) Can arrange jeep, trekking and tailor-made tours, as well as homestays, OVIR registration (US$45), GBAO permits (US$35), letters of invitation (US$50) and airport pickup (US$25). Located at the Adventurer's Inn (p386). Formerly Great Game Travel. Contact Ruslan.
Tajikaviatour (☎ 227 47 25; www.tajikaviatour.tj; dmelnichkov@hotmail.com; Bukhoro 32) For tailor-made top-end tours contact Dimitri Melnichkov.
Tajikintourservice (☎ 221 71 84; www.tis.tj; Pushkin 85) Air tickets, GBAO permits (US$35), OVIR registration (US$36) and tours, plus the only place to book charter Tajik Air flights to Ürümqi. Credit cards accepted.
Vostok Trading Tour (☎ 221 10 22; vtt_travel@mail.tj; Pushkin 14) Irregular opening hours but can arrange OVIR registration (US$60), GBAO permits (US$35), visa extensions and re-entry permits (US$15).

SIGHTS
Museums

The **National Museum of Antiquities of Tajikistan** (☎ 227 13 50; www.afc.ryukoku.ac.jp/tj; Ak Rajabov 7; adult/student 15/5TJS; ♥ 10am-5pm Tue-Fri, to 4pm Sat, to 2pm

DUSHANBE

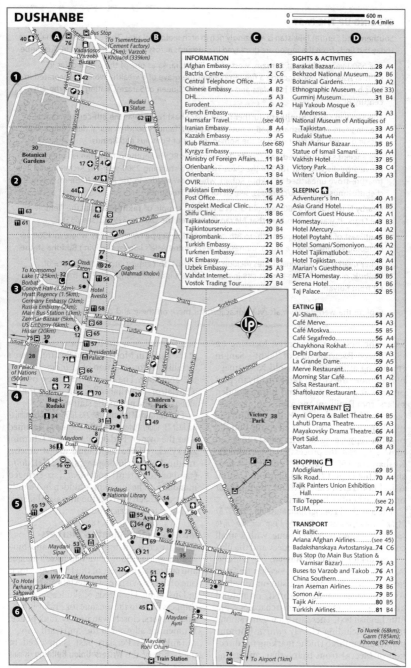

0 ────── 600 m
0 ────── 0.4 miles

INFORMATION
Afghan Embassy...................................1 B3
Bactria Centre......................................2 C6
Central Telephone Office.....................3 A5
Chinese Embassy..................................4 B2
DHL...5 A3
Eurodent..6 A2
French Embassy....................................7 B4
Hamsafar Travel.......................(see 40)
Iranian Embassy...................................8 A4
Kazakh Embassy...................................9 A5
Klub Plazma..............................(see 68)
Kyrgyz Embassy..................................10 B2
Ministry of Foreign Affairs................11 B4
Orienbank...12 A3
Orienbank...13 B4
OVIR...14 B5
Pakistani Embassy..............................15 B5
Post Office..16 A5
Prospekt Medical Clinic.....................17 A2
Shifu Clinic..18 B6
Tajikaviatour......................................19 A5
Tajikintourservice..............................20 B4
Tajprombank......................................21 B5
Turkish Embassy.................................22 B6
Turkmen Embassy..............................23 A1
UK Embassy..24 B4
Uzbek Embassy...................................25 A3
Vahdat Internet..................................26 A3
Vostok Trading Tour...........................27 B4

SIGHTS & ACTIVITIES
Barakat Bazaar...................................28 A4
Bekhzod National Museum.................29 B6
Botanical Gardens..............................30 A2
Ethnographic Museum.............(see 33)
Gurminj Museum................................31 B4
Haji Yakoub Mosque &
    Medressa.......................................32 A3
National Museum of Antiquities of
    Tajikistan.......................................33 A5
Rudaki Statue.....................................34 A4
Shah Mansur Bazaar...........................35 B5
Statue of Ismail Samani.....................36 A4
Vakhsh Hotel......................................37 B4
Victory Park..38 C4
Writers' Union Building......................39 A3

SLEEPING
Adventurer's Inn................................40 A1
Asia Grand Hotel................................41 B5
Comfort Guest House.........................42 A1
Homestay..43 B3
Hotel Mercury....................................44 A2
Hotel Poytaht.....................................45 B6
Hotel Somani/Somoniyon..................46 A2
Hotel Tajikmatlubot...........................47 A2
Hotel Tojikistan..................................48 B4
Marian's Guesthouse..........................49 B4
META Homestay..................................50 B5
Serena Hotel.......................................51 B6
Taj Palace...52 B5

EATING
Al-Sham..53 A5
Café Merve...54 A3
Café Moskva.......................................55 A3
Café Segafredo...................................56 A4
Chaykhona Rokhat.............................57 A4
Delhi Darbar.......................................58 A3
La Grande Dame.................................59 A5
Merve Restaurant...............................60 B4
Morning Star Café..............................61 A2
Salsa Restaurant.................................62 B1
Shaftoluzor Restaurant......................63 A2

ENTERTAINMENT
Ayni Opera & Ballet Theatre..............64 B5
Lahuti Drama Theatre.........................65 A3
Mayakovsky Drama Theatre...............66 A4
Port Saïd...67 B2
Vastan..68 A3

SHOPPING
Modigliani..69 B5
Silk Road..70 A4
Tajik Painters Union Exhibition
    Hall..71 A4
Tillo Teppe.................................(see 2)
TsUM..72 A4

TRANSPORT
Air Baltic..73 B5
Ariana Afghan Airlines.............(see 45)
Badakhshanskaya Avtostansiya..........74 C6
Bus Stop (to Main Bus Station &
    Varnisar Bazar)..............................75 A3
Buses to Varzob and Takob................76 A1
China Southern...................................77 A3
Iran Aseman Airlines..........................78 B6
Somon Air...79 B5
Tajik Air..80 B5
Turkish Airlines...................................81 B4

TAJIKISTAN

DIGGING UP THE PAST

Southern and Central Tajikistan is amazingly rich in archaeological sites. There's little to actually see today but finds from the region are displayed in museums across the world, including in Dushanbe.

- The 5500-year-old site of **Sarazm**, west of Penjikent, ranks as one of the oldest cities in Central Asia. The finds include a fire temple and the grave of a wealthy woman, decorated in lapis beads and seashell bracelets and dubbed the 'Queen of Sarazm', dating from the 4th century BC.

- The Sogdian site of **Bunjikath**, further north near Shakhristan, was the 8th-century capital of the kingdom of Ushrushana, and is noteworthy for a famous Sogdian mural depicting a wolf suckling twins, in a clear echo of the Roman legend of Romulus and Remus.

- The ancient site of **Kobadiyan** (7th to 2nd centuries BC) in southern Tajikistan is famed for the nearby discovery in 1877 of the Oxus Treasure, a stunning 2500-year-old Archaemenid treasure-trove unearthed at Takht-i Kobad, which now resides in the British Museum (www.thebritishmuseum.ac.uk/compass, search for 'Oxus Treasure').

- Nearby is the ruined 2300-year-old Graeco-Bactrian temple of **Takht-i Sangin**, the 'Temple of the Oxus'. It was close to here that Alexander crossed the Oxus in 329 BC (see p35).

- Southeast of Kurgonteppa is 7th- to 8th-century **Ajina Teppe** (Witches Hill), where in 1966 archaeologists unearthed a stupa, monastery and Central Asia's largest surviving Buddha statue.

- Other nearby archaeological sites include the 9th- to 11th-century citadel and palace of **Hulbuk**, once the fourth-largest city in Central Asia. It is at Khurbanshaid, 7km from Vose, not far from Kulyab.

Explore the website www.afc.ryukoku.ac.jp/tj for more on these and other sites.

Sun) is the best in the country, focusing on the Graeco-Bactrian sites of Takht-i-Sangin (including a tiny 3000-year-old ivory image of Alexander the Great) and Kobadiyan, plus original Sogdian murals and burnt wooden pillars from Penjikent and a 6th-century scabbard and hilt in the shape of a griffin. The highlight is the 13m-long sleeping Buddha of Ajina Teppe, excavated in 1966 (and sliced into 92 pieces in the process). It dates from the Kushan era, 1500 years ago, and is now considered the largest Buddha figure in Central Asia. Photos aren't allowed and you must put on plastic booties before entering.

The attached **Ethnographic Museum** (☎ 227 87 51; Ak Rajabov 7; admission 15TJS; ☺ 10am-4pm Tue-Fri, to 4pm Sat, to 2pm Sun) is poorer value, with a small collection of clothes, embroidery and the like.

The **Bekhzod National Museum** (☎ 221 60 36; Maydoni Ayni; admission 20TJS; ☺ 9am-4pm Tue-Sat, to 3pm Sun), on a commanding site on Maydoni Ayni, includes standard exhibits on natural history, art, ethnography and archaeology, but little English text. There are a few gems among the filler, including a lovely *minbar* (mosque pulpit) and mihrab (niche marking the direction of Mecca) from Istaravshan and a fine painting of Lenin meeting oppressed women of the world in Moscow's Red Square. There's a chilling reconstruction of a *zindan* (jail) on the 2nd floor. The top floor is given over to a Soviet/presidential collection – look for the alabaster carvings in the stairwell.

The **Gurminj Museum** (☎ 223 10 76; www.gurminj.tj; Bokhtar 23; adult/student 5/1TJS; ☺ 11am-6pm) is named after the owner, Badakhshani actor Gurminj Zavkybekov. The antique musical instruments are the draw, including a *gijak* (fiddle), *doira* (tambourine/drum) and *rabab* (six-stringed mandolin). The museum is hidden in a family compound across from the mosaic of justice and next to a district court.

Mosques, Monuments & Markets

With its crescent-topped minaret and burnished golden dome, the **Haji Yakoub mosque** and **medressa**, just west of the Hotel Avesto, is one of the few visible manifestations of Islam in Dushanbe. Hundreds of skullcapped worshippers file into the mosque for Friday lunchtime prayers, closely watched by Tajik police. Women are allowed in the courtyard only.

Tajikistan's Persian past is invoked in the facade of the **Writers' Union Building** (Ismoili

Somoni). It's adorned like a medieval cathedral with saintly, sculpted-stone figures of Sadruddin Ayni, Omar Khayam, Firdausi and other writers from the Persian pantheon.

Dushanbe's most visible monument to nation-building is the surprisingly clean-shaven sorcerer-like **statue of Ismail Samani** (Ismoili Somoni), the 10th-century founder of the Samanid dynasty, occupying prime place on Maydoni Dusti. His statue ousted Lenin's from the top spot in 1999 on the 1100th anniversary of the Samanid dynasty. Look behind the statue for a map of the Samanid empire at its height.

A large statue of Rudaki now dominates the rather soulless remodelled **Bag-i Rudaki**, just to the north. Just behind the park is the Palace of Nations, an opulent new presidential palace whose construction allegedly cost more than the country's annual health budget.

The bustling and colourful **Shah Mansur (Green) Bazaar** (cnr Lokhuti & Nissor Muhammed) is the heartbeat of Dushanbe trade and the best place to stock up on travel snacks from dried fruit to Korean kimchi.

Less exotic is the large, covered **Barakat Bazaar** (Ismoili Somoni), northwest of the Hotel Tajikistan, where you might pick up an embroidered *tupi* (skullcap) or stripy *chapan* (cloak). The market will eventually be replaced by a new national museum and theatre complex.

Other notable buildings include the **Ayni Opera & Ballet Theatre** (p387) and the **Vakhsh Hotel** (Rudaki 24) on its south side. During the civil war the hotel was occupied by bands of bearded mujaheddin rebels and peppered with bullet holes. Now it's one of the city's nicest places to grab an open-air beer.

Parks

Several places in town offer green space for some down time, including the peaceful **Botanical Gardens** (admission 1TJS; 8am-7pm), which is a favourite of canoodling couples. The north end spotlights some finely carved examples of Tajik architecture.

For the best views over the city, take the creaking Soviet-era cable car up to **Victory Park** (cable car 1TJS; until 8pm) and watch the sun set over a draft Simsim Beer. The impressive WWII monument here is worth a look.

Liveliest of the parks on weekends and holidays is family-friendly **Komsomol Lake** (Ismoili Somoni), offering outdoor shashlyk, draft beer,

a Ferris wheel and pedalos on the water. It's one bus stop east of Rudaki, opposite the zoo. A huge new chaikhana is under construction next door.

ACTIVITIES

Director Goulya Petrova of **Goulya's Outdoor Adventures** (93-505 0122; goulya.petrova@gmail.com) runs popular weekend hiking trips to destinations around Dushanbe for around US$20 per person. Contact Goulya or Artyom. Goulya also organises skiing trips to the Takob ski base in the Varzob Valley.

The Dushanbe Hash House Harriers ('drinkers with a running problem') organise runs every Saturday. See the website http://sites.google.com/site/dushanbeh3/home for details.

SLEEPING

Dushanbe's accommodation options aren't great. Homestays exist but are hard to track down. The main midrange and top-end choices are either ageing Soviet-era hotels or pricey private modern mansions that cater mostly to local *biznezmen* and consultants on an expense account.

Budget

Hotel Poytaht (221 96 55; Rudaki 7; d per person 44TJS, half lux per person 110TJS, lux 220-352TJS) The plain 4th- and 5th-floor simple *(prastoi)* rooms in the former Hotel Dushanbe are the cheapest in town, but are stiflingly hot in summer, the bathrooms are shared and single travellers may have to share rooms. The midrange rooms here capture the dubious charms of a 1970s Soviet apartment block but you get nice leafy views of Maydoni Ayni, plus TV, air con and fridge and the bathrooms are surprisingly clean. The fearsome dressing-gown-clad floor ladies have retained their impressive ability to ignore their guests. Some travellers have complained about a lack of security in the shared rooms.

Hotel Farhang (223 31 57; Negmat Karaliev 2; s/d 50/100TJS) You can get better rooms for your buck here. Rooms are clean and decent (the upper floor is best) and there's a shared hot-water bathroom for every two rooms. The location is inconvenient but transport is easy, there are supermarkets and restaurants across the road and the hotel has a cafe for beer and breakfast. Get here on bus No 2 or trolley bus No 4 from Ayni, or bus No

18 from Ismoili Somoni and Rudaki; get off opposite the UFO-shaped circus and walk 100m south.

META Homestay (☎ 221 20 83; Bez Proezd 11, Zekhni; dm US$15, breakfast US$2, dinner US$6) The house of Makhbuba Mansurova offers clean mattresses, a tea bed in the garden and access to a hot water bathroom, though the top-floor room can be hot in summer. Be warned: it's hard to find, down an alley *(proezd)* on the south side of the obvious TV transmitter.

Homestay (☎ 224 57 81, 90-109 7404; Mirzo Tursunzoda 178; dm US$15) This simple private home offers three beds in a stuffy spare room, with access to a clean, tiled bathroom with hot shower. Ask for English-speaking Farzona.

Adventurer's Inn (☎ 228 00 93; www.hamsafar -travel.com; Pulod Tolis 5/11; s/d incl breakfast US$25/40; ☎) Despite a temperamental shower and the occasional grubby sheet, this is still our pick for the best sleeping spot in town. Major pluses are the two shared bathrooms, the excellent breakfasts and the relaxed vibe. There are only four rooms (named after Pamiri explorers), so book in advance, especially in July and August. The guesthouse is run by Hamsafar Travel (p382). It's well hidden in the backstreets behind the Vadanosos (Varzob) Bazaar, across a bridge over the sewer pipe behind the US ambassador's residence (!), so you'll need some help finding it the first time.

Midrange & Top End

Hotel Tajikmatlubot (☎ 224 64 87; Rudaki 137; r incl breakfast US$40-80; 🖵 ⊠) You'll feel like you're a guest of the government at this small, off-beat, 11-room place, offering spacious rooms and good bathrooms. This is good value for Dushanbe, especially for singles.

Hotel Mercury (☎ 224 44 91; www.hotel-mercury. tj; Tolstoy 9; r US$80-100, lux US$100-140; ⊠ 🖵 Ⓟ ☎) This privately run, villa-style hotel is one of the best value top-end places in town. The 20 spacious modern rooms come with satellite TV, computer and a kettle, and the reception can order in food from a variety of local restaurants. The half-lux rooms (US$100) offer the best value. Credit cards are accepted and the hotel has its own ATM. There's even a kitschy garden waterfall.

Marian's Guesthouse (☎ 223 01 91; www.marians guesthouse.com; Shotemur 67/1; r €70-80; ⊠ 🖵 🙀 Ⓟ ☎) Visiting consultants love this comfortable refuge, so reserve a room in advance (there

are only eight) or you won't even get past the security guards. There's laundry, satellite TV and airport transfer, breakfast included and evening driver service. One room has its bathroom down the hall. The guesthouse is hard to find; head down the little alley just after the TV-station building (with its satellite dish) across from the Children's Park and look for the black-and-white gates. Contact Gulnura Razukova.

Comfort Guest House (☎ 228 9645; ghcomfort@mail. ru; Hamza Hakimzade 61; r incl breakfast US$80-85; 🖵 ☎) Another well-run private guesthouse in the north of town, with seven spacious rooms and immaculate bathrooms. Join the family for a shared *plov* on weekends.

Hotel Tojikiston (☎ 44-600 99 33, 221 62 62; www. hoteltojikiston.com; Shotemur 22; s US$150, half lux tw US$240, lux $250; ⊠ ☎) This former Soviet-era hotel has been renovated to five-star standard but is a big step down from the Hyatt. Standard single rooms are ridiculously small; the fresh and modern half-lux twins are a better bet. A gym and pool are under construction. Credit cards are accepted and registration is included in the price.

Hyatt Regency (47-377 12 34; www.dushanbe.regency. hyatt.com; Ismoili Somoni 26/1; s/d US$210/230, plus 18% tax; ⊠ ⊠ Ⓟ ☎ 🙀) Opened in 2009 beside Komsomol Lake, this half-empty place clearly focuses on business over pleasure, though the rooms are stylish with perks like open-plan bathrooms and iPod docks. Internet access and tax alone cost an extra US$70.

Two new five-star places were set to open in 2010; the 95-room **Serena Hotel** (www.serena hotels.com; Rudaki) and the 19-storey **Hotel Somani/ Somoniyon** (Rudaki), further north on Rudaki. Other top-end places include the attached and almost identical four-star **Asia Grand Hotel** (☎ 44-600 7777; www.asiagrandhotel.tj; Mirzo Tursunzoda 21A; ☎) and **Taj Palace** (☎ 48-701 7171; www.taj-pal ace.tj; Mirzo Tursunzoda 21B; ☎), both with flash restaurants and rooms from US$110 to US$150.

EATING
Cafes & Chaikhanas

The cheapest eats are to be found at the chaikhanas in the markets.

our pick Café Merve (☎ 221 94 09; Rudaki 92; mains 9-12TJS, snacks 2-4TJS; ⏱6am-midnight; Ⓔ Ⓥ) Our favourite eatery in town is this bright and bustling cafeteria, churning out Turkish kebabs, pizza, salads, cakes and instant coffee (but no alcohol), plus the best breakfast bets in town (feta and olives). It can be hard to get a seat at lunchtime.

Merve Restaurant (☎ 221 80 02; Drujba Naradov 47) Plusher branch of Café Merve, with similar prices and pleasant outdoor seating at the foot of Victory Park.

Chaykhona Rokhat (☎ 221 76 54; Rudaki 84; mains 7-11TJS; ☺ lunch & dinner) This unusual, Soviet-era attempt at a grand Persian-style chaikhana is great for people-watching but is perhaps better for a drink or snack than a full meal. Lose yourself in the ceiling paintings while you wait for your waiter.

Morning Star Café (☎ 228 94 64; www.morning starcafe.net; Said Nosir 47; sandwiches 9-13TJS, coffee 6-9TJS; ☺ 8am-5pm Mon-Sat; ⓖ ⓔ ⓥ) This American-style cafe is a fine place to refuel on locally roasted coffee and a slice of cheesecake, or choose from lunch options like carrot soup, salads and sandwiches (try the Greek wrap with yoghurt and olives). The breakfast stops are pulled out on Saturdays with an entire menu of American-style pancakes and biscuits.

Shaftoluzor Restaurant (Said Nosir; mains 6-9TJS; ☺ 11am-4pm Mon-Fri) Opposite the Morning Star, this simple, local, open-air eatery is one of the best places in town to try *kurtob*, a Tajik dish of flatbread, yoghurt, onion and parsley served in a wooden bowl.

Café Moskva (Ayni Park; mains 8-14TJS) The nicest of several pleasant open-air restaurants dotted around town, serving up shashlyk, *borek* (pies), salads and samosas, plus local beer on tap and live music.

Café Segafredo (☎ 701 57 77; Rudaki 70; coffee 15TJS; ⓔ) This open-air cafe is currently the chic-est place for well-heeled NGO staff to recharge over real espresso.

Restaurants

Dushanbe restaurants add a service charge of 10% to 12%.

Delhi Darbar (☎ 224 66 11; delhi@tajik.net; Rudaki 88; mains 10-20TJS; ☺ lunch & dinner; ⓥ ⓔ) The spice factor here might not be 100% subcontinental but the Indian standards like chicken tikka masala, veggie curries and cooling lassis are tasty, plus there are thalis (set meals) and a popular Friday-night buffet (35TJS).

Al-Sham (☎ 227 12 00; Ak Rajabov 11; starters 6-10TJS, mains 12-15TJS; ☺ lunch & dinner; ⓥ ⓔ) This Lebanese and Syrian restaurant (Al-Sham is the Arabic name for Damascus) has sophisticated decor, outdoor seating and an

authentic range of *mezze* (starters), plus all your main-dish grills and kebabs. There's an English menu but no translations of the dishes, so take a knowledgeable friend if you don't know your *kubba* (croquettes of lamb and cracked wheat) from your *baba ganoush* (smoky eggplant dip).

Salsa Restaurant (☎ 224 88 57; cnr Karamov & Omar Khayam; starters 4-9TJS, mains 15-23TJS; ⓥ ⓔ) Just what you didn't expect in Dushanbe; an Ecuadorian restaurant serving everything from carrot cake and cocktails to Tex-Mex, complemented by a decent selection of wines, real coffee and a soup of the day. This is definitely your only chance in Central Asia to try Ecuadorian *llapingachos* (fried potato and mozzarella cheese with peanut sauce).

La Grande Dame (☎ 93-501 0089, 227 62 74; www. lagrandedamecafe.com; cnr Bukhoro & Shevchenko; mains 22-45TJS; ☺ 8am-11pm; ⓔ) If you need a slice of Western familiarity to go with your Lavazza coffee, try this low-key, French-style brasserie, run by Marian's Guesthouse. The menu (available online) offers everything from lunchtime baguettes to salmon blinis with sour cream and caviar (29TJS), fine desserts and a Sunday brunch with treats like French toast and eggs Benedict.

ENTERTAINMENT

Dushanbe's outdoor cafe-bars are particularly pleasant on a warm summer evening, when locals catch up on the day over a locally brewed draft Simsim or Dushanbinsky Beer. Our favourite places are the Café Moskva (p387), the seats beside the fountains of the Ayni Opera & Ballet Theatre, the balcony of the Chaykhona Rokhat (p387) or at Victory Park (p385).

Other nightlife is hit and miss. You'll have to try to decipher the Cyrillic notice boards outside the following theatres to find out what's on.

There's still life left in the classy **Ayni Opera & Ballet Theatre** (☎ 221 44 22, 221 62 91; Rudaki 28; ☺ closed Jul), with the odd opera and classical music concert, plus it has possibly the finest interior in Dushanbe. Tickets cost from 10TJS.

The **Borbat Concert Hall** (☎ 223 5186; Ismoili Somoni 26) hosts occasional Tajik music concerts. Ask at the Gurminj Museum (p384) about their weekly Pamiri music concerts featuring traditional band Samo.

There are Tajik plays at the **Lahuti Drama Theatre** (☎ 221 37 51; Rudaki 86) and the nearby

TAJIKISTAN

Mayakovsky Drama Theatre (☎ 221 31 32; Rudaki 76), the latter with a Russian emphasis.

There are several nightclubs, including **Port Saïd** (☎ 224 88 02; Rudaki 114; admission 10TJS; ☺ 9pm-4am Mon, Wed & Fri) and the flashier **Vastan** (☎ 224 09 36; Rudaki 88; admission 10TJS; ☺ closed Mon). Prostitutes frequent these clubs so solo female travellers will get less hassle if they go with a friend.

SHOPPING

TsUM (☎ 221 51 11; Rudaki 83; ☺ 8.30am-5pm Mon-Sat) This central department store has some souvenirs among the shampoo and mobile phones. Items include *suzani* embroidery, stripy cloaks, hats, Pamiri socks, ceramic Central Asian figures, musical instruments and lots of *ikat* silks, plus practical items such as camera batteries, memory sticks and print film.

Tillo Teppe (☎ 221 81 34; Mirzo Rizo 22; ☺ 9am-6pm Mon-Fri) This shop in the Bactria Centre (p382) sells a good range of Pamiri handicrafts from the Yak House (p413), as well as *ikat* cloth, embroidered bags, Marcus Hauser's map of the Pamirs (US$15), music CDs and museum guidebooks.

Modigliani (☎ 227 04 74; art_modigliani@yahoo.com; Nissor Muhammed 4A; ☺ 10am-6pm Mon-Fri, 10am-5pm Sat) A small shop crammed with carpets, paintings, embroidery, pottery and especially jewellery, plus products from De Pamiri (p406) and some nice *ikat* scarves.

Silk Road (☎ 227 43 05; Shotemur 32; ☺ 9am-6pm Mon-Fri) One of the best souvenir shops, particularly good for Tajik robes, embroidery, carpets, scarves and those hard-to-find postcards.

Tajik Painters Union Exhibition Hall (cnr Rudaki & Ismoili Somoni; ☺ 10am-5pm Mon-Fri, to 3pm Sat) Worth a visit for three floors of modern Tajik art, much of which is for sale.

GETTING THERE & AWAY
Air

Tajik Air (p388) theoretically has flights to Garm, Penjikent, Ayni, Isfara, Vanj (Vanch) and Kulyab, most of them in winter only. In practice the only reliable regular services are to Khojand (US$65, three daily) and Khorog (US$80, daily).

To try for a ticket on the 8am flight to Khorog, visit the airport ticket office the afternoon before, or turn up around 6am on the day of the flight. Flights are grounded at the first sign of bad weather (see p406).

Tajik Air has three flights weekly to Bishkek (US$200) and Almaty (US$188) but none to Ashgabat or Tashkent. For more on international flights, see p421. Nissor Muhammed (former Chekhov) street is lined with *aviakassa* (travel agencies).

AIRLINE OFFICES
Air Baltic (☎ 227 10 55; Lokhuti 16; ☺ 9am-noon, 1-5pm Mon-Fri) Represented by GlobalTrans; you're better off buying tickets online.
Ariana Afghan Airlines (☎ 227 27 09; ariana5duy@yahoo.com; Rudaki 7; ☺ 8am-3.30pm Mon-Sat) Located in the lobby of Hotel Poytaht. Weekly flight to Kabul (US$160, cash only). Confirm any booking as soon as you arrive in Dushanbe.
China Southern (☎ 224 1765; Rudaki 98; ☺ 9am-5pm Mon-Fri) Weekly to Ürümqi.
Iran Aseman Airlines (☎ 221 97 03; cnr Ayni & Adkhamov; ☺ 8.30am-1pm & 2-5pm Mon-Wed & Fri, 8.30am-noon Thu, 8.30am-2pm Sat) Weekly to Mashhad.
Somon Air (☎ 93-560 0000; Nissor Muhammed; ☺ 8am-7pm Mon-Sat, closed Sun) Flies to Khojand, plus international flights.
Tajik Air (☎ 229 82 06; Nissor Muhammed 5, cnr Lokhuti; ☺ 8am-6pm)
Turkish Airlines (☎ 48-701 15 01; kaynak@gsakaynak.tj; Vefa Centre, Bokhtar 37/1; ☺ 8.30am-5.30pm Mon-Fri, 9am-3pm Sat) Popular twice-weekly flight to İstanbul.

Minibus & Shared Taxi

Frequent minibuses to Varzob (2TJS) and Takob (3TJS), and irregular taxis to Khoja Obi Garm depart from the bus stand west of the Vadonasos (Varzob) Bazaar in the north of town.

Shared taxis to Penjikent, Ayni, Istaravshan and Khojand leave in the morning from the Tsementzavod (Cement Factory) stand in the north of town. A seat to Khojand or Penjikent costs anywhere from 100TJS to 120TJS, depending on the car and the price of fuel, and takes about eight hours. Choose your car with care as there are some real rattletraps out there. Take minibus 24 or bus 3 here from along Rudaki or from near the Vadonasos (Varzob) Bazaar.

UAZ minibuses and 4WDs to Khorog (180TJS to 220TJS, 14 to 16 hours, 555km) and Kala-i Khum (120TJS) leave early in the morning from the **Badakshanskaya avtostansiya** (Badakhshan bus stand) transport yard on Ahmad Donish (the road to the airport), near the railway bridge. Minibuses 1 and 8 pass here. Visit the day before to score a front seat and expect to hang around for hours for the vehicle to fill up. See p402 for more on the roads to Khorog.

Routes to southern Tajikistan (Kurgonteppa, Kulyab and as far down as Shahr-i Tuz, Dusti and Pyanj) leave in the morning from the **main bus station** in the western suburbs, 3km from the centre, though some services also leave from the Sahowat Bazaar in the 63rd *mikrorayon* (microregion) in the southwestern suburbs. Bus 29 and 18 run to the main bus station from Ismoili Somoni, or take a taxi (7TJS); bus 18 continues to Sahowat Bazaar.

GETTING AROUND

Buses (50 to 60 dirham) and private minibuses (1TJS) buzz around town. Bus/minibus 3 and trolleybus 1 shuttle up and down Rudaki, stopping frequently; others such as bus 18, trolleybus 11 and minibuses 8 and 22 turn west along Ismoili Somoni. Faster shared taxis (2TJS per seat) also run the popular routes; look for the numbered sign stuck furtively in the front window.

The airport is a quick ride on buses 2, 8 or 12, all caught along Rudaki and marked фурудгох (*furudgoh*). Trolleybus 4 runs here from Ayni. A taxi will cost 10TJS to 15TJS, a little more in the middle of the night. To order a cab, call ☎ 233 33 33.

AROUND DUSHANBE

The main M34 winds north through the valley of the Varzob River, past dozens of villas built in recent years by the city's nouveau riche. There's no one particular place to head for but there are plenty of picturesque locations, including the Varzob Reservoir which offers a popular place to cool off in summer. Minibuses run up the valley to the villages of Varzob and Takob.

Popular hiking destinations in Varzob Valley include the pretty 20m **Gusgarf Waterfall**, a 2½-hour walk up a side valley 7km south of Varzob (31km from Dushanbe), and further north, the Khoja Obi Garm Valley (behind the industrial-sized sanatorium of the same name) and Siama Valley. There's also good hiking around the ski resort at **Takob**, whose turn-off is 36km north of Dushanbe, just before the President's dacha.

For a day or weekend hike, expatriates recommend the **Karatag Valley**, located 80km east of Dushanbe (turn north from the Dushanbe–Tursanzade road at Shakhrinav). From the village of Hakimi, 18km from the junction, it becomes a two- to three-hour (or 6km) hike to **Timur Dara Lake**. **Payron Lake** is about 8km further north, up the main Karatag Valley and then northeast up a side valley.

In the same region, the **Shirkent Valley** has tricky-to-see, difficult-to-reach and hard-to-forget dinosaur footprints a 90-minute hike from the trailhead. You'll need a guide to find them.

Hissar

☎ 3139

On a wide mountain-fringed plain, 30km west of Dushanbe, are the remains of an 18th-century **fortress** (admission 1TJS; ☒ 8am-6pm), that was occupied until 1924 by Ibrahim Beg, the local henchman of the Emir of Bukhara. Once a *basmachi* stronghold, the fortress was destroyed by the Red Army and all that remains is a reconstructed stone gateway (Darvaza-i-Ark) in the cleavage of two massive grassy hillocks. A scramble up the hill on the right (the former residence of the *beg*, or landlord) offers excellent views. The fort is depicted on the 20TJS note.

In front of the fortress are two plain medressas, the 16th-century **Medressa-i-Kuhna** and the 17th-century **Medressa-i-Nau**, a later overspill (*nau* means 'new'). The older medressa (facing the fortress gate) contains a small **museum** (admission 3.50TJS; ☒ 8am-6pm), whose mildly interesting displays include an 1800-year-old ceramic tomb discovered nearby. Next door are the foundations of a caravanserai built in 1808 and, in the former Registan Square front of the medressa, the remains of the town *taharatkhana* (bathhouse). A short walk down the road behind the medressas is the **mausoleum** of 16th-century Sufic teacher Makhdum Azam.

At the foot of the slopes around the fortress is a **holy spring** and pleasant chaikhana.

Getting There & Away

To get here from Dushanbe, take bus 8 west on Ismoili Somoni to Zarnisar Bazaar, then a minibus (1.50TJS) or shared taxi (3TJS per seat) to Hissar (30 minutes). In Hissar bazaar take a shared taxi (1TJS per seat) across from the bazaar to the fort, some 7km further, past cotton fields. Ask for the *qala* (fortress; *krepast* in Russian).

TAJIKISTAN

NORTHERN TAJIKISTAN

Tajikistan in the north squeezes between Uzbekistan and Kyrgyzstan before oozing across the mouth of the Fergana Valley, the Uzbek heartland.

South of Istaravshan, the twin Turkestan and Zerafshan (Zeravshan) ranges sever northern Tajikistan from Dushanbe and the bulk of the country's landmass. The scenic M34 connects the two parts of the country via Iranian- and Chinese-built tunnels that bypass the spectacular old route over the 3378m Shakhristan Pass and 3372m Anzob Pass. The road was upgraded by the Chinese in 2009 and is now a smooth ride.

Possible stops en route are the homestays of the Yagnob and Zerafshan valleys, beautiful Iskander-Kul lake (see p396) and the heavily eroded 13.5m-tall 10th-century Varz-i-Minor (Tall Minaret) in Ayni village.

KHOJAND
ХОДЖАНД/ХУЧАНД
☎ 3422 / pop 164,500

Khojand (or Khojent, former Leninabad) is the capital of northern Tajikistan's Sughd province and the second-largest city in the country. It's also one of Tajikistan's oldest towns, founded on the banks of the Syr-Darya by Alexander the Great as his easternmost outpost, Alexandria-Eskhate. Commanding (and taxing) the entrance to the Fergana Valley, Khojand built palaces, grand mosques and a huge citadel before the Mongols bulldozed the city into oblivion in the early 13th century. Today the economically booming town is of marginal interest to visitors, useful mainly as a springboard to the spectacular overland route south to Dushanbe.

Khojand, made up mostly of Uzbeks, has more in common with the Uzbek Fergana Valley than Dushanbe, although it always provided Tajikistan's Soviet elite. When President Nabiev, a Khojand man, was unseated in 1992 and Tajikistan appeared to be becoming an Islamic republic, Khojand (Leninabad) province threatened to secede. Secure behind the Fan Mountains, it managed to escape the ravages of the civil war and remains the wealthiest part of the country, producing two-thirds of Tajikistan's GDP, with 75% of the country's arable land and only one-third of the population.

Information
Agroinvestbank (www.agroinvestbank.tj/eng; Lenin 41A; ☾ 8am-noon & 1-4pm Mon-Fri) The ATM here accepts foreign cards.

Orienbank (Kamoli Khojandi; ☾ 8am-noon & 1-5pm Mon-Fri) Cash advances on a Visa or MasterCard for 2% commission.

OVIR (Firdausi; ☾ 10am-noon & 1-5pm Mon-Fri) If you need to register (see p419) you'll need a photocopy of your passport, one photo and the equivalent of US$15 plus perhaps 32TJS, paid into the nearby Amonat Bank. The office is known in Tajik as 'Khadamoti Muhokirat Dar Bilyoti Sugd' and is the cream building with the big brown gate.

Post Office (Rajabov; ☾ 8am-6pm Mon-Fri, to 3pm Sat, to noon Sun)

Sights
The city's oldest remains are the formless baked-earth walls of the 10th-century **citadel**, which once boasted seven gates and 6km of fortifications. This was also the site of Alexander's original settlement. The fort was the site of pitched battles in 1997 between rebel Uzbek warlords and government troops, during which 300 people were killed. The reconstructed eastern gate houses the **Museum of Archaeology and Fortifications** (M Tanbyri 4; admission 1TJS; ☾ 8am-noon, 1-5pm Mon-Fri, 9am-4pm Sat & Sun), which has some interesting 19th-century photos and plans of the original citadel. You can climb the ramparts but be careful when photographing, as the citadel behind is occupied by the military.

At the other end of the reconstructed city walls, the **Historical Museum of Sughd Province** (admission 6TJS; ☾ 8am-4pm Tue-Fri, 9am-4pm Sat & Sun) has prominent displays on Timur Malik, the local hero who battled the Mongol onslaught from an island in the Syr-Darya, but suffers from a chronic lack of actual artefacts.

At the south end of Lenin kuchai is **Panchshanbe Bazaar**, one of the best-stocked markets in Central Asia, especially on Thursday (*panchshanbe* in Tajik). The core of the bazaar is an elegant, purpose-built hall (1954) with arched entrance portals and a pink-and-lime-green neoclassical facade – think Stalin meets *1001 Nights*.

Opposite the bazaar is the **mosque, medressa** and **mausoleum of Sheikh Massal ad-Din** (1133–1223), a modest, relatively modern complex that is quietly busy with serious young men clutching Qurans. Take a look at the carved wooden pillars lining the side *aivans* (covered porticoes). The impressive

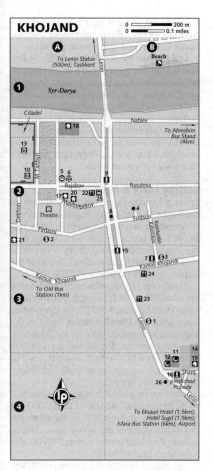

KHOJAND

ously in the middle of Lenin street, not far from an extinguished eternal flame.

Sleeping

Hotel Sharq (☎ 6 78 83; Sharq; dm 12-15TJS) Hard-core travellers can bunk down with Tajik traders on the top floor of this friendly but pretty basic bazaar hotel. Rooms are spacious but there's only one toilet and no hot water (staff can direct you to a *banya* nearby). It's good for groups of three or four. Women might feel uncomfortable here.

Eksaun Hotel (☎ 6 69 84; Lenin 171; r 30TJS, half lux 50TJS, lux 100-130TJS) This is the obvious choice for budget travellers, though gruff staff will shepherd you away from the cheapest high-rise rooms with shared bathroom. The half-lux and lux options offer private hot-water bathrooms and several bizarrely unfurnished rooms (the building was meant to be an apartment block). The hotel is about 1.5km south of the Panchshanbe Bazaar, at the fork in the road.

Hotel Leninabad (☎ 6 55 35; Nabiev 51; s/d 47/94TJS, half lux/lux 68/120TJS) This unfashionably named state hotel is well placed on the corniche beside

khaki-coloured mausoleum was built in 1394. The stubby 21m-high minaret was added in 1865. The complex is currently under expansion, as clear a sign as any of Islam's regional rebirth.

Since the removal of its giant rival in Tashkent, Khojand's 22m-tall **statue of Lenin** is now the largest in Central Asia. It was moved here from Moscow in 1974. It's on the north side of the river, 500m beyond the bridge.

Other eye-catching Soviet leftovers include the bright red **hammer and sickle** in the centre of Lenin kuchai, a **bust of Marx and Lenin** on the side of an apartment block on Kamoli Khojandi and the impressive **WWII monument** across from the Panchshanbe Bazaar. A statue of the poet **Komil (Kamoli) Khojandi** sits studi-

STALIN'S BUM DEAL

The crazy jigsaw boundaries of northern Tajikistan are in fact the result of sober thought. Before 1929 Tajikistan was an autonomous republic within the Uzbek ASSR, but because of its sensitive location on the edge of the Islamic world, Stalin wanted it upgraded to a full republic. But there weren't enough Tajiks; full-republic status required one million inhabitants. They simply topped up numbers by adding the (mainly Uzbek) population of the Khojand region (then Leninabad) to Tajikistan's. There may also be some truth in the theory that this was in partial recompense for the loss of the culturally Tajik cities of Bukhara and Samarkand – a bum deal if ever there was one.

the Syr-Darya but is in a state of neglect, with only a couple of floors in operation. The rooms are Soviet hangovers, with dim lighting and a broken lift, but some rooms have been slightly renovated. The cheaper rooms have a bathroom but only cold water.

Hotel Vatan (☎ 4 20 80; Dekhon 2A; s/d 180/250TJS, lux 300-500TJS; 🕸) NGO staff like the large, clean and fresh rooms here. The singles are especially good value.

Hotel Sugd (☎ 4 11 88; hotel_sugd@mail.ru; Lenin 179A; s/d 245/310TJS, half lux 270-320TJS, lux 360TJS; 🕸) This new three-star place near the Eksaun is an excellent choice, with fresh, neat, carpeted rooms with fridge, kettle, hair dryer and friendly English-speaking staff. Breakfast is included.

Other central midrange options include the **Hotel Khujand** (☎ 6 59 97; Mavlonbekov 1; lux 220TJS; 🕸), with five absurdly large rooms overlooking the opera house, and the very similar next-door **Hotel Vahdat** (☎ 6 51 01; Mavlonbekov 3; half lux/ lux 220/280TJS; 🕸). Both places offer only rooms with one double bed.

Eating

The bread is particularly good in Khojand; glazed and sprinkled with cardamom or sesame seeds. There are many chaikhanas, shashlyk grills and vats of *plov* around the bazaar.

Oshkhona-i Parhezy (Kamoli Khojandi; dishes 1-2TJS; 🕑 6am-3pm) You can afford to load up at this proletarian cafeteria, since nothing costs more than 2TJS. Simple salads, fruit and iced

tea make for an ideal light lunch, or choose from stodgy main dishes unchanged from the Soviet Union (and with similar prices).

Café Ravshan (Rajabov 102; mains 5-7TJS; 🕑 7am-10pm Mon-Sat) The great chicken kebabs (shashlyk *okaroshka*) here make this our favourite place in town. The cheaper *plov* and shashlyk stalls outside have the added attraction of beer on tap.

Kavsar Café (Lenin; mains 5-7TJS; 🕑 7am-10pm Mon-Sat; 🕸) The wide range of salads, cakes and breakfast blinis are the draw here and it's a nice place for a quiet break.

Getting There & Away

From Khojand there are daily flights to Dushanbe (US$65), plus flights to Moscow, St Petersburg and various Siberian cities. **Tajik Air** (☎ 6 40 67; Lenin 56; 🕑 8am-noon & 1-6pm) is near the Panchshanbe Bazaar, from where taxis (15TJS to 20TJS) and minibus 80 run to the airport, around 16km south of the city.

Minibuses to Kanibadam/Kanibodom (minibus 328; 2.50TJS), for Uzbekistan, and to Isfara (minibus 301; 3.50TJS), for Kyrgyzstan, leave from the **Isfara bus station** (Lenin) in the southeast suburbs, on the road to Chkalovsk. There are also quicker shared taxis (10TJS per seat) from here to both destinations. For more details on getting to/from Uzbekistan or Kyrgyzstan, see p422.

There are frequent minibuses (minibus 314; 4TJS, 90 minutes) and shared taxis (7TJS per seat) south to Istaravshan from the **old bus station** (Kamoli Khojandi) in the west of town. Shared taxis to Penjikent (seven hours, 100TJS) also leave from here when full.

For shared taxis to Dushanbe (120TJS to 150TJS per seat, eight hours) you need to take minibuses 29, 36, 45 or 55 in the early morning from Lenin street to the Abreshim bus stand in the northeastern suburbs. Minibuses 389 and 55 also run from here to Buston (3TJS to 4TJS), from where you can take a taxi to the Oybek border crossing with Uzbekistan.

Getting Around

For the Isfara bus station, take minibus 35 or 55. To get to the old bus station on Kamoli Khojandi, take minibus 29. You can catch all of these buses at the stand on the corner of Lenin and Rajabov. To get off in the centre, alight at the bus stand by the hammer and sickle monument.

TAJIKISTAN

ISTARAVSHAN ИСТАРАВШАН

☎ 3454 / pop 50,000

Called Kir by the Parthians, Cyropol by Alexander the Great and Ura-Tyube by the Russians and Soviets, this small historic town has one of the best preserved old towns in Tajikistan, punctuated with some lovely traditional architecture. Bukhara it's not, but then there aren't any tourists either.

You can easily visit Istaravshan as either a day trip from Khojand or as an overnight stop en route to Dushanbe.

Sights

The **Shahr-e-kuhna** (old town) is an interesting maze of alleys west of the main drag, Lenin, which connects the bus station and bazaar. Alleys disappear into the old town from the **Hazrat-i-Shah Mosque and Mausoleum** (Lenin 98), the town's main Friday mosque. Buildings to track down include the working 15th-century **Abdullatif Sultan Medressa**, also known as the Kök Gumbaz (Blue Dome) after its eye-catching turquoise Timurid dome, and the nearby 19th-century **Hauz-i-Sangin Mosque**, with its fine ceiling paintings, dried *hauz* (pool) and tomb of Shah Fuzail ibn-Abbas.

West of the old town, the four tin cupolas of the **Mazar-i-Chor Gumbaz** conceal Tajikistan's most impressive painted ceilings. To get here, walk west from the Abdullatif Sultan Medressa for five minutes to the main road and then take marshrutka 3 north to the tomb. If you're keen, you could also take a taxi from here for the short ride to the 17th-century **Sary Mazar** (Yellow Tomb), a complex of two tombs, a mosque and some 600-year-old *chinar* (plane) trees in the southwest of the old town.

The hill to the northeast of town is **Mug Teppe**, the site of the Sogdian fortress stormed by Alexander the Great in 329 BC (there are faint remains in the northwest corner). The imposing entry gate was actually built in 2002 during Istaravshan's 2500th anniversary celebrations. To get to the hill, take the road just north of the Istaravshan Hotel.

The colourful central **bazaar** is one of the biggest in the region and well worth a visit, especially on Tuesday.

Sleeping

The town's former budget mainstay, the **Istaravshan Hotel** (Lenin 80), was closed at the time of research.

Homestay of Zafar Rajibov (☎ 2 04 05; Holik Rajibov 6; dm incl breakfast US$15) This private homestay offers the normal mattresses on the floor, as well as a nice garden and tea bed and even car rental. It's hard to find on the northeastern edge of the bazaar. Take the street behind the Lenin statue next to the bazaar for 200m, take the first road to the right and it's 100m on the right. Dinner and lunch are an extra US$5 each.

Hotel Jasnovar (☎ 2 49 61; r without bathroom 40-50TJS; r with bathroom 80-120TJS) The simple rooms here are a bit grubby but the pleasant courtyard seating area and hot showers make this the best hotel in town (though this is hardly a boast in Istaravshan). It's 500m south of the bazaar, along the road to Dushanbe.

Eating

Istaravshan is famed for its pears and sweet *kishmish* grapes. Buy a kilo and retire to the **Aka Musa Choykhana**, a nice Soviet-era chaikhana with fine tea beds but lacklustre service. It's next to the car-parts market, 200m north of the bazaar; the entrance is marked by a large mosaic.

There are lots of kebab places in front of and at the back of the bazaar. **Bar Sohil**, across the main road from the bazaar, serves up roast chicken and beer.

Getting There & Around

Shared taxis to Dushanbe (100TJS per seat, eight hours, 276km) leave from the southern end of the bazaar. Cars to Penjikent (80TJS to 90TJS, seven hours) leave from 100m further south. A taxi to Dushanbe via an overnight in Iskander-Kul starts at around US$140.

The best option to Khojand is one of the shared taxis (7TJS per seat, 1½ hours) across from the bazaar, otherwise minibuses (4TJS) run from the main bus stand, 3km north of the centre. Marshrutkas 4, 6 and 18 shuttle up and down Lenin between the bazaar, Hotel Istaravshan and the bus station.

PENJIKENT ПЕНДЖИКЕНТ

☎ 3475 / pop 50,000

On a terrace above the banks of the Zerafshan (Zeravshan) River, 1.5km southeast of the modern, pleasant but somewhat dull modern town, are the ruins of **ancient Penjikent**, a major Sogdian town founded in the 5th century and abandoned in the 8th century. At its height the settlement was a rich trading centre and one of the most cosmopolitan cities on the Silk Road.

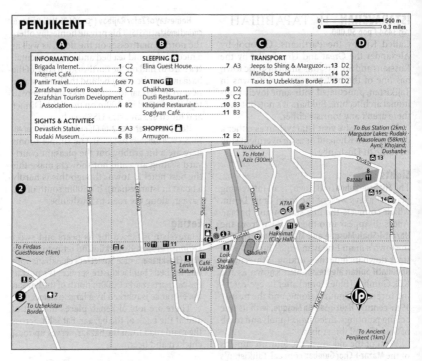

PENJIKENT

INFORMATION
Brigada Internet.....................1 C2
Internet Café..........................2 C2
Pamir Travel.......................(see 7)
Zerafshan Tourism Board........3 C2
Zerafshan Tourism Development
   Association..........................4 B2

SIGHTS & ACTIVITIES
Devastich Statue......................5 A3
Rudaki Museum........................6 B3

SLEEPING
Elina Guest House....................7 A3

EATING
Chaikhanas.............................8 D2
Dusti Restaurant.......................9 C2
Khojand Restaurant.................10 B3
Sogdyan Café........................11 B3

SHOPPING
Armugon...............................12 B2

TRANSPORT
Jeeps to Shing & Marguzor....13 D2
Minibus Stand.......................14 D2
Taxis to Uzbekistan Border....15 D2

Today the ruins are largely limited to sun-baked walls but they are worth a look, and the modern city is becoming increasingly popular as a springboard to visit the nearby Fan Mountains.

Information

Brigada Internet (Rudaki; 8.30am-10pm; 3TJS per hr) Internet access next to the Tourist Information Centre, with other places near the post office.

Pamir Travel (5 50 88; www.travel-pamir.com; Elina Guest House, Rudaki 20/16) Good for local transport, treks and visa paperwork. Contact Sadoullo Khasanov.

Zerafshan Tourism Board (5 36 80; Rudaki 125; www.zerafshan.info) Offers all kinds of tourist information and can book local tours, accommodation, transport and guides.

ZTDA Information Centre (5 63 39; www.ztda-tourism.tj; Sherozi 47; 9am-5pm Mon-Fri) This helpful centre can arrange regional homestays, transport, treks and guides (see p395 for details of its community tourism program) and it also sells its own 1:100,000 Fan Mountains and 1:400,000 Zerafshan Valley maps. The attached Armugon shop sells handicrafts from across the Zerafshan region.

Sights

Most travellers make it to **ancient Penjikent**. You can make out the faint foundations of houses, two Zoroastrian temples and the shop-lined bazaar of the main *shakhristan* (town centre), as well as the obvious citadel to the west. The palace was originally decorated with ornate hunting scenes and pillars carved in the shape of dancing girls. Surrounding the site are scattered remains of a *rabad* (suburb) and necropolis. A small **museum** (admission 3TJS; 10am-5pm) at the site chronicles the excavations but the best of the frescoes (some of them 15m long), sculptures, pottery and manuscripts were long ago carted off to Tashkent and St Petersburg. There's a useful map at the site entrance. The ruins are a 15-minute walk from the bazaar, or you could take a taxi. Visit in the early morning or afternoon to avoid the heat. For a plan and archaeological details of the site see www.orientarch.uni-halle.de/ca/pandzh.htm.

Some more finds and reproduction frescoes are on display at the **Rudaki Museum** (Rudaki 67; admission 10TJS; 8am-5pm), 1.5km west of the bazaar in modern Penjikent. There are also tools from the nearby Neolithic site of Sarazm and a copy of documents found at Mt Mug, where the Sogdians made their last stand against the Arab invaders. (A statue of Devastich, the last Sogdian leader, dominates the roundabout at the west end of town.) The museum's name arises from the claim that Penjikent was the birthplace of Abu Abdullah Rudaki (858–941), the Samanid court poet considered by many to be the father of Persian poetry. His modern **mausoleum** (Map p396), a popular pilgrimage place, is located 58km east of Penjikent in the village of Panjrud, along with a small museum and guesthouse.

The best local excursion is to the picturesque **Marguzor Lakes** (p396), up in the Fan Mountains.

Sleeping & Eating

Elina Guest House (☎ 5 31 34; www.travel-pamir.com; niyozkul@mail.ru; Rudaki 20/16; r per person US$10) This comfortable guesthouse is easily the most popular place to stay. The rooms are clean and the modern shared bathrooms boast hot water and a washing machine. Local manager Niyazov Niyozkul can also arrange transport and treks as part of Pamir Travel (see p394 and p114). The guesthouse is at the west end of town, about 700m from the Rudaki Museum, before the roundabout; ask for the '*ostanovka Samarkand*' and look for the colourful mural on the side of the apartment block.

Firdaus Guesthouse (☎ 92-765 0685; firdaus772004@ mail.ru; per person US$20) You'll never find this new four-roomed compound by yourself but its traditional courtyard architecture and communal kitchen warrant the schlep out to the far west of town. Book in advance or arrange through Hamsafar Travel (p382) in Dushanbe.

Hotel Aziz (☎ 5 52 24, 92-780 3331; Devastich 4; r per person US$10) Ask around at the museum and you'll be pointed to this good-value private guesthouse with half a dozen rooms, clean, tiled private bathrooms and a private billiard table. It's slightly off the beaten track, near a lakeside park, so you may have to call to find the owners.

For food you can cobble together salads, shashlyk and melon at either the **Khojand Restaurant** or **Sogdyan Café**, on Rudaki near the museum, or try the cavernous Soviet-style **Dusti Restaurant** in the central square. There are also several chaikhanas around the bazaar.

Getting There & Away

Shared taxis run along the scenic mountain roads to Khojand (80TJS per seat, seven hours) and Dushanbe (100TJS per seat, eight hours, 225km) from the bus station, 2km east of the central bazaar.

Buses leave at around 9am for Panjrud and the Rudaki Mausoleum (6TJS, one hour), returning at 2.30pm, and you might also find white minivans headed this way. Three other

---

OFF THE MAP: MOUNTAIN VILLAGE HOMESTAYS

The **Zerafshan Tourism Development Association** (ZTDA; www.ztda-tourism.tj) is the latest community-based tourism program to hit Tajikistan. Set up with German assistance in 2008 to bring economic benefit to remote villages overlooked by conventional tourism. According to project adviser Valeriya Tyumeneva, the project works with 20 homestays and 200 service providers, with economic benefits filtering down to an estimated 12,000 people.

Homestays are currently located in the Zerafshan Valley (Veshab and Langar; see p398); Yagnob Valley (Magrib Bolo; p398); at Sarytag and Narvad near Iskander-Kul (p396); at Shing, Nofin, Padrud (at the fifth lake, 2km from Nofin) and Marguzor in the Marguzor Lakes area (p396) south of Penjikent; and at three locations on the approach routes to Alauddin Lake in the Fan Mountains (p397). Each homestay offers simple rooms, meals and some form of hot water for washing, plus a welcome booklet that explains the host's family history.

Homestays cost US$10 per person with breakfast, with meals an additional US$5 each. One slight irritation is that lower-quality accommodation and food in places like the Zerafshan and Yagnob Valleys are the same price as better places, though this may change. Guides (per day US$20) and pack donkeys (per day US$16 with donkey man) can be arranged through the office in Penjikent (and the planned centre in Ayni), as can tents, mats and sleeping bags, opening up lots of scope for adventurous overnight treks.

For more information and potential itineraries, contact the information centre in Penjikent (see p394) or see its website.

buses departing at 8am, 12.30pm and 2pm also make a stop here before continuing 9km to Artush (8TJS), for access to treks in the Fan Mountains.

Taxis cost around 80TJS per car to Mazar-e Sharif, 150TJS to Shing or Artush, or 200TJS to Ayni.

For details of getting to Samarkand, in neighbouring Uzbekistan, see p422.

Getting Around

Minibuses 1 and 4 run along Rudaki from Elina Guest House, past the museum to the bazaar and on to the bus station.

FAN MOUNTAINS
ФАНСКИЕ ГОРЫ

The Fannsky Gory (Russian for Fan Mountains) are one of Central Asia's most popular trekking and climbing destinations, being only a couple of hours from both Samarkand and Dushanbe. See the boxed text (p397) for trekking route overviews.

If you don't have time for a trek, a great way to get a taste of the Fans is to make a day or overnight trip from Penjikent to the

Marguzor Lakes, known in Tajik as the Haft-Kul, or Seven Lakes, a 20km-long chain of turquoise pools strung along the western end of the range. Try to make it to the last lake (Hazor Chashma), 2km beyond Marguzor village and 63km from Penjikent, from where you can hike along the dramatic lakeshore (bring a picnic).

Shoestringers could take the bus to **Shing**, which departs Penjikent at 2pm (5TJS to 8TJS), or try the impossibly cramped afternoon jeeps to Marguzor (25TJS), which depart from Penjikent's Takhta Bazaar, just downhill from the main Penjikent bazaar. Jeeps return the next morning at 6am. You can hire an entire jeep for around 200TJS. An easier option is to hire a car for the day trip through Nematov Niyozkul (see p395) for between US$60 and US$70. There are good ZTDA homestays at Shing, Nofin, Padrud and Marguzor (see p395).

Iskander-Kul

One other gem accessible to nontrekkers is Iskander-Kul, a gorgeous mountain lake 24km off the main road, at the southeastern

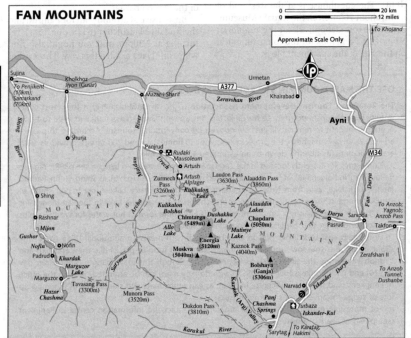

end of the range. The lakeside **turbaza** (Soviet-era holiday camp; per person 30TJS) is rundown (with pit toilets and cold showers) but enjoys a lovely spot, with 30 quiet chalets and a great lakeside picnic area. Bring food and warm clothes as the lake is at 2195m. You can get great views of the main lake and smaller black Zmeinoe (Snake) Lake behind, from the hill behind the *turbaza*. A 25-minute walk leads downstream along the north bank

---

DIY TREKKING IN THE FAN MOUNTAINS

The Fan Mountains (Fannsky Gory) – located in Tajikistan but easily accessed from Samarkand – are one of Central Asia's premier trekking destinations. The rugged, glaciated mountains are studded with dozens of turquoise lakes, on whose shores Tajik shepherds graze their flocks.

Many Uzbek and Tajik travel agencies offer trekking programs here, as do some overseas trekking companies (see p114), though it is a possible destination for experienced and fit do-it-yourselfers. To get to the Fans as an excursion from Uzbekistan you will need a Tajik visa and a double-entry Uzbek visa.

Daily buses run from Penjikent to Artush or Shing/Rashnar, the main trailheads. You can get decent supplies in Penjikent, though it's better to bring your own lightweight foodstuffs. The region can be very hot and dry at the end of summer (August to early September). It's possible to hire pack donkeys at the trailheads for US$10 to US$17 per day.

The best maps are the hard-to-find 1:100,000 *Pamir Alay – Severno-Zapadnaya Chast* (1992 Tashkent), the 1:100,000 map from the ZTDA tourist information centre in Penjikent or the 1:100,000 *Fan Mountains Map and Guide* published abroad by EWP (www.ewpnet.com).

Routes from Artush
From Artush it's a two-hour (6km) walk up to the *alplager* (mountaineers' camp) where rooms and food are generally available but overpriced (dm US$20, plus US$5 to US$8 for meals). Alternatively, Pamir Travel (p394) can arrange a homestay in Artush for around US$10 with meals. From Artush it's a hard three-hour uphill hike into the Kulikalon bowl, home to a dozen deep-blue lakes. Excellent camping can be found near Dushakha Lake, at the foot of Chimtarga (5489m – the highest peak in the region).

Then it's a hard slog up and over the Alauddin Pass (3860m) to the Alauddin lakes, where you can find good camping and sometimes a teahouse tent in summer. From here you can make a long day-hike up to Mutinye (Muddy) Lake and back.

From Alauddin Lakes you can head downstream to the Chapdara Valley and then west up to Laudon Pass (3630m) and back down into the Kulikalon bowl.

An alternative from Mutinye Lake takes you over the difficult Kaznok Pass (4040m, grade 1B), where you may need an ice axe and rope, even in summer. From here head down the long Kaznok Valley to a hot meal and sauna at Sarytag village (p398), near Iskander-Kul.

There are daily buses from Penjikent to Artush at 8am, 12.30pm and 2pm. Four-wheel drives can normally get as far as the *alplager*.

Routes from Shing/Marguzor
The other main trailhead is at Shing or Marguzor (see p396). After visiting the Marguzor Lakes, trails lead over the Tavasang Pass (3300m) to the Archa Maidan Valley. Trails continue down the valley to the foot of the Zurmech Pass (3260m) and then over to Artush.

Alternatively, when you hit the Archa Maidan Valley, you can climb up to the Munora Pass (3520m) and down into the valley, and then up over the Dukdon Pass (3810m) into the Karakul Valley and, eventually, Sarytag and Iskander-Kul.

There are daily buses from Penjikent to Shing and afternoon jeeps to Marguzor – see p396.

Routes from the South
From Dushanbe it's possible to take a taxi to Karatag or Hakimi and start a three-day trek north over Mura Pass (3787m), crossing the Hissar range, to drop down into the Sarytag Valley and Iskander-Kul. Bring your passport, as you're close to the Uzbekistan border.

TAJIKISTAN

of the river to a rickety platform overlooking an impressive waterfall.

On the far side of the lake, 5km away, are the Panj Chashma springs and the President's *dacha* (holiday bungalow), from where a road branches right uphill for 5km to **Sarytag** (Saratag) village. Sarytag has four comfortable **homestays** (US$10 incl breakfast, plus $5 per meal, sauna US$5), of which our favourite is **Dilovar's** (☎ 92-788 2235). The village is a great base for hikes up the Kaznok (Arg) Valley, or hire a guide (US$17) for the long hike around nearby Kyrk Shaitan (Forty Devils) peak. You can also rent mountain bikes (US$6 to US$10) and even boats (US$2 per hour) for fun on the lake.

There's no public transport to the lake or Sarytag. It's generally possible to find a taxi at the M34 turn-off but it would be much easier to hire a car between Dushanbe and Penjikent/ Khojand and visit en route. Hitching is easiest on weekends when Dushanbe partygoers head to the *turbaza*. Note that the road to Iskander-Kul branches off the larger road (to the mine) 300m after leaving the main M34, by the defunct Zerafshan II factory site, and crosses the river. From Sarytag you might find a car headed to Dushanbe for 50TJS per seat.

A taxi from Penjikent to Dushanbe via a night in Iskander-Kul costs around US$150.

ZERAFSHAN & YAGNOB VALLEYS
ЗЕРАФШАНСКАЯ ДОЛИНА, ЯГНОБ

These two remote and little-visited mountain valleys to the east and southeast of Ayni offer adventurous travellers plenty of scope to ditch the guidebook and do some serious exploring. Travel here is rough and ready but both valleys now offer homestays and guides (see p395) and the mountains offer a deliciously cool summer escape from the baking plains of Dushanbe. For maps of the region see the 1:400,000 ZTDA *Zerafshan Valley* map (p394) or Marcus Hauser's 1:500,000 *Northern Tajikistan* map (www.geckomaps.com).

Barren khaki walls and splashes of intense irrigated green characterise the wide Zerafshan Valley to the north. The most promising destination here is the traditional village of **Veshab**, 47km from Ayni. There's good hiking behind the village to the summer pastures at Tagob (two hours), or try the steep two- to three-day trek to Hshirtob in the

Yagnob Valley (via Darg). The mosque and tomb of Shams-i Tabrizi below the village are also worth a visit. There are more trekking opportunities further up the valley, around Langar and Past-i-Gov in the wild region of Gorno Matcha. Pamir Travel (p394 and p114) runs an interesting six-day trek here between the Zerafshan and Yagnob valleys, via the alpine lakes of Sar-i Pul.

The **Yagnob Valley** to the south is the narrower and wilder of the two valleys and yet is closer to Dushanbe. The upper valley is famous as the last home of several hundred native speakers of Sogdian, the last echo of a language largely unchanged since the time of Alexander the Great. The village of **Magrib Bolo** has a particularly dramatic location surrounded by jagged peaks, with the giant Zamin-Karor rock wall looming over it from behind. The wall attracts climbers from around the world and the valley and peaks to the south offer fine hiking if you enjoy walking uphill.

The road ends at Bedev, 22km past Magrib, where trekking trails continue to camping spots at Kironte and then over the mountains to the Takob ski resort or Romit Valley.

Sleeping

In Zerafshan, Veshab has three **homestays**, with the Atoev, Khojiev and Sultanov families, and there's also a homestay (with the Kholov family) in Langar, 62km further up the valley.

In Yagnob, Bolo (upper) Magrib has three homestays, at the Rasulov, Dustbekov and Malikov families, and one shop. All homestays cost US$15, including breakfast and dinner (see p395).

If you are stuck in Ayni, try the **Agro-Action Guest House** (Tukhtamuradov 11; US$10pp) or the **Aziz Homestay** (☎ 92-775 5669, Tukhtamuradov 37-39) For the Aziz, contact Aziz, also known as Bobo, or his son Bakhtiyor; for Agro Action you'll need to get permission first from the Agro-Action office (☎ 83479-22 56 36), above the derelict Zerafshan Hotel at the north end of town.

Getting There & Away

The turn off to the Zerafshan Valley is a couple of miles south of Ayni, by the river crossing to Dushanbe. A taxi from Ayni to Veshab costs 100TJS to 200TJS, though you might just find a shared taxi during weekdays (25TJS per seat). From Ayni a shared taxi to Dushanbe costs 60TJS to 70TJS.

For Yagnob, make your way hitching or by taxi to Takfon, from where it's 18km east to Anzob village. A couple of kilometres east of Anzob, the old road to Dushanbe over the Anzob Pass branches south, while the turn off east leads to Magrib, 6km up the valley. Cars run most days from Magrib to Dushanbe (50TJS per seat).

Now that most road traffic uses the Anzob tunnel, the old road over the Anzob Pass is traffic-free and makes for a challenging mountain bike trip. You could hire a vehicle to take you to the top and cycle down for a fabulously scenic ride.

THE PAMIRS

The plain is called Pamier, and you ride across it for twelve days together, finding nothing but a desert without habitations or any green thing, so that travellers are obliged to carry with them whatever they have need of. The region is so lofty and cold that you can not even see any birds flying. And I must notice also that because of this great cold, fire does not burn so bright, nor give out so much heat as usual.

Marco Polo, Description of the World

Locals refer to the Pamirs as the Bam-i-Dunya (Roof of the World), and once you're up in the high Pamirs it's not hard to see why. For centuries a knot of tiny valley emirates lost in the blank of imperial maps, the Pamirs feel like a land a little bit closer to heaven.

The word *pamir* means 'rolling pasture-land' in ancient Persian, in reference to the eastern Pamirs, but there is not one obvious Pamir range, rather a complex series of inter-connected ranges separated by high-altitude valleys. The Chinese called the mountains the Congling Shan, or 'Onion Mountains'.

The western half of the region, Badakhshan, is characterised by deep irrigated valleys and sheer peaks reminiscent of the Wakhi areas of far northern Pakistan (which are also ethnically Tajik). The eastern half of the region is the high, arid and sparsely inhabited Pamir plateau, home largely to Kyrgyz herders and their yurts. For the most part, the Pamirs are too high for human settlement.

The Pamirs contain three of the four highest mountains in the former Soviet Union,

the apex of which is Koh-i Somoni (former Pik Kommunizma) at 7495m. Less than an Empire State Building shorter is Pik Lenin (sometimes known as Koh-i-Istiqlal, or Independence Peak) at 7134m. The Pamir is drained by the numerous tributaries of the Vakhsh and Pyanj Rivers, which themselves feed into the Amu-Darya, Central Asia's greatest river.

Kohistani Badakhshan (still most commonly known by its Soviet-era name the Gorno-Badakhshan Autonomous Oblast, or GBAO) accounts for 45% of Tajikistan's territory but only 3% of its population. The 212,000 souls who do live here are divided between Pamiris in the west and Kyrgyz in the east. Culturally speaking, Badakhshan extends over the Pyanj River well into Afghan Badakhshan.

The slopes and high valleys are inhabited by even hardier creatures, near-mythical animals such as the giant Marco Polo sheep, which sports curled horns that would measure almost 2m were they somehow unfurled, and the rarely seen snow leopard. During the Soviet era several scientific teams tried to track down the similarly elusive 'giant snow-man', but in vain.

Chance encounters with yetis aside, the Pamir region is generally safe to travel in, despite a strong KGB presence and a healthy penchant for red tape. Tajik border guards have the unenviable task of keeping a lid on Central Asia's heroin-soaked border with Afghanistan and are best avoided if possible.

History
THE LEGACY OF ISOLATION
With no arable land to speak of and no industry, Gorno-Badakhshan has always relied heavily on Moscow and Dushanbe for its upkeep, with most of its processed goods and all of its fuel coming from outside the region.

The collapse of the USSR was a particularly hard blow for the region. As money and fuel supplies dried up in the early 1990s, the region's markets, state farms, irrigation channels and bus routes slowly ground to a halt. Local farmers and herders suddenly had to relearn traditional farming techniques and skills that had been suppressed for decades. The largely Russian Soviet scientists packed up and left behind half-abandoned mines, research stations and observatories scattered across the Pamirs.

TAJIKISTAN

Frustrated by its marginal position and seeing no future in a collapsing Tajikistan, GBAO nominally declared its independence in 1992 and chose the rebel side in the civil war. Since then, the government has not sent much in the way of aid or reconstruction its way.

Through most of the 1990s, humanitarian aid convoys kept the region from starvation, while establishing agricultural and hydro-electric programs in an attempt to create some degree of self-sufficiency. In 1993 the region grew 16% of its basic food needs; by 2006 that figure had risen to 80%. The next stage is to create employment, much of which depends on education and tourism (see p414).

Despite this, 80% of the local population still earns less than US$200 per year. The region's largest employer, the Russian military, pulled out of the region in 2005, further worsening the situation. Over 15,000 Badakhshanis have left their homes in search of work outside the region.

It is hoped that the highway between Murgab and Tashkurgan in China over the Qolma Pass will help lift the region out of its isolation, though it's hard to see quite what the region currently has to export. Meanwhile to the south the Aga Khan Foundation has been busy rebuilding bridges, literally, with Afghan Badakhshan on the other side of the Pyanj River, reuniting communities severed since the formation of the USSR.

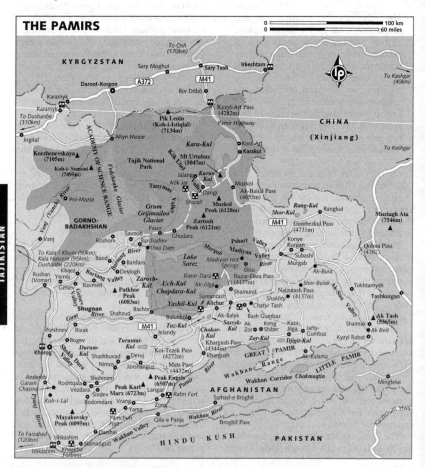

THE PAMIRS

PAMIRI HOUSES

If the chance arises it is worth accepting an offer to look inside a traditional *huneuni chid* (Pamiri house). Guests are received in the large, five-pillared room with raised areas around four sides of a central pit, but there is also a smaller living space, a kitchen and a hallway. There are few, if any, windows; illumination comes through a skylight in the roof *(tsorkhona)*, which consists of four concentric squares, representing the elements of earth, fire, air and water. Carpets and mattresses take the place of furniture and also serve as decoration along with panels of photographs – the most prominent of which is often a portrait of the Aga Khan.

The five vertical pillars symbolise the five members of Ali's family (Fatima, Ali, Mohammed, Hassan and Hussein), as well as the five pillars of Islam and, some say, the five deities of Zoroastrianism (the structure of Pamiri houses goes back 2500 years). In a further act of symbolism, the number of roof beams relates to the seven imams and six prophets of Ismailism. The place of honour, next to the Hassan pillar (one of two pillars joined together), is reserved for the *khalifa* (village religious leader), so visitors should avoid sitting there. For some pointers on etiquette when visiting a Central Asian home, see p90 and p70.

People

Centuries of isolation in high-altitude valleys has meant that the Pamiris of Gorno-Badakhshan speak languages different not only from those of lowland Tajiks but from one another. Each mountain community has its own dialect of Pamiri, a language that, although sharing the same Persian roots as Tajik, is as different as English is from German. Shugnani (named after the emirate of Shugnan once based in the Gunt Valley) is the dialect spoken in Khorog, the Gunt Valley and among Badakhshani Tajiks in Murgab. Other languages in the mosaic include Wakhi, Ishkashimi and Rushani. *Khologh* is 'thank you' in Shugnani.

The mountain peoples of the eastern Pamirs are, however, solidly bound by their shared faith: Ismailism, a breakaway sect of Shiite Islam, introduced into Badakhshan in the 11th-century by Nasir Khusraw (see p379). Ismailism has no formal clerical structure, no weekly holy day and no mosques (rather multipurpose meeting halls called *jamoat khana*, which also double as meeting halls and community guesthouses). Ismailis greet each other with *yo-ali madat* (may Ali bless you), rather than the standard Islamic *asalam aleykum*. Each village has a religious leader known as a *khalifa*, who leads prayers and dispenses advice, assisted by a *rais* (community leader).

One of the few visible manifestations of the religion are the small roadside *oston* (shrines), covered in ibex horns, burnt offerings and round stones, at which passers-by stop to ask for a blessing. The horns are often the remnants of hunting trips and ensuing community meals known as *khudoi*. The shrines also act as charity stations; in return for a blessing, the Ismailis customarily leave some money or bread for anyone in need.

The spiritual leader of the Ismailis is the Swiss-born Aga Khan, revered by Pamiris as a living god and the 49th imam. He's no remote, abstract deity – it's the Aga Khan's charity that has kept almost certain starvation at bay over the last 15 years.

Pamiri hospitality is legendary and you can expect a warm welcome and a place to stay in almost any village.

Information
PERMITS & REGISTRATION

It is essential to have both a Tajik visa and a GBAO permit to travel in the Pamirs. Many Tajikistan embassies will now issue the GBAO permit at the same time as your visa, generally for an extra US$50, though sometimes for free. If you can't get one at the embassy, almost any travel agency in Dushanbe, Khorog or Murgab can arrange one for US$30 to US$40. It's best to apply a couple of weeks in advance. There are rumours that the GBAO permit may be discontinued.

If you can't get a permit from a Tajik embassy and can't pick one up in Dushanbe (eg if you want to travel from Osh in Kyrgyzstan), you'll have to ask the travel agency to email you a scan of the permit. You can then travel with a colour printout in its original size (around 6.5cm by 11cm) as far as Khorog and pick up the original there. Munduz Travel (p358) and the Osh Guesthouse (p359), both in Osh, can also arrange GBAO permits.

TAJIKISTAN

The GBAO permit lists the districts to be visited, so make sure you get all the regions you want to visit (these are Ishkashim, Murgab, Vanj, Darvaz, Shugnan, Rushan and Roshtqala). Like registration, the GBAO permit is valid only for the duration of your visa. If you extend your visa, you will need to extend the GBAO permit to remain in the region.

Passports and permits are checked sporadically throughout the Pamirs, including possibly at Kala-i Khum, Khorog airport, just outside Murgab, Kara-Kul, Tokhtamysh, Rang-Kul, Khargush and the Kyzyl-Art border post.

You need an additional nature reserve permit if you want to visit Zor-Kul lake (see p415).

WHAT TO BRING
Khorog has a well-stocked bazaar but Murgab's is limited to Chinese beer and expired Snickers bars, so bring some snacks from home, especially if you're trekking or travelling off the beaten track. Gifts of photos of the Aga Khan go down very well. Sunscreen, sunglasses and a torch (flashlight) are essential. Water purification tablets are advisable.

It's essential to have warm clothing, though a fleece and windproof shell should generally suffice in midsummer. Strong winds can pick up very quickly in the Pamirs, something even Marco Polo moaned about. A sleeping bag is useful but not essential, as most homes and yurts can provide plenty of duvets. A tent is only really useful for wilderness treks.

Despite the high altitudes, mosquitoes can be voracious during early summer in the river valleys of Murgab and Ak-Suu and around Rang-Kul, so bring repellent if travelling in June, July or August (they are largely gone by September).

There's little electricity in the eastern Pamirs and reliable batteries are impossible to buy, so bring enough camera batteries to last until Osh or Dushanbe.

Maps
Cartographer Marcus Hauser has produced an essential 1:500,000 colour tourist map to the Pamirs. It is for sale at Tillo Teppe (see p388) in Dushanbe, less reliably from META (p413) or Pamir Bikes (p413) in Murgab, or directly from www.geckomaps.com.

MONEY
It's wise to bring enough cash for your entire Pamir trip. It's possible to change cash (US dollars) in Khorog and Murgab and there's an ATM in Khorog. Kyrgyz som are accepted between Murgab and the Kyrgyz-Tajik border.

Sleeping
Most of the tourist accommodation in the Pamirs is in homestays or yurtstays, which are simple but comfortable. Homestays generally have an outdoor toilet and a place to wash. Yurts don't supply toilets or bathrooms so you'll have to find a spare rock to squat behind. For a rundown on the structure of a yurt, see p337. Formal homestays cost around US$15 per person including three meals, less at remoter villages. For informal invitations we suggest offering around US$10. The ecotourism organisation META offers accommodation throughout the eastern Pamirs – see p414.

If you are getting off the beaten track in the eastern Pamirs, check with the Pamirs Ecotourism Association Information Centre (see p404) in Khorog for a list of homestays in the region. Khorog's travel agencies can also arrange homestays throughout the region.

Tourists can also stay at the **MSDSP office** (dm US$10, meals US$3-5) in Kala-i Khum if it is not being used by staff. MSDSP in general is a good resource for finding homestays and transport. To find the local MSDSP office in any village ask for 'Hazina' (treasure chest), the name by which the organisation is known locally.

Getting There & Around
The major transport options for the 728km Pamir Hwy between Khorog and Osh are hitching on Chinese trucks, renting a 4WD with driver or cramming in the occasional minibus.

MINIBUS
There are daily-ish minibuses between Murgab and Khorog and, less frequently, between Osh and Murgab. In Kyrgyzstan daily public buses run from Osh to Sary Tash (see p361). From Khorog, minivans and shared 4WDs shuttle to villages in the surrounding valleys such as Jelandy, Ishkashim, Rushan, Langar and Roshtqala, though the timings generally require an overnight stay.

CAR HIRE
Hiring a private vehicle (normally a Russian UAZ jeep but possibly a Lada Niva) and a

driver is relatively expensive, but gives you a flexibility that you will value on this scenic and fascinating trip. Please note that the transport rates listed in this section will doubtless change over time.

The availability and cost of fuel is a significant factor in the cost of transport (prices generally rise in autumn, when supplies are scarcer), but what really counts is whether you have to pay for the vehicle's return trip; this essentially doubles the cost.

At the time of research, META (p413) in Murgab was offering 4WDs at between US$0.45 to US$0.75 per km, plus 15% commission, which worked out at US$315 from Murgab to Osh (420km), or US$330 from Murgab to Khorog via the Wakhan Valley (you have to pay for the car's return trip to Murgab). Private drivers are cheaper. To shave costs from Osh you could take a shared taxi to Sary Tash in Kyrgyzstan and arrange for a META 4WD to pick you up there. Travellers have recommended Osh-based driver **Abdulaziz Nemat** (☎ 555-633643).

Hamsafar Travel (p382) charges US$0.80 per km for Land Cruiser hire. Prices in Khorog start at around US$0.50 per km for a Lada Niva. Independent car hire from Dushanbe to Khorog costs around US$200 for a Lada Niva. One Dushanbe-based Pamiri driver/guide recommended by travellers is **Pamirbek** (☎ 93-531 4593; www.pamirbek.com), who has his own UAZ minivan (seats six) and can arrange treks.

Private drivers based in Murgab include **Tatik Kalandarkhonov** (☎ 91-948 4966; tatik_66@mail.ru), **Mamadiev Altynbek** (☎ 93-558 8596; altynbek11@mail.ru) and **Mamadiev Asilbek** (☎ 93-547 5679; aska-m06@mail.ru). All three have Mitsubishi Pajeros and basic English. Asilbek also puts up guests in his house.

Hiring a 4WD independently costs less than going through an agency but you'll need to negotiate hard and speak decent Russian. Generally speaking, car hire is cheaper in Murgab than in Khorog. Make sure any rate includes petrol, vehicle maintenance and the driver's pay, food and accommodation. For every extra day that the driver waits for you (for day hikes etc), add about US$10. Give the vehicle the once-over, check that the 4WD is operational and, if coming from Osh, check that the driver has a GBAO permit.

As a rough guide, a Russian UAZ jeep needs around 20L of petrol per 100km, which works out at around US$0.20 per km for the petrol alone. Lada Nivas use around 10L per 100km so are generally cheaper, though the spiffier Chrysler Nivas cost more. The main problem with Russian jeeps is the limited visibility from the back seat.

Finding petrol can be a problem in the Pamirs. A trip into remoter corners of the region generally involves at least one dash around town to find a obliging local with a jerry can of diluted fuel and a bucket.

HITCHING

Traffic is light along the Pamir Hwy and hitching is hard work. The main commercial vehicles these days are the Chinese trucks which shuttle between the Qolma Pass, Murgab and a terminal 30km east of Khorog. It helps if you speak a few words of Chinese. If you break a journey you could end up waiting a long time for another ride. Controls at checkpoints are particularly tedious for trucks.

Hitching from Osh is possible but finding a ride from Sary Tash to Murgab is problematic, as most vehicles are full by the time they get here.

DUSHANBE TO KHOROG

If you are hiring a car between Dushanbe and Khorog, you have the choice of two routes; the main, summer-only route via Tavildara and the 3252m Sagirdasht Pass to Kala-i Khum, or the longer but year-round southern route via Kulyab and the Afghan border road. Minibuses generally take the shorter Tavildara route, though political violence closed that route temporarily in 2009.

The condition of the Tavildara road is particularly bad and without prospect of improving any time soon. The southern route is longer but slowly being upgraded by Turkish road crews (there is a surreal three-lane stretch of highway at Zigar), plus there are great views of the amazing cliffside footpaths (known as *owrings*) and traditional villages on the Afghan side of the river, often less than 100m away. **Yoged** is one of several lovely Tajik villages en route and has signposted homestays (Soukrihusein Sukronov and Kalandarsho Dodarsjonov). Signs warn of mines along parts of this route so don't go wandering by the river bank.

The best place to break the trip is in **Kala-i Khum** (also known as Kalaikhum, Darvaz or Darwaz). The **homestay of Bakhrom Sangkakuf**, by the bridge, is a good accommodation bet, as

TAJIKISTAN

is the **homestay of Katya Khudoyidodova**. There's also an **MSDSP guesthouse** (dm US$15), 1km down the road to Kulyab. There's a signed homestay (Dilshod Ibronov) at Togmay, 44km east of Kala-i Khum.

KHOROG ХОРОГ
☎ 3522 / pop 27,800 / elev 2100m

A small mountain-valley town, Khorog is the capital of the autonomous Gorno-Badakhshan (GBAO) region. It is strung out on either side of the dashing Gunt River and penned in by dry, vertical peaks. A few kilometres downstream, the Gunt merges with the Pyanj, marking the border with Afghanistan.

Until the late 19th century, present-day Khorog was a tiny settlement that loosely belonged to the domain of local chieftains, the Afghan Shah or the Emir of Bukhara. Russia installed a small garrison here following the Anglo-Russian-Afghan Border Treaty of 1896, which delineated the current northern border of Afghanistan on the Pyanj River. Khorog was made the administrative centre of GBAO in 1925.

Khorog suffered badly in the wake of independence (at the depths of the economic crisis money disappeared altogether, replaced by barter) but things have picked up in recent years. In 2003 the Aga Khan pledged US$200 million to establish one of the three campuses of the University of Central Asia in Khorog's eastern suburbs. Khorog has one of the brightest and best educated populations of any town in Central Asia.

Note that the town largely closes down on Sunday, when open restaurants and transport can be hard to find.

Information
EMBASSIES
Afghanistan consulate (☎ 2 24 92; Gagarin; ◷ 9am-2pm Mon-Fri) Tourist visas cost US$30, require a photocopy of your passport and take a couple of days to process. Pay visa fees at the Tojik Sodirot Bank at Lenin 60.

INTERNET ACCESS
Karavan Internet Café (Lenin 50; per hr 3TJS; ◷ 8am-8pm Mon-Sat) One of two places at the post/telecom office.

MONEY
Agroinvestbank (Lenin 101; ◷ 8am-noon & 1-5pm Mon-Fri, 8am-noon Sat) Changes cash US dollars and Russian roubles and has an ATM.

Amonat Bank (Lenin 115; ◷ 8am-noon & 1.30-5pm Mon-Fri) Changes cash US dollars and euros.

REGISTRATION
OVIR (Lenin; ◷ 8am-noon & 1-5pm Mon-Fri, 8am-noon Sat) If you need to register (see p419), do so here, next to the Amonat Bank.

TOURIST INFORMATION
Pamirs Ecotourism Association Information Centre (PECTA; ☎ 2 24 69; www.pamirspecta.com; Central Park, Elchibek 10) This loose affiliation of drivers, guides and tour operators offers travel information, a list of guides, drivers and homestays in the western Pamirs and rents simple trekking gear (40TJS for five days). It's an essential stop to plan your Pamir adventure.

TRAVEL AGENCIES
All the following can arrange GBAO permits, transport, guides and homestays:
Pamir Silk Tour (☎ 91-927 9982, 2 22 99; pst_pamirs@yahoo.com; Azizbek 1) Can arrange horse treks and Wakhan trekking. Contact Mullo Abdo Shagarf.
Pamir Tourism (☎ 93-500 9947, 2 52 99; www.pamirs-tourism.org; Lenin 55) Treks, tours and homestays throughout the eastern Pamirs. Contact Ismoil Konunov.
Tour De Pamir (☎ 93-500 7557, 2 66 61; tourdepamir@yahoo.com) Contact Ergash or Abrigol.

Sights
Khorog's surprisingly good **Regional Museum** (Lenin 105; admission 5TJS; ◷ 8am-noon & 1-5pm Mon-Fri) is well worth an hour of your time, if only to see the fabulous cross-bow mousetrap and early crampons, as well as the first Russian piano to arrive in Badakhshan (10 Russian soldiers spent two months carrying it over the mountains from Osh in 1914).

It's hard to believe that Khorog's **Central Park** (◷ 6am-11pm) was dug up to grow crops during the famine of the 1990s. It's since been renovated by the Aga Khan Trust for Culture and is now a delightful place to read a book or take a riverside stroll after visiting the nearby tourist information centre.

Tourists can visit the **Saturday market** by the bridge on the border with Afghanistan, by the Serena Inn, 5km west of town, but it's not as big as the Saturday market in Ishkashim (p409).

The **Pamir Botanical Gardens** (Botanicheskii Sad; ◷ 9am-4pm), 5km east of town at the entrance to the Shokh Dara Valley, has a couple of hundred hectares of parkland and is apparently the world's second highest botanical garden.

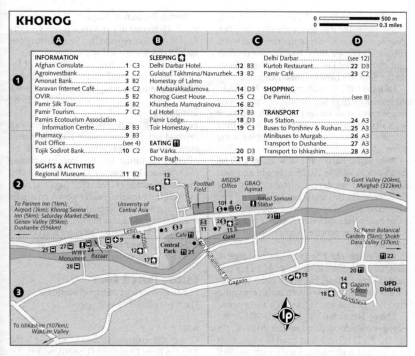

KHOROG

Minivan 3 runs to the front gate (a few turn round before the gate) or take a taxi for 6TJS. Take a picnic to savour the excellent views over the town.

Sleeping

The best places to stay are the town's homestays, though a couple of midrange hotels now offer more comfort and privacy.

HOMESTAYS

There are two main concentrations of homestays; in the centre of town east of the football pitch, and out in the pleasant UPD district, a half-hour walk (2km) southeast of town. Most homestays cost US$10 per person without meals, unless otherwise noted. PECTA (p404) can supply a full list of homestays.

Gulaisuf Takhmina/Navruzbek (☎ 2 45 54; Kirmonsho 25; US$8, breakfast US$1) Nice Pamiri-style house, garden and tea bed but basic toilet and very basic shower.

Homestay of Lalmo Mubarakkadamova (☎ 2 69 99; Bandalieva 61/10; dm US$8, meals US$3) Our new favourite homestay, with a clean modern bathroom and friendly family vibe. It's in the UPD district next to the Pamir Lodge.

Khursheda Mamadrainova (☎ 2 47 54; Kirmonsho 38; dm US$10, meals US$5) Good central place with real beds, an upper balcony and good bathroom but distant toilet and pricey meals.

Toir Homestay (☎ 2 57 97; Gagarin 80; US$10, plus US$2 breakfast) A ramshackle META-affiliated homestay that is hopefully building a new toilet and bathroom.

HOTELS

Pamir Lodge (☎ 2 65 45; http://pamirlodge.com; Gagarin 46; US$6 per person, breakfast & dinner US$3; P) Overlanders and independent travellers flock here, making this the best place in the Pamirs to swap travel tips and share transport. Rooms are simple, with mattresses on the floor, but the garden is a pleasant spot and the hot shower a luxury. A new block of rooms was built in 2009. For dinner ask in advance for the homemade *kurtob* – layered bread, yoghurt, onion and coriander. The lodge was established to fund the local *jamoat khana* (Ismaili prayer hall), which is in the grounds. It's just past the football pitch of the Gagarin School.

Khorog Guest House (Atobek 25; r per person US$15, breakfast US$3.50) Clean pine furniture, some nice design touches and the best breakfast in Tajikistan make this an excellent central bet, despite an occasionally temperamental water supply. There are three rooms: two doubles and a traditional Pamiri room with mattresses on the floor. It's hard to find down a side alley.

Lal Hotel (☎ 2 91 92; lalhotel@inbox.ru; Azizbek 5/1; r incl breakfast US$25-50; 🖳) Rooms in this private house vary but all are cosy and clean and come with shared bathrooms and access to the little kitchen and washing machine. Look for the silver gate.

Delhi Darbar Hotel (☎ 2 12 99; Azizbek 2; s/d incl breakfast US$30/50) The 10 clean, bright and neat rooms, with modern bathrooms and free laundry, make this a safe bet, especially if you like hard beds. The spacious double rooms offer easily the best value. Order a tikka masala from room service to spice up the bland atmosphere.

Parinen Inn (☎ 2 54 17; parinen_hotel@mail.ru; Lenin 193; r incl breakfast US$40-60; ℗ ✗) This private midrange hotel has seven clean modern rooms with (shared) Western bathrooms, plus riverside garden seating, but it's overpriced.

Khorog Serena Inn (☎ 2 32 28, 93-5008224; rita. kurbonbekova@akdn.org; s/d incl breakfast US$80/100, plus 18% tax; ℗) This is the best hotel in town, built in boutique Badakhshani style with modern amenities for the visit of Aga Khan. The six rooms are spacious and only used occasionally by consultants and the odd tour group. Credit cards are not accepted. It's by the bridge to Afghanistan, 5km northwest of Khorog Bazaar.

Eating

The best bet for dinner is your homestay or guesthouse.

Delhi Darbar (☎ 2 12 99; Azizbek 2; mains 10-20TJS; 🕙 11am-10pm; Ⓔ) Often the only place open in the evenings, the Indian veg and nonveg curries here hit the spot. There's a lunch buffet (25TJS) on Friday.

Bar Varka (☎ 93-5014143; Gagarin; mains 6-10TJS; 🕙 closed Sun; Ⓔ) Out in the UPD district, this slightly Mafiosi-looking place has spuriously dim lighting but a good range of salads and Russian dishes. Perfect for a date or a drug deal.

Chor Bagh (☎ 2 90 57; Central Park; 🕙 10am-10pm; Ⓔ) The best restaurant in town is run by the Serena, with a great riverside location in a pavilion in Central Park. Multicuisine.

Pamir Café (Lenin; pizzas 12-15TJS; 🕙 closed Sun & Sat night) Acceptable fast food, including greasy pizza and 'gamburger', plus salads.

Kurtob Restaurant (Gagarin) This informal place, 100m east of Bar Varka, promises tasty *kurtob* but was repeatedly closed during our visits. Look for the stripy awnings.

Look out in the bazaar for bottles of locally made sea-buckthorn juice and tart, high-vitamin dog-rose juice *(shipovnik sok)*.

Shopping

De Pamiri (☎ 2 48 29; www.depamiri.org; Central Park; 🕙 closed Sun) This impressive NGO initiative aims to revive traditional Pamiri crafts by offering an outlet for 100 Pamiri artisans (80% women) to market and sell their crafts. Products include excellent felt rugs and bags, musical instruments, *palas* (woven goat-hair carpets) and embroidered skullcaps; view a selection of products at the website or at www. pamirs.org/handicrafts. Prices are marked and fixed, and 80% of earnings go to the artisans. Contact Yorali or Vatani.

Getting There & Away

For an overview of transport along the Pamir Hwy, see p402.

AIR

One of the main attractions of Khorog is the flight in from Dushanbe (US$80), which, depending on your confidence in the pilots of Tajik Air, will be one of the most exhilarating or terrifying experiences of your life. For most of the 45-minute flight the aircraft scoots through (not above) mountain valleys, flying in the shadow of the rock face with its wingtips so close you could swear they kick up swirls of snow. In Soviet days this was the only route on which Aeroflot paid its pilots danger money.

Flights originate in Dushanbe and, in theory, run daily but they are grounded at the first sign of bad weather (which is frequent outside of the summer months). Passengers must then take their chances the next day, tussling for seats with those already booked on that flight. After a run of bad weather, hundreds can turn up to fight for the first flight's 40 available seats. You should budget an extra day or two into your itinerary in case flights are cancelled and be prepared to travel overland if need be.

The **airport ticket office** (🕙 8am-12.30pm & 1.30-4pm) is 3km west of town and minivan 1 runs to/from the centre. To buy a ticket, turn up at the airport at around 8am to see if the plane is coming. Only when the plane actually arrives will you be allowed to check in. Baggage allowance is 10kg; excess is around 1% of the air ticket per 1kg. There's no pre-assigned seating; seats look left to views of Afghanistan, right towards the peaks of the Pamirs.

MINIBUS
Sturdy 4WD vans and Pajero jeeps leave from the bazaar and a stand 100m west of the bazaar for Dushanbe (200TJS, 16 to 20 hours) when full. Get there in the morning and be prepared to hang around for hours before finally leaving. You might score a ride in a Land Cruiser for 150TJS per seat.

Minibuses to Murgab (50TJS, nine hours) depart when full from 200m east of the bazaar, assuming there are enough passengers.

Four-wheel drives and minibuses to Ishkashim (30TJS, three hours) leave in the late morning from a lot just across the river from the bazaar.

There are also daily minivans to the outlying villages of Roshtqala, Jelandy, Rivak, Shahzud, Porshnev, Rushan and Basid. Some depart from the bus station, others from two stands a couple of hundred metres west. Note that very little transport runs on Sunday.

Getting Around
Minibus 3 (1TJS) runs from the bazaar to the UPD district. The same trip by taxi costs around 6TJS.

BARTANG VALLEY
The stark and elemental Bartang Valley is one of the wildest and most beautiful in the western Pamirs and offers a fine opportunity for an adventurous multiday 4WD adventure. At times the fragile road inches perilously between the raging river below and sheer cliffs above. Only the occasional fertile alluvial plain brings a flash of green to the barren rock walls.

HOMESTAY HIKING IN THE WESTERN PAMIRS

Several village homestays in the western Pamir offer the chance to get a taste of some of the region's finest scenery without the need to drag along a tent or stove. Perhaps the best short trekking destination from Khorog is the **Geisev Valley**, a lovely string of traditional Pamiri villages set beside multicoloured lakes. A sustainable tourism project has created seven **homestays** (dm US$6, meals US$2-3) in the valley's three villages, equipped with solar electricity and heating, where travellers can buy food and hire donkeys (US$5 per day) and a guide (US$15) if needed.

From the suspension bridge, 23km from the turn-off to the Bartang Valley, it's a 2½-hour walk uphill to the first village, by the second lake. From the first village it's an easy half-hour walk to the second village, where you'll find the majority of the homestays, and a further 30 minutes to the third village. From here it's an hour to the large third lake. Beyond the third lake, you'll need tents to continue to the fourth and fifth lakes, summer pastures and glacier. A two-night excursion is the best way to soak up the gorgeous scenery.

Car travel from Khorog to Geisev is 85km each way, which costs around US$80, plus a daily rate for the driver to wait for you, or take the crowded daily minibus from Khorog to Basid. Cars should park 1.5km past the suspension bridge, up a small side road.

The Ravmed Valley also has a fledgling homestay program, with two homestays in Khijez at the houses of Odina Davlatmamadov and Ramazan Mirzoev. From here it's an 18km walk to Ravmed village, via an unmanned hut offering basic accommodation below some petroglyphs. Ravmed has three homestays (houses of Murodbek Fuzailov, Durbannasein Zaurbekov and Mubarakqadam Bakhtibekov). All homestays cost around US$15 per person per day with three meals and can arrange guides (US$10 to US$15 per day) and donkeys (20TJS per day). It's possible to trek to Ravmed over the ridge from the Geisev Valley in two or three tough days, or you can continue up to the head of the Ravmed Valley in a day or two for views of Patkhor Peak (6083m). Camping is the only option for these last two trips.

Less-visited homestay hiking destinations include **Devlogh** (p407) in the Bardara Valley, which offers day hikes to high *ayloks* (summer pastures), and the remote village homestay of **Bodomdara** (p408) in the Shokh Dara Valley, which offers the chance to day-hike out to views of 6095m Mayakovsky Peak. If you have a tent consider using the three homestays of **Rivak**, 40km from Khorog and 5km off the main Pamir Hwy, as a springboard to the three-day trek to Nimos in the Shokh Dara Valley, via Zirdgok-Kul and Rivak-Kul lakes.

The road into the Bartang branches off the main road to Dushanbe, just before the village of Rushan, 61km from Khorog. After the village of **Yemts**, famous for its musicians, look for the footbridge that marks the start of the wonderful hike up the **Geisev Valley** (p407). A further 9km up the main valley is the village of Khijez, which offers more hiking routes.

The lovely village of **Basid**, 50km further, boasts two shrines (tourists can't visit the upper one) and scenic forests, good hiking and a homestay 5km up a side valley at Devlogh.

About 9km from Basid, it's worth taking the very rough side road 9km up to **Bardara**, at the junction of two gorgeous valleys. The hospitable village has homestays, two ancient shrines and foot trails that lead up to summer pastures and over the high Bardara Kutal pass to Zarosh-Kul (see p412). Ask to see the village *khalodelnik* (fridge).

The road to **Savnob** switches back high up the valley side and then down into a protected bowl. The ruined fort (sadly used as a village toilet) and the hillside caves here served as protection against raids by Afghans, Kyrgyz or neighbouring Yazgulomis. The village of **Roshorv**, high above the valley, is another possible detour. From Savnob the road continues to the start of trekking routes near Ghudara.

Up a side valley are the villages of Nisar and **Barchadiev**, which is the trailhead for treks up to **Lake Sarez** (p409), currently off-limits to foreigners.

Odina Nurmamadov (basid@mail.ru) is a Bartang-based trekking guide who has experience in organising treks in the region.

Sleeping

There are seven homestays in the Geisev Valley (p407). In Basid, tourists can stay at the homestays of Qozi Mastonov, Sebak Mardonaeva or Niyazbek Niyazbekov, the latter the head of the local *jamoat* (village committee).

In Savnob, stay at the homestays of Mamodsho Guliev, Mulkabek Alifbekov or garrulous English teacher Tobchibek Bekov. There are also homestays in Bardara (Muborakadam Muborakadamov and Mamadior Kazakov), Nisar (Niyazov Hosil), Devlogh (Gulbein Vataniev) and Barchadiev (Nurmamad Raziqov). Expect to pay around US$10 to US$15 per person, with dinner and breakfast.

Getting There & Away

Minibuses run between Basid and Khorog most days (40TJS), leaving Khorog at lunchtime, but there's little other traffic. The easiest way to visit the Bartang Valley is by hire car. A trip from Khorog to Savnob and back, via Bardara, eats up about 420km. Make sure your driver has a spare jerry can of fuel, as there is little, if any petrol available en route. High river flows often wash away sections of the road in early summer.

Past Savnob, a road of sorts continues on to Kök Jar (p415) and Murgab but the road is in *very* bad condition and only worth contemplating at the end of summer and with a reliable 4WD. Check beforehand whether the road is open. As one local told us, 'The road to Kök Jar is fine but at the end of the trip both the car and driver will be destroyed.'

SHOKH DARA VALLEY ШОХ ДАРА

The Shokh Dara Valley southeast of Khorog offers a fine overnight excursion from Khorog or, with your own transport, a loop route option, connecting with the Pamir Hwy and returning to Khorog via the Gunt Valley or the Wakhan.

About 34km from Khorog (7km before Roshtqala) you'll see an alluvial plain on the right that until 2002 was the village of **Dasht**. The huge mud slide killed 24 and diverted the river. Due to the lack of arable land, most Pamiris live on such volatile alluvial plains.

The main town in the valley is **Roshtqala** (Red Fort), named after the ruined fort above the town. The village has a small bazaar and frequent transport from Khorog.

About 11km past Roshtqala a road branches right at Bidiz/Shavoz and climbs on a *very* rough track for 14km to **Bodomdara** and the welcoming homestay of Khandongul Dorobshoeva. Trekking routes lead from here to Darshai in the Wakhan Valley and Garam Chashma, or you can day hike to fine views of 6095m Mayakovsky Peak in around four hours each way.

One other potential detour is the day-long walk from Vrang to scenic Durum-Kul. Alternatively, drive part of the way (6km), past great views over Vrag village, and make it a half-day hike (90 minutes each way). Further up the Shokh Dara Valley, look out for **forts** at Shashbuvad and Deruj.

Just before **Javshanguz** are dramatic views of peaks **Engels** (6507m) and **Karl Marx** (6723m),

---

AN ACCIDENT WAITING TO HAPPEN

As if Tajikistan didn't have enough to worry about, geologists warn that the country faces a potential natural disaster of Biblical proportions. The liquid ticking bomb lies high in the Pamirs in the shape of Lake Sarez, a 60km-long body of disarmingly pretty turquoise water half the size of Lake Geneva. Lake Sarez was formed in 1911 when an earthquake dislodged an entire mountain side into the path of the Murgab River, obliterating the villages of Usoi and Sarez. A 500m-deep lake gradually formed behind the 770m-high natural dam of rocks and mud known as the Usoi Dam. The dam is currently considered stable but if a regional earthquake were to break this plug or create a wave to breach the dam, as some experts think could happen, a huge wall of water would sweep down the mountain valleys, wiping away roads and villages deep into Uzbekistan, Turkmenistan and Afghanistan, with flood waters reaching as far as the Aral Sea. Experts warn that it would be the largest flood ever witnessed by human eyes.

---

offering fantastic camping opportunities. One enticing trekking route follows an old 4WD track over the 4432m Mats Pass into the Pamir Valley.

From Javshanguz the scenery blurs from the jagged valleys of the western Pamirs to the plateau scenery of the eastern Pamirs, as the rough 4WD road runs to **Turuntai-Kul**, 29km away and 6km off the main road. From here the main road winds down to the Pamir Hwy just beyond Jelandy, but there is a difficult river crossing en route for which you'll need a high-clearance 4WD. It's generally easier to cross near the lake; ask herders for the best route.

Sleeping

There are signed homestays at Javshanguz (Sabrigul Nazarkhudoeva and Firichtamo Shohnavruzova), as well as at the villages of Vezdara, Shohirizm, Sindev and Bodomdara.

Getting There & Away

Minivans to Roshtqala (5TJS) depart from Khorog fairly frequently, except on Sundays. Occasional transport continues further up the valley, or travellers can arrange to pay for the extra leg to Javshanguz (around US$15 for the vehicle).

Car hire to Javshanguz from Khorog costs around US$120.

WAKHAN VALLEY

The Tajik half of the superbly remote Wakhan Valley, shared with Afghanistan, is a fantastic side trip from Khorog, either en route to Murgab or as a loop returning via the Gunt or Shokh Dara Valleys. The route's many side valleys reveal stunning views of the 7000m peaks of the Hindu Kush (Killer of Hindus)

range, marking the border with Pakistan, and there's a thrill from knowing that Marco Polo travelled through the valley in 1274. You will need to have Ishkashim marked on your GBAO permit to travel this road. The Tajikistan side is also the perfect gateway to the Afghan Wakhan (see p488).

Some 46km south of Khorog, and 7km from the junction at Anderob, the hot springs and turquoise pool of **Garam Chashma** make for a nice soak.

Continuing south of Anderob towards Ishkashim, you'll see the **Koh-i-Lal ruby mine** from the road. The region's gem mines were mentioned by Marco Polo (who called the region Mt Shugnon) and Badakhshani rubies are still famed throughout the region. There are good views of Afghanistan from here, with its pyramid-shaped hay stacks and donkey caravans.

Ishkashim is the Wakhan's regional centre and largest village. The Saturday transborder market bustles with Afghan traders in turbans and *pakol* (flat caps) and boasts a superb location on an island in the Pyanj River (upper Oxus) at the border crossing to Afghanistan, 3km west of town. Bring your passport.

Some 15km from Ishkashim, near the village of Namadguti, is the impressive Kushan-era **Khaakha fortress**, dating from the 3rd century BC and rising from a platform of natural rock. The fort is currently occupied by Tajik border guards, so ask before taking pictures, though the lower parts of the fort are generally accessible. Just 300m further on is the interesting Ismaili *mazar* (tomb) and nearby museum of Shah-i-Mardan Hazrati Ali, one of many places in Central Asia that claims to be the final resting place of the Prophet's son-in-law.

Seven kilometres from Namadguti is another ruined fortress and a further 20km, is the village of **Darshai**, where trekking routes lead over the mountains to the Shokh Dara Valley.

A further 57km from Khaakha, 3km past Ptup village at Tuggoz, is the turn-off for the ruined 12th-century **Yamchun Fort** (also known as Zulkhomar Fort), the most impressive in the valley, complete with multiple walls and round watchtowers. The site is a 6km switch-backed drive from the main road and sits about 500m above the valley. Climb up the hillside west of the fort for the best views. About 1km further uphill from the fort are the **Bibi Fatima Springs** (local/foreigner 1/10TJS; 5am-9pm), probably the nicest in the region and named after the Prophet Mohammed's daughter. Women believe they can boost their fertility by visiting the womblike calcite formations. Bring a towel and keep an eye on your valuables as there are no lockers. Men's and women's bath times alternate every half hour.

Yamg village is worth a brief stop for the **tomb** and **reconstructed house museum** of Sufi mystic, astronomer and musician Mubarak Kadam Wakhani (1843–1903). You can see the stone that he used as a solar calendar. If the museum is closed, ask around for Aydar Malikmadov. The museum is 500m off the main road.

Vrang is worth a stop for its fascinating 4th-century Buddhist stupa (some sources describe it as a fire-worshipping platform). All around the ruins are the sulphurous remains of geothermal activity, as well as dozens of hermit caves. Walk through the village, cross the water channel and it's a steep scramble to the site. Locals can show you the village's traditional water-driven mill. There's a small museum and shrine at the base of the hill.

Four kilometres further on, along the Wakhan plain, is distant Umbugh Qala, used by the Tajik military and therefore off-limits. The views south of the mountains bordering Afghanistan and Pakistan are superb. Some 20km from Vrang, near Zugband, look across the river to the ruined Afghan fort of Qala-i-Panja, once the largest settlement in the Wakhan.

A further 5km (5km before Langar) is **Abrashim Qala** (Vishim Qala in Wakhi), the 'Silk Fortress' of **Zong**, built to guard this branch of the Silk Road from Chinese and Afghan invaders. The fort offers perhaps the most scenic views of all those in the valley. It's a steep 45-minute hike up the hillside, though 4WDs can drive part way via a looping road to the east.

Langar (population 1800) is strategically situated where the Pamir and Wakhan Rivers join to form the Pyanj, marking the start of Afghanistan's upper Wakhan, or Sarkhad region. It's an excellent base to visit surrounding sites. For a half-day hike, hire a local guide (US$5) for the hour-long walk uphill (500m vertical ascent) to a collection of over 6000 petroglyphs. The village *jamoat khana* is easily recognisable by its colourful wall murals. Across the road is the *mazar* of Shoh Kambari Oftab, the man credited with bringing Ismailism to Langar. There are rumours that the border with Afghanistan here will open soon.

Ratm Fort has a strategic location, surrounded on three sides by cliffs. It's 5.5km from Langar and a 15-minute walk off the main road through bushes. Its name means 'first' as it is the first fort in the valley.

From Langar the road continues 77km to a military check post at **Khargush**. En route keep your eyes peeled for Bactrian camels on the far (Afghan) side of the Pamir River. At Khargush the main road leads uphill over the 4344m Khargush Pass (look behind for stunning views of the Koh-i-Pamir massif in Afghanistan) to the salt lake of **Chokur-Kul**, 25km from Khargush, which is normally teeming with birdlife. From here it's 12km to the main Pamir Hwy.

The protected area of Zor-Kul, further up the Pamir Valley from the Khorgush check post, can only be visited with a permit from Dushanbe or Khorog and permission from the border guards (though there are actually no checks if you approach the lake from its eastern end, via Jarty-Gumbaz – see p415). The lake was determined to be the source of the Oxus River during the 1842 expedition of Lieutenant Wood, when it was named Lake Victoria.

Sleeping

In Ishkashim, the **Hanis Guesthouse** (3553-2 13 55; per person US$8, incl breakfast & dinner US$13-15) is a popular place at the west end of town, next to the *militsia* (police) station. The Western toilet and hot shower feel pretty luxurious, and owner Sanavbar can provide information about onward travel in Afghanistan.

A few intrepid travellers have discovered the homestay of **Akdod Muradaliev** (☎ 3553-2 11 41; Khairoloieva Dom 2; dm incl breakfast & dinner 15TJS-25TJS), a friendly family home with two rooms, a hot bath of sorts and a pit latrine. It's one block west of the Ishkashim central bazaar, opposite the Bahodor Restaurant.

There are blue signposted homestays in Ptup/Navobad (two); at the simple homestays of Otashbek Nazirov, Mirshakar Nazirov or Alifkhan Makonshoev in the village of Vitchkut, below Yamchun Fort; and at Yamg (two), Vrang (two) and Zong, where the homestay of Mavluda Baharieva is recommended

At Yamchun, it's possible to overnight at the nearby small **sanatorium** (dm incl 3 meals 30TJS).

In Langar, it's possible to stay at the Yodgor homestay, run by the local *khalifa* Yodgor Molleijev, or at the homestays of Nasab Talgunsho, Nigina Avassronova or Zumrat Shambiyeva (US$15 with breakfast and dinner), all are a five-minute drive away.

Transport

Ishkashim has transport to Khorog (25TJS, three hours) every morning. There are buses (15TJS) from Langar to Ishkashim on Monday and Thursday at 6am, as well as daily private minibuses (20TJS), all returning in the afternoon.

PAMIR HIGHWAY
ПАМИРСКОЕ ШОССЕ

The Pamir Hwy from Khorog to Osh (a section of the M41) was built by Soviet military engineers between 1931 and 1934, in order to facilitate troops, transport and provisioning to one of the remotest outposts of the Soviet empire. Off-limits to travellers until recently, the extremely remote high-altitude road takes you through Tibetan-style high plateau scenery populated by yurts and yaks and studded with deep-blue lakes.

Blue kilometre posts line the way, with the distance from Khorog marked on one side and from Osh on the other.

Khorog to Murgab
GUNT VALLEY TO KOI-TEZEK PASS

The initial 120km stretch out of Khorog climbs the attractive and well-watered Gunt Valley. At the east end of town, by the campus site of the planned University of Central Asia, look for a monument to the Pamir Hwy in

the form of the first car ever to make the trip from Osh to Khorog, in 1925. Just past here a large concrete overhang protects the road from landslides.

At Bogev village, 17km from centre of Khorog, it's possible to visit **Kafir-Qala** (Fortress of the Infidels), a faint ruined citadel with two circular Aryan fire temples. A further 5km you pass the truck terminal for Chinese vehicles from Xinjiang; a modern-day Silk Road transit spot.

As the main road continues to climb, there are spectacular views back to the dramatic vertical peaks of the Gunt Valley. About 8km before Jelandy, just past a concrete ibex statue, a dirt road branches left to a **hot springs** complex, where you can soak in the curative hot-water pool.

At **Jelandy**, at the 120km post, is a larger **Sarez Sanatorium** (dm 10-15TJS) with more hot pools. It's a bit off the road; ask for the *kurort* (sanatorium).

A further 12km past Jelandy a 4WD-only road branches right over a flimsy bridge uphill to eventually join the Shokh Dara Valley (p408). A side track on this road offers a challenging detour to the impressive high-altitude lake **Turuntai-Kul** (p409).

The main road switchbacks to the 4272m **Koi-Tezek Pass**, after which the mountains pull back from the road to reveal the lunar-like high-altitude desert, framed by snowy peaks, that marks the start of the Pamir plateau. Some 16km on from the pass a metal silhouette of a Marco Polo sheep and giant Cyrillic letters mark the entry to Murgab *rayon* (district).

BULUNKUL TO MURGAB

Just 36km after the pass, a dirt road shoots off to the left for 16km, to the end-of-the-world Tajik settlement of **Bulunkul**, reportedly the coldest place in Tajikistan. Accommodation is available at the META-supported **homestay** (dm US$6) of Mahbuba Nabieva or the Sharaf or Pokiza families.

From the village it's a short drive or a one-hour walk to get views of **Yashil-Kul** (Green Lake, 3734m), a surreal turquoise lake framed by ochre desert. Look for warm springs on the southern side. Archaeological sites by the lake include the 4000-year-old stone circles at the mouth of the Bolshoi Marjonai River and the **mausoleum of Bekbulat** on the north bank of the Alichur River. The area was once the

HIGH-ALTITUDE ADVENTURES AROUND BACHOR

The small village of Bachor in the upper Gunt Valley is fast becoming one of the Pamirs' most popular trekking spots, either on foot or on horseback.

The most popular option is the week-long loop route via Zarosh-Kul, Uch-Kul and Chapdara-Kul, a series of spectacular high-altitude lakes nestled in the heart of the Pamirs. Other route options include the five-day lollipop loop to Chapdara-Kul, or the adventurous trek from Bartang to Zarosh-Kul and Bachor over the 5200m Bardara Kutal Pass. Note that Zarosh-Kul is at an altitude of 4518m, so you shouldn't attempt this trek unless you are well acclimatised, preferably after a warm-up trek or trip to the eastern Pamirs. The route is generally clear of snow between July and September.

Alternatively, DIY adventurers could spend a couple of days hiking and hitching down the Gunt Valley from Bulunkul, along the northern shore of Yashil-Kul lake to the Pamir Hwy near Shahzud. Another possible route, by foot or 4WD, follows the dirt track across the Sumantash plain between Alichur and Bulunkul, passing the hot spring at Ak-Jar.

Bachor is 18km off the Pamir Hwy (turn off at Varshedz), 120km (three hours) from Khorog. To get here from Khorog you'll have to hire a vehicle, though to shave costs you could take a Jelandy-bound minivan to Shahzud and hire a car there. Homestay options in Bachor include those of Shoidonboi Tursunbaev, Sangnanad Narodmamadov and the Sultanshah family. It's possible to hire donkeys, horses and trained guides at Bachor (US$20 per horse, US$30 for guide with horse, donkeys are half price). **Aslisho Qurboniev** (☎ 93-566 1504; aspamir@gmail.com) is a good, English-speaking guide from Bachor who knows the region well.

major trade route between the eastern and western Pamirs.

Back on the main highway, just past the turn-off to Bulunkul, pause at the impressive viewpoint overlooking the salt lakes of the sweeping Alichur plain. The highway descends to the turn-off right to Khargush and the Wakhan, then passes **Tuz-Kul** (Salt Lake) and **Sassyk-Kul** (Stinking Lake), before reaching **Alichur** village. The plain around Alichur is one of the most fertile in the region and is dotted with Kyrgyz yurts in summer.

Just 14km past Alichur, stop at the remarkable holy **Ak-Balyk** (White Fish) spring by the side of the road. The **fish restaurants** (fish 3-5TJS) here and at Alichur are popular with Chinese truck drivers.

Just past Ak-Balyk a 4WD track branches north to the remote 11th-century ruins of a silver mine and caravanserai at **Bazar-Dara**, 40km from the highway in a side valley over the 4664m Bazar-Dara Pass. A visit to the site entails a five-hour, 90km return drive along a very rough road. The site was once home to 1700 miners and you can just about make out raised dais and fireplaces and the remains of nearby baths, complete with underfloor heating. Climb above the site for the best overview. Just 5km further from the ruins are the Bronze-Age **Ak-Jilga petroglyphs**, some of the world's highest at 3800m, which depict

miniature chariots, archers, ibex and skeletons. META offers a yurtstay in the Shamurat Valley, on the south side of the pass, 12km from the Pamir Hwy.

About 20km further along the highway, 3km outside the village of **Bash Gumbaz** (itself 7km off the main highway) is a photogenic **Chinese tomb**, marking the high tide of Chinese influence on the Pamir. Five kilometres further down the main highway you'll pass **Chatyr Tash** (Tent Rock), a large square stone that can be seen for miles.

A further 50km on is another turn-off to the right, this time to the Jarty-Gumbaz region. Around 25km down this track and well worth the detour is the wonderfully preserved Neolithic cave painting of **Shakhty** (see p415).

Back on the main road, there is a police check before you cross the Madiyan Valley and sweep into Murgab.

Murgab
☎ 3554 / pop 6500 / elev 3576m

The wild-east town of Murgab is a day's drive (310km) from Khorog. A former Tsarist garrison like Khorog but rougher around the edges, Murgab isn't exactly charming but it is a good base from which to explore the eastern Pamirs. The town itself is half-Kyrgyz, half-Tajik (the surrounding communities are almost all Kyrgyz) and there is some tension between the two communities. On clear days, the 7546m-high Chinese peak of Muztagh Ata is visible to the northeast of town.

Electricity alternates daily between the two halves of town but is of such low voltage as to be of marginal use, so don't expect to recharge batteries here. Murgab operates on Badakhshani time, which is an hour after Dushanbe, and the same as neighbouring Kyrgyzstan.

Murgab House, in the northern outskirts of town, houses META (see p414) and the Yak House (see p413). The cleverly-designed building incorporates architectural elements from both a Kyrgyz yurt and a Pamiri house.

INFORMATION
Agroinvest Bank (Pamir Hwy; 8am-noon & 1-5pm Mon-Fri, 8am-noon Sat) This modern, two-storey building in the northern part of town changes cash only.

Kizmat-i-Amniyat-i-Milli (National Security Service, or KGB) Travellers no longer need to report here automatically, though you might need advance approval to visit border regions like Shaimak or Rang-Kul. META can advise. It's located across from the Ismail Somoni statue.

Murgab Ecotourism Association (META; 2 17 66, 93-593 1449; ubaidulla46@mail.ru, aiymgulk@yahoo. de; Murgab House; 9am-6pm) This is an essential address; for details on META see the boxed text (p414). Apart from arranging trips, the office offers internet access (TJS5 for the first hour), sells an interesting brochure on archaeological sites in the eastern Pamir and has a detailed Soviet map of the region on the wall. Ask for Ubaidullah or Aimgul.

Pamir Bikes (2 13 38; Syemdyesat Let Murgab 62) Sells Marcus Hauser's map of the Pamirs (US$15), operates a book exchange and rents bikes (per day/half-day US$7/4). It's tricky to find; head east towards the bazaar from the sign on the Pamir Hwy, en route to Murgab House. Ask about the half-day return pedal to Konye Kurgan.

SLEEPING & EATING
META can arrange good **homestays** (dm US$9, breakfast US$2, meals US$4) in town, including those of Apal Doskulieva, Aizada Murzaeva, Yrys Toktobekova, Arzybai Matarozov and Gulnamo Nosirshoeva. Apal is just off the main Pamir Hwy, Yrys and Arzybai are in the southwest Jar-Bashy district near the bridge and Gulnamo (the only Tajik family) is near the bazaar. Expect to get a mattress on the floor, tasty homemade food, a clean outside squat toilet, an *umuvalnik* (hand basin), hot water in buckets and a warm welcome.

Hotel Mariya (2 11 93; Ayni 49; dm incl 3 meals 25TJS) Owners Zhora and Mariya offer the town's cheapest digs in their house just south of the bazaar. Accommodation is a ragtag collection of beds and mattresses in various rooms but it's a welcoming place and excellent value.

Sary Kol Lodge (2 17 89, 93-569 7101; Sorok Let Pobieda; dm US$9, breakfast US$2.50, lunch & dinner US$3-4) Travellers have recommended this new private guesthouse between Murgab House and the bazaar.

Suhrab's Guesthouse (2 16 53; per person US$10, full board US$15) This comfortable private guesthouse is run by English-speaking Suhrab and has comfortable rooms, with an inside toilet and *banya*. Choose between beds or traditional mattresses on the floor. Look for the half-wooden building northwest of the centre.

Ibrahim/Anara Guest House (2 13 24; Frunze 30; dm US$10, hot bath US$2) This guesthouse offers such Pamiri luxuries as a good hot-water supply, clean toilet, generator, nice sitting area and a kitchen but lacks the family feel of the homestays. Owner Ibrahim Gambarov can arrange local transport.

You can buy basic foodstuffs at the converted containers of the bazaar but your best bet for a meal is at your homestay.

SHOPPING
Yak House (Murgab House; 9am-6pm) A showroom for Acted's crafts project, selling traditional Pamiri-style *jurabi* socks, plus table mats, pillow cases, felt *shyrdak* and wool rugs, all decorated with traditional Kyrgyz motifs. Prices are marked, as are the names of the craftswomen.

GETTING THERE & AWAY
The easiest way to arrange transport is to band together a small group and hire a 4WD from META. The rate at the time of research was US$0.45 to US$0.55 per km, but this will doubtless change over time with the price of fuel. Private drivers also hang around the bazaar. See the Pamirs transport overview on p402.

Minibuses and jeeps to both Khorog (80TJS, nine hours, 320km) and Osh (100TJS to 120TJS, 12 hours, 420km) depart most days when full. Expect to wait forever for the vehicle to fill up.

If you are thinking of hitching, most Chinese trucks headed to/from the Qolma

---

ECOTOURISM ON THE ROOF OF THE WORLD

Created by the French NGO Acted as part of its Pamir High Mountain Integrated Project (http://phiproject.free.fr), the **Murgab Ecotourism Association (META)** has revolutionised independent travel in the Pamirs. Through a network of 60 community-based tourism providers, ranging from 4WD drivers to camel owners, the organisation essentially links travellers and locals, helping to spread the economic benefits of tourism throughout the impoverished Murgab region. Recent reports suggest that the organisation isn't working as well as it once did but it's still a good place to organise a Pamir adventure, so try to budget a couple of extra days to take advantage of the program.

The program offers yurtstays in the Pshart and Madiyan Valleys and can arrange homestays in Karakul, Bulunkul, Rangkul, Shaimak and Alichur. There are more yurtstays further away at Rang-Kul, the Jalang Valley, Kök Jar/Shurali, Ak Zor and Keng Shiber (in the southern Pamirs) and in the Shamurat Valley (south of Bazar-Dara). Note that yurts only occupy the higher mountain valleys between mid-June and mid-September.

Costs are US$5 per person in a yurt, US$6 to US$10 in a homestay, plus US$10 for three meals. English-speaking guides (US$15 per day) and treks can also be arranged (ask about the three-day trek from Elisu in the Madiyan Valley to Shamurat near Bazar-Dara, via herders' yurts in Chat and Koburgun), and it also organises 4WD hire and even camel trekking. META collects a reasonable 15% fee on all services to cover its running costs.

Bear in mind that META is an association of locals, not a professional tour agency. Despite the relative high prices for transportation, you can expect jeep breakdowns, guides with imperfect English, fairly basic conditions and the occasional logistical mess-up; it's part of the nature of travel in the Pamirs. For a top-end tour try a Dushanbe- or Khorog-based agency.

Acted has also protected several archaeological sites and helped set up the **Yak House** (see p413), which trains around 250 local women in Tajik and Pamiri crafts to provide much-needed additional income to marginalised families.

Pass stop at a depot 2km northeast of town along the road to the Qolma Pass.

Around Murgab

GUMBEZKUL VALLEY

One excellent short, but adventurous, trip is to hike up the **Gumbezkul Valley** from its junction with the Pshart Valley, 35km northwest of Murgab. The 9km hike takes you from a META yurtstay (see p414) over the 4731m Gumbezkul Pass, steeply down the southern Gumbezkul Valley to another META yurtstay, from where a rough 4WD road leads 7km down to the Madiyan Valley, 22km from Murgab. The path is easy to follow and there are stunning views in both directions from the pass, though it's a steep scramble on either side. It's a half-day hike from yurt to yurt. A 4WD hire to drop you off at the northern yurts and pick you up the next morning on the other side of the pass costs around US$80 through META. META also offers yurtstays at Kyzyl Jilga and Jar Jilga (*jilga* means 'high pastures') further up the Pshart Valley. The turn-off to the Pshart Valley is 6km north of Murgab, by some Saka (Scythian) graves.

For a post-hike soak, the **Madiyan hot springs** (admission 1TJS), 35km from Murgab, are just up the Madiyan Valley from its junction with the southern Gumbezkul Valley – ask for the *issyk chashma* ('hot spring' in Kyrgyz).

RANG-KUL

The scenic **Rang-Kul** area, 65km from Murgab, is a potential detour en route to Karakul. Five kilometres after you turn off the Pamir Hwy are some Saka tombs. Further on are the lakes of Shor-Kul and Rang-Kul, with fine views of Muztagh-Ata peak over the border in China.

META (p414) runs camel treks between yurtstays in the three valleys to the south of Rang-Kul. A three-day trek costs around US$135 per person for camel hire, food and accommodation, plus around US$100 per vehicle (not per person) to get you to Rang-Kul and back.

The nearby border with China was recently delimited, ceding a 10km strip to China, so you may have trouble getting beyond the border checkpost at Rangkul village, 15km past the lake.

SHAIMAK

To really get off the beaten track, take the road up the Ak-Suu Valley to Shaimak, 126km from Murgab, at the strategic junction of the borders of Tajikistan, Afghanistan, China and Pakistan. This is about as Great Game as it gets! You may need KGB approval to travel past the checkpoint before Tokhtamysh.

After crossing the lovely Subashi plain, the road passes the turn-off to the Qolma Pass (see p422), Tajikistan's only border crossing with China (currently closed to foreigners). You may be rewarded with views of Muztagh-Ata from here.

At the village of Tokhtamysh you could detour 1km across the river to a damaged bow-shaped geoglyph and the faint ruins of a 19th-century caravanserai. The scenery gets increasingly impressive, passing rolling Pamiri peaks, seasonal lakes and scenic yurts.

There's not much to **Shaimak** village (3852m), located below the impressive 5365m bluff of Ak Tash, except for its striking mosque and exciting views of the Little Pamir. The Chinese border is only 10km from here. You might get permission to continue to the geoglyphs and the 2500-year-old Saka *kurgan* (tombs) at Ak Beit, 3km south of Shaimak. Three days a year in June the border is opened to cross-border trade with Kyrgyz herders living in the very remote Little Wakhan region of Afghanistan.

If you have time on the way back, stop for a quick look at the beehive-shaped tombs at **Konye Kurgan** (Old Tomb), 7km from Murgab.

Return 4WD hire, through META, to Shaimak costs about US$150 (240km trip).

SHAKHTY & ZOR-KUL

The impressive Neolithic cave paintings of **Shakhty** (4200m) are 50km southwest of Murgab, 25km off the Pamir Hwy, in the dramatic Kurteskei Valley. Soviet archaeologists apparently took shelter in the cave during a storm one night in 1958, only to awake the next morning open-mouthed in front of the perfectly preserved red-ink paintings of a boar hunt. Check out the strange birdman to the left. Don't get too close to the paintings to avoid damaging them. The cave is a five-minute scramble up the hillside; you'll never find it without a knowledgeable driver.

META offers a day tour that takes in Shakhty, the Shor-Bulak observatory (currently closed to foreigners) and Shor-Bulak pass, with fine views of Muztagh-Ata, to the meteorite site of Ak-Bura in the Ak-Suu valley, and back to Murgab.

For a longer trip, continue south over two minor passes and past a seasonal lake rich in birdlife to the Istyk River and the remote Jarty-Gumbaz region. A hunting camp (currently closed in a battle over hunting revenues) is marked by a small Kyrgyz cemetery and a depressing stack of Marco Polo sheep horns.

Basic accommodation is available at yurt-stays in Ak-Kalama, 13km south of the hunting camp near the Afghan border, but it's better to continue 17km over a low pass to the impressive yurt camps at **Kara-Jilga**. The superb scenery here is classic Wakhan, with epic views over a string of glorious turquoise lakes (Kazan-Kul and Djigit-Kul) to the snowcapped Wakhan range that borders Afghanistan. Continue east to the end of these lakes and you will be rewarded with rare views of **Zor-Kul** (elevation 4125m) stretching into the distance. To continue on to Khargush you'll need permits to get past the border posts and watch towers.

From Jarty-Gumbaz it's possible to take an alternative route northwest to join the Pamir Hwy 3km east of Chatyr Tash. En route you can stop over at the META yurtstay of **Ak Zor** (White Cliff) in the lake-filled Uchkol Valley, from where you can trek along Marco Polo sheep migration routes towards Zor-Kul and another yurtstay at **Keng Shiber**; ask at META for more details. From Murgab to Jarty-Gumbaz and Zor-Kul and on to Chatyr Tash is about 225km.

Note that this region can be wet and boggy in June and July, making transport difficult.

JALANG & KÖK JAR

North of Murgab and southwest of Karakul are several interesting sites, including the petroglyphs and pastures of **Jalang** (150km from Murgab), which make an adventurous overnight trip from Murgab.

META can arrange a yurtstay at Jalang. Alternatively, stay at the yurt of Baba Nazar at Tora Bulak, 4km before Jalang. There are petroglyphs near the *aul* (yurt camp) at Jalang and in half a day it's possible to climb the 5129m peak to the southwest for fine views of the Pamirs.

The dirt road to Jalang branches off the Pamir Hwy near Muzkol and passes south of Mt Urtabuz (5047m). Fit and acclimatised hikers can climb the peak for dramatic views of Kara-Kul, but you'll need most of the day and a guide to find the right route up. The dirt road swings into the Kök Ubel Valley, past the small lake of Kurun-Kul and fine views towards the impressive peaks of Muzkol (6128m) and Zartosh (6121m).

Fifty kilometres further, down the Kök Ubel Valley, are the geometric stone symbols of **Kök Jar** (also known as Shurali), which are thought to have acted as a Stonehenge-like solar calendar as far back as 2500 years ago.

From here, the remote Tanymas Valley offers demanding trekking access to the **Fedchenko Glacier**, one of the world's longest. A very rough road continues southwest to meet the Bartang Valley (p407) at Ghudara, but you should check that the road is passable before considering this very remote route.

If you are heading on to Karakul after Jalang, it's possible to take a short cut along the southern shores of the lake.

Murgab to Sary Tash

North of Murgab, the road passes the turn-offs to the Pshart Valley (6km) and then Rang-Kul (24km), before swinging close to the Chinese border. In places the twin barbed-wire-topped fences run less than 20m from the road.

Soon the mountains close in as the road climbs towards the **Ak-Baital** (White Horse) Pass, at 4655m, the highest point of the journey. From here it's a long descent of some 70km to Kara-Kul, the highest lake in Central Asia. Just after the pass there are nice views back up a side valley leading to Muzkol Peak.

About 20km from the pass are the remains of a 19th-century Russian military post, later used by the Red Army in battles with White Russians and *basmachi* rebels. After another 6km a dirt track to the left offers access to Jalang and Kök Jar (p415).

Created by a meteor approximately 10 million years ago, **Kara-Kul** (3914m) has an eerie, twilight-zone air about it. The Chinese pilgrim Xuan Zang passed by the lake in 642, referring to it as the Dragon Lake, and both Sven Hedin and Austrian traveller Gustav Krist later camped on its shores. Local Kyrgyz call the deep-blue, lifeless lake Chong Kara-Kul (Big Black Lake), compared to Kishi Kara-Kul (Lesser Black Lake) along the Karakoram Hwy in China. Although salty, the lake is frozen and covered in snow until the end of May.

The only settlement of any significance here is the lakeside village of **Karakul**, where META can arrange a homestay at the houses of Saodat Kasymbekova or Tildakhan Kozubekova. Karakul lies right next to the Chinese border security zone and there's a passport check just before the village. Around 7km north of Karakul at Kara-Art, 500m off the road, there are some *kurgan*s (burial mounds) and faint geoglyphs.

The border between Tajikistan and Kyrgyzstan is 63km from Karakul, just before the crest of the **Kyzyl-Art Pass** (4282m), but the Kyrgyz border post is a further 20km at **Bor Döbö**. Don't forget to look behind you here for a stunning panorama of the Pamir. Kyrgyzstan is one hour ahead of Tajikistan time (but the same as Murgab time). Kyrgyz border controls can take a long time, especially if you are travelling by truck.

At **Sary Tash**, 23km further, the A372 branches off southwest to the Pamir Alay Valley (p361) of Kyrgyzstan and the A371 heads northeast to the Kyrgyz–Chinese border post of Irkeshtam (p362).

TAJIKISTAN DIRECTORY

ACCOMMODATION

Tajikistan has patchy accommodation. The Pamir, Fan and Zerafshan mountains now have a good network of homestays but elsewhere formal accommodation is quite limited. Dushanbe is particularly short on good, cheap accommodation.

The Pamir region has an excellent network of home- and yurtstays, which offer easily the best accommodation, and there are often informal homestays along many other mountain roads. If you hire a car, your driver will most likely know a family where you can all bunk down at night. If you are invited to stay at someone's house, a reasonable amount to offer is the equivalent of US$10 per person, including breakfast and dinner.

As with much of Central Asia, accommodation rates are often quoted in US dollars but you can pay in either US dollars or somani.

ACTIVITIES

Trekking options are fantastic in Tajikistan, principally in the Fan Mountains and western Pamirs, though these are demanding, remote routes. Trekking guides are available in Khorog for around US$20 to US$40 per day. Mountaineers will be in heaven and even a few hardcore kayakers are discovering Tajikistan's remote white water. Horse trekking to Zarosh-Kul is an option and camel trekking is available in the eastern Pamirs. Rock climbers should head for the Yagnob's Zamin-Khoror wall, a sheer 1km high slice of rock that you'll likely have to yourself.

The most obvious treks outside of the Fan Mountains include the following:

Bazar-Dara (four days) Loop trek to archaeological site and petroglyphs, heading in over the Bazar-Dara Pass and out via the 4918m Ak-Jilga Pass. See p411.

Darshai Valley (three to four days) Up the Darshai Valley to summer pastures and views of Mayakovsky Peak. Back the same way or over a 4941m pass and down valley to Bodomdara. See p408.

Grum Grijimailoo Glacier (four to five days) Two routes, from Kök Jar in the east up the Tanymas Valley, or north up the Khavraz Dara Valley from Pasor in the upper Bartang Valley.

Gumbezkul Valley and Pass (one day). See p414.

Javshanguz to Langar (two days) Following a former 4WD track over the 4432m Mats Pass into the Pamir Valley.

Karatag Valley (two to three days) To Timur Dara and Payron lakes, see p389.

Zarosh-Kul Loop (six to seven days) From Bachor village via Zarosh-Kul, Vikhinj, the three Uch-Kul lakes, the Langar Valley and Yashil-Kul. See p412.

DANGERS & ANNOYANCES

Tajikistan is a generally safe travel destination. Don't drink the tap water in Dushanbe, as there are occasional water-spread typhoid outbreaks.

The remote mountain passes between Tajikistan and Uzbekistan have been land-mined, as have parts of the Pyanj River banks that form the border with Afghanistan, so don't go for a stroll in these areas.

If you're going to be travelling the Pamir Hwy, particularly if you are headed from Osh to Karakul or Murgab in one day, there are serious risks associated with altitude sickness (see p535) for more information). A few lone cyclists (particularly women) have been hassled or assaulted while pedalling the remote border roads between Dushanbe and Khorog.

Southern Tajikistan has a malaria risk along the Afghan border and along the lower Vakhsh Valley as far north as Kurgonteppa. See p533.

EMBASSIES & CONSULATES

For a full list of embassies see www.tjus.org/embassies.htm or the website of the Ministry of Foreign Affairs (http://mfa.tj).

Tajik Embassies in Central Asia

There are Tajik embassies in the cities of Almaty (Kazakhstan; p194), Ashgabat (Turkmenistan; p462), Tashkent (Uzbekistan; p828), Bishkek

(Kyrgyzstan; p366) and Kabul (Afghanistan; p491). Bishkek and Almaty are good places to get a Tajik visa; Kabul is said to be trickier.

Tajik Embassies & Consulates in Other Countries

Austria (☎ 1-409 82 66 11; www.tajikembassy.org; Universitätesstrasse 8/1A, 1090 Vienna) Covering Austria and Switzerland.

Belgium (☎ 02-640 69 33; www.taj-emb.be; 16 Blvd General Jacques, 1050 Brussels)

China (☎ 10-6532 2598; www.tajikembassychina.com; LA 01-04 Liangmaqiao Diplomatic Compound, 22 Dongfang Donglu, Chaoyang, Beijing 100 600; ⏱ 9am-noon Mon, Tue & Thu)

Germany (☎ 30-347 93 00; www.botschaft-tadschikistan .de; Otto-Sühr Allee 84, 10585 Berlin)

India (11-2615 4282; www.tajikembassy.in; E-12/6, Vasant Vihar, New Delhi 110057)

Iran (☎ 21-229 9584; tajemb-iran@tajikistanir.com; Block 10, 3 Shahid Zinali, 610 Maidan-é Niyovaron, Tehran)

Pakistan (☎ 51-2293462; www.tajikembassy.pk; House 295, Street 35, F-11/3, Islamabad)

Russia (☎ 095-690 61 74; www.tajembassy.ru; 13 Granatniy Pereulok, Moscow, 103001)

Turkey (☎ 312-491 1607; tajemb_turkey@inbox.ru; Ferit Recai Ertugrul Cad 20, Oran 25009 Ankara)

UK (☎ 0208-600 2520; www.tajembassy.org.uk; 27 Hammersmith Grove, London W6 0NE; ⏱ Mon & Thu)

USA (☎ 202-223 6090; www.tjus.org; 1005 New Hampshire Ave NW, 20037 Washington DC)

Embassies & Consulates in Tajikistan

All of the following embassies are located in Dushanbe (Map p383):

Afghanistan (☎ 221 64 18; afembtj@tjinter.com; Mirzo Tursunzoda 124, cnr Turdiev; ⏱ 9am-noon & 2-4pm Mon-Fri)

China (☎ 224 21 88; fax 224 41 22; Rudaki 143; ⏱ 9am-1pm Wed & Fri)

France (☎ 221 50 37; http://ambafrance-tj.org; Rakhim-zade 17, proezd/alley No 2)

Germany (☎ 221 21 89; www.duschanbe.diplo.de; Ismoili Somoni 59/1; ⏱ 8.30am-12.30pm Mon-Fri) Represents those EU citizens without an embassy.

Iran (☎ 221 00 72; fax 221 04 54; Tehran 18; ⏱ 8.30am-12.30pm) Enter on the northeast side, on Bokhtar.

Kazakhstan (☎ 221 11 08; www.kazakhembassy.tj; Husseinzoda 31/1; ⏱ 9am-noon Mon, Wed & Fri) Look for the pastel-blue building set back from the main road.

Kyrgyzstan (☎ 224 26 11; www.kgembassy.tj; Said Nosir 50; ⏱ 9am-noon & 2-5pm Mon, Tue & Thu, 9am-noon Fri)

Pakistan (☎ 223 01 77; www.mofa.gov.pk/tajikistan; Azizbekov 20A; ⏱ 10am-1pm Mon-Fri) Behind the Asia Grand Hotel.

TAJIKISTAN

Russia (☎ 235 98 27; www.rusemb.tj; Abuali Ibn-Sino 29/31; ◷ 10am-12.30pm & 3-5.30pm Mon, 9am-12.30pm & 3-5.30pm Wed-Fri)

Turkey (☎ 221 22 08; turemdus@tajik.net; Rudaki 15)

Turkmenistan (☎ 224 11 62; fax 221 68 84; Akhunbabaev 10; ◷ 9am-noon & 2-4pm Mon-Fri)

UK (☎ 224 22 21, emergency 91-770 8011; http://ukin tajikistan.fco.gov.uk; Mirzo Tursunzoda 65)

USA (☎ 229 23 00; http://dushanbe.usembassy.gov; 109 Ismoili Somoni, Zarafshan district) Way out in the western suburbs.

Uzbekistan (☎ 224 15 86; www.uzembassy-tadjik. mfa.uz; Ozodi Zanon 9; ◷ 9am-1pm Mon-Fri) Near Hotel Avesto and chaotic.

Visas for Onward Travel

The following visas are available in Dushanbe:

Afghanistan A 30-day visa (US$30) requires a letter of introduction (written by yourself!), one photo and a copy of your passport, and takes two to four days from either Dushanbe or Khorog. In Dushanbe you may have to pay the visa fee into the nearby Orienbank.

China Visas cost US$30 (up to two weeks processing time) and often require an invitation from a Xinjiang tourism company. The embassy is only open two days a week and queues are long; one passport photo is required. Try somewhere else.

Kyrgyzstan A 30-day visa costs US$40, paid into the Orienbank on Rudaki, takes four days and requires two photos, a copy of your passport and Tajik visa.

Uzbekistan Visas take a week with a letter of invitation.

FESTIVALS & EVENTS

Eid-e Qurban and Ramadan are celebrated in Tajikistan. See p503 for dates.

Ismaili communities in Badakhshan celebrate 24 March as Ruz-i-Nur, the Day of Lights, celebrating the first visit of the Aga Khan in 1995, as well as 11 July, the Aga Khan's birthday (Day of the Imam).

With its links to a Persian past, Navrus (Nawroz, p503) is the year's biggest festival and you are likely to see song and dance performances, and even *buzkashi* (a polo-like game; see p64), during this time (the latter most easily seen at Hissar).

July sees the annual Roof of the World festival in Khorog, which features music, singing and dance from across the region. The third weekend in July has a horse festival in Murgab, part of Kyrgyzstan's At Chabysh festival (see p330), aimed at reinvigorating horse traditions among the Pamiri Kyrgyz. Expect horse races, *Manas* recitals and plenty of *kymys* (fermented mare's milk).

HOLIDAYS

1 January New Year's Day
8 March International Women's Day
21-23 March Nawroz, or Navrus (Persian New Year), called Ba'at in Badakhshan
1 May International Labour Day
9 May Victory Day
27 June Day of National Unity and Accord
9 September Independence Day
6 November Constitution Day

INTERNET ACCESS

Internet cafes are widespread in Dushanbe and Khojand, and cost around 5TJS per hour. Khorog has some internet access and you might get online in Murgab.

INTERNET RESOURCES

Asia Plus (www.asiaplus.tj/en) A news service focusing on Tajikistan.

Khorog – Gateway to the Pamirs (www.khorog.com) Hotels and travel information for Khorog in Badakhshan.

National Museum of Antiquities (www.afc.ryukoku. ac.jp/tj) Superb introduction to Tajikistan's history and the country's best museum.

Pamirs.org (www.pamirs.org) Excellent travel guide to the Pamirs, with virtual itineraries and good trekking information.

Tajik Maps (www.geocities.com/tajikmap/index.html) Collection of links to online maps of Tajikistan.

Tajik Tourism (http://tajiktourism.com) Private site aimed at independent travellers.

Tajikistan Tourism Development Centre (www. tourism.tj/en) Government tourism information.

US Embassy in Dushanbe (http://dushanbe.usembassy. gov) Has good travel tips under 'Citizens Services', including visa information and 'Travel Routes'.

Zerafshan Tourism Board (http://zerafshan.info) For travel information on the Zerafshan region around Penjikent, including a map of Penjikent town.

Send an email to gulya@mariansguesthouse. com to subscribe to 'What's on in Dushanbe', a weekly miniguide to Dushanbe, with restaurant listings, job openings and classified ads from the expat community.

MAPS

Marcus Hauser's 1:500,000 map of the Pamirs (see p418) is the best map of that region. It's available from www.geckomaps. com. A less detailed version is on view at www.pamirs.org/images/maps/pamir-gr.jpg. Gecko also produce two detailed 1:500,000 maps to *Northern Tajikistan* and *Southern*

Tajikistan, which are useful if headed off the beaten track.

If you are trekking, Firma Geo in Almaty (p127) is the best shot for 1:500,000 scale Soviet military maps covering Tajikistan (J-42 Dushanbe and J-43 Kashgar) from a series called *Generalnii Shtab*. See the map numbering at www.topomaps.eu/asia/tadj_100k.shtml. **Därr Expeditionsservice** (☎ 089-282032; www.daerr.de; Theresien Str 66, 80333 Munich) is one of the few places outside the region to sell these Russian topo maps. The website is in German only.

The University of Berne's Centre for Development and Environment has fascinating interactive topo and satellite maps of the Pamirs online at http://cdegis.unibe.ch/pamir.

See p397 for information about trekking maps of the Fan Mountains.

MONEY

The Tajik somani (TJS) is divided into 100 dirham. Somani notes come in one, five, 10, 20, 50 and 100 denominations. Dirham come in coins and notes.

You'll find a credit card and cash the most practical ways to carry your money, especially if you are headed into the Pamirs. Cash in US dollars, euros and Russian roubles are easily changed at numerous exchange booths. There is no black market for currency transactions.

In Dushanbe, Khojand and Khorog you can access ATMs but at the time of research it was still impossible to cash travellers cheques. Both Uzbek and Kyrgyz som are accepted in border areas.

Exchange rates, current at the time of research, are listed below (Uzbek rate not given due to instability):

Country	Unit	Somani
Afghanistan	Afg10	0.88TJS
Australia	A$1	3.79TJS
China	Y1	0.55TJS
euro zone	€1	6.12TJS
Kazakhstan	10 T	0.23TJS
Kyrgyzstan	10som	0.81TJS
Russian	R10	1.30TJS
UK	£1	6.70TJS
US	US$1	4.42TJS

POST

Tajikistan's postal service is ropey and it's not uncommon for mail to take a month or more to reach its destination, if it arrives at all.

An international letter/postcard up to 20g costs around 2.15/1.35TJS to all countries except Russia. A package up to 1kg/2kg costs a pricey 83/120TJS. Rates to Russia are half this.

Couriers are the only reliable way to send important documents, though they charge up to US$70 for a 500g package. DHL has offices in **Dushanbe** (☎ 221 02 80) and **Khojand** (☎ 4 06 17).

REGISTRATION

The good news is that tourists staying in Tajikistan for less than 30 days no longer need to register. If you have a nontourist visa such as a business *(delovaya)* visa, have a double-entry visa or are staying for longer than 30 days, you will need to register at some point during your stay (after 30 days if on a tourist visa). Registration is easiest in Khojand, Penjikent or Khorog, and is also possible in Murgab. Registering in Dushanbe (p401) is a real pain and is best avoided if possible. You get a piece of paper in your passport when you register and this is checked when you exit the country, especially at Dushanbe airport. The fine for not registering is theoretically around US$300 per day.

Registration costs US$15, plus 23TJS. The main hotels in Dushanbe can register you for a small fee, which makes their rates a better deal. Travel agencies will generally register you but in Dushanbe you'll have to hang around for up to three or four days.

TELEPHONE

To call internationally (including to other Central Asian republics) dial ☎ 10, followed by the country code, the area code (without the 0) and the number.

International rates are around US$1 per minute. Cheaper are the Internet Phone (IP) cards sold at telecom offices, with per minute costs as low as US$0.05. Buy a card, dial ☎ 009, then the card's pin number, ☎ 8-11 and then your number.

Most internet cafes in Dushanbe and Khojand offer headsets, webcams and Skype software for around 5TJS per hour.

Dual-band GSM phones work in Tajikistan. Mobile network providers include **MLT** (www.mlt.tj), the Tajik-American joint venture **Indigo** (www.indigo.tj), **Beeline** (www.beeline.tj) and **Babilon-M** (www.babilon-m.com); websites are in Russian only. Indigo supposedly has roaming agreements with Cingular, O2 and Vodafone, and Babilon-M has similar arrangements with

T-Mobile and Bell Wireless. For more details see www.gsmworld.com.

There are dozens of places in Dushanbe (with a concentration around TsUM, p388) where you can buy a SIM card for your phone. Cards cost around 180TJS, which includes 150 minutes of local calls and free incoming calls for a month.

TRAVEL PERMITS

Tajikistan has many internal checkpoints, particularly in Gorno-Badakhshan (GBAO), and the *militsia* in all towns are keen to check a foreigner's papers, so make sure you have impeccable documents.

For travel in the Pamirs you will need a GBAO permit; see p401. Many embassies abroad will now issue a GBAO permit alongside a visa, which will save you time and hassle in Dushanbe. Most embassies charge around US$50 but a few issue it for free.

To visit Zor-Kul (which is theoretically a nature reserve) you need a US$50 permit from the Ministry of Environment *(Vazorati Tabiyat)*. Even then you'll need permission from the local border guards. Agencies in Khorog and Murgab can help obtain this.

Lake Sarez is currently off limits to foreign trekkers for security reasons; check with the trekking agencies on p114 to see if this has changed.

VISAS

Tajikistan visa requirements seem to change every five minutes, though in general the process is becoming increasingly streamlined. These days most Tajik embassies abroad (see p417) will issue a 30-day tourist visa without a letter of invitation (LOI). There aren't many Tajik embassies abroad so you may have to post your passport to an embassy in a neighbouring country and arrange return postage and a method of payment (often in a foreign currency). Budget plenty of time for this.

Visas from the embassies in the US and UK are particularly expensive and British citizens are supposed to get their visa in person, though this is not always strictly enforced. Bishkek, Vienna, Berlin, Ankara and Delhi are all good places to get a Tajik visa; Moscow and Tashkent are more difficult. **Pamir Travel** (p114; ☎ 37-224 09 06, 771 86 46; www.travel-pamir.com) is good at expediting visas at the embassy in Tashkent.

A useful regulation entitles tourists from 80 countries (including the EU, Australia and the US) to obtain a 30-day visa on arrival at the airport without the need for a Ministry of Foreign Affairs–approved letter of invitation. Even so, it's a good idea to get a LOI and have the travel agency inform the airport immigration officer of your impending arrival (consular officials only reliably greet the Turkish Airlines flight from İstanbul). Bring one photo, a photocopy of your passport and US$50 in cash. Visas are not issued at land borders. Note that you can't get a GBAO permit or a double-entry visa at the airport. The safest option is to apply for a visa in your home country.

Tourist visas longer than a month are often available at embassies in Europe, though they may request a LOI and many travel companies are unable to provide a LOI for longer than one month. The visa specifies exact dates (you have to travel within those dates but not on those dates), but not the towns to be visited.

If you need a LOI, Tajikintourservice (p382) charges US$30, Stan Tours (p130) charges US$30 to US$45 and Hamsafar Travel (p382) charges US$50; cheapest is **Tajikistan Visa Company** (www.tajikistanvisa.land.ru) at €12. See p511 for contact details of these and other travel companies. LOIs are generally issued within two weeks.

For details on getting visas in Dushanbe for neighbouring countries, see p418.

Visa Extensions & Re-Entry Permits

Visa extensions are a pain so try to avoid one if you can. If you extend your visa, you'll also need to separately extend any existing registration (and possibly your GBAO permit) at OVIR.

To try an extension by yourself, head to Dushanbe's Ministry of Foreign Affairs **Consular affairs office** (Map p383; ☎ 221 61 03; ku@mfa.tj; Pushkin 22; ☯ 8am-noon & 1-5pm). You'll need to fill in two forms, pay the relevant fees into the Amonat Bank on Rudaki and return after two days. Extensions require two photos and a photocopy of your passport and cost US$30/40 and 35TJS for a one/two-week extension. Join the scrum at the entry at the back of the building.

Vostok Trading Tour in Dushanbe (see p382) can arrange visa extensions for around US$40/50/60 for seven/14/30 days and they take about a week to process.

It's technically possible to add a re-entry permit (US$10) to your visa, for example if you decide to visit the Afghan Wakhan and will return to Tajikistan.

TRANSPORT IN TAJIKISTAN

GETTING THERE & AWAY

With a limited number of flights and international border crossings, Tajikistan isn't the easiest republic to get to. This section concentrates on getting to Tajikistan from other Central Asian countries; for details on flying to Tajikistan from outside Central Asia see p515.

Entering Tajikistan

As long as your documents are in order you shouldn't have any major problems. Expect a certain amount of delay and chaos, even at the airport, where visa queues can take an hour.

Uzbek–Tajik border crossings are hostage to the current state of political relations between the two republics (which are often poor) and sudden unannounced closure by the Uzbeks.

Air

The most popular routes into Tajikistan are the twice-weekly flights with budget airline Air Baltic (www.airbaltic.com) via Riga and on Turkish Airlines (www.thy.com) via İstanbul, though both arrive at an ungodly hour (plenty of taxis meet the flights).

Tajik Air (www.tajikair.tj) is the national airline, though most consider the new Tajik airline Somon Air (www.somonair.com) a more reliable option – see p516 for flight connections. Sample one-way fares include Moscow (US$320), Dubai (US$280), Tehran (US$230) and Ürümqi (US$350). One-way flights to İstanbul cost US$445 with Tajik Air or US$550 with Turkish Airlines.

Regional flight connections to/from Dushanbe are limited to Bishkek (US$200, four weekly) and Almaty (US$188, four weekly). Ariana has a weekly flight to Kabul (US$160). There are no flights between Dushanbe and Tashkent; most people fly to Khojand (US$65) and then travel overland to the Uzbek capital (five hours; see p422). From Khojand there are weekly flights to Moscow.

> **DEPARTURE TAX**
>
> Dushanbe has no international departure tax, whether by air or land.

Land

As is the case throughout Central Asia, there is almost no cross-border bus transport between Tajikistan and its neighbours, so you have to take a combination of minibuses and taxis to get to and from the borders.

BORDER CROSSINGS
To/From Afghanistan

It's possible to travel between Dushanbe and Kunduz (Afghanistan) in a long day but check the security situation in Kunduz before making this trip as it was a centre of insurgency at the time of research. The main and easiest crossing is at Panj-e-Payon (formerly Nizhniy Panj) in the south; don't confuse this with the town of Pyanj (or Pyanzh), 75km further east. To get to Panj-e-Payon take a shared taxi or, alternatively, a minibus to Dusti (12TJS, six hours) from Dushanbe or Kurgonteppa (Kurgan-Tyube) and then a taxi 27km to the border. A taxi between Dushanbe's Sahowat Bazaar and the border costs around US$50, or US$15 per seat if sharing.

After Tajik immigration and customs checks, cross the US-funded bridge and take a bus (US$1) 1km to the Afghan border controls at Shir Khan Bandar. After another short transfer, you'll find transport (taxi 80Afg, one hour) running from here to Kunduz. Travellers report that the border is closed on Sunday.

The crossing at Ishkashim in Badakhshan is one of the wildest entries into ex-Soviet Central Asia. You will need to show a GBAO permit (see p401) to enter Tajikistan here so make sure you get one of these when you get your visa. The crossing is open from 8am to 4pm but closed lunchtime, Sunday and public holidays. The Afghan village of Ishkashim is 4km (and about four centuries) uphill from the border crossing and you'll have to arrange private transport or walk, as there's little transport at the border. Tajik immigration may try to charge you a bogus US$10 for your entry declaration form. There's a daily minibus between Afghan Ishkashim and Faizabad (eight hours) via Baharak. Locals advise not stopping at Varduj for security reasons.

A bridge over the Pyanj River at Khorog connects the Afghan and Tajik sides of Badakhshan at the Sheghnan crossing (closed Sunday) to offer 4WD access to remote Lake Shiva but you will need to have transport pre-arranged on the Afghan side. The region is snowbound from October to June and roads are often washed out in early summer.

To/From China

A road exists from Murgab over the 4362m Qolma Pass to the Karakoram Hwy in Xinjiang north of Tashkurgan. The border is open to Chinese and Tajiks but currently not open to foreigners, though rumours persist that this may change in the future. If the pass does open, you'll have to find a way through the 7km of no-man's-land between customs posts. The border is currently only open 15 days per month but again this is expected to change.

To/From Kyrgyzstan

From the Pamir Alay Valley you can cross into Tajikistan just north of the Kyzyl-Art Pass (south of Sary Tash). The Kyrgyz authorities sometimes don't stamp your passport when you enter Kyrgyzstan here at Bor Döbö, so keep some evidence that indicates when you arrived in Kyrgyzstan.

The border crossing into the Garm region at Karamyk between Daroot-Korgon and Jirgital is closed to foreigners.

From Khojand you need to get to Isfara (not Isfana, which is in Kyrgyzstan) and then take a shared taxi or bus across the border to Batken. Onward transport to Osh normally travels through the Uzbek enclave of Sokh and this creates visa headaches if you don't have multiple-entry Uzbek and Kyrgyz visas. (One way to avoid this is to pay a taxi driver extra to detour around the checkposts). If you are headed directly to Osh from Khojand and have an Uzbek visa it's easiest to just take taxis through the Uzbek Fergana Valley to Kokand, Andijon and the border at Dostyk (see p422).

To/From Uzbekistan

Most travellers making a beeline between Tashkent and Dushanbe drive to Khojand and then take a domestic flight (US$65). It's also possible to drive via Samarkand and Penjikent, or even fly to Termiz and then drive to Dushanbe.

From Dushanbe the closest border crossing is 55km west of the capital, near Tursanzade/Regar, crossing to Denau. Taxis from Dushanbe's Zarnisar Bazaar to the border cost 8TJS per seat (1½ hours), or take a bus to Tursanzade (3.50TJS) from the main bus station. En route you pass the huge aluminium factory, the world's third largest, which allegedly sucks up three-quarters of the nation's entire electricity supply. At the border, minibuses run to Denau, where you may find a shared taxi direct to Samarkand, or take one of three local trains to Termiz from the Uzbek border town of Sariosiyo.

From Khojand there are two main border crossings; Oybek in the northwest for Tashkent, and Kanibadam in the northeast for Kokand and the Fergana Valley. From Tashkent's Kuyluk Bazaar get a bus headed to Bekabad (note that foreigners cannot currently cross at Bekabad) and get off at Oybek (90 minutes), near Chanak village. The border post is visible from the road. Once across the border take a taxi to Khojand (US$15) or a taxi to nearby Buston (5TJS) and then a minibus to Khojand (3TJS to 4TJS). From Khojand to Tashkent it's easiest to take a taxi (US$15) to the Oybek border post, cross and then take an Uzbek taxi onwards. For a marshrutka (US$3) to Tashkent, walk a short way to the main crossroads.

For Kokand and the Fergana Valley take a bus to Kanibodom (4TJS), passing the massive Kairakum Reservoir en route, and then a minibus 9km to the border, cross the border by foot and then take multiple onward minibuses in Uzbekistan from Tamozhnaya to Besh Aryk (Beshariq) and then Kokand. You'll save a lot of time by taking a taxi direct from the border to Kokand.

It's easy to travel between Samarkand and Penjikent through a combination of minibuses and taxis. Shared taxis run from opposite the Penjikent bazaar 22km to the border (30 minutes) for 6TJS per seat, from where there are plenty of shared taxis on to Samarkand (a further 48km). The whole trip takes less than two hours. Change your Tajik somani into Uzbek som in the Penjikent bazaar.

GETTING AROUND
Air

Tajik Air pretends to operate domestic flights from Dushanbe throughout the country, but in reality this is limited to Khorog (US$80) and Khojand (US$65). Flights out of Khorog are notoriously unreliable so if you are headed to Dushanbe to catch an international flight, budget an extra day or two in the capital and be prepared for a possible 16-hour overnight drive.

Bus, Minibus & Shared Taxi
The bus/minibus network is limited to towns around Dushanbe, southern Tajikistan and villages around Khorog. Outside these areas

you'll find shared taxis making the mountain run from Dushanbe to Penjikent and Khojand, as well as shared 4WDs and minibuses heading east to Khorog. Beyond this, you'll need a combination of hitching, vehicle hire and luck.

Taxis are available in Khojand and Dushanbe for both local and long-distance runs and are the best option if you can afford them. See p402 for specific details of transport along the Pamir Hwy.

Turkmenistan

By far the most mysterious and unexplored of Central Asia's 'stans, Turkmenistan became famous for the truly bizarre dictatorship of Saparmyrat Niyazov, who ruled as 'Turkmenbashi' ('leader of the Turkmen') until his death in 2006, covering this little-known desert republic with golden statues of himself and grandiose monuments to the achievements of his 'golden age'. But the least-visited of Central Asia's countries is actually far more than the totalitarian theme park it's often portrayed as being, and is an ancient land of great spirituality, tradition and natural beauty.

The ancient cities of Merv, Misrian and Konye-Urgench inspire visions of slow-moving caravans plodding along the ancient Silk Road, while the haunting beauty of the Karakum desert and other quirky natural phenomena, from vast coloured canyons and dinosaur footprints to burning gas craters, are less expected but equally mesmerising sights. But the full Turkmen experience is ultimately about mingling with the Turkmen themselves, only a couple of generations removed from a nomadic lifestyle and a welcoming people whose hospitality is the stuff of legend. Women are seen decked out in colourful headscarves and ankle-length dresses decorated with Turkmen motifs, while everyone from young boys to *aksakal* (literally 'white beards', revered elders) will greet you warmly with a two-handed clasp and a slight bow.

Xenophobia runs deep in the upper echelons of Turkmen authority, which constricts independent travel. Anyone with a tourist visa is required to hire a guide to accompany them through the country. While this may dampen your independent spirit, it is for now the only way to fully experience the country.

FAST FACTS

- **Area** 488,100 sq km
- **Capital** Ashgabat
- **Country code** ☎ 993
- **Famous for** Multiple personality cults, gas reserves, Akhal-Teke horses, carpets
- **Off the map** Pretty much anywhere, but for true adventure try the Yangykala Canyon
- **Languages** Turkmen, Russian, Uzbek
- **Money** manat (M); US$1 = 2.85M, €1 = 3.64M
- **Phrases in Turkmen** *salam aleykum* (peace be with you/hello); *sagh bol* (thanks); *siz nahili?* (how are you?)
- **Population** 4.88 million

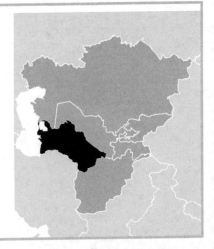

HIGHLIGHTS

- **Konye-Urgench** (p457) Ancient minarets, mausoleums and palaces that stand testament to the former glories of the Khorezm-shah empire.
- **Darvaza Gas Craters** (p442) A bizarre combination of human accident and natural phenomenon, and a vision of hell amid the incredible lunar landscapes of the Karakum desert.
- **Ashgabat** (p430) Extraordinary Turkmen capital laden with marble palaces, golden statues and more fountains than Las Vegas; home to the wonderfully chaotic Tolkuchka Bazaar.
- **Yangykala Canyon** (p445) A painted desert that wouldn't look out of place in a John Ford film, great for camping and exploration.
- **Merv** (p451) Extensive ruins of Merv, littered with ancient foundations and pottery shards, with Gonur, the largest archaeological excavation in the Near East, nearby.

ITINERARIES

- **Three days** Arriving on a transit visa, see Ashgabat (p430) in a day and wander Tolkuchka Bazaar. Cross the Karakum desert (p442) and then wrap things up with a visit to historic Konye-Urgench (p457).
- **One week** Spend at least three days around Ashgabat before heading east to visit the ancient sites of Merv (p451) and Gonur (p453). From here, return to Ashgabat and travel north to Konye-Urgench, camping en route at the unforgettable Darvaza Gas Craters (p442).
- **Two weeks** Along with the sights mentioned above, head west to Dekhistan

(p445), the Yangykala Canyon (p445) and Turkmenbashi (p446). While in the Karakum desert, scope out some remote villages for the chance to overnight in a yurt.

- **Three weeks** Explore the above sights at a slower pace and take the time for some activities, such as horseback riding in Geok-Dere (p436), cave exploration in Kugitang Nature Reserve (p456) and hiking in Nokhur (p443).

CLIMATE & WHEN TO GO

Turkmenistan is the hottest country in Central Asia, although its dry desert climate means that it's not always uncomfortably warm. That said, only the insane or deeply unfortunate find themselves in Ashgabat in July and August, when the temperature can push 50°C. The best times to visit are between April and June, and September to early November. Winters can be very cold throughout the country and aren't a great time to visit, though you may equally find bright blue skies and spring-like warmth even in the depths of December, but it's a gamble.

HISTORY
From Conquerors to Communists

Stone Age sites have been identified in the Big Balkan Mountains but the first signs of agricultural settlements appeared in Kopet Dag in the 6th millennium BC. More Bronze Age sites have been located in the Margiana Oasis, where archaeologist Viktor Sarianidi has identified a sophisticated culture that encompassed several villages and an extensive capital. Rivers that shifted over the centuries caused the abandonment of these settlements, but paved the way for a great civilization around Merv. Alexander the Great established a city here on his way to India.

Around the time of Christ, the Parthians, Rome's main rivals for power in the West, set up a capital at Nissa, near present-day Ashgabat. In the 11th century the Seljuq Turks appropriated Merv, Alexander's old city and a Silk Road staging post, as a base from which to expand into Afghanistan.

Two centuries later Chinggis (Genghis) Khan stormed down from the steppes and through Trans-Caspia (the region east of the Caspian Sea) to lay waste to Central Asia. Entire city-states, including Merv and Konye-Urgench, were razed and their populations

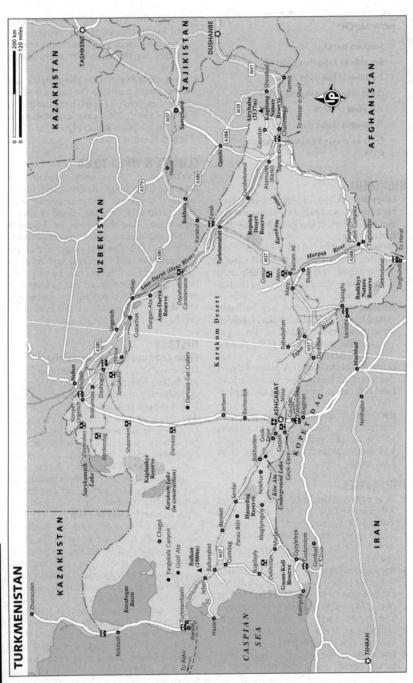

TURKMENISTAN

slaughtered. Unlike Samarkand and Bukhara, the cities to the south failed to recover.

It's not known precisely when the first modern Turkmen appeared, but they are believed to have arrived in modern Turkmenistan in the wake of the Seljuk Turks some time in the 11th century. A collection of displaced nomadic horse-breeding tribes, possibly from the foothills of the Altay Mountains, they found alternative pastures in the oases fringing the Karakum desert and in Persia, Syria and Anatolia (in present-day Turkey). Being nomads, they had no concept of, or interest in, statehood and therefore existed in parallel to the constant dynastic shifts that so totally determined Central Asia's history.

Terrorising the Russians, who had come to 'civilise' the region in the early 19th century, Turkmen captured thousands of the tsar's troops, and sold them into slavery in Khiva and Bukhara. This invited the wrath of the Russian Empire, which finally quelled the wild nomads by massacring thousands of them at Geok-Depe in 1881.

After the Bolshevik revolution in 1917, the communists took Ashgabat in 1919. For a while the region existed as the Turkmen *oblast* (province) of the Turkestan Autonomous Soviet Socialist Republic, before becoming the Turkmen Soviet Socialist Republic (SSR) in 1924.

The Turkmen SSR

Inflamed by Soviet attempts to settle the tribes and collectivise farming, Turkmen resistance continued and a guerrilla war raged until 1936. More than a million Turkmen fled into the Karakum desert or into northern Iran and Afghanistan rather than give up their nomadic ways. The Turkmen also fell foul of a Moscow-directed campaign against religion. Of the 441 mosques in Turkmenistan in 1911, only five remained standing by 1941.

Waves of Russian immigrants brought with them farming technology and blueprints for cotton fields. Turkmenistan's arid climate was hardly conducive to bumper harvests, and to supply the vast quantities of water required the authorities began work in the 1950s on a massive irrigation ditch – the Karakum Canal. The 1100km-long gully runs the length of the republic, bleeding the Amu-Darya (Oxus River) to create a fertile band across the south. Cotton production quadrupled, though the

consequences for the Aral Sea have been catastrophic (see p100).

In 1985 the relatively unknown Saparmurat Niyazov was elected General Secretary of the Communist Party of Turkmenistan (CPT) and retained power until the collapse of the Soviet Union. Although totally unprepared for the event, Niyazov was forced to declare independence for Turkmenistan on 27 October 1991.

Independence & the Golden Age

Determined to hold on to power, Niyazov renamed the CPT the Democratic Party of Turkmenistan for the sake of appearances before banning all other parties. His cult of personality began to flourish, starting with an order that everyone call him Turkmenbashi, which translates as 'leader of the Turkmen'. The president erected gold statues of himself and plastered buildings with his image. His slogan 'Halk, Watan, Turkmenbaşi' ('People, Nation, Me' – an eerie echo of Hitler's 'Ein Volk, Ein Reich, Ein Führer) was ubiquitous.

Tapping Turkmenistan's vast oil and gas reserves, Niyazov promised a Kuwait-style economy with enormous private wealth. Most of the profits, however, ended up funding ostentatious public-works projects. Public dissent was somewhat placated by enormous government subsidies for gas, water and electricity. The free ride was part of Niyazov's much touted 'Turkmen Golden Age' (Altyn Asyr), though its less benevolent side was the Orwellian control of the media that caused Reporters Without Borders to rank Turkmenistan second to last in its press freedom index (one spot ahead of North Korea).

At the height of his personality cult and power, Niyazov's life was almost ended when gunmen opened fire on his motorcade on the morning of 25 November 2002. The assassination attempt failed but provided grounds for an immense bloodletting of the remaining political opposition, including Niyazov's outspoken critic Boris Shikhmuradov. The one-time ambassador and dissident leader was tried for treason and remains jailed today.

Despite avoiding an assassin's bullet, President Niyazov proved mortal when he passed away on 21 December 2006, aged 66, the result of a massive heart attack. Having groomed no heir, the death left a power vacuum that for a brief moment opened the door for democratic reform and the return of exiled dissidents. Instead, a surprisingly smooth transfer of power occurred when Deputy Prime Minister Gurbanguly Berdymukhamedov grabbed the reins of power and won backing from Niyazov's inner circle. He was rubber stamped into power after elections in February 2007 (having won 90% of the popular vote in elections where only the Democratic Party of Turkmenistan fielded candidates, and when even Berdymukhamedov's 'rivals' openly supported him). Berdymukhamedov had been Turkmenistan's health minister and rumours that he is the former president's illegitimate son have being doing the rounds for some time. While this is unlikely – Niyazov was only 17 years old when Berdymukhamedov was born – the two men do bear an uncanny resemblance.

CURRENT EVENTS

On assuming the presidency, Berdymukhamedov made some initial reforms that toned down some of his predecessor's policies. The most egregious initiatives, such as renaming the months of the year and the days of the week after Turkmenbashi's family members, a ban on ballet and even the prohibition on listening to music in cars, were all lifted. Yet despite these small signs of reform, nothing more has been forthcoming. While the pathological state paranoia that so thrived under Niyazov has also been toned down, travellers wishing to visit the country continue to go through the same rigorous visa channels and must be accompanied by guides in most cases.

Turkmenistan's foreign policy is also unchanged; good news for Russia, which secured promises that its lucrative energy contracts would be honoured by the new regime. Berdymukhamedov has also retained Niyazov's declaration of neutrality, and his ability to keep out radical Islam in a volatile region has allowed the country to safely fend off harsh criticism from the West.

The latest phase of Turkmenistan's development is called 'the New Era', superseding Niyazov's 'Golden Age', and while the personality cult of Turkmenbashi still survives in the form of monuments and statues throughout the country, there's a mood of moving on in the air, with few people even wanting to talk about the man who dominated every aspect of daily life for the past two decades.

Yet portraits of Berdymukhamedov are ubiquitous and while the new president hasn't exhibited the same lust for adoration as his predecessor, he himself enjoys no meagre personality cult.

With its enormous oil and gas reserves generating billions a year for the government, Turkmenistan today has the potential to be a very wealthy country, though for the time being these massive revenues are being used not for much needed education and infrastructure investment, but on largely unnecessary vanity projects. A new gas pipeline connecting Turkmenistan to China opened in late 2009, ensuring access to the world's fastest growing economy and more economic stability beyond the control of Russia, yet it continues to look unlikely that this economic progress will be matched by political reform and democratisation any time soon.

PEOPLE

Turkmen remain nomadic at heart, if not still in practice, and carry themselves in a simple yet dignified manner that reflects their rural lifestyle. Nomadic rules, including the treatment of guests, still dominate home life.

Turkmen are guided spiritually by a unique form of Central Asian animism. Holiday breaks are thus used for pilgrimage time. Women in particular use these pilgrimages as an opportunity to take a break from their home life, and you may see caravans of women on buses, headed to places like Parau Bibi (p443).

Women who live outside Turkmenistan's towns are generally homemakers and mothers, and men the breadwinners. The oldest woman in the household, however, wields the most authority in decision making.

For more on the Turkmen people, see p65.

Population

The population of Turkmenistan is just under five million. Uzbeks, who make up about 5% of the population, live in the border cities of Konye-Urgench, Dashogus and Turkmenabat. Russians have left in huge numbers since independence, as it becomes increasingly hard to work without speaking Turkmen. Today they make up around 4% of the population. Turkmen ethnic groups make up 85% of the population, with other groups accounting for 6% of the population.

RELIGION

Turkmen are deeply religious people; their traditional animist beliefs have been blended over centuries of time with Islam. Evidence of this is clear at mosques and mausoleums, which are often decorated with animist features such as snakes and rams' horns. Likewise, pilgrims arrive at these sites bearing tokens such as crib models, indicating a desire for children.

Sunni Islam is the state religion, though despite Turkmenistan's constitutional guarantee of free practice for all faiths, in reality Islam and Orthodox Christianity are the only freely practised religions. Others, mainly Christian sects, have been forced to curtail their activities under government pressure, although the state-sponsored repression seen in the 1990s has eased somewhat.

ARTS

Turkmen carpets are world famous and can be seen just about everywhere, although the best place to see them is in the bazaar. Silk, embroidery and jewellery are other crafts that have been perfected over the centuries. Museums often have fine displays of traditional silverwork used to decorate women's clothing.

Certain forms of Western art were frowned upon by Niyazov, resulting in a ban on opera and ballet. Film making and cinema-going are nonexistent, though foreign DVDs can be bought with no problem in Ashgabat. Theatres do remain active, albeit with Turkmen-only song and dance acts, concerts and drama performances. The most impressive traditional singing, *bakhshi*, deals with folklore, battles and love, and is accompanied by a *dutar* (two-stringed guitar). Shukur Bakhshi, singing competitions, can be heard at festivals.

Between the Soviets and Niyazov, contemporary Turkmen literature has been all but destroyed. Rahim Esenov was Turkmenistan's best literary hope until he was jailed (in 2004) following publication of his book *The Crowned Wanderer*, which portrays a history of Turkmenistan different from that espoused by Turkmenbashi's *Ruhnama*, the 'book of the soul' that until recently was required reading for all Turkmen. Esenov, in his late 70s, was arrested for attempting to smuggle copies of his book into the country. While in jail the books were burned although he did win an award from the PEN American

Centre (2006). Turkmen are encouraged to read the writings of poet Magtymguly Feraghy (1733–83) and, increasingly, those of President Berdymukhamedov.

ENVIRONMENT

Effectively a giant desert ringed by oases along the country's border, Turkmenistan is home to far more varied landscapes than you might expect. To the east are the canyons and lush mountains of the Kugitang Nature Reserve, while to the south the Kopet Dag range rises up in a line towards the Caspian Sea. The territory along the Caspian is particularly unusual – vast mud flats, coloured canyons and the enormous bulk of the Big Balkan massif make this one of the more bleakly beautiful places in the country.

Wildlife

The most famous of Turkmenistan's many interesting species is the Akhal-Teke horse, a beautiful golden creature that is believed to be the ancestor of today's purebred. Dromedaries (Arabian camels) are everywhere, wandering scenically between villages and towns. Many of the Karakum's nastiest inhabitants are really exciting to see in real life – most importantly the grey *zemzen*, or *varan*, a large monitor lizard – though these are extremely rare. Despite its large size and particularly painful bite, Turkmen have traditionally welcomed the giant lizard as it devours or scares away snakes (such as cobras), eats mice and eradicates colonies of sandflies.

You are also likely to see desert foxes, owls and the very common desert squirrel.

Tarantulas and black widows are both indigenous to Turkmenistan, although you are unlikely to see them. Snake season is from April to May. Cobras, vipers and scorpions can all be found in the desert, so tread with caution. Turkmen folklore has it that once a snake has looked at you, you'll die shortly afterwards unless you kill it first.

Environmental Issues

Turkmenistan has paid a heavy price for the irrigation of its southern belt, using source water bound for the Aral Sea. While the Aral Sea is in Uzbekistan and Kazakhstan, its disappearance has led to desperate environmental problems in northern Turkmenistan, with the salination of the land taking its toll on the health of local people. Overfishing is another concern, as caviar-bearing sturgeon become rarer in the Caspian Sea. There is very little environmental consciousness in Turkmenistan, where no one bothers to save gas, electricity or water because all are subsidised by the government. The result in Ashgabat is a thin layer of semipermanent smog.

Nature Reserves

Turkmenistan's eight nature reserves are not designed for public use – they have been set aside for scientific research, as per the Soviet model. A permit is required to visit a reserve and these are available from the **Ministry of Nature** (Map p432; ☎ 39 60 02; 2035 köçesi 102, Ashgabat). Your travel agency will need to apply for this on your behalf, but the process is usually a straightforward one.

FOOD & DRINK

Similar to other Central Asian countries, *plov* (rice, meat and carrots) and shashlyk are the staple dishes across Turkmenistan. *Plov* is produced with cottonseed oil, which provides its distinctive aroma, while shashlyk is considered at its best when cooked over the branches of a saxaul tree. Other favoured snacks include *samsa* (samosa, meat-filled pastries) and a variation on the meat pastry called *fitchi*, which is larger and round in shape.

Dograma, made from bread and pieces of boiled meat and onions, is a traditional

Turkmen meal. Other soups include *chorba* (soup of boiled mutton with potato, carrot and turnip, known elsewhere in the region as *shorpa*). *Manty* (steamed dumplings) served with sour cream is another popular dish.

Bread (*çörek*) is round, flat and delicious when it's fresh out of the oven, although it does harden quickly. Çörek holds a place of honour in Turkmenistan and it is surrounded by superstition; it must be handled with utmost respect and never served or left upside down, even crumbs are collected and left in a safe place. Never throw bread away and if you must discard it, don't leave it where it could be kicked or stepped on. Çörek is cooked in a *tamdyr,* a large earthen oven that is also considered holy. It's bad luck to destroy an old *tamdyr,* so these are simply left to disintegrate.

At breakfast you'll be served sour milk or *chal* (fermented camel's milk) in the desert. Mineral water is sold everywhere and is of good quality, while beer and vodka – a legacy of the Russians – are popular alcoholic drinks. There are several decent Turkmen brands of both, although the most common beers are Berk and Zip.

ASHGABAT

☎ 12 / pop 650,000

With its lavish marble palaces, gleaming gold domes and vast expanses of manicured parkland, Ashgabat ('the city of love' in Arabic) has reinvented itself as a showcase city for the newly independent republic. Built almost entirely off the receipts of Turkmenistan's oil and gas revenues, the city's transformation continues at break-neck speed, with whole neighbourhoods facing the wrecking ball in the name of progress, although the more outlandish projects so favoured by Niyazov have been replaced in recent years by more sober ones under President Berdymukhamedov.

Originally developed by the Russians in the late 19th century, Ashgabat became a prosperous, largely Russian frontier town on the Trans-Caspian railway. However, at 1am on 6 October 1948, the city vanished in less than a minute, levelled by an earthquake that measured nine on the Richter scale. More than 110,000 people died (two-thirds of the population), although the official figure was 14,000; this was the era of Stalin, when socialist countries didn't suffer disasters.

Ashgabat was rebuilt in the Soviet style, but its modern incarnation is somewhere between Las Vegas and Pyongyang, with a mixture of Bellagio fountains and Stalinist parade grounds. At its heart it's a surprisingly relaxed city, with a varied dining scene and no shortage of quirky sights, making it a pleasant place to spend a few days absorbing Turkmenistan's bizarre present before heading into the rest of the country to discover its fascinating past.

ORIENTATION

The main arteries of the city are Turkmenbashi şayoli (avenue), running all the way from the train station to the new area of Berzengi, and Magtymguly şayoli, running east to west. Many of the city's landmarks and institutions are on or near these streets.

In 2002 former President Niyazov renamed all the streets with numbers. This pointless exercise has only served to confuse, as nobody seemed to know the names of the streets anyway – some have changed as many as four times since the 1990s. In this chapter we have used the most commonly used local name for each street, be it Soviet, Turkmen or number.

INFORMATION
Bookshops

Turkmen bookshops are little more than propaganda storefronts to promote national glory.

Miras Bookshop (Turkmenbashi şayoli 29; 🕑 10am-7pm) Find some novels in Russian among copies of the *Ruhnama* and various other pieces of dictatorship ephemera.

Emergency

The operators will speak Turkmen or Russian only.

Ambulance (☎ 03)
Fire service (☎ 01)
Police (☎ 02)

Internet Access

There are now several internet cafes in Ashgabat, though they're not cheap and they are state run, so bring your passport, know that anything you view or write can be monitored and expect news websites to be blocked.

Ak-Altyn Hotel (Magtymguly şayoli 141/1; per hr 14.25M; 🕑 24hr) Unreliable wireless available in the lobby.

Grand Turkmen Hotel (Görogly köçesi 50; per hr 20M; 🕑 24hr) Expensive internet access is offered in the hotel's business centre.

Internet Café (Karl Liebknecht köçesi; per hr 6M; 🕑 9am-1pm & 2-9pm) The most conveniently located is behind the international call centre. It has seven modern and fast terminals and you're able to connect your laptop here too.

Yimpaş (Turkmenbashi şayoli 54; per hr 6M; 🕑 7am-11pm) There are internet cafes on the 3rd floor here.

Laundry

Floor maids at most hotels will do a load of laundry for around 10M.

Brilliant (☎ 39 06 39; Magtymguly şayoli 99) Dry-cleaning can be done for reasonable rates here.

Yimpaş (Turkmenbashi şayoli 54; 🕑 9am-11pm) Dry-cleaning at this Turkish department store is more expensive than at Brilliant.

Medical Services

Central Hospital (☎ 45 03 03, 45 03 31; Emre köçesi 1) This large and excellent hospital is the main medical provision in Ashgabat. There's an accident and emergency section and pharmacy, both of which are open 24 hours a day. Foreigners have to pay for their treatment, so insurance is essential. The facility also includes a dental clinic.

Lechebny Hospital (Shevchenko köçesi) This Soviet-era hospital in the city centre is less well equipped than Central Hospital.

Money

There are several banks in the city centre, but they're not of much use to travellers as they don't have ATMs or change travellers cheques. Most places change US dollars, and euros too, even though the euro rate is not always displayed. As the exchange rate is fixed, there's no advantage in going to one place over another and there is no longer a black-market rate. There are just two banks that can do credit and debit card advances:

Senagat Bank (☎ 45 31 33; Turkmenbashi şayoli 42; 🕑 9am-1pm & 2-6pm Mon-Fri, 9.30am-1pm Sat & Sun) For MasterCard and Maestro advances, go to the Western Union office inside this bank. It's located next to the Yimpaş department store and charges a 3% commission on withdrawals.

State Bank for Foreign Economic Affairs (Türkmenistanyň Daşary Ykdysady Döwlet Banky; ☎ 40 60 40; Garaşsyzlyk şayoli 32; 🕑 9.15am-1pm & 2-4pm Mon-Fri, 9.15am-12.30pm Sat) If you have a Visa card, use this bank, 2.5km south of downtown and 2km north of the Berzengi Hwy (Archabil şayoli). The bank charges a 5% commission on withdrawals. Go to desks 31 or 32. This is also one of the few banks where you can change currencies other than dollars and euros.

TURKMENISTAN

ASHGABAT

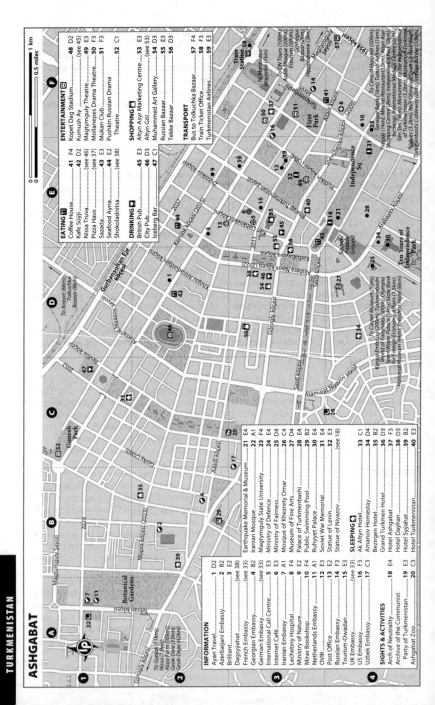

Post

Post office (☎ 35 15 55; Mopra köçesi 16; ☼ 9am-5pm Mon-Fri, 9am-2pm Sat, 9am-1pm Sun) This main post office is in the city centre. A postcard to anywhere in the world costs 2M. Letters by airmail cost 2.2M.

Registration

OVIR (State Service for the Registration of Foreign Citizens; ☎ 39 13 37; 2011 köçesi 57; ☼ 9am-noon & 2-5pm Mon-Fri, 9am-noon Sat) For tourist registration see p464.

Telephone & Fax

Most hotels offer international direct dialling (IDD) and fax facilities, although the **International Call Centre** (Karl Liebknekht köçesi 33; ☼ 8am-7pm) offers better calling and fax rates than hotels.

Travel Agencies

Any traveller not simply in transit through Turkmenistan will usually make contact with one of the following agencies to organise their letter of invitation (LOI). The following companies offer comprehensive services including LOIs, guides, drivers, hotel bookings, city tours and other excursions.

Aşgabatsyýahat (☎ 21 05 56, 35 20 15; fax 21 05 61; www.ashgabatravel.com; Garaşsyzlyk şayoli, Olimp 76)

Ayan Travel (☎ 35 29 14, 35 07 97; www.ayan-travel.com; Magtymguly şayoli 108-2/4)

Dagsyýahat (☎ 39 04 63, 39 04 51; tss@online.tm; Hotel Daýhan, Azadi köçesi 69)

DN Tours (☎ 39 58 28; www.dntours.com; Magtymguly şayoli 48/1)

Stantours (☎ in Kazakhstan 7 705 1184619; www.stantours.com; Almaty) Though not based in Turkmenistan, Stantours consistently get excellent feedback from travellers who travel with their local staff on the ground in Turkmenistan.

Tourism-Owadan (☎ 39 18 25; www.owadan.net; Azadi köçesi 65)

DANGERS & ANNOYANCES

Be aware that all top-range hotel rooms are bugged, as are many offices, restaurants and anywhere foreigners meet, though it's extremely unlikely that anyone is interested in your conversations unless you happen to be a senior diplomat or politician. However, it's best to reserve sensitive conversations, especially any with Turkmen citizens (who are far more likely to get into trouble than you), for safe places, preferably outside. Also take care when photographing public buildings; ask the nearest police officer for permission first.

SIGHTS

Ashgabat has plenty to occupy visitors for a day or two, though its often very good museums are ridiculously overpriced, which will put many travellers off going. Despite this, some sights are free (such as wandering the new city, the Earthquake Museum or a visit to Tolkuchka Bazaar) or very reasonably priced (eg the Turkmenbashi Cableway), so you won't always spend a fortune.

Central Ashgabat

Being all but wiped from the earth in 1948, Ashgabat was rebuilt into a ho-hum, low-rise Soviet city of no great beauty. However, since independence the city has again been demolished in vast swathes and is unrecognisable as the Soviet provincial capital of two decades ago. While many of Niyazov's stranger schemes have indeed now been abandoned, there's no sign of a slowing of the building program, which is at least keeping the world's marble industry afloat.

At the centre of Niyazov's monolithic Ashgabat is the embarrassingly large **Arch of Neutrality** which, while standing at the time of writing, was scheduled for demolition and removal in the near future. The arch marks the Turkmen people's unsurprisingly unanimous endorsement of Turkmenbashi's policy of neutrality in 1998, though it looks more like a rocket primed for take-off. Above the arch itself is the real gem, a comic 12m-high polished-gold **statue of Niyazov**, which revolves to follow the sun throughout the day. As a symbol of Niyazov's sun-king complex, it's perhaps unsurprising that the post-Niyazov regime has decided to remove it as the biggest and most prominent Turkmenbashi monument in the country.

The arch gives commanding views of the enormous **Independence Square**, on which sits the golden-domed **Palace of Turkmenbashi** (the place of work of the former president), the **Ministry of Fairness**, the **Ministry of Defence** and the **Ruhyyet Palace**, all of which were built by the French corporation Bouygues Construction, the court builder to Niyazov. Behind this is the **Majlis** (parliament).

Next to the Arch of Neutrality is the **Earthquake Memorial**, a bombastic bronze rendering of a bull and child (the baby Niyazov), under which lurks the **Earthquake Museum** (admission free; ☺ 9am-6pm). This is perhaps Ashgabat's most touching museum and the display includes once-banned photos of the 1948 earthquake and its aftermath as well as information about the five-year clean-up effort, the burying of 110,000 bodies and the building of a new city. Unfortunately the museum is usually locked (asking a guard nearby might get you inside).

Further down this long and manicured strip is the **Soviet war memorial**, a pleasingly subtle structure with an eternal flame at its centre. The strip ends with **Magtymguly State University**, the country's leading educational institution.

The **statue of Lenin**, off Azadi köçesi, is a charmingly incongruous assembly of a tiny Lenin on an enormous and very Central Asian plinth surrounded by Bellagio-style fountains of the sort so beloved by Niyazov. Behind Vladimir Illych is the new Magtymguly Theatre (p439), where traditional Turkmen performances can be seen. Across the road, Lenin faces an austere concrete building that was once the **Archive of the Communist Party of Turkmenistan**. Its walls feature modernist concrete sculptures made by Ernst Neizvestny, the Russian artist who lived and worked in Ashgabat during the 1970s.

Also in the vicinity is the overpriced **Museum of Fine Arts** (☎ 39 61 42; Alishera Navoi köçesi 88; admission 33M; ☺ 9am-6pm Wed-Mon), located in an impressive building with a big rotunda, two tiers and lots of gold. The collection contains some great Soviet-Turkmen artwork: happy peasant scenes with a backdrop of yurts and smoke-belching factories. There is also a collection of Russian and Western European paintings and a fine selection of Turkmen jewellery and traditional costumes. Guided tours in English are available for an expensive US$10 per person.

Further south from here is the large new **Carpet Museum** (☎ 44 68 09; Atamurat Nyazov köçesi 158; admission 33M, tour 33M; ☺ 10am-1pm & 2-6pm Sun-Fri, 10am-1pm & 2-3pm Sat), which along with its white marble facade now has very high entrance fees, though these are worth paying if you're interested in Turkmen carpets. While there's a limit to the number of rugs the average visitor can stand, the central exhibit, the world's largest handwoven rug, really is something to see (though you can see it hanging from the lobby when you enter – you don't even

have to buy a ticket). For a really detailed English-language tour, call ahead and check that Kamila will be working when you visit. The 'expert commission' here is the place to have your carpets valued and taxed, and the necessary documentation issued for export.

Central Ashgabat

More a statement of foreign-policy leanings than a sign of religious awakening, the **Azadi mosque** stands just south of Magtymguly şayoli, 600m east of the junction with Turkmenbashi. Similar in appearance to the Blue Mosque in İstanbul, the mosque sees few worshippers because of several accidental deaths during its construction.

The modern **mosque of Khezrety Omar**, off Atamurat Niyazov köçesi, is also worth visiting for its wonderfully garish painted ceilings. The angular, futuristic **Iranian mosque**, illuminated with green neon, is on Tehrn köçesi on the western outskirts of the city on the way to Nissa.

The **Ashgabat Zoo** (2011 Azadi köçesi; admission 1M; ☺ 8am-7.30pm Tue-Sun) is a curious diversion if you happen to be walking nearby, although animal-lovers may be appalled by the tiny living quarters set aside for the animals. The resident lion and bear in particular look severely downtrodden. At the time of writing, a new zoo was being planned, in which case this one will likely close.

Berzengi

South of Moskovsky şayoli the surreal world of Berzengi begins – an entirely artificial brave new world of white-marble tower blocks, fountains, parks and general emptiness that culminates in the Berzengi Hwy (Archabil şayoli), which is home to a huge number of hotel complexes.

Altyn Asyr Shopping Centre, the curious pyramidical shopping centre at the northern end of **Independence Park**, is reputedly the biggest fountain in the world. Inside it's rather less than impressive – an all but empty two-floor shopping centre, although there's a restaurant on the 5th floor (Minara, p438) that's popular for weddings.

The **Monument to the Independence of Turkmenistan**, known universally for the foreign community as 'the plunger' (for reasons obvious as soon as you see it), is a typically ostentatious and tasteless monument that houses the **Museum of Turkmen Values** (☎ 38 16

25; admission 28.5M; ⊙ 9am-12.30pm & 2-5.30pm Wed-Mon), another overpriced museum that is rarely troubled by visitors. Its displays are divided into four sections: independence, weapons, numismatics and jewellery. This is a popular spot for wedding groups to take photographs with a golden statue of Turkmenbashi, and the fountains are pleasant enough (a kind of totalitarian *Waterworld*, if you will).

Further south is the **Palace of Knowledge**, three large buildings that include a library, concert hall and the **Turkmenbashi Museum** (☎ 48 95 79; Archabil şayoli; admission 28.5M; ⊙ 9am-6pm Wed-Mon), which, taking a leaf out of Kim Jong-Il's book, houses all the gifts and awards presented to former President Niyazov by various people around the world. Expect to see lots of gold.

Looking like a lost palace in the urban desert, the **National Museum** (☎ 48 25 90; Archabil şayoli 30; admission per museum 28.5M; ⊙ 9am-5pm Wed-Sun) occupies a striking position in front of the Kopet Dag. It's actually a collection of three overpriced museums – the History Museum, the Nature & Ethnographic Museum and the Presidential Museum. The History Museum is the only one of the three that approaches value for money, so give the others a miss. The lavish Ancient History Hall includes Neolithic tools from western Turkmenistan and relics from the Bronze Age Margiana civilisation, including beautiful amulets, seals, cups and cult paraphernalia. There is also a model of the walled settlement uncovered at Gonur (p453). The Antiquity Hall houses amazing rhytons – horn-shaped vessels of intricately carved ivory used for Zoroastrian rituals and official occasions.

Between the National Museum and downtown is **Turkmenbashi World of Fairytales** (Garaşsyzlyk şayoli; ⊙ irregular). The US$50-million amusement park (dubbed 'Turkmen Disneyland' by locals) was unveiled with great fanfare in 2006, just in time for the nation's 15th anniversary celebrations. The park has 34 attractions, including a roller coaster that swoops over a giant map of the Caspian Sea. Despite taking up a huge amount of space in the centre of modern Ashgabat, it's rarely open.

Tolkuchka Bazaar

The sight of withered men haggling for shaggy sheepskin hats, a braying camel suspended in midair by a crane or a sheep being driven away in a sidecar are a few of the oddities you can expect from the Tolkuchka Bazaar, one of Central Asia's most spectacular sights. The enormous market sprawls across acres of desert on the outskirts of Ashgabat, with corrals of camels and goats, avenues of red-clothed women squatting before silver jewellery, and villages of trucks from which Turkmen hawk everything from pistachios to car parts. Whatever you want, it's sold at Tolkuchka. At some point in 2010 the market will relocate to a new site – with, of course, white marble gates and a general grandeur rather incongruous with such a bustling, noisy entity. Hopefully the market's soul will survive in the new location. The New Tolkuchka market will be approximately 2.5km north of the old site but on the right side of the road if you're coming from Ashgabat.

Expect to haggle. A *telpek* (sheepskin hat worn by Turkmen males) should go for around 30M, although the best *telpek* go for 40M or more. A fair price for a *khalat* (the attractive red-and-yellow striped robe worn by Turkmen men) is roughly 40M, while sequined skullcaps and embroidered scarves cost between 5M and 8M.

Above all, Tolkuchka is the place for carpets. Predominantly deep red, most are the size of a double bed or a bit smaller, and the average price ranges from 500M to 750M. Remember you'll still need to get an export certificate for the carpet before taking it out of the country (see p461); these are available at the 'expert commission' at the Carpet Museum (p434).

Tolkuchka is in full swing every Saturday and Sunday from around 8am to 2pm and, on a slightly smaller scale, on Thursday morning. Watch out for pickpockets. The current site is about 8km north of Ashgabat, past the airport and just beyond the Karakum Canal, while the new site is 3km further away.

A taxi should cost around 4M. Buses go there from the corner of Magtymguly şayoli and 1958 köçesi (1958 is a block east of Turkmenbashi şayoli).

Turkmenbashi Cableway

For some spectacular views of Ashgabat and the surrounding desert, take a ride up the **Turkmenbashi Cableway** (return ticket 2M; ⊙ 10am-6pm Tue-Sun). The US$20-million cable-car system, opened in 2006, starts from the base of the Kopet Dag (south of the National Museum) and climbs to a height of 1293m above sea

THE EVER-CHANGING FACE OF ASHGABAT

Ashgabat's post-Soviet facelift is a work in process. Niyazov spent the better part of his presidency transforming the capital into an all-marble 'White City', and still today whole neighbourhoods are being demolished to make way for palaces, apartments, fountains and enormous sculptures.

The demolitions have left hundreds of people homeless and the city authorities have no provision for rehousing or compensation. Turkmenbashi World of Fairytales (p435), an enormous amusement park in the heart of the new city that for most of the year sits empty and unused, was one of many projects that required the eviction of hundreds of families.

The destruction of old buildings is not limited to Ashgabat. During one trip to the Karakum desert, President Niyazov stopped at the town of Darvaza and, not pleased with its dilapidated state, had the village razed to the ground à la Chinggis Khan. Apparently it was not living up to the lofty standards of the 'Golden Age'. The people living there were moved to other villages and the name 'Darvaza' was deleted from the maps.

Be aware that the Ashgabat map is particularly vulnerable to change during the lifetime of this book.

level on a lower peak of the Kopet Dag. The upper terminal has souvenir shops, a restaurant, cafe, picnic spots, several high-powered telescopes for sightseeing and an 80m-high artificial waterfall. It takes 10 minutes to travel the 3.5km-long cableway. To get here your only option is to take a cab. Ask to be taken to the *kábelnaya daróga* (in Russian) or *asma ýoly* (in Turkmen). You'd be best off paying the driver to wait as there's no passing traffic here, or it's a 25-minute walk back to the main road. A taxi from the centre of Ashgabat and back including waiting time should be around 10M to 12M.

ACTIVITIES

Akhal-Teke horses are Turkmenistan's pride and joy, and many visitors come to Turkmenistan specifically to ride one. Highly recommended is the **Alaja Farm**, run by Katya Kolestnikova and located in Geok-Dere (also called Nizhny Chuli). This is a professional stable, where the horses are well cared for and well fed (not always the case elsewhere). Riding here costs 80M an hour, and it's normal to ride for four hours in one day, well worth the price for the beautiful golden stallions and some wonderful riding in the canyons around Geok-Dere. Contact Katya (☎ 866 330 362), or call her colleague Gulya Yangebaeva (☎ 42 63 58, 866 340 198); otherwise you can just turn up as the farm operates seven days a week. Take the Geok-Depe road out of Ashgabat and turn left at the sign for Geok-Dere. Continue through the village and Alaja is at the end on the right.

The only ice-skating rink in the country, **Milli Olimpiya Sport Ice Rink** (☎ 48 92 70; Berzengi; admission 1M; 🕑 9am-7pm) is hugely popular with locals so if you want to skate there you may need to call and make a reservation. It's on the Berzengi Hwy, a couple of hundred metres north of the Independence monument.

Bowling and **billiards** are both available on the 3rd floor of the Yimpaş department store (p439).

Swimmers may want to check out the **Olympia Sport Water Palace**, a brand-new pool facility located on Garaşsyzlyk şayoli, opposite the puppet theatre, or they can try the far less impressive Soviet era **Public Swimming Pool** (Görogly köçesi).

SLEEPING

Ashgabat has a range of affordable accommodation options, although it's thin in the midrange category. The government's ongoing obsession with building hotels has left an enormous number of perfectly comfortable but desolate hotels in the suburb of Berzengi. Most tour companies suggest that their clients stay in these, although we've found them depressingly isolated and many of them are overpriced.

Budget

Amanov Homestay (☎ 39 36 72; 2028 köçesi 106; dm 30M) Continuing to defy the odds stacked against it is this eccentric homestay in a neighbourhood of 'old Ashgabat' that was miraculously still standing in early 2010, despite the daily further encroachment of yet more white marble palaces on all sides. Just a five-minute walk from the city's main square, the rooms here are functional and clean, with constant hot water and decent shared toilets. Not an option for people with tourist visas as this is an unofficial hotel, but great for people who are transiting. Taxi drivers still know this street as ulitsa Shaumyana. Ask for Murat when you arrive, and call ahead in case it's been bulldozed.

Hotel Syýahat (☎ /fax 34 45 08; Görogly köçesi 60a; dm/r/lux US$8/30/40; ☒) Rather remotely located, this place isn't a bad deal if you're looking for a cheap-but-official bed. Rooms come in varying states of decay and each seems to have its own wallpaper pattern. The bathrooms are not a highlight. For an extra US$10 you get a half-lux room that comes with TV. Hotel amenities include a bar and sauna. It's located a short taxi ride from downtown, or take bus 10.

Bezirgen Hotel (☎ 34 06 44; Mopra köçesi 45; r/lux US$20/30; ☒) Despite its large exterior, this hotel now has just seven rooms on the 4th floor and they have seen decidedly better days. Despite this, it's not a bad budget option, each room coming with a large balcony, hot water and private bathroom. If you need to pass the time there is a billiards hall in the basement.

Hotel Ashgabat (☎ 35 74 02, 35 74 05; fax 39 47 38; Magtymguly şayoli 74; s/d unrenovated US$20/30, s/d/lux renovated US$35/50/60; ☒) Ashgabat's old Soviet standby has recently given its lobby a marble makeover, but the renovations have thus far only made it to selected rooms. Those that have been redone are comfortable and even cosy, while those that haven't are pretty grim but entirely bearable, given the low price and great location. All rooms have balconies, and those designated lux are made up of two rooms.

Hotel Daýhan (☎ 35 73 44; Azadi köçesi 69; r/lux US$30/40; ☒) This tired old Soviet joint has passable accommodation in a great location. Expect nothing special here – rooms have not been refurbished since Brezhnev's time, but they are perfectly adequate and the bathrooms are not actively revolting. The 'lux' rooms are two normal rooms joined together and are no newer in design or better in upkeep, but they have a TV. All rooms have fridges.

Midrange

Hotel Turkmenistan (☎ 35 05 44/43; fax 35 05 93; Bitrap Turkmenistan şayoli 19; s/d/tr/lux/ste US$40/50/55/60/70; ☒) With the classiest facade in Ashgabat, this old timer has some atmosphere and a cosy feel to its rooms. Redone bathrooms are good and the location can't be beaten.

Hotel Aziya (☎ 48 01 80; Archabil şayoli 31; s/d US$45/50; ☒ P) Rooms here are enormous by local standards, and since a 2009 refit, come complete with flat-screen TV, good Turkmen carpets and eye-wateringly tasteless furniture. Despite the Aziya's large size, there are just eight rooms – the rest of the building is offices. There's an excellent Chinese restaurant here too, which makes this a relatively popular local hangout come the evenings. To get into town, take bus 19 to Görogly köçesi or bus 34 to the station.

Top End

Ak Altyn Hotel (☎ 36 37 00; fax 36 34 94; akaltyn@online.tm; Magtymguly şayoli 141/1; s/d/ste US$70/82/93; ☒ P ☒ ☎) The golden-rust facade of this 109-room hotel a short distance to the west of downtown suggests an era of bygone splendour, and that's just what you get here, though the interior is somewhat more impressive than the exterior. The rooms are anonymously styled and comfortable, and there's an outdoor pool, a nightclub and temperamental wireless access in the lobby (US$5 per hour). Breakfast is included.

ourpick Grand Turkmen Hotel (☎ 51 05 55; fax 51 12 51; grandhtl@online.tm; Görogly köçesi 50; s/d/ste US$85/96/108; ☒ ☐ ☒) Blessed with a fantastic location, the Grand Turkmen is a great choice. The standard rooms are in good shape and all have balconies. The suites are divided into a bedroom and cosy living room. It's a lively downtown place, within easy walking distance of many restaurants and shops, and in-house amenities include a fitness centre and sauna. Before checking in, make sure your room can be properly air-conditioned, as it's not terribly effective in all rooms and windows don't open. The business centre offers internet access for US$7 per hour.

President Hotel (☎ 40 00 00; presidenthotel@online.tm; Archabil şayoli 54; s/d/ste US$180/200/250; ☒ ☐ P ☒) The lobby at Ashgabat's top hotel says it all – the blur of gold, crystal and marble is enough to make even Donatella Versace exclaim 'too much!' – but if you want to impress, this place is for you. Rooms are large and extremely comfortable, and gold effect fittings predominate throughout. Breakfast costs an extra US$10 and internet is available for US$7 per hour, but the two pools, gym and sauna are free for guests. The Italian restaurant on the top floor is one of the best in town.

EATING

With the best range of eating options in the country, Ashgabat may not be Paris, but after a long trip through the desert the hungry traveller will be spoiled for choice. Few restaurants open for breakfast and all shut by 11pm, so it's best to get to a restaurant by 10pm at the latest.

Restaurants

Erzurum (☎ 27 53 71; Shevchenko köçesi 53; mains 8-26M; ⏰ 9am-10.30pm; **E**) Brusque service and no alcohol may put some punters off this simple Turkish eatery, but the food is good and includes *pide* (Turkish pizza) and delicious kebabs. The service is attentive and swift, although it can get very hot in the summer months due to the wood-fired oven.

Pizza Haus (☎ 39 56 00, 39 56 30; Magtymguly şayoli 74; mains 10-40M; ⏰ 9am-11pm; **E**) Just outside the Hotel Ashgabat, this cosy and popular place serves up the best pizza in town, though that's not a huge culinary achievement, admittedly. Try to come before 9pm, as it tends to 'run out' of pizza by then. There's a big non-pizza menu too, and free delivery citywide.

Nissa Truva (☎ 35 22 88; Alishera Navoi köçesi 54a; dishes 10-36M; ⏰ 9am-10.30pm; **E**) The surprisingly posh restaurant behind the decidedly down-to-earth City Pub (right), Nissa Truva offers its customers a wide range of Turkish, European and American dishes. The food is on the greasy side but crowd pleasing nonetheless.

Minara Restaurant (☎ 47 74 64; Altyn Asyr Shopping Centre, Independence Park; mains 12-28M; ⏰ 10am-11pm; **E**) This rather odd restaurant located on the 5th floor of the enormous waterfall-mall in Independence Park is well known locally for its good food. The views are great and the menu is so large it could be used as a weapon. Dishes on offer include an encyclopaedia of salads, lamb with aubergine caviar and Thai chicken with honey and nuts.

Sim Sim (☎ 45 33 43; Andaliba köçesi 50/1; 20-86M; ⏰ 10am-11pm; **E**) Hidden among apartment blocks near the Mir Bazaar, Sim Sim serves some of the best food in the city, though a recent renovation has made its interior rather on the bright side, and a once slightly quirky and cool eatery decidedly mainstream. The

menu is enormous and takes in modern European flavours. Take a taxi to get here.

Coffee House (☎ 39 60 06; Turkmenbashi şayoli 15A; dishes 30-50M; ⏰ 9am-11pm; **E**) One of the best choices in the city, this place is about a lot more than coffee – its inventive yet rather vegetarian-unfriendly menu is of excellent quality (we recommend the Greek salad with fried feta and olive tapenade), and service is unusually friendly. The bar is a masterwork of kitsch and must be seen, its breakfasts are solid and this is a prime hang-out for the foreign community.

Seafood Ayna (☎ 39 10 56; Kemine köçesi 156a; dishes 30-60M; ⏰ 10am-11pm Mon-Sat, 11am-11pm Sun) With its fabulously '90s interior and Yeltsin-era feeling of luxury, Seafood Ayna is one of Ashgabat's best restaurants, flying in all its ingredients from Moscow and Dubai (global warming anyone?). There's a sushi menu on top of the seafood menu, which includes dishes such as lobster thermidor (35M per 100g) and even shark fin soup (to be ordered 48 hours in advance, 24M).

Quick Eats

Kafe Süÿji (☎ 35 57 87; Magtymguly şayoli 113; cake from 5M; ⏰ 8am-11pm) Dessert-lovers will appreciate this cake, ice-cream and coffee shop. Look for the sign 'Tortlar' – as the cafe's name is not displayed on the street.

Shokoladnitsa (☎ 39 09 84; Azadi köçesi 69; cake from 7M; ⏰ 9am-11pm) Nothing to do with the Russian chain of the same name that thrives throughout the former Soviet Union, this lovely place exudes that rarest of traits in Central Asian cafes – charm. Choose from an impressive array of cakes, teas and coffees.

Nurana (☎ 47 45 52; Andalyp köçesi 80, Santa Barbara; mains 10-20M; ⏰ 8am-11pm) This smart and popular canteen in the faintly ridiculously named 'Santa Barbara' neighbourhood between the city centre and Berzengi, serves up delicious kebabs and other Turkish-style delights. There's no alcohol though.

Şazada (☎ 35 09 58; World Trade Centre, Seidi köçesi; 15-40M; ⏰ 10.30am-10.30pm Mon-Sat; **E**) This cosy patisserie and restaurant has its charm, despite being housed in a rather anaemic shopping centre. As well as coffee and cake there's a big menu offering everything from steaks to seafood tempura. There's another branch opposite Hotel Ashgabat (☎ 39 57 64; Turkmenistan Söwda Merkazi, Magtymguly şayoli; open 10.30am to 10.30pm Monday to Saturday).

DRINKING

There are few dedicated bars in Ashgabat, and those that do exist tend to be aimed at the wealthy and foreigners. For a cool drink on a hot summer day, check out one of the patio bars located in First Park. One last reminder: pouring your own drink is bad form, wait for a friend to fill your cup.

Iceberg Bar (☎ 36 18 08; cnr Kemine köçesi & Revfov köçesi; ☾ 10am-11pm) This tranquil beer garden, located behind the circus, serves up frothy pints of microbrewed beer and sizzling sticks of shashlyk.

British Pub (☎ 39 33 36; Görogly köçesi 8; ☾ 10am-4am) If it's pub grub, expats and large mugs of imported beer you're after, then step into British Pub, which has been around for quite a while, albeit under different names and management. The low-lit, dark-wood atmosphere is a bit sombre, but gets going at night with live music and free-flowing alcohol. The menu (dishes US$3) includes burgers, fish and chips, and steak; the fajitas are recommended.

City Pub (☎ 35 22 88; Alishera Navoi köçesi 54a; ☾ 9am-11pm) In a worrying trend, City Pub is another 'real British pub' that while looking nothing like one, has found its way to Central Asia. Like a home from home it contains scarves of every imaginable English football team, and is popular with both locals and expats.

ENTERTAINMENT

Live Music

The best place to try for live music is the British Pub (p439), which hosts local rock bands a few nights a week. Fun, yet extremely tourist-oriented 'folk evenings' are organised by most travel agents for around US$20 per person, including dinner and a full program of traditional dancing and singing.

Nightclubs

Following a fatal nightclub fire in Perm, Russia, in late 2009 all of Ashgabat's nightclubs were closed for safety inspections at the time of writing, with nobody knowing when they would reopen. Some of the most popular places in town before the closures were the following.

Kumush Ay (Florida; ☎ 39 33 36, 39 33 51; Görogly köçesi 8; ☾ 11pm-4am) The biggest, brashest nightclub in Ashgabat is this venue, located above the British Pub and owned by the same people. Note that some taxi drivers may know this place by its alternative name, the Florida Nightclub.

Mukan Club (☎ 35 18 54; First Park; ☾ 10am-11pm) Lively local bar that attracts an enthusiastic crowd of regulars and has a rather arty air.

ABC Disco Club (☎ 48 00 91/92; Archabil şayoli 41, Berzengi; ☾ 11pm-4am) Popular Berzengi disco aimed at a smart local crowd.

Sport

Ashgabat is a great place for horse-lovers. Every Sunday from the end of March until May, then again from the end of August until mid-November, the **Hippodrome** plays host to dramatic Turkmen horse races. It's 5km east of the city centre – either bus 4 down Magtymguly or a 3M taxi ride.

The local football team is Kopet Dag, which plays at the **Kopet Dag stadium**. You should have no trouble picking up a ticket on match days.

Theatres & Concert Halls

Ashgabat offers some excellent venues for watching music and drama productions centred on Turkmen folklore and traditional music. If you'd like to watch Turkmen drama then the **Mollanepes Drama Theatre** (☎ 35 74 63; Magtymguly şayoli 79; admission 15M) is the place to go. Performances are held Wednesday to Sunday at 7pm, although in summer (July to October) the theatre will probably be shut. For Turkmen musical performances, visit the **Magtymguly Theatre** (☎ 35 05 64; Shevchenko köçesi; admission 15M), which has shows Friday to Sunday at 7pm. It is also usually shut during the summer months.

While Turkmen productions flourish, the Russian Theatre is dying a slow death. No longer supported by the government, the once-proud **Pushkin Russian Drama Theatre** (☎ 36 42 81; Magtymguly şayoli 142; admission 3M) has seen its original home demolished and has been moved into a smaller facility near Gunesh Park. Performances are held 7pm Friday to Sunday.

SHOPPING

The biggest and best supermarket in town is the **Yimpaş** (☎ 45 42 66; Turkmenbashi şayoli 54; ☾ 7am-11pm), a huge Turkish shopping complex featuring, among other things, the only escalators in Turkmenistan. Here you can buy everything from frozen lobster to Doritos over several floors. If you want to buy carpets or inexpensive cotton clothing, visit the **Altyn Asyr Marketing Centre**, opposite the Grand Turkmen

TURKMENISTAN

Hotel, which has outlet shops for the carpet and textile industry. The carpets here are sold with all the documentation needed to be exported from the country, making it a lot simpler to buy them here. The best selection is available in **Altyn Göl** (☎ 39 21 56; Görogly köçesi 77; ◷ 9am-7.30pm Mon-Fri, to 6pm Sat & Sun).

If you are looking to buy some locally produced art, try **Muhammed Art Gallery** (☎ 39 59 31; Görogly köçesi 12a), run by artist Allamurat Muhammedov. The unique collection has Muhammedov's own works set around his studio, plus a museum of ancient artefacts. The gallery is next to City Pub (look for the metal gate with the stained-glass horse design). Muhammedov, who speaks English, has displayed his art in galleries worldwide and welcomes foreign visitors in for tea.

The best shopping experiences are to be had at one of Ashgabat's many markets. While Tolkuchka Bazaar (p435) is possibly the most fabulous in Central Asia, there are others in the town centre. The **Russian Bazaar** is great for food of all kinds, especially fresh fruit and vegetables, as well as for stationery. The **Tekke Bazaar** is also recommended for foodstuffs and fruit as well as flowers.

GETTING THERE & AWAY
Air
For information about flights from outside Central Asia, see p515. Within Central Asia, Uzbekistan Airways links Ashgabat and Tashkent in both directions every Wednesday. Turkmenistan Airways flies between Ashgabat and Almaty three times a week (one way 220M).

Domestic Turkmenistan Airlines flights are heavily subsidised to make the ticket prices amazingly low. Consequently, demand is high and flights need to be booked in advance. Timetables also change regularly but there are approximately five daily flights to Dashogus (48M), three daily to Turkmenabat(50M), two daily to Mary (42M) and two daily to Turkmenbashi (54M), as well as regular flights to Kerki (also known as Atamurat, 58M, via Turkmenabat) and three weekly connections to Balkanabat (38M).

AIRLINE OFFICES
The following airlines fly to/from Turkmenistan and have offices in Ashgabat.
Lufthansa (☎ 51 06 84; www.lufthansa.com; Main Concourse, Saparmurat Turkmenbashi Airport) Several weekly flights to Frankfurt via Baku.

Turkish Airlines (☎ 45 66 47/48/49/50; www.turkishairlines.com; Yimpaş Business Centre, Turkmenbashi şayoli 56) Daily flights from İstanbul to Ashgabat.
Turkmenistan Airlines (☎ 39 39 00; www.turkmenistanairlines.com; Magtymguly şayoli 82) From Ashgabat to Abu Dhabi, Almaty, Amritsar, Bangkok, Beijing, Birmingham, Delhi, Dubai, Frankfurt, İstanbul, Kiev, London, Moscow and St Petersburg.
Uzbekistan Airways (☎ 37 82 03; Main Concourse, Saparmurat Turkmenbashi Airport) Flies from Tashkent to Ashgabat and back every Wednesday.

Bus, Marshrutka & Shared Taxi
Bus stands in Ashgabat are organised by destination, and are used by shared taxis and marshrutki as much as buses. Fares for private cars fluctuate by demand and the make of the car – bargain hard and ask several drivers before agreeing to a price.

Transport for Mary and Turkmenabat leaves from a makeshift bus station known to locals as the *Mariiskaya stoyanka* about 3km east of the centre on the main road out of the city. There are marshrutki to Mary (four hours, 12M) and Turkmenabat (6½ hours, 20M). There is also one daily bus to Seraghs from here (five hours, 14M).

Transport for Dashogus and Konye-Urgench leaves from the Dashogus Bazaar (also called Azatlyk Bazaar). A marshrutka to Konye-Urgench costs 28M (seven to eight hours), while a seat in a shared taxi is 30M. Chartering a whole taxi will cost 120M. Prices to Dashogus are slightly higher: regular daily buses take around nine hours for the trip (30M), while marshrutki (35M) make the trip in six hours. A place in a taxi will cost 36M and the trip takes 5½ hours.

Short-distance destinations west of Ashgabat (eg Old Nissa) depart from the western side of Tekke Bazaar. A spot in a minibus to Bagyr (for Old Nissa) costs 0.5M.

Train
The brand new Ashgabat **train station** (☎ 39 38 04) is at the northern end of Turkmenbashi şayoli, a short taxi ride from downtown. Following large investment in the network and a fleet of new Chinese trains, this is now a good way to get around the country if you don't mind taking things slowly. There are daily trains in both directions to Turkmenbashi (15 hours, 4.76M/7.66M), Balkanabat (seven hours, 3.84/6.20M), Mary

(7½ hours, 3.22M/5.24M), Turkmenabat (12 hours, 4.76M/7.66M), and Dashogus (20 hours, 5.08M/9.58M). There are also trains to the Iranian border at Saraghs (nine hours, 3M/5.74M) twice a week in both directions. Prices quoted above are for *platskartny/kupeyny* (hard/soft sleeper). Note that tickets are not sold in the main station building, but in the ticket office a short distance away down the platform.

GETTING AROUND
To/From the Airport
The best way to get into central Ashgabat from the airport is to take a taxi. They are both plentiful and cheap, especially if you choose to go with a shared one. You should expect to pay 10M, but agree before getting in, as drivers are likely to try their luck and ask for much more.

Public Transport
A fleet of new, white **buses** now serves the local populace, making this a quick and cheap way to get around. Tickets cost 0.2M and can be bought on board. There are however no maps or lists of routes, so you'll need to ask locals which bus to take wherever you want to go.

As with almost every other city in the former Soviet Union, you can just hold out your arm on the street and a **car** will soon stop and give you a lift to wherever you need to go. Short hops in the city cost 2M, rising to 3M for longer journeys. Agree a price before you get in, or hand over the money with supreme confidence when you get out. To order an official **taxi** call ☎ 35 34 06. Ashgabat has no metro or tram system.

AROUND ASHGABAT
Nissa & Around
Founded as the capital of the Parthians in the 3rd century BC, in its prime **Nissa** (admission incl guide 22.80M; 8am-sunset) was reinforced with 43 towers that sheltered the royal palace and a couple of temples. It was surrounded by a thriving commercial city. One ruling dynasty replaced another until the 13th century when the Mongols arrived, laid siege to the city and after 15 days razed it to the ground.

The ridges surrounding the plateau were the fortress walls; the steep, modern approach road follows the route of the original entrance. In the northern part of the city are the remains

of a large house built around a courtyard, with wine cellars in nearby buildings.

The main complex on the western side includes a large circular chamber thought to have been a Zoroastrian temple. Adjoining it is the partly rebuilt 'tower' building. On the far side of the western wall are the ruins of a medieval town, today the village of Bagyr.

Coming by car from Ashgabat it is possible to take the road past Berzengi along the presidential highway. On the way you'll pass the **Palace of Orphans**, another bizarre project by Niyazov (who was himself an orphan), with massive futuristic marble buildings, sporting facilities and its own mosque. The children in this village are educated to be government officials.

Gypjak
The boyhood home of Turkmenbashi, Gypjak is 11km west of Ashgabat. The major sight here is the gleaming **Turkmenbashi Ruhy Mosque**; the biggest structure of its kind in Central Asia (it can hold 10,000 worshippers). Four minarets soar above the gold-domed mosque, each 91m tall, representing the year of Turkmenistan's independence. The inscription over the main arch states '*Ruhnama* is a holy book; the Quran is Allah's book' and there are quotes from the *Ruhnama* etched into the minarets. Inside, you can contemplate the grandeur and extravagance of it all while sitting on enormous hand-woven carpets. Next to the mosque is a surprisingly modest **mausoleum** containing the tomb of former President Niyazov. As in life, Turkmenbashi's death is a gold- and marble-intensive affair. He is buried alongside his two brothers and his mother; the marker for his father is ceremonial.

The mosque and mausoleum are clearly visible from the main Ashgabat–Balkanabat road. Parking shouldn't be a problem – there is an enormous underground car park big enough for 400 vehicles.

Geok-Depe
Midway on the main road between Ashgabat and Bakharden is the village of **Geok-Depe** (Green Hill), site of the Turkmen's last stand against the Russians. During the Soviet era the uncommemorated site of the breached earthen fortress, where 15,000 Turkmen died, was part of a collective farm. Today the large, futuristic **Saparmurat Hajji Mosque**, and its

sky-blue domes, stands beside the telltale ridges and burrows. The mosque's name refers to Niyazov's pilgrimage to Mecca, from which he returned with US$10 billion in aid from the Saudi government.

KARAKUM DESERT

The Karakum desert is a sun-scorched expanse of dunes and sparse vegetation in the centre of Turkmenistan. It's Central Asia's hottest desert but manages to support a handful of settlements, including the oasis town of **Jerbent**, 160km north of Ashgabat. A ramshackle collection of homes, battered trucks, yurts and the occasional camel, Jerbent is being slowly consumed by the desert as sands continue to blow off the overgrazed dunes. While it doesn't look like much, the village does offer a glimpse of rural Turkmen life, and you can watch traditional cooking methods and sit down for tea inside a yurt.

If you have time, money and a sense of adventure, a travel agency can organise 4WD trips further into the desert towards ever more remote villages. As this requires much time, extra fuel and possibly a backup vehicle, you'll need to request that your guide lists agreed details of your trip on the itinerary. Off-road trips usually require at least two vehicles, which costs around US$200 per day (depending on how many people are travelling, but this price is for groups of three or four people).

Although the village of **Darvaza** was demolished in 2004 on the orders of President Niyazov, who apparently didn't like what he saw while inspecting the new Ashgabat–Dashogus highway, you'll still see it marked by the road on some maps. Slowly local herders are returning to the area, if not to the site of the village itself, which is well worth a visit for a chilling illustration of Niyazov's total power – nothing of the village survives save the odd vehicle chassis and the ubiquitous bread ovens, considered too holy in Turkmenistan to be destroyed.

Darvaza, whether the village of the same name continues to exist or not, is the halfway post between the capital and Konye-Urgench. It's also at the heart of the Karakum desert and draws visitors for the **Darvaza Gas Craters**, one of Turkmenistan's most unusual sights. Apparently the result of Soviet-era gas exploration in the 1950s, the three craters are artificial. One has been set alight and blazes with an incredible strength that's visible from miles away. The other two craters contain bubbling mud and water. However, on a visit here in April 2010, President Berdymukhamedov ordered that the burning gas crater be extinguished to enable exploration for gas in the area, so that while at the time of research the crater was still accessible, it's important to check the latest news with a travel agency in Ashgabat.

The fire crater is of course the most impressive, and it's best seen at night, when the blazing inferno can only be compared to the gates of hell. There is a naturally sheltered camping place behind the small hill, just south of the crater. Getting to the crater is an off-road ride and drivers frequently get lost or get stuck in the dunes. There is no one around to give directions, so make sure you go with somebody who knows the way. If you intend to walk from the road, think twice. While the walk only takes two hours through the dunes, you'll have to spend the night here, as finding your way back to the road without the reference of a huge burning crater is very hard. Even in daylight you may get lost – it's much better to pay for a tour. There are no hotels in the area, but most of the chaikhanas that line the main road just north of the turn-off to the crater offer beds for the night, provide meals and even sell petrol. As there are no signposts for either the turn-off or the chaikhanas, the landmark to look for is where the train line crosses the main road. If coming from Ashgabat, the turn-off for the crater is about 1km before the railway line, and the chaikhanas are a few kilometres afterwards. If you plan to camp at the crater, make sure you sleep a good distance back from its edges, as breathing in the gas all night long can make you very ill.

All buses and marshrutki heading from Ashgabat to both Konye-Urgench and Dashogus go through Jerbent and pass nearby the Darvaza Gas Craters on the main road.

WESTERN TURKMENISTAN

Driving west from Ashgabat, the main road skirts the edges of the Kopet Dag and the Iranian border before opening up into a vast, featureless landscape that is wonderfully Central Asian. This region of haunting moonscapes, ruined cities and minority tribes such as the mountain-dwelling Nokhurians is often raced through on the way between Ashgabat and the boat to Azerbaijan, though for those with time and inclination, it's possible to see some of the country's best natural phenomena including the Kopet Dag mountains, the Yangykala Canyon, and the ruins of Dekhistan.

KÖW ATA UNDERGROUND LAKE

Like entering Milton's underworld, only with changing rooms and a staircase, a visit to the **Köw Ata Underground Lake** (admission 40M; ☿ dawn-dusk) is a unique experience. You enter a cave at the base of a mountain and walk down a staircase, 65m underground, which takes you into a wonderfully sulphurous subterranean world. At the bottom awaits a superb lake of clear water naturally heated to about 36°C. Underground swimming is one of Central Asia's more unusual activities, and worth it if you don't mind the steep entry fee – particularly annoying given that the facilities here are all in poor condition.

Follow the main road to Balkanabat from Ashgabat for the best part of an hour; the turn-off to the lake is clearly marked to the left with a large sign for Köw Ata. By marshrutka or bus to Balkanabat or Turkmenbashi you could easily ask the driver to stop at the Köw Ata turn-off, although it's a good 90-minute walk from the road. There's a good shashlyk restaurant on site here, making this a great lunch stop.

NOKHUR

Wedged into the mountains just a few kilometres from Iran, this village offers a unique opportunity to hike in the hills and soak up some rural life. Nokhur was once a byword among Soviet Turkmen for everything rural and backwards. Thanks to their isolation, Nokhuris have retained unique traditions and a particular dialect of Turkmen. They claim ancestry from Alexander the Great's army and prefer to marry among themselves rather than introduce new genes to the tribe.

There are two sights in this fascinating village. One is the town's **cemetery**, where each grave is protected by the huge horns of the mountain goats that locals consider sacred – indeed many houses in the village have a goat's skull hanging on a stick outside to ward

off evil spirits. You should not enter the cemetery, as it's for locals only, although photography is perfectly acceptable. A short walk beyond the cemetery is **Qyz Bibi**, a spiritualist-Muslim shrine, where people from all over the country come on pilgrimage. Qyz Bibi was the pre-Islamic patroness of women and the goddess of fertility. She is believed to dwell in the cave (the entrance of which is just 30cm to 40cm in diameter) at the end of a winding pathway that passes a huge, ancient tree where pilgrims tie colourful material in the hopes of conceiving a child.

There are four impressive waterfalls in the mountains beyond Nokhur, all of which can be visited by hiring a UAZ 4WD in Nokhur (ask your guide to ask around for you). The routes are fairly arduous, but great fun for day-tripping and taking in the impressive scenery.

For accommodation, it is possible to stay with a local family. The best homestay is with Gaib and Enebai, a local couple who welcome guests to their large mountain house (complete with satellite TV). They charge 45M per person per night. Ask anywhere for Kinomekanik Gaib – he was the village's cinema projectionist before he retired.

There is a daily bus from Tekke Bazaar in Ashgabat to Nokhur (3M, two hours).

PARAU BIBI

The **Mausoleum of Parau Bibi** has been an important place of pilgrimage since ancient times. According to lore, Parau Bibi was a virtuous young woman living in the area. During a time of enemy siege, Parau Bibi prayed that the mountain would open up and swallow her, lest she be carried off by the barbarian tribes. The mountain heard her pleas and accordingly engulfed her in the nick of time.

Locals later honoured her selfless act by creating a fertility shrine on the spot. The small white tomb, built from a cave in the cliffs, contains offerings such as model cribs, indicating the desire of the pilgrim. It is located at the top of a staircase 269 steps high, which you trudge up with other devotees. The mystical surrounds are enhanced by the steppe behind you, stretching endlessly into the distance.

Nearby, on the hillside, you can spot holes in the ground, delineating the underground *karyz* (irrigation canals). A century

TURKMENISTAN

ago there were more than 500 such canals in Turkmenistan, but only 10 remain today.

The turn-off for Parau Bibi is 19km west of Serdar – follow the road another 8km to reach Parau Bibi. If it's late it's possible to spend the night under the pilgrim tents, although it does stay busy most of the night, so don't expect to get much sleep.

BALKANABAT
☎ 222 / pop 110,000

Tucked below a range of imposing mountains and the only sign of civilisation as far as the eye can see, Balkanabat is the logical stopover on the long haul across western Turkmenistan. Oil was discovered in the vicinity in 1874 and a small refinery was built, only to be abandoned for 50 years after being bankrupted by competition from Baku. Today no oil remains in the town itself, though it's still a small centre for the oil industry, as reserves nearby are still to be exhausted.

Originally called Nebit Dag ('Oil Mountains'), Balkanabat is a staging point for trips to Dekhistan and Yangykala Canyon, though annoyingly accommodation ranges between wretched and plush with nothing in-between.

The main axis is Magtymguly şayoli, running east–west and parallel to the railway. At its midpoint is Niyazov Sq, watched over by a lonely statue of the former president. Note that Balkanabat uses both street names and block (kvartal) numbers.

Balkansyyahat (☎ 7 70 39; Hotel Nebitçi; Kvartal 198) is a travel agency that, while mainly organising trips abroad for locals, can organise trips to Dekhistan or Balkan Mountain at somewhat inflated prices (a trip to Dekhistan costs around US$200).

Sights
There's nothing worth seeing in Balkanabat, but if in a bizarre set of circumstances you need to pass some time here, then the largely uninteresting **Regional History Museum** (☎ 4 91 26; Gurtgeldi Annayew köçesi; admission 2.5M; ☒ 9am-6pm) is for you. It contains ethnography, archaeology and wildlife exhibits of the Balkan region including a display of local carpets (look for the anchor designs, symbols of the Caspian-dwelling Yomut Turkmen). There are also photos of Dekhistan to whet your appetite if you are headed that way. The museum is

located opposite the Cultural Palace of Oil Workers.

On the west side of the city, you can take a look at the pretty **Russian Orthodox Church**, which stands just north of the defunct oil rig. Heading west, just off the road to Turkmenbashi, is the **Monument to the Builders of Nebit Dag**, a handsome concrete statue of caravan men urging forward their obstinate camel in the midst of a fierce sandstorm.

Sleeping & Eating
Nebitdag Hotel (☎ 6 71 92; Kvartal 115; dm 4M) This may be the town's cheap option – and how – but it's anything but cheerful and will appal even the most seasoned backpackers. Rooms are just about functional, with four uncomfortable beds and a balcony in each. The real highlight is the bathrooms, where disgusting showers spew forth cold water and the smell from the toilets will haunt you. Make sure if you do stay here that you're as far from them as possible.

Hotel Nebitchi (☎ 7 70 31; www.balkansyyakhat.com; Kvartal 198; s/d/ste US$70/100/150; ☒ 🖳 Ⓟ 🖳) As if it were needed, here is further evidence of the madness of the Turkmenistan tourism industry – one of the country's best hotels has been built in a place almost nobody visits. The 38 rooms are spacious, extremely comfortable and come with cable TV and minibars. The enormous place is empty though, and you'll usually be the only person in the bar or restaurant. There's also a loud nightclub downstairs that can make some rooms noisy. The pool is outdoors and only open in summer, while the internet hadn't been working for two months when we stayed here.

Victoria (Kvartal 197; dishes 2-20M; ☒ 9am-11pm) Generally held to be the best eatery in town (albeit with a competition of approximately one), Victoria has a cosy downstairs section where it serves up tasty Russian and Turkmen dishes, including a large selection of sturgeon. Rather surprisingly there's a little swimming pool on the rather makeshift roof terrace, so you can absorb Balkanabat in style.

Ruslan Restaurant (☎ 7 07 50; Kvartal 200; dishes 10-20M; ☒ 11am-11pm) The only other option in town is this standard-issue Turkmen restaurant that does a good range of food from veal schnitzel to shashlyk. In the evenings you are sometimes treated to live music acts. Expect service to be on the surly side.

Getting There & Away

The wonderful old Soviet **train station** (☎ 7 09 35) is 1km west and 400m south of Niyazov Sq. There is one train a day to Turkmenbashi (3½ hours), and two to Ashgabat (seven hours), one of which continues to Dashogus.

Marshrutkas and shared taxis gather in the lot in front of the train station. These travel to Ashgabat (30M per place, 120M per car, six hours) throughout the day. The zip to Turkmenbashi costs 20M per place and 80M per car and takes around an hour and half.

Turkmenistan Airlines flies between Balkanabat and Ashgabat (38M) on Tuesday, Thursday and Saturday. The airport is 2km east of the city. The **booking office** is on Magtymguly şayoli in the centre of town.

DEKHISTAN

If you seek the true definition of a ruin, then look no further than the mysterious land of Dekhistan, once a thriving Silk Road state whose grand capital Misrian rivalled Merv and Konye-Urgench. The city-state even managed to revive itself after destruction by the Mongols, finally collapsing when the region suffered an ecological catastrophe sometime in the 15th century. The forests of the Kopet Dag to the east had been exploited for centuries until the water supply failed and the well-watered slopes finally became a barren, deeply eroded lunar landscape, one that still dominates the region today.

Dekhistan lies deep in the barren mudflats south of Balkanabat, midway between the tumbledown villages of Bugdayly and Madau. Not much remains on the 200-hectare site of **Misrian** (N 38°15.975′, E 54°37.322′), apart from two truncated 20m-high **minarets** from the 11th and 13th centuries, and the decorated remains of a **portal** that once stood before the Mosque of the Khorezmshah Mohammed. Rudimentary excavations here have also revealed the remains of several caravanserais that once served the Silk Road traders. The entire site is littered with porcelain, coins and other fragments of life at the time of the city's collapse. If you're an archaeologist looking for your life's work, this Klondike of unearthed treasure is worth considering. Much of the city is literally buried in sand, clay and mud with dune-like lumps that were once houses lying all over the place, while the city walls have been reduced to giant verges surrounding the site. Inside the citadel a small section

of the city has been excavated, revealing what is thought to have been a medressa. You can climb both minarets for good views of the city's layout, though this is a guano-intensive experience.

The **cemetery**, 7km north of Dekhistan at Mashat, features five semi-ruined mausoleums, including the Shir-Kabir Mosque-Mausoleum, the earliest mosque in the country, being slowly restored and excavated on our last visit.

Unless you have your own vehicle, Dekhistan is difficult to get to, and even if you do, you'll need a guide. Public transport is nonexistent, and although you should be able to get a taxi from Balkanabat, bear in mind that very few locals even know of the site's existence. On the road south of Bugdayly there's a single green marker pointing you off road (there's nothing written on it) – from here, in good weather, you should be able to see the minaret towers around 6km away. In dry weather you can make this trip in a normal car with no problems, but a 4WD is needed if there's been any recent rain, and after heavy rains Dekhistan is all but unreachable in any vehicle.

GOZLI ATA & YANGYKALA CANYON

A respected Sufi teacher in the early 14th century, Gozli Ata had a large following until his untimely death at the hands of Mongol invaders. His **mausoleum** (N 40°20.051′, E 54°29.249′), located in a natural depression of rocky desert, is now a popular place of pilgrimage. Gozli Ata's wife is buried in an adjacent mausoleum and according to custom visitors must first pray at her last resting place. A cemetery has sprung up nearby where gravestones contain a notch in the top where water can collect to 'feed' the soul of the deceased. Gozli Ata is 135km north of Balkanabat; an experienced driver is needed to find it.

From the turn-off to Gozli Ata (marked with a 9km sign), another road continues north to **Yangykala Canyon** (N 40°27.656′, E 54°42.816′). With bands of pink, red and yellow rock searing across the sides of steep canyon walls, Yangykala is a breathtaking sight and one of the most spectacular natural attractions in Turkmenistan. Just as alluring as the beautiful views is its solitary isolation in the desert; few Turkmen are aware of its existence.

Canyons and cliffs slash for 25km towards the Garagogazgol basin and lie approximately

165km north of Balkanabat and about 160km east of Turkmenbashi, making it easy to slot the canyon between the two cities. It's possible to camp on the plateau above the canyon, although it can get windy here. While most tour companies run trips here, not all include it on their standard itineraries, so make inquiries when planning your trip.

TURKMENBASHI
☎ 243 / pop 60,000

Turkmenbashi is the end of the line for travellers heading on to the Caucasus, and the first taste of Turkmenistan for those arriving on the ferry from Baku. Either way, it serves its function fairly well – there's nothing much to actually keep you here for any length of time, but it's a pleasant and friendly town with a more Russian feel than most Turkmen cities and an enjoyable Caspian Sea location.

The first settlement here, Krasnovodsk, was established when a unit of Russian troops under Prince Alexander Bekovich set ashore in 1717 with the intention of marching on Khiva. They chose this spot because it was close to the place where the Oxus River (now the Amu-Darya) had once drained into the Caspian Sea, and the dry riverbed provided the best road across the desert. But the mission failed, Bekovich lost his head and the Russians didn't come back for more than 150 years. In the late 1800s, Krasnovodsk grew in importance with the arrival of the Trans-Caspian railroad. Thousands of Japanese POWs were dumped here after WWII and ordered to construct roads and buildings. Since then the town has become somewhat cosmopolitan, with a mix of Russians, Turkmen, Azeris, Turks and a handful of Western oil workers.

Sights

The **Museum of Regional History** (☎ 2 59 94; off Garayeva köçesi; admission 1.85M, guided tour 5.70M; ⊙ 9am-1pm & 2-6pm) is located in a quaint old structure west of Magtymguly Sq. The collections include disintegrating taxidermy, some interesting maps, models of the Caspian Sea, traditional Turkmen clothing and a yurt. In the last room a photo exhibition recalls an expedition made in 1936 by a group of fishermen from Krasnovodsk to Moscow.

There's a charming **Russian Orthodox church** set back from the sea front, a testament to the city's past as a Russian fortress town. All that remains of the fortress itself are the gates – distinct creations with red stars mounted about them – which can be found in the park below the museum.

Japanese travellers often pay their respects to their dead countrymen at a **Japanese memorial** located near the airport. The monument commemorates the thousands of Japanese POWs who spent years in Krasnovodsk constructing roads and buildings. A Japanese graveyard is nearby.

The beaches near town are a bit rocky and not great for swimming, considering the proximity of the town oil refinery. There are better beaches at Awaza, 8km west of the city. North of Awaza it's a 20-minute drive to some spectacular sand dunes, sea views and an abandoned lighthouse, but you'll need a 4WD and a driver who knows the way.

Sleeping

Hotel Hazar (☎ 2 13 64, fax 2 46 36; Azadi köçesi; s/d 55/85M; 🐾) Any foreigner who stays at this Soviet-era hotel needs to produce a certificate from Turkmenbaşybank proving that your Manats were purchased there. The rooms aren't bad value, though. All were renovated in 2009, although many still have nasty old bathrooms. Another strange touch is that one person sleeping in a double room is 42M, cheaper than taking a single room. Enjoy!

Hotel Çarlak (☎ 2 13 64, fax 2 13 75; Bahri-Hazar köçesi; s/d/ste incl full board 140/200/285M; 🐾 🛜 Ⓟ 🛆) The newest hotel in Turkmenbashi is this flashy white marble number overlooking the naval base and the Caspian. The rooms are good and of international business standard, though some are a little on the small side. Wireless is available throughout the hotel for 14M per 10 megabytes (whatever that means) and the vast lobby portrait of the President in naval get-up and binoculars is priceless.

Hotel Turkmenbashi (☎ /fax 2 17 17, 2 13 14; Bahri-Hazar köçesi; s/d/ste US$100/120/150; 🐾 🖥 Ⓟ 🛆) Four-star-quality rooms with sea views and a range of facilities make this a great choice, especially from October to May when prices fall 50%. The 90-room hotel includes a gym, bar, decent restaurant, laundry and internet access. It's about 2km west of the station, on the road to Awaza.

Eating

At first glance Turkmenbashi is a culinary desert – finding a restaurant is a tough call,

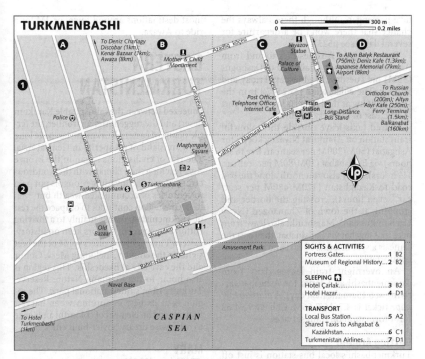

TURKMENBASHI

SIGHTS & ACTIVITIES
Fortress Gates........................1 B2
Museum of Regional History...2 B2

SLEEPING
Hotel Çarlak..........................3 B2
Hotel Hazar...........................4 D1

TRANSPORT
Local Bus Station....................5 A2
Shared Taxis to Ashgabat &
Kazakhstan.........................6 C1
Turkmenistan Airlines.............7 D1

but there are actually several decent options, though few are conveniently located. The colourful **Kenar Bazaar**, also called Cheryomushki, is located on Magtymguly şayoli in the western part of town. You can buy black caviar here for around US$400 per 500g.

Deniz Kafe (☎ 2 88 51; Azadi köçesi 54; mains 4-28M; 8am-11pm; E) Definitely the best place in town, this small, Turkish-run cafe is a delightful find by local standards, with a pleasant decor, friendly (if rather easily confused) waitresses and excellent meals. Their kebab with yoghurt and the lentil soup are both excellent. To get here simply follow Azadi köçesi 1.5km up the road from the Hotel Hazar.

Altyn Asyr Kafe (☎ 2 07 52; Gahryman Atamurat Niyazov şayoli; mains 5-15M; noon-11pm) This standard-issue Russian-style restaurant is conveniently located 600m east of the train station and fills up in the evenings. The menu is Russian through and through – chicken Kiev, beef Stroganov and sturgeon dominate. It's housed in a pink building on the embankment.

Altyn Balyk Restaurant (☎ 2 64 49; Puşkin köçesi 21; mains 6-35M; 10am-11pm) The golden fish,

or *zolotaya ribka* as local Russian speakers know it, is now housed in a large building a short distance out of the immediate town centre. The dining experience is posh Russian, complete with the inevitable live music each evening. Think pink walls, a disco ball and 'Lady in Red'. The brilliantly translated menu runs from 'amateur chicken' to pizza.

Entertainment
Deniz Charlagy Discobar (☎ 2 56 53; Magtymguly şayoli; entry 20M; 11pm-4am) The city's main nightclub is a great place for a night out with locals. It plays a mix of Turkish and Russian pop. There is plenty of alcohol upstairs and a small restaurant downstairs.

There's also a popular nightclub with pool tables in the basement of the **Hotel Turkmenbashi** (Bahri-Hazar köçesi; entry 10M; 11pm-3am), which is popular with foreign oil workers and local prostitutes.

Getting There & Away
From the Turkmenbashi **ferry terminal** (☎ 2 44 91) there are frequent untimetabled cargo ships to Baku in Azerbaijan, most of which

take passengers, although there's always the chance that there won't be a departure for several days (see p523).

Turkmenistan Airlines flies to and from Ashgabat (54M) twice daily and to Dashogus (58M) on Tuesday, Wednesday, Friday and Sunday. The **airline office** (☎ 2 54 74) is in the same building as the Hotel Hazar. The airport is 8km east of the ferry terminal.

Shared taxis leave outside the colourful train station on Atamurat Niyazov köçesi for Ashgabat (50M/200M per seat/car, five to six hours) via Balkanabat (20M/80M per seat/car, 1½ hours). They also run north along the bad road to Kazakhstan (120M/480M per seat/car, seven hours), crossing the border and stopping at the town of Zhanaozen (Novy Uzen in Russian). Marshrutki also leave from here to Ashgabat via Balkanabat; they cost the same as a seat in a shared taxi and are far less comfortable.

An overnight train leaves daily from Turkmenbashi at 3.35pm for Ashgabat (arriving at 6.15am the next day). A *platskartny/kupe* ticket is 4.76M/7.66M. Call ☎ 9 94 62 for information on train services.

Getting Around

Turkmenbashi's local bus station is just off Balkan köçesi, about 500m west of the museum. From here you can catch infrequent transport to the airport, the seaport and Awaza at prices that are almost negligible. Taxis also hang around here, as well as near the train station, and charge around 1M for most destinations around town, or 2M for a ride to Awaza.

EASTERN TURKMENISTAN

Squeezed between the inhospitable Karakum desert and the rugged Afghan frontier, the fertile plains of eastern Turkmenistan have long been an island of prosperity in Central Asia. The rise of civilisations began in the Bronze Age, reaching their climax with the wondrous city of Merv. The invading Mongols put paid to centuries of accumulated wealth but even today the region continues to outpace the rest of Turkmenistan, thanks mainly to a thriving cotton business. For visitors keen on history, eastern Turkmenistan offers some of the best sights in the country, including Merv, Gonur and the cave city at Ekedeshik. This region is also home to the Kugitang Nature Reserve, Turkmenistan's finest national park. The region is at its best in autumn when harvest festivals add an element of colourful ambience to otherwise dreary Soviet-built cities.

MARY

☎ 522 / pop 123,000

The capital of the Mary region is a somewhat spartan Soviet confection of administrative buildings and vast gardens disproportionate to the size of the city. Mary (pronounced mah-rih) is also the centre of the major cotton-growing belt, which gives the city an air of prosperity; the markets bustle on weekends and commerce is surprisingly brisk.

Mary's history dates back to the 1820s when the Tekke Turkmen erected a fortress here, preferring the site to ancient Merv, 30km east. In 1884, a battalion of Russian troops, led by one Lieutenant Alikhanov, convinced the Turkmen to hand over control of the fort before things got bloody. Cotton production quickly picked up and the guarantee of continued wealth came in 1968 when huge natural gas reserves were found 20km west of the city.

Apart from the excellent regional museum there is nothing much of note to see in the town itself, although it makes for a handy base to explore the nearby ancient cities of Gonur and Merv. The city has accommodation for all budgets, good transport links and some of the best shashlyk joints in the country.

KARABOGAS

From Turkmenbashi there is a good road to Karabogas (formerly Bekdash), with spectacular views of the Caspian Sea and the Karabogas Basin. En route you cross a bridge that spans the 5km-long channel which connects the Caspian Sea and the inland gulf. The distance between the bridge and Karabogas town is around 60km.

Karabogas is a nearly-abandoned Soviet industrial city, filled with vacant apartment blocks gutted for anything usable. The city is surrounded by surreal-looking salt lakes; the remnants of a once profitable sodium sulphate business gone belly up. From here is a 40-minute drive to the Kazakhstan border on a rough dirt track.

Orientation & Information

The town's main thoroughfare is Mollanepes şayoli, where you'll find the decaying seven-storey Hotel Sanjar and the train station at the heart of the Soviet town. Further down Mollanepes is the modern town, replete with vast white marble buildings. Here you'll find the Zelyony (Green) Bazaar and the Murgab River. Crossing the river en route to Merv you'll see the enormous Turkmenbashi Hajji mosque and the new Mary Regional Museum building. The central **post office** is 1km east of the Sanjar off Mollanepes, while the central **telephone office** is 50m northwest of the post office, with the town's **internet cafe** (per hr 6M; 9am-1pm & 2-6pm Mon-Sat;) opposite.

Yevgenia Golubeva (6 03 05, 866 393 958; evgenia golubeva@yahoo.com) is an experienced, English-speaking tour guide, who used to be the deputy director of the Mary Museum. She can organise highly recommended tours to nearby Merv and Gonur.

The **OVIR** (State Service for the Registration of Foreign Citizens; 4 50 40, 4 41 22; Turkmenbashi köçesi; 9am-6pm Mon-Fri, 9am-1pm Sat) handles registration.

Sights

The highlight of the city is the collection of the excellent **Mary Regional Museum** (3 99 55; admission 11.40M, camera 20M; 10am-1pm & 2-5pm Tue-Sun) which, at the time of writing, was still housed in the 100-year-old mansion built by a Russian brick baron near the river. However, with a new (you guessed it) white-marble palace being finished off to house the museum at the time of writing, the staff were expecting to move to the new premises next to the Hotel Margush some time in 2010. There are several English-speaking guides working here, and a tour is included in the ticket price.

Wherever the collection is, make an effort to see it. There's an extensive ethnography section, including a large collection of Turkmen jewellery, carpets, stuffed animals, a fully decorated yurt and pottery from the time of the Mongol occupation. But best of all is the archaeological section, bringing together arte-facts found at both Merv and Margush, including pottery, weapons, household implements and jewellery. The fine quality and design of household items from Margiana is striking and rivals the collection of the National Museum in Ashgabat. A skeleton of a Margiana priestess was once also on display, though a series of deaths and misfortunes among museum staff

persuaded them to have the original returned to where it was found.

The other main sight in Mary is **Pokrovskaya Church**, a handsome red-brick affair built in 1900. The church is surrounded by pleasant parkland and its interior is crammed with religious icons. Walk a few hundred metres west and you'll spot a **MiG aeroplane** on display, a legacy of the Soviet period. To get to the church and aeroplane, head east on Mollanepes şayoli, cross the bridge over the Murgab River, take the first left over the rail-road tracks, and after two streets you'll see the MiG on your right.

In the town centre there are several **statues** of former President Niyazov; the seated statue on the corner of Saparmurat Niyazov köçesi and Gurbansoltan Eje köçesi bears a striking resemblance to US President Kennedy. Behind the statue is a mosaic of a Turkmen carpet.

You can get your shopping done at the enormous **Zelyony Bazaar** (Mollanepes şayoli). This is a great place to stock up on fresh fruit and just about anything else you need. If you're still looking for something to do, you can

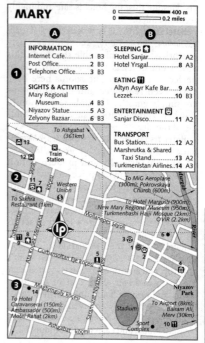

MARY

0 — 400 m
0 — 0.2 miles

INFORMATION	
Internet Cafe	1 B3
Post Office	2 B3
Telephone Office	3 B3

SIGHTS & ACTIVITIES	
Mary Regional Museum	4 B3
Niyazov Statue	5 A3
Zelyony Bazaar	6 B3

SLEEPING	
Hotel Sanjar	7 A2
Hotel Yrsgal	8 A3

EATING	
Altyn Asyr Kafe Bar	9 A3
Lezzet	10 B3

ENTERTAINMENT	
Sanjar Disco	11 A2

TRANSPORT	
Bus Station	12 A2
Marshrutka & Shared Taxi Stand	13 A2
Turkmenistan Airlines	14 A3

To Ashgabat (361km)

Train Station

Western Union

To Sakhra Restaurant (1km)

To MiG Aeroplane (300m); Pokrovskaya Church (600m)

To Hotel Margush (900m); New Mary Regional Museum (950m); Turkmenbashi Hajji Mosque (2km); OVIR (2.2km)

Mollanepes şayoli

Gurbansoltan Eje köçesi

Saparmurat Niyazov köçesi

Magtymguly köçesi

To Hotel Caravanserai (150m); Ambassador (500m); Motel Rahat (2km)

Ashgabat köçesi

Niyazov Park

To Airport (8km); Bairam Ali; Merv (30km)

Stadium

Sport Complex

TURKMENISTAN

walk around **Niyazov Park**, which contains some amusement rides, bumper cars and a handful of cafes. The park is a short walk east of the museum.

Sleeping

Hotel Caravanserai (☎ 3 34 64; Nisimi köçesi 25; 30M per person) A private hotel run in the house of a Turkmen family, this is definitely the place to come for some local atmosphere, though it's only an option for those on transit visas, as you can't be registered here. Several large rooms with multiple beds in them surround a pleasant courtyard. The facilities are shared, but are clean and have hot water.

Motel Rahat (☎ 6 42 04; Serkhetabat köçesi; r/lux 60/90M; ☒ Ⓟ) Despite the slightly out of the way location (2km from the town centre, a 1M taxi ride), the Rahat offers surprisingly excellent value for money. The spacious rooms are built around a courtyard of lemon trees and each comes with TV and a decent bathroom. The motel is built next to a truck stop on the road to the southern border and as such attracts plenty of Iranian truck drivers who can be found most nights in the bawdy bar downstairs, along with a gaggle of local hookers. Despite this, the hotel is safe and highly recommended.

Hotel Sanjar (☎ 7 10 76; Mollanepes şayoli 58; s/d/tr US$30/40/45, lux US$50-70; ☒) Outrageously overpriced for its miserable standards, this Soviet-era hotel is your standard pile of neglected concrete. The rooms here have never been renovated and the bathrooms are simply ghastly. The only real reason to stay here is the location, smack in the middle of the city.

Hotel Yrsgal (☎ 7 21 27/31; Ata Kopek Mergana köçesi 2; s/d/tr/q incl breakfast 109/166/182/220M; ☒ ▣) This friendly and modern option in the centre of town is pricey for what it is, but offers comfortable, clean rooms with good bathrooms and little seating areas by the windows, many of which have lots of light streaming in. There's internet access for 6M per hour.

Hotel Margush (☎ 6 03 86/7; fax 6 03 88; Gowshuthat köçesi 20; s/d/ste US$40/60/150; ☒ ▣ Ⓟ ☎) Mary's only top-end accommodation is located near the Murgab River, 1km east of the town centre, and despite being open for five years, it still feels strangely empty and lacking any atmosphere. The 30 rooms are built around a pleasant lobby, and each room contains a TV,

fridge and small desk. Other facilities, such as the sauna, fitness centre, swimming pool and internet cafe, are extra.

Eating & Drinking

Altyn Asyr Kafe Bar (☎ 7 09 49; cnr Turkmenistan şayoli & Gurbansoltan Eje köçesi; mains 1-6M; ☒ 9am-10.30pm) A friendly and atmospheric spot in the centre of town that serves up delicious shashlik, the Altyn Asyr may just be the best place in town for a meal. There's a pleasant patio to sit out on by the barbeque.

Sakhra (☎ 7 49 95; Magtymguly köçesi 40; mains 2-6M; ☒ 9am-11pm) This appears to be a vodka shop when you enter, but has two dining rooms that serve good Turkmen and Russian dishes, running the gauntlet from shashlyk and goulash to *kharcho* (Georgian meat soup) and even vegetarian dishes.

Lezzet (☎ 3 57 67; Ashgabat köçesi; mains 3-6M; ☒ 7am-9pm) This Turkish restaurant is rather too brightly lit and doesn't serve alcohol but, despite these flaws, it serves up passable kebabs and other Turkish dishes, albeit with noticeable Turkmen accents. The restaurant also delivers orders over 30M.

Entertainment

Ambassador (Podeby köçesi; admission 3M; ☒ noon-3.30am) This anomalously rowdy place for Turkmenistan is definitely the place to head for if you want a night out. Though closure always threatens it, this strip and dance club is the only place you can drink late in town.

Sanjar Disco (Mollanepes şayoli; admission 2M; ☒ 8-11pm) This tamer option, next to the eponymous hotel, can be a fun evening out in a dark room with ear-splitting music full of local teenagers.

Getting There & Away

Mary is 3½ hours by car from Ashgabat and two hours from Turkmenabat. There are three scheduled daily buses to Ashgabat (12.60M, four hours) from the modern **bus station** (☎ 7 1171), and one 2pm departure to Turkmenabat (7.40M, three hours). There is also a daily bus at midday to Serkhetabat (6M, six hours) on the Afghan border (p466). Shared taxis and marshrutki leave from a lot next to the bus station. Marshrutki link Mary to both Ashgabat (12M, four hours) and Turkmenabat (10M, 2½ hours), while shared taxis run the same routes, costing 20M/80M per seat/car for both destinations.

Mary's modern **train station** (☎ 9 22 45) has trains to Ashgabat (*platskartny/kupe* 3.22/5.24M, 7½ hours), as well as to Turkmenabat (3.61/6.51M, four hours). There is no left-luggage facility, but the station does have an international phone office and exchange facilities.

Turkmenistan Airlines (☎ 3 27 77; Magtymguly köçesi 11) has at least two flights per day to Ashgabat (42M). If time is short, you could even take the morning flight, visit Merv and return on the same day to Ashgabat. The airport is 8km east of the city, on the road to Merv.

MERV

In its heyday it was known as Marv-i-shahjahan, 'Merv – Queen of the World', and it stood alongside Damascus, Baghdad and Cairo as one of the great cities of the Islamic world. A major centre of religious study and a lynchpin on the Silk Road, its importance to the commerce and sophistication of Central Asia cannot be underestimated. Today, almost nothing of the metropolis remains.

Before the sons of Chinggis Khan laid waste to the great city and slaughtered its population, Merv had been a melting pot of religious faiths and ethnic groups. Its buildings of fired brick towered over the green oasis, and included palaces, mosques, caravanserais and thousands of private homes.

The scattered ruins left today include fortified walls, brick foundations and gazillions of shards of pottery. It became a Unesco World Heritage site in 1999 and is deservedly considered the most impressive historical site in the country. Merv can easily be visited on a day trip from Mary but it's essential to have your own transport, and preferably a guide to make sense of it all.

History

Merv was known as Margiana or Margush in Alexander the Great's time. Under the Persian Sassanians, it was considered religiously liberal, with significant populations of Christians, Buddhists and Zoroastrians cohabiting peacefully. As a centre of power, culture and civilisation, Merv reached its greatest heights during the peak of the Silk Road in the 11th and 12th centuries, when the Seljuq Turks made it their capital. Legendary Merv may even have been the inspiration for the tales of Scheherazade's *Thousand and One Nights*.

Merv suffered a number of attacks over the course of its history, but instead of being rebuilt on top of the older ruins, Merv slowly spread west. In total, five cities were constructed next to each other, largely because of the shifting rivers. The oldest section was the Erk Kala and in later centuries most people lived in the vast walled city called Sultan Kala.

All of this was completely eradicated in 1221 under the onslaught of the Mongols. In 1218 Chinggis Khan demanded a substantial tithe of grain from Merv, along with the pick of the city's most beautiful young women. The unwise Seljuq response was to slay the tax collectors. In retribution Tolui, the most brutal of Chinggis Khan's sons, arrived three years later at the head of an army, accepted the peaceful surrender of the terrified citizens, and then proceeded to butcher every last one of them, an estimated 300,000 people.

Merv made a small comeback in the 15th century and was soon at the centre of a territorial dispute between the rulers of Bukhara, Khiva and Persia. Persian influence eventually won out when a noble named Bairam Ali rebuilt the dam, which allowed the irrigated region to prosper, and encouraged free trade. The Emir of Bukhara struck back with military force, captured the city, and utterly destroyed it in 1795.

Russia annexed Merv in 1884 and the Turkmen settlement became known as Bairam Ali. Russians monitored events from Mary, their newly built town 30km to the west.

Sights

Coming from Mary you pass through the town of Bairam Ali, and turn left on a road heading north from the Central Bazaar. After 4km a sign points right towards the Merv complex. On the road towards ancient Merv is a small ticket office for the **Merv complex** (admission 11.40M, camera 5.70M, video camera 70M; ☉ 7am-dusk) and the **Margush Archaeological Museum** (admission free; ☉ 7am-dusk), which houses a tiny collection of artefacts and old photos.

MAUSOLEUM OF MOHAMMED IBN ZEID

From the ticket office, continue east and take your first left (north) to an early-Islamic monument, the 12th-century **Mausoleum of Mohammed ibn Zeid**. The small, unostentatious earthen-brick building, which was heavily restored in the early 20th century, benefits

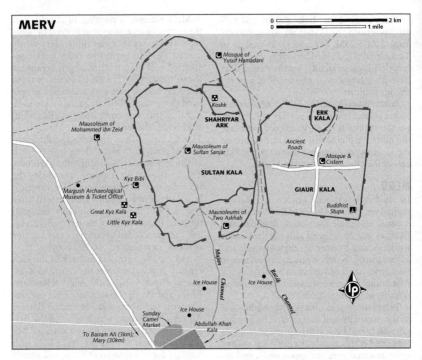

greatly from an attractive setting in a hollow that is ringed by spindly saxaul trees. Like the other Sufi shrines (Gozli-Ata and Kubra), this shrine is also an important site for Sufi pilgrims.

There's confusion as to who's actually buried under the black marble cenotaph in the centre of the cool, dark shrine. It's definitely not Ibn Zeid, a prominent Shiite teacher who died four centuries before this tomb was built and is known to be buried elsewhere.

EARLIEST REMAINS

The oldest of the five Merv cities is **Erk Kala**, an Achaemenid city thought to date from the 6th century BC. Led by Alexander the Great, the Macedonians conquered it and renamed it Alexandria Margiana. Under Parthian control (250 BC to AD 226) Zoroastrianism was the state religion but Erk Kala was also home to Nestorian Christians, Jews and Buddhists.

Today Erk Kala is a big earthen doughnut about 600m across. There are deep trenches that have been dug into the ramparts by Soviet archaeologists. The ramparts are 50m high, and offer a bird's-eye view of the surrounding savannah-like landscape. On the ramparts it's easy to see small hills that were once towers.

From this vantage point you can see that Erk Kala forms part of the northern section of another fortress – **Giaur Kala**, constructed during the 3rd century BC by the Sassanians. The fortress walls are still solid, with three gaps where gates once were. The city was built on a Hellenistic grid pattern; near the crossroads in the middle of the site are the ruins of a 7th-century mosque. At the eastern end of the mosque is an 8m-deep water cistern that's been dug into the ground.

In the southeastern corner of Giaur Kala a distinct mound marks the site of a Buddhist stupa and monastery, which was still functioning in the early Islamic era. The head of a Buddha statue was found here, making Merv the westernmost point to which Buddhism spread at its height.

SULTAN KALA

The best remaining testimony to Seljuq power at Merv is the 38m-high **Mausoleum of Sultan Sanjar**, located in what was the centre of Sultan Kala. The building has been recently restored with Turkish aid and rises dramatically in the open plain.

Sanjar, grandson of Alp-Arslan, died in 1157, reputedly of a broken heart when, after escaping from captivity in Khiva, he came home to find that Chinggis Khan's soldiers had laid waste to his beloved Merv.

The mausoleum is a simple cube with a barrel-mounted dome on top. Originally it had a magnificent turquoise-tiled outer dome, said to be visible from a day's ride away, but that is long gone. Interior decoration is sparse, though restoration has brought back the blue-and-red frieze in the upper gallery. Inside is Sanjar's simple stone 'tomb' although, fearing grave robbers, he was actually buried elsewhere in an unknown location. The name of the architect, Mohammed Ibn Aziz of Serakhs, is etched into the upper part of the east wall. According to lore, the sultan had his architect executed to prevent him from designing a building to rival this one.

The **Shahriyar Ark** (or Citadel of Sultan Kala) is one of the more interesting parts of Merv. Still visible are its walls, a well-preserved *koshk* (fort) with corrugated walls, and the odd grazing camel.

North of the Shahriyar Ark, outside the city walls, lies the **Mosque of Yusuf Hamadani**, built around the tomb of a 12th-century dervish. The complex has been largely rebuilt in the last 10 years and turned into an important pilgrimage site; it is not open to non-Muslims.

Archaeologists have been excavating a number of sites around Sultan Kala, revealing the foundations of homes. If you have an experienced guide they should know the location of recent digs.

KYZ KALA

These two crumbling 7th-century *koshk* outside the walls of Merv are interesting for their 'petrified stockade' walls, as writer Colin Thubron describes them, composed of 'vast clay logs up-ended side by side'. They were constructed by the Sassanians in the 7th century and were still in use by Seljuq sultans, 600 years later, as function rooms. These are some of the most symbolic and important structures in western Merv archaeology and they have no analogies anywhere else.

MAUSOLEUMS OF TWO ASKHAB

One of the most important pilgrimage sites in Turkmenistan are the mausoleums built for two Islamic *askhab* (companions of the prophet), Al-Hakim ibn Amr al-Jafari and Buraida ibn al-Huseib al-Islami. The two squat buildings sit in front of reconstructed Timurid *aivans* (*iwans,* portals) that honour the prophets. In front of the mausoleums is a still-functioning water cistern.

ICE HOUSES

South of Sultan Kala and Giaur Kala are three ice houses built during the Timurid era. The giant freezers, made from brick and covered by a conical-shaped roof, were used to keep meat and other foods frozen during the summer. The ice house closest to Giaur Kala is perhaps the best-preserved structure. They now sit in a fairly neglected state, but are worth a quick look.

Getting There & Away

The only way to see the site without an exhausting walk is by car. From Mary expect to pay 20M for a car and driver for four hours (the minimum amount of time needed to see the main monuments). Buses go between Mary and Bairam Ali every half hour or so; the journey takes about 45 minutes. Guided tours are available from any travel agency and this is the way most people see Merv. Yevgenia Golubeva (see p449) in Mary includes Merv on her tour of the area.

GONUR

Long before Merv raised its first tower, Bronze Age villages were assembling along the Murgab River in what is called the Margiana Oasis. The greatest of these ancient settlements, currently being excavated around **Gonur Depe** (Gonur Hill; admission 3M, camera 4M), has stunned the archaeological world for its vast area and complex layout.

The discoveries were first made in 1972 by Russian-Greek archaeologist Viktor Sarianidi, who still works at the site, continually uncovering new findings. Sarianidi considers Gonur to be one of the great civilisations of the ancient world and while this claim may be disputed, it certainly is a fascinating site. What is certain, however, is that Gonur is one of the oldest fire-worshipping civilisations, parallel to the Bactrian cultures in neighbouring Afghanistan. The first agricultural settlements appeared in the area around 7000 BC and developed a strong agriculture. It is believed the city was slowly abandoned during the Bronze

Age as the Murgab River changed course, depriving the city of water. The current excavations have been dated back to 3000 BC.

Sarianidi believes that Gonur was the birthplace of the first monotheistic religion, Zoroastrianism, being at some point the home of the religion's founder, Zoroaster. The adjacent sites have revealed four fire temples, as well as evidence of a cult based around a drug potion prepared from poppy, hemp and ephedra plants. This potent brew is almost certainly the *haoma* (soma elixir) used by the magi whom Zoroaster began preaching against in Zoroastrian texts.

The excavations are ongoing and during your visit you may have a chance to speak with the archaeologists and inspect the most-recent findings. There is also significant effort being put into conservation, although the work being done (sealing the ruins with mud bricks) is covering up some of the most photogenic portions of the city. The Royal Palace and necropolis are the most fascinating sites to visit.

Gonur is a two-hour drive from Mary and you'll need at least two hours there. A 4WD is required and the final 20km of road is little more than a rough track in the dirt. You can organise a trip through any travel agency or call Yevgenia Golubeva (see p449) in Mary. Expect to pay 120M to hire a driver, and a further 90M for an in-depth guided tour. There is nowhere in the area to buy food or water, so pack a lunch before setting off.

TAGTABAZAR

The peaceful town of Tagtabazar lies 215km south of Mary on the road to Afghanistan. On the fringe of the former Russian Empire, it was here that the tsar locked horns with British-backed Afghanistan in one of the salvoes of the Great Game (see p50). A brief battle near the town (then called Pandjeh) left more than 800 Afghans dead and Russia hanging onto victory by a thread. The battle ultimately forced Afghanistan and Russia into negotiations that delineated a border.

If you happen to be passing through Tagtabazar en route to Afghanistan, it's worth stopping to see the extraordinary **Ekedeshik cave complex** (admission 6M; tours 3M, camera 9M; ⏰ 9am-5pm), located in the hills north of town. The main cavern is reached through a metal gate where a caretaker sells you a ticket. From here the cave stretches back 32m and includes

44 rooms on two levels. One room, containing a vaulted ceiling and a carved doorway, may have been used by a chief or priest. The curator will show you a staircase to more caverns below, but this section is off-limits.

The caves are sometimes locked, so before you go there inquire about the key-holder at the local governor's office. The caves are 3km north of town and accessible by private car or taxi. There's no hotel in town though, so you're best off continuing to either Mary or Herat for the night.

TURKMENABAT

☎ 422 / pop 203,000

Lying on the banks of the mighty Amu-Darya, between the Karakum desert and the fertile plains of Uzbekistan, sprawling Turkmenabat sits at a crossroads of cultures. On its streets you'll hear as much Uzbek as Turkmen and will likely be enjoying Uzbek produce, driven across the border a few kilometres to the north. The town itself feels as if it's in the geographic centre of nowhere, yet after the mind-numbing drive through the desert from either Dashogus or Mary, it's something of a surprise to find such a large city appear out of the sand.

The Silk Road city of Amul prospered here until its destruction by the Mongols in 1221, and was reborn under the Russian empire as Charjou, a name you'll still hear used by the remaining Russian-speaking locals. In 2009 a new gas pipeline opened here taking Turkmen gas to China, thus ensuring the city's economic prosperity. Despite being the second-largest city in the country, there's nothing much to see or do here, though it's an obvious stopover on the long journeys to Kugitang Nature Reserve, Mary, Dashogus or Uzbekistan.

You'll find an internet cafe and international call centre in the post office building on Niyazov şayoli, the town's main drag, that curves around to the left connecting the city centre to the bus and train station.

Sights

The **Lebap Regional Museum** (Shaidakov köçesi 35; admission 2.85M; ⏰ 9am-1pm & 2-6pm) is well worth visiting for its building – a unique Shia mosque built in the early 20th century and turned into a museum by the Soviets in the 1960s. It's a brick structure with a rectangular tower and two brick minarets and it may

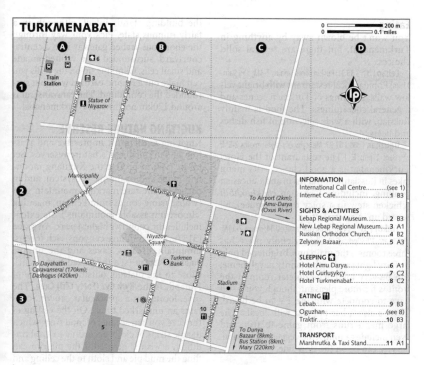

TURKMENABAT

0 —— 200 m
0 —— 0.1 miles

INFORMATION
International Call Centre............(see 1)
Internet Cafe.............................1 B3

SIGHTS & ACTIVITIES
Lebap Regional Museum...............2 B3
New Lebap Regional Museum......3 A1
Russian Orthodox Church.............4 B2
Zelyony Bazaar...........................5 A3

SLEEPING
Hotel Amu Darya........................6 A1
Hotel Gurluşykçy........................7 C2
Hotel Turkmenabat.....................8 C2

EATING
Lebab.......................................9 B3
Oguzhan..............................(see 8)
Traktir....................................10 B3

TRANSPORT
Marshrutka & Taxi Stand..........11 A1

become a mosque again once the museum moves to new premises that were being built opposite the train station at the time of writing. Downstairs, an ethnography section includes a fully furnished yurt, a diorama of a silversmith workshop and the requisite room full of quietly disintegrating taxidermy. The 2nd floor is surreal, with displays including randomly collected coins from foreign currencies (most long since superseded by the euro), two enormous cakes, a collection of children's clothing, a few Berdymukhamedov hagiographies and a collection of wares produced by the Charjev Leased Chemical Enterprise.

A couple of blocks northeast of the museum is the **Russian Orthodox Church** (Magtymguly şayoli), built to honour St Nicolas. Built in the late 19th century, the church is painted canary yellow and decorated on the interior with a rich collection of icons.

Turkmenabat has a couple of busting bazaars. The most convenient is **Zelyony Bazaar**, near the telephone office. A better choice if you are looking for carpets is the **Dunya Bazaar**, 8km south of downtown.

Sleeping

Hotel Gurluşykçy (☎ 3 81 85; Magtymguly şayoli; s/d 50/100M;) This unpronounceable hotel is an old Soviet-era place, but friendly and decently looked after. The rooms are large apartments with a living room, a couple of bedrooms, and rather awful bathrooms, though there's usually hot water. The air con fails to keep the large rooms cool in summer, but on the plus side there's a kitchen guests are free to use. It is located behind the Hotel Turkmenabat.

Hotel Amu Darya (☎ 3 14 30; Niyazov şayoli 14; s/d/tr/lux US$30/80/90/100;) Finally reopening in 2010 after several years of renovations, the Amu Darya has re-emerged looking surprisingly similar to how it did before it went under the knife. Admittedly rooms are nicely painted now, and are as spacious as ever, but there are still no holders for the showerheads.

Hotel Turkmenabat (☎ 3 82 92; Magtymguly şayoli; s/d US$40/80;) Although a little overpriced, the Turkmenabat offers very comfortable rooms. Each has high ceilings, fridges and comfy beds, but the TVs are tiny. There is a pleasant bar and a good restaurant, the Oguzhan.

TURKMENISTAN

Eating

You won't be blown away by anything in Turkmenabat, but there are several solid choices.

Lebap (☎ 3 35 21; Puşkin köçesi; mains 2-4M; ☻ 9am-11pm) Popular local restaurant with bright yellow walls, paintings of Turkmen scenes and a general cheerfulness. The food is mainly Russian, with a wide selection of fish dishes and beers.

Oguzhan (☎ 3 82 92; Magtymguly şayoli; mains 2-5M; ☻ 8am-11pm; **E**) The restaurant of the Hotel Turkmenabat is a good choice – its menu takes in Russian, Central Asian and Caucasian cooking, including Georgian *chakhokhbili* (chicken stew in a spicy tomato sauce), all served up in a cosy setting.

Traktir (☎ 3 14 38; Arsarybaba köçesi 14; mains 7-11M; ☻ 11am-10.30pm; **E**) This friendly place has three rooms – the main one, brightened only by fairy lights and with a jaunty naval theme, can be very loud. The quieter room at the front is far more pleasant, though you'll still have to compete with the TV to be heard. There's also a bar popular with locals. The large menu runs from game to fish, and even includes a miniscule vegetarian section. Service can be on the slow side.

Getting There & Away

There are around three flights a day between Turkmenabat and Ashgabat (50M, one hour). The airport is 2km east of the Hotel Turkmenabat. The brand new **train station** (☎ 3 60 62), in the centre of town, has two daily trains to Ashgabat (4.76/7.66M, 12 hours) via Mary (3.61/6.51M, four hours). Outside the station you can catch marshrutki or taxis to Mary (20M per place, 80M per taxi), Ashgabat (60M per place, 240M per taxi) and to Dashogus (600M per taxi). A ride to the Uzbek border will cost 3M per seat, but you may need to bargain hard as starting prices can be much higher. There is another, more formal bus station 9km south of the centre of town, near Dunya Bazaar, but the transportation links from the lot outside the train station are just as good.

DAYAHATTIN CARAVANSERAI

This Silk Road caravanserai stands on the ancient route between Amul and Khorezm and dates to around the 12th century (give or take a couple of hundred years). Although abandoned around 500 years ago, most of the building stands intact, although in a fairly ruinous state. Pick your way through the enormous arched gateway into a central courtyard, surrounded by a vaulted arcade and small cells. Climbing up on the walls you can make out a second earthen wall that surrounded the compound. The caravanserai is around 170km northwest of Turkmenabat.

KUGITANG NATURE RESERVE

Kugitang is the most impressive and pristine of Turkmenistan's nature reserves. Set up in 1986 to protect the Kugitang mountain range and its unique ecosystem, and in particular the rare markhor mountain goat (whose name comes from Persian, meaning 'almost impassable mountains'). Its extent includes the country's highest peak, Airybaba (3137m), several huge canyons, rich forests, mountain streams, caves and the unique **Dinosaur Plateau** (see the boxed text, right). Close to the plateau, outside the village of Hojapil, is the **Kyrk Gyz (Forty Girl) Cave**. The cave, located in a spectacular canyon, contains an unmarked tomb. On the ceiling of the cave you can see bits of mud from which dangle strips of cloth; according to local tradition, a wish is granted if the pilgrim can fling the mud pie and cloth to the ceiling and make it stick.

Visiting one of the **Karlyuk Caves** is also an incredible experience. The limestone caves are considered the most extensive network of caves in Central Asia. They have been known since ancient times, having been mentioned in Greek texts, but the Soviets were the first to fully explore and exploit the caves; it was during their rule that onyx was harvested from the caves. The caves are also home to the blind cave loach, a sightless fish.

As the caves have not been readied for the tourist masses, only the **Kapkytan Cave** is accessible for visitors. Walking deep into the caves with one of the park rangers is both spooky and exciting, with some astonishing stalactites and stalagmites. Some of these natural wonders have been named by locals according to their form, including Medusa, a maiden and others of more phallic nature.

You'll need to organise a trip here through a travel agent who can get you a permit to visit and provide a driver. Accommodation is usually in a homestay with rangers or at a newly built hotel. Expect to pay US$40 per person per night for full board.

TURKMENOSAURUS REX

Looking like someone took a giant stamp of a footprint and pounded it into the ground, the dinosaur footprints of Kugitang Nature Reserve seem almost too perfect to be real. But the tracks are indeed legit, and were left here by ambling dinosaurs some 155 million years ago.

According to local legend, the prints were left by elephants used by the armies of Alexander the Great. Scientists, however, will tell you that the prints were left during the Jurassic period by a species called Megalosauripus.

The location of the tracks is a plateau (Dinosaur Plateau) that is presumed to be the bottom of a shallow lake that dried up, leaving the dinosaur prints baking in the sun, after which a volcanic eruption sealed them in lava. There are more than 400 prints visible on a steep incline of limestone, the largest of which has a diameter of 80cm. Around Kugitang, more than 2500 prints have been found.

The giant dinosaurs were apparently joined by smaller dino creatures that left imprints resembling a human foot. In 1995 a Russian newspaper stirred up controversy when it reported incorrectly that the prints were in fact human, which has fuelled Creationist claims that the dinosaurs are just a figment of Darwinist imagination.

NORTHERN TURKMENISTAN

Stalin's modus operandi in Central Asia sought the division of its people, thus resulting in the split of the Khorezm (an ancient kingdom centred around the Amu-Darya delta) oasis – the northern section around Khiva going to Uzbekistan and the southern portion going to Turkmenistan. It remains this way today, with the Amu-Darya river wriggling its way in and out of the Uzbek and Turkmen borders. As part of historic Khorezm, the Turkmen portion still contains a sizable Uzbek minority and retains a culture apart from the rest of the country. Sadly, the region has not escaped the Aral Sea disaster (p100) and suffers from air, soil and water pollution. It's also the poorest part of the country, with little commerce apart from the smuggling of subsidised petrol to Uzbekistan. Still, it's worth visiting the area to explore some unique historical sights, especially if you are travelling to or from Uzbekistan.

KONYE-URGENCH
☎ 347 / pop 15,000
The modern town of Konye-Urgench (from Persian 'Old Urgench') is a rural backwater with empty plazas, wandering livestock and back roads that end in agricultural fields. Yet centuries ago, this was the centre of the Islamic world, not the end of it.

Khorezm fell to the all-conquering Seljuq Turks, but rose in the 12th century, under a Seljuq dynasty known as the Khorezmshahs, to shape its own far-reaching empire. With its mosques, medressas, libraries and flourishing bazaars, Gurganj (the Persian name for Konye-Urgench) became a centre of the Muslim world, until Khorezmshah Mohammed II moved his capital to Samarkand after capturing that city in 1210.

Chinggis Khan arrived in 1221, seeking revenge for the murder of his envoys in Otrar as ordered by Mohammed II. Old Urgench withstood the siege for six months, and even after the Mongols broke through the city walls the residents fought them in the streets. The Mongols, unused to cities, burnt the houses but the residents still fought from the ruins. In the end, the Mongols diverted the waters of the Amu-Darya and flooded the city, drowning its defenders.

The Mongol generals went in pursuit of Mohammed II who eluded them for months until he finally died of exhaustion in 1221 on an island in the Caspian Sea. The tombs of his father, Tekesh, and grandfather, Il-Arslan, survive and are two of Old Urgench's monuments.

In the following period of peace, Khorezm was ruled as part of the Golden Horde, the huge, wealthy, westernmost of the khanates into which Chinggis Khan's empire was divided after his death. Rebuilt, Urgench was again Khorezm's capital, and grew into what was probably one of Central Asia's most important trading cities – big, beautiful, crowded and with a new generation of monumental buildings.

Then came Timur. Considering Khorezm to be a rival to Samarkand, he comprehensively finished off old Urgench in 1388. The city was partly rebuilt in the 16th century, but it was abandoned when the Amu-Darya changed its course. (Modern Konye-Urgench dates from the construction of a new canal in the 19th century.)

Today, most of Old Urgench lies underground, but there is enough urban tissue to get an idea of its former glories. Its uniqueness was acknowledged in 2005 when Unesco named it a World Heritage Site. The modern town is somewhat short on tourist facilities and most travellers overnight in Dashogus.

Sights

NEJAMEDDIN KUBRA MAUSOLEUM & AROUND

The sacred Nejameddin Kubra Mausoleum is the most important of a small cluster of sights near the middle of the town and is the holiest part of Konye-Urgench.

The simple **Konye-Urgench Museum** (☎ 23 57 71; admission 11.40M; ☽ 8am-6pm Wed-Mon) is housed in the early-20th-century Dash Mosque, just before the main mausoleum complex. It includes some ancient Arabic texts and a few interestingly labelled artefacts from Old Urgench (eg 'blue polished eight-cornered thing'). Note the Christian symbols carved onto some of the stone pieces. Off the medressa courtyard are several rooms containing ethnographic displays of Turkmen culture, including a pottery workshop and carpet looms.

To one side of the mosque is the **Matkerim-Ishan Mausoleum**, which is also early 20th century.

The path past here leads to the **Nejameddin Kubra Mausoleum** on the left, and the **Sultan Ali Mausoleum** facing it across a shady little courtyard. Nejameddin Kubra (1145–1221) was a famous Khorezm Muslim teacher and poet who founded the Sufic Kubra order, with followers throughout the Islamic world. His tomb is believed to have healing properties and you may find pilgrims praying here. The building has three domes and a tiled portal that appears on the brink of forward collapse. The tombs inside – one for his body and one for his head (which were kindly separated by the Mongols) are quite extraordinarily colourful with floral-pattern tiles.

SOUTHERN MONUMENTS

The city's most striking **monuments** (admission 11.40M, camera 5.70M; ☽ 8am-6pm) are dotted like a constellation across an empty expanse straddling the Ashgabat road, 1km south of the main town.

Turabeg Khanym Complex, opposite the ticket office, is still the subject of some debate. Locals and some scholars consider this a mausoleum, though no-one is too sure who is buried here. Some archaeologists contend that it was a throne room built in the 12th century (it appears to have a heating system, which would not have been used in a mausoleum). Whatever its function, this is one of Central Asia's most perfect buildings. Its geometric patterns are in effect a giant calendar signifying humanity's insignificance in the march of time. There are 365 sections on the sparkling mosaic underside of the dome, representing the days of the year; 24 pointed arches immediately beneath the dome representing the hours of the day; 12 bigger arches below representing the months the year; and four big windows representing the weeks of the month. The cupola is unusual in early Islamic architecture and has its equal only in Shiraz, Iran.

Crossing the road to the side of the minaret, the path through a modern cemetery and the 19th-century **Sayid Ahmed Mausoleum** leads to the **Gutlug Timur Minaret**, built in the 1320s. It's the only surviving part of Old Urgench's main mosque. Decorated with bands of brick and a few turquoise tiles, its 59m-tall minaret is not as tall as it once was, and leans noticeably. It's interesting to note that there is no entrance to the minaret – it was linked to the adjacent mosque by a bridge 7m above the ground. Since that mosque was destroyed, the only way into the minaret is by ladder. There are 144 steps to the top, although you can't climb it now.

Further along the track is the **Sultan Tekesh Mausoleum**. Tekesh was the 12th-century Khorezmshah who made Khorezm great with conquests as far south as Khorasan (present-day northern Iran and northern Afghanistan). It is believed that he built this mausoleum for himself, along with a big medressa and library (which did not survive) on the same spot. However, some scholars theorise that the building had earlier existed as a Zoroastrian temple. After his death in 1200 Tekesh was apparently buried here, although there is no tomb. There are recent excavations of several early Islamic graves near the entrance to the building.

Nearby is the mound of graves called the **Kyrk Molla** (Forty Mullahs Hill), a sacred place where Konye-Urgench's inhabitants held their last stand against the Mongols. Here you'll see young women rolling down the hill in a fertility rite – one of Konye-Urgench's more curious attractions.

Continue along the track to the **Il-Arslan Mausoleum**, Konye-Urgench's oldest standing monument. The conical dome, with a curious zigzag brick pattern, is the first of its kind and was exported to Samarkand by Timur. Il-Arslan, who died in 1172, was Tekesh's father. The building is small but well worth a close look. The conical dome with 12 faces is unique, and the collapsing floral terracotta moulding on the facade is also unusual. Further south lies the base of the **Mamun II Minaret**, which was built in 1011, reduced to a stump by the Mongols, rebuilt in the 14th century and finally toppled by an earthquake in 1895. At last you'll arrive at the so-called **portal of an unknown building**. The structure is now thought to have been the entrance to the palace of Mohammed Khorezmshah, due to its ornateness and the thickness of its walls.

Sleeping

Ruhbelent Hotel (☎ 2 10 45; Turkmenistan köçesi; r 40M) On the road from the Uzbek border into town, this pink-purple building houses a boisterous downstairs chaikhana popular with wedding groups, and has four comfortable rooms upstairs, with mattresses on the floor, TV, and shared bathroom and sauna downstairs. Prices are negotiable.

Ürgenç Hotel (☎ 2 24 65; Dashogus köçesi; bed US$20) This once state-run hotel opposite the town's bus station is now mercifully in private hands, and while so far four rooms have been renovated, progress is glacial; full renovation is promised. The slightly overpriced rooms have bathrooms with hot water, and there are plans to install air con too. There's a small chaikhana here too, offering breakfast and hot meals.

Eating

Bedev Café (☎ 2 10 44; Azadi köçesi; mains 3M; ☺ 7am-10pm) On the road from the main ruins into town, this is one of the most reliable places in town to grab a meal. It specialises in *samsa* (samosa), fresh *gatik* (yoghurt) and *manty*. There's no sign – look for the small Pepsi logo on a brick building.

Mekan (☎ 2 26 81; VKLSM köçesi; dishes 3-4M; ☺ 8am-9pm) This large, tiled restaurant near the bazaar is a consistent fall-back, with decent food and questionable cleanliness, though we've only ever seen cockroaches scuttling about and never found them in our food. Private booths are available.

Getting There & Away

The town's bus station, where taxis, marshrutki and buses meet and pick up passengers, is opposite the Ürgenç Hotel and a taxi ride from the town centre.

Frequent buses and marshrutki go to Ashgabat (28M, seven to eight hours) and to Dashogus (15M, two hours). Taxis leave for Ashgabat (seat/car 30M/120M) and Dashogus (seat/car 5M/20M) at all times of day. Those not in a hurry can take the daily 5.40pm train to Dashogus (1.50M, 4½ hours).

A taxi to the border with Uzbekistan (20km away) should cost 5M and can be picked up anywhere.

Getting Around

The main sights of Konye-Urgench are spread out so it's best to use a car. There is no public transport as such, but you can flag down a taxi on the main roads or by the market. The trip to the southern monuments and back, with waiting time, is 6M.

DASHOGUS

☎ 322 / pop 160,000

A creation of the Soviet Union, Dashogus is a sprawling industrial city with a neat, soulless centre and nothing to attract visitors. Even its one semi-sight, some idiosyncratic dinosaur statues, was recently removed by the authorities for reasons best known to them. The centre itself consists of an enormous boulevard lined with concrete buildings separated by empty lots. Despite this most travellers end up spending a night here, as it's a useful stopover between Ashgabat and Uzbekistan. For some local colour, head to the excellent **Bai Bazaar**, where you can buy pretty much anything. There's an **internet cafe** (per hr 6M; ☺ 9am-9pm) on the main drag, between the Dashogus and Diyarbekir hotels.

Sleeping

Hotel Dashogus (☎ 5 55 06; Turkmenbashi şayoli 5; per person 40M; 😊) The requisite Soviet dinosaur still chugs along, accommodating budget travellers in rickety old rooms shot through with despair. The decrepit air is slightly relieved by nice balconies and friendly management. The Dashogus has a bar and a small restaurant and hot water is available twice a day.

Hotel Uzboy (☎ 2 60 16; Turkmenbashi şayoli 19/1; s/d/lux US$30/50/70; 😊 P) Dashogus' newest hotel is a white-tile construction on the western side of town. Rooms are rather cramped but have good bathrooms and are generally comfortable. Breakfast is included in the price.

Hotel Diyarbekir (☎ 5 90 37; Turkmenbashi şayoli; s/d/ste US$35/35/70; 😊) This Turkish-owned venture has 40 ridiculously large rooms with TV and balcony. Other amenities include a sauna and restaurant. Despite its relatively recent construction there is already plenty of wear, including stained carpets, cracked mirrors and neglected bathrooms worthy of a Soviet-era hotel.

Eating

Kafé Marat (☎ 5 06 00; Turkmenbashi şayoli 15; mains 3-5M; 🕙 10am-11pm) Decorated with faux torches, red curtains and Christmas lights year-round, this festive restaurant is a lively downtown institution. The occasional live band adds to the atmosphere.

Kafé Bereket (Atamurat Niyazov köçesi; mains 3-5M; 🕙 9am-10pm) Outside Dashogus's train station, this welcome addition to the eating scene serves up good kebabs in its garden and has an interior decor from some kind of a modern Arabic fantasy.

Şatugi (☎ 5 97 42; Al Khorezmi köçesi 6; mains 3-12M; 🕙 10am-11pm) This rather ostentatious restaurant is popular with weddings and groups, and serves up pizza, kebabs, roast chicken and a large selection of salads. The loud music and disco lighting rather detract from the experience. Find it on the edge of a park behind the Hotel Diyarbekir.

Chaikhana (Mudsavod Shorva, Irfimenko 13; set menu 12M; 🕙 9am-11pm) This is by far the most atmospheric place in town to eat – a simple, Turkmen-run chaikhana where you'll eat good homecooked soups and fresh bread and be made to feel very welcome. It's some way from the hotels – take a taxi.

Getting There & Away

Dashogus airport is 14km south of the city. Flights from Ashgabat to Dashogus (48M, five daily) take about 50 minutes, although you should book early as this is a very popular route. Turkmenistan Airlines also flies to Turkmenbashi (58M, four weekly) and Mary (57M, three weekly).

The bus station is near the Bai Bazaar, in the north of the city. Buses regularly go from here to Konye-Urgench (3M, two hours) and Ashgabat (30M, nine hours). Buses for Turkmenabat were not available at the time of research. Shared taxis go from outside the train station and cost 36/150M per place/car to Ashgabat. The arduous journey to Turkmenabat will set you back 70/280M per place/car.

The **train station** (☎ 4 68 75) is on Woksal köçesi, about 600m east of Gurbansoltan köçesi. One painfully slow train per day goes from here to Konye-Urgench (1.5M, four hours) at 7.05am daily and one to Ashgabat at 11.15am daily (*platskartny/kupe* 5.08M/9.58M, 20 hours). The rail line to Ashgabat was built on sand without foundation, forcing trains to crawl at agonisingly slow speeds. There is a rail line to Turkmenabat but a lack of demand has suspended services and currently trains from Turkmenabat only go as far as Gazachak.

TURKMENISTAN DIRECTORY

ACCOMMODATION

In 2009 a rule confining hotel ownership to the state was rescinded, meaning that finally some private enterprise can enter the local hotel market, which at present is in a fairly dire state. As a rule hotels throughout the country are easily divided into dilapidated Soviet-era behemoths and newer three- and four-star ventures built since independence. Turkmen citizens can stay at a hotel at a discounted rate, which is usually 60% to 80% less than the price that foreigners are charged. So while you may have to pay for the lodging of your guide, this shouldn't cost more than a few dollars. Expect to pay for any extra services – breakfast is not usually included in the room rate and you'll be charged to use the gym or the pool.

It's illegal for tourists to sleep in a private home if a licensed hotel exists in the same city; some travellers have got in trouble for staying with a family or unlicensed guesthouse. This law does not apply for travellers on a transit visa.

Turkmenistan's wide open spaces make for good camping and there is nothing to stop you from pulling off the road and pitching a tent in the desert. Some of the best places for camping include Yangykala Canyon (p445) and the Darvaza Gas Craters (p442).

ACTIVITIES

Horse-lovers from around the world flock to Turkmenistan to ride the unique Akhal-Teke thoroughbreds. Many travel agencies offer specialist horse-trekking tours with these beautiful creatures. For further information on riding these horses near Ashgabat, check out p436.

Turkmenistan has wonderful potential for hiking, although the concept of the pastime is not widely understood (this is after all the country that built concrete staircases into its mountainsides). However, if you have permission to visit one of the nature reserves, walking is of course no problem whatsoever. Some of the best places to explore are the Kugitang Nature Reserve (p456) and the mountains around Nokhur (p443).

CUSTOMS REGULATIONS

In Turkmenistan official regulations state that you need permission to export any carpet over 6 sq m, though trying to export a smaller one without an export licence is also likely to be problematic. In all cases it's best to take your carpet to the Carpet Museum (p434) in Ashgabat, where there is a bureau that will value and tax your purchase, and

provide an export licence. This can take up to a few days. There are several fees to pay. One certifies that the carpet is not antique, which usually costs US$10 to US$30, while a second is an export fee that costs around US$50 per square metre. As with all government taxes on foreigners, these are paid in US dollars. When you buy a carpet at a state shop, these fees will be included in the price, but double check before handing over your money. Those in a hurry are best advised to buy from one of the many government shops in Ashgabat, where all carpets come complete with an export licence. Despite being more expensive than purchases made at Tolkuchka Bazaar, this still works out as very good value.

Antiques are difficult to impossible to export. If you are transiting through the country carrying antiques bought in Iran, Uzbekistan or elsewhere, make sure to list those items on your customs form when you enter the country. Anything that looks remotely old, used or scrubby could be considered an antique.

DANGERS & ANNOYANCES

Take care when photographing public buildings, especially in Ashgabat. Local police take this seriously and you may have your documents checked even if simply strolling near the Presidential Palace with a camera in your hand. There are no 'no photo' signs anywhere, so you'll need to ask the nearest policeman if it's OK to take a picture.

EMBASSIES & CONSULATES
Turkmen Embassies in Central Asia

There are Turkmen embassies in the cities of Tashkent (Uzbekistan; p282), Dushanbe (Tajikistan; p418), Kabul (Afghanistan; p491) and Almaty (Kazakhstan; p194).

Turkmenistan Embassies & Consulates in Other Countries
Azerbaijan (☎ 012 465 4876; Shamsi Rahimov 14, Genclik, Baku)
China (☎ 65326975/6/7; www.turkmenembassy.cn; King's Garden Villas, D-1, Xiaoyunlu 18, 100016, Beijing)
France (☎ 0147550536; fax 0147550568; 13 rue Picot, 75016, Paris)
Germany (☎ 30 30102451; www.botschaft-turkmenistan .de; Langobardenalle 14, D-14052, Berlin)
Iran Mashhad (☎ 511 8599940, 8547660; fax 511 8547660; Kucheye Konsulgari 34, Mashhad); Tehran

(☎ 21 2542178, 2548686; fax 2540432; 39 Pardaran Ave, Golestan-5 St, Tehran)
Pakistan (☎ 2278699, 2214913; fax 278799; Nazim-ud-Din Rd, 22-a, F-7/1, Islamabad)
Russia (☎ 095 2916591/636; www.turkmenistan.ru; Filipovsky pereulok 22, 121019, Moscow)
Turkey Ankara (☎ 312 4417122; fax 312 4417125; Koza sokak 28, Chankaya 06700, Ankara); İstanbul (☎ 212 6620221/2/3; fax 212 6620224; Gazi Evrenos Jadesi Baharistan sokak 13 Eshilkoy, İstanbul)
UK (☎ 020 7255 1071; fax 020 7323 9184; www. turkmenembassy.org.uk; St George's House, 14-17 Wells St, W1T 3PD, London)
USA (☎ 202 588 1500; fax 202 280 1003; www. turkmenistanembassy.org; 2207 Massachusetts Ave, NW 20008, Washington DC)

Embassies & Consulates in Turkmenistan

All the following legations are in Ashgabat. The British embassy looks after the interests of Commonwealth nationals in Turkmenistan.
Afghanistan (☎ 48 07 57; fax 48 07 26; Garaşsyzlyk şayoli 4/4, Berzengi; ☽ lodging 9.30am-12.30pm, collection 3.30-4pm Mon-Fri)
Azerbaijan (☎ 36 46 08; fax 36 46 10; www.azembassy ashg.com; 2062 köçesi 44; ☽ 10am-1pm & 4-6pm Mon-Fri)
China (☎ 48 81 05; fax 48 18 13; Archabil şayoli 45, Berzengi; ☽ 3-5pm Tue & Fri)
France (☎ 36 35 50, 36 34 68; 3rd fl, Ak Altyn Hotel, Magtymguly şayoli; ☽ 9am-1pm & 2-5pm Mon-Fri)
Georgia (☎ 33 08 28; fax 33 02 48; Azadi köçesi 139a; ☽ 9am-6pm Mon-Fri)
Germany (☎ 36 35 15/17-20; fax 36 35 22; 1st fl, Ak Altyn Hotel, Magtymguly şayoli; ☽ 9am-noon Mon-Fri)
Iran (☎ 34 14 52; fax 35 05 65; Tehran köçesi 3; ☽ 9.30am-12.30pm Mon-Fri)
Kazakhstan (☎ 48 04 72, 48 04 69; fax 48 04 74; Garaşsyzlyk şayoli 11/13, Berzengi; ☽ lodging 9am-noon, collection 5-6pm Tue-Fri)
Kyrgyzstan (☎ 48 22 95; Garaşsyzlyk şayoli 17, Berzengi; ☽ 9.30am-12.30pm Mon-Fri)
Netherlands (☎ 34 67 00; fax 34 42 52; Tehran köçesi 17; ☽ 9am-6pm Mon-Fri)
Pakistan (☎ 48 21 28/9; fax 48 21 30; Garaşsyzlyk şayoli 4/1, Berzengi; ☽ 8.30am-4pm Mon-Fri)
Russia (☎ 35 39 57, 35 70 41; fax 39 84 66; Turkmenbashi şayoli 11; ☽ 9am-12.30pm Mon, Tue, Thu & Fri)
Tajikistan (☎ 48 01 63; Garaşsyzlyk şayoli 4/2, Berzengi; ☽ 3-6pm Mon-Fri)
UK (☎ 36 34 62/3/4; www.britishembassy.gov.uk/turkmenistan; 3rd fl, Ak Altyn Hotel, Magtymguly şayoli; ☽ 8.30am-12.30 & 1-4.30pm Mon-Fri)

USA (☎ 35 00 45; http://turkmenistan.usembassy.gov; 1984 köçesi 9; ☽ 9am-noon & 1-6pm Mon-Fri)
Uzbekistan (☎ 33 10 62; Görogly köçesi 50A; ☽ 10am-1pm Mon, Wed & Fri)

Visas for Onward Travel

The following countries have embassies and consulates in Turkmenistan that can provide information and visas for travel to them.
Afghanistan Can issue one-month business visas for US$60 or three-month business visas for US$90. You need to show a letter from your employer or organisation. Tourist visas are not issued.
Azerbaijan Issues tourist visas (US$40) and transit visas (US$40) in two to three days. You'll need a copy of your passport, two photos and either an LOI or a letter from your own embassy asking them to issue you a visa.
China Currently only issues visas to Turkmen citizens.
Iran Offers transit visas in 10 days (€21) or 24 hours (€42), as well as one-month tourist visas in 10 days (€42) or 24 hours (€84). However at the time of research it advised US citizens not to apply here.
Kazakhstan Issues one-month tourist visas (US$40) in three days. Transit visas (US$20) are ready the following day. You'll need a photo and a copy of your passport and Turkmen visa.
Kyrgyzstan Issues one-month tourist visas (US$50) in seven days. Urgent processing in one or two days costs double that.
Tajikistan One-month tourist visas are available 'in 10 minutes' at an eye-watering US$111. Bring your LOI, passport, copy of passport and one photo.
Uzbekistan Issues one-month tourist visas (US$42) in seven days to EU citizens, no invitation needed. Australians, Canadians and New Zealanders are charged the same but require an invite. US citizens are charged US$133 and require an invite.

GAY & LESBIAN TRAVELLERS

Homosexuality is illegal in Turkmenistan. There are no gay or lesbian bars in Ashgabat, but gay men sometimes meet in the park in front of the Lenin statue. Lesbianism remains an entirely alien concept in Turkmenistan.

HOLIDAYS

Turkmenistan has a great number of holidays, though the country largely continues to work as normal during most of them.
1 January New Year
12 January Remembrance Day (Battle of Geok-Depe)
19 February Flag Day (President's Birthday)
8 March Women's Day
21 March Navrus (spring festival; p503); date varies
April (first Sunday) Drop of Water is a Grain of Gold Day

April (last Sunday) Horse Day
9 May Victory Day
18 May Day of Revival & Unity
19 May Magtymguly Poetry Day
May (last Sunday) Carpet Day
August (second Sunday) Melon Holiday
6 October Remembrance Day (1948 Earthquake)
27 & 28 October Independence Day
November (first Saturday) Health Day
November (last Sunday) Harvest Festival
7 December Good Neighbourliness Day
12 December Neutrality Day

INTERNET ACCESS

Internet access, once horrendously slow, expensive and limited to top hotels in Ashgabat, is now available in all big towns through state-run internet cafes. Prices are standardised at 6M per hour, and you'll need to leave your passport with the administrator while you surf. As all internet access is via the state-run www.online.tm, bear in mind that out-going emails may be monitored and many websites (mainly news and politics sites) are blocked, so save any plotting to overthrow the government until you're back home.

INTERNET RESOURCES

While most commentary on Turkmenistan has some sort of agenda, there are several interesting websites about the place.
www.chaihana.com For general information and archived articles.
www.gundogar.org The opposition website is invaluable for news and politics.
www.stantours.com A great introduction and aid for planning your trip.
www.turkmenistan.gov.tm Turkmenistan's government news and information page. It pops up in Russian but there is an English link.
www.turkmenistaninfo.ru News and features site with an English-language tab.
www.turkmens.com A huge and rather eccentric collection of Turkmenistan-related websites about culture, music, politics and history.

MONEY

The currency in Turkmenistan is the manat (M, sometimes also abbreviated to DTM), which is made up of 100 tenge. It's a new currency that replaced the previous manat, whose value had become miniscule. From 1 January 2010, it was the only legal tender in the country, one new manat being equal to 5000 old manats.

There is no longer a black market currency exchange in Turkmenistan, which has made everything far more expensive for visitors. All exchange offices change dollars at the fixed rate of 2.84M to the US$. Exchange offices are everywhere, take no commission, and will freely exchange US dollars and euros back and forth (you don't need to worry about having official certificates in order to change your money back when you leave the country, for example). US dollars remain the currency of choice for Turkmenistan. Euros are also generally easy to change, though less so outside Ashgabat. You can change pounds, yen, rubles and yuan at banks in Ashgabat too, but rates aren't great and you'll have no luck elsewhere in the country.

Confusingly, many people still speak in old manats, and when they do so they usually leave off the thousands, as they were implied for years. For example you may ask how much something is and be told '20M' – this means 20,000M, which is 4M. Confused? You will be. To make things even trickier, more and more people are speaking in new manats every day. To clarify which currency you're being quoted in, simply ask *novimi ili starimi manatami?* (new or old manats?).

Everything bought in Turkmenistan will be paid for in manats, but travel agencies and hotels still usually require payment in dollars, so it's best to keep a supply of both currencies. Throughout this chapter prices are listed in the currency they are charged in – all state taxes and state-run hotels are charged in US dollars, while private hotels and nearly everything else can be paid only in manats.

Cash advances on credit cards are only available in Ashgabat (p431) and ATMs taking international cards are nonexistent. Outside Ashgabat emergency money can be wired through Western Union only. Credit cards are accepted by a few luxury hotels in Ashgabat but by few other places, and you'd be ill advised to rely on them anywhere. Travellers cheques are not accepted anywhere. It's best to bring US dollars in all sorts of denominations. Ones, fives and 10s will prove handy when paying for just about anything; they are especially helpful around borders when you may need just a little cash for a taxi or a customs fees. Note that notes need to be in pristine condition to be accepted.

TURKMENISTAN

The only time you'll ever need to show an exchange receipt is if you plan to stay at Hotel Hazar in Turkmenbashi (p446).

Country	Unit	Manat
Afghanistan	Afg1	0.06M
Australia	A$1	2.54M
Canada	C$1	2.78M
China	Y1	0.41M
Euro zone	€1	3.57M
Iran	100 rials	0.02M
Japan	¥1	0.03M
Kazakhstan	10 T	0.19M
Kyrgyzstan	1som	0.06M
New Zealand	NZ$1	2.02M
Pakistan	Rs 1	0.03M
Russia	R1	0.09M
UK	£1	4.15M
USA	US$1	2.85M

Uzbek rate not included above due to instability.

POST

Your post may be read first, but at some stage it should still be delivered unless your postcard is truly offensive. Sending a postcard anywhere in the world costs 2M and a 20g letter costs around 2.20M. There are post offices in all towns, usually in the same place as the international phone centre and state-run internet cafe.

REGISTRATION

Anyone entering Turkmenistan on a tourist or business visa must be registered within three working days with the State Service for the Registration of Foreign Citizens (aka OVIR) via the local bureau of the state tourism company. The tour company that invited you will undoubtedly organise this. You will need two passport photos and your entry card, which you'll need to pick up at the airport. As well as this initial registration, you will automatically be registered by any hotel you stay at in the country for each night you stay with them – this service is included in the room price, and you won't have to do anything. However, travellers on tourist visas are therefore only able to stay in hotels with licences to register foreigners, the only exceptions being when you spend the night in a place without such an establishment, making these the only legal opportunities to stay in a homestay. Transit visa holders do not need to be registered, and transit visa holders can sleep wherever they please.

TELEPHONE

You can call internationally, nationally and send faxes from most big towns at the telegraph station, often referred to by its Russian name, *glavny telegraf*, or main telegraph office.

The major mobile phone provider is MTS (look for the sign MTC – MTS in Cyrillic). Prepaid SIM cards are available from their offices, though at the time of writing foreigners were only able to purchase them at the main MTS office at the back of the World Trade Centre in Ashgabat. In 2010 we were told that foreigners had to buy and recharge their cards in US dollars (US$7 per card). This makes it problematic to recharge your card as only the main office in any town (including Ashgabat) will accept dollars. By far your best bet would be to ask your guide to buy one for you in their name, as this can be easily recharged anywhere in the country using manats.

TRAVEL PERMITS

Permits are needed to visit the border regions of Turkmenistan. Given that the centre of the country is largely uninhabited desert and the population lies on the periphery, you need permits for some of the most interesting areas. Ashgabat, Mary, Merv, Turkmenabat and Balkanabat are not restricted, but anywhere outside these areas should be listed on your visa, thus giving you permission to go there. Travellers on transit visas can usually transit the border zones along the relevant main road, if they correspond to the country they are supposed to exit to.

Nature reserves are likewise restricted to the public unless you have a special permit. If you think you might want to visit one, you'll need to put in a request to your travel agent well in advance (see p430).

The following areas are termed 'class one' border zones and entry without documentation is theoretically not possible, though since the removal of the roadblocks that strictly controlled traffic movement during the Niyazov years, there's actually surprisingly little chance you'll have your documents checked:

Eastern Turkmenistan Farab, Atamurat (Kerki) plus adjoining areas, Kugitang Nature Reserve, Tagtabazar, Serkhetabat.

Northern Turkmenistan Entire Dashogus region including Konye-Urgench, Dargan-Ata, Gazachak.

Western Turkmenistan Bekdash, Turkmenbashi, Hazar, Dekhistan, Yangykala, Gyzyletrek, Garrygala, Nokhur and surrounding villages.

VISAS

All foreigners require a visa to enter Turkmenistan and transit visas are the only visas issued without a letter of invitation (LOI). Prices for visas vary enormously from embassy to embassy.

As a general rule, plan on getting a visa at least six weeks ahead of entry to Turkmenistan, as the process (even for transit visas) is lengthy. Ideally work through a Turkmen travel agent you trust. On entry every visa holder will need to pay an additional US$12 to US$14 fee for an entry card that will list your exit point in Turkmenistan.

For details on getting visas in Ashgabat for neighbouring countries see p462).

Transit Visas

The only visa that allows unaccompanied travel for tourists is the transit visa. Relatively easy to come by, they are normally valid for three days, although sometimes for five days and in rare cases, seven and even 10 days. Turkmen embassies in Europe (as opposed to Central Asia or Iran) are more likely to grant longer visas. Transit visas can be obtained at any Turkmen consulate, although if you apply without an LOI, the application will need to be forwarded to the Ministry of Foreign Affairs in Ashgabat, meaning a processing time of around 10 to 14 days.

No transit visa is extendable, save in the case of serious illness. The penalty for overstaying a transit visa is US$200, and you may be taken back to Ashgabat and deported on the next available flight at your expense.

Your route will normally not be indicated on the visa, but your entry and exit point (unchangeable) will be, and you may therefore run into trouble going anywhere not obviously between the two points (eg Nokhur or Kugitang), though as document checks on the roads are relatively few and far between these days, you can often get away with it. Transit visas are usually not valid if you are dealing with a Kazakh routing, a double-entry Uzbekistan visa or even an air ticket out of Ashgabat. Turkmen embassies regularly refuse transit visa applications, so don't count on getting one.

Note that the five-day transit visa is not enough time to cycle across the country, (ie from Turkmenbashi to the Farab border point), as you're likely to lose at least one day at Turkmenbashi (the boat may be delayed).

Tourist Visas

Tourist visas are a mixed blessing in Turkmenistan. While they allow the visitor to spend a decent amount of time in the country (up to three weeks as a rule), they require accompaniment by an accredited tour guide, who will meet you at the border and remain with you throughout your trip. This obviously has cost implications, as you will have to pay your guide a daily rate (usually between US$30 and US$50), as well as pay for their meals and hotels. The latter cost is very small, however, as Turkmen citizens pay a local rate that is at least 60% to 80% less than the foreigner rate. Guides will allow you to roam free in Ashgabat and the immediate environs unaccompanied, as well as around any other large town – there's no legal requirement for them to be with you throughout the day, but you're not legally allowed to travel in Turkmenistan without them. Most tour companies insist on travelling in private transport with the guide. But a few allow you to ride public transport with the guide, which drops the prices.

You can only get a tourist visa by going through a travel agency. Only travel agencies with a licence from the Turkmen government can issue LOIs. Many unaccredited agencies still offer LOI services, however, simply by going through an accredited agency themselves. The LOI will be issued with a list of all restricted border regions you are planning to visit. In turn, these are the places that will be listed on your visa, and so therefore it's essential to decide what you want to see before applying so that the appropriate restricted regions can be listed. The LOI is approved by the OVIR and takes five days. Rejections are neither common nor rare. Anyone working in the media, human rights or for political organisations had better not state this on their application, as it's certain to be rejected. Employers are rarely called and asked to verify an applicant's position, but it can happen, so have a good cover story.

Once the LOI is issued (usually faxed or emailed to you by your travel agent), you can take it to any Turkmen embassy to get your visa. The original LOI is not needed. The issuing of the visa itself is purely a formality, once the LOI has been issued. Normal processing time is three to seven working days depending on the embassy, but most Turkmen embassies offer an express service for a hefty surcharge, reducing processing time to between 24 hours and three days. When you apply for the visa, you will be asked for exact dates of entry and exit, which will be put on the visa. While you may leave before the exit date, you cannot leave any later or enter earlier than the entry date .

Armed with an LOI there is also the possibility of getting a visa on arrival at Ashgabat airport, Turkmenbashi and Farab by prior arrangement with your travel agent. In the case of Turkmenbashi and Farab, the agent needs to arrange for the consul to be present. In any case the original LOI must be taken to the relevant border and the visa will be issued for a maximum of 10 days.

On arrival in Turkmenistan, you must be met by your guide (*geed* in Russian) who will bring you a small green travel document, the Entry Travel Pass (*putyovka* in Russian). You should only exit the country at the point indicated on the travel permit, although if you alter your route there is the possibility of changing this in Ashgabat. To do this you will have to speak to your travel agent or guide and they can see what they can do. It is often possible to extend tourist visas in Ashgabat, again, only with the assistance of your travel agent.

TRANSPORT IN TURKMENISTAN

GETTING THERE & AWAY

For information on getting to/from Central Asia see p515.

Entering Turkmenistan

Entering the country overland tends to invite more scrutiny than arriving by air. Baggage checks can be very thorough at lonely border posts, while the undermanned airport in Ashgabat seems more interested in processing people quickly rather than in pawing through your underwear. You'll need to pay your arrival tax and collect your Entry Travel Pass if you're travelling on a tourist or business visa.

Air

The only international airport in Turkmenistan is **Saparmurat Turkmenbashi Airport** (☎ 37 84 11) in Ashgabat. For the contact details of airlines that fly in and out of Turkmenistan, see p440.

Land

Visitors with visas can enter Turkmenistan from all bordering countries, although the borders with Uzbekistan and Iran are the most frequently used. There are no international train or bus services to or from Turkmenistan. All land borders are open from 9am to 6pm daily.

BORDER CROSSINGS
To/From Afghanistan

Serkhetabat (formerly known as Gushgi) is the border town with Afghanistan. Crossing here is now a fairly hassle-free prospect, although be prepared to be thoroughly searched by both Turkmen and Afghan border guards. If you arrive late it's OK to overnight with a local family as there are no hotels in town.

The border post is 3km south of Serkhetabat. Leaving Turkmenistan, there's a 1.5km walk to the first Afghan village of Torghundi and it's a two-hour taxi journey onwards to Herat. If you are coming to Turkmenistan, you'll need to catch a ride from Herat to Torghundi (US$20 in a shared vehicle). Here you need to pay a US$12 to US$14 customs fee at a bank in town (1.5km south of the border), or you might be able to pay an extra US$4 to the border guard to do this for you.

The Saparmurat border crossing (called Imam Nazar) near Atamurat (also known as Kerki) is used by UN staff, but was not recommended for independent travellers at the time of writing.

To/From Iran

The simplest exit point is Gaudan/Bajgiran, due south of Ashgabat and a corridor between the Kopet Dag into Iran. From Ashgabat, take a taxi (40M to 50M) for the 20km ride to Yablonovka checkpoint. Here you'll have your passport checked, after which you take a marshrutka shuttle to the border. Once

---

ENTRY & DEPARTURE TAX

For entry into Turkmenistan there is a US$12 to US$14 fee per person, depending on your nationality. Bring cash in US dollars for this; change is normally available. International air departure tax is now included in all airline ticket prices. There is no domestic departure tax, nor by land or sea.

through, it's a taxi (US$2.50) across some 20km of no-man's-land to Bajgiran where you can get buses or taxis (US$20, four hours) to Mashhad.

There are also borders with Iran at Saraghs (there is a Mashhad–Saraghs train, but no international trains into Turkmenistan) and Gudurolum (which is reachable by car or taxi only).

To/From Kazakhstan

Shared taxis (120M/480M per seat/car) go from Turkmenbashi, via Karabogas, across the Kazakh border and on to Zhanaozen (Novy Uzen), where there is further transport to Aktau. From Karabogas to the border the road's a rough dirt track. Delays at the border can occur when caravans of traders appear together. Note that there is absolutely nothing on either side at this remote border – do not try to save money by paying for a taxi to the border post alone, as you'd be extremely lucky to find any onward transport from here.

To/From Uzbekistan

There are three crossings from Uzbekistan. Each crossing requires a walk of about 10 to 20 minutes across no-man's-land. Shared taxis are sometimes available to shuttle travellers across, the cost of which is approximately US$1. Whether they are operating or not when you visit is a matter of luck.

The Farab crossing is closest to Bukhara (Uzbekistan) and Turkmenabat (Turkmenistan). The 45km taxi ride to Farab from Turkmenabat should cost 15M for a taxi (or 4M for a seat in a shared taxi). From the border, take a taxi (US$20) to Bukhara, or hire a taxi as far as Uzbek Olot (or Karakol), where you can change to a shared taxi.

The Dashogus crossing is best if you are headed for Khiva or Urgench. A taxi from Dashogus to the Uzbek border is no more than 5M. From the border to Khiva expect to pay around US$10.

Less used is the Hojeli crossing, a 10-minute taxi ride (6M) from Konye-Urgench. Once across the border it's a half-hour drive to Nukus in Karakalpakstan. From the border, take public transport to Hojeli (US$2) or a taxi

all the way to Nukus (US$10). For more Uzbek border info, see p288.

Sea

You can enter Turkmenistan by boat from Azerbaijan. See p523 for details.

GETTING AROUND
Air

Turkmenistan Airlines serves most main cities with a fleet of modern Boeing 717s. As the main hub, most flights go in and out of Ashgabat, though there are also flights from Dashogus to Turkmenbashi, Mary and Turkmenabat, a Mary–Turkmenbashi flight and Turkmenbashi–Turkmenabat flight. Flights are extremely cheap and generally very reliable. Flights are generally full, but relatively large price increases of late have meant that fewer locals fly and so demand is not as ridiculous as it was before, when your only chance to get a seat was to book months in advance.

Car & Motorcycle

Driving through Turkmenistan is perfectly possible, but expensive and full of hassles. A carnet is not needed, though you'll need to pay the following: US$30 transit fee; US$50 obligatory third-party liability insurance; US$2 bank fee; US$5 documentation fee; and also US$10 for disinfection of your vehicle. Significantly, there's also a road tax calculated by the kilometre for your route through the country. Usually this totals around US$75 for cars and up to US$250 for larger vehicles. This effectively raises the cost of petrol (gas) from US$0.02 at the pumps to around US$1.50 in reality. Be aware that taking your vehicle on the ferry to/from Baku is an invite to be bribed.

Driving in Turkmenistan is a veritable freestyle sport, with drivers weaving indiscriminately through traffic and drag racing off green lights – you can do nothing but adapt. The drivers of Mary are notoriously bad – even Ashgabat drivers avoid cars with Mary tags. One last warning: fines can be imposed if you enter a city with a dirty car; make sure your vehicle is spotless after hauling it across the desert.

Afghanistan

Throughout its history, Afghanistan has been a country united against invaders but divided against itself. Its allure, spread by Great Game romantics and travel literature alike, has only been heightened by its inaccessibility over the last 30 years.

The most recent cycle of violence started with the Soviet invasion of 1979, a bloody 'David and Goliath' conflict, with the underdogs eventually besting the superpower. But the war's dividend wasn't peace, but a ruinous civil war – a morass that came back to haunt the West in the shape of the medieval Taliban and the smoking rubble of 9/11. The subsequent ouster of the Taliban promised another new start, but Afghanistan's rebirth as an infant democracy been troubled at best. Despite early promise, stability has proved difficult to find, with patchy reconstruction and the south of the country in particular bleeding from a deep-rooted insurgency.

Yet before all this bloodshed, Afghanistan had formed part of the original overland hippy trail, beguiling its visitors with great mountain ranges, a rich mix of cultures – and the Afghan people themselves, who greeted all with an easy charm and ready hospitality.

A battered, but beautiful and proud country, Afghanistan's road to recovery lies as strewn with pitfalls as ever, and the resilience of its people remains under strain.

FAST FACTS

- **Area** 650,000 sq km
- **Capital** Kabul
- **Country code** ☎ 93
- **Famous for** civil war, the Taliban, carpets
- **Languages** Dari (Afghan Persian), Pashto
- **Money** afghani (Afg); US$1=45.52Afg, €1=57.26Afg
- **Population** 28.4 million (2009 estimate)

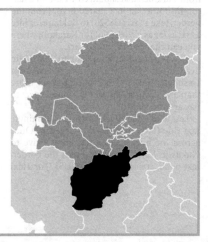

HOW MUCH?

- **Snickers bar** US$0.80
- **100km shared taxi ride** US$2
- **Internet connection per hour** US$1
- **Afghan pakol (hat)** US$2
- **Homestay** US$25
- **1L bottled water** US$0.40
- **1L petrol** US$1

HIGHLIGHTS

- **Kabul** (p476) Afghanistan's hectic capital, permanently buzzing on the cusp of change.
- **Bamiyan** (p481) Home to the giant Buddha niches, and the nearby sapphire waters of the Band-e Amir lakes.
- **Herat** (p483) The Silk Road heart of the country, with an astounding Friday Mosque and Citadel.
- **Mazar-e Sharif** (p486) The blue domes of the Shrine of Hazrat Ali make this Afghanistan's most important pilgrimage site.
- **Wakhan Corridor** (p488) The remote plateaus of the High Pamirs are perfect for trekking with yaks.

ITINERARIES

- **One week** Arriving in Kabul (p476), take a couple of days to explore the city, be-

fore heading out to the Bamiyan Valley (p481) and the lakes of Band-e Amir (p483).
- **Two weeks** Add a few days to the above itinerary, and then fly to Herat (p483) to explore the riches of its old city before either crossing into Turkmenistan or Iran, or returning to Kabul.
- **One month** Slow the pace down and then head into the north, checking out Mazar-e Sharif (p486) and Balkh (p487), before making a trek into the Wakhan Corridor (p488) and exiting the country to Tajikistan.

CLIMATE & WHEN TO GO

There's fine weather in spring (March to May), but rain and snowmelt can make many roads difficult to traverse. Summer (June to August) can be blisteringly hot, although Kabul and Bamiyan enjoy pleasantly cool nights. Autumn (September to November) is warm and dry, with plenty of delicious Afghan fruit. From the end of November winter arrives, and snow is common across much of the country making travel difficult.

HISTORY

Afghanistan's history as a country spans little more than two centuries, but in the past it has been part, or the centre, of many great empires. As with much of the region, the rise and fall of political power has been inextricably tied to the rise and fall of religions.

SAFE TRAVEL IN AFGHANISTAN?

The British Foreign & Commonwealth Office and US State Department both currently advise against travel to Afghanistan. The situation in Afghanistan continues to deteriorate and there's every reason to believe that things will remain unpredictable for some time to come. Due to the continuing instability affecting Afghanistan, we were unable to do on-the-ground research for this edition, and relied on friends and contacts residing in the country.

If you must travel to Afghanistan, it's imperative that you get the most up-to-date safety advice available. Check on security before setting out – the political situation can change quickly and without warning. A list of good news sources can be found on p492.

Bloody attacks inside Kabul (including the targeting of hotels) have become a favoured Taliban tactic, and the road to the Pakistan border at Torkham is not considered safe for travel. All points south of the capital remain firmly out of bounds, and the only secure way of reaching Herat is by air. Bamiyan remains an oasis of calm, as does Mazar-e Sharif, but the north is increasingly unstable, including Kunduz and parts of Badakhshan. Only the Wakhan Corridor, isolated by its remoteness, can be considered truly calm, but is best accessed via Tajikistan.

Always remember that Afghanistan is one of the most heavily mined countries in the world, and land mines and unexploded ordnance (UXOs) claim dozens of victims a month. It's common to see murals on buildings identifying different types of land mine and UXO.

It was in Afghanistan that the ancient religion of Zoroastrianism began in the 6th century BC. Later, Buddhism spread west from India into the country, where it remained strong in the Bamiyan Valley until the 10th century AD. The eastward sweep of Islam reached Afghanistan in the 7th century and to this day the entire country remains Muslim.

Empires & Invaders

Afghanistan has weathered invasions by such historical superstars as Darius of Persia, Alexander the Great, the Kushans, Sassanids, the Arabs, the Mongols, Timur (Tamerlane), Babur (the founder of the Mughals), the British and even the Soviet Red army. Between 1220 and 1223 Chinggis (Genghis) Khan tore

through the country reducing its cities to rubble. When the damage was finally repaired Timur swept through in the early 1380s and reduced the region to rubble again.

In contrast to Chinggis, Timur's reign ushered in a golden era, when poetry, architecture and miniature painting reached their zenith. Timur's descendants devoted much wealth and energy to the arts from their capital in Herat; building shrines, mosques and medressas from Balkh to Mashhad (in modern-day Iran) before the empire fell apart.

The rise of the Mughals returned Afghanistan to heights of power. Babur made Kabul his capital in 1512, after fleeing Central Asia (see p47), but as the Mughals extended their power into India, Afghanistan's status

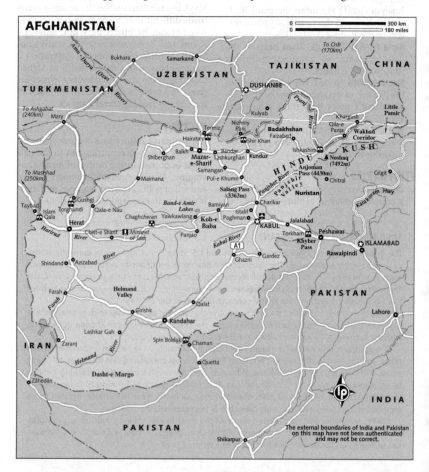

declined to the peripheries of empire. In 1747 Ahmad Shah Durrani broke free to found the kingdom of Afghanistan.

The Afghan Wars

The Afghan kingdom was under pressure almost from the outset. The Afghan summer capital of Peshawar was quickly lost to the Sikhs, while a greater worry was being caught between the attentions of the ever-expanding Russian and British empires. Afghanistan soon found itself at the heart of the Great Game (p50).

The first took place between 1839 and 1842. Britain contrived to put a friendly amir on the Afghan throne, backed up with an arm of redcoats. But in 1841, the Kabul garrison found itself under attack after British officer Alexander 'Bukhara' Burnes was hacked to pieces by an Afghan mob. The British attempted to retreat to India and were almost totally wiped out – out of 15,000 persons barely a handful survived. The British eventually reoccupied Kabul but were forced to put Dost Mohammed – who they'd originally overthrown – back in power.

Afghanistan agreed to become more or less a protectorate of the British, happily accepting an annual payment to keep things in shape and agreeing to another British resident in Kabul. But history repeated itself when striking soldiers murdered the British envoy, provoking another uprising. After being given another bloody nose on the battlefield by the Afghans, the British withdrew again, satisfied to keep control over Afghanistan's external affairs, but to leave the internal matters strictly to the Afghans themselves.

Later treaties between Britain and Russia took much of the heat out of the Great Game, when they agreed that Afghanistan would be a buffer between them, and they formalised its borders. In 1893 the British also drew Afghanistan's eastern boundaries with the so-called Durand Line and neatly partitioned a large number of the Pashtun tribes into imperial India, in what is Pakistan today. This has been a cause of Afghan-Pakistani strife for many years and is the reason that many Afghans refer to the western part of Pakistan as Pashtunistan.

The 20th Century

Britain and Afghanistan fought their last war in 1919, a brief affair that brought Afghanistan's first experience of air war, with the bombing of Kabul and Jalalabad by the Royal Air Force (RAF). Weary from the exertions of WWI, the British sued for peace and Afghanistan finally gained its independence.

From the 1920s onwards the US replaced Britain in worrying about Russian influence. Afghanistan was firmly in the Soviet sphere of influence and the Russian presence was strongly felt. Afghanistan's trade tilted heavily towards the USSR and Soviet aid to Afghanistan far outweighed Western assistance.

Internally Afghanistan remained precariously unstable. Attempts to encourage Turkish-style progress in the country failed dismally between WWI and WWII. The postwar kingdom ended in 1973 when King Zahir Shah was overthrown while in Europe by his cousin Daoud. Afghanistan's new ruler was scarcely any more progressive than his cousin had been, but the situation under him was far better than what was to follow.

After the bloody pro-Moscow revolution that took place in 1978, Afghanistan slid into turmoil and confusion. Its procommunist, antireligious government was far out of step with the countryside and soon the population was up in arms. A second revolution brought in a government leaning even more heavily on Soviet support and the country took another lurch towards anarchy.

The Soviet Invasion

Finally in late 1979, the Soviet regime decided that enough was enough. Another 'popular' revolution took place and a government was installed in Kabul, with what looked like half the Soviet army lined up behind it. Despite an ineffectual storm of Western protests it soon became clear that the Soviets were there to stay. An Islamic jihad (holy struggle) was called and seven competing mujaheddin factions emerged. The Soviets soon found themselves mired in what later became known as 'Russia's Vietnam'. They had the advantage of short supply lines, no organised protests from home and a divided enemy, but the Afghans were every bit as determined as the Vietcong.

The war ground on through the 1980s. The Afghan resistance remained disorganised and badly trained but to their determination and bravery they also began to add modern weaponry; the US CIA pumped up to US$670 million a year into the conflict in one of the

AHMAD SHAH MASSOUD – 'LION OF THE PANJSHIR'

Arriving in Kabul for the first time, you could be forgiven for confusing the identity of Afghanistan's president. Pictures of Ahmad Shah Massoud vastly outnumber those of Hamid Karzai.

Hailing from the Panjshir Valley north of Kabul, Massoud was the most formidable mujaheddin leader to fight against the Soviets. Largely ignored by the Pakistanis and Americans, he built a formidable guerrilla army that repulsed 10 Russian offensives against the Panjshir, often by evacuating its entire civilian population. His natural charm, fluent French and moderate Islam made him a hugely popular figure with Western journalists.

Following the capture of Kabul in 1992, Massoud became the real power behind the throne. While militarily brilliant, Massoud was no politician, and his inability to form alliances with other factions did much to prolong the civil war.

The Taliban reduced Massoud to a rump of power in the northeast. His assassination two days before 11 September 2001 has since cast him permanently in the role of martyr and saviour, his image reproduced everywhere in the style of an Afghan Che Guevara. Politically he has become more influential dead than when he was alive.

Not everyone idolises Massoud. Many Pashtuns resent him as a symbol of Tajik rule, Hazaras for his massacres of their kin, and others yet for the part he played in reducing Kabul to rubble in the 1990s. While Massoud will surely remain Afghanistan's number one poster boy for the foreseeable future, he's also a useful reminder that in civil wars few people emerge without any blood on their hands.

largest covert operations in history. Soon the Soviet regime held only the cities, but even supplying those became difficult as convoys were ambushed and aircraft brought down with surface-to-air missiles. In the late 1980s Gorbachov's policy of *perestroika* (restructuring) weakened the Russians' will to fight such an intractable opponent and suddenly they wanted out.

The decade-long war had cost the Soviets over 15,000 men, produced a wave of nationalism in the Central Asian republics and contributed significantly to the collapse of the USSR. In Afghanistan 1.5 million Afghans lay dead, and four times that many had fled the country.

Civil War in the 1990s

The Soviet withdrawal in 1989 weakened the Russian-backed government of President Najibullah. In an attempt to end the civil war, he proposed a government of national unity, but the mujaheddin refused to participate in any government that included the communist leader. In April 1992 Kabul finally fell to the mujaheddin, who immediately started fighting among themselves for control of the capital. Burhanuddin Rabbani, leader of the Northern Alliance faction, emerged as president.

His accession did nothing to stop the fighting. While the civilian population suffered,

the disparate mujaheddin groups and their international backers turned Afghanistan into an ever-bloodier playground, devastating the country and carving it into private fiefdoms. The civil war did more damage than the Soviet occupation and reduced much of Kabul to ruins.

The Taliban

War breeds terrible offspring and in the mid-1990s the Pakistan secret service acted as midwives to a group of Islamist Pashtun fighters calling themselves the Taliban. Largely borne of the refugee camps and medressas in Pakistan (Taliban means 'religious student'), they spectacularly captured Kandahar in 1994, Herat a year later, and in 1996 entered Kabul largely unopposed, where their first act was to drag Najibullah from hiding for a public lynching.

Many initially applauded the Taliban, and their illiterate one-eyed leader Mullah Omar, for bringing security, but their stringent Islamist vision also mean harsh penalties for anyone not meeting their vision of their Islamic 'emirate' – women were banned from working and forced under the burqa, while beards became compulsory for men, who could be flogged for not attending prayers five times a day. Their hardline policies later brought more international condemnation following their destruction of the giant statues of the Buddha at Bamiyan in March 2001.

By 1999 the Taliban were in control of 90% of Afghanistan, having pushed back their opponents (led by Ahmad Shah Massoud) to the far northeast of the country. Yet recognition as Afghanistan's new rulers eluded them. Instead, UN sanctions isolated the regime for its refusal to hand over Osama bin Laden, who the Taliban became increasingly tied to.

Bin Laden had to come Afghanistan in the mid-1980s, as part of the influx of Islamic militants who arrived to fight in the jihad against the Soviets. These so-called 'Arab-Afghans' later took their experience to conflicts ranging from Algeria to Chechnya, but Bin Laden stayed behind to form Al-Qaeda (The Base), an organisation dedicated to worldwide violent jihad. As the Taliban's isolation grew, Mullah Omar became increasingly reliant on Al-Qaeda, both financially and militarily. The Arab-Afghans were responsible for some of the worst atrocities against Afghan civilians, particularly the massacres in Bamiyan and Mazar-e Sharif of the minority Hazara population.

On 9 September 2001, two suicide bombers posing as journalists assassinated Massoud, an act heavily suspected to be the work of Al-Qaeda. Two days later, hijackers flew planes into New York's Word Trade Centre and Washington's Pentagon, killing over 3000 people.

The Taliban's days were numbered. Still refusing to hand over Bin Laden, the regime crumbled in the face of the US-led military campaign, Operation Enduring Freedom. The Taliban melted away, with Mullah Omar fleeing to the hills. A major offensive against Al-Qaeda at Tora Bora similarly failed to capture Bin Laden. On 13 November 2001 a resurgent Northern Alliance entered Kabul.

Reconstruction challenges

Although huge gains have been made since the Taliban's ouster, peace has barely been less rocky than the fighting that preceded it. Afghanistan in 2002 was effectively at 'Year Zero', its people traumatised and the infrastructure of the state destroyed. Huge attention was paid to getting the country back on its feet and assistance pledged by international donors. Girls returned to school and men shaved off their beards. Yet for every gain made, a step back was taken elsewhere.

Remembering the dark days of the civil war, Afghans craved security more than anything, but requests to expand international peacekeepers outside the capital were repeatedly blocked by the Americans. Instead, many of the warlords and mujaheddin were allowed to creep back into power through either direct support or the turning of blind eyes. The failure to properly control the south left the back door open for the return of the Taliban and the opium mafias. As the security situation there deteriorated, reconstruction efforts ground to a halt, further alienating a Pashtun population wondering where their peace dividend had gone.

A *loya jirga* (grand council) appointed Hamid Karzai as the new Afghan leader, and after the introduction of a new constitution in 2004 he became the country's first democratically elected president. A year later, parliamentary elections took place, with reserved seats for women, although many were dismayed that not only known human rights abusers were not disbarred from standing, several found their way into Karzai's cabinet. Meanwhile, the aid effort struggled with the massive reconstruction effort, and corruption, which had flourished in the absence of a strong state, has challenged the re-emergence of civil society.

Afghanistan today

A fitful peace has returned to most of the country, but international neglect of the south has proved the worm in the bud. Pakistan's border regions have provided safe haven for the Taliban leadership and fighters launching cross-border raids. Suicide bombs, previously unknown in Afghanistan, are now commonplace. Stuck in the death-grip of drugs and insurgency, south Afghanistan looks increasingly like a separate country, with the armies of the USA and Britain paying an ever-higher cost in blood and treasure in their attempts to pacify the Taliban heartland, particularly around Helmand province.

At the same time, the controversial election of 2009 returned Karzai as president amid allegations of vote-rigging on a massive scale. With war in the south and the rest of the nation continuing along its unsteady path, Afghanistan's immediate future is hard to divine.

PEOPLE

Afghanistan's location at the crossroads of Asia has produced a jigsaw of nationalities.

The largest ethnic groups are the Pashtun, Tajik and Hazara (see p62), but over a dozen smaller nationalities also live within Afghanistan's borders, from the Uzbek Baluchi and the blue-eyed Nuristanis, to the nomadic Kuchi and Kyrgyz. More than two decades of war has enflamed ethnic divisions. Afghanistan's ethnic mix breaks down into Pashtun: 42%, Tajik: 27%, Hazara: 9%, Uzbek: 9%, Aimaq 4%, Turkmen: 3%, Baluchi: 2%, and other: 4%.

Much of the recent Afghan experience has been framed by population flight. At the time of the Soviet withdrawal, there were over six million Afghan refugees, mainly living in Pakistan and Iran, and comprising over half the world's refugee population.

Afghans are famed for their hospitality. Foreigners experience this everyday, but war has severely damaged the structures of Afghan society. Displacement, violence and the absence of law for prolonged periods have helped produce a county riddled with corruption – according to Transparency International in 2009, the world's second most corrupt country.

Afghanistan is an agrarian society, but the majority of returning refugees have headed for the cities in search of employment, rather than returning to their home villages. The drought of the 1990s reduced may families to dependency on outside aid, while the failure to invest in agricultural reconstruction helped fuel the return of widespread opium cultivation, particularly in the south.

RELIGION

Afghanistan is majority Sunni Muslim. Around 15% of the population, mostly the Hazaras, follows Shiite Islam, and also in Badakhshan where much of the population are Ismailis. Sufism has always been an important strand in traditional Afghan Islam, with high importance attached to local saints and shrines.

The experience of war hardened the political role of Islam, and all mujaheddin groups espoused their Islamic ideals against secular communism. With much funding going to the most radical Islamist groupings, this eventually deepened ethnic and social divisions across the country and had a major effect on lengthening the civil war.

The Taliban movement was born in the medressas of Pakistan, particularly those teaching the hardline Deoband doctrine. This was combined with a Pashtun tribal code fractured through the experience of refugee camps, to produce a highly conservative interpretation of Islam – one rejected by most Afghans. The Taliban particularly discriminated against Shiites, whom they viewed as infidels, and forbade them to celebrate the central Shiite festival of Ashura.

ARTS
Music

Traditional Afghan music follows many of the same strands as the rest of Central Asia, with influences imported from north India. After the mujaheddin takeover of Kabul in 1992,

---

RECOMMENDED READING

The Sewing Circles of Herat by Christina Lamb wonderfully stitches together accounts of the author's time with the mujaheddin (including a young Hamid Karzai) with a return to post-Taliban Afghanistan to produce a beautifully balanced mix of reportage and travel writing.

The Places In Between by Rory Stewart is the account of an incredible journey walking across central Afghanistan in mid-winter, months after the fall of the Taliban. Pensive and well-observed, it's a great companion for anyone heading for that part of Afghanistan.

Ostensibly a quest for the roots of Islamic architecture, *The Road to Oxiana* by Robert Byron remains our favourite travel book on Afghanistan (and Persia), more than 70 years after it was written. Few characters in the travel literature genre are as memorable as the show-stealing Afghan ambassador to Tehran.

A Short Walk in the Hindu Kush by Eric Newby is one of the modern classics of travel writing. It describes the misadventures of two Englishmen who trekked to the remote Nuristan region in the 1950s. It has one of the best (and funniest) endings of any travel book.

A Bed of Red Flowers by Nelofer Pazira is a lyrical memoir of life growing up in 1970s Kabul, the Soviet occupation and her family's flight to Pakistan and Canada as refugees. The denouement, in Kabul and Moscow, is highly moving.

LANDAYS

Pashtun women are typically thought of as being the most voiceless of all Afghan communities, but they are also composers of one the most vibrant forms of poetry in the country – the *landay*. Landay is the Pashto word for a small venomous snake, and these poems follow suit: short, but with a lot of bite.

Like haiku, *landay* is a stylised poetry with a set number of syllables. The authors are usually unknown, but in almost all examples the woman addresses the man. Touching on the universal themes of love and war, the *landays* reveal a strong thread of pride, passion, longing and anger from beneath the burqa. Unrequited love and illicit love affairs are used by the women to taunt the weakness and virility of their men, for it is the women alone who carry the risks and consequences of their love. Some *landays* have even reached into history, such as the maiden Malalai's taunt to her menfolk credited, with inspiring a famous Afghan victory over the British army in 1880: ' My love! If you do not fall in the battle of Maiwand/Someone is saving you as a symbol of shame!'

Here are some of our other favourites:

'My beloved returned unsuccessful from battle/I repent the kiss I gave him last night'

'May you turn into a riverside flower/So that I may come on the excuse of taking water and smell you'

'O passing traveller!/Are you satiated with my sight or should I turn my face again?'

'You started loving, not I/Now the scandal has come into the open you blame me'

'Call it romance, call it love, you did it/I am tired now, pull up the blanket for I want to sleep'

many Afghan musicians fled into exile, as the militias often viewed musical performances as un-Islamic; the Taliban ban on music brought events to a close.

Traditional music has slowly made a return to the country, although Hindi pop is popular with many Afghans. The greatest of all modern Afghan musicians was Ahmad Zahir, the so-called 'Afghan Elvis', who died in 1979. More recently, the reality show 'Afghan Star' has sought to promote popular music forms, with a modern reality TV format that has infuriated the more conservative elements of society.

Poetry

Poetry is vital to Afghan culture and many of the greatest Persian poets, such as Jami and Rumi, were Afghan, while Iran's national epic, the *Shah Nama* by Firdausi, was actually composed for the Ghaznavid sultans in the 10th century.

Around the same time, Balkh produced the first female Persian poet, Lady Rabi'a Balkhi. Punished for her love of a slave, she was bricked up to die in a prison by her brother. Her tomb is still visited by young women and her name is popularly given to girls' schools and hospitals.

Pashtun poets are similarly revered, and the 17th-century warrior-poet Khushal Khan Khattak is often held up as a national ideal. His famous couplet sums up the martial spirit of his people:

'The Pashtun name spells honour and glory/Without that what is the Afghan story?'

Architecture

Afghan building has harnessed the vitality of the Central Asian steppe to the refinement of Persian culture to produce some masterpieces of world architecture (see also p77). Afghanistan's historical buildings suffered massively in more than two decades of fighting, but the war left one indelible architectural legacy – the metal shipping container, seen everywhere across the country, pressed into service as shops, workshops and temporary accommodation, often covered with mud brick to insulate against the heat and cold. Reconstruction has seen the rise of the 'poppy palace', modern confections of mock-Grecian pillars and plate glass – the name derived from the commonly held belief that those who have most profited from the new political order have been the most corrupted by opium money.

KITE FIGHTING

Of the Taliban's many prohibitions, the ban on kite flying seemed one of the most needlessly cruel. Any visitor to Afghanistan will soon become accustomed to seeing kites flapping above the streets. Kite flying is a favourite obsession of Afghan boys, one recently revealed to the outside world through Khaled Hosseini's haunting novel *The Kite Runner*.

The smallest kites are tiny affairs, homemade from plastic or paper scraps and a wire frame. There's no tail to increase manoeuvrability, and fliers can get their kites aloft in the barest waft of air, with patient tugs of the line. Being Afghanistan of course, there's a martial element to the pursuit and kites are fought against each other for supremacy of the skies. In kite fighting (*gudiparan bazi*), the kites' strings are covered with a mix of paste and ground glass. As the kites fly together, the flier attempts to position his kite to rub against the string of his opponent, to cut the kite loose. As the vanquished kite flutters to earth, a mad race breaks out to claim the prize. Trees and power lines take their share of the winnings too. Winter, with its strong winds, is the most popular time for kite fighting, while Kabul hosts a kite-fighting festival around Nauroz (Navrus; p503).

ENVIRONMENT

Afghanistan is a country of high mountains and sweeping steppes – a geography that has played a key part in its history. The flat north and west open out to the grass plains of Central Asia and the Iranian plateau – well-trodden invasion routes throughout the centuries. The massive spine of the Hindu Kush that bisects Afghanistan has given refuge to its people, and made the country hard to conquer completely.

War has left a high environmental toll on Afghanistan. The population upheavals caused by refugee flight have strained the land immensely, particularly in the pollution of water supplies and deforestation for firewood and shelter. The country as a whole suffered terribly as the result of a huge drought that lasted for much of the Taliban's reign, and the water table is still recovering.

Deforestation continues in the guise of illegal logging in the wooded provinces of Kunar and Paktia in the east. Mujaheddin groups, and now local warlords, have greatly profited by smuggling timber across the border into Pakistan. Massive erosion has been the result.

Afghanistan's wildlife continues to suffer. Rare falcons are caught and sold to Gulf Arabs for hunting, while in Badakhshan and Nuristan the snow leopard population remains under severe pressure from poaching.

FOOD & DRINK

Food shares much with the rest of Central Asia (see p85), with plenty of rice, kebabs and nan. Mounds of steamed rice with meat (*pulao*) are eaten everywhere from commu-

nal plates, most usually as *qabli pulao*, topped with almonds, raisins and grated carrot. In the north steamed dumplings are served with yoghurt sauce. They're either stuffed with meat (*mantu*) or leeks (*ashak*). Also look for *shorwa* (soup), and streetside *boloni* (vegetable-stuffed pancakes). Afghanistan is also famous for its fruit – particularly *angur* (grapes) from the Shomali Plain, northern *tarbuza* (melons) and Kandahari *anaar* (pomegranates).

The national drinks are either green tea (*chai sabz*) or black tea (*chai siah*) – both highly sweetened and scalding hot.

Bottled water is available everywhere, and fruit juices are very popular. It's illegal for Afghans to drink alcohol, but it is possible to buy it in some shops and upmarket restaurants in Kabul.

KABUL

☎ 020 / population 3 million (estimated) / elevation 1800m

Kabul has come a long way since the Taliban's 2001 ouster. Once a stop on the old hippy trail to India, then ruined by the civil war, the city has boomed in recent years, with endless new buildings being thrown up, fancy restaurants, busy bazaars and an air thick with the sound of mobile phones. But scratch the surface and things aren't always so rosy – the infrastructure creaks, electricity and clean water remain an aspiration for too many, and the background thrum of security alerts and road barriers remind you that Kabul's path to reconstruction continues to be rocky. As an introduction to Afghanistan it's exciting, frustrating, inspiring and shocking in equal measure.

HISTORY

Known in antiquity as Kabura, Kabul grew under the rule of the Greeks, Kushans, Hindus, Arabs and Timurids. Babur, the first Mughal, rhapsodised about its beauty, although it didn't become capital of the Afghan kingdom until 1772.

In the 19th century, Kabul became the centre of Russian and British rivalry. The British tried to install a puppet ruler in 1839, but their resident was hacked to pieces by a mob, and the Kabul garrison massacred as it tried to retreat from the city. The British returned to plunder the city in retribution, then blinked, amazed, when the same scenario replayed in 1878.

At the start of the 20th century King Amanullah led an ambitious modernising program. Cold War competition between the USA and Soviet Union later provided massive aid, and Kabul became a cosmopolitan city, then one under siege when war arrived. The downhill slide really started with the fall of Kabul in 1992, as the victorious mujaheddin fell into a murderous battle for control of the city. At different times, all the major factions fought with or against each other, but this meant little to Kabul's suffering population. Around 50,000 civilians lost their lives between 1992 and 1996 and the city was devastated.

The Taliban captured Kabul in September 1996 and quickly squeezed the remaining life out of Kabul, beating women for wearing high heels under their *burqas,* and imprisoning men whose beards were too short.

Under American bombardment, the Taliban fled Kabul in November 2001. The Northern Alliance walked back into power. Another army followed, this time of aid workers, contractors and returning refugees. Reconstruction has been a slow and often frustrating process.

ORIENTATION

Kabul sits on a plain ringed by the mountains of the Hindu Kush. The Kabul River divides the city. To the north is prosperous is Shahr-e Nau area, while east of this is Wazir Akbar Khan, home to many embassies.

The bustle of the city increases the closer you get to the river. Kabul's commercial heart beats around Pul-e Khishti bridge, and Jad-e Maiwand, badly damaged in the war. Also levelled in war was the model district of Darulaman, in west Kabul, home of the former palace and the Kabul Museum. New buildings are springing up everywhere.

Kabul International Airport is northeast of the city.

The **Afghanistan Information Management Service** (AIMS; ☎ 070-248 827; www.aims.org.af; Salang Wat) sells detailed city and country maps produced mainly for government and NGOs, while the **Afghanistan Research & Evaluation Unit** (www.areu.org.af) produces the useful *A-Z Guide,* with a directory of NGOs, ministries and embassies.

INFORMATION
Bookshops

Shah M Book Co (Charahi Sadarat) Also has a branch at the InterContinental Hotel. Excellent selection of books on the region.

Emergency

Ambulance (☎ 020 112/0799 357 049)
Kabul Police (☎ 911)

Internet Resources

Survival Guide to Kabul (www.kabulguide.net) Has a very useful bulletin board for news among the expat community.
What's on in Kabul (kabul.news@caritas.org) Weekly newsletter with news and listings.

Medical Services

Blossom Group Hospital (☎ 0790 298 397; www.blossom-group.org; Hanzala Mosque Rd, Shahr-e Nau; ⏲ clinic, 24hr emergency) Private Indian-run hospital with walk in general practice clinic and emergency treatment.
German Medical Diagnostic Centre (☎ 0799 136 211; www.medical-kabul.com; St 3, Charahi Ansari; ⏲ 9am-5pm, closed Fri) Offers wide range of laboratory diagnostic tests, vaccinations and x-rays. Treatment requires a deposit of US$100/5000Afg.

Money

To change money, ask first at your hotel or guesthouse; banks aren't much help.
Afghanistan International Bank (Behind Amani High School, Wazir Akbar Khan; ⏲ 9am-5pm Sun-Thu, 9am-1pm Sat) ATM. Also has 24-hour ATMs at Kabul airport, InterContinental Hotel, Kabul City Centre and Chelsea Supermarket, issuing US dollars and afghanis.
Standard Chartered Bank (St 10, Wazir Akbar Khan; ⏲ 9am-6pm) ATM issues US dollars and afghanis.

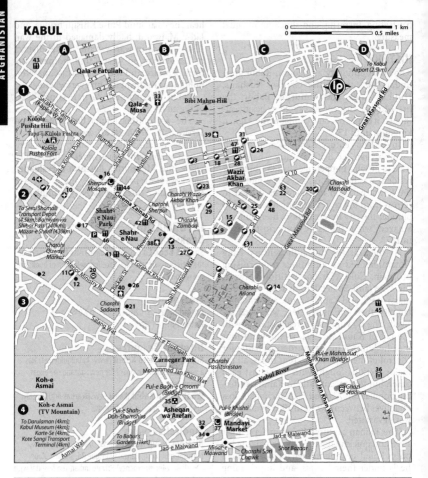

KABUL

Post

DHL (☎ 0799 750 750; Charahi Sherpur; ☒ 9am-6pm Sat-Thu)

Federal Express (☎ 020 250 0525; Sarakh-e Khai, Karte Se; ☒ 8am-5pm, Sat-Thu)

Post Office (Interior Ministry Rd)

TNT (☎ 020 220 0266; Charahi Torabaz Khan; ☒ 8am-5pm, Sat-Thu)

SIGHTS
Babur's Gardens

This formal **park** (Bagh-e Babur; admission 100Afg; ☒ 7am-sunset) was created in the 16th century by the first Mughal emperor, Babur. The walled gardens climb a series of terraces to give views over west Kabul. Babur is buried at the top of the garden. Below Babur's grave is a fine white marble mosque built by Shah Jahan (who built the Taj Mahal).

Gardeners have worked hard to replant the trees and rose bushes lost to neglect and war, resulting in one of the most peaceful and beautiful spots in Kabul. At the entrance there's a restored caravanserai, while a 19th-century pavilion looks out from the centre of the garden.

Kabul Museum

The **Kabul Museum** (Darulaman; admission 20Afg, camera 100Afg; ☒ 8am-3.30pm) was once one of the greatest museums in the world. It was greatly plundered during the civil war, when it found itself on a mujaheddin frontline, but has since been rebuilt. There's a surprising amount on display, including a series of huge wooden deities from Nuristan, several Graeco-Bactrian Buddha statues and a giant marble basin from Kandahar. Unfortunately, continued security concerns mean that the great gold treasures of the Bactrian Hoard, and the intricate Kushan-era Bagram Ivories are not on display and have instead been sent on an extended tour of word museums.

The ruins of **Darulaman Palace** sit on a rise opposite the museum. Built by Amanullah in the 1920s in grand European style, the palace is now little more than a war-ravaged shell.

National Gallery

The **National Gallery** (Asmai Wat; admission 250Afg; ☒ 8am-4pm) contains a mix of historic pictures and paintings by modern Afghan artists. It didn't escape the Taliban's zealous attentions, as the cabinet displaying ripped-up watercolour portraits attests. Amazingly however,

the gallery's staff fought against the Taliban's juncture against images of living things, overpainting many pictures with watercolours, hiding a horse behind a tree, or turning a person into a mountain view.

European Cemetery

This **cemetery** (Kabre Ghora; Shahabuddin Wat; donation requested; ☒ 7am-4pm) was established to bury the British killed in the second Anglo-Afghan war in the 1880s. A few of the headstones have been mounted in the right-hand wall, with more recent memorials added by the British, German and other NATO contingents.

The cemetery's most famous grave belongs to Sir Aurel Stein, acclaimed Silk Road archaeologist, who died in Kabul in 1943.

Old City

Virtually none of old Kabul survives, but it is still possible to get a taste of the traditional life of the city. **Pul-e Khishti Mosque** is a good place to start, then follow the bustle to the crossroads at **Minar-e Maiwand** and the old commercial thoroughfare of **Jad-e Maiwand.**

Off Jad-e Maiwand is **Ka Faroshi**, the old bird market. There has been a bazaar here for around 300 years. Most popular are *kowk* (partridges; used for fighting), as well as pigeons and songbirds, which are sold in beautiful handmade wooden cages.

Close by is the **Carpet Bazaar**, a good place to hunt for rugs. The lane leads up to the **Mausoleum of Timur Shah**. Built in the late 18th century in Mughal style, it has been beautifully restored by the Aga Khan Trust for Culture.

Chicken Street

Since the days of the hippy trail, Chicken Street has been a focus for Afghanistan's tourists. All kinds of handicrafts are available here, from jewellery to carpets. The eastern end turns into Flower Street, where you'll often see cars being decorated with bouquets and ribbons for wedding celebrations.

OMAR Land Mine Museum

This small **museum** (www.landmineclearance.org; bottom of Teppe Maranjan; ☒ Sun-Thu), run by the Organisation for Mine Clearance & Afghan Rehabilitation, it acts as a training and education centre for landmine clearance. It holds over 50 types of mine found in Afghanistan, and has information about demining and safety. Most sobering are the Russian 'butterfly' mines often picked up by children, mistaking them for plastic toys.

SLEEPING

Mustafa Hotel (☎ 0702 760 21; www.mustafahotel.com; Charahi Sadarat; r US$35-50, half board supplement US$10; 🖳) Truly a Kabul institution, the Mustafa was the main post-Taliban hang-out for journos, 'security consultants' and other would-be adventurers. Its high-rolling days have passed but it's still a decent place to stay, with small, adequate rooms, hot water and satellite TV in the lounge. No security.

Heetal Heritage Hotel (☎ 0797 001 002; heetal kabul@yahoo.com; St 14, Wazir Akbar Khan; r US$70-90; 🔀 🖳) On the edge of Wazir Akbar Khan, this place gets cleaner air than others in the city. It's laid out in a decent approximation of a caravanserai. Rooms could be bigger, but there's a good restaurant serving everything from Tex-Mex to Indian and a weekly film night to keep you entertained.

Gandamack Lodge (☎ 0798 511 111; www.ganda macklodge.co.uk; next to UNHCR, Charahi Sherpur; r US$115-143; 🖳 🔀) A perennially popular option with visiting media. There's a nice garden and rooms are comfy and tastefully decorated in colonial fashion. The restaurant is excellent, and worth visiting for the full English cooked breakfast alone, plus there's the Hare & Hounds pub in the cellar.

InterContinental Hotel (☎ 020 2201 320; reserv ations@intercontinentalkabul.com; Karte Parwan; r from 5000Afg; 🅿 🖳 🖳) This venerable institution was Afghanistan's first international luxury hotel. It's a 20-minute drive from the centre if the traffic allows, but the hilltop location gives great views of Kabul. Rooms are fine, but some can be musty.

Safi Landmark Hotel (☎ 020 2203 131; safiland markhotel@yahoo.com; Charahi Ansari; r from 200Afg; 🖳)

A SECURE BED FOR THE NIGHT

Taliban attacks in Kabul have recently targeted hotels and guesthouses used by foreigners, often with lethal effect. Although we have endeavoured to list the most secure accommodation, be aware that many of these hotels have been the focus of attacks, and no accommodation in Kabul can be regarded as truly secure.

You can't miss the Safi, part of the Kabul City Centre tower block in bright green glass. The lobby speaks of understated service, and a glass elevator whisks you to your room, many of which overlook the shopping mall. Everything is laid on, but for the money the rooms are a bit small and cramped.

Kabul Serena Hotel (☎ 0799 654 000; www.serena hotels.com; Jad-e Froshgah; r from US$275; 🅿 🔀 🖳) Serena is now owned by the Aga Khan. It has undergone a massive renovation to transform it into Kabul's swankiest hotel by some stretch. The public areas are all light and space, while rooms have all mod-cons and a sprinkling of traditional Afghan decor.

EATING

Herat (Cinema Zainab Rd, Shahr-e Nau; meals 60-150Afg; ☒ 10am-10pm) A really great Afghan place which positively bursts at lunchtime, when half of Kabul appears to eat here. The *mantu* (steamed dumplings) will set you back 80Afg, but save some room for the sticky sweets at the end with your tea.

Taverna du Liban (☎ 0799 828 376; Lane 3, St 14, Wazir Akbar Khan; mezze from US$3, mains from US$8; ☒ 11.30am-midnight) Several Lebanese restaurants have come and gone in Kabul; this one has stayed the course. Tables are easily laden with mezze, load up before hitting the grill for your main.

Flower Street Café (☎ 0700 293 124; St 2, Taimani; snacks from US$4; ☒ 8am-8pm) The name is momentarily confusing, as this cafe is nowhere near Flower Street. It's worth finding though, as it does some great sandwiches and burgers served in a flowery garden, with cake for afters.

Delhi Darbar (☎ 0799 324 899; Muslim St; mains from US$5; ☒ 10am-9pm) A popular choice for Indian food, with branches in Mazar-e Sharif and even Tajikistan. The focus is on north Indian cuisine, fiery curries and lots of vegetarian options, washed down with a cold lager.

Red Hot Sizzlin' (☎ 0799 733 468; Microrayon 1; meals from US$9; ☒ 10am-9.30pm) Slightly out of the way, this restaurant is the place to go if you're after a steak, American-style. It's all Tex-Mex here, with juicy T-bones, piles of fries and a cold one to wash it down with.

Chelsea Supermarket (Jad-e Torabaz Khan) The biggest (and dare we say most expensive?) supermarket selling imported food and toiletries in Kabul. It's handy though, and has an ATM. Who can argue with its proud motto over the door: 'Be happy all the time'.

GETTING THERE & AWAY
Air
Kabul is the main gateway to Afghanistan, and has the country's only international **airport** (☎ 020 2301344). For more information on international flight connections see p515.

AIRLINE OFFICES
Ariana Afghan Airlines (☎ 0752 023 494; www.flyariana.com; St 10, Wazir Akbar Khan)
Kam Air (☎ 020 2301753; www.flykamairline.com; Kabul Business Centre, Shahr-e Nau)
Pamir Airways (☎ 0700 151 000; www.pamirairways.af; St 13, Wazir Akbar Khan)
Safi Air (☎ 020 2222 222; www.safiairways.aero; Charahi Quwayi Markaz, Shahr-e-Nau)

Pamir has the largest domestic network, with daily flights from Kabul to Herat, Mazar-e Sharif, Kandahar, and several weekly to Kunduz and Faizabad. Kam Air operates to Mazar-e Sharif, while Ariana flies to most major cities, but chops and changes its schedule without warning.

Minibus & Shared Taxi
Several terminals serve Kabul, though in reality they are little more than massed ranks of vehicles, with drivers shouting out the destinations and leaving when they are full, rather than by any set timetable. If you do have to wait, there's always somewhere to get tea or juice and a plate of kebabs. At the time of writing, only the highway north to Mazar-e Sharif could be regarded as secure.

Minibuses heading north through the Salang Tunnel depart from Serai Shomali, a 20-minute taxi ride to the Khair Khana district on the edge of Kabul. Minibuses from here include Mazar-e Sharif (eight hours), Kunduz (10 hours) and Faizabad (1½ days).

To travel to Bamiyan (10 hours), catch a minibus from Kote Sangi (sometimes called Pul-e Sokhta) in west Kabul, but ensure you travel only via the Shomali Plain/Shibar Pass route; the southern route (via the Hagijak and Unai Passes) is too dangerous to travel.

Faster shared taxis also depart from the same terminals, and cost up to a third more. Long-distance transport can start leaving from 5am or 6am, so arrive early.

GETTING AROUND
To/From the Airport
A taxi between the airport and the centre of Kabul should cost 200Afg, a 20-minute trip given good traffic. Security at the airport is extremely tight, with vehicles subject to security checks on arrival and all luggage searched. Always factor in extra time when flying out.

Local transport
There are plentiful yellow taxis. **Afghan Logistics & Tours** (☎ 079 8443 311/077 7443 311; www.afghanlogisticstours.com; per trip US$7 6am-6pm, US$5 6pm-6am, airport transfer US$15) operates secure 24-hour, radio-controlled taxi services in Kabul, as well as renting cars and 4WDs.

CENTRAL AFGHANISTAN
Known as the Hazarajat, this region is high and isolated in the knot of the Koh-e Baba mountains. It is one of the most beautiful areas of Afghanistan and contains some its best attractions – the Bamiyan Valley and the incredible blue lakes of Band-e Amir. Beyond these is the Minaret of Jam, hidden deep in the folds of the mountains.

BAMIYAN
elev 2500m
Once a place of Buddhist pilgrimage, Bamiyan is now more closely associated with the destruction visited on Afghanistan's culture by war. The two giant statues of the Buddha that once dominated the valley now lie in rubble, victims of the Taliban's iconoclastic rage. Despite this, the Bamiyan Valley remains one of the most beautiful (and stable) places in Afghanistan, and a must-see for any visitor. The valley was made a World Heritage site in 2003.

Bamiyan is a one-street town, dominated by the sandstone cliffs that form the northern wall of the valley. The Buddha niches are visible from everywhere in Bamiyan; they are a short walk over the river from the town centre. Bamiyan sees heavy snow from November through to spring, and nights can be cold even in the height of summer. Take care with well-marked mined areas.

The first annual Bamiyan Silk Road Festival was held in July 2009, attracting many visitors with music, art and other cultural events. For more information, contact the Bamyan Ecotourism office, or the official Bamiyan visitor's **website** (www.bamyantourism.org).

Information
Bamiyan's scanty amenities – telephone offices, moneychangers and the **Bamiyan Business**

Centre (internet cafe) are all found on the main street.

Bamyan Ecotourism Office ☎ 077 8227 935; amir. foladi.@akdn.org; Shahr-e Nau) Excellent tourism development office run by the Aga Khan Development Network, has pamphlets and trained guides.

Sights

THE BUDDHA NICHES

Bamiyan's two Buddhas, standing 38m and 55m respectively, were the tallest standing statues of the Buddha ever made, created around the 6th century AD.

The statues weren't simply carved out of the sandstone cliffs. The rough figures were hewn from the rock, which was then covered in mud and straw to create the intricate folds of the robes, before being plastered. Each statue was then painted, and the faces covered with gilded masks.

The walls of the niches were covered in paintings, with symbolism borrowed from Greek, Indian and Sassanid art. The fusion of these traditions gave the Buddhist art of Bamiyan its vitality.

The surrounding cliffs are honeycombed with monastic cells. These were decorated with frescoes, although almost all have been lost. Passages and stairways link a warren of chambers and halls surrounding the Buddhas, which you are free to explore – buy a ticket at the **Director of Information and Culture** (entry to Buddha niches, Shahr-e Gholghola & Shahr-e Zohak 200Afg; ☾ 8am-5pm), located in front of Large Buddha niche. Entrance includes a guide.

At the foot of the cliff, a series of stupas and monasteries further served the complex. The Chinese monk Xuan Zang visited Bamiyan at the height of its glory in the 7th century and noted 10 convents and over 1000 priests. Of the statues themselves, he wrote, 'the golden hues sparkle on every side, and its precious ornaments dazzle the eye by their brightness'.

Following Bamiyan's conversion to Islam, memories of its past faded and locals imagined that the statues were of pagan kings. Amazingly Chinggis Khan left them untouched. In the 17th century the Mughal Aurangzeb smashed their faces, and 100 years later the Large Buddha had its legs chopped off.

During the civil war, the niches and caves were used as ammunition dumps; the statues suffered under pot shots from the soldiers. The final indignity came with their complete demolition by the Taliban – an indelible testament to Afghanistan's many cultural losses in recent decades.

SHAHR-E GHOLGHOLA

The impregnable walls of this citadel were Bamiyan's last bastion against the Mongol hordes. The ruling king, Jalaludin didn't reckon on the treachery of his daughter. In a fit of pique at her widowed father remarrying, she betrayed the fort's secret entrance to the invaders, expecting to be well rewarded. Chinggis put her to the sword anyway, along with the rest of the defenders, hence the citadel's modern name – 'City of Screams'.

Shahr-e Gholghola lies 2km southeast of Bamiyan. The climb to the top gives excellent views of the Bamiyan Valley. You need a ticket from the Director of Information and Culture.

SHAHR-E ZOHAK

The ruins of Shahr-e Zohak, perched high on the cliffs at the confluence of the Bamiyan and Kalu Rivers, guard the entrance to the Bamiyan Valley.

The citadel is still relatively intact and it's possible to see the barracks, stables and defensive towers. There are mines around the ruins, so stick to the clearly marked path.

Shahr-e Zohak is 17km east of Bamiyan on the road to Kabul. Take your ticket from the Director of Information and Culture for entry.

Sleeping & Eating

Zohak Hotel (☎ 079 9235 298; Shahr-e Nau; s/d US$20/40) Bamiyan's reliable budget option. Rooms are compact and basic, but clean. Shared bathrooms have hot showers and squat toilets. Food is good, with large plates of rice, vegetables and meat for around 150Afg.

Roof of Bamiyan Hotel (☎ 079 9235 292; Sir Asyab; r US$40-60) If it's location you're after, head here – this hotel offers fantastic views over the Bamiyan Valley. Clean bathrooms are shared, with the cheaper rooms in a separate annex plus a series of yurts. The manager, an Afghan veteran of the hippy trail, can organise reliable vehicle hire and the like.

Hotel Silk Road (☎ 079 8405 486; www.silkroadbami yan.com; Foladi Rd; s/d US$100/200) This new hotel is a venture run by a Japanese ex-journalist and her Afghan husband. It's an impressive modern venture, with comfy rooms, and a good rooftop cafe with excellent food (dinner US$15) that looks towards the Buddha niches.

Aside from hotel restaurants, there are several chaikhanas on the main street serving kebabs and *pulao*.

Getting There & Away

Minibuses depart early morning for Kabul (nine hours). There are two roads to Kabul – the northern (via the Shibar Pass and Shomali Plain) and the southern (via the Hagijak and Unai Passes and Wardak province). The latter route is extremely dangerous due to Taliban activity and must be avoided. There are minibuses most days to Band-e Amir (three hours), and west to Yawkawlang. Snowfall and floods can make the route west from Bamiyan extremely difficult from November to as late as May.

There are no commercial flights to Bamiyan.

BAND-E AMIR

Afghanistan's first national park, the lapis-blue lakes of Band-e Amir, deep in the Koh-e Baba mountains, glitter like jewels against their dusty surrounds. The most accessible is Band-e Haibat – the suitably named Dam of Awe.

Over the millennia, sulphur deposits have formed huge curtain walls that contain the waters of the lakes. These natural dams stand over 10m tall, and must be Afghanistan's greatest natural wonder. Indeed, locals credit the creation of the lakes to miracles performed by the Prophet Mohammed's son-in-law Ali, and pilgrims visit to enjoy the water's reputed healing powers. There is a small mosque dedicated to Ali on the shore of Band-e Haibat.

Eating & Sleeping

There are a number of chaikhanas near the edge of Band-e Haibat, offering simple food and a very rough bed for the night for 100Afg.

Getting There & Away

There are minibuses most days to Band-e Amir from Bamiyan. Hiring a vehicle for a day trip will cost around US$60.

THE MINARET OF JAM

This fabulous **minaret** (Minar-e Jam; admission US$5, still/video camera US$5/10, vehicle US$10, translator US$15) sits in the remote valleys of the Koh-e Baba. Forgotten by the outside world until the mid-20th century, it remains a holy grail for many travellers to Afghanistan. Dating

from the late 12th century, the minaret is the visible remnants of the Ghorid capital of Firuzkoh, destroyed by the Mongols. The minaret has undergone emergency work to protect its foundations from the river. It became Afghanistan's first World Heritage site in 2002.

Three tapering cylindrical storeys rise 65m from an octagonal base, the whole completely covered in intricate raised cafe-au-lait brick decoration. Interlocking chains, polygons and medallions wind delicately around the shaft, interspersed with text from the Quran. A ladder allows you to crawl through a narrow entrance hole to climb the interior to an upper gallery. There are two staircases, winding around each other like a DNA double-helix. The views are astounding.

There's a simple government-run guesthouse (room US$30, dinner US$10, breakfast US$5) next to the minaret.

WESTERN AFGHANISTAN

Afghanistan's western provinces feel a world away from the mountains that dominate much of the country. The land here is flat and open, stretching out to the Iranian Plateau and the Central Asian steppe. Such geography means that its principal city, Herat, has both prospered from trade and suffered from the designs of foreign invaders. Road connections to the rest of Afghanistan are poor or dangerous (there are flights to Kabul), but from the main city of Herat, it's possible to cross into either Turkmenistan or Iran.

HERAT

One-time capital of the Timurid empire and seat of learning and the arts, Herat has flourished throughout history as a rich city-state, and been repeatedly fought over. The city is as much Persian as it is Afghan, and wears an air of independence as the country's old cultural heart.

Herat's place in history has often been overlooked in favour of Samarkand and Bukhara, but its inhabitants are proud of their past and the city's reputation as a place of culture. Many of Herat's historic monuments are in a sorry state, ruined by British and Russian invaders, but with its Friday Mosque the city

CROSSING CENTRAL AFGHANISTAN

A trip through the Hazarajat to see the Minaret of Jam is one of the most adventurous trips possible in Afghanistan. The roads are appalling, the region remote, and outside June to September snow and spring melt can make the roads difficult or impossible to traverse. There are several passes over 3000m that are frequently closed, cutting off the region from the outside world. Always check the security situation before attempting this route.

Minibuses west from Bamiyan to Yawkawlang (six hours) depart most days. It's a typical town of the Hazarajat, set in a well-watered valley. The Park Hotel and Newab Hotel offer standard chaikhana fare. Minibuses west to Chaghcheran (one day) leave less frequently; you may need to head to Panjao and change there.

The road through the heart of the Koh-e Baba is spectacular. It's often possible to see the Aimaq, a seminomadic people who share the area with the Hazaras, herding their flocks. After Lal-o Sar Jangal, the poor road deteriorates further. You'll often drive along dry riverbeds and see more animal traffic than other vehicles.

Chaghcheran is the largest town in the region. The town was once a major bazaar for nomads, and in the summer months Aimaq and Kuchi nomads still bring their livestock to market here. Hotel options are limited to the chaikhanas near the bazaar, but transport connections are decent, including 4WD hire to Jam and minibuses to Herat (1½ days).

There is no direct transport to the Minaret of Jam. Take any transport heading west and get off at the junction town of Garmao (10 hours). Trucks regularly take the road north to Kamenj and will be able to take you to Jam.

The approach to the minaret is beautiful. After crossing the Garmao Pass, the road descends to the waters of the Hari Rud. The mountain walls twist and close in, until the minaret is finally revealed, hidden in the narrow cleft of the valley.

From Garmao, the road continues west to Herat via Chist-e Sharif and Obey – both reasonably sized towns and transport hubs. The latter has hot springs that are worth a visit. With an early start you'll reach Herat in one day. At Obey, the sealed road leads to Herat in a couple of hours.

still possesses one of Islam's great buildings. The insecurity of the Herat–Kandahar highway occasionally ripples back to disturb the city, while a long-term Iranian influence is never far from the surface.

Orientation

Only the core of Herat's old city remains, around the crossroads of Chahar Su and the Friday Mosque. The citadel dominates the northern edge of the old city, looking out to the minarets of the ruined Musalla Complex. West of this the wasteland created by Soviet carpet bombing is being replaced by a building boom.

The new town (Shahr-e Nau) is east and north of the walled city and home to the majority of government and NGO offices. The streets are lined with tall pine trees.

Herat's airport is 8km south of the city, on the same road as the new bus station.

Information

Street moneychangers remain the best option in Herat: there are stands between Darb-e Malik and Chowk-e Gulha. There are several internet cafes on Jad-e Walayat.

AIMS (www.aims.org.af) Has an excellent downloadable map of Herat.

Ariana Afghan Airlines (☎ 040 222315; Park-e Gulha)

Herat Hospital (☎ 040 223412; Jad-e Walayat)

Kabul Bank (cnr Park-e Gulha & Jad-e Ghomandani) Has a branch of Western Union inside.

Police (☎ 040 222200; Jad-e Ghomandani) Located opposite the Friday Mosque.

Sights

OLD CITY

Herat's Old City, measuring approximately 1200 sq metres, is the most complete traditional medieval city in Afghanistan, although modern development is putting it under extreme pressure. Four main streets radiate out from the bazaar of Chahar Su to the old gates that pierced the city walls, which were pulled down in the 1950s. A few of the vaulted covered bazaars survive, along with the great brick cisterns that kept the city supplied with water, recently restored by the Aga Khan Trust for Culture.

Plenty of the character of the Old City remains. Entrances off the main street lead into old caravanserais, now used as warehouses for carpet sellers and cloth merchants, and donkey carts make up much of the traffic in side streets too narrow for cars.

FRIDAY MOSQUE
Over 800 hundred years old, Herat's **Friday Mosque** (Masjid-e Jami; ☽ closed to non-Muslims during Friday prayers) is Afghanistan's finest Islamic building. The mosque is laid out in the classical four-*aivan* (arched portal) plan. Two huge minarets dominate the courtyard, with every square centimetre covered in fabulous mosaic.

Of the original decoration, only a section of floral stucco remains in the south *aivan*. In a cell on the east side is a huge ceremonial bronze cauldron from the 13th century, which now takes donations for the mosque's upkeep.

The lavish tiling that covers the mosque is the product of the tile workshop set up in the 1940s. The workshop is based near the east entrance, and the craftsmen will readily show off their work.

Mosque attendants are normally happy for you to take photos, but this should be avoided during prayer times.

THE CITADEL
Towering over the Old City, the Citadel, or **Arg** (Qala-ye Ikhtiyaruddin; admission 250Afg; ☽ 8am-5pm) has foundations dating back as far as Alexander the Great. Shah Rukh built the present fort early in the 15th century.

The Citadel has been much rebuilt and restored with fired brick by successive rulers. It was originally covered in bright tiling, and some Timurid decoration remains on the northwest towers. The biggest attraction is the Citadel's huge curtain wall topped with battlements, offering tremendous views over Herat, looking south towards Chahar Su, and north to the minarets of the Musalla Complex. It's also possible to make out the last remains of the old city walls.

MUSALLA COMPLEX & MINARETS
Herat's Musalla Complex was Gowhar Shad's masterpiece, comprising a mosque, medressa and mausoleum, and over 20 minarets. The British dynamited most of the complex in 1885, with the rest falling to earthquakes and war.

One minaret of the Musalla survives, with a mortar hole bitten out of it. Gowhar Shad's mausoleum stands in the middle of the grounds, topped by a huge ribbed dome. The caretaker may unlock it for you to see her tombstone. The cupola is beautifully painted in blue and rust-red. A smaller building next door holds the tomb of Mir Ali Shir Nawai (Alisher Navoi), Sultan Baiqara's prime minister.

Opposite, four minarets, leaning at dangerous angles, mark the corners of Baiqara's long-gone **medressa** (admission free; ☽ 7am-sunset). The minarets were covered in delicate blue lozenges framed in white and set with flowers. A little tiling remains – war and the abrasive wind have done away with the rest.

GAZAR GAH
This Sufi shrine, 5km northwest of Herat, is one of Afghanistan's holiest sites, dedicated to the 11th-century saint Khoja Abdullah Ansari. It's also the most complete Timurid building in Herat, dominated by a 30m-high portal. The courtyard inside the shrine is filled with gravestones, and decorative tiling covers the walls and arches. At the far end, under an ilex tree, is the saint's tomb.

Locked in a cell on the left side of the tomb is the Haft Qalam (Seven Pens) sarcophagus, named for its intricate carving. The tomb of Amir Dost Mohammed, who died soon after capturing Herat in 1863, sits in front.

The shrine is a popular place for both men and women to visit, and you'll see people offering prayers to the tomb before turning around to perform the full prayer ritual facing Mecca. There's no entrance fee, but the Sufis who tend the shrine appreciate a small donation.

Sleeping & Eating
Marco Polo Hotel (☎ 0799 206 192; heratmarcopolo@ yahoo.com; Jad-e Badmurghan; s/d from US$25/44, with bathroom US$40/70; ☒ ▣) An ever friendly option, the Marco Polo isn't elaborate, but there's 24-hour hot water, free internet, helpful staff and a generous breakfast.

Nazary Hotel (☎ 0799 345 100; www.nazaryhotel.com; Jad-e Walayat; s/d US$66/88; ☒ ☎) By some degree Herat's best hotel, you can't miss this shiny tower-block on the main road. Rooms are very comfortable, with all the mod-cons, plus a restaurant, coffee shop, gym and vehicle/ security hire.

Arghawan Restaurant (☎ 040 221919; Chowk-e Cinema; kebab meal 200Afg; ☽ 8am-11pm) Popular with middle-class Heratis and internationals alike, the attraction here isn't so much the formal dining room as the outside seating area, strewn with bolsters to slump against and shade for the heat of the day. The set meals are excellent value, comprising soup, salad, bread, rice, kebabs, tea and a soft drink.

Yas Restaurant (Park-e Girdha; menu from 60-200Afg; ☺ 9am-10pm) Always busy, this is one of the few places we found in Herat serving *mantu*. Yas also has a decent range of kebabs with rice, salad and yoghurt. The pizzas are disappointing in comparison.

There are some good juice bars are Park-e Gulha, while kebab sellers and chaikhanas cluster around Darb Khosh.

Shopping

Herat is famous for its blue glass, handmade by Sultan Hamidy and his family for generations in a tiny factory north of the Friday Mosque. Ask at his shop if you may watch the glass being blown.

Getting There & Away

Herat is poorly connected by road – the highway to Kabul via Kandahar passes through a warzone and countless Taliban checkpoints, while the two-day slog to Maimana (and on to Mazar-e Sharif) passes through similarly risky territory. There are daily flights to Kabul (3500Afg, one hour) and several weekly to Mazar-e Sharif (3000Afg, 45 minutes) and Chaghcheran (3000Afg, 45 minutes) with Pamir Airways.

There are several daily buses to Mashhad in Iran (see p493 for more information).

NORTHERN AFGHANISTAN

North of the Hindu Kush is a rather different Afghanistan – akin to the Central Asian steppes. Indeed, prior to the modern obsession about borders, the Afghan nomads were quite at home on both sides of the Amu-Darya, which now separates Afghanistan from both Tajikistan and Uzbekistan. The Salang Tunnel through the Hindu Kush connects the region to Kabul.

The shimmering blue domes of Mazar-e Sharif, and ancient Balkh draw traveller's interest, while the Wakhan Corridor in the high Pamirs offers trekking as remote as anyone could desire.

MAZAR-E SHARIF

North Afghanistan's biggest city, Mazar-e Sharif was long overshadowed by the power of its neighbour Balkh. It took a 12th-century mullah to change that. He claimed to have found the hidden tomb of Ali, the Prophet Mohammed's son-in-law, buried in a local village. Balkh declined and Mazar grew as a place of pilgrimage. Its shrine today is the focus of the national Nauroz (Navrus) celebrations, and is a great place to see *buzkashi* (a pololike game played with a headless goat carcass).

The blue domes of the Shrine of Hazrat Ali dominate Mazar-e Sharif. The shrine sits in a large park in the centre of the city, with four main roads radiating out to the cardinal points. Mazar is a good place to pick up gilims and embroidery – the shops along the east side of the shrine have the best stock.

Sights

SHRINE OF HAZRAT ALI

Popular Muslim tradition contends that Ali is buried in Najaf in Iraq, but in the 12th century he visited a local mullah in a dream, revealing his true tomb to be hidden in a village near Balkh. A shrine was subsequently built on the site, which was renamed Mazar-e Sharif (Tomb of the Exalted). The building was levelled by Chinggis Khan, who had heard rumours of gold buried beneath its domes. Balkh's Timurid rulers rebuilt the current shrine in the 15th century.

The shrine has undergone repeated extensions and restoration, and most of the current decoration is modern. The complex is also home to hundreds of white pigeons; the site is so holy it's said that if a grey pigeon flies here, it will turn white within 40 days.

There's no entrance fee, but non-Muslims are not permitted to enter the tomb itself.

Festivals & Events

NAWROZ

Mazar-e Sharif is the centre of Afghanistan's Nauroz celebrations. A *janda* (religious banner) is raised in the courtyard of the shrine, which families visit to picnic at, celebrating the arrival of spring. *Buzkashi* is played at Mazar Stadium, or on a large, open expanse, south of the city, called Meidan-e Buzkashi.

Sleeping & Eating

Barat Hotel (☎ 0799 015 229; Chowk-e Mukharabat; r US$20-80; 🔌) This is a modern hotel, with carpeted rooms, squashy beds and decent furniture. Bathrooms are shared but are kept spotlessly clean and have lashings of hot water. Rooms on the upper floors are nicer, and are more expensive; management also ask for more if you want a view of the shrine.

Delhi Darbar (☎ 0705 05417; Jad-e Maulana Jalaluddin Balkhi; 🕙 noon-10pm) Sister to the restaurant in Kabul, and Mazar-e Sharif's best dining. Eat inside or in the walled garden in summer. The *thali* (meat or vegetarian) is good value at US$5, and goes well with a US$2 beer. Popular with NGO expats. You'll find it opposite the military hospital.

Kebab shops, chaikhanas and juice stands line the side streets near the shrine. *Mantu* is popular in Mazar-e Sharif, so take a break from kebabs and *pulao*. Bread comes in heavy round loaves rather than the usual flat nan.

Getting There & Away

There are daily flights to Kabul (2500Afg, 45 minutes). Road transport to Kabul (eight hours) and all points south and east leaves from the Ah Deh depot; westbound transport (including Balkh) leaves from Charahi Haji Ayoub.

BALKH

The town of Balkh is one of Afghanistan's oldest. Zoroaster, founder of the world's oldest monotheistic religion, was born here in the 6th century BC, Alexander the Great camped here, and the Arabs dubbed it 'the Mother of Cities'. Despite a Timurid flowering, Balkh never recovered from its sacking by Chinggis Khan, and today it is little more than a large village. The main road from Mazar-e Sharif turns right into Balkh through the old city walls, which stretch for 10km around the town.

Sights

SHRINE OF KHOJA ABU NASR PARSA

Built in the mid-15th century, this shrine ('Khoja Parsa' for short) is dedicated to a famous theologian. A classic of Timurid architecture, it's also a symbol of Balkh's final flourish before sliding into decay. The shrine is dominated by its massive portal entrance, flanked by twisted cable pillars and decorated in blue tiles and plain brick. The whole is

topped with a turquoise ribbed melon dome. It's currently under renovation.

Opposite the shrine is the tomb of the first female Persian poet, Rabi'a Balkhi.

NO GOMBAD MOSQUE

This ruined 9th-century mosque is the oldest in Afghanistan. The name refers to its originally nine-domed structure, although little more than the arcade piers now remain. The columns are covered in delicate stucco influenced by Samarra in Iraq.

The mosque lies a 2km walk south of the intersection for Balkh on the road from Mazar-e Sharif. It's also known locally as Masjid-e Haji Piyada (Mosque of the Walking Pilgrim).

Getting There & Around

Plenty of minibuses (30 minutes) link Balkh and Mazar-e Sharif, 20km away. Balkh is small enough to explore by foot.

KUNDUZ

The largely Uzbek town of Kunduz lies amid rich agricultural land. It's a transport hub to reach Tajikistan and Badakhshan, but the province itself is increasingly insecure due to insurgent activity, so even passing through by road can't be recommended.

FAIZABAD

elev 1200m

Badakhshan's largest town sits in a valley surrounded by high peaks and alpine meadows. Its remoteness has been a virtue – it sat out the Soviet occupation and civil war completely. Even today, animal traffic seems to outnumber vehicles. Faizabad has an interesting bazaar and lapis lazuli and local knitted goods make good souvenirs. The whole area tempts you to start trekking, but be aware that opium production is rife in the province.

Faizabad is a base from where to organise treks into the Wakhan (see p488).

Sleeping & Eating

Hotel Ishan Awliyan (west of main square, Old Town; r 300Afg) One step up from a chaikhana, this 1st-floor hotel has a handful of private rooms with two beds and a beaten-up sofa apiece – a little dingy but perfectly serviceable. Meals are in the main restaurant.

Pamir Club (☎ 0799 443 117; Kokcha River, Old Town; r US$40) If there's a hotel with a better location in Afghanistan, we'd like to know about it. On a promontory surrounded on three sides by the rushing Kokcha River, this government hotel has a hard spot to beat. Rooms are large and reasonably decent, with balconies looking over the water and shared bathrooms (don't hope too hard for hot water).

Aria Guest House (☎ 0799 178 661; ahmadshukran@ yahoo.com; New Town, Sange Muhar; s/d US$40/50) The 18 comfortable rooms with bathrooms and decent security make this a good choice. Manager Ahmad Shukhran rents out 4WDs for US$150 per day. There's a branch in Ishkashim.

A host of chaikhanas are clustered along the southern edge of the main square – offering exactly what you'd expect from such places.

Getting There & Away

Pamir Airways flies between Faizabad and Kabul (2500Afg, one hour).

Minibuses and shared taxis for all points outside Badakhshan depart from the Bandar-e Takhar station. To get further into Badakhshan, including Ishkashim (eight hours) go to Bandar-e Baharak in the old town.

ISHKASHIM

elev 3030m

The only reason you'll visit this tiny town is to cross the Tajik border, or a stop en route to the Wakhan. A bridge over the Pyanj River marks the border. There isn't much traffic on to Faizabad, so take whatever's going. Town Ace minivans run sporadically to Baharak (650Afg, six hours) and Faizabad (800Afg, eight hours). For more information on the border, see p494.

Aria Guest House (☎ 0799 372 449; r US$25) has eight rooms in a villa just off the main bazaar. There are also half a dozen private guesthouses in town, all of which cost around US$25 with meals, though they can be hard to track down. Places include **Juma's** (☎ 0795 770 104), **Boz Mahmud's** (☎ 0797 744 330) and **Nur Mohammed's** (☎ 0795 587 271). Just outside town are **Ayanbeg's** (☎ 0797 649 931), 2.5km from the bazaar, **Noor's**, 3km from the bazaar and with a western bathroom, and **Wafai's** (☎ 0797 798 504), 5km from the bazaar.

For the latest accommodation options contact Wakhan Tourism (wakhan.tourism@ gmail.com) in the centre of town, part of the Pamir Business Service Centre (pamirbsc@ gmail.com), or visit the Mountain Unity Welcome Centre (www.mountainunity.org).

WAKHAN & THE AFGHAN PAMIR

Afghanistan's Wakhan District is a narrow strip of land jutting eastwards 350km between Tajikistan and Pakistan to touch the Chinese border. It has two distinct parts – the Wakhan Corridor and the Afghan Pamir. The deep valley of the Wakhan Corridor is formed by the Panj River as it courses between the lofty mountains of Tajikistan to the north and the snowcapped Hindu Kush to the south. The Hindu Kush, Karakoram and Pamir Ranges converge in the Afghan Pamir, known in Persian as the Bam-e Dunya ('roof of the world'). *Pamir*, U-shaped, high-elevation valleys with lush seasonal meadows and vivid blue lakes, are renowned as summer grazing grounds, but lie snow-covered more than six months of the year.

Trekking is by far the most popular way to experience the natural beauty and cultural diversity of Wakhan, and the only way to visit the roadless Afghan Pamir.

Practicalities

Permission is required for travel anywhere in Wakhan District. This is best done through an agency who can issue paperwork for Faizabad and Ishkashim. There are two agencies in Faizabad who work with communities in the Wakhan in developing sustainable local tourism: **Aga Khan Development Network** (AKDN, ☎ 0799 400 135; najmuddin.najm@akdn.org), **Great Game Travel** (☎ 0799 062 033; www.greatgametravel.com) in Faizabad, and **Mountain Unity** (www.mountainunity. org) in Ishkashim.

As well as organising permissions, the agencies can arrange guides, pack animals (donkey, horse, yak or camel) and vehicles. A local guide costs from 500Afg per day, and pack animal with handler from 800Afg per day. A 4WD to get you into the Wakhan is the big ticket expense, starting from US$180 per day.

May to September is the optimal trekking season. Snowmelt in July and early August, however, swells rivers whose high water can block the sole road. In later summer, the **Pamir Festival** is held at Sarhad-e-Broghil. It's a celebration of local Wakhi and Kyrgyz culture, with polo and *buzkashi* matches, folk music and other events – possibly the most remote festival in the world. Contact the AKDN for dates and more information.

Tourism infrastructure in Wakhan is developing quickly. Newly built guest houses and camping grounds are in Qazideh, Khandud, Goz Khun, Qila-e Panja and Sarhad-e Broghil, with prices around 500Afg per night. A fee of 100Afg per tent is appropriate for pitching your tent in village camping grounds.

There are now over 25 homestay/guest houses and camping grounds in the valley; in Qazideh, Kishni Khan, Khandud, Goz Khun, Qila-e Panja, Uzed, Qila-e Hurst, Sargaz, Kret, Nirs, Sarhad-e Broghil and others. Guesthouses cost US$15 to US$25 per person per night, including meals.

Juldu (www.juldu.com) is a useful online guide to visiting the Wakhan, as is www.mockand oneil.com/wakhan.htm.

Lower Wakhan

More than 5000m of vertical relief commands the southern horizon of Lower Wakhan, the villages between Ishkashim and Qila-e Panja, where the valley is only 2km across at its widest point. Snowcapped peaks soar majestically above villages and glaciers descend precipitously to feed the Panj River in this land of immense scale. Afghan urial and ibex thrive in numerous steep and arid side valleys.

Upper Wakhan

The Wakhi villages in Upper Wakhan between Qila-e Panja and Sarhad-e Broghil lie along the narrow Wakhan River, which opens to a dramatic 3km-wide river basin at Sarhad-e Broghil. Wetlands along the river are nesting grounds for geese, ducks and ibises, as well as stopovers for migratory waterfowl and raptors, and marshy flats provide year-round habitat for wading birds.

Wakhi, who depend on livestock to supplement their agriculture, take their herds to seasonal pastures as high as 4500m, where they greet guests with a warm smile, cup of tea and bowl of yoghurt.

Big Pamir

The 60km long Big Pamir nestles between the Southern Alichur Range to the north and the Wakhan Range to the south. The Big Pamir or Great Pamir is called Past Pamir in Wakhi, and Pamir-e Kalan or Pamir-e Buzurg in Persian.

Little Pamir

The Little Pamir, at 100km long and 10km wide, is actually larger in area than the Big Pamir, yet the more rugged Big Pamir has a higher elevation and so earns its name. The Little Pamir or Small Pamir is called Wuch Pamir in Wakhi, and Pamir-e Khurd or Pamir-e Kochak in Persian. Its most remote valleys, no longer used for grazing, are pristine alpine grasslands. Tombs called *gumbaz*, with distinctive conical mud cupolas, mark Kyrgyz graves. Wildlife watchers will find the area home to Marco Polo sheep, snow leopard, and brown bear.

EASTERN AFGHANISTAN

Predominantly Pashtun, the east of the country is heavily influenced by its crumpled border with Pakistan, running along the Northwest Frontier and the fractious Tribal Areas. In happier times, adventurous travellers would head for the high trekking country of Nuristan, immortalised in Eric Newby's *A Short Walk in the Hindu Kush*. Current politics restricts the east to transit only – taking the road from Kabul through Jalalabad to the border, at the foot of the fabled Khyber Pass.

JALALABAD

The Mughal emperor Akbar founded Jalalabad, and its warm winter climate helped it become a popular retreat for Afghan kings. The region was once littered with Buddhist sites, but most have been destroyed – the loss of **Hadda**, site of over 1000 stupas, to Soviet bombing was particularly grievous. The caves around Hadda were used as caches by the mujaheddin and later hosted Al-Qaeda training camps.

The **Spinghar Hotel** (sarakh-e Kabul; r $50), set in large gardens in the centre of town, is the most secure sleeping option. There are plenty of stands and chaikhanas in the centre, around the bazaar and Chowk-e Mukharabat.

Minibuses to Kabul (three hours, 250Afg) and the border at Torkham (two hours, 100Afg) run through the day. Shared taxis are faster and cost more. The road to Kabul follows the Kabul River past Sarobi Dam and up the stupendous Tangi Gharu Gorge to the Kabul Plateau.

TORKHAM

There's no reason to stick around in this border town, it's all auto shops and moneychangers. As Afghanistan's busiest border post, there's plenty of transport – see p494 for more information.

SOUTHERN AFGHANISTAN

Afghanistan's south is dry, dusty and very dangerous. Largely Pashtun, it's the centre of the Taliban insurgency against Kabul, while Helmand province is the largest producer of opium in the world. The US and UK military are active throughout the region, which blows hot and cold as a warzone according to the season. We strongly advise against all travel to this area.

GHAZNI

The modern town of Ghazni is a pale shadow of its former glory. In the 11th century the city was home to the Ghaznavid empire. Sultan Mahmud filled his court with poets and artists, his stables with elephants, and whenever the treasury was bare, he raided Delhi – introducing Islam to India in the process.

Ghazni's most visible monuments to this history are it's two massive 11th-century minarets on the road from Kabul. Mahmud's tomb lies nearby.

KANDAHAR

Kandahar sits at the crossroads where the Kabul road branches northwest to Herat and southeast to Quetta in Pakistan. It lies in the Pashtun heartland and was Afghanistan's first capital under Ahmad Shah Durrani in the 18th century. More recently it was the spiritual capital of the Taliban.

Kandahar's great treasure, a cloak which once belonged to the Prophet, is safely kept in the Mosque of the Sacred Cloak. Prior to the Taliban's capture of Kabul in 1996, Mullah Omar wrapped himself in the cloak in front a cheering Taliban crowd, declaring himself Amir al-Momineen (Commander of the Faithful). Ahmad Shah Durrani's mausoleum sits nearby.

A few kilometres west from the centre of Kandahar are the Chihil Zina (Forty Steps). They lead up to a niche, guarded by two stone lions, carved in the rock by Babur to celebrate the Mughal's achievements.

AFGHANISTAN DIRECTORY

ACCOMMODATION

Most levels of accommodation are available in Afghanistan, from simple hotels to private guesthouses. Outside the cities quality drops off considerably, and basic hotels are the order of the day. Long bus trips are often broken with an overnight stay at a chaikhana, sleeping on the floor with fellow passengers.

ACTIVITIES

The mountains of Afghanistan could rival Nepal for trekking opportunities. There's no infrastructure and you'll be unsupported in very remote areas. The best potential areas for treks are the Wakhan Corridor, Bamiyan and the Panjshir Valley. Remember that land mines are present throughout the country.

BUSINESS HOURS

Afghan businesses generally open from 8am to 4pm. The official weekend is on Friday, although government offices (and many businesses) close around noon on Thursday. Official business is better conducted in the mornings. Shops and offices have restricted hours during Ramazan. Chaikhanas tend to open in the early morning (restaurants follow suit a few hours later), staying open until late evening.

DANGERS & ANNOYANCES

Afghanistan presents unique potential risks in comparison with the rest of Central Asia. The continuing insurgency by the Taliban and other groups has left few parts of the country unaffected. It's essential to keep abreast of the current political and security assessments both before travelling and while in the country. For more information, see Travelling Safely in Afghanistan, p469.

EMBASSIES & CONSULATES

There are Afghan embassies in Almaty (Kazakhstan; p194), Bishkek (Kyrgyzstan; p366), Dushanbe (Tajikistan; p417), Ashgabat (Turkmenistan; p462) and Tashkent (Uzbekistan; p282).

Afghan Embassies & Consulates

Australia (☎ 02-6282 7311; www.afghanembassy.net; PO Box 155, Deakin West, Canberra, ACT 2600)

Belgium (☎ 02-761 3166; ambassade.afghanistan@
skynet.be; 281 Rue Francoise Gay, B-1150, Brussels)
Canada (☎ 613-563 4223/65; www.afghanemb-canada.
net; 240 Argyle Ave, K1P 5E4, Ottawa)
China (☎ 010-6532 1582; afgemb.beijing@gmail.com; 8
Dongzhimenwai Dajie, Beijing)
France (☎ 01-45 25 05 29; www.ambafghane-paris.
com; 32 Ave Raphael, 75016, Paris)
Germany (☎ 030-224 87229; afghanische-botschaft@
t-online.de; Wilhelmstrasse 65 D, 10117, Berlin)
India (☎ 011- 410 331; afghanspirit@yahoo.com; Plat
No. 5, Block 50F, Chanakyapuri, 110021, Delhi)
Iran Tehran (☎ 021-873 7050; afghanembassytehran@
hotmail.com; 4th St, Dr Beheshti Avenue, Tehran); Mashad
(☎ 0511-854 4829; Afghanistan_ge_con_mashad@
samanir.net; Sevom Isfand Sq, off Doshahid St, Emam
Khomeini Ave)
Italy (☎ 06-8621 6111; afghanembassy.rome@flashnet.
it; Via Nomentana 120, 00161, Rome)
Japan (☎ 03-5465 1219; www.afghanembassyjp.com;
3-37-8-B Nishihara, Shibuya-ku, 151-0066, Tokyo)
Netherlands (☎ 20-6721311; afconsulholland@yahoo.
com; Wellemsparkweg 114, Amsterdam)
Norway (☎ 22 83 84 10; www.afghanemb.com; 17
Kronprinsens Gt, 0244, Oslo)
Pakistan Islamabad (☎ 051-282 4505/6; House 8, St
90, G-6/3); Peshawar (☎ 091-285962; The Mall, Saddar
Bazaar); Quetta (☎ 081-843364; 45 Prince Rd)
Russia (☎ 095-9287581; safarat_moscow@yahoo.com;
Sverchkov Per 3/2, Moscow)
UK (☎ 020-7589 8891/2; www.afghanembassy.org.uk;
31 Prince's Gate, SW7 1QU, London)
United Arab Emirates Abu Dhabi (☎ 2-665 5560; PO
Box 5687); Dubai (☎ 4-398 8229; PO Box 113233)
USA Washington DC (☎ 202-416 1620; www.embassy
ofafghanistan.org; 2341 Wyoming Ave NW, 20036); New
York (☎ 212-972 2276; info@afghanconsulateny.org; 11th
fl, 360 Lexington Ave, CA 10017)

Embassies & Consulates in Afghanistan
Canada (☎ 0788 742800; House 258 St 15, Wazir Akbar
Khan)
China (☎ 020 2102548/9; Shah Mahmoud Wat, Shahr-e
Nau)
France (☎ 0700 284032; near Charahi Zambak &
Charahi Ariana, Shahr-e Nau)
Germany (☎ 020 2101512; Charahi Zambaq, Shahr-e Nau)
India (☎ 020 2200185; Malalai Wat, Shahr-e Nau)
Iran (☎ 020 2101396; Charahi Sherpur, Shahr-e Nau;
Herat (☎ 040 220015), Jad-e Walayat); Mazar-e Sharif
(Kheyaban-e Nasir Khusrau)
Italy (☎ 020 2103144; Charahi Ariana, Shahr-e Nau)
Japan (☎ 0700 224451; St 15, Wazir Akbar Khan)
Kazakhstan (☎ 070277450; House 1, St 10, Wazir
Akbar Khan)

Netherlands (☎ 0700 286640/1; Ghiyassudin Wat,
Shahr-e Nau)
Norway (☎ 020 2300900, Lane 4, St 15, Wazir Akbar
Khan)
Pakistan (☎ 020 2300911/3; St 10, Wazir Akbar Khan);
Jalalabad (Charahi Marastoon); Kandahar (☎ 070 302520;
Noorzo Shah Bridge, District 2)
Russia (☎ 020 2300500; Darulman Wat, Karte Se)
Sweden (☎ 020 2301416; House 70, Lane 1, St 15,
Wazir Akbar Khan)
Switzerland (☎ 020 2301565; House 486, Lane 3, St
13, Wazir Akbar Khan)
Tajikistan (☎ 0799 327744; House 41 St 15, Wazir
Akbar Khan, Kabul) Also has a consulate in Mazar-e Sharif.
Turkmenistan (☎ 020 2302550; Lane 3, Street 13,
Wazir Akbar Khan); Herat (☎ 040 223534; Jad-e Walayat);
Mazar-e Sharif (☎ 050 5023; Darwaza-ye Tashkurgan)
UK (☎ 070 102000; St 15, Wazir Akbar Khan)
USA (☎ 0700 108278; Charahi Massoud)
Uzbekistan (☎ 020 2500431; Karte Se, Kabul); Mazar-e
Sharif (☎ 050 3042; Darwaza-ye Tashkurgan)

Visas for onward travel
Visas for the following places are technically
available in Kabul, but costs and requirements
can change frequently so check with the relevant embassies: Iran, Pakistan, Tajikistan,
Turkmenistan, Uzbekistan.

FESTIVALS & EVENTS
Nauroz (Navrus; see p503) is greatly celebrated in Afghanistan; Mazar-e Sharif is the
centre of the national holiday.

Ramazan (Ramadan elsewhere) is taken
a lot more seriously here compared with the
rest of Central Asia, and travellers may find
things harder work at this time, as chaikhanas
and restaurants are closed during the day. Lots
of businesses (and government offices) close
early during Ramazan.

Shiites celebrate Ashura, to commemorate
the martyrdom of Hussain during the month
of Moharram. Men parade and whip themselves as a mark of their grief.

See p502 for the dates of major Islamic
holidays.

HOLIDAYS
21 March Nauroz
28 April Celebration of the Islamic Revolution in
Afghanistan
1 May National Labour Day
4 May Remembrance Day for Martyrs and the Disabled
19 August Independence Day
9 September Ahmad Shah Massoud Day

AFGHANISTAN

INSURANCE

Political instability (and advice from government travel advisories) means that some insurance companies may be reluctant to issue insurance for a trip to Afghanistan. Check the fine print on the policy before signing up.

INTERNET ACCESS

The internet has caught on in a big way in Afghanistan. All major towns have cybercafes or 'internet clubs', with prices varying between 50Afg and 80Afg.

INTERNET RESOURCES

Afghan News Network (www.afghannews.net) Useful news portal covering Afghan current affairs.

Institute for War and Peace Reporting (www.iwpr.net) Runs the useful weekly *Afghan Recovery Report*, written by Afghan journalists.

Juldu.com (www.juldu.com) Comprehensive travel site for trekking in the Wakhan Corridor and the Afghan Pamir.

Lonely Planet (www.lonelyplanet.com) The dedicated Central Asia branch of the Thorn Tree bulletin board is one of the best places to get up-to-date travellers' reports on Afghanistan.

Moby Capital (www.mobycapital.com) Hard to beat daily email service, collating news on Afghanistan from the world's media.

Relief Web (www.reliefweb.int) Provides excellent coverage from a humanitarian slant, with news and press releases from the UN and many NGOs.

Survival Guide to Kabul (www.kabulguide.net) Aimed primarily at expat workers and with a useful bulletin board for up-to-the-minute goings-on.

MAPS

Afghanistan is a good 1:1.5 million map produced by Nelles, as is GeoCenter's 1:2 million *Afghanistan & Pakistan* map. AIMS (www.aims.org.af) has excellent free downloadable maps, including topographic and detailed city maps.

MONEY

Afghanistan's currency is the afghani (Afg). Paper notes come in denominations of one, two, five, 10, 20, 50, 100, 500 and 1000Afg. There are one, two and five afghani coins.

Afghanistan's banking system keeps improving, but the country remains primarily a cash-only economy. The majority of people change their currency at the moneychangers bazaar in each town. The US dollar is king, and currencies of neighbouring countries are readily changeable. Payment for hotel bills (along with airline tickets) is often requested

in US dollars. Euros are hard to change outside the main cities.

Credit cards are accepted at a limited number of hotels and businesses in Kabul. There are some ATMs wired to MasterCard and Visa. Don't even think of bringing travellers cheques.

Exchange rates, current at the time of research, are listed below (Uzbek rate not included due to instability):

Country	Unit	Afghani
Australia	A$1	38.56Afg
euro zone	€1	57.26Afg
Iran	1000rials	4.55Afg
Pakistan	Rs10	5.31Afg
Tajikistan	1TJS	10.38Afg
Turkmenistan	1M	15.97Afg
UK	UK£1	68.78Afg
USA	US$1	45.52Afg

POST

Mail is best sent from Kabul. A postcard to anywhere in the world costs 16Afg. International letters cost from 60Afg. Mail generally arrives at its destination in less than two weeks.

Sending packages is a daylong process and customs-declaration paper chase. It's more efficient (if more expensive) to use a courier like DHL, TNT, FedEx and UPS, all of whom have offices in Kabul.

SHOPPING

Afghanistan is best known for its carpets, mostly produced in the north and west of the country. Prices are best in Mazar-e Sharif, Kunduz and Herat. As well as traditional styles, carpet patterns move with the times – modern designs include the Soviet army retreating from Afghanistan, and the World Trade Centre attacks.

Other good souvenirs include lapis lazuli from the mines of Badakhshan, handmade blue glass from Herat, pottery from Istalif, Uzbek embroidery, quilted silk coats *(chapans)*, and the pancake-flat *pakul* hats.

TELEPHONE

A limited fixed-line telephone network exists in the major cities, but most people and companies use mobile phones. Five networks jostle for business: Roshan, Afghan Wireless, Etisalat, Areeba and MTN. Coverage is generally good, and a local sim card can be picked up for less than 500Afg.

Public Call Offices (PCOs) are everywhere should you need to make a call – typically 5Afg per minute for local calls, and around 20Afg per minute for international calls.

Due to the proliferation of different networks all telephone numbers in this guide are listed with their prefixes.

TRAVEL PERMITS

Travel permits are not required for general travel in Afghanistan, although they are needed for trekking in the Wakhan – see p488 for details.

VISAS

Visas are easy to obtain. Tourist-visa applications do not require a letter of support, while those travelling for work purposes require a supporting letter from their office.

A one-month single-entry visa in London costs UK£50 (longer multiple entry visas are only issued under 'exceptional' circumstances); the embassy in Washington charges US$50 for the same. Visas take two weeks to process, with a premium charged for same-day issue.

In neighbouring countries, New Delhi, Peshawar, Tehran, Mashhad and Tashkent are good places to apply for an Afghan visa. One-month single-entry visas cost US$30 and are generally issued on the same day.

Visa Extensions

Visas can be extended in Kabul at the **Interior Central Passport Department** (Passport Lane, off Interior Ministry Rd). Tourists require one passport photo and a letter requesting an extension from the head office of the **Afghan Tourist Organisation** (ATO; ☎ 020 2300 338, atokabul@yahoo.com; Great Massoud Rd). The letter costs US$10 per month requested, with a maximum three-month extension possible.

If you're working in Afghanistan, you'll need a letter of support from your organisation, or in the case of journalists, a letter from the **Ministry of Information and Culture** (☎ 020 2101301; Pul-e Bagh-e Omomi, Kabul). Visa extensions cost US$30 for three months, which must be paid into the central branch of **Da Afghanistan Bank** (Jad-e Froshgah, Kabul), and the receipt presented at the passport office along with one passport photo.

WOMEN TRAVELLERS

Afghanistan has a conservative culture where attitudes to women are bound up with the protection of honour, and society generally seeks to minimise contact between unrelated men and women.

Foreign women may be treated as an 'honorary male' by local Afghan men, although it's best to wait for them to offer a hand to shake rather than offering your own. If you're travelling with a man, Afghan men will talk to him rather than you.

It's not compulsory for women to wear a headscarf, but you'll attract a lot of attention if you don't. In keeping with local sensibilities, wear long shirts that hide the shape of the body; bare arms should be also avoided by both sexes.

TRANSPORT IN AFGHANISTAN

GETTING THERE & AWAY
Entering Afghanistan

When entering the country by air, formalities are fairly simple, but be prepared for long queues and a scrum at baggage reclaim. Crossing land borders is also usually straightforward, although customs checks on leaving Afghanistan to neighbouring countries – particularly the Central Asian republics and Iran – can often be exceedingly thorough.

Air

Kabul is increasingly well-connected to international flight hubs. The most common connections are to Dubai, Delhi, Frankfurt, Moscow and Islamabad. For a full list of airlines flying to/from Afghanistan, see p516.

Regional flight connections to/from Kabul are limited to weekly flights Dushanbe (Ariana and Kam Air) and Almaty (Kam Air).

Land

Afghanistan shares its border with six countries, maintaining official border crossings with all except China. Bear in mind that Afghanistan has 30 minutes' time difference with all its neighbours, and that some borders are closed on certain days.

BORDER CROSSINGS
To/From Iran

Crossing the Iranian border is straightforward. There are direct buses between Mashhad to Herat (IR70,000, seven hours), which are

AFGHANISTAN

---

quicker (and cheaper) than taking a bus from Mashhad to the border at Taybad, and arranging onward transport from the Afghan side at Islam Qala. Herat–Mashhad buses cost 300Afg; there are also plentiful shared taxis to Islam Qala (60Afg/90 minutes).

Customs checks can be rigorous on entering Iran, and remember that female travellers need to adhere to a stricter dress code – covering the head and body shape.

The border crossing at Zaranj is closed to foreigners.

To/From Pakistan

The crossing from Peshawar in Pakistan over the Khyber Pass to Afghanistan is one of the most evocative border crossings in the world.

The road to the border runs through Pakistan's Tribal Areas, where the government's writ has no power. You'll need to arrange a permit to go to the border at Torkham from the **Home & Tribal Affairs Dept** (Civil Secretariat, Saddar Rd; 9am-2pm Mon-Sat) in Peshawar. This is free, but you'll need photocopies of your passport and Afghan and Pakistan visas. You can arrange the permit 48 hours before travel, but on the day you must pick up an armed escort from the **Khyber Political Agent's Office** (Stadium Rd, Peshawar) to accompany you to the border.

A taxi (it's not permitted to take public transport) to the border, 55km away, will cost around US$15/Rs1200, and your guard will expect a tip of around Rs200. Once across the border, there's plenty of onward transport – expect to pay around 300Afg for a minibus to Kabul. If you leave Peshawar early, you can reach Kabul in one go.

Entering Pakistan, you'll be assigned an armed guard after immigration, and you must take a taxi to Peshawar.

The road from Quetta to Kandahar, crossing from the Pakistani border town of Chaman to Spin Boldak is not safe for travel.

To/From Tajikistan

There are three crossing points between Afghanistan and Tajikistan, two of which are in Badakhshan. The most straightfor-

ward is the bridge at Shir Khan Bandar to Panj-e-Payon (formerly Nizhniy Panj). The Badakhshan border posts are at Ishkashim and Khorog. Border posts are closed on Sundays.

On the Afghan side, it's one hour by shared taxi to Kunduz (80Afg). There's plentiful transport on the Tajik side. It's just about possible to travel overland between Dushanbe and Kunduz in one long day.

In Badakhshan the bridge over the Pyanj River is open to travellers at Ishkashim. Entering Afghanistan here is easy, but the Tajik side lies in the restricted region of Gorno-Badakhshan, which requires a permit (see p401). Afghan Ishkashim is a 4km walk from the border posts, with little transportation; from the towns there's a daily minibus to Faizabad (800Afg, eight hours).

The largest town in Tajik Badakhshan, Khorog also has a border crossing on the bridge across the Pyanj, but transport options on the Afghan side are thin.

To/From Turkmenistan

There are two open crossings into Turkmenistan. Torghundi in Afghanistan to Serkhetabat in Turkmenistan (formerly Gushgi) is the more commonly used, due to its proximity to Herat (200Afg, two hours by shared taxi). A more obscure alternative is at Imam Nazar, near Andkhoi. You must have your point of entry listed on your Turkmen visa and (for tourist visas) be met by an official guide. There's an entry tax of US$12 to US$14 according to nationality. On the Afghan side, allow around 500Afg for customs fees. In both directions, the Turkmen customs will probably take your luggage apart. For more information, see p466.

A more border obscure alternative is at Imam Nazar to Saparmurat (near Kerki). A 4WD is recommended.

To/From Uzbekistan

The Friendship Bridge across the Amu-Darya links Hairatan in Afghanistan to Termiz in Uzbekistan. Although open to travellers, the Uzbek authorities are prone to unannounced closures, usually citing security concerns. Contacting the Uzbek embassy in Kabul in advance isn't a bad idea; in the opposite direction contact OVIR (p217) or a reliable travel agency in Tashkent. The easiest way to get to Hairatan is from Mazar-e Sharif by private taxi (500Afg, 30 minutes). The bridge is 10km from the centre of Termiz, and there are a few minibuses (*marshrutka*) that make the run into town (S200, 20 minutes).

Tours

Two reputable Kabul-based companies offer tours and transport logistics:

Afghan Logistics & Tours (☎ 0700 442211; www. afghanlogisticstours.com)

Great Game Travel (☎ 0799 489120; www.greatgame travel.com) Also has a Faizabad office.

GETTING AROUND

Air

Ariana, Kam Air and Pamir Airways link Kabul to the Herat, Mazar-e Sharif and Kandahar, plus smaller destinations like Kunduz and Faizabad. A typical one-way ticket costs around 3500Afg/US$70. Always recheck the time of departure the day before you fly. Schedule changes are both common and unexplained. If you're in the provinces you'll probably depart late anyway, as you'll have to wait for the plane to arrive from Kabul.

Bus

Afghanistan is held together by the Toyota HiAces minibus (*falang*). There are no time-tables – minibuses tend to start rolling out at the crack of dawn, leaving when they've collected enough passengers. Drivers frequently stop for prayer time, and at chaikhanas for food – where you might end up overnight on a really long trip.

Clunky old German buses also ply Afghanistan's roads. Painfully slow and over-crowded, they're only used by the poorest locals – and by those unconcerned about time or comfort.

Car & Motorcycle

Afghanistan doesn't recognise carnets so bringing in your own vehicle is a legal grey area. Foreign vehicles are highly visible and may present a target if there are security problems. The country runs on diesel and petrol can be hard to find. Road rules are lax, but most vehicles aspire to drive on the right.

Taxi

Yellow-and-white shared taxis are a popular way to travel between towns. They leave from the same terminal as minibuses. They're faster than minibuses and, with fewer seats, fill up and leave sooner. Fares are around a quarter to a third more expensive than the equivalent minibus.

Central Asia Directory

CONTENTS

Most of this chapter refers to general information on travelling through the ex-Soviet republics of Central Asia. For country-specific information, refer to the individual country directories in each country chapter. For Afghanistan-specific information see p490.

ACCOMMODATION

Accommodation alternatives are springing up all over Central Asia, so thankfully the smoky, disintegrating Soviet-era leftovers need only be used as a last resort. Private places are almost always preferable to government-run places.

Options are somewhat uneven across the region. The excellent homestays of Kyrgyzstan and Tajikistan and the B&Bs of Uzbekistan offer the best alternatives to the few remaining Soviet-era fossils. Budget travellers in Kazakhstan will still find the latter a regular companion, alongside railway and bus-station hotels, though there are now plenty of good midrange options. Tajikistan's Pamir region in particular has an informal network of homes and yurts that offer a fascinating and intimate look at the way local people live.

Oddball accommodation options include sleeping in a former medressa in Khiva (p275) or an astronomical observatory outside Almaty (p144).

In this book, budget accommodation is considered anything under around US$25 for a double room in high season. Midrange options run up to around US$70 (US$100 in Kazakh cities) and top-end choices are above that.

B&Bs

These are small private guesthouses, as opposed to homestays, though the distinction can be a fine one. The majority are to be found in the Uzbek cities of Bukhara, Khiva and Samarkand, where the best are stylish boutique-style hotels. Rates tend to be around US$15 to US$25 per person and include breakfast. Meals are extra but can normally be provided for around US$5 each.

Camping

In the wilds there's normally no problem with you camping, though there is always an inherent security risk with this. If you are obviously on someone's land then you should try to ensure that you have permission. Staying anywhere near habitation will result in an immediate audience. Popular trekking routes have established camping areas, frequented by Soviet alpinists during the Soviet era. You can normally camp at a *turbaza* (Soviet-era holiday camp) or yurt camp for a minimal fee.

Homestays

These are happily on the rise. For a bed of duvets on the floor and some type of breakfast you'll probably pay between US$10 (in rural Tajikistan and Kyrgyzstan) to US$15 per person (in Uzbekistan and cities) per night. Travel in Tajikistan and Kyrgyzstan in par-

---

BOOK YOUR STAY ONLINE

For more accommodation reviews and recommendations by Lonely Planet authors, check out the online booking service at www.lonelyplanet.com/hotels. You'll find the true, insider low-down on the best places to stay. Reviews are thorough and independent. Best of all, you can book online.

---

ticular has been revolutionised by the homestay networks of the Murgab Ecotourism Association (META; p413), Community-Based Tourism (CBT; p302) and Shepherd's Life organisations (p302). Kazakhstan also has some homestays at between US$25 and US$35 per person with all meals.

Do not expect hotel-style comforts; rural toilets, for example, are likely to be squatters in the garden. Don't expect anything exotic either – in larger towns you may well end up in a block of flats, in front of a TV all evening. Levels of privacy vary. You might get access to a kitchen, especially if you are in an apartment.

Potential hosts may accost you as you alight at a station or enter a tourist hotel; older people, generally women, tend to be the best to deal with. Sympathetic hotel reception staff may put you in touch with private homes in some cities. Many local private travel agencies can set you up with someone, though prices may be double local rates.

Even though prices are listed in this book as 'dorms' you will usually not be expected to share rooms with strangers; however, friends travelling together will be expected to share a room.

Locals you meet on the road may invite you home and ask nothing for it, but remember that most ordinary people have very limited resources, so offer to pay anything from US$5 to US$10 (rural Tajikistan and Kyrgyzstan) to US$10 in larger towns (add on around US$5 for dinner and breakfast in rural areas). Another option in regions without formal homestays is to contact locals or expats through sites like CouchSurfing (www.couch surfing.com), or social networking sites like Facebook (www.facebook.com) or its regional equivalent V Kontakte (www.vkontakte.ru). Accommodation is free or cheap and it's often a good way to meet locals and get an inside perspective on a place.

In Turkmenistan and Uzbekistan, staying with someone who hasn't gone through official channels with the Office of Visas & Registration (OVIR; *Otdel Vis i Registratsii* in Russian) could put them at risk, especially if your own papers aren't in order. For details on potential registration problems for homestayers and campers in Uzbekistan, see p285.

Hotels

Though some are better than others, you often don't get what you pay for in government or Soviet-era tourist hotels, largely because tourists pay higher rates than locals. Windows that don't open or close properly, chronically dim or missing light bulbs and toilets that leak but don't flush are common problems. All beds are single, with pillows the size of suitcases. That said, a lot of Soviet-era hotels have spruced themselves up in recent years and the situation is constantly improving.

Uzbekistan leads the way in stylish private hotels, which are popping up all over the place. There is also a limited number of party or government guesthouses, *dacha* (holiday bungalows) and former government sanatoria, which are now open to all. Most cities have a choice of several modern and comfortable private-sector hotels catering mostly to local and international *biznezmen*, where nouveau riche is the dominant style.

If you're staying at a budget hotel that doesn't have hot water, ask about the local *banya* (public bath), which will.

Some hotels will take your passport and visa for anywhere from half an hour to your entire stay, to do the required registration paperwork and to keep you from leaving without paying.

LATE-NIGHT TELEPHONE CALLS

Those late-night calls to your room aren't wrong numbers. All hotels with significant numbers of foreigners attract prostitutes, especially, it seems, in Kazakhstan (or was that just us?). Women guests rarely seem to get unexpected calls but several men have received calls from someone who knew their name, so somebody at the front desk knows what's going on. All you can do is work out how to temporarily disable your telephone and don't answer the door.

FLOOR-LADIES

On every floor of a Soviet-style hotel a *dezhurnaya* (floor-lady) is in charge of handing out keys, getting hot water for washing, or *kipitok* (boiled water) for hot drinks, sometimes for a small fee. Even the most god-awful hotel can be redeemed by a big-hearted floor-lady who can find someone to do your laundry, find a light bulb or stash your bags while you're off on an excursion. Others can be a bit eccentric (one floor-lady in a hotel in Bishkek insisted on wiping the room clean with several old pairs of women's panties).

Don't forget them when you leave – no one is likely to remind you.

Budget-hotel room rates range from a few dollars in the countryside to around US$20 in the cities. We do not mention all of a hotel's price options in our reviews; even the worst hotels often have a few *lux* (deluxe) or half-*lux* (semideluxe) suites for about twice the price of a basic room, sometimes with a sofa, bathtub and hot water. Strangely, a room with a large double bed often costs more than two single rooms.

Midrange hotels and B&Bs will have air con, satellite TV, an internet connection (often wi-fi) and a decent breakfast and range from US$25 to US$70 per night (US$50 to US$100 in capitals like Tashkent, Almaty and indeed much of Kazakhstan).

For top-end places you may get a better room rate by booking through a local travel agent or online booking service, though most hotels offer their own discounts.

Yurtstays

It's easy to arrange a yurtstay in central Kyrgyzstan and the eastern Pamirs region of Tajikistan. Yurts range from comfortable tourist camps with beds, electricity and a nearby toilet, to the real McCoy owned by shepherds who are happy to take in the occasional foreigner for the night. The CBT and Shepherd's Life organisations in Kyrgyzstan (see p302) and Murgab Ecotourism Association (META: p414) in Tajikistan offer yurtstays in the mountain pastures of the Tian Shan and Pamirs. Don't expect a great deal of privacy or much in the way of toilet facilities, but it's a fantastic way to get a taste of life on the high pastures (including the freshest yoghurt

you've ever tasted!). For upmarket yurtstays try Ecotour in Kyrgyzstan (p304).

There are also yurts at a half-dozen locations in Kazakhstan, including Aksu-Zhabagyly (p155) and Sayram-Ugam national parks, plus scenic Kolsay Lakes, Burabay, Kaskasu and Mamyr. Uzbekistan has a yurt camp in the Kyzylkum desert near Ayaz-Qala (see p270) and several yurtstays at Lake Aidarkul (p256).

BUSINESS HOURS

In general most government offices and banks are open from 9am to 5pm Monday to Friday, with an hour (or two) off for lunch between noon and 1pm, and possibly 9am to noon on Saturday. All offices and some shops are closed on Sunday. Exchange offices keep longer hours, including weekends. Telephone offices are often open 24 hours.

In Afghanistan the official weekend is on Friday, with many offices closing early on Thursday lunchtime or afternoon. Most Afghan business also shorten office hours during the month of Ramadan.

Museum hours change frequently, as do their days off, though Monday is the most common day of rest. Some just seem to close without reason and a few stay that way for years.

Many restaurants outside the capitals close quite early (around 9pm). In rural areas it is often worth telling a restaurant a couple of hours beforehand that you would like to eat there, to give them some time to prepare and to ensure that they are open.

CHILDREN

Children can be a great icebreaker and a good avenue for cultural exchange, but travelling in Central Asia is difficult even for the healthy adult. Long bus and taxi rides over winding mountain passes are a sure route to motion sickness. Central Asian food is difficult to digest no matter what your age, and extreme temperatures – blistering hot in the city, freezing in the mountains – lead to many an uncomfortable moment. Islamic architecture and ruined Karakhanid cities may well leave your children comatose with boredom. A few places of added interest to children in summer include the amusement and aqua parks in Tashkent (p221), Astana (p173) and Almaty (p133).

If you are bringing very young children into Central Asia, nappies are available at department stores, but bring bottles and medicines. Forget about car seats, high chairs, cribs or anything geared for children, though you'll always find a spare lap and helpful hands when boarding buses. It's possible to make a cot out of the duvets supplied in most homestays. *Lux* hotel rooms normally come with an extra connecting room, which can be ideal for children.

For more advice on travelling with children, pick up Lonely Planet's *Travel with Children*.

We're Riding on a Caravan: An Adventure on the Silk Road by Laurie Krebs is a children's picture book aimed at four- to eight-year-olds that describes a trader's life on the Chinese section of the Silk Road.

Stories from the Silk Road by Cherry Gilchrist is a story book aimed at a similar age group.

CLIMATE CHARTS

CUSTOMS REGULATIONS

Barring the occasional greedy official at a remote posting, few Western tourists have major customs problems in Central Asia. When they do, it's usually over the export of 'cultural artefacts'.

Declaring money on entry to a former Soviet republic is an awkward matter – total honesty reveals how much cash you're carrying to possibly dishonest officials, while fudging can create problems later. In Uzbekistan you should declare everything (cash and travellers cheques) to the penny; officials at Tashkent airport will likely ask you to pull out your money and seize and fine you for the difference between what you have and what you declared. Count up your money privately before you arrive. You won't have a problem unless you are trying to leave with more money than you arrived with, so don't withdraw hundreds of dollars from ATMs in

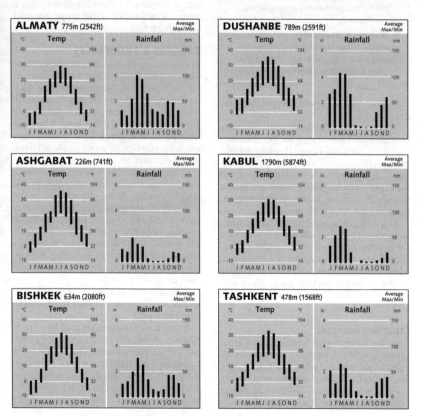

Uzbekistan that you intend to spend elsewhere in Central Asia.

There are no significant limits on items brought into Central Asia for personal use, except on guns and drugs. Heading out, the main prohibitions are 'antiques' and local currency. Every country's regulations prohibit the export of endangered animals and plants, though few officials would recognise an endangered species if it bit them.

You may well be asked for the customs declaration you filled out when you first entered the country, so save all official-looking documents. The main exception is Kazakhstan, where customs forms don't need to be filled in unless you are carrying goods above normal duty-free limits or cash worth more than US$3000.

Exporting Antiques

From the former Soviet republics, you cannot export antiques or anything of 'historical or cultural value' – including art, furnishings, manuscripts, musical instruments, coins, clothing and jewellery – without an export licence and payment of a stiff export duty.

Get a receipt for anything of value that you buy, showing where you got it and how much you paid. If your purchase looks like it has historical value, you should also have a letter saying that it has no such value or that you have permission to take it out anyway. Get this from the vendor, from the Ministry of Culture in the capital, or from a curator at one of the state art museums with enough clout to do it. Without it, your goodies could be seized on departure, possibly even on departure from another Commonwealth of Independent States (CIS) state.

In Uzbekistan any book or artwork over 50 years old is considered antique. In Turkmenistan 'cultural artefacts' seems to embrace almost all handicrafts and traditional-style clothing, no matter how mundane, cheap or new.

To export a carpet from Turkmenistan you'll need to get the carpet certified (for a fee) at Ashgabat's Carpet Museum or buy it from one of the state carpet shops. See p461 for more on this.

DANGERS & ANNOYANCES

Travel in Central Asia is a delight for those who are ready for it, but a potential nightmare for the unprepared. We get letters from readers chastising us for overplaying the hassles of travel in Central Asia, and an equal number describing a litany of police hassles, violence and rip-offs. Most people have a problem-free trip but inexperienced travellers should travel with their radar up.

Crime is minimal by Western urban standards, but visitors are tempting, high-profile targets. Central Asian officials and police generally create more problems than they solve. Local and regional transport can be unpredictable, uncomfortable and occasionally unsafe. Don't be surprised if the visa process doesn't quite go according to plan. For emergency phone numbers see the inside front cover of this book.

Afghanistan is in a league of its own. For specific warnings on travelling there, see the boxed text, p469.

If you have an emergency or have your passport stolen, you must immediately contact the nearest embassy (which might be in a neighbouring republic, or even Moscow). It will help if you have a photocopy of your passport to verify who you are. It's a good idea to register with your embassy upon arrival in

Central Asia and to carry the telephone numbers of your embassies in the region.

This section, all about the headaches, is not meant to put you off. Rather, it is intended to prepare you for the worst. Here's hoping you don't run into any of these problems.

Alcohol

Whether it's being poured down your throat by a zealous host, or driving others into states of pathological melancholy, brotherly love or violent rage, alcohol can give you a headache in more ways than one. This is especially true in economically depressed areas, where resentment hovers just below the surface and young men may grow abruptly violent, seemingly at random. The Islamic injunction against alcohol has had little obvious impact in ex-Soviet Central Asia, unlike in Afghanistan.

Crime

You can cut down on the potential for crime by following these tips:

- Be especially alert in crowded situations such as bazaars and bus station ticket scrums, where pockets and purses may be easily picked.
- Avoid parks at night, even if it means going out of your way.
- Take officially licensed taxis in preference to private ones. At night don't get into any taxi with more than one person in it.
- Travellers who rent a flat are warned to be sure the doors and windows are secure, and never to open the door – day or night – to anyone they do not clearly know.

If you're the victim of a crime, contact the *militsia* (police), though you may get no help from them at all. Get a report from them if you hope to claim on insurance for anything that was stolen, and contact your closest embassy for a report in English. If your passport is stolen, the police should also provide a letter to OVIR, which is essential for replacing your visa. See p506 for some tips on how to minimise the danger of theft of credit cards or travellers cheques.

Crooked Officials

The number of corrupt officials on the take has decreased dramatically since the first edition of this book and most travellers make

---

---

their way through Central Asia without a single run-in with the local *militsia*. The strongest police presence is in Uzbekistan (particularly in the Tashkent metro), followed by Turkmenistan and Tajikistan, where there are police checkpoints at most municipal and provincial borders. Take a long-distance taxi ride anywhere in the region and you'll see your driver paying off traffic cops after being waived down by an orange baton, up to a dozen times in a trip. It's a near certainty that you'll meet a gendarme or two in bus and train stations in Uzbekistan, though most only want to see your papers and know where you're going. Uzbek police are particularly inquisitive in Termiz and the Fergana Valley.

If you are approached by the police, there are several rules of thumb to bear in mind:

- Your best bet is to be polite, firm and jovial. A forthright, friendly manner – starting right out with an *asalam aleykum* (peace be with you) and a handshake for whomever is in charge – may help to defuse a potential shakedown, whether you are male or female.
- If someone refers to a 'regulation', ask to see it in writing. If you are dealing with lower-level officers, ask to see their *nachalnik* (superior).
- Ask to see a policeman's ID and, if possible, get a written copy of the ID number. Do not hand over your passport unless you see this ID. Even better, only hand over a photocopy of your passport; claim that your passport is at your hotel or embassy.
- Try to avoid being taken somewhere out of the public eye, eg into an office or into

the shadows; it should be just as easy to talk right where you are. The objective of most detentions of Westerners is simply to extort money, and by means of intimidation rather than violence. If your money is buried deeply, and you're prepared to pull out a paperback and wait them out, even if it means missing the next bus or train, most inquisitors will eventually give up.

- If you are detained at a police station, insist on calling the duty officer at your embassy or consulate. If your country has no diplomatic representative in the country you're in, call the embassy of a friendly country – for example the UK if you're from Australia or New Zealand.
- Make it harder for police on the take by speaking only in your own language.
- If officers show signs of force or violence, and provided they are not drunk, do not be afraid to make a scene – dishonest cops will dislike such exposure.
- Never sign anything, especially if it's in a language you don't understand. You have the right not to sign anything without consular assistance.
- Antinarcotics laws give the police powers to search passengers at bus and train stations. If you are searched, never let the police put their hands in your pockets – take everything out yourself and turn your pockets inside out.
- If police officers want to see your money (to check for counterfeit bills) try to take it out only in front of the highest-ranking officer. If any is taken insist on a written receipt for it.
- If you have to pay a fine, insist that you do so at a bank and get a receipt for the full amount.

DOCUMENTS

Besides your passport and visa, there are a number of other documents you may need to keep track of:

- Currency exchange and hard currency purchase receipts – you may need to show these when you sell back local money in a bank (not needed for money changers or in Kazakhstan).
- The customs form or entry form that you were given on entering the country.
- Vouchers – if you prepaid accommodation, excursions or transport, these are the only proof that you did so.

- Hotel registration chits – in Uzbekistan you may need to show these little bits of paper (showing when you stayed at each hotel) to OVIR officials.
- Letters of invitation and any supporting documents/receipts for visa and permit support.

It's wise to have at least one photocopy of your passport (front and visa pages), a copy of your OVIR registration (especially if your passport is at an embassy or hotel front desk), your travel-insurance policy and possibly your airline tickets on your person. It's also a smart idea to leave a photocopy of your passport, travel insurance and airline ticket with someone at home, or scan and store them in a webmail account.

Student and youth cards are of little use, though they can be helpful as a decoy if someone wants to keep your passport.

EMBASSIES & CONSULATES

Listings of embassies and consulates can be found in the directories of each country chapter.

GAY & LESBIAN TRAVELLERS

There is little obvious gay/lesbian community in Central Asia, though there are a couple of gay bars in Almaty. It's not unusual to see young women showing affection towards each other, nor is it uncommon to see men holding hands. However, this is a reflection of Asian culture rather than homosexuality.

In Uzbekistan, Turkmenistan and in Tajikistan, gay male sex is illegal, but lesbian sex does not seem to be illegal (it is seldom spoken about). Kazakhstan and Kyrgyzstan have lifted the Soviet-era ban on homosexuality. However, whether you're straight or gay, it's best to avoid public displays of affection.

The website www.gay.kz has information on gay life in Kazakhstan, but in Russian only.

Homosexuality is illegal in Afghanistan and penalties can be harsh – the Taliban spent much time debating whether being pushed off a cliff or crushed under a toppled wall was the appropriate punishment. Afghan men often hold hands in public but this is an accepted form of platonic friendship.

HOLIDAYS

See the Holidays section of the relevant country Directory for details of each country's public holidays. Turkmenistan has some par-

---

TOP CELEBRATIONS IN CENTRAL ASIA

- Independence Day in any ex-Soviet capital, but particularly in Tashkent (the only day of the year even the police don't demand bribes).

- Navrus (p503), the region's biggest festival, with celebrations ranging from wild games of *buzkashi* (a polo-like game played with a goat's carcass, p64) to lame funfairs. The region's biggest celebrations are at Mazar-e Sharif in Afghanistan.

- Summer horseback wrestling and other nomadic games on the *jailoo* (summer pastures) of Song-Köl (p340), Sarala-Saz (p339) or Murgab (p412), or Sunday horse races (spring and autumn) in Ashgabat's hippodrome (p439).

- The At Chabysh horse festival ((p330; www.atchabysh.com) in early November at Barskoön in Kyrgyzstan.

- Eagle-hunting competitions (hunting with eagles) at the August Birds of Prey Festival (p332), on the south side of Lake Issyk-Köl in Kyrgyzstan.

- Badakhshani music, dance and handicrafts at Khorog's Roof of the World Festival (p418) in the Tajikistan Pamirs.

---

ticularly wacky holidays, including Melon Day and 'A Drop of Water is a Grain of Gold' Day.

The following Islamic holidays are observed lightly in ex-Soviet Central Asia but more fervently in Afghanistan. Dates are fixed by the Islamic lunar calendar, which is shorter than the Western solar calendar, beginning 10 to 11 days earlier in each solar year. Future holy days can be estimated, but are in doubt by a few days until the start of that month, so dates given here are only approximate. The holidays normally run from sunset to the next sunset.

Ramadan and Eid al-Azha are observed with little fanfare in most of Central Asia (where you shouldn't have major problems finding food during the daytime) but are becoming more popular. Almost all restaurants in Afghanistan shut between dawn and dusk during Ramadan and you should avoid eating in public during the day.

Moulid an-Nabi (15 February 2011, 4 February 2012, 24 January 2013, 13 January 2014) The birthday of the Prophet Mohammed. A minor celebration in Central Asia, though you might notice mosques are a little fuller.

Ramadan (1 August 2011, 20 July 2012, 9 July 2013, 28 June 2014) Also known as Ramazan, the month of sunrise-to-sunset fasting. Dates mark the beginning of Ramadan.

Eid al-Fitr (31 August 2011, 19 August 2012, 8 August 2013, 28 July 2014) Also called Ruza Hayit in Uzbekistan and Orozo Ait in Kyrgyzstan. This involves two or three days of celebrations at the end of Ramadan, with family visits, gifts, a great banquet (known as Iftar) to break the fast and donations to the poor.

Eid al-Azha (16 November 2010, 6 November 2011, 26 October 2012, 15 October 2013) Also called Eid-e Qurban,

Korban, Qurban Hayit or Qurban Ait in Central Asia. This is the Feast of Sacrifice, commemorating Ibrahim's willingness to sacrifice his only son Ismael (paralleled in the Biblical story of Abraham and Isaac), and is celebrated over several days. Those who can afford it buy and slaughter a goat or sheep, sharing the meat with relatives and with the poor. This is also the season for the haj (pilgrimage to Mecca). Afghanistan largely shuts down for three days.

If you are crossing an international border it may be useful to know that Russian national holidays fall on 1 and 7 January, 8 March, 1 and 9 May, 12 June and 7 November. If heading to China don't cross the border on the Chinese national holidays of 1 January, 8 March, 1 July, 1 August, spring festival (some time in February) and the weeks following the major holidays of 1 May and 1 October.

Navrus

By far the biggest Central Asian holiday is the spring festival of Navrus ('New Days' – transliterated as Nauryz in Kazakh, Novruz in Turkmen, Nooruz in Kyrgyz and Nauroz in Dari). Navrus is an adaptation of pre-Islamic vernal equinox or renewal celebrations, celebrated approximately on the spring equinox, though now normally fixed on 21 March (22 March in Kazakhstan). Navrus was being celebrated in Central Asia before Alexander the Great passed through.

In Soviet times this was a private affair, even banned for a time (as it was in Afghanistan during the Taliban era). In 1989, in one of several attempts to deflect growing nationalism, Navrus was adopted by the then Soviet Central Asian republics as an official two-day festival, with traditional games, music and drama festivals, street art and colourful fairs, plus partying, picnics and visiting of family and friends. Families traditionally pay off debts before the start of the holiday.

Mazar-e Sharif's Shrine of Hazrat Ali (p486) is the epicentre of Nauroz celebrations in Afghanistan. Around 100,000 people come to visit the shrine and attend *buzkashi* games that are held in the southern outskirts, and accommodation is at a premium.

INSURANCE

Central Asia is an unpredictable place so insurance is a good idea. A minimum of US$1 million medical cover and a 'medevac' clause or policy covering the costs of being flown to another country for treatment is essential, as few reliable emergency services are available in the CIS. See p531 for more information on health insurance.

Some policies specifically exclude 'dangerous activities', which can include skiing, motorcycling, even trekking or horse riding. If these are on your agenda, ask about an insurance amendment to permit some of them (at a higher premium).

Likewise, many insurance companies will not insure for a trip to Afghanistan, citing it as a conflict zone, so double check with your insurance company, including what it defines as an 'active' and 'passive' conflict zone.

Few medical services in Central Asia will accept your foreign insurance documents for payment; you'll have to pay on the spot and claim later. Get receipts for everything and save all the paperwork. Some policies ask you to call back (reverse charges) to a centre in your home country where an immediate assessment of your problem is made.

Insurance policies can normally be extended on the road by a simple phone call, though make sure you do this before it expires or you may have to buy a new policy, often at a higher premium.

INTERNET ACCESS

Internet access is widely available throughout the region; just look for a roomful of pasty teenagers playing games like *Counterstrike*. The only place where you can't get reliable internet access is Turkmenistan. Most computers in the cities are loaded with Skype and instant messaging software. Wi-fi is available in many midrange and top-end hotels, especially in Kazakhstan, and is marked in this book with a ⊚ symbol.

You may find your keyboard set to Cyrillic; pressing 'shift' + 'alt' should change the keyboard language from Cyrillic to English.

LEGAL MATTERS

Visitors are subject to the laws of the country they're visiting. It's unlikely that you will ever actually be arrested, unless there are supportable charges against you. If you are arrested, authorities in the former Soviet states are obliged to inform your embassy (*pasolstvah* in Russian) immediately and allow you to communicate with a consular official without delay. Most embassies will provide a list of recommended lawyers.

MAPS

Buy your general maps of Central Asia before you leave home. For a search of the available maps try www.stanfords.co.uk.

German publisher Reise Know How (www.reise-know-how.de) produce good and long-lasting travel maps to Central Asia (*Zentralasien*, 1:700,000), Kazakhstan (*Kasachstan*) and Afghanistan.

Central Asia (Gizimap, 1999) is a good 1:750,000 general elevation map of the region (plus Kashgar), though it excludes northern Kazakhstan and western Turkmenistan. It usefully marks many trekking routes.

Central Asia – The Cultural Travel Map along the Silk Road (Elephanti) is a similar 1:1.5 million Italian map, which concentrates on Uzbekistan and Tajikistan. Nelles' 1:750,000 *Central Asia* map is also good.

Reliable, locally produced city and regional maps can be found in Kazakhstan and Kyrgyzstan, but are hard to find elsewhere. Especially in Uzbekistan, where many street names have been changed three or four times since independence, any map older than a couple years will drive you crazy.

In Ashgabat's top-end hotels you'll be able to purchase good Turkish-made maps of Ashgabat, Balkanabat, Dashogus, Mary and Turkmenbashi.

MONEY

The 'stans' banking systems have improved greatly in the last few years, with credit-card transactions, wire transfers (particularly Western Union) and regulated foreign exchange available in most towns. In the countryside there are few facilities, so change enough cash to get you back to a main city.

If you plan to travel extensively in the region, it's worth bringing a flexible combination of cash in US dollars or euros (particularly in Kazakhstan), a few US-dollar or euro travellers cheques and a credit card or two, to cover every eventuality.

ATMs

Most cities in ex-Soviet Central Asia have ATMs (bankomat) that accept Western credit cards, as does Kabul. (Ashgabat, and in fact the whole of Turkmenistan, is the main exception.) It makes sense to get your cash during working hours, since the last thing you need is to watch your card get eaten alive by an Uzbek ATM. Some ATMs charge a service fee of around 2%.

Black Market

The existence of licensed moneychangers in every town has done away with the black market in all republics except Uzbekistan, where it is very much alive (see p284).

Cash

Cash in US dollars is by far the easiest to exchange, followed by euros. Take a mixture of denominations – larger notes (US$100, US$50) are the most readily accepted and get a better rate, but a cache of small ones (US$10, US$5) is handy for when you're at borders, stuck with a lousy exchange rate or need to pay for services in US dollars. Cash is particularly useful in Uzbekistan, due to the black market (see p283).

Make sure notes are in good condition – no worn or torn bills – and that they are dated post-1994. Taxi drivers and market-sellers often fob off their own ragged foreign notes on tourists as change, so of course you should refuse to accept old notes too. At the time of research US$100 gave you a pile of Uzbek som as thick as an airport paperback.

Credit Cards

It's an excellent idea to bring a credit card as an emergency backup, though you shouldn't rely on it completely to finance your trip as there are still only a limited number of places where it can be used. Kazakhstan is the most useful place in Central Asia to have a credit card, and Afghanistan is the least useful.

Major credit cards can be used for payment at top-end hotels and restaurants, central airline offices, major travel agencies and a few shops throughout the region. Visa is the most widely recognised brand, but others (American Express, JCB, MasterCard) are accepted in most places, as are the Cirrus and Maestro systems.

If you can't find an ATM to accept your card, it's possible to get a cash advance against a Visa card or MasterCard in capitals for commissions of 1% to 3%. You will need your PIN to access the ATMs but not for a cash advance. Asking for the 'terminal' (the handheld machine that processes the card transaction) indicates that you want a cash advance. Always get a receipt, in case you are asked for proof of changing money at customs or if there is any discrepancy when you get home.

Remember that by using credit cards in Uzbekistan you fail to make use of the black market (see p283).

International Transfers

Bank-to-bank wire (telegraphic) transfers are possible through major banks in all capitals. Commissions of 1% to 4% are typical, and service takes one to five days. Millions of Central Asians work in Russia and wire money back home. Western Union (www.westernunion.com) has partners in banks and post offices everywhere and remains the easiest way to send money.

DOLLARS & SOMS

Prices in this book are sometimes given in US dollars or euros, when that is the most reliable price denominator or if that's the currency you'll be quoted on the ground. Even when a price is quoted in dollars you can normally pay in local currency (and technically in Tajikistan and Uzbekistan you actually have to).

You may need cash in US dollars to pay for visas, registration and some services with a private travel agency, though many of those now accept credit cards. Although officially you cannot spend foreign currency anywhere in Uzbekistan, private hotels and homestays normally accept US dollars and often give you change in local currency at the market rate. Most other homestays and drivers expect payment in local money.

Moneychangers

Dealing with licensed moneychangers is the easiest way to change cash in Kyrgyzstan, Kazakhstan, Tajikistan and Afghanistan. They are readily found in small kiosks on nearly every block, and some will give a receipt if you ask them; rates vary by 1% to 2% at most. Licensed changers are completely legal. Moneychangers are marked by signs such as ОБМЕН ВАЛЮТЫ (*obmen valyuty;* currency exchange) and ОБМЕННЫЙ ПУНКТ (*obmenny punkt;* exchange point).

Nearly all tourist hotels have branch/bank-exchange desks where you can at least swap cash US dollars for local money.

In convoluted border areas you may need to deal with several currencies simultaneously; when trekking in southern Kyrgyzstan it's necessary to carry a mixture of Tajik somani, Uzbek som, US dollars and Kyrgyz som.

Try to avoid large notes in local currency (except to pay your hotel bills), since few people can spare much change.

EXCHANGE RECEIPTS

Whenever you change money, ask for a receipt (*kvitantsiya* or *spravka* in Russian) showing your name, the date, the amounts in both currencies, the exchange rate and an official signature. Not everyone will give you one, but if you need to resell local currency through the banks (in Uzbekistan or Turkmenistan) you may need enough receipts to cover what you want to resell. You will not need a receipt to sell local currency into US dollars with money-changers in other countries. Customs officials may want to see exchange receipts at crossings to non-CIS countries but it's unlikely.

At the time of research you had to sell Uzbek som back at a main city office of the National Bank – not at the airport or the hotels, or the border. The easiest thing, of course, is to spend it up before you leave, change it to neighbouring currencies on the black market or swap it with travellers going the other way.

Travellers Cheques

Travellers cheques can now be cashed in all the major Central Asian capitals, except Dushanbe. American Express and Thomas Cook are the most widely recognised flavours, although only Visa travellers cheques can be changed in Turkmenistan. US-dollar travellers cheques are the best currency to bring. Commissions run between 1% and 3%. It is possible to get your money in dollars instead of local currency, though the commission rate may be a little different.

Travellers cheques can also make good decoy money if pressed for a bribe, as most people don't know what to do with them. If visiting Uzbekistan you need to list your travellers cheques on your customs declaration form or you won't be able to cash them.

Security

Thankfully, credit cards and travellers cheques are becoming more common in Central Asia, but you may still end up carrying large wads of cash.

Don't leave money in any form lying around your hotel room. Lock it deep in your luggage or carry it securely zipped in one or more money belts or shoulder wallets buried deep in your clothing, with only what you'll immediately need (or would be willing to hand over to a thief or to an official on the take) accessible in an exterior pocket, wallet or purse.

When paying for anything substantial (eg a hotel bill or an expensive souvenir) or changing money on the street at an exchange kiosk, count out the money beforehand, out of public sight; don't go fumbling in your money belt in full view. There are tales of thieves targeting people coming out of banks with fat cash advances, so keep your eyes open.

Make sure you note the numbers of your cards and travellers cheques, and the telephone numbers to call if they are lost or stolen – and keep all numbers separate from the cards and cheques.

Tipping & Bargaining

Tipping is becoming increasingly common in Central Asian cities. Most cafes and restaurants in the capitals add a 10% service charge to the bill, or expect you to round the total up. This doesn't always actually go to the staff so add some extra if you want to reward particularly good service.

Bribery is a fact of life in Central Asia but try to avoid it where possible – it feeds the already-widespread notion that travellers all just love throwing their money around, and makes it harder for future travellers. In fact a combination of smiles (even if over gritted teeth) and patient persistence can very often work better.

Shops have fixed prices but in markets (food, art or souvenirs) bargaining is usually expected. Press your luck further in places like art and craft markets, which are heavily patronised by tourists, and when negotiating transport hire. In Kyrgyzstan bargaining is usually reserved only for taxi drivers. In the markets asking prices tend to be in a sane proportion to the expected outcome. Sellers will be genuinely surprised if you reply to their '5000' with '1000'; they're more likely expecting 3500, 4000 or 4500 in the end. The Russian word for 'discount' is *skidka*.

PHOTOGRAPHY & VIDEO
Film & Equipment
Memory cards for digital cameras are quite prevalent in Central Asia these days. Most internet cafes can burn your photos onto a CD, as long as the burner works. Electricity is quite reliable for charging batteries, except in the remote Pamirs or in Afghanistan. Good quality batteries are hard to find in rural areas.

There are no significant customs limits on camera equipment and film for personal use. Declare video cameras on customs forms and carry by hand through customs, but don't leave the tape, memory stick or disk in it as it may be confiscated.

Photographing & Videoing People
Most Central Asians are happy to have their picture taken, though you should always ask first. A lifetime with the KGB has made some older people uneasy about having their picture taken. Many people are also touchy about you photographing embarrassing subjects like drunks or run-down housing. You may find people sensitive about you photographing women, especially in rural areas. Women photographers may get away with it if they've established some rapport. Don't photograph an Afghan woman without express permission, even if she is only in the background or in a burqa. By contrast Afghan men generally love having their picture taken.

The Russian for 'may I take a photograph?' is *fotografirovat mozhno*? (fa-ta-gruh-*fee*-ra-vut *mozh*-na?). The Dari equivalent is *aks gerefti*?

POST
The postal systems of Central Asia are definitely not for urgent items – due in part to the scarcity of regional flights. A letter or postcard will probably take two weeks or more to get outside the CIS. Kyrgyzstan and Kazakhstan are probably the most reliable places from where to send packages.

Central post offices are the safest places to post things. It can help to write the destination country in Cyrillic too. See the Post entries in the individual country Directories for postal rates.

If you have something that absolutely must get there, use an international courier company. DHL (www.dhl.com) and FedEx (www.fedex.com) have offices in major cities. A document to the US or Europe costs from US$40 to US$60 and takes about four days.

Express Mail Service (EMS) is a priority mail service offered by post offices that ranks somewhere between normal post and courier post. Prices are considerably cheaper than courier services.

REGISTRATION
This relic of the Soviet era allows officials to keep tabs on you once you've arrived. In Uzbekistan the hotel or homestay in which you stay the night is supposed to register you. Kyrgyzstan has ended the need to register, in Kazakhstan tourists who fly into the country are generally registered automatically (see p196 if entering overland) and tourist-visa holders in Tajikistan only need to register if staying for over 30 days.

The place to register is at OVIR. There's one in every town, sometimes in each city district, functioning as the eyes and ears of the Ministry of the Interior's administration for policing foreigners. Though it has a local name in each republic (eg Koshi-Kon Politsiyasi in Kazakhstan, OPVR in Tajikistan, IIB in Uzbekistan, UPVR in Kyrgyzstan), everybody still understands the word OVIR. In some remote areas where there is no OVIR office you may have to register at the *passportny stol* (passport office).

SHOPPING
In general Uzbekistan offers Central Asia's best shopping; in fact most of central Bukhara is now one big souvenir stall.

Potential Central Asian buys include carpets, hats, musical instruments, felt rugs, wall hangings, silk, traditional clothing, ceramic figurines and even nomadic accessories such as horse whips and saddles.

Turkmenistan is the place for a 'Bukhara-style' carpet, though getting it out of the country can be a problem (see p461). The best places for a *shyrdak* (Kyrgyz felt carpet) are the women's cooperatives in Kochkor and elsewhere in Central Kyrgyzstan. CBT can often put you

---

TOP PLACES FOR CRAFTS

For those interested in learning about local handicrafts, with an eye to purchasing, see the following in the main text. See also the boxed text 'Responsible Shopping' on p249.

- **Ak Orgo yurt workshop, Barskoön** (p330) If you have a lots of cash and a generous baggage allowance, the ultimate Kyrgyz souvenir is your very own yurt.
- **Altyn Kol, Kochkor** (p338) Local *shyrdak* (Kyrgyz felt carpet) cooperative.
- **Bukhara Artisan Development Centre, Bukhara** (p267) Watch artisans at work here.
- **Caravan & Caravan One, Tashkent** (p224) Browse for stylish handicrafts over lunch or a cappuccino.
- **De Pamiri, Khorog** (www.depamiri.org; p406) Felt carpets, musical instruments and more from the western Pamirs.
- **Kochkor Kutu, Kochkor** (p338) Some of the country's best *shyrdak*.
- **Rishton, Fergana Valley** (p239) Easily the best place to learn about and buy Uzbek ceramics.
- **Tolkuchka Bazaar, Ashgabat** (p435) Turkmen crafts, shaggy *telpek* hats and 'Bukhara' carpets at this wonderful bazaar, soon to be relocated.
- **Silk-carpet workshop, Khiva** (p276) Hand-made Khivan carpets that incorporate local designs with natural dyes.
- **Unesco silk-carpet workshop, Bukhara** (p266) Watch how carpets are made.
- **Yak House, Murgab** (p413) For Pamiri-style crafts, bags and socks.
- **Yodgorlik (Souvenir) Silk Factory, Margilon** (p238) Silk for US$4 per square metre, as well as *ikat* (brightly coloured cloth) dresses, carpets and embroidered items.

---

in touch with local *shyrdak* producers. You can find more Kyrgyz felt souvenirs at the Yak House (p413) and De Pamiri (p406), both in Tajikistan's Pamir region.

See p500 about exporting antiques or items that look antique.

Central Asian bazaars are enjoyable, even if you're just looking, with everything from Russian sparkling wine to jeep parts. Tolkuchka Bazaar (p435), outside Ashgabat, has acres of carpets, handicrafts and silks. Another surprising souvenir source right under your nose is the local TsUM department store.

Afghanistan offers some fine potential trophy souvenirs, including stripy *chapan* cloaks, a *pakul* cap, a chunk of lapis lazuli, some blue Herati glass (well-packed), a poster of Ahmad Shah Massoud, an old-style portrait from a pin-hole camera studio or, of course, an Afghan carpet.

SOLO TRAVELLERS

There are no real problems travelling alone in Central Asia. There isn't much of a traveller scene here but you'll meet other travellers in backpacker guesthouses in Bishkek, Osh, Khorog and the main towns in Uzbekistan.

It's generally not too difficult to find travellers to share car hire costs for the Torugart, Irkeshtam or Pamir Hwy trips. Local travel agents and community tourism providers can often help link you up with other travellers or try a post on the **Thorn Tree** (http://thorntree.lonelyplanet.com).

Travelling alone in Turkmenistan can be expensive. Hotel rooms cost almost the same whether you have one of two people in your party and if you are on a tourist visa you'll have to bear the burden of hiring a guide for yourself.

TELEPHONE
International Calls

The easiest and cheapest way to make international calls in Central Asia is in an internet cafe through a service like Skype (www.skype.com). Calls are free to other Skype users and as low as US$0.02 per minute to landlines or mobile phones in most countries.

Other ways to make cheap internet phone calls include through private communication centres or, in Tajikistan and Kazakhstan, through prepaid internet phone (IP) cards which you can buy at telephone offices and use at any public phone. These cost a fraction of a conventional international phone call (from around US$0.10 per minute) and the quality is usually as good as through the old Soviet-era landlines.

In smaller towns you place international calls (as well as local and intercity ones) from the central telephone and telegraph offices. You tell a clerk the number and prepay in local currency. After a wait of anything from half a minute to several hours, you're called to a booth. Hotel operators also place calls, but for a hefty surcharge. International calls in the region generally cost between US$0.50 and US$2 per minute.

Calls between CIS countries are now treated as international calls, though they have a different rate. Thus to call Uzbekistan from, say, Kyrgyzstan, you would need to dial Kyrgyzstan's international access code, the Uzbek country code, then the Uzbek city code.

See the inside front cover for individual country codes, and the individual city entries in the country chapters for their telephone codes.

Local Calls

Placing a local or trunk call on Central Asia's telephone systems is usually harder than placing an international one, one reason why most locals use mobile phones. None of the old Soviet-era token-operated telephones work any more but entrepreneurs often fill the gap in the market by setting up a telephone on a very long extension cable (pay cash to the small Uzbek boy seated by the phone). Some shops have a phone available for calls. Kazakhstan has card-operated phones. Local calls are free from many hotels.

Mobile Phones

Several Central Asian companies have roaming agreements with foreign providers but if you have an 'unlocked' GSM phone it's generally much cheaper to buy a local sim card and top that up with local scratch cards or at top-up booths. Local calls and texts with a local sim card cost as little as US$0.02 in Uzbekistan. You will probably need a copy of your passport to buy a sim card and may need a local's help.

Note that Central Asian mobile phones work on 900/1800 MHz frequencies. European phones generally share these frequencies but most US cell phones use 850/1900 frequencies so you will probably need an unlocked quad-band American phone if you want to use it in

Central Asia. You might find it cheaper to buy a cell phone on arrival. See www.gsmworld.com/roaming for details.

TIME

The official time in most of Central Asia is Greenwich Mean Time (GMT) plus five hours. Transcontinental Kazakhstan straddles GMT plus five and six hours and Afghanistan uses GMT plus 4½ hours.

None of the Central Asian republics has Daylight Savings Time.

TOILETS

Public toilets are as scarce as hen's teeth. Those that you can find – eg in parks and bus and train stations – charge the equivalent of US$0.10 or so to use their squatters. Someone may be out front selling sheets of toilet paper. Most toilets are awful, the rest are worse. You are always better off sticking to top-end hotels and restaurants or shopping malls. Carry a small torch for rural restaurant toilets, which rarely have functioning lights, and for trips out to the pit toilet. *Always* carry an emergency stash of toilet paper.

Out in the *jailoo* (pastures) of Kyrgyzstan and Tajikistan there are often no toilets at all. You'll have to go for a hike, find a rock or use the cover of darkness. Always urinate at least 50m from a water source (and downstream!) and dig a hole and burn the paper after defecating.

Toilet paper is sold everywhere, though tissues are a better bet than the industrial strength sandpaper that is ex-Soviet toilet paper. Flush systems and pit toilets don't like toilet paper; the wastepaper basket in the loo is for used paper and tampons (wrapped in toilet paper).

Before bursting in, check for the signs 'Ж' (Russian: *zhenski*) for women or 'М' *(muzhskoy)* for men.

TOURIST INFORMATION

Intourist, the old Soviet travel bureau, gave birth to a litter of Central Asian successors – Intourist Tojikistan in Tajikistan, Turkmensiyahat in Turkmenistan, and Uzbektourism in Uzbekistan. Few are of any interest to independent travellers. You are almost always better off with one of the growing number of private agencies or community-based-tourism projects.

That said, there are useful tourist information centres in Almaty in Kazakhstan, at Khorog in Tajikistan and also at Karakol in Kyrgyzstan, with new centres planned for Dushanbe (Tajikistan) and Karaganda (Kazakhstan). In remote areas local NGOs can often offer advice on accommodation, transport and ecotourism initiatives.

TRAVEL PERMITS

Uzbek, Kazakh, Tajik and Kyrgyz visas allow access to all places in the republics, save for a few strategic areas that need additional permits. See the Travel Permits section in the Directory of the individual country chapters for details. Generally you should apply for these permits through a travel agency a few weeks before arrival.

In Kazakhstan some interesting areas near the Chinese border, such as the Altay and Zhungar Alatau mountains, require special permits that take up to six weeks to procure. Baykonur Cosmodrome (p159) can only be visited on tours organised through agencies and you need to start the paperwork process about two months ahead. Visits to the Semey Polygon nuclear-testing site and its command town Kurchatov need to be organised through agencies or Kazakhstan's National Nuclear Centre (see p192).

In Kyrgyzstan any place within 50km of the Chinese border (such as the Inylchek Glacier, Alay Valley and Pik Lenin) requires a military border permit that is fairly easy to obtain through a trekking agency.

The Gorno-Badakhshan region of Tajikistan needs a separate permit, which you can get at most embassies abroad or through a travel agency in a couple of days.

Turkmenistan presents a more complicated picture, as much of the country outside the main cities (restricted border zones) has to be listed on your visa for you to be able to visit it. You'll need a travel agency to get the visa in the first place so your visa acts as your permit.

Travel in the Wakhan Corridor of Afghanistan requires permission from Faizabad, the capital of Afghan Badakhshan, though you can sometimes arrange this through an agent in Ishkashim if travelling from Tajikistan.

VISAS

Visas can be the single biggest headache associated with travel in ex-Soviet Central Asia, where the bureaucracy seems designed to actually hinder tourism and regulations mutate frequently. Collecting visas for a multicountry trip through Central Asia can take months and cost hundreds of US dollars.

Things are, however, getting easier. Visas for Kazakhstan, Tajikistan and Kyrgyzstan are now a formality for most nationalities and no letter of invitation (LOI) is required for single-entry visas of 30 days (double entry for Kazakhstan). It's even possible to get a visa on arrival at Bishkek or Dushanbe airports. The difficulty involved in getting an Uzbekistan visa generally depends on how loudly your country criticises their human-rights record, but is generally not too big a problem. Turkmenistan requires you to jump through the largest number of hoops.

The steps to obtain a visa and the attention it gets after you arrive differ for each republic, but their outlines are similar. The following information is general, with individual country variations detailed in the Directories of the relevant country chapters.

Letters of Invitation

The key to getting a visa for Turkmenistan and, for many nationalities, Uzbekistan, as well as longer duration, multiple-entry visas or sometimes visas on arrival for other countries, is 'visa support', which means an invitation (LOI), approved by the Ministries of Foreign Affairs and/or Interior, from a private individual, company or state organisation in the country you want to visit. After obtaining ministry approval, your sponsor sends the invitation to you, and when you apply at a consular office for your visa it's matched with a copy sent directly to them from the Ministry of Foreign Affairs.

The invitation should include your name, address, citizenship, sex, birth date, birthplace and passport details; the purpose, proposed itinerary and entry/exit dates of your visit; and the type of visa you will need and where you will apply for it. A business visa always requires a letter of invitation.

The cheapest way to get a visa invitation is directly, by fax or email, through a Central Asian travel agency. Many Central Asian agencies will just sell you a letter of visa support for between US$20 and US$40, which you pay when you arrive in the country. See the boxed text on p511 and also the Travel Agencies sections of capital cities for some trustworthy agencies in Central Asia. A few Western travel agencies can arrange visa invitation but charge up to five times the local fee.

Try to apply for letters of invitation a month, or preferably two, in advance. Individual sponsors may need months to get their invitations approved before they can even be sent to you.

Afghanistan sometimes requires a letter of introduction stating your purpose and itinerary but this can be from your employer or even from yourself.

Applying for a Visa

Visa applications can be made at some or all of the republics' overseas embassies or consulates, the addresses of which are listed in this book's Directories in individual country chapters. If your country doesn't have Central Asian representation you'll have to courier your passport to the nearest embassy, arrange a visa on arrival (p512), or arrange your itinerary to get the visa

in another Central Asian republic. Kazakh embassies will often issue visas for Kyrgyzstan if there is no Kyrgyz representation, though you need an LOI for this (whereas no invitation is required at a Kyrgyz embassy).

In addition to a letter of support, embassies may want a photocopy of the validity and personal information pages of your passport, two or three passport-size photos and a completed application form. Some may want more.

For Kyrgyzstan, Uzbekistan, Tajikistan, Kazakhstan and Afghanistan, visas do not list the towns to be visited and you are free to travel almost everywhere in these countries (see p510). The tourist-visa application for Turkmenistan requires you to list the name

---

VISA WEB CONTACTS

Embassies
Useful embassy websites:

- www.embassyofafghanistan.org, www.afghanembassy.net, www.afghanistanembassy.org.uk
- www.kazakhembus.com, www.kazconsulny.org, www.kazembassy.org.uk
- www.kyrgyzembassy.org, www.kyrgyz-embassy.org.uk, www.botschaft-kirgisien.de
- www.tjus.org, www.tajikembassy.org, www.taj-emb.be, www.tajembassy.org.uk
- www.turkmenistanembassy.org, www.turkmenembassy.org.uk
- www.uzbekconsulny.org, www.uzbekistan.org, www.uzbekistan.de, www.uzbekembassy.org, www.ouzbekistan.fr (in French)

Travel Agencies
The following travel agencies can arrange letters of invitation for their republic and in most cases the surrounding republics. Fees are around US$25 to US$35. Stantours is recommended by many travellers for impartial regional visa information.

- Valentina Guesthouse, Almaty (http://valentina-gh.narod.ru)
- Jibek Joly, Almaty (www.jibekjoly.kz)
- Otrar Travel, Almaty, Astana and 15 other Kazakh cities (www.otrar.kz)
- Stantours, Almaty (www.stantours.com)
- Ayan Travel, Ashgabat (www.ayan-travel.com)
- DN Tours, Ashgabat (www.dntours.com)
- Celestial Mountains, Bishkek (www.celestial.com.kg)
- ITMC, Bishkek (www.itmc.centralasia.kg)
- Salom, Bukhara (www.salomtravel.com)
- Hamsafar Travel, Dushanbe (www.hamsafar-travel.com)
- Somon Travel, London & Dushanbe (www.somontravel.com)
- Sogda Tour, Samarkand (www.sogda-tour.com)
- Advantour, Tashkent (www.advantour.com)
- Arostr Tourism, Tashkent (www.arostr.uz)
- Oriental Express Central Asia, Tashkent (www.orexca.com)

CHINESE VISAS

Chinese visas can be arranged in Tashkent but are a real pain to organise elsewhere in Central Asia, since embassies often demand a letter of invitation. These are available for around US$50 from travel agencies but can take a couple of weeks to arrange. The best advice is to get a Chinese visa before you set off, though remember that you must normally enter China within 90 days of your visa being issued.

of every town you want to visit, and these will normally be printed on your visa. It's a good idea to ask for every place you might conceivably want to see, unless these are sensitive border towns or off-limits to foreigners. There's no charge for listing extra destinations.

Bear in mind that many visas have either fixed-entry dates (Turkmenistan) or fixed-validity dates (Tajikistan), so you may have to plan the dates of your itinerary closely in advance. If you are weaving in and out of republics, ie from Uzbekistan to Tajikistan's Pamir Hwy, Kyrgyzstan and then back to Uzbekistan, you'll need to ensure that the first visa is still valid for when you return to that republic (and that it's a double- or multiple-entry visa).

Even the most helpful Central Asian embassies in the West normally take a week or two to get you a visa. Most embassies will speed the process up for an express fee (often double the normal fee). Central Asian embassies within the CIS seem to be quicker, eg a couple of days at Kyrgyz embassies in other Central Asian republics (slightly longer in Almaty), three working days or less at Kazakh embassies.

Visas can be more difficult to get in the run-up to elections and national days (the latter in Turkmenistan only).

Try to allow time for delays and screw-ups. Errors do happen – check the dates and other information on your visa carefully before you hit the road, and try to find out what the Cyrillic or other writing says.

Visas on Arrival

If there's no convenient embassy in your country, you can get a visa on arrival at Bishkek airport without an invitation, at Dushanbe airport if you have travel agency support and at Almaty, Astana, Uralsk, Atyrau, Tashkent and Ashgabat airports if this has been arranged in advance with a travel agency in that country and you have a letter of invitation to prove it. It's possible to get a five-day transit visa on arrival at Almaty airport for US$25 without an LOI but you should have proof of an onward air ticket and an onward visa.

Responsible sponsors and agencies send representatives to meet their invitees at the airport and smooth their way through immigration. Even so, consular officials at the airport can be notoriously hard to find, especially if your flight arrives in the middle of the night, and may not be able to find your records scribbled in their big black book. You may also need to persuade the airline that you are guaranteed a visa as many are keen to avoid the costs and fines associated with bringing you back if your papers aren't in order. Try to get a visa in advance if possible.

You can't get a tourist visa at a land border of any Central Asian republic, though Kyrgyzstan plans to introduce this at some point.

Getting Central Asian Visas in Central Asia

Some (not all) visas are simpler and cheaper to get after you arrive. It's relatively easy, for example, to get a Kazakh or Uzbek visa in Bishkek (Kyrgyzstan), or a Kyrgyz visa in Dushanbe.

This could make your pretrip visa search much simpler, if you're willing to take some chances and have a week or so in a Central Asian republic to deal with the bureaucracy. It is theoretically possible (though not recommended) to leave home without any visas at all – eg fly to Bishkek and get a visa on arrival, then get a Kazakh or Uzbek visa in Bishkek and continue your trip there. This will work if you contact local travel agencies in advance to prepare any LOIs you might need. In general, though, you are better off getting at least one visa (Kyrgyz and Kazakh are the easiest, followed by Uzbekistan or Tajikistan) before you board a plane to Central Asia.

Transit & Multiple-Entry Visas

Even if you are just passing through a republic (eg flying into Almaty and transferring to Bishkek) you will need a transit visa. If you are also flying out this way you will need to apply for another transit visa (in this case in Bishkek). It is possible to get a five-day Kazakh transit visa for US$25 on arrival at Almaty airport (see p512).

You will need transit visas for some trips even if you're not stopping in the country. For example you will need a Kazakh transit visa to travel overland (by bus or train) from Tashkent to Bishkek (which goes through Kazakhstan). You may also need a re-entry visa to get back into the first country if your bus or train transport dips temporarily into a neighbouring republic.

Train trips can be particularly tricky. New routings mean that you no longer need a Turkmen transit visa to take the Uzbek train between Tashkent and Urgench. Less convenient connections such as Tashkent to the Fergana Valley (which requires a Tajik transit visa and a double-entry Uzbek visa) are worth avoiding.

Uzbekistan and Kazakhstan now even require other Central Asians to have a visa, in a move planned to boost security, which will only add to the visa queues at the respective embassies of those two countries.

A 2008 regulation allows Kazakh tourist visa holders one entry to neighbouring areas of Kyrgyzstan (Chuy, Talas and Issyk-Köl oblasts), and Kyrgyz tourist visa holders one entry to districts of Kazakhstan's Zhambyl and Almaty oblasts that adjoin Kyrgyzstan. You cannot return to the first country without a new visa and some border officials do not know about it or ask for bribes, so it's still best to get two separate visas.

Getting Current Information

As with all official mumbo jumbo in Central Asia, the rules change all the time, so the info here may be out of date by the time you read it. Kyrgyzstan is even thinking of getting rid of visas entirely for some nationalities. Check Central Asian embassy websites (see the boxed text, p511), Lonely Planet's Thorn Tree (www.lonelyplanet.com/thorntree) and with one or more CIS-specialist travel or visa agencies.

Visa Extensions

Extending an ordinary tourist visa after you get there is relatively easy in Kyrgyzstan and Afghanistan, a bureaucratic tussle in Tajikistan and Uzbekistan (you can get a week's extension at Tashkent airport) and almost impossible in Kazakhstan and Turkmenistan. Travel agencies can normally help for a fee. You may find it easier to travel to a neighbouring republic and arrange another tourist visa.

WOMEN TRAVELLERS

Despite the imposition of Soviet economic 'equality', attitudes in the Central Asian republics remain fairly male-dominated. Many local men cannot understand why women (in groups of any size, for that matter) would travel without men, and assume they have ulterior sexual motives. Although harassment is not so unrelenting as in some Middle Eastern countries, it tends to be more physical. Macho Uzbekistan tops the list, with Kyrgyzstan by far the least sexist. As always, Afghanistan is in a league of its own (see p493).

Both men and women should seek permission before entering a mosque, particularly during prayer times when non-Muslims will feel uncomfortable. Women are generally not allowed in mosques in Tajikistan and the Fergana Valley. Most mosques in cities and the major tourist areas are open to all.

In bigger cities there is no taboo on unaccompanied local women talking to male visitors in public. Local men addressed by a woman in a couple direct their reply to the man, out of a sense of respect, and you should try to follow suit. Local women tend not to shake hands or lead in conversations. Because most local women don't drink in public, female visitors may not be offered a shot of the vodka or wine doing the rounds. But these are not taboos as such, and foreigners

---

THE INVISIBLE HUSBAND *Kelli Hahn*

In some parts of Central Asia men are unused to seeing women travelling by themselves and you'll be continually asked where your husband is, and the system can often work in the lone woman's favour. So slip on a fake wedding ring and invent the invisible husband (in Russian, 'moy muzh' means 'my husband'), who can then be used in uncomfortable situations. When being pressured to buy something in a shop, cast your eyes downward and murmur 'moy moozh' (my husband doesn't give me any money). When a strange man tries to befriend you and you can't shake him, give a frantic glance at your watch and shout 'moy moozh' (I am meeting my husband at any moment). When officials, guards or policemen demand a bribe, shrug your shoulders helplessly and cry 'moy moozh' (my husband has left me here and there's nothing I can do!).

usually tend to be forgiven for what locals might consider gaffes.

Keen sensibilities and a few staunch rules of thumb can make a solo journey rewarding:

- Clothes do matter: a modest dress code is essential (even if local Russian women don't seem to have one).
- Walk confidently with your head up but avoid eye contact with men (smile at everybody else).
- Never follow any man – even an official – into a private area. If one insists on seeing your passport, hand over a photocopy as well as a photocopy of your OVIR registration (have quite a few of these); if he pushes you to follow him, walk away into a busy area.
- When riding in shared taxis choose one that already has other female passengers.
- Sit at the front of the bus, preferably between two women, if you can.
- When seeking information, always ask a local woman. Most matronly types will automatically take you under their wing if you show enough despair.
- If you feel as though you are being followed or harassed, seek the company of a group of women, or even children; big smiles will get you a welcome.
- If you are arranging a trek or car hire, ask the agency to include female travellers.
- Some local men will honestly want to befriend and help you; if you are unsure and have a difficult time shaking them, mention your husband even if he's imaginary (see boxed text, p513).
- Wear a whistle around your neck in case you get into trouble. Blow on it relentlessly if you are absolutely in danger.

But it isn't all bad! The opportunities for genuine cross-cultural woman-to-woman interactions can generally be had during homestays, and usually outside the cities. Everyone loves to have their children cooed over and doing so will gain you friends as well as unique experiences. You may well see a side of Central Asia hidden to male travellers.

WORK, STUDY & VOLUNTEERING

There aren't many casual work opportunities in the region. What work *is* available is probably limited to English teaching and aid work, both of which are best arranged prior to your arrival in the region. The US Peace Corps has a strong presence in the region, except in Uzbekistan, and the UK Voluntary Service Overseas (VSO) operates in Tajikistan.

You may find teaching positions in the region's universities, particularly the American University in Bishkek (www.auca.kg), the Samarkand State Institute of Foreign Languages (www.sifl.50megs.com) and the planned University of Central Asia (www.ucentralasia.org) campuses in Khorog (Tajikistan), Naryn (Kyrgyzstan) and Tekeli (Kazakhstan).

For those with a TEFL or CELTA certificate, the **London School in Bishkek** (www.tlsbi.com) offers teaching posts for a minimum of 6 months for the academic year, or four months for the summer. The school also offers intensive Kyrgyz or Russian language tuition for travellers, with both classroom and homestay environments.

The Practical Centre Bishkek (p304) also offers month-long language classes in Russian and Kyrgyz.

Volunteers headed to Central Asia should read *Taxi to Tashkent: Two Years with the Peace Corps in Uzbekistan* by Tom Fleming, or *Chai Budesh? Anyone for Tea?*, by Joan Heron, which is subtitled 'A Peace Corps Memoir of Turkmenistan'. Another useful read is the novel *This Is Not Civilization*, by Robert Rosenberg, which chronicles the travails of a Peace Corps volunteer and is partly set in Kyrgyzstan. Prospective mothers and Bishkek expats might like *Revolution Baby* by Saffia Farr, an account of three years of expat life raising a baby in Kyrgyzstan.

The Alpine Fund (www.alpinefund.org) in Bishkek accepts six-month volunteers. You could also volunteer at Habitat Kyrgyzstan Foundation (www.habitat.elcat.kg). Volunteer teachers can help out with the Sworde-Teppa (www.sworde-teppa.org.uk) organisation in Kurgonteppa in southern Tajikistan. Some travellers have helped out at community-based tourism projects in Kyrgyzstan (see p302).

The American organisation CDC Development Solutions (www.cdcdevelopmentsolutions.org) sometimes have a need for volunteers in its Central Asian tourism projects.

Other good volunteer resources are www.volunteer.kz, www.jashtar.kg, www.unv.org and www.worldvolunteerweb.org.

American Councils (☎ 202-833-7522; www.americancouncils.org; 1776 Massachusetts Ave., NW, Suite 700, Washington, DC 20036) organises summer- and year-long academic exchanges and language study programs in Central Asia.

Transport in Central Asia

GETTING THERE & AWAY

This chapter deals with travel into or out of Central Asia and includes general getting around advice for the region. For details of travel between and within Central Asian countries, see the transport sections of the individual country chapters.

ENTERING CENTRAL ASIA

The region's main air links to the 'outside' are through the main cities of Almaty (Kazakhstan), Bishkek (Kyrgyzstan), Tashkent (Uzbekistan), Ashgabat (Turkmenistan) and, to a lesser extent, Dushanbe (Tajikistan) and Astana (Kazakhstan). A few cities in Kazakhstan have international links to Europe and smaller cities in other republics have connections to Commonwealth of Independent States (CIS) countries outside of Central Asia, especially Russia. Kabul is the only international air gateway to Afghanistan.

The long-distance rail connections are mostly with Mother Russia – from Moscow or the Trans-Siberian Railway to Tashkent, Almaty and Astana. The only other rail link is the Silk Road express between Astana/Almaty and Ürümqi (and beyond) in China.

The other main overland links are three roads from China – one accessible year-round via Ürümqi to Almaty, and two warm-weather

routes from Kashgar to Kyrgyzstan, over the Torugart or Irkeshtam Passes into Kyrgyzstan. A fourth mountain route may open soon over the Qolma Pass between Murgab in Tajikistan and Tashkurgan in China. A road link connects Mashhad in Iran to Ashgabat at two locations.

Afghanistan's main overland gateways are from Iran (Mashhad to Herat) and Pakistan (Peshawar to Jalalabad over the Khyber Pass), the latter dependent on security concerns.

Finally there is the offbeat journey from Turkey through the Caucasus Mountains by bus to Baku (Azerbaijan), across the Caspian Sea by ferry to Turkmenbashi (Turkmenistan) and by train to Ashgabat, Bukhara and beyond (or alternatively to Aktau in Kazakhstan). See 'From Turkey' (p520) for details.

AIR

Many European and Asian cities now have direct flights to the Central Asian capitals and Almaty but connections are still limited. Of the many routes in, two handy corridors are via Turkey (thanks to the geopolitics of the future) and via Russia (thanks to the geopolitics of the past). Turkish Airlines has the best connections and in-flight service but is at the higher end of the fare scale, while Russian and Central Asian carriers have the most connections. The budget airline Air Baltic has quickly become popular for its low fares and good European connections. Turkey also has the advantage of a full house of Central Asian embassies and airline offices. Moscow has four airports and connections can be inconvenient.

> **THINGS CHANGE...**
> The information in this chapter is particularly vulnerable to change. Check directly with the airline or a travel agent to make sure you understand how a fare (and ticket you may buy) works and be aware of the security requirements for international travel. Shop carefully. The details given in this chapter should be regarded as pointers and are not a substitute for your own careful, up-to-date research.

Airports & Airlines

Tashkent – seven hours from London, 3½ hours from Moscow, Tel Aviv and Delhi, 4½ hours from İstanbul, 5½ hours from Beijing and 6½ hours from Bangkok – may have the most central airport in Eurasia. More flights go to Tashkent than to any other city in the region.

Almaty is a useful gateway to both Kazakhstan and Kyrgyzstan (Bishkek is just three hours by road and shared taxis and a shuttle bus operates this route – see p370.

Ashgabat is less well connected, most reliably by Lufthansa and Turkish Airlines, and Tajikistan is the least connected, with popular weekly connections with Turkish Airlines and Air Baltic. For Dushanbe it's possible to fly to Bishkek and take a regional flight, or fly to Tashkent and travel overland to Khojand and then take a domestic flight.

For Kabul, Dubai is the main transit hub for flights from Europe and North America, though Safi Airways and Ariana Afghan now have direct flights from Frankfurt. Other transit hubs include Delhi and Islamabad. The only connections between Kabul and the rest of Central Asia are the weekly Ariana flight to Dushanbe and an irregular Kam Air flight to Almaty. You can normally book Ariana and Kam Air tickets online.

If flying to Kabul via Dubai it is unlikely you will be able to check your luggage all the way through, which is not a bad thing as it frequently gets lost in transit. You will likely have to transfer terminals in Dubai (Emirates uses its own Terminal 3, whereas Safi Airways uses Terminal 1 and Ariana uses Terminal 2).

The following are the main Central Asian airlines, of which Uzbekistan Airways and Air Astana are probably the best:

Air Astana (www.airastana.com; airline code KC; hub Almaty) Flies Almaty to Amsterdam, Baku, Bishkek, Bangkok, Beijing, Delhi, Dubai, Frankfurt, İstanbul, Kuala Lumpur, London, Moscow and Seoul; Astana to Dubai, İstanbul, Frankfurt, Moscow, Novosibirsk, and Ürümqi; Atyrau to Amsterdam and İstanbul; Kostanay to Hanover; Uralsk to Amsterdam.

Air Company (AC) Kyrgyzstan (www.air.kg; airline code QH; hub Bishkek) Flies to Moscow, Delhi, Dubai, Dushanbe, Tashkent and other Russian destinations, plus seasonal flights to Germany. Formerly known as Altyn Air.

Itek Air (www.itekair.kg; airline code GI; hub Bishkek) Kyrgyz airline flies to Ürümqi and Moscow.

SCAT (www.scat.kz in Russian; airline code DV; hubs Almaty, Astana, Shymkent) Kazakh airline flies from Aktau to Astrakhan, Baku, İstanbul, Moscow, Tbilisi and Yerevan among others; from Atyrau to Baku and Mineralnye Vody; from Aktobe and Shymkent to Moscow; from Almaty to Tashkent and Dushanbe; and from Ust-Kamenogorsk to Bayan-Ölgii (Mongolia) and Novosibirsk.

Somon Air (www.somonair.com; airline code 4J; hub Dushanbe) Flies to Dubai, Frankfurt, İstanbul, Moscow, St Petersburg, Sochi and Krasnoyarsk, with Ürümqi, Bishkek and Orenberg planned.

Tajik Air (www.tajikair.tj; airline code 7J; hub Dushanbe) Flies to Moscow (Domodedovo), Sharjah, Tehran, Sochi, İstanbul, St Petersburg, Ürümqi, Bishkek, Almaty and various Siberian cities.

Turkmenistan Airlines (www.turkmenistanairlines.com; airline code T5; hub Ashgabat) Flies to Abu Dhabi, Almaty, Amritsar, Bangkok, Beijing, Birmingham, Delhi, Dubai, Frankfurt, İstanbul, Kiev, London, Moscow and St Petersburg.

Uzbekistan Airways (www.uzairways.com; airline code HY; hub Tashkent) Flies to Amritsar, Athens, Baku, Bangkok, Beijing, Delhi, Dubai, Frankfurt, İstanbul, Kiev, Kuala Lumpur, Lahore, London, Milan, Moscow, New York, Osaka, Paris, Riga, Rome, Seoul, Sharjah, Tel Aviv, Tokyo, Ürümqi and several Russian cities; as well as Astana, Almaty, Ashgabat and Bishkek.

Airlines in Afghanistan include:

Ariana Afghan Airlines (www.flyariana.com; airline code FG; hub Kabul) Flies to Ankara, Baku, Delhi, Dubai, Dushanbe, Frankfurt, Islamabad, İstanbul, Jeddah, Kuwait, Mashhad, Moscow, Riyadh, Sharjah, Tehran, Ürümqi; plus Dushanbe (weekly).

Kam Air (www.flykamair.com; airline code RQ; hub Kabul) To Almaty, Delhi, Dubai, Mashhad and Ürümqi.

Safi Airways (www.safiairways.aero; airline code 4Q; hub Kabul) To Abu Dhabi, Dubai, Frankfurt, Kuwait and Sharjah.

Pamir Airways (www.pamirairways.af; airline code NR; hub Kabul) To Delhi, Dubai, Jeddah and Riyadh.

Other international airlines that fly into Central Asia:

Aeroflot (www.aeroflot.ru; airline code SU; hub Sheremetyevo-2, Moscow) To Tashkent and Bishkek four times weekly.

Air Arabia (www.airarabia.com; airline code G9; hub Sharjah) To Almaty.

Air Baltic (www.airbaltic.com; airline code BT; hub Riga) To Almaty, Dushanbe and Tashkent twice weekly; meals not included.

Asiana Airlines (www.flyasiana.com; airline code OZ; hub Kimpo Airport, Seoul) To Tashkent and Almaty.

Austrian Airlines (www.aua.com; airline code OS; hub Vienna) To Astana.

Azerbaijan Airlines (www.azal.az; airline code AHY; hub Baku) To Aktau.

CLIMATE CHANGE & TRAVEL

Climate change is a serious threat to the ecosystems that humans rely upon, and air travel is the fastest-growing contributor to the problem. Lonely Planet regards travel, overall, as a global benefit, but believes we all have a responsibility to limit our personal impact on global warming.

Flying & Climate Change

Pretty much every form of motor travel generates CO_2 (the main cause of human-induced climate change) but planes are far and away the worst offenders, not just because of the sheer distances they allow us to travel, but because they release greenhouse gases high into the atmosphere. The statistics are frightening: two people taking a return flight between Europe and the US will contribute as much to climate change as an average household's gas and electricity consumption over a whole year.

Carbon Offset Schemes

Climatecare.org and other websites use 'carbon calculators' that allow jetsetters to offset the greenhouse gases they are responsible for with contributions to energy-saving projects and other climate-friendly initiatives in the developing world – including projects in India, Honduras, Kazakhstan and Uganda.

Lonely Planet, together with Rough Guides and other concerned partners in the travel industry, supports the carbon offset scheme run by climatecare.org. Lonely Planet offsets all of its staff and author travel.

For more information check out our website: lonelyplanet.com.

BMI (www.flybmi.com; airline code BD; hub London Heathrow) To Almaty and Bishkek three times weekly.

China Southern (www.cs-air.com/en, www.flychina southern.com; airline code CZ; hub Guangzhou) Ürümqi to Almaty, Ashgabat, Dushanbe, Tashkent and Bishkek.

Czech Airlines (www.czechairlines.com; airline code OK; hub Prague) Flies to Almaty and Tashkent twice weekly.

Etihad Airways (www.etihadairways.com; airline code EY; hub Abu Dhabi) Twice weekly to Almaty and Astana.

Indian Airlines (www.indianairlines.in; airline code IC; hub New Delhi) To Kabul.

Iran Air (www.iranair.com; airline code IR; hub Tehran) To Tashkent, Almaty and Ashgabat (via Mashhad).

Iran Aseman (www.iaa.ir; airline code EP; hub Tehran) From Tehran and Mashhad to Ashgabat, Bishkek and Dushanbe (Mashhad only).

KLM (www.klm.com; airline code KL; hub Schiphol Airport, Amsterdam) Four weekly to Almaty.

Korean Air (www.koreanair.com; airline code KE; hub Seoul) To Tashkent thrice weekly.

Lufthansa (www.lufthansa.com; airline code LH; hub Frankfurt) To Almaty (daily), Astana (three weekly), Ashgabat (three weekly via Baku) and Munich to Tashkent.

Pakistan International Airlines (www.piac.com.pk; airline code PK; hub Karachi) Islamabad and Peshawar to Kabul.

Rossiya Russian Airlines (www.rossiya-airlines.com; airline code FV; hub St Petersburg) To Almaty, Dushanbe, Khojand, Samarkand, Tashkent and Bishkek, plus maybe Namangan, Fergana and Osh.

Transaero (www.transaero.ru; airline code UN; hub Domodedovo Airport, Moscow) To Almaty, Astana, Atyrau, Aktau, Karaganda, Shymkent, Uralsk, Tashkent and Bukhara.

Turkish Airlines (www.turkishairlines.com; airline code TK; hub İstanbul) To Tashkent (five weekly), Ashgabat (daily), Almaty (daily), Astana (two weekly), Bishkek (three weekly) and Dushanbe (twice weekly) from İstanbul.

Ukraine International Airlines (www.flyuia.com; airline code PS; hub Kiev) To Almaty twice weekly.

Tickets

Finding flights to Central Asia isn't always easy, as travel agents are generally unaware of the region (you'll have to help with the spelling of most cities and airlines) and many don't book flights on Russian or Central Asian airlines. You may need to contact the airlines directly for schedules and contact details of their consolidators, or sales agents, who often sell the airlines' tickets cheaper than the airlines themselves. For airline offices in Central Asia see Getting There & Away in the relevant capital city in each country chapter.

One thing to consider when arranging your itinerary is your visa situation. You may find it easier flying into, for example, Bishkek if that's the easiest place to arrange a visa from home.

You might also consider that it's worth paying a little extra for a reliable airline such as KLM or Turkish Airlines, rather than a cash-strapped one such as Tajik Air.

Always check how many stopovers there are, how long these are and what time the flight arrives (many airlines arrive in the dead of night) as well as any restrictions on the ticket (ie on changing the return date, refunds etc).

Fares to the region tend to be 10% to 20% higher in peak travel season (roughly July to September and December in North America and Europe; December to January in Australia and New Zealand).

Online ticket agencies such as www.cheap-flights.com, www.expedia.com, www.kayak.com and www.travelocity.com have links on their webpages to their specific country websites.

Visa Checks

You can buy air tickets without a visa or a letter of invitation (LOI; see p510), but in most places outside Central Asia you will have trouble getting on a plane without one – even if embassies and travel agents tell you otherwise. Airlines are obliged to fly anyone rejected because of improper papers back home and are fined, so check-in staff tend to act like immigration officers. If you have made arrangements to get a visa on arrival, have your LOI handy at check-in and check with the airline beforehand.

Airline Safety

Aeroflot, the former Soviet state airline, was decentralised into around 400 splinter airlines and many of these 'baby-flots' now have the worst regional safety record in the world, due to poor maintenance, ageing aircraft and gross overloading. In general though, the Central Asian carriers have lifted their international services towards international safety standards, at least on international routes.

In 1993 a Tajik Air Yak-40 crashed on take-off from Khorog; it had 81 passengers in its 28 seats. In 1997 another Tajik Air plane crashed in Sharjah, killing 85 passengers, and an Air Kazakhstan (now defunct) plane collided with a Saudi jet over Delhi, killing 350 people. In January 2004 an Uzbekistan Airways Yak-42 crashed in Termiz killing 37 passengers. In 2005 a Kam Air flight crashed near Kabul, killing 104. In 2008 an Itek Air flight to Tehran crashed at Bishkek killing 65 passengers.

Most Kazakh airlines (except Air Astana) and all Kyrgyz airlines are currently banned from flying into EU airspace. See www.airsafe.com/events/airlines/fsu.htm for an overview of recent air accidents in the former Soviet Union.

Kam Air had a catastrophic crash in 2005 between Kabul and Herat, due to a heavy snowstorm over the mountains, killing all 104 passengers and crew. At the time of research, Ariana Afghan was banned from landing in the EU due to safety concerns, whereas Safi Airways has a modern fleet and seems well regarded.

From Asia

From Beijing there are twice weekly flights to Tashkent on Uzbekistan Airways, and five weekly to Almaty on Air Astana and to Bishkek on Kyrgyzstan Airlines.

Ürümqi in China's Xinjiang province has several flights a week to/from Almaty, Astana (US$450), Tashkent, Bishkek, Osh, Dushanbe and Ashgabat. Uzbekistan Airways also operates a weekly Fergana–Ürümqi connection. One-way prices are between US$250 and US$350.

Kazakhstan's SCAT (www.scat.kz in Russian) runs a little-known weekly flight between Almaty and Bayan-Ölgii in western Mongolia (US$280) via Ust-Kamenogorsk (Oskemen; US$170 to Bayan-Ölgii).

New Delhi is a minor hub for flights to Kabul, and both Ariana and PIA fly from Islamabad.

From Australia & New Zealand

Most flights to Central Asia go via Seoul (to pick up Asiana or Korean Air flights to Tashkent and Almaty or Air Astana to Almaty), Kuala Lumpur (Uzbekistan Airways to Tashkent, Air Astana to Almaty), Bangkok (Uzbekistan Airways to Tashkent, Air Astana to Almaty or Turkmenistan Airlines to Ashgabat) or İstanbul).

Sample routes include Sydney to Tashkent on Malaysia Airlines and Uzbekistan Airways via Kuala Lumpur, and Sydney to Almaty via

---

DEPARTURE TAX

Departure taxes are figured into your air ticket so you won't face any extra charges when you fly out of Central Asia, except in Afghanistan where there's a US$10 departure tax. Turkmenistan is odd as usual, with an arrival tax of around US$14.

Seoul on Asiana or Korean Air. For Dushanbe and Bishkek you'll probably have to go via İstanbul.

Online agencies include:

Flight Centre (☎ Australia 133 133, New Zealand 0800 24 35 44; www.flightcentre.com)

Gateway Travel (☎ 02-9745 3333; www.russian-gate way.com.au; 48 The Boulevarde, Strathfield NSW 2135) Ex-USSR specialists with experience in booking flights to Central Asia.

STA Travel (☎ Australia 134, New Zealand 0800 474 400; www.statravel.com.au, www.statravel.co.nz)

Trailfinders (☎ 1300 780 212; www.trailfinders.com.au)

www.travel.com.au (www.travel.com.au)

From Continental Europe

The best fares from Europe to Central Asia are with Air Baltic via Riga, though the best range of connections are with Turkish Airlines, via İstanbul. Air Astana offers some of the other best fares to Almaty, from Amsterdam and Frankfurt, or try KLM and Ukraine International (via Kiev).

Safi Airways and Ariana Afghan have direct weekly flights from Frankfurt to Kabul. Somon Air has a direct Frankfurt–Dushanbe flight, costing around €350 one way.

Flightbookers (www.ebookers.com) and **LastMinute** (www.lastminute.com) have online sites tailored to countries across Europe. **STA** (www.sta.com) has branches across Europe.

Other recommended agencies include:

Airfair (☎ 0900 7717 717; www.airfair.nl) In the Netherlands.

Anyway (☎ 0892 302 302; www.anyway.fr) In France.

Barcelo Viajes (☎ 902 200 400; www.barceloviajes. com) In Spain.

CTS Viaggi (☎ 06 441 1166; www.cts.it) In Italy.

Nouvelles Frontières (☎ 01 49 20 64 00; www. nouvelles-frontieres.fr) In France.

From Russia

There are daily flights from Moscow to most Central Asian cities, including Almaty, Tashkent, Dushanbe, Khojand (weekly), Ashgabat, Bishkek, Osh and many Kazakh cities. One-way fares range from US$220 to US$300. There are slightly fewer connections from St Petersburg. Major Siberian cities such as Novosibirsk also have connections to the Central Asia capitals. You can often get seniors, student and under-30s discounts of 25% on Russian flights.

Uzbekistan Airways flies from Moscow to Samarkand, Bukhara, Urgench, Termiz,

---

> **SAMPLE ONE-WAY AIR FARES FROM CENTRAL ASIA:**
>
> These fares are a rough guide only.
>
> - Tashkent–Bangkok US$500
> - Tashkent–Baku/Delhi US$290
> - Tashkent–Frankfurt/London/Paris US$460
> - Bishkek/Dushanbe/Almaty–İstanbul US$428/440/420
> - Bishkek–London US$675
> - Bishkek–Dubai US$360
> - Ashgabat–İstanbul US$200
> - Ashgabat–London/Beijing/Birmingham US$175
> - Dushanbe–Moscow US$320
> - Dushanbe–Tehran US$230
> - Dushanbe–Ürümqi US$350
> - Almaty–Frankfurt/London US$450/550
> - Aktau–Baku US$190
> - Kabul–Dubai/Frankfurt/Delhi/İstanbul US$190/715/270/300

Andijon and several others several times weekly for around US$230. Aeroflot fly from Moscow to Tashkent and Bishkek.

Transaero (☎ 495-788 8080; http://transaero.ru/ en; 18/1 Sadovaya-Spasskaya, Moscow) is an international-grade airline that flies from Moscow Domodedovo (www.domodedovo.ru) to Astana, Almaty, Tashkent, Bukhara and several other cities in Kazakhstan, and has connections to European destinations.

Note that Moscow has two main international airports: Sheremetyevo (http://svo.aero/ en) and Domodedovo. Sheremetyevo is itself divided into several terminals: Terminal B (Sheremetyevo-1), the international Terminal F (Sheremetyevo-2), and newly renovated terminals C, D and E (opens in 2010).

At the time of research Aeroflot (international flights) and Air Astana operated from Sheremetyevo (Terminal F), Ariana Afghan operated from Sheremetyevo (Terminal C), while Transaero, Tajik Air, Turkmenistan Airways, SCAT, Uzbekistan Airways and Kyrgyzstan Airlines used Domodedovo airport. You will need to get a Russian transit visa in advance to transfer between airports and even between Sheremetyevo's two terminals.

A bus service runs between Domodedovo and Sheremetyevo (terminal 1 and 2), costs around US$8 per person and takes at least two hours. A free transit bus links Sheremetyevo terminals B and F.

Travel agencies in Moscow include **Unifest Travel** (☎ 495-234 6555; http://unifest.ru/en.html; Komsomolsky prospekt 16/2) for rail and air tickets and Central Asia packages, affiliated with the Travellers Guest House.

From Turkey

Turkish Airlines flies from İstanbul to Almaty (daily), Astana (two to four weekly), Bishkek (daily), Dushanbe (twice weekly), Tashkent (five weekly) and Ashgabat (daily). The various republics' national airlines also fly once or twice a week. Alternatively you could fly from İstanbul or Trabzon to Baku, take the ferry to Turkmenbashi and a 12-hour train ride across the desert to Ashgabat.

One-way flights to İstanbul cost around US$400 from most Central Asian capitals.

From the UK

The best return summer fares are with Air Baltic, weighing in at around £360 to Tashkent, £470 to Almaty and £430 to Dushanbe, and there's lots of scope for open-jaw fares, such as in to Tashkent and out of Dushanbe.

The cheapest flights to Bishkek are probably with Aeroflot or BMI at around £560 return and are therefore somewhat more expensive than Almaty.

Other fares to Almaty are about £500 return on KLM via Amsterdam or Transaero via Moscow. Air Astana's direct flights from London to Almaty can also be good value. To Tashkent the cheapest return fares are often with Aeroflot or Transaero, with Turkish Airlines or Lufthansa costing more. Uzbekistan Airways' London–Tashkent–Delhi run (four weekly, £500 return) is comfortable, with good service and decent food (but the return is no match, with exhausted Delhi passengers sprawled everywhere and poor food from Tashkent). For details and prices contact **HY Travel** (☎ 020-7935 4775; 69 Wigmore St, London).

The best flights to Ashgabat are with Lufthansa or Turkish Airlines. A cheaper but harder-to-book option is **Turkmenistan Airlines** (☎ London 020-8577 2211, Birmingham 0121-558 6363; fax 8577 9900), which flies two times a week to Ashgabat from London and also four times a week from Birmingham. Most pas-

sengers are headed either to/from Amritsar. For cheap fares contact **Amritsar Travel** (www.ashgabatflights.com).

The best way to Dushanbe is via Air Baltic. Connections on Turkish Airlines via İstanbul are much more expensive at around £680 return but flights still fill up weeks in advance.

For Kabul you will likely have to fly first to Dubai (Emirates is a good choice) and then connect. Agents selling Ariana and Kam Air tickets include **Ariana Travel** (☎ 020-8843 0011; www.arianatravel.co.uk; 136 The Broadway, Southall, UB1 1QN) and **Afghan Travel Centre** (☎ 020-8983 0700; www.afghantravelcentre.co.uk; ste 719, Crown House, North Circular Rd, London NW10 7PN).

Online agencies include www.cheapflights.co.uk, www.ebookers.com, www.opodo.co.uk, www.expedia.co.uk and www.travelocity.co.uk.

Discounted travel agencies include:
Flight Centre (☎ 0870-499 0040; www.flightcentre.co.uk)
STA Travel (☎ 0870-1600 599; www.statravel.co.uk)
Trailfinders (☎ 0845-058 5858, 020-7938 3939; www.trailfinders.com)

From USA & Canada

From North America you generally have the choice of routing your trip via İstanbul (Turkish Airlines), Riga (Air Baltic), Moscow (Aeroflot) or a major European city (KLM, British Airways, Lufthansa etc). Stopovers can be lengthy. From the west coast it's possible to fly to Almaty or Tashkent via Seoul on Asiana or Korean Air.

From New York, the best return fares to Central Asia at the time of writing were with Aeroflot (via Moscow) to Tashkent for as low as US$700, or Turkish Airlines for around US$1000 return. Fares are similar to Almaty and around US$700 more to Ashgabat with Turkish Airlines or Lufthansa. Flights from the west coast are around US$500 more expensive.

Uzbekistan Airways (☎ 201-944 4474) flies from New York (JFK airport) to Tashkent (via Riga) once a week, an 18-hour flight. **Brand New Travel** (☎ 800-790 8960; www.flyfromusa.com) and **East Site** (☎ 877-800 6287; www.east-site.com) sometimes offer discounted Central Asian fares, including on Uzbekistan Airways.

General discounted agencies include **STA Travel** (☎ 800-781 4040; www.statravel.com) in the US and **Travel CUTS** (☎ 416-979 2406; www.travelcuts.com) in Canada.

Online booking services include www.expedia.com, www.orbitz.com, www.kayak.com and www.travelocity.com.

LAND
Border Crossings
Cross-border roads that are open to foreigners (by bus, taxi or hired car) are listed in the table on p522) and covered in the Transport sections of the relevant country chapters. There are literally dozens of crossings between Russia and Kazakhstan.

For details of crossing between Central Asia countries see the Transport sections of the country you wish to depart from (ie from Uzbekistan to Tajikistan see the Transport section of the Uzbekistan chapter p287).

Bus
From China, there are twice-weekly buses (Monday and Tuesday) from Kashgar to Osh (US$70, plus 100 som) via the Irkeshtam Pass (p371 and p362), and also direct buses from Ürümqi (daily except Sunday) and Yining (twice weekly) to Almaty (p200). Foreigners are still not allowed to take the twice-weekly bus between Kashgar and Bishkek, via Naryn.

There are also direct buses between Ust–Kamenogorsk in eastern Kazakhstan and the towns of Ürümqi (twice weekly) and Altay (twice weekly) in Xinjiang province (see p187 for details).

Direct buses run daily from Mashhad to Herat (seven hours) via the border crossing at Taybad (Islam Qala in Afghanistan). There are also direct Herat–Tehran buses (two days). It's also possible to take shared taxis to and from the border crossings.

Car & Motorcycle
Although car or motorbike is an excellent way of getting around Central Asia, bringing your own vehicle is fraught with practical problems. Fuel supply is uneven, though modern petrol stations are springing up throughout the region. Prices per litre swing wildly depending on supply. Petrol comes in four grades – 76, 93, 95 and 98 octane. In the countryside you'll see petrol cowboys selling plastic bottles of fuel from the side of the road, often of very poor quality.

The biggest problem is the traffic police (Russian, GAI). Tajikistan's roads have almost as many checkpoints as potholes. In Uzbekistan and Kazakhstan there are police skulking at every corner, most looking for excuses to wave their orange baton and hit drivers (local or otherwise) with a 'fine' (straf). There are no motoring associations of any kind.

The state insurance offices, splinters of the old Soviet agency Ingosstrakh, have no overseas offices that we know of, and your own insurance is most unlikely to be valid in Central Asia. You would probably have to arrange insurance anew at each border. See Getting Around (p526) for more information on hiring a car within Central Asia.

Many Kazakh cities have motorbike clubs which will often welcome foreign bikers – and in some cases drivers (see p164). Almaty is easily the best place in Central Asia for getting motorbike repairs done. The website www.horizonsunlimited.com is a good resource for bikers.

Train
There are three main rail routes into Central Asia from Russia. One comes from Moscow via Samara or Saratov, straight across Kazakhstan via Aktobe and Kyzylorda to Tashkent (3369km), with branch lines to Bishkek and Almaty (4057km). Another, the Turkestan–Siberian railway or 'Turksib' (see www.turksib.com for timetables) links the Trans-Siberian railway at Novosibirsk with Almaty. A third route goes around the other side of the Aral Sea via Volgograd, Atyrau, Kungrad, Uchquduk, Navoi and Samarkand to Tashkent, with a branch line to Dushanbe.

These 'iron roads' don't have quite the romance or the laid-back feel of the Trans-Siberian railway, but they are usually cheaper than flying, and allow Central Asia to unfold gradually, as you clank through endless plains, steppe and desert.

Several other lines enter northern Kazakhstan from Russia and meet at Astana, from where a line heads south to Karaganda and Almaty. From the Caspian Sea yet another line crosses Turkmenistan – the Trans-Caspian route. No international trains run to or from Turkmenistan. A line connects Mashhad in Iran with Ashgabat in Turkmenistan, but no passenger trains run along this line at present.

Completed in 1992, after being delayed almost half a century by Russian-Chinese geopolitics, is a line from China via Ürümqi to Almaty and Astana in Kazakhstan, joining the Turksib for connections on to Siberia.

CLASSES

A deluxe sleeping carriage is called *spets-vagon* (SV, Russian for 'special carriage', abbreviated to CB in Cyrillic; some call this *spalny vagon* or 'sleeping carriage'), *myagkiy* (soft) or 1st class. Closed compartments have carpets and upholstered seats, and convert to comfortable sleeping compartments for two.

An ordinary sleeping carriage is called *kupeyny* or *kupe* (which is the Russian for compartmentalised), *zhyosky* (hard) or 2nd class. Closed compartments are usually four-person couchettes and are comfortable.

A *platskartny* (reserved-place) or 3rd-class carriage has open-bunk (also known as hard sleeper) accommodation. *Obshchiy* (general) or 4th class is unreserved bench-type seating.

With a reservation, your ticket normally shows the numbers of your carriage *(vagon)* and seat *(mesto)*. Class may be shown by what looks like a fraction: eg 1/2 is 1st class two berth, 2/4 is 2nd class four berth.

FROM CHINA

The 1363km Silk Road express between Ürümqi and Almaty leaves twice a week and takes about 32 hours, which includes several hours at the border for customs checks and to change bogies. Sleeper tickets cost around US$110 and should be booked a couple of weeks ahead, in either Ürümqi or Almaty. There is also a weekly Astana–Ürümqi service (US$115, 39 hours). See p200.

FROM RUSSIA

Most trains bound for Central Asia depart from Moscow's Kazan(sky) station. Europe dissolves into Asia as you sleep, and morning brings a vast panorama of the Kazakh steppe.

Train connections between Russia and Central Asia have thinned out in recent years but are still a favourite of by seasonal workers, tourists and drug smugglers. At the time of writing, fast trains left three times a week to/from Tashkent (No 5/6, 70 hours),

MAJOR BORDER CROSSINGS INTO CENTRAL ASIA

Border	Crossing	Means of Transport	Page	Comments
Iran–Turkmenistan	Gaudan/Bajgiran	car	p466	From Mashhad to Ashgabat; change transport at the border
Iran–Turkmenistan	Saraghs	car/rail	p466	The best bet if you want to head straight for Mary/Merv
Azerbaijan–Turkmenistan	Turkmenbashi	boat	p523	Upgrade to a cabin when on board
China–Tajikistan	Qolma (Kulma) Pass	car		Currently closed to tourists but might open soon
China–Kazakhstan	Khorgos	bus	p200	Direct buses run from Yining and Ürümqi to Almaty, or change buses at the border
China–Kazakhstan	Dustyk	rail	p200	Twice-weekly direct trains between Alashankou, Almaty and Ürümqi take 32 hours and cost US$110
China–Kazakhstan	Bakhty/Tacheng	bus	p187	Little-used crossing taken by direct buses between Ürümqi and Ust-Kamenogorsk
China–Kazakhstan	Maykapsha-gay/Jeminay (Jimunai)	bus	p187	Little-used crossing but direct buses between Altai (China) and Ust-Kamenogorsk
China–Kyrgyzstan	Torugart Pass	car	p371 & p348	Relatively expensive as you must hire your own transport in advance on both sides
China–Kyrgyzstan	Irkeshtam Pass	car/bus	p371 & p362	Weekly bus between Kashgar and Osh (US$70) or take a taxi, closed weekends
Pakistan–Afghanistan	Khyber Pass/Torkham	taxi	p494	You'll need an armed guard and a tribal area permit. Security is a concern
Iran–Afghanistan	Islam Qala/Taybad	bus or shared taxi	p493	The old Hippy Trail from Mashhad to Herat is relatively straightforward

---

SILK ROAD BY RAIL

Silk Road romantics, train buffs and nervous flyers can cross continents without once having to fasten their seatbelt or turn off their cell phones. From Moscow (or even St Petersburg) you can watch Europe turn to Asia on the three-day, 4000km train trip to Tashkent or Almaty. From here you can add on any number of side trips to Samarkand, Bukhara or even Urgench (for Khiva), the last two of which are on spur lines. Then from Almaty it's possible to continue on the train to Ürümqi in China and even to Kashgar. From Ürümqi you can continue along the Silk Road by train east as far as Beijing, Hong Kong or even Lhasa or Saigon, making for an epic transcontinental ride. It's not always comfortable and it will take some time, so why do it? Because like Everest, it's there.

---

every other day to/from Almaty (No 7/8, 80 hours), daily to/from Astana (Nos 71/72 and 83/84, 55 hours) and twice weekly to/from Bishkek (Nos 17/18 and 27/28, 76 hours). Other offbeat connections include the St Petersburg–Astana (every other day) and Saratov–Nukus–Tashkent (weekly) lines. There are other, slower connections but you could grow old and die on them. Trains out of Moscow have even numbers; those returning have odd numbers.

Typical fares for a 2nd-class (*kupeyny*) berth are US$250 Moscow–Tashkent, US$200 Moscow–Almaty and US$280 Moscow–Bishkek.

For a useful overview of international trains to/from Central Asia see www.seat61.com/silkroute.htm. For an online timetable see www.poezda.net. To buy tickets from Moscow try **Way to Russia** (www.waytorussia.net), **Real Russia** (www.realrussia.co.uk/trains) or **G&R International** (www.hostels.ru).

You will need to check visa requirements carefully. Trains from Moscow to Tashkent demand a Kazakh transit visa and some trains between Russia and Kazakhstan require a multiple-entry Russian visa. Trains to/from Dushanbe are impractical because you will need a Kazakh, multiple-entry Uzbek and a Turkmen visa.

SEA

The Baku (Azerbaijan) to Turkmenbashi 'ferry' route (seat US$80 to US$90, 12 to 18 hours) across the Caspian is a possible way to enter and leave Central Asia. Buy the cheapest seat: once on board you'll likely be offered a cabin by a crewmember, for which you could pay anything up to US$50. The best cabins have private bathrooms and are comfortable, although all are cockroach infested.

Boats usually leave several times a day in both directions, but there is no timetable. You'll simply have to arrive and wait until the ship is full of cargo. You should leave with a couple of days left on your visa in case the boats are delayed, which is common. Some travellers have found themselves waiting for a couple of days to dock in Turkmenbashi, using up valuable time in their fixed-date visa. Stock up on food and water beforehand, as there is little food available on board. Crossings can end up taking 32 hours.

There are irregular boats every week or 10 days between Baku and Aktau (US$55 to US$75, 18 to 24 hours) in Kazakhstan. One of these ferries sunk in October 2002, killing all 51 people aboard.

Boats also sail occasionally from Turkmenbashi to Astrakhan in Russia.

GETTING AROUND

Flying is the least interesting and arguably the least safe mode of transport in Central Asia, but to some destinations and in some seasons it's the only sensible alternative. Trains are slow but crowded and generally not very convenient outside Kazakhstan. Buses are the most frequent and convenient way to get between towns cheaply, though trips can be cramped and vehicles are prone to breakdowns. The best option in many areas is a car: shared taxis or private drivers are often willing to zip you between cities for little more than a bus fare (see p526).

The biggest headache for travellers crossing the region is that most inter-republic bus services have been cut. Travellers generally have to get a shared taxi or minibus to and from both sides of the border (see the boxed text p527). Crossings to/from Uzbekistan are generally the most tightly controlled.

AIR

Flying saves time and takes the tedium out of Central Asia's long distances. It's also the only sensible way to reach some places, particularly in winter. But the Central Asian airlines have some way to go before meeting international safety standards on their domestic routes. Flights are particularly good value in Turkmenistan, where a domestic flight costs between US$10 and US$15!

You generally have to pay for air tickets in local currency (there's often an exchange booth nearby), though you can pay in US dollars in Kyrgyzstan. Some airline offices and travel agencies accept credit cards.

Apart from the national Central Asian airlines (see p516), there are a couple of domestic airlines, such as Kyrgyzstan's Itek

Air and Altyn Air (www.altynair.kg/en) and Kazakhstan's SCAT. Domestic and inter-republic services are no-frills; you might get a warm glass of Coke if lucky. For long flights consider packing lunch.

At the time of writing there were no Dushanbe–Tashkent services. Major internal connections still run daily.

Flights between the biggest cities generally stick to their schedules, but those serving smaller towns are sometimes delayed or cancelled without explanation. Printed schedules are unreliable; routes and individual flights are constantly being cancelled or reintroduced. The only sure way to find out what's flying is to ask at an air booking office. In any case, confirm any flight 24 hours prior to departure.

TRAVEL AGENCIES & ORGANISED TOURS

Throughout this book, in the relevant city sections, we list reliable Central Asian travel agencies who can help with the logistics of travel in Central Asia – whether it be visas, a few excursions or an entire tailored trip.

The following agencies outside the region can arrange individual itineraries and/or accommodation, tickets and visa support.

Australia
Passport Travel (☎ 03-9500 0444; www.travelcentre.com.au; Level 1, 12-14 Glenferrie Rd, Malvern, VIC 3144) Silk Road by rail tours.
Russian Gateway Tours (☎ 02-9745 3333; www.russian-gateway.com.au; 48 The Boulevarde, Strathfield NSW 2135) Airfares to Central Asia, hotel bookings, homestays, visa invitations and airport transfers.
Sundowners Overland (☎ 03-9672 5300; www.sundownersoverland.com; Level 1, 51 Queen St, Melbourne 3000) Small-group and independent tours into Central Asia.

The UK
Regent Holidays (☎ 0845-277 3317; www.regent-holidays.co.uk; Froomsgate House, Rupert St, Bristol BS1 2QJ) Offers tours, and can cobble together an individual itinerary.
Scott's Tours (☎ 020-7383 5353; www.scottstours.co.uk; 141 Whitfield St London W1T 5EW) Hotel bookings, visas and more.
Silk Road and Beyond (☎ 020-7371 3131; www.silkroadandbeyond.co.uk; 371 Kensington High St, London, W14 8QZ)
Somon Travel (☎ 020-7101 9226; www.somontravel.com; 72 Hammersmith Rd, London W14 8TH)

The US
Mir Corporation (☎ 800-424 7289; www.mircorp.com; Suite 210, 85 South Washington St, Seattle, WA 98104) Independent tours, homestays and visa support with accommodation.
Red Star Travel (☎ 206-522 5995; www.travel2russia.com; Suite 102, 123 Queen Anne Ave N, Seattle, WA 98109) Organises tours, individual itineraries, accommodation, train tickets, visa support with booking.

For Afghanistan contact **Afghan Logistics & Tours** (☎ 0700-442211; www.afghanlogisticstours.com) or **Great Game Travel** (☎ 0799-489120; www.greatgametravel.com; in Kabul and Faizabad). Foreign companies running tours or treks to Afghanistan include **Wild Frontiers** (www.wildfrontiers.co.uk) and **Hinterland Travel** (www.hinterlandtravel.com).

Tickets for Central Asian airlines are most easily purchased from private travel agents *(aviakassa)*. You'll often need your passport and visa. Many booking offices have a special window for international flights. Air Astana has useful online booking for both international and domestic flights.

The airfare diagram shows approximate one-way fares in US-dollar equivalents for the major regional connections. Expect these fares to change over time.

Seating is a bit of a free-for-all (there are often no assigned seats), especially if the flight is overbooked. To minimise the risk of loss or theft, consider carrying everything on board.

Helicopter flights were once popular in the Tian Shan and Pamir Ranges but rising fuel

costs have made most services prohibitively expensive (around US$1300 per hour for a chopper). Maintenance is also patchy; avoid them except in summer and go only if the weather is absolutely clear.

BUS

This is generally the best bet for getting between towns cheaply. The major transport corridors are served by big long-distance coaches (often reconditioned German or Turkish vehicles), which run on fixed routes and schedules, with fixed stops. They're relatively problem-free and moderately comfortable, with windows that open and sometimes with reclining seats. Luggage is locked safely away below. Journey times depend on road

TRANSPORT IN CENTRAL ASIA

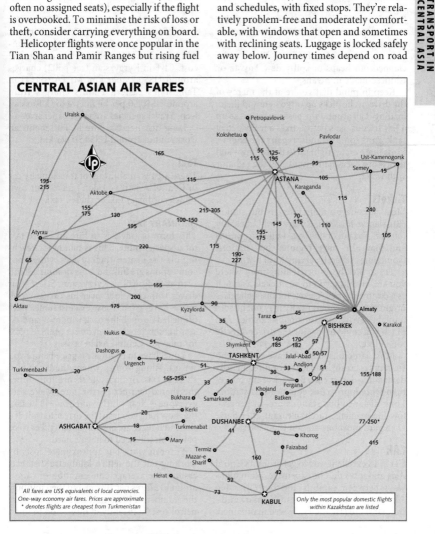

CENTRAL ASIAN AIR FARES

*All fares are US$ equivalents of local currencies. One-way economy air fares. Prices are approximate. * denotes flights are cheapest from Turkmenistan*

Only the most popular domestic flights within Kazakhstan are listed

conditions but are somewhat longer than a fast train.

Regional buses are a lot less comfortable and a bit more…interesting. Breakdowns are common. They are also used extensively by small-time traders to shift their goods around the region, and you could gradually become surrounded by boxes, bags, and both live and dead animals.

Private minibuses, generally called marshrutka (Russian for 'fixed route'), are a bit more expensive, always faster, and usually more hair-raising. They generally have fixed fares and routes but no fixed timetable (or no departure at all if there aren't enough passengers to satisfy the driver), and will stop anywhere along the route. They can be clapped-out heaps or spiffy new Toyota or Chinese-made minivans.

Keep in mind that you're at the mercy of the driver as he picks up cargo here and there, loading it all around the passengers, picks up a few friends, gets petrol, fixes a leaky petrol tank, runs some errands, repairs the engine, loads more crates right up to the ceiling – and then stops every half-hour to fill the radiator with water.

Tickets

Most cities have a main intercity bus station (Russian: avtovokzal, Kyrgyz and Uzbek: avtobekat, Kazakh: avtobeket, Tajik: istgomush) and may also have regional bus stations (sometimes several) serving local towns.

Try to pick buses originating from where you are, enabling you to buy tickets as much as a day in advance. Tickets for through buses originating in a different city may not be sold until they arrive, amid anxious scrambles. At a pinch you could try paying the driver directly for a place.

Most large bus stations have police who sometimes create headaches for foreigners by demanding documents. Be wary of any policeman who approaches you at a bus station. Long-distance bus stations are, in general, low-life magnets, rarely pleasant after dark. Disregard most bus-station timetables.

CAR

Car is an excellent way to get around Central Asia and it needn't be expensive. Main highways between capitals and big cities (eg Almaty–Bishkek–Tashkent–Samarkand–Bukhara) are fast and fairly well maintained.

Mountain roads (ie most roads in Kyrgyzstan and Tajikistan) can be blocked with snow in winter and plagued by landslides in spring.

See Car & Motorcycle (p521) for advice about driving your own vehicle through Central Asia.

Hire

Almaty and Bishkek have a Hertz franchise and travel agencies can hire you out a Mercedes or 4WD, but you are almost always better off hiring a taxi for the day.

Community-based tourism organisations and travel agencies hire 4WDs for remoter areas of Kyrgyzstan and Tajikistan. Hiring a car unlocks some of Central Asia's best mountain scenery and is well worth it, despite the cost. CBT in Kyrgyzstan (see p302) charges around US$0.25 per km, META (p414) in Tajikistan's eastern Pamirs charges from around US$0.50 per kilometre for a Russian jeep. Travel agencies are more expensive.

Long-distance taxi hire in Turkmenistan works out to around US$0.10 per km.

Taxi

There are two main ways of travelling by car in Central Asia if you don't have your own vehicle: ordinary taxi or shared taxi.

ORDINARY TAXI

This form of travel is to hire an entire taxi for a special route. This is handy for reaching off-the-beaten-track places, where bus connections are hit-and-miss or nonexistent, such as Song-Köl in Kyrgyzstan. Select your driver with care, look over his car (we took one in Kyrgyzstan whose exhaust fumes were funnelled through the back windows) and assess his sobriety before you set off. See p528 for more on Central Asian taxis.

You'll have to negotiate a price before you set off. Along routes where there are also shared taxis, ordinary taxis are four times the shared taxi per-person fare. Make sure everyone is clear which route you will be taking, how long you want the driver to wait at a site and if there are any toll or entry fees to be paid. You will need to haggle hard.

You can work out approximate costs by working out the return kilometre distance; assume the average consumption of cars is around 12 litres per 100km and then multiply the number of litres needed by the per litre petrol cost (constantly in flux). Add to this a

JIGSAW BORDERS

When Stalin drew the borders between the different republics in 1924 no-one really expected them to become international boundaries. Areas were portioned off on the map according to the whims and horse-trading of Party leaders, without much regard to the reality on the ground. As these crazy jigsaw borders solidify throughout post-Soviet Central Asia, many towns and enclaves are finding themselves isolated, as the once complex web of regional ties shrinks behind new borderlines.

The Fergana Valley has been particularly affected. Travellers (and locals) may find it tricky to get to more remote areas or trekking bases by public transport. Borders sometimes close, especially between Uzbekistan and Tajikistan. Cars with Tajik number plates can no longer cross into Uzbekistan, and Uzbek border guards often give locals the third degree.

Buses no longer run from central Uzbekistan into the Fergana Valley along the natural route via Khojand but rather take the mountain road from Tashkent over the Kamchik Pass. Only train connections exit the Fergana Valley through its mouth.

Trains are not immune to these border shenanigans, as many lines cross into neighbouring republics. Trains between Dushanbe and Khojand (both in Tajikistan) route via Uzbekistan (twice) and Turkmenistan, making the line impractical to foreign travellers. Trains running from Aktobe to Uralsk, and Semey to Ust-Kamenogorsk, pass through Russian territory and foreigners are either not allowed on these trains or must have a Russian visa. Uzbekistan has built miles of train track in recent years to avoid routing its trains to Urgench and Nukus through Turkmenistan.

The bottom line is that there are now border checks at many hitherto disregarded borders and you need a visa any time you cross into another republic. If you are just transiting in another republic before heading back into the first you should invest in a double- or multiple-entry visa.

Some problems are short-lived as new transport connections spring up across the region. Uzbekistan has built a railway line to bypass Turkmenistan and roads have sprung up in Kyrgyz parts of the Fergana Valley to avoid Uzbek border guards. But these are just a few of the thousands of ties that bind the ex-Soviet republics to one another and to Russia, and disentangling them will take decades.

daily fee (anything from US$5 up to the cost of the petrol) and a waiting fee of around US$1 per hour and away you go.

SHARED TAXI

Shared taxi is the other main form of car travel around Central Asia, whereby a taxi or private car does a regular run between two cities and charges a set rate for each of the four seats in a car. These cars often wait for passengers outside bus or train stations and some have a sign in the window indicating where they are headed. Cars are quicker and just as comfortable as a bus or train, and are still very affordable. Some fares are so cheap that two or three of you can buy all four seats and stretch out. Otherwise smaller cars can be a little cramped. The most common car is the Russian Zhiguli, fast being replaced by modern Daewoo models such as the Nexia (the most comfortable) and the smaller and cheaper Tico, both made in Central Asia. The front seat is always the one to aim for; only lemons get the middle back seat.

These services are particularly useful in Kyrgyzstan along certain major routes such as Bishkek–Almaty, Bishkek–Osh, and Naryn–Bishkek. Other useful shared taxi routes are Bukhara–Urgench/Khiva, Samarkand–Termiz, Dushanbe–Khojand and Ashgabat–Mary.

HITCHING

In Central Asia there is generally little distinction between hitching and taking a taxi. Anyone with a car will stop if you flag them down (with a low up-and-down wave, not an upturned thumb) and most drivers will expect you to pay for the ride. If you can negotiate a reasonable fare (it helps to know the equivalent bus or shared taxi fare) this can be a much quicker mode of transport than the bus. There's also a good chance you'll be invited to someone's house for tea.

Hitching to parks and scenic spots is generally much easier on the weekends but you'll lose some of the solitude at these times.

Normal security rules apply when trying to arrange a lift; don't hitch alone, avoid flagging down cars at night and try to size up your driver (and his sobriety) before getting in.

LOCAL TRANSPORT

Most sizeable towns have public buses, and sometimes electric trolleybuses. Bigger cities also have trams, and Tashkent and Almaty have a metro system (Almaty's first line opened in 2010). Transport is still ridiculously cheap by Western standards, but usually packed because there's never enough money to keep an adequate fleet on the road; at peak hours it can take several stops for those caught by surprise to even work their way to an exit.

Public transport in smaller towns tends to melt away soon after dark.

Bus, Trolleybus & Tram

Payment methods vary, but the most common method is to pay the driver or conductor cash on exit. Manoeuvre your way out by asking anyone in the way, *vykhodite?* (getting off?).

Marshrutka

A marshrutka, or marshrutnoe taxi (marsh-*root*-na-yuh tahk-*see*), is a minibus running along a fixed route. You can get on at fixed stops but can get off anywhere by saying '*zdes pozhaluysta*' (zd-*yes* pa-*zhal*-stuh; here please). Routes are hard to figure out and schedules erratic, and it's usually easier to stick to other transport. Fares are just a little higher than bus fares.

Taxi

There are two kinds of taxis: officially licensed ones and every other car on the road. Official taxis are more trustworthy, and sometimes cheaper – if you can find one. They rarely have meters and you'll have to negotiate a fare in advance. Or let a local friend negotiate for you – they'll do better than you will.

Unofficial taxis are often private cars driven by people trying to cover their huge petrol costs. Anything with a chequerboard logo in the window is a taxi. Stand at the side of the road, extend your arm and wait – as scores of others around you will probably be doing. When someone stops, negotiate destination and fare through the passenger-side window or through a partially open door. The driver may say '*sadytse*' (sit down) or beckon you in, but sort the fare out first. It helps a lot if you can negotiate the price in Russian, even more so in the local language.

TAXI TIPS

- Avoid taxis lurking outside tourist hotels – drivers charge far too much and get uppity when you try to talk them down.

- Never get into a taxi with more than one person in it, especially after dark; check the back seat of the car for hidden friends too.

- Keep your fare money in a separate pocket to avoid flashing large wads of cash.

- Have a map to make it look like you know your route.

- If you're staying at a private residence, have the taxi stop at the corner nearest your destination, not the specific address.

A typical fare across Dushanbe at the time of research was around US$3; less in Tashkent and Bishkek, and less than half that in Ashgabat. Fares go up at night and extra charges are incurred for bookings.

TRAIN

Lower-class train travel is the cheapest but most crowded way to get around Central Asia. Travel in the summertime is best done at night. Kazakhstan and to a lesser extent Uzbekistan are probably the only countries where you'll find yourself using the train system much.

Connections

Trains can be useful to cover the vast distances in Kazakhstan. Certain corridors, such as the Turksib (Semey–Almaty) are well served by three or four fast trains a day. The morning fast trains from Tashkent to Samarkand and Bukhara are faster than the buses and feature airplane-style seats. There's also a useful overnight Tashkent–Bukhara run. Other intriguing links include a Nukus–Almaty connection and a summertime Tashkent–Bishkek train (via Kazakhstan). As an indication of journey times, Urgench–Tashkent is 20 hours and Tashkent–Almaty is 25 hours (three weekly).

Turkmenistan has slow but new trains running to most corners of the country. Travel times are long but fares are low, with an overnight berth between Ashgabat and the Caspian Sea costing less than US$3.

Elsewhere, connections are drying up as fast as the Aral Sea; few trains run to Dushanbe any more (those that do take a very roundabout route and multiple transit visas) and there are no direct lines, for example, between Ashgabat and any other Central Asian capitals.

Many trains to and from Russia can be used for getting around Central Asia, and may be faster and in better condition. But any train originating far from where you are is likely to be filthy, crowded and late by the time you board it.

Tickets

Book at least two days ahead for CIS connections, if you can. You will probably need to show your passport and visa. A few stations have separate windows for advance bookings and for departures within 24 hours; the latter is generally the one with the heaving mob

around it (beware of pickpockets). You may also find a city train-ticket office (Russian: *zheleznodorozhnaya kassa* or *Zh D Kassa*) where you can buy train tickets for small or no markup, without going to the station. Many tourist hotels have rail-booking desks (including their own mark-up).

If you can't get a ticket for a particular train, it's worth turning up anyway. No matter how full ticket clerks insist a train is, there always seem to be spare *kupeyny* (2nd-class or sleeping carriage) berths. Ask an attendant.

A few sample *kupeyny* fares (one-way) from Tashkent are US$23 to Urgench and US$18 to Bukhara. A seat on the high-speed daytime train costs US$8.50/13 to Samarkand/Bukhara (these fares are 30% cheaper if converting at black market rates – see p283). Fares from Almaty include Semey (US$30), Taraz (US$16) and Astana (US$20 or US$92 express).

Health Dr Trish Batchelor

CONTENTS

Stomach and digestive problems are by far the most common problem faced by visitors to Central Asia. A diet of mutton, bread and *plov* seems to induce diarrhoea and constipation in equal measure!

Since independence, health rates across the region have dropped and many diseases formerly eradicated or controlled in the time of the USSR, such as tuberculosis (TB) and diphtheria, have returned.

Minor risks such as malaria, rabies and encephalitis depend largely upon the location and/or months of travel. More common during the searing summer months is heat exhaustion, so make sure you keep cool and hydrated in the 35°C heat. Most short-term travels to the main tourist areas remain problem-free.

BEFORE YOU GO

Pack medications in their original, clearly labelled containers. A signed and dated letter from your physician describing your medical conditions and medications (using generic names) is also a good idea. If carrying syringes or needles, be sure to have a physician's letter documenting their medical necessity. If you have a heart condition, bring a copy of your ECG taken just prior to travelling.

If you take any regular medication, bring double your needs in case of loss or theft. In most Central Asian countries you can buy many medications over the counter without a doctor's prescription, but it can be difficult to find some of the newer drugs, particularly the latest antidepressant drugs, blood pressure medications and contraceptive methods.

Make sure you get your teeth checked before you travel – there are few good dentists in Central Asia. If you wear glasses take a spare pair and your prescription.

INTERNET RESOURCES

There is a wealth of travel-health advice on the internet. It's also a good idea to consult your government's travel-health website before departure, if one is available.

- Australia (www.dfat.gov.au/travel/)
- Canada (www.travelhealth.gc.ca)
- New Zealand (www.mfat.govt.nz/travel)
- South Africa (www.dfa.gov.za/consular/travel_advice.htm)
- UK (www.doh.gov.uk/traveladvice/)
- USA (www.cdc.gov/travel/)
- Lonely Planet (www.lonelyplanet.com) – good basic health information
- World Health Organization (WHO; www.who.int/country) – a superb book called *International Travel & Health* is revised annually and available online
- MD Travel Health (www.mdtravelhealth.com) – provides complete travel-health recommendations for every country and is updated daily

MEDICAL CHECKLIST

Recommended items for a personal medical kit:

- Antibacterial cream (eg muciprocin)
- Antibiotics for diarrhoea (eg norfloxacin, ciprofloxacin or azithromycin for bacterial diarrhoea; tinidazole for giardiasis or amoebic dysentery)
- Antibiotics for skin infections (eg amoxicillin/clavulanate or cephalexin)
- Antifungal cream (eg clotrimazole)
- Antihistamine – there are many options (eg cetrizine for day and promethazine for night)
- Antiseptic (eg Betadine)
- Antispasmodic for stomach cramps (eg Buscopan)
- Decongestant (eg pseudoephedrine)
- DEET-based insect repellent
- Diamox if going to high altitude
- Elastoplasts, bandages, gauze, thermometer (but not mercury), sterile needles and syringes, safety pins and tweezers
- Ibuprofen or another anti-inflammatory
- Indigestion tablets (eg Quick Eze or Mylanta)
- Laxative (eg Coloxyl)
- Oral rehydration solution for diarrhoea (eg Gastrolyte), diarrhoea 'stopper' (eg loperamide) and antinausea medication (eg prochlorperazine)
- Paracetamol
- Permethrin to impregnate clothing and mosquito nets, for some regions, see p533
- Steroid cream for allergic/itchy rashes (eg 1% to 2% hydrocortisone)
- Thrush (vaginal yeast infection) treatment (eg clotrimazole pessaries or Diflucan tablets)
- Ural or equivalent if prone to urine infections

INSURANCE

Even if you are fit and healthy, don't travel without health insurance – accidents do happen. Declare any existing medical conditions you have – the insurance company *will* check if your problem is pre-existing and will not cover you if it is undeclared. You may require extra cover for adventure activities such as rock climbing. If you're uninsured, emergency evacuation is expensive – bills of over US$100,000 are not uncommon.

Make sure you keep all documentation related to any medical expenses you incur.

RECOMMENDED VACCINATIONS

Specialised travel-medicine clinics are your best source of information; they stock all available vaccines and will be able to give specific recommendations for you and your trip. Most vaccines don't produce immunity until at least two weeks after they're given, so visit a doctor four to eight weeks before departure. Ask your doctor for an International Certificate of Vaccination (otherwise known as the yellow booklet), which will list all the vaccinations you've received.

The only vaccine required by international regulations is yellow fever. Proof of vaccination will be required only if you have visited a country in the yellow-fever zone within the six days prior to entering Kazakhstan.

Uzbekistan, Kazakhstan and Kyrgyzstan all require HIV testing if staying more than three months (two months for Uzbekistan). Foreign tests are accepted under certain conditions, but make sure to check with the embassy of your destination before travelling.

The World Health Organization recommends the following vaccinations for travellers to Central Asia:

Adult Diphtheria & Tetanus Single booster recommended if none in the previous 10 years. Side effects include sore arm and fever.

Hepatitis A Provides almost 100% protection for up to a year; a booster after 12 months provides at least another 20 years' protection. Mild side effects such as headache and sore arm occur in 5% to 10% of people.

Hepatitis B Now considered routine for most travellers. Given as three shots over six months. A rapid schedule is also available, as is a combined vaccination with hepatitis A. Side effects are mild and uncommon, usually headache and sore arm. In 95% of people lifetime protection results.

Measles, Mumps and Rubella Two doses required unless you have had the diseases. Occasionally a rash and flulike illness can develop a week after receiving the vaccine. Many young adults require a booster.

Polio Afghanistan had 38 cases of polio in 2009. Only one booster is required as an adult for lifetime protection.

Typhoid Recommended unless your trip is for less than a week. The vaccine offers around 70% protection, lasts for two to three years and comes as a single shot. Tablets are also available; however, the injection is usually recommended as it has fewer side effects. Sore arm and fever may occur.

Varicella If you haven't had chickenpox discuss this vaccination with your doctor.

These immunisations are recommended for long-term travellers (more than one month) or those at special risk:

Meningitis Recommended for long-term backpackers aged under 25.

Rabies Side effects are rare (headache and sore arm).

Tick-borne Encephalitis (Kyrgyzstan, Uzbekistan) Sore arm and headache are the most common side effects.

Tuberculosis Adult long-term travellers are usually recommended to have a TB skin test before and after travel, rather than vaccination.

FURTHER READING

Lonely Planet's *Healthy Travel – Asia & India* is a handy pocket size and is packed with useful information, including pretrip planning, emergency first aid, immunisation and disease information, and what to do if you get sick on the road. Other recommended references include *Traveller's Health* by Dr Richard Dawood and *Travelling Well* by Dr Deborah Mills – check out the website (www.travellingwell.com.au).

IN TRANSIT

DEEP VEIN THROMBOSIS (DVT)

Deep vein thrombosis (DVT) occurs when blood clots form in the legs during plane flights, chiefly because of prolonged immobility. Though most blood clots are reabsorbed uneventfully, some may break off and travel through the blood vessels to the lungs, where they can cause life-threatening complications.

The chief symptom of DVT is swelling or pain of the foot, ankle or calf, usually but not always on just one side. When a blood clot travels to the lungs, it may cause chest pain and difficulty in breathing. Travellers with any of these symptoms should immediately seek medical attention.

To prevent the development of DVT on long flights, you should walk about the cabin, perform isometric compressions of the leg muscles (ie contract the leg muscles while sitting), drink plenty of fluids, and avoid alcohol and tobacco.

JET LAG & MOTION SICKNESS

Jet lag is common when crossing more than five time zones; it results in insomnia, fatigue, malaise or nausea. To avoid jet lag try drinking plenty of fluids (nonalcoholic) and eating light meals. Upon arrival, seek exposure to natural sunlight and readjust your schedule (for meals, sleep etc) as soon as possible.

Antihistamines such as dimenhydrinate (Dramamine), promethazine (Phenergan) and meclizine (Antivert, Bonine) are usually the first choice for treating motion sickness. Their main side effect is drowsiness. A herbal alternative is ginger, which works like a charm for some people.

IN CENTRAL ASIA

AVAILABILITY OF HEALTH CARE

Health care throughout Central Asia is basic at best. Any serious problems will require evacuation. The clinics listed in the relevant country chapters can provide basic care and may be able to organise evacuation if necessary. In Central Asia a pharmacist is known as an *apoteka* in Russian or *dorikhana* in Turkic. Clinics are widely known as *polikliniks*.

Self-treatment may be appropriate if your problem is minor (eg travellers' diarrhoea), you are carrying the relevant medication and you cannot attend a recommended clinic. If you think you may have a serious disease, especially malaria, travel to the nearest quality facility immediately to receive attention. It is always better to be assessed by a doctor than to rely on self-treatment.

Buying medication over the counter is not recommended, as fake medications and poorly stored or out-of-date drugs are common.

To find the nearest reliable medical facility, contact your insurance company, your embassy or a top-end hotel.

INFECTIOUS DISEASES
Brucellosis
Risk: Kazakhstan, Kyrgyzstan, Tajikistan, Uzbekistan, Turkmenistan. It is rare in travellers but common in the local population, it's transmitted via unpasteurised dairy products. Common symptoms include fever, chills, headache, loss of appetite and joint pain.

Hepatitis A
Risk: all countries. A problem throughout the region, this food- and waterborne virus infects the liver, causing jaundice (yellow skin and eyes), nausea and lethargy. There is no specific treatment for hepatitis A, you just need to allow time for the liver to heal. All travellers to Central Asia should be vaccinated.

Hepatitis B
Risk: all countries. The only sexually transmitted disease that can be prevented by vaccination, hepatitis B is spread by contact with infected body fluids, including via sexual contact. The long-term consequences can include liver cancer and cirrhosis.

HIV
Risk: all countries. HIV is transmitted via contaminated body fluids. Avoid unprotected sex, blood transfusions and injections (unless you can see a clean needle being used) in Central Asia.

Influenza
Risk: all countries. Present particularly in the winter months, symptoms of the flu include high fever, muscle aches, runny nose, cough and sore throat. Vaccination is recommended for those over the age of 65 or with underlying medical conditions such as heart disease or diabetes. There is no specific treatment, just rest and painkillers.

Leishmaniasis
Risk: Kazakhstan, Turkmenistan, Uzbekistan, and in particular Afghanistan. This sandfly-borne parasite is very rare in travellers but common in the local population. There are two forms of the disease – one which only affects the skin (causing a chronic ulcer) and one affecting the internal organs. Avoid sandfly bites by following insect avoidance guidelines.

Malaria
Risk: southern Tajikistan, southeastern Turkmenistan, Afghanistan and far southern Uzbekistan; only present in the extreme south in the warmer summer months (June to October). Malaria is caused by a parasite transmitted by the bite of an infected mosquito. The most important symptom of malaria is fever, but general symptoms such as headache, diarrhoea, cough or chills may also occur. Diagnosis can be made only by taking a blood sample.

Two strategies should be combined to prevent malaria – general mosquito/insect avoidance and antimalaria medications. Before you travel, it is essential you seek medical advice on the right medication and dosage. In general, Chloroquine is recommended for Turkmenistan and southern Uzbekistan. Some resistance to Chloroquine is reported in southern Tajikistan (mainly Khatlon province), so get your doctor's advice on whether to take Chloroquine, Larium (Mefloquine), Doxycycline or Malarone. Chloroquine is not effective in Afghanistan (Mefloquine, Malarone and Doxycycline are effective). See the World Malaria Risk Chart (www.iamat.org/pdf/world malariarisk.pdf) for detailed information.

To prevent mosquito bites, travellers are advised to take the following steps:

- Use a DEET-containing insect repellent on exposed skin. Natural repellents such as citronella can be effective, but must be applied more frequently than products containing DEET.
- Sleep under a mosquito net impregnated with permethrin.
- Choose accommodation with screens and fans (if not air-conditioned).
- Impregnate clothing with permethrin in high-risk areas.
- Wear long sleeves and trousers in light colours.
- Use mosquito coils.
- Spray your room with insect repellent before going out for your evening meal.

HEALTH

Rabies

Risk: all countries. Still a common problem in most parts of Central Asia, this uniformly fatal disease is spread by the bite or lick of an infected animal – most commonly a dog. Having a pretravel vaccination (three shots over a one month period) means the postbite treatment is greatly simplified. If an animal bites you, gently wash the wound with soap and water, and apply iodine-based antiseptic. If you are not vaccinated you will need to receive rabies immunoglobulin as soon as possible and seek medical advice.

STDs

Risk: all countries. Sexually transmitted diseases most common in Central Asia include herpes, genital warts, syphilis, gonorrhoea and chlamydia. People carrying these diseases often have no signs of infection. Condoms will prevent gonorrhoea and chlamydia but not warts or herpes. If after a sexual encounter you develop any rash, lumps, discharge or pain when passing urine seek immediate medical attention. If you have been sexually active during your travels, have an STD check upon your return.

Tuberculosis (TB)

Risk: all countries. Medical and aid workers, and long-term travellers who have significant contact with the local population should take precautions against TB. Vaccination is usually given only to children under the age of five, but adults at risk are recommended pre- and post-travel TB testing. The main symptoms are fever, cough, weight loss, night sweats and tiredness.

Typhoid

Risk: all countries. This serious bacterial infection is spread via food and water. It gives a high and slowly progressive fever and headache, and may be accompanied by a dry cough and stomach pain. Be aware that vaccination is not 100% effective so you must still be careful what you eat and drink. Dushanbe had typhoid outbreaks in 2003 and 2004.

Travellers' Diarrhoea

Travellers' diarrhoea is defined as the passage of more than three watery bowel actions within 24 hours, plus at least one other symptom, such as fever, cramps, nausea, vomiting or feeling generally unwell. It is by far the most common problem affecting travellers – between 30% and 50% of people will suffer from it within two weeks of starting their trip.

Travellers' diarrhoea is caused by a bacterium and, in most cases, treatment consists of staying well hydrated; rehydration solutions such as Gastrolyte are the best for this. It responds promptly to treatment with antibiotics such as norfloxacin, ciprofloxacin or azithromycin. Loperamide is just a 'stopper' and doesn't get to the cause of the problem. It can be helpful, for example, if you have to go on a long bus ride. Don't take loperamide if you have a fever, or blood in your stools. Seek medical attention quickly if you do not respond to an appropriate antibiotic.

Amoebic Dysentery

Amoebic dysentery is actually rare in travellers but is often misdiagnosed. Symptoms are similar to bacterial diarrhoea, ie fever, bloody diarrhoea and generally feeling unwell. You should always seek reliable medical care if you have blood in your diarrhoea. Treatment involves two drugs: tinidazole or metronidazole to kill the parasite in your gut, and a second drug to kill the cysts. If left untreated, complications such as liver or gut abscesses can occur.

Giardiasis

Giardia is a parasite that is relatively common in travellers. Symptoms include nausea, bloating, excess gas, fatigue and intermittent diarrhoea. 'Eggy' burps are often attributed solely to giardia, but research in Nepal has shown that they are not specific to giardia. The parasite will eventually go away if left untreated, but this can take months. The treatment of choice is tinidazole; metronidazole is a second option.

Other Diseases

Kazakhstan occasionally reports outbreaks of human plague in the far west (the last was in 2003). Outbreaks are often caused by eating diseased meat but are also transmitted by the bites of rodent and marmot fleas.

In 2009 there were outbreaks of anthrax in Afghan Badakhshan, Uzbekistan and Kazakhstan.

Crimean Congo haemorrhagic fever is a severe viral illness characterised by the sudden onset of intense fever, headache, aching limbs, bleeding gums and sometimes a rash of red dots on the skin, a week or two after being bitten by an infected tick. Though not all ticks are infected, it's a minor risk for trekkers and campers in Central Asia during the summer months. Insect repellent will help keep the blighters off you. There were Crimean Congo haemorrhagic fever outbreaks in Afghanistan in 2008 and 2009, Southern Kazakhstan in 2009 and Tajikistan in 2009.

Afghanistan suffered a cholera outbreak in 2009.

ENVIRONMENTAL HAZARDS
Altitude Sickness

This is a particular problem in high-altitude regions of Kazakhstan, Kyrgyzstan and Tajikistan. With motorable roads (such as the Pamir Hwy) climbing passes of over 4000m, it's a problem not just restricted to trekkers.

Altitude sickness may develop in those who ascend rapidly to altitudes greater than 2500m. Being physically fit offers no protection. Risk increases with faster ascents, higher altitudes and greater exertion. Symptoms may include headaches, nausea, vomiting, dizziness, malaise, insomnia and loss of appetite. Severe cases may be complicated by fluid in the lungs or swelling of the brain.

To protect yourself against altitude sickness, take 125mg or 250mg of acetazolamide (Diamox) twice or three times daily, starting 24 hours before ascent and continuing for 48 hours after arrival at altitude. Possible side effects include increased urinary volume, numbness, tingling, drowsiness, nausea, myopia and temporary impotence. Acetazolamide should not be given to pregnant women or anyone with a history of sulfa allergy. For those who cannot tolerate acetazolamide, the next best option is 4mg of dexamethasone taken four times daily. Unlike acetazolamide, dexamethasone must be tapered gradually upon arrival at altitude. Dexamethasone is a steroid, so it should not be given to diabetics or anyone for whom steroids are contraindicated. A natural alternative is gingko.

When travelling to high altitudes, avoid overexertion, eat light meals, drink lots of fluids and abstain from alcohol. If your symptoms are more than mild or don't resolve promptly, see a doctor.

The Murgab Ecotourism Association (META; see p413) in Tajikistan's eastern Pamirs has a hyperbaric chamber in case of altitude-related emergencies.

DRINKING WATER

- Never drink tap water, especially in Karakalpakstan, Khorezm, Dushanbe and remoter Kazakhstan.
- Bottled water is generally safe – check the seal is intact at purchase.
- Avoid ice.
- Avoid fresh juices – they may have been watered down.
- Boiling water is the most efficient method of purifying it.
- The best chemical purifier is iodine. It should not be used by pregnant women or those with thyroid problems.
- Water filters should also filter out viruses. Ensure your filter has a chemical barrier such as iodine and a small pore size, eg less than four microns.

Food

Eating in restaurants is the biggest risk factor for contracting travellers' diarrhoea. Ways to avoid it include eating only freshly cooked food, avoiding food that has been sitting around in buffets, and eating in busy restaurants with a high turnover of customers. Peel all fruit, cook vegetables and soak salads in iodine water for at least 20 minutes.

Insect Bites & Stings

Bedbugs don't carry disease but their bites are very itchy. They live in the cracks of furniture and walls, and then migrate to the bed at night to feed on you. You can treat the itch with an antihistamine.

Lice inhabit various parts of your body but most commonly your head and pubic area. Transmission is via close contact with an infected person. They can be difficult to treat and you may need numerous applications of an anti-lice shampoo such as permethrin. Pubic lice are usually contracted from sexual contact.

Ticks (*kleshch* in Russian) are contracted after walking in rural areas. They are commonly found behind the ears, on the belly and in the armpits. If you have had a tick bite and experience symptoms such as a rash at the site of the bite or elsewhere, fever or muscle aches, you should see a doctor. Doxycycline prevents tick-borne diseases.

Anyone with a serious bee or wasp allergy should carry an injection of adrenaline (eg an Epipen) for emergency treatment. For others, apply ice to the sting and take painkillers.

Skin Problems

Take meticulous care of any cuts and scratches to prevent complications such as abscesses. Immediately wash all wounds in clean water and apply antiseptic. If you develop signs of infection (increasing pain and redness) see a doctor.

Sunburn

Even on a cloudy day sunburn can occur rapidly, especially at high altitudes. Always use a strong sunscreen (at least factor 30), and always wear a wide-brimmed hat and sunglasses outdoors. If you become sun-burnt stay out of the sun until you have recovered, apply cool compresses and take painkillers for the discomfort. One percent hydrocortisone cream applied twice daily is also helpful.

WOMEN'S HEALTH

Supplies of sanitary products may not be readily available in rural areas. Birth control options may be limited so bring adequate supplies of your own form of contraception.

Heat, humidity and antibiotics can all contribute to thrush. Treatment is with anti-fungal creams and pessaries such as clotrima-zole. A practical alternative is a single tablet of fluconazole (Diflucan). Urinary tract infections can be precipitated by dehydration or long bus journeys without toilet stops; bring suitable antibiotics.

Language

CONTENTS

Central Asia is a multilingual area, and so this chapter includes words and phrases from seven different languages that you may find useful. The official languages of the former Soviet Central Asian countries are Kazakh, Kyrgyz, Tajik, Turkmen and Uzbek, but Russian is still the language of government and academia. Therefore the one language most useful for a visitor in these countries is still Russian; you'll find that it's the second language for most adults, who were taught it in school. A few words of the local language will nonetheless give a disproportionate return in good will. Learning the Russian Cyrillic alphabet is a very good idea, as most of the Cyrillic-based alphabets of Central Asia will then be familiar as well (see The Russian Cyrillic Alphabet on p538 and Non-Russian Cyrillic Letters on p540).

Dari and Pashto are the official languages of Afghanistan, but Dari is the one most commonly used as a lingua franca. Dari (as well as Pashto) is written using a modified alphabet of the cursive Arabic script.

Tajik, Uzbek, Turkmen, Kyrgyz, as well as Wakhi, are also spoken by minorities in northern Afghanistan.

For a comprehensive guide to Russian, get a copy of Lonely Planet's *Russian Phrasebook*. For an excellent guide to the other languages of Central Asia, get a copy of Lonely Planet's *Central Asia Phrasebook*.

RUSSIAN

Two words you're sure to use during your travels are здравствуйте (*zdrastvuyte*), the universal 'hello' (but if you say it a second time in one day to the same person, they'll think you forgot you already saw them!), and пожалуйста (*pazhalsta*), the multipurpose word for 'please' (commonly used with all polite requests), 'you're welcome', 'pardon me', 'after you' and more.

To turn a statement into a question just use a rising tone and a questioning look, or follow it with *da?*, eg 'Is this Moscow?', Это Москва, да? (*eta maskva da?*). A sentence is made negative by putting не (*ni*) before its main word, eg 'This is not Moscow', Это не Москва. (*eta ni maskva*).

Two letters have no sound, but modify others. A consonant followed by the 'soft sign' ь is spoken with the tongue flat against the palate, as if followed by the faint beginnings of a 'y'. The rare 'hard sign' ъ after a consonant inserts a slight pause before the next vowel.

Greetings & Civilities

Hello.
  zdrast·vuy·te   Здравствуйте.
Goodbye.
  da svi·da·ni·ya   До свидания.
How are you?
  kak di·la?   Как дела?
I'm well.
  kha·ra·sho   Хорошо.
Yes./No.
  da/net   Да./Нет.
good/OK
  kha·ra·sho   хорошо
bad
  plo·kha   плохо
Thank you (very much).
  (*bal'sho·ye*) *spa·si·ba* (Большое) Спасибо.
What's your name?
  kak vas za·vut?   Как вас зовут?
My name is …
  mi·nya za·vut …   Меня зовут …
Where are you from?
  at·ku·da vy?   Откуда вы?
Australia
  af·stra·li·ya   Австралия
Canada
  ka·na·da   Канада
France
  fran·tsi·ya   Франция
Germany
  ger·ma·ni·ya   Германия

Ireland
ir·*lan*·di·ya   Ирландия
New Zealand
no·va·ya ze·*lan*·di·ya   Новая Зеландия
the UK (Great Britain)
ve·li·ka·bri·*ta*·ni·ya   Великобритания
the USA
se she a/a·*me*·ri·ka   США/Америка

Language Difficulties
I don't speak Russian.
ya ni ga·va·*ryu* pa *ru*·ski   Я не говорю по-русски.
I don't understand.
ya ni pa·ni·*ma*·yu   Я не понимаю.
Do you speak English?
vy ga·va·*ri*·te pa   Вы говорите
ang·*liy*·ski?   по-английски?
Could you write it down, please?
za·pi·*shi*·te pa·*zhal*·sta   Запишите пожалуйста.

Transport & Travel
Where is …?
gde …?   Где …?
When does it leave?
kag·da at·prav·*lya*·   Когда отправляется?
et·sya?
What town is this?
ka·*koy* e·ta *go*·rat?   Какой это город?
How much is a room?
skol'·ka *sto*·it *no*·mer?   Сколько стоит номер?

airport
ae·ra·*port*   аэропорт
bus
af·*to*·bus   автобус
hotel
gas·*ti*·ni·tsa   гостиница
railway station
zhi·lez·na da·*rozh*·nyy   железнодорожный
vag·*zal*   вокзал (abbr. ж. д.)
square/plaza
plo·shchat'   площадь (abbr. пл.)
street
u·*li*·tsa   улица (abbr. ул.)
toilet
tua·*let*   туалет
train
poy·ezt   поезд

Money & Shopping
How much is it?
skol'·ka *sto*·it?   Сколько стоит?
Do you have …?
u vas est' …?   У вас есть …?

THE RUSSIAN CYRILLIC ALPHABET

Cyrillic	Roman	Pronunciation
А, а	a	as the 'a' in 'father' (in stressed syllable); as the 'a' in 'ago' (in unstressed syllable)
Б, б	b	as the 'b' in 'but'
В, в	v	as the 'v' in 'van'
Г, г	g	as the 'g' in 'god'
Д, д	d	as the 'd' in 'dog'
Е, е *	e	as the 'ye' in 'yet' (in stressed syllable); as the 'yi' in 'yin' (in unstressed syllable)
Ё, ё **	yo	as the 'yo' in 'yore'
Ж, ж	zh	as the 's' in 'measure'
З, з	z	as the 'z' in 'zoo'
И, и	i	as the 'ee' in 'meet'
Й, й	y	as the 'y' in 'boy'
К, к	k	as the 'k' in 'kind'
Л, л	l	as the 'l' in 'lamp'
М, м	m	as the 'm' in 'mad'
Н, н	n	as the 'n' in 'not'
О, о	o	as the 'o' in 'more' (in stressed syllable); as the 'a' in 'hard' (in unstressed syllable)
П, п	p	as the 'p' in 'pig'
Р, р	r	as the 'r' in 'rub' (rolled)
С, с	s	as the 's' in 'sing'
Т, т	t	as the 't' in 'ten'
У, у	u	as the 'oo' in 'fool'
Ф, ф	f	as the 'f' in 'fan'
Х, х	kh	as the 'ch' in 'Bach'
Ц, ц	ts	as the 'ts' in 'bits'
Ч, ч	ch	as the 'ch' in 'chin'
Ш, ш	sh	as the 'sh' in 'shop'
Щ, щ	shch	as 'sh-ch' in 'fresh chips'
Ъ, ъ		'hard sign' (see p537)
Ы, ы	y	as the 'i' in 'ill'
Ь, ь	'	'soft sign'; (see p537)
Э, э	e	as the 'e' in 'end'
Ю, ю	yu	as the 'u' in 'use'
Я, я	ya	as the 'ya' in 'yard' (in stressed syllable); as the 'ye' in 'yearn' (in unstressed syllable)

* E, e are transliterated *ye* when at the beginning of a word

** Ё, ё are often printed without dots

bookshop	*knizh*·nyy	книжный
	ma·ga·*zin*	магазин
currency exchange	ab·*men* val·*yu*·ty	обмен валюты
market	*ry*·nak	рынок
money	*den*'gi	деньги
pharmacy	ap·*te*·ka	аптека
shop	ma·ga·*zin*	магазин

70	sem'di·*syat*	семьдесят
80	vo·sim·di·*syat*	восемьдесят
90	di·vya·*no*·sta	девяносто
100	sto	сто
1000	*ty*·sya·cha	тысяча

KAZAKH

Kazakh is a Turkic language. Since 1940 it has been written in a 42-letter version of the Cyrillic alphabet (see p538 and p540). It's spoken by 64% of the population, whereas almost everyone speaks Russian. Any political tension over language issues has been rather neatly sidestepped by making Kazakh the state language, but giving Russian the status of an official language and permitting the predominant language in local regions to be used in written government business.

Russian is the first language for some urban Kazakhs, as well as the large Russian minority, who form 24% of the population. Few people speak English or other Western languages, but those who do tend to work in the tourist industry or with foreigners.

Street signs are sometimes in Kazakh, sometimes in Russian, sometimes in both. In this book we use the language you're most likely to come across in each town.

Kazakh Basics

Peace be with you.	*assalamu aleykum*
And peace with you.	*wagaleykum ussalam* (response)
Hello.	*salamatsyz be*
Goodbye.	*kosh-sau bolyndar*
Thank you.	*rakhmet*
Yes./No.	*ia/zhok*
How are you?	*khal zhag dayynyz kalay?*
I'm well.	*zhaksy*
Do you speak English?	*agylshynsa bilesiz be?*
I don't understand.	*tusinbeymin*
Where is…?	*… kayda?*
How much?	*kansha?*

airport	*auezhay*
bus station	*avtovokzal/avtobeket*
doctor	*dariger*
friend	*dos*
hospital	*aurukhana*
hotel	*konak uy/meymankhana*
police	*politsia*
restaurant	*meyramkhana*
toilet	*daretkhana*
train station	*temir zhol vokzal/ temir zhol beket*

EMERGENCIES – RUSSIAN

I need a doctor.

mne *nu*·zhin vrach	Мне нужен врач.

hospital

bal'*ni*·tsa	больница

police

mi·*li*·tsi·ya	милиция

Fire!

pa·*zhar*!	Пожар!

Help!

na *po*·mashch'!/	На помощь!/
pa·ma·*gi*·ti!	Помогите!

Thief!

vor!	Вор!

Time & Days

Dates are given as day-month-year, with the month usually in Roman numerals. Days of the week are often represented by numbers in timetables; Monday is 1.

When?	kag·*da*?	Когда?
today	si·*vod*·nya	сегодня
yesterday	vchi·*ra*	вчера
tomorrow	zaf·tra	завтра
Monday	pa·ni·*del'*nik	понедельник
Tuesday	ftor·nik	вторник
Wednesday	sri·*da*	среда
Thursday	chit·*verk*	четверг
Friday	*pyat*·ni·tsa	пятница
Saturday	su·*bo*·ta	суббота
Sunday	vas·kri·*sen*'e	воскресенье

Numbers

How many?	*skol*'ka?	Сколько?
0	nol'	ноль
1	a·*din*	один
2	dva	два
3	tri	три
4	chi·*ty*·ri	четыре
5	pyat'	пять
6	shest'	шесть
7	sem'	семь
8	*vo*·sim'	восемь
9	de·vit'	девять
10	de·sit'	десять
20	*dva*·tsat'	двадцать
30	*tri*·tsat'	тридцать
40	*so*·rak	сорок
50	pyat'di·*syat*	пятьдесят
60	shest'di·*syat*	шестьдесят

NON-RUSSIAN CYRILLIC LETTERS

Cyrillic	Common	Transcription

Kazakh

Ә, ә	a	as the 'a' in 'man'
Ғ, ғ	g	as the 'gh' in 'ugh'
Қ, қ	k	a guttural 'k'
Ң, ң	n	as the 'ng' in 'sing'
Ө, ө	o	as the 'u' in 'fur'
Ұ, ұ	u	as the 'u' in 'full'
Ү, ү	u	as the 'oo' in 'fool'
Һ, һ	h	as the 'h' in 'hat'
І, і	i	as the 'i' in 'ill'

Tajik

Ғ, ғ	gh	as the 'gh' in 'ugh'
Й, й	ee	as the 'ee' in 'fee'
Қ, қ	q	as the 'k' in 'keen'
Ӯ, ӯ	ö	as the 'u' in 'fur'
Х, х	kh	as the 'h' in 'hat'
Ҷ, ҷ	j	as 'j' in 'jig'

Uzbek

Ғ, ғ	g	as the 'gh' in 'ugh'
Қ, қ	k/q	a guttural 'k'
Ӯ, ӯ	u	as the 'oo' in 'book'
Х, х	kh	as the 'ch' in 'Bach'

Kyrgyz

Ң, ң	ng	as the 'ng' in 'sing'
Ө, ө	ö	as the 'u' in 'fur'
Ү, ү	ü	as the 'ew' in 'few'

bad	zhaman
boiled water	kaynagan su
bread	nan
expensive	kymbat
good	zhaksy
meat	yet
rice	kurish
tea	shay

Monday	duysenbi
Tuesday	seysenbi
Wednesday	sarsenbi
Thursday	beysenbi
Friday	zhuma
Saturday	senbi
Sunday	zheksenbi

1	bir	7	etti
2	yeki	8	sakkiz
3	ush	9	togyz
4	tort	10	on
5	bes	100	zhus
6	alty	1000	myn

KYRGYZ

Kyrgyz is a Turkic language that has been written using a Cyrillic script since the early 1940s. Along with neighbouring countries Uzbekistan and Turkmenistan, Kyrgyzstan is in the process of changing over to a modified Roman alphabet.

Russian has official-language status, but there is also a strong push to promote Kyrgyz as the predominant language of government, media and education.

Kyrgyz Basics

Peace be with you.	asalamu aleykom
And peace with you.	wa aleykum assalam (response)
Hello.	salam
Goodbye.	jakshy kalyngydzar
Thank you.	rakhmat
Yes./No.	ooba/jok
How are you?	jakshysüzbü?
I'm well.	jakshy
Do you speak English?	siz angliyscha süylöy süzbü?
I don't understand.	men tüshümböy jatamyn
Where is …?	… kayda?
How much?	kancha?

airport	aeroport
bus station	avtobiket
doctor	doktur
friend	dos
hospital	oruukana
hotel	meymankana
police	militsia
restaurant	restoran
toilet	darakana
train station	temir jol vokzal

bad	jaman
boiled water	kaynatilgan suu
bread	nan
expensive	kymbat
good	jakshy
meat	et
rice	kürüch
tea	chay

Monday	düshömbü
Tuesday	seyshembi
Wednesday	sharshembi
Thursday	beishembi
Friday	juma
Saturday	ishembi
Sunday	jekshembi

1	bir	7	jety
2	eki	8	segiz
3	üch	9	toguz
4	tört	10	on
5	besh	100	jüz
6	alty	1000	ming

TAJIK

Tajik, the state language of Tajikistan since 1989, belongs to the southwest Persian group of languages and is closely related to Dari (the principal language of Afghanistan) and Farsi (the language of Iran). This sets it apart from most other Central Asian languages which are Turkic in origin. Tajik was formerly written in a modified Arabic script (similar to the Farsi alphabet) and then in Roman, but since 1940 a modified Cyrillic script has been used.

Tajik Basics

Peace be with you.	assalomu aleykum
And peace with you.	valeykum assalom (response)
Hello.	salom
Goodbye.	khayr naboshad
Thank you.	rakhmat/teshakkur
Yes./No.	kha/ne
How are you?	naghzmi shumo?
I'm well.	mannaghz
Do you speak English?	anglisi meydonet?
I don't understand.	man manefakhmam
Where is …?	… khujo ast?
How much?	chand pul?

airport	furudgoh
bus station	istgoh
doctor	duhtur
friend	doost
hospital	bemorhona/kasalhona
hotel	mekhmon'hona
police	militsia
restaurant	restoran
toilet	khojat'hona
train station	istgoh rohi ohan

bad	ganda
boiled water	obi jush
bread	non
expensive	qimmat
good	khub/naghz
meat	gusht
rice	birinj
tea	choy

Monday	dushanbe
Tuesday	seshanbe
Wednesday	chorshanbe
Thursday	panjanbe
Friday	juma
Saturday	shanbe
Sunday	yakshanbe

1	yak	7	khaft
2	du	8	khasht
3	seh	9	nukh
4	chor	10	dakh
5	panj	100	sad
6	shish	1000	khazor

TURKMEN

Turkmen, the state language of Turkmenistan since 1990, belongs to the Turkic language family. There's been a significant infiltration of Russian words and phrases into Turkmen, especially in this century (particularly words to do with science and technology). In Turkmenistan almost everyone speaks Russian or Turkmen. English speakers are generally only found in the tourist industry and at some universities.

Four different scripts have been used to write Turkmen; first Arabic, then a Turkish-Roman alphabet, then the Cyrillic alphabet took over from 1940. On 1 January 1996, Turkmen Cyrillic was officially replaced by another modified Roman alphabet called Elipbi, and the changeover to this is complete.

Turkmen Basics

Peace be with you.	salam aleykum
And peace with you.	waleykum assalam (response)
Hello.	salam
Goodbye.	sagh bol
Thank you.	tangyr
Yes./No.	howa/yok
How are you?	siz nahili?
Fine, and you?	onat, a siz?
I don't understand.	men dushenamok
Do you speak English?	siz inglische gepleyarsinizmi?
Where is …?	… niredeh?
How much?	nyacheh?

airport	aeroport
bus station	durolha
doctor	lukman
friend	dost
hospital	keselkhana

hotel	*mikmankhana*		
police	*militsia*		
restaurant	*restoran*		
toilet	*hajat'hana*		
train station	*vokzal*		
bad	*ervet*		
boiled water	*gaina d'lan su*		
bread	*churek*		
expensive	*gummut*		
good	*yakhsheh*		
meat	*et*		
rice	*tui*		
tea	*chay*		
Monday	*dushanbe*		
Tuesday	*seshenbe*		
Wednesday	*charshanbe*		
Thursday	*penshenbe*		
Friday	*anna*		
Saturday	*shenbe*		
Sunday	*yekshanbe*		

1	*bir*	7	*yed*
2	*ikeh*	8	*sekiz*
3	*uch*	9	*dokuz*
4	*durt*	10	*on*
5	*besh*	100	*yuz*
6	*alty*	1000	*mun*

UZBEK

Uzbekistan's three major languages are Uzbek, Russian and Tajik. Uzbek, a Turkic language, is the country's official language and, with 15 million speakers, it is the most widely spoken of the non-Slavic languages of all the former Soviet states.

Uzbek was written in Roman letters from 1918 to 1941. Since then it has used a modified Cyrillic alphabet, but the country has been moving to a Roman alphabet.

Uzbek Basics

Peace be with you.	*salom alaykhum*
And peace with you.	*tinch berling* (response)
Hello.	*salom*
Goodbye.	*hayr*
Thank you.	*rakhmat*
Yes.	*kha*
No.	*yuk*
How are you?	*kanday siz?*
Do you speak English?	*inglizcha bila sizmi?*
Where is ...?	*... kayerda?*
How much?	*kancha/nichpul?*

airport	*tayyorgokh*
bus station	*avtobeket*
doctor	*tabib*
friend	*urmok/doost*
hospital	*kasalhona*
hotel	*mehmon'hona*
police	*militsia*
restaurant	*restoran*
toilet	*hojat'hona*
train station	*temir yul vokzali*
bad	*yomon*
boiled water	*kaynatilgan suv*
bread	*non*
expensive	*kimmat*
good	*yakhshi*
meat	*gusht*
rice	*guruch*
tea	*choy*
Monday	*dushanba*
Tuesday	*seyshanba*
Wednesday	*chorshanba*
Thursday	*payshanba*
Friday	*juma*
Saturday	*shanba*
Sunday	*yakshanba*

1	*bir*	8	*sakkiz*
2	*ikki*	9	*tukkiz*
3	*uch*	10	*un*
4	*turt*	11	*un bir*
5	*besh*	100	*yuz*
6	*olti*	1000	*ming*
7	*etti*		

DARI

Dari is so similar to Farsi (the language of Iran) that even Afghanis will often refer to it as Farsi. The principal difference between the two is that Farsi contains more loan words from Arabic and Turkish.

Dari is an Indo-Iranian language and a member of the Indo-European language family. While it is written in Arabic script, and runs from right to left, it isn't related to Arabic at all.

Dari Basics

Greetings.	*salam aleykom*
Hello.	*salam*
Goodbye.	*khoda hafez*
How are you?	*haletan chetor hast?*
Yes.	*bala*

No.	na	Is it dangerous?	khatar hast?
Please.	lotfan	Are there landmines?	mayn hast?
Thank you.	tashakor	aid-worker	komakgar
You're welcome.	khahesh mikonam	bomb	bam
Excuse me./I'm sorry.	bebakhshid	gun	tofang
It is God's will.	mashallah	landmine	mayn
Where is the …?	… koja st?	refugee	panahanda
How much is it?	Kimatesh chand hast?	rocket	rakat
Help!	komak!	security (forces)	amniyat
Stop!	tavaghof!	soldier	asgar
Go away!	gom sho!	war/fighting	jang
Do you speak English?	shoma ingilisi midanin?		
I (don't) understand.	(na) mifahman	Monday	dushanba
I'm sick.	mariz am	Tuesday	se shanba
		Wednesday	chahar shanba
		Thursday	panj shanba
		Friday	jom'a
ambulance	ambulans	Saturday	shanba
chemist	davakhana	Sunday	yakshanba
doctor	daktar		
hospital	shafakhana		
hotel	hotal		
lodging house	mosaferkhana		
market	bazar		
mosque	masjed		
police	polis		
toilet	tashnab		

0	sifir	7	haft
1	yak	8	hasht
2	du	9	noh
3	se	10	dah
4	chahar	100	sad
5	panj	1000	hazar
6	shash		

LANGUAGE

Glossary

ABBREVIATIONS

A – Arabic
D – Dari
Kaz – Kazakh
Kyr – Kyrgyz
R – Russian
Taj – Tajik
T – general Turkic
Tur – Turkmen
U – Uzbek

-abad (T) – suffix meaning 'town of'
aivan – covered portico or vaulted portal
aiwan – see *aivan*
ak (T) – white
ak kalpak (Kyr) – felt hat worn by Kyrgyz men
akimat (T) – regional government office or city hall, also *aqimat*
aksakal (T) – revered elder
akyn (Kyr) – minstrel, bard
ala-kiyiz (Kyr) – felt rug with coloured panels pressed on
alangy (Kaz) – square
alplager (R) – mountaineers camp, short for *alpinistskiy lager*
apparatchik (R) – bureaucrat
apteka (R) – pharmacy
arashan (T) – springs
asalam aleykum (A) – traditional Muslim greeting, meaning 'peace be with you'
ASSR – Autonomous Soviet Socialist Republic
aul (T) – yurt or herders' camp
aviakassa (R) – air ticket office
avtobus (R) – bus
avtostantsia (R) – bus stop or bus stand
azan (A) – Muslim call to prayer

babushka (R) – old woman; headscarf worn by Russian peasant women
bagh (Taj, D) – garden
balbal (T) – totemlike stone marker
banya (R) – public bath
basmachi (R) – literally 'bandits'; Muslim guerrilla fighters who resisted the Bolshevik takeover in Central Asia
batyr (Kyr, Kaz) – warrior hero in epics
beg (T) – landlord, gentleman; also spelt *bay* or *bek*
berkutchi (Kyr) – eagle hunter
beshbarmak (Kaz, Kyr) – flat noodles with lamb, horse meat or vegetable broth (served separately)

Bi (Kaz) – honorific Kazakh title given to clan elders
bishkek (Kaz, Kyrg) – see *pishpek*
bosuy (Kyr) – see *yurt*
bufet (R) – snack bar selling cheap cold meats, boiled eggs, salads, breads, pastries etc
bulvar (R) – boulevard
bulvary (Kyr) – boulevard
burqa (D) – body-length shuttlecock-shaped veil worn by many Afghan women
buzkashi (T, D) – traditional pololike game played with a headless calf, goat or sheep carcass *(buz)*

caravanserai – travellers inn
chabana (Kyr, Kaz) – cowboy
chaderi (D) – see *burqa*
chaikhana (T) – teahouse
chapan (U, Taj) – traditional stripy Uzbek/Tajik cloak
chay (T) – tea
chaykhana (T) – see *chaikhana*
chong (T) – big
chorsu (T) – market arcade
chowk (D) – crossroads or town square
choy (U, Taj) – see *chay*
choyhona (T) – see *chaikhana*
chuchuk (Kaz) – see *kazy*
chuchvara (T) – dumplings
CIS – Commonwealth of Independent States; the loose political and economic alliance of most former member republics of the USSR (except the Baltic states and Georgia)
CPK – Communist Party of Kazakhstan

dacha (R) – a holiday bungalow
dangyly (Kaz) – avenue
Dari – national language of Afghanistan, closely connected to Farsi
darikhana (Kaz) – pharmacy
darya (T) – river
dastarkhan (T) – literally 'tablecloth'; feast
depe (Tur) – see *tepe*
dezhurnaya (R) – floor-lady; the woman attendant on duty on each floor of a Soviet-style hotel
dom (R) – building
dom otdykha (R) – rest home
doppe (U) – black, four-sided skullcap embroidered in white and worn by men; also *dopi, doppa, dopy* or *doppilar*
dutar (T) – two-stringed guitar

eshon (A) – *Sufi* leader, also spelt *ishan*

GAI (R) – traffic police

geoglyph – geometric pattern of stones, often used in astrological observations

ghanch (T) – carved and painted plaster

gillam (T) – carpet, also *gilim*

glasnost (R) – 'openness' in government that was one aspect of the Gorbachev reforms

gorod (R) – town

Graeco-Bactrian – Hellenistic kingdom and culture centred on northern Afghanistan, southern Uzbekistan and Tajikistan following the conquests of Alexander the Great

Great Game – the geopolitical 'Cold War' of territorial expansion between the Russian and British empires in the 19th and early-20th centuries in Central Asia

Hadith (A) – collected acts and sayings of the Prophet Mohammed

haj (A) – the pilgrimage to Mecca, one of the five pillars of Islam, to be made by devout Muslims at least once during their lifetime

hakimat (T) – see *hakimyat*

hakimyat (Kyr) – municipal administration building

hammam (A) – bathhouse

hammomi (U) – baths

hanako (U) – see *khanaka*

hauz (T) – an artificial pool

Hazara – Shiite ethnic group of Central Afghanistan

hazrat (A) – honorific title meaning 'majesty' or 'holy'

Hejira – flight of the Prophet Mohammed and his followers to Medina in AD 622

hijab (A) – Muslim woman's veil or headscarf (literally 'modest dress')

hoja (U) – lord, master, gentleman (honorific title)

ikat (U) – tie-dyed silk

IMU – Islamic Movement of Uzbekistan

IRP – Islamic Renaissance Party; grouping of radical activists dedicated to the formation of Islamic rule in Central Asia

ISAF – International Security Assistance Force, lead by NATO

Ismaili (A) – a branch of *Shiite* Islam

iwan – see *aivan*

jailoo (Kyr) – summer pasture

jami masjid (A) – Friday mosque

jamoat khana (Taj) – Ismaili prayer hall and meeting hall

jihad (A) – struggle, or holy war

juma (U) – Friday, see *jami masjid*

kala (T) – fortress

kalon (Taj) – great

kara (T) – black

kassa (R) – cashier or ticket office

kazan (T) – large cauldron (used to cook *plov*)

kazy (Kaz) – horse-meat sausage

-kent (T) – suffix meaning 'town of'

khanaka (A) – a *Sufi* contemplation hall and hostel for wandering ascetics; the room of an *eshon* in which he and other *Sufis* perform their *zikr*

khanatlas (U) – see *ikat*

khiyeboni (Taj) – avenue

kino (R) – cinema; also kinoteatr

köçesi (Tur) – street

kochasi (U) – street

köchösü (Kyr) – street

koh (Taj, D) – mountain

kok (T) – blue

kökör (T) – *kumys* storer

kokpar (Kaz) – see *buzkashi*

kolkhoz (R) – collective farm

koshesi (Kaz) – street

koshk (U, Tur) – fortress

koshma (Kaz) – multicoloured felt mats

kozha (Kaz) – see *hoja*

kuchai (Taj) – street

kumys (Kyr) – fermented mare's milk (also *kymys*)

kupeyny (R) – 2nd-class or sleeping carriage on trains; also *kupe*

kupkari (U) – see *buzkashi*

kurgan (T) – burial mound

kurort (R) – thermal-spring complex

kurpacha (U) – colourful sitting mattress for a *tapchan*

kvartal (R) – district

kymyz (Kaz) – see *kumys*

kyz-kumay (Kyr) – traditional game in which a man chases a woman on horseback and tries to kiss her

kyz-kuu (Kaz) – see *kyz-kumay*

kyzyl (T) – red

laghman (T) – noodles

lepyoshka (R) – bread, see *nan*

LOI – letter of invitation

lungi – turban

lux (R) – deluxe

mahalla (U) – urban neighbourhood

Manas (Kyr) – epic; legendary hero revered by the Kyrgyz

manaschi (Kyr) – type of *akyn* who recites from the Kyrgyz cycle of oral legends

manty (T) – small stuffed dumplings

marshrutka (R, T) – short term for *marshrutnoe* and *marshrutny avtobus*

marshrutnoe (R, T) – small bus or van that follows a fixed route but stops on demand to take on or let off passengers, with fares depending on distance travelled

marshrutny avtobus (R, T) – large bus that follows a fixed route but stops on demand to take on or let off passengers, with fares depending on distance travelled

maydoni (U, Taj) – square

mazar (T) – tomb or mausoleum

medressa (A) – Islamic academy or seminary

mihrab (A) – niche in a mosque marking the direction of Mecca

mikrorayon (R) – micro region or district

militsia (R, T) – police

minor (T) – minaret

MSDSP – Mountain Societies Development Support Project

muezzin (A) – man who calls the Muslim faithful to prayer

mufti (A) – Islamic legal expert or spiritual leader

mujaheddin (A) – Muslim freedom fighter engaged in *jihad*

mullah (A) – Islamic cleric

nan (T) – flat bread

Naqshband – the most influential of many *Sufi* secret associations in Central Asia

Navrus (A) – literally 'New Days'; the main Islamic spring festival; has various regional transliterations (Nauroz, Nauryz, Nawruz, Norruz or Novruz)

non (U, Taj) – see *nan*

oblast (R) – province, region

oblys (Kaz) – province, region

OVIR (R) – Otdel Vis i Registratsii; Office of Visas and Registration

Oxus – historic name for the Amu-Darya river

pakhta (T) – cotton

pakhtakor (T) – cotton worker

panjara (T) – trellis of wood, stone or *ghanch*

pattu – woollen blanket carried by many Afghan men

perestroika (R) – literally 'restructuring'; Gorbachev's efforts to revive the economy

piala (T) – bowl

pirhan tonban – traditional male clothes of Afghanistan, knee-length shirt and baggy trousers

pishpek (Kaz, Kyr) – churn for making *kumys*

pishtak – monumental entrance portal

platskartny (R) – hard sleeper train

ploshchad (R) – square

plov (T) – a rice dish with meat, carrots or other additions (traditionally prepared by men for special celebrations), also known as pilau

pochta (R) – post office

pol-lux (R) – semideluxe

polyclinic – health centre

propusk (R) – permit

prospekt (R) – avenue

pulao (D) – see *plov*

qala (U) – see *kala*

qymyz (Kaz) – see *kumys*

rabab (T) – six-stringed mandolin, also *rubab*

rabad (T) – suburb

rabat (T) – caravanserai

rayon (R) – district

samovar (R) – urn used for heating water for tea, often found on trains

samsa (T) – samosa

sary (T) – yellow

şayoli (Tur) – street

shahr (D) – town, city

sharq (Taj, U) – east

shashlyk (T) – meat roasted on skewers over hot coals

shay (Kaz) – see *chay*

shaykhana (T) – see *chaikhana*

Shiite (A) – one of the two main branches of Islam

shubat (Kaz, Taj) – fermented camel's milk

shyrdak (Kyr) – felt rug with appliquéd coloured panels

skibaza (R) – ski base

SSR – Soviet Socialist Republic

stolovaya (R) – canteen, cafeteria

Sufi (A) – mystical tradition in Islam

suzani (U) – bright silk embroidery on cotton cloth

tapchan (Taj) – tea bed

tash (T) – stone

tebbetey (Kyr) – round fur-trimmed hat worn by men

telpek (Tur, U) – sheepskin hat worn by men

tepe (T) – fort or fortified hill, also *depe*

teppe (D) – see *tepe*

tim (T) – shopping arcade

toi (T) – celebration

Transoxiana – meaning 'the land beyond the Oxus'; historical term for the region between the Amu-Darya and Syr-Darya rivers

TsUM (R) – *Tsentralny universalny magazin*; central department store

tubiteyka (R) – see *doppe*

tugai – dense forest endemic to Central Asian river valleys and flood plains

turbaza (R) – holiday camp typically with Spartan cabins, plain food, sports, video hall and bar, usually open only in summer

Turkestan – literally 'the Land of the Turks'; covers Central Asia and Xinjiang (China)

UAZ (R) – Russian jeep

ulak-tartysh (Kyr) – see *buzkashi*

ulama (A) – class of religious scholars or intellectuals

ulitsa (R) – street
umuvalnik (R) – portable washing basin
univermag (R) – universalny magazin; department store
uulu (Kyr) – meaning 'son of'

viloyat (U) – province
vodopad (R) – waterfall
vokzal (R) – train station

wat – street

ylag oyyny (Karakalpak) – see *buzkashi*
yurt – traditional nomadic 'house', a collapsible cylindrical wood framework covered with felt

zakaznik (R) – protected area
zapovednik (R) – nature reserve
zhyostky (R) – hard carriage on trains
ziarat – shrine
zikr (A) – recitation or contemplation of the names of God; recitation of sacred writings; one part of traditional *Sufi* practice

The Authors

BRADLEY MAYHEW
Coordinating Author, Tajikistan

It must be a taste for ropey mutton that has driven Bradley repeatedly to almost every corner of inner Asia since spending six months in Uzbekistan for guidebook research. He has coordinated the last four editions of Central Asia and is the co-author of Lonely Planet guides to *Nepal, Tibet, Bhutan* and *Trekking in the Nepal Himalaya*, as well as several guides to the Silk Road. He has lectured on Central Asia to the Royal Geographical Society and was recently the subject of an Arte/SWR documentary film retracing the route of Marco Polo from Venice to Beijing. An expat Brit, Bradley lives in Yellowstone County, Montana. Check out his blog at www.bradleymayhew.blogspot.com.

GREG BLOOM
Uzbekistan

On Greg's first mission to Tashkent, in 2003, he trained newspaper reporters for the International Centre for Journalists, an American NGO. That was before most NGOs and all Western journalists were kicked out of the country after the Andijon incident. He returned to update the previous edition of this guide, narrowly escaping deportation after staying in an illegal hotel in Termiz. The Uzbek police seem more foreigner-friendly these days and this trip went without a hitch. Formerly the editor of Ukraine's Kyiv Post, Greg is now based in Cambodia and writes for Lonely Planet about Southeast Asia and former Soviet places. He blogs about his research trips at www.mytripjournal.com/bloomblogs.

PAUL CLAMMER
Afghanistan

Once a molecular biologist, Paul spent several years kicking around the Islamic world from Casablanca to Kashgar, eventually becoming a tour guide in Morocco, Turkey and Pakistan. Having watched *The Man Who Would Be King* at an impressionable age, the Khyber Pass was always in his sights, and in 2001 he made it to Afghanistan, only to find himself having dinner with two Taliban ministers a fortnight before the 9/11 attacks. He has since returned many times. He has worked on a dozen Lonely Planet guides, including writing 2007's groundbreaking *Afghanistan* and covering the North-West Frontier for the *Pakistan* guide.

LONELY PLANET AUTHORS

Why is our travel information the best in the world? It's simple: our authors are passionate, dedicated travellers. They don't take freebies in exchange for positive coverage so you can be sure the advice you're given is impartial. They travel widely to all the popular spots, and off the beaten track. They don't research using just the internet or phone. They discover new places not included in any other guidebook. They personally visit thousands of hotels, restaurants, palaces, trails, galleries, temples and more. They speak with dozens of locals every day to make sure you get the kind of insider knowledge only a local could tell you. They take pride in getting all the details right, and in telling it how it is. Think you can do it? Find out how at **lonelyplanet.com**.

MICHAEL KOHN   Kyrgyzstan

A journalist by profession and a traveller by nature, Michael has been churning out news articles and guidebooks from the far corners of the globe. He first visited Central Asia in 2003 to update Kazakhstan and Uzbekistan for Lonely Planet. On a second tour he covered Afghanistan and Turkmenistan, eventually taking the ferry to Azerbaijan. This time he traded deserts for mountains and took on Kyrgyzstan. Michael has also worked on Lonely Planet books to China, Mongolia, Tibet and Russia. In the off-season he calls San Francisco home, and when the weather is warm, Ulaanbaatar. He can be found online at www.michaelkohn.us.

JOHN NOBLE   Kazakhstan

With colleague John King, John helped destroy the Soviet Union by writing a Lonely Planet guide to it. Hoping to put independent travellers off the scent, the KGB engineered the disintegration of the country so that when Lonely Planet's *USSR* hit the bookshops in 1991 it was about a country that no longer existed. Undeterred, John has since written or co-written seven Lonely Planet guides to Soviet successor states, including three bites at Kazakhstan, which gets better and better to travel in every time. He is trying to find a way of basing himself in fascinating Central Asia for an extended period.

ANONYMOUS   Turkmenistan

The author of the Turkmenistan chapter has chosen to remain anonymous to protect the people who helped him/her during research.

Behind the Scenes

THIS BOOK

The 1st edition of this book was researched and written by John King, John Noble and Andrew Humphreys. Bradley Mayhew coordinated the 2nd, 3rd and 4th editions. This 5th edition was yet again coordinated by Bradley Mayhew, who also researched and wrote the Tajikistan chapter, and all the front and back chapters. Other authors for this edition were John Noble (Kazakhstan), Greg Bloom (Uzbekistan), Michael Kohn (Kyrgyzstan), Paul Clammer (Afghanistan), and another anonymous Turkmenistan author. Dr Trish Batchelor wrote the Health chapter. This guidebook was commissioned in Lonely Planet's Melbourne office, and produced by the following:

Commissioning Editors Will Gourlay, Suzannah Shwer
Coordinating Editor Elisa Arduca
Coordinating Cartographer Jolyon Philcox
Coordinating Layout Designer Yvonne Bischofberger
Managing Editor Bruce Evans
Managing Cartographer Herman So
Managing Layout Designer Indra Kilfoyle
Assisting Editors Carolyn Boicos, Barbara Delissen, Penelope Goodes, Charlotte Harrison, Elizabeth Swan, Helen Yeates
Assisting Cartographers Corey Hutchison, Valentina Kremenchutskaya, Anthony Phelan
Cover Research Naomi Parker, lonelyplanetimages.com

Internal Image Research Jane Hart, lonelyplanet images.com
Language Content Laura Crawford
Thanks to Daniel Corbett, Brigitte Ellemor, Lisa Knights, Annelies Mertens, Adrian Persoglia, Averil Robertson, Gerard Walker, Celia Wood

THANKS
BRADLEY MAYHEW

Special thanks to Marielle and Pamirbek for letting me crash in their apartment – twice. Valeria Tyumenova was very helpful in offering information on the ZDTA homestays in Penjikent. Cheers to Tanya Keim and the staff of MSDSP in Khorog and ace photographer Matthieu Paley for trips in the Pamirs and thanks to Rohilla at PECTA and Ubaidullah and Aimgul in Murgab for their help. Suzannah Shwer was a wonderful commissioning editor and my regular band of Stanophile co-authors were, as always, totally on the ball. *Katta rakhmat.*

GREG BLOOM

Thanks as always to my wife, Karin, for her love and support and for tolerating another brutal deadline, and to my daughter, Anna, for the needed distractions. I received plenty of help from my new posse in Tashkent. A special nod to Chris Van H, Livy, Murod and TIS gurus Ronald and Alex. No less inval-

THE LONELY PLANET STORY

Fresh from an epic journey across Europe, Asia and Australia in 1972, Tony and Maureen Wheeler sat at their kitchen table stapling together notes. The first Lonely Planet guidebook, *Across Asia on the Cheap*, was born.

Travellers snapped up the guides. Inspired by their success, the Wheelers began publishing books to Southeast Asia, India and beyond. Demand was prodigious, and the Wheelers expanded the business rapidly to keep up. Over the years, Lonely Planet extended its coverage to every country and into the virtual world via lonelyplanet.com and the Thorn Tree message board.

As Lonely Planet became a globally loved brand, Tony and Maureen received several offers for the company. But it wasn't until 2007 that they found a partner whom they trusted to remain true to the company's principles of travelling widely, treading lightly and giving sustainably. In October of that year, BBC Worldwide acquired a 75% share in the company, pledging to uphold Lonely Planet's commitment to independent travel, trustworthy advice and editorial independence.

Today, Lonely Planet has offices in Melbourne, London and Oakland, with over 500 staff members and 300 authors. Tony and Maureen are still actively involved with Lonely Planet. They're traveling more often than ever, and they're devoting their spare time to charitable projects. And the company is still driven by the philosophy of *Across Asia on the Cheap*: 'All you've got to do is decide to go and the hardest part is over. So go!'

uable were the efforts of my posse in cyberspace – Airat, Sevara and Charles in Tashkent; Denis, Farruh and Nargiza in Samarkand; Abdurahmon in Bukhara; Muhammad in Khiva; Daniel Lepetit in Nukus; and visa guru David in Almaty. *Spacibo bolshoy* to Nellifa for the Tashkent tips, and to other travellers who shared tips with me along the way, especially obsessive note-taker Tim Harford-Cross. Lastly, thanks to Fahkmuddin, Shahina and Co for looking out for me.

PAUL CLAMMER

Events on the ground meant that I was unable to travel to Afghanistan for this edition of *Central Asia*, and had to live vicariously through emails from friends and contacts in Kabul, who rose valiantly to my requests for information. Particular thanks in this regard to Andre Mann. Thanks also Muqim Jamshady, and the staff of the AKDN. A couple of other correspondents remain nameless, but no less appreciated.

At Lonely Planet, thanks to my co-authors, especially coordinating supremo Bradley Mayhew. On the editorial side, thanks to Suzannah Shwer and Will Gourlay.

MICHAEL KOHN

Firstly, thanks to the many Kyrgyz drivers, families and passers-by who saved my hide on a number of occasions – there are too many to name. Special thanks to Ian Claytor at Celestial Mountains for logistical help and for answering my many questions, Sandro Henschel for help all over the place (I owe you a beer, mate) and travel mate Ran Finkelstein. Thanks also to Taalai Janybekov (Karakol), Daniyar Abdurahmanov (Osh) and CBT coordinators everywhere. I received tons of support from the Peace Corps volunteers of Kyrgyzstan, especially in Osh, Talas, Karakol, Kochkor and Naryn; special thanks to Lynnie Moore and Cameron Blume. In Bishkek, thanks to Ala at the Sabrybek Guesthouse and Jack Losh, formerly of the *Times of Central Asia*. Much support also came from Bradley Mayhew, my fellow Lonely Planet scribes and Suzannah Shwer. And back home, thanks to my wife Baigal and baby Molly.

JOHN NOBLE

Very many thanks to the many who shared their knowledge and time, gave me rides and invited me into their homes and gatherings, especially: David Berghof, Timur and Ruslan from Kyzylorda, John Saunders and crew in Atyrau, Svetlana Baskakova, Karla Makatova, David Andrews and the Mongol Rally crew, Robert Manson and

friends in Almaty, Dagmar Schreiber and colleagues at the EIRC, Perry Teicher, Melanie Siler, Vitaly Shuptar and all at the Ecological Museum in Karaganda, Joe Urbanas, Zach Scheid, Vicente Escriva, Leah Engle, Marat Ainsanov, Joe Mizener, Andrew Smith, Anne-Marie (Ust), Blake Reinhold, Casey Meyering, Uighur Tour (Kashgar), Timothy Cope, Niall O'Donoghue, Alikhan Abdeshev, Jeffrey Mason, Ryskul Bokisheva, John O'Neill, and not least commissioning editors Will Gourlay and Suzannah Shwer, coordinating author Bradley for his guiding hand and patience, and all my other fellow authors for their cross-border cooperation and email fellowship.

OUR READERS

Many thanks to the travellers who used the last edition and wrote to us with helpful hints, useful advice and interesting anecdotes:

Miree Abrahamsen, Stephan Beck, Oleg Belkov, Elisabetta Bonino, Sofie Boogaerdt, Didier Bourguignon, Andrew Brady, Ken Brandon, Graeme Brock, Faith Cabanilla, Alan Calder, Courtney Calvin, Duncan Cannon, Michael Cavey, Ying Chou Chen, Ernst Christen, Johan Collier, Roslyn Coltheart, Erin Cunningham, Marc Dankers, Lilian de Boer, Bjorn Dettwiler, Frederike Diersen, Aybek Djuraev, Nadja Douglas, Anne Edwards, Stephen Edwards, Alun Evans, Victoria Evans, Timothy Eyre, Saffia Farr, Margot Fonteyne, Martin Godau,

---

SEND US YOUR FEEDBACK

We love to hear from travellers – your comments keep us on our toes and help make our books better. Our well-travelled team reads every word on what you loved or loathed about this book. Although we cannot reply individually to postal submissions, we always guarantee that your feedback goes straight to the appropriate authors, in time for the next edition. Each person who sends us information is thanked in the next edition and the most useful submissions are rewarded with a free book.

To send us your updates – and find out about Lonely Planet events, newsletters and travel news – visit our award-winning website: **www.lonelyplanet.com/contact**.

Note: We may edit, reproduce and incorporate your comments in Lonely Planet products such as guidebooks, websites and digital products, so let us know if you don't want your comments reproduced or your name acknowledged. For a copy of our privacy policy visit www.lonelyplanet.com/privacy.

Celine Heinbecker, Mathis Hemberger, James Hodgson, Curran Hughes, Adam James, Ute Kellermann, David Kerkhoff, Shabbir Khambaty, Peter Klomp, Matthew Kovacs, Sylvia Kranz, Holger Krausse, Katherine Landers, John Latham, Waheb Lekhal, Ralf Liekmeier, Brad Lindenbaum, Ann Lond-Caulk, Stefan Loose, Jack Losh, Francis Macdonnell, Stephen Macleod, Isabella Moore, Christina Mueller, Barbara Myczko, Iona Naismith, Bernhard Nemec, Jussi Niemelainen, Lewis Nightingale, Robert Norman, David Oates, Christian Obermeier, Shannon O'Brien, Kevin O'Flynn, Greg O'Hern, Jeremy Parsons, Simon Penner, Rick Porter, Meghan Redd, Corinne Reinhard, Julian Roemer, Laziza Salikhbaeva, Pascale Saravelli, Thomas Sarosy, Mikel Sauhansen, Michael Schena, Nadia Sknar, Leo Sluis, Tanadini Stefano, Robert Sukup, Laurel Sutherland, John Usmonov, Frank van der Heyden, Christian Vignali, Saija Vuola, Bill Weir, David Whiting, Helena Wilde, Katherine Wilde, Sophie Willingale, Klaus Winterling, Rainer Winters, Mirjam Wouters, SR Yelda, Maria Zavala

ACKNOWLEDGMENTS
Many thanks to the following for the use of their content:

Globe on title page ©Mountain High Maps 1993 Digital Wisdom, Inc.

Index

INDEX

INDEX

INDEX

INDEX

000 Map pages
000 Photograph pages